Child & Adolescent Development

AN INTEGRATED APPROACH

Karen B. Owens

Barat College

Australia • Canada • Mexico • Singapore • Spain
United Kingdom • United States

Psychology Publisher: Edith Beard Brady
Developmental Editor: Sherry Symington
Assistant Editor: Rebecca Heider
Editorial Assistant: Maritess A. Tse
Marketing Manager: Kandis Mutter
Marketing Assistant: Megan E. Hansen
Technology Project Manager: Michelle Vardeman
Project Manager, Editorial Production: Lisa Weber
Print/Media Buyer: Karen Hunt
Permissions Editor: Robert Kauser

Production Service: Joan Keyes/Dovetail Publishing Services
Text Designer: Lisa Buckley
Photo Researcher: Linda L Rill
Copy Editor: Lura Harrison
Illustrator: B & B Illustrators
Cover Designer: Stephen Rapley
Cover Image: Ken Fisher/Tony Stone Images
Cover Printer: Phoenix Color Corporation
Compositor: New England Typographic Service
Printer: R. R. Donnelley & Sons, Willard

Printed in the United States of America

1 2 3 4 5 6 7 05 04 03 02 01

Library of Congress Cataloging-in-Publication Data
Owens, Karen.
Child & adolescent development : an integrated approach / Karen B. Owens.
p. cm.
Includes bibliographical references and index.
ISBN 0-534-36618-X
1. Child psychology. 2. Child development. 3. Adolescent psychology. 4. Adolescence.
I. Title: Child and adolescent development. II. Title.

BF721 .O96 2001
305.231—dc21 2001046581

Wadsworth/Thomson Learning
10 Davis Drive
Belmont, CA 94002-3098
USA

For more information about our products, contact us:
Thomson Learning Academic Resource Center
1-800-423-0563
http://www.wadsworth.com

International Headquarters
Thomson Learning
International Division
290 Harbor Drive, 2nd Floor
Stamford, CT 06902-7477
USA

UK/Europe/Middle East/South Africa
Thomson Learning
Berkshire House
168-173 High Holborn
London WC1V 7AA
United Kingdom

Asia
Thomson Learning
60 Albert Street, #15-01
Albert Complex
Singapore 189969

Canada
Nelson Thomson Learning
1120 Birchmount Road
Toronto, Ontario M1K 5G4
Canada

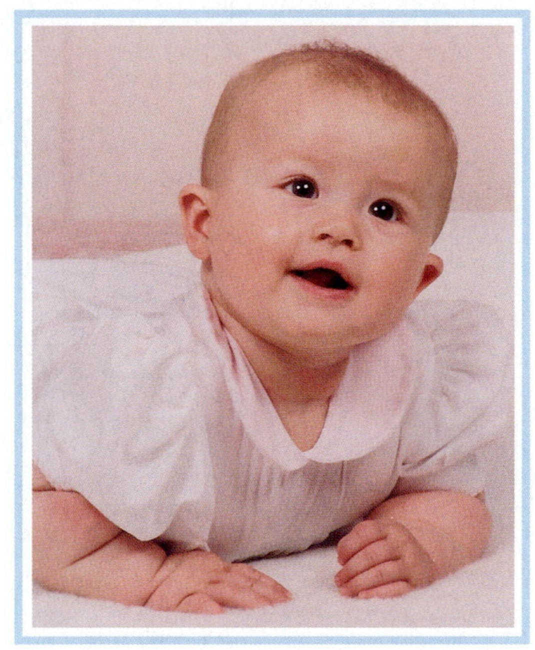

To Caitlin Meade Owens

BRIEF CONTENTS

PART ONE
Historical and Cultural Contexts 2

Introduction ▪ *John Ogbu, University of California, Berkeley* 2
Chapter One ▪ Introducing Child Development: History, Theory, and Research 5
Chapter Two ▪ Cultural and Ethnic Influences on Children's Development 49

PART TWO
Genetic and Environmental Contexts 80

Introduction ▪ *Robert Plomin, Social, Genetic, and Developmental Psychiatry Research Centre, London, England* 80
Chapter Three ▪ Heredity and Environment 83
Chapter Four ▪ Parenthood, Prenatal Development, and Birth 115

PART THREE
Developmental Contexts: Infancy and Toddlerhood 154

Introduction ▪ *Michael E. Lamb, National Institute of Child Health and Human Development* 154
Chapter Five ▪ Physical Development: Infancy and Toddlerhood 157
Chapter Six ▪ Cognitive Development: Infancy and Toddlerhood 195
Chapter Seven ▪ Socioemotional Development: Infancy and Toddlerhood 227

PART FOUR
Developmental Contexts: Early Childhood 264

Introduction ▪ *Alison Clarke-Stewart, University of California, Irvine* 264
Chapter Eight ▪ Physical Development: Early Childhood 264
Chapter Nine ▪ Cognitive Development: Early Childhood 299
Chapter Ten ▪ Socioemotional Development: Early Childhood 339

PART FIVE
Developmental Contexts: Middle Childhood 376

Introduction ▪ *James Garbarino, Cornell University* 376
Chapter Eleven ▪ Physical Development: Middle Childhood 379
Chapter Twelve ▪ Cognitive Development: Middle Childhood 413
Chapter Thirteen ▪ Socioemotional Development: Middle Childhood 455

PART SIX
Developmental Contexts: Adolescence 488

Introduction ▪ *Jeanne Brooks-Gunn, Columbia University Teachers College* 488
Chapter Fourteen ▪ Physical Development: Adolescence 491
Chapter Fifteen ▪ Cognitive Development: Adolescence 531
Chapter Sixteen ▪ Socioemotional Development: Adolescence 569

TABLE OF CONTENTS

PART ONE
Historical and Cultural Contexts 2

Introduction *John Ogbu, University of California, Berkeley* 2

Chapter One Introducing Child Development: History, Theory, and Research 5

A Historical Overview of Attitudes Toward Children 6
- Childhood in Ancient Times 6
- Children in Medieval Times 7
- Views of Children in the American Colonies 7
- Native American Views of Children 8
- The Advent of Humanistic Views of Children 8
- Views of Children in the Industrial Revolution 9

CHILD DEVELOPMENT ISSUES:
Are We Witnessing the Disappearance of Childhood? 10

The Emergence of Developmental Theories 11

SELF-INSIGHT: *Your Personal Theory on Personality* 12

- The Psychoanalytical Perspective 13
- Behaviorism and Social Learning Theories 18
- Cognitive-Developmental Theory 22
- Assessing Theories 24

Contexts of Development 27
- Bell and Reciprocating Influences 27
- Minuchin and the Family Systems Model 27
- Bronfenbrenner and Ecological Contexts 28
- Vygotsky's Sociocultural Contexts 30

Conducting Child Development Research 31
- Research Strategies 31

CULTURAL VARIATIONS: *Vygotsky on the Importance of Cultural Contexts* 32

- Research Designs 38

FIRST PERSON: *Longitudinal Research* 39

Contemporary Issues and Future Concerns 40
- Developmental Issues 40
- Improving Children's Lives 43

About This Book 44
- An Integrated Approach 44
- Chronological Understandings 44
- Domains of Development 45

Reviewing Key Points ■ Answers to Concept Checks ■ Key Terms ■ InfoTrac College Edition ■ Child Development CD-ROM 46

Chapter Two Cultural and Ethnic Influences on Children's Development 49

A Multicultural Perspective 50
Goals of Understanding Multiculturalism 50
Within-Group Variations 51
Socializing Children for Competency 52
Collectivism and Individualism 54
Conducting Cross-Cultural Research 55

SELF-INSIGHT: *Collectivism–Individualism Scale* 56

Children in Various Cultures 57
Japan: Fostering Academic Achievement 57

CULTURAL VARIATIONS: *Fathers Around the World* 60

China: Traditionalism and Moderism 61

FIRST PERSON: *A Visit to Peking University* 63

Sweden: Social Welfare Systems 65

U.S. Ethnic Groups: Beliefs and Concerns 67
Cultural Beliefs 67
Ethnicity: A Central Concern? 68
Vulnerable Families? 68

Children in Various Ethnic Groups 69
African American Families 69

CHILD DEVELOPMENT ISSUES:
Are Those Children Yours?—Mixed-Ethnic Adoption 70

Asian American Families 72
Native American Families 73
Latino Families 76

Reviewing Key Points ▪ Answers to Concept Checks ▪ Key Terms ▪ InfoTrac College Edition ▪ Child Development CD-ROM 78

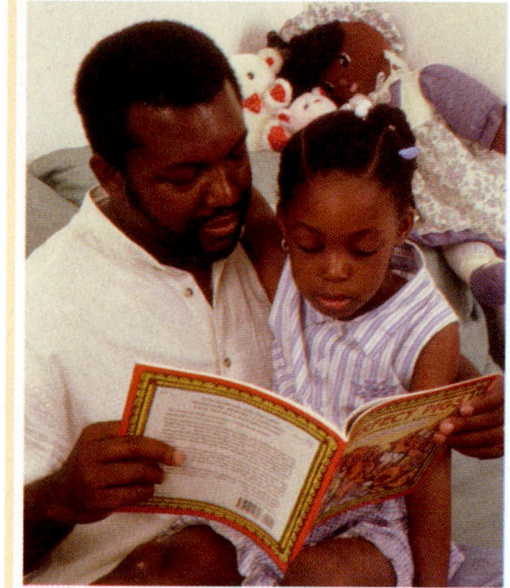

PART TWO Genetic and Environmental Contexts 80

Introduction *Robert Plomin, Social, Genetic, and Developmental Psychiatry Research Centre, London, England* 80

Chapter Three Heredity and Environment 83

The Basics of Genetics 84
Heredity in Action 84
Mechanisms of Genetic Inheritance 86
The Determination of Sex 88

Genetic Disorders and Abnormalities 89
Disorders Causing Mental Retardation 89
Abnormalities of Autosomes 91

Abnormalities of Sex Chromosomes 93
Diagnosing Disorders 93
The Synchrony of Genes and Environment 96
The Nature–Nurture Pendulum 96
Directness and Indirectness of Heredity 97
Canalized Traits 97
The Genetics of Human Traits 98
Current Research Tools 98

FIRST PERSON: *Being an Identical Twin* 99

Personality 100

CHILD DEVELOPMENT ISSUES:
Other Than Depositing Their Genes, Do Parents Matter? 102

SELF-INSIGHT: *The Big Five Inventory* 104

Intelligence 106

CULTURAL VARIATIONS: *Assessing Intelligence* 109

Creating Optimal Environments 109

Reviewing Key Points ▪ Answers to Concept Checks ▪ Key Terms ▪
InfoTrac College Edition ▪ Child Development CD-ROM 112

Chapter Four

Parenthood, Prenatal Development, and Birth 115

Psychological Factors in Becoming Parents 116
Motivational Factors for Parenthood 116

SELF-INSIGHT: *Why I May (or May Not) Want to Have Children* 118

How Your Life Changes 120
Factors Leading to Positive Transitions 122
Infertile Couples 122
Causes of Infertility 123
Artificial Fertilization 123
Surrogate Mothers 125

FIRST PERSON: *In Vitro Fertilization* 125

CULTURAL VARIATIONS: *Sex Preferences for Firstborn Children* 126

Prenatal Environmental Hazards 127
Diseases: AIDS and Measles 127
Immunological Effects: Rh Factor 129
Diet and Caffeine 130
Age and Emotions 131
Prescription and Nonprescription Drugs 131
Smoking 132
Alcohol 133
Illicit Drugs 134
Chemical Hazards to Sperm 136

Conception and Prenatal Development 138
Conception 138
The Infant's Gestation Period: Three Stages 139
The Parents' Experience 142
The First Trimester 142

CHILD DEVELOPMENT ISSUES: *Fathers—The Forgotten Parent?* 143

The Second Trimester 143
The Third Trimester 144
The Birth Process 145
Contemporary Childbirth 145
Stages of Childbirth 147
Life Begins: The Newborn 149
Neonatal Assessment Techniques 149
The Newborn's Appearance 150
Born Too Small, Born Too Soon 150
Postpartum Period 151

Reviewing Key Points ▪ Answers to Concept Checks ▪ Key Terms ▪ InfoTrac College Edition ▪ Child Development CD-ROM 152

PART THREE Developmental Contexts: Infancy

Introduction *Michael E. Lamb, National Institute of Child Health and Human Development* 154

Chapter Five Physical Development: Infancy and Toddlerhood 157

Brain Development During Infancy and Toddlerhood 158
A Baby's Brain—A Work in Progress 158

SELF-INSIGHT: *Recognizing the Infant's Competencies* 159

The Brain's Pruning System 161
Brain Plasticity 163
The Emotional Brain 163
Applications: Fostering Brain Growth Development 163

FIRST PERSON: *The Geniuses of Tomorrow* 165

Physical and Motor Development 167
Physical Growth Patterns 167
Principles of Motor Development 168
Applications: Toilet Training 171

CULTURAL VARIATIONS: *Cross-Cultural Differences in Motor Development* 172

The World of Sights, Sounds, and Smells 174
Sensory Systems 174
Depth Perception 178

Intermodal Perception 179
Applications: Making Sure the Infant Can Hear 180
Behavioral States 181
Crying 181
Sleep 182
Sleep Apnea 184
Applications: Symptoms of and Recommendations for Infants at Risk for SIDS 185
Health 187
Immunizations 187
Nutrition 187

CHILD DEVELOPMENT ISSUES: *Breast or Bottle Feeding?* 189

Undernutrition 190
Applications: Overnutrition 190

Reviewing Key Points ■ Answers to Concept Checks ■ Key Terms ■ InfoTrac College Edition ■ Child Development CD-ROM 192

Chapter Six Cognitive Development: Infancy and Toddlerhood 195

Piaget's Sensorimotor Thinker 196
The Mechanisms of Thought 196

SELF-INSIGHT: *Learning About Learning* 197

Understanding Their World 198
Criticisms of Piaget's Theory 200
Looking Beyond the Challenges 202
Applications: A Piagetian Approach to Fostering the Infant's Cognitive Competence 203

FIRST PERSON: *Everyday Learning* 204

Information-Processing Views of Cognition 204
The Structure of Memory 205
Habituation and Dishabituation 205
The Infant's Memory Skills 206
Early Imitation 206
Evaluation of Information-Processing Theory 207
Applications: The Perils of Overstimulation 207
Psychometric Assessment 208
Gesell's Developmental Quotient 209
Bayley's Scales of Infant Development 209
Applications: Early Intervention for At-Risk Infants and Toddlers 210

CHILD DEVELOPMENT ISSUES: *Do Smart Infants Become Smart Children?* 211

Language Development 212
Language in Its Cultural Setting 212
Language: A Rule-Governed System 213

Theories of Language 214
The Infant's First Communications 216
First Words 218
Caregiver Speech 220
Applications: The Growth of Shared Understandings 221

CULTURAL VARIATIONS: *The Language We Speak: The Message We Give* 222

Reviewing Key Points ■ Answers to Concept Checks ■ Key Terms ■ InfoTrac College Edition ■ Child Development CD-ROM 224

Chapter Seven Socioemotional Development: Infancy and Toddlerhood 227

Attachment Relations 228
Developmental Progression of Attachment 228
Assessing Attachment Relations 230

CHILD DEVELOPMENT ISSUES: *Is There a Critical Period for Establishing Attachment Relations?* 231

Strange Situation Attachment Classifications 232
Developmental Significance of Attachment 235
The Mother's Contributions to the Attachment Process 236
The Father's Contributions to the Attachment Process 237

CULTURAL VARIATIONS: *Attachment Relations* 238

Applications: Fostering Strong Attachment Relations 240

Understanding Others and Self 242
How Infants Learn About Their Social World 242
Gender-Based Socialization of Infants 242
The Emerging Self 243
Applications: Developing a Sense of Self 243

Emotional Development 244
Emergence of Emotional Displays 244
Social Referencing 245
Imitating Others' Emotions 246
Autism 246
Patterns of Emotionality: Temperament 249

SELF-INSIGHT: *Analyzing Your Own Temperament* 250

Applications: Recognizing and Accepting the Infant's Temperament 252

Family Influences 254
Maternal Employment 254
The Effects of Child Care on Attachment 255
Overall Effects of Maternal Employment 255
Fathers in Dual-Wage Families 256
Applications: Generative Fathering 258

FIRST PERSON: *Chris, A "Stay-At-Home" Dad* 259

Reviewing Key Points ■ Answers to Concept Checks ■ Key Terms ■ InfoTrac College Edition ■ Child Development CD-ROM 261

PART FOUR
Developmental Contexts: Early Childhood 264

Introduction *Alison Clarke-Stewart, University of California, Irvine* 264

Chapter Eight Physical Development: Early Childhood 267

Physical Transformations 268
The Developing Brain 268
The Nature of Physical Growth 270
Applications: Factors Affecting Growth 273

Motor Development 274
Movement and the Young Child 274
Perceptual Development 275
Gross and Fine Motor Skills 276
Assessing Children's Gross and Fine Motor Development 279
Applications: Enhancing Children's Motor Development 279

Health Factors in Early Childhood 282
Safety Concerns 282
Illness and Infectious Diseases 283

CHILD DEVELOPMENT ISSUES:
Does Poverty Influence Child Development Outcome? 284

Nutrition 284

FIRST PERSON: *Breaking Away From Poverty* 286

Applications: Meeting the Preschooler's Nutritional Needs 287

Health-Related Issues 288
Sleeping Patterns 288
Bed-Wetting 289
Sexuality 290
Applications: Sex Education for Preschoolers 291

SELF-INSIGHT: *Sexuality Comfort Inventory* 292

CULTURAL VARIATIONS: *Sex Education* 294

Reviewing Key Points ▪ Answers to Concept Checks ▪ Key Terms ▪ InfoTrac College Edition ▪ Child Development CD-ROM 296

Chapter Nine Cognitive Development: Early Childhood 299

The Young Child's Thinking Skills 300
Piaget's Preoperational Thinker 300
Vygotsky's Sociocultural Theory 306
Information-Processing Theory 310
The Young Child's Theory of Mind 313
Applications: Supporting the Child's Developing Theory of Mind 316

Language Development 317
The New "Second Word" 317
Multiple-Word Utterances 317

Speech and Hearing Problems 319
Applications: Learning a Second Language 320

Early Education 322
Child Care 322

FIRST PERSON: *Child Care in Sweden* 324

CULTURAL VARIATIONS: *Child Care* 325

School Readiness 326

SELF-INSIGHT: *Child Development Expectations* 327

Reading Readiness 329

CHILD DEVELOPMENT ISSUES:
School Phobia: What Is It and What Can Be Done About It? 330

Learning and Television and Videos 332
Applications: Helping Children Make a Successful Adjustment to School 333

Reviewing Key Points ▪ Answers to Concept Checks ▪ Key Terms ▪ InfoTrac College Edition ▪ Child Development CD-ROM 336

Chapter Ten

Socioemotional Development: Early Childhood 339

Social Understandings 340
The Young Child's World of Play 340

CULTURAL VARIATIONS: *Play* 342

Preschool Friendships 344
Understanding Self 347
Gender Roles 349

CHILD DEVELOPMENT ISSUES: *Who's Socializing Whom?* 355

Applications: Socializing Children into Gender Equality 356

Emotional Development 358
Culture and Emotion 358
Emotional Understandings in Early Childhood 360
Applications: Helping Children Deal Effectively with Anger 362

Family Influences in Early Childhood 364
Parents as Guidance Engineers 365

SELF-INSIGHT: *Assessing Parenting Styles: What Would You Do If Your Child Did This?* 366

Guidance Strategies 369

FIRST PERSON: *The Best Disciplinarian Ever!* 369

When Punishment Goes Awry: Child Abuse 371
Applications: Helping Abused Children 373

Reviewing Key Points ▪ Answers to Concept Checks ▪ Key Terms ▪ InfoTrac College Edition ▪ Child Development CD-ROM 374

PART FIVE
Developmental Contexts: Middle Childhood 376

Introduction *James Garbarino, Cornell University* 376

Chapter Eleven Physical Development: Middle Childhood 379

How the Body Changes 380
Height and Weight 380
Skeletal and Muscular Growth 382
Vision and Hearing 382
Perceptual Development 382
Brain Development 382

CHILD DEVELOPMENT ISSUES: *How Adaptable Is the Human Brain?* 384

Applications: Exercising Growing Intelligences 385

Motor Development 387
Basic Skills Expanded and Refined 387
Motor Fitness 387
Play 390

FIRST PERSON: *Being Physically Fit* 390

CULTURAL VARIATIONS: *Games and Sports Around the World* 392

Applications: Physical Fitness 392

Health in Middle Childhood 395
Illnesses, Injuries, and Accidents 395
Death 396
Precursors for Undereating Disorders 399
Obesity 400
Applications: Helping Obese Children 402

Stress 403
Is This a Stressful Situation or Not? 403

SELF-INSIGHT: *Stress Test* 404

Common Childhood Stressors 405
Daily Hassles 406
Stress and Illness 407
Applications: Stress Management 407

Reviewing Key Points ■ Answers to Concept Checks ■ Key Terms ■ InfoTrac College Edition ■ Child Development CD-ROM 410

Chapter Twelve Cognitive Development: Middle Childhood 413

The School Child's Thinking Skills 414
Piaget's Concrete Operational Thinker 414
Information-Processing Skills 416
Creativity 419
Applications: On Academic Success 421

SELF-INSIGHT: *Do You Have an Internal Locus of Control?* 424

Technology, Culture, and Achievement 425
The Impact of Video Games 425
Education and Technology 426
The Hidden Curriculum 429
Culture, Ethnicity, and Achievement 432

CHILD DEVELOPMENT ISSUES: *Will Extending the School Year Lead to Growth in Academic Achievement?* 434

CULTURAL VARIATIONS: *Meet Miss Ying* 436

Applications: Multicultural Education 439

Children with Special Learning Needs 441
Mentally Challenged Children 441
Gifted and Talented Children 442
Children with Learning Disabilities 444

FIRST PERSON: *Working with Learning Disabled Children* 445

Attention Deficit Hyperactivity Disorder 446
Applications: Helping Children with ADHD 447

Refinements in Language Development 449
Understanding Sarcasm 449
Pragmatics of Language 450
Children's Sense of Humor 450
Applications: The Gift of Laughter 450

Reviewing Key Points ■ Answers to Concept Checks ■ Key Terms ■ InfoTrac College Edition ■ Child Development CD-ROM 452

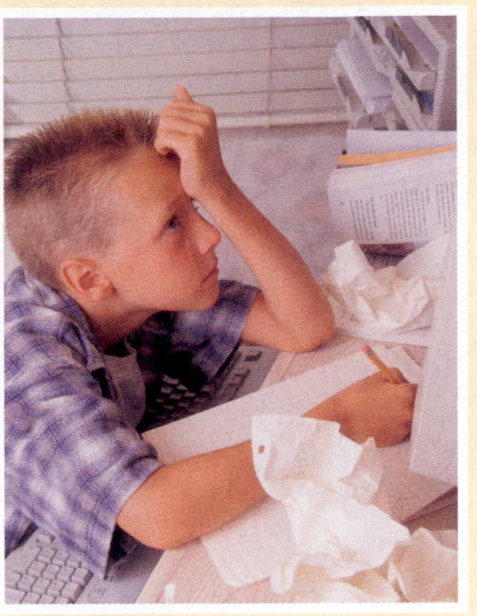

Chapter Thirteen Socioemotional Development: Middle Childhood 455

Understanding Self and Others 456
Changes in Self-Systems 456
Friendships 458
Group Acceptance: Popular Children 461
Group Difficulties: Neglected Children 462

CULTURAL VARIATIONS: *Cultural Meanings of Social Behavior* 464

Group Difficulties: Rejected Children 464

CHILD DEVELOPMENT ISSUES: *Does Viewing Media Violence Increase a Child's Aggression?* 466

Stability of Peer Adjustment 468
Consequences of Peer Relationships 468
Applications: Helping Children with Peer Difficulties 468

Moral Development 472
What Is Morality? 472
Piaget's Theory of Moral Development 472
Kohlberg's Theory of Moral Reasoning 474
Applications: Promoting Morally Competent Behavior in Children 476

SELF-INSIGHT: *How Empathic Are You?* 479

Family Influences in Middle Childhood 480
When Parents Divorce 480
Single-Parent Families 482
Blended Families 482
Applications: Helping Children Adjust in Single-Parent and Blended Families 484

FIRST PERSON: *Single Parenting after Divorce* 485

Reviewing Key Points ▪ Answers to Concept Checks ▪ Key Terms ▪ InfoTrac College Edition ▪ Child Development CD-ROM 486

PART SIX: **Developmental Contexts: Adolescence** 488

Introduction *Jeanne Brooks-Gunn, Columbia University Teachers College* 488

Chapter Fourteen Physical Development: Adolescence 491

Physical Transformations 492
Defining Adolescence 492
Pubertal Changes 493
Early- and Late-Maturing Males and Females 497
The Ideal Masculine and Feminine Physiques 498
Adolescents and Nutrition 498
Eating Disorders 499
Applications: Helping Anorectic and Bulimic Teenagers 502

Sexuality Issues 503
Physical Attractiveness 503
Dating and Intimacy 505
Sexual Awakenings 505

CULTURAL VARIATIONS: *Sexuality* 506

Sexually Active Teenagers 507

CHILD DEVELOPMENT ISSUES: *Is Risk-Taking Part of Being an Adolescent?* 508

Sexually Transmitted Diseases 511
Teenage Pregnancy 513
Applications: Helping Teenage Parents 516

Health-Related Issues 518
Youths and Violence 518
Drugs 521

FIRST PERSON: *Making Money the Wrong Way* 524

Why Do Teenagers Use Drugs? 524
Treatment 525
Applications: Peers—Should Adults "Buzz Off" or "Butt In"? 525

SELF-INSIGHT: *Coping with Stress* 526

Reviewing Key Points ▪ Answers to Concept Checks ▪ Key Terms ▪ InfoTrac College Edition ▪ Child Development CD-ROM 528

Chapter Fifteen — Cognitive Development: Adolescence 531

The Adolescent's Thinking Skills 532
- Piaget's Formal Operational Thinker 532
- The Adolescent's Information-Processing Skills 536
- A Psychometric Look at Intelligence 539

CHILD DEVELOPMENT ISSUES: *Are Girls Getting Shortchanged in School?* 542

SELF-INSIGHT: *How Smart Are You?* 544

- Applications: Possible Solutions to Underachievement 547

Possible Outcomes of the Adolescent's New Thinking Skills 549
- Imaginary Audience 549
- Personal Fable 549
- Idealism 550
- Argumentativeness 551
- Applications: Managing Argumentativeness 553

Adolescents and School 555
- Curriculum: Rigor or Relevance? 555

CULTURAL VARIATIONS: *Occupational Training* 556

- Occupational Role Development 557
- Adolescent Employment 558
- Dropping Out of School 559
- Applications: Helping Potential High School Dropouts 561

Language Development 562
- Refined Understandings of Language 562
- Communication Patterns 563
- Typical Ways of Responding 564
- Applications: Conversing with Adolescents 565

FIRST PERSON: *A Mother and Daughter on Communication* 565

Reviewing Key Points ▪ Answers to Concept Checks ▪ Key Terms ▪ InfoTrac College Edition ▪ Child Development CD-ROM 566

Chapter Sixteen — Socioemotional Development: Adolescence 569

Understanding Self and Others 570
- Self-Understandings 570
- Friendships in Adolescence 573

FIRST PERSON: *Cliques and Friendships* 574

- Identity Issues 577

CHILD DEVELOPMENT ISSUES: *Rites of Passage: Are They a Necessary Step to Fostering Adult Identity Status?* 580

Gender Roles in Adolescence 582
Applications: Rewriting Gender Scripts 583

SELF-INSIGHT: *How Androgynous Are You?* 584

Emotional Concerns in Adolescence 587
Juvenile Delinquency 587
Teenage Suicide 589
Applications: Warning Signs of a Potentially Suicidal Teenager 589

Moral Development 591
Moral Reasoning in Adolescence 591

CULTURAL VARIATIONS: *Culture as a Context for Moral Development* 592

Moral Feelings: Guilt 594
Morality and Peers 595
Applications: Morality and the Power of Parents 595

Family Influences During Adolescence 597
Emotionality 597
Emotional Separateness from Parents 598
Emotional Connectedness to Peers and Parents 598
Applications: Fostering the Adolescent's Emancipation Proclamation 599

Reviewing Key Points ■ Answers to Concept Checks ■ Key Terms ■ InfoTrac College Edition ■ Child Development CD-ROM 601

Glossary G-1

References R-1

Photo Credits C-1

Name Index I-1

Subject Index I-16

ABOUT THE AUTHOR

Courtesy of John Whitt

Dr. Owens has researched the topic of children's self-esteem and published scholarly books and journal articles on this topic. One of her current works is *Raising Children's Inner Self-Esteem*. Recently, she was a visiting professor in England and lectured at several universities on this topic. Among her other research interests are rejected children and childhood aggression. She is the past Director of Preventative Diagnostic Services, a testing assessment service designed to give parents foresight into their preschooler's academic, emotional, and social strengths and weaknesses to help them succeed in these domains. Her professional career spans both therapy and academia. She has advanced degrees in psychology from Saybrook Institute, Lake Forest College, and Northwestern University. She has served as a psychological consultant for several school districts and as a special services coordinator for the federal government. Her passion is travel, which has enabled her to observe children's development in a wide range of cultures and to bring these multicultural understandings to this text and her students in the psychology courses she teaches.

PREFACE

The Hotel Bonaventure in Los Angeles has a glass elevator that climbs the exterior of the building. As you ascend to your room, you are offered a nice but somewhat restricted view of the city. In contrast, the 1000-foot-high Tokyo Tower in Japan offers a more sweeping, 360-degree view from its glass-enclosed carousel.

The glass elevator is analogous to past and rather constrained approaches to understanding children; they gave us, at best, limited views of children. What was needed to gain a more complete picture of children was an integrated approach to studying child development. The integrated approach can be likened to the view the Tokyo Tower's design provides.

An Integrated Approach

The integrated approach draws from multiple contexts and disciplines; highlights the influence of culture and ethnicity; and stresses the applications of empirical research to the study of children's growth and development.

Multiple Contexts and Disciplines

The integrated approach draws from multiple contexts and disciplines of development and stresses the interplay between them. Past research often overlooked the impact of biological (neuroscience), genetic, and cultural contexts of children's behavior. Thus these influential components generally were not incorporated into the overall picture of children's development. Similarly, the reciprocal and mutual actions among these contexts were not taken into consideration. Just six years ago, for example, child development textbooks talked about how infants' and toddlers' thinking skills and behaviors emerged, yet the corresponding changes in brain development that orchestrate many of these achievements were never mentioned.

One cannot study cognitive processes, for example, without appreciating the contribution of brain development. In this text's chapters on cognition (Chapters 6, 9, 12, and 15), the context of neuroscience is intertwined with cognitive development, enabling students to see how brain development is linked to the development of more sophisticated thinking processes in children. Similarly, one cannot study personality development without considering the influence of genetic and environmental contexts (Chapter 3). Biological, social, genetic, and historical contexts all impact children's development singularly and in concert.

Further, the integrated approach strives to unite developmental psychology with other related fields of study, for example, anthropology, sociology, and history. These disciplines have in the past often been considered separate domains of research. Until recently, the science of child psychology was generally compartmentalized, but contemporary research is striving to break down these old barriers—permitting this text to include comparative developmental data generated by these allied fields.

Diversity: Culture and Ethnicity

One context of development, culture, has received a great deal of deserved attention in recent years. It is probably safe to say, however, that not long ago, child development textbooks could have been described as "The study of the white middle-class American child with a brief mention of others outside this 'norm.'" Psychologist Marc Bornstein of the National Institute of Child Health and Human Development (NICHD) stated recently that it is a truism of psychological study that often cultural contexts are neglected, despite the central role they play. Developmental psychologists are currently addressing this gap as evidenced by the growing number of research projects examining the cultural and ethnic variations that influence children's development.

Culture becomes our "design for living"; it is the "human made" part of the environment, which also, in turn, helps to "make" humans. Culture and children's development are as inseparable as heredity and environment; each is the expression of the other. Understanding *diversity* in children's development helps students to recognize the value of differences that exist between people as a function of their culture and ethnicity. Cross-cultural views of children's development also make students aware of the striking universals and shared understandings that exist among children worldwide. Although we will travel to distant parts of the world throughout the text, we will not ignore the differing ethnic groups found in our own backyard.

Issues of culture and ethnicity are so integral to the study of children's development that a separate chapter (Chapter 2, *Cultural and Ethnic Influences on Children's Development*) sets the stage for this multicultural/ethnic understanding of children in cultures outside the United States as well as within our own borders. Further, throughout the text, students will encounter *Cultural Variations*—inserts that will help them see that their own culture's "design for living" is just one among many. In Chapter 7, we will discuss cultural variations in attachment relations; Chapter 10 looks at play around the world; and Chapter 14 discusses teenage sexuality in various parts of the world. Less immediately visible are numerous multicultural/ethnic research findings incorporated throughout the text.

Applications

At the end of the spring semester, I made my usual pilgrimage to the local bookstore in search of some great summer reading material. I chose a book from the biography section, A. N. Wilson's *Tolstoy,* even though the book was massive and expensive. Wilson, however, made Tolstoy come alive. The reader could see how Tolstoy's life experiences shaped and molded the vividness of his main characters in his most notable literary works, *War and Peace* and *Anna Karenina*. The book was terrific—and was certainly money and time well spent. I want this text to provide students with a similar reading experience. One of the best ways for this to happen is to make this text's principal characters, children, come alive and to provide information about children's development that will be meaningful to students—personally and, perhaps, professionally. Thus, I have integrated chapter contents with real-world applications throughout.

Many students who take a course in child development often do so for personal or future professional reasons. Some take the course because they plan to become parents; some already are parents. Many plan to engage in applied work with children as educators, counselors, social workers, and medical professionals. This text strives to make pragmatic information an integral part of the organizational design. Its objective is to draw a parallelism between theoretical views, empirical works, and the implications of this research. By including the practical side of information about children, we complement students' needs for understanding important theoretical concepts with their need to see the personal value of research and theory.

To this end, each of the main sections in the developmental chapters begins with a discussion of the current research pertaining to the topic at hand and concludes with "Applications" that reflect the practical implications of the material discussed. In Chapter 7, dual-wage family structures are discussed, and the section ends with an Applications section on "generative fathering"—the type of father involvement and responsible caring that will facilitate the needs of the next generation of children. In Chapter 15, for example, we discuss "Possible Outcomes of the Adolescent's New Thinking Skills," addressing imaginary audience, idealism, and argumentativeness in adolescents. The Applications section then explores issues in "Managing Argumentativeness." This organizational format clearly reflects how theory/research is translated into action. In this text, applications go beyond the confines of boxed inserts and applied reading segments and receive the prominence they deserve.

"College matters, but only insofar as it yields something that can be used once students leave."

In reflecting on the courses that he took as an undergraduate, my son Gordon commented on one that was required for entering freshman—a "college survival" course that covered everything from health issues to time management. It was the "best course," because it taught him "valuable information" that he could "actually use and apply—even after graduating!" Another purpose of this text, then, is to provide knowledge about children's development along with the applied correlates of that knowledge that go beyond the classroom confines and will be relevant to students in the future.

Features of the Text

This text is organized chronologically; it chronicles children's development from birth through adolescence. Within each developmental stage, we examine the physical, cognitive, and socioemotional development of children. This focus on skill development within each chronological stage of development enhances students' appreciation of how various aspects of children's development are interrelated and integrated. The text also includes several recurring inserts and learning aids to enhance students' understanding.

Self-Understandings

To understand children, students need to discover more about own their attitudes, expectations, and values. As an aid to developing self-understanding, each chapter offers a *Self-Insight* section. For example, "What Would You Do If Your Child Did This!" helps students gain insight into their child-rearing philosophies. These inventories help students learn more about themselves in a variety of areas, such as "How Stressed Are You?" "Do You Have an Internal Locus of Control?" and "Measuring Your Own Temperament." The more foresight students achieve in terms of understanding their thoughts and ideas about themselves and children, the more capable they will become in helping children grow in beneficial ways.

Humanizing Objectivity

To emphasize real voices as a counterpoint to our objective discussions, I have included *First Person* inserts in each chapter. These rich commentaries, written by individuals who have firsthand experiences with the issue discussed, complement the research-based text by humanizing the data with personal experiences. A marvelous description of the in vitro fertilization process is offered by Jennifer in Chapter 4; Chris, a stay-at-home dad, describes his trials and tribulations in Chapter 7; and Ann discusses working with "learning different" children in Chapter 12.

Critical Thinking

Each chapter features a *Child Development Issues* insert, which highlights a significant child development issue currently being debated. Topics such as "Are We Witnessing the Disappearance of Childhood? "Other Than Depositing Genes, Do Parents Matter?" and "Do Smart Infants Become Smart Children?" are explored. Throughout every chapter, I have also created *Thought Challenges,* designed to stimulate thinking about topics related to chapter content and generate class discussions. For example, in Chapter 6, readers are challenged to consider "Should criminal charges be brought against pregnant women who abuse drugs?" and "If preconception sex selection became 100% accurate and inexpensive, what do you think the consequences would be?"

Learning Aids

Pedagogical features such as key terms, glossary terms, and reviews of key points in the chapter are designed to help students focus their attention on important concepts in each chapter. Further, each main heading in the chapters starts with a *Before Beginning* feature that focuses on the section's objectives. *Concept Checks,* which close each section, help students review what they just read through multiple-choice, true/false, and matching questions. Students are encouraged to do further research using the free online database, InfoTrac College Edition, and to expand their understanding through the Child Development CD-ROM that accompanies this text.

Advice from a Hockey Great

Every once in a while a great sports hero captures the attention of others because of his or her unparalleled playing ability. Wayne Gretzy, with his innovative playing style, was considered by many to be one of hockey's greatest players. Shortly before his retirement,

Wayne Gretzky was asked why he was such a great hockey player. He responded, "I don't skate to where the puck is but to where it is going."

Similarly, every once in a while dramatic and innovative changes in research designs take place in the science of child psychology. Certainly, decompartmentalizing the study of children, incorporating culture and ethnic understandings of children's growth and development, and applying research to real-life applications are three tremendously exciting changes. These shifts in experimental paradigms have helped me to achieve important objectives in writing this text. The format of this text highlights a range of contexts and disciplines; presents multicultural/ethnic views of children; and focuses on applications that link research to its serviceable applications. This integrated approach will not only help students skate to where the puck is going but will provide a panoramic perspective of children's development in all its richness and complexity.

Dr. Karen Owens
Barat College

ACKNOWLEDGMENTS

It is hard to estimate the sheer volume of research articles and books that have been collectively produced by the scholars who generously wrote the introductions to the six parts of this text. It is not hard, however, to estimate the enormous impact their work has had in their respective disciplines—anthropology, sociology, genetics, and developmental and applied psychology—and subsequently to the field of child development. I heartily thank the following individuals for their skillfully written essays for this text: John Ogbu, University of California, Berkeley; Robert Plomin, Social, Genetic, and Developmental Research Centre, London; Michael E. Lamb, National Institute of Child Health and Human Development, Maryland; Alison Clarke-Stewart, University of California, Irvine; James Garbarino, Cornell University; and Jeanne Brooks-Gunn, Columbia University's Teachers College.

In the course of writing this text countless little questions and problems arose for which I needed to seek the expert help of our reference librarians Joe Beckwith, Michelle Carter, and Jean Suter. As difficult as some of these problems were, thanks to them, I never left the library without my questions being answered thoroughly, efficiently, and with a smile! A colleague, Dr. Carol Huntsinger, provided help and counsel throughout this entire project.

I would also like to thank the great team at Wadsworth Publishing: Edith Beard Brady, publisher; Lisa Weber, project editor; Michelle Vardeman, technology project manager; and Maritess Tse, editorial assistant. I owe immeasurable gratitude to Sherry Symington, the developmental editor, and Lura Harrison, the copy editor, of this text. If any author has the hubris to think "What a great writer I am," these self-honorific thoughts are brought down a notch or two when an edited chapter is returned. Sherry's work went beyond editing; her organizational skills and suggestions were invaluable. It has been a joy working with her. In addition, I'd like to express my appreciation to Joan Keyes at Dovetail Publishing Services.

Finally, I wish to thank the following reviewers for their thoughtful suggestions and guidance in the preparation of this book: Karen Bartsch, University of Wyoming; Pearl Berman, Indiana University of Pennsylvania; Lynn L. Coffey, Minneapolis Community and Technical College; Ramie Cooney, Creighton University; Katrina Daytner, Ball State University; Jill Dohrmann, Northern Arizona University; Ruth H. Doyle, Casper College; Jerry Dusek, Syracuse University; Bernard S. Gorman, Nassau Community College; Roxane Gudeman, Macalester College; Catherine L. Harris, Boston University; Daniel Houlihan, Minnesota State University; Marie P. Hume, Florida State University; Wendy Kliewer, Virginia Commonwealth University; Melissa A. Koenig, The University of Texas at Austin; Mary Langenbrunner, East Tennessee State University; Dennis A. Lichty, Wayne State College; Rebecca K. Loehrer, Blinn College; Jane A. Rysberg, California State University, Chico; Russell A. Sabella, Florida Gulf Coast University; and Ali Sharf-Matlick, Iona College.

Dr. Karen Owens
Barat College

Let me introduce you to
John Ogbu

On a hot day in May on the University of California, Berkeley campus, students were rushing to class by foot or on bike. Most students were carrying the Library of Congress in their backpacks, some were engaged in animated conversations, while others were quietly contemplative. This scene is common on campuses across the United States, but to John Ogbu who entered Berkeley as a student shortly after leaving his rural Igbo farming village in Southeastern Nigeria, this urban, academic setting was a decidedly different culture.

Courtesy of John Ogbu

Understanding cultural diversity and its impact on development is of special interest to Dr. Ogbu, now a professor in the Department of Anthropology at Berkeley. Professor Ogbu has published a number of papers and books on cross-cultural development, education and culture, and minority education. In one representative example, "Cultural Context of Children's Development" (1999), Dr. Ogbu makes us aware of the enormous impact our cultural surroundings have on determining what we become. His works help us to see the importance of developing a multicultural understanding of children's development that transcends a "white-urban-middle-class-centric" point of view—an important theme of this text.

PART 1

Historical and Cultural Contexts

The Importance of a Multicultural View of Children's Development

by John Ogbu, Department of Anthropology, University of California, Berkeley

It is appropriate that Part One of this book focuses on history and culture in child development. From time immemorial, there has always been social construction of childhood in every society and at every historical period. The ways societies construct childhood and bring up their children, however, have not always been ideal. The first phase of child development was ushered in by philosophers such as Confucius, Plato, Locke, and Rousseau—each of whom advocated particular ways of viewing and raising children. The next distinctive phase emerged as ideas about children's development were no longer being based on armchair speculation or perceived wisdom but on scientific experimentation.

For a long time, research was limited to dominant group children in Western societies, which, in reality, represented "white American" children. There was little, if any, inclusion of African American, Asian American, Hispanic American, Native American, or other nonwhite children in the United States in these empirical accounts of children's development. Toward the end of the 1960s, when minority children began to be included in research designs, the primary goal of researchers was to determine if minority children were developing the same cultural attributes that white middle-class children were developing, and if minority parents were using the same child-rearing practices that white middle-class parents were using. Both the attributes acquired by white middle-class children and the child-rearing practices of their parents were regarded as the correct ones, and the different patterns found among minorities were invidiously compared with those used by white middle-class parents. Differences found among minorities were considered to be evidence of "cultural deprivation" and "deficient development." Relatedly, research findings concluded that minority parenting patterns were incorrect and in need of remediation. A considerable problem plaguing research was a lack of understanding of what culture is and how culture shapes children's development.

Culture is an adaptive way of life shared by members of a population. It is the social, economic, and psychological adaptation worked out in the course of a people's history. The culture of any population (for example, white middle class, African Americans, Native Americans) includes customary ways of behaving and frames of reference that encompass standard ways of making a living, expressing affection, getting married, and getting ahead in society. Culture also includes artifacts—things that members of the population make or have made that have meanings for them, such as cars, clothes, family homes, and music. All these imperatives of culture form a kind of "cultural world" for people of a given society or population, and they help shape children's development.

Cultural diversity, or cultural differences in valued behaviors; assumptions about such behaviors; patterns of social relations; patterns of communication; and the like result in differences, or diversity, in child development. Thus, in the United States, minority children who live in more or less separate cultural worlds of their groups develop different customary behaviors. Diversity among groups, however, does not mean that some groups are substandard. People of various cultures have unique views on appropriate child behavior and successful maturity, and these distinctive views are not necessarily inferior, as once proclaimed.

Chapter Two underscores the fact that child development can only be understood by taking into consideration the particular cultural context in which it occurs. The research cited by Owens in this chapter indicates a significant shift toward recognition of the role of cultural diversity in child development and a movement away from negative comparisons. But cultural diversity still challenges the researcher in two ways. One challenge is for the researcher to start from a good knowledge of the culture (for example, customary behaviors, language and communication patterns, patterns of social relations, and social competencies). Another challenge is for the researcher to become familiar with the formulae that exist in the culture or group for transmitting and acquiring the cultural attributes that children learn, facilitating them to grow up as competent adults in their culture. This knowledge enables the researcher to interpret his or her findings more accurately and better understand how well the children in the sample are developing.

It is clear that there are multiple ways to socialize children, and these specific practices arise from the culture's deep values and traditions. Although contrasting parental strategies produce children with different capacities, goals, and expectations, it is also evident that children of all cultures become relatively well prepared for the culture in which they are being raised.

PART OUTLINE

Chapter One
Introducing Child Development: History, Theory, and Research

Chapter Two
Cultural and Ethnic Influences on Children's Development

cdRiSTiAV

CHAPTER ONE

Introducing Child Development: *History, Theory, and Research*

CHAPTER OUTLINE

A Historical Overview of Attitudes Toward Children
- Children in Ancient Times
- Children in Medieval Times
- Views of Children in the American Colonies
- Native American Views of Children
- The Advent of Humanistic Views of Children
- Views of Children in the Industrial Revolution

The Emergence of Developmental Theories
- The Psychoanalytical Perspective
- Behaviorism and Social Learning Theories
- Cognitive-Developmental Theory
- Assessing Theories

Contexts of Development
- Bell and Reciprocating Influences
- Minuchin and the Family Systems Model
- Bronfenbrenner and Ecological Contexts
- Vygotsky's Sociocultural Contexts

Conducting Child Development Research
- Research Strategies
- Research Designs

Contemporary Issues and Future Concerns
- Developmental Issues
- Improving Children's Lives

About This Book
- An Integrated Approach
- Chronological Understandings
- Domains of Development

Reviewing Key Points

Christian is 4 years old—a neighbor of mine. From time to time, he'll bring over a prized drawing that he created at "Little Hands Child Center." Although he takes great pride in his drawing (which is of me and my garden), it is his name printed in the center of the page that causes him to beam with self-glory. Christian's favorite thing to wear in the afternoon (almost every afternoon) is his Superman costume, made for last Halloween. His chest is engulfed in a huge *S* and his shoulders are draped with a flowing crimson cape. In glancing out my den window, I often notice a blur of red as Christian dashes through the green bushes. Each day brings a new adventure. Today, as he related to me, he is searching for "evil aliens." Somehow one just has to feel a bit safer when Christian travels from yard to yard as our Superman protector.

Manang lives in the Bamenda Grassfields of Cameroon in West Africa. Although she is only one year older than Christian, she is her baby brother's "little mother." Manang, like all the children in the village, spends most of her day sharing necessary responsibilities that will help her family as well as her community. The daily routines of her mother and father keep them away from home most of the day. So, Manang interacts primarily with peers and older siblings who act as her teachers, with adults exerting very little control. Peer-mentoring affords Manang opportunities to learn a particular task or service as well as social skills such as cooperation, leading and following, and obedience to others—including older peers and siblings.

Christian and Manang are being exposed to a set of experiences that channel their development with different purposes and in different directions, often leading to diverse outcomes. No child is untouched by his or her surroundings. As such, children's development is influenced by many interconnected *contexts*, which include not only the basic physical context of our inherited traits but the larger environmental contexts created by our family, society, and culture. This text will explore all of these influences and the theories that have emerged to unlock the mysteries of human development from conception through adolescence.

We begin our introduction to the field of child development by exploring children's past, present, and future. A number of great thinkers, from Confucius to Rousseau, offer their interesting armchair philosophical musings about children—opening windows of understanding to children in times past. The twentieth century ushered in a more scientific view of children's development. No doubt, you are very familiar with many of these developmentalists whose theories have significantly influenced our views on children. Sigmund Freud is a name well known to us all—even to a delightfully precocious 5-year-old who said he plays Frazier's father on the television series of the same name. Many other developmentalists, such as Erikson, Skinner, Bandura, and Piaget followed Freud, and their theories shall be highlighted as well.

Often, however, these theorists focused on the family context as *the* context in influencing children's development—a rather constricted context, according to such theorists as Uri Bronfenbrenner and Lev Vygotsky. An overview of the contextual theorists will help to expand our understandings of the many extrafamilial contexts, such as school and culture, which impact children's development. Our understanding of children, although guided by theory, is dependent on research—more precisely—empirical research strategies and designs. As such, we need to examine the "nuts and bolts" in studying children; this is vital to constructing accurate knowledge about children. The chapter concludes with a look to children's future by seeking answers to such questions as, What are the needs of children in the twenty-first century? and How can we improve the lives of children?

meritocracy
Plato's belief that regardless of the child's position in life or gender, each should be educated to the full extent of his or her abilities.

A Historical Overview of Attitudes Toward Children

Before Beginning . . .

After reading this section, you will be able to

- examine the various ways in which societies, from the eras of Confucius to the Industrial Revolution, have viewed and treated children.

What was it like to be a child in times past? How have our conceptions of children changed over the centuries? Beginning in 551 B.C. and progressing into the nineteenth-century Industrial Revolution, views of children represented a kaleidoscope of changing perspectives; they have, in turn, been seen as linked with others in a web of interrelatedness, parents' property, miniature adults, innately evil, blank slates, and needed workers.

Childhood in Ancient Times

More than 2000 years ago lived a wise prophet, near the state of Wei, along the Yellow River in China. He was known as Chungni K'ung and later as Confucius, or K'ung, the Master. Confucius emphasized that the duty of man was to cultivate and practice *Tao* (the way), which promotes virtues such as loyalty, sincerity, good faith, justice, and kindness (Gabrenya & Hwang, 1996). Confucius believed children were not independent entities but linked to others in a web of interrelatedness. To this end, he urged parents to raise their children with firm parental control, obedience, and strict discipline. He emphasized the importance of a child's education, respect for elders, reverence for tradition, and maintenance of harmony toward others and within oneself (Chang, 1997).

In contrast, the Greek philosopher Plato (427–347 B.C.) emphasized the importance of promoting the individualism and innate abilities of children. His ideal society was a **meritocracy**, in which an individual's position in life (regardless of a child's gender or economic position) would be decided by objectively determined merits (Geddes, 1994). Each child should be treated as special, and each should be educated to the full extent of his or her ability.

Plato's views were the exception, however. The most common perception of children in ancient Western cultures was that they were simply the property of their parents. In ancient Greece and Rome, children were often sold into slavery (Aries, 1962), beaten, and even killed without consequences for the parents. There were even bloody Spartan flagellation contests, which often involved whipping boys to death. Whipping children was quite common in school as well; one teacher proudly reported that in the course of two school years, he had given 911,527 strokes with the stick, 124,000 lashes with the whip, 136,715 slaps with the hand, and 1,115,800 boxes on the ear (de Mause, 1995).

Infanticide, the deliberate murdering of infants, was also common practice in ancient Greece and Rome, and neither law nor public opinion condemned it. A child that was not perfect in shape or size, or that cried too much, might readily be killed. In fact, in Athens, Greece, a pamphlet entitled "How to Recognize the Newborn That Is Worth Rearing" was widely distributed and read (Langer, 1973). The firstborn was generally allowed to live—particularly if it was a boy. Girls were considered of little value, which resulted in large numbers of females being killed. Sometimes children were sacrificed for religious purposes. Parents would offer up their own children—even legitimate children of wealthy parents—for these bloody religious rites. Those who had no children would buy little ones from poor people and cut their throats for religious sacrifices as if they were lambs or young birds.

Confucius contended that children need to learn that we are all equal and all interdependent.

Children in Medieval Times

Ancient times came to an end with the fall of Rome in the fifth century, ushering in the medieval period, also known as the Middle Ages. The Middle Ages were a period of superstition, ignorance, brutality, and disease. Children were generally deemed of little importance, not even worthy of record once born, and their lives continued to be hard even after infancy. Older children, for example, were beaten, neglected, and afforded no rights at all. Legally, children were put in the same class as servants who had no civil rights, and they were considered to be their parents' personal property.

Infant mortality was extremely high during the Middle Ages. Influenza, bubonic plague, and smallpox epidemics, to name a few, targeted young children. If children survived the first seven years of life, their daily activities consisted of the same laborious work their parents did. Everyone, even the youngest children, had work to do. There was much to do: bread to bake, beer to brew, fish to catch, animals to butcher, tables to set, houses to build, ships to sail, and pots to peddle. With few exceptions, children ate the same food, wore the same clothing, played the same games, used the same language, and performed the same labor; in short, they were treated like adults. As late as 1780 in England, 7-year-olds could be convicted (and were), for any of the more than two hundred crimes for which punishment was hanging (Borstelmann, 1983).

Views of Children in the American Colonies

The colonial period stretched from the early 1600s, with the Puritan settling of New England, to the mid-1800s and the Industrial Revolution. Puritans were highly influenced by the religious leader John Calvin's (1509–1564) ideas that children are born sinful and must be forced to be good. Children were viewed as being filled with the "pollutions of sin." Similarly, parents viewed the first strivings of a 2-year-old toward independence as a clear manifestation of that original sin (Beekman, 1977). Children were taught to revere their parents and to fear not living up to their parents' expectations (Hwang, Lamb, & Sigel, 1996).

infanticide
During antiquity, the deliberate murdering of young children.

© Lawrence Migdale/Photo Researchers Inc.

A primary goal promoted by Native American cultures is to teach children respect for all living things, including themselves.

Calvinist parents were faced with two tasks: instruction and discipline. They saw their role as being strict, and they worked diligently to break the child's will, subdue the evil spirit within, and provide scriptural foundations. Perhaps, an appropriate label for seventeenth-century America would be the "age of the whip." Although parents believed that children were evil and sinful, they also believed that children were at least partly rational creatures who with proper training could learn to act piously and according to reason. The belief that human effort could eradicate sin and ignorance was one of the rays of light that occasionally broke through the clouds of seventeenth-century Calvinism.

Native American Views of Children

The Puritans discovered that Native American families differed in their view of children as being ignorant and sinful, for many Native Americans believed in the inherent worth, goodness, and dignity of each child. Values that were traditionally expressed by Native American parents included harmony with nature, respect for elders and traditional ways, centrality of family and tribal life, cooperation, humility, and sharing wealth (Dilworth-Anderson & Marshall, 1996). The primary goal of Navajo parents (and society) was to inculcate "good thought," which included fostering "respect" for any living thing or person—including oneself.

tabula rasa
Locke argued that children's minds were like a "blank tablet" on which experience writes, creating their personalities.

The Advent of Humanistic Views of Children

In eighteenth-century England and France, this view of inherently sinful children was challenged as the values of society shifted from obedience to self-reliance and the influence of philosophers such as John Locke and Jean Jacques Rousseau rose. Unlike the Calvinists, these philosophers believed that children were not born evil. During the Age of Enlightenment, the writings of Locke and Rousseau were widely read and accepted, helping to usher in the great and innocent "age of the child" and a child-rearing mode of helping children (see Table 1.1).

The British philosopher John Locke (1632–1704) agreed that children should be disciplined but suggested abandoning the harsh philosophy of "spare the rod and spoil the child." Instead, Locke (1964) recommended that parents use "praise and commendation" for children's successes and a "cold and negative countenance" for their failures. Locke argued emphatically that the environment in which children were raised determined what they became. Children's minds were like a *blank tablet,* a **tabula rasa**, on which experience writes, thereby creating the child's personality (Locke, 1693/1964). Locke urged parents to carefully observe each of their children and try to adjust their education to help them form their unique personalities. His basic approach to child rearing was one of encouragement and support, rather than punishment.

In France, Jean Jacques Rousseau's (1712–1778) views were also gaining in popularity. Rousseau, however, disagreed with Locke on several important matters. Whereas Locke viewed children as passive (experience "writes" on the child's blank mind, which influences his or her personality and intellect), Rousseau argued that children come into this world equipped with many positive traits and are busy, motivated explorers who shape their own development. Further, Rousseau believed that children were naturally good—all children could develop into paragons of virtue (Rousseau, 1762/1911). To Rousseau, nature provided children with the necessary learning tools, and, as such, parents and schools needed to become more flexible and less rule-governed. However, when it came to education for girls, his

TABLE 1.1

Modes of Parental–Child Relations

Mode	Period	Description
Infanticide	Antiquity to fourth century A.D.	For various reasons—want of money, religious sacrifice, child deformity, child gender, and simply the idea that parents could do what they wanted with children—many children were deliberately put to death.
Abandonment	Fourth to thirteenth century A.D.	Once parents began to accept children as having a soul, the only way they could escape from their children was through abandonment to the wet nurse, the monastery or nunnery, foster families, or nobility where children would serve as slaves or hostages, or through severe emotional abandonment at home.
Ambivalent	Fourteenth to seventeenth centuries	Parents believed it was their duty to mold children. Children were seen as soft wax, plaster, or clay to be beaten into shape.
Intrusive	Eighteenth century	Parents tried to conquer their children's minds to control their anger, needs, and will.
Socialization	Nineteenth to mid-twentieth centuries	The process of raising children became less one of conquering their will than of training them, guiding them into proper paths, teaching them to conform, and socializing them.
Helping	From mid-twentieth century	The proposition that children know better than their parents what they need at each stage of their lives, led to full involvement by both parents in children's lives as they worked to empathize with and fulfill their expanding and particular needs.

From "The Evolution of Childhood," in *The History of Childhood* (pp. 51–52), by L. de Mause, 1995, New York: The Psychohistory Press. Reprinted by permission.

tone changed from that of the Enlightenment to that of the Middle Ages, for Rousseau believed that higher education for girls was useless because they were incapable of logical reasoning. Girls, instead, were bound by tradition to bring comfort and love to those around them.

Views of Children in the Industrial Revolution

Children have always worked, but they generally did so in the fields and shops near their homes. Radical changes occurred, however, during the historical period in the United States and Europe known as the Industrial Revolution (1780–1900). Because of widespread economic changes, towns and cities that were once solely dependent on farming and crafts quickly became industrialized. Subsequently, great numbers of children began working in airless, insect-infested factories, meatpacking plants, and coal mines for 14 to 16 hours a day. In 1880, the U.S. census revealed that one million children between the ages of 10 and 15 were holding jobs (Robertson, 1995).

Things were even worse in London. Children as young as 4 were being used as chimney sweeps or working in the coal mines because their small bodies could fit into the narrow flues and coal seams. If they survived the hazardous work and grew too big, they were simply turned out into the streets to become the little, begging urchins that adults frequently encountered on the street. At age 7, poor children were often indentured to textile mills (often until age 21) virtually without pay. As inmates of poorhouses, 50 or more children were crammed into bare barracks and fed so poorly that they often raided pigsties to get food (Greenleaf, 1978). A small but bright note was the passing in 1802 of the Factory Act; it included a 12-hour-per-day work limit for children working in factories, along with some provisions for schooling and changes in factory hygiene. Although this act only applied to orphans, it was the first act of legislation intended to ensure the well-being of young children.

It took many centuries for the thought to germinate that children are beings with special needs because of their helplessness and vulnerability. It may seem quite obvious, as you compare today's child

Child Development Issues

Are We Witnessing the Disappearance of Childhood?

It doesn't take a social scientist's keen eye and experimental expertise to observe that children are growing up faster and faster. One can observe today how the language, games, clothing, sexuality, and taste of children and adults have become barely distinguishable. Precocious knowledge, independence, assertiveness, and "adultness" characterize many children today. Sometimes it's easy to get the impression that children are just more mature these days. However, many doubt this is so, especially, if maturity is characterized as the ability to share, to sacrifice, and to love unselfishly.

Elkind (1998) maintains that the changes in society and family lifestyles are prominent reasons for the disappearance of childhood. We are witnessing a rise in two-career families and a mounting divorce rate that has led to many single-parent families. Moreover, the media place children and adults in the same symbolic world. Media, including books, films, and television, portray young people as precocious and present them in explicitly sexual or manipulative ways. The darker areas of sex, violence, and human aberrations are revealed all at once by media that do not and cannot exclude any audience.

Adults may believe that children should be readied for each new "milestone" in their development by being given systematic practice. Our preschoolers, for example, are given practice in the technical requirements of the reading process (known as "reading readiness") because to "be prepared" a child must read as soon as possible. The push to early academic achievement is but one area of the contemporary pressures on children. Another may be "Be somebody—be a superkid!" Be a star basketball player, tennis hero, and so on. Sometimes children go to practice these skills before and after school. Sometimes they go to specialized training summer camps, such as the Michael Jordan Basketball Camp. Increasingly, we are hearing that childhood should not be "frittered away" by engaging in activities merely because they are fun.

Further, children are often exposed to life events in the media that are frightening and certainly difficult for them to assimilate. Exposing them to evil, violence, sexuality, and injustice is questionable. Have you ever seen a movie, even as a young adult, that was frightening and had enduring and negative effects on you? When I was 10 years old, my friends and I went to see *The Invasion of the Body Snatchers* —a movie about alien pods taking over the minds and bodies of people as they slept. I had nightmares for weeks! To this end, it is suggested that children should be protected from life's ugly vicissitudes. They need to feel the protectiveness of their parents.

Under the parent's careful supervision, children can sense that

with those in times past, that children have come a long way since the days of antiquity. After all, children are no longer in service from dawn until dusk. Whereas some may say that children "never had it so good," others maintain that we are regressing to some of the ideas of the Middle Ages. David Elkind (1998), for example, suggests that increasingly childhood in the United States is no longer considered to be a sheltered, special, and formative time. Are we, as Elkind might suggest, witnessing "the disappearance of childhood"? (See Child Development Issues.)

Concept Checks

Matching:

___ 1. Calvin	a. Children are naturally good.
___ 2. Plato	b. The child's mind is a blank slate.
___ 3. Rousseau	c. Children are naturally evil.
___ 4. Confucius	d. Every child is equal.
___ 5. Locke	e. Children are interconnected to others.

they are separate, protected, and special. Children need to feel secure in the certainty that children are children and adults are adults and that in spite of the "wretchedness" they might glimpse in their world, they can still remain in a different state, untouched by it. Children should be allowed the simple pleasures of play, imagination, curiosity, and pursuit of adventure—even in the most adverse circumstances. As Elkind notes, perhaps the recognition that a highly complicated civilization such as ours cannot afford to shorten the period of nurture and protection of its immature members will restore a real childhood to the children of coming generations.

AP/Wide World Photos

Search Online

Explore InfoTrac® College Edition, your online library. Go to **http://www.infotrac-college.com/wadsworth** and use the passcode that came on the card with your book. Try these search terms: super kid, child nature, early puberty.

The Emergence of Developmental Theories

Before Beginning . . .

After reading this section, you will be able to

- explain the developmental theories of Freud, Erikson, Watson, Skinner, Bandura, and Piaget.
- discuss the legacies, strengths, and weakness of each developmental theory.

A large array of twentieth-century theories has ushered in a more scientific and insightful view of children's development. Theorists, however, necessarily narrow the focus of their investigations to aspects of child development they consider most important. The main theories that continue to have a prominent impact on our views of children's development and adults' treatment of children are the psychoanalytic theories of Sigmund Freud and Erik Erikson; the behaviorist and social learning theories of John B. Watson, B. F. Skinner, and Albert Bandura; and the cognitive developmental theory of Jean Piaget.

Your Personal Theory on Personality

INSTRUCTIONS For each of the following statements, circle the number that corresponds most closely to your point of view.

1. Human behavior results primarily from *heredity*, what has been genetically transmitted by parents, or from *environment*, the external circumstances and experiences that shape a person after conception has occurred.

   1 2 3 4 5 6 7
   heredity ________________ environment

2. An important part of every person is a *self*, some central aspect of personality referred to as "I" or "me," or there really is *no self* in personality.

   1 2 3 4 5 6 7
   self ________________ no self

3. Personality is relatively *unchanging*, with each person showing the same behavior throughout a lifetime, or personality is relatively *changing*, with each person showing different behavior throughout a lifetime.

   1 2 3 4 5 6 7
   unchanging ________________ changing

4. The most important influences on behavior are *past* events, what has previously occurred to a person, or *future* events, what a person seeks to bring about by striving to meet certain goals.

   1 2 3 4 5 6 7
   past ________________ future

5. The most important characteristics about people are *general* ones, those commonly shared by many people, or *unique* ones, those that make each person different from every other person.

   1 2 3 4 5 6 7
   general ________________ unique

6. People are motivated to cooperate with others mainly because they are *self-centered*, expecting to receive some personal gain, or mainly because they are *altruistic*, seeking to work with others only for the benefit of doing things with and for others.

   1 2 3 4 5 6 7
   self-centered ________________ altruistic

7. People learn best when they are motivated by *reward*, involving pleasure, or by *punishment*, involving pain.

   1 2 3 4 5 6 7
   reward ________________ punishment

8. The main reason you behave as you do (for example, attend college) is because of conscious *personal* decisions to do so, or because *social* factors outside your control leave you little real choice in the matter.

   1 2 3 4 5 6 7
   personal ________________ social

During the twentieth century, several prominent scholars began to propose individual theories charting the course of children's development—each having a significant impact on our views about children, each emphasizing a different aspect of children's development. The psychoanalytic theories of Sigmund Freud and Erik Erikson emphasized personality development and stressed the importance of unconscious conflicts and biological instincts in the determination of children's development. Erikson's theory expanded our understanding of the psychosocial challenges that occur during each developmental stage. The behaviorist theories of John B. Watson, B. F. Skinner, and Albert Bandura focused on environmental determinants of behavior and stressed the role of reinforcement and imitation in shaping a child's behavior. The cognitive theory of Jean Piaget concerned the development of thought processes or reasoning from infancy to adolescence and stressed the child's active role in determining his or her developmental level.

Before beginning our discussion with Sigmund Freud's theory, it may be interesting to first analyze

9. Human nature is essentially *constructive*, with people showing positive, personal growth and a desire to help others fulfill their potentials, or *destructive*, with people showing behavior that is ultimately self-defeating and a desire to keep others from improving themselves.

   1 2 3 4 5 6 7
   constructive ______________ destructive

10. Human beings have *no purpose* or reason for their existence other than what they experience on a day-to-day basis, or human beings have some *purpose* for living that is outside themselves.

   1 2 3 4 5 6 7
   no purpose ______________ purpose

From *Personality: Theory, Research, and Application*, by C. R. Potkay and B. P. Allen, 1986, Monterey, CA: Brooks/Cole.

Theorist's Assumptions

1. heredity (1 2 3 4 5 6 7) environment
   Freud — Skinner, Bandura
2. self (1 2 3 4 5 6 7) no self
   Erikson — Bandura
3. unchanging (1 2 3 4 5 6 7) changing
   Freud — Skinner
4. past (1 2 3 4 5 6 7) future
   Freud — Bandura
5. general (1 2 3 4 5 6 7) unique
   Watson, Skinner — Piaget, Bandura
6. self-centered (1 2 3 4 5 6 7) altruistic
   Freud — Piaget, Bandura
7. reward (1 2 3 4 5 6 7) punishment
   Skinner, Bandura, Freud — Watson
8. personal (1 2 3 4 5 6 7) social
   Piaget — Skinner, Bandura
9. constructive (1 2 3 4 5 6 7) destructive
   Piaget — Freud
10. no purpose (1 2 3 4 5 6 7) purpose
    Skinner, Watson, Bandura — Erikson

ANSWERS 1, 2, and 3 indicate views of personality that are indicative of the respective theorists listed on the left; answers 5, 6, and 7 indicate views of personality closer to the theorists on the right; answer 4 signifies a middle-of-the-road stance on these theories of personality.

your personal views or theory of children's development in the Self-Insight segment.

The Psychoanalytical Perspective

It is hard to imagine what psychology would be like without having had Sigmund Freud (1856–1939) at its helm. So much of what he gave to us (for example, talking cure therapy) is just taken for granted today. At the turn of the twentieth century, prior to Freud, those who were considered "insane," or suffering from dementia praecox (schizophrenia), were literally thrown into pits. Treatment consisted of bloodletting with leaches or boring holes in their heads. These methods were thought to release the demon spirits within them. That our unconscious mind, a mental receptacle for ideas that are too anxiety-producing for the conscious mind to acknowledge, influences our behavior is another fact that many accept with a rather ho-hum attitude today. But, 100 years ago Freud's belief that we

psychosexual stages
Freud's notion of five stages in which sexual instincts are associated with different erogenous zones.

id
Freud's level of personality that contains all human motives and emotions such as love, aggression, fear, and so on. It is primitive and illogical and wants immediate gratification.

unconscious mind
Freud defined it as a sort of mental receptacle for ideas too anxiety-producing for the conscious mind to acknowledge.

ego
Freud's rational level of personality that slowly emerges and becomes noticeable after the child's first birthday. It is the executive branch of personality, mediating between the id and superego.

superego
Freud's level of personality that represents ideals on morals and manners.

libido
The sexual energy that Freud believed children expended during each of their five psychosexual stages.

fixation
According to Freud, leaving too much libido in one psychosexual stage, results in stagnation, or fixation, within that stage.

American Museum, Bath, Avon, UK/Bridgeman Art Library

Freud developed his psychoanalytic theory in an environment of sexual repression and male dominance typical of the Victorian era.

need to analyze the deep inner unconscious mind to understand behavior was just short of revolutionary.

Freud's theory was formulated initially on an intuitive basis, drawn from his own experiences and memories. It was then constructed along more rational lines through his work with patients, examining their childhood experiences and memories. As Freud's practice continued to grow, more and more people paid respectful attention to his work. Freud held that biologically based sexual instincts motivate behavior and steer development through five **psychosexual stages**, in which children learn to expend their sexual energy. The major tenets of his theory pertained to children's sexual and aggressive drives, the importance of early experiences to later development, and to the ways the unconscious mind—the seething cauldron of our innate pleasurable instincts—influences our adult behavior.

Freud's Pleasure-Seeking Child

In Sigmund Freud's view, the **id** is our **unconscious mind**. As such, it contains our human motives and emotions such as love, aggression, fear, and so on. It is primitive and illogical. The childlike id wants immediate gratification; it wants what it wants now! The id's inability to always produce the desired objective leads to the development of the *ego,* the mind's avenue to the real world. The **ego** is the rational level of personality that slowly emerges and becomes noticeable after the child's first birthday. It guides the basic impulses for behavior that arise from the id. In a sense, it functions as the executive in dealing with real-life events and balances the irrational demands from the id and the higher guidance of the *superego* (Freud, A., 1974). The **superego** is that aspect of personality that represents ideals on morals and manners. It consists of the conscience, which reminds us of our "shoulds" and "should nots"; it is our internal judicial system. The superego strives for perfection and is not satisfied with less. It is, like our id, unrealistic. Let's say, for example, that you have been invited to a party tonight, but unfortunately, you have an exam tomorrow. The superego might say, "Stay home and study all day so you can get an "A." In contrast, the id would prompt, "You have been working so hard; you need to relax and have fun!" The mediating ego might advise, "If you study all afternoon, maybe you can attend the party for awhile." In conflict situations, these three aspects of our personalities each will struggle for control (Freud, 1920/1957).

Psychosexual Stages One of Freud's most influential notions is that our adult personality is shaped by early childhood experiences. He proposed that children travel through several psychosexual stages. Freud (1973) believed that the psychological disorders he observed in his patients were the result of inadequate solutions to problems they had faced as children at one or more of these stages. He labeled these phases *psychosexual stages,* because he believed the development of the personality—the *psyche*—was influenced by the way in which children learned to expend *sexual* energy (**libido**) from one period of life to the next (Fine, 1979).

If children's progress through the stages is arrested—that is, if they become **fixated** at any point in psychosexual growth—then they may evidence such fixation as adults. Freud proposed that the most significant emotional experiences during childhood are those associated with expending libido in relation to a series of particularly sensitive zones of the body. These *erogenous zones,* in chronological sequence, are the mouth, the anus, and the genital organs. If fixation occurs, the person is predisposed to seek tension reduction later in life by resorting to forms of behavior that were of greatest significance during earlier stages of development. If the child fixates in the oral stage, for example, as an adult he or she may experience urges to eat and drink to excess or develop a pattern of "biting" criticism of others. Table 1.2

TABLE 1.2

Sigmund Freud's Psychosexual Stages

Stage	Behavior	Fixation	Developmental Outcome
Oral (birth to 2 years)	Child gums, mouths, bites everything in sight	Child weaned from bottle or breast too early or too late	As adult, will be dependent, gullible, ready "to swallow" anything; excessive eating, drinking, kissing, and smoking behaviors
Anal (2 to 3 years)	Anus is a source of pleasure	Child is severely toilet trained or undertrained	As adult, overly neat, always on time, stingy, stubborn, never disobeys orders; excessive sloppiness
Phallic (3 to 6 years)	Phallus, or penis, is most important body part	Child fails to identify with the same-sex parent	Homosexuality*
Latency (6 to 12 years)	A period of suspended sexual activity; energies shift to physical and intellectual activities	No psychosexual fixations during this stage	If development has been successful during the early stages, it leads to marriage, mature sexuality, and the birth and rearing of children

* Author's note: Freud believed that homosexuality was caused by "arrested development" in the Phallic stage. The "cause" of homosexuality—learned behavior or biological destiny—has not been empirically resolved. See, for example, *Taking Sides: Clashing Views on Psychological Issues* (pp. 52–64), B. Slife, 1998, New York: Dushkin/McGraw-Hill.

summarizes Freud's scheme of the psychosexual stages and the developmental outcomes of fixation at each stage.

How well a child comes through each stage, according to Freud, depends on how the child's sexual impulses and behavior are handled. If children receive too much gratification or too little in each of the stages, they fixate. To pass through these stages successfully, with no psychological conflicts or tensions, they need an optimal amount of gratification at each stage. The first three psychosexual stages were particularly important. Freud believed that how mothers raised their children was crucial. (See Table 1.3, which offers Freud's advice on caregiving.)

Erikson's Identity-Seeking Child

Erik Homburger Erikson (1902–1994), a student and an avid follower of Freud, expanded and refined Freud's notions of personality development, emphasizing the role that social and cultural factors play in personality development. Although Erik Erikson was strongly influenced by Freud, their theories differ in important ways. Whereas Freud was concerned with personality development in the psycho*sexual* stages of the first five to six years of life, Erikson (1968) was concerned with personality development in psycho*social* stages throughout the total life cycle. Erikson's scheme centered on acquiring different aspects of our social selves, unlike Freud's, which centered on sexuality. Whereas Freud was primarily concerned with the unconscious mind, Erikson focused on the social aspects of personality and emphasized the role of the ego in children's development. Erikson changed the focus of psychodynamic theory from an emphasis on the gratification of pleasure (id) to an emphasis on successful adaptation (ego). Indeed, Erikson saw the ego as a powerful and positive force as it actively "negotiates" in each of the "eight stages of man" (Erikson, 1959).

The Psychosocial Stages Erikson proposed that human development consists of a series of periods in which some issue is particularly prominent and important. In his view, individuals experience a psychosocial crisis, or conflict, during each of these eight **psychosocial stages**. A *crisis* is a turning point, a period when the potential for growth is high but the person is also quite vulnerable. Erikson saw a crisis as a struggle between attaining some adaptive psychological quality versus failing to obtain it. Individuals negotiate each stage by developing a balance, or ratio, between the two qualities for which that stage is named. Successful negotiation of a stage, however, does imply that the balance is weighted more toward the positive value

psychosocial stages Erikson's notion that during our life span, we pass through eight psychosocial stages, each representing a turning point with a potential for growth as well as vulnerability.

TABLE 1.3

Freud's Child Development Advice

- Provide at each developmental stage enough opportunities for the child to satisfy instinctual drives within an atmosphere of understanding but not so many that the child becomes fixated at that point and is unwilling to move on to the next stage.
- Don't be too soft or too harsh. During the anal stage, for example, parents need to achieve a balance between not being overly strict in toilet training ("You will sit on this potty-chair until you go!") or too lenient ("What do you mean my child cannot attend kindergarten unless he's potty trained?")
- Recognize that children's emotional adjustment is dependent on the way they were treated during the first five years of life.
- Be aware of the potential harm done to young children when their needs, drives, wishes, and emotional dependencies are not met early in life.
- Become aware of children's sexual fantasies.
- Recognize the roles of conflict, conscience, and anxiety in the development of children.
- Acknowledge the need for children to express aggression.
- Develop an awareness of the importance of the mother–child relationship; it is the mother's role to be an auxiliary ego for the growing child.

than the negative value. A summary of the eight psychosocial stages is offered in Table 1.4.

Successful resolution in each of these stages strengthens the ego and prepares one to face the next crises. Inadequate resolution invariably continues to haunt a person and affects his or her ability to function and to cope. Failure or difficulty in establishing what is required at one stage does not condemn a person to complete failure in the next stage, although developmental progress can be slowed or made more difficult to achieve. Thus, a crisis is not resolved once and then forgotten. Rather, resolutions of previously encountered conflicts are reshaped at each new stage of psychosocial development. Early psychosocial crises in Erikson's theory are similar to the psychosexual stages articulated by Freud, but Erikson's interpretation adds a strong social element.

The first psychosocial stage, which Erikson labeled the "cornerstone of the vital personality," is known as *Basic Trust vs. Mistrust* (birth to age 2). Infants reach out to their social environment for nurturance with the expectation that their longing will be satisfied. The degree of trust that the infant develops depends on the quality of care he or she receives. Erikson (1950) would advise parents to cuddle, play, and talk to their infants. They need to meet children's physical and psychological needs when they arise and remove discomforts quickly, so that children can develop a vital sense of trust that the world is safe and reliable. Infants who receive inconsistent and unreliable care from their parents develop a basic mistrust, which may lead, in adulthood, to a basic fear and withdrawal from interpersonal contact and a dread that one's social needs cannot or will not be met. An adult who experienced the conditions for trust during infancy greets the world with fundamental hope; one who did not greets the world with a sense of doom. Table 1.5 offers advice on further child-care throughout the psychosocial stages by Erikson.

The last three Eriksonian stages are concerned with adulthood. *Intimacy versus Isolation* is the time when young adults seek companionship and love with another person, or they become isolated from other people. During the *Generativity versus Stagnation* stage adults either become productive and perform meaningful work or stagnant and inactive. Late adulthood, the *Integrity versus Despair* stage, is when people either look back and see their lives as meaningful or experience despair at goals never reached (Erikson, 1968). Each stage of development contributes its own unique virtue to the human personality:

- Infancy contributes to faith.
- Early childhood contributes to power.
- Preschool contributes to purposefulness.
- School age contributes to efficiency.
- Adolescence contributes to commitment.
- Young adulthood contributes to love.
- Adulthood contributes to responsibility.
- Old age contributes to wisdom.

The Psychoanalytic Perspective and Culture

Freud's theory emphasized "universals" in personality development rather than cultural specificity, and he believed that his psychosexual stages of development applied to everyone worldwide. For example, Freud maintained that during the Phallic stage, pleasurable sensations begin in the genital areas and other erogenous zones and after that there is a lessening of such interest until the coming of puberty. However, Bronislaw Malinowski (1953) observed families and children of the Trobriand Islanders of the western Pacific and found some cross-cultural differences that contradict Freud's notion that Latency is a period of sexual quiescence. Trobriand children grow up with much freedom, including sexual freedom. Children play sexual games in imitation of adult copulation, which is regarded with amused tolerance by adults.

TABLE 1.4

Summary of Erik Erikson's Psychosocial Stages

Stage	Description of Task	Major Characteristics
Trust vs. mistrust: Infancy (first year)	The infant learns to feel safe and secure with a minimal amount of fear.	If the infant's basic physical and psychological needs are met by a responsive, sensitive caregiver, the infant develops a basic sense of trust.
Autonomy vs. shame: Infancy (second year)	The toddler strives to learn independence and self-confidence.	If infants are able to assert independence by not being restrained too much or punished too severely, they are able to develop a sense of autonomy.
Initiative vs. guilt: Preschool years (ages 3 to 5)	The preschooler learns to initiate tasks and grapples with self-control.	Preschoolers assume more responsibility for their behavior. Children need to be able to initiate projects and ask questions. Learning to be responsible without feeling too guilty leads to a sense of initiative.
Industry vs. inferiority: Middle childhood (ages 6 to 12)	The child learns to feel effective in mastering academic skills.	Energies are now directed at gaining knowledge and doing well in school, leading to feelings of competence and productiveness.
Identity vs. role confusion: Adolescence (ages 13 to 19)	The teenager works at refining a sense of self.	Teenagers explore where they are going and who they are. By testing roles and integrating them, they are able to form a sense of identity.
Intimacy vs. isolation: Early adulthood (ages 20s to 30s)	The young adult struggles to form intimate relationships with others.	When young adults are able to form close relationships and gain a capacity for loving others and being loved, their sense of intimacy is enhanced.
Generativity vs. stagnation: Middle adulthood (ages 40s to 50s)	The middle-age person seeks a sense of contributing to the world through family and work.	When adults have achieved a sense of succeeding in domestic and/or occupational domains, their sense of generativity is enhanced.
Integrity vs. despair: Late adulthood (ages 60 on)	The older person feels life has been productive and worthwhile.	Looking back on their lives, when older adults feel a sense of contribution, their sense of integrity is enhanced.

According to Malinowski's observational data, Trobriand children continue to maintain their curiosity and interest in sex throughout childhood—including during the Latency period.

Moreover, in Freud's (1974) model "biology is destiny," meaning that by virtue of the fact that boys have penises, they are destined to be powerful and superior. Because girls lack this impressive organ, they are destined to be dependent and subservient. However, in *matrifocal* societies, this doesn't appear to be the case. The term "matrifocal" is commonly used to refer to households composed of key female decision makers. Cross-cultural variations of the status of men and women reveal that in the matrifocal society of Tahiti, notions of male superiority and female inferiority are not accepted (Lockwood, 2001). Members of this society continue to see women in a largely egalitarian, interdependent way that affords mutual respect for both sexes. Consequently, women own and control land and other resources, control the income they earn, and play an important role in decision making in their society. Further, in societies characterized by *matrilineal* descent (descent through the female line from a common female ancestor), women, having access to and control over resources and authority to make community and household decisions, are viewed as powerful (Prior, 2001). For example, on the island of Rurutu in the South Pacific, women in this matrilineal culture are the breadwinners in their families, which translates into enhanced authority and decision-making prerogatives (Lockwood, 2001).

Feminists argue that in cultures where females are seen as dependent, controlled, and subservient, it is society not biology that contributes to their second-class status (Chodorow, 1989). For example, girls in most cultures are still being predominantly socialized for family roles. Further, cultural ideologies that associate women with motherhood and their critical "instinctual" role as nurturing constrain women from

TABLE 1.5

Child-Care Advice from Erik Erikson	
Stage	**Advice**
Autonomy vs. shame and doubt (2 years)	Recognize children's needs to climb, open and close, push and pull, and hold on and let go. Protect children from excesses, while granting them autonomy in matters they can handle. Avoid overprotection, lack of support, restricting children's freedom of movement, impatience, or continually doing things for children that they can do for themselves.
Initiative vs. guilt (3 to 5 years)	Reward children's explorations, projects, and activities. Don't consider children's motor activity bad, their questions bothersome, or their play activities frivolous; children develop a sense of guilt over self-initiated activities in general.
Industry vs. inferiority (6 years to puberty)	Encourage children to build things, cook, and experience, and offer praise for their results.
Identity vs. role diffusion (10 to 20 years)	Establish firm but fair rules. Be supportive of children, and encourage them to explore their life's goals. Establish a warm and positive relationship. Don't always be the all-knowing one. Don't place undue restrictions on the adolescent.

participation in other areas—namely, in educational and occupational pursuits—and this is what leads to subordinance, dependence, and control.

Considering Erikson's life experiences, it is not surprising that he was alerted to the importance of culture. Erikson's national status, for example, changed from Dane to German to American. He was born of Danish parents; brought up by his mother and the German pediatrician she had married when Erik was a few years old; and moved to the United States where he taught the rest of his life in some of America's finest universities (Coles, 1970; Stevens, 1983). In 1938, only four years after arriving in America, Erikson visited the Sioux Indian Reservation in South Dakota. His work with the Sioux Indians marked the beginning of a lifelong effort to demonstrate how the events of childhood are affected by the inevitable encounter within a given culture. To Erikson, cultural customs affect a number of socialization patterns, from the way mothers hold and feed infants to how they bring up children to behave later on.

Day after day, Erikson came to know the Indian mothers and their children and noted how the character of the Sioux culture shaped children at the various stages of psychosocial development. For example, in his first stage, Trust versus Mistrust, Erikson observed the permissive warmth that many Sioux mothers showed toward their offspring. According to Erikson, meeting the infant's need for love and acceptance lays the foundation for developing a sense of trust. He also noted that the general features of the Sioux child-rearing practices fostered a sense of individual autonomy during the years of 2 to 4. Sioux mothers influenced their children through praise and attitudes of acceptance when displaying valued behaviors, such as girls demonstrating cooking and sewing skills and boys exhibiting good hunting techniques.

To both Freud and Erikson, Mother played the key role in children's development. It was she who guided children successfully (or unsuccessfully) through the first psychosexual and psychosocial stages (Friedman, 1998). Indeed, to Freud, no one could take her place. However, Barry S. Hewlett's (2001) research among the Aka pygmies contradicts both Freud's and Erikson's belief in the centrality of mothering as well as its corollary notion that fathers play distant, primarily moralistic roles in children's development. Aka pygmies are a group of foragers who live in the tropical forests of central Africa. Aka fathers spend a significant portion of their day caring for and nurturing their children. A good father, among the Aka, is a man who stays near his children, shows them affection, and assists the mother with her work. Although there are many cultures that give women the primary responsibility for family matters, there are a number of other cultural systems where men are the active, intimate, and nurturing caregivers (Menon, 2001).

Behaviorism and Social Learning Theories

In the early twentieth century, many American psychologists dismissed such hidden, internal agents as Freud's "id" and "ego" as unfortunate leftovers from the magical thinking of the Middle Ages. The first American psychologists ushered in a new era of pragmatic adherence and scientific preciseness to fact rather than speculative imagination.

Watson's Conditioned Child

John Broadus Watson (1878–1959) was an American psychologist who sought to bolster the scientific character of psychology. Contrary to Freud's and Erikson's theories, Watson (1914) argued that any science of behavior must be based on observable events. His approach to studying behavior is known as **behaviorism**. Watson (1914) set out to demonstrate the relevance of purely behavioral procedures to the study of child behavior. He began his work with newborn infants and the analysis of the conditioning of emotional responses.

Watson's work was heavily influenced by Russian psychologist Ivan Pavlov (1948–1936). Pavlov was the first to scientifically demonstrate the process of **classical conditioning**, a type of learning that results from the repeated pairing of two stimuli. Pavlov taught dogs to salivate to the sound of a bell by pairing it with the presentation of food. In classical conditioning, the response that naturally follows one stimulus (the presentation of food) begins to occur following the other stimulus (a bell), after the two stimuli are repeatedly paired (see Figure 1.1). Watson wondered, "Can classical conditioning be applied to children's behavior?" The experiment with "Little Albert" on which he then embarked was to become an enduring classic.

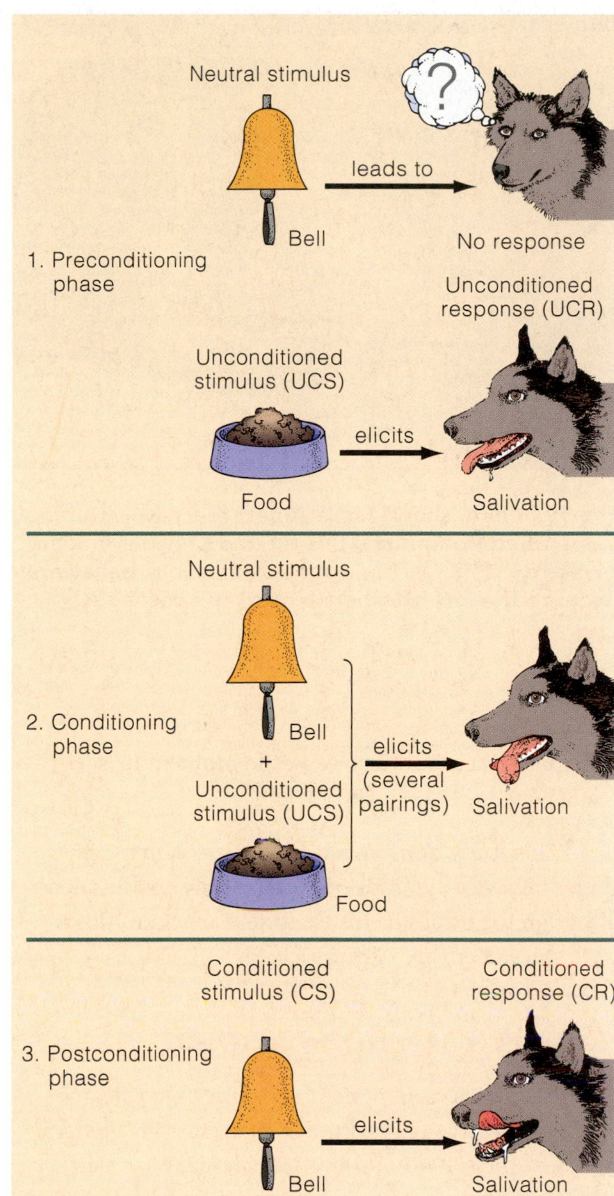

FIGURE 1.1 *Pavlov's Classical Conditioning Experiment*

The three phases of classical conditioning. In the preconditioning phase, the unconditioned stimulus (UCS) always elicits an unconditioned response (UCR), whereas the conditioned stimulus (CS) never does. During the conditioning phase, the CS and UCS are paired repeatedly and eventually associated. At this point, the learner passes into the postconditioning phases, in which the CS alone elicits the original response (now called a conditioned response, or CR).

behaviorism A psychology movement begun by J. B. Watson and embellished by B. F. Skinner, which emphasizes the importance of the environment in shaping behavior via classical and operant conditioning.

classical conditioning Learning that involves the modification of a reflex; the conditioning stimulus, which is neutral at the start, eventually initiates the same behavioral response as the unconditioned stimulus (reflex reaction).

Classical Conditioning Albert, an 11-month-old child, was shown a small, white rat, which he reacted to with pleasure and curiosity. However, just as Little Albert reached out to touch the rat, Watson banged on a steel bar with a hammer. As Watson describes the experiment, "The infant jumped violently, and fell forward, burying his face in the mattress." As the infant reached for the rat again, Watson banged again. "Again the infant jumped violently, fell forward and began to whimper." Three times Albert reached for the rat; three times Watson made a loud noise as he did. Watson describes what happened next:

> [The child] puckered his face and cried. Then I let him quiet down. Again the assistant brings in the rat. This time something new develops: No longer do I have to rap the steel bar. He shows fear at the sight of the rat. He makes the same reaction to it as he makes to the sound of the steel bar. He

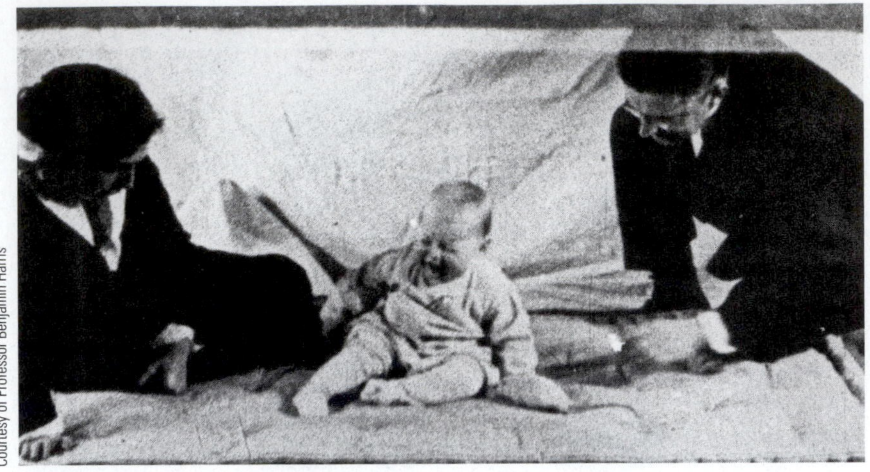

Courtesy of Professor Benjamin Harris

This photo, taken from a 1920 film, shows Little Albert reacting with dismay to a white rat. As described in the text, this rat had previously been paired with a very unpleasant noise. On the right is the famous behavioral psychologist John Watson; to the left of Albert is Watson's colleague, Rosalie Rayner.

begins to cry and turn away the moment he sees it. (Watson, 1928, pp. 52–53)

This study demonstrated to Watson that children's behavior can indeed be classically conditioned—although the ethics of his treatment of Little Albert have since been strongly criticized.

Skinner's Mechanical Child

operant conditioning According to Skinner, a process of learning in which reinforced behaviors tend to be repeated and occur more frequently.

positive reinforcement A consequent event that occurs after a desired behavior, increasing the probability the behavior will recur.

negative reinforcement Removing a condition previously in effect to increase the probability of a response.

By the time his career ended, no American research psychologist was better known than Burrhus Frederic Skinner (1904–1990). Proceeding along Watsonian lines, B. F. Skinner (1974) did not concern himself with studying internal motives to explain behavior. Skinner (1972) maintained that all behavior is a result of classical and *operant conditioning* with the larger part of behavior being learned via the latter. In **operant conditioning**, the subject is active; that is, he or she operates on the environment. Moreover, the subject's behavior is voluntary and is determined by its consequences. If the consequences of a particular behavior are rewarding, the child will likely repeat this behavior. However, if a behavior leads to consequences that are not rewarding or are painful, the child is less likely to repeat the behavior. If a friend says to you, "I love that green sweater you're wearing, the color looks great on you!" the odds are that you'll wear it more frequently. If, however, a friend says, "Are you feeling sick today, you look so tired and pale—maybe it's that green sweater you're wearing," you may stuff the sweater in your bottom drawer.

At the same time, Skinner (1948) argued that individuals have very little control over their environment. Just as we deserve no credit for inherited qualities, Skinner maintained we can take no credit for what we become after being born; external factors simply exist and have effects on us. We cannot freely choose nor decide what conditions will affect us or what we become. For Skinner, there is no ego that eventually will enable us to take over and give deliberate, conscious, rational directions to our lives. We are never really free; our "choices" are dependent on our exposure to a multitude of environmental conditions (Skinner, 1981).

Reinforcement Skinner emphasized the importance of rewards in shaping behavior. *Reward,* however, is a term that Skinner would find imprecise. What most of us think as a reward is a form of **positive reinforcement**, which can be anything that makes it more likely that a person will repeat a response. Words of praise, bear-hugs, money, a piece of candy are all potential reinforcers. For example, a mother may increase the probability that her son will eat his spinach if she reinforces him with his favorite chocolate bar when he cleans his plate. In this case, the chocolate bar is a positive reinforcer; it is a consequent event after a desired behavior that increases the probability that the behavior will recur.

In contrast, **negative reinforcement**, involves removing something unpleasant to influence a child's behavior. If, for example, a parent is screaming at her children to come to dinner, to stop their mom's tirade, they may all scramble to the table. The unpleasant screaming stops as soon as the children are all seated at the table, so the act of sitting down stops the unpleasant situation. The pleasant state of quiet is, for the children, a negative reinforcer for sitting down. The next time the mother starts calling the children to dinner, they can be expected to come to the table more promptly because sitting down produced the happy state of quiet the first time. Both positive and negative reinforcement, then, are rewarding. Negative reinforcement is not the same as punishment. As you will see in Chapter 10, punishment involves inflicting some kind of pain—either physical or emotional.

Behaviorists, such as Watson and Skinner, see children as raw material that must be molded into shape. Children's natural impulses have to be controlled or shaped as firmly as bed-wetting and thumb-sucking.

An effective way to shape children's behavior is through reinforcement—either positive or negative. A child's personality, as defined by Skinner, is the result of that individual's reinforcement history and genetic makeup. Skinner never actually set forth a scientific theory of children's development, but he presented in his novel *Walden Two* (Skinner, 1948) his fictionalized notions of how children should be raised. In a mythical American town he called Walden Two, children were not to be raised by their parents (whom Skinner deemed incapable) but by professionally trained "behavioral engineers" who were capable of shaping children's behavior systematically by reinforcing desired actions and ignoring undesirable ones, a technique known as **behavior modification**.

Bandura's Imitating Child

Albert Bandura (1925–) became the best-known advocate of **social learning theory**—a viewpoint that got its name from the emphasis it placed on social variables as determinants of behavior and personality. Whereas Skinner held that the environment influences behavior directly, Bandura (1977; 1991) maintains that the child is the active agent who interacts with his or her surroundings. The behavior of the child and environmental events are interconnected determinants of each other; the environment may affect the child's behavior, but the child may also influence the environment. Children are, therefore, freer to monitor and control their own actions.

Did you ever model your behavior after some hero when you were a young child—perhaps, Wonder Woman, the Bionic Woman, He-Man, or Spider Man? Bandura (1977, 1991) stresses that many kinds of behavior are learned simply by observation and **imitation**, or emulating, based on self-interest. Children learn from models how the observed behavior might aid or hinder them in fulfilling their needs in the future. The appearance of social learning had a refreshing, immediate appeal, for the theory saw children as social creatures who do learn a great deal—language, eating habits, or mischief—from observing what others say and do and then emulating them. Later, Bandura refined his theory further by pointing out the influence of cognition in modeling. He gave additional weight to the children's ability to decide for themselves which behaviors to model, based on their own personal standards (Bandura, 1997).

Whereas Skinner maintained that children will only reproduce behaviors that are directly reinforced, Bandura contends that children will also learn when reinforcement is only vicarious or indirectly reinforced. For example, if Lin observes that Kendall is rewarded by her dad for saying "please," she too will say please in a similar circumstance. This nonreinforced type of learning, **vicarious reinforcement**, plays a central role in social learning theory.

Bandura (1991) further asserts that adequate attention must be given to cognitive and motivational factors as determinants of behavior. Cognitive processes play a central role in regulating what children attend to, how they describe or think about what they see, and whether they repeat it to themselves or lodge it in memory. Some developmental trends in imitation then are apparent. Young infants' modeling, or imitative behaviors, are mainly instantaneous, whereas older children, because of their more sophisticated cognitive functioning, can store and recall after extended periods of time. As language and memory skills become more advanced, children's abilities to profit from models are enhanced. Children without an adequate coding system will fail to store what they have seen or heard. Older children are able to pay attention to pertinent cues in a modeling situation.

The Behaviorists and Culture

Watson placed a great deal of emphasis on raising an emotionally independent child. Some interesting differences emerge, however, when "emotional independence" is examined cross-culturally. In a study comparing a sample of mothers of preschoolers in Japan and in Israel, Israeli mothers tended to emphasize a child's ability to be alone as an example of emotional independence (Osterweil & Nagano, 1991). They appreciated this type of emotional dependence because they valued initiative in self-expression and the capacity for self-occupation. Japanese mothers, however, valued the development of the capacity for establishing social relationships and viewed this as the measure of emotional independence. The authors concluded that emotional independence "is viewed as a manifestation of separateness in Israel, but in Japan it indicates a close relationship with mother and compliance with her wishes" (p. 373). What constitutes emotional independence can be culturally based.

Similarly, attitudes toward punishment can vary among cultures. Skinner's concept of behavior modification stressed avoiding the use of punishment in socializing children. To Skinner inflicting some kind of

behavior modification
A technique, defined by B. F. Skinner, that would shape children's behavior by reinforcing desired actions and ignoring undesirable ones.

social learning theory
A theory by Bandura that emphasizes social variables as determinants of behavior and personality.

imitation
Many kinds of behavior are learned by observing and then mimicking the behavior of others.

vicarious reinforcement
A central tenet of social learning theory that says learning will take place even when reinforcement is indirectly applied.

verbal or physical pain does not teach the child appropriate ways of responding. Thus, he preferred the technique of noticing and praising children for positive behaviors and ignoring, when possible, negative behaviors. Whether or not adults use punishment relates to their attitudes about its effectiveness; those with positive attitudes about the effectiveness of punishment tend to use it more frequently (Durrant, Broberg, & Rose-Krasnor, 1999). In a study, both foreign-born and native-born Mexican American mothers tended to have negative views about the use of punishment, and rarely used it as a control method when children misbehaved (Buriel, Mercado, Rodriguez, & Chavez, 1991). Praising children for good behavior was their chief socializing method in disciplining children. When some sort of disciplinary action was necessary, withdrawal of privileges, rather than punishment, was used. Similarly, mothers from Mamachi, Japan used considerable indulgence, praise, and permissiveness in their early child socialization practices (Vogel, 1996). Close emotional bonding was used to shape children's behavior and maintain discipline without resorting to punishment, which they believed would provoke rebellion.

However, a study of Rajput mothers from Khalapur, India (Rajputs are a caste in India, which consists of landowners) found they did believe in the effectiveness of punishment and were more apt to use it more frequently. Praise, they tended to believe, was not very effective in training children, and so they used it very infrequently in socializing their children (Minturn & Lambert, 1964). The absence of praise, the experimenters noted, was the result of a disciplining policy designed to train "compliant personalities" in children. Further, Rajput mothers tended to believe that if children were praised, they would become spoiled because they would think their parents "love[d] them too much." Physical punishment was used more frequently for shaping the behavior of boys and to a lesser extent girls.

Cognitive-Developmental Theory

Piaget's Problem-Solving Child

For more than 50 years Jean Piaget (1896–1980) studied how children of different ages solved reasoning problems. Categorizing this continuous process of cognitive development into four periods of cognitive growth, he labeled them the Sensorimotor (ages birth–2); Preoperational (ages 2–7); Concrete Operational (ages 7–11); and Formal Operational (ages 11–15). According to Piaget, each stage is associated with the appearance of certain kinds of behaviors and reasoning strategies (as can be seen in Table 1.6). Although each new stage represents an advancement in the way children reason about their environment, limitations are also apparent until children reach the last stage of "formal thinking." How do children develop more sophisticated reasoning strategies that allow for cognitive growth and enable them to progress from one stage to the next?

TABLE 1.6

Piaget's Stages of Cognitive Development

Stage	Ages	Major Characteristics
Sensorimotor	0–2	All knowledge is acquired through senses and movement (such as looking and grasping). Thinking occurs at the same speed as physical development. Object permanence develops.
Preoperational	2–7	Thinking separates from movement and increases greatly in speed. The ability to think in symbols and nonlogical, "magical" thinking begins. Animism—all objects have thoughts and feelings—and egocentric thinking—being unable to see the world from others' points of view—develop.
Concrete operational	7–11	Logical thinking develops, including classifying objects and mathematical principles, but only as they apply to real, concrete objects. The abilities to grasp conservation of liquid, area, and volume concepts and to infer what others may be feeling or thinking develop.
Formal operational	11 and up	Logical thinking extends to hypothetical and abstract concepts. Reasoning using metaphors and analogies begins. Exploration of values, beliefs, and philosophies begins. Not all people use formal operations to the same degree, and some don't use them at all.

How Children's Minds Come to Know the World

When discussing a particular system reflecting some specific knowledge, Piaget (1929) used the term *scheme.* **Schemes** reflect a particular way of interacting with the environment. They reflect children's knowledge at all stages of development—their "old information," or what they know. A scheme may be as simple as knowing how to pick up a chess piece, or as complex as applying a strategy for beating a particular chess opponent. The process of taking in or understanding events of the world by matching the perceived features of those events to one's existing schemes is known as **assimilation**. Children are continually working toward establishing harmony, *equilibrium* in Piagetian terms, between themselves and their environment.

If they encounter some task, experience, or situation that cannot be readily assimilated, one of two consequences can be expected. The first is that the event is not assimilated at all. It is ignored or passed by. The encounter with the environment simply does not register on the child. The second possible consequence between perceived environment and available schemes is not outright rejection but dissatisfaction or disequilibrium and continued efforts to achieve a match.

So it is that schemes, under pressures from perceived realities of the environment, are altered in form or multiplied to accommodate for the lack of an adequate match. Piaget used the term **accommodation** to identify this process of altering or modifying existing schemes to permit the assimilation of events that would otherwise be incomprehensible. As children get older, more sophisticated schemes form, providing them with more efficient reasoning skills and adaptability to their surroundings. If the structural components of the child's cognition do not change with differential exposure and learning, development will not occur.

Although Piaget is not considered to be a personality theorist, he worked extensively with children in trying to understand their patterns of learning. It is from his work in cognition that we receive vivid impressions of not only how children learn but what children are like. In this sense, we can profit from his child development advice (see Table 1.7).

TABLE 1.7

Piaget's Child Development Advice
▪ Remember that children are active, curious creatures and give them opportunities to actively explore their environment.
▪ Expect active children to find it difficult to make fine distinctions in what they can or cannot do. Therefore, they delight in pulling the cord on their "Speak and Say" and see very little difference between that and pulling on the cord to the television set.
▪ Give them extensive opportunities to engage in discovery learning, so they can actively construct their worldviews.
▪ Allow children to engage in spontaneous interactions with the environment; these experiences are critical to their progressing toward a more accurate view of the world.

Piaget and Culture

Piaget sent forth the notion that cognitive development is universal and follows the same path. In particular, he believed that the same cognitive stages will occur and follow each other in the same order of succession everywhere in the world. However, in traditional cultures, there is commonly a time lag of about two years before concrete operations come to be attained (Jahoda, 1998). The original Piagetian tasks dealing with physical and mathematico-logical problems, however, are not suitable for cross-cultural studies, because they presume a background of Western-type schooling.

Piaget (1950) also suggested that the relative difficulty of tasks remains constant across cultures. The outcome here is quite clear: There are wide performance variations in different tasks domains, so that relative difficulty does not remain constant. For example, when comparing Inuit children from Cape Dorset in Canada and Baoule children (West African agriculturists) on Piagetian tasks, interesting differences in their performance are apparent (Dasen, 1984). Piaget's beaker problem is often used to assess children's understanding of the concept of conservation of liquids. Following the classic procedure, the child is shown two identical, tall, linear beakers that contain the same amount of liquid. The child agrees that the amount of liquid is the same in both beakers. Then the experimenter pours the content from one of the tall beakers into a shallow, wide beaker. The child is then asked if the beakers now contain the same amount of liquid. The children's understanding of horizontality was also assessed. Horizontality tests require children to understand that when a glass containing a liquid is tilted in various angles the surface of the liquid will always be horizontal.

As one can see in Figure 1.2a, 90 percent of Inuit children understood horizontality by age 8 and 100

scheme A particular system, in Piaget's theory, that reflects what the child knows—his or her arsenal of knowledge.

assimilation According to Piaget, the method of applying old information (schemes) when encountering new learning situations.

accommodation According to Piaget, the process of modifying a scheme or adding a new one.

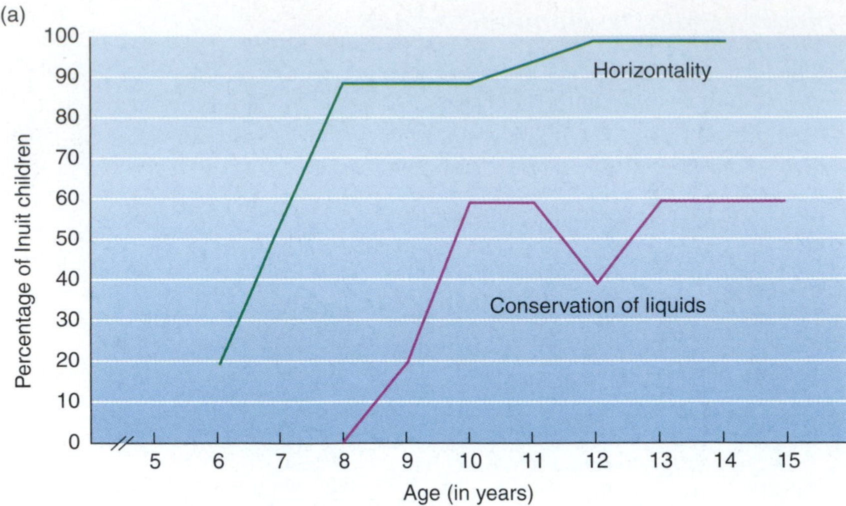

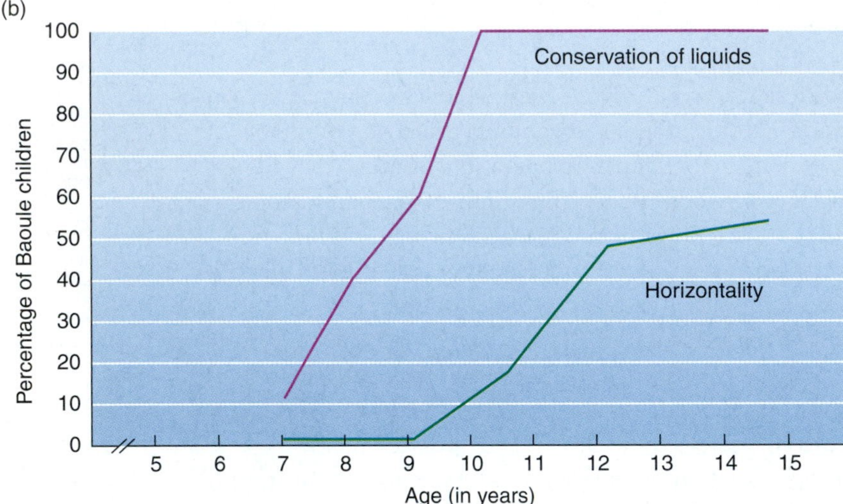

FIGURE 1.2 ***Comparisons of Performances of Inuit and Baoule Children on Conservation of Liquids and Horizontality Tasks***

Achievement of horizontality and conservation of liquids between the ages of 6 and 15 among Inuit and Baoule children

From "The Cross-Cultural Study of Intelligence: Piaget and the Baoule," by P. R. Dasen, 1984, *International Journal of Psychology, 19,* 407–434.

percent by age 12, but only 60 percent grasped the conservation of liquids even by age 15. In contrast, approximately 55 percent of the Baoule children understood horizontality by age 15, but 100 percent had an understanding of the conservation of liquids by the age of 10 (Figure 1.2b).

In these cultures, and worldwide as well, cognitive skills that are considered adaptive are taught and their importance is stressed. The Inuit are a nomadic, hunting tribe that value spatial skills and subsequently acquire ideas like horizontality quite readily. The Baoule are an agricultural people, who produce food and thus assign value to quantitative concepts. The lesson here is that individual differences in cognitive abilities are fostered by culture-specific experiences—a lesson that is accepted by neo-Piagetians today (Segall, Dasen, Berry, & Poortinga, 1999).

A number of legacies are left behind by the psychologists of the twentieth century. The main contributions that Freud, Erikson, Skinner, and Piaget gave to the field of child development are summarized in Table 1.8.

Assessing Theories

We have discussed the most influential early theories about the nature of children's development. An important question that remains is, Why is it important to study these classic theories—or any theories? One reason is that they provide a framework for studying children. Given the vast number of events and conditions that influence children's development, we need theories to help give shape to an otherwise large and unmanageable collection of data. As such, theories can be likened to a special pair of glasses through which children and their development are observed.

A look at a hypothetical example will help you to see how these special lenses work. Seventeen-year-old Renee is continually having fights with her parents about her schoolwork. The main area of dissension is her poor grade in English. If you don your "Erikson glasses," you may explain her behavior in this way: Renee is more than likely going through an identity crisis, trying to find herself and establish her sense of independence. If you exchange these glasses for your Skinnerian horn rims, you will see Renee from a different perspective: Renee's argumentative behavior undoubtedly is being reinforced; maybe the only time she gets attention at home is when she brings home a poor grade in English. Your Piagetian lenses enable you to focus on another perspective: Renee is struggling with her Formal Operational stage and is having difficulty mastering some of the abstract concepts associated with literary criticism. Thus, she is doing poorly in English.

The situation—Renee doing poorly in English—remains the same, but the way you perceive that situation changes with each switch of eyeglasses. Understanding theories will show how variations in perspective can lead to markedly varied interpretations of development. You must also be aware, however, that theorists propounding a certain philosophy on children's development may be somewhat nearsighted; a

TABLE 1.8

Contributions of Four 20th Century Psychologists

Psychologist	Major Area of Concern	Premise	Conceptions	Sources of Problems	Legacy
Freud	Personality development	Human beings are motivated to reduce tensions produced by sexual and aggressive drives; the unconscious mind directs and controls behavior; children go through psychosexual stages	Psychosexual stages; the first five years are important to later behavior	Fixation during psychosexual stages; repressed sexual and aggressive drives	Early experiences may influence later behavior. Made us aware that children have sexual pleasures and fantasies long before they reach adolescence. Before Freud, children were thought of as innocent and sexless creatures. Made us realize how important parental love and acceptance are to children's development. Gave to the field of child development a wealth of ideas about children's behavior.
Erikson	Ego development through the psychosocial stages	Each stage of life produces a psychosocial crisis that children must solve to effectively function at a later stage of development	Psychosocial stages, spanning a lifetime	Too much attention or not enough in each stage, resulting in maladjustment	Relationships with parents and peers important. Strongly emphasized social and cultural influences on development. His delineation of development and crises of the healthy personality emphasized normal, not abnormal, development.
Skinner	Environmental effects on behavior	Environment is a crucial factor in determining behavior; the consequences of our behavior (positive, negative, neutral) shape our personality	Environment continually acts on the individual; no stages of development	Excessive punishment, leading to undesirable behavior	Underscored the importance of environment and reinforcement in shaping children's behavior. Behavior modification—ignoring negative behavior and rewarding positive behavior—considered his greatest legacy. Brought "science" into studying children's behavior.
Piaget	Development of thought and reasoning in children	Children are active explorers seeking to establish harmony between what they know and what they experience	Qualitative cognitive stages; sensorimotor to formal	Nonstimulating environment; not recognizing the child's cognitive developmental level	Gave us the rudiments of human cognitive development. His assimilation/accommodation model of cognitive development emphasized the active, constructive nature of the child. Helped us to accept the idea that children's cognitive behavior is intrinsically, rather than extrinsically, motivated. Theory has produced thousands of studies on cognition around the world.

specific theory may be shortsighted in that it only focuses on a particular subset of the entire domain of variables. For example, behaviorists believe that in studying children's behavior, you need to be concerned with only observable events. Therefore, unobservable aspects of behavior such as motivations or emotions may be ignored. Theories are a way of seeing children's behavior—and their behavior is often interpreted in light of that orientation.

Any theory has positives and negatives, strong points and weaknesses. Freud, on the positive side, made us aware that children have sexual pleasures and fantasies long before they reach adolescence (Fromm, 1980). One of the most significant ideas in Freud's theory was the realization of the need for maternal acceptance and affection. Some problems in accepting Freud's theory as a valid reflector of children's development include the source of his data (a small sample of an atypical group of adults); his methodology (theory based on recollections of his patients' childhood memories); and the fact that he did not directly test children during their years of growth. These factors along with the vagueness and lack of empirical proof of such ideas as the Oedipus complex, have significantly reduced the status of psychoanalytic theory among contemporary scholars.

Erikson's theory is subject to similar mythological criticisms. He relied on subjective data built out of his own experiences and recollections of patients in therapy. However, one of his strongest contributions relates to his emphasis on the importance of social and cultural influences on children's development. This perspective is still prominent today.

Perhaps the most salient weakness of the behaviorist approach associated with Watson and Skinner is the assumption that development is a mechanistic process. The behaviorist assumption that human beings function *as if* they are machines is improbable and has led to an overly narrow focus of observable and measurable behaviors that fit best into a mechanistic model. Watson's work did, however, open up a new era in psychology. His theory effected a complete change from Freud's nonempirical approach to an objective study of behavior. One weakness of Skinner's theory is that it fails to explain behavior that doesn't fit neatly into the controlled experimental situation. One of his greatest contributions, however, is behavior modification, in which undesirable behavior is changed through positive reinforcement.

The legacy of Bandura's social learning theory is the acknowledgment that human beings imitate the behaviors of others and have cognitive, symbolic capacities that allow them to regulate their own behavior and, to some degree, control their environment rather than being completely controlled by it.

See if you can answer the question in the *Concept Check* about this photo.

Piaget's (1950) theory breathed fresh life into how thought and logic develop in children. Criticisms of Piaget's theory center on the particulars of his descriptions of children's cognitive development at each of his four stages of cognitive development, as well as his basic concept of distinct cognitive stages. These criticisms shall be covered in more depth in the chapters that follow.

It is apparent that no one theory offers a complete, comprehensive picture of children's development. Each theory has, however, something to contribute to the field as a whole: unique ideas, observations, and evidence. Taken together, they can give us considerable insight into understanding children's development.

Concept Checks

1. How would Freud, Skinner, and Piaget analyze the children's (ages 4–7) activities in the photo above?
2. Matching: Link the major strengths with each of the following theorists:

___ 1. Freud	a. expounded the power of positive reinforcement
___ 2. Skinner	b. noted the role that observation plays in development
___ 3. Erikson	c. saw children as curious, exploratory creatures
___ 4. Bandura	d. emphasized the need for maternal affection
___ 5. Watson	e. emphasized social and cultural influences on behavior
___ 6. Piaget	f. first emphasized the objective study of behavior

Contexts of Development

Before Beginning . . .

After reading this section, you will be able to

- explain the contextual models of R. Q. Bell, Patricia Minuchin, Urie Bronfenbrenner, and Lev Vygotsky.

As the field of child development became more empirical, and the theorists we just discussed looked closely at many aspects of the developing child, it became clear that children's physical, cognitive, and socioemotional development are strongly shaped and molded by the principal caregiver which, in most cases, is Mother. Further insight into children's development comes from R. Q. Bell, Patricia Minuchin, Urie Bronfenbrenner, and Lev Vygotsky who moved beyond the confines of studying children from a mother-to-child influential perspective as well as underscoring the importance of a number of powerful contexts that impact children's development.

Bell and Reciprocating Influences

For many years, developmentalists assumed that variations in parents' behavior cause variations in children's behavior. For example, they assumed that children are more prosocial when their parents act in warm and loving ways toward them. But, could this causal arrow go in the opposite direction? It could, and it does. Richard Q. Bell (1979) was one of the first to suggest that researchers should focus on the mutually interactive effects of the mother and child. As evidence became available that children are not passive creatures, the idea of the actively thinking child was brought quickly to bear on the study of parenting and children's development. Rather than being faithful recorders of adult directions, children are now seen as capable of eliciting, maintaining, and modifying their environment and the behavior of others.

Current developmental theorists suggest that children create their own experiences from the opportunities afforded by their rearing environment. It is further recognized that parents and children engage in a constant two-way flow of influence, and that the relationship between the parent and the child is interactive. As Robert Cairns (1998) points out, however, the idea of bidirectionality does not assume that parents and children exercise equal influence over each other. The evidence from the past 20 years indicates that if influence is a two-way street, one direction is a four-lane expressway (caregivers) and the other an alleyway (children). Moreover, the weight of influence of parent or child is affected by the type of interaction, and the age and developmental status of the participants. Thus, in recent years, a more interactive, fluid, and complex point of view about parenting and children's behavior has emerged. Bell's model has made us aware that socialization depends on the reciprocal influences of each person in the system on every other person.

Minuchin and the Family Systems Model

Whereas Bell focused on the reciprocating influences between mother and child, Patricia Minuchin's (1985) **family systems model** underscores the bidirectional influences and reciprocal relationships among all family members. It is interesting to note that for many years fathers were not part of the family system. In fact, prior to the 1970s, fathers were virtually ignored in developmental research, as they were not considered potent forces in influencing children's development. The father was seen simply as a secondary figure and at the very most played a supporting role for the mother. These earlier researchers may have been inclined to agree with the bemused view of the famous anthropologic, Margaret Mead, who quipped, "Fathers are a biological necessity, but a social mistake!" Today, we have broadened the scope of research to include the study of not only father's influence but that of siblings and other family members as well.

Minuchin (1988) regards the family as a complex system in which the behavior of each member of the nuclear family affects those of others. Therefore, to fully understand children's development, it is necessary to recognize the interdependence among the roles and functions of all family members. From a systems perspective, an open system such as the family is a complex, integrated whole, with organized patterns of interaction. Family members are not detached and self-contained; each member very much influences other members and, in turn, is influenced by them (Minuchin, 1988).

Minuchin's model underscores that children's socialization depends on the reciprocal influences of each person in the system on every other person. As such, she makes us aware that children's behavior is due more than just to their parents' treatment of them. For example, a child's whining does not necessarily

family systems model
A theory that emphasizes that each member of the family influences other members and is influenced by them. It underscores the bidirectional and reciprocal nature of family relationships.

cause the parent to give in to its coercion. Parents and children can, however, create a pattern of interaction, a coercive cycle, that has negative consequences for all.

Bronfenbrenner and Ecological Contexts

A theory contains broadly applicable knowledge, **generalizability**, and certainly the classic theories such as Freud, Skinner, and Piaget can claim this quality. Two theories, rather than taking the position of developmental universals, emphasize *context specificity.* **Context** refers to the social relationships in which children are involved, the features of their particular society or culture, and the social institutions that affect the beliefs and behavior of parents and other caregivers. One early theorist in this group is Urie Bronfenbrenner (1989), whose **ecological approach** stresses that development takes place in a variety of contexts that extend from the immediate physical environment of the child out to the society and culture. He has also recently further refined his theory to include basic biological contexts of the child (1995). These contexts, as seen in Figure 1.3, are best viewed as concentric networks of five interrelated systems: the microsystem, mesosystem, exosystem, macrosystem, and chronosystem.

generalizability Refers to the extent to which research findings may be applied to broader populations or settings.

context This refers to the social relationships in which children are involved, the features of their particular society or culture, and the social institutions that affect the beliefs and behavior of parents and other caregivers.

ecological approach Bronfenbrenner's model, which emphasizes five environmental subsystems that influence the child's development.

The Microsystem

Bronfenbrenner calls the innermost environmental setting the *microsystem.* It includes family, peers, school, and neighborhood. All relationships within it are bidirectional and reciprocal; the environment influences the child, and the child affects the environment. Children are active in constructing their worlds. For example, 4-year-old Michael's microsystem changes because his mother has gone back to work full time after being home for the first three years of his life. This decision, of course, affects Michael's immediate environment. The microsystem is also affected by what Bronfenbrenner called "third parties." In this case, as a result of his mother's working, Michael's grandparents, may decide to help care for him while she is gone.

The Mesosystem

The next level of the environment, according to Bronfenbrenner, is the *mesosystem,* which includes links between home, school, and neighborhood. For optimal development to occur in children, says Bronfenbrenner, child-rearing supports must exist in a larger environment. He emphasizes the importance of connections or relationships among microsystems to mesosystems. To illustrate, as a result of his mother's working, Michael now attends a child-care program three mornings a week. Michael's mother and his teacher keep in constant touch about how he is doing. Michael's experiences at school will affect his behavior in the microsystem.

The Exosystem

The next environmental system, the *exosystem,* consists of settings that do not include the child but that affect the child, such as city government, the workplace, school board, and mass media. For example, Michael's mother works at a firm that allows flexible working hours and paid absence when Michael is sick. These work policies affect Michael in positive ways. Further, as a result of her new job, Michael's family decides to move to a small community, which has great schools and a village government that sponsors community improvements, such as parks, tennis courts, and a pool. Again, Michael's microsystem is affected in positive ways.

Some children, such as Linda, may not be as fortunate as Michael. Linda's mother also works, but she works very long hours and is away from home for most of the day. Linda's family may not have the support of loving grandparents, and she may have to stay with a caregiver that doesn't pay much attention to her. Her community also may be poor and lack the tax base to support tennis courts and pools.

The Macrosystem

The *macrosystem* involves the dominant attitudes and ideologies of the child's culture. In the United States, Michael's mother is not considered a "bad mother" because she works. In Japan, however, there are still some strong cultural messages that convey to mothers that they should stay home and help to educate the child; working in Japan may be seen in a less favorable light. Thus the values, laws, and customs of a particular culture are also an important environment affecting children's development. In Sweden, most mothers work and the government supports high-quality child care for a nominal fee to working parents. Other countries, such as the United States, may believe that child-care benefits are not a governmental issue but a private one. Many children in the United States receive poor-quality child care because their parents cannot afford to pay for more expensive, quality care.

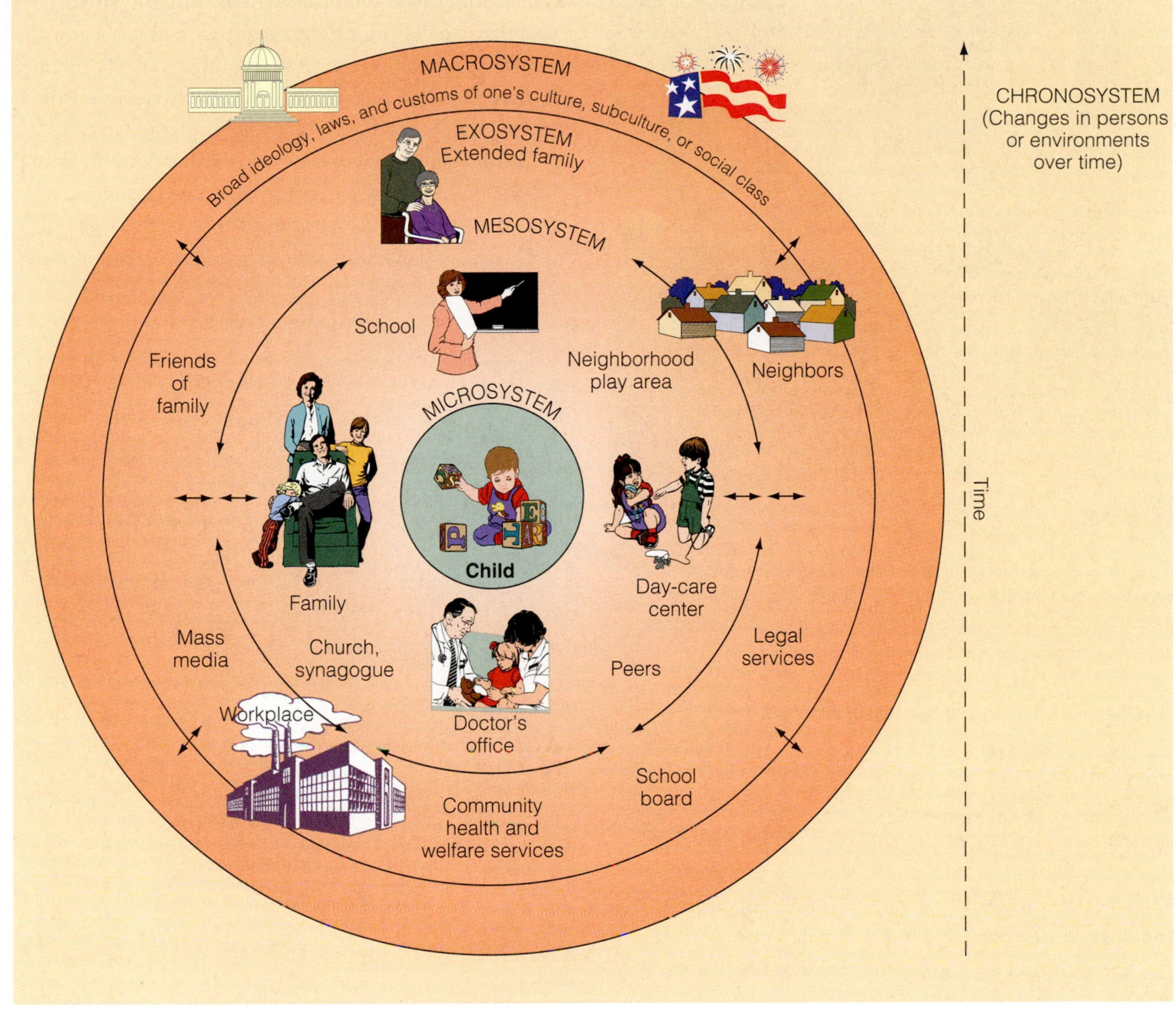

FIGURE 1.3 ***Bronfenbrenner's Model of Ecological Systems***

Bronfenbrenner's ecological model of the environment as a series of nested structures. The microsystem refers to relations between the child and the immediate environment, the mesosystem to connections among the child's immediate settings, the exosystem to social settings that affect but do not contain the child, the macrosystem to the overarching ideology of the culture, and the chronosystem to changes in persons or environments over time.

Based on Bronfenbrenner, 1979.

The Chronosystem

The *chronosystem* is the context of time and includes patterns of stability and change in children's environment over time. Michael's mother after working for a little over a year is quitting because she is going to have twins. Michael's world changes because his mother is now home; he is not going to child care anymore. He sees his grandparents less frequently, and, shortly, he will have to adjust to two tiny new siblings. So, children are affected not only by their current environment but by changes that occur in that environment.

More than any other theorist, Bronfenbrenner makes us aware of the environmental specificity in children's development. As such, we gain a broader picture of the environmental systems that affect children's development which, in turn, has enabled researchers to gain a more comprehensive understanding of children's development in social as well as cultural context. The weakness of his theory, however, is overlooking the role of maturational processes in children's development.

© Sean Sprague/Stock Boston

The most global of all systems is the macrosystem, which involves the culture in which a child lives, according to Bronfenbrenner's ecological approach.

Vygotsky's Sociocultural Contexts

Whereas Bronfenbrenner sees children's development occurring in a number of complex environmental contexts, a second contextualist theory was presented by Russian psychologist Lev Vygotsky (1896–1934). Over the past decade there has been a major upsurge of interest in Vygotsky's ideas, reflected in the dramatic rise in citations of his publications, new translations of his writings and research, and books about his life and work. Several factors seem to have played a role in the current interest in Vygotsky in the United States.

It is only relatively recent that Vygotsky's writings have become available. In 1934, shortly before his death, Vygotsky wrote *Thought and Language* (1962). Two years after its publication, the book was suppressed in the Soviet Union because of disputes within the nation's psychological community. When the disputes ended in 1962, it was once again distributed. So, it has only been since then that Vygotsky's theory has been read, scrutinized, and researched.

zone of proximal development
Vygotsky's phrase to describe the range of skills a child has not yet mastered, but could accomplish with the assistance provided by adults and more knowledgeable peers.

culture
A culture reflects the values, ideals, and beliefs of a particular group of people that are passed on from one generation to the next.

Another possible reason for new interest in Vygotsky's ideas is that they are directly relevant to issues in education. Prior to Vygotsky's theory, the child's cognitive developmental level was often determined on the basis of how he or she answered questions or solved problems posed by some assessment measure or Piagetian task. Tests and Piagetian tasks reveal the current mode of the child's cognitive capabilities. Vygotsky disagreed with this way of thinking and proposed that we consider two developmental levels in determining the child's level of cognitive development. The first level he called the child's *actual developmental level,* one that is established by tests or Piagetian tasks, which shows completed levels of cognitive development.

The second and more important level, argued Vygotsky, is the child's *potential developmental level,* one that is currently evolving. This sort of learning potential cannot be revealed by traditional tests. Rather, the child's potential developmental level of intellectual functioning is best understood when a sensitive instructor *extends* the child's actual developmental level by working slightly above the child's actual level. He called this the **zone of proximal development**, which defines those cognitive functions that have not yet matured but are in the process of maturation. The zone of proximal development will be addressed in Chapter 9. Such a notion of learning potential and learning readiness have significant implications for teaching as well as how we measure children's cognitive competencies.

In addition, researchers were looking for theories that considered cultural and social contexts as influential factors impacting children's cognitive development, and Vygotsky's theory emphasized uniquely three ecological contexts—culture, social, and historical contexts—as powerful determinants in shaping children's behavior.

Cultural Contexts

Whereas Piaget's theory ignored the culturally specific nature of children's learning, Vygotsky made culture an important feature of his theory. One's **culture**, according to Vygotsky, comprises the environment that humans have created and continue to perpetuate in their caregiving practices. Culture consists of human "designs for living," which are embodied in beliefs, values, customs, and activities. His theory emphasized the collective wisdom of each culture that is then passed on to its children (Ratner, 2000).

As cultures develop, people create a number of tools necessary to master their environment. Each culture targets different behaviors and selects different skills for children to learn. In an agricultural community, for example, this may mean children learn such skills as the proper use of farming tools or how to take care of the animals. In another culture, for example, the Zinacanteco Indians in southern Mexico, girls learn how to weave wool into beautiful blankets. Each culture transmits the appropriate learning tools necessary to their culture.

Social Contexts

Vygotsky also emphasized that learning occurs in an interpersonal, social context. To Vygotsky, thinking is a process of social interaction between children and more experienced and knowledgeable members of society. These social interactions help children to master culture-specific skills and behaviors that will enable them to successfully adapt to their particular community. Development then is largely due to social processes. As will become apparent to you in later chapters, learning to Vygotsky is a collaborative enterprise. Through formal and informal instruction, adults and peers play an important role in transmitting cultural knowledge and helping children develop more complex cognitive and behavioral skills. In this way, children acquire the unique tools necessary for successful adaptation to their culture (see Cultural Variations).

Historical Contexts

From Vygotsky's viewpoint, the history of the society in which a child is reared as well as the child's own developmental history in terms of his or her experiences in that society are both very important in determining the ways in which the child will think. Furthermore, advanced modes of thinking—conceptual thinking—must be transmitted to children via words, so language becomes a crucial cognitive tool for deciding how children learn to think.

Vygotsky died prematurely from tuberculosis at the age of 38. Despite his short life, Vygotsky published more than 180 books and articles on his theory and research. In the early years of the communist regime, Vygotsky was considered the chief architect of Soviet developmental psychology. Today, his writings and research are also significantly impacting the thinking of developmental psychologists in the United States, and the popularity of his theory continues to grow.

Concept Checks

Matching:

___ 1. Bell: reciprocating influences	a. recognizes interdependence of family members
___ 2. Minuchin: family system model	b. focuses on multiple contexts influencing development
___ 3. Bronfenbrenner: ecological contexts	c. underscores the power of the cultural context
___ 4. Vygotsky: sociocultural model	d. emphasizes interactive effects between family members

Conducting Child Development Research

Before Beginning . . .

After reading this section, you will be able to

- examine the different types of research designs (longitudinal, cross-sectional, cross-sequential) and their usefulness and limitation.

As the focus of understanding children switched from the armchair advice offered by philosophers to more scientific endeavors, a number of effective techniques for gathering information about children were developed. Research strategies, from case studies to experimental methods, improved our knowledge—and the accuracy of that knowledge—about children. Similarly, a number of research designs were devised that helped to illuminate how children develop over time.

Research Strategies

Your term paper is due at the end of the week. Due to previous academic commitments, you know that meeting this deadline is an impossible feat. You are thinking of asking your professor for an extension but are not quite sure of her reaction. You observe her reaction to two students who came to class late, and she seemed to be annoyed by their late entrance to class. You begin to construct a theory about her based on your observational impressions. You thus hypothesize that she will not give you an extension. But, you are not exactly sure that your observations are absolutely accurate. So, after class you meet with her and casually discuss a friend who is so overwhelmed with midterm requirements that he may not finish his paper on time. The professor laughs and suggests that the friend ask for an extension. You then reveal that you are the person who needs the extension, and the professor grants you one. In this example, you are doing exactly what psychologists do when conducting research:

- Observe a phenomenon.
- Construct a theory.
- Use the theory to develop a hypothesis.
- Measure psychological processes.
- Test the hypothesis.

Cultural Variations

Vygotsky on the Importance of Cultural Contexts

According to Vygotsky (1978), culture influences caregiving processes and child development through such factors as when and how parents care for their children, how nurturant and restrictive parents are, and which behaviors parents emphasize as important for their children to learn. Vygotsky made us aware that children growing up in different cultures are likely to show differences in behavioral outcomes, how they think, how they solve problems, and how cognitive development occurs.

Manang, from West Africa, who was introduced earlier, is being socialized in ways that will minimize her disturbance to adults' work in the field or market. As a result, obedience and passivity are encouraged and Manang, like all the babies and children in her community, is quiet by U.S. standards. Further, children are encouraged to be dependent upon the wider family and are taught the importance of obedience and respect for elders. Mothers tend not to respond to children's demands for attention, and children are less apt to experience such attention as rewarding. Caregiving strategies tend to encourage compliant behavior in children because these types of behaviors are most adaptive for survival in hazardous environments.

Diversity in the amount of verbal interaction between mothers and children also varies in different cultures. Studies on samples of mothers from Mexico City, Mexico, for example, reveal that the mothers typically use limited verbal interaction with their young children (Arcia & Johnson, 1998). When children do interact with adults, they are expected to show politeness and respect, as in the following exchange:

> Rosa was instructed by her parents to greet her grandparents and then be silent. Rosa walked into the kitchen and sat down at the table where there was a big plate of tortillas and cheese. Rosa asked, "May I have some?" Her mother said, quietly, *"Quiero de esa tortilla con queso, se dice por favor, Rosa. Pedir asi no mas es falta de respecto."* ("If you want some of the tortilla and cheese, you say please. To ask just like that is nothing more than a lack of respect"). When Rosa was finished eating, her mother told her to go outside to play. "This is an adult conversation, not for children. It's lack of respect for you to keep talking."

In contrast, parents in the United States tend to be verbally responsive to their children (Stevenson, 1998). In fact, many of us have at some point found ourselves frustrated in our attempts to carry on an uninterrupted conversation with a friend when his or her child was present. If the child interrupts the conversation, the parent typically attends to the child.

Why do Mexican parents tend to be verbally inactive with their children and American parents verbally active? Again, cultural beliefs appear to translate into parental actions. Many American parents believe that verbal responsiveness to children helps them to develop critical thinking skills, and that these are best fostered when parents promote skills in verbal analysis, verbal questioning, and verbal argumentation. In the United States, we assume that practice and stimulation in critical speaking will ultimately translate into success in the classroom and in later occupational endeavors. In contrast, Mexican parents tend to believe that children will succeed in the classroom if they are quiet and polite (Solis & Fox, 1996) and thus engage in less-extensive verbalization with their children.

These findings lend support to Vygotsky's theory that each culture can be thought of as setting priorities for adaptive behavioral development that guide socializing agents (parents, teachers, peers) to select some of the children's potentials for realization and neglect others.

hypothesis A specific prediction of behavior based on scientific theory that can be tested.

Psychologists, however, are likely to be more systematic and are able to choose from a number of research methods to test their **hypothesis**, a prediction of behavior based on scientific theory. Their methods include case studies, surveys, questionnaires and interviews, naturalistic observations, correlational research, and the experimental method. Moreover, researchers may be interested in events that have immediate effects or long-term consequences. There are several ways in which they can study development over a period of time, using a longitudinal, cross-sectional, or cross-sequential design. Let's begin with studies that involve a sample size of one.

Case Studies

> I have been working with Peter for six months, and during this time he has shed a great deal of light on autistic children. Peter does not like to be touched but he does like sitting right next to me and often rocks back and forth. He does not tolerate change well. Yesterday, the school was going on an excursion to the zoo. Our usual yellow van was not available and when a green van pulled up Peter started crying hysterically and refused to get on the bus. He was terrified. After much coaxing and calming him down, he apprehensively entered the strange new vehicle.

The distinguishing feature of a **case study** is that it focuses intensely on a defined unit (a person or community); it could have a sample size of one person, one organization, one society, or one church. With a case study, the researcher can examine a particular individual or group in great detail and depth. Yet, the limited nature of the sample has drawbacks. To what extent can the findings about a case be generalized? Clearly, the findings of a case study could simply represent idiosyncrasies, and thus provide little general explanation or prediction.

Also, using one case alone obviously prohibits comparison. If a researcher is interested in the differences between high-quality and low-quality child care, she needs at least two cases to make a comparison. Even with two case studies, the question remains: Can we generalize these findings to the larger population of all high- or low-quality child-care centers? Case studies are also limited in their ability to find causal relationships. They can, however, stimulate hypotheses and systematic research.

Surveys

Whereas the case study has a sample of one well-defined unit, the **survey** is designed to investigate many cases at once. The researcher using a survey method wishes to know how a particular phenomenon is distributed throughout the population of interest. Basically, to *survey* means to describe the characteristics of any given phenomenon in a population. Surveys may address whether variables are related to each other, and in surveys covered over time, whether some variables change. For example, a team of researchers embarked on a massive study of over 2200 Americans to see whether conceptions of mental health and attitudes about treatment for emotional problems had changed since the administration of a similar survey twenty years earlier (Veroff, Douvan & Kulka, 1981).

The strength of the survey lies in the generalizability of its findings; a great deal of information can be obtained from a large population. Although surveys tend to be more expensive than laboratory experiments, for the amount and quality of information they yield they are economical. However, with these advantages go inevitable disadvantages. Survey information ordinarily does not penetrate very deeply below the surface; as such, surveys seem to be best adapted to extensive rather than intensive research.

Surveys commonly use *questionnaires* and *interviews* to gather data. Although both the interview and questionnaire make use of questions to determine facts, beliefs, feelings, and attitudes, they differ in important ways. In an interview, data are commonly collected through face-to-face or telephone interaction. In the following example, Piaget (1929) is exploring a 5-year-old's understanding of dreams using the interview method:

> P: Where does the dream come from?
> C: I think you sleep so well that you dream.
> P: Does it come from us or from outside?
> C: From outside.
> P: When you are in bed and you dream, where is the dream?
> C: In my bed, under the blanket. I don't really know. If it was in my stomach, the bones would be in the way and I shouldn't see it.
> P: Is the dream in your head?
> C: It is I that am in the dream: it isn't in my head. (pp. 97–98)

With a questionnaire, respondents give written responses to a list of questions.

Each method has advantages and disadvantages. For example, the interview provides flexibility and allows the interviewer to observe the subject and the situation in which he or she is responding. Further, questions can be repeated or their meanings explained. The interview can also press for additional information if the subject's response is confusing or incomplete. Interviews also have a greater completion rate. The low return rate of the questionnaire (typically around

case studies
Research done on a sample of one: one person, one institution, one society, and so on.

survey
A research design that investigates many cases at once via questionnaires and/or interviews.

40%) may not only reduce the sample size but also may bias the results. The important question for the researcher is how these nonresponses affect the generalizability of the findings. If you are surveying attitudes toward working mothers, for example, and have a large number of female nonrespondents who were too busy or not at home, you might suspect that those who failed to respond to the questionnaire differ significantly from those who cooperated. The main disadvantage of interviews is that they are more expensive and time-consuming than questionnaires.

Another problem with questionnaires and interviews is the possibility that respondents are not telling the truth or are distorting their beliefs or facts about their lives. A socially rejected child may respond that she has "lots of friends" because she knows this is a more flattering response than "I am lonely and have no friends." In such instances, the respondent may be more concerned with answering "the right way" or the socially desired way than in giving true attitudes or answers regarding behaviors. Researchers need to be concerned about such matters as the representativeness of the population being surveyed and the reliability and validity in assessing the questionnaires and interviews used in surveys.

Naturalistic observation involves watching subjects in their natural environment.

Naturalistic Observation

> I am observing children at the middle school during their lunch recess time. I notice that the girls stay near the building and the teacher; they are playing jump rope and some kind of marble game. The boys tend to run and explore farther away from the teacher and the school building. They play tag and are often seen pushing and shoving to see who can be first to go down the slide.

Any analysis of behavior requires observation, a basic tool and method used in gathering information. At times, observation is done in a laboratory setting, but because many psychological variables cannot be observed there, it is sometimes better to turn to **naturalistic observation**: watching children in their natural environments (home or school, for example). In conducting this kind of research, no attempt is made to change or control the environment of the children being studied. You can, however, select both the subjects and situations you wish to observe.

naturalistic observation
A study in which the researcher observes subjects in their natural habitat.

Reed Larson and Maryse Richards (1994) used naturalistic observation as a means to gain detailed information about the kinds of activities adolescents engage in at home as well as their moods and thoughts. Seventy-five fifth-through-ninth-grade adolescents were asked to carry an electronic beeper with them for a week, from the time they woke up in the morning until they went to bed at night. At random intervals the subjects were "beeped" (approximately eight times per day) which served as a reminder for them to fill out a standard report about what they were doing and experiencing.

Naturalistic observation may also be used when it is unethical to subject children to various experimental situations. For example, if you wanted to study the effects of maternal separation, you might use a sample of children who are enrolled in child-care centers and observe and compare their behavior with children who remain at home with their mothers.

Information about children in natural settings is crucial for a complete science of children's development. It does, however, suffer from some drawbacks. The main disadvantage of this method is that it does not indicate cause and effect. Because you cannot manipulate or control the environments, you cannot be sure which factor (or factors) is determining the outcome. A second disadvantage may be observer bias. For example, if researchers are observing boys and girls on the playground to see who is more aggressive, their observations may be clouded by their own thoughts, feelings, and ideas. Having more than one observer helps to lessen observer bias. When two or more observers agree, the observations are more likely to be reliable. *Systematic observation* also helps to objectify observable phenomena. For example, observers may use checklists or detailed coding systems in conjunction with systematic time sampling procedures.

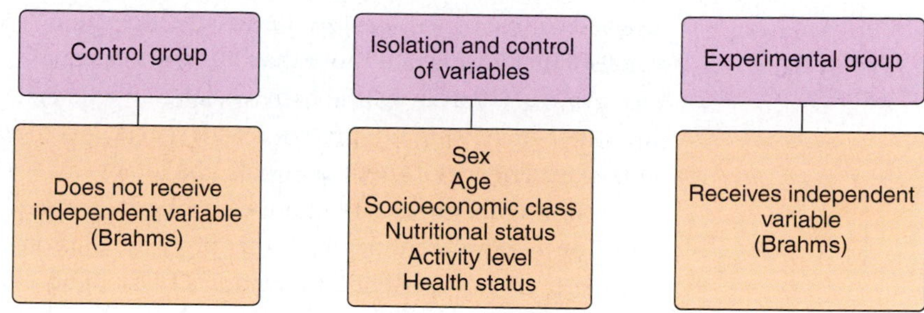

FIGURE 1.4 *The Experimental Method*

To determine whether there is a causal relationship between two variables, researchers use the experimental method. Controlling for confounding variables enables the experimenter to determine if the independent variable (listening to Brahms) is *the* variable affecting the dependent variable (the types of children's play activities).

The Experimental Method

An experiment differs from other types of scientific investigation in that, rather than searching for naturally occurring situations, the experimenter *creates* conditions necessary for observation. By using the **experimental method**, you can manipulate the environment to provide a precise test of your hypothesis. Thus, the link between cause and effect is clearer than in naturalistic observation. Generally, in the experimental method, you observe the effects of a particular variable(s) under study. *Variables* are factors that are controlled and measured in an experiment. The researcher tries to establish a causal link between two variables—that is, to show that one variable is *the* variable causing the observable effect in the subjects.

To do this, the experimenter manipulates and controls one variable, known as the **independent variable**. Then they note how that change affects some particular behavior they are studying, which is known as the **dependent variable**. It is called dependent because the experiment is designed so that any change in this factor *depends* on change in the independent variable.

Researchers gather data on two samples that are similar in every important aspect except one—the independent variable. An experimental and control group are often used in this type of design. The **experimental group** receives the experimental treatment (the independent variable). Research subjects in the control group are comparable with those in the experimental group in every relevant dimension, except they do not experience the special condition or treatment that is the key variable of the experiment. The **control group** is used for comparison.

The experimental method works something like this: Suppose you wanted to test the hypothesis "If nursery school children are exposed to soft, relaxing music (Brahms, for example), then they will tend to participate in quiet activities (working with puzzles, looking at books) during free play." First, you select your sample of children and place half in the experimental groups and half in the control group. Each of your subjects in these groups is as alike as possible so that you can make sure that it is your independent variable (relaxing, soft music) that is producing the behavior. The experimental group hears Brahms music during free-play time, and the control group does not (see Figure 1.4).

During your experiment you record the types of activities in which the children from the experimental group and the control group participate. You note from your statistical analysis of the data that there is a *significant* difference in their activity levels, with the experimental group engaging in more quiet activities. (Significant here means that the different behaviors observed in the two groups are unlikely to have occurred by chance.) Have you proved your hypothesis? In this experiment you have. Conclusions are not based on the results of one study, however. Further replication is necessary to establish the validity of the hypothesis.

Bennett Bertenthal and his colleagues (Bertenthal, Campos, & Barrett, 1984) provide another example that demonstrates how the experimental method works. For many years it was believed that the fear of heights is innate in the human infant. Bertenthal, however, believed that fear of heights develops as a result of the kinds of experiences infants acquire as they become ambulatory. To test this hypothesis, 92 six-month-old infants who were just beginning to crawl were randomly

experimental method A method in which one can manipulate the environment to provide a precise test of the hypothesis. This is the only experimental method that allows us to draw cause-and-effect relationships.

independent variable In an experimental design, the variable that is manipulated and controlled by the experimenter. It is received by the experimental group.

dependent variable The performance or behavior of the subjects in the experimental research design.

experimental group In experimental research design, the group of subjects who receives the experimental treatment.

control group In an experimental design, the group of subjects that does not receive the experimental treatment; they are used for comparison.

assigned to one of two groups. In the *experimental group,* infants were given more than 40 hours of experience moving about in special baby walkers. Infants in the *control group* were not provided with special locomotion experiences. In separate trials, the infants in the experimental group and in the control group were placed on a transparent platform that gives the illusion of a sharp drop. If Bertenthal's hypothesis was right, the infants in the experimental group, subjected to the *independent variable* (special moving experiences) should respond differently to the visual cliff than the control group of infants who received no special movement experiences. Although responses varied somewhat, the infants in the experimental group with more crawling experience showed fear in crossing over the "cliff," whereas the control group infants did not demonstrate such fear (*dependent variable*). Thus, the study provides evidence that locomotion does play a role in the development of the fear of heights.

The chief advantage of the experimental method is that it allows researchers to control for *confounding variables,* thus providing clues to causal relationships. A **confounding variable** is a factor(s) that is known to influence the independent variable. The presence of confounding variables compromises the validity of the study by making inferences about causality impossible.

Suppose an experimenter concluded from his research that watching violence on television causes aggressive behavior in children. You might comment, "But what if the children who watch violent programming are naturally more aggressive?" Children's preexisting levels of aggressiveness is a confounding variable. To be sure that one's interpretation of the results is correct, the researcher must make sure that he has controlled for variables that may influence the dependent variable. Thus, the subjects in the experimental and control groups need to be as similar as possible on all variables known to have an influence on the dependent variable.

confounding variables
Factors that could confuse or confound the effects of the independent variable.

multivariate analysis
Experimental designs that utilize information about the relationship among two or more variables.

The disadvantage is that experiments conducted in this situation can be rather artificial. As a result, the structured laboratory situation may elicit behaviors from children different from those evoked in the natural setting. In the previous example, children may react differently in their home surroundings when Brahms is played. Although much information can be obtained about the relations between discrete aspects of children's behavior, the experimental situation, by design, does not begin to approximate the total environment in its intricate complexity.

Field Experiments

Although many people tend to associate experiments with highly controlled laboratory settings, it is not necessarily so. A field experiment, for example, is one that takes place in a naturally occurring situation. A field setting might be a classroom in which a new teaching method is introduced. The dependent variable might be students' knowledge of a particular academic subject after exposure to the teaching method. The major advantage of this setting over that of a laboratory experiment is its increased reality.

Quasi-Experimental Designs

Researchers are sometimes unable to randomly assign individuals to experimental and control conditions; they may be required to utilize only one group or to use intact, preexisting groups. Studies that have independent and dependent variables but do not use randomization to assign subjects to groups are called quasi-experimental studies. Because random assignment is not used, the groups compared are likely to differ in many ways aside from the treatment. For example, medical researchers may measure the physical and psychological functioning of a group of patients *before* the administration of a new drug and at various times *after* the administration of the drug. This strategy allows for comparison of individual patient's functioning before and after the drug is prescribed. Should symptoms subside, the researchers can be somewhat confident that the drug was the cause of improvement. Quasi-experimental studies, although sharing the logic and many features of the experimental method, do not afford the experimenter as much control over all relevant variables, and, thus, generalizability is limited.

Multivariate Analysis

Although the experimental method is designed to answer cause-and-effect questions (Can the presence of the independent variable x cause a change in the dependent variable y?) rarely can children's behavior be attributed to a single cause or variable. Rather, behavior is a result of interconnected effects. Researchers seek to describe these effects with procedures that are sensitive to these complexities. The effects of two or more different variables are considered in these experimental designs rather than just one. The advantage of these designs, called **multivariate analysis**, is that they utilize information about the relationship among variables.

For example, you may wish to know the relationship of several background characteristics, such as social class, urban-rural residence, parental relationship, gender, and age, to drug addiction. In this case, there are many independent variables, and one dependent variable for which explanation is sought. Or, you may wish to know the relationships of gender and age to drug addiction and juvenile delinquency. This problem has two dependent variables. Obviously, these designs are quite complex, but so is children's behavior. Behavior is determined by multiple variables, and multivariate analysis research is designed to analyze the behavior in terms of multiple causes and effects.

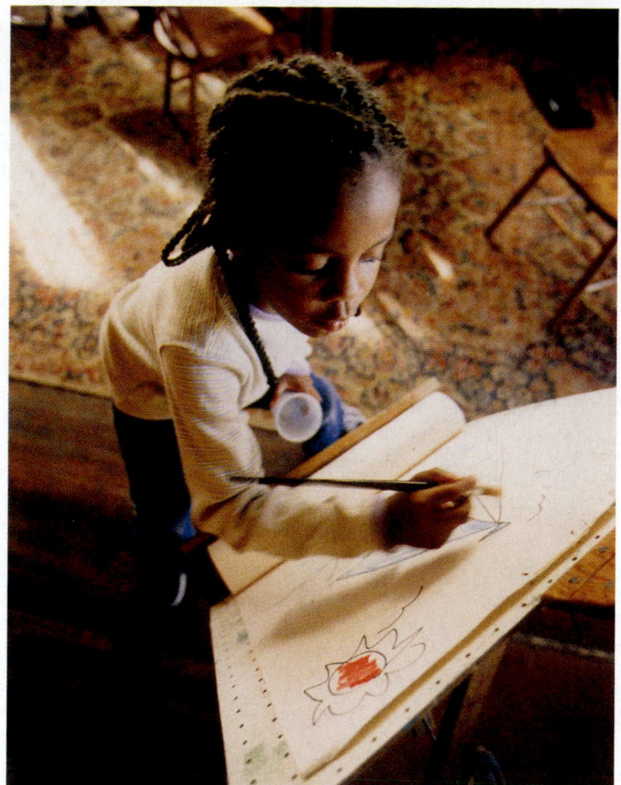

© Dwayne Newton/PhotoEdit, Inc.

Do creative children have high IQs? In a correlational study, the researcher tries to find a link or correlation between variables such as these.

The Correlational Method

Do creative children have high IQs? Studies in which the investigator is looking for a relationship between two or more variables that can be measured but not controlled are called **correlational** studies. For example, if you want to find out if there is a relationship between IQ and creativity, neither one can be manipulated by the researcher. In this case, all you can do is measure IQ and see how it compares (correlates) with creativity. The relationship between these variables is expressed in terms of a direction (positive or negative) and size of the relationship. For example, if you tested five children (in practice, you would use a larger sample), you might find their scores as follows:

Child	*IQ Test Score (Average = 95–105)*	*Creativity Test Score (Highest Score = 15)*
Dominque	125	14
Dave	118	11
Xavier	100	7
Dan	98	6
Chris	95	4

In analyzing the scores, you would compute a *correlational coefficient,* which would tell you the direction and power of the connection between variables. A +1.0 is a positive, perfect correlation, which means that when a child receives a high score on the IQ test, he or she also receives a high score on the creativity test. In contrast, a –1.0 correlation coefficient indicates a negative, perfect correlation. In this case, low IQ scores are correlated with high scores on creativity tests. It is rare or almost impossible for variables to receive these kinds of correlation coefficients. Your data indicate a +.50 which, in psychology, is considered to be a strong correlation between IQ and creativity.

Correlational methods can only describe relationships among variables. When two variables correlate with each other, the researcher must infer the relationship between them: Does one cause the other, or does some third variable explain the correlation? Media reports on research often disregard the fact that correlation does not imply causation. For example, some studies have shown a correlation between pornography and crimes against women. The media reported, "A new study shows that pornography leads to rape." Just because rapists read pornography, however, does not prove that pornography leads to rape. The correlational method simply points out that an association between two variables has been found. Table 1.9 summarizes research methods in developmental psychology.

Thought CHALLENGE

Why can't correlational studies show causality between two variables?

correlational method
A method that attempts to measure the relationship between two or more variables. The association does not imply a causal link between the variables.

TABLE 1.9

Methods of Research

Method	General Approach	Advantages	Disadvantages
Case study	Describes carefully all relevant aspects in a sample size of one	Examines a particular case in great depth and detail	Provides little general explanation or prediction
Survey	Measures many cases at once; considered synonymous with the use of questionnaires and interviews	Examines how a particular phenomenon is distributed throughout the population	Respondents may refuse to participate; in assessing validity and reliability, need to be concerned about representativeness of the sample
Naturalistic observation	Analyzes behavior through observation without intrusion	Provides information from "real life" situations	Causal inferences are speculative
Interview	Subjects give verbal responses on their thoughts, attitudes, and behaviors	Allows generation of systematic data	Verbal responses of subjects may be inaccurate
Experimental	Manipulates the environment to provide precise test of hypothesis	Allows control for confounding variables, thus providing clues to causal relationships	In a testing situation, responses from subjects may differ from those encountered in a natural setting
Correlational	Determines relationships among variables	Allows discernment of relationships among variables	Cannot show causality

Research Designs

A number of research designs are available to researchers. For example, in studying developmental changes, an investigator might decide to focus on behaviors that accompany age change with the same individuals over time—a *longitudinal* study. Or, the investigator may focus on behaviors that reflect age differences among individuals at given points in time—a *cross-sectional* study.

Longitudinal Studies

Studies that follow people over time are called **longitudinal studies**. You may ask the question, "Do children who are verbally proficient at a young age continue to display high language skills?" To test the hypothesis that they do, you may make repeated observations and give language proficiency tests to the same group of children over an extended period of time. By doing so, you gain valuable information regarding the stability or instability of a behavior (see First Person, where Carol Huntsinger discusses the nature of longitudinal designs).

The main advantages of this method are that it allows direct analysis of age changes and, because individuals are compared with themselves at different periods of time, there are fewer problems with the sample itself. Subjects do not have to be carefully sorted out and matched each time, for example. The major disadvantage is that it is costly in money and time. Another limiting factor is that over time original subjects may move, get sick, or drop out of the experiment. Changeovers in staff can also occur. In addition, the fact that children are taking tests over a period of four or five years could enable them to become quite proficient test takers; that is, the repeated testing itself could cause an increase in performance.

longitudinal studies Study done on a group of subjects over a period of time.

cross-sectional research design A study that compares groups of individuals of different ages on some particular behavior at one point in time.

cohort A generation of individuals used to make comparisons in cross-sectional research.

cohort effect Differences between cohorts that reflect unidentified cultural or historical factors.

Cross-Sectional Studies

Another method that is quick and less expensive is the **cross-sectional research design**. In this design, groups of individuals of different ages are observed and/or measured on some particular behavior at one point in time (see Figure 1.5 on page 40). It is assumed that when large numbers of children are chosen at random, the difference found in the older age groups are a reflection of how the younger children will develop, given time. In this case, we can test children's language proficiency skills by using a sample, of fourth-, fifth-, and sixth-graders. Each of these groups is referred to as a *cohort*. A **cohort** represents a generation of individuals, and comparisons are made between generation groups.

One drawback to the cross-sectional design is that not all the differences observed between the cohorts are the result of age; differences between cohorts may reflect other cultural or historical factors that distinguish members of different cohorts. This is known as the **cohort effect**. If, for example, you tested groups of people at ages 20, 30, 40, 50, and 60 about their attitudes toward sex, you might find that as people get older they tend to become more conservative. Can these differences be a result of age, or could they be a result of the experiences peculiar to each of the cohorts? A 60-year-old, for example, was raised in a more conservative cultural milieu.

Thus, it is often difficult to separate the effects of age from those of the historical period. Similarly, this method does not allow you to study continuity in behavior changes in a particular child, only behavioral differences among groups of individuals. Moreover, if you do not control for important variables in making your subjects similar (health, education, socioeconomic class) your results may not be valid. Therefore, it is important to use similar groups of people at different age levels being investigated. The greatest advantage of the cross-sectional design is its efficiency. A researcher can study children's development across several years in no more time than it takes to collect data on several groups of children.

Cross-Sequential Studies

The **cross-sequential research design**, which incorporates cross-sectional and longitudinal studies, may eliminate either's disadvantages. Suppose you wondered if children's conceptions of friends change over time. You could conduct a study to test this idea. Let's say that in 2000, a group of 4-, 5-, and 6-year-olds were asked to describe their friends. You noted that these children used highly personal and concrete constructs to describe their friends: "We play together." "She gives me things."

A longitudinal component will be added when these same children are tested four years later at ages 8, 9, and 10. Then you may note that these children now use less personal and more abstract constructs, such as "She is kind when she wants to be." Using cohorts at different age levels greatly reduces the amount of time needed to gather information about a particular behavior, and, at the same time, provides useful information about behavioral differences at different ages and within a given age group.

FIRSTPERSON

Longitudinal Research

Many Asian Americans experience superior achievement at the college level. Through my observations of younger Chinese American children, it became apparent that even preschool children I observed showed advanced mathematic skills compared with their European American children counterparts. I began my research in the early 1990s guided by research questions, What do Chinese American parents do to foster this early achievement? How do their experiences differ from European American children? From my initial interviews with Chinese American immigrant parents, it became apparent that young children are being exposed to systematic and formal teaching techniques during their preschool years such as learning to count to 100, reading and writing numerals to 100 and higher, doing simple addition and subtraction. Chinese American parents spend approximately 55 minutes everyday in these kinds of exercises and drills. On the other hand, European American parents tend to rely to a greater extent on everyday experiences (weighing produce at the grocery store, measuring ingredients for a recipe) and only spend about 6 minutes a day in focused practice. It appears from testing children at the kindergarten level, that these kinds of experiential differences do matter; Chinese American kindergartners outperform European American children in mathematics knowledge and skills.

These findings are interesting, but research, once begun, often generates new hypotheses, requiring an analysis that goes beyond a one-point-in-time analysis. I now became interested in whether these early systematic mathematics instructions by Chinese parents will continue to impact on children's performance. I have continued to study my original sample of Chinese and European American children; they are now beginning their fifth year of school. The Chinese American children are still outperforming the European American children in mathematics. It seems that systematic parental teaching of mathematics to young children reaps long-term benefits, but this only could have been discovered through a longitudinal research design.

—***Carol Huntsinger, Ph.D.***

Dr. Huntsinger does research on mathematical development in Chinese American children. Her findings have been published in a number of scholarly journals.

Concept Checks

1. The key advantage of using the experimental method over other designs is that
   a. relationships between two variables can be determined.
   b. cause-and-effect relationships between variables can be identified.
   c. the results can be applied to real life situations.

2. An investigator tests the effectiveness of a new reading program by testing the reading skills of a third-grade class and a fifth-grade class at the beginning and end of the first semester. The investigator is using a ________________ design.
   a. cross-sequential
   b. cross-sectional
   c. time sampling

cross-sequential research design A study that incorporates cross-sectional and longitudinal designs.

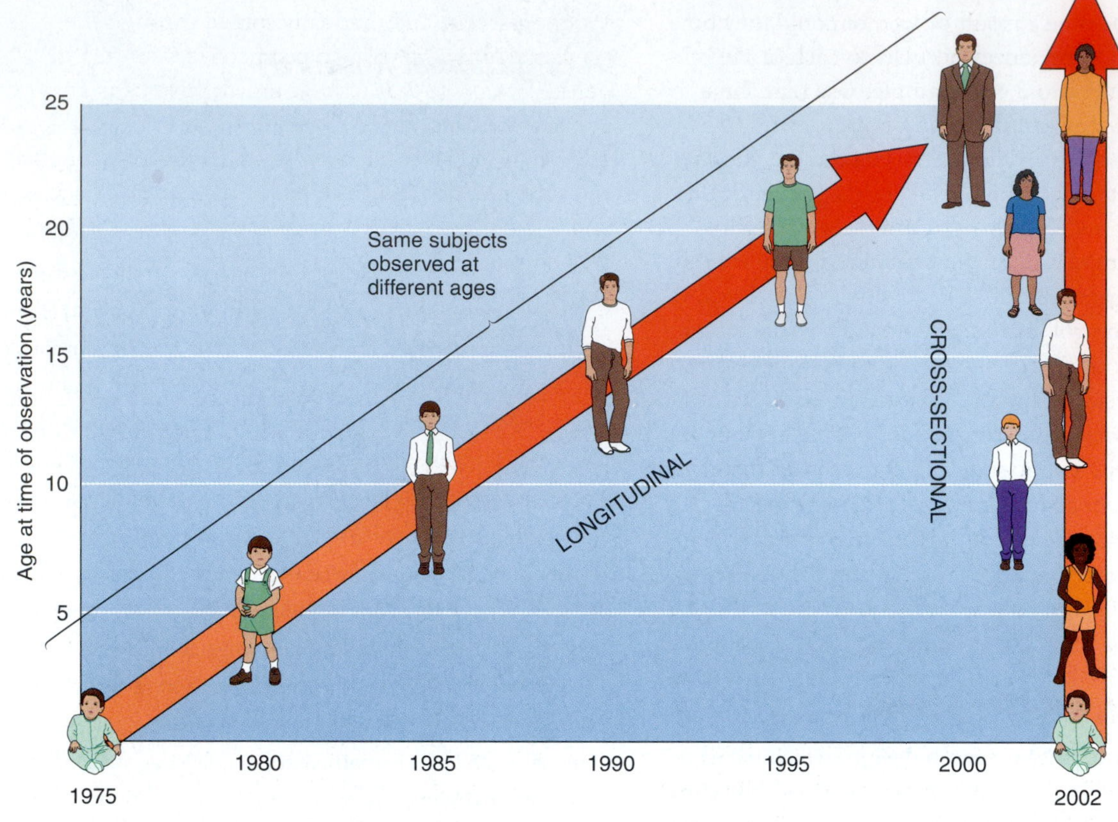

FIGURE 1.5 ***The Difference between Longitudinal and Cross-Sectional Designs***

In longitudinal designs, the same subjects are followed over several years, enabling researchers to focus on the processes of development. In cross-sectional designs, subjects of different ages are studied at one point in time, allowing experimenters more time-efficient assessments.

Contemporary Issues and Future Concerns

Before Beginning . . .

After reading this section, you will be able to

- examine the developmental issues in child development research.
- focus on factors that will improve children's lives.

Developmental Issues

As you have seen in our overview of the history of childhood, philosophers pondered many issues. Lively debates occurred over such questions as:

- Do human beings have free will, or are we victims of unconscious forces?
- Is the personality of each individual unique, or are there broad universal personality patterns?
- Are human beings kind and compassionate, or cruel and merciless?

Today, developmental psychologists continue to address issues of human nature and individual differences.

Nature or Nurture?

Are you a product of your genes, or is behavior more influenced by the environment?

Ramon was a good friend of yours in eighth grade, but you have not seen him since. Last week, you most surprisingly ran into him and spent some time together reminiscing. You thought as you walked away, "Good old Ramon, still the same funny guy."

You remember a quote by Socrates in Plato's Dialogues (350 B.C./1952) . . . some men—the best men are made of gold, others of silver, and still others of brass and iron. Socrates asserted that these characteristics generally will be preserved in their children, meaning that our genetic lotteries play a key role in determining our behavior. Thinking of Socrates' statement makes you wonder if perhaps Ramon's humor is determined by something in his genetic constitution.

But, as you walk on, you also remember a contradicting thought from Locke's works. He made a point of emphasizing that impressions are made during our "tender infancies" and have lasting and important consequences. Now you wonder if Ramon's environment was the main contributing factor in making him the funny person that he is. Which view is correct?

The defenders of the **nature** position believe that behavior is largely inherited; each species is born with a number of behavioral traits that are largely inborn. In contrast, the **nurture** viewpoint suggests that we are free from the chains of biology, and behavior is fully a product of our environmental experiences. Even though the nature/nurture debate centered on these either/or issues and was heatedly argued for a number of decades, today, we know that heredity and environment impact each other in determining personality traits—such as Ramon's sense of humor.

Currently, the **evolutionary psychology** movement has gained prominence because it so clearly rests on a combination of nature and nurture in explaining behavior. Evolutionary psychologists recognize that some behaviors are learned and easily modified, whereas others are biologically based and thus resistant to modification. Learning to speak, for example, is preprogrammed in our brains (nature); but it is also a socially constructed phenomena (nurture). To develop speech, we need to be exposed to language and to communicate with others (nurture). Evolutionary psychologists also add a special twist to the nature *and* nurture position; they stress that our present ways of behaving and the structure of the human mind are linked to our evolutionary past—a rather distant past—back to the Pleistocene Era when our human ancestors lived in hunter-gatherer groups (Panter-Brick, 1998). Our current behavioral tendencies and ways of thinking have been designed by evolution over millions of years through a process known as *natural selection*.

Natural selection, according to Charles Darwin, works like this. As the human mind evolved, certain combinations of genes proved successful at reproducing themselves, and gradually spread through the species. From a Darwinian perspective, "successful genes" are those that provide an adaptive edge and continue to be selected. Thus, humans are seen as *adaptation executors* carrying out programs written into our brains a long time ago (de Waal, 1999). Our early ancestors whose genetic constitutions provided them with language abilities more often made a successful adaptation to the environment and thus survived to spread their genes. Similarly, diverse behaviors such as nurturing young, fear of heights, and preference for nutritious foods prepared our ancestors to survive and conferred a reproductive advantage upon them. Over time, behaviors that once were developed for adaptive purposes came to prevail and exist within our genetically hard-wired brains today. From an evolutionary psychology perspective one can see the universality of certain behaviors because of the similarity in our prehistoric genetic legacies. But this perspective also speaks to the issue of diversity: each individual is adapted to a specific way of life in a specific environment. For example, although we all learn to communicate with others, we all learn the language indigenous to our particular culture.

Continuity or Discontinuity in Development

Is development a smooth continuous process or does it occur in abrupt, discontinuous stages?

While you notice Ramon is still his same funny self, you also notice some new traits that he didn't have in eighth grade. For example, you are amazed at his quick and accurate memory. Ramon didn't seem to have these great memory skills several years ago when you were friends. What is the best way to explain the differences in his memory then and now?

Developmentalists all agree that children's behavior and abilities change, but there is less of a consensus on how to explain these changes. Some view development as a *continuous* process—such as planting an acorn and watching an oak tree grow progressively and steadily taller over time (see Figure 1.6a). The phrase "as the twig is bent, so grows the tree," captures the essence of continuity—once children start on a path, they more than likely stay on the same path. So Ramon's "new" memory skills would be viewed as occurring gradually and steadily in small quantitative advances. For example, as Ramon grew older, his memory skills continued to improve as a result of his being able to store and retrieve

nature
Genetic and biological influences on children's development.

nurture
Environmental influences on children's development.

evolutionary psychology
The study of evolution of behavior using the principles of natural selection. Certain behavioral traits and ways of thinking are selected by conferring a reproductive advantage upon them. Those traits, over time, come to prevail.

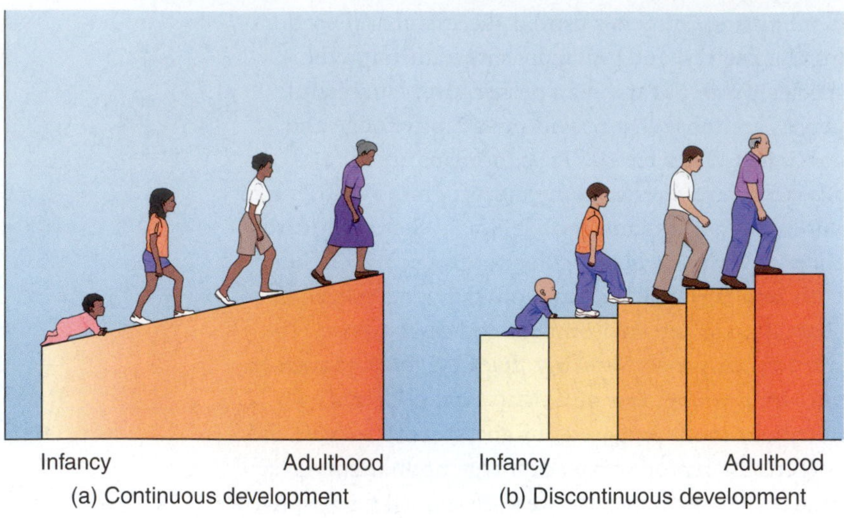

FIGURE 1.6 *Continuous and Discontinuous Views of Development*

(a) According to the continuity view of development, children's development is a gradual, even process; (b) whereas the discontinuity view sees development as occurring in a series of stagelike progressions.

more and more pieces of information. Other developmentalists view great instability in individual differences over time. Those who emphasize *discontinuity* in development would explain that Ramon's memory feats emerged at a particular period in time and would see him as moving through a series of developmental sequences (see Figure 1.6b) until he reaches a final transformation—much like a caterpillar emerging from its cocoon as a butterfly. The discontinuous perspective sees children's behavior as going through various stages—such as Piaget's four stages of cognitive development. Stages are believed to be additive (each stage building on previous stages) and universal.

Are children active beings or are they passive recipients of their environment? The interesting thing about Ramon is that he came from a very poor family. His parents could not speak English and felt it was the school's job to educate Ramon. His home environment was impoverished and unstimulating. Now look at him—he's a sophomore at one of our most prestigious universities. Was Ramon able to "overcome" the effects of his earlier nonenriched environment because of something within him? Did he play an active role in surmounting earlier impoverishment? For example, Ramon may have possessed such traits as curiosity and a desire to learn. Or, was the change stimulated by the environment—some external source acting on Ramon—such as an enthusiastic and involved teacher or grandparent. Once again, however, the either/or position is put aside and in this case the child *and* the environment are both viewed as active in producing behavioral outcomes.

Early Experiences

Do early experiences (particularly in infancy and toddlerhood) leave everlasting marks on children? Is it true that "By the mother's forming hand the child receives its shape to a great extent for future existence"? From Plato (who maintained that rocking infants will turn them into skilled athletes) to Freud (who stressed the notion that the first five or six years of life are crucial determinants of later behavior), the notion of early experiences has led to proclamations that nothing of good or evil is ever lost; every early experience is written indelibly in the brain to be counted for or against the individual. Although proclamations about the strength and stability of early experiences appear throughout the history of developmental psychology, research findings offer meager support for the idea of "infant/toddler determinism" (Cairns & Hood; 1983 Kagan, 1996). To the contrary, current research on the brain, for example, clearly demonstrates continuous alterations in the brain are produced by ongoing environmental experiences. As you will see, research findings on attachment relations between caregiver and infant also suggest that substantial psychological change in insecure attachment relations is possible when children's environments change. Further, evidence from longitudinal studies suggests that it is not until 6 or 7 years of age that a large number of adult behaviors becomes largely predictable (Kagan, 1999).

Some childhood experiences disappear like mere trifles; others, though, particularly those that tend to be traumatic, intense, and frequent, tend to endure for longer periods of time. But, even in these situations there is some support that substantial psychological change is possible when children's environments change (Carlson & Sroufe, 1995; Sroufe, 1996). Ramon, for example, may have encountered a teacher who stimulated his desire to learn and become a good student despite a less-than-optimal home environment. Another dramatic example would be those children of the Holocaust who turned out to be productive, successful adults.

In the majority of cultures around the world the notion of early-experience determinism is not supported (Lamb & Sternberg, 1992). This belief is more prevalent in Western cultures where Freudian beliefs are stronger. Moreover, as a result of overemphasizing the importance of early experiences on children's outcome, the role of later experiences, which also impact children's development, has been overlooked. Despite the fragility of confirming evidence for the lasting effects of early experiences, there remains considerable allegiance to this notion and resistance to awarding influence to experiences that occur after the first few years of life.

This is not to discount early experiences—all children profit, when, from the very beginning, they receive warm and loving treatment and stimulating environments. However, today, psychologists do not view development from the extreme positions of nature / nurture, continuous / discontinuous, active / passive, or early / later experiences; rather, they see the merits of both sides of the argument.

Improving Children's Lives

- Roughly 23 percent (58 million) of the U.S. population is composed of children under the age of 15.
- Approximately 75 percent of mothers with children work in outside paid employment.
- There are more than 14.5 million children living in poverty.
- Children are far more likely to play indoors with ready-made toys and computers than they are to play outdoors.
- An estimated 135,000 children take guns to school.

In the 1940s, public school teachers listed their top disciplinary concerns (Bear, 1998); compare them with the disciplinary concerns of today's educators:

1940	*2001*
talking out of turn	drug abuse
chewing gum	alcohol abuse
making noise	pregnancy
running in the halls	suicide
cutting in line	rape
dress-code violations	robbery
littering	assault

These are but a few current statistics and concerns about children, but they tell us a variety of things about children's development in the twenty-first century. By combining our past knowledge with our present information about children, we are then in a better position to gain greater insight into how we can effectively meet their future needs. Certainly, meeting children's *educational needs* is a current concern—the society of the future is a society of knowledge. This issue concerns all children—for all children, as the saying goes, represent our society's future. Improving the lives of children then involves helping every child reach his or her potential; those who fail to do so are destined to become noncontributing members of that society.

A second issue relates to children's gender:

> In my day, women were a lot different than they are today. We were quieter, and we put other people ahead of ourselves. We knew our place, and we didn't try to be equal with men. Today's women are very different. Some of the younger women in my classes put their careers ahead of marriage, some don't want children, and many think they should be as much the head of a family as the man. Sometimes I feel they are all wrong in what they want and how they are, but I have to admit that a part of me envies them the options and opportunities I never had.

On the surface, it appears that we value the full range of human qualities; however, we still hand out cultural labels of feminine and masculine and continue to create differing emotional worlds for boys and girls.

Because messages that reinforce cultural views of gender pervade our daily lives, most of us seldom pause to reflect on whether they are as "natural" as they have come to seem. Improving the lives of children involves learning to reflect on *cultural prescriptions for gender* and enlarging our awareness of the arbitrary and not always desirable nature of cultural expectations. Equally important is Plato's marvelous concept of meritocracy. In his ideal ancient society, an individual's position in life—regardless of race, ethnicity, or economic position—should be determined by individual merit. This 2000-year-old idea is something we still need to strive for in our contemporary times.

Health issues represent another domain that we must address in improving the lives of children. Health issues encompass broader problems such as poverty, homelessness, disease, and hunger. To this end, we need public policies, laws, and government programs that will enable us to improve the health conditions and the lives of many children and families in our country and throughout the world.

Finally, *parent education,* involving knowledge about children's development and how to enhance that development, is an important prerequisite to improving the lives of children. Here, again, perhaps we give superficial importance to caregiving. Although most agree that parenting is the most important profession that we

Calvin and Hobbes © 1987 Watterson. Dist. by Universal Press Syndicate. Reprinted by permission of the publisher.

have, it requires no advanced training—we confer no degrees and award no certificates. A knowledgeable parent, wise in the ways of understanding and enhancing children's development, is another vital ingredient to improving the lives of children.

Concept Checks

1. The perspective that Ramon's sense of humor developed progressively over time is known as
   a. the discontinuity view of behavior.
   b. the continuity view of behavior.
   c. a combination of discontinuity and continuity views of behavior.
2. In your opinion, what is an important issue today that needs to be addressed to improve children's lives?

About This Book

An Integrated Approach

What exactly is an *integrated* approach? It means that our discussions about children's growth and development will incorporate research findings from a number of various disciplines—anthropology, sociology, and history, to name a few. In the past, each of these fields of study was isolated and segmented from the others—like individual pieces of a puzzle. It is only recently that the old barriers between these disciplines have begun to break down. Thanks to a lot of exciting new research, this text brings these puzzle pieces together and incorporates research from various fields, giving you a much more comprehensive picture of children's development.

"Integrated" also means that we will discuss how children's behavior is influenced by many different contexts, such as biology, genetics, and culture. In the past, these contexts were also largely ignored when studying children. Researchers, reflecting the integrated approach, are now looking at how all these contexts influence children, and the results of their research will enable you to see children in all their richness and complexity.

Chronological Understandings

One of my least-cherished tasks is gardening. Christian, whom you met in the introductory paragraphs, watched as I started plucking out green growths. I grumbled to Christian, "I really hate this—I can't tell if these are flowers or weeds." Four-year-old Christian, without hesitation and with great authority, began pointing, "This is a weed. That is a weed. This one is a flower." Christian has been a special friend of mine for many years and I've enjoyed getting to know him as he has progressed through the developmental periods of prenatal, infancy, early childhood, middle childhood, and adolescence. We discuss these chronological periods, used to organize this text, next.

Prenatal (Conception to Birth)

The first developmental stage is known as the *prenatal period*. All our lives began as a single cell, and in the course of the nine-month-gestation period, this fertilized cell developed from a microscopic entity to a highly developed, generally, 7- to 8-pound baby.

Infancy (Birth to 2)

Christian's parents sent birth announcements complete with a photo of their newborn son—who, in all honesty, looked like a miniature Winston Churchill—a round little face with a fringe of dark hair encircling his head. The infancy period, birth to 24 months, is a period of "firsts"—first tooth, first steps, first words. During this period, infants move from babyhood to first forms of personhood; personalities become clearer, more stable, and more individual. The first two years of life are filled with progressively refined development in physical, motor, and manipulative skills. The baby's brain is being "soft-wired" by the environment and is highly dependent on caregivers providing windows of opportunities for its development. We have a sensorimotor, highly action-oriented thinker capable of effectively processing information and retaining it. During this period, infants move from a symbiotic relationship with their principal caregiver to establishing a separate sense of self.

Early Childhood (Ages 2 to 6)

This period has been correctly labeled, "the Declaration of Independence," for young children between the ages of 2 to 6 years are busy exerting their self-initiated drives for autonomy and separateness. During early childhood, the body becomes more agile and controlled. Thought at this stage is based on mental representation; the child learns to represent the world mentally by means of language or symbols. Thinking, however, is heavily influenced by children's visual perceptions of the problem-solving event. In many ways, early childhood is an imaginative, creative, fanciful time. "Will you read this?" asks 4-year-old Christian. I am handed a piece of paper with scribbly lines down the entire page.

"I think I need your help reading this, Christian." It is his letter to Santa Claus and the things that he is requesting from him this year.

"Okay, this first line says, Santa, I want a wagon. Now you read the second line."

Children branch out socially, as they learn to adapt to ever-widening social networks, and friends become increasingly important—although friends tend to change rather quickly.

Middle Childhood (Ages 7 to 12)

As a fourth grader, Christian has become quite interested in playing soccer in his school-league and often relates, in a play-by-play description, how the game went. Children generally exhibit a strong desire to engage in vigorous physical activities, which reflects their increasing size and strength of muscles. During these developmental years, children can reason logically about objects, events, and relationships. Their thinking is bound, however, to a concrete world in which they can only reason about objects they can see or manipulate. Children's all-consuming interests in parents begin to subside as they withdraw some of their emotional energy from adults and begin to unite with their society of peers. As such, middle childhood is a time when peer relationships play an increasingly complementary role to that of parents.

Adolescence (Ages 13 to 19)

There is a knock on the door. It's Christian who is on his way to the eighth-grade graduation dance—looking perfect in the hair department and smelling vaguely of—Can it be? Yes, it's aftershave lotion. "How do I look?" he asks in his voice that vacillates between sounds of a little boy and sounds of a young man. The teenage years represent a period of transition in many areas. Physically, adolescents are embarking on maturing both physically and sexually; cognitively, their concrete world of thinking becomes unhinged as they can now reason abstractly; and socially, friendships become more enduring and more intimate.

Domains of Development

As developmental psychologists follow children through these chronological periods, they have concentrated on the physical, cognitive, and socioemotional aspects of each period.

- *Physical development:* This area studies the basic changes in the child's body, such as height and weight, and health factors that include nutrition and health-related issues, such as safety concerns. The physical domain also includes motor development, from the infant's earliest grasping reflexes to highly skilled execution of complex athletic feats during later childhood and adolescence. The development of the brain and genes inherited from parents is also a part of children's physical development.
- *Cognitive development:* This reflects all the mental processes related to how children come to know and understand their world—how they think, decide, and learn. Cognition encompasses thought, intelligence, perception, imagination, memory, and language.
- *Socioemotional development:* This area studies changes in emotions, temperament, moral reasoning, self-understandings, and peer relationships.

These physical, cognitive, and socioemotional domains are intricately entwined. Changes in one domain involve changes in other domains as well. For our purposes of study, we shall examine each important aspect of children's development in these domains like individual pieces of a complex puzzle. Upon completion of the puzzle, one can see the interrelatedness of each of these facets of development forming a holistic picture of children as they grow.

Also, although these three domains are important at every stage of development, researchers have tended to vary their focus to mirror the dominant features of each stage. For example, in the infancy period, a primary concern of physical development is the infant's perceptual world of sights, sounds, and smells; cognitive development centers on curiosity; and social development is primarily concerned with attachment relationships with caregivers. In contrast, understanding the adolescent involves looking at rapid biological and hormonal transitions in the physical domain; the development of formal, logical, idealistic reasoning in the cognitive domain; and the growing sophistication of friendships and dating in the social domain.

In addition, when developmental psychologists describe children's development, they focus on both typical patterns of change, or *normative development,* as well as on individual variations, or *ideographic development.* This enables us to understand how children resemble one another and how they are likely to differ as development proceeds.

Reviewing Key Points

A Historical Overview of Attitudes Toward Children

- Confucius believed that children should be raised with firm parental control and strict discipline so that they would show respect for elders, reverence for tradition, and maintenance of harmony. Beginning in ancient Greece, children were subjected to a low level of care. Infanticide occurred, children were put out in the fields to work when they were very young, and parents had complete control over their children's lives.
- Children in the New World were considered first and foremost as workers. Adults took for granted that they were ignorant and sinful. The job of parents was to discipline and instruct them. After several centuries, and through the influence of the works of Locke and Rousseau, childhood came to be seen as a separate and special time.

The Emergence of Developmental Theories

- Sigmund Freud viewed the infant as being born with a collection of unconscious sexual and aggressive drives that supply energy and direction for behavior. All development may be seen as the result of changes in the way psychic energy is channeled and organized as the child journeys through the first three psychosexual stages. Freud maintained that the bulk of our personality is unknown to us; it resides in the unconscious mind.
- Erikson emphasized the role of the ego developing throughout the psychosocial stages. According to Erikson, adults need to meet children's physical and psychological needs at each psychosocial stage of development.
- John B. Watson believed that stimuli in the environment force organisms to behave or incite them into initial action. He proposed that classically conditioned responses were the key to understanding human behavior. Skinner agreed that behavior is controlled by the eliciting stimuli (classical conditioning) and by stimuli that reinforce responses (operant conditioning). Bandura's social learning theory stressed the importance of observation, imitation, and cognitive factors in producing various behaviors.
- Jean Piaget traced the development of the intellect, beginning with reflexive behavior in early infancy to the abstract thinking found in late adolescence. Piaget made adults aware that children are active problem solvers who should be encouraged to explore their environment.

Contexts of Development

- Today, children are viewed as active problem solvers, who construct their own life experiences. It is further recognized that parents and children engage in a constant flow of influence. Moreover, researchers using a family systems perspective are studying the reciprocal influences among all family members.
- Bronfenbrenner made us aware of the importance of studying children in several environmental subsystems, or contexts, of development (microsystem, mesosystem, exosystem, macrosystem, chronosystem).
- Vygotsky underscored the power of the cultural context and explained the growth of children's knowledge in terms of the guidance provided by the more knowledgeable adults in each culture.

Conducting Child Development Research

- Scientific methods and procedures used in studying children are case studies, surveys, questionnaires, the experimental method, naturalistic observation, and the correlational method.
- In research designs, a longitudinal approach, in which behavior is observed at successive time periods, can be used. In cross-sectional designs, groups

of children of different ages (cohorts) are observed at one point in time. Sometimes a combination of these two methods is used, which helps to cancel out the drawbacks of each.

Contemporary Issues and Future Concerns

- Psychologists do not view developmental issues from the extreme positions of nature/nurture, continuous/discontinuous, active/passive, or early/later experiences; rather, they see the merits of both sides of the argument.
- Improving the lives of children involves issues of education, health, gender, and family issues. This includes equal educational opportunities so that all children can fulfill their potential; physical well-being; fulfillment, without regard to gender or ethnicity; and caregivers more knowledgeable about children's development and how to enhance it.

Answers to Concept Checks

A Historical Overview of Attitudes Toward Children

1. c   2. d   3. a   4. e   5. b

The Emergence of Developmental Theories

1. Freud: (possible answers) These children are "acting out" their sexual fantasies. The picture is demonstrating Freud's notion of men's superiority over women because the boy in the picture is playing the doctor.

   Skinner: (possible answers) These children are emulating behavior that has been reinforced by caregivers.

   Piaget: (possible answers) These children are assimilating their newly formed schemes about doctors and nurses.

2. 1. d   2. a   3. e   4. b   5. f   6. c

Contexts of Development

1. d   2. a   3. b   4. c

Conducting Child Development Research

1. b   2. b

Contemporary Issues and Future Concerns

1. b
2. discuss children's educational needs, gender issues, health, and parent education

Key Terms

accommodation
assimilation
behaviorism
behavior modification
case studies
classical conditioning
cohort
cohort effect
confounding variables
context
control group
correlational method
culture
cross-sectional research design
cross-sequential research design
dependent variable
ecological approach
ego
evolutionary psychology
experimental group
experimental method
family systems model
fixation
generalizability
hypothesis
id
imitation
independent variable
infanticide
libido
longitudinal studies
meritocracy
multivariate analysis
naturalistic observation
nature
negative reinforcement
nurture
operant conditioning
positive reinforcement
psychosexual stages
psychosocial stages
random sampling
reality principle
scheme
social learning theory
superego
survey
tabula rasa
unconscious mind
vicarious reinforcement
zone of proximal development

InfoTrac College Edition

For additional readings, explore InfoTrac College Edition, your online library. Go to **http://www.infotrac-college.com/wadsworth** and use the passcode that came on the card with your book. Try these search terms: Jean Piaget, research ethics, experimental design, Sigmund Freud.

Child Development CD-ROM

Go to the Wadsworth Child Development CD-ROM for further study of the concepts in this chapter. The CD-ROM also includes quizzes and additional activities to expand your learning experience.

CHAPTER TWO

Cultural and Ethnic Influences on Children's Development

CHAPTER OUTLINE

A Multicultural Perspective
- Goals of Understanding Multiculturalism
- Within-Group Variations
- Defining Terms
- Socializing Children for Competency
- Collectivism and Individualism
- Conducting Cross-Cultural Research

Children in Various Cultures
- Japan: Fostering Academic Achievement
- China: Traditionalism and Modernism
- Sweden: Social Welfare Systems

U.S. Ethnic Groups: Beliefs and Concerns
- Cultural Beliefs
- Ethnicity: A Central Concern?
- Vulnerable Families?

Children in Various Ethnic Groups
- African American Families
- Asian American Families
- Native American Families
- Latino Families

Reviewing Key Points

Tina, who is the mother of 4-year-old Christian (my neighborhood Superman protector you met in Chapter 1), relates, "I want to raise my son to be independent, self-assertive, and able to stand up for his own rights. I want him to do well in school and become successful in his occupation."

Sung Liu, mother of Manang, has very different goals for her daughter: "My goal as a mother is to raise my daughter to be obedient, reliable, and a good worker. I want her to approach life with patience, accommodation, and respect for others."

Culture is the "man made" part of the environment that greeted Christian and Manang from birth. In this sense, *culture*, as noted in Chapter 1, is a particular form of civilization involving a set of shared values, assumptions, behavioral patterns, and customs that has evolved over many years and will be passed down from generation to generation. Children learn many things from the way they are handled, held, and talked to and from the daily rhythm of life that goes on around them. For example, Tina gleamed with delight when Christian spoke his first word and praised his problem-solving skills and independent thinking, but Sung Liu was most delighted with her daughter's evolving social and nurturing skills.

Different cultures, different philosophies. In every culture around the world, adults, consciously or unconsciously, try to teach children to behave in valued ways that will enable them to become socially competent adults. What is seen as social competency is diverse and varies with different cultures and ethnic groups. As will become apparent to you in reading this chapter, each of us acquires a different *design for living* from the respective societies that structure our lives.

In this chapter, we will travel across geographic and cultural boundaries to learn about children's development from a multicultural/ethnic perspective—an important theme that we will revisit throughout the text. I find cross-cultural studies fascinating, and I think you will, too. Examining the similarities and sometimes striking differences among children worldwide opens up whole new vistas in understanding children.

First, we will travel to Japan, China, and Sweden. Although each of these countries has been studied extensively, researchers tend to focus on each for different reasons. Japan is often studied because of the academic excellence achieved by its children. Although this tends to be true of Chinese children as well, China is included here because it represents a changing country that is in a rapid state of evolution and modification of tradition. China is also unique because of its government-mandated one-child policy, which gives us a particularly unique perspective on children's development. Finally, Sweden has earned recognition as a pacesetter for pioneering changing roles for mothers and fathers and for research focusing on the health and welfare social services needed to support working parents. Although we will travel to distant lands, we will not ignore our own backyard. In the second half of this chapter, we will also examine the richness and complexity of the various ethnic groups—African Americans, Asian Americans, Native Americans, and Hispanic Americans, to name a few—that are found within our own U.S. borders.

A Multicultural Perspective

Before Beginning . . .

After reading this section, you will be able to

- see the importance of understanding children from a multicultural perspective.
- discuss how caregivers in various parts of the world socialize children for competency in their adult roles.
- examine collective and individualist cultural perspectives.

ethnocentrism
The belief that one's culture is preferable or superior.

Goals of Understanding Multiculturalism

We have two major goals for presenting childhood from a multicultural perspective throughout the text: first to develop a less ethnocentric view of children and, second, to increase recognition of and respect for cultural diversity.

Develop a Less Ethnocentric View of Children

USA! USA! USA! Our country is the best! It is not just here in the United States that we view our country—our culture—as the center of everything and rate all others by referencing our standards and beliefs. People in cultures around the world regard their own particular habits and customs as right and therefore, presumably, superior. The notion is an old one. In the 1700s, the Greenland Eskimos, for example, thought the Europeans who arrived on their shores had come to learn virtue and good manners from them (Brown, 1963). **Ethnocentrism**, the belief that one's culture is preferable or superior, is not all bad. In fact, it may serve a very useful service. The very existence of a culture depends on a high degree of consensus.

Sometimes, however, this ethnocentric notion is carried too far when peoples of various cultures begin to impose their own values on others and judge others' behavior and beliefs as inferior to their own. When this happens, diverse family patterns are often misunderstood or judged as "deviant" rather than simply different. By studying children in various cultural and ethnic contexts, we gain a richer and more accurate understanding of the complexity of children's development.

Increase Our Recognition of and Respect for Cultural Diversity

There was a time when understanding people in other cultures was the sole province of ambassadors, diplomats, military personnel, and businesspeople with cross-cultural interests. Today, understanding the various cultures of the world is everybody's business. We live in an age of continuous change and ever-increasing global interdependence. The internationalization of economies, governments, and cultures creates a compelling need for examining the diversity of children and family life in other countries. Within the United States, we continue to be an increasingly diverse population as African Americans, Hispanics, Chinese, Japanese, Vietnamese, and many other segments of the population continue to grow. As such, it is imperative to understand the ways of peoples both outside and inside of our own particular culture or ethnic group. Through a cross-cultural/ethnic approach to studying children, we increase the probability that we will respect cultural diversity and recognize that our beliefs and practices do not always reflect optimal and normative child development. In addition, multicultural/ethnic understandings of children help us to develop an awareness of how culture contributes to divergent pathways to children's development and cultivates a sensitivity and understanding of the customs and lifestyles of other cultures.

Danny Lehman/Corbis

Worldwide, children learn behaviors and skills that enable them to adapt successfully to their society.

Within-Group Variations

Cross-cultural research may help to illuminate our understanding of others, but there is no way that *all* the people composing a culture or ethnic group can be neatly and precisely "categorized." As we look at peoples from Japan, China, and Sweden and explore ethnic groups such as African Americans, Hispanics, and Pacific Islanders in the United States, we have to always keep in mind that there is considerable variation among members of these cultures and ethnic groups. Although there may be some unifying cultural themes, clearly not all Japanese children excel in finite math and quantum physics; not all Hispanic families are family-centered, with strict sex and age roles; and not all African American families emphasize children's compliance with authority. Such a narrow view leads to stereotyping rather than understanding. Thus, within-group differences need to be underscored.

Ideally, the sample populations that psychologists use to examine various cross-cultural behaviors should be representative of the population as a whole. This enables researchers to generalize their findings to a larger group with a certain degree of confidence. No study, however, can describe an entire nation of people. Studies can only describe the specific communities within these nations that were the focus of the research. But even then, it is important to remember that there will be exceptions to the data reported.

Defining Terms

Key terms such as *race, ethnic* or *ethnic group*, and *minority* have become a part of everyday conversation and description. The term **race** is linked with superficial *physical* differences. Classifying people "racially" presents several problems. First, there is not a consensus among physical anthropologists on how many races exist. Textbooks frequently designate three broad categories: Mongoloid, or Asian; Negroid, or African; and Caucasoid, or European. Caucasians are differentiated by light skin pigmentation, prominent chins, and relatively long trunks, for example. Despite these and many more precise characteristics of each of the three races, many groups, some sizable, defy fixed classification. For example, Native Americans do not fit into one of the three racial classifications, and diverse peoples such as Arabs and Hindus, although physically different, are grouped as Caucasians. Some physical anthropologists have created up to 200 classification categories to describe exceptional groups (Schaefer, 1988).

The second problem in defining human races is that given frequent migration, exploration, and invasions, pure gene frequencies have not existed for quite some time—if they ever did. There are no mutually exclusive races. The notion of "race" persists in popular discourse, but inherently pure divisions of mankind do not exist in reality (Rodriguez & Cordero-Gusman, 1992).

The third problem is deciding what characteristics will be chosen to classify people into racial categories.

race
Technically, a race is an interbreeding population whose members share a greater number of traits with one another than they do with people outside the group.

Why are some physical characteristics, such as skin color, selected as a basis for distinguishing human groups, while other characteristics, such as eye color, are seldom used to distinguish groups from one another? Basically, because skin color was so noticeable, it was one of the more frequently explained traits, and most systems of racial classification were based on it. All physical anthropologists who have attempted to classify people according to race have *arbitrarily* selected the traits they used—whether it was blood type; structure of noses, mouths, or eyes; or hair (Montague, 1963). Although biological differences among human groups do exist, the human species cannot be sorted into a small number of biologically fairly discrete groups.

As a scientific concept, then, race is not terribly significant. In fact, most anthropologists no longer view racial classifications as valid given the current state of genetic and evolutionary science. However, to some people, it appears to make little difference that beliefs about race have no scientific basis; the term has become socially significant. Race relations and stratification based on race are affected by people's beliefs, not necessarily by scientific facts. Thus, the term has become significant because people have given it significance. People often speculate that if human groups have obvious physical differences, then they must have corresponding mental or personality differences. When this belief is coupled with the feeling that certain groups or races are inherently superior to others, it is called *racism*—the most detrimental outcome of racial classification.

By contrast, the term **ethnic** is used primarily in context of *cultural* differences. Indeed, the word *ethnic* comes from the Greek *ethnos*, originally meaning "nation." "Ethnic group" usually describes a group that is socially distinguished or set apart by others, and/or by itself, primarily on the basis of cultural or nationality characteristics. These cultural or national traits may include commonly perceived shared ancestry, language, and national or regional origin (Fenton, 1999). Members of an ethnic group perceive themselves as sharing these (and perhaps other) cultural characteristics (Ferraro, 2001).

ethnicity, or ethnic group
Groups having a unique system of beliefs and practices that overlap but differ in some respects from that of other ethnic groups.

Currently, the majority of the people in the United States are perceived as ethnically "white," despite the great variation displayed among the 53 categories of white subgroups identified by the 2000 U.S. Census. This population currently represents about 70 percent of the child population under the age of 18 (see Figure 2.1). These people were labeled "Caucasian"; today they are referred to as European Americans. Approximately 60 percent of the Europeans who came to the United States during colonial times were English, and the dominant culture of the United States was built on their language, lifestyle, values, and social institutions.

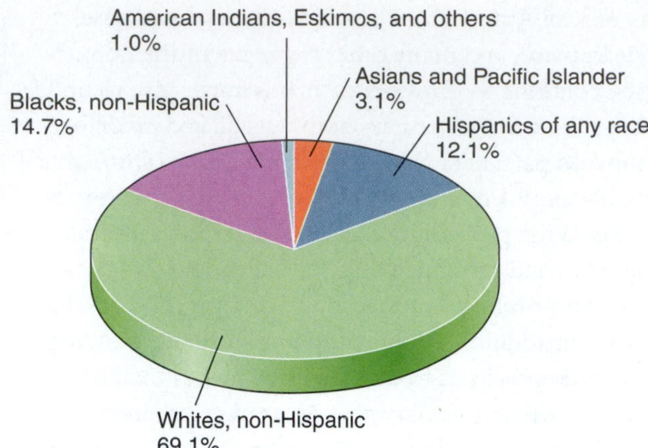

FIGURE 2.1 ***Composition of Child Population Under the Age of 18 in the United States***

From *The Experience of Parenting*, by M. J. Muzi, 2000, Upper Saddle River, NJ: Prentice-Hall.

Among the other terms that have been used to describe ethnic groups is *minority group*. "Minority" means the smaller number of a group or society. Like *race*, a powerful set of social ideas and beliefs accompany terms such as ethnic or minority group. The terms refer to groups who share unique cultural traditions and a heritage that persists across generations, but too often *minority*, *ethnic*, and *ethnic group* are used to stigmatize group members whose experiences may have included political victimization, economic disadvantage, oppression, and difficulty blending into mainstream social institutions (Ogbu, 2000).

Socializing Children for Competency

Culture is an adaptive mechanism. A universal goal in every culture is for its children to become competent members of a society (Ingoldsby & Smith, 1995), and child-rearing processes may be seen as "successful" to the extent that children internalize their society's values and traditions. Eventually, the child comes to see the routines of the society as natural and right. Children, then, depend on their culture to help define who they are, who other people are, and their "proper" role.

In the process of **socialization**, adults teach their children how to become acceptable members of society. Members of any one society usually share clear ideas about the means and ends of child rearing (Super & Harkness, 1999). Basically, the behaviors of children most valued are those that are functional for the larger society (Ogbu, 2000). This does not imply, however, that socialization only works one way, with passive children simply soaking up the lessons of their caregivers. Rather, it is a two-way street involving interaction and influence between children and their caregivers, family members, teachers, and peers.

What Behaviors Are Valued?

Recently while waiting in a European airport, I found myself observing other travelers. Across the aisle from me was a Turkish family—a father, a mother, and their two sons. I guessed the children's ages at 4 and 6 years. The older boy was trying to get his dad's attention, constantly tugging at his pant leg. The child was holding a one-sided conversation, telling his dad what he saw in the airport and asking him questions; the father, however, looked aimlessly into space. The child then tried to get his mother's attention; and like his father, she was nonresponsive. After many attempts, the boy gave up and turned to his younger brother who appeared to be a more eager audience.

Were these just travel-weary parents? Not necessarily, according to Cigdem Kagitcibasi (1996), who has studied the Turkish culture intensively. After studying samples of parents from various urban and rural parts of Turkey, Kagitcibasi reported (1994) that these parents' verbal responsiveness to their children was infrequent and the parents tended to be less child-centered. In a sample of 5000 Turkish mothers, 73 percent reported that a child interrupting adult conversation was simply "not tolerated." Another study lends support to these findings. In this nationwide study, 6000 Turkish mothers were asked how often they gave their full attention to the child outside of mealtimes (Macro, 1993). Those who said, "never" or "almost never" accounted for 22 percent. When combined with those who said "seldom," low involvement was found among more than 40 percent of the mothers. Approximately, 90 percent of the mothers stated that household chores were the main focus at home and that they had little direct interaction with their children.

Moreover, according to Kagitcibasi, a positive social orientation and an obedient disposition were highly valued among her sample of Turkish parents. Traits such as respect, good relational behavior (with being good to mother mentioned most frequently), and social behavior (showing affection and getting along with others) were cited as the most esteemed ways of behaving. Being independent was rarely mentioned as a valued behavior (Kagitcibasi, 1996).

A different line of research sought to gain insight into culturally valued behaviors by examining the words parents used to praise children (Super & Harkness, 1999). The sample consisted of urban-dwelling Kenyans and a cross-section of European American parents in the United States. The Kenyan parents tended to use words to praise their children that emphasized obedience and helpfulness, such as "respectful, polite, good-hearted." In comparison, the American parents were more likely to use words that frequently referred to children's cognitive capacities, such as "intelligent, smart, curious, inquisitive." The differences in words used in parental talk, suggest the authors, relate to the traits valued and the behavior expected of their children. Charles Super and Sara Harkness further noted that parental communications were often translated into action. The authors reported that the American children studied were far more verbally precocious and adept at imaginative play than the Kenyan children. The Kenyan children, however, were far more socially responsible. For example, they noted 5-year-old children supervising babies and children as young as 8 cooking the family dinner.

Socially Prescribed Caregiver Roles

Whether or not caregivers see themselves as active players in child rearing appears to be important in determining their socialization practices. For example, in India, people commonly refer to the child "growing-up" (*buyur*) rather than "being brought up" (*yetistirlir*). According to several researchers, the Indian mothers they studied saw themselves as not playing a critical role in molding the child. Instead, they tended to see the child as on his or her own developmental path, over which parents had little or no control (Kakar, 1978; Saraswathi & Pai, 1997). If parents mentioned child rearing, it was more in the sense of enabling the physical growth of the child, or *buyytmek*, which literally means "to get bigger." Relatedly, in terms of academic growth, the Indian mothers sampled did not appear to see themselves so much as "teachers" but as supportive helpers who applied little pressure to instruct the child.

In a similar light, Concha Delgado-Gaitan (1994) suggests that the Mexican American mothers she studied

socialization
Refers to how parents rear their children and how children learn to become acceptable members of society.

did not see themselves as "academic teachers." Delgado-Gaitan observed Mexican American mothers in a small city in California and noted that although they were eager to be helpful to their children, they did not tend to contribute directly to their children's academic achievement. These mothers helped their children indirectly by providing quiet places for them to do their homework, setting regular meal and bedtimes, and stressing to them the importance of doing well in school but did not tend to coach them directly.

In contrast, Harold Stevenson (1998) compared a sample of American mothers from Minneapolis and mothers from Taipei, Taiwan, and noted that both groups played a highly direct role in promoting their children's academic achievement. The American mothers, he reported, tended to believe that they should play a crucial role in preparing the child for school and future educational achievements. They believed their academic involvement with their children would help them to succeed in their future occupations. Similarly, the Taiwanese mothers also expressed the belief that it was important for them to help their children through coaching and giving specific instructions regarding schoolwork (Coll, 1990), but they did so for slightly different reasons. They believed that their children's academic success would bring pride to their family and to their country.

Parental roles and self-definitions of their roles may also have implications for parent–child relationships extending throughout the life cycle. For example, in his study of the Minneapolis and Taipei mothers, Stevenson reports that the American mothers' definition of their term of parental responsibility was relatively short and lasted only until late adolescence. To these parents, independence and self-sufficiency were valued as traits in their offspring. In Taiwan, noted Stevenson, the mothers he studied believed that their maternal responsibility lasts a lifetime. In general, conceptualizations of such lifelong parental responsibilities go hand in hand with more *collectivist* socialization patterns that emphasize interdependence.

collectivism
A cultural philosophy that emphasizes the interconnectedness of persons; valuing the social and the group. Collective societies tend to emphasize obedience, reliability, and proper behavior in children.

Socializing girls to do well academically is typical in many technologically advanced societies. In contrast, in many developing or rural economics, the roles for females tend to emphasize domestic accomplishments more than academic achievement (Smith, 1995). For example, consider the girls from Varanasi, India—a community of weavers:

> Most of the girls by the time they are six years old are adept at sweeping, cleaning and washing dishes and looking after siblings. . . . Young, unmarried girls, by and large, lead a life of domesticity unhampered by school routines or tasks. The day's routine runs an uninterrupted course of spooling, interspersed with domestic chores, the care of younger siblings and gossiping and giggling to the background noise of film music on the radio." (Anandalaksmy & Bajaj, 1988, pp. 34, 37–38)

For these girls, formal education in their rural Indian village was not deemed essential because all that they had to do was to "manage the household." Further, the adults believed that education might lead to the girls becoming clever and nonconforming. These studies show how children's competence in culturally valued domains gets promoted, whereas development in other domains lags behind if it is recognized at all.

There is infinite variety in the roles and skills that children learn in different cultures, but there are two cultural perspectives that have a broad, unifying effect on socialization practices. These two dimensions of cultural variation, the collectivist and the individualist philosophies, have a key effect on parental belief systems, and subsequently, children's developmental outcomes (Goodnow, 1998).

Collectivism and Individualism

About 70 percent of the population of the world (for example, China, Egypt, Russia, Venezuela, Columbia, Pakistan, Peru) live in collectivist cultures (U.S. Bureau of the Census, 1998). **Collectivism** is a social norm that emphasizes the interconnectedness of people—one that places a high value on harmony in interpersonal relations and the ability to cooperate with others (Lonner, Dinnel, Forgays, & Hayes, 1999). In a collectivist society, the social, the collective, and the group are valued over the personal, the familial, and the individual (Azuma, 1998). Collectivist cultures value harmony within the group, politeness, and security. This philosophical viewpoint emphasizes a preference for a tightly knit social framework in which each individual can expect their relatives, clan, and other "in-group" members to look after them in exchange for unquestioning loyalty (Cheung & Liu, 1997). Collectivist societies tend to emphasize obedient, reliable, and proper behavior in children. Children are encouraged to follow rules and conform to norms (Sastry & Ross, 1998).

Although diversity exists within each culture, two broad cultural perspectives are apparent worldwide: individualism and collectivism.

A culture of **individualism** is prominent in highly industrialized countries, such as the United States, France, Germany, Sweden, England, Australia, and Canada, and represents a preference for a loosely knit social framework where individuals are supposed to take care of themselves and their immediate families only. The individualistic philosophy tends to place emphasis on such behaviors as self-reliance, personal reliance, independence, personal freedom, competition, and distance from groups. Child-rearing beliefs in an individualistic culture tend to be dominated by the notion that "each of us is an entity separate from the other and from the group and as such is endowed with natural rights" (Spence, 1985, p. 1288). In contrast to the virtues of patience, persistence, and accommodation promoted by collectivist societies, the traits admired by individualist cultures tend to be originality, exploration, and self-assertion. Collectivism embraces a positive attitude toward ancestors, whereas individualism tends to emphasize the importance of youth and the future (Triandis, 1997). Table 2.1 summarizes the key differences between collectivism and individualism.

Individualism and collectivism reflect, in part, core values. Of course, they do not reflect the beliefs of all who reside within these respective types of cultures. There is more than one variety of individualism or independence orientation and more than one variety of collectivism or interdependence orientation across and within cultures (Greenfield, 1994). Your basic cultural values, needs, and beliefs, however, do strongly influence your attitudes about how children should be socialized. The Self-Insight exercise will help you to identify whether your beliefs are more reflective of collectivism or individualism.

Conducting Cross-Cultural Research

Cultures may be studied from two perspectives: *emic* and *etic*. When conducting research from an **emic** perspective, the objective is to describe behavior *within* a certain cultural setting. For example, if I am interested in understanding political leadership among the Ashaninka, an Amazonian group living in the rugged foothills of the Andes, I would talk to the *pinkatsari*, which literally translated means "big man" or chief. In this sense, the emic approach tries to view another culture through the eyes of a cultural insider or native. As such, we gain an understanding of that culture from the participants—in this case, the pinkatsari's point of view. In carrying out research in the emic mode, my concern would be to describe behavior in ways that

individualism
A cultural philosophy that emphasizes independence, self-assertiveness, and competitiveness.

emic
When conducting research from an *emic* perspective, the objective is to describe behavior *within* a certain cultural setting.

TABLE 2.1

Key Differences Between Collectivism and Individualism

Collectivism	Individualism
"We" consciousness	"I" consciousness
Collective identity	Autonomy
Emotional dependence	Emotional independence
Group solidarity	Individual initiative
Sharing	Right to privacy
Duties and obligations	Pleasure seeking
Need for stable and predetermined friendship	Financial security
Group decision	Need for specific friendship

Self-Insight

Collectivism–Individualism Scale

Rate each of the items below using the following scale:

Strongly disagree	Moderately disagree	Slightly disagree	Slightly agree	Moderately agree	Strongly agree
0	1	2	3	4	5

____ 1. If a husband is a sports fan, a wife should also cultivate an interest in sports.

If the husband is a stockbroker, the wife should also be aware of current stock trends.

____ 2. It is better for a husband and wife to have their own bank accounts rather than to have a joint account.

____ 3. The decision of where one is to work should be jointly made with one's spouse, if one is married.

____ 4. When making important decisions, I seldom consider the positive and negative effects my decisions have on my father.

____ 5. Teenagers should listen to their parents' advice on dating.

____ 6. The bigger a family, the more family problems there are.

____ 7. When deciding what kind of education to have, I would pay absolutely no attention to my uncle's advice.

____ 8. Each family has its own problems, unique to itself. It does not help to tell relatives (beyond one's immediate family) about one's problems.

____ 9. I can count on relatives (beyond my immediate family) for help if I find myself in any kind of trouble.

____ 10. I would rather struggle through a personal problem by myself than discuss it with my friends.

____ 11. I like to live close to my good friends.

____ 12. I would pay absolutely no attention to my close friends' views when deciding what kind of work to do.

____ 13. I am not interested in knowing what my neighbors are really like.

____ 14. One need not worry about what the neighbors say about whom one should marry.

____ 15. I don't really know how to befriend my neighbors.

____ 16. There is everything to gain and nothing to lose for classmates to group themselves for study and discussion.

____ 17. I would help if a colleague at work told me that he/she needed money to pay utility bills.

____ 18. In most cases, to cooperate with someone whose ability is lower than one's own is not as desirable as doing the thing alone.

C. Harry Hui (1988) wrote the Individualism–Collectivism Scale. These items represent a sample of the items from each of the subscales in the scale. To score the scale, reverse your scores for items 2, 4, 6, 7, 8, 10, 12, 13, 14, 15, and 18 (0 = 5, 1 = 4, 2 = 3, 3 = 2, 4 = 1, 5 = 0). Higher scores reflect a greater collectivist tendency. If you are from the United States, which is an individualistic country, you may find that your scores are rather low. The culture in which we are raised impacts our values, socialization strategies, and expectations and the goals we have for our children.

etic
Refers to *outside* the cultural setting. Researchers interested in studying political leadership across several cultures might adopt an *etic* approach.

are important to that culture or ethnic group, without making generalizations across cultures.

If, however, I am interested in studying political leadership across several cultures, I may adopt an **etic** approach. "Etic" refers to *outside* the cultural setting. If I apply the outsider etic approach, my observational point of view is the ultimate interpreter of political leadership in various cultural settings. Edward Tronick and his colleagues (Tronick, Morelli, & Ivey, 1992) used the etic approach when studying the Efe pygmies in the tropical rainforests of Zaire. The research team, armed with their laptop computers, recorded minute-by-minute observations of the social life of Efe infants and toddlers in the camps.

The authors observed that Efe children were constantly surrounded by other people—almost every waking moment of their day. They concluded that, in contrast to many U.S. children who are groomed for independence, the Efe children appeared to be socialized for their interdependent and communal lifestyles. The emic approach is culture-specific; the etic approach is culture-universal. Of course, both emic and etic approaches can be applied when conducting cross-cultural research.

Researchers may rely on other methods, such as the correlational or experimental methods, to investigate psychological phenomena. For example, one researcher noted that harsh childhood discipline seemed to correlate with a society's belief in evil and spiteful deities (Rohner, 1986). Experimental methods have been used in other countries to test whether the findings of studies of phenomena like the development of "formal operational thinking" replicates cross-culturally. (For a discussion of Piaget's concept of formal operational thinking, see Chapter 15.)

Cross-cultural research, however, presents a number of challenges. For example, it is important to define and classify what is comparable from one society to another. The same stimulus may mean very different things to people in different cultures. For example, "abstract reasoning" in the United States typically refers to logical-mathematical problems; these same problems may not be applicable in measuring abstract reasoning in other cultures. In addition, researchers must be particularly alert to their own ethnocentrism and culturally biased value judgments for or against such traits as independence or community orientation.

Similarly, researchers must be careful about translations as well. For example, if I learned that a pinkatsari was a prominent person with a forceful personality and applied the outsider etic category "chief" to the Ashaninka, I would have completely misunderstood his cultural role. As John Bodley (1997) points out, a pinkatsari can harangue or persuade others, but he has no coercive authority over his followers. In fact, the Ashaninka reject this kind of central political authority implied by the outsider word *chief*. Moreover, when employing questionnaires, even minor changes or ambiguities in the wording of questions could make cross-cultural comparisons invalid. There are hurdles to climb when conducting cross-cultural research, but we have to learn to surmount them if we want to have a fuller understanding of children's development.

Concept Checks

1. A particular culture selects child-training practices that will tend to produce a particular behavior because
   a. this behavior makes parents' lives easier.
   b. children will be successful in their expected adult roles.
   c. children will do well in school and get along with others.
2. A young child is brought up in a culture in which obedience and strong interconnectedness with other people are emphasized. He is probably being raised in
   a. Paris, France.
   b. St. Louis, Missouri.
   c. Shanghai, China.

Children in Various Cultures

Before Beginning . . .

After reading this section, you will be able to

- examine the child-rearing goals of Japanese caregivers.
- discuss the changes underway in China and how its one-child policy impacts children's development.
- identify social policies in Sweden that help working parents.

We begin our journey in Japan. Considerable research has focused on the outstanding academic performance of an impressively high percentage of Japanese children—particularly in mathematics and science. In Chapter 12, we will examine these achievements and possible factors for students' exemplary scholastic performance; in this chapter we will look at the beginning socialization patterns that may set these high-performing children on a trajectory for academic excellence.

Japan: Fostering Academic Achievement

Yukimi is 4 years old. She lives in Tokyo with her mother Li and her father Chen Ichiro. Mrs. Ichiro holds a strong position in the family; it is her exclusive domain, and Yukimi is her mother's first priority. Mrs. Ichiro feels responsible for her daughter's unhappiness,

© Elizabeth Crews

The traditional expectation in Japan is that women will curtail their outside employment once they have children, but many remain in the workforce.

whether it is expressed in sickness, fussing, crying, sadness, or doing poorly in school. To avoid criticism from her husband and neighbors, she does whatever is possible to keep her child calm and happy. Mrs. Ichiro's major goal is to make sure that her child will do well in school. The community's perception of a Japanese mother's socialization success is strongly linked to her children's performance in the academic setting.

Hiroshi Azuma (1998) suggests that Japanese students' superior performance in school is supported by a variety of factors that stem from the influence of "Japanese collectivism,'" which supports communal, societal, and specifically educational achievement. Azuma argues that these values are imparted to children very early in life, setting children on a positive trajectory to academic success. The child must never bring shame to his or her mother, and one of the worst things a child could do to cause a mother humiliation is not do well in school. Children learn this lesson very early in life, and the key architect in fostering academic excellence is the mother.

For these reasons, the traditional Japanese expectation is that mothers will curtail their employment once they have children. Japanese women are significantly less likely than U.S. women to think that women can handle both home and career and more likely to think that problems with their children or marriage would arise if they were employed (Engel, 1998). Thus, it is largely still the ideal in Japan for mothers not to work in outside paid employment (Shwalb & Shwalb, 1996).

Although some Japanese mothers of young children do work outside the home, they do so primarily to allow their children to attend nursery school (Hirayama, 1999). Because many day nurseries have openings only for employed mothers, a growing number of mothers are taking jobs just so their children can be enrolled in nursery school (Zahn-Waxler, Friedman, Cole, & Mizuta, 1996). Moreover, contemporary financial demands often make it more difficult for Japanese women to see mothering as a full-time, lifetime job. Today, providing children with an appropriate education is expensive in Japan, and some mothers are obliged to take part-time jobs for additional income for the family. The majority of Japanese mothers' participation in the labor force, however, tends to conform to the "M-shaped model" (Hayashi, 1991). For example, young women enter the workforce after they complete their formal education and continue to work after marriage. Women discontinue working after they have their first child. They then return to the labor force as part-time workers after their children are in school and stay there until their children complete their education.

What about fathers? What is their role in socializing their children? Both mothers employed outside the home and those who remained at home expressed beliefs that they are responsible for "family care," and husbands should be the sole breadwinners (Hirayama, 1999). This belief tends to be held much more widely in Japan than in the United States (Shwalb, Kawai, Shoji, & Tsunetsugu, 1997). Although the father as the formal head of the family is accorded respect, he does not tend to exert much control over daily affairs. In many ways, Japanese fathers are treated like high-status guests in their homes, a friendly and even jovial guest, but one who stands on the periphery of the intimate relationship between mothers and children (Hara & Minagawa, 1996). As stated by one Japanese mother, "A woman does not need a husband except as a supplier of money" (Lebra, 1994). There is some evidence, however, of shifting society values in support of greater paternal involvement (Crystal,

Watanabe, Weinfurt, & Wu, 1998). Thus, the father's role in Japan may be changing, with more emphasis on both parents making joint contributions to caring for children (Muzi, 2000). This trend appears to be evident in many contemporary cultures. (See Cultural Variations.)

When traditional Japanese fathers and mothers go out for the evening, they are likely to bring along their young children. Indeed, the reason for going out is to bring some cultural enrichment into their children's lives. The concept of hiring a baby-sitter to allow the parents some time off from child care is almost unheard of in Japan (Morinaga, 1995). Although many American parents would not doubt their right to enjoy themselves away from their children, in Japan, leaving children with outsiders, for such frivolous reasons, would likely be frowned on.

Child-Rearing Goals and Methods in Japan

Patterns of socialization in Japan attempt to foster politeness, attentiveness to others, concentration, patience, and a strong sense of family and group identity. Similarly, the Japanese culture has traditionally emphasized harmonious relationships within and between groups, and childhood socialization stresses this spirit of interdependence (Hara & Minagawa, 1996).

Japanese mothers' message to their children is, "I am one with you, we can be and will be of the same mind." Children then are likely to develop a social sensitivity to their mother's feelings, and, through her, to other people's feelings. The ideal is for children to love their parents and very early in life to develop a strong desire to bring them honor through their social sensitivity and academic successes (Behrens, 2001).

These valued behaviors are fostered through mothers' indulgence and devotion. The family assumption, however, is that as children mature, they will need to reciprocate the unconditional support provided by their parents by fulfilling various responsibilities (Kim & Choi, 1994):

- *Obeying*: Respect parents' opinions and authority through daily behavior, such as seeking parental agreement before making decisions.
- *Attending*: Take care of parents' needs, for example, taking care of them when they are ill.
- *Supporting*: Provide materialistic comforts for parents, such as being sure that parents are comfortably housed, fed, and cared for.
- *Comforting*: Create psychological ease and entertainment, by not worrying parents. For example, children must let their parents know their coming in, going out, and general whereabouts.
- *Honoring*: Even after parents die, honor the parents' achievements, fulfill their intentions, complete their undertakings, and sustain their social networks.

One important goal for many Japanese mothers is to protect their feelings of closeness with their children (Kazui, 1997). Mothers are likely to promote empathic harmony and work hard to avoid escalation of conflict, confrontation, and depreciation of children's self-esteem. Mothers promote closeness through practices such as prolonged breast-feeding, co-bathing, and co-sleeping. Moreover, if the child is obstinate, the mother will more than likely give in rather than injure the relationship. For example, if a child does not like what her mother has prepared for dinner, and refuses to eat, the mother may simply clear away the plate and prepare the child's preferred dish. The most important concern of traditional Japanese mothers is preservation of closeness between mother and child rather than absolute obedience (Azuma, 1998).

Traditional Japanese mothers establish control over their children through devotion and indulgence. The sequence works much like this:

indulgence ► dependence ► identification ► controllability

Children are expected to be childlike, which means natural and spontaneous, and Japanese mothers are expected to accept this childish behavior. The child's natural spontaneity merges with the mother's indulgence leading to **amae**, a feeling of dependency by children coupled with their expectation of indulgence from their mothers (Lebra, 1994). Children also generally attempt to sense what pleases their mothers and try to behave accordingly (Azuma, 1998).

Disciplining techniques are also designed to bring about children's dependency on their mothers. Mothers frequently appeal to their children's sense of empathy, presenting themselves as victims of ridicule and humiliation if their children misbehave or do poorly in school (Crystal, Watanabe, Weinfurt, & Wu, 1998). A mother, for example, might employ the technique of announcing that she feels hurt when her child misbehaves and happy when the child behaves appropriately.

Japanese mothers may even use fear to discipline their children (Vogel, 1996). For example, if a child did something her mother disapproved of, the mother

amae
Refers to one's inclination to depend on or accept another's nurturing and indulgence, including one's dependency; typically used to describe the mother–child relationship in Japan.

Cultural Variations

Fathers Around the World

The notion that culture is synonymous with cultural differences is very prevalent. However, culture in human development has universal mechanisms as well. This is quite apparent when looking at fathers cross-culturally. Several commonalities about fathers are found across a variety of cultures, including France, Italy, Great Britain, and Australia (Bronstein, 1999; Dollahite, Hawkins, & Brotherson, 1997; Furman, 1999; Lamb, 1997, 1998).

FATHER'S INFLUENCE

In general, fathers tend to rate their influence on children as *less than mothers,* particularly in the areas of

- getting along with others.
- developing sensitivity to others' feelings.
- developing attitudes and morals.
- learning to be expressive.
- shaping manners and appearance.

In contrast, fathers tend to rate their influence as being greater than mothers over children's

- sense of humor.
- problem-solving skills and efforts.
- coping with rough play or fighting.
- independence.
- competitiveness.
- being good at a sport.

WHAT FATHERS ENJOY THE MOST AND THE LEAST

The things that fathers tend to *enjoy most* are

- watching children grow and develop.
- the status and achievement associated with being a parent.
- the stimulation and fun of having personal growth/learning experiences.
- the expression of love and affection.

In contrast, the majority of fathers from these cultures noted the following as the aspects they *disliked the most:*

- the costs of raising children.
- the anxiety their children cause them.
- the constancy of their children's demands.
- their loss of freedom.
- time conflicts.

IMAGES OF FATHERS' ROLE

Samples of fathers in all four cultures found that they are expected to be the breadwinner, head of the household, family protector, and disciplinarian (especially in more serious matters). They are expected to represent a masculine model and to spend time and play with their children when they can, especially with sons (for example, playing rough-and-tumble games). The organization of family life remains the mother's responsibility, even if she is employed in a position of high salary and prestige. The father, in contrast, plays a marginal role in the care of his children. The majority of fathers, however, express a desire to spend more time with their children and to become more patient or tolerant with their children.

One of the most consistent findings in these various cultures is fathers' beliefs that mothers are by nature better suited to care for children. They believe that mothers have a biological advantage over fathers and are more competent, sensitive, and patient with children, and perhaps above all, that children (particularly younger ones) need their mothers. Fathers see themselves as competent enough, but only if the situation demands it. As such, the demonstrations of affection for and care of the children officially revert to the mother. A mother shows her devotion to her child through affection; in the father–child relationship, devotion is shown through strictness. Another consistent finding in all these cultures, including the United States, is that there is a slow but nevertheless significant shift in father participation (Cole, 1999). This topic is further discussed in Chapter 7.

might threaten to report her to the teacher or a policeman. At the same time, parents demonstrate to their children that they will be there to comfort them, thereby encouraging children to remain close and dependent. Japanese mothers may also use teasing, shaming, and ridiculing as disciplining techniques. They can appeal to children's duties, responsibilities, and guilt. In general, mothers control their children's behavior calmly and without anger (Lanham & Garrick, 1996). In this way, they ensure that children do not develop feelings of resentment that might weaken the bonds of love and filial gratitude.

However, this lack of discipline—letting children be natural, free, and spontaneous—coupled with fear and love-withdrawal techniques may result in contradictory patterns of behavior (Kim & Choi, 1994). Japanese children, for example, tend to be spoiled yet disciplined, spontaneous yet programmed, unruly yet reserved, and free but conforming.

Fostering Social Relationships

A primary purpose of preschools in Japan is to help children learn how to get along with others and develop a love for learning—two powerful prerequisites to academic success (Gu, Cen, Li, Gao, Li, & Chen, 1997). The importance and pleasure of being with others and the acquisition of social skills to facilitate acceptance by others are central themes that Japanese adults and preschool teachers emphasize. Through lessons and activities, skills such as thoughtfulness, hard work, endurance, fairness, and cooperation are taught.

While observing children in a Japanese preschool, I noticed one group of children sitting in a circle and the teacher was asking each child a favorite nickname they would like to be called by the other children. The teacher told the children that good names make children feel good. Another group of children were busily engaged in the "turtle game." Ten children were huddled close together on their hands and knees. A big green cloth (the turtle's shell) was placed over the children with only the two front children able to see. The object was for the children to travel *en masse* to the treat table located at the other side of the room. As they progressed across the room, you could hear their giggles as they moved toward the cookies and lemonade. The game appeared to be quite successful in promoting cooperation and social coherence among the children—first vital steps to academic success.

China: Traditionalism and Modernism

I remember two things my mother told me over and over again when I was a little girl—"eat well so you won't get sick," and "remain strong so that you will do well in school." This is all I remember from my early years, and I told my children to do these things as well.

Because China, like Japan, has a collectivist society heritage, similarities exist between these two cultures. Core values and beliefs, such as parents stressing the importance of children doing well in school, are apparent in both countries (Stevenson, 1998). However, there are some important differences as well. In China, unlike Japan, most mothers work in outside paid employment. Further, although communist China has had a long history as a stronghold for collectivist beliefs, today, there is a growing trend toward an individualistic philosophy among China's youths. These factors, along with the one-child philosophy in China call for different parenting needs and practices.

The Changing Face of China

Under the influence of social change in China, two important changes are occurring: the first relates to values and ways of behaving, and the second involves a decline in traditional filial piety (Chen, Rubin, & Sun, 1992; Ho, 1998). The first change is a central trend among many Chinese youths, who are moving away from a social, collectivist value orientation to one that is more reflective of a Western individualism orientation.

Chinese high school and college students, for example, are placing higher values on personality measures for such traits as sociability (extroversion), dominance, flexibility, tolerance, and masculinity and lower values on their emotionality (anxiety), self-restraint (cautiousness), friendliness (harmonious relationship), conscientiousness, and perseverance (Ho, 1998). Moreover, a growing number of young Chinese have a higher need for exhibition and autonomy and lower needs for deference, order, abasement, nurturance, and social approval. They also appear to be more free of the traditional inhibitions against associating with people of the opposite sex. Younger Chinese also are tending to express less interest in helping and giving sympathy to others, persevering in a task or activity until finished, seeking approval or admiration from others or society, or striving to achieve goals set by their society. They have been developing a greater concern with self-expression, self-assertion, independence, and personal achievement (Cheung & Liu, 1997). (In the First Person box, Dr. Yi Qing Liu, a professor at the University of Peking, discusses the growing individualistic views and ways of behaving that she has observed among her students.)

TABLE 2.2

The Impact of Societal Modernization on Chinese Personality

Decreasing	Increasing
Motivational Characteristics	
Deference	Exhibition
Order	Autonomy
Endurance	Achievement
Achievement (social-oriented)	Achievement (individual-oriented)
Social approval	Self-approval
Evaluative–Attitudinal Characteristics	
Preference for inner development	Preference for achievement
Preference for collectivism	Preference for individualism
Preference for social restraint and self-control	Preference for self-indulgence and enjoyment
Theoretical value	Aesthetic value
Religious value	Democratic value
External control beliefs	Internal control beliefs
Temperamental Characteristics	
Self-restraint	Sociability and extroversion
Friendliness and harmoniousness	Dominance
Conscientiousness	Flexibility
Femininity	Masculinity

From "Chinese Personality and Its Change" (pp. 106–170), by K. Yang, 1996, in M. H. Bond (Ed.), *The Psychology of the Chinese People,* New York: Oxford University Press. Used by permission.

"I was at my sister's today. They have two pots."

Today's youths in China, then, are exhibiting more of an *individual-oriented achievement motivation* as opposed to a social-oriented achievement motivation (Goodwin & Tang, 1998). Individual-oriented achievement values the standards of excellence set and evaluated by oneself. In contrast, social-oriented achievement motivation values the standards of excellence set and evaluated by significant others, such as the family, group, or the society as a whole. Striving for profit, achievement, and other forms of regard are becoming principal motivating forces for many Chinese (Lee, 1999). Table 2.2 summarizes the impact of societal modernization on Chinese personality and behavior.

The second change involves a weakening in familial piety among Chinese youths. Generally, middle-age adults still uphold the traditional value of taking care of aging parents and sharing economic assistance among siblings. This traditional perspective was evident in a 1987 study that described Chinese families as "obsessed with social order and the need to do the right thing" for their extended family members (Yu, 1987, p. 211). In families, this requires children, no matter how old, to remain loyal to their elders and to value them. An old Chinese saying goes, "The elderly are a family's greatest treasure." Filial piety requires children to give priority to the parents' need for material comfort not only while they are alive but also after death. Not to accept responsibility for one's parents or siblings goes against the cardinal Confucian principle of devotion to the family (Chuang, 2001). Family is considered the prototype of all relationships. The decline in filial piety among Chinese youths then signifies a radical change in the Chinese view of intergenerational relationships (Chan & Lee, 1995).

Modern prevailing family norms among adults in China are derived both from traditional Chinese *and* modern Western influences. For example, traditional views still espouse that the ideal child should exhibit the following types of attributes:

- *Family-related:* good parent–child relations and fulfillment of family responsibilities
- *Academic-related:* good academic outcome, positive attitude toward studying, fulfillment of responsibility in studying, and high education attainment
- *Conduct-related:* good character, self-discipline when going out, obedience to the law, no acquaintance with undesirable peers, and no naughtiness
- *Others:* such as, having good relations with others and being mature (Shek & Chan, 1999)

But, in other ways, urban, middle-age parents also reflect the trend toward a changing Chinese philosophy. A growing number of parents appear to oppose the traditional idea that children should be highly conforming and unquestionably obey authority. To illustrate, on a sample of urban Chinese middle-class parents from Beijing, Hong Xiao (1999) found that these parents were more likely to endorse children's independence. The weakness of conformity and other traditional attitudes and ideas about child rearing and training has been substantiated in a number of studies (Chen, Rubin, & Li, 1997; Tao, Dong, Lin, & Zeng, 1997).

Similarly, while many Chinese families were traditionally patriarchal, modern family life is no longer conducted along the same absolutist lines. The father is still considered the head of the family, but his authority is less autocratic and more egalitarian (Lee, 1999). The modern Chinese family, then, is a mixture of traditionalism and modernism. Traditionally, Confucianism, which emphasizes personal virtue, justice, and devotion to the family, has been the ideal philosophical and moral guidance. It, however, has been shaken by a growing modern philosophy emphasizing material and economic gain.

Relatedly, economic and material advantages come from having smaller families. In an attempt to foster these advantages and to curb China's explosive population growth, families are "allowed" to have only one child. The one-child policy, however, is not proving to be very successful.

FIRSTPERSON

A Visit to Peking University

Nowadays in China, college or university students are becoming more individualistic and pragmatic. One big difference is shown in their loss of interest in collective activities organized by schools and in the national goals, which used to be upheld by young people as sacred. They no longer care that much about whether the unemployed workers can find jobs or the poor peasants' children can go to school. What they are most concerned about is their own future, and this future is almost always seen in terms of their individual gain and fame. Of course, most students still love China and believe they should do something to make China strong and prosperous, but the difference now is that they tend to put their own interest before that of the country. Therefore, many of them would not readily give up their personal benefit or opportunities to meet any urgent need of the country or community unconditionally as many young people once did.

Another noticeable change among Chinese youths toward individualism is that the bright students do not help the slower ones; this was once the usual practice. Everyone is busy trying to do well at courses, so that later they can secure good jobs or study abroad. Now, young people keep a loose and friendly relation with each other, but even students living in the same room do not share useful information. In this way, they stand a better chance to get these coveted positions.

In the past, professors and students always had a nice friendship. Students often would come back to visit us or send greetings back to us. This rarely occurs today, and professors sometimes feel that students use them. For instance, students come to sweet-talk teachers into writing recommendation letters for them and never talk or write to teachers again. Wiping the blackboard clean after each lecture used to be a tradition for our students to show their respect, but now they sit there and watch their gray-haired professors do that. Students are beginning to recognize their individual identity and fulfillment at the cost of some important traditions—some big, some small; we professors react strongly to this change because we have the comparison with the past in our minds.

—***Yi Qing Liu, Ph.D.***

China's One-Child Policy

"Carry Out Contraception and Family Planning Measures Voluntarily"

This sign is printed on the wall in a rural town of Zhongguan, China.

Zhongguan and five other pilot counties have been selected to participate in an experiment that could change the face of China's one-child policy. The exercise of free choice over family size does not mean that the Chinese government is abandoning its one-child policy. Rather, it is attempting to encourage Chinese citizens to choose to have one child when they are given information about the economic and material merits of smaller families. The program has not been highly publicized in China; officials fear that this "relaxed" child policy may cause an explosion in the birth rate (Ho, 1998).

This new approach appears to have evolved out of a realization that the one-child policy in its current form is not working—for various reasons. One factor may be that the policy only applies to the national majority, the Han, and so-called minority Chinese (Tibetans and Mongolians, for example) are exempt. Further, population control appears to be more successful in urban than in the rural areas of China. Whereas the educated Chinese tend to want smaller families and thus may be more inclined to follow the one-child rule, less-educated families continue to want more children—in many cases to assist with their farming economy as well as to be a source of pride. Perhaps, the most important reason for the lack of effectiveness of the one-child policy is the government

© Rhoda Sidney/Stock Boston

The current population of China is 1.4 billion; China's one-child policy has been an attempt to reduce the birth rate.

does not consistently enforce this policy through the administration of negative sanctions.

The current program gives rewards for couples in China who have only one child and negative sanctions against those who have more than one child. Couples who have one child are issued a "Planned Parenthood Glory" coupon, which enables them to receive free medical treatment and hospitalization. They also receive a monthly subsidy to help pay for their expenses. Moreover, they are provided with special housing—an apartment in Hankow, for example, with two bedrooms, a living room, and a kitchen—very spacious by Chinese standards.

However, if a couple has a second child, all the benefits are immediately taken away and the family receives sanctions for disobeying the one-child policy (see Table 2.3). Even with the negative sanctions for having a second child, 64,000 babies are born every day in China, and overpopulation continues to be a paramount national problem. Twenty-four million children were born in 1994—a number slightly less than the population of Canada (Lee, 1999).

The 4-2-1 Syndrome

For those families who have adhered to the one-child policy, there is some concern that the single child might be overindulged or "spoiled." Chinese preschools are expected to provide an antidote to this potential spoiling. Although studies suggest that children in China generally exhibit high academic achievement (Doh & Falbo, 1999), other studies indicate that children tend to be low in behavioral control, cooperation, and peer prestige and high in self-identity and egocentrism—a shift away from traditional Chinese values (Falbo & Poston, 1993; Jiao, Ji, & Jing, 1996).

In effect, the one-child policy may be fostering the rising individualistic trends toward a stronger self-focused ideology seen in Chinese youths. The problem has been labeled the "4-2-1 syndrome," (4 doting grandparents and 2 indulgent parents, pinning all their hopes and ambitions on 1 child). Such a configuration is thought to "spoil" children and lead them to behave like "little Emperors" and "little Empresses." And, there appears to be some truth in this; with neither brothers nor sisters, some of these children are more inclined to become loners who do not learn to share or develop a sense of community involvement (Zhang

TABLE 2.3

Sanctions for Having More Than One Child

Sanctions
1. The planned parenthood glory coupon will be withdrawn and all the child's health expenses or supplementary work points recovered.
2. Five percent (in some provinces the fine exceeds 25 percent of family income for over four years) of total family wages or income will be deducted from welfare expenses, 6 percent deducted for a fourth child, and 7 percent for a fifth child.
3. For third and additional children, confinement medical expenses must be paid by parents, and children will be unable to participate in comprehensive medical schemes.
4. No coupons for commodities or subsidiary foodstuffs will be available for third or fourth children; no extra housing space in urban areas or additional land in rural areas will be provided.
5. Couples who undergo sterilization will receive economic rewards and public recognition.

From Yi Qing Liu, Ph.D., personal communication.

& Liao, 1998). Therefore, preschool in China is officially viewed as the major institution for socialization and transmission of desirable cultural values. Further, the socialist ideal has long been for the state to take away the responsibility of child rearing from mothers. Because most Chinese mothers work in full-time outside employment, another purpose of preschools is to help liberate mothers for the working forces and to ease the burdens of working parents (Wu, 1992; 1996).

Sweden: Social Welfare Systems

Karen Jorgensen is the mother of a 2-year-old boy, Jonas. She, along with roughly 86 percent of Swedish women with preschool children, is working full time outside the home. Sven, the father of Jonas, has been living with Karen for the past five years. Sven is a highly involved father; in fact, it was Sven who stayed home and cared for his newborn son for the first six months of his life.

In contrast to China, Sweden is primarily an urban-industrial society with a low fertility rate and a low infant mortality rate. As such, Swedish couples are being *encouraged* to have children and the government provides benefits to encourage women to have more children, including a parental insurance program that covers the mother and child through pregnancy, childbirth, and infancy. It subsidizes one parent for a nine-month period at 90 percent of his or her salary to take care of the newborn child (Ingoldsby & Smith, 1995).

Sweden is on the low end on the global continuum of reproductive rates. Its first-time mothers are among the world's oldest, averaging 26.4 years of age. Most Swedish women begin their occupational careers before their reproductive lives. Close to 80 percent of mothers with young children are employed. Most Swedish women have only one or two children, and only 2 percent of the families with children have as many as four children, compared with 12 percent in the United States (Bjoenberg, 1998). Marriage has become more optional and cohabitation has increased.

Cohabitation

It is estimated that close to 1 in 4 Swedish couples living together are not married compared with an estimated 1 in 20 couples in the United States (Popenoe, 1998). Higher numbers of cohabiting couples in Sweden may be due to a number of factors. Unlike the United States, cohabiting couples enjoy many of the same legal and social privileges as married couples, and most of these Swedish couples see their relationship as on a par with marriage. Moreover, having a child is no longer an incentive to marriage in Sweden, as witnessed by the high rates of children born to unmarried mothers—close to 50 percent, compared with 18 percent in the United States (Berggren, 1997). Nearly all of the children born to unmarried mothers, however, are born to cohabiting parents.

Unfortunately, neither love and marriage nor parenthood and marriage necessarily go together in Sweden (Moen, 1989). Dissolution rates, although high for married couples, are estimated to be as much as three times higher for cohabiting couples (Bjoenberg, 1998). The high divorce rates in Sweden in conjunction with even higher separation rates for cohabiting couples means that significant numbers of children live with only one parent. The Swedish scene has been summarized in this way, "We have a new pattern of male–female interaction, characterized by an increasing prevalence of informal cohabitation rather than formalized marriage, including dissolution rates and a lessening economic dependence on the part of the women in a partner relationship" (Bernhardt, 1987, p. 27).

Working Mothers

Women entered the labor market because of plentiful job opportunities (especially in the public and service sectors), high wages (the result of union efforts to lessen class differences by raising the wages of the lowest-paid workers), and a tax system that taxes their incomes separately from their spouses. In the homes of working parents, fathers of children under 5 spend an average of 7 hours a week in basic child care; mothers spend approximately 16.5 hours (Bjoenberg, 1998). In addition, fathers average 0.8 of an hour and mothers spend 2 hours per week in transporting children (Sandqvist, 1997). Research shows that Swedish men have been doing more housework and child care over time (since 1957, when the first measurements were taken), both relative to women and in an absolute sense. Their levels of participation appear higher than those for men in other societies. Swedish men are not equal partners in the home, but they come closer than men in other industrial societies (Haas, 1993). Fathers are close to taking an equal share in "food-related work" and "general responsibility for children" (Jensen, 1998).

SuperStock

The majority of Swedish mothers work in outside paid employment.

Thought CHALLENGE
Should the U.S. government subsidize child-care programs for working parents?

Sweden is often depicted as a socialist country. The label, however, more accurately refers not to its economic system but to its comprehensive social welfare system, which provides general social insurance, child allowances, free education, and guaranteed health care for all permanent residents. There is a concerted effort made by the government, organized labor, and other institutions to distribute the responsibilities of child rearing evenly between men and women and to facilitate the employment of all adults, including those caring for infants and children. Thus, because of the high rate of working mothers and the new pattern of male and female relationships, parents in Sweden have different needs and the government has responded to those needs in the form of social welfare policies.

Social Welfare Policies in Sweden

Swedish parenting policies have three major components: direct economic family subsidies; significant paid family leave; and an extensive network of high-quality subsidized and regulated childcare facilities (Gustafsson & Stafford, 1998). Sweden has done much to acknowledge that both mothers and fathers have legitimate economic and caregiving roles. Fathers as well as mothers work fewer hours in the labor market when they have young children. Sweden was the first country in the world to introduce a system of a six-month paid parental leave that enabled either the mother or the father to stay home from work and take care of their child. This leave can be used on a full-time or part-time basis any time before the child is 8 years old. Also, the leave can be split between the two parents. Due to extended parental leave opportunities, a declining proportion of children under 1 use public child care—approximately 2 percent.

A cornerstone of the Swedish universal social welfare system is the nontaxable child allowance, which is paid to couples and 1 million other families with children under the age of 16, regardless of income, at a rate of about $10,000 per year in U.S. dollars. In addition, single parents with children under the age of 18 can receive an advanced maintenance (child support) payment, tax-free, on application if the noncustodial parent fails to pay the maintenance allowance (Barnett & Boocock, 1998). These allowances are determined by voluntary agreement or court order and depend on the income of both parents. Moreover, low-income families with children can obtain a nontaxable monthly housing allowance. The size of the allowance depends on family income, number of children, and housing costs.

The policies afforded parents of young children in Sweden help parents to make a more positive transition to parenthood and to alleviate some of the frustrations and problems that occur in dual-wage families. As such, Sweden recognizes that the resources that individuals bring to the parenting years, in the form of energy level and freedom from psychological strain, have an important influence on the well-being of children. Sweden is a country that recognizes that working outside the home and caring for children may be particularly difficult for parents and subsequently their children (Rydell, Hagekull, & Bohlin, 1997). Because of the country's economic policies (reviewed in Table 2.4), Sweden is viewed as a pacesetter in confronting the changing nature of men's and women's roles.

Concept Checks

1. Japanese children are taught very early in life to ________, and this may propel them later on to do very well in school.
   a. learn to read and memorize facts
   b. be competitive
   c. never bring shame to the family

TABLE 2.4

Is Child Care a Public or a Private Issue? Sweden's Policy

Benefit	Description
Parental insurance permits	Father or mother to take a six-month paid leave of absence on the birth of a child and to receive, typically, 90 percent of his or her normal wage.
Parental leave benefit	Paid for by the Riksforsakringsverket (Social Insurance Board) rather than by employees directly.
Reduced working time	Parents with children under the age of 8 can work from two to six hours a day with a proportional reduction in wages. There is a high degree of flexibility and discretion available over work schedules.
Fringe benefits	Two-thirds of mothers with preschoolers are working part time; however, they receive all the benefits of full-time employees.
Variety of government-supported child-care assistance	Day nurseries (children 6 months to 7 years); part-time groups (3 hours of activities); recreation centers (providing before- and after-school care); small, home-day nurseries (child care for up to four children); open preschools (which enable unemployed parents and children to meet together under trained leadership). The responsibilities for these child-care programs are assigned to the local government and are located in residential neighborhoods.

Note: Sweden stands at the forefront of advanced, industrialized societies in its recognition of the dilemmas of employed parents as a public rather than a private issue and its adoption of a number of structural child-care reforms.

2. Cheng Ling argues with his parents and questions their authority, which exemplifies the fact that
   a. filial piety is declining in China.
   b. Cheng is questioning his beliefs in the individualist philosophy.
   c. Chinese parents were never authority figures.
3. Swedish parents are fortunate because as a working family
   a. they receive cash bonuses for each child born.
   b. are eligible for glory coupons they can cash in for food and housing.
   c. receive significant paid family leave.

U.S. Ethnic Groups: Beliefs and Concerns

Before Beginning . . .

After reading this section, you will be able to

- see the role ethnicity plays in the socialization of children.
- identify the cultural beliefs of many minority families.

Differences and similarities are found between countries as well as within countries. For example, the United States comprises a wide range of divergent and unique cultures and ethnic groups in which children grow up. Consider, for example, the variety of values, customs, beliefs, and traits one can find among the Native American child of the Southwest, the child from Appalachia, and the daughter from Amish country.

Increases in the proportion of ethnic minorities are occurring and are expected to continue for several decades in the American population—the technical definition of minority will soon no longer apply. African American children, for example, make up the largest percentage of ethnic youths in the United States, but minority numbers are changing. Between 2000 and 2010, it is projected that the Latino, African American, East Asian, and Native American populations will increase by 30, 12, 42, and 14 percent respectively (McLoyd, 1999). In contrast, only a 2.8 percent increase is projected for the non-Latino white population. The increases in the proportion of ethnic minorities in the American population are driven by two factors: higher immigration rates and slightly higher fertility rates.

Cultural Beliefs

Many of the child-rearing patterns of various ethnic populations in the United States reflect the kinds of parental conceptions of competence that are reminiscent of the collectivist philosophy. For example, African American and Hispanic American families generally embrace an extended family model (going

© Will Hart/PhotoEdit

Traditionally, Native American cultures feature collective, cooperative social networks that extend from the family to the tribe.

beyond the nuclear family of parents and their children to include wider kinship networks). In addition, these two ethnic groups have tended to promote children's compliance and to be more conservative in terms of gender roles and child-rearing values and practices than Americans with a European heritage (Masten, 1999). Moreover, many members of ethnic groups in the United States espouse collectivistic beliefs that emphasize loyalty to the family group in some form and have well-defined, unilaterally organized, highly interdependent, cohesive, and often father-dominated families. The majority of Latino families, for example, display strong feelings of identification, loyalty, and solidarity with parents and extended family and are characterized by strong familism (Masten, 1999).

Ethnic families that emphasize a collectivist ideology tend to be oriented toward group affiliation, interdependence, and sharing versus individualism, independence, and competition (Guerra & Jagers, 1998). This is associated with an acceptance of, and respect for, authority figures and hierarchical relationships versus a more egalitarian view that promotes greater questioning of authority. As a result of this ideology, individuals may be inhibited in expressing their views or asserting their own authority. In effect, this may create a "misfit" between their cultural conceptions of competence and that of the dominant culture (Guerra & Jagers, 1998).

Ethnicity: A Central Concern?

For some families, ethnicity is one of their central concerns in raising their children. These parents are conscious that they are not simply raising an American child but an African American, Native American, or Hispanic American whose situation and experiences are different from that of other ethnic groups as well as from the dominant culture. A primary goal of some families is to prepare their offspring for succeeding in an oppressive environment (Richards, 1997). In effect, being a "minority" means that their children should learn how to survive and cope with prejudice; acquire self-respect and pride; grasp the importance of a good education; and understand that fair play, while important, is not necessarily reciprocated by those members of the dominant culture (Thornton, Chatters, Taylor, & Allen, 1990). Because ethnic identity is so important to promoting self-esteem and a sense of belonging, some scholars believe that failure to develop constructive group identities will have an adverse effect on the African American child's mental health (Ogbu, 1997).

This issue is made particularly salient in the case of so-called transracial adoptions. (See discussion on p. 51 about the concept of "race.") The focus of most studies has been on the adoption of African American infants by European American families. The Child Development Issues feature examines these types of adoptions, exploring this complex, emotional, and value-laden issue.

Vulnerable Families?

In the United States, there is still disturbing evidence that being a member of an ethnic "minority" can mean increased vulnerability to poverty and discrimination. According to a recent study, one-third of the nation's ethnic minorities are afflicted by the ills of poverty and discrimination (Brody & Flor, 1998). The percentage of young African American men in jail is much higher than other groups. Roughly 68 percent of African American children live in poverty (Steele, Forehand, Armistead, Morse, Simon, & Clark, 1999). Fifty-six percent of Mexican Americans have less than a high school education (Greenfield, 1999). Native Americans are among the most impoverished groups in the United States, with over half living in very poor conditions on reservations. These statistics are bleak; and these conditions certainly warrant change. At the same time, there are some encouraging signs, as well, that members of various ethnic groups are reaching the highest pinnacles of achievement in the United States and succeeding in breaking down bias and ignorance in the larger culture (Hrabowski, Maton, & Greif, 1998).

Concept Checks

1. The fastest growing minority group in the United States is ________________.
2. Minorities in the United States tend to believe more closely in the ________________ philosophy.

Children in Various Ethnic Groups

Before Beginning . . .

After reading this section, you will be able to

- discuss African American child-rearing practices.
- identify socialization techniques of Chinese Americans.
- understand the Navajo's child-rearing views.
- examine Mexican American child-rearing practices.

African American Families

Although a large number of ethnic groups exist in the United States, researchers have focused predominantly on individuals belonging to ethnic "minority" groups, with African Americans being the most frequently studied. African American children compose approximately 14 percent of the population (34.4 million) (see Figure 2.1). Although as Americans they have been socialized within the dominant, individualistic culture, many maintain collectivist values.

Diverse, recent immigration patterns are further shaping the picture of the African American family. People, for example, who have emigrated from Caribbean islands (formerly owned by England) will have assimilated some of the customs and beliefs of the British. Families from Central and South America will have been influenced by the Spanish. Families who came from Africa are a diverse group because of geographic origins and religious background. Despite these significant differences, there are some commonalities.

According to researchers, traditional African American families have tended to place emphasis on the family and the broader kinship network. As such, one goal of the socialization practices among many African American families is to foster a positive orientation among children toward their ethnic group as a means of promoting biculturalism and acceptance of this ancestral worldview (Tucker, 1999). Many African American children are taught to view their role within the family and society in terms of relationships and obligations to the family. Kinship networks are believed to serve as a source of strength, trust, and survival. Children tend to learn to place a high value on respecting, obeying, and learning from the elders in the kinship community. Similarly, organized religion and spirituality have been emphasized as a confirmation of their personal identity and worthiness as well as a means of social support and belongingness (Boyd-Franklin, 1989).

Many African American parents stress interdependence by teaching children to think, feel, and act in ways that involve the development of a cooperative view of life, rather than one of a singularly competitive nature. As such, many African American children come to view themselves as an integral part of the totality of their families and the larger social structure (Ogbu, 2000). Cooperation, obligation, sharing, and reciprocity are essential elements of their social interactions with others (Hrabowski, Maton, & Greif, 1998). These values sharply contrast with Western ideals of competition, autonomy, and self-reliance.

Child-Rearing Practices

Many African American fathers frequently have strict behavioral expectations for their children and emphasize parental control in their child-rearing attitudes (Kelley, Power, & Wimbush, 1992). There are, however, differences in child-rearing practices among different socioeconomic classes. Middle-income African American fathers, for example, tend to be significantly more responsive to their children's needs than are lower-income African American fathers. The level of responsiveness of African American fathers from the middle-income groups is identical to that of middle-income European American fathers (McAdoo, 1997).

According to one research study of middle-class African American fathers, 75 percent of the fathers sampled were ranked as predominantly warm, loving, and nurturing in their interactions with their children (McAdoo, 1997). The remaining 25 percent of the African American fathers were identified as predominantly restrictive. The children of these restrictive

Child Development Issues

Are Those Children Yours? Mixed-Ethnic Adoption

One of the more controversial issues in adoption concerns the appropriateness of placing children in families that differ in ethnic background from the child's birth parents. In the United States, this typically involves placing children from minority ethnic groups into European American families. Both the professional literature and the public discussion about so-called transracial adoption entwine two matters—ethnicity and self-esteem—into one phenomenon called "identity," and scholars concur that positive ethnic identity is at the core of healthy development (Ogbu, 1997).

Opponents of cross-ethnic adoption argue that this leads to identity confusion in African American children, which will result in poor psychological adjustment. Concerns center on such questions as, "How can it be sound to place children in a foreign setting and expect them to develop a healthy sense of African American identity when they are so different from the family in which they are being raised?" "How can a white family help a black child realize, *feel,* and know his true heritage?" Having a family that is not *what* they are will leave them troubled about *who* they are. As 12-year-old Marcus relates, "I didn't really view myself as a black child. I saw my color as different from other blacks. It was a very shattering experience for me having grown up in a white world with white parents to be told that I was black."

According to this argument African American children belong in African American families, so that they can receive the total sense of themselves and develop a sound projection of their future (Russell, 1995). A corollary argument is that European American families cannot prepare African American children to cope with the problems of living in a "racially divided" or "white racist" society. White parents cannot give African American children the survival education they need or interpret the society of racism to them honestly (Hollingsworth, 1998).

In principle, such "mixed" adoptions are allowed only when waiting children do not have access to parents who share their ethnic heritage. For example, historically there have tended to be more African American children waiting to be adopted than African American families who wish to adopt. While proponents of "transracial" placements see such adoptions as the solution for children from various ethnic minorities who are waiting to be adopted, those opposed believe that there are actually adequate minority families wishing to adopt. Rather, they argue, it is the adoption agencies who do not put out enough effort to identify appropriate minority families and also unjustifiably reject them (Association of Black Social Workers and Allied Professions, 1993).

Proponents of mixed-ethnic placements argue that large numbers of minority children who are in foster care, combined with the relative scarcity of available ethnically matched families willing to adopt, demand that children be placed in nurturing homes without respect to cultural heritage (Simon, Altstein, & Melli, 1995). They argue that these kinds of placements are not inherently negative and that a child's need for a stable, permanent family is paramount. They also point out that these adoptions will promote integration—an ideal toward which society should strive. The child's possible confusion about his or her identity is seen as avoidable, provided the adopting parents take care to provide the child with a sense of his or her cultural heritage.

At the most general level, research findings show that children who have a different ethnic background from their adoptive parents grow up to be emotionally and socially adjusted and aware of and comfortable with their identity. They perceive themselves as integral parts of their adopted families and expect to retain strong ties to their parents and siblings in the future (Andujo, 1988; Binder, 1998; Brodzinsky, Smith, & Brodzinsky, 1998; Grow & Shapiro, 1974). As Laticia relates, "I do think if you are a minority with white parents that it makes you a more interesting person. It gives you a lot of depth. You think about racial issues and become more reflective. In my family, we feel and act like any other everyday family—so we keep forgetting that we don't look like one another." In a longitudinal investigation involving over 200 adoptees placed with parents of a different ethnic background by private agencies, both the adoptive parents and adopted children expressed considerable satisfaction in their roles (Simon & Alstein, 1987). Other researchers report no differences in self-esteem between children whose heritage matches that of their adoptive parents and those whose heritage is different, suggesting that a shared cultural heritage between child and parents is not necessary for the development of the child's healthy view of self (DeBerry, Scarr, & Weinberg, 1996).

© Taeke Henstra/Petit Format/Photo Researchers, Inc.

Other investigations, working directly with young children, have evaluated ethnic identity through project assessment measures such as the Doll Preference Test (Simon & Alstein, 1977). In this procedure, children are shown dolls of their own and different ethnic groups and asked to identify the doll they think is more attractive, least attractive, and so on. The preferences are presumed to reflect the degree to which children have positive attitudes and feelings about their own versus other ethnic groups. In comparing children who had the same ethnic heritage as their adoptive parents to those who did not, it was found both groups of children initially picked the white doll. Around the age of 8 years, however, the majority of African American children with adoptive African American parents showed a preference for black dolls (Shireman & Johnson, 1986). African American children adopted by European American parents did not show the same change over time. The authors concluded that these children exhibited a more negative view of their own ethnic heritage, presumably as the result of being raised in white families.

The research base on this controversy has not been developed adequately and the potential benefits and drawbacks of cross-ethnic placements remains elusive leaving us with a number of thought-provoking issues: What is the motivation of European American couples wishing to adopt minority children? Is it better for these children to be placed in long-term foster care with same ethnic-group parents than to be adopted by parents of a different ethnic group? Does adoption of an African American child by a European American family present more problems than the adoption of children from other ethnic groups such as Native American, Japanese American, or Chinese American?

Conditions that contribute to all adoptive children's well-being are marital stability, tolerance of differences, flexible roles and rules, an open communication system, acceptance of the child and his or her membership in the family, and acceptance of the adopted child's family of origin, the child's background, and his or her past links (Berry, Dylla, Barth, & Needell, 1998). These conditions apply to all adoptions along with instilling an appreciation of and pride in the child's ethnic heritage (Richards, 1997).

Search Online

Explore InfoTrac College Edition, your online library. Go to **http://www.infotrac-college.com/wadsworth** and use the passcode that came on the card with your book. Try these search terms: racial adoptions, international adoptions, mixed families.

Many African American families believe in a collectivist philosophy and socialize their children to be cooperative, obliging, and respectful of their elders.

fathers, however, were generally more restless and made repeated demands for their father's attention. Thus, the interactions between restrictive fathers and their children seems to have been a reciprocal process, with the children playing an active role; that is, the children's misbehavior and demands for attention tended to evoke restrictive parental responses. Both African American mothers and fathers appeared to favor child-rearing strategies that involve some combination of warmth and support, as well as firm control (Cochran, 1997).

Research on a sample of African American mothers from lower socioeconomic classes found that they generally expected their children to show unquestioning obedience to parental rules (Kelley, Power, & Wimbush, 1992). Perhaps, however, this is a more adaptive parenting style for children growing up in dangerous neighborhoods. These children are at a greater risk for involvement in antisocial acts (either as victims or as perpetrators). As such, mothers may be forced to make a greater effort to prevent their children from getting involved in the first place. Consequences of disobedience in low-income environments are more serious. Moreover, these mothers expressed concern for not spoiling their children by giving them too much attention and saw one of their major child-rearing objectives as keeping children "in line" and out of trouble (Brody & Flor, 1998).

In addition, mothers from all socioeconomic classes are more likely than fathers to educate their child about race (Thornton et al., 1990). Moreover, older African American parents are more likely than younger parents to view information regarding ethnic identity as a necessary element of the socialization process. In general, African American parents are more likely to socialize their children to ethnic matters when they live in "mixed" neighborhoods as compared with those who live in all-black communities (Pearson, Hunter, Ensminger, & Kellam, 1990). The socialization messages given about their ethnicity is reflective of the African American cultural experience emphasizing African American heritage, history, and tradition.

Asian American Families

African American families represent the largest minority group, but Asian American families compose the fastest growing minority. Asian Americans, currently representing 4 percent of the population (10.5 million), are a diverse group comprising 28 subgroups, including Chinese, Filipino, Japanese, Korean, Laotian, Pacific Islander, Thai, Cambodian, and Vietnamese families (see Figure 2.2). From this broad group, we will focus our discussion on Chinese Americans.

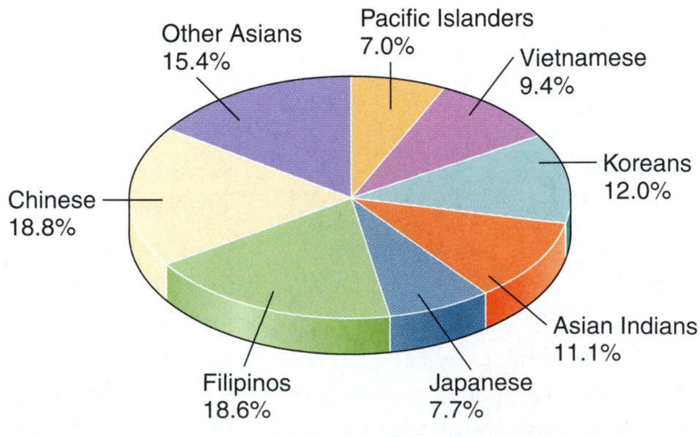

FIGURE 2.2 ***Composition of Asian Americans***

From *The Experience of Parenting,* by M. J. Muzi, 2000, Upper Saddle River, NJ: Prentice-Hall.

Chinese American Child-Rearing Practices

According to several studies, the first generation of an individual Chinese family immigrating to the United States often followed the traditional Chinese model of the family, which was characterized by male dominance, a rigid division of labor, priority given to filial relations over the marital bond, and emotional restraint (Vogel, 1996). In this traditionalist view, marriage was a relationship that brought together two very different but complementary gender domains. Wives would take care of the inside—the home or family; husbands would take care of the outside—economic responsibilities. Thus, the genders were both separate and unequal. Because the male participated in both inside and outside spheres, he was accorded more power and was considered the head of the family (Slaughter-Defoe, Nakagawa, Takanishi, & Johnson, 1990).

Research indicates Chinese American families today have created more of a balance between that rigid prototypical family and the more egalitarian marital idea, so that Chinese American families now more closely approximate the European American pattern (Lee, 1996). Studies show that contemporary Chinese American families give priority to the marital relationship over the parent–child relationship (Crystal, Watanabe, Weinfurt, & Wu, 1998). Although they have retained the notion of male and female domains, these domains are considered complementary and equal.

Researchers have attributed several Chinese American child-rearing practices to the influence of Confucianism, which taught that the "proper development of character" should be a primary goal of child rearing. Proper character involves academic achievement, hard work, and obligation to reach one's fullest potential. Emphasis placed on academic achievement and effort, parents believe, will lead to higher social status, wealth, and overcoming discrimination. Proper character also requires that children learn obedience, piety, respect for elders, and reverence for tradition (Kelley & Tseng, 1992).

How do Chinese American mothers respond when their children act in unacceptable ways, such as engaging in aggressive or socially withdrawn behavior? Charissa Cheah and Miao Li (2001) presented a sample of mothers with vignettes that depicted acting-out and socially withdrawn behaviors. When responding to the acting-out story ("Your child took a toy from another child and pushed him down"), mothers said they would not tolerate such behavior and would use strong disciplinary techniques to control it. They responded to these stories with disappointment and anxiety. Socially withdrawn vignettes depicted two different scenarios. In one story, the child was fearful of others and played alone. The second story characterized a child acting in humble, nonassertive ways with others. Mothers saw the "fearful" behavior as unacceptable; their reactions to the second story were positive and often evoked praise from the mothers.

Although traditionally the father in China is relatively uninvolved in child-rearing matters, he is commonly seen by his children as a powerful figure and is usually accorded much respect.

Interestingly, mothers saw all these behaviors as being externally caused. According to Cheah and Li, Chinese mothers tend to see a child's behavior as being exclusively influenced by environmental factors and believe that they are responsible for shaping the child's behavior. As such, their socialization strategies tended to concentrate on more training strategies to promote "harmony with others."

Native American Families

Terms such as "American Indian" or "Native American" encompass a variety of cultures, nationality groups, languages, and family systems. Thus, it is very difficult to generalize about such groups. There are over 400 tribal groups in every state in the United States (Joe & Malach, 1992). The Navajo of Arizona and New Mexico are the largest of these tribal groups (160,000); the Chumash of California are the smallest with fewer than 100 people. Native American families range on a continuum that includes traditional, nontraditional, transitional, and acculturated (a culture change that results from continuous firsthand contact between two distinct cultural groups) family types (Red Horse, 1988).

In general, the traditional family system was derived from the village structure that was common among tribal groups. Such groups were small, ranging from 200 to 350 residents, and prevailing values revolved around village and kinship structures. All residents of a village were members of an extended kin system. Elders, particularly males, were to be respected and exercised considerable power and control over the family. The Navajo provide an interesting example of Native American families. James Chisholm (1983, 1989, 1996) has given us a great deal of insight into the Navajo nation.

The Navajo Nation

The Navajo, who refer to themselves in the Navajo language as *Dine*—"The People"—differ considerably, like other ethnic groups, from one another. Just as there is no single Navajo culture, there is no single "true" Navajo image of the child. Moreover, there is considerable variation in the sizes and types of camps on the Navajo reservation. Some camps consist of isolated nuclear-family camps. Navajo infants in these camps have very few opportunities for social interaction. In many isolated nuclear-family camps, children have only their parents and siblings to interact with and are likely to have little or no contact with strangers until they are a few years old. In larger extended family camps, children typically have more playmates but also more caretakers and the opportunity for meeting more strangers (Chisholm, 1996).

The Navajo live in a difficult terrain; the soil is poor, rainfall is sparse, and there is rampant unemployment (in some communities it approaches 75 percent). In the vast majority of the reservation's rural areas, sheepherding continues as the primary subsistence activity. Poor grazing conditions and widely scattered water holes dictate that the Navajo must reside in well-dispersed clusters.

Navajo families have been depicted as an extended family system that integrates several generations into a cohesive whole. In traditional Navajo society, women exercise a role that is equal to, if not greater than, that of men. Women assume a prominent role in the subsistence economy; their duties consist of making pottery, baskets, and clothes; weaving blankets; and taking care of their hogan (home) (Chisholm, 1996). Sheep are owned by the women, and inheritance is passed on through the female line. Women are responsible for the care and maintenance of children, but they also make many of the financial decisions in the home.

Most other Native American tribes have *patrilineal kinship* systems, whereby descent, affiliation, and inheritance pass through males; this renders less power to women in these tribes. The Navajo, however, are a *matrilineal kinship system*, or a system of kinship in which descent, affiliation, and inheritance pass along the female line. In this regard, the Navajo and Navajo women are not representative of American Indians (Ogbu, 2000). Contact with the white culture, however, has greatly diminished the power of the Navajo women. Under allotment, land policy has been altered, so that only married men are considered eligible for land ownership. Similarly, the move from a subsistence to a wage market economy has reduced the influence of Navajo women. Thus, Navajo women have lost much of their influence and security, and Navajo men have become increasingly important.

Child-Rearing Practices

Within their first week of life, Navajo infants are commonly placed on a cradleboard that the mother carries on her back; they spend most of their time there until they are just over 10 months. In the first 3 months of life, infants are generally on the cradleboard 15 to 18 hours a day, during most of which they are asleep. With each succeeding quarter, they spend approximately 3 hours less each day within its confines. The cradleboard provides a measure of protection for the infant, promotes mother–infant proximity, makes travel easier, and promotes infant sleep. In addition to promoting sleep, the location of the cradleboard on the mother's back makes interactions between mother and child short, and therefore, less intense. Taken together, these cradleboard functions seem to have been successful adaptations by the

Navajo to the demands of child care in a hunting–gathering society where movement is great, social organization is fluid, women's labor is vital, and the environment is harsh.

In general, Navajo infants are less likely to cry or fret; slower to reach a crying state; less likely to respond to aversive stimuli with a cry; more easily consoled if they do cry; and less likely to show numerous or rapid changes from one state to another than are European American babies. Studies have consistently shown that Navajo newborns are quieter and less irritable than European American newborns (Chisholm, 1996; Freedman, 1969; 1979).

While recognizing the possibility of a genetic influence on these traits, Chisholm also notes that the child-rearing techniques used by Navajo mothers tend to maintain these behavioral styles. Quiet, nonintrusive parenting styles are considered by the Navajo appropriate and good.

In the Navajo value system, "showing respect" for a thing or person is a manifestation of taking care of that thing or person. Moreover, good thought has the power to cause good things to happen. It follows that good thought is thus good (moral) action (Chisholm, 1996). As one Navajo described this, "The goal of the Navajo people is to first learn to take care of yourself—then some things, then some animals, then your family. Then you help all your people and the whole world." This view of development as fundamentally a process of moral maturation is clearly seen in Navajo concepts of developmental states shown in Figure 2.3.

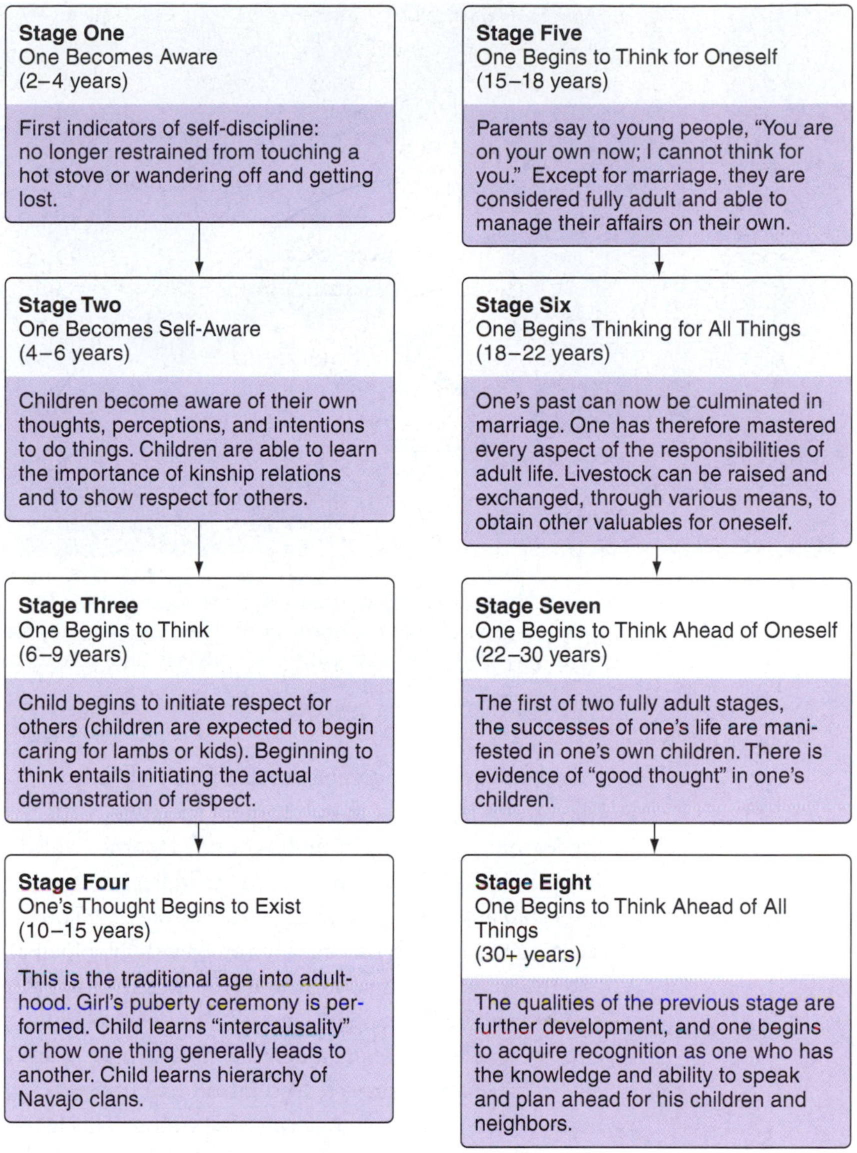

Stage One
One Becomes Aware
(2–4 years)

First indicators of self-discipline: no longer restrained from touching a hot stove or wandering off and getting lost.

Stage Two
One Becomes Self-Aware
(4–6 years)

Children become aware of their own thoughts, perceptions, and intentions to do things. Children are able to learn the importance of kinship relations and to show respect for others.

Stage Three
One Begins to Think
(6–9 years)

Child begins to initiate respect for others (children are expected to begin caring for lambs or kids). Beginning to think entails initiating the actual demonstration of respect.

Stage Four
One's Thought Begins to Exist
(10–15 years)

This is the traditional age into adulthood. Girl's puberty ceremony is performed. Child learns "intercausality" or how one thing generally leads to another. Child learns hierarchy of Navajo clans.

Stage Five
One Begins to Think for Oneself
(15–18 years)

Parents say to young people, "You are on your own now; I cannot think for you." Except for marriage, they are considered fully adult and able to manage their affairs on their own.

Stage Six
One Begins Thinking for All Things
(18–22 years)

One's past can now be culminated in marriage. One has therefore mastered every aspect of the responsibilities of adult life. Livestock can be raised and exchanged, through various means, to obtain other valuables for oneself.

Stage Seven
One Begins to Think Ahead of Oneself
(22–30 years)

The first of two fully adult stages, the successes of one's life are manifested in one's own children. There is evidence of "good thought" in one's children.

Stage Eight
One Begins to Think Ahead of All Things
(30+ years)

The qualities of the previous stage are further development, and one begins to acquire recognition as one who has the knowledge and ability to speak and plan ahead for his children and neighbors.

FIGURE 2.3 *Navajo Concepts of Children's and Adult's Developmental States*

The Navajo view of development is fundamentally a process of moral education—one of learning to respect self, others, and all living things.

From "Learning 'Respect for Everything': Navajo Images" (pp. 167–184), by J. S. Chisholm, 1996, in C. P. Hwang, M. E. Lamb, & I. E. Sigel (Eds.), *Images of Childhood,* Mahwah, NJ: Erlbaum.

The Rough Rock Navajo School

Located deep in the Navajo reservation where sheepherding and ranching remain prominent, the Rough Rock School lies in the shadow of Black Mesa. Many of the ancestors of the Navajo who lived here took refuge in the Black Mesa's recesses and thus escaped Kit Carson's drive against the Navajo people. Today, the Navajo reservation consists of a trading post, a mission, a small health clinic, a fire station, and a school. Most of the students of Rough Rock come from traditional Navajo families living within a 20-mile radius of the school.

Conditioned by years of the federal government's policy of preventing parental involvement with education, many Navajo families are still reluctant to question and/or visit their children's schools (Joe, 1994). Some Navajo are still fearful of sending children to schools being controlled by non-Navajo who are unfamiliar with their beliefs and customs. With this type of experience, it is not difficult to understand why formal schooling and learning remain "outside" the Navajo family circle.

This is not to say that learning is not valued in the Navajo culture. It is. The Navajo culture promotes the

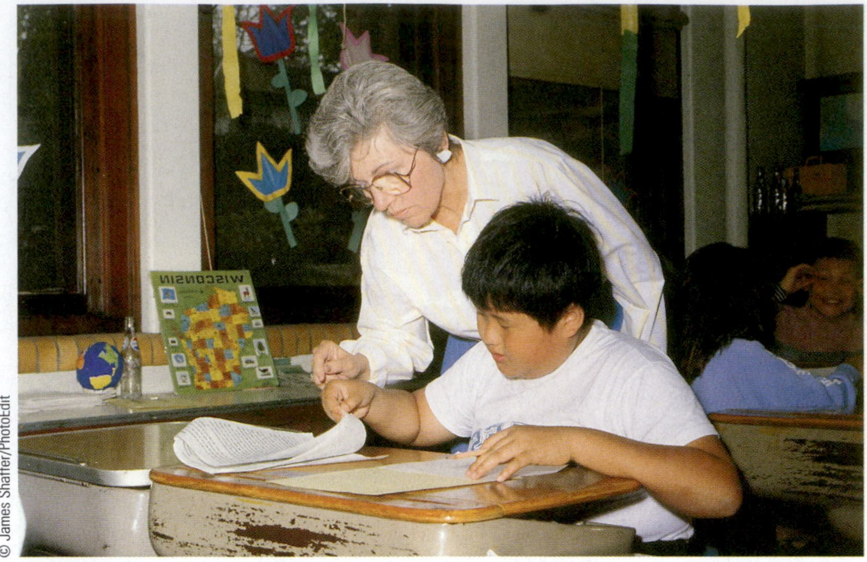

© James Shaffer/PhotoEdit

Some Navajo are concerned about sending their children to government schools controlled by non-Navajo who may be unfamiliar with their beliefs and customs.

idea that learning encompasses three different arenas that cannot be taught in government schools. One is the learning that lasts throughout one's lifetime, which originates at birth and helps mold the individual into a respected and useful member of Navajo society. The learning methods in this instance are generally informal, and teaching may come from many sources. Within this context are the learning of language, kinship, religion, customs, values, beliefs, nature, and the purpose of life.

This learning process also introduces ways to make a living, the second arena of learning. This learning often requires an apprenticeship to become a farmer, a sheepherder, a weaver, or other profession. The third type of learning is reserved for those who are interested or have some special talent and will become healers or religious leaders. These specialists make a lifetime commitment to training and serving.

In the government-run school, however, these areas of learning respect for the Navajo nation, apprenticeship to a useful trade, or becoming a religious leader are not part of the school curriculum. What is taught often goes against Navajo beliefs (LaLonde, Chandler, Hallett, & Paul, 2001).

> Mrs. Clarke, who teaches third grade at Rough Rock, begins the first day of school by asking each of her students to come up to the front of the room and tell their classmates what they did over the summer. Mr. Jacobs tells his sixth-grade boys to be more aggressive on the soccer field. "Be tough! Be competitive." Miss Philips holds a contest in her fourth-grade class to see who can be the first student to finish a math problem.

Navajo children are traditionally taught that they should never push themselves forward and never try to win at games or to get ahead of their playmates. The teacher who encourages children to see who can finish an assignment first, or who organizes competitive games, is asking these children to act in accord with a set of values that is not only foreign but repugnant to them. The Navajo way, as is true in many other Native American tribes, is a way of cooperation, and competition is alien to their whole system of values.

The academic achievement of Native American students declines throughout their elementary school careers; it becomes particularly pronounced after third grade. Part of the problem may lie with the differing views of learning that Native Americans have. For example, schooling requires obedience and assertiveness on the part of students. It requires that students accept that knowledge is important to their survival and their future. However, education may not be viewed in that context by Native American students, which may lead to their increasingly poor performance in school (Clarke, 1997).

Native American children's optimal development in school certainly depends on "ethnosensitivity"—understanding how they feel about competition, their religious beliefs and incorporating these cultural patterns into the school curriculum (McCubbin, Thompson, & Thompson, 1998). Native Americans may be required to change and adapt, but preserving their traditional beliefs is equally important.

Latino Families

Hispanic and *Latino* are terms that have been used to refer to individuals with a common language (Spanish) and historical (colonized by Spain) heritage. Hispanics or Latinos are a heterogeneous population; Latino families, for example, may come from Puerto Rico, the Dominican Republic, Cuba, Spain, Colombia, Guatemala, Mexico, Belize, Argentina, Chile, Ecuador, Peru, Nicaragua, El Salvador, and many other Central and South American countries (see Figure 2.4). In the United States, Latinos constitute

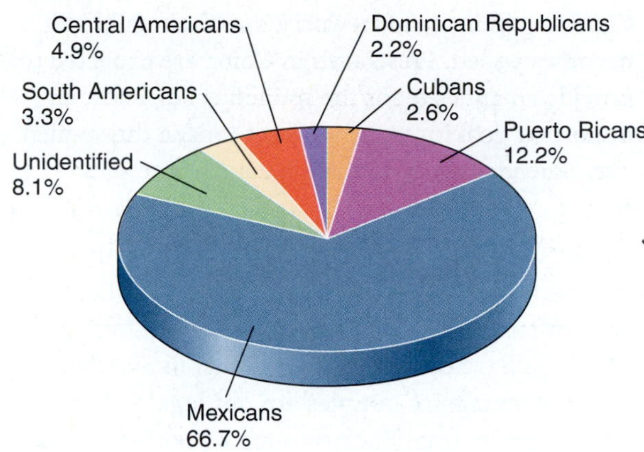

FIGURE 2.4 ***Composition of Latinos***

From *The Experience of Parenting,* by M. J. Muzi, 2000, Upper Saddle River, NJ: Prentice-Hall.

approximately 11 percent of the population (30.3 million), and it is expected that in the next few years they will become the largest minority group (U.S. Bureau of the Census, 1998).

Traditional values of Latino families include a deep sense of family loyalty; extended family and social support networks; and emphasis on interpersonal relatedness, relationships, and mutual respect (Pernice-Ducas, Harrison, & Martin, 2001). Latinos tend to be more collectivist than non-Latinos in the United States but become increasingly individualistic as they become acculturated (Garcia-Preto, 1996). Latinos in the United States pay more attention to the needs of in-group members, avoid interpersonal competition, and stress family obligations. Although Latino and Hispanic are the preferred references to the individuals composing these ethnic groups, it is apparent that the large and diverse nature of this population clearly render this as an overly general label. We will limit our discussion to Mexican Americans as an example of the Latino population.

Mexican American Child-Rearing Practices

Despite current trends toward less patriarchal and more egalitarian family structures, Mexican American women are still seen as being primarily responsible for the domestic realm and subordinate to men (Sanchez-Ayendez, 1988). Patriarchal norms notwithstanding, Mexican American women, however, exercise considerable influence in the domestic sphere (Malgady & Costantino, 1999). The emergent literature includes a number of studies of marital decision making and action taking in Mexican American families that report that domestic decisions are usually shared by husbands and wives.

One study of Mexican American mothers suggested that they tended to be more controlling and demanded more compliance and deference from their children than European American mothers (Delgado-Gaitan, 1994). In contrast, fathers were observed as being a great deal more playful and companionable with children than mothers (Bronstein, 1999). In their nonworking hours and days off, these fathers spent a significant amount of time in recreational family activities. Both fathers and mothers, however, tended to place strict rules on dating and sexual relations (Knight, Tein, Shell, & Roosa, 1992). Many Mexican American young people comply with parental rules, particularly in the areas of dating and marrying within their ethnic and religious group; having parental approval and some supervision of dating, and complete abstinence from sexual intercourse before marriage (Kephart & Jedlicka, 1991).

Mexican American children are more group-oriented and more reliant on authority figures for solving problems than are European American children (Malgady & Costantino, 1999). Hispanic cultures have been characterized as group-oriented, which is reflected in parental socialization techniques that focus on sharing, affiliation, and cooperation. Parents tend to emphasize that children be sensitive to others, loyal, respectful, dutiful, gracious, and conforming (Malgady & Costantino, 1999). As such, these children tend to adapt to an interpersonal challenge rather than trying to change situations, are less assertive in expressing themselves to peers and adults, and rely more on authority figures to resolve interpersonal problems (Gutierrez & Sameroff, 1990).

Concept Checks

Matching:

___ 1. African American
___ 2. Native American
___ 3. Latino
___ 4. Asian American

a. more likely to socialize children in racial matters
b. believe in self-discipline
c. school learning remains "outside" the family
d. avoid interpersonal competition

Reviewing Key Points

A Multicultural Perspective

- Each culture has a set of customs that relate to the physical and geographical setting and the economic activities of the group. Parents in various cultures engage in child-rearing techniques that encourage the development of those behaviors, qualities, and attitudes that children will need as adults to be successful members of the community. One important dimension of cultural variation that determines socialization strategies is a culture's belief system.
- Collectivism pertains to societies in which people from birth are integrated into strong, cohesive in-groups that throughout their lifetime continue to protect them in exchange for unquestioning loyalty. Collectivist cultures, such as Japan and China, value harmony within the group, politeness, obedience, conformity, and respect for others.
- Individualism pertains to societies in which the ties between individuals are loose; everyone is expected to look after himself or herself and his or her immediate family. Individualist cultures, such as the United States, value independence, personal freedom, competition, and distance from groups.

Children in Various Cultures

- In Japan, being a mother is a highly prestigious profession. Children are the mother's first priority. A major parenting goal in Japan is to ensure that children are doing well in school. In addition, fostering politeness, attentiveness to others, and a strong sense of family and group identity are stressed. Disciplining techniques are designed to bring about children's dependency on their mothers and foster a close mother–child bond. Japanese children excel in math and science. The reasons for children's academic excellence may be due to a more egalitarian educational philosophy, a more academically demanding classroom, and higher parental involvement and expectations.
- China is a collectivist society and as a result, the Chinese share many common beliefs with the Japanese. Parental beliefs about child rearing can be traced to the philosophical views of Confucius. In an attempt to deal with an impending population explosion, China, in the 1980s, implemented the one-child policy. Rewards are given to one-child families; sanctions are imposed against those who do not comply. Chinese parents tend to worry that their child will become spoiled. Preschools in China are expected to provide an antidote for the spoiled child. Thus, an important goal for preschools is to make the spoiled, overdependent child less spoiled and more self-reliant.
- Unlike China, Sweden has a low fertility rate, subsequently the government offers extensive health and welfare services in support of reproduction. Marriage has become more optional in Sweden; a high percentage of couples are not legally married but are cohabiting. Because such a high percentage of women work, Sweden has adopted a number of social welfare policies to help working parents.

U.S. Ethnic Groups: Beliefs and Concerns

- The United States is characterized by a diverse system of ethnic groups who have a unique system of beliefs and practices. Ethnic minorities such as African Americans, Chinese Americans, Native Americans, and Mexican Americans tend to believe in a collectivist rather than an individualist philosophy. These ethnic families emphasize group affiliation, interdependence, and sharing.
- Because the dominant culture was used as the standard upon which to base societal standards, minority family forms were often found to be vulnerable, deficient, and maladaptive. Minority families when analyzed from their unique social, historical, economic, and political histories are found to be adaptive and viable.

Children in Various Ethnic Groups

- African American parents tend to emphasize more control in their child-rearing techniques. Current research suggests that children are expected to be compliant and conforming and that parents are also warm and responsive to their children. Many African American parents stress interdependence by teaching children to think, feel, and act in ways that involve the development of a cooperative view of life rather than one of a singularly competitive nature.
- Chinese American parents emphasize the importance of the mother–son relationship, family pride, and ancestor worship. A good child is one who is mild, gentle, obedient, cooperative, and smart. Socialization techniques emphasize self-control, social inhibition, and compliance with social norms. Asian American parents tend to be highly involved

in their children's academic achievement. Subsequently, many of these children do very well in the academic setting.

- Native American families are among the least studied. The Navajo represent an interesting example of the Native American family. Navajo families have an extended family system. Many Navajo live in isolated nuclear-family camps in which parents and children have little contact with outsiders. Most Navajo infants spend the first 10 months of their life on cradleboards, which protect the infant and make it easier for mothers to work in the market or the field. Navajo infants tend to be quieter, less irritable, and more easily consoled than European American infants.
- Mexican American families currently reflect an egalitarian view in gender roles, which is reflected in women sharing in decision making with men. Mexican American children have been characterized as group-oriented, which is reflected in parental socialization techniques that focus on sharing, affiliation, and cooperation. Parents tend to emphasize that children be sensitive to others, loyal, respectful, dutiful, gracious, and conforming.

Answers to Concept Checks

A Multicultural Perspective

1. b   2. c

Children in Various Cultures

1. c   2. a   3. c

U.S. Ethnic Groups: Beliefs and Concerns

1. Latino   2. collectivist

Children in Various Ethnic Groups

1. a   2. c   3. d   4. b

Key Terms

amae
collectivism
emic
ethnicity, or ethnic group
ethnocentrism
etic
individualism
race
socialization

InfoTrac College Edition

For additional readings, explore InfoTrac College Edition, your online library. Go to **http:/www.infotrac-college.com/wadsworth** and use the passcode that came on the card with your book. Try these search terms: culture, collectivism, ethnicity, socialization.

Child Development CD-ROM

Go to the Wadsworth Child Development CD-ROM for further study of the concepts in this chapter. The CD-ROM also includes quizzes and additional activities to expand your learning experience.

Let me introduce you to
Robert Plomin

More than likely, you will find Dr. Plomin in his laboratory at the Social, Genetic, and Developmental Psychiatry Research Centre in London, England, trying to decipher genetic markers on DNA segments. His work in genetics has resulted in countless books and publications; a book that you might find particularly interesting is *Behavioral Genetics* (1997). His findings are among the most important in behavioral genetics. His studies on family environmental influences in genetically sensitive designs—such as twin and adoption studies—shed new light on how the environment works to make each child special and unique. Further, his identification of specific genes enables us to understand the widespread influence of genetics in children's development. Most important, Dr. Plomin makes us aware of how nature (genetics) and nurture (environment) collectively impact children's development. In this introduction to Part Two, Dr. Plomin helps us to see the conjunction between nature and nurture; it is truly nature *and* nurture—not *versus*.

Courtesy of Robert Plomin

PART 2

Genetic and Environmental Contexts

The Genetic–Environmental Analysis of Behavior

by Robert Plomin, Social, Genetic, and Developmental Psychiatry Research Centre, London, England

As the name implies, behavioral genetics involves the genetic analysis of behavior. The name behavioral genetics, however, does not adequately convey the important role of the field in investigating environmental influences. A more informative name for the field might be genetic–environmental analysis of behavior. This is an important distinction because behavioral genetic research has not only demonstrated the importance of genetics, it has also given us our strongest evidence for the importance of environmental influences in behavioral development.

For example, consider schizophrenia. Your risk of becoming schizophrenic—the risk of anyone who does not have a schizophrenic first-degree relative (parent or sibling)—is about 1 percent. If you had a first-degree relative or a fraternal twin who became schizophrenic, your risk would jump to 10 percent. However, if you had an identical twin who was schizophrenic your risk would be about 50 percent, meaning that you would have a 50–50 chance of becoming schizophrenic.

Back in the sixties, environmental factors were emphasized; schizophrenia was thought to be due entirely to early childhood experiences. More than forty years later, the importance of genetics has become widely accepted, and we now know that genetic factors have been incorrectly emphasized. Both genetic constitution and environmental factors contribute to this disorder.

Further, as you will learn in Chapter 3, these environmental factors operate in a strange way: they make siblings growing up in the same family different from one another. This type of environmental influence is described as a non-shared environment. *Using the example of schizophrenia among twins, pairs of identical twins have grown up in the same family and yet half the time one is schizophrenic and the other is not. The environment impacts differently on each of these twins, causing one to contract schizophrenia and the other not to. The environment is important—at least as important as genetic factors for most behavioral domains—but the way the environment works is nonshared—that is, not shared.*

New knowledge can create many new controversies, especially recent molecular genetic findings that pinpoint the genetic contribution to behaviors such as reading disability. For example, could evidence for genetic influence be used to justify the status quo? Will people at genetic risk be labeled and discriminated against? As specific genes are found for psychological traits, will parents use them prenatally to select "designer" children? New knowledge, however, also presents new opportunities. For example, knowing that certain children have increased genetic risk for a disorder could make it possible to prevent the disorder before it appears, rather than trying to treat the disorder after it appears and causes other problems.

My hope for the future is that the next generation of psychologists will wonder what the nature–nurture fuss was all about. I hope they (you!) will say, "Of course, we need to consider nature as well as nurture in understanding children's development."

PART OUTLINE

Chapter Three
Heredity and Environment

Chapter Four
Parenthood, Prenatal Development, and Birth

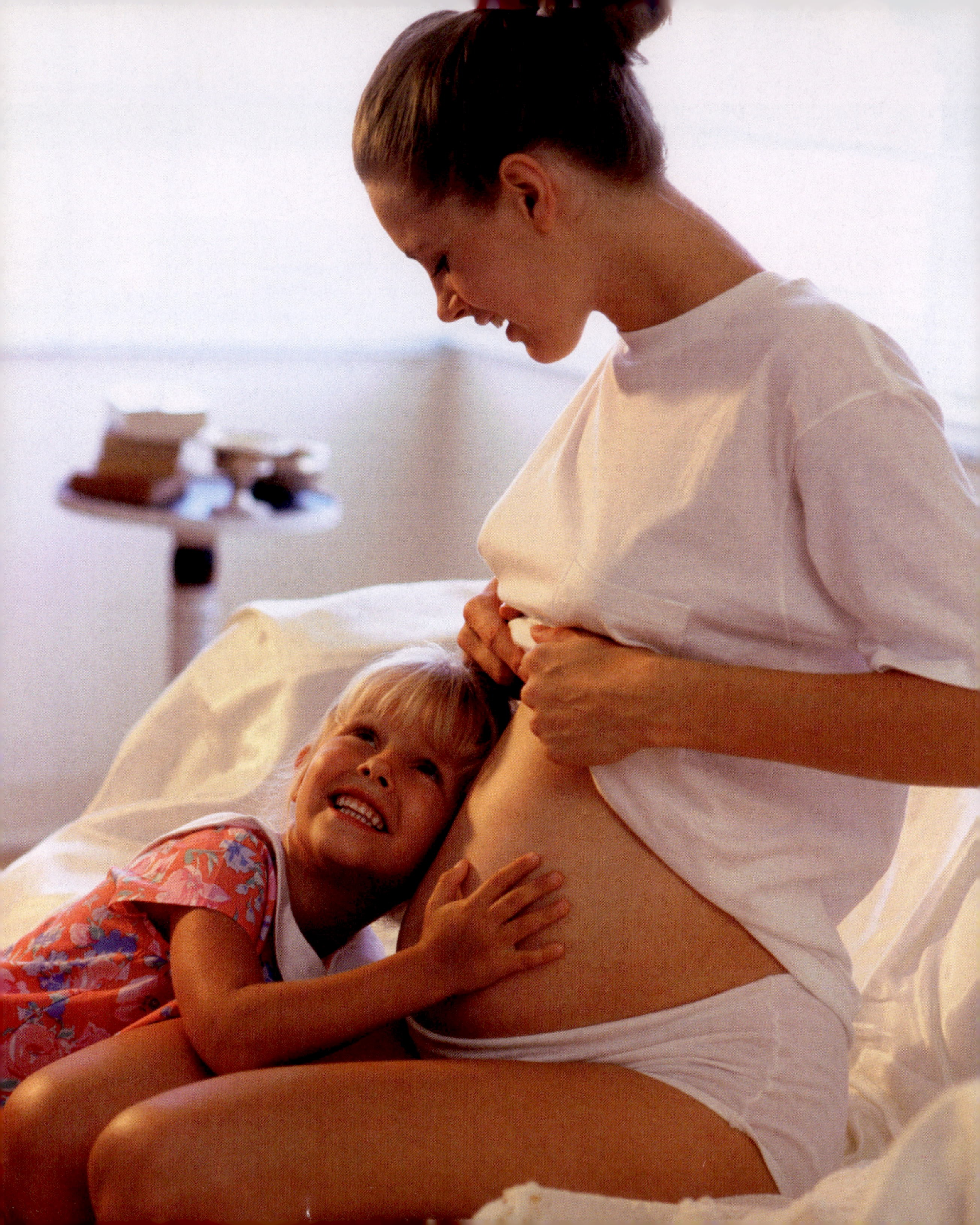

CHAPTER THREE

Heredity and Environment

CHAPTER OUTLINE

The Basics of Genetics
- Heredity in Action
- Mechanisms of Genetic Inheritance
- The Determination of Sex

Genetic Disorders and Abnormalities
- Disorders Causing Mental Retardation
- Abnormalities of Autosomes
- Abnormalities of the Sex Chromosomes
- Diagnosing Disorders

The Synchrony of Genes and Environment
- The Nature–Nurture Pendulum
- Directness and Indirectness of Heredity
- Canalized Traits

The Genetics of Human Traits
- Current Research Tools
- Personality
- Intelligence
- Creating Optimal Environments

Reviewing Key Points

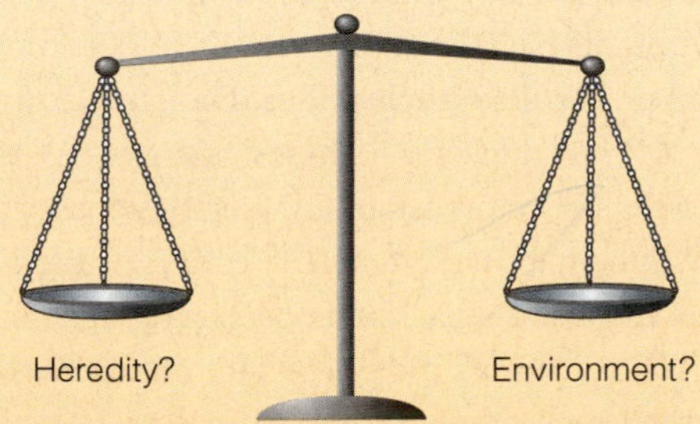

Antonio was recently elected president of the student body at the University of Wisconsin. Ever since Antonio was in preschool, he has had lots of friends. Perhaps, his *outgoingness* and his *helpful* ways contribute to his popularity. Just about anyone who has ever known Antonio describes him as *warmhearted, happy,* and *self-confident*. Still, although his *IQ* is above average, Antonio maintains a "gentlemen's C" average at school. His grades would perhaps be higher if he were not quite so *disorganized* and sometimes *careless*. Antonio has many interests and prefers to be involved in a *variety* of activities.

The environment and heredity do not influence personality and behavior in isolation, but rather, their combined effect determines what we become. Some behaviors appear to be more influenced by our genetic foundations and others more environmentally determined, but which behaviors fall into each category?

How we become what we are is the focus of this chapter. For decades it was believed (and, in many cases, substantiated by research) that only environmental factors shape and mold us into our uniquely different selves. Most notably, B. F. Skinner (1974), the leading behaviorist, when asked about possible genetic influences on behavior, replied that they played an extremely minuscule role in determining behavior—so much so that such factors need not even be studied. We might refer to this one-way directional influence of environment on behavior as "environmental determinism."

Parents, for a long time, have noticed differences in their children from the moment of birth. Their first-born, for example, may have been placid and easygoing, whereas their second-born behaved more like Ivan the Terrible. Even though researchers noticed what appeared to be inherited behaviors, they continued to give more weight to the power of the environment in shaping behavior. However, behavioral geneticists are now providing compelling evidence on the prominent role that genes play in determining who we are. However, genes work in concert with the environment, and vice versa. This is an important point because the theory of "genetic determinism" (with very few exceptions) is as incorrect as that of "environmental determinism."

First, to understand the nature and organization of our genetic structures, we will explore the body's microscopic world of chromosomes, genes, and the mighty architect that makes you distinctively you—DNA. Unfortunately, however, our genetic constitutions are not flawless, and, in some cases, abnormalities occur. We classify and discuss these DNA "miscodes," or genetic and chromosomal abnormalities, as disorders causing mental retardation, abnormalities of the autosomes, and abnormalities of the sex chromosomes.

We conclude this chapter by exploring two heavily investigated areas of genetic research—personality and intelligence. Which of the italicized traits describing Antonio would you put on the left side of the scale on page 83 as being more influenced by heredity, or genetics, and which traits would you put on the right side—tipping the scale toward a heavier environmental impact? Did you categorize Antonio's IQ or his outgoingness and self-confidence as being more influenced by genes? or does the environment play a more predominant role in influencing these traits? or is it a 50–50 influence?

chromosome Threadlike structures in the body's cells made up of genes.

homologous chromosomes Matched chromosomes that are virtually identical in shape, size, and function and that pair during meiotic cell division.

deoxyribonucleic acid, or DNA DNA is a long threadlike molecule shaped like a double helix that runs along the length of each chromosome.

nucleotide A chemical subunit composed of a sugar, phosphate, and base, which makes up the nucleic acids of DNA and RNA.

The Basics of Genetics

Before Beginning . . .

After reading this section, you will be able to

- describe the difference between and general function of chromosomes and genes.
- discuss the function of autosomes and sex chromosomes.
- define terms such as *alleles, dominant* and *recessive genes, genotype,* and *phenotype*.
- examine the unique properties of DNA and RNA.

Natalie is 31 years old. She and her husband both work full time and have worked hard to buy a small home. Natalie wants to start a family and thinks *now* is the time. Andy wants a family as well, but does not quite feel the immediacy that Natalie does. They have used the home-pregnancy tests a few times, but each time the results have been negative. Natalie feels a bit different this time, and her hunch is right—this time the test shows that Natalie is pregnant.

Heredity in Action

At conception, the fertilized cell inside Natalie's uterus was microscopically small; and yet, it contained the complete genetic blueprint that will transform it into a distinctive and special human being.

Chromosomes

In the nucleus of this cell we find 46 elongated, threadlike "colored bodies" called **chromosomes**. In Greek, *chromo* means color and *soma* refers to body. These structures are so named because when a cell is stained with certain chemicals, the chromosome takes on a deep color. There are 23 chromosomes from Andy's sperm and 23 chromosomes from Natalie's egg, or ovum. For each sperm chromosome there is a corresponding egg chromosome that is closely related functionally. The two chromosomes of each of these pairs are called **homologous** because of their similar sizes and shapes. This does not mean, however, that they physically exist in pairs; they are randomly placed in the nucleus of the cell.

Deoxyribonucleic Acid (DNA)

Chromosomes are made up of sequences of **deoxyribonucleic acid**, or **DNA**. The amount of DNA is less than one-billionth of a gram, but the genetic information coded within its bases is enormous. DNA is composed of individual units called **nucleotides**. Each nucleotide contains one of four nucleic acid bases: adenine (A), thymine (T), guanine (G), or cytosine (C). It is these bases that carry the information content, or "code," of the DNA molecule. DNA has a backbone consisting of two strands of sugar (deoxyribose) and phosphate molecules that twist around each other. Between the two strands, linking them together, are nucleotide *bases* that resemble rungs on a twisted rope ladder.

TABLE 3.1

Common Dominant and Recessive Traits

Dominant Trait	Recessive Trait	Dominant Trait	Recessive Trait
Brown eyes	Gray, green, hazel, or blue eyes	Short fingers	Fingers of normal length
Hazel or green eyes	Blue eyes	Double fingers	Normally jointed fingers
Normal vision	Nearsightedness	Double-jointedness	Normal joints
Farsightedness	Normal vision	Type A blood	Type O blood
Normal color vision	Red–green color blindness	Type B blood	Type O blood
Brown or black hair	Blond hair	Rh-positive blood	Rh-negative blood
Nonred hair	Red hair	Normal blood clotting	Hemophilia
Curly or wavy hair	Straight hair	Normal protein metabolism	Phenylketonuria (PKU)
Full head of hair	Baldness	Normal blood cells	Sickle-cell anemia
Normal hearing	Some forms of congenital deafness	Normal physiology	Tay-Sachs disease
Normally pigmented skin	Albino (completely white skin)	Huntington's disease	Normal central nervous system functioning in adulthood
Facial dimples	No dimples	Immunity to poison ivy	Susceptibility to poison ivy

Genes

It is amazing to note that each chromosome consists of roughly 20,000 genes. A **gene** is a segment of a chromosome that gives chemical instructions for individual characteristics. These genes follow one another on a chromosome like words composing a very long sentence. As each word in a sentence has a different function—some are nouns, verbs, or adjectives, for example—genes vary in function as well. Some genes will direct the process by which some cells of the body grow into skin and others into nerves or muscles. Genes also control the process by which cells become grouped into organs such as the heart, liver, or stomach. They are responsible for such aspects of development as the color of eyes and the length of bones. Most traits are **polygenic**, which means they do not usually result from a single gene pair but from a combination of many genes that interact in a number of ways to produce a particular result. Genes vary in size as well. Some genes are made up of many thousands of pairs of bases (the ladder rungs on the DNA molecule); others contain perhaps only 100.

Just as each chromosome is paired, so is each gene. Traits are determined by pairs of genes. We refer to each member of a pair of genes as an **allele**. When alleles are identical—for example, when both code for brown eyes—the individual is **homozygous** for that trait. When the paired genes have contrasting traits—one gene for blue eyes and one gene for brown eyes—the individual is **heterozygous** for that trait.

Dominant and Recessive Genes

There are several possible outcomes when someone is heterozygous for a trait. One is that the **dominant** gene will be expressed. Dominance is a principle first observed by Gregor Mendel (1866), a monk who studied the inherited characteristics of plants, particularly garden peas. Dominance means that one gene may prevent the expression of another gene. It does not mean that it is a superior trait, or even the one that will always be transmitted. For example, Natalie has blue eyes; blond, straight hair; and dimples. Andy has brown eyes; brown, wavy hair; and no dimples. What will their baby look like? Andy's brown eyes and brown, curly hair are dominant, and Natalie's blue eyes and blond, straight hair are **recessive** (nondominant). (See Table 3.1 for a list of dominant and recessive traits.) The influence of a recessive gene cannot be observed unless the person is homozygous for that trait—that is, has two recessive

gene The basic physical and functional unit of heredity that is transmitted from one generation to the next.

polygenetic (polygenic) inheritance The joint operation of several genes in producing a particular phenotype.

allele One of two or more alternative forms of a gene that exist at a specific gene location on a chromosome, giving rise to alternative hereditary characteristics.

homozygous An individual whose genotype is characterized by identical alleles of a gene.

heterozygous An individual whose genotype is characterized by two different alleles of a gene.

dominant Said of an allele that expresses its phenotype even in the presence of a recessive allele.

recessive Said of an allele that must be present in a homozygous pair to be phenotypically expressed.

genes paired at the same **locus**, or position, on the same chromosome. As a result, there are many possible outcomes for children as illustrated in Figure 3.1.

What also is apparent from Figure 3.1 is that some inherited genetic traits are expressed visibly, whereas others are not. For example, we may have curly hair that is directly observable, but we may also carry the gene for straight hair, which is not observable. A child's complete genetic constitution is defined as his or her **genotype**, which refers to the actual genetic composition of the organism, regardless of whether or not it is expressed. **Phenotype** refers to the individual's observable traits. As shown in Figure 3.1, genotype refers to an individual's genetic *potential* and phenotype refers to the *actual expression* of genes. For example, three of the four children in Figure 3.1 have curly hair (phenotype); however, the genetic compositions (genotype) are different in each of these children.

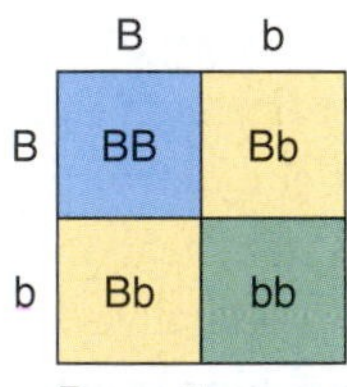

B
b
B
BB
Bb
b
Bb
bb
Punnett square

FIGURE 3.1 *Inheritance of Curly or Straight Hair*

If both the father and mother have curly hair but carry the recessive gene for straight hair, they are heterozygous for this trait. Their offspring have a 25 percent chance of having curly hair and being homozygous for this trait; a 50 percent chance of being like their parents (curly hair, heterozygous); and a 25 percent chance of having straight hair and being homozygous for this trait.

locus
The term in genetics for the position of a specific gene on a chromosome.

genotype
An individual's genetic makeup underlying a specific trait or constellation of traits.

phenotype
The detectable characteristics associated with a particular genotype.

ribonucleic acid (RNA)
An RNA molecule that has been transcribed from a gene-bearing DNA molecule and will later be translated into a protein.

mitosis
A mode of cell division in which a single parent cell gives rise to two genetically identical daughter cells.

meiosis
A mode of cell division in which a diploid parent cell gives rise to haploid reproductive cells or gametes.

Mechanisms of Genetic Inheritance

At conception, the child's DNA coding is locked into one tiny cell; how, then, does this single cell develop into roughly 60 trillion cells of a complete human body? One of DNA's unique properties is that it can reproduce, or copy, itself. As shown in Figure 3.2, during cell division, the DNA molecule "unzips" along the weak-paired bases. Then each half duplicates itself by attracting new material from the cell to synthesize a second chain and form a new DNA molecule.

When the DNA molecule unzips, it creates a second kind of nucleic acid, **ribonucleic acid (RNA)**. Although DNA contains the complete blueprint of the living organism, it cannot move out of the nucleus of the cell. But RNA, which acts as a messenger to carry out the instructions of the DNA, can. DNA directs the functions of RNA. The remarkable duplicating ability of DNA makes it possible for the genetic code of each of the parents to be passed on to their offspring, thus creating a unique individual. This duplication of DNA normally occurs during a process of cell division called **mitosis**, which occurs in the production of all new *somatic cells*. Somatic cells will make up the child's various organs and body systems (digestive, respiratory) and carry on life-giving processes: These cells carry the oxygen, rebuild the tissue, feed cells, and so on. The first step in mitosis is the duplication of DNA, and thus, the formation of duplicate copies of each chromosome. In mitotic cell division, an identical copy of the original single cell is reproduced. After the process is complete, the resulting daughter cells have the same material and genetic potential as the parent cell. Sometime between 24 and 60 hours after conception, the first cell begins to divide. Gradually, as the process continues, the resulting *sister chromatids*, or daughter cells, begin to form duplicate copies.

A second form of cell division, **meiosis**, enables a couple to produce a daughter or a son. New life is cre-

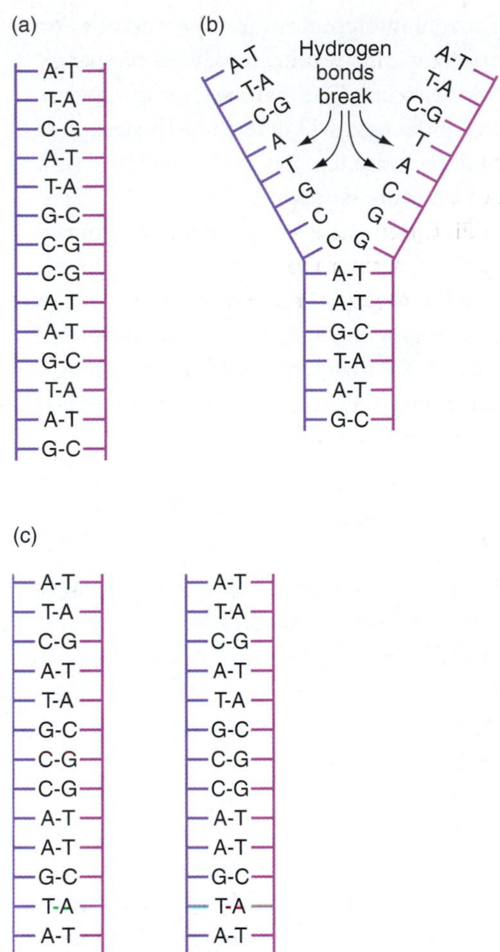

FIGURE 3.2 *DNA Replication*

(a) Portion of one DNA molecule. (b) The two strands separate at the hydrogen bonds, and free bases attach to the appropriate base in the original strand. (c) Two new DNA molecules, each identical to the original molecule.

ated when two special cells known as **gametes** (egg and sperm cell) combine. This form of cell division is reserved just for gametes. Instead of containing the usual 46 chromosomes, these cells contain only 23. Meiosis means *to make smaller*; that is, the developing sperm or ovum relinquishes its duplicate set of chromosomes so that the mature gamete has 23 pairs of chromosomes (see Figure 3.3). Thus, the mathematics of meiosis is relatively straightforward. **Diploid** somatic cells (a cell containing two full sets of chromosomes) require 46 chromosomes—two homologous sets of 23—to fulfill a wide range of specialized body functions. Gametes—eggs and sperm—require precisely half that number, one set of 23 chromosomes, to carry out their singular mission of sexual union to form a diploid fertilized egg (zygote).

Clearly, if gametes arose by mitosis, each would bring a full complement of 46 chromosomes to the zygote, bloating it with 92 chromosomes, or two complete sets of human chromosomes. Assuming it managed to survive, a most unlikely prospect, the next generation of mitotically produced gametes would double its 92 chromosomes to 184 following fertilization. Instead, through a variety of ingenious steps, it produces **haploid** cells (a cell containing only one set, or half the usual diploid number, of chromosomes) endowed with a novel mix of parental genes.

Additional variability in the pattern of genetic information results from **crossing over**. When the cells divide during meiosis, some of the material from the male and female chromosome strands may cross over and exchange places. The resulting sequence of specific genetic information on a chromosome is unlike that in either the original maternal or paternal code. Through crossing over, new arrangements of genetic information may be passed on to offspring. This variation in the patterning of genetic information adds to the diversity of offspring.

During this crossing-over process in meiosis, segments of matching chromosomes break off and trade places with each other. Crossing over plays an important role in reassorting genes into new combinations.

gamete
A haploid reproductive cell—for example, a sperm or an egg cell—in sexually reproducing organisms.

diploid cell
A cell containing two full sets of chromosomes.

haploid cell
A cell containing only one set, or half the usual diploid number, of chromosomes.

crossing over
Creation of new genetic information in offspring through the exchanging of places by male and female chromosome strands during meiosis.

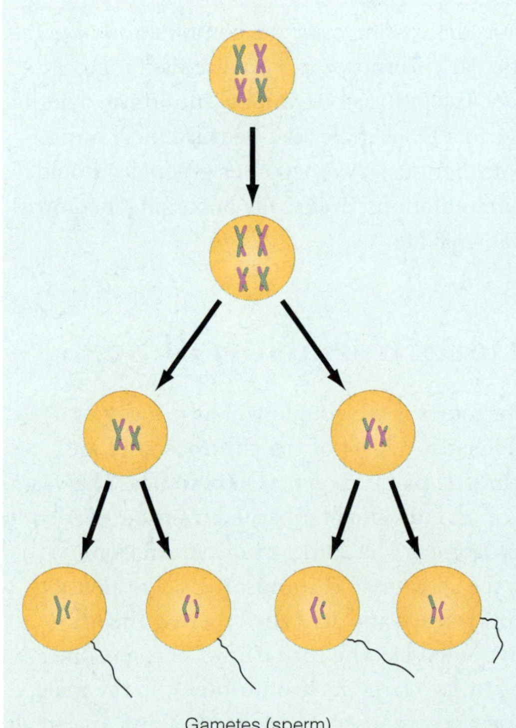

Step 1. Each of the germ cell's original chromosomes duplicates itself, and the duplicate remains attached. (To simplify, we only show four chromosomes and their duplicates. In human germ cells, there are 46 chromosomes.)

Step 2. Crossing over takes place among adjacent chromosomes, thus creating new hereditary combinations.

Step 3. The original cell now divides to form two parent cells, each of which has 23 duplicated chromosomes (some of which have been altered by crossing over).

Step 4. Finally, each chromosome and its duplicate now split and segregate into separate gametes. Thus, each gamete has but half the chromosomes of its parent cell.

FIGURE 3.3 *Meiosis*

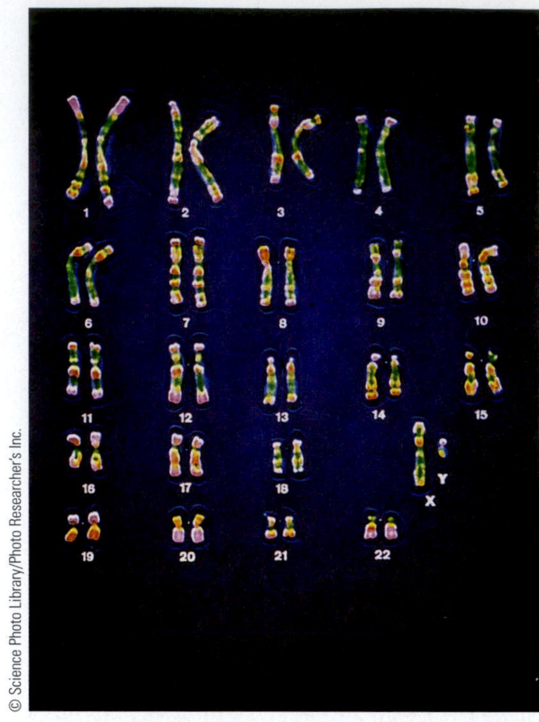

Every cell includes 23 pairs of chromosomes. The last pair, the sex chromosomes, are distinct in males and females. The female has two elongated X chromosomes, and the male (shown here) has one X chromosome and one smaller Y chromosome.

Were it not for crossing over, the combination of genes on a particular chromosome would remain together indefinitely except for an occasional **mutation**, a heritable change in a DNA molecule. Because most mutations are deleterious, chromosomes gradually would accumulate mutations, eventually becoming incompatible with normal life.

mutation A heritable change in a DNA molecule.

autosome Any chromosome that is not a sex chromosome.

sex chromosome See *gamete*.

sex-linked characteristics Those that depend on X and Y chromosomes.

hemophilia An X-linked disorder that prevents blood from clotting.

The Determination of Sex

What determines if the couple will have a boy or a girl? Within each cell, 44 of the chromosomes are grouped into 22 pairs, known as **autosomes**. The vast majority of an individual's inherited traits are carried on the autosomes. The 23rd pair of chromosomes (bringing the total to 46 chromosomes) is responsible for determining sex and are called the **sex chromosomes**. In the female, the 23rd pair of chromosomes is composed of two large X chromosomes. In the male, the 23rd pair is composed of one large X and one small Y. Whereas every gamete a female produces will carry just the X chromosome, half of a male's sperm will carry an X and half Y.

During sexual intercourse, the male's ejaculation of sperm into the vagina results in millions of sperm racing toward the ovum. The "winner," or the sperm first to penetrate the egg, will determine the sex. If an X is first, it will be a girl; if a Y is first, it will be a boy. Actually, it is a bit more complicated than that. The *testes-determining factor* refers to a genetic segment usually found on the Y chromosome, and it is this stretch of genetic material that actually determines the sex of the child. If this segment is missing, we will have an XY female; in cases of XX males, the testes-determining factor segment hooks onto the X. These are rare chromosomal abnormalities, however.

X-Linked Inheritance

Characteristics that depend on these X and Y chromosomes are called **sex-linked characteristics**. Hemophilia, color blindness, and some forms of baldness are examples of sex-linked characteristics. These chromosomal characteristics are much more likely to appear in males than in females. Why is this so?

Hemophilia, a disease that interferes with normal blood clotting, is caused by a gene that appears only on the X chromosome. The female has two X chromosomes and so is protected from having this disorder by the fact that she has a normal gene on the other X chromosome. She must have two genes for this trait to appear. The male, however, has only one X chromosome. If the male receives the gene for hemophilia X, he has no second X chromosome; thus, he inherits the disorder from his mother. See Figure 3.4 for a visual example of sex-linked color blindness.

Concept Checks

1. Chromosomes serve as the carriers of the actual units of genetic transmission known as ________________.
2. Which of the following behaviors or traits are determined by autosomes, and which are determined by sex chromosomes?
   a. Baldness ________________
   b. Sex of the child ________________
   c. Eye color ________________
3. Charles has blue eyes; both of his parents have brown eyes. What is his phenotype?
   a. Blue eyes
   b. Brown eyes
   c. Brown and blue eyes

4. A unique feature of deoxyribonucleic acid, or DNA, is that it can
   a. replicate itself.
   b. move out of the nucleus of the cell.
   c. receive "orders" from ribonucleic acid or RNA.

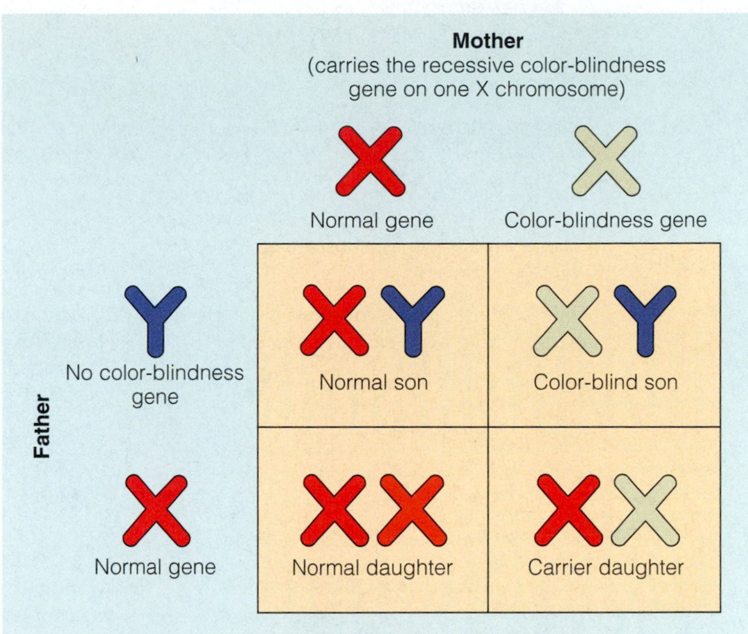

FIGURE 3.4 *Sex-Linked Transmission of Color Blindness*

In this example, the mother is not color blind but is a carrier because one of her X chromosomes contains a color-blind allele. Notice that her sons have a 50 percent chance of inheriting the color-blind allele and being color blind, whereas none of her daughters would display the trait. A girl can be color blind only if her father is, and her mother is at least a carrier of the color-blindness gene.

Genetic Disorders and Abnormalities

Before Beginning . . .

After reading this section, you will be able to

- identify genetic disorders causing mental retardation.
- identify abnormalities of the autosomes.
- discuss sex chromosome abnormalities.
- discuss genetic screening and diagnostic tests.

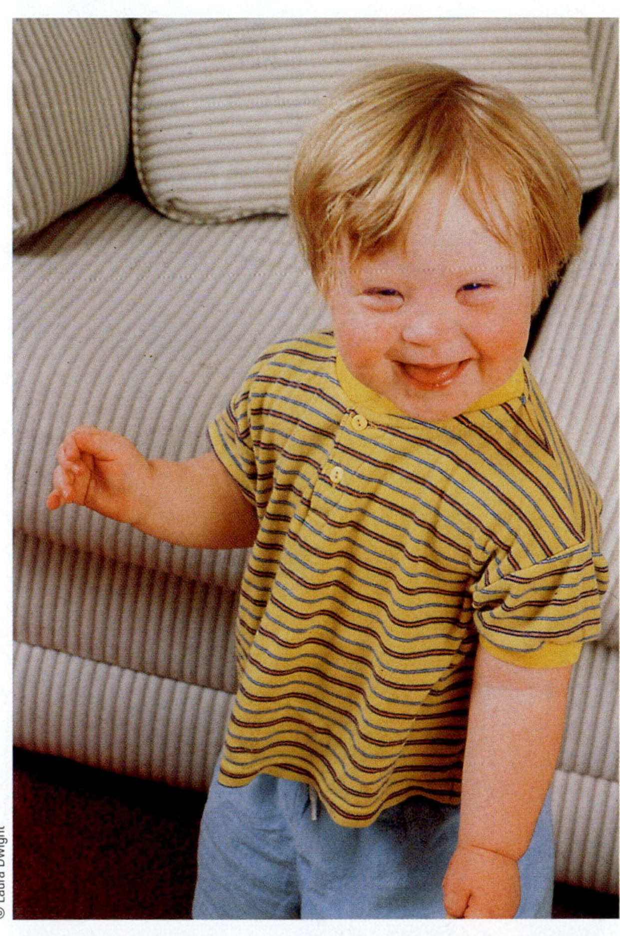

© Laura Dwight

Children with Down Syndrome are often characterized by a number of distinctive physical features such as almond-shaped eyes, a flattened nose, and a sloping forehead.

The ability to reproduce ourselves and to preserve our genetic diversity is truly miraculous. However, are these processes of genetic transmission always fail-safe? Unfortunately, the answer is no. None of us is perfect, and in some cases abnormalities of the autosomes, or sex chromosomes, occur and cause various types of disorders.

Disorders Causing Mental Retardation

Down Syndrome

The child with **Down syndrome** has distinctive facial features—a large, broad skull and slanting eyes. After birth, the child's rate of growth continues to be slow, with shortness of stature common. These children rarely attain sexual maturity. Like other genetic birth defects, Down syndrome is not correctable; every cell of the individual's body carries the same error. Individuals with this disorder usually have 47 chromosomes instead of 46; this extra chromosome is responsible for the syndrome. All the chromosomes of a Down syndrome child are in pairs except the 21st pair, which is represented in triplicate and known as Trisomy 21. Having an extra chromosome 21

Down syndrome A genetic disorder, which leads to mental retardation, caused by an extra chromosome on the 21st pair.

TABLE 3.2

Down Syndrome Myths

Myth	Truth
Down syndrome is a rare genetic disorder.	One in every 1000 live births is a child with Down syndrome, representing approximately 5000 births per year in the United States alone. Today, Down syndrome affects more than 250,000 people in the United States.
People with Down syndrome are severely retarded.	Most people with Down syndrome have IQs that fall into the mild to moderate range of retardation.
Children with Down syndrome must be placed in separate special education programs.	Children with Down syndrome have been included in regular academic classrooms in schools across the country. In some instances, they are integrated into specific courses; in others, they are fully integrated into the classroom for all subjects.
People with Down syndrome are perennially happy.	People with Down syndrome have feelings just like everyone else in the population; they respond to positive expressions of friendship, and they are hurt and upset by inconsiderate behavior.
Down syndrome can never be cured.	Research is making great strides in identifying the genes on chromosome 21 that cause the features of Down syndrome. Scientists now feel strongly that it will be possible to improve, correct, or prevent many of the problems associated with Down syndrome in the future.

From *Genetic Disorders Sourcebook* (pp. 15–17), by K. Bellenir (Ed.), 1996, Detroit: Omnigraphics, Inc.

Thought CHALLENGE

Should children with Down syndrome be mainstreamed into the regular classroom, or should they be a part of a special education system?

fragile X syndrome A genetic disorder resulting from an abnormal chromosomal structure.

phenylketonuria (PKU) An autosomal recessive disorder that leads to an excess of phenylalanine. If untreated through proper diet, children will suffer from severe mental retardation.

affects many aspects of development; the most salient is a decreased rate of intellectual development. Physical abnormalities, such as heart and intestinal defects, cause an increased mortality rate during the first few years of life, and about 1 percent of children with Down syndrome develop leukemia. However, treatment can relieve or improve some of the most severe problems. Despite general familiarity with this syndrome, a number of myths still prevail (see Table 3.2). We will take a more in-depth look at Down syndrome in Chapter 12.

Fragile X Syndrome

> When he was 4 years old, Sam was identified as having fragile X syndrome during his evaluation for entry into a preschool program for children with special needs. He had been diagnosed as having mental retardation, requiring limited supports. His behavior showed marked hyperactivity, self-stimulatory behavior, and language skills that were more delayed than his cognitive abilities.

Some genetic disorders do not involve changes in the number of chromosomes children have but rather are a result of an abnormal chromosomal structure. Such is the case with **fragile X syndrome**, which ranks just behind Down syndrome as the leading cause of heritable mental retardation (Mazzocco, Kates, Baumgardner, Freund, & Reiss, 1997). Its incidence is 1 in 1250 males and 1 in 2500 females (Plomin, 1997). Males with fragile X show more serious problems than females do and may have unusual responses to sensory stimuli as well as social and communications problems. Physical manifestations include a long face with large ears (Steward, Bakker, Wilems, & Oostra, 1998). The effects of fragile X syndrome range from normal IQ and subtle learning disabilities to severe mental retardation and the social and language difficulties called autism.

Fragile X syndrome receives its name from the fact that the region near the tip of the long arm of the X chromosome is pinched in. The abnormal structure of this region makes the tip of the chromosome more fragile or vulnerable to breaking off. As one of the major X-linked disorders, it is more prevalent in boys, which helps to explain why mental retardation in males is 25 to 35 percent higher than in females. Evidence exists that the defective gene at the fragile site is expressed only when it is passed from mother to child.

Phenylketonuria (PKU)

Phenylketonuria (**PKU**) is another well-known inherited condition that causes mental retardation. PKU is known as an autosomal recessive disorder, because it is caused by inheriting two recessive genes. If both parents carry one copy of this recessive gene, they will not themselves display the trait, but their children could inherit a defective allele from each parent and thus display the trait. PKU affects one in 10,000 to 20,000 live births. It is a genetically caused disease characterized by a deficiency in an enzyme normally produced in the liver. This enzyme, phenylalanine hydroxylase, is responsible for breaking down phenylalanine, an amino acid found in many foods (Hanley, Demshar, Preston, & Borczyk et al., 1997). In the absence of this enzyme, excess phenylalanine from protein in the diet is not utilized and accumulates in the body. As a result, the excess phenylalanine produces toxic by-products that are detrimental to the development and growth of the central nervous system. High concentrations of phenylalanine and other chemical by-products result in reduced brain development and irreversible mental retardation (Batshaw, 1997).

Untreated or late-treated babies with PKU usually develop mild to severe mental retardation. Therefore, it is imperative that the diagnosis of PKU be established within the first days of life, before the onset of mental damage. All U.S. states and Canadian provinces have blood-screening programs to detect PKU shortly after birth, and similar programs are in place in many other countries.

The treatment for PKU is simple—almost completely eliminating the intake of phenylalanine. Milk, for example, has high levels of phenylalanine; thus, its intake must be curtailed. The diet prescribed by a physician must be appropriate for the child and thus needs to be monitored carefully in the first few years of life. Too high a level of phenylalanine in the system and mental retardation occurs; too low a level and lethargy and poor physical growth may result. In general, studies of treated PKU children indicate that early dietary restrictions alter the biochemical abnormality and result in the attainment of at least average intellectual abilities (Griffiths, Smith, & Harvie, 1997). Dietary restrictions generally continue only through the early school years. After the brain is sufficiently developed, excess phenylalanine will not hurt it (Plomin, 1990).

Abnormalities of Autosomes

Sickle-Cell Anemia

Sickle-cell anemia is another autosomal recessive disorder that occurs when a child inherits two recessive alleles. With this disorder, children experience problems with their red blood cells. Normally oval, the red blood cells take on a curved "sickle" shape. This makes it difficult for the cells to move through the blood vessels and can lead to clogging of the arteries. The sickle-shaped cells can lodge in small blood vessels, causing painful swelling of joints or even bleeding into the brain. It is a worldwide health problem, affecting many individuals from various countries and ethnic groups. The World Health Organization estimates that each year more than 250,000 babies are born worldwide with this inherited blood cell disorder. About 1 in 400 African American newborns in the United States have sickle-cell anemia, but the disease is also prevalent in Africa and many Spanish-speaking regions of the world, such as South America, Cuba, and Central America.

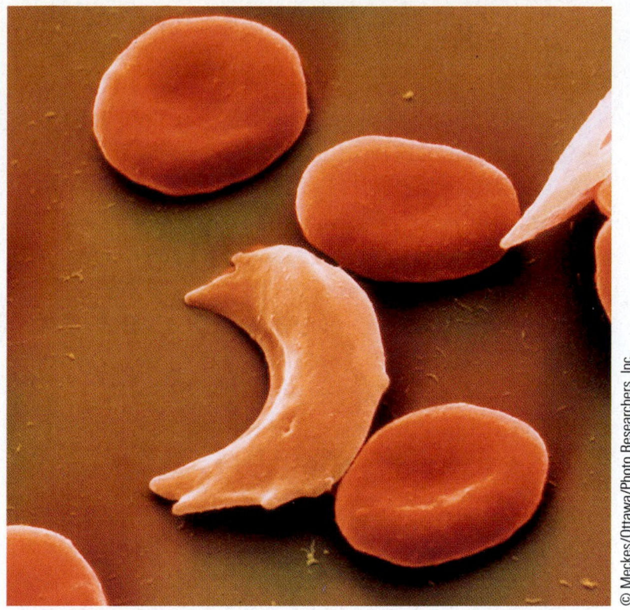

Individuals with sickle-cell anemia have red blood cells that take on a rigid, sickle shape rather than the normal round, doughnut shape.

In African countries where malaria is common, carriers for sickle-cell anemia are actually protected against contracting a severe form of malaria. So in these countries, children born with the sickle-cell trait tend to survive. They grow up, have their own children, and pass the gene for sickle-cell anemia on to their offspring. Thus, sickle-cell anemia is more common in Africa.

For African Americans in the United States, sickle-cell anemia results in chronic pain and life-threatening infections. Currently, there is no cure. However, one of the most important advances in recent years has been the proof of our ability to decrease the severity of illness and the death rate in young children with this disorder. Infants are at great risk for overwhelming infection

sickle-cell anemia A genetic disorder in which the blood cells become curved or sickle-shaped, causing clotting in joints or body organs.

and death from the age of 3 months to 5 years. Infection is the main cause of death from sickle-cell anemia, and as many as 40 percent of the children with these infections die. Now, this does not have to occur. First, all babies should be screened at birth to find out if they have sickle-cell disease. It is a simple test and very inexpensive. If the baby has sickle-cell anemia, it is very important that the baby be entered into a pediatric program, seen frequently, and most important, placed on penicillin by mouth every day. Studies have shown that babies given penicillin every day have their risk of infection reduced by 84 percent, and among those studied no deaths occurred (Suzuki & Knudtson, 1989).

Thought **CHALLENGE**

If you inherited the gene for Huntington's disease, which is always fatal, would you want to know? Why? or Why not?

Tay-Sachs Disease

Tay-Sachs disease (TSD) is another autosomal recessive disorder, and it is fatal. This genetic disorder in children causes the progressive destruction of the central nervous system. It is caused by the absence of a vital enzyme called hexosaminidase A (hex-A). Without hex-A, a fatty substance builds up abnormally in the cells, especially in the nerve cells of the brain. This destructive process begins in the fetus early in pregnancy, although the disease is not clinically apparent until the child is several months old. By the time a child with TSD is 4 or 5 years old, the nervous system is so badly affected that life itself cannot be supported. Even with the best of care, TSD children die by the age of 5.

In the past, prenatal diagnosis of these disorders could be accomplished only after a family had already produced at least one affected child. Now, a blood test can identify carriers of this disease (as well as cystic fibrosis and sickle-cell anemia) before they have an affected child. If a couple is screened and both are found to be carriers, they know that in each pregnancy there is a one in four risk of having an affected child. They then can consider a number of reproductive options, including artificial insemination with donor sperm or egg, adoption, or monitoring the pregnancy with prenatal diagnostic techniques.

Tay-Sachs screening has been particularly successful because it can be limited to a relatively small number of people, the Ashkenazic Jewish population. The chance of a Jewish couple bearing a child affected with Tay-Sachs disease is about 1 in 2500. Among non-Jewish couples, the risk is about 1 in 360,000 (Batshaw & Rose, 1997).

Tay-Sachs disease (TSD)
A fatal genetic disorder in children that causes the progressive destruction of the central nervous system.

Huntington's disease
A dominant autosomal disorder that leads to death.

Huntington's Disease

As noted, disorders like PKU and sickle-cell anemia are caused by recessive alleles, which means that the child must inherit both recessive alleles from each parent to inherit the disorder. If a disorder, however, is caused by a dominant allele, the individual who inherits even one allele will show the disorder—such is the case with **Huntington's disease**. Huntington's disease is a rare autosomal dominant disorder that results from a dominant allele linked to a genetic marker on chromosome 4. The chances of passing on the dominant allele are relatively small, however, because this disorder also limits the person's ability to reproduce. Individuals with Huntington's disease show normal development until they are between 35 and 50. Symptoms include muscle spasms, irritability, depression and other personality disorders, memory impairments, and other signs of brain deterioration. Death usually follows within 15 years after diagnosis. Despite the severity of the disorder, the dominant allele remains in the gene pool because some individuals with Huntington's bear children before any symptoms appear.

Huntington's disease and PKU constitute examples in the field of psychopathology. These diseases are properly termed "genetic conditions," because environmental factors play no role in the *cause* of the underlying psychophysiology. In contrast, most medical conditions, such as asthma, diabetes, hypertension, Alzheimer's disease, and coronary artery disease and almost all personality disorders, such as schizophrenia and clinical depression, are not purely genetic (Botstein, 1999). Although twin, adoption, and family studies often show a strong genetic influence (Plomin, DeFries, McClearn, & Rutter, 1997), the aforementioned personality disorders are regarded as "complex" and "multifactorial" (not just "genetic"), because environmental factors are also important in their etiology. A study that dramatically demonstrates this point has shown that schizophrenia is six times more likely to appear when the twins share a placenta than when they do not, suggesting that some intrauterine environmental process can affect the development of this psychological disorder (Davis, Phelps, & Bracha, 1995). Moreover, it is usual for several different genes to be involved, and because of this, understanding the interplay between genes and environment in the causal processes is quite complicated (Plomin & Rutter, 1998).

Abnormalities of the Sex Chromosomes

Abnormal sex chromosomes are more common but have less serious consequences than abnormal autosomal disorders. In particular, children with abnormal sex chromosomes do not consistently suffer from mental retardation. They do tend, however, to differ in their physical features, biological functioning, and social behavior.

Turner's Syndrome

Turner's syndrome occurs only in females. Girls with Turner's syndrome are short as adults (rarely more than 5 feet tall) and are without sexual development; a web of skin also may be present on the sides of their neck. These girls are described as immature and unassertive. In Turner's syndrome, the sperm cell fails to produce sex chromosomes, and the zygote becomes a female who has one instead of two X chromosomes, resulting in a total of 45 chromosomes, instead of the normal 46. Turner's syndrome results in higher rates (about 20 percent) of mild retardation and is strongly associated with substantial space-form perceptual deficiencies. Many are not diagnosed until adolescence, when sex development fails to occur and short stature is noted. Others are diagnosed at birth when certain physical abnormalities, such as webbing of the neck, are noted. Although these women are sterile because they lack functional ovaries, development of secondary sex characteristics is possible with the administration of female hormones.

Klinefelter's Syndrome

Actually, the term **Klinefelter's syndrome** has fallen out of favor with medical researchers. Most prefer to describe men and boys having the extra chromosome that causes this condition as "XXY males." Klinefelter's syndrome is another chromosome abnormality that occurs when a normal ovum is fertilized by a sperm that has both an X and a Y chromosome instead of having only one or the other. This produces a zygote with an extra X chromosome (XXY); however, their appearance is unequivocally male. There are approximately 2 cases per 1000 males. Often having small testes and prostates, they also have diminished body and facial hair. Some breast development may also show at puberty. These males are frequently infertile. Mental retardation occurs in 25 to 50 percent of the cases, but it is usually mild with no outstanding deficits.

Hemophilia

Hemophilia is a genetic blood-clotting disorder that affects about 20,000 Americans. There is no cure; people with hemophilia require lifelong treatment. Contrary to popular belief, people with hemophilia do not bleed to death from minor cuts or injuries, nor do they bleed faster than what is considered normal. However, people with hemophilia do bleed longer, because their blood cannot develop a firm clot. Often bleeding is internal, into joints, and results in arthritis or crippling.

Hemophilia is carried by females, but those affected are almost always males. Hemophilia is a good example of the incomplete expression of the genotype in the phenotype. There is a 50 percent chance, for example, that sons of a female carrier will have hemophilia and a 50 percent chance that daughters will be carriers. All daughters of men with hemophilia are carriers, but their sons are unaffected.

Color Blindness

Another X-linked disorder is red–green color blindness. Males are two times more likely to be affected than are females. For the daughter to exhibit this trait, she must be homozygous for it; that is, she must have a father who is red–green color blind and a mother who is either color blind or heterozygous for the trait. If a son receives the gene for color blindness on the X chromosome, he inherits it from his mother and will be unable to distinguish red from green because there is no corresponding gene on the Y chromosome to counteract the recessive gene.

Diagnosing Disorders

None of us has a totally "error free" genetic system, and it is unrealistic to expect this in our offspring. There are, however, some genetic abnormalities that can be treated and some that place severe limits on the child's future health and happiness. For these reasons, some couples may choose to see a genetic counselor for **genetic screening**.

Turner's syndrome A chromosomal abnormality that results from the presence of only one sex chromosome, an X. Children with this syndrome are female but sterile.

Klinefelter's syndrome A chromosomal abnormality that usually results from the presence of two X chromosomes and one Y chromosome. Children with this syndrome are male but never produce sperm.

genetic screening The process of systematically scanning individual genotypes for possible defects or abnormalities.

TABLE 3.3

Prenatal Diagnostic Tests

Test	When Performed	Description	Risk
Ultrasound	6-weeks gestation	High-frequency sound waves are beamed at the uterus. Their reflection is transmitted to a video screen, which reveals the placement of the fetus, gross physical defects, fetal age, and multiple fetuses.	No risk factors
Chorionic villus sampling	6 to 8 weeks	A thin tube is inserted into the uterus through the vagina, or a hollow needle is inserted through the abdominal wall. A small plug of tissue is removed from the end of one or more chorionic villi (the hairlike projections on the membrane surrounding the fetus). Cells are examined for genetic defects.	Slightly greater risk of miscarriage
Amniocentesis	14 to 16 weeks	A hollow needle is inserted through the abdominal wall to obtain a sample of the amniotic fluid. Cells are then evaluated for genetic defects.	Small risk of miscarriage
Alpha-fetoprotein test	16 weeks	Some of the baby's cells enter the maternal blood; a sample of the mother's blood is screened for Down syndrome and neural tube defects.	No risk

Genetic Screening

There are two basic strategies for spotting genetic abnormalities. The first strategy depends on the *biochemical analysis* of substances in the body to reveal the presence of abnormal genes indirectly. For example, Tay-Sachs disease can be detected by examining the biochemical fetal fluids. The second basic strategy of genetic screening involves the direct *examination of chromosomal DNA* in human body cells to detect defects that range from major chromosomal anomalies like Down syndrome to minute differences in the DNA sequences characteristic of diseases like sickle-cell anemia (Plomin, 1998).

Many genetic problems can be avoided with genetic counseling and testing. Couples, particularly those who already have a child with a condition that might be genetic, who have relatives who have genetic problems, or who have had several miscarriages, should be aware of the importance of consulting a genetic specialist. Once he or she knows the couple's personal and family histories, the specialist may then accurately diagnose the risk of their conceiving an affected child. Some individuals may believe that the purpose of genetic screening leads to the intention of abortion; the genetic counselor's ultimate responsibility, however, is to help prospective parents digest the information about genetic disorders and to make the right decisions for themselves (Furr & Seger, 1998).

A strong belief in personal autonomy, then, is a cornerstone of genetic counseling offered here in the United States. This nondirective and value-free type of information offered may conflict with the expectations of some ethnic groups (Greb, 1998), for example, Chinese and Japanese American couples. Stanley Sue (Sue & Zane, 1987) suggests that families of Asian descent and other traditional cultures seek help from and develop trust in professionals who respond with directive advice, because this is more consistent with the authority relations and role expectations from their cultures. Cross-cultural research illustrates the need to appreciate couples' cultural values (Wang & Marsh, 1992).

Diagnostic Tests

For a woman who is already expecting a child, there are a number of tests that can determine if the fetus is developing properly. Although prenatal technology has largely brought hope and comfort into parents' lives, the waiting period can be stressful for many parents, even those couples who would not consider abortion. Many couples put themselves in a kind of limbo zone, afraid to invest emotionally in their pregnancies until the results confirm their child's well-being. Based on the couple's health history, doctors may suggest various tests (see Table 3.3). Most expectant mothers, however, will have an ultrasound test.

Ultrasound Tests An ultrasound test can be performed at about the sixth gestational week. The test is painless and safe: the doctor moves a microphone-like device called a transducer across the abdomen. As the sound waves reflect off the fetal tissue and organs a computer translates them instantly into an image on a video screen. The test may be performed to detect gross structural anomalies, such as missing or deformed limbs, implantation in the fallopian tube instead of the uterus, date of conception, and multiple fetuses.

At 8 weeks, Natalie has an ultrasound test. Both she and Andy are mesmerized by the image they see on the screen, which, according to Andy, resembles a lima bean with a pulsating blip in the middle. As Andy looks a bit closer, he notices two pulsating blips. The obstetrician informs the couple that they are going to have twins, and these "blips" are the heartbeats of two viable fetuses.

By 15 weeks, a trained eye can discern major organs. While the parents happily count toes and fingers, a physician may measure the length of the leg bones or check facial features for signs of Down syndrome. Locating the position of the fetus by means of ultrasound enables the doctor to perform another diagnostic test—amniocentesis.

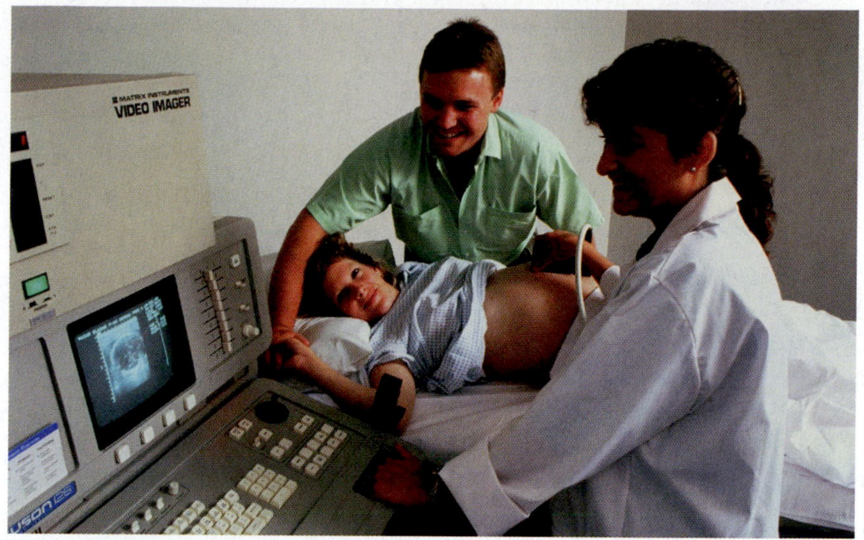

High-frequency sound waves are beamed at the uterus in an ultrasound prenatal diagnosis. Their reflection is translated into a picture on a video screen that reveals the size, shape, and placement of the fetus.

Amniocentesis Over 50 biochemical inherited disorders and close to 300 chromosomal disorders can be detected through amniocentesis. It is a technique of withdrawing some of the amniotic fluid that bathes the developing fetus to diagnose disorders. The amniotic fluid is obtained by carefully inserting a hollow needle through the mother's abdominal wall and into the amniotic sac (see Figure 3.5). Fetal cells floating in the fluid are grown and examined for chromosomal abnormalities, such as the extra chromosome 21 that causes Down syndrome. Biochemicals in the fluid also provide diagnostic clues to several inborn errors of metabolism. Amniocentesis usually is performed between the 14th and 16th week of gestation (the volume of amniotic fluid is insufficient before this time), and results are not available for 3 or 4 weeks.

Chorionic Villus Sampling Chorionic villus sampling can be performed early (6 to 8 weeks and results are available within 24 hours) and is an important alternative to amniocentesis. Cells can be suctioned from the developing placenta via a small tube passed through the vagina and cervix. These cells then can be analyzed to determine the fetus's genetic makeup.

The Alpha-Fetoprotein Test The alpha-fetoprotein test (AFP) is performed at 16 weeks. A sample of the mother's blood is screened for Down syndrome and neural tube defects, such as spina bifida, in which the

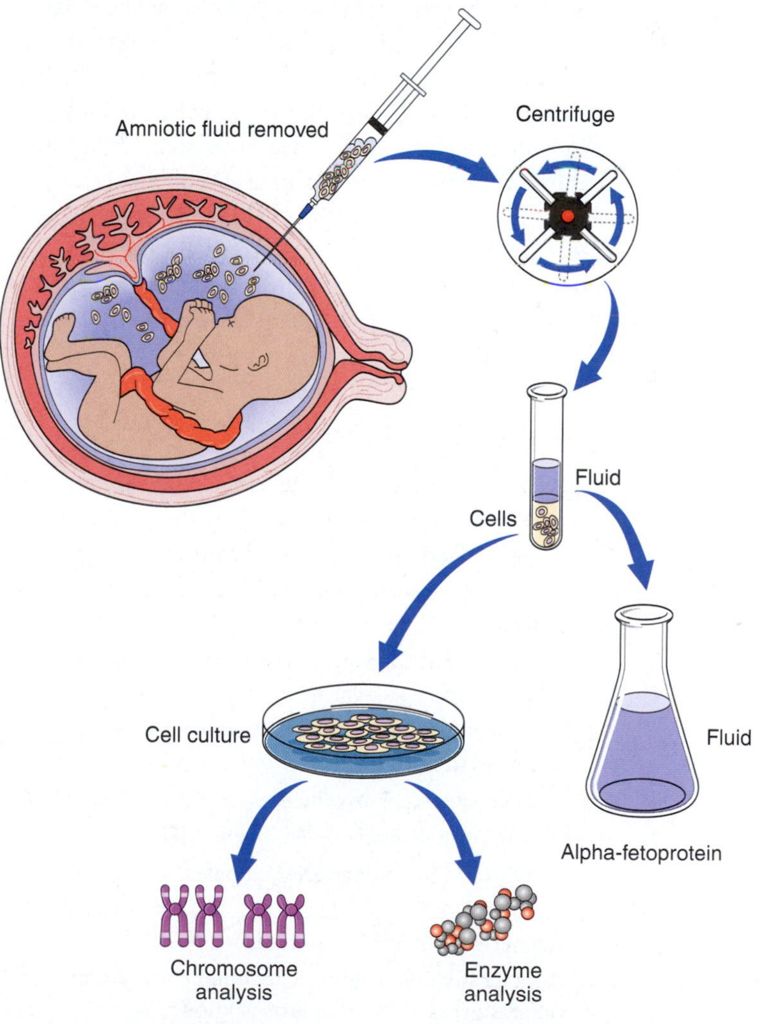

FIGURE 3.5 *Amniocentesis*

TABLE 3.4

Questions to Ask Your Obstetrician

1. **What are the dangers of the test?** Does it involve a trivial or nonexistent risk, like that involved in taking blood or urine, or could it cause physical harm to you or your baby? How much does the procedure cost, and does insurance cover it? Is it regularly performed in your area, or do you have to search for an experienced clinic? Would the test ever have to be performed twice?
2. **What information does the test provide?** How long does it take for the results to come back, and will another test center give a quicker reading? Is the information reliable? Are there frequent false positive (the test says something is abnormal when it is not) or false negative (the test is read as normal when there is actually a problem) results?
3. **Would the test results alter treatment?** Does the information gained enable doctors to save your child in utero or help them arrange for prompt treatment at birth?
4. **If you and your partner would choose to terminate a problem pregnancy, would knowing sooner be important?** If abortion is not a consideration, would diagnosing a defect early on still offer an emotional benefit, allowing you and your partner to prepare for the baby's arrival?

From Dr. Gerald Lasin, M.D., personal communication.

vertebrae that normally protect the spinal cord fail to form properly. The AFP test measures a protein manufactured in the liver of the fetus. When the level is abnormally low, it can mean the baby has Down syndrome; when AFP levels are too high, it may indicate that the baby carries a neural tube defect. A summary of diagnostic tests is provided in Table 3.3. Questions that may be beneficial to ask the doctor before couples gear up for the tests are highlighted in Table 3.4.

Concept Checks

1. Phenylketonuria, PKU, which may cause severe retardation, is due to
   a. each parent displaying the disorder.
   b. both parents carrying one allele of a recessive gene.
   c. one parent carrying a dominant gene for the disorder.
2. Sickle-cell anemia, an autosomal disorder, would most likely occur in individuals
   a. with two recessive alleles.
   b. with one recessive allele.
   c. who live in cold-weather climates.
3. ____________ ____________ describes an infertile female who is small in stature.
4. A generally safe diagnostic technique that often detects gross physical defects is known as ________________________.

The Synchrony of Genes and Environment

Before Beginning . . .

After reading this section, you will be able to

- identify the synchrony of genes and environment.
- discuss directness and indirectness of heredity.
- define terms such as *reaction range* and *canalized traits*.

For decades, a frequently pondered and debated question was "Is it nature or nurture?" Is our behavior a product of the genes we inherit or the environment to which we are exposed? Asking the right question is always an important achievement. In research, the questions we ask become the guiding force in directing what we seek to find. As noted in Chapter 1, for many years, the wrong question—nature or nurture—guided researchers in a quest to find out if genes or environment determined behavior. The inevitable answer was that the truth lies somewhere in between these two polarities. It is nature *and* nurture—genetic differences as well as environmental differences—that contribute to individual differences in behavior.

The Nature–Nurture Pendulum

Over the past century, the nature–nurture pendulum has swung back and forth several times. Each swing of the pendulum often was triggered by some new revelation. For example, William James's (1890/1907) highly influential book, *Principles of Psychology*, set the agenda for a nurturing view of psychology for the next century—James did not even mention genetics. There the pendulum remained until the early 1900s, when the rediscovery of Gregor Mendel's (1866) experiments in genetics and the influence of Sir Francis Galton led to its swing toward the nature side. It was Galton who actually coined the alliterative phase *nature–nurture*; he argued that nature prevails enormously over nurture. As new discoveries emerged, the pendulum continued to vacillate. Today, one point upon which all serious investigators agree is that both genes and environments play essential roles in human development.

Thus, the question is which psychological characteristics are most or least vulnerable to biological forces. Serious depression falls into the first category, whereas preference for camping in Yosemite belongs to the second. Having genetic traits for these behaviors, however, does not mean that we are programmed. Genes, for many behaviors, have a powerful influence but not a deterministic one. In this sense, genes influence the *propensity* or probability that certain behaviors may develop, which may be supported by a detrimental environment or buffered by a secure one.

Directness and Indirectness of Heredity

Perhaps a good way to view the nature–nurture controversy is in terms of a directness and indirectness scale (Anastasi, 1958). The more directly heredity influences traits, the narrower will be the range of their possible outcomes. For certain traits such as mental retardation, or hereditary blindness or deafness, the boundaries set by heredity appear to be very narrow, and environment does not exert a great influence. For example, in the case of hereditary blindness, irrespective of the environment, sight cannot be restored. By the same token, there is much more room for the environment to influence a child's characteristics that are not directly dependent on genetic factors.

The **reaction range** for a genetically influenced trait is the range of possibilities that the genetic code allows. Thus, the reaction range reflects the interaction of genetic potential and environmental factors. Thus, we can see that there is more leeway for the influence of environmental factors in determining the child's emotional control than there is for determining height.

Thus, the general consensus is that inheritance determines certain outside or upper limits that a person may attain, and a maximally stimulating environment can allow one to reach these genetically set heights. Heredity then determines what we can do, environment determines what we do do.

Canalized Traits

Antonio is 6′2″, weighs 200 pounds, has an IQ of 110, and is an easygoing kind of guy. All these traits—height, weight, intelligence, temperament—appear to reflect genetic inheritance to a substantial degree (Bouchard, 1990; Bouchard & Pedersen, 1999). The relative contribution of genes to a given trait is called **heritability**. Heritability tells us what proportion of individual differences in a population can be ascribed to genes. If we say, for example, that 50 percent of intelligence is heritable, we are in effect saying that half of this trait is linked to heredity. Heritability, then, is a way of explaining what makes people different, not what constitutes a given individual's intelligence. A trait that stems entirely from genes is defined as 100 percent heritable. Height is 90 percent heritable; that is, 90 percent of the variation in height is accounted for by genetic variation, and the other 10 percent is accounted for by diet and other environmental factors. Characteristics that are fairly resistant to environmental effects are said to be **canalized** (Waddington, 1968). These traits are "fated" or predetermined on a virtually fixed, developmental pathway.

Gottlieb (1991) suggests that canalization does not just take place only at the genetic level but at all levels of the developing system. Gottlieb's *experienced canalization theory* suggests that genes are part of the developmental system and are not immune to influences from other levels of the system. Gottlieb's developmental systems theory, in contrast to Waddington's view of canalization, reflects the integration of experiential and genetic factors. The most important feature of Gottlieb's view is the recognition that the genes are an integral part of the system and that their activity (genetic expression) is affected by events at other levels of the system, including the developing organism's environment. A good example of the bidirectional influences of genes and environment is PKU (discussed earlier in this chapter). PKU is caused by a genetic defect; however, if caught early enough, its devastating mental retardation affects can be alleviated by restricting the amount of phenylalanine in the child's diet.

Concept Checks

1. The statement that best describes the nature–nurture issue is that
   a. genes act in concert with one another in determining behavior.
   b. psychological characteristics are most vulnerable to genetic influences.
   c. genes influence the probability that certain behaviors may develop.
2. The more directly heredity influences behavior, the narrower will be the range of environmental influences. True or False?
3. An example of a canalized trait would be
   a. a desire to travel.
   b. PKU.
   c. temperament.

reaction range The degree to which variations in environments can affect the development of children within the boundaries of the genetic code.

heritability The relative contribution of genes to a given trait, which tells us what proportion of individual differences in a population can be ascribed to genes.

canalized traits Traits that are fated or predetermined on a virtually fixed, developmental pathway.

The Genetics of Human Traits

Before Beginning . . .

After reading this section, you will be able to

- give an overview of genetic methodology.
- discuss how environmental and hereditary forces influence intelligence.
- discuss how environmental and hereditary forces impact personality.
- identify important environmental variables that promote optimal development.

Current Research Tools

By far, the most common design in human behavior–genetic studies is the comparison of identical and same-sex fraternal twin pairs. It remains a basic approach today. Twin, as well as adoption studies serve as experiments of nature that can help researchers disentangle the complex genetic and environmental influences.

Twin and Adoption Studies

Identical twins (**monozygotic twins**) develop from one fertilized egg that produces two embryos that are an exact genetic duplicate of one another and are enclosed in a single fetal membrane. Because identical twins have the same genetic structure—they have a 100 percent gene complement—differences observed in identical twins reared apart are thought to be caused by the environment. The term *identical* is somewhat misleading because even genetically identical twins can be surprisingly different right from infancy. (See the First Person box.)

Commonly, genetically identical twins exhibit a wide range of similar traits, but much of this may be

© Ann Clark

© Ann Clark

Identical twins (monozygotic twins) are an exact duplicate genetically because they come from the same fertilized egg (zygote). Fraternal, or dizygotic, twins develop from separate zygotes and have no more genes in common than other siblings.

monozygotic twins Identical twins have the exact same genotype and have shared the same fetal environment.

influenced more by environment than genetics. For example, evidence from observational studies has shown that identical twins are more likely to be treated similarly (wear similar clothes, given comparable toys) by parents and peers than nonidentical twins. Further, identical twins are also more likely to imitate one another. As a result, heritability estimates may then become inflated.

Fraternal twins result when two ovum are released and each is fertilized by a different sperm, each enclosed in its own fetal membrane. Although they share the same intrauterine environment and are born at the same time, these **dizygotic twins** are usually no more alike than siblings born at different times. Fraternal twins, like siblings, have a 50 percent gene complement. Researchers often use comparisons of fraternal twins with identical twins on various traits and cognitive functioning to hypothesize about the latter group; if, for example, identical twins are more similar on a trait such as sociability, this would indicate that inherited factors play a role in the development of sociability.

The question that comparisons of twins seek to answer is how much of some trait—height, for example—can be ascribed to heredity or to environment. To answer this question we might measure the heights of a large number of twins. Calculating the difference in height between the members of each pair, we will probably find that the identical twins are, on average, closer in height than the fraternal twins. We then conclude, according to the methodology of behavioral genetics, that height is predominantly, though not exclusively, a genetic trait. This procedure of comparing monozygotic and dizygotic twins provides the database for the study of genetic differences in intelligence and personality traits.

Another way to separate the impact of genetics from environmental influences is to study children brought up by parents other than those who conceived them and to compare their psychological characteristics with those of both their biological and their adoptive parents. Similarity to the biological parents is assumed to indicate genetic influences; similarity to the adoptive parents indicates environmental influences. This research strategy is not altogether problem-free; first, biological parents cannot always be traced or may not wish to be tested. Also, selective placement often occurs whereby children are assigned to adoptive parents who resemble the biological parents.

FIRSTPERSON

Being an Identical Twin

I am an identical twin. But, from birth my sister and I began growing into two different people. You might say we were a pair of complementary differences. We are physically alike; it's just like seeing yourself in a mirror—only this isn't a reflection—it's my sister. We both have light brown hair, and green eyes; we are the same height; and we wear the same size clothes and same size shoes. But, there are ways in which we are very comfortably different. I tend to be a bit more impulsive than she and would like to spend my life traveling around the world; she's more patient and has no interest in travel. I know my sister as her own vibrant person, whom I also regard as separate and different from me. If our similar genetic codes were the only thing influencing us, my sister would be my clone—alike in every way—but she is not. Our random environmental influences modified her development and mine in small but distinctive ways.

—*Jackie McKnight*

Gene-Linkage Analysis

Gene-linkage studies focus on detailed family trees with many affected individuals in the hope of finding the major gene(s) responsible for a particular disorder. Chromosome analysis then allows researchers to search for genetic abnormalities that tend to occur together in families. Gene-linkage analysis procedures were used in the study of Huntington's disease (described on p. 92). It was discovered that a high number of cases of this disease have occurred in Venezuela. Through the study of a family tree that included over 10,000 individuals afflicted with the disease, the disease was traced back to a European man living in Venezuela seven generations ago.

Molecular Genetics

The most exciting way in which genetic research is moving beyond the nature–nurture question is in beginning to harness the power of *molecular genetics* to identify specific genes responsible for the substantial influence of genetics on behavior. **Molecular genetics** is the study of gene structure and function. The genetic quest is not to find *the* gene for a behavioral trait but the many genes that affect the trait in a probabilistic rather than a predetermined manner. Genes are the direct cause of many diseases such as cystic fibrosis and sickle-cell anemia, and they regulate our tendency toward cancer, heart attacks, or

dizygotic twins Fraternal twins are no more alike than siblings, but they do share the same fetal environment.

molecular genetics The study of the molecular basis of gene structure and function.

One human
body cell

contains 23 pairs of chromosomes

for a total of about 100,000 genes

that are segments of DNA

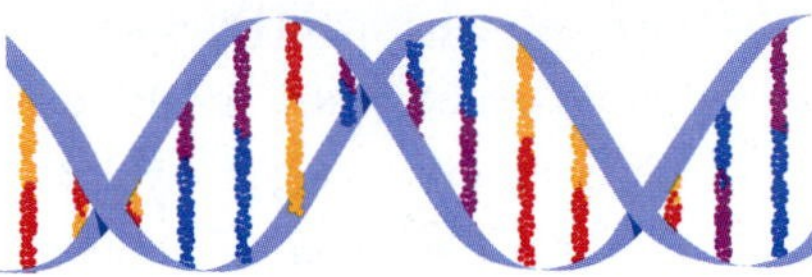

which, in the total human genome,
compose about 3.3 billion pairs of the
chemical bases
A-T, T-A, C-G, and G-C.

FIGURE 3.6 ***Genetic Material***

What's in a human cell? Mapping the human genome means determining the entire sequence of the more than 3 billion pairings of the chemical bases that make up DNA. Knowing the chemical sequence of a gene allows scientists to deduce its corresponding protein.

Alzheimer's disease. Humans are afflicted by more than 3000 known inherited diseases, but we have identified only the genes responsible for less than 3 percent of these (Cunningham-Burley & Boulton, 2000). So there is much to explain about the human genome.

The Human Genome Project is a worldwide research effort that ultimately will lead to an understanding of the structure and function of the genetic information in each human cell (see Figure 3.6). A **genome** is all the genetic information encoded in a complete strand of DNA as it lies coiled inside a cell. A completed genetic map for a chromosome would contain all of the genes on that chromosome in their correct linear order. The project is a massive undertaking considering that the human genome contains approximately 100,000 genes, though numbers as low as 50,000 and as high as 150,000 have been suggested by scientists working on the Human Genome Project (Cohen, 1997). Currently, they have mapped more than 38,000 human genes, with at least 99.9 percent accuracy (Travis, 2000). Nearing its expected completion date in 2003, it is now said to be 85 percent complete. Its central aim is to decipher the approximately 3.3 billion letter code that constitutes the DNA of our genes (Powledge, 2000; Tuohy, 2000).

genome
All the genetic information encoded in a complete strand of DNA as it lies coiled inside a cell.

Why is the Human Genome Project so important? First, the current perception is that genome sequences are the key to the continued development of not only molecular biology and genetics but also those areas of biochemistry, cell biology, and physiology now described as the molecular life sciences. A catalog containing a description of the sequence of every gene in a genome is immensely valuable in terms of opening the way to a comprehensive description of the molecular activities of living cells and the ways in which these activities are controlled. The implications of the rough draft of the Human Genome Project for medicine and pharmacy may revolutionize 21st century healthcare on fronts ranging from improved diagnostics to the prospect of molecular surgery. The genome project may also lead to the development of "customized drugs"; that is, the prescription of drugs to treat illness will transform from an art to an almost exact science in the context of knowing an individual's genetic profile prior to treatment.

Pertinent ethical and social questions, however, are almost as numerous as the genome's three billion chemical letters and nearly as difficult to resolve (Clarke, 2000). One concern is the possibility that once the sequence is known, individuals whose sequences are considered "substandard," for whatever reason, might be discriminated against. The dangers range from increased insurance premiums for individuals whose sequence includes mutations predisposing them to genetic diseases, to the possibility that racists might attempt to define good and bad sequence features, with depressingly predictable implications for the individuals unlucky enough to fall into the "bad" category (Efran & Greene, 2000). Many scientists, however, argue in support of the Human Genome Project, and insist that data resulting from their research will emphasize the unity of the human race by showing that patterns of genetic variability do not reflect the geographical and political groupings that humans have adopted during the last few centuries (Brown, 1999; Efran & Greene, 2000).

Personality

How did you develop your sense of humor or your serious demeanor? Why do you tend to be outgoing or shy? Why are your siblings so different from you? Research supplies some interesting answers to these questions. Pinpointing genetic factors in shaping our personalities, however, is difficult because personality characteristics are difficult to define and measure. Further, personality characteristics are rarely an all-or-nothing phenomena; individuals express degrees of certain traits such as friendliness, outgoingness, or shyness. Moreover, the dynamic interaction between the individual and the environment that shapes personality is highly complex.

Data from the Texas Adoption Project (Loehlin, 1997; Loehlin, Willerman, & Horn, 1981) show that a greater similarity in twins' experiences (environment) accounted for only a small fraction of the monozygotic twins' similarity in personality. The authors suggest that genetic factors not only contribute directly to children's personality, but also mediate the effects of the environment. Other studies suggest a greater role of genetics in influencing personality. For example, Anke Tellegen and his colleagues (Tellegen, Lykken, Bouchard, Wilcox, Segal, & Rich, 1988) in a study of monozygotic and dizygotic twins reared together and reared apart, conclude that personality differences are more influenced by genetic diversity than they are by environmental diversity. Personality differences, these results suggest, are due more to genetic than to environmental factors.

Extending the analysis of the impact of genetics on personality, Sandra Scarr (1992, 1998) argues that, within the range of "good-enough parenting," children's development depends primarily on heredity. Children, of course, require supportive and affectionate parenting; in the absence of opportunities to use their inherent capabilities, they cannot develop fully. The notion that ordinary differences between families have few effects on children's development is an unpalatable argument for many and has aroused some fierce opposition (Baumrind, 1993). For example, Diana Baumrind warns that when we assign primary responsibility for child outcomes to genetic factors (the effect of which parents believe they cannot change) we may undermine parents' beliefs in their own effectiveness. Conversely, when we attribute to parents primary responsibility for their children's outcomes, parents are more likely to try to be effective caregivers, which, in turn, is associated with more positive outcomes for children. The environmentalist perspective advocated by Baumrind is intended to empower parents and to reinforce their sense of responsibility to the children they choose to conceive, and in the case of foster or adoptive parents, to raise. (See the Child Development Issues box.)

The Big Five

There are some convergent findings from a number of studies that confirm the significant influence of genetics on children's social characteristics. Almost all knowledge regarding the relative impact of environmental and genetic influences on stable personality traits comes from studies of twins reared together. On the genetic side, regardless of the trait studied, genes appear to account for about 50 percent of any given personality trait (Plomin & Caspi, 1998). Of course, if that figure is correct, then that leaves 50 percent of personality due to environmental influences, measurement error, and nonsystematic changes in the trait over time. A personality trait can be just about anything—a desire to make a lot of money, sharp-wittedness, flexibility, honesty, tolerance. Fortunately, this never-ending list can be boiled down to five general supertraits—labeled the "Big Five" (John, Donahue, & Kentle, 1991; Slotboom, Havill, Pavlopoulous, & De Fruyt, 1998; Trull & Geary 1997).

- Extroversion—the tendency to be sociable, adventurous, and energetic
- Agreeableness—the tendency to be affectionate and kind
- Conscientiousness—the tendency to be reliable and organized
- Emotional stability—the tendency to be calm
- Openness to experience—the tendency to be insightful and inventive

There is also impressive evidence, ranging from studies of temperament in infants to investigations of personality dimensions in adults, that these five personality characteristics have a high genetic component (Eaves, Eysenck, & Martin, 1989; Eysenck, 1998; Rowe, 1997; 1998). Further, these five traits appear to be universal variants of human nature, for they are found in cultures throughout the world, each with different traditions, worldviews, and languages. For example, the Big Five pattern is found in samples of children from societies such as China (Trull & Geary, 1997); Belgium, Netherlands, Germany, Greece, Poland (Slotboom, Havill, Pavlopoulos, & De Gruyt, 1998) and the United States (Cohen, 1999; Trull & Geary, 1997). The meaning of each trait as well as the desirability of that trait, however, appears to be different in each culture.

One dimension of the Big Five personality traits that has been studied extensively is extroversion (see

Child Development Issues

Other Than Depositing Their Genes, Do Parents Matter?

Sandra Scarr (1992) asserts that being reared in one family, rather than another, within the range of "normal," makes few differences in children's personality and intellectual development. She argues that most families provide sufficiently supportive environments that enable children's individual genetic differences to develop. She points out that children create their own environments based on their genetic makeup. For example, if a child has the genetic propensity for shyness, as young children they will avoid playing boisterous games with others and choose more solitary, quiet play. She concludes that "good enough," ordinary parents probably have the same effects on their children's development as culturally defined superparents.

Scarr reports that causal assumptions about the direction of effects between parental behavior and children's outcomes have been called into question even more strongly by research in developmental behavioral genetics which has shown, for example, that the heritability for a wide variety of traits, including intelligence, specific cognitive abilities, and personality, is between .40 and .70.

Diana Baumrind (1993) has responded to Scarr's "good enough" parent by arguing that parents do matter and being a good-enough parent is not good enough. She points out that children will respond differently to similar genetic factors and genetically different children will respond differently to the same environment. For example, by engaging Down syndrome children in a carefully graduated series of learning activities in a supportive relationship, a parent or teacher can enable many of these children to master more cognitive regulatory functions themselves than they could previously, so that their performance approaches normal (Feuerstein, Rand, & Rynders, 1998).

In addition, when parents of preschool children are highly involved with their children's academic work and engage in "high level distancing behaviors" (anticipating, proposing alternatives, and evaluating outcomes) that challenge their children's representational abilities, these children outperform children *with equivalent IQs* on anticipatory and memory tasks. The remarkable achievement of American children with Korean, Japanese, Chinese, and Taiwanese heritages is attributable, in part, to their parents' "tremendous efforts," fueled by their Confucian-based belief that differences in children's experiences, actively shape children's character and intellect (Huntsinger, Jose, Liaw, & Ching, 1997).

Baumrind (1991) defines seven parent types on the basis of their patterns of scores that assess facets of demandingness and responsiveness. Three of these patterns of child rearing are of relevance to this discussion: authoritative (high-demanding, high-responsive); good-enough (medium demanding, medium-responsive), and unengaged (low-demanding, low-responsive).

Authoritative parents put forth exceptional effort, encouraging and modeling responsibly interpersonal behavior, and their adolescents are exceptionally competent (mature, prosocial, high internal locus of control, low internalizing and externalizing problem behavior, low substance use). Unengaged parents put forth minimal effort, virtually abdicating their parental role, and their adolescents are relatively problematic and lacking in competence. Good-enough parents put forth mediocre effort with mixed results. Generally, sons from good-enough homes are themselves "good enough," achieving average scores on most competence and problem behavior scales. Daughters, however, manifest internalizing problem behavior and low self-esteem or abuse illicit substances, suggesting that these girls needed more from their "good enough" parents.

Baumrind concludes that the high level of investment in parenting that characterizes authoritative parents is especially important when both parents work. Invested parents are more willing to provide explanations, more sensitive to their children's needs, and firmer. Current research findings support the claim that the current social milieu requires something more than "good-enough" parenting. Minimally sufficient adult investment in children is seldom good enough to ensure optimum outcomes.

Search Online

Explore InfoTrac College Edition, your online library. Go to **http://www.infotrac-college.com/wadsworth** and use the passcode that came on the card with your book. Try these search terms: parenting and genes, genes and intelligence, do parents matter.

TABLE 3.5

The "Big Five" Personality Traits

Extroversion	Agreeableness	Conscientiousness	Emotional Stability	Openness to Experience
Affectionate vs. reserved	Softhearted vs. ruthless	Conscientious vs. negligent	Worrying vs. calm	Imaginative vs. down to earth
Joiner vs. loner	Trusting vs. suspicious	Hardworking vs. lazy	Temperamental vs. even-tempered	Creative vs. uncreative
Talkative vs. quiet	Generous vs. stingy	Well-organized vs. disorganized	Self-pitying vs. self-satisfied	Original vs. conventional
Active vs. passive	Acquiescent vs. antagonistic	Punctual vs. late	Self-conscious vs. comfortable	Prefer variety vs. prefer routine
Fun-loving vs. sober	Lenient vs. critical	Ambitious vs. aimless	Emotional vs. unemotional	Curious vs. uncurious
Passionate vs. unfeeling	Good-natured vs. irritable	Persevering vs. quitting	Vulnerable vs. hardy	Liberal vs. conservative

From *Personality in Adulthood* (p. 3), by R. R. McCrae & P. T. Costa, 1996, New York: Guilford Press. Reprinted by permission.

Table 3.5). The core of extroversion is sociability, or gregariousness, which is the extent to which individuals prefer to do things with others rather than alone. Longitudinal studies of children from birth to adolescence and studies of twins and adopted children suggest that the inclination to be friendly, outgoing, and sociable (extroverted) is influenced by heredity (Goldsmith & Campos, 1990; Henderson, 1982; Wilson & Matheny, 1986). In a related cluster of studies conducted on extroversion with monozygotic and dizygotic twins, in Great Britain, the United States, Sweden, Australia, and Finland, there was a significantly larger link between the extroversion levels of identical twins than those of fraternal twins. Again, these results indicate high genetic influences on this trait.

Emotional stability is another global trait that has received recent research attention. The key component of emotional stability (the tendency not to become aroused easily to fear and anger) is measured by personality questionnaires in which subjects note how much they agree or disagree with statements like "I am not a worrier" or "Frightening thoughts sometimes come into my head." Researchers suggest that emotional stability is roughly 50 percent heritable, meaning that 50 percent of individual differences in the trait (from strong to weak) likely come from genetic differences. As a case in point, monozygotic twins show more similarity on this trait than do dizygotic twins, which underscores its genetic component. From infancy to adulthood, both emotional stability and extroversion have been proposed as the most heritable components of personality (Plomin, 1998).

Activity level is another behavioral trait that also shows a high degree of heritability. Activity level is the preference for different kinds and amounts of stimulation. Some individuals seem to crave excitement and activity; others prefer a more tranquil existence. It appears that monozygotic twins are more similar than dizygotic twins in seeking (or not seeking) stimulation (Bouchard, 1997; Hur & Bouchard, 1997). There is also evidence that altruism may be influenced by heredity as well (Rushton, Fulker, Neale, Nias, & Eysenck, 1986). Nancy Segal (1990; 1997) compared monozygotic and dizygotic twins as interactive participants in a variety of social contexts.

© Bob Daemmrich/The Image Works

Why are some children more extroverted than others? Studies indicate that the tendency to be friendly, outgoing, and sociable is influenced by heredity.

Self-Insight

The Big Five Inventory

Here are a number of characteristics that may or may not apply to you. For example, do you agree that you are someone who likes to spend time with others? Please write a number next to each statement to indicate the extent to which you agree or disagree with that statement.

Disagree strongly	Disagree a little	Neither agree nor disagree	Agree a little	Agree strongly
1	2	3	4	5

I see myself as someone who

____ 1. is talkative.
____ 2. tends to find fault with others.
____ 3. does a thorough job.
____ 4. has a wide range of interests.
____ 5. is depressed, blue.
____ 6. is original, comes up with new ideas.
____ 7. is reserved.
____ 8. is helpful and unselfish with others.
____ 9. prefers the conventional, traditional.
____ 10. can be somewhat careless.
____ 11. is relaxed, handles stress well.
____ 12. is curious about many different things.
____ 13. is full of energy.
____ 14. prefers work that is routine and simple.
____ 15. starts quarrels with others.
____ 16. is a reliable worker.
____ 17. can be tense.
____ 18. is clever, sharp-witted.
____ 19. tends to be quiet.
____ 20. values artistic, aesthetic experiences.
____ 21. tends to be disorganized.
____ 22. is emotionally stable, not easily upset.
____ 23. has an active imagination.
____ 24. perseveres until the task is finished.
____ 25. is sometimes rude to others.
____ 26. has unwavering self-confidence.
____ 27. is inventive.
____ 28. is generally trusting.
____ 29. tends to be lazy.
____ 30. is clear-thinking, intelligent.
____ 31. worries a lot.
____ 32. wants things to be simple and clear-cut.
____ 33. is sometimes shy, inhibited.
____ 34. has a forgiving nature.
____ 35. is idealistic, can be a dreamer.
____ 36. does things efficiently.
____ 37. can be moody.
____ 38. is ingenious, a deep thinker.
____ 39. generates a lot of enthusiasm.
____ 40. can be cold and aloof.
____ 41. enjoys thinking about complicated problems.
____ 42. makes plans and follows through with them.
____ 43. remains calm in tense situations.
____ 44. likes to reflect, play with ideas.
____ 45. is considerate and kind to almost everyone.
____ 46. seeks adventure and excitement.
____ 47. gets nervous easily.
____ 48. is sophisticated in art, music, or literature.
____ 49. has an assertive personality.
____ 50. is insightful, sees different possibilities.
____ 51. likes to cooperate with others.
____ 52. is easily distracted.
____ 53. is outgoing, sociable.
____ 54. has few artistic interests.

Monozygotic twins provided striking evidence of greater cooperation with each other. They expended significantly greater efforts for their partners on the different tasks than dizygotic twins, strongly suggesting that a more altruistic spirit was operative between pairs. It also appears that monozygotic twins show considerable similarity on the Big Five personality dimensions.

SCORING FOR THE SELF-INSIGHT BIG FIVE INVENTORY

Extroversion: Reverse the numbers placed in front of items 7, 19, and 33 (1 = 5, 2 = 4, 3 = 3, 4 = 2, 5 = 1). Then add all the numbers for items 1, 7, 13, 19, 33, 39, 46, 49, and 53. Total scores can range from 9 to 45, with higher scores reflecting greater extroversion.

Agreeableness: Reverse the numbers placed in front of items 2, 15, 25, and 40 (1 = 5, 2 = 4, 3 = 3, 4 = 2, 5 = 1). Then add all the numbers for items 2, 8, 15, 28, 34, 40, 45, and 51. Total scores can range from 9 to 45, with higher scores reflecting greater agreeableness.

Conscientiousness: Reverse the numbers placed in front of items 10, 21, 29, and 52 (1 = 5, 2 = 4, 3 = 3, 4 = 2, 5 = 1). Then add all the numbers for items 3, 10, 16, 21, 24, 29, 36, 42, and 52. Total scores can range from 9 to 45, with higher scores reflecting greater conscientiousness.

Emotional Stability: Reverse the numbers placed in front of items 5, 17, 31, 37, and 47 (1 = 5, 2 = 4, 3 = 3, 4 = 2, 5 = 1). Then add all the numbers in front of items 5, 11, 17, 22, 26, 31, 37, 43, and 47. Scores can range from 9 to 45, with higher scores reflecting greater emotional stability.

Openness to Experience: Reverse the numbers placed in front of items 9, 14, 32, and 54 (1 = 5, 2 = 4, 3 = 3, 4 = 2, 5 = 1). Then add all the numbers in front of items 4, 6, 9, 12, 14, 18, 20, 23, 27, 30, 32, 35, 38, 41, 44, 48, 50, and 54. Total scores can range from 18 to 90, with higher scores reflecting greater openness to experience.

Source: John O. P., Donahue, E. M., & Kentle, R. L. (1991). The "Big Five" Inventory—Versions 4a and 54 (Tech. Report). Berkeley, CA: Institution of Personality Assessment and Research.

How do these Big Five dimensions of personality apply to you? Are you more outgoing or quiet? more irritable or good-natured? more late or punctual? See how you fare on the Self-Insight Big Five Inventory.

Personality and Shared and Nonshared Family Environments

If you have a sibling, take a few minutes to compare yourself with him or her on the following traits:

Characteristic	*The Same*	*Different*
Academic goals		
Clothes		
Future occupation		
Favorite car		
Special talents		
Music		
Favorite courses in school		
Favorite books		

Shared and Nonshared Family Environment

Shared family environments are those experiences that are common to all children growing up in the same family. For example, they include such family characteristics as social class, educational level, number of books in the home, and childrearing philosophy, all of which act to make members of the family *similar* to each other. **Nonshared family environments**, on the other hand, are those that are not common to all family members. These environmental influences tend to make each of us living in the same family different from one another. As such, they represent those experiences that are unique to each sibling: the parents' preference for one child over another; their differential treatment of each child because of the child's own inherent characteristics; the position each child occupies within the sibling constellation; the child's exposure to particular familial influences outside the home such as peers and teachers; and idiosyncratic experiences like accidents or illnesses (Dunn & Plomin, 1998).

shared family environment Factors such as parental attitudes, education, socioeconomic factors, experiences, and the effects of those experiences that family members have in common.

nonshared family environment Experiences and the effect of experiences that are unique to each family member.

variance The percentage of individual differences on certain traits that can be accounted for or explained by another factor or factors is something behavioral geneticists try to explain.

Chances are you are more different from your sibling than you are similar. In fact, siblings often appear no more alike than individuals selected at random from the population (Turkheimer & Waldron, 2000). Why is that so? Contrary to what most of us would think, less than 1 percent of individual differences in personality is explained by shared family environment (Cohen, 1999). Environmental **variance**, the percentage of individual differences on certain traits that can be explained by other factors, works in a way very different from how

Separated at birth, the Mallifert twins meet accidentally.

the environment was thought to work. The environment primarily operates to make children growing up in the same family *different from*, rather than similar to, one another (Dunn & Plomin, 1998; Wright, 1999). Growing up together in the same family does not make siblings similar in personality. Even an event that affects every individual in the family will not be experienced in the same manner by each individual. The event or experience may be the same, but nonshared environment refers to what you get out of the experience—not what you are given.

Let's take a family experience common to many in the United States, such as celebrating Thanksgiving. Will everyone in the family experience this event the same? You may say, "I love celebrating Thanksgiving. The smell of the turkey roasting in the oven, seeing my relatives; it's just a very happy occasion." Your sibling, however, may have very different views of this event. "Thanksgiving is boring; there is too much food, and Dad wants to control everything."

Sometimes parents wonder why their children are often wildly different. Of course, part of the differences are due to their differing genetic lotteries, but not so obvious, part are due to their nonshared family environments. Each child experiences different aspects of the family environment, and that in turn influences his or her personality (Loehlin, 1992; Plomin, 1998). Basically, there is no such thing as parents' treating their children "the same," and there is no such thing as being raised in exactly the "same" family environment. What makes all the difference is not only how one is treated but how one digests the experience, and how one digests is strongly influenced by his or her genetic endowment (Cohen, 1999).

IQ
Intelligence quotient measured by the ratio of children's chronological age and their mental age.

intelligence
Capacities, including social intelligence, mechanical ability, abstract reasoning, musical ability, and others.

Intelligence

How heritable are children's intellectual abilities (those measured by IQ tests)? First, we need to distinguish between IQ and intelligence. **IQ** (intelligent quotient) is a ratio of children's chronological age (CA) and their "mental age" (MA) as determined by their responses to the IQ test, which usually measures the child's knowledge of vocabulary, understanding of basic math, problem solving abilities, and other learned factors (Sternberg, 2000). The more items a child passes beyond his or her chronological age, the higher the IQ score. Of course, **intelligence** is not merely confined to the abstract reasoning abilities measured in IQ tests but, rather, includes a number of different capacities, such as social intelligence, mechanical ability (understanding machines), and musical ability, to name a few (see multiple intelligences, Chapter 12).

We could assume that if genetic factors do play a role in intelligence, then we would find that monozygotic twins' IQs would be more highly correlated than dizygotic twins' IQs. This is supported by a number of research studies (Cherny, Fulker, & Hewitt, 1997; Plomin, DeFries, McClearn, & Rutter, 1997). In fact, researchers have demonstrated a link between the percentage of genes in common and resemblance in IQ. According to these findings, we would predict that identical twins would be closer in IQ than nontwin brothers and sisters.

IQ and Twins

Studies do confirm this; identical twins reared together tend to have similar IQs (Plomin, 1998; Reiss, 1995; Saudino, 1997). Further, Thomas Bouchard (1990; 1997) reports that the correlations between IQ scores of identical twins reared apart are quite substantial and appreciably greater than those for fraternal twins reared in the same home. Such findings are typically interpreted as testifying to the primacy of genetic influences in the determination of the qualities of intelligence measured by IQ tests. Analyses of twin data indicate that approximately 50 to 60 percent of the variance in IQ is associated with genetic differences among individuals. The error surrounding this estimate may be as high as 20 percent, so we can only say with confidence that the heritability of IQ scores is between 30 and 70 percent (Plomin, DeFries, McClearn, & Rutter, 1997). Underlying this interpretation is the assumption that twins reared apart are experiencing widely different environments, so that substantial similarity between them must be attributable primarily to their common genetic endowment.

What is interesting is that it is not only the absolute *level* of intelligence as measured by IQ tests but also the *pattern* of intellectual growth that appears to be linked to children's genetic lottery. In the Louisville twin study (Wilson, 1983), which followed nearly 500 pairs of twins and their siblings from infancy to adolescence, it was found that the profiles of developmental spurts and lags in IQ over time showed considerably greater resemblance in monozygotic pairs than in dizygotic pairs. This was particularly marked in early childhood, when the rate of gains is sharpest and the spurts and lags more pronounced. According to Wilson, the message from these results seems clear: there is a strong developmental thrust in the growth of IQ that continues through adolescence and is guided by some kind of genetic ground plan.

Tony Freeman/PhotoEdit

IQ tests have been criticized as culturally biased in favor of urban, middle-class, and European American children.

IQ and Adopted Children

Adoption provides yet another opportunity to evaluate the impact of heredity and environment. Marie Skodak and Harold Skeels's (1949) classic longitudinal adoption study of IQ found that the correlation between the IQ of biological mothers and their adopted-away children indicate increasing hereditary influence as the child develops. In early childhood, the adopted children's IQs were closer to that of their adoptive parents; however, by early adolescence the child's IQ tended to be more in sync with their biological parents. Other more recent studies confirm this finding (Cherney, Fulker, & Hewitt, 1997; Feldman & Otto, 1997). Thus, adopted children resemble their adoptive parents slightly in early childhood but much less by middle childhood or adolescence.

The results of another ongoing longitudinal study of cognitive development, known as the Texas Adoption Study (Horn, Loehlin, & Willerman, 1979; Loehlin, 1997; Loehlin, Horn, & Willerman, 1997), also showed that the average IQ score of the children is more similar to that of their adoptive parents. But, interestingly, it also showed that moving a young child from an unstimulating home environment to a more stimulating one could raise IQ scores by as much as 15 to 20 points, demonstrating the importance of environmental effects.

IQ and Verbal and Spatial Abilities

Thomas Bouchard, Jr., at the University of Minnesota, and Nancy Pedersen, at the Karolinska Institute in Stockholm (Bouchard & Pedersen, 1999), have concluded from their research that heritabilities for verbal and spatial abilities is about 50 percent. The Colorado Adoption Study (Plomin, DeFries, McClearn, & Rutter, 1997) is providing a growing body of evidence that verbal and spatial abilities are substantially influenced by genetics, which accounts for 40 percent and 50 percent of the variance, respectively.

IQ and Ethnicity

The pragmatic importance of understanding how genes and environment influence development is demonstrated in claims of group differences among IQ test scores of various ethnic groups. On average African American children score 15 points below European American children on standardized IQ tests (Anastasi, 1989; Neisser, Boodoo, Bouchard et al., 1996). These, however, are group *differences*. Group differences refers to patterns of IQ scores among these populations and does not mean that every European American child performs higher than every African American child. Within-group differences are substantial; trying to explain these differences led to the "heredity/environment controversy."

Arthur Jensen (1969; 1985), Hans Eysenck (1998; Eysenck & Eysenck, 1969), and Philip Vernon (1997) are three psychologists that have championed and promoted the view that individual differences in human IQ can only be fully understood through investigations of their genetic and biological bases. Jensen wrote an article entitled "How much can we boost IQ and scholastic achievement?" The answer, according to Jensen, was not much. He suggests that the differences on IQ tests are primarily due to genetic factors. Unfortunately, such comments foster ethnic-group stereotypes and ignore the impact of the environment.

Critics of the "hereditary" position, argue that although genetics play a role in determining intelligence, the environment also makes a substantial contribution to the IQ gap between African American and dominant-group children (Fischer, Hout, Jankowski, Lucas, Swidler, & Voss, 1996; Nisbett, 1998; Stevenson, 1998). These researchers contend that IQ differences can be attributed to various environmental inequalities that disadvantaged African American children encounter, such as in prenatal and postnatal health care, income, education, and general living conditions.

Moreover, we have to look at the measuring instruments themselves. Although IQ tests attempt to measure general reasoning qualities and knowledge, they also contain biases. They tend to be culturally biased in favor of urban, middle-class, and European American children (Sternberg, 2000). For example, one question might ask "What is a garden hose?" which implies having backyards and gardens. "What is a concerto?" assumes that the child has been exposed to these types of experiences. In addition, the norms for many IQ tests are generally based on white middle-class children. In light of these cultural biases, one must question how meaningful IQ differences between ethnic groups actually are. Is there an IQ test that adequately and fairly measures individuals from different ethnic groups or cultures? Or, are we instead measuring a kind of dominant-culture literacy?

Before we can measure IQ, we must be able to define it. Is there some universal definition of intelligence that is applicable across cultures? What sorts of behaviors are considered as intelligent or cognitively competent in a given cultural setting? Each society considers certain behavior as highly valuable for its members, and its socialization processes tend to inculcate those valued behavioral repertoires. There appears to be a great deal of evidence suggesting that the meaning of intelligence varies across cultures. (This is highlighted in Cultural Variations.)

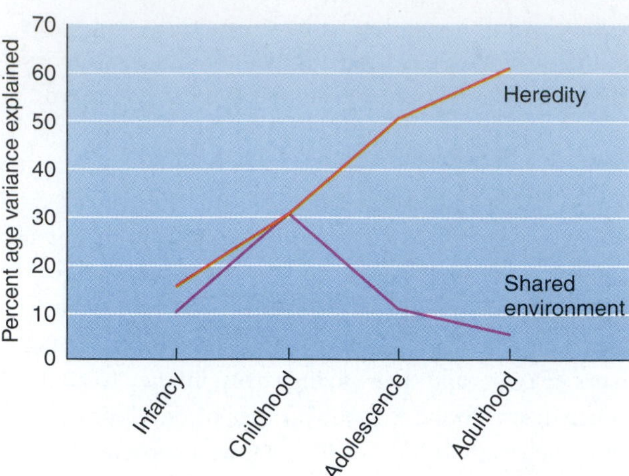

FIGURE 3.7 ***Life-Span Profile of Genetic and Shared Environmental Influences on IQ***

Heritability increases substantially during childhood and may increase further during adolescence. Genetic effects account for about 15 percent of the variance in infant mental test scores and, by the early school years, increase in importance to about 40 percent of the variance.

From *Nature and Nurture: An Introduction to Behavioral Genetics,* by R. Plomin, 1990, Belmont, CA: Wadsworth.

Changing Role of Genetics and Environment

Probably one of the most intriguing results from several studies concerns the changing role of genes and environment on IQ (Loehlin, 1997; Plomin & Petrill, 1997). The environment has its greatest impact on IQ during the early years of life. As children get older, we see a diminishing effect of environment and an increasing effect of genetics. Increasing heritability means that individual differences in IQ are increasingly due to genetic differences (see in Figure 3.7). This means that if we want to have some kind of positive environmental impact on the infant's intelligence, we need to provide this optimal environment as soon as possible. Here we will discuss general factors in creating optimal environments; Chapter 5 will examine more focused activities that will enhance the infant's cognitive development.

Cultural Variations

Assessing Intelligence

Are there some universal aspects of children's intelligence? Do smart children around the world share some common characteristics? The problems of assessing intelligence worldwide are many. One first must be able to define intelligence before one can measure it, and there is no consensus among scientists concerning an appropriate definition of "intelligence." Earlier researchers defined intelligence as good sense or initiative, to be able to judge and comprehend well (Binet & Simon, 1905). Others saw it as consisting of basic skills and general strategies for solving problems—the *g* factor (Spearman, 1927). More recent researchers have included verbal and logical thinking skills as the cornerstones of intelligence (Gardner, 1983; Sternberg, 2000).

According to Lev Vygotsky's theory, intelligence is largely "context" specific. To Vygotsky (1978), an individual's intelligence cannot be understood without taking social and cultural processes into consideration. Individuals in different cultures, he asserted, are likely to define intelligence in different ways. In Kenya, for example, *ng'om* is the closest approximation to the English word *intelligent* (Harkness & Super, 1995). This word means "obedient and responsible." Smart children are those who conform and are capable of providing help to the family at an early age. The Guatemalan term *listura* is the equivalent of intelligence and is used to describe children who engage in high physical activity and independence. Ugandan villages associate intelligence with being slow and careful when solving problems, whereas in the United States intelligence tends to be associated with speed in processing information (Rogoff & Chavajay, 1995).

Another problem in assessing intelligence across different cultures is the cultural validity of assessment measures. To Western cultures, a strong component of intelligence may relate to abstract or logical thinking. In other cultures, however, it may be linked to engaging in self-help skills at an early age or being able to track animals. Therefore, measurements of "intelligence" must be appropriate to that particular cultural setting. This would require that tests measure traits (intellectual competencies) that have meaning in the context of a local culture. Even where Western assessment instruments have been adapted to employ materials and concepts that appear to be native to a culture, it is not always clear whether "successful" test performance actually equates to local definitions of intelligence. The test-givers may, instead, just be measuring Western standards of ability.

A "culture fair" assessment is one in which each child taking the test (regardless of their cultural or ethnic background) has an equal chance of performing successfully. By definition then, a test without cultural bias would actually measure some inherent quality of human capacity equally well in all cultures. However, there can be no such test (Cole, 1999), because even IQ tests designed by psychologists to be culture-neutral actually may ignore many subtle cultural variations that lead to differences in groups' scores. Because of these limitations, cross-cultural comparison of children's abilities is a difficult task. As such, there are many important factors to consider before we can effectively measure and compare the abilities of individuals from other cultures as well as when assessing IQ among different ethnic groups within the United States.

Creating Optimal Environments

Suppose that 100 percent of the variation in scores on IQ tests is genetic in a particular population. We could then conclude that

1. efforts to teach children to be more intelligent are a total waste of time.
2. the environment can have no effect on intelligence.
3. to know one's parents would be to know one's IQ.
4. all of the above.
5. none of the above.

The correct answer is (5). Given this fact, Robert Sternberg (1997) asks, why do people care so much about what proportion of IQ is heritable? Well, there

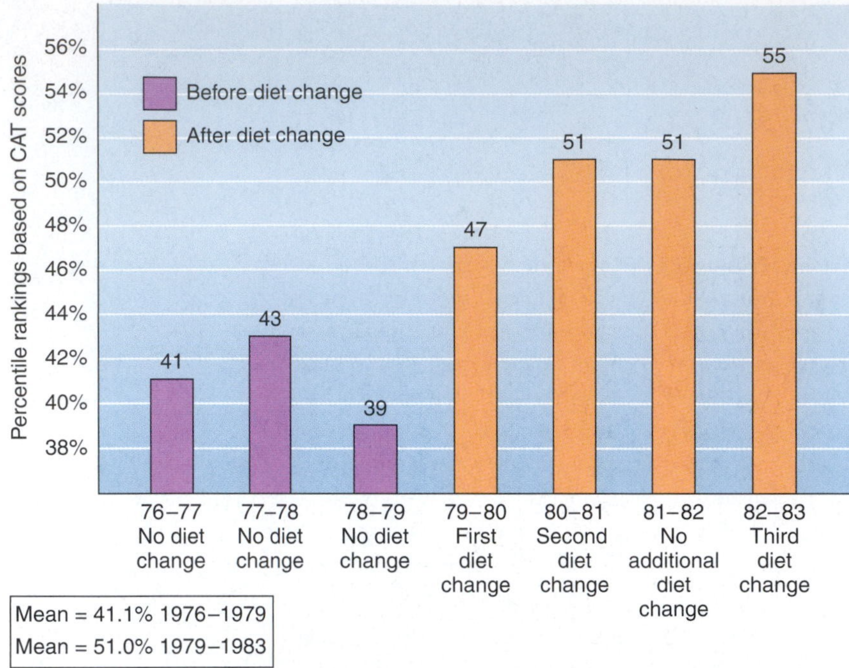

FIGURE 3.8 ***Percentile Ranking of Schools in New York State Before and After Introduction of Diet Change***

From *A New Look at Intelligence* (p. 105), by H. Eysenck, 1998, New Brunswick, NJ: Transaction Publishers. Reprinted by permission of the publisher.

are a number of reasons, but the main one may be to educate individuals on how to optimize *intelligence*. Intelligence is not predetermined.

Children's Diet

Hans Eysenck (1998) has suggested that the answer to improving children's intelligence, lies not in psychological or educational areas but in biological ones. He believes that through vitamin and mineral supplementation of a child's diet and relieving micronutrients deficiencies considerable increases in intelligence can be produced. Proper diet could improve children's ability to take in information, reason abstractly, and solve problems, which would then translate into higher scholastic performances. The effect, Eysenck notes, is likely to be greatest in the very young, less in the secondary school, and least in the late teens.

The results of a large-scale study in the New York schools gives evidence of the important effects of dietary improvement. The schools revised the type of food supplied to the children, eliminating preservatives, synthetic colors, and synthetic flavors. They also diminished progressively high use of sucrose foods and supplemented children's diet with micronutrients. The scholastic results of the schools involved are graphically illustrated in Figure 3.8. As one can see, there was considerable improvement in the scholastic achievement of hundreds of thousands of children due to slight improvements in their diets.

Robert Bradley (1995) suggests that there are several other aspects of the caregiving environment that promote optimal development of intelligence, including sustaining and stimulating, warm and supportive relationships, and providing direction and guidance.

Sustaining and Stimulating

The first component of an optimal family system is for parents to sustain or ensure the viability of the child through proper food, shelter, and conditions that maintain the health of children and protect them from harm. Second, adults need to provide stimulating environments; books, trips to culturally enriching places, and communicating with children are necessary to foster the child's potential. Providing support—when parents respond to their child's human social and emotional needs—is another vital environmental condition.

Warm and Supportive Relationships

Substantial evidence exists that children's development is more nearly optimal in an environment where their requests for assistance are dealt with in a timely, predictable, and satisfying way. Warm, supportive relationships help to promote good adjustment, a sense of well-being, good health, and a wealth of other positive developmental outcomes.

Providing Direction and Guidance

An optimal environment also provides control. Parents play an important role in providing direction and guidance to their children. Parental management practices that provide predictability and order are important.

All children deserve supportive environments that nurture their development and enable them to be the best and happiest people they can become. Beyond loving support, children need opportunities to develop their own individual abilities, talents, and personalities. Parents' most important job is to provide support and opportunities, not to try to shape children's enduring characteristics.

Stanley Greenspan (1998) maintains that creating optimal environments for promoting children's intelligence is about adult's establishing strong, positive, emotional relationships with children to help them grow up with an openness to learning and the ability to process, understand and experience emotion with compassion and resilience. These are the building blocks of intelligence and successful learning. It is the emotional quality of the relationship between infant and adult that will stimulate the infant's brain for optimum emotional and intellectual growth. Creating optimal environments is not about pushing babies to learn words, numbers, colors, and shapes; it is not about supplying the baby with ready-made "computer" type toys; it is not about teaching the baby "tricks" that will impress others. It is about the emotional quality of the relationship between parent and infant—a relationship that maximizes the baby's delight and minimizes her frustrations. It is about rocking, touching, soothing, talking, and singing; it is about being in sync with the baby's emotional needs. Greenspan notes that positive emotional interactions stimulate the baby's brain to make the neuronal connections he needs to process the sensory information the environment provides. It is emotional nurturing that maximizes the infant's potential.

Concluding Comments

The study of human behavioral genetics is still at a very early stage. Nevertheless, a number of conclusions have risen from the findings on IQ and personality presented here:

1. *Virtually all psychological traits show some evidence of genetic influence.* Recent findings show that individual variability in virtually all behavioral aspects examined is to some extent under genetic influence, including behaviors that are believed to be highly influenced by environment, such as television-viewing time or caregiving practices.
2. *Genetic influences increase with age.* It is also becoming apparent from both twin and adoption studies that genetic influences, particularly intellectual development, increase with age. Robert Plomin concludes from a review of relevant studies that whenever the relative magnitude of genetic variance changes during development, its impact increases rather than decreases. Physical and intellectual characteristics show this increasing genetic influence to a more marked degree than social or personality characteristics.
3. *Nonshared environmental influences are of greater importance than shared environmental influences.* Research has consistently substantiated that most of the environmental influences critical to psychological development are of the nonshared kind, not the shared influences, which have received most attention from psychologists.
4. *Children's genetic makeup directly affects their rearing environment.* Traditional psychological theory that parental socializing techniques cause the nature of individual development may be challenged by the results of several studies. The cause–effect sequence may run both ways. For example, it is proposed that each child constructs a reality from the opportunities afforded by caregivers *in keeping with their own talents.* The child then elicits responses from others according to its genotype. For instance, active, social babies tend to receive more attention than more quiet or introverted babies. A colleague of mine took her one-year-old grandchild Pascale out to dinner with the family. As Pascale, seated in her highchair, smiled and waved to all those passing their table, those passing by, of course, stopped, smiled, and said hello to this very sociable little girl.
5. *Genetic factors influence environmental measures.* When some aspect of the child's environment is measured and then related to some aspect of the child's behavior, it appears that the environment is influenced by the individuals' (both parent and child) genetic structure. To illustrate, the parents' disciplinary practices are a function of the parental personality and are therefore similarly linked to the child's behavior via genetic factors. A quiet, sensitive parent may find it abhorrent to resort to physically punishing the child, for example. Similarly, aspects of a caregiving environment are related to the caregiver's genetic makeup; for example, the number of books in the home may reflect the parents' intelligence. Thus, we cannot assume that the types of environments we create and in which we are raised are totally free of genetic influences.

Current findings from the field of behavioral genetics do not imply that the quality of the home environment is inconsequential. The contribution of the parents, whether natural or adoptive, is in helping children reach the fullest extent of their cognitive abilities and personality strengths. As Wilson notes,

> The wide diversity within families emphasizes the importance of giving each child full opportunity for development and indeed of making sure that the opportunity is taken. The ultimate goal is the maximum realization of each child's personality strengths and intelligence coupled with a sense of

satisfaction and personal accomplishment. There is no better way to foster such development than by supportive and appropriately stimulating caregiving. (1983, p. 313)

Concept Checks

1. Hemophilia was traced to several members of the same extended family. The most likely method used to discover this would be
   a. molecular genetics.
   b. gene-linkage studies.
   c. twin and adoption studies.
2. Which pair of individuals is most likely to have similar personality traits?
   a. Monozygotic twins reared apart
   b. Dizygotic twins reared together
   c. Siblings reared together
3. On which side of the pendulum do Antonio's personality traits—outgoing, helpful, warmhearted, happy, self-confident, disorganized, and careless—belong?
4. The strongest conclusion that one can reach about creating optimal environments appears to be:
   a. Caregivers should provide warm, supportive, and stimulating settings for children.
   b. Environments are inconsequential because genetic factors play a bigger role in children's intelligence and personality.
   c. Caregivers shape children's talents very early in life.

Reviewing Key Points

The Basics of Genetics

- Each human cell contains 46 elongated, threadlike "colored bodies" called chromosomes. Of the 23 pairs of chromosomes in the nucleus of the cell, 22 are called autosomes. The 23rd pair of chromosomes is responsible for determining the sex of the baby. Approximately, 20,000 genes are found on each chromosome.
- Genes are the basic transmitters of heredity. Each gene has a partner gene, or allele. If the alleles have contrasting effects, the individual is said to be heterozygous for that trait. If the genes have the same trait, the individual is said to be homozygous for that trait. Genes are composed of a complex chemical called deoxyribonucleic acid (DNA).
- Although DNA contains the complete blueprint of the living organism and the genetic code to regulate the functioning and development of the organism, it cannot move out of the nucleus into the cytoplasm. RNA can, however, and acts as a messenger to carry out the instructions of DNA to the cytoplasm; it thus guides the synthesis of thousands of proteins needed to create and sustain life processes in a cell or organ.
- Human beings have two kinds of cells, somatic (body cells) and gametes (germ or sex cells). Both types of cells reproduce in number via mitosis, which results in an identical copy of the parent cells. Gametes are produced via meiosis, in which the duplicate set of chromosomes is relinquished, resulting in a mature gamete with only 23 single chromosomes rather than 46.

Genetic Disorders and Abnormalities

- Down syndrome is characterized by severe mental retardation, congenital heart disease, short stature, and a large tongue. Fragile X syndrome is another example of complex genetic transmission associated with effects ranging from normal IQ and subtle learning disabilities to severe mental retardation. Phenylketonuria (PKU) is an inherited condition that results when the child inherits two recessive genes. Mental retardation can be prevented by eliminating phenylalanine from the child's diet.
- Sickle-cell anemia results from the child inheriting two recessive alleles that cause the normally round blood cells to develop an elongated hooked-shaped appearance. Extreme pain results when sickled cells cause clots to occur in various organs and joints. Tay-Sachs disease is a fatal genetic disorder that progressively destroys the central nervous system.
- A dominant allele disorder, Huntington's disease, like Tay-Sachs, is fatal. However, whereas children with Tay-Sachs generally die before the age of 5, symptoms for Huntington's disease appear between 35 and 50, and death occurs approximately 15 years later.
- Turner's syndrome occurs when a sperm cell fails to produce a sex chromosome, resulting in a female with one X chromosome. These females are sterile. XXY (Klinefelter's syndrome) occurs when the male offspring has two X chromosomes and one Y. Characteristics include small testes, diminished body and facial hair, and infertility. Individuals with hemophilia require lifelong treatment because they do not have normal blood-clotting abilities. Red–green color blindness is another X-linked disorder.
- Genetic counseling may be appropriate for couples with a history of genetic abnormalities in their family

history. Other prenatal tests designed to examine the integrity of the developing fetus include ultrasound (6 weeks gestation); amniocentesis (14th–16th week gestation); chorionic villus sampling (8–12 weeks gestation); and alpha-fetoprotein tests (16 weeks gestation).

The Synchrony of Genes and Environment

- Neither genes nor environment exists in a vacuum. Genes influence the propensity or probability that certain behaviors may develop, which may be supported by a deleterious environment or buffered by a benevolent one. Some traits are more influenced by environment, and some are more influenced by genetics.
- Cognitive function and personality traits have a reaction range, which determines the range of possibilities that the genetic code allows. Those traits that allow little environmental influence are known as canalized traits.

The Genetics of Human Traits

- Geneticists study human traits through twin and adoption studies, analysis of pedigrees (traits running in families), and molecular genetics.
- The shared family environment appears to have a decreasing influence on IQ as children get older. Convergent findings suggest that genetic factors make a contribution to personality characteristics such as extroversion, emotional stability, activity level, inhibition or fearfulness, altruism, and cooperation.
- A consistent finding is that the common shared family environment accounts for only about 1 percent of the variance in personality. Personality differences are more influenced by the nonshared family environment—unique experiences that children share with nonfamily members.
- Behavioral genetics explores the role played by genetics in influencing IQ and personality. Research has shown that approximately 50 percent of individual differences in IQ scores is accounted for by genetic factors. In support of this statement, studies have shown that identical twins' IQs are more highly correlated than fraternal twins' IQs. Other studies have demonstrated that adopted twins resemble their biological mothers' IQ more than lifelong providers.

Answers to Concept Checks

The Basics of Genetics

1. genes 2. a. sex chromosomes, b. sex chromosomes, c. autosomes 3. a 4. a

Genetic Disorders and Abnormalities

1. b 2. a 3. Turner's syndrome 4. amniocentesis

The Synchrony of Genes and Environment

1. c 2. true 3. c

The Genetics of Human Traits

1. b 2. a 3. with the exception of happiness, all belong on the heredity side 4. a

Key Terms

allele
autosome
canalized traits
chromosome
crossing over
diploid cell
deoxyribonucleic acid
dizygotic twins
dominant
Down syndrome
fragile X syndrome
gamete
gene
genetic screening
genome
genotype
haploid cell
hemophilia
heritability
heterozygous
homologous chromosomes
homozygous
Huntington's disease
intelligence
IQ
Klinefelter syndrome
locus
meiosis
mitosis
molecular genetics
monozygotic twins
mutation
nonshared family environment
nucleotide
phenylketonuria (PKU)
phenotype
polygenetic inheritance
reaction range
recessive
ribonucleic acid (RNA)
sex chromosome
sex-linked characteristic
shared family environment
sickle-cell anemia
Tay-Sachs disease (TSD)
Turner's syndrome
variance

InfoTrac College Edition

For additional readings, explore InfoTrac College Edition, your online library. Go to **http://www.infotrac-college.com/wadsworth** and use the passcode that came on the card with your book. Try these search terms: behavioral genetics, amniocentesis, Huntington's chorea, phenylketonuria, Turner's syndrome.

Child Development CD-ROM

Go to the Wadsworth Child Development CD-ROM for further study of the concepts in this chapter. The CD-ROM also includes quizzes and additional activities to expand your learning experience.

CHAPTER FOUR

Parenthood, Prenatal Development, and Birth

CHAPTER OUTLINE

Psychological Factors in Becoming Parents
- Motivational Factors for Parenthood
- How Your Life Changes
- Factors Leading to Positive Transitions

Infertile Couples
- Causes of Infertility
- Artificial Fertilization
- Surrogate Mothers

Prenatal Environmental Hazards
- Diseases: AIDS and Measles
- Immunological Effects: Rh Factor
- Diet and Caffeine
- Age and Emotions
- Prescription and Nonprescription Drugs
- Smoking
- Alcohol
- Illicit Drugs
- Chemical Hazards to Sperm

Conception and Prenatal Development
- Conception
- The Infant's Gestation Period: Three Stages

The Parents' Experience
- The First Trimester
- The Second Trimester
- The Third Trimester

The Birth Process
- Contemporary Childbirth
- Stages of Childbirth

Life Begins: The Newborn
- Neonatal Assessment Techniques
- The Newborn's Appearance
- Born Too Small, Born Too Soon
- Postpartum Period

Reviewing Key Points

Fumi finishes her letter to her mother-in-law in Shanghai telling how her pregnancy is progressing and gets ready for a new class she is taking. A child's disposition, Fumi believes, begins to develop before birth and during gestation—a condition that suggests a need for *tai-jiao,* or "womb education." In her first class, Fumi learns that if she is affected by good things, the child will be good, if by bad the child will be bad. "The woman should seek to shape the character of the coming child by restricting her activities and avoiding bitter and spicy foods. She should listen to refined music and elevated moral discourse," her teacher imparts to the class. (Hawes & Hiner, 1991)

The ancient Chinese theories of child development emphasize that the foundation of learning to become an adult with reverent manners and moral tenets begins before the child is born. One of Confucius' most basic assumptions was that a child's disposition is exclusively derived from environmental influences that begin in the womb. In one sense, this chapter can be thought of as being dedicated to "womb education."

It is said that a good parent is a knowledgeable one; that knowledge begins with gaining insight into your attitudes and feelings about becoming a parent. Thus, the first objective of this chapter will be to explore motivational issues for wanting or not wanting to have children. It is estimated that 60 percent of couples who want to have children become pregnant within 3 months, but 40 percent do not. What help is available to couples who want to have children but are having difficulties conceiving? The causes of infertility, and what can be done about it, is our next topic of investigation.

In some ways, the information presented in this chapter is in agreement with what Fumi is learning in class—the intrauterine world is a delicate one. Scientific evidence may not help you turn your unborn child into a reverent adult, but research has given us a great deal of information about how the unborn child's physical being is affected by the intrauterine environment. We used to believe that the developing embryo/fetus only took what was good from the mother and was somehow immune from the bad. Today, we know that the mother's lifestyle has an important bearing on the health and physical integrity of the child. The next objective of this chapter is to understand preventable prenatal environmental hazards.

We then follow the infant's development as it grows from one tiny cell into several trillion cells and the new experiences the expectant couple encounters in each new trimester. As the 266-day gestation period nears its end, the excitement builds as the parents make their final preparations for the arrival of their child. We will complete our discussion by examining childbirth and its glorious finale—the newborn child.

Psychological Factors in Becoming Parents

Before Beginning . . .

After reading this section, you will be able to

- evaluate possible motivational factors for wanting or not wanting to have children.
- examine how one's life changes during first parenthood.
- explain the factors that lead to a positive transition to parenthood.

Whether or not to have a child is a daunting question for some, an obvious choice for others, and for still others, a surprise decision seemingly out of their control.

Motivational Factors for Parenthood

> I wish I could decide once and for all to have a baby, or even figure out whether I want one. Then I could plan the rest of my life. . . . One day I'm so absorbed by my career that I think I can't possibly have a child. Then the next day, I'm staring somewhat jealously at pregnant women. I see mothers and babies everywhere. It looks good to me. But I always scare myself away before I actually do anything about it. (Faux, 1984)

There are no guaranteed benefits of either having or not having children. The motivation for having (or not having) children involves many factors (socioeconomic status, ethnicity, mother's employment, and so forth), but generally speaking, there are nine value categories that encompass why both men and women may want to have children and the needs children fulfill for parents. These are highlighted in Table 4.1. (See Self-Insight on page 118 to evaluate your own feelings about having children.)

Women tend to have slightly different motivations for having children than most men. Some of the strongest motivational factors cited by women include (Cowan & Cowan, 1992):

- having the opportunity to establish a close affiliation with another human being.
- having the experience of participating in the education and training of a child.
- producing a grandchild for their parents.

Thus, both socialization to the role of parent and family expectations appear to be important motivational factors for having a first child for women. They often regard childbearing as the primary means to a fulfilling and rewarding life.

The reasons men commonly cite for wanting to be a parent include (Cowan & Cowan, 1998a):

- establishing a close affiliation with another human being.
- to affirm their virility.
- expanding themselves by achieving immortality through their children.

Both men and women, however, cite fulfillment as an important reason for wanting to have children.

TABLE 4.1

Reasons for Wanting to Have Children

Reason	Need Satisfied
Adult status and social identity	To be accepted as responsible and mature
Expansion of the self	To have someone carry on for me after my own death, as well as to have new growth and learning experiences and add meaning to my life
Moral values	To improve morally, including becoming less selfish and learning to sacrifice, making a contribution to society, or satisfying my religious beliefs
Primary group ties and affection	To express affection and attain intimacy with another person and to be the recipient of such feelings from someone else
Stimulation and fun	To add the interest to my life that children can provide
Achievement and creativity	To realize the accomplishment, achievement, and creativity that can come from having children and helping them grow
Power and influence	To have influence over another person
Social comparison	To have prestige or a competitive advantage over others through comparing the behavior, appearance, or accomplishments of my children with those of other children
Economic utility	To gain an economic advantage; children can sometimes help with the parents' work or add their own income to the family's

They want to experience the honesty and freshness of children and watch them grow and develop. Children, they believe, will make life more interesting. Some people cite mutual dependency—having someone who needs you, looks up to you, and depends on you—as an important reason for having children. Others cite traditional reasons—such as "it's part of being a man or woman," "it seems odd not to," and "to be like other couples"—for wanting to have children.

Are fathering incentives congruent across ethnic groups? Samples of Hispanic American, European American, Chinese American, and African American men revealed that the responses of the first three groups were virtually interchangeable. These men strongly indicated that they wanted to enter into the father role for psychological reasons such as close affiliation with another human being (Coney & Mackey, 1998). Among African American men, the most important reason cited was their wife wanted children.

Reasons for Not Wanting to Have Children

The disadvantages of having children have been less extensively studied. Following are some reasons why individuals may choose not to have children:

- Their lives would be restricted (not as free to leave house, to travel, loss of privacy, and little personal time).
- Children might be a disappointment (might turn out badly through no fault of my own).
- They might not be able to create the right environment for children (both parents and society may not provide an environment in which healthy development of a child takes place).

Factors of greatest concern to women generally cluster around their emotional and physical fatigue, interrupted sleep, worry about personal appearance, and feelings of emotional upset (Sewell, 1999). Fathers do see interrupted sleep and rest as a concern, but many also see in-laws, increased money problems, changed plans, and the additional work that comes with fatherhood as troublesome.

Some choose not to have children because they are apprehensive that a child will have a negative impact on their lifestyle and intrude on their relationship with their partner or spouse. Some women worry that pregnancy and motherhood will tip their delicate domestic balance, throwing them into a traditional role of housekeeper. Women also express discomfort with the idea of financial dependence should they opt to stay at home (Sewell, 1999).

Why I May (or May Not) Want to Have Children

Imagine that you are deciding today whether to have children, then answer the following questions. Read each statement and record on the right the degree to which you agree or disagree with it. If the statement is not applicable to you, go on to the next question. There are no right or wrong answers; there is no answer key. The inventory is intended not as a test but as an exercise to help you recognize your present feelings about having children. If you are already a parent, use the inventory to examine, in retrospect, what some of your reasons were for wanting to have a child. After finishing the questionnaire, analyze your responses. What questions did you strongly agree or disagree with? Is there a point when people are "ready" to start a family? If so, what factors may make one "ready"?

I might want to have children because . . .	Agree Strongly	Agree Somewhat	Disagree Somewhat	Disagree Strongly
■ I enjoy being around children.	_____	_____	_____	_____
■ having children will create stronger bonds between my partner and me.	_____	_____	_____	_____
■ my child will realize aspirations I couldn't fulfill.	_____	_____	_____	_____
■ my child will look after me in my old age.	_____	_____	_____	_____
■ I should help populate the world.	_____	_____	_____	_____
■ my child will make a contribution to this troubled world.	_____	_____	_____	_____
■ I would be a good mother/father.	_____	_____	_____	_____
■ my present/anticipated partner wants children.	_____	_____	_____	_____
■ I have children and I want them to have brothers and/or sisters.	_____	_____	_____	_____
■ my child would live on after me.	_____	_____	_____	_____
■ I would never want to terminate a pregnancy.	_____	_____	_____	_____
■ having a child would prove I'm a mature woman or man.	_____	_____	_____	_____
■ I want to continue the family name.	_____	_____	_____	_____
■ parenthood would open up new realms of my life.	_____	_____	_____	_____
■ it would please my parents/in-laws.	_____	_____	_____	_____
■ I think pregnancy and childbirth are fulfilling experiences.	_____	_____	_____	_____
■ I could give nice things to my children.	_____	_____	_____	_____
■ I have stepchildren or adopted children, but I want children of my own.	_____	_____	_____	_____
■ I know a lot about raising children.	_____	_____	_____	_____
■ having children is more important to me than having a career.	_____	_____	_____	_____
■ I would love to take care of a child.	_____	_____	_____	_____
■ it would be selfish for me *not* to have children.	_____	_____	_____	_____
■ I have a social obligation to have children.	_____	_____	_____	_____

I might not want to have children because . . .	Agree Strongly	Agree Somewhat	Disagree Somewhat	Disagree Strongly
■ being around children makes me nervous.	____	____	____	____
■ having children will separate my partner and me.	____	____	____	____
■ I might pressure my child to accomplish things I couldn't.	____	____	____	____
■ I want to be independent in my old age.	____	____	____	____
■ I want to help relieve the world of overpopulation.	____	____	____	____
■ I don't want to bring a child into this troubled world.	____	____	____	____
■ my present/anticipated partner doesn't want children.	____	____	____	____
■ I am satisfied with the number of children I have.	____	____	____	____
■ I don't need a child to demonstrate that I'm a mature man or woman.	____	____	____	____
■ being a parent would interfere with my freedom to do things I enjoy.	____	____	____	____
■ I shouldn't be a parent just to please my parents/in-laws.	____	____	____	____
■ I think pregnancy and childbirth are frightening.	____	____	____	____
■ I don't think I'm physically up to having children.	____	____	____	____
■ children would be too much of a financial burden to me.	____	____	____	____
■ I already have stepchildren or adopted children, so I don't need more.	____	____	____	____
■ I know nothing about raising children.	____	____	____	____
■ my child might have birth defects.	____	____	____	____
■ children would interfere with my career.	____	____	____	____
■ I don't want the added responsibility.	____	____	____	____
■ I would have to give up too much of myself if I had children.	____	____	____	____
■ I don't anticipate having a partner of the opposite sex.	____	____	____	____

TABLE 4.2

Advantages of Being Parents or Nonparents

Parents	Nonparents
Children give as well as receive love.	Couples can more fully pursue their careers, finding more fulfillment in their professional lives.
Their presence may enhance the love between couples as they share in the experiences of raising children.	They can find more intimacy in an adult relationship.
Successfully managing the challenges of parenthood can also build self-esteem and provide a sense of accomplishment.	They don't have to worry about providing for the physical and psychological needs of children.
Children provide an opportunity for discovering new and untapped dimensions of one's self that can give one's life greater meaning and satisfaction.	There is less conflict in "who does what" around the house.
Children offer ongoing stimulation and change as they develop throughout childhood.	

In addition, many individuals may have unconscious reasons for beginning a family (competing with a sister who is pregnant, hoping for acceptance by parents, helping the marital relationship). These reasons or values traditionally do not appear on any inventories given to couples to assess their attitudes about having children, and thus, are rarely cited as possible motivating factors for or against having children. Having children or remaining childless each has potential advantages (discussed in Table 4.2).

Childbearing and Culture

Reproduction in many Third World countries such as sub-Saharan Africa, North Africa, and west Asia, is so central to a woman's social status that choosing not to have children is simply not an option. Currently, 77 percent of the world's population lives in the Third World, and by 2025, five out of six people will live in Latin America, Africa, Asia, and the Middle East (U.S. Bureau of the Census, 1998). In many industrialized nations, couples' abilities to make choices about becoming parents have increased because of such factors as lower infant mortality rates, longer life spans, growth in demand for female labor, postponement of marriage, and increased availability of contraception. These factors also increase the couple's ability to limit the number of children they will have.

In contrast, a shorter life expectancy, higher infant mortality rate, lower literacy levels, an agriculture-based economy, and earlier age of marriage for individuals in many Third World countries mean that women's lives tend to be defined by marriage and having children (U.S. Bureau of the Census, 1998). The Baganda, for example, are one of the larger Bantu tribes living in Uganda in East-Central Africa. They are an agricultural people. Wives are valued for two things: economic production and producing children (Ingoldsby, 1995).

The total fertility rate, which refers to the average total number of births per woman at the end of childbearing age, is between three and six children in many parts of the Third World. However, in sub-Saharan Africa and west Asia, the average number of children is more than six (Smith, 1995). Whereas in the past few decades, families with children have declined in industrialized societies, this is not the case in Third World countries, where approximately 30 percent of women are pregnant at any given time in large part because their social position depends on their ability to bear children (United Nations, 1991).

How Your Life Changes

The transition to parenthood is unsettling for both parents, and their relationship as a couple may suffer (Chapman, 1997). Negative changes often outweigh the positive changes in parents' lives during the early postpartum period (Lamb, 1998). Couples who are welcoming their first child into the family are likely to experience change in four major areas: (1) division of labor, (2) self-esteem, (3) marital satisfaction, and (4) relationships with the couples' parents (Cowan & Cowan, 1998a). These areas of relationship encompass individual, couple, and baby concerns, as well as involving third-generation, or extended family parties and other social systems.

Division of Labor

> Don and Melinda are a dual-career couple. Despite their socialization in a sexist culture, they express an intellectual commitment to gender equality. Don and Melinda begin their marriage with a similar level of education, and both start out at entry-level jobs. In the early years of their marriage, they establish an equitable division of household tasks. However, after their first child is born, the power relations between the spouses change.

Given the typical gender "ideology" common in the United States, it is presumed that mothers are naturally more responsive to and nurturing toward infants than fathers, and that fathers are better at breadwinning (Carter, 1992). Melinda begins to limit her commitment to paid work through part-time employment, thus reducing her level of job responsibility. Because Don earns more than his wife, this division of labor seems to make economic, as well as biological, sense. By the time their second child arrives, Don has been promoted and is earning a significantly larger salary than Melinda. Because her earning capacity is now diminished, and the cost of child care is so great, Melinda is motivated to work outside the home as little as possible. As she now contributes a smaller proportion of the family's income, it seems only natural that she continue to assume a higher proportion of the housework and child care. In this cycle, men and women's division of labor in the home becomes increasingly different during this transition to parenthood.

After the birth of a child, parents are less likely to share participation in household tasks and decision making (Lavee, Sharlin, & Katz, 1996). The transition to parenthood generally brings with it a shift toward a more traditional division of labor. Women handle more of the child care and domestic home chores. Men do fewer household chores, but they tend to give themselves more credit for participation in household chores than do their wives (Deutsch, Lozy, & Saxon, 1993). Not surprisingly, couples report a decline in satisfaction with the "who does what" of life and subsequently experience an increase in marital disagreement and conflict.

Self-Esteem

Overall levels of self-esteem tend to be similar between couples with children and couples who are child-free. However, certain aspects of self-systems do change (Cowan & Cowan, 1997). Couples who remain childless, for example, show a significant increase in the "partner/lover" aspect of self. For new parents, "being a parent" becomes a larger part of their psychological selves and the "partner/lover" becomes a lesser part for both partners. Similarly, one's sense of self as "worker" or "student" becomes a much smaller part of self-identity for women, but for men it remains virtually unchanged. This appears to be true in other cultures, such as Sweden and Norway, as well (Roenkae & Pulkkinen, 1998).

Although many fathers still largely define themselves in terms of their occupation, they often succeed in broadening their conceptions of self to include a sense of "father" as well (Cowan & Cowan, 1988; 1992; 1998b). These new fathers may find themselves becoming more aware of the needs of others, experiencing a pull to be caring and empathic even when their own resources are depleted. Many fathers describe themselves as more aware of their personal relationships on the job.

Marital Satisfaction and the Couple's Parents

Expectant mothers tend to experience their greatest decline in marital satisfaction from the beginning of pregnancy to six months after giving birth (Broom, 1998; Miller & Sollie, 1990). Their partners' level of satisfaction, however, tends to remain relatively stable during that period. Couples also experience the transition to parenthood in different ways. In heterosexual couples, women tend to show less satisfaction with themselves and their mutual role arrangements than do men (Grossman, Eichler, Winickoff, Anzalone, Gorseyeff, & Sargent, 1990). This may be explained by the fact that the women usually have more responsibility in managing the home and caring for the child and are more likely to put aside work and outside studies after giving birth.

Parenthood brings about changes in the couples' relationships with their parents. The birth of a child may lead to a closer relationship between the new mother and her own mother. The younger woman may feel there are more common interests and call upon her own mother's experience. Further, sons and daughters are often treated more like adults by their parents once they become parents themselves (Cowan & Cowan, 1998b).

© David Young-Wolfe/PhotoEdit

The birth of a child may lead to a closer relationship between the new mother and her own mother.

Factors Leading to Positive Transitions

Positive transitions occur when new parents meet their individual needs for *autonomy* (independence) and *affiliation* (connectedness). Basically, new parents need to discover how each can satisfy their individual needs and develop independence and autonomy, while maintaining closeness and connectedness with the other (Cowan & Cowan, 1998a). Although individuality and connectedness are equally desirable goals, taken to the extremes, either can interfere with the development of the individual and the relationship.

For example, if one or both partners are devoted to fostering only individuality, the relationship can be severely strained. It is, perhaps, less obvious that emphasis only on the relationship may lead to a state of fusion that can interfere with the individual growth of the partners. Thus, the balance between the two orientations, rather than the adoption of either one, constitutes positive relationship development. The greatest challenge is for two spouses to work out a way to maintain a sense of individuality and mutuality while becoming a family.

Thought CHALLENGE

What are some ways in which you will be able to meet your needs for automony and affiliation with your spouse?

For some individuals, parenthood leaves them feeling fragmented and powerless in their identities, and their self-esteem suffers as well. These parents seem unable to solve problems, take perspective, and regulate their emotions. Other new parents, however, exhibit an increased maturity that appears to be a direct outcome of their transition into parenthood. What accounts for these differences in couples experiencing first parenthood? Factors that can help couples make a positive transition to their new roles as parents are highlighted in Table 4.3.

When does the transition period into parenthood begin and end? Answers vary greatly. Some couples suggest that the beginning of the transition occurs long before conception, and some still have "not quite got the hang of being parents" by the time their first child enters kindergarten (Cowan, Cowan, Heming, & Miller, 1991). On average, however, the transition involved in becoming parents ends by the time the first child is 2 years old.

Concept Checks

1. Women and men tend to share which key reason for wanting to have children?
   a. Achieving immortality through children
   b. Establishing close affiliation with another human being
   c. Having an impact on the world
2. When welcoming their first child into the family, couples are likely to experience change in one of the following ways:
   a. They are more likely to report an increase in marital satisfaction.
   b. Their self-esteem is likely to change in significantly negative ways.
   c. New parents are less likely to share participation in household tasks.
3. One factor that can contribute to new parents' positive transition to parenthood is:
   a. The couple agrees about having a child.
   b. The couple agrees about the roles their in-laws will play with their new grandchild.
   c. The couple agrees to have children when they are quite young when the transition to parenthood will be less severe.

Infertile Couples

Before Beginning . . .

After reading this section, you will be able to

- recognize the possible reasons for infertility.
- discuss reproductive choices.

TABLE 4.3

Factors Leading to Positive Transitions to Parenthood

Factor	Explanation
Agreement about having a child	Expectant couples who fail to agree about having a child tend to have more difficulties in their marriage (Giguere, Fortin, & Sabourin, 1999).
Preparation	Couples who believe they are ready to become parents adapt best to new parenthood. Preparing for parenthood by attending classes, reading books, or caring for others' children is more positively associated with assisting men's transition to parenthood than women's.
Quality of marriage	Men and women who are more satisfied with themselves, their marriage, or their jobs before becoming parents are less stressed as parents (Cowan, Cowan, Heming, & Miller, 1991). Babies do not appear to create severe marital distress where it was not present before, nor do they tend to bring already mutually dissatisfied couples closer together (Cowan & Cowan, 1998a).
Age	The transition to parenthood may be less severe when the parents are older or have been married a longer time before conceiving.
Division of labor	When both the husband and wife are satisfied with the others' contribution to the family, there is a greater satisfaction with the marital relationship and an easier transition to parenthood (Lamb, 1998).
Tolerance	When both spouses can show tolerance for ambiguity, flexibility, adaptability, and a good sense of humor, the transition to parenthood is a positive one (Rice, 1999). Similarly, the availability of social support from friends, neighbors, relatives, co-workers, and their spouse helps make the transition easier.

When attempts to become pregnant are unsuccessful after one year, it is generally recommended that a couple consult a physician. **Infertility** can be defined as the inability to conceive after one full year of normal, regular heterosexual intercourse without the use of any contraception. The odds that a woman will get pregnant without medical assistance when she has failed to do so after a year or two of unprotected intercourse are extremely low (Eriksen, 2001). It has been estimated that one in six couples encounters problems conceiving. In 1997, more than one million new patients sought fertility treatment, 6 times as many people as are treated for lung cancer and 10 times the number of reported cases of AIDS (Chandra & Stephen, 1998). In what has become a booming industry over the last 20 years, there are now 350 fertility clinics in the United States.

Causes of Infertility

The two most common causes in women are reduced egg production and blocked fallopian tubes. To correct blocked fallopian tubes, delicate microsurgery is necessary, and unfortunately, it is successful only about 50 percent of the time (Greil, 1997). Failure to ovulate at regular intervals can also make conception difficult. There also are "preventable" causes for infertility. Women, for example, who smoke cigarettes are less fertile and take longer to become pregnant than nonsmokers (Curtis, Savitz, & Arbuckle, 1997). Alcohol and drug abuse also reduce fertility in women (Sheynkin & Schlegel, 1997).

Women have historically been accorded the lion's share of the blame when a marriage was "barren," but when reproductive specialists looked more closely into the problem, they discovered that men are wholly or partly responsible for a couple's infertility problem 40 to 60 percent of the time (Becker, 1997). In men, infertility may be caused by a low sperm count. In this case, sperm may be collected, concentrated, and frozen in sperm banks to be used later for artificial insemination. Another common cause of infertility in men is *motility;* this is when the sperm cells do not propel themselves with sufficient vigor. Smoking, alcohol, and drug use and abuse can also reduce fertility in males (Curtis, Savitz, & Arbuckle, 1997).

Some women delay beginning a family until they are at least 30 for a variety of reasons: to establish their careers, to be sure they and their partner can afford it, because they married relatively late, or because they want to have a child with a new partner. However, in spite of the medical profession's increasing ability to stretch the limits of a woman's reproductive years, it is statistically more difficult for a woman in her mid-thirties to conceive a child than it is for a younger

infertility
When a couple is unable to conceive after one year of unprotected intercourse; also when a woman is unable to carry a pregnancy to term.

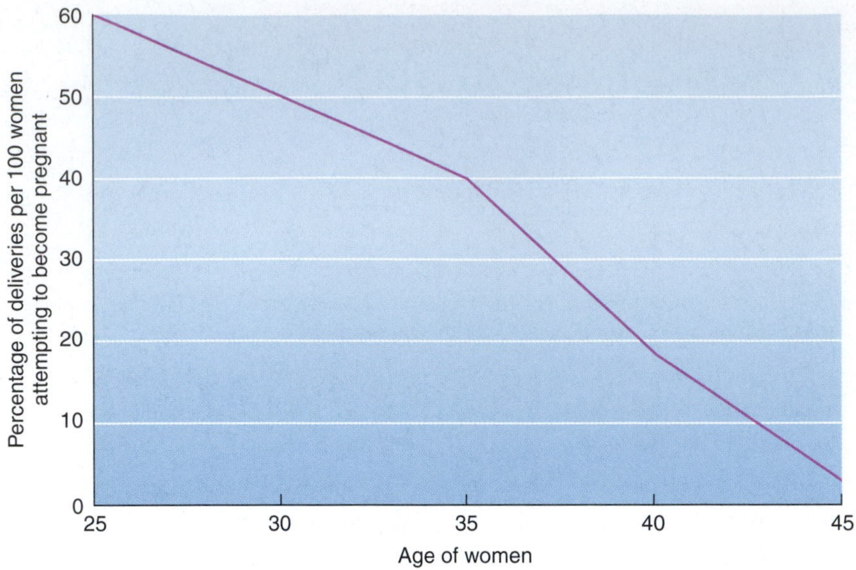

FIGURE 4.1 ***Increasing Age = Declining Fertility***

Fertility in women exhibits a substantial decline after the age of 35.

From "The Reproduction Cycle" (p. 16), by B. Cohen, in *Management of Infertility: A Clinician's Manual* (2nd ed., 1991), Durant, OK: Essential Medical Information Systems. Used by permission of Brian M. Cohen, M.D., modified from Behrman, S. J. and Kistner, R. W. *Progress in Infertility* (1975).

woman (Eriksen, 2001) (see Figure 4.1). Fertility in women declines substantially after 35 (Epstein & Rosenberg, 1997). Aging increases the likelihood that accidents and/or a wide range of illness will occur that will ultimately affect fertility. The limited supply of eggs is another reason why fertility decreases with age (Rosenthal & Kingsberg, 1999).

Recent studies of egg donation provide strong evidence that it is the age of the eggs, and not the age of the rest of the reproductive system, that causes fertility to decline sharply after age 35. Older women who receive eggs from younger women get pregnant at rates comparable to the age of the egg donor, not the age of the recipient (Leiblum & Greenfeld, 1997). Contrary to what most people believe, men also experience problems when they get older; their hormone levels drop and the number of sperm they produce is affected by a longer exposure to environmental chemicals, infections, disease, and stress (van Balen, Verdurmen, & Ketting, 1997).

in vitro fertilization
Ova are removed from the woman when they are just about to rupture; they are then mixed with the sperm and if the eggs develop and begin to divide, they are placed inside the woman's uterus.

A considerable body of evidence illustrates that men and women are affected differently by the experience of infertility (Sewell, 1999). Women are more likely to worry that something is wrong even before seeking treatment, to initiate discussion with their partners, and to assume personal responsibility when efforts to conceive prove unsuccessful (Newton, 1999). They also are more likely to reach out for social support and to use certain escape strategies (wishing, hoping, fantasizing) than men. Not surprisingly, women express greater openness to counseling than men. Men, by contrast, are more likely to view infertility as a "problem" to be solved.

Artificial Fertilization

Artificial fertilization reflects the advances that have been made in our knowledge of human fertility genetics and understanding of prenatal development, most of it very recently. In July 1978, Patrick Steptoe and Robert Edwards topped decades of work by delivering by cesarean section 5-pound, 12-ounce Louise Joy Brown, the first "test-tube baby" to be carried to term. Human reproduction was changed forever. Since Baby Louise, about 26,000 babies in the United States alone have been born by artificial fertilization.

In Vitro Fertilization

The **in vitro fertilization** procedure was developed to bypass a woman's infertility due to blocked fallopian tubes. First ova, or eggs, are obtained from the woman. To do this the maturation of the ova is carefully monitored, and when they are just about to rupture from the ovaries (ovulation), the eggs are surgically removed. The ova are then mixed with the sperm (conception) and, if the eggs develop and begin to divide, a number are placed inside the woman's uterus (implantation). It is common to implant more than one fertilized egg in the hope of increasing the chances of establishing a pregnancy. Because in vitro fertilization is a difficult process, there is a high chance of failure at every stage (Rosenthal & Goldfarb, 1997). It is expensive (about $7,800 to $10,000 per attempt; three or four attempts are often needed to achieve success) and not covered by many insurance plans. The high price of in vitro treatments means that generally only the rich and well insured can afford them. Finally, the procedure produces children for only 18 percent of the couples who try it; despite these odds, each year some 40,000 do try it. For both men and women in vitro fertilization treatments offer excitement at the prospect of pregnancy and emotional disappointment when attempts prove to be unsuccessful (as Jennifer Zell points out in the First Person box). The waiting for the outcome of the in vitro fertilization treatment and an unsuccessful outcome are the most stressful factors (Eugster & Vingerhoets, 1999). Common reactions during these treatments are anxiety and depression; after an unsuccessful attempt, feelings of sadness, depression, and anger prevail. Those who have gone through in vitro attempts but have not been able to conceive need to grieve for their losses and resolve issues of infertility before they can successfully move on (Salzer, 1999). For some couples, an infertility counselor may help them address these issues as well as discuss possible alternatives such as adoption.

Sometimes artificial insemination is used to select the sex of a child when a couple is at risk for passing on X-linked diseases to their children. For example, the couple may want a girl because a boy would be at-risk for hemophilia. In these situations, laboratory techniques are used to separate X- from Y-bearing sperm. Once the laboratory separation process is complete, the desired X or Y fraction is introduced into the vagina by artificial insemination. Success rates are about 80 percent. If you could choose the sex of your first child, would it be a boy or a girl? What about couples in other countries? Is there a sex preference? (See Cultural Variations.)

FIRSTPERSON

In Vitro Fertilization

My husband and I went through four cycles of in vitro fertilization in a period of a year and a half; none was successful. From start to finish one cycle takes about six weeks. The process involves several visits to the doctor's office for monitoring, taking drugs, giving yourself shots, and receiving shots from your spouse. Each time we went through it I looked at it like it was a job; it was very structured and required that we adhere to specific instructions. I never got wrapped up in the thought of "I know this time it will work." I just did what was required of me and went about doing the other things in my daily life. After the pregnancy test, we had to wait two weeks for the results. During this time, I simply avoided the subject. I never wanted to give myself false hopes. Our friends and family would say, "I know this time it will work," or "I had a dream you were pregnant." I would always remain realistic, remembering my 25 percent chance of conceiving.

Each time the results came back negative we were sad for a few days. My husband was very sweet and supportive each time, giving me cards and flowers when he, too, was feeling the pain. It brought us closer together. I would feel that it wasn't meant to be and that some day, somehow, we would have a family. Only after the fourth in vitro cycle did I stand firm and say "enough"! I felt like we had given it our all and had stayed positive through each unsuccessful cycle. It also helped having such wonderful doctors and nurses working with us and for us, and of course, our caring and supportive families and friends. We knew that we would be wonderful parents. Our wishes and hopes came true recently when we adopted a beautiful baby boy. He is the reason that the in vitros didn't work.

—*Jennifer Zell*

Intracytoplasmic Sperm Injection (ICSI)

Until a few years ago, couples in which the man was infertile were told to find a sperm donor or to consider adoption; their choices were minimal. In 1992, a new technique known as ICSI (**intracytoplasmic sperm injection**), in which sperm was injected into an egg, was successfully performed in Belgium. Injecting a sperm cell into an egg may sound like a simple procedure, but attempts had failed until researchers figured out how to manipulate the sperm and egg without damaging them. U.S. clinics now do thousands of ICSI procedures each year, with a success rate of about 24 percent. The technique can help men with low sperm counts, or motility, and even those who cannot ejaculate or have no live sperm in their semen as a result of vasectomy, chemotherapy, or a medical disorder. The cost for this procedure ranges from $10,000 to $12,000.

Surrogate Mothers

Sometimes infertile couples use surrogate mothers. Here one woman contracts to carry and give birth to a child for another woman. The surrogate mother gives birth to the child who is then brought up by the receiving parents. It is similar to adoption, except that the agreement between the surrogate and receiving mothers is made prior to conception rather than after birth. Surrogate mothers typically receive a fee of $12,000 (Foote, 1998). The personal and legal issues of such arrangements remain complex and unresolved.

Concept Checks

1. ***True or False:*** Alcohol, drug use, and cigarette smoking do not significantly reduce fertility in either men or women.
2. ***True or False:*** In vitro fertilization was developed to bypass a woman's infertility due to blocked fallopian tubes with a success rate of approximately 50 percent.

Thought CHALLENGE

If preconception sex selection became 100% accurate and inexpensive, what do you think the consequences would be?

intracytoplasmic sperm injection
Technique in which a sperm cell is injected into an egg; used for infertile couples.

Cultural Variations

Sex Preferences for Firstborn Children

The preference for firstborn sons over daughters is worldwide (Kim, Kim, & Rue, 1997; Mwageni, Ankomah, & Powell, 1998). In fact, throughout the world, preference for males is so strong that there would probably be twice as many boys as girls if parents were allowed to choose. In countries such as the United States, Germany, France, and Great Britain, parents, in general, prefer a boy for their firstborn child. Reasons for preferring a boy, for men, are to carry on the family name. Women often prefer a son to please their husbands. In other countries, however, the desire for sons is extremely important. In China and South Korea, for example, until a woman bears a male child, she is only a provisional member of her husband's household—merely a daughter-in-law. With the birth of a son, however, she becomes the mother of the family's descendants, a position of prestige and respect (Kim, Kim, & Rue, 1997). In more extreme incidences, such as in Egypt, bearing no son is considered sufficient reason for a man to leave his wife (Zeidenstein & Moore, 1996).

So strong is the preference for a son in China, with its one-child policy, that selective abortion of female fetuses is common (Faison, 1997). Although there are laws banning prenatal testing for sex and subsequent selective abortion, it still occurs illegally. In India, firstborn girls are given boys' names in the hope that this will bring a boy the next time (Dosanjh & Ghuman, 1996). In some countries where there is a high preference for boys, couples practice certain sex practices, pregnant women eat certain foods, and couples say special prayers so that their firstborn child will be a boy (Mwageni, Ankomah, & Powell, 1998).

Several factors lead to this preference for firstborn sons:

- *Economic* Girls require the expense of a dowry; boys do not. Sons will provide for parents in old age (and sons are legally entitled to larger shares of the inheritance for this reason).
- *Religion* In Confucian and Hindu religions, only sons can pray for the release of the souls of dead parents.
- *Patrilineal* In patrilineal societies, all property is passed from father to son. Having a son is a sign of the father's virility.
- *Assigned gender roles* Girls will belong to the family into which they marry. Males have more opportunity for advancement in society.

Are there any societies that prefer girls, and, if so, what are their reasons? In societies where daughters make significant economic contributions to the society, they are viewed as a source of wealth and support. Some societies that prefer girls are matrilineal, which means all property is passed to the daughter upon the death of the parents. Among the Mundugumor of New Guinea, who have a strong preference for girls, the marriage system uses women as a medium of exchange. Every man is supposed to obtain a wife by giving his sister in return for another man's sister, resulting in men constantly fighting over wives (Siegmund, Tittel, Schiefenhoevel, 1994). Finally, girls tend to be preferred in some societies because they provide companionship to the mother and can participate in jobs such as child rearing, household work, agriculture, or home industries.

Latin American and Caribbean countries have low preferences for sons, which is rather surprising because these areas are usually stereotyped as placing a strong value on masculinity. Some express the belief that girls are easier to take care of. The cultural assumption is that once a girl is properly socialized, she will be humble and less likely to fight, be noisy, or get into trouble. It is believed that boys, however, have a tendency to cause discipline problems for the parents. In the Filipino society, there is a slight preference for girls, but the responsibility for caring for aged parents goes to the eldest child—whether it is a male or female (Santos, 1997).

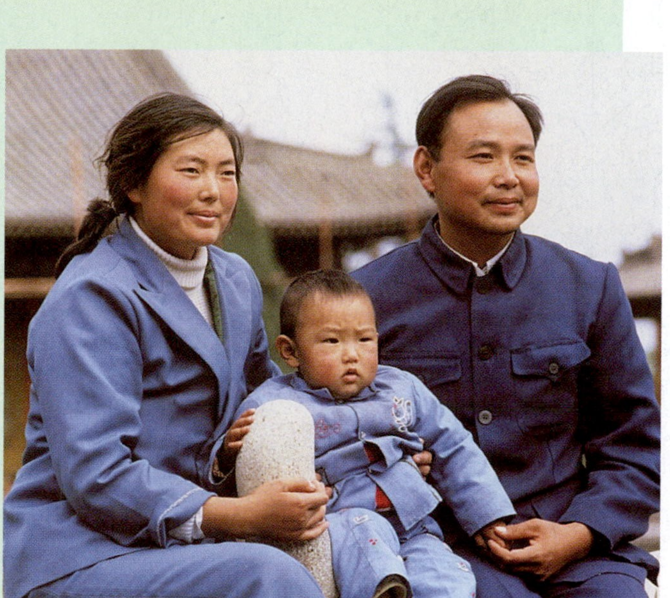

Christopher Arnesen/Tony Stone Images

Some countries have made purposeful attempts to create a preference for girls because infant boys outnumber infant girls, causing an imbalance. Educational programs under planned parenthood organizations in South Korea issue pamphlets explaining the advantages of having girls. A sign posted in Taipei, Taiwan, informs its readers, "Daughters and Sons Without Distinction." In many countries the expectation that girls have a responsibility to parents, even after marriage, is becoming more prevalent. Further, today, unmarried girls often contribute financially to the family income, and the expectation of a large dowry is no longer necessary. Despite all these changes, however, firstborn sons are still preferred throughout the world.

Prenatal Environmental Hazards

Before Beginning . . .

After reading this section, you will be able to

- explain the deleterious effects of environmental teratogens during prenatal development.
- discuss how prescription and nonprescription drugs can affect the developing embryo/fetus.

The idea that some specific experience that occurs at one time in utero will affect the development of an organism more than it would at other times led to a branch of study called *teratology*. A **teratogen** is any substance or environmental agent that can interfere with or permanently damage an embryo's growth; it causes birth defects or even death. Teratogens may include medicinal and nonmedicinal drugs; chemicals; harmful environmental influences, such as radiation; and diseases (virus and bacteria).

All nine months of prenatal development may be critical periods in some respects, but much of the damage produced by various teratogens takes place during the *embryonic* period. During the **embryonic period** (third through eighth week), the formation of body parts and organs takes place (organogenesis). Figure 4.2 shows when these critical periods of primary organs occur. When these body parts and organs are undergoing a rapid state of development, known as "critical periods," they are particularly vulnerable.

Babies, however, have a marvelous filtering system known as the *placenta* and subsequently most turn out to be healthy. The placenta is a truly amazing organ that makes it possible for the embryo (and later, the fetus) to receive nutrients and oxygen from the mother. Although the placenta prevents some kinds of bacteria and viruses from passing into the embryo's bloodstream, some, including the human immunodeficiency virus (HIV), do cross through.

Diseases: AIDS and Measles

Recently, **acquired immunodeficiency syndrome (AIDS)**, a disease that shuts down the immune system, in infants has received considerable attention. HIV is the virus associated with the pathogenesis of AIDS. The first cases of pediatric AIDS were seen in the

teratogens External agents, such as viruses, drugs, chemicals, and radiation, that can impair prenatal development and lead to abnormalities, disabilities, or even death.

embryonic period The third to eighth weeks of gestation; the growing organism is no longer a blastocyst but an embryo. The prominent task of this period is differentiation and development of organs.

placenta The membranous structure that supplies the fetus with nourishment before its birth and to which the fetus is attached by the umbilical cord.

acquired immunodeficiency syndrome (AIDS) The shutting down of the immune system; caused by human immunodeficiency virus (HIV).

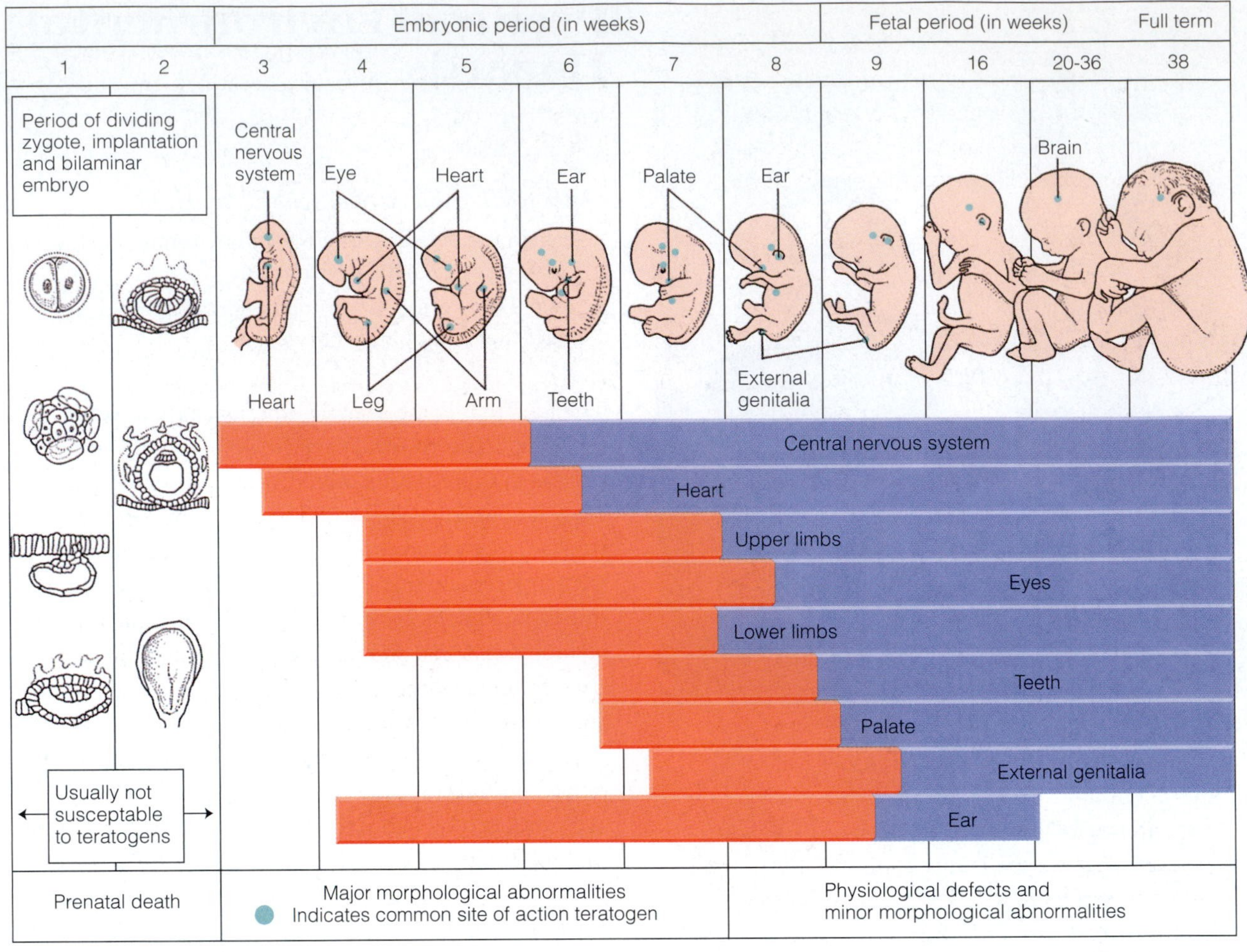

FIGURE 4.2 ***Critical Periods of Primary Organs***

Sensitivity to teratogens reaches its peak at roughly four weeks after conception. After organogenesis is complete, susceptibility to anatomical defects diminishes (light color).

From *The Developing Human: Clinically Oriented Embryology,* by K. L. Moore & T. V. N. Persaud, 1998. Philadelphia: W. B. Saunders. Used by permission of W. B. Saunders.

United States as early as 1979, although an official case definition to include criteria for diagnosing children was not developed by the Centers for Disease Control (CDC) until seven years later. The CDC reports a total of 1230 cases of pediatric AIDS (diagnosed between birth and 12 years of age) (Sogolow, Kay, Doll, Neumann, Mezoff, Eke, Semaan, & Anderson, 2000).

Pediatric AIDS constitutes less than 2 percent of the total reported AIDS cases in the United States, but it is predicted to become the leading cause of death in the near future (Clatts, Davis, Sotheran, & Atillasoy, 1998; Lowenthal, 1997). Severe HIV infection leaves the child vulnerable to illnesses that might not occur in a child with a healthy immune system. These illnesses are called "opportunistic" infections, because a weakened immune system gives opportunities for these infections to proliferate (Beverly, 1995). Minority children are disproportionately affected, with African Americans constituting 53 percent of the pediatric AIDS cases, and Latinos, 23 percent. A higher birth rate among African Americans and Latinos has contributed to these disproportionately higher rates of pediatric HIV and AIDS (Boyd-Franklin, Aleman, Jean-Gilles, & Lewis, 1995). More than half the cases have been reported from only three states (New York, New Jersey, and Florida), but the epidemic among children is spreading geographically (Goicoehea-Balbona, 1998).

A significant number of women are infected through heterosexual contacts with HIV-positive sexual partners. The population of women infected in such a manner is steadily increasing (Stephenson, 1999).

The transmission of HIV to the newborn may occur in utero, with the virus crossing the placenta; during the birth process through exposure to infected genital fluid; or through breast feeding. Nineteen percent of the CDC-reported cases of pediatric AIDS have resulted from transfusions with HIV-contaminated blood and blood products. With screening of the blood supply and heat treatment of blood products, however, this mode of infection has dropped significantly. Seventy-eight percent of the pediatric AIDS cases involve perinatal transmission from an infected mother to her child. Approximately 90 percent of the children with HIV from ages birth to 12 years have mothers who are HIV positive (Jessee, Nagy, Gresham, & Poteet-Johnson, 1996). Whether infection can occur by exposure to HIV known to be present in the blood and secretions in the birth canal in a vaginal delivery is a matter for speculation until more definitive data are available. At present, the data do not support routine cesarean deliveries for infected mothers (Armistead, Forehand, Steele, & Kotchick, 1998).

The developmental progress for babies infected with HIV or at risk for AIDS is very chaotic, and they do not respond well to the medication used for detoxification. Indeed, this symptom may be one of the first markers that the infant has AIDS (Cole, 1991). These infants show abnormal posturing; fluctuating tone; undulating, uncontrolled movement patterns; and very flat affect (unanimated facial expression). Other symptoms include, but are not limited to, failure to thrive, recurrent or intermittent fevers, swollen lymph nodes, recurrent pulmonary disease (such as pneumonia), and skin rashes (Armistead, Forehand, Steele, & Kotchick, 1998). They do not present much positive emotional feedback for their caregivers.

In the battle to medically prevent HIV in the unborn child, one of the most recent and exciting findings is that two anti-retroviral drugs, zidovudine and nevirapine, reduce the rate of mother-to-infant transmission of the virus by as much as 67 percent when administered pre-, peri-, and post-natally (Marseille, Kahn, Mmiro, Guay, Musoke, Fowler, & Jackson, 1999). Both are antiviral medications that reduce the reproductive capacity of the HIV virus and increase the immunological protection for the child. However, as significant as this discovery is, there remains a need for additional prevention strategies because there is no present cure or vaccine for HIV or AIDS (Glazer, Goldfarb, & James, 1998).

The only means to prevent further spread of the virus to children is through education and counseling sexually active women of child-bearing age and their partners. In particular, women who use or have used intravenous drugs, or have partners who do; wives of infected hemophiliacs; and women with multiple sexual partners living in regions of the country with a high incidence of HIV infection should be targeted (Wiener & Taylor-Brown, 1998).

Viral diseases such as German measles (rubella) also can affect the fetus during early stages of pregnancy. Rubella is one of the best-known examples of viral disease. Depending on when the virus enters the mother's body, infants with rubella may be born deaf or blind, have heart defects, have central nervous system damage, or experience mild retardation. Rubella leads to a 70 percent chance of deformity in the first trimester and 50 percent in the second trimester, dropping to nearly 0 percent in the last trimester. Fortunately, a vaccination for rubella, given before pregnancy, prevents the disease.

Immunological Effects: Rh Factor

During the final weeks of pregnancy, the mother transfers to the fetus immunities to such diseases as polio, chicken pox, measles, hepatitis, and diphtheria. The antibodies for such diseases cross the placenta and immunize the child for several months after birth. Other antibodies can cause serious problems, however. The most common problem is **Rh factor**. The Rh factor is a protein substance in the red blood cells of about 85 percent of the population. It is a genetically dominant blood trait named for the rhesus monkey, which is always positive for this trait.

Rh factor
A protein that when present in the fetus's blood but not in the mother's causes the mother to build up antibodies. In any subsequent pregnancies, these antibodies can be passed on to the fetus, destroying its red blood cells and reducing oxygen supplies to vital organs and tissues.

As can be seen in Figure 4.3, when an Rh-positive father and an Rh-negative mother have a child who is Rh-positive, the child's blood is incompatible with the mother's. If this is the woman's first pregnancy there is rarely a problem. However, subsequent children may be endangered because during the birth (or miscarriage) of the first child, some of the fetus's blood may mingle with the mother's when the membranes of the

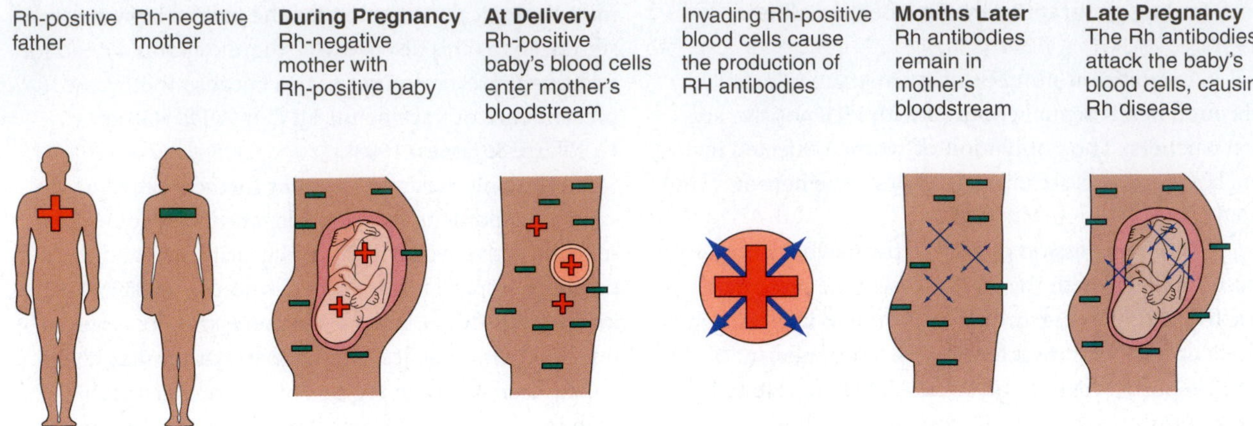
Rh-positive father
Rh-negative mother
During Pregnancy
Rh-negative mother with Rh-positive baby
At Delivery
Rh-positive baby's blood cells enter mother's bloodstream
Invading Rh-positive blood cells cause the production of RH antibodies
Months Later
Rh antibodies remain in mother's bloodstream
Late Pregnancy
The Rh antibodies attack the baby's blood cells, causing Rh disease

FIGURE 4.3 *How Rh Disease Develops*

placenta are ruptured. Because the fetus's blood is incompatible with the mother's, her body starts producing antibodies to combat the foreign blood of the fetus. These antibodies continue to exist throughout subsequent pregnancies. If subsequent pregnancies produce another Rh-positive infant, the mother's antibodies attack the red corpuscles in the blood of the fetus, causing erythroblastosis fetalis, or Rh disease. Possible outcomes of Rh incompatibility are fetal anemia, fluid retention in the fetus, brain damage, nutrition deficiencies, and death. Rh disease poses no threat to the mother.

An anti-D globulin, Rhogam, is given to the mother within 72 hours after every delivery or miscarriage (or in the seventh month of pregnancy with the first child). Rhogam is usually effective in reducing the buildup of antibodies, so that other children can then be carried by the mother with little risk of fetal erythroblastosis. Rhogam is Rh-negative blood that already has antibodies, which eventually dissipate; they also prevent the formation of additional antibodies.

Diet and Caffeine

Eating well during pregnancy makes good sense. After all, the growing fetus's food comes from the mother's bloodstream via semipermeable membranes of the umbilical cord and the placenta. Both the amount and the vitamin balance of the food a pregnant woman eats are important. The fetus stores none of the necessary substances except iron. A pregnant woman needs at least 100 grams of protein per day to promote the normal growth of the baby and maintain her health as well. The most complete protein foods are meat, fish, eggs, and cheese. On average, expectant mothers need a daily additional 300 calories and an extra serving of high protein foods.

Nearly two-thirds of pregnant women in the Third World are thought to be anemic, possibly due to a lack of protein and iron-rich foods (Ingoldsby, 1995). These nutritional deficiencies compromise their health, physical development, and ability to bear healthy children. Their children are also at greater risk for infant and child mortality. In an attempt to compensate for these losses, women often continue bearing children for as long as possible. This further increases the stress on their bodies and traps them and their children in a cycle of poor health and nutrition (United Nations, 1991). In many cases, cultural beliefs and practices result in a tendency for women and girls to consume smaller amounts and less nutritious food. Further, in some countries, food taboos discourage pregnant women from eating fruit, vegetables, milk, rice, and other high-calorie foods, which increases their susceptibility to illness, pregnancy complications, and death during childbirth.

Research directly linking caffeine to teratogenic effects in humans is limited, but some evidence does exist. An increased incidence of spontaneous abortions, stillbirths, and premature births has been associated with maternal consumption of more than 500 mg of caffeine per day, approximately eight cups of coffee (Schuetze & Zeskind, 1997). However, these findings have not been replicated with larger samples.

Other studies found no relationship between low birth weight, gestation, or malformations and drinking four cups of coffee per day (Linn, Schoenbaum, Monson, Rosner, Stubblefield, & Ryan, 1992). However, the researchers did not consider other sources of caffeine, such as cola or tea, and they did not control for changes in behavior during pregnancy. There is also evidence that prenatal caffeine exposure is predictive of higher heart rates overall both prenatally and postnatally (Schuetze & Zeskind, 1997). It should be noted that the half-life of caffeine (the amount of time required for half the amount of caffeine to dissipate from the system) triples during the third trimester of pregnancy (Crain & Bennett, 1996). Consequently, the same amount of caffeine results in much higher blood levels in the last trimester. The long-term effects of caffeine exposure in utero may be exaggerated stress in uncertain situations and increased fearfulness in general (Reznick, 1999).

Age and Emotions

Women under the age of 18 and older than 35 have a higher probability of experiencing a high-risk pregnancy. Although it is still suggested that the optimal age for childbirth is 20 to 29, current research indicates that mothers who are delaying motherhood until their thirties or later are giving birth to healthy infants (Rogers & White 1998). The most consistent findings for pregnant teens are that they are more likely to experience labor complications, have a higher prematurity rate, and bear babies with low birth weight. The fetal mortality rate is nearly 2½ times higher than that for babies of mothers in their early twenties. Teenagers' immature reproductive apparatus, lifestyle, and nutritional decisions, combined with inadequate prenatal care and psychological factors, are commonly cited as the causes (Welles, 1997).

As age increases, so does the risk of the infant developing abnormalities—having stillborns, miscarriages, and complications in pregnancy. For example, women over 40 have twice the fetal mortality rate of women between the ages of 20 and 35. The chances of having a Down syndrome child are highest in women over 40. The chances of having fraternal twins, which may be regarded as good by some and not desirable by others, also increases with age. As women get older and their ovulation becomes more irregular, they may be more likely to produce no egg one month and two the next.

Although the mother and fetus have separate nervous systems, maternal emotions probably affect the fetus. During a strong emotional state, the endocrine system releases the hormones epinephrine and norepinephrine into the bloodstream; these hormones can then pass through the placenta into the bloodstream of the fetus. Such endocrine changes may alter the fetal environment by producing a more rapid heart rate, constricting the blood vessels, and increasing uterine contractions as well as restlessness, sleeplessness, and indigestion in the mother (Glover, 1997). It has also been found that the effects of prolonged chronic anxiety, upset, and unhappiness during pregnancy have been linked with hyperactivity, irritability, crying, feeding difficulties, and sleeping problems in their offspring (Janus & Dowling, 1997). James Chisholm provides some rather suggestive data implicating high blood pressure resulting from the stress of living in fast-paced and generally unsupportive urban centers as the cause of increased infant irritability. In contrast, Navajo women, who, he argues, tend to lead less stressful lives, have less irritable babies (Chisholm, 1989).

Prescription and Nonprescription Drugs

An estimated three-quarters of the 4 million U.S. women who give birth each year receive at least one prescription while pregnant (Hutchins, 1997). Concerned about fetal risk, most physicians prescribe safe medications. The ten most often prescribed drugs for pregnant women are the antibiotics amoxicillin, ampicillin, erythromycin, metronidazole, cephalexin, and nitrofurantoin; codeine, a narcotic; docusate sodium, a stool softener; acetaminophen products, painkillers; and terconazole, a vaginal antifungal. Pregnant women metabolize drugs differently from other women. Like anyone else deciding whether to take medication, pregnant women must balance what is known about the potential risks and benefits.

An extensive use of aspirin (eight tablets a day) during the first half of pregnancy has been associated with as much as a 10-point decrement in IQ of the offspring at 4 years of age (Streissguth, Treder, Barr, Shepard, Bleyer, Sampson, & Martin, 1987). Mark Klebanoff and Heinz Berendes (1988), however, found no adverse effect of aspirin exposure on IQ. Aspirin (but not acetaminophen use) taken during the first half of pregnancy is also associated with poorer balance and fine motor unsteadiness in the offspring (Henderson, Jorm, Christensen, Jacomb, & Korten, 1997).

Smoking

Another serious health threat for the fetus is cigarette smoking. Estimates of the percentage of pregnant women who smoke cigarettes range from 14 to 29 percent (Kallen, 1997). Nicotine in tobacco products does cross the placenta and directly impacts the developing fetus. Passive smoking—or secondhand smoke from others—can also affect the fetus (Ahluwalia, Grummer-Strawn, & Scanlon, 1997). Smoking cigarettes also has been associated with sudden infant death syndrome (SIDS) (Fullilove & Dieudonne, 1997); but more commonly it is related to lower average birth size (Aaronson, & Macnee, 1989). Smoking is a contributing factor in 20 to 40 percent of the cases of low birth weight infants in the United States and, in general, is associated with a 9-ounce (about a 250-gram) reduction in infant birth weight (Wakschlag, Lahey, Loeber, Green, Gordon, & Leventhal, 1997). Some 20 to 25 percent of pregnant women, or approximately one million, smoke during pregnancy, which results in low weight gain for some of the mothers as well (Ahluwalia, Grummer-Strawn, & Scanlon, 1997).

Further, smoking-related outcomes are dose-related. The more women smoke during pregnancy, the lower the weight of the newborn at delivery. The odds of a woman delivering an infant weighing less than 5½ pounds increases by 26 percent for every five cigarettes she smokes per day (Christianson, 1990). Smoking may be especially harmful during the last three months (particularly the last month) when the fetus normally gains weight. Specifically, smoking may affect birth weight by directly interfering with nutrition through physiologically depressing the mother's weight gain or indirectly through decreasing her nutritional intake. Smoking causes inadequate nutrition by causing difficulties in absorbing and/or metabolizing calcium, vitamin B12, and vitamin C (Diebel, 1990). The fetus may be compromised from poor assimilation of nutrients rather than the toxic effects of tobacco alone.

In addition, smoking may increase the chance that the placenta will separate too soon from the womb, causing a miscarriage (Mills, 1999). Babies born to smoking mothers are twice as likely to have heart anomalies (Batshaw & Conlon, 1997). Nicotine, a powerful stimulant, also appears to restrict blood vessels in the placenta. Smoking increases the carbon monoxide level in the blood, which slows blood flow through the placenta, in turn, causing the blood to absorb less oxygen. Thus, smoking may be linked to impaired fetal brain development. Peter Fried and Barbara Watkinson (1990) found in examining children for whom prenatal exposure to cigarettes had been previously ascertained that exposure to cigarette smoking was significantly associated with poorer language development and lower cognitive scores.

© David Young-Wolfe, PhotoEdit

Smoking is associated with low birth weight infants, perhaps caused by the infant's inability to absorb and metabolize nutrients from the mother.

In investigating the long-term consequences of pregnant mothers who smoked, those who did not smoke, and those who were exposed to second hand smoke, researchers found that at ages 6 to 9, the children of nonsmoking mothers performed better than children of smoking mothers on tests of speech and language skills, intelligence, visual/spatial abilities, and on the mother's rating of behavior (Makin, Fried, Watkinson, 1991). The performances of children exposed to passive smoke, in most areas, fell between those of children of the active smoking and nonsmoking mothers.

Although the long-term effects of smoking have not been established conclusively, one must conclude that smoking is harmful to fetal development. Despite the fact that the nicotine and tar content of cigarettes has decreased, there has not been a significant beneficial effect on birth weight or perinatal mortality (Naeye, 1998). Protection of the fetus can come about only by the mother's quitting smoking.

Alcohol

Varying levels of alcohol use during the *entire* pregnancy have been associated with a variety of fetal problems (Maier, Chen, Miller, & West, 1997), such as an increased incidence of stillbirths, midtrimester spontaneous abortions, congenital abnormalities, growth retardation, and delayed physical and mental development (Chen & West, 1999).

Blood ethanol levels in the fetus are compatible with those of the mother (Roebuck, Simmons, Mattson, & Riley, 1998). However, alcohol may stay in the fetus's system longer than in the mother's because the immature liver of the fetus is only half as effective in breaking down alcohol. Of course, the degree to which intrauterine exposure to any drug affects the fetus will depend on the type of drug ingested, the amount consumed, and individual or genetic factors in the mother and the fetus. The type of teratogenic effects on the developing organism can range from death to malformation, growth deficiency, and behavioral abnormalities.

Large quantities of oxygen are required to metabolize alcohol. When a pregnant woman drinks heavily, she draws oxygen away from the fetus that is vital for cell growth in the brain. Thus, it is not surprising that a wide variety of problematic classroom behaviors can be seen later in childhood. Attentional, activity, information-processing, and academic difficulties all show a significant correlation with prenatal alcohol exposure (Olson, Sampson, Barr, Streissguth, & Bookstein, 1992). The long-term effects of maternal binge drinking and drinking in the very early stages of pregnancy still can be seen in their children's later school performance.

Fetal Alcohol Syndrome (FAS)

> Hal is the fourth child born to Krista, who had problems with alcoholism during her pregnancy. Born at term, Hal weighed only four pounds. He displayed the typical features of FAS—small head, widely spaced eyes, an upturned nose, large ears, and a small chin. He had a ventricular heart defect. When tested at age 4, he was found to have mental retardation, requiring intermittent supports. (Batshaw, 1997)

Children born with fetal alcohol syndrome are those who are genetically vulnerable and whose mothers were heavy drinkers (five or more drinks daily) during pregnancy.

The term **fetal alcohol syndrome** (FAS) describes the symptoms observed in infants subjected to high levels of alcohol in utero; it is the leading cause of developmental disabilities and birth defects in the United States (Kaemingk & Paquette, 1999). It is now well established that heavy alcohol consumption during pregnancy (over eight units a day; a unit of alcohol is equivalent to half a pint of ordinary lager, beer, or cider; a single measure of spirits; or a single glass of wine) can result in a child being born with FAS (Fullilove & Dieudonne, 1996). The Centers for Disease Control estimate that more than 8000 alcohol-affected babies are born each year in the United States and that a further 36,000 infants are affected by fetal alcohol effects (FAE). Children who do not have enough characteristics for a diagnosis of FAS are often called possible FAS, or *fetal alcohol effects* (FAE) (Abel, 1998).

fetal alcohol syndrome (FAS) A condition in which a child suffers from growth deficiency, dysmorphogenic characteristics, and central nervous system manifestations; caused by alcohol consumption during pregnancy.

As many as 86 percent of women drink at least once during pregnancy, and experts estimate that between 20 to 35 percent of pregnant women drink regularly (Olson, 1998). Elisabeth Rosenthal (1994) discovered in her sample of highly educated women (39 percent had postgraduate degrees) that 30 percent consumed more than one drink a week during pregnancy; only 11 percent smoked.

FAS is a birth defect consisting of three types of features: facial characteristics, growth deficiency, and central nervous system manifestations. To be diagnosed with FAS, it is necessary to have some manifestations from each of the three categories and a history of heavy in utero exposure to alcohol. The facial characteristics include a flat midface, a thin upper lip, and/or a small chin. The height and/or weight growth deficiency originates in the womb and continues postnatally. Alcohol influences the developing fetus directly because it crosses the placenta and enters the fetal bloodstream, but it also has indirect effects by disturbing the functions and interactions of maternal and fetal hormones (Gabriel, Hofmann, Glavas, & Weinberg, 1998). The indirect adverse effects interfere with the activities of the growth hormone, which promotes body growth.

Research presents evidence that the central nervous system (CNS) is also sensitive to the effects of alcohol. Characteristics demonstrating that the child's central nervous system has been affected include small head, tremulousness, seizures, slow development, hyperactivity, learning problems, attentional deficits, and/or memory problems (Roebuck, Simmons, Mattson, & Riley, 1998; Streissguth, Sampson, & Barr, 1989). FAS results in a decrease in the overall size of the brain and, because the total number of cells is reduced, diminished thickness of the outer layers of the brain (the cortex), as well as reductions in the volume of deep cerebral white matter. There is also evidence that some parts of the brain are more sensitive to the teratogenic impact of alcohol than others (Roebuck, Mattson, & Riley, 1999). Findings suggest that the parts of the brain that are most susceptible to damage are those that are involved in language, verbal learning, fine-motor skills, and visual-motor integration (Mattson, Riley, Gramling, Delis, & Jones, 1998).

There appears to be a relationship between the amount of alcohol consumed and the severity of the syndrome (Ott, Tarter, & Ammerman, 1999). Mild symptoms can occur if the mother ingests two drinks daily, and most often includes low birth weight as one of its features. Of women who drink moderately (1–1.5 oz/day) in the first trimester, 11 percent gave birth to children with alcohol-related abnormalities. Infants born to social (or moderate) drinkers also have been born with low birth weights, abnormal heart rates, and lower IQs (Allan, Weeber, Savage, & Caldwell, 1997). Women who consume 2 to 4 ounces of hard liquor daily have a 10 percent chance of producing a child with FAS; the percentage increases to 50 percent if the woman consumes 10 ounces or more of whiskey or a six-pack of beer. Approximately 30 to 40 percent of infants born to alcoholic mothers develop complete fetal alcohol syndrome (Fullilove & Dieudonne, 1997). Eight drinks a day will produce the full FAS syndrome for most babies (Barr, Streissguth, Darby, & Sampson, 1990). Although eight drinks per day constitute a major risk, no safe levels of alcohol ingestion have been established and, therefore, it is probably best that pregnant women abstain from drinking. Damage caused by alcohol seems to be permanent.

Thought CHALLENGE

Should criminal charges be brought against pregnant women who abuse drugs?

Illicit Drugs

Heroin

Heroin, a narcotic or opiate, may cause deafness, heart defects, and malformed limbs, as well as behavioral disorders and neurological defects (Wilson, 1989). It has been established that infants born to heroin-addicted mothers are, on the average, small for gestational age, with approximately 50 percent below 5½ pounds at birth (Fricker & Segal, 1988).

Fetuses have been observed to kick violently when their addicted mother is denied heroin. This is seen as evidence of intrauterine stress on the developing fetus (Chavkin & Breitbart, 1997). The fetus may be undergoing periodic withdrawal in utero; this kicking subsides when the mother is given the proper dose of the heroin. Researchers believe these repeated withdrawals could create a risk of lack of oxygen to the fetus' brain that may result in brain damage or neurological impairment (Householder, Hatcher, Burns, & Chasnoff, 1992).

An estimated 70 to 90 percent of the infants born to opiate-addicted mothers also undergo some degree of withdrawal (Cornelius, Day, Richardson, & Taylor, 1999). Heroin withdrawal is manifested by a number of symptoms. The most frequent are those of the central nervous system restlessness; incessant, shrill crying; inability to sleep; and breathing difficulties), increased muscle tone, hyperactive reflexes, tremors, and in severe cases generalized convulsions (Mayes, Feldman, Granger, Haynes, Bornstein, & Schottenfeld, 1997). Infants exposed to heroin, or methadone, are significantly smaller at birth and have a higher incidence of intrauterine growth retardation than infants born to drug-free mothers (Wilson, 1989).

Cocaine

> Jon was born at term to a 24-year-old who was a crack-cocaine user up to the time of delivery. Jon weighed only 4½ pounds, and his head circumference was small. In the first days of life, he was irritable and ate poorly. He often sucked his fists as if very hungry but failed to drink his formula. He cried inconsolably and did not like to be held. He did best when swaddled in a blanket and rocked. Even then, he had a hard time sleeping and exhibited startled responses to the slightest noise.

Cocaine is reportedly used by 4 to 5 percent of pregnant women nationwide (Field, 1998). This figure, however, varies significantly in different urban areas; for example, in Washington, D.C., use of cocaine is almost three times this amount (14.7 percent) (Visscher, Bray, & Kroutil, 1999). Linda Mayes (1999) reports that from 17 to 50 percent of women who receive prenatal care at Yale New Haven Hospital use cocaine or crack cocaine two or three times a week throughout their pregnancies. Mayes estimates that nationwide, at least 40,000 and perhaps as many as 375,000 infants born each year have been exposed to cocaine in utero.

The severity of the symptoms is directly related to the drug dosage taken by the mother. Gastrointestinal symptoms are frequent. Infants may frantically mouth their hands as if in extreme hunger, yet feedings are taken poorly, and vomiting, diarrhea, and progressive weight loss are common. Other symptoms include yawning, sneezing, stretching, sweating, nasal stuffiness, and skin pallor. Poor temperature regulation and fever often signal severe withdrawal symptoms.

Cocaine is now believed to be more harmful to the fetus than any other drug, heroin included, and irrevocably affects the infant's brain chemistry, altering neurochemical transmitters in the brain and putting the infant at terrible risk both for his or her life and developmental outcome (Behnke, Eyler, Conlon, Casanova, & Woods, 1997; Martin, Barr, Martin, & Streissguth, 1996; Mirochnick, Meyer, Cole, & Zuckerman, 1991).

Ira Chasnoff and his colleagues (Chasnoff, Anson, Hatcher, Stenson, Iaukea, & Randolph, 1998) report that mothers who use cocaine have higher rates of spontaneous abortions, abruptio placentae (separation of the placenta from the uterine wall prior to delivery), and neonatal neurobehavioral deficiencies. They also suffer from a higher rate of premature labor and delivery, and intrauterine growth retardation (Fulroth, Phillips, & Durant, 1989). Cocaine use during pregnancy is related to reductions in infant birth weight, length, and head circumference, and an increase in sudden infant death syndrome (Batshaw & Conlon, 1997).

Cocaine is a stimulant; however, in the infant it depresses the central nervous system and causes a drowsy "shut down" behavior, sometimes described as hypersomnolence. The cocaine-exposed infant's responses to stimuli are delayed; once the stimulus breaks through the infant's hypersomnolent state, he or she is difficult to console. Although irritable, these infants rarely become aroused enough to sustain a vigorous cry, the result of a depressed central nervous system (Woods, Eyler, Behnke, & Conlon, 1993).

The majority of cocaine-exposed infants can be classified as "fragile" infants who are easily overloaded by environmental stimuli (Inciardi, Surratt, & Saum, 1997; Kramer, Locke, Ogunyemi, & Nelson, 1990). Cocaine-exposed infants have very few self-protective mechanisms for avoiding overstimulation and require considerable assistance from caretakers to maintain control of their hyperexcitable nervous systems. When using the Brazelton Neonatal Test (Brazelton, 1984) shortly after birth, cocaine-exposed newborns often make abrupt state changes that are inappropriate for the level of stimulation being presented. One pattern that was quite common in these newborns is the inability to sleep or cry to shut themselves off from external stimulation (Richardson, Conroy, & Day, 1996).

Marijuana

Perhaps the only definitive statement to be made about marijuana use during pregnancy and its consequences upon the offspring is that there is a surprising scarcity of consistent results. Some studies reveal no difference between marijuana users and control subjects who are matched in terms of alcohol consumption, cigarette use, and family income on outcome measures such as type of presentation at birth, Apgar status (a behavioral assessment test given to newborns), and the frequency of complications or major physical anomalies at birth (Fried, 1989; Fried, Watkinson, & Siegel, 1997). Other studies, however, have shown that marijuana use during pregnancy is associated with a variety of adverse outcomes, including prematurity, low birth weight, decreased

Thought **CHALLENGE**

The infant has rights as soon as it is born. Should it have rights before it is born?

TABLE 4.4

Prescription and Other Frequently Used Drugs and Their Known or Suspected Effects

Prescription	Effects
Alcohol	Mental retardation, growth retardation, facial and heart defects, behavioral problems
Amphetamines	(Stimulants for the central nervous system; some types frequently used for weight control) Fetal intrauterine growth retardation; increased amounts and duration of exposure prenatally found to be correlated with aggressive behavior in 8-year-olds
Antibiotics (streptomycin, tetracycline)	Streptomycin associated with hearing loss. Tetracycline associated with staining the baby's teeth if exposure occurs during the second or third trimester
Aspirin	Possible IQ decrement, poorer balance, and fine-motor unsteadiness
Barbiturates	(Sedatives and anxiety reducers) Newborns may show withdrawal symptoms. No consistent long-term effects in humans have been found
Benzodiazepines	(Tranquilizers) Not shown to have teratogenic effects; newborns may show withdrawal symptoms
Caffeine	Low birth weight, miscarriage, stillbirths
Cigarettes	Low birth weight, premature delivery, learning disorders
Cocaine	Stillbirth, neurological and behavioral problems
Heroin, morphine, methadone	Motor and attentional deficits, low birth weight, prematurity
Lithium	(Treatment for bipolar disorder) Strong suggestive evidence of increased cardiovascular defects in human infants
Marijuana	Premature delivery, failure to habituate
Thalidomide	(Reduces morning sickness or anxiety) Deformities of the limbs, depending on the time of exposure, often accompanied by mental retardation
Vitamins	Vitamin A in large amounts may cause birth defects. Excessive amounts of other vitamins may also cause prenatal malformations

maternal weight gain, complications of pregnancy, difficult labor, increased stillbirths, and perinatal mortality (Nahas, Sutin, Harvey, Agurell, Pace, & Cancro, 1999). A summary of the possible effects of teratogens is found in Table 4.4.

Chemical Hazards to Sperm

Kate and Raul had one healthy child, and shortly after Raul was hired for a new job working for a manufacturing company that used a chemical derived from benzene, a known carcinogen, they began trying to have a second. Although they had no trouble conceiving their first child, their attempts at having a second child were unsuccessful; Kate had two miscarriages. Kate remembered hearing that two other men in Raul's small office were also suffering from unexplainable infertility. After a year, Raul found a new job in a chemical-free workplace, so the couple decided to try once more to have a baby. Kate conceived immediately, and last August she gave birth to a healthy boy.

Some scientists are challenging the double standard that leads women to overhaul their lives before pregnancy—avoiding stress, champagne, cigarettes—while fathers are left with the misconception that what they do has little or no bearing on their child's future health and physical well-being. Evidence is accumulating that challenges this assumption. Male-mediated abnormalities have been reported after exposure to therapeutic and recreational drugs and to chemicals in the workplace and environment. The impact on their child's outcome includes an increased risk for congenital malformations, spontaneous abortions, low birth weight, and increased risk for childhood cancers (Friedler, 1996).

Some of the best-known evidence that chemicals can harm sperm comes from research on male U.S. veterans of the Vietnam War. These soldiers were exposed

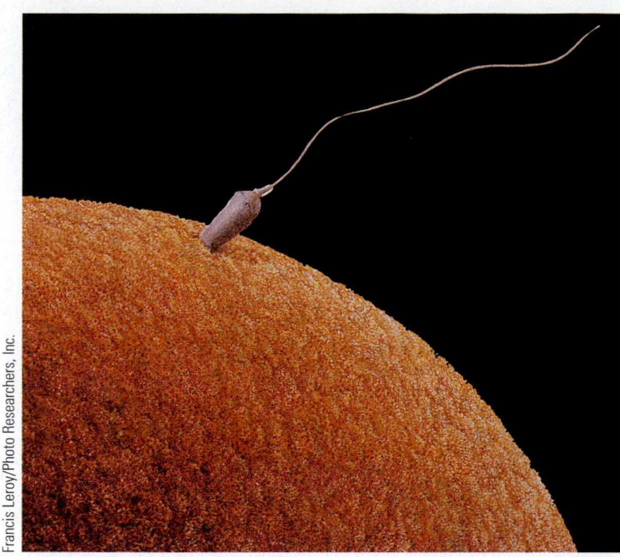
Francis Leroy/Photo Researchers, Inc.

Conception occurs when a sperm cell penetrates an egg cell, forming a zygote. Almost immediately, the wall of the new zygote changes so that no other sperm can enter.

to the herbicide Agent Orange (dioxin), and studies have shown that these veterans had almost twice the risk of other men of fathering infants with one or more major malformations (Rosenheck & Fontana, 1998). Babies born to fathers who work in unsafe chemical environments in the months before conception are at significantly higher risks for physical and developmental problems (Paul, 1997; Schnitzer, Olshan, & Erickson, 1995). Paternal marijuana and cocaine use appear to contribute to risk for heart problems in their offspring (Ewing, Loffredo, & Beaty, 1997).

Preimplantation Genetic Testing

Despite the fact that fathers may contribute to the health and physical integrity of the developing fetus, there are no tests available to pre-identify sperm likely to cause defects. Risk factors for men, however, can be easily prevented. Because new sperm supplies occur every 90 days (King, 1999), it takes a comparatively short time to start creating healthy sperm. Equally important, however, is acknowledging the father's role in producing healthy children. As evidence accumulates that the father's sperm is delicate and influential in determining the physical integrity of the developing fetus the balance of responsibility may shift and fathers-to-be may become more mindful of their role in producing healthy offspring.

Assessing the healthiness of the woman's egg, however, is possible through *preimplantation genetic testing*. **Preimplantation genetic testing** enables doctors to examine the health of the egg before fertilization. It works like this: as the egg prepares itself for fertilization, the cells' original second set of 23 maternal chromosomes is discarded in what is called a *polar body*. In the first of a two-step cell division that produces an egg with 23 chromosomes, division of the 46-chromosome germ cell distributes 23 chromosomes to each of the two daughter cells. But one cell, destined to develop into the egg, receives the lion's share of nutrients, while the other, called the first polar body, is deprived and scrawny by comparison. The egg and its first polar body are stuck together in the ovary.

An egg can carry either an unhealthy gene for a particular disease or the normal gene, but not both. By examining the chromosomes in the polar body, the health of the egg can be deduced. If the woman is a carrier for a genetic disease, when the chromosomes are divvied up between the polar body and the egg, one normal gene goes to one, and the disease-causing gene to the other. So, if the polar body is examined and found to have the disease-causing gene for cystic fibrosis, then it can be inferred that the corresponding egg does not. The healthy egg can then be artificially fertilized and implanted in the woman's body.

Knowledge about the harmful effects of teratogens and abstaining from their use renders, in most cases, a healthy environment for the developing fetus. Even in cases of pregnant drug users, detoxification followed by drug-free living leads to a statistically significant improvement in the birth outcome (Kyei, Acker, & MacBain, 1998). There are, of course, occasions when the fetus does not develop properly because of genetic and unpreventable reasons. Still, prenatal care is essential in promoting the health of the mother and the fetus.

preimplantation genetic testing
In this experimental procedure, ova and sperm from the parents are collected, fertilized, and grown in the laboratory. Then a number of developing preembryonic cells are subjected to DNA analysis. A healthy preembryo is selected and implanted into the mother, where it can complete its prenatal development.

Concept Checks

1. The transmission of HIV infection from mothers to infants most likely occurs through
   a. cesarean section delivery.
   b. fetal blood transfusions with contaminated blood.
   c. the virus crossing the placenta.

2. Infants who are fragile and exhibit tremors, irritability, and a shrill cry most likely had mothers who abused ______________ while pregnant.
   a. marijuana
   b. heroin
   c. PCP dust
3. Mary Ella smoked heavily during pregnancy. Her newborn will most likely be
   a. underweight.
   b. mentally retarded.
   c. hyperactive.

Conception and Prenatal Development

Before Beginning . . .

After reading this section, you will be able to

- discuss fertilization processes.
- identify the germinal, embryonic, and fetal phases of gestation.

Conception

An author of a recent best-selling book on sexuality wrote to her readers, "The safest time to have sex in terms of not getting pregnant is shortly after ovulation." Several thousand copies were printed before the error was discovered; this is the time when pregnancy is most likely to occur! Many young individuals learn about sexuality from their well-meaning but, perhaps, misinformed friends. So to avoid any misconceptions about fertilization processes, a brief review follows.

The Female Reproductive System

The sex cell of the female is call an *ovum,* or egg, and is one of the largest cells in the human body. It is about 0.006 inch (or 0.15 millimeter) in diameter. The ova are produced by two oval-shaped ovaries that are located in the pelvic cavity. During embryonic development of a human female, several hundred minute structures known as *ovarian follicles* form in the ovaries. Each follicle consists of a cell, which is destined to become an ovum. When a female reaches sexual maturity, one of these follicles matures approximately each month. When the cell enlarges into a primary oocyte it bursts, releasing the ovum (a process known as **ovulation**), which then enters one of the fallopian tubes. Each tube is 4 to 5 inches long and from 0.2 to 0.6 inch in diameter.

ovulation Producing and discharging ova.

The Male Reproductive System

The main parts of the male reproductive system are the testes, which produce the hormones testosterone and androsterone. These hormones are responsible for the development at puberty of secondary sex characteristics: lowering of the voice, facial and pubic hair, and thick muscles. The testes also produce millions of sperm cells. These individual sperm are small, approximately 0.002 inch from head to tail. *Spermatozoa,* when combined with secretions from other internal organs, form semen, which is ejaculated by the penis during intercourse. The sperm cell, with its long tail and pointed head, swims 6 or 7 inches on its journey to reach the ovum (King, 1999).

Fertilization

Ovulation occurs during mid-cycle, and conception is most likely to occur during a six-day period ending on the day of ovulation (Wilcox, Weinberg, & Baird, 1995). If conception does not occur, the ovum disintegrates and conception cannot occur until the next ovulation. However, if in the ovum's journey down the fallopian tube, it encounters healthy spermatozoa and one of the sperm manages to penetrate the wall of the egg, life processes begin.

As noted in Chapter 3, occasionally, two ova are released during ovulation instead of one. If both are fertilized, fraternal, or dizygotic, twins result. Occasionally, a fertilized egg will split and two separate embryos will develop. Because they originated from the same zygote, they have the same genetic structure and are called identical, or monozygotic, twins. Triplets, quadruplets, and quintuplets may be identical, fraternal, or a combination.

The chances of having twins are 1 in 96. The chances of having triplets are 1 in 9216, quadruplets 1 in 900,000, and quintuplets 1 in 85 million (Leiblum & Greenfeld, 1997). Giving birth to more than one child depends on many factors: the mother's age, the history of multiple births in the family, and the use of fertility drugs. These drugs are generally given to females who have reduced egg production. Fertility drugs, however, cause superovulation, in which the woman releases several ova, increasing the odds of multiple births.

An astounding 300 to 500 million sperm are released in a single ejaculation. This is a large, but necessary number, because only a few hundred sperm are able to reach the fallopian tube, which harbors the ovum. The sperm, upon penetrating the ovum, releases a substance that makes the surface of the egg impermeable to other sperm. After penetrating the egg, the sperm loses its tail, and the head becomes a cell nucleus. Typically, conception takes place in the fallopian tube, from which the fertilized egg, or zygote, travels down into the uterus and implants in the lining of the uterus. The nuclei from the egg and the sperm lose their nuclear membranes and unite into a single set of 23 pairs of chromosomes (46)—and a new life begins.

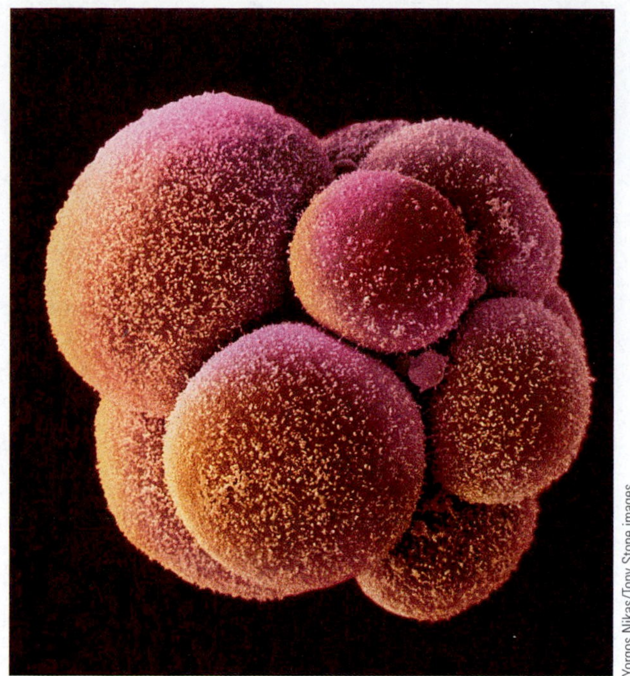

Yorgos Nikas/Tony Stone images

At fertilization, sperm and ovum combine to form a zygote with forty-six chromosomes in twenty-three pairs.

The Infant's Gestation Period: Three Stages

Prenatal life can be divided into three phases. The first phase of development, the **germinal period**, lasts from fertilization until the time the zygote is firmly implanted in the wall of the uterus, a process that takes between 10 and 14 days. This phase of development is followed by the *embryonic period,* which begins in the third week in utero and lasts through the eighth week. The **fetal period** lasts from the ninth week until delivery.

Germinal Period

During the *germinal period,* the process of cell division begins a few hours after fertilization of the ovum and produces two cells. The zygote wanders through a fallopian tube and the uterus for up to eight days. As it free-floats, the original cells divide until they become a 60-to-70-cell mass called a **blastocyst**, a hollow ball of cells. During the formation of the blastocyst, the cells begin the processes of differentiation; that is, they separate into groups according to their future function. The blastocyst secretes a hormone that inhibits menstruation, allowing itself to continue to grow.

Implantation, the major developmental task of the germinal period, then begins. The colony of cells does not simply attach itself to the uterine wall but actually digs into it. Small, rootlike extensions have begun to grow outside the blastocyst, and it is by means of these tendrils that it will rupture the small blood vessels of the uterine wall to obtain nourishment. At the time of implantation, the blastocyst is about the size of a pinhead. Implantation enables the developing organism to absorb nutrients from the blood vessels of the endometrium for its subsequent growth and development. The process of implantation is difficult; more than half of the blastocysts never become implanted, usually because they are abnormal in some way. The blastocyst that fails to implant is lost in the normal menstrual cycle. If implantation is successful, growth continues. (See Figure 4.4.)

Embryonic Period

After the blastocyst successfully attaches itself to the uterine wall, development enters the *embryonic period.* The growing organism is no longer called a blastocyst but an embryo. The prominent task of this

germinal period
In the first two weeks of gestation, the process of cell division begins; implantation is the major developmental task of this period.

fetal period
Lasts from the ninth week of gestation until delivery; a period marked by the continued elaboration and growth of the basic systems and ossification.

blastocyst
The zygote three days after fertilization; the tiny mass of cells forms a hollow, fluid-filled sphere that looks like a miniature mulberry.

implantation
Takes place during the germinal period when the trophoblast burrows itself into the uterine wall to obtain nourishment.

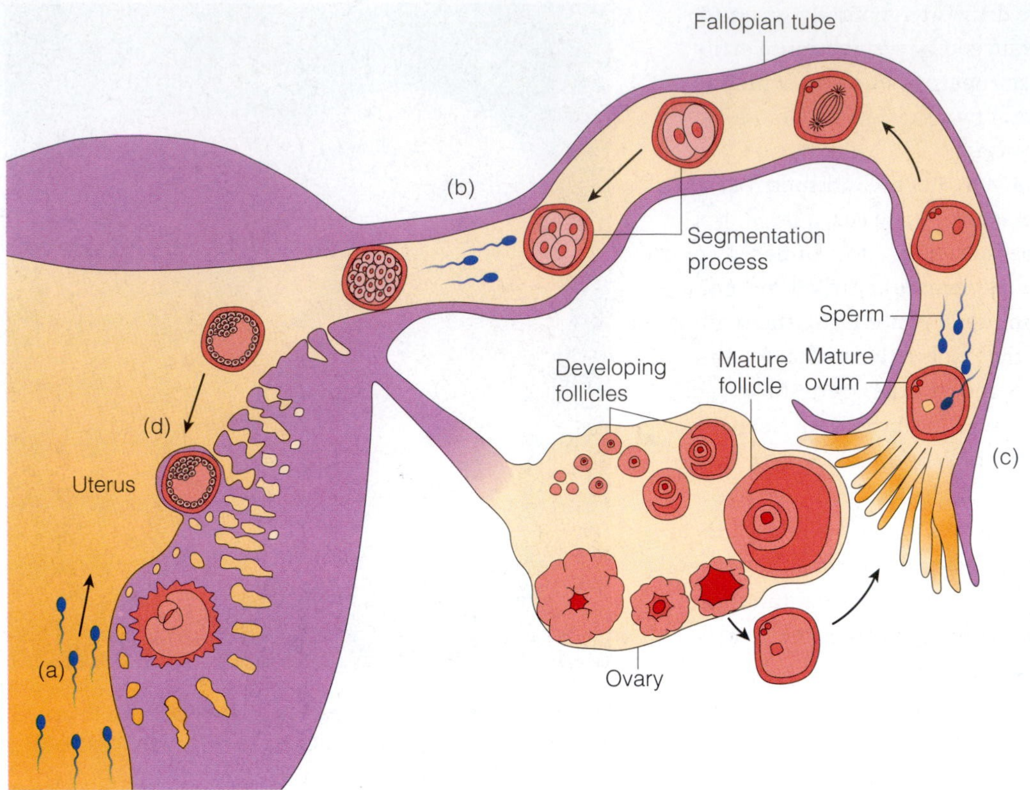

FIGURE 4.4 *Fertilization and Implantation*

(a) Millions of sperm cells have entered the vagina and are finding their way into the uterus. (b) Some of the spermatozoa are moving up the fallopian tube (there is a similar tube on the other side) toward the ovum. (c) Fertilization occurs. The fertilized ovum drifts down the tube, dividing and forming new cells as it goes, until it implants itself in the wall of the uterus (d) by the seventh or eighth day after fertilization.

period is differentiation and development of organs. By the end of this period, differentiation is complete but organ development is not. Cells become so rapidly differentiated that the organism's features become distinctly human. Differentiation of body structures is now 95 percent complete. By the third week, a primitive heart has developed and begun to beat. (The heart is one of the larger organs of the body.) By the end of four weeks, the embryo is 3⁄16 of an inch (0.6 cm). A system for digesting food has begun to form and the first series of kidneylike structures emerge. The embryo's skeleton is flexible cartilage. Sometime during the eighth week bone cells begin to replace the cartilage cells, a process called *ossification*.

By the end of this period, the tiny being has the rudimentary beginnings of arms, legs, fingers, and toes, a heart that beats, a brain, a liver that secretes bile, lungs, and all the other major organs—all of this before many mothers even know they are pregnant! The organism, however, could not survive outside the womb because it still lacks the ability to breathe.

The single most crucial phase of embryonic development is the emergence of the future brain, and early brain development is stunningly fast. As Marian Diamond and Janet Hopson (1998) describe it:

> Let's say the fertilization of an egg took place on a Monday. By Thursday, the embryo would consist of thirty cells clustered together like a colorless blackberry no bigger than a pinpoint. By Saturday, the cluster would have burrowed into the woman's uterine wall, and by Tuesday of the second week, a layer would have emerged within the cluster, des-

tined to become the ectoderm, or future skin, sense organs, and the nervous system, brain included. (p. 39)

By the time the embryo is just 4 weeks old, three sections of the embryo's fore-, mid-, and hindbrain have already begun to form: At 7 weeks, the organism's forebrain balloons out into two delicate little bubbles, each a future cerebral hemisphere. At this stage, however, they are no larger than a pea and have two-layered walls no thicker than a human hair. Neurologists estimate that between 50,000 and 100,000 new brain cells are generated *each second* between the 5th and 20th weeks of gestation (Shore, 1997). As brain cells continue to form, a second great drama unfolds—migration. As the organism develops, brains cells have to find their way up the cerebral wall, sliding up elongated cells called glial fibers until they reach their precise position within the cerebral cortex—our thinking brain.

The sequence and timing of this process must adhere to a very precise schedule if normal development is to occur. As a cell climbs this cortical "ladder," it comes into contact with the numerous cells that it passes on its rise to the top. This contact activates various *genes* that define the cell's identity, location, and mission. (Roughly 60 percent of genes in the human body are dedicated to brain development!) But, if anything interrupts or sidetracks this journey—such as exposure to adverse environmental conditions or lack of nutrition—the effects can be devastating. The delicate nature of this cell migration process explains, in part, why substance abuse or poor nutrition can have a long-lasting impact on the developing child.

These astounding feats of development could not take place without the aid of the placenta, which until birth will supply the developing child with oxygen and nutrients. The umbilical cord connects the embryo to the placenta. This lifeline consists of three large blood vessels, one to provide nutrients from the mother and two to carry the embryo's waste products into the mother's body—a process that continues until the child is born.

It is important to note that the mother and child do not actually share the same blood system and that the exchange of nutritive and waste materials occurs across cell membranes in the placenta. These semipermeable membranes keep bloodstreams separate and selectively allow certain substances such as oxygen, salts, drugs, vitamins, some nutrients (protein and sugar), and other substances of small molecular size to pass through to nourish the embryo. Blood cells are too large to pass through these membranes, so there is no direct link between the circulatory system of the mother and that of the embryo. Bodies carrying immunity also pass through the membranes from the mother to the embryo, thus giving the child some protection for several months after birth from diseases to which the mother is immune.

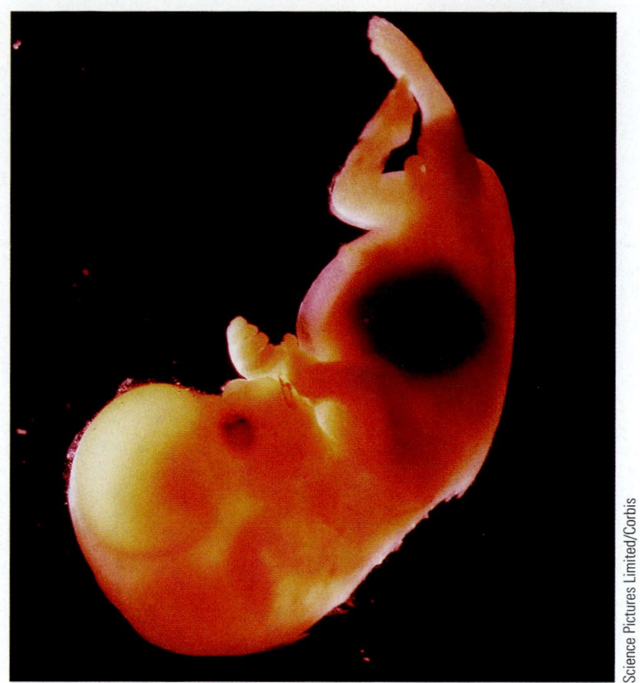
Science Pictures Limited/Corbis

At 10 to 12 weeks after conception, the head is one-third of the body size.

Fetal Period

The *fetal period* is marked by continued elaboration and growth of the basic systems and ossification. Growth proceeds in two directions: cephalocaudal (head to tail) and proximodistal (spine to extremities). At birth, the head will make up 22 percent of the infant's height, a proportion that changes dramatically with age. The fetus increases in size and maturation so that it begins to show some independent functioning. Organs, limbs, and muscles become functional. Even with eyes sealed shut, the infant can frown and squint. It is able to open and close its mouth and by doing so swallow a few small gulps of amniotic fluid. Table 4.5 summarizes intrauterine development.

TABLE 4.5

Milestones in Fetal Development	
Milestone	**Development**
End of third month	3 in.; 1 oz. Head is one-third of body size. First external sign of gender differentiation becomes apparent: the penis and scrotum in the male and the beginning of the labia in the female. Small buds for teeth form. Nose bridge develops. Ossification continues. Fetus moves spontaneously.
End of fourth month	6½–7 in.; ½–1 lb. At the beginning of the 4th month, fetus weighs 1 oz and is roughly 3½ in. tall; no month shows a comparable growth rate. Physician can detect heartbeat (120–160 beats per minute). Although eyes are fused shut, frowning occurs. Hands become capable of gripping.
End of fifth month	10–12 in.; ½–1 lb. Fetus increases the amount of force of its movement; mother will be able to feel an elbow, foot, or head. Sleep cycle organizes, as do reflexes for swallowing and hiccupping. Eyelashes and eyebrows appear. Soft hair (lanugo) grows over body. Fetus undergoes process of skin-cell replacement. Skin cells mix with fatty substances from oil glands to form white, cheesy coating called vernix caseosa, which helps prevent the skin from hardening in the mineral-laden amniotic fluid.
End of sixth month	10–14 in.; 1¼–1½ lb. Ossification is still taking place. Head becomes less disproportionate to rest of body. Eyelids separate. Skin is wrinkled.
End of seventh month	13–17 in.; 2½–3 lb. Age of viability (if the fetus is born, it has a reasonable chance to survive, although special care is required). Premature infants born at this stage still have poorly developed sleep-wake cycles, and breathing is irregular.
End of eighth month	16–18 in.; 4½–5 lb. Skin is less wrinkled. Bones of head are soft. Subcutaneous fat is deposited.
End of ninth month	20 in.; 7–7½ lb. Additional subcutaneous fat accumulates. Lanugo hair is shed. Antibodies are received from mother's blood. Movement is quite restricted. Fetus begins to turn to a head-down position in preparation for birth.

Concept Checks

1. ***True or False:*** Typically, conception takes place in the female's fallopian tube.
2. ***True or False:*** During the germinal period, the process of cell division begins and a blastocyst is formed.

The Parents' Experience

Before Beginning . . .

After reading this section, you will be able to

- identify the psychological and physical changes that expectant couples experience in the three trimesters of pregnancy.

Pregnancy is a unique and significant experience for both the woman and her partner. In the following pages, we will look at the experiences they may encounter during the nine-month gestation period.

The First Trimester

Several changes occur during the first three months of pregnancy. Menstruation ceases. As the milk glands in the breasts develop, the breasts increase in size. During the initial stages of pregnancy, women may feel tired, bloated, and sometimes, nauseous. Following a good nutritional diet may help modify some of these symptoms. Vaginal secretions may change or increase. Urination may become more frequent and bowel movements less regular. There is little increase, however, in the size of the woman's abdomen.

The first trimester is initially a time of adjustment to the idea of pregnancy and then a time of coping with the emotional and physical changes that occur over the next six or seven months. Trying to involve the male partner may be difficult at this stage. Many men react to the news of pregnancy by increasing their involvement with work or retreating to special interests, such as hobbies. Fathers-to-be adjust more slowly to their partner's pregnancy; the impact on mothers-to-be, however, is quicker.

Child Development Issues

Fathers—the Forgotten Parent?

Psychologically, men are just as pregnant as their wives, but, of course, in a sympathetic way. The extra support, understanding, and caring that are rightfully offered to his pregnant partner, however, are rarely accorded to the "pregnant dad." Fathers often get mixed messages as well, such as "Be an involved Dad" and the amendment "Be strong and silent." Fathers are told, "Thou shalt not upset the person carrying thy child." So, being supportive is okay; expressing anxiety or worry is not okay. We are often not very supportive of the impending fathers' concerns and feelings.

EXPECTANT FATHERS' CONCERNS

- He suddenly finds that his partner is unavailable emotionally.
- She may also be unavailable physically and sexually.
- He reflects on the impending changes the new baby will make in his and his partner's life.
- He believes that he should be strong enough to handle concerns but sometimes wonders if he is.
- He worries about financial or job concerns.
- He feels disconnected from sources of support (mainly his wife). (Shapiro, 1995)

EXPECTANT FATHERS' FEARS

- Although fathers may desire to be a part of childbirth, they often fear that they may not be able to "keep it together" in the delivery room.
- Usually during the second trimester, a powerful fear may develop surrounding the feeling that something might happen to his partner or baby.
- It is common and important for pregnant women to turn inward and begin bonding with the life growing inside of them. At such times, however, husbands may feel neglected.

EMOTIONAL CHANGES

It is important for fathers to expect, accept, and pay attention to the emotional changes they feel. They need to expect to be confronted with double messages from others indicating a desire for their presence and a simultaneous discomfort with their true feelings. Once fathers are aware of their concerns about the pregnancy, they need to share them with their pregnant partner. It is important that fathers have opportunities to talk about their concerns and joys about the pregnancy. Finally, fathers need to understand as well as they can their pregnant partner's shifting moods, fatigue, and physical symptoms (Garbarino, 1993).

Search Online

Explore InfoTrac College Edition, your online library. Go to **http://www.infotrac-college.com/wadsworth** and the passcode that came on the card with your book. Try these search terms: being father, father and parent, family leave.

As the pregnancy progresses, fathers do become quite involved—even physically. It is interesting to note that toothaches are so common among men whose wives are pregnant that dentists have been advised to ask men between the ages of 20 and 40 if their wife is pregnant when the cause of the tooth pain cannot be determined. Supportive fathers may have food cravings similar to their pregnant wives as well. Kyle Pruett (1995) finds that significant quantities of ice cream, eggs, milk, and cheeses enter men's diet during the second trimester of their wife's pregnancy. Fathers are sometimes seen as the forgotten parent (see Child Development Issues).

Second Trimester

During the second trimester, the mother experiences movement of the fetus and it becomes physically obvious that she is pregnant. Her waist thickens, and her abdomen begins to protrude. She now wears maternity clothes and adjusts to her new body image. Some women worry about weight gain. Obstetrical advice about the optimal amount of weight to gain has varied, but most medical professionals believe that a gain of 22 to 45 pounds is normal. Fetal movements may be felt in the fourth and fifth month—an exciting event for the parents-to-be. The breasts may now begin to secrete a thin yellowish fluid called colostrum. Women sometimes feel pressured because everything they do from taking an aspirin to eating a slice of pepperoni pizza is critically reviewed by others. However, men are not immune from social pressures; many may feel pressured by their wives or family to cut down on all-male social activities in recognition of their upcoming family responsibilities.

During the second trimester, in the Quiche community of Guatemala, mothers-to-be and their husbands tell the leaders of their village that they are going to have a child (Menchu, 2000). The child will not only belong to them but to the whole community and must follow their ancestors' traditions. The leaders then pledge the support of the community and become *abuelos* or "grandparents." It is also the custom for the pregnant mother's neighbors to visit her every day until the birth of the child and take her little things, no matter how simple. They stay and talk to her, and she tells them about her pregnancy.

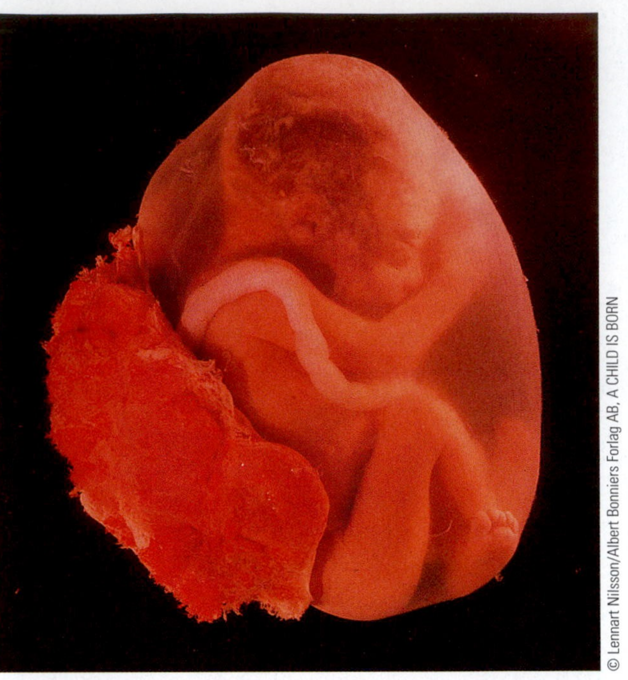

At 24 weeks in utero, the fetus increases the force of its movement. Mother can now feel an elbow, foot, or head.

Third Trimester

By the third trimester, the uterus and abdomen increase in size. The muscles of the uterus begin to occasionally contract, but this is painless. The enlarged uterus produces pressure on the woman's stomach, intestines, and bladder, which may cause an intensification of physical discomforts, such as tiredness, heartburn, muscle aches, and disturbed sleep. Couples are now generally busy buying baby supplies and making arrangements for space for the newborn. During this time, many mothers may be fearful that something will be wrong with their baby; this seems to be a universal fear. Some may experience ambivalence about having a baby. Participation in childbirth education classes may help to diminish these fears and concerns.

Guatemalan mothers, like the Chinese, believe that learning begins in the womb. In their third trimester, Guatemalan mothers will introduce their unborn babies to the natural world. The mother goes out into the fields or walks over the hills to show the baby the kind of life she leads. As she does her chores and tends to the animals, she believes her unborn child is learning about her—and its—future way of life (Menchu, 2000). She talks to the child continuously while it is in the womb, telling the child how hard life will be. It is a duty to her child that a mother must fulfill. It is as if she is a guide explaining things to a tourist, "You must never abuse nature and you must live your life as honestly as I do," she tells the fetus.

Concept Checks

Matching: Identify the trimester during which the following events take place.

a. first trimester

b. second trimester

c. third trimester

___ 1. Men may react to the pregnancy by increasing their involvement with work.

___ 2. Women's breasts enlarge and may secrete colostrum.

___ 3. The father may get "cravings" for ice cream.

___ 4. The abdomen increases in size and the woman is now wearing maternity clothes.

___ 5. Physical discomforts intensify for women.

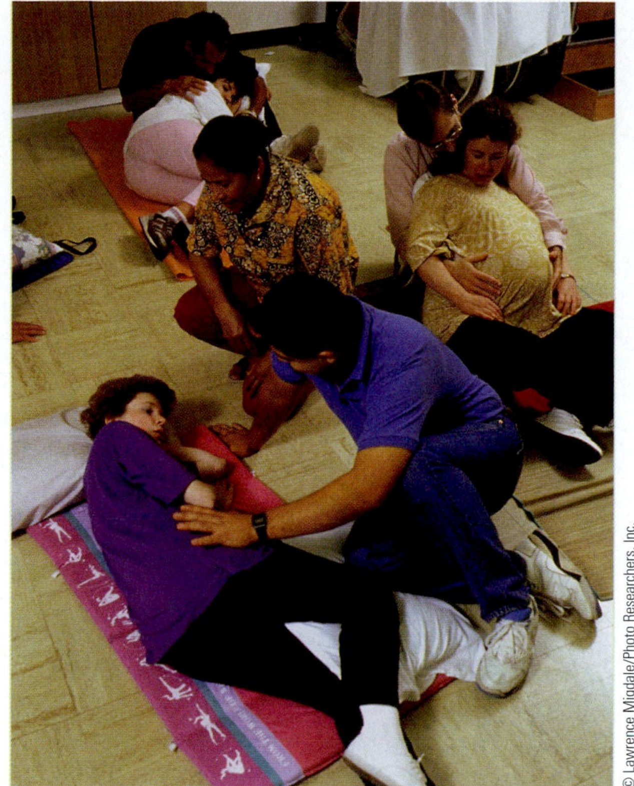

Fathers and other partners are welcome in Lamaze childbirth classes which teach relaxation techniques to reduce childbirth pain.

The Birth Process

Before Beginning . . .

After reading this section, you will be able to

- note the contemporary methods of childbirth.
- identify the three stages of the birth process.

Today, couples can make choices about where and how they want to deliver their child. In the past, delivering a child was a process with few choices. Fifty years ago, women "gratefully" received general anesthesia when going through the birthing process in a white, sterile, often austere, hospital environment (with an average 10-day hospital stay). The father, seen as a threat of infection, was not admitted into the delivery room. Couples, today, have many more birthing options, and the view of the father's presence has changed from one of a source of *infection* to a source of *affection* in the delivery room.

Contemporary Childbirth

The term *natural childbirth* has been applied with considerable variation. Most recently, it has come to mean the use of breathing or relaxation techniques during labor and delivery to provide the mother with psychological and physical tools for dealing with pain. Because these breathing and relaxation techniques require concentrated effort and hard work on the part of the parents, perhaps *prepared* or *educated childbirth* are more accurate terms for the process.

Painless, Relaxed Childbirth

Approaches to contemporary childbirth began when Grantly Dick-Read (1959) observed, as an obstetrician, that some women suffered horribly during labor and birth, whereas others experienced very little pain. What distinguished the relatively painless labors, he came to realize, was that these mothers were calm and relaxed. Fear and expectation of pain, Dick-Read pointed out, cause the body to become tense and, that tension increases and emphasizes the pain response. Dick-Read maintained that a program of education with breathing and relaxation exercises would eliminate or greatly reduce the need for drugs during labor and delivery. This advice may not be particularly earthshaking today, but it was in the late 1950s when he made these statements. At that time, the trend was to administer general anesthesia in labor to the mother to obliterate sensation entirely.

The best-known and most widely used system of breathing and relaxation exercises is the **Lamaze method**. These exercises teach a precise set of breathing techniques associated to the various stages of labor. Fernand Lamaze, like Dick-Read, also stresses the importance of factual education in preparation for childbirth. In a study of couples that attended childbirth classes in the United States, Italy, Germany, and France, the women felt more in control of the birth process and, in turn, had higher rates of

Lamaze method A series of exercises designed to teach breathing techniques associated with different stages of labor to ease the pain of delivery.

natural childbirth (Scopesi, Zanobini, & Carossino, 1997).

The father plays a crucial role in the Lamaze program as the exercise coach, timer of contractions, and major supporter. His support to his partner during labor may be the crucial factor. Several studies show the existence of a positive correlation between mothers' well-being and husbands' emotional support, as well as the link between mothers' mental health and other relatives' and friends' support (McKay & Yager Smith, 1993; Scopesi, Zanorini, & Carossino, 1997). In Mexico, for example, women are generally not accompanied by fathers but rather by a *doula*—a woman who provides continuous support to a woman during labor, delivery, and the immediate postpartum period. When comparing women in labor who are accompanied by a doula and those that are not, the former have a more positive and easier childbirth experience (Campero, Garcia, Diaz, Ortiz, Reynoso, & Langer, 1998).

The effectiveness of the Lamaze method has been supported by a variety of research studies, which suggest that women who attend classes have shorter labors, fewer complications, less anxiety, less medication, and healthier babies than other motivated women who do not take classes (Hughey, McElin, & Young, 1988). One criticism of the Lamaze training, however, is that the issue of pain medication is rarely addressed. The mother and father are encouraged to have strong, positive thoughts about labor and delivery and learn to envision an easygoing time. However, this could lead to unrealistic expectations in the woman regarding labor pain (Scopesis, Zanobini, & Carossino, 1997).

Thought CHALLENGE

By discouraging medication for pain during labor, does the Lamaze method lead mothers who decide they need some relief from the pain to emerge from the birth experience with a sense of failure?

Choosing a Birthing Center

Choosing a birthing center is an important decision. For some couples, a hospital delivery with complete medical backup systems seems optimal. Others, however, may desire the hominess and safety of an out-of-hospital birth center. Others may feel that home is the best place to deliver their child.

The overwhelming benefit of a hospital birth is the security of having medical help in the event of birth complications. Some women, however, complain of the "dehumanizing" atmosphere where they are often confined to a bed during labor, subjected to an overenthusiastic use of medication, and routinely separated from their families. As a result, some women are opting for what they see as a more humanistic environment. Most hospitals, in trying to humanize the childbirth experience, have "rooming-in" facilities, in which the mother and newborn are together continuously. In addition, an increasing number of hospitals have "birthing rooms," which are decorated to resemble more homelike settings. There are also homelike, birthing centers located outside the hospital. In these settings, there is always a nurse/midwife in attendance.

A nurse/midwife's training generally entails a course of study of one to two years after the nursing degree. During training, the midwife will attend approximately 150 births. Licensed midwives do not practice independently but rather are found on the staff of a clinic, health center, maternity center, or hospital. In the United States, they are always members of a health-care team.

In Japanese hospitals, midwives carry out labor support and attend all normal deliveries; obstetricians do not routinely appear during normal labor but are always present in the delivery room to perform any interventions that may be required (Hatta, Kawakami, Goto, Kadobayashi, & Iwamoto, 1999). In Japan, birth is viewed as best handled with a minimum of obstetrical technological intervention. The coexistence of the midwifery and "just-in-case" obstetrical care in Japan serves to limit the widespread and routine application of obstetrical technology in hospital births. In the United States, birth in the hospital is supported by a great deal of complex technology during labor and birth—a hospital bed during labor, an IV and a pump to infuse an oxytoxic agent to induce labor contractions, an electronic fetal monitor. The woman's connection to the hospital staff is also mediated through specialized equipment, such as an intercom or call bell system.

For some U.S. women, then, their own home seems the best place to give birth to their child because it provides a more relaxed and warm atmosphere. The home birth provides the least disruption of family life and the maximum opportunity for intimacy with the newborn. The greatest risk is the absence of emergency equipment, however. Therefore, in describing a low-risk candidate for home birth, one stipulation is that she be 10 miles or less from the hospital. Further, the mother should have no evidence of hypertension,

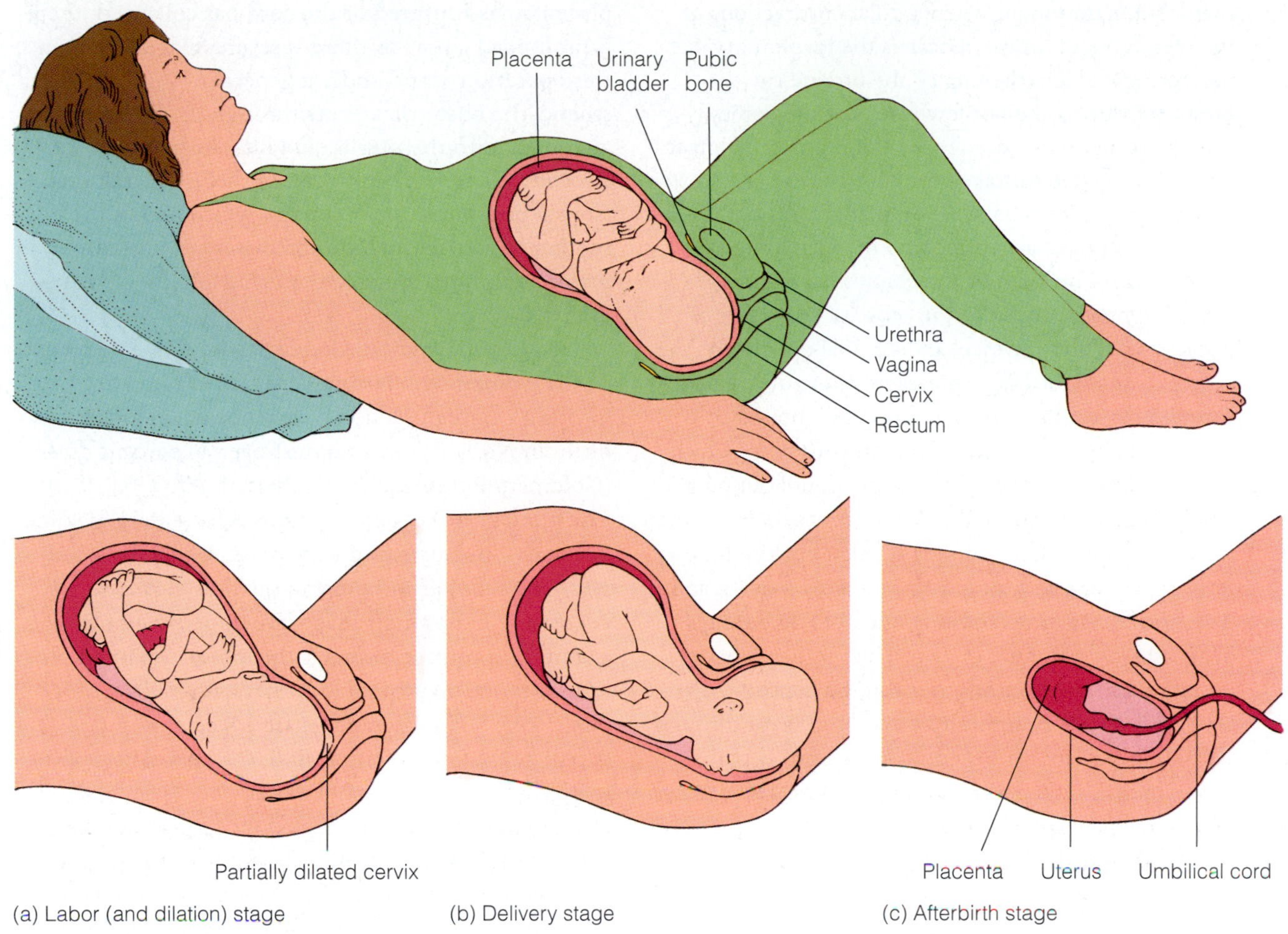

(a) Labor (and dilation) stage

(b) Delivery stage

(c) Afterbirth stage

FIGURE 4.5 ***The Four Stages of Childbirth***

Chiras, 1993.

epilepsy, Rh problem, severe anemia, diabetes, history of multiple births, or previous cesarean sections.

Stages of Childbirth

The mother's and child's experiences at birth vary considerably across societies of the world according to cultural traditions that prescribe the procedures to be followed in preparation for, during, and after the birth. In a few societies, birthing is treated as a natural process that requires no special preparation or care. For example, a !Kung woman living in the Kalahari desert may simply walk a short way out of the village, sit down against a tree, and give birth (Cole, 1999). For pregnant women in Third World countries, it is uncommon for births to be attended by trained personnel and there are few backup services for high-risk pregnancies. The result is that pregnant Third World women are 80 to 600 times more likely to experience death due to complications of childbirth than are pregnant women in industrialized societies where birthing is treated with more preparation and specialized help (Smith, 1995). Despite variations in childbirth, there are three generally recognizable stages in the birth process: labor, delivery, and afterbirth (see Figure 4.5).

Labor

During the last month, the fetus drops down into the lower part of the abdomen. A woman can often tell that labor is imminent when regular contractions of the uterus begin. (A *contraction* is the involuntary narrowing and lengthening of the uterine cavity.) However, during the last few weeks of pregnancy, women sometimes experience mild muscular contractions that may be mistaken for labor. These are *Braxton Hicks contractions,* or false labor, that are felt as the uterus enlarges to accommodate the increasing size of the fetus. The birth of the child is not far off.

The precise cause of the onset of true labor is not known. Labor involves the gradual opening of the cervix to allow the baby to pass from the uterus and through the vagina. The beginning of labor often is announced by the release of the mucous plug, which has sealed off the cervical opening throughout pregnancy. Women commonly refer to this as their "water breaking." Then, the amniotic sac that enclosed the fetus may break and some amniotic fluid may escape. The first contractions begin about 15 to 20 minutes apart and last a minute or two. The mother cannot initiate these contractions, nor can she control their onset, regularity, or intensity—except perhaps through relaxation. As labor proceeds, contractions become more intense and appear more frequently. The uterus works hard to expand the cervix to its full 8- to 10-centimeter diameter.

Delivery

The expulsion, or delivery stage, includes the time from full dilation of the cervix to the birth of the child and lasts between one and two hours for first births and a few minutes to a half hour for subsequent births. The baby is pushed by the uterus through the cervix and down the birth canal. As the head passes through the pelvis, a curvy, bony passageway, it rotates, helping to protect the baby's head from being injured. The baby's head crowns (becomes visible) at the vaginal opening, and the mother experiences an incredible urge to push and bear down. The baby is born in a face-down position. Once the head appears, shoulders and then the trunk and legs follow quickly. The average first labor and delivery is about 14 hours.

In some cases, the mother has to undergo a surgical childbirth, or a cesarean section. This is performed in cases where the baby's head is larger than the mother's pelvis can accommodate; there is a breech birth, where the child's head emerges last; the placenta has ruptured or the cord has collapsed; there is prolonged labor; or there is severe fetal distress. In this operation, done under a general or local anesthetic, the obstetrician cuts through the layers of the abdomen, into the uterus, and lifts the baby out. Recently, there has been a rise in the use of regional (spinal) anesthetic for cesareans, which allows the mother to see her infant immediately. In any case, it is major abdominal surgery, requiring intensive postoperative care.

In Canada and the United States, only 8 percent of the women who become pregnant again after having a cesarean section have a normal vaginal birth. In Norway, however, just over 40 percent do so (Goldman, Pineault, Potvin, Blais, & Bilodeau, 1993). The number of cesarean sections is increasing in some hospitals—mainly those who serve middle-class couples. The number of cesarean sections, however, is decreasing in hospitals that serve poorer patients. For example, in private hospitals the rate of cesarean sections is twice that found in church and military hospitals. Lisa McKenzie and Patricia Stephenson (1993) speculate that doctors may have a financial incentive to perform cesarean sections in private hospitals because they will be reimbursed for surgery and longer hospital care, which is generally not the case for poorer patients such as those in church or military hospitals.

After the birth of the child, parents may beam with delighted relief at the little bundle as the attending health-care professional proudly holds the tiny baby. The only one in this quartet who does not seem to be relaxed and contented is the newborn. For this reason, Frederick Leboyer (1975) suggests an alternate method of childbirth. He maintains that birth is a violent, painful, and traumatic experience for the newborn. The task of obstetrics, therefore, according to Leboyer, is to impose fewer demands on the baby. Rather than thrust the newborn into a brightly, fluorescent-lighted room, the baby should be delivered in a darkened room. The delivery room should be as quiet as possible. The newborn should be placed on the mother's abdomen before the cord is cut, and then given a bath as a first independent experience. The bath experience has received the most criticism. Some say it puts too heavy a demand on the temperature-regulating system of the newborn. Others point out that rather than being reassuring to the newborn, it may be sensorily confusing once the transition out of the wet, warm uterus has already been accomplished.

Afterbirth

About 10 minutes after the birth of the baby, the uterus contracts once again and the placenta and membranes, as well as any remaining amniotic fluid, will be expelled. This stage, the afterbirth, is painless and generally lasts 10 to 20 minutes. At the time of birth, the umbilical cord contains as much as 100cc of blood, about half the total blood supply of the newborn. Postponing the clamping and cutting of the cord for a few minutes allows this blood to drain into the baby's system and helps prevent anemia in the newborn. Complete drainage of the cord's arterial blood into the baby requires perhaps 7 minutes at the most.

Concept Checks

1. Prepared childbirth programs are based on the belief that
   a. difficult births are largely caused by mother's tension and anxiety.
   b. delivering babies in the home provides mother with a sense of control.
   c. educating girls about childbirth when they are young enhances painless delivery later in their lives.
2. An indication of the first stage of labor is
   a. descent of the infant into the birth canal.
   b. regular contractions of the uterus.
   c. cervical effacement of 15 cm.

Life Begins: The Newborn

Before Beginning . . .

After reading this section, you will be able to

- describe neonatal assessment procedures.
- distinguish between infants who are born too small and born too soon.
- explain the postpartum period of childbirth.

Among the Australian Aborigines, the newborn's life commonly begins with the father, or a shaman, trying to determine who the child really is, and then naming it accordingly. Traditionally, most Aborigines believe in a form of reincarnation in which the souls of the deceased stay in some sacred and secret location for some time, until one of them jumps into the womb of a pregnant woman passing nearby. A baby then is a respected ancestor; hence, it comes with a full-fledged personality that has to be respected. In Guatemala, the purity with which the child comes into the world is protected for eight days (Menchu, 2000). Customs prescribe that the newborn baby should be alone with his mother in a special place, without any visitors except those who bring her food. This is the baby's period of integration and membership into the family. The community takes over all the household expenses for these eight days and the family spends nothing.

In the United States, most infants are born in hospital settings. After the newborn is welcomed into the world, clinical testing of nervous functions begins. The recognition of injury to the nervous system at this time depends mainly on the demonstrations of disorders of responsiveness, instability of temperature, respiration, and blood pressure—all of which are under the control of the brain stem and spinal mechanisms.

Neonatal Assessment Techniques

Neurological assessments are done to test the infant's reflexes; the infant's responsiveness to stimulation; and muscle tone, physical condition, and general state. From evaluation of the infant's behavior, state, and responsiveness, a diagnosis is typically made about the maturity and functioning of the infant's central nervous system and sensory functioning. The most widely used tests in the United States are the Apgar Scale, the Gesell Developmental Schedules, the Bayley Scales of Infant Development, and the Brazelton Neonatal Behavioral Assessment Scale.

The Apgar Scale (Apgar, 1953) is given to the infant 60 seconds after birth and then again at 5 and 10 minutes after birth. The infant is rated for five signs: heart rate, respiratory effort, reflex irritability, muscle tone, and color. A score of 2 is given if the infant is in the best possible condition for a particular sign; a 0 is given if the sign is not present; and a 1 is given for all conditions between 0 and 2. Thus, the optimal score an infant can obtain is 10.

The Brazelton Neonatal Assessment Scale (NBAS) was developed to assess the dynamic processes of behavioral organization and development in the neonate, or newborn. It is a psychological scale that views the infant as part of a reciprocal, interactive feedback system between infant and caregiver. Although the exam includes the assessment of reflex responses, it focuses on the infant's capability to respond to the kind of stimuli that caregivers present in an interactive process. The scale assesses 16 reflexes and 26 behavioral items. The examiner plays the role of the caregiver and systematically manipulates the baby from sleep to alert to crying states and back down to quiet states to bring the infant through an entire range of situations that captures the baby's coping and adaptive strategies.

The Newborn's Appearance

Fumi, who was introduced at the beginning of the chapter, looks at her newborn daughter, barely minutes old. She and her husband begin to inspect their miraculous little one. Compared with the rest of the body, the newborn's head is quite large. The important bones of the baby's head are separated by sutures, membranous spaces that feel soft to the touch. The space where several sutures meet is called a *fontanelle*. As Fumi strokes her newborn's arms, she discovers that her baby's skin is extremely soft and wrinkly. As they touch the infant's arms and bowed-little legs, the infant responds with a quick, jerky movement—Fumi and her husband giggle with surprise. They discover the infant's minute hands with tiny little fingernails. As her father strokes the palm of his daughter's hand, she grasps it with decisive firmness. Fumi can feel her baby's heartbeat as she gives her child the first of many tender hugs.

The baby's heart, prior to birth, had an opening between the right and left ventricles that kept the blood from flowing into the nonfunctioning lungs. This opening between the ventricles closes at birth, and the heart begins its normal functioning. Most newborns breathe spontaneously at birth. Their breathing, however, is irregular, shallow, rapid, and punctuated frequently with coughs and sneezes to clear the air passages and lungs. After birth, blood begins to flow into the lungs and oxygenation begins. The newborn also changes from taking in nutrients through the placenta to ingesting food into its mouth and stomach, while eliminating wastes through its own elimination system.

Newborns are surprisingly self-regulatory organisms. This means that their behavior processes tend to minimize deprivations; defend against the intrusion of noxious stimulation; correct imbalances; thwart disturbances; and otherwise perpetuate life, protect limbs, and protect against extremes of emotional excitement. All in all, the newborn is quite a miracle! Fumi's child weighs 7½ pounds, which is in the normal range for newborns, but some infants are born too soon and some are born too small and weigh considerably less.

Born Too Small, Born Too Soon

Low birth weight infants are born at the proper gestation time but weigh less than 5½ pounds (2500 grams). African American infants have double the rates of low birth weight as European American infants (Collins & David, 1990); the reasons are unknown (Chomitz, Cheung, & Lieberman, 1995). Among infants of Hispanic origin, the rate of low birth weight is relatively low. Latinos represent a very diverse group and their low birth weight rates vary considerably by national origin, ranging from approximately 10 percent among Puerto Rican mothers to 5.6 percent among Cuban mothers. Among East Asian infants, the incidence of low birth weight ranges from about 5 percent for Chinese births to 7 percent for Filipino births (National Center for Health Statistics, 1993).

Infants who are born too soon (before the 266-day gestation period) are labeled premature infants. A number of maternal factors increase the likelihood of a "preterm delivery" (see Table 4.6). The largest single factor is maternal age, with adolescent mothers accounting for 20 percent of all premature births. There may be short-term as well as long-term consequences of prematurity. The most immediate problem is simply the infant's struggle to survive. The primary problem is breathing. These infants have not had a chance to develop *surfactin,* a substance that coats the lungs during the last few weeks of gestation and helps to keep them from collapsing. The respiratory system of a preterm infant is not ready to cope with breathing outside the womb. Because of the fragile physical systems, low birth weight infants are kept in isolettes (similar to incubators) to keep them warm and prevent infections. Technological advances have dramatically improved the life chances of preterm infants. Consequently, there is a significant increase in the number of high-risk infants who survive the neonatal period.

Some long-term consequences may result from inadequate oxygen to the brain. Thus cognitive deficits, language, and learning problems may be seen during the school years (Bernbaum & Batshaw, 1997). However, it is possible to overcome these problems to some extent through an advantaged environment (Shaffer, 1999). With improved prenatal care and an increased number of neonatal intensive care units, the prognosis for low birth weight infants should continue to improve.

Premature infants are assessed while they are hospitalized and following discharge. Five subsystems are analyzed: physiologic, motoric, state, attentional-interaction, and self-regulation. The examiner determines how well the infant adapts to various manipulations and also determines the infant's tolerance for stimulation. Within each subsystem, signs of stability and instability are assessed.

The best treatment for low birth weight babies is prevention, including the early identification of women at high risk for premature delivery (for example, adolescents, women with substance abuse or chronic illness) and providing these women with education, comprehensive health care, and early detection of preterm labor.

Once the child comes home, the challenges of caring for this very dependent and needy infant become apparent. Premature infants tend to be irritable, and many cry for long periods of time. They often have poor sleep–wake cycles and typically sleep for only short periods of time. Fortunately, however, a premature infant's condition stabilizes within two to three weeks. By then, adequate nutrition is possible and weight gain begins. Because of the many stressors involved in caring for a premature infant, however, it is important that the parents be provided with adequate support systems. These should include close medical supervision in a follow-up clinic; home care services, such as a visiting nurse; and a social worker to advocate for financial resources and provide emotional support to the family. In addition, parents should be encouraged to enroll their infants in early intervention programs that will provide support and training for the child and parent.

TABLE 4.6

Possible Causes of Prematurity

▪ Amniotic fluid/membrane infection	▪ Multiple gestation
▪ Drug/alcohol abuse	▪ Placental bleeding
▪ Fetal distress	▪ Excessive amniotic fluid
▪ Maternal age (adolescent or older mother)	▪ Poor prenatal care
▪ Maternal bacterial vaginosis	▪ Premature rupture of the membranes
▪ Maternal kidney infection	▪ Uterine abnormalities/incompetent cervix

Postpartum Period

The first several weeks after birth, known as the **postpartum period**, are a time of intensified emotional highs and lows. The newness of parenthood, the sheer fatigue associated with caring for the infant, and interrupted sleep present many new adjustments to each parent. As such, a certain amount of depression is common just after giving birth. Most women experience "the blues" for a day or two after delivery because of pain, emotional upheaval, the inconvenience of hospital care, and possibly hormonal changes. About 20 percent experience a moderately serious postpartum depression —that is, a depression after giving birth (Lee, 1997).

Postpartum depression occurs when women are unable to experience, express, and validate their feelings and needs within supportive, accepting, and nonjudgmental interpersonal relationships (Mauthner, 1999). For most women who suffer from postpartum depression, depression generally appears during pregnancy, which is called *prepartum depression* (Manzano, Righetti-Veltema, & Perreard, 1997). This syndrome is quite frequent among pregnant women (19.8%). Such current findings make it possible to detect the majority of women at risk for postpartum depression and to undertake preventive measures.

The wonder, however, of sharing in the power of creating this new life is often overshadowed by these early challenges. As Fumi expressed it:

> That calm, sure, unambivalent woman who moved through the pages of the manuals I read seemed as unlike me as an astronaut. Nothing, to be sure, had prepared me for the intensity of relationship already existing between me and a creature I had carried in my body and now hold in my arms.... No one mentions the strangeness of attraction—which can be as single-minded and overwhelming as the early days of a love affair—to a being so tiny, so dependent, so folded-into itself—who is, and yet is not, part of oneself.

postpartum period
Refers to the first several weeks after giving birth when the mother undergoes intensified positive and negative emotions.

Concept Checks

1. Which of the following neonatal tests assesses reflexes and interactive reactions?
   a. Bayley Motor Scale
   b. Denver Developmental Screening Test
   c. Brazelton Neonatal Behavioral Assessment Scale

2. Yolanda gave birth to a preterm baby. She should
   a. minimize physical contact until the baby's sensory systems are stronger.
   b. provide social and physical support when the infant leaves the hospital, not before.
   c. provide social and physical contact during the infant's hospitalization.
3. Which statement best reflects our scientific knowledge about postpartum depression.
   a. It is a state of the "blues" brought on by the stress of giving birth.
   b. It is strictly produced by hormonal changes.
   c. It is a combination of biological and psychological changes accompanying childbirth.

Reviewing Key Points

Psychological Factors in Becoming Parents

- The reasons why men and women want to have children focus on obtaining adult status, expanding the self, group ties and affection, power and influence, and close affiliation with another human being.
- Reasons cited for not wanting to have children tend to relate to loss of freedom and privacy, economic deprivations, worry about childhood outcomes due to improper parenting, or the additional work parenting may bring.
- Many changes occur in parents' lives as they adjust to the birth of their child. Most researchers contend that the transition to parenthood is unsettling for men, for women, and for their relationship as a couple. Five areas, in particular, are affected: division of labor, self-concept/self-esteem, marital relationships, three-generational relationships, and stress and social support.
- For parents to make a positive transition into parenthood, they need to be adaptable, flexible, and tolerant. They need to discuss division of labor and to be satisfied with who does what and when. Each couple also has to work on their needs for individuality and mutuality while becoming a family.

Infertile Couples

- The two most common causes of infertility in women are reduced egg production and blocked fallopian tubes; for men, it is low sperm count and motility.
- Thanks to modern technology, a number of procedures can be employed to increase the chances of having a baby. These procedures are artificial insemination, enlisting a surrogate mother, preimplantation genetic testing, and intracytoplasmic sperm injection.

Prenatal Environmental Hazards

- When organs are undergoing rapid development, they are particularly sensitive to various teratogens, such as viral diseases, radiation, alcohol, nicotine, and narcotics.
- Threats to the infant's development can be prevented if the mother is aware of the harmful effects of these teratogens and abstains from use of alcohol, narcotics, smoking, and other environmental hazards.

Conception and Prenatal Development

- The nine-month gestation is divided into three phases of development: the germinal period lasts from fertilization until the time the zygote is firmly implanted in the wall of the uterus, a process that takes between 10 and 14 days. This phase is followed by the embryonic period, which begins in the second week in utero and lasts until the eighth week. During this period, the embryo germ layers form and differentiation of body parts is almost completed. The fetal period, which lasts from the eighth week until delivery, is marked by continued elaboration and growth of basic systems.

The Parents' Experience

- During the first trimester, the couple adjusts to the pregnancy (which takes a bit longer for men than for women). They seek obstetrical advice and care. The woman adjusts to her new body image during the second trimester. In the third trimester, couples prepare for the arrival of their child by making sleeping arrangements and buying clothes and needed baby supplies. Fathers' emotional needs are often overlooked during pregnancy. They are expected to be the strong ones upon whom mothers depend. Having opportunities to express their concerns and fears is important for expectant fathers as well as expectant mothers.

The Birth Process

- The best-known and most widely used system of precise breathing and relaxation exercises is the Lamaze method. These exercises teach a precise set of breathing techniques associated to the various stages of labor. Choosing a birthing center is an important decision. For some couples, a hospital delivery, with complete medical backup systems, seems optimal. Others, however, may desire the hominess and safety of an out-of-hospital birth center. Still others may feel that home is the best place to deliver their child.

- The stages of childbirth are labor (onset of uterine contractions), delivery (passage of the baby through the birth canal, or vagina, and delivery into the world), and afterbirth (expulsions of the placenta, blood, and fluid).

Life Begins: The Newborn

- To assess the newborn's health and developmental status, a neurological exam is given. Quite commonly, the Apgar Scale or the Brazelton Neonatal Assessment Scale is administered.
- The prognosis for infants born too soon or too small is looking better thanks to the ability to identify mothers who are at risk and better intensive-care procedures. Short-term consequences mainly relate to the child's surviving; long-term consequences relate to learning impairment for the child due to lack of oxygen to the brain. It is recommended that parents enroll preterm and low birth weight babies in special programs to overcome these possible learning impairments.
- The first several weeks after birth, known as the postpartum period, are a time of intensified emotional highs and lows. The newness of parenthood, the sheer fatigue associated with caring for the infant, and interrupted sleep present many new adjustments to each parent. As such, a certain amount of depression is common just after giving birth.

Answers to Concept Checks

Psychological Factors in Becoming Parents
1. b 2. c 3. a

Infertile Couples
1. false 2. false

Prenatal Environmental Hazards
1. c 2. heroin 3. a

Conception and Prenatal Development
1. true 2. true

The Parents' Experience
1. a 2. b 3. a 4. b 5. c

The Birth Process
1. a 2. b

Life Begins: The Newborn
1. c 2. c 3. c

Key Terms

acquired immunodeficiency syndrome (AIDS)
blastocyst
embryonic period
fetal alcohol syndrome (FAS)
fetal period
germinal period
implantation
infertility
intracytoplasmic sperm injection
in vitro fertilization
Lamaze method
ovulation
placenta
postpartum period
preimplantation genetic testing
Rh factor
teratogens

InfoTrac College Edition

For additional readings, explore InfoTrac College Edition, your online library. Go to **http://www.infotrac-college.com/wadsworth** and use the passcode that came on the card with your book. Try these search terms: in vitro fertilization, pregnancy, childbirth, fathers.

Child Development CD-ROM

Go to the Wadsworth Child Development CD-ROM for further study of the concepts in this chapter. The CD-ROM also includes quizzes and additional activities to expand your learning experience.

Let me introduce you to
Michael E. Lamb

For the past 24 years, Dr. Lamb has been head of the Section on Social and Emotional Development at the National Institute of Child Health and Human Development in Bethesda, Maryland. Because of his varied interests, his name appears quite often throughout this text as we discuss fathers, child abuse, and child care in their respective chapters. But it is Dr. Lamb's work on social and emotional development in infancy that is a special area of concern to him and of particular interest to us in Part Three of this book. Michael Lamb's book *Development in Infancy* is a classic in our field. This work, however, is just one among his many scholarly books and widely published articles. Dr. Lamb refers to the first two years of life as the "magic years." The appropriateness of this label will become apparent as you read his introduction and the chapters that follow.

Courtesy of Michael E. Lamb

PART 3

Developmental Contexts: *Infancy and Toddlerhood*

Infancy: The Magic Years

by Michael E. Lamb, Director, Section on Social and Environmental Development, National Institute of Child Health and Human Development

To psychologists like myself, infancy is the most exciting phase of life because so many and such extraordinary changes take place in so brief a period of time. It is exciting because it provides some of the most compelling examples of the ways in which inborn tendencies work together with diverse and distinctive experiences to shape the child's unique emergent characteristics. But, how can we learn about these amazing beings? After all, infants cannot tell us what they are seeing, hearing, feeling, or thinking. Or can they? Psychologists have developed numerous techniques—transparent and ingenious, simple and complex—to study the inner and unspoken lives of infants. Armed with their research tools, investigators have accumulated a remarkable understanding of infancy, and the readers of the next three chapters of this book will gain insight into this exciting phase of life and the ways in which it has been explored.

Perhaps, to the casual observer, the newborn infant seems to do little more than sleep, eat, cry, urinate, and defecate. The infant does specialize in these activities, of course, but he or she is also a "sensory

sponge," constantly taking in sensory information through five remarkable, mature sensory channels. Much of what we have learned about early sensory capacity and perceptual organization has been learned by exploiting two of the most basic tendencies—the tendency to pay attention to novel stimuli and the parallel tendency to cease paying attention to boring old stimuli. All organisms, from earthworms to humans, pay attention when they become aware of new sensations. In most vertebrates (including humans), heart rates decline when we pay attention, returning to baseline when we come to see the stimuli as old rather than new. This basic pattern of responding has been exploited by countless researchers eager to explore infants' capacities.

For example, when researchers flash a bright red light in front of a baby, he will look at it and his heart rate will drop. However, after repeated flashes, the red light becomes uninteresting and the baby's attention drifts. What if we then flash a bright green light in the same location? If the child immediately stares and attends, we know that he can tell the difference between the red and green lights and, thus, is capable of color discrimination. By varying the similarity between the two lights, or sounds, or smells, we can probe further into the acuity or sensitivity of the child's capacities.

Remarkable as their sensory precocities are, infants learn about social relations as well. Mom and Dad are not simply defined by specific sounds, smells, and visible features, they are also characterized by their repeated and predictable associations with a very desirable state—the relief of the baby's state of distress. Parents, for example, pick up a crying infant and, as she is soothed, she moves to a quiet alert state. But, much more is happening here. Repeated pairings of the parent's much-welcomed relief of distress helps the infant learn that she can count on, or trust, the parent to intervene in appropriate ways when necessary and that she can personally influence what happens to her. These three concepts—the notion that both objects and people are characterized by specific sounds and smells and tactile sensations and visible features, trust in specific people, and a sense of personal efficacy—are three of the most fundamental and important lessons to be learned, and infants learn these phenomenal achievements remarkably early in life.

About a century ago, William James (America's first and most distinguished psychologist) described the infant's world as a "booming, buzzing confusion," but his many heirs and pretenders have shown that the infant's capacities are both more remarkable and more rapidly organized than James could have ever imagined.

PART OUTLINE

Chapter Five
Physical Development: Infancy and Toddlerhood

Chapter Six
Cognitive Development: Infancy and Toddlerhood

Chapter Seven
Socioemotional Development: Infancy and Toddlerhood

CHAPTER FIVE

Physical Development: *Infancy and Toddlerhood*

CHAPTER OUTLINE

Brain Development During Infancy and Toddlerhood
- A Baby's Brain—a Work in Progress
- The Brain's Pruning System
- Brain Plasticity
- The Emotional Brain
- Applications: Fostering Brain Growth Development

Physical and Motor Development
- Physical Growth Patterns
- Principles of Motor Development
- Applications: Toilet Training

The World of Sights, Sounds, and Smells
- Sensory Systems
- Depth Perception
- Intermodal Perception
- Applications: Making Sure the Infant Can Hear

Behavioral States
- Crying
- Sleep
- Sleep Apnea
- Applications: Symptoms of and Recommendations for Infants at Risk for SIDS

Health
- Immunizations
- Nutrition
- Undernutrition
- Applications: Overnutrition

Reviewing Key Points

You hold your newborn so his eyes are just inches from the brightly patterned wallpaper. *ZZZt:* A neuron from his retina makes an electrical connection with one in his brain's visual cortex. You gently touch his palm with a clothespin; he grasps it, drops it, and you return it to him with soft words and a smile. *Crackle:* Neurons from his hand strengthen their connection to those in his sensory-motor cortex. He cries in the night; you feed him, holding his gaze because nature has seen to it that the distance from a parent's crooked elbow to his eyes exactly matches the distance at which a baby focuses. *Zap:* Neurons in the brain's amygdala send pulses of electricity through the circuits that control emotions. You hold him on your lap and talk . . . and neurons from his ears start hardwiring connections to the auditory cortex. And you thought you were just playing with your child. (Begley, 1999)

The first year of life, according to Erik Erikson, is crucial for infants' developing a sense of trust in themselves and their environment. Erikson believes that this is the single most important goal in getting a child off to a good start in life. As infants reach out to the social environment for nurturance and their expectations are met, as they receive reliable and consistent responding from their caregivers;

and as caregivers cuddle, affectionately stroke, play, and talk with their infants a sense of trust is established. As the infant's physical and psychological needs are met, he or she is then able to perceive the world as predictable, safe, and reliable; and, equally as important, infants are then able to develop a sense of efficacy—a belief that they have some control over that world. Trust enables children to act on their capabilities and curiosities and explore the exciting world that caregivers are opening up to them.

The first two years, the period of infancy and toddlerhood, is a critical time for brain development. Current research tells us that healthy brain development is determined by the infant's environment. Part of the baby's brain is "natural," shaped by evolution; it is hardwired and governs such things as breathing and heartbeat. Part of the baby's brain, however, is "cultural," shaped by the environment; it is soft-wired and manages such things as learning to weave a blanket or solve a complex math problem. Researchers now believe that the soft-wiring that takes place in the first two years of life is more rapid and extensive than was previously realized and the environment plays a bigger role in brain development than was once thought. From the infant's first few minutes of life, very impressive feats of engineering are taking place in its brain. During the early years of life, for example, neurological foundations for rational thinking, problem solving, and general reasoning are established. These facts might have shocked the renowned psychologist William James (1890). As Michael Lamb pointed out in his introduction, James concluded that infants were rather incapable little creatures. This view of infants as inactive, reflexive little organisms has changed dramatically thanks to exciting discoveries in child development research.

This chapter also surveys other impressive feats that take place during the infancy period, such as infants' and toddlers' physical and motor achievements; their growing sensory sophistications; their perceptual competencies; and their active, daily quest to comprehend the environment. Later in the chapter, we will examine common behavioral states, such as crying and sleeping during the infancy period and also discuss the unexplainable death of some infants—a phenomenon known as sudden infant death syndrome, or SIDS. Health issues, such as immunizations and nutrition, conclude the chapter. As you explore the pages that follow, it will soon become apparent that we have come a long way from James' turn-of-the-century view of infants and toddlers as inactive, incapable beings.

neurons
Brain cells.

soma
The cell body of the neuron.

dendrites
Fine, wirelike extensions that receive messages from adjacent neurons and conduct them to the soma, or cell body.

Brain Development During Infancy and Toddlerhood

Before Beginning . . .

After reading this section, you will be able to

- understand the processes of synaptic connections and dendrite branching and their relation to sophisticated mental activity.
- characterize the brain's pruning process.
- understand the difference between hard- and soft-wiring of the brain.
- describe ways in which brain development can be enhanced during infancy.

Infants were once viewed as rather primitive physiological beings with sleep–wake, hunger–satiation cycles. The first few months of life were labeled the "normal–autism" phase. Most of us recognize that infants are more than just reactive creatures on automatic pilot, but what behaviors are they actually capable of executing during the infancy period? We will examine this issue throughout this chapter. (See the Self-Insight, which offers a list of developmental milestones that occur during the infancy period. Test your knowledge of when these competencies occur.)

A Baby's Brain—A Work in Progress

Infants display quite remarkable skills—but most new parents can tell you that. Jessica was born almost a year ago. As each month went by, her proud parents told their friends of yet another amazing milestone—first smiles, rolling over, her babbling little dialogues, crawling—and now Jessica is on the verge of taking her all-important first step. Orchestrating these advancing skills are the 100 billion **neurons**, or brain cells, that compose the human brain and spinal cord. Although neurons have different functions—the motor neurons enable Jessica, in part, to sit, stand, crawl, and walk, and the sensory neurons enable her to see and to hear—the chief workers in the brain, however, are the association neurons located in the higher centers of the brain. These neurons will enable Jessica to engage in progressively more complex thinking skills. As a newborn, these parts of the brain, which are responsible for complex cognitive functions like language and spa-

Recognizing the Infant's Competencies

After each of these developmental milestones, check the appropriate age column that corresponds to when you believe the child is capable of this skill.

Developmental Milestone	Birth to 2 Months	3 to 4 Months	5 to 7 Months	8 to 11 Months	12 Months	After 12 Months
Laughs spontaneously	✓					
Sits with support			✓			
Walks unassisted					✓	
Thinks about things that cannot be seen					✓	
Seeks adult approval for "cute" behaviors					✓	
Recognizes own voice and face			✓			
Crying becomes intentional				✓		
Recognizes Mom and Dad			✓			
Engages in fantasy behavior (pretending to talk on phone)					✓	

ANSWERS Laughs (2 months); sits with support (5–6 months); walks unassisted (12 months); thinks about things that cannot be seen (12 months); seeks adult approval (12 months); recognizes voice and face (6 months); crying becomes intentional (9 months); recognizes Mom and Dad (5 months); engages in fantasy behavior (12 months).

Note: To those who received a perfect score, please contact me about co-authoring the next edition of the book.

tial orientation, are relatively dormant. By the time the candle is lighted on Jessica's first birthday cake, however, these higher centers of the brain will become much more dominant.

Each neuron, while differing in function as well as size, consists of a **soma**, or cell body; the dendrites and the axon extend from the cell body (see Figure 5.1a). **Dendrites** are fine, wirelike extensions that receive messages from adjacent cells and conduct them to the cell body. The **axon** is the long extension from the cell body that transmits messages away from the cell body to other neurons across the gap

axon
The long extension from the cell body that transmits messages away from the cell body to other neurons across the synapse.

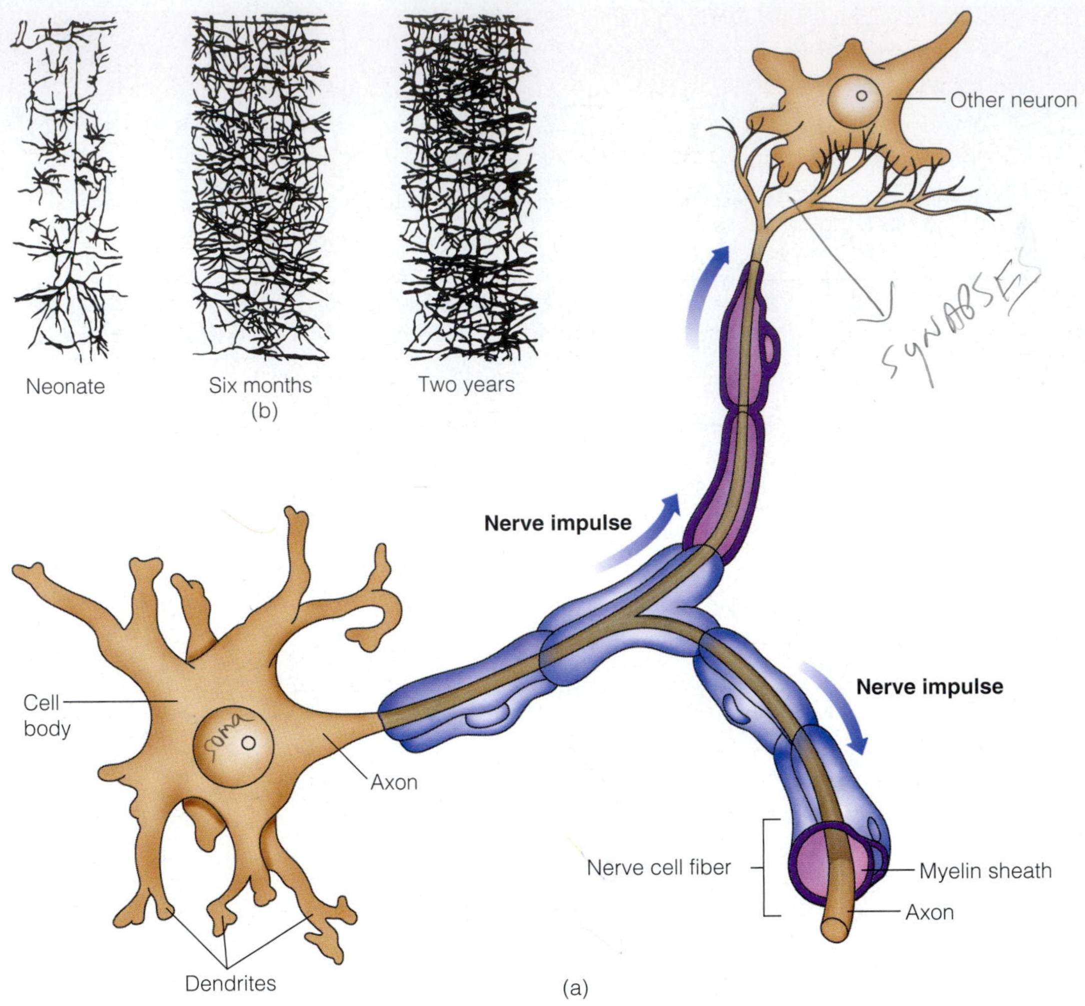

FIGURE 5.1 *Parts of a Neuron*

(a) Although neurons differ in size and function, all brain cells contain three main parts: the dendrites, which receive messages from adjacent neurons; the cell body, or soma; and the long extension from the soma called the axon. (b) The formation of dendrites leading to new connections among existing neurons, as well as the myelination of neural pathways, accounts for much of the increase in brain weight during a baby's first two years.

known as the **synapse**. Neurons communicate with each other by transmitting chemical impulses across the synapse.

synapses Microscopic gaps that exist between neurons; where communication between neurons takes place.

For the brain, birth is just a momentary pause along the developmental continuum, but ironically, the size of the brain helps to determine the timing of a baby's arrival into the world. The newborn brain is only one-quarter of its adult size and weight so that the baby's head can fit through the birth canal. It will nearly triple its weight within 3 years and quadruple to its mature weight of roughly 3 pounds by 6 to 14 years. Most of our brain growth takes place after birth, so what exactly keeps growing inside the child's head to enlarge his or her brain size (see Figure 5.1b)?

Until recently, researchers believed that brain growth did not involve the growth of new neurons and that we acquired all the neurons that we will ever have before we are born. However, biologists Elizabeth Gould (1999; Gould, Reeves, Graziano, & Gross, 1999) and Charles Gross (1998) made the astonishing discovery that thousands of new neurons are formed each day in the brains of macaque monkeys, and they make their migration to the prefrontal cortex—the seat of intelligence (see Figure 5.2). New neurons appear to grow in the frontal cortex, used for decision making, and two areas on the side of the brain implicated in memory. Though their research is based on monkeys, as fellow primates, it is likely to be true of human beings as well. What do these newly formed neurons do? Researchers speculate that the continuum of newly formed neurons, arriving one after another, might be the brain's way of storing memories in a chronological order—something like pages of each individual's neurological memory book. Our memory systems also may weave in the new neurons as well (Honer, 1999). This research creates a whole new ballgame for addressing brain diseases, by harnessing the brain's own restorative potential. These new findings certainly challenge the long-lasting and never-disputed belief that human beings never generate new brain cells. As such, scientists will have to make major revisions in their theories of how memory works (Bruer, Johnson, Kirlik, North, Rissland, Bray, Reilly, Huffman, Grupe, Villan, Fletcher, Anumolu, Brewer, & Mishra, 1998).

Besides the possible multiplication of nerve cells, how does a baby's brain grow? The major portion of brain growth is due to the growth of *glial cells,* which provide neurons with nourishment and structural support (*glia* literally translated means glue). Most important, to the growth of the brain, glial cells produce a lipoprotein substance known as *myelin.* The quadrupling of brain weight after birth comes mostly from accumulating myelin that covers the axons of neurons. This process, called **myelination**, helps to preserve energy in the axon, enabling neurons to communicate quickly and efficiently despite the increasing distances that impulses must travel as the baby's body continues to grow.

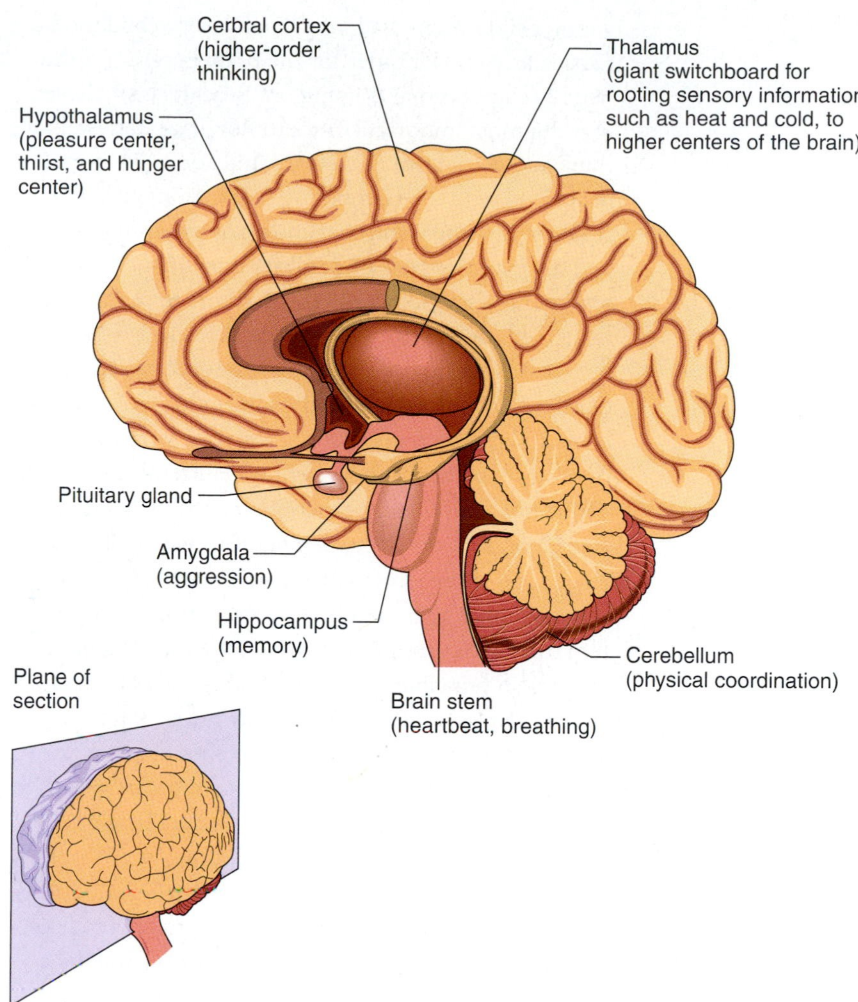

FIGURE 5.2 *The Human Brain*

Each part of the brain performs important functions. The crowning achievement, however, is the cerebral cortex, which enables us to solve complex problems.

The Brain's Pruning System

By the best estimates, natural cell death can eliminate 50 percent of the neurons in the brain before the baby is born and up to 40 percent of the synaptic connections between nerve cells by the age of 21 months (Diamond & Hopson, 1998). This so-called naturally occurring cell death in the brain is one way of clearing up developmental mistakes—for example, a cell that migrated to the wrong address, or that connected with the wrong targets or with targets that were already filled. But programmed elimination is more than just a predator on weak cells; it is nature's way of shaping each individual brain. Many of our abilities, talents, and reactions get soft-wired in childhood and become the neural platform upon which we stand and grow for the rest of our lives.

Fortunately, the brain produces many times more neurons and more synapses than it will eventually need. During childhood, there is a gradual decline in synapse density. In fact, by the time the child is 14, half of all the synapses in her brain will have been discarded—leaving about 500 trillion. Brain development then is a process of pruning; the brain selectively eliminates excess synapses. But how does the brain "know" which connections to keep and which to discard? When some kind of stimulus activates a neural pathway, all the synapses that form that pathway receive and store a chemical signal. Repeated activation increases the strength of that signal, and it becomes exempt from elimination and retains its protected status into adulthood. If synapses are not used repeatedly, or often enough, they are eliminated.

Connectivity, Synapses, and Dendrites

Research findings thus confirm that brain development is a "use it or lose it" process. As such, environmental experience (or input) plays a crucial role in wiring a

myelination The process of covering the axon of the neuron with a protein covering called the myelin sheath.

young child's brain, and infancy and early childhood are particularly crucial times for the brain because of the neural sculpting that is going on. Researchers believe that the most important clues to how, and how well, we think and learn both as children and adults has a great deal to do with the number of connections each neuron makes with other neurons, known as **synaptogenesis**, and the extensiveness of dendrite branching, known as **sprouting** (Greenough, 2001). Both processes are highly dependent on environmental experiences.

Research findings suggest, for example, that an enriched environment can actually increase the number of neural connections that children can form as well as the density of dendrite branching (Huttenlocher, 1998). These rich, stimulating experiences result in more efficient "connectivity" between neurons which, in turn, results in a more streamlined and efficient communication system. The more effective the communication system that exists among pathways, the more potential there is, in principle, for highly sophisticated mental activity (Nelson, 1998), enabling us to be smart, creative, and adaptive. As William Greenough (2001) points out, it is not necessarily the number of synapses an individual has that results in more productive thinking. Individuals with fragile X syndrome, which causes mental retardation (see Chapter 3), actually have more synapses than is normal. Neuronal patterning and connectivity are what is important for complex mental activity.

A child's environment and daily experiences determine which brain neurons will be used and how.

Environmental Input

Some neurons have already been hardwired for breathing or controlling the heartbeat by the genes in the fertilized egg; they are not susceptible to the brain's pruning processes. Millions of neurons, however, are "soft-wired," which means they are waiting for instructions from their environment and the experiences provided by that environment to program them into neural circuits that will enable them, one day, to write a symphony or play chess or compute a problem in finite math. As an engineer wires circuits in a computer, the child's environment determines not only which neurons are used but how they will be used.

synaptogenesis
The formation of synapses or connectivity between neurons; implicated in behavior functions and higher-order mental functioning.

sprouting
The extensiveness of dendrite branching in the neurons.

We have long understood that factors other than genetic programming affect brain development—nutrition, for example. We now know, however, that the first 18 months of life are an especially significant period of brain development. "It can now be said with far greater confidence than before, that the brain responds to experience, particularly in the first years of life. That means that by ensuring a good start in life, we have more opportunity to promote learning and prevent damage than we ever imagined" (Carnegie Task Force, 1994, p. 9).

Soft-Wiring the Brain

Windows of opportunity emerge as children develop; if they are not provided with appropriate stimulation these windows close (Chugani, 1996; Chugani & Phelps, 1986; Mueller, Rothermel, Behen, Muzik, Mangner, & Chugani, 1997). For example, taping one eye shut of a newborn kitten rewires its brain so that almost no neural connections from the shut eye to the visual cortex develop. The animal is blind even after its eye is untaped. Such rewiring does not occur in adult cats whose eyes were taped shut because the neural circuitry took place early in life. Similarly, a baby whose eyes are clouded by cataracts from birth, despite cataract-removal surgery at the age of 2, will be forever blind.

Further, new studies are showing that spoken language has an astonishing impact on brain development (Huttenlocher, 1998). The number of words an infant hears each day from an attentive, caring adult is an extremely important indicator of later intelligence. Betty Hart (Hart & Ridley, 1995) studied children from professional, working-class, and welfare families.

Children with professional parents hear, on average, 2100 words an hour; children of working-class parents hear 1200 words, and those with parents on welfare hear only 600 words an hour. Professional parents talk three times as much to their infants. Moreover, children with professional parents get positive feedback 30 times an hour—twice as often as working-class parents and five times as often as parents on welfare. At age 3, when the children were given standard tests, the children of the professional parents scored the highest. Spoken language, reports Hart, is the key variable. Vocabulary words are a magnet for a child's thinking and reasoning skills.

In researching the development of speech sounds, Patricia Kuhl (Kuhl, Williams, & Lacerda, 1992) notes that by the age of six months, infants in English-speaking homes already have different auditory maps (as shown by electrical measurements that identify which neurons respond to different sounds) from those infants in Swedish-speaking homes. Children are functionally deaf, she notes, to sounds absent from their native tongue. The map is completed by the first birthday.

This helps to explain why it is so difficult to pronounce words with sound units that are not a part of our native tongue. To illustrate, a few semesters ago, I had a student from Hong Kong. His name was indeed a difficult name for me to pronounce, and I knew that I would have some trouble. So, I asked him if there was some nickname I could call him. "Please call me," he said with an indulgent grin, ". . . John Wayne."

Brain Plasticity

Even though the brain has its greatest growth in utero and in the first 18 months of life, research consistently points out that there is room for modification in the brain later in life. Marian Diamond and her colleagues at the University of California at Berkeley have shown that brain structures are modified by the environment (Diamond & Hopson, 1998). There is now ample scientific support for the view that the brain is not a static entity and that a person's capacities are not fixed at birth.

Brain plasticity is especially remarkable up to age 8 or 9, after which plasticity declines (Chugani, 1996). For example, if damage occurs to the language center of the brain during the early years, uncommitted neurons (those that are not already engaged in a particular function), will "take over" language functions, and the child will develop normal speech. If an adult suffers from the same damage to the language center from a stroke for example, he or she is unlikely to recover to the same degree.

The Emotional Brain

Experience can also wire the brain's emotional circuity (Greenspan, 1998). If the baby's squeal of delight at seeing her mother is met with a smile and a hug, the circuits for these positive emotions are reinforced. The brain uses the same pathways to generate an emotion as to respond to one. When emotions are reciprocated, the electrical and chemical signals that produce it are reinforced (Cahill & McGaugh, 1997; Greenspan, 1998). But if emotions are *repeatedly* met with conflicting responses—the child is proud of his sculpted work of art made out of mother's new dishes, and mother does not share the child's enthusiasm—those circuits become confused and do not strengthen (Van Stegeren, Everaerd, Cahill, McGaugh, & Gooren, 1998).

Emotions play an important role in learning. Joseph LeDoux (1994; 1996) reports that sensory input reaches the amygdala part of the brain (implicated in emotions: fear, anger, aggression) before they get to the rational, higher center of the brain, the cerebral cortex. If a sight or experience has proved painful—for example, the child's attempts to explore and create are habitually met with parental anger—then the amygdala floods the brain circuits with neurochemicals before the higher centers of the brain know what is happening. After these events occur repeatedly, the sight of the mother may induce fear or a negative feeling in the infant.

APPLICATIONS:

Fostering Brain Growth Development

Just 10 years ago, child development textbooks talked about how infants' and toddlers' thinking skills and behaviors emerged, and yet they never mentioned the brain. Today, the new field cognitive neuroscience links brain processes to human behavior. Kurt Fischer (1994, 1997), a neo-Piagetian (whom you shall learn more about in the next chapter) and a cognitive neuroscientist, presents a more brain-oriented model of child development. In Fischer's model, various regions of the brain undergo rapid periods of development. During these "growth spurts" of particular brain regions, we see the emergence of new behaviors and skills. He also associates the growth of particular brain regions with the emergence of particular behaviors.

Consider, for example, the following brain growth spurts and the new skills that accompany them:

- Prior to birth, growth spurts occur in the cerebellum and hypothalamus, which enable all the infant's basic survival functions, such as breathing, a heartbeat, body temperature, reflexes, and sensation, to work fairly efficiently early in life.
- At the 7- to 8-week brain growth spurt, the baby starts to build reflex upon reflex; hearing his mother's voice triggers staring in her direction.
- At the 10- to 11-week spurt, the reflex chain grows another link longer: The baby hears Mom's voice, looks at her, and responds by smiling or cooing; or she sees a ball, reaches toward it, and opens her fingers.
- At about 2 months, growth spurts occur in the motor cortex; correspondingly, the infant will lose reflex rooting (turning its cheek in the direction of a touch) and startle responses (throwing its arms outward in response to a loud noise) and begin to make purposeful motor movements.
- At about 8 or 9 months, growth spurts occur in the hippocampus, which is implicated in memory, allowing infants to form explicit memories, such as remembering to kick at the mobile in the crib to make it move.
- By the end of the infancy period, the toddler has piled up experiences provided by chains of reflexive and sensorimotor actions, and these have helped the brain reach a new level of potential; the infant now has the ability to represent objects, people, or events through mental symbols.

When a child is about 2 years old, new growth spurts in the cerebellum and midbrain are reflected in his growing coordination and ability to walk, run, and manipulate objects. Finally, the last areas in the brain that undergo growth spurts are the **cerebrum** and **cerebral cortex**, which are responsible for higher-order thinking, complex reasoning, and problem solving. These take the longest to mature—about 10 years or more. These long cycles explain why our ability to memorize, recall information, generate complex thoughts, plan strategies, or formulate hypotheses begins to unfold in toddlerhood but continues to mature well into our teenage years.

Thought **CHALLENGE**

If positive early experiences are crucial for healthy brain development and deprivation leads to unhealthy brain development, what should society do to intervene in cases of deprived children?

cerebrum and cerebral cortex Higher centers of the brain implicated in higher-order thinking, complex reasoning, and problem solving.

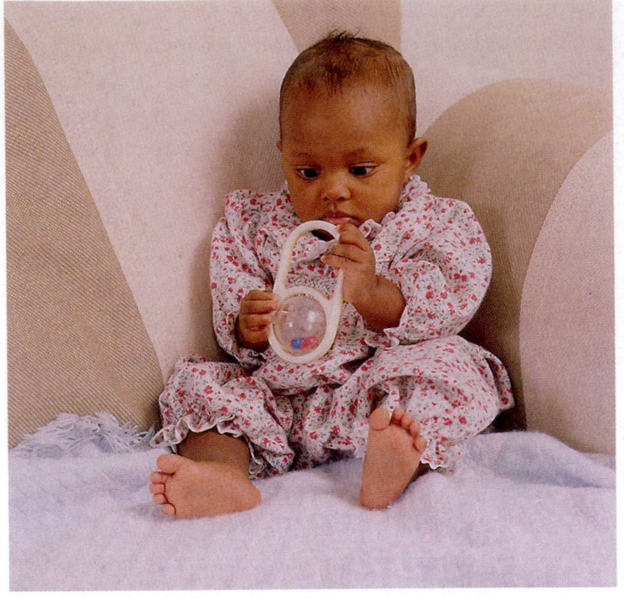

In Kurt Fischer's model of child development, various regions of the brain undergo growth spurts during which we see the emergence of new behaviors and skills such as the ability to manipulate objects.

Providing an Enriched Environment

Through their constant touching, looking, tasting, listening, and moving, babies provide themselves with experiences they need for the brain to develop normally. By instinct, babies and toddlers are creatures of learning, and of play, exploring every detail of their surroundings with intense curiosity. But to foster the child's fullest development, babies' caregivers must provide certain kinds of experiences, particularly in the realm of emotional support and language.

In Charles Dickens' *David Copperfield,* Mrs. Micawber conveys her father's sage advice to young David, "*Experentia* does it." And, when it comes to the brain, experience is important. For adults hoping to promote children's healthiest development, it is critical to pick the *right* experience at the *right* time. For the early years of life, there are a variety of physical and social characteristics of the child's home environment that are particularly critical for early brain development. Aspects of the physical environment that are positively related to healthy brain development include availability and variety of stimuli, responsivity of the physical environment, and organization of regularity of scheduling in the home (Wachs, 1992). Table 5.1 identifies the common threads in all enriched environments.

In contrast, evidence consistently suggests that high levels of ambient background noise, overcrowding, and too many people coming and going in the house are negatively related to healthy brain development. A nonenriched environment is also one that has a vacillating or negative emotional climate, deprives the child of sensory stimulation, is characterized by unchanging conditions lacking novelty, provides passive rather than active involvement of the child, or affords little chance for fun and a sense of exploration and the joy of learning to the young child (Diamond & Hopson, 1998).

An "At Risk" Curriculum

A new group of parents arrives at the Institutes for the Achievement of Human Potential in a Philadelphia suburb. They have come to take a seven-day course in "How to Multiply Your Baby's Intelligence." In their first meeting, they meet the director, who then introduces them to 4-year-old Gunther, a former graduate. Gunther plays the violin, speaks Hungarian, reads in two languages, and excels in gymnastics. His mother began his training very early in Gunther's life, and according to her, "he *loved* every minute of it!"

Infants are capable little beings, and as such, some adults believe that infants should be exposed to rigorous, structured learning. (In the First Person section, Gunther's mother talks about the lessons she taught him as an infant.) However, in the opinion of many experts (Rovee-Collier, 1996; Ramey, Breitmeyer, Goldman, & Wakeley, 1996) babies do not profit from regimented drills. Craig Ramey and his colleagues (Ramey & Ramey, 1998) advise against the view that infants are receptacles waiting to be filled up with information.

A growing number of parents believe, however, that toddlers should be exposed to computers. The idea: Buy the computer and the software and the brain will grow. Without an early start, they believe, children will never catch up. Out of the ten best-selling children's CD-ROM titles, four are marketed for toddlers (Healy, 1998). Some parents are convinced that connecting children to computers will somehow make them smarter, and the earlier they begin their computer literacy programs, the better.

> Perched on her mother's lap, 2-year-old Marta pounds the keyboard, and the pleasant computer-synthesized voice says, "Car starts with the letter C." Marta stares at the keyboard, ignoring the toy trucks and plastic dolls on the floor around her. Her tiny fist taps the keyboard again—"Rain begins with the letter R."

TABLE 5.1

Enriched Environments for Infants and Toddlers

An enriched environment: ▪ Includes a steady source of positive emotional support ▪ Provides a nutritious diet with enough protein, vitamins, minerals, and calories ▪ Stimulates all the senses (but not necessarily all at once!) ▪ Has an atmosphere free of undue pressure and stress but is suffused with a degree of pleasurable intensity	▪ Presents a series of novel challenges that are neither too easy nor too difficult for the child at his or her stage of development ▪ Allows for social interaction for a significant percentage of activities ▪ Promotes the development of a broad range of skills and interests that are mental, physical, aesthetic, social, and emotional	▪ Gives the child a chance to assess the results of his or her efforts and to modify them ▪ Creates an enjoyable atmosphere that promotes exploration and fun-filled learning ▪ Above all, allows the child to be an active participant rather than a passive observer

From *Magic Trees of the Mind* (pp. 107–108), by M. D. Diamond & J. Hopson, 1998, New York: Dutton. © 1988 by Marian Diamond & Janet Hopson. Used by permission of Dutton, a division of Penguin Putnam, Inc.

FIRSTPERSON

The Geniuses of Tomorrow

I would attend the School for Early Development once a week and learn how to teach Gunther reading, math, and encyclopedic knowledge, and then I would teach him these skills at home. When first teaching him to read, for example, I made hundreds of big cards, each bearing a letter of the alphabet "A," "B." For approximately 3 to 5 minutes a day, I would flash these cards very quickly and as I was doing so, I pronounced each letter. In the math course, I would expose Gunther to cards holding various numbers of red dots and as he gazed at the cards, I would flip them in rapid succession, and call out "63," "21," "88." When Gunther was about 8 months old, I taught him about birds, their names, identification, and scientific classifications. Sometimes I would bring Gunther to the Institutes for Physical Excellence, the staff (through the parents) would help infants learn how to swim—and when Gunther was a toddler, how to run and do Olympic routines, ballet, and a host of other physical activities superbly.

Some days we would work on foreign languages. Although Gunther could not talk when he was 7 months old, he could understand speech. I would write words from various languages in red ink on separate pieces of white cardboard and place them in a pile at the other end of our living room. Holding Gunther on my lap, I would say, "Gunther, crawl over there to the words and bring me the Japanese word for 'mother' or the Hebrew word for 'door.'" He would enthusiastically crawl and retrieve the cardboard with the correct word. Although he couldn't talk he could read hundreds of words in three different languages. I do believe that young children are ready to begin learning and the sooner the training begins, the more capable they will be later on. In today's highly competitive world, we've got to give our kids a head start, or they will fall behind and never catch up.

—***Colleen Brown***

TABLE 5.2

The Infant's Brain: Stimulating Development

Period	Development
1 month	A low level of stimulation reduces stress and increases the infant's wakefulness and alertness. The brain essentially shuts down the system when there is overstimulation from competing sources. Thus, when talking to an infant, filter out distracting noises, for example, like a radio.
1–3 months	Light/dark contours, like high-contrast pictures or objects, foster development in neural networks that encode vision. The brain also starts to discriminate among acoustic patterns of language, like intonation, lilt, and pitch. Speaking to the infant, especially in an animated voice, aids this process.
3–5 months	The infant relies primarily on vision to acquire information about the world. Make available increasingly complex designs that correspond to real objects in the baby's environment.
6–7 months	The infant becomes alert to relationships like cause and effect, the location of objects, and the functions of objects. Demonstrate and talk about situations such as how the turning of a doorknob leads to the opening of the door.
7–8 months	The brain is oriented to make associations between sounds and some meaningful activity or object. For example, parents can deliberately emphasize in conversation that the sound of water running in the bathroom signals an impending bath or that a doorbell means a visitor.
9–12 months	Learning adds up to a new level of awareness of the environment and increased interest in exploration; sensory and motor skills coordinate in a more mature fashion. This is the time to let the child turn on a faucet or a light switch, under supervision.
13–18 months	The brain establishes accelerated and more complex associations, especially if the toddler experiments directly with objects. A rich environment will help the toddler make such associations, understand sequences, differentiate between objects, and reason about them.

From *Brain under Construction: Experiences That Promote the Intellectual Capabilities of Young Toddlers,* by W. H. Staso, 1995, Orcutt, CA: Great Beginnings. Reprinted by permission of Will Staso, M.D.

Researchers agree that computers are not for toddlers; however, they tend to disagree about what is the ideal time to introduce children to computers. Some researchers support the notion that children around the age of 7 can be introduced to computers with parental guidance and for short periods of time (Case, 1996). Others favor postponing computer use until children develop conceptual abilities, at around the sixth grade at the earliest (Healy, 1998). Most learning specialists suggest that the best learning tool or toy is 90 percent child and 10 percent toy.

Adults do not need to rush to do more and more "things" for infants and young children. Stimulation does not equate to regimented exercises. It is wise to avoid the feeling that simply because an infant has an impressionable brain awaiting information that more and more information should be pumped into it (Haith, Wass, & Adler, 1997). The "curriculum" most beneficial to infants is not the type discussed in the First Person box. Rather exposing them to lots of sounds, sights, smells, and experiences that enhance their innate curiosity is most appropriate (Greenspan, Wieder, & Simons, 1998). These types of activities are what infants need, not regimented drills. A timetable of different kinds of stimulation that should be emphasized at different ages in the first 18 months of life is presented in Table 5.2.

As noted in Chapter 1, in Creating Optimal Environments, we now know that the baby's participation in creating solid emotional bonds with parents is crucial. The parents' loving gaze is reciprocated by the baby's broad, toothless grin. Parents, taking their cues from the infant, fine-tune their activity to be in sync with that of the child. Periods of play and interaction are followed by restful and quiet periods of nonplay. Play periods stimulate the brain's periods of alertness; inactivity allows the infant's developing brain to process the stimulation and the interaction (Greenspan, 1998). It is the emotional quality of the relationship that parents have with their babies that will stimulate brain development for optimal emotional and intellectual growth.

Concept Checks

1. At the end of the first year of life, regions in the __________ cortex become __________, which is reflected in the young child's ability to walk.
2. Whereas the phenomenal growth of neurons ceases after birth, __________ keep on growing.

3. *True or False:* Neurons stimulated by the environment continue to establish new connections after birth.
4. If the infant's emotions are repeatedly met with conflicting responses,
   a. circuits in the emotional brain for negative emotions (fear, anger) become reinforced.
   b. the child will be incapable of expressing his or her emotional feelings.
   c. nothing will happen because emotional circuits in the brain are not formed until toddlerhood.
5. Which statement best sums up the most effective way of enhancing brain development during infancy?
   a. Infants are active creatures. Their spontaneous activities provide enough brain stimulation.
   b. Infants need to be exposed to vigorous, structured learning.
   c. Infants prosper when adults expose them to environmental events that will enhance their innate curiosity.

Physical and Motor Development

Before Beginning . . .

After reading this section, you will be able to

- index weight and height changes during infancy.
- describe cephalocaudal and proximodistal patterns of growth.
- review the development of reflexes.
- characterize reaching, grasping, and manipulative skills.
- discuss effective methods for toilet training young children.

Where once reflexes dominated the infant's motor capabilities, in a few short months, the infant will engage in purposeful motor movements. Independent locomotion is a dramatic step in the parade of the infant's new motor skills. In a brief 24 months, the infant progresses from his first wobbly steps to one who is able to navigate in, over, under, around, and through his environment with surprising agility and ease.

Physical Growth Patterns

The gestation period is the most rapid period of physical growth. At conception, the embryo is smaller than the dot over an "i"; at birth the average infant weighs 7½ pounds and is about 20 inches long. That is a pretty impressive growth rate. Amazingly enough, the developmental transformations that take place in the next two years of life come in a close second. Children's physical development in the infancy period happens so rapidly that their size and skills appear to change daily. One way of noting the rapid sequence of physical development is by looking at their changing height and weight. During the first two years of life, the child grows about 14 inches, topping the height charts at about 34 inches in length, and gains about 20 pounds, tipping the scales at about 28 pounds.

Weight changes are much more dramatic than height changes during the first year after birth. The human baby doubles its weight during the first 3 months of life and almost triples it in the first year. From birth to 6 months of age, babies increase in weight almost .1 ounce, (about 2 grams) every 24 hours. From 6 months to 2 years, the daily increase averages about .01 ounce (.35 gram) per day (DiGirolamo, Geis, & Walker, 1998). The growth rate is faster in the first 6 months of life than it will ever be again; in fact, during the second year of life, it is already beginning to slow down (Tanner, 1998).

Growth is not steady or constant in all areas; different parts of the body grow at different times and rates. From birth to 1 year, the trunk is the fastest-growing portion, accounting for about 60 percent of the total increase in body length during this time. From age 1 to the onset of adolescence, legs grow the fastest, accounting for 66 percent of the total increase in height (Tanner, 1998). Changing proportions are perhaps even more dramatic than total growth. During the first year, the head is disproportionately large. The pot-bellied look is normal and has nothing to do with overfeeding or malnutrition in healthy babies. The infant's liver is relatively large at this age, and the immature abdominal muscles lack the strength to hold in the abdominal contents.

Many aspects of physical growth during infancy, such as height and weight, vary widely around the world, depending upon genetic pools, nutrition, and other environmental factors. At age 1, infants living in different regions of the world differ as much as 5.5 inches in average height and 9 pounds in average weight (Tanner, 1998). The shortest and lightest infants come from South-Central and Southeast Asia (India, Vietnam, Pakistan). The tallest and heaviest come from the United States and Europe. In the United States, African American infants tend to be slightly smaller at birth than European American infants, but their skeletal development is slightly more advanced. African

American infants soon surpass European American infants in size and are a little taller and heavier throughout childhood as long as socioeconomic factors are equivalent (Tanner, 1998).

Principles of Motor Development

The infant's motor development has been described as progressing in a **cephalocaudal** (head-to-toe) and **proximodistal** (from close to the midline of the body to away from the midline) direction. In the first pattern, cephalocaudal, the head and the body initially grow faster and reach mature size earliest, whereas the "tail" end takes longer to develop. In proximodistal growth patterns, areas closer to the center of the body, like the shoulders, grow and mature earlier than do more distant parts, like the hands.

Complex Reflexive Actions

Much of the complex motor behavior children use later on is anticipated in early infancy in the form of **reflexes**—unlearned, involuntary, and autonomic responses that become the building blocks of later motor behavior. Newborns are capable of an amazingly complex series of reflex activities that are present at birth. These early reflexes are slow, generalized, patterned movements of the head, trunk, and extremities.

Infants are a mixture of volition and reflexes. At birth the infant exhibits a sucking reflex, which means that the child will make sucking motions when lips are touched or something is inserted into the mouth. Putting your finger in the palm of a newborn will cause that infant to grasp it with firmness and unbelievable strength—in fact, newborns have such a strong grasp that they can actually hang from a bar. A newborn who thinks he is falling will throw his arms back and spread his fingers as if to clutch the air and then bring his arms back to hug his chest. This is known as the *Moro reflex.* The *startle reflex,* often confused with the Moro reflex, is elicited by loud noises or unexpected stimuli. The response is similar. When babies are held up vertically with their feet touching a flat surface such as a table, they will alternately lift each knee up high, as if trying to take some steps. This *stepping reflex* disappears in the second or third month.

cephalocaudal
An organized pattern of physical growth, which literally means from "head to foot"; that is, the body develops from the head end downward.

proximodistal
Development proceeds from the middle of the organism out to the periphery; that is, growth proceeds from the midline of the body outward.

reflexes
Unlearned responses that involve a reaction of an organism to a specific, eliciting stimulus.

Why do reflexes, such as the stepping reflex, disappear? For a long time, neurobiologists believed that increasing activity in the cerebral cortex was responsible for inhibiting reflex activity. Primitive reflexes governed by the older structures of the brain drop out or disappear when the cerebrum, or higher centers of the brain, begin to dominate. While it is true that maturation in the higher centers of the brain is required for the onset of true walking, the real reason why reflexive walking disappears in early infancy is much more mundane—relatively heavy heads and short legs make balance excessively difficult for infants. A summary of the infant's primitive reflexes is found in Table 5.3.

Posture

Posture represents the adjustments of the body in relation to the forces of gravity. Postural abilities an infant must develop include head control, rolling over, sitting, and standing. The first step toward sitting upright and independent locomotion is establishing *head control.* With amazing strength, the newborn will lift his head for just a few seconds at a time, an amazing feat considering the weight and size of his head and the fact that his neck muscles are quite weak.

Rolling from one side to another represents the infant's first attempt at locomotion. Ordinarily, an infant can roll from stomach to back around 16 weeks of age, while the more difficult task of rolling from back to stomach is typically performed about six weeks later. Currently, however, many infants are only positioned to sleep on their backs because it appears to be advantageous in reducing sudden infant death syndrome. In a recent study, however, pediatricians found that babies who only sleep on their backs display slower progress in learning to roll over as well as to sit, crawl, and pull themselves to stand than babies who sleep on their stomachs (Davis, 1998). The delay is minor and may not justify abandoning back-sleeping but the experimenters advise that caregivers should give infants some time on their stomachs to exercise their arm and neck muscles.

As the infant gradually gains control over the muscles in the trunk of the body, *sitting* alone becomes possible. Most babies are able to sit alone momentarily without support at around 5 months (Bayley, 1993). By 6 or 7 months, an infant can maneuver into a sitting position and sit alone steadily. Shortly thereafter, a number of action achievements follow, beginning with toddlers pulling themselves

TABLE 5.3

Newborn Reflexes

Reflex	Description	Usual Age of Disappearance
Hand grasp	Place objects in the newborn's hands, and the infant grasps the object tightly.	3 months
Rooting	Stroke the corner of the infant's mouth and he turns his head toward the side of the stimulation.	Weakens by 2 months; disappears by 5 months
Sucking	Place a nipple or a finger in the newborn's mouth, and she sucks it.	7 months
Babinski	Stroke the sole of the infant's foot and his toes spread out.	12–18 months
Moro	With the infant on her back, remove her head support. Her arms move in toward the body, then extend, and then move in again.	4 months
Foot withdrawal	Lightly prick the sole of his foot with a pin and he withdraws with leg flexion.	8–12 months
Walking reflex	Hold the infant upright with the soles of her feet touching a surface. She will make a walking movement when moved forward.	8 weeks

up on the furniture and standing for a few shaky moments, which helps them learn the fine art of balancing (Adolph, Vereijken, & Denny, 1998). At age 1, they can stand alone, usually followed shortly thereafter by crawling and walking.

Becoming Ambulatory

Infants are physically active little beings, with an insatiable urge to explore. These young children invent all sorts of strategies to get that sought-after toy or just to see what there is to see. For many infants, their first success at mobility is crawling, which generally begins at about 10 months. Most likely, this begins with clumsy attempts to move forward with his stomach dragging on the ground and ends several weeks later in stable, proficient travel with his body being propped firmly on hands and knees, or various versions thereof. Some children, for example, roll over and over; some do the old Marine crawl; some scoot on their seats—but all these methods of locomotion serve the same purpose.

From the time they begin to walk until they achieve a stable pattern of walking around 24 months of age, infants are often referred to as **toddlers**. And, what an achievement walking is! Onlookers offer their oohs and ahs, and the child beams with delight in taking those first jerky, unstable, flat-footed steps. Although the onset of walking generally occurs around 13 to 15 months, it is not until about age 4 that the child assumes the adultlike walk with the smooth, rhythmical transfer of weight from heel-to-toe and the rhythmical swing of the arms in opposition to leg action.

At 18 months, children can walk upstairs in a "mark-time" pattern, that is, the lead foot steps up, followed by the other foot, which is placed beside it. The alternating foot pattern does not occur until around age 3. Going upstairs is easier than coming down. Children generally are unable to descend stairs using the alternating foot pattern without support until age 4, perhaps 5. Two-year-olds can climb, run forward and backward, and seemingly have unlimited powers to get where they want to go. It should be pointed out that the average age at which a child masters a certain

toddlers
The term applied to infants from the period when they begin to walk until they achieve a stable pattern at about 24 months.

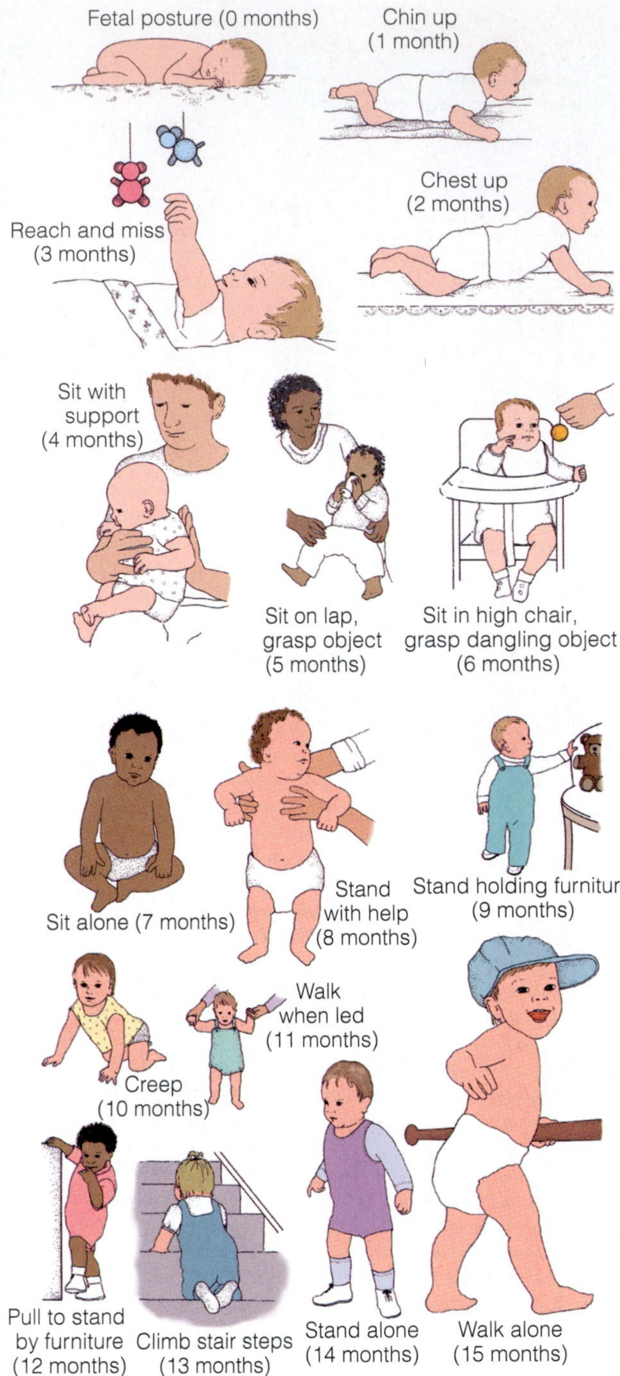

FIGURE 5.3 ***Sequence of Motor Development Leading to Walking***

In a short 15 months, children progress from an immobile state to being capable of navigating their environment with unsteady, flat-footed steps.

Shirley, 1933

motor task has a wide range. Figure 5.3 highlights the sequence of the infant's motor development and the average ages for these milestones.

Reaching, Grasping, and Manipulative Skills

Success at last! Five-month-old Michael has finally succeeded in grasping the brightly colored rings on the mobile over his crib. But this feat, the first in a long succession of manipulative milestones, has taken a lot of diligent practice. In a sense, reaching can be said to begin before Michael was born. All those random arm movements performed in utero were first steps toward refining the motor systems responsible for reaching. Reaching takes another gigantic leap after birth. At 1 month after birth, Michael stared at the rings in his field of vision. At a little over 2 months, he made swiping motions at it. By 4 months, he was able to glance at the ring and his hand and then touch the ring and grasp it (Rochat & Goubet, 1995). (What sometimes happens, however, is that the child gets so absorbed in staring at its hand that it forgets about the object.) By 5 months or so, Michael was an expert; he could not only reach for the object but could make efficient contact with it. One problem exists, however, the young infant doesn't know how to let go. Usually what happens is that the infant eventually loses interest, the hand relaxes, and the object, unnoticed by the infant, drops. By 6 months, most children are able to intentionally release an object.

Once infants develop the ability to grasp objects, they spend a large amount of time engaging in manipulative activities. In the early stages, infants use only the fingers and the palm in picking up an object, a small cube, for example. Picking up small objects is more problematic, and an infant will generally just rake at a tiny object without picking it up. As soon as the ability to use the thumb (finger-thumb opposition) is acquired at approximately 9 months, grasping skills develop faster. By age 1, an infant can pick up cubes and small objects in an adultlike fashion with a thumb and forefinger pincer grasp. Figure 5.4 takes a look at the progressive development of the infant's manipulative skills.

Maturation, Experience, and Motor Skills

As reflexive motor abilities come under voluntary control, they are elaborated on to produce new, more sophisticated and effective motor skills. The increasing ability to perform complex motor functions tends to be linked to the increase in body size; brain development;

the growth of various body parts, bones, and muscles; and maturation of neural pathways.

Investigators have found early development (precocity) in motor skills in literally dozens of cultures around the world—in tribes in Africa, in many societies in Latin America and Asia, and within ethnic groups in the United States (LeVine, Dixon, LeVine, Richman, Leiderman, Keefer, & Brazelton, 1994). In Africa and Latin America, infants display more advanced motor development than European American infants. In these societies, infants are often encouraged to stand and begin to walk at early ages. The Bayley Scales (see Chapter 4) are often used to study intercultural differences in infant motor development. These scales, measuring both mental and motor development, have been standardized with large populations of infants in the United States, Europe, and other countries around the world. Based on Bayley Scales assessments, it was found that Israeli infants in the Kibbutz tend to develop early motor skills. Motor precocity is also found among Kikuyu infants from Nairobi, the capital of Kenya, Africa. Kikuyu infants score significantly higher than would be expected for American infants of the same ages. In the United States, African American infants' motor development tends to be more advanced than European American infants (Malina, 1988). Motor precocity found in ethnic groups in the United States, however, is not as great as that in African infants in rural, preindustrial societies.

In Mexico, where infants are reared quite passively and are kept bundled up, motor development is generally less advanced than that of Western infants. Rigoberta Menchu (2000), a Mayan native of Guatemala, describes the infant's first year. For a good part of this time infants are kept indoors in small, dark, windowless huts. Only when they can walk are they allowed outdoors. Guatemalan women do not work in the fields but spend their days at home preparing meals, weaving, and looking after their babies. They usually keep the baby in their laps, or in a cloth on their backs, or close to them on a floor mat or in a hammock. Mothers believe sun, air, and dust are harmful to babies, so they keep them inside. These infants are not trained to stand, crawl, or walk, because they are believed to be incapable of learning.

Overall, the greatest motor precocity has been found in black infants, both in Africa and in the United States, followed by Indian infants in Latin America and infants in Asia. European American infants rate lowest on the precocity scale. Why are some infants more advanced motorically than others? Are these advancements due to their genetic structure, or does the environment influence the appearance of early motor skills? There is some disagreement as to what role learning and maturation play in the development of motor skills. (This issue, along with further cross-cultural comparisons of motor development, is discussed in Cultural Variations.)

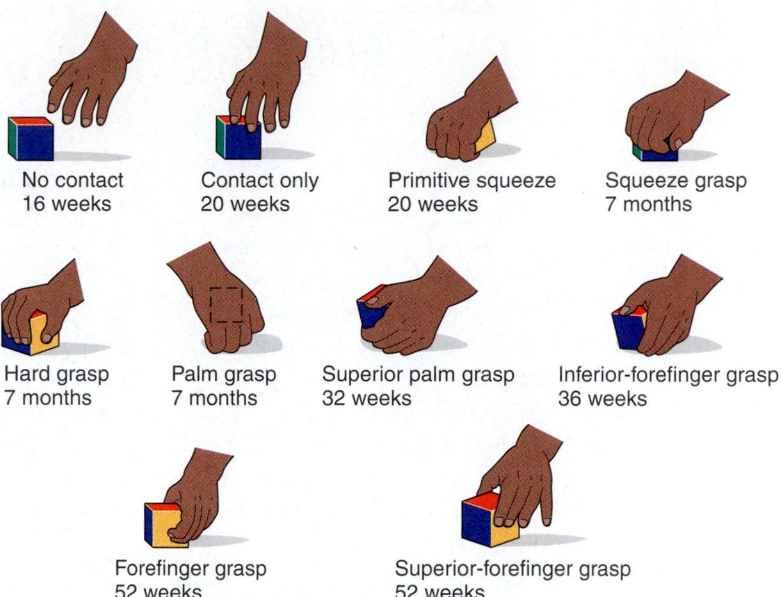

FIGURE 5.4 *Development of Grasping Skills*

As fine muscles develop, children's grasping skills become progressively more sophisticated—eventually culminating in the superior-forefinger grasp at 52 weeks.

From "An Experimental Study of Prehension in Infants by Means of Systematic Cinema Records" (pp. 212–215), by H. M. Halverson, 1931, *Genetic Psychological Monographs,* 10. Reprinted by permission of Helref Publications.

APPLICATIONS: Toilet Training

Being toilet trained is another physical and motor skill that, in the United States, is expected to be attained by age 3.

> Lorenzo, age 2, dashes to the bathroom. With his *Barney* easy-pull-down diapers, he loves to play the game of sinking the Cheerios as he takes aim and achieves another success keeping himself dry. Controlling bladder and bowel functions, commonly known as toilet training, depends on the child's physical, motor, and motivation skills—and, perhaps, some clever engineering tricks from his parents.

Cultural Variations

Cross-Cultural Differences in Motor Development

Many observers have reported that African infants have an accelerated rate of motor development. Indeed, the findings of some 50 studies point to a generalized accelerated pace of motor development among non-Western infants. The infants of the Gusii tribe living near the equator in western Kenya, Africa, for example, are reputedly more advanced in motor functioning than Caucasian age norms would predict (LeVine, Dixon, LeVine, Richman, Leiderman, Keefer, & Brazelton, 1994). These infants show remarkable control over motor reactions: they are able to be pulled to sit by extended arms; they not only maintain excellent head control in bringing their heads up parallel to their bodies but also turn their heads to look around the room as they sit. They also stand and walk earlier than American babies.

The mothers in many African cultures, however, work to promote their infants' motor skills. Often they spend time, for example, in "early walking" exercises (Zelazo, Zelazo, Cohen, & Zelazo, 1993). When infants are just 2- to 8-weeks old, mothers help them practice their stepping reflex. Similarly, infants are put in holes that mothers dig in the ground. These holes encase the infant up to his neck and the sides of the hole support his back. These experiences in upright posturing and various forms of walking practice appear to influence the age at which maturational capabilities are achieved and translated into action.

Brian Hopkins (Hopkins & Westra, 1989) has also done experiments comparing white infants from England with black infants from Jamaican families who recently emigrated to England. Like their African counterparts, Jamaican mothers also tend to use techniques for nurturing more precocious motor behavior. The Jamaican mothers' expectation of when their infants would achieve sitting and walking alone was significantly earlier than their English counterparts. As expected, the Jamaican infants, who receive early motor training, are more advanced in standing, sitting, and walking skills than white infants and Jamaican infants who did not receive early motor training.

It appears, then, that cross-cultural differences in motoric behavior exist early in life. But, we need to ask, are these differences attributed to culturally different child-rearing practices, or do these differences reflect some kind of genetic predisposition of a group? Traditionally, developmental changes in motor abilities were attributed to maturational processes in the central nervous system.

According to the *biologically related model,* cultural differences in motor behavior are presumed to be a matter of different genetic predispositions. According to this theory, maturation of the central nervous system is the primary catalyst for stagelike transitions in motor development (Gesell & Ames, l940). In general, studies use twins to determine the role of learning in motor skills. In each case, one of the twins receives a great deal of training in a particular skill such as walking upstairs. The other twin is not given such extensive training but rather is given only a brief period of practice later in development. The results of these studies have shown that both of the twins perform equally well. No matter how much training the first twin receives, she will not learn the particular skill until she is maturationally ready to walk upstairs.

Models of standard learning theory, the *learning-experience model*, have also been employed to explain motor development. In these accounts, motor development is viewed as a derivative of training and it is argued that essentially no meaningful biological differences distinguish black babies from white babies. Rather, a culture-mother-infant chain of cause and effect best explains the relation between culture and individual behavior. Infant activities develop under maternal influences, which are in turn guided to conform to culturally preferred patterns. A number of common features in the first year of life of all these precocious infants have been identified: many caregivers, usually in extended families; fairly constant contact with caregivers either in sleeping or in being held and carried; lack of restrictive clothing and of set routines for feeding, elimination, and sleeping; and frequent stimulation from adult activities carried on in the infant's presence.

Some researchers, however, have turned to a *dynamic systems* approach as a more adequate account for many aspects of early motor development. Esther Thelen (1998) argues, for example, that motor development is not programmed in our genes nor is it just

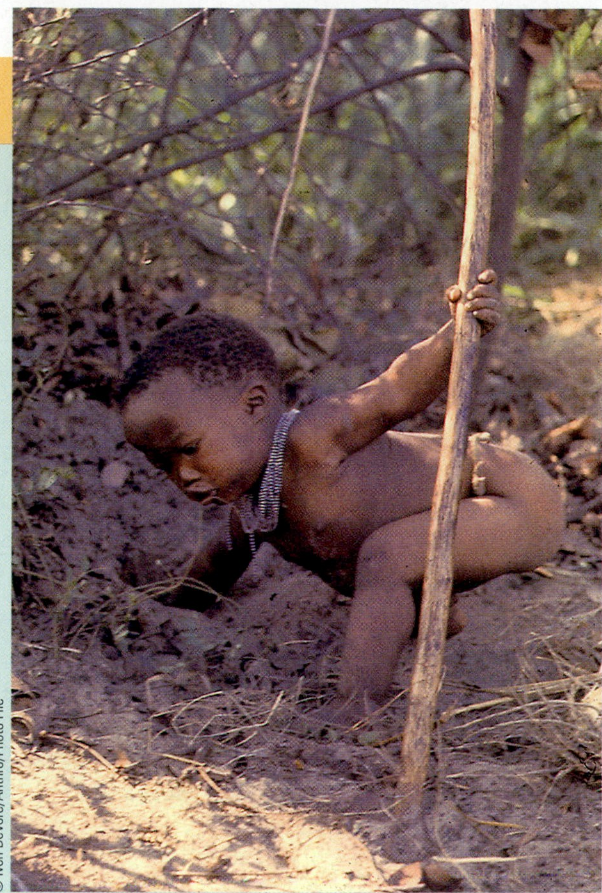
© Iven DeVore/Anthro/Photo File

a consequence of early experience. In this model, the child's world of motor development forms a system that is dynamic (constantly in motion). Any change in that system, whether it results from their genetic endowment (maturation) or from environmental inputs (experience), upsets the balance in the system, which causes the child to actively reorganize his or her behavior in a more complex manner. Thus, the child's motor activity level is influenced in part by genetic endowment and the environment. Once the proper maturational level is reached in the muscles, bones, and central nervous system *and* the child is given some opportunity to move about and to explore the environment, the development of a particular motor activity occurs. Thus, patterns of motor behavior are assumed to be the product of *self-organizing* systems involving many component processes.

Toilet training is actually an inappropriate label because it implies that the caregiver will "train" the child to perform this task. It is more effective to see toilet training as the child's own learning process, one that is achieved by the child in accordance with his or her own maturation (Thienemann, 1998). Around age 2, children will usually train themselves in a relatively short period of time.

Waiting for the Optimal Moment

Attempts at mastering toilet training before the age of 2 tend to result in much effort on the parents' part and little success on the children's part. As such, pediatricians advise that "training" the child between the ages of 14 and 24 months is not the optimal time. Further, this time period may be less than optimal because these months tend to coincide with a rise in negativism in children; attempts at conquering toilet training may, thus, prove quite difficult. When parents are unable to wait and impose toilet training as their idea, children see this as an invasion.

Waiting until the child is ready does not mean doing nothing. It is important for caregivers to look for readiness signs and explain to children what is expected of them. Children should be capable of physical skills such as being able to pull their pants down all by themselves. Independence issues are paramount to two-year-olds, and if they have to keep running to caregivers for aid in getting their clothes off so they can go to the bathroom, they are likely to feel dependent and rebellious. It is helpful for parents to get a potty chair, talk about its purposes, and encourage the child to sit on it and play with it. While children are playing and exploring with it, they are learning. If there are older siblings, two-year-olds can observe their very talented, toilet-trained brother or sister. Children often train themselves quite readily by imitating older siblings.

Staying Dry at Night

By the time children are 3, they can control their bowel movements and can stay dry during the day. Staying dry at night may take a few more years. In fact, many pediatricians feel that staying dry at night should not be considered a problem until after the fifth birthday for girls and the sixth birthday for boys. Mistakes made by the child, pediatricians advise, should not be taken very seriously by the parent because the child takes them very seriously. Repeated failures are likely to occur because adults have punished or overreacted to mistakes and have put too much pressure on the child.

Concept Checks

1. ***True or False:*** Height changes are more dramatic than weight changes in the first two years of life.
2. The fact that infants can control their heads before they can control their arm and hand movement is an example of ________________ motor development.
3. The disappearance of reflexes is a sign that
   a. the older centers of the brain have been damaged.
   b. the higher centers of the brain are beginning to dominate.
   c. flexibility in the brain is decreasing.
4. If you believe that maturation plays a bigger role in the development of motor skills than learning, which of these statements would you believe is true?
   a. The growing sophistication of the motor cortex results in more advanced motor skills.
   b. Despite maturation, young children still need a great deal of training to learn a specific skill.
   c. Children need to be given lots of opportunity to explore their environment.
5. To teach children to control bladder and bowel functions, pediatricians generally advise that parents
   a. train the child before the "terrible twos" set in.
   b. wait until the child shows signs of readiness.
   c. be relaxed and laid back about training the child.

The World of Sights, Sounds, and Smells

Before Beginning . . .

After reading this section, you will be able to

- identify the visual, auditory, olfactory, gustatory, and tactile accomplishments of infants.
- explain the process of organizing and interpreting sensory information.
- understand signs of normal and impaired hearing.

The senses—sight, sound, smell, touch, and taste—provide infants with rich understandings of their world, enabling them to become purposeful problem solvers who are able to organize their behavior in meaningful ways.

Sensory Systems

After nine months in intrauterine darkness, a baby is plunged into a world of lights, sounds, movement, touch, taste, and smell, which is nothing short of a sensory extravaganza! Sight, sound, smell, taste, and touch are the doorways into the brain. Each converts its chosen category of information from the outside world into the electrical signals that are the brain's common language. It is on these sensory systems that many developmental researchers have concentrated their efforts to understand the infant's world.

Although all this sensory information is exciting and stimulating to newborns, their very first challenge is to learn to regulate their responses to this sensory panorama and remain calm. Gradually, the newborn does just that. Soon she focuses her interests on her mother's face, on her father's voice, and the soft texture of the blanket. Little by little, the infant learns to *balance* an awareness of these sensations and acquires the ability to *self-regulate* her arousal level. This pair of skills is one of the most basic building blocks of emotional, social, and intellectual health.

The Visual System

At birth an infant's senses of sight, sound, touch, taste, and smell are nearly complete and improve rather rapidly in the first six months of life. Vision provides newborns with most of their information about their world. At birth, however, the infant's visual system has some limitations. For example, they have a fairly rigid distance of focus—approximately 8 to 10 inches—the distance from their mother's breast to her face. Many people do not know this, yet, almost all adults (and children) will unknowingly accommodate to the infant's limited field of vision by bending over close to the baby's face or bringing the baby close to their faces when communicating with the young infant.

Do infants have the ability to see clearly? Normal acuity for adults is 20/20; estimates of newborn acuity range from 20/400 to 20/600, making the neonate legally blind. Acuity improves gradually over the next several months. This slow process of the development of the visual system, however, helps protect the infant from too much stimulation. Visual acuity reaches adult levels by 6 months.

A young infant lying in his crib may not be able to actively explore with his hands and feet, but he is extremely busy exploring with his eyes. When infants encounter an interesting stimulus, they appear to

To an adult with good vision, the details of the woman's face on the left are clear. In contrast, with vision of 20/400 to 20/600, newborns are legally blind. When looking at their mother's face (right), they see only areas of contrast.

explore the areas of greatest contrast and are particularly sensitive to contrasting edges and contours, for example, the edge of a black line on a white background. Similarly, 1-month old infants, when viewing a human face, scan the areas of most contrast—the hairline of the face, angles, and edges (Johnson, Dziurawiec, Ellis, & Morton, 1991). It appears that infants do not respond to or perceive total form but instead react to some feature of the stimulus. At 2 months, children track an individual trait of the face such as a bright red mouth or shiny eyes.

Faces Are Special Human infants are marvelously social individuals and appear to enjoy looking at faces more than any other visual form. One view is that babies are attracted to faces from birth because of the varied stimulation they provide to the visual system (Slater, 1997). Another argument is that "faces are special," and that infants have an innate predisposition to respond to faces as faces, over and above the stimulation they offer (Johnson, Dziurawiec, Ellis, & Morton, 1991). For example, if we present 2-month-old Raphael with head-shaped designs, one with a face, one upside-down face, and one blank, he prefers the facelike pattern the most, followed by the upside-down one; the least favored is the blank head. These findings appear to demonstrate that Raphael, like all newborns, prefers a facelike pattern.

Further, if we now present Raphael with six flat disks, each painted differently with a face, a bull's-eye, a patch of printed matter, or plain red, fluorescent yellow, and white, his response is consistent. Once again, the face pattern is overwhelmingly his favorite, followed by the printing and then the bull's-eye. The three brightly colored disks without patterns trail far behind and are never their first choices (Fantz, 1961).

Laura is seated opposite her 3-month-old daughter, Tonya. Laura remains silent and expressionless. When Laura fails to greet her daughter, Tonya begins to look sober and warily at her mother, giving a brief smile. When Tonya's smile is not reciprocated, she looks away. She alternates brief glances at her mother and then glances away, occasionally smiling but in an increasingly wary manner. The glances away become longer and longer, until Tonya becomes overtly distressed.

Real human faces seem to be the most interesting to young infants (Fagan & Haiken-Vasen, 1997; Fantz, Fagan, & Miranda, 1975; Neisser, 1995) whose vision is a bit blurry. For example, when Tonya is presented with a real face, she gets quite excited—more so than when looking at a plain old cardboard face—and quickly smiles. Even more amazing, Tonya "expects" some interaction with this "real" face. If that is not forthcoming, newborns, in the United States, like Tonya, look worried, frown, and turn away—a wonderful indication that we are truly social creatures from the moment of birth. The nonhuman or stylized face attracts infants but does not carry this kind of expectation with it; they will, therefore, stare at it for longer periods of time (Legerstee, Anderson, & Schaffer, 1998).

When a sample of Chinese American infants was compared with a sample of infants from the United States and Canada, the researchers noted that the infants tended to respond to their silent mothers with distress; thus demonstrating the universality of the still-face effect (Kisilevsky, Hains, Lee, Muir, Xu, & Fu, 1998). It was also noted, however, that when Chinese American mothers interacted with their infants, the infants would smile, but they took longer to do so than European American or Canadian infants. Perhaps, this is so because of cross-cultural differences. The sample mothers from the United States and Canada tended to encourage their infants to verbally interact with them; this mutual regulation created a dancelike synchrony between the infant and the mother. Further, these mothers tended to interact with their infants to stimulate them in an effort to elicit positive exchanges, such as smiling and cooing. The sample of Chinese American mothers, however, did not engage in these types of behaviors but, rather, used more nonverbal visual stimulation.

Infants Prefer Attractive Faces

Several researchers have found that when attractive faces are paired with faces judged to be less attractive, infants prefer to look at the former (Langlois, Ritter, Roggman, & Vaughn, 1991; Samuels, Butterworth, Roberts, & Graupner, 1994). This is found also with African American, Asian American, and European American infants (Rhodes, Sumich, & Byatt, 1999). It is possible that newborn infants' preferences for attractive faces result from an innate representation of faces that infants bring into the world with them.

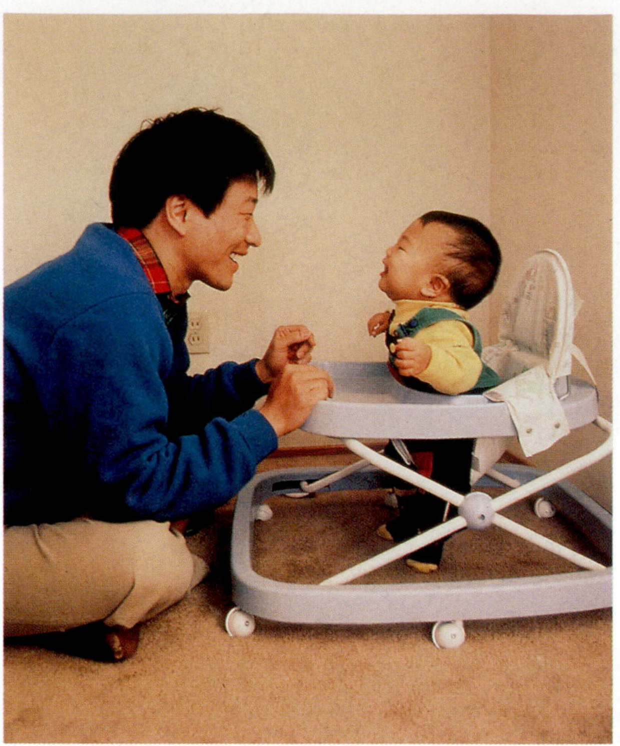

Infants prefer looking at smiling rather than frowning faces.

Recognizing Their Own Faces and Other Feats

Not only do infants prefer human faces during the first six months of life, they seem to recognize their own faces and voices as familiar stimuli (Bahrick, 1995). Young infants can also discriminate the facial expressions of others (Legerstee, 1997). Tonya will look more at facial expressions of joy than anger. Infants as young as 10 weeks old react to maternal facial and vocal displays of anger with anger but have fewer angry responses when their mothers pose sadness. Moreover, infant reactions are even influenced by an appreciation of the context surrounding the event. If Tonya's mother, for example, peers at her wearing a mask, Tonya laughs with delight. If a stranger does the same thing, she shows distress and fear. It appears, then, that from the moment of birth, infants are tuned to their social world; they find the stimuli coming from the social world very interesting, and they have a preference for the social stimuli with which they are accustomed.

Do mothers in other cultures engage in these exciting social interactions with their infants? Take the mothers of Gusii of Kenya. The relationship between these Kenyan mothers and their infants is marked by comparatively little face-to-face interaction (LeVine, Dixon, LeVine, Richman, Leiderman, Keefer, & Brazelton, 1994). According to the researchers who studied these mothers, the reason for little face-to-face action between mother and infant is to dampen the excitement of social interactions and to keep the infant calm at all times because these behaviors work best in this culture. The mother follows the cultural agenda because of her need to return to working in the fields at an early stage of the child's life and for the infant to be handed over to the care of older children. Therefore, the young child must be sufficiently calm and manageable for them.

Seeing Colors It is quite customary in many homes to provide colorful surroundings for young infants, such as brightly colored Disney characters parading across the infant's sheets and blankets. But, can they see the bright reds, greens, and yellows? Mickey and his friends, for a period of time, are perceived in only black, white, and gray. So, when do infants see color?

Marc Bornstein (1992) observed as 4- and 5-month-old infants viewed pairs of colored circles projected on a screen in front of them. Each circle of a pair was of a different color, and their preference for one over the other was measured in terms of gazing time. The infants showed marked differences in their gazing time. Infants were more "taken" with the primary colors blue and red. The boundary colors blue-red and yellow-red came next. Green, yellow, and green-yellow were liked least and were least gazed at by the infants. Such preferences suggest that the first color infants see is blue, followed by red, yellow, and green. By 6 months, their color perception equals that of an adult. This striking agreement between the color preferences of infants may have far-reaching implications. It could mean that color preferences are to some extent innate and not entirely the result of cultural influence.

The Auditory System

Unlike the visual system, the auditory system is functional from 5 months gestational age onward (DeCasper & Fifer, 1999; DeCasper, Lecanuet, Busnel, Granier-Deferre, & Naugeais, 1994). Early auditory competency may serve a variety of developmental functions such as learning to talk and parent–infant bonding. It has also been shown that it does not take a particularly loud sound to penetrate the womb and amniotic sac. Thus, the fetus may hear normal conversational sounds. Without being aware of it, parents may begin to sensitize the child to their voices even before a child is born. Perhaps, this explains why babies recognize their parents' voices as familiar sounds once they are born.

> Lillian is just 3 days old. She's tucked in her bassinet, earphones are secured over her ears, and a nonnutritive nipple is placed in her mouth. She has the programming options of hearing her mother or a stranger read Dr. Seuss's, *To Think I Saw It on Mulberry Street.* Lillian is sucking quite fast, but by doing so, she is hearing her mother's prose—not the stranger's. Shortly after birth, then, infants not only can discriminate their mother's voice from a stranger's, they also work harder to produce her voice in preference to the voice of another female (DeCasper & Fifer, 1999).

Lillian demonstrates another auditory feat, she is also able to localize sounds. Even when she is sleeping, one may see a slight stir to a quiet voice near her ear. Her breathing changes; she may open her eyes slightly or even briefly grin in response. The softest sound that a newborn can hear is 10 to 20 decibels (Trehub, Schneider, Thorpe, & Judge, 1991), approximately the amount you hear when you have a head cold. Infants are anywhere between 10 and 30 decibels less sensitive to sound than adults.

Newborns also respond to auditory stimulation. They respond to the loudness or intensity of different sounds and to sounds within the range of the human voice and make identifiable reactions to sudden loud noises (Jusczyk, Kennedy, & Jusczyk, 1995). Infants can also discriminate between loud and soft sounds and high and low ones and can detect nuances of sounds made in foreign languages that adults cannot hear. For example, Japanese babies have no trouble with hearing the "L" "R" distinction that their parents find difficult if not impossible. Adults apparently have had long practice at learning not to hear many sounds that are not significant in their own language. This effect sets in early. Even at age 1, infants have more trouble than they did earlier distinguishing sounds that are not used in their own language (Simion & Butterworth, 1998).

The Olfactory System

Smell is another way newborns gather information about their environment. Newborns are able to react to different smells and different tastes. They are able to discriminate among odors on the first day after birth. Young infants have the ability to detect **pheromones**, chemical signals given off by others of the same species that communicate various messages such as fear, identification, and so forth. Within two weeks of their birth, for example, sleeping children will turn instinctively toward the breast pads worn by their own mother or a strange mother—food, any food, is essential. A month later, however, one observes reduced head and arm movements in breast-fed infants when their noses come into contact with breast pads worn by their mothers, signifying that the newborn can recognize the smell of his mother (Schaal, 1986). This calming effect does not occur in response to odors from unfamiliar mothers.

Taste

Taste is a relatively simple sense in human beings, and the fine discriminations that we think we can make by taste alone, we actually smell. The neonate's sense of taste, however, is reasonably well developed.

> Cassandra Hurley, newly named, rests quietly in her bassinet, practicing breathing through her nose. She is just 12 hours old, and no food has yet appeared. But suddenly there is this stick, with a wisp of cotton on the end, waving under her nose. A luscious scent of ripe bananas is in the air. Her lips smack; up go the corners of her mouth. Here is another stick with yet another wisp of cotton waving back and forth. This time Cassandra shoots out a minute pink tongue and emphatically spits.

Video tapes of infants' responses to various tastes reveal that newborns display different facial expressions, tongue movements, and physiological responses for each of the four basic tastes of sweet, sour, salty, and bitter. A "down-in-the-mouth" look and protrusion of the tongue follow bitter tastes. Sour tastes cause pursing of the lips and swallowing. Sweet tastes elicit a relaxed, smiling expression. The expressions appear almost instantly. Infants also show preference for some tastes—sweetness over saltiness, for example (Harris, 1997). In fact, when babies are just 2 to 3 days old and given a tiny amount of sugar water every time they make a sucking motion, they tend to suck more slowly and their heart rates tend to increase. Why did they suck more slowly? Perhaps, to savor the sweeter liquid, and perhaps the excitement of tasting it increases the heart rate.

pheromones
Chemical signals given off by others of the same species that communicate various messages such as fear and identification.

Tactile Stimulation

Infants are born with the ability to respond to tactile stimulation. When touched, neonates show heart rate changes. Tactile sensitivity is particularly higher around the mouth and hands. Little research has been done on the baby's perception of pain—after all, no one wants to hurt tiny newborns. However, if you have ever observed an infant's reaction to a blood test (usually done by pricking the baby's heel with a small stilette), you could assume, as he jerks back his foot and wails with anguish, that he is aware of pain. Similarly, after circumcision, a newborn's sleeping patterns are often disturbed, and there is a prolonged period of fussiness. We know that babies are sensitive to touch because most of their early reflexes are triggered by touching various parts of their body.

It is rather interesting to note that cultures vary in terms of how they rank the senses. Vision appears to predominate in the United States with many Americans believing that the eyes are the window into one's true feelings. In contrast, the Ongee of the South Pacific are said to place more importance on smell (Pandya, 1987, as cited in Claussen, 1993) and believe even personal identity is wrapped up in the nose. Among the Ongee, one person greets another by asking, literally, "How is your nose?" and one refers to oneself by pointing at the nose.

Depth Perception

Although it takes some time for children to acquire skills that enable them to make sense of the information carried via the senses, most researchers agree that infants can discriminate depth as soon as they can crawl (Kellman & Arterberry, 1998). In the "visual cliff" experiments, a child crawls out onto a checkerboard pattern stretched out from a table (see Figure 5.5). One area of the checkerboard is optically distorted so that the squares appear smaller, thus creating the illusion of being farther away. The infant, perceiving the illusion as true depth, will not crawl over the "cliff." Some infants will pat the glass on the deep side, but nevertheless they refuse to cross it, even though their touch tells them it is solid.

Do infants in the precrawling stage display depth perception? When 8-month-old crawling infants are placed on the "deep" side of the cliff (directly on the protective glass), they show a rapid increase in heart rate. When precrawling infants are placed in the same position, they show a decrease in heart rate. What do these differences mean? Although infants younger than 8 months do notice the deep side and pay attention to it (heartbeat tends to slow down when an infant is attentive to something), they are essentially fearless (Sorce, Emde, Campos, & Klinnert, 2000). More than likely, perception and cognitive maturation are necessary to know what the edge of the cliff means. Perhaps, too, babies have to fall or nearly fall before fear develops.

Neonates are highly responsive to touch because of the density of their skin receptors in relation to skin surface.

Intermodal Perception

You are driving down the road and hear a police siren. You immediately check your rearview mirror to see if the officer is signaling you to pull over. In this situation you have combined stimulation from more than one of your senses, or modalities—hearing and vision. Can young infants do the same? Piaget claimed that

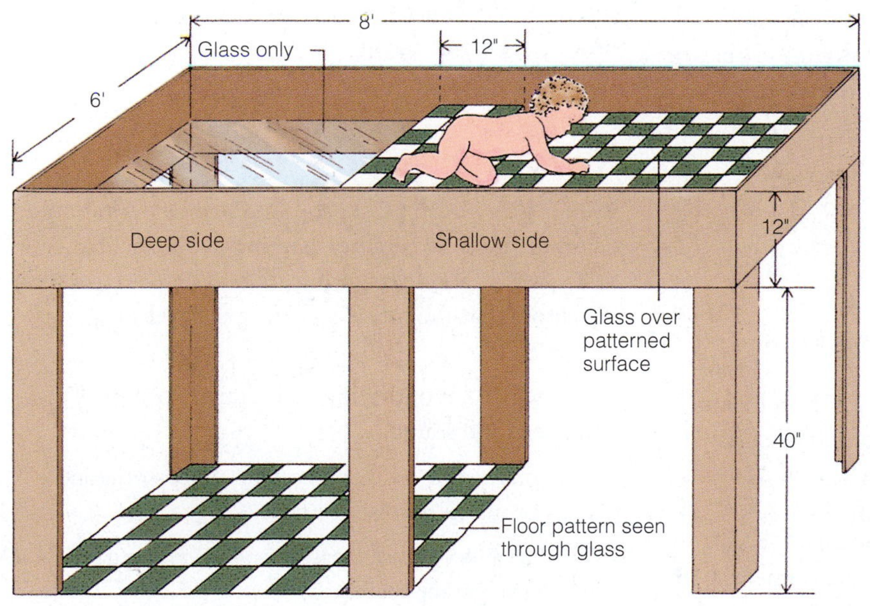

FIGURE 5.5 ***The Visual Cliff***

A crawling infant's actions on a visual cliff reflect its knowledge and feelings about depth.

Gibson & Walk, 1960.

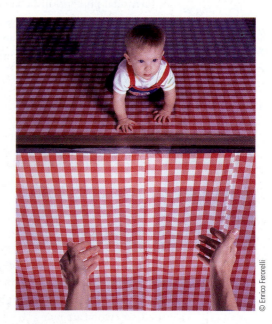

perceptual abilities such as vision or hearing are completely uncoordinated at birth and, as such, young infants are amodal; in other words, they cannot integrate two or more senses, rendering them incapable of **intermodal perception**.

Some rudimentary forms of intermodal perception, however, do appear to exist in infants. To illustrate, infants as young as 4 months old are able to perceive a relationship between puppets and the sounds they make, thus combining the two modalities of vision and hearing (Spelke, 1991). The infant observes as two puppets, a kangaroo and a donkey, jump up and down at different times. When the kangaroo hits the floor a clinking sound is made; when the donkey hits the floor a low thud is heard. The infant's attention is drawn to the kangaroo when she hears the clinking sound but switches to the donkey when she hears the thud. The study suggests that babies are able to integrate information across senses and that these abilities occur quite early in life.

Infants, however, do not demonstrate intermodal perception between other more complex sights and sounds, such as hearing a siren and looking for a police car, because they lack experience with these stimuli. Thus, one may conclude that enrichment may be a key factor in the development of more complex intermodal perception behaviors. It appears that the integration of two or more senses depends on specific experiences, which in later months enable infants' to become more proficient in their use of multisensory skills.

Thought CHALLENGE

Is the infant actually associating sights and sounds with the kangaroo and donkey and the visible noises they make, or is she just perceiving something interesting and orienting visual and hearing receptors to it?

intermodal perception
Relating or coordinating two or more senses such as hearing and vision.

APPLICATIONS:

Making Sure the Infant Can Hear

The auditory sense plays a significant role in infants' learning to speak. When a hearing problem exists, speech and language are delayed. Each year, 24,000 infants are born with some degree of hearing loss. Experts have known for years that hearing loss can cause major problems in children's development, with the first two years being the most important in terms of language development. The longer it takes to discover a hearing loss, the more damage that hearing loss can cause in terms of language development. Thanks to modern technology, within hours of birth, families can find out if their infants have hearing problems and, thus, give them a chance to go through life with little or no disability.

The OAE Test

A very accurate hearing test, called the OAE test (otacoustic emissions test), can be administered to infants shortly after birth. It is a simple, five-minute procedure that evaluates hearing by measuring the vibration of the small hair cells in the cochlea, a part of the inner ear, when exposed to sound. A plastic probe, which contains both a transmitter and a microphone, is nestled in the child's ear. A sound is sent down into the baby's ear and the vibration made by the child's hair cells in response to the sound is measured.

Babies found to have minor hearing loss can be fitted with hearing aids as early as 3 months of age, and sometimes that is all it takes to give them normal hearing. When the child reaches 18 months, surgeons can perform a cochlear implant, a procedure that can provide lifetime corrections for hearing problems. In cases of profound hearing loss, caregivers can be taught early on to spend extra time with the infant, using visual cues and examples to teach the baby about the world. Further, adults and deaf infants can learn to communicate effectively with each other by learning American Sign Language.

Normal Hearing Behaviors

Even if a newborn passes the OAE, caregivers should be on the alert for signs of hearing problems that can be caused by an illness or infection. There are certain indicators that the infant's hearing is developing normally:

- At birth to 3 months, the baby startles or jumps at a sudden loud sound.
- The infant stirs, awakens, or cries when someone talks or makes a noise.
- The baby recognizes a parent's voice and quiets when the parent speaks.
- From 3 to 6 months, the baby turns his eyes toward interesting sounds and appears to listen.
- From 6 to 12 months, the infant understands "no," "bye-bye," and his or her own name.

- The baby begins to imitate speech sounds and enjoys rattles and similar toys for their sounds, not their visual appearance.
- From 12 to 18 months, the child says her first words, such as "Da-Da," "Ma-Ma," and "bye-bye."
- From 18 to 24 months, the baby sings and hums spontaneously and has a vocabulary of approximately 20 words.

Concept Checks

1. A 1-month-old baby will probably look at your ____________ or ____________.
2. Human infants are naturally drawn to human faces. Interestingly,
   a. they will expect some sort of interaction from them.
   b. they respond the same way to objects as to human faces.
   c. they prefer brightly moving objects to human faces.
3. When precrawling infants are placed on the "deep" side of the cliff in depth perception experiments, they
   a. are fearful and will not cross.
   b. are fearless.
   c. look to their mother for cues about what they should do.
4. A 3-month-old infant that may have a hearing impairment will
   a. not give a startle response to a loud noise.
   b. still recognize his parent's voice.
   c. awaken when someone talks.

Behavioral States

Before Beginning . . .

After reading this section, you will be able to

- understand the child's first form of communication, crying.
- describe the infant's waking and sleeping patterns.
- discuss the theories of what causes sudden infant death syndrome (SIDS).
- identify symptoms and recommendations for infants at-risk for SIDS.

TABLE 5.4

Newborn Behavioral States

Stage	State	Description
1	Quiet sleep	Characterized by no movement; startles; eyes closed; regular breathing
2	Active sleep	Bursts of movement; rapid eye movement (REM); respiration irregular
3	Drowsy	Eyelids closed; increasing activity level; irregular breathing
4	Quiet alert	Few body movements; regular breathing; eyes open for more than 15 seconds
5	Active alert	Eyes open; spontaneous motor activity; bursts of fussiness
6	Crying	Cries for longer than 15 seconds; skin color changes; body movements

From *Neonatal Behavioral Assessment Scale,* by T. B. Brazelton, by 1973, National Spastics Society Monograph. Philadelphia: J. B. Lippincott. Reprinted by permission.

In the first few days of life, infants spend almost 17 hours sleeping, averaging only an hour of alertness a day (about 3 minutes an hour). Periods of wakefulness will lengthen slowly over the next month of life. Infants exhibit a range of behavioral states from blissful sleep to fretful crying (see Table 5.4). Infants are unusually sensitive, and it is perfectly normal for them to startle and cry at any abrupt change in stimuli during the first few weeks of life (Bornstein, 1996).

Crying

Have you ever been around an infant that would not stop crying? On hearing infants cry, most of us experience physiological arousal or uncomfortableness and usually we translate this into an attempt to relieve the infant's distress. This reaction is found worldwide. The first three months of the baby's life may be particularly distressful for new caregivers, because it is during these months that babies cry the most. Fortunately, in most cases, picking up the infant usually terminates the crying, which helps caregivers feel relieved and more confident in their role. Moreover, if the distress–relief sequence is sufficiently predictable, infants may develop expectations concerning the probability of their caregivers' responses, permitting them to develop a sense of their own efficacy.

Are crying infants trying to purposely communicate with their caregivers? Certainly, the infant's crying communicates an unmet infant need (cold, wet, hungry), but parents are the experts in deciphering just what that need is. As such, an infant's crying is thought to be a response to an inner need, not intentional communication. At around 9 to 10 months of age (for most infants), however, intentional communication begins (Bates, 1979; Bates, Bretherton, & Snyder, 1988). How do we know that? If we observe a child, a wanted toy, and her mother, prior to 9 months the child cries but does not look at her mother. At 9 or 10 months something interesting changes; now the infant will not only cry but look at her mother and then the toy, as if to say, will you please get that toy for me?

The implication of these findings is that prior to the age of 9 months, crying infants will not become "spoiled" if they are picked up. Further, crying does not increase when they are picked up; in fact, infants who are picked up and rocked and soothed, soon cry less than those infants whose cries go ignored. What about infants who are seemingly inconsolable and cry for no apparent reason?

> You can't really understand how frustrating it is to have a small infant crying and you cannot console the child. You feel so helpless. I would put Justin in his crib, and just seconds later he would be crying—really crying. Nothing seemed to work. I would put him in his buggy and walk around the apartment; sometimes my husband and I would take him for a ride in the car. That would work most of the time, but it gets to be a problem when the windchill is below zero. I have discovered something that works; Justin is tucked snugly in his bassinet and I place it on the dryer and turn it on. The warmth and vibrations are all that it takes to help him get to sleep and stay asleep.

Some babies wake up during the night and "self-sooth," then go back to sleep. Parents may not be aware of this; researchers are because they have recorded these periods. Other babies cry whenever they awaken. Some are consolable, but others cry inconsolably; these babies are considered to be "colicky." Between 3 to 12 weeks, many infants develop a fussy period (most often toward the end of the day) known as **colic**. Colic is an inconsolable crying for which no physical cause is apparent, which lasts for more than three hours a day, occurs at least three days a week or more, and continues for at least three weeks. This irritable, fussy crying seen at the end of the day occurs in 20 percent of infants. Colic can be a frustrating nightmare to parents, but it is not the parent's fault. It is not due to the parent's anxiety, inexperience, or personality. Colic usually disappears between 5 and 10 months (Stifter & Braungart, 1992), which may help adults cope more effectively.

colic
An extremely fussy period of crying usually disappearing between 5 and 10 months.

Most doctors do not attribute colic to gastrointestinal disturbances or indigestion but to an immature nervous system (Stein, 1996). The immature nervous system of the infant can only handle limited amounts of stimuli. At the end of the day, the infant is overloaded with stimuli and finally blows off steam in the form of a fussy period. After this is over, the nervous system can reorganize for another 24 hours. Parents usually are advised to pick up and rock the infant to soothe the overloaded nervous system.

Sleep

Some adults prepare for sleep by shutting the bedroom door, turning off the radio, lying down quite motionless, and covering themselves with blankets that provide a constant temperature. To reduce their state of arousal and get to sleep, they find it necessary to exclude as many external stimulations as possible. However, in a classic study (Blackbill & Fitzgerald, 1969), it was found that the conditions that lead to sleep in infants are reversed. Perhaps, you have observed an infant sleeping in her bassinet with the television blasting. The infant, however, continues to sleep. Nearly any continuous, moderately intense stimulus will tend to reduce the infant's level of arousal and induce sleep. Loud sounds, strong lights, above normal temperatures, the continuing tactile stimulus of tight swaddling from neck to toes in strips of flannel, or even constant swinging or jiggling have been found to reduce infant arousal. It is not recommended, however, that parents quiet babies by such constant high-intensity stimulation.

As adults, we respond to a circadian rhythm. Our waking and sleeping patterns correspond to a 24-hour period of time that organizes diurnal (day) and nocturnal (night) cycles for wake and sleep patterns, as well as synchronizes other physiological functions such as body temperature and urine excretion. It takes about four months for infants to establish this circadian rhythm wake and sleep pattern. A nocturnal sleep pattern continues to solidify progressively until the infant reaches 6 or 7 months of age.

Active and Passive Sleep Patterns

Ultradian rhythms are shorter biological cycles (defined as less than a day). Ultradian organization related to sleep refers to alternating cycles of REM (rapid eye movement) and NREM (nonrapid eye movement) sleep. REM, or active sleep, is characterized by higher brain wave activity and is usually the time when dreams occur. During this period of sleep, muscle tone is actually suppressed. Eye movement is typically rapid and sharp. NREM, or passive sleep, will eventually differentiate into four separate stages (from light to heavy sleep) by 4 months of age. Initially, infants spend about 50 percent of their total sleep time in REM states. Does the high percentage of REM sleep observed in infants mean that they dream right after they are born?

This seems unlikely because they probably lack the ability to hold images in memory. REM sleep, more than likely, involves the exercise of newly forming sensorimotor schemes. It is thought that infants do not begin to dream with visual images until object permanence (knowing that objects continue to exist even though they cannot be seen) is established (around 18 to 24 months). At age 1, the amount of REM sleep decreases to 30 to 35 percent, and at 2 to 5, it decreases further to 20 to 25 percent of total sleep time, which is the average amount seen in adulthood. As REM sleep decreases, so do the infant's normal motoric movements, such as facial twitches and grimaces.

Co-Sleeping

Co-sleeping is another factor that directly affects a child's and parents' sleep patterns. Definitions of co-sleeping vary, but generally, this refers to children sleeping in the same bed as their parents. The shared amount of sleeping time also varies—it could be minutes, hours, part of the night, or all night. Frequency varies as well from as often as nightly to a few times a week, to once a month, and so forth. Despite the variables in definitions, questions often arise over this controversial topic.

Cultural variables make the topic of co-sleeping particularly complex and important. In the United States, primary care providers often frown on co-sleeping. Many reputable pediatrics associations and groups support separate sleeping quarters for children and adults, which they perceive as the norm. At one time, almost all U.S. hospitals separated the mother from the child at birth. Although neonates in hospitals often stay with their mothers, they still do not share the same bed; instead, they have their own hospital crib. The beliefs surrounding these sleeping arrangements center on interfering with the child's independence, intruding on parental privacy, and causing more sleep problems (Wolf, Lozoff, Latz, & Paludetto, 1996).

Co-sleeping is not as common in the United States as it is in other cultures.

Although co-sleeping may be considered "aberrant" by many in the United States, it has been a common and normal practice in most other societies. In these cultures, it is believed that mothers need to attend to an infant's need for dependency by allowing a child to sleep with her. In doing so, the mother is creating a secure base for her child from which later independence, autonomy, and exploration can grow (Gonzalez-Mena, 1991). Thus, it is important for adults to look at the overall picture and bring the family and child's cultural perspective into making an assessment of co-sleeping. Despite pediatric advice to the contrary, as many as 50 percent of parents eventually co-sleep, with rates varying from 12 to 70 percent. Seventy percent of African American toddlers co-sleep with their parents, and approximately 45 to 50 percent of Hispanic American toddlers do (Stein, 1997).

co-sleeping When young children share the same bed with their parents.

The question of "who sleeps with whom" reflects deeply held cultural convictions about the family and the nature of human development. Parents' ideas about independence or separation and dependence and social bonding lie at the core of sleeping arrangements. European American parents often favor sleeping alone as a practice to foster healthy independent development (Super & Harkness, 1997), whereas in other cultures and ethnic groups in which co-sleeping is a common practice, parents tend to believe that co-sleeping fosters dependence and social cohesion between the parents and the child (Shweder, Jensen, & Goldstein, 1995). Thus, socially constructed moral convictions appear to be systematically related to sleep management practices.

Sleeping through the Night

When we talk about infants sleeping "through the night," we generally mean uninterrupted sleep from about midnight to 5:00 A.M. When infants accomplish this feat is highly variable. Some will sleep through the night at an early age, and some will not. Getting up in the middle of the night is never a favorite part of parenting. But, experts note that there are ways to come to terms with the situation (Brazelton, 1992). One is to develop an attitude of greater acceptance about interrupted sleep. If parents have a resentful attitude, they face the next day more frustrated and try harder to fit the baby into their sleep pattern. By contrast, if they develop a mental attitude of acceptance, they will find themselves able to enjoy those quiet moments at night nursing, holding, and loving their infants. According to research on the normal sleeping pattern of babies, 70 percent of American children sleep through the night by 3 months, and 83 percent are likely to be doing so by 6 months. By 1 year, only 10 percent do not sleep through the night (Bornstein, 1996). Breast-fed babies sleep less than others and continue to wake frequently into the second year of life if they have not been weaned by that time.

Prematurity and limits on the infant's ability to nurse may play a role when children are not sleeping through the night by 1 year of age. There may also be parental factors such as a reluctance to encourage independence in the child and let her work her way back to sleep. Some working mothers and fathers may feel guilty about being away all day and may get up to rock the child to sleep. Similarly, a single parent may feel the loneliness of having to face the daily adjustments of parenting by herself and might not want to give up night feedings. In this sense then, the development of an organized sleep–wake cycle in young infants is influenced by characteristics of both the infant and the parent and by the nature of their dyadic interaction. Mothers who report higher levels of psychological well-being and calmness tend to have infants with more organized sleep–wake cycles than mothers who report lower states of psychological well-being as well as depression (Goodlin-Jones, Eiben, & Anders, 1997).

Developing Self-Comforting Behaviors

Issues of autonomy (child should sleep in own bed) and interdependence (child should sleep with parents) may lie at the root of sleep problems. It may seem natural to cling and be clung to, but children profit when parents help them learn how to get back to sleep on their own when they awaken in the middle of the night (Wolfson, 1996). If parents rush to comfort them, children will not learn self-comforting patterns, and this prolongs night waking. Some children learn to self-comfort by stroking their blankets, wiggling their feet, or snuggling with a stuffed animal. Light sleep cycles occur frequently during the night and are self-limited as long as the child can quiet himself and then bring himself down into deeper sleep again. When the parents rush in at the child's first whimper, she may become stimulated by their presence, or if she uses their presence to wake up and start playing, she may turn night into day, and a vicious circle may easily be set in motion.

Sleep Apnea

Most infants periodically stop breathing (apnea) for a few seconds throughout the night; some infants, however, may stop breathing for longer periods of time. Researchers suspect that these apneic periods may be related to a tragedy of monumental proportions—the sudden death of a child, known as **sudden infant death syndrome (SIDS)**. For those who lose a child to SIDS, the profound and overwhelming sense of loss is compounded by the fact that no clear-cut evidence has

sudden infant death syndrome (SIDS)
The unexplainable death of an infant. It is the leading cause of infant mortality.

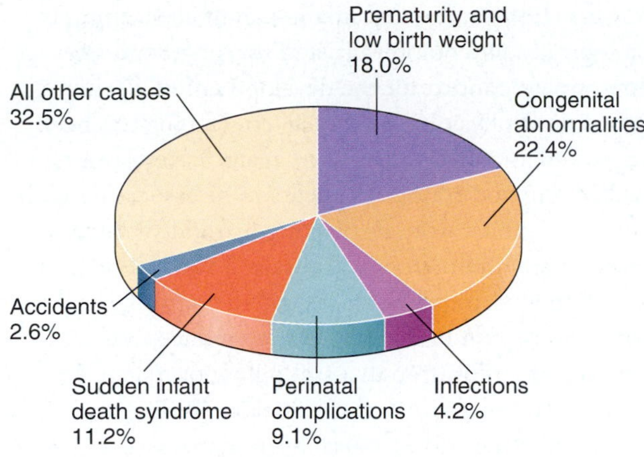

FIGURE 5.6 ***Causes of Death in the First Year of Life***

From "The First Weeks of Life (pp. 93–114), by J. R. Evans, 1997, in M. L. Batshaw (Ed.), *Children with Disabilities,* Baltimore, MD: Paul H. Brookes. Used by permission of M. L. Batshaw.

connected SIDS to sleep apnea and no medical explanation is available to account for what went wrong, even after an autopsy.

Every year 8000 to 10,000 babies in the United States alone die of this unexplained disorder, sometimes referred to as crib death; the incidence is 2 to 3 per thousand live births (Boyle, Vance, Najman, & Thearle, 1996). Ninety percent of these deaths occur before 6 months of age, with 2 to 4 months being the peak ages (Cornwell, 1992). SIDS accounts for about 11 percent of the 38,000 babies born in the United States who die before their first birthday (see Figure 5.6).

Causes

The cause(s) of SIDS is unknown. Studies have shown that SIDS involves a developmental disability involving a learning deficit. This deficit jeopardizes infants' ability to defend themselves with appropriate behavioral adjustments when they have difficulty breathing or during apneic episodes (cessation of breathing) (Lipsitt, 1990). Many of the unconditioned reflexes that infants have at birth undergo marked changes between 2 and 4 months of age. Involuntary reflexive functioning is slowly superseded by slower, more voluntary, learned patterns of behavior, mediated by higher centers of the brain. This transitory period, which is characterized by disorganized behavior, occurs at 100 to 150 days old—just the age period when infants are most at risk of crib death.

To illustrate, infants have an innate respiratory defense system at birth; newborns are biologically equipped to respond when their breathing is obstructed. When a newborn's face is covered with a cloth, the infant reacts with an almost enraged response, which escalates as the stimulus is prolonged. The response culminates in crying, which frees the respiratory passages. The behavioral pattern is essentially fail-safe. This innate respiratory defense system will, however, diminish with the passage of time and is gradually supplanted by a slower, more deliberate, cortically mediated response pattern (Lipsitt, 1990). It may be possible that the SIDS infant has not adequately learned to respond to respiratory difficulties once the unlearned protective reflexes have diminished. Thus, SIDS may be due to maturational delays in the brain.

APPLICATIONS:

Symptoms of and Recommendations for Infants at Risk for SIDS

Although the causes of SIDS remain unknown, studies have demonstrated a consistent pattern of factors and characteristics of infants at risk for SIDS (summarized in Table 5.5). Most deaths occur in the winter and spring. Colds and sniffles have been observed in infants a few days prior to death. Most deaths occur when the infant is sleeping, usually between midnight and 9:00 A.M. Death occurs rapidly, and the child turns blue and limp. There is usually no evidence of any suffering, no

TABLE 5.5

Infants at Risk for SIDS

Studies have demonstrated a consistent pattern of risk factors:

- Low socioeconomic status
- Young maternal age
- High number of births
- Multiple births
- Maternal smoking during pregnancy
- Short interval between births
- Being a male child
- African American or Native American heritage
- Low birth weight
- Frequent respiratory difficulties
- Lower Apgar test scorings (measurement of vital signs) at 1, 2, and 5 minutes after birth
- Infant requires more intensive care, is hospitalized longer, and requires more resuscitative measures

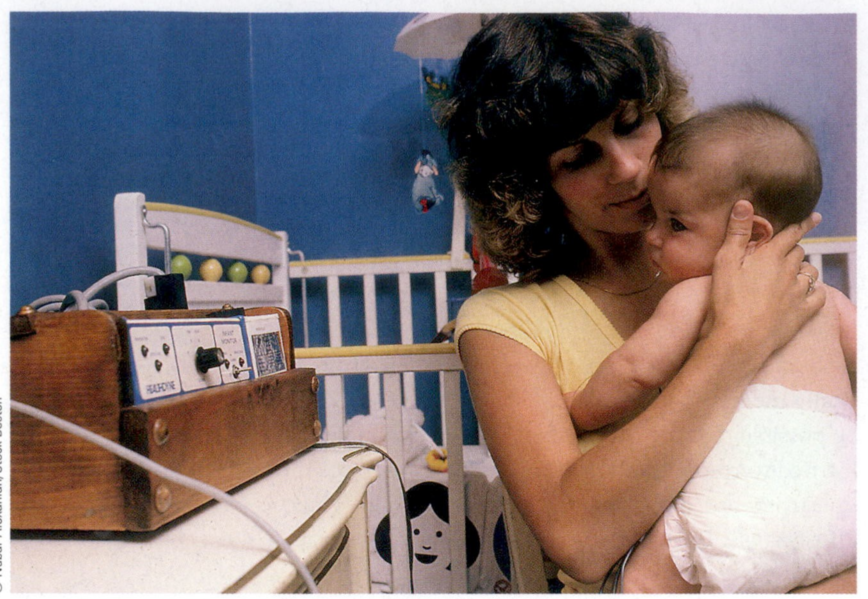

© Nubar Alexanian/Stock Boston

A monitor is often used for infants at risk for SIDS. An alarm goes off if the baby stops breathing for longer than a few seconds.

sign of pain or struggle (DeVries, 1997). One may be tempted to conclude that there are some telltale precursors in SIDS infants, but these infants do survive the neonatal period and seem quite well at birth, as well as immediately preceding death. Moreover, many infants with similar symptoms survive.

Using a Monitor

In some cases, the use of a monitor is recommended for infants who have been diagnosed as at risk for apnea, but there is much controversy about that use. Physically, it is quite simple: electrodes are placed on the baby's diaphragm to monitor the baby's breathing and signal an alarm if the baby ceases to breathe for longer than 20 seconds. However, there are some difficulties surrounding the use of a monitor: first, it has not been proven that apnea or cessation of breathing is the single cause of SIDS, and second there is no 100 percent guarantee that the infant will not succumb to SIDS, even with a monitor.

Sleeping Arrangements and Sleeping Positions

Infants' sleeping arrangements may play a role in reducing SIDS risks. James McKenna (1996) and Nancy Powers (1997) argue that infant–parent co-sleeping is biologically, psychologically, and socially the most appropriate context for the development of healthy infant sleep physiology. As such, co-sleeping has been suggested as a protective factor against sleep apnea. Bedsharing, for example, appears to be associated with enhanced infant arousals (waking up) and synchronized infant and maternal arousals (Powers, 1997).

Other recommendations include putting the baby to sleep on his back or side to reduce the chances of suffocation in a soft pillow or mattress (which also may trap carbon dioxide) (Willinger, Hoffman, & Hartford, 1994). Firm mattresses are recommended as preventative measures as well. Other suggestions include avoid overheating; provide adequate room ventilation (which disperses carbon dioxide); and do not use medications that contain sedatives that are found in some cold remedies.

Mother's Diet

Marten de Vries' (1997) and Letten Saugstad's (1997) research findings suggest a connection between a maternal diet low in polyunsaturated fatty acids in the third trimester of pregnancy and a subsequent delay in fetal myelination and brain maturation in infants. A rising number of women favor a low-calorie, low-fat diet, especially in the third trimester when the fetus is most susceptible. However, this may lead to a depressed birth weight and delayed somatic growth and neuronal maturation, such as is observed in SIDS victims. The authors conclude that to prevent death from SIDS, it is necessary to ensure optimal development by promoting fetal growth, avoiding unnecessary dieting, and favoring a diet high in polyunsaturated fatty acids.

Concept Checks

1. Which statement best describes crying prior to 9 months?
   a. From the beginning, crying is a form of purposeful, but not intentional, communication.
   b. Crying behavior becomes more frequent when adults constantly pick up a crying infant.
   c. Picking up a distressed infant advances his or her sociability.
2. Night waking may be prolonged because the infant
   a. is spoiled.
   b. is genetically programmed to be a light sleeper.
   c. has not learned self-comforting behaviors.

3. ***True or False:*** SIDS is a tragic occurrence that affects infants similarly across their ethnic group or socioeconomic status.
4. The infant most at risk for SIDS is
   a. Sandra, who was born to a teenage mother.
   b. Luke, who was born to a mother who smoked during pregnancy.
   c. Tina, who had low-average Apgar scores one minute after birth.

Health

Before Beginning . . .

After reading this section, you will be able to

- note the necessary immunizations during the infancy period.
- explain the importance of good nutrition in the first two years of life.
- identify causes for and types of malnutrition.
- trace the possible repercussions of overnutrition during infancy.

Health issues in the infancy and toddlerhood period also focus on immunizations, nutrition, and undernutrition.

Immunizations

The infant's immune system fights against infection by defending the body against "foreign" molecules like those present when infectious agents invade the body. Circulating *antigens* are substances that stimulate the production of *antibodies,* which defend the body against infection. During the eighth month in utero, the infant receives antibodies from the mother's blood that protect against illnesses, because the newborn's own immune system will not work well until several months after birth. After birth, however, the mother may act as an auxiliary immune system for the baby if she breast-feeds, because her milk contains large doses of antibodies (Dermer, 1998). Further, if the mother is exposed to a new infection, the mother's body will quickly begin to produce the appropriate antibody and will pass it on to the baby in her milk.

Allergic reactions occur when a foreign protein (from certain foods, for example) triggers the production of certain protein antibodies. Once such a reaction has occurred, the infant's body is sensitized to the protein and will more and more readily respond to it with itching, wheezing, sneezing, and so on. There appears to be a strong genetic factor that predisposes infants to allergies (Seachrist, 1994). Cow's milk and wheat products are common causes of allergic sensitization when fed to an infant too early.

To keep infants and toddlers free from dangerous diseases, they are given a series of immunizations. Some parents are anxious about the possible side effects that may occur as a result of a vaccination; the risk of complications, however, is extremely small compared with the harmful effects from the diseases (Seachrist, 1994). Infants do not receive immunizations if they are running a fever or have a subclinical infection such as an earache or sore throat. If the infant does develop side effects from a previous vaccination, the pediatrician may delay or stop further immunizations. Table 5.6 gives an overview of the immunizations given in the infant's first year of life.

Nutrition

According to Carolyn Rovee-Collier (2000), the infant's primary "occupation" is to eat. The infant begins life as a *Body Builder* (birth to 9 weeks), where its task is to minimize activity to convert calories to optimal growth. The infant accomplishes this by maximizing caloric intake and minimizing caloric expenditure. Infants display a number of behaviors that are normally associated with eating, for example the sucking and rooting reflex. Those behaviors that require more energy expenditure, such as looking, are not displayed frequently. The very young infant, therefore, works to acquire energy and minimize energy loss. First-time mothers frequently ask, "Which method is best: the breast or the bottle?"

It is interesting to note that cross-culturally, many countries have traditions surrounding the treatment of new mothers that make it easier for her to nurse her child. For example, in Oaxaca in southern Mexico, new mothers are allowed a 40-day rest period (*la cuarantena*) in which they avoid all heavy work and are encouraged to relax and spend their time in extended interaction with their infants (Hannon, Willis, Bishop-Townsend, Martinez, & Scrimshaw, 2000). This extended-interaction period makes way for more successful breast feeding. Women in many rural areas of Third World countries might even wonder why there is a "bottle/breast"

TABLE 5.6

Immunizations Given in the First Year of Life

Age Due	Vaccination	How Given	Side Effects
Newborn	Hepatitis B	Injection	None
1 month	Hepatitis B	Injection	None
2 months	Polio (IPV) DTP (diptheria, tetanus, and pertussis)	Injection Combined injection	Possible lump at injection site; fever; slight risk of high fever and convulsions
4 months	Polio (IPV) Hepatitis B DTP	Injection Injection Combined injection	None Possible lump at injection site; fever; slight risk of high fever and convulsions
6 months	Polio (IPV) Hepatitis B DTP	Oral Injection Combined injection	None Possible lump at injection site; fever; slight risk of high fever and convulsions
12–18 months	MMR (measles, mumps, rubella)	Combined injection	Fever; rash; slight risk of high fever and convulsions

question. Most infants are breast-fed, and the process continues for at least the first 18 months of the infant's life (Whitman, White, O'Mara, & Goeke-Morey, 1999).

The answer to the breast or bottle question for many women in the United States is a complicated one often involving several factors. If, for example, the mother returns to work after a short leave of absence, it is difficult for her to continue nursing without extreme dedication. (Other factors that may enter into this decision to breast- or bottle-feed, are discussed in Child Development Issues.) Although the clear majority of pediatricians and health personnel recommend breast feeding if possible, there is little research to show that breast feeding makes a difference in the forming of important attachment relations between the infant and the mother.

Gradually (and sometimes abruptly), the infant is weaned from the bottle or breast. The weaning process means offering the infant nonmilk foods, which in the United States, usually means cereal. Although most cultures complete weaning from the breast much later than is common in the United States, there is a good deal of variation across cultures. As in the United States, the mother's lifestyle often determines when the weaning decision is made. For example, if a woman in Yoruba is a market trader, she may take the infant to work and continue to nurse. If she must work in some domestic situation, however, this may not be conducive to continued nursing so the baby is weaned. Most often, cross-culturally, weaning occurs when the woman has another baby. In the United States, mothers generally nurse for 6 to 8 months (Mercer, 1998).

As infants get older and move to solid foods, nutritionists advise giving young children generous amounts of fruits and vegetables and limiting starches and sugars to moderate amounts. Chicken and fish are recommended to be eaten twice a week. Foods containing protein are important, and wheat and oat cereals have better quality protein than corn cereals. Similarly, wheat bread has more nutritional value than white bread. It needs to be pointed out, however, that human beings are *omnivores*—meaning, we can eat different kinds of foods and thus there are different ways of achieving a good diet. With the possible exception of milk, there is no single food that has to be eaten to guarantee good nutrition (Mercer, 1998). However, for most people, mere intuition is an insufficient guide for getting an adequate diet. It is for this reason that basic food guides have been created and that recommended daily allowances of specific nutrients have been determined.

Toddlers need to receive complex carbohydrates, and they can get them from a variety of foods such as sugar-free cereal, whole-wheat bread, potatoes and other vegetables, rice, and pasta; protein from lean white meat, fish, and legumes such as beans, and after she's about six months, eggs and cheese; and the vitamins and minerals contained in fresh fruits and vegetables. Infants and toddlers need some fat, but they should be able to get enough for their nutritional needs

Child Development Issues

Breast or Bottle?

Advocates of breast feeding point out that no baby is allergic to breast milk. The ratio of protein and sugar is ideal; the milk is loaded with antibodies that will boost the level of immunity with which the baby is born. Fetuses receive immunity from their mothers across the placenta, but this diminishes shortly after birth unless breast milk keeps up the level. Protection against allergy is another advantage a baby receives from his mother's milk (Golding, Rogers, & Emmett, 1997).

In some cases, a food that a breast-feeding mother eats will cause a reaction in her baby. The protein from cow's milk, eggs, or some other food in the mother's diet may penetrate her gastrointestinal tract. These "stray" proteins in her blood can find their way into her milk. If her baby reacts to these proteins, it is an indication of a pronounced sensitivity to that food and that the baby has a strong tendency toward developing allergies. In such a case, the answer is for mothers to exclude the food containing the specific protein from their diet.

Breast feeding is more economical, is readily available, and does not cause constipation in young infants. The disadvantages may be inconvenience, particularly for mothers who have returned to the workforce full time; it is sometimes difficult to establish; it does not involve the father (although he may give substitute bottles to his infant); and it may be painful at times for some nursing mothers.

The chief advantage of bottle feeding is that if frees mothers and may involve the father on a more frequent basis. Disadvantages of bottle feeding are that it is expensive; it requires a thorough cleaning of the bottles; it may lead to constipation in the infant; and the formula may have allergy-causing properties.

FEEDING: AN EARLY FORM OF COMMUNICATION

Whether to bottle-feed or breast-feed needs to be resolved by each mother based on her preferences, schedules, and needs. There are positive and negative points to each method. The important thing, however, is that the infant is held in a loving way while feeding, with the parent gently talking and stroking him as he nurses from the bottle or the breast. A great deal more than receiving nourishment goes on when feeding infants; a parent–infant relationship is being formed. Over time, soft words and strokes help establish a loving and secure parent–child relationship, and fewer eating problems.

Relaxed, calm feeding times also enable infants to establish a rhythm of sucking for approximately 8 to 10 seconds and then pausing for 3 to 5 seconds. During the pause, parents usually stroke, pat, or talk to the baby. This interaction of sucking and pausing helps infants to learn cause and effect; when they pause parents will talk or pat them. Over time, the more the parent does during the pause, the more the baby pauses (Gill, Behnke, Conlon, McNeely, & Anderson, 1988).

The infant will actually pause more often waiting for those all-important soft words and gentle strokes. These forms of affection and mild stimulation are as important to the infant's health as the food they are consuming.

Search Online

Explore InfoTrac College Edition, your online library. Go to **http://www.infotrac-college.com/wadsworth** and use the passcode that came on the card with your book. Try these search terms: breast feeding, breast versus bottle, bottle feeding.

from other foods they are given, especially milk. Once young children are accustomed to a variety of tastes, adults can plan their diets to include a combination of foods.

Nutritionists tell us that giving babies fresh fruits and vegetables, processed in a processor or blender, is more nutritious than using processed baby food. If the young child refuses to eat certain vegetables, most advise that we not force them to eat these foods. If adults continue to offer the disliked food, the child only becomes more obstinate in his or her refusal. Most young children generally like fruits, which contain the same minerals, roughage, and (some of the) vitamins as vegetables.

At 7 months, new motor skills—sitting, exploring, and the fascinating pincer grasp—are major touchpoints of development affecting all aspects of a child's life. They enhance a child's independence in the feeding area as well. Learning to play with a cup and to handle it herself is one exciting goal for the child. With his newly developed pincer grasp, the child can be given small bits of finger food, which help him feel more independent about this eating process.

Undernutrition

Milk provides the infant with the needed proteins, vitamins, and minerals to sustain her until about 6 months of age. After that, she needs suitable weaning foods, which for many infants of the world are not available. For most infants, then, the greatest concern for nutritional deficiency occurs after weaning from the breast—making undernutrition the most serious obstacle to adequate growth throughout the world. Even today, in many parts of the world, mothers' inability to breast-feed still condemns many infants to poor health—and perhaps an early death. A child is considered to be malnourished if his or her body weight is less than 60 percent of the average for his or her age.

Because growth occurs at such a rapid pace, malnutrition is especially damaging during infancy. Malnourished infants are often listless and passive. This may help the infant conserve his or her limited energy, but the lack of appropriate stimulation may have a significant negative impact on the developing brain. Recent World Health Organization statistics indicate that 40 to 60 percent of the world's children suffer from mild to moderate undernutrition and 3 percent to 7 percent are severely malnourished in some parts of the world. Although undernutrition is more prevalent in developing nations, it does exist in affluent countries such as the United States as well. In the United States, undernutrition is most prevalent among ethnic minorities from low socioeconomic levels. In the past few decades, health care systems around the world have substantially improved their ability to provide infants with proper diets; despite that, however, the infant mortality rate due to malnutrition is staggering.

marasmus
A form of starvation found in children under 1 who are severely deprived of necessary proteins and calories.

kwashiorkor
Malnutrition found in toddlers whose diet consists of carbohydrates and little or no protein.

The infant mortality rate in the United States and Canada is three times lower than in Third World countries (United Nations International Children's Emergency Fund, 1995). Even so, the infant mortality rate in the United States is higher than in Japan Sweden, France, or Great Britain. In these countries, health-care support takes several forms such as, free prenatal care, medical care after the birth of the child, and provisions for proper nutrition for the child (United Nations International Children's Emergency Fund, 1995). Distribution of infant health-care services, it appears, is far from ideal in the United States.

Children under 1 who are severely deprived of necessary proteins and calories suffer from a form of starvation called **marasmus**. In its primary form, it results from too little food. The main clinical features include wasting of muscles, diarrhea, and anemia. The weight of the child is often less than 60 percent of that considered normal for the child's chronological age. Marasmic infants gain very little or no weight, hardly grow, and, if they survive, remain unresponsive.

Toddlers whose diet consists of carbohydrates and little or no protein may suffer from **kwashiorkor**. The word is derived from a tribe in Ghana; literally translated, it means "the sickness that the older child gets when the next baby is born." The condition often develops when the child is taken from the breast and placed on a starchy diet. Kwashiorkor manifests itself by growth failure, muscle wasting, edema (especially a tightly swollen potbelly), loss of hair pigmentation, and mental changes, such as apathy and irritability. The mental changes may lead to alterations in the attitude of the mother to her child and may reduce her responsiveness and warmth.

APPLICATIONS:

Overnutrition

Infants should consume 50 calories per day for each pound they weigh (more than twice what adults need). Some babies are extremely enthusiastic eaters; similarly, some parents may be overzealous in encouraging their infants to consume every morsel of food and every drop of formula. In these situations, the consumption of calories may far exceed the recommended amount. Subsequently, these infants are overweight. Although weight in infancy correlates little with weight in childhood and adulthood, and some of the "chubbiness"

© Myrleen Ferguson/PhotoEdit

Extremely overweight infants are those who are above the 85 percent mark on weight charts.

observed in some infants disappears during the high-activity toddlerhood and early childhood years, extremely overweight infants may be at some added risk of remaining overweight.

Overweight Infants

Obese infants may be more prone to becoming overweight adults because of the greater number of fat cells developed early in life (Hirsch, 1997). Fetal fat does not appear until quite late in gestation (30 weeks) and then increases quite rapidly. During the first year of life, body fat increases from 40 to 53 percent. In fact, 67 percent of weight gain during the first four postnatal months is adipose tissue, or fat cells.

Adipose Tissue

If the mother overeats during the last trimester of her pregnancy, the infant is overfed in the first few years, or the child overeats during pubescence, the number of fat cells increases. With the exception of these three growth periods, the number of fat cells in the body remains the same throughout life—no matter how much a person does or does not eat. Once fat cells are formed, however, they do not disappear but remain storage places for any future extra calories. People become thinner because each fat cell becomes emptier, not because fat cells are lost; people become fatter because each fat cell becomes fuller, not because new fat cells are formed. It has been found that obese children of all ages have a greater amount of adipose tissue than do children of normal weight. These observations suggest that overeating while expecting, particularly in the last trimester, overfeeding during early infancy, or overeating during pubescence may be important etiologic factors in some forms of obesity.

High-Calorie Foods

This does not mean that infants and toddlers should be put on diets, which may lead to malnutrition. However, it has been observed that overweight infants tend to have diets high in calories. What infants eat affects how much they weigh. For this reason, it is recommended that children's diets should contain very limited amounts of sugary juices (including apple juice); high-calorie foods loaded with sugar; salt, or saturated fats. Even in infancy and toddlerhood, if these types of foods are offered, children will prefer them later on. By offering nutritious foods, good eating habits are promoted, and the risk of becoming overweight is lowered.

Concept Checks

1. Substances that stimulate the production of antibodies are known as ______________.
2. ***True or False:*** When the infant is given solid foods, certain foods such as vegetables must be consumed for healthy nutrition.
3. The greatest concern for the world's families is
   a. providing an ideal diet for their infants.
   b. preventing malnutrition.
   c. providing better quality, energy-enriched foods.
4. A possible concern of overnutrition during the infancy period is the growth of an overabundance of ______________ ______________.

5. The most accurate statement about the differences between breast-fed and bottle-fed babies is
   a. there is little or nothing to say about differences in attachment relations.
   b. that bottle-fed babies get more milk.
   c. breast-fed babies are often allergic to mother's milk.

Reviewing Key Points

Brain Development during Infancy and Toddlerhood

- New research suggests that brain development that takes place in the first few years of life is more rapid and extensive than was previously realized. Further, critical windows of time exist during which the infant must learn certain skills, or they may never do so. "Connectivity" of neurons—the number of connections each neuron makes with other neurons—is responsible for the appearance of various behavior functions and underlies the development of higher-order, complex thinking. Stimulation from the environment enables the brain to form more extensive connections. Research also points out that the brain has the power of adaptive plasticity, which is greatest during the developmental years up to age 8 or 9.
- Infants prosper when parents provide a variety of sensory stimulation (vision, hearing, touch, taste, smell). Responsivity on the part of caregivers and organization in the home also foster brain development. Talking to children enriches their vocabulary and enhances brain development. The "curriculum" most beneficial is not regimented drills but enriching infants' lives by enhancing their innate curiosity.

Physical and Motor Development

- During the infancy period, birth to age 2, children will grow approximately 14 inches and increase their birth weight of 7 or 8 pounds to a full 28 pounds. Changing proportions are more dramatic than total growth.
- Infants are capable of a number of involuntary, autonomic responses, known as reflexes, which are the building blocks of later motor behavior. Early motor development is largely concerned with reaching, grasping, and manipulating objects.
- Toilet training, which is learning to control bowel and bladder movements, requires physical and motor maturity. It is not something that caregivers "train" children to do, but rather, should be seen as the child's own learning process. It is achieved by the child in accordance with his or her own maturation.

The World of Sights, Sounds, and Smells

- The neonate has a number of sensory and perceptual capabilities that develop rapidly over the first 6 months. Newborns appear to be more attentive to contrasting edges and contours and prefer complex patterns and the human face. Young infants are able to localize sounds and prefer high-pitched voices. They have the ability to smell and detect pheromones. Infants are able to taste the differences between various substances and do react to pain.
- Perception is the process of organizing and interpreting sensory information. In visual cliff experiments, crawling infants appear to perceive depth and will not crawl over the "cliff." Precrawling infants, while noticing the depth, are essentially "fearless," suggesting that babies have to fall or nearly fall before fear develops.
- Some rudimentary forms of intermodal perception, the ability to relate/integrate two or more senses together, are seen in infants as young as 4 months old. Complex intermodal perception abilities, however, appear to depend on enrichment or experiences that the child encounters. As such, in later months infants become more proficient in their use of multisensory skills.
- Hearing is significantly tied to the infant's language development, and for this reason it is important for caregivers to make sure the infant can hear. A simple test, the OAE test (otacoustic emissions test), can be administered to infants shortly after birth to determine if they have even a minor hearing loss.

Behavioral States

- Crying in young infants indicates an unmet need. Crying does not become intentional until around 8 or 9 months. Therefore, prior to this time infants who are picked up when crying cannot be spoiled.
- Newborn's sleeping patterns are made up of complex, intertwined behavioral states ranging from crying to quiet sleep. The infant's sleep is also characterized by active (REM) and passive sleeping (NREM) patterns. At around 4 months, NREM sleep patterns differentiate into four stages. The point when infants are able to sleep through the night is highly variable;

however, approximately 70 percent of infants sleep through the night by 3 months. Even though they may be sleeping eight hours a night, infants will wake up several times in the course of the evening. They need to be allowed to establish their own patterns of self-comfort (rocking, snuggling a blanket, wiggling a foot); this will allow them to go back to sleep on their own.

- Sleep apnea refers to periods of nonbreathing. When it lasts 20 seconds or longer, it may be a factor in causing sudden infant death syndrome, or SIDS. SIDS is a label applied to an infant's death when a satisfactory explanation for that death cannot be found. These infants appear to have a fragile beginning that, when compounded with experiential conditions, makes them especially vulnerable.
- Findings that have led to recommendations for lowering the risk of SIDS include using an apnea monitor, co-sleeping, putting the baby to sleep on his or her back, ensuring proper room ventilation, and not overheating the child. Mothers should also consume a diet that is high in polyunsaturated fatty acids during pregnancy.

Health

- There are advantages and disadvantages to breast and/or bottle feeding. However, the most important factor in feeding is not the method chosen, but that the child is stroked, talked to, and cuddled during feeding.
- Dietary habits are formed early in life and tend to persist. For this reason, caregivers can provide infants with complex carbohydrates from such things as sugar-free cereal, whole-wheat bread, potatoes, and other vegetables and protein from lean white meat and fish and legumes such as beans.
- Undernutrition is one of the most serious obstacles to adequate growth throughout the world. Children under 1 who are severely deprived of necessary proteins and calories suffer from a form of starvation known as marasmus. Toddlers whose diet consists of carbohydrates and little or no protein suffer from kwashiorkor.
- Overnutrition may put extremely fat babies (those over the 85th percentile on weight charts) at risk for becoming overweight adults more easily because of the greater number of fat cells developed in early infancy. Once fat cells are formed, they do not disappear but remain storage places for any future extra calories. However, it is not recommended that children be put on a diet. Children should not be "forced" to consume every last drop of formula or food. Also, high-calorie foods loaded with sugar, salt, and saturated fats should be restricted in their diets.

Answers to Concept Checks

Brain Development
1. motor; myelinated 2. dendrites 3. true 4. a 5. c

Physical and Motor Development
1. false 2. proximodistal 3. b 4. a 5. b

The World of Sights and Sounds
1. mouth; eyes 2. a 3. b 4. a

Behavioral States
1. a 2. c 3. false 4. b

Health
1. antigens 2. false 3. b 4. fat cells 5. a

Key Terms

axon
cephalocaudal
cerebrum and cerebral cortex
colic
co-sleeping
dendrites
intermodal perception
kwashiorkor
marasmus
myelination
neurons
pheromones
proximodistal
reflexes
soma
sprouting
sudden infant death syndrome (SIDS)
synapses
synaptogenesis
toddler

InfoTrac College Edition

For additional readings, explore InfoTrac College Edition, your online library. Go to **http://www.infotrac-college.com/wadsworth** and use the passcode that came on the card with your book. Try these search terms: brain development, sudden infant death syndrome, breast feeding, colic.

Child Development CD-ROM

Go to the Wadsworth Child Development CD-ROM for further study of the concepts in this chapter. The CD-ROM also includes quizzes and additional activities to expand your learning experience.

CHAPTER SIX

Cognitive Development: *Infancy and Toddlerhood*

CHAPTER OUTLINE

Piaget's Sensorimotor Thinker
- The Mechanisms of Thought
- Understanding Their World
- Criticisms of Piaget's Theory
- Looking Beyond the Challenges
- Applications: A Piagetian Approach to Fostering the Infant's Cognitive Competence

Information-Processing Views of Cognition
- The Structure of Memory
- Habituation and Dishabituation
- The Infant's Memory Skills
- Early Imitation
- Evaluation of Information-Processing Theory
- Applications: The Perils of Overstimulation

Psychometric Assessment
- Gesell's Developmental Quotient
- Bayley's Scales of Infant Development
- Applications: Early Intervention for At-Risk Infants and Toddlers

Language Development
- Language in Its Cultural Setting
- Language: A Rule-Governed System
- Theories of Language
- The Infant's First Communications
- First Words
- Caregiver Speech
- Applications: The Growth of Shared Understandings

Reviewing Key Points

Observation 110 at 6 months: Laurent grasps a new rattle made of three parts: the handle, a middle ball of medium size, and the end ball, a large one. He looks at the object quite a long time while passing it from one hand to the other. . . . He moves the object in the air, at first slowly, then more and more rapidly, and finally he shakes it. I offer him various new objects to see if he will resume his attempts at spatial exploration. He takes hold of a doll, looks at it for a moment without investigating either its shape or clothing; he rubs it against the wicker of his bassinet, and then shakes it in the air.

Observation 146 at 1 year 2 months: In her bath, Jacqueline engages in many experiments with celluloid toys floating on the water. For example, not only does she drop her toys from a height to see the water splash or displace them with her hand in order to make them swim, but she pushes them halfway down in order to see them rise to the surface. (Piaget, 1952)

How do infants learn? How do seemingly helpless infants become the complex, fascinating organisms who not only learn about their environment to survive but learn to comprehend and control that environment?

These questions were very important to Piaget, and he set out to find the answers, initially, by observing (in great detail as the opening excerpts depict) his own children, Lucienne, Laurent, and Jacqueline, as they grew up in the family's home in Geneva, Switzerland. It was on hundreds of such notations that he based his theory of the development of the infant's mind.

Whereas philosopher John Locke believed that knowledge had its sources *outside* (experiences "write" and leave their indelible imprint as the child grows), Piaget's constructivist view of learning was that much of learning originates *inside* the child (children actively select and interpret their environment in the construction of knowledge). Rather than debating the issue philosophically, however, Piaget decided to study it scientifically. He believed that to understand the nature of knowledge, one must study its formation and not the end product. As a result of his work, babies come alive when we read Piaget's rich overview of how infant's think—our first topic of discussion.

We also focus on information-processing views of children's cognitive development. They provide us with a wealth of information about children's ever-changing memory and imitative skills. From yet another perspective, the psychometric approach, we learn about assessing children's capabilities.

Next, we turn to language development. Even though infants can make only a few verbal signals in the form of sounds, sighs, and grunts, from the very beginning, they exhibit a passionate desire to communicate.

Darin is 8 days old. As his mother enters his visual field, they look at each other—the mother smiling and the baby bright-eyed. Darin begins to vocalize for a second or two, pauses, gurgles, and again vocalizes. He looks at his mother the whole time. His face is alive and, occasionally, he smiles. Mother talks in a sing-song pattern that Darin seems to like.

Even though he is just days old, Darin's behavior suggests to us that social interaction and social communication are destined to play a very special role throughout the course of his life. The establishment of a dialogue between infants and those who care for them is a matter of critical importance. As we will see, the tiny infant (with the caregiver's skillful interpretation) is quite a communicator, and shortly after birth he embarks upon the never-ending program of social communication with other human beings.

intelligence
According to Piagetian theorists, organization and adaptation, or the ability to deal with the complexities of one's environment; according to information-processing theorists, the ability to solve problems and adapt effectively to the environment; according to psychometric theorists, information a child possesses at a given point in time.

equilibrium
A Piagetian term that refers to the cognitive balance between assimilation and accommodation.

Piaget's Sensorimotor Thinker

Before Beginning . . .

After reading this section, you will be able to

- identify the mechanisms of thought: equilibrium, schemes, organization, adaptation, assimilation, and accommodation.
- discuss the six substages of Piaget's sensorimotor period.
- explain the strengths and weaknesses of Piaget's theory.
- relate Piaget's theory of how children's cognitive development can be enhanced.

The Mechanisms of Thought

How do infants think? When does memory begin? What does an infant know? These and other questions about the development of **intelligence** in infants have been the focus of numerous inquiring minds, such as Jean Piaget's. Piaget (1952) never used the term "learning" to describe the development of children's thought processes; rather, he saw all behavior as adaptation to the environment. Piaget identified four stages of cognitive development (see Chapter 1): sensorimotor (birth to 2 years), preoperational (2 to 7 years), concrete operational (7 to 11 years), and formal (11+ years). As we trace children's progress through these four stages of cognitive development, we will see infants who begin by acquiring their knowledge through the manipulation of objects become adolescents who acquire their knowledge through the manipulation of ideas. Through these predictable cognitive stages, the developing child gradually comprehends, ever more realistically, how the world functions. (See Self-Insight to analyze your beliefs about how infants and toddlers learn.)

Equilibrium

There were times while writing this book that to finish a chapter, I had to let other things go—from important things such as grading papers to more mundane matters such as household chores. It would gnaw at me that other factors in my life were such a disheveled mess. Upon completing the chapter, I would finally take care of all the neglected activities and feel a sense of structure return to my life. A pivotal Piagetian idea is that we all need some sort of order or a state of balance; Piaget (1955) called this **equilibrium**.

Self-Insight

Learning About Learning

The purpose of this questionnaire is to determine your beliefs about the development of infants and young children. There are no right or wrong answers. Read each item and decide which answers are most important. Then number your choices as follows: 1 = best response, 2 = second best response, 3 = third best response.

1. How do infants acquire their knowledge about the world?
   ______ Parents and teachers must explain concepts to them.
   ______ They discover things on their own by experimenting and exploring.
   ______ They learn to know things as they grow and mature.
2. What good does playing with others serve 2-year-olds?
   ______ They are afforded opportunities to test and develop their ideas.
   ______ Playmates teach each other new ideas and behaviors.
   ______ During play young children demonstrate the skills that are appropriate for their age.
3. How do infants come to realize that objects (and people) continue to exist even though they cannot see them (object permanence)?
   ______ Parents or adults must explain the concept to them.
   ______ They discover the concept by exposure to people and objects.
   ______ With time, they demonstrate this skill at the appropriate age.
4. How do infants learn to talk?
   ______ Caregivers must constantly interact with them.
   ______ They discover this themselves.
   ______ They are genetically programmed to do so.
5. What makes young children act independently?
   ______ They reach a stage when they can do things alone.
   ______ Parents praise them for doing things on their own.
   ______ They have a desire to experiment with new ideas and actions.
6. When do children learn to follow rules?
   ______ They learn when they want the approval of others or they fear punishment.
   ______ They learn when the rules are appropriate for their age level.
   ______ Children learn when they understand the reasons for the rules.
7. How do young children make decisions?
   ______ They make decisions by weighing all the alternatives.
   ______ They rely on adults to help them decide.
   ______ They decide on the basis of what a child their age usually knows.

This instrument was developed to assess adult's general beliefs about the nature of children and how they change over time. The response options represent learning, maturational, and cognitive-development perspectives. According to Carole Martin and James Johnson (1992; Martin, 1983), if you have ranked the first response as number 1 for most items, you tend to emphasizing *learning*. You tend to believe that children are shaped by their social environment (parents, teachers, peers) and the physical environments (toys, situations). You would tend to use the following mechanisms in socializing infants and young children: direct instruction, reinforcement, reward, punishment, imitation, and modeling.

If you ranked the second items number 1, you tend to emphasize *cognitive-developmental* factors. You tend to believe in the dynamic interaction between the child's existing knowledge and the environment as important keys to children's development. You tend to believe that knowledge is the result of active processing on the child's part. As such, the primary mechanisms you will use to socialize children will capitalize on the child's own curiosity, exploration, discovery, self-regulation, and experimentation.

If you ranked the third items number 1, you tend to emphasize *maturational* factors. You tend to believe that the characteristics of the child emerge spontaneously as a result of a natural biological growth. As such, you tend to follow the child's lead as his or her genetic potential unfolds. The timing and patterning of the child's behavior changes are, in your opinion, independent of training or experience.

Equilibrium is an act of searching for a state of *mental balance*. Individuals try as they encounter new experiences to reconcile them with their existing understanding. For example, when you first entered college you might have expected, based on your high school experiences, that teachers would announce in class what chapter to read and when to read it. If this happened in your college classes, then you remained at equilibrium. However, if readings and dates were just noted in the syllabus and never mentioned by the professor, your expectations were not met. Hopefully, only a brief period of disequilibrium followed before you adjusted your behavior and resolved the inconsistency.

Schemes

Thus, equilibrium is achieved when our "mental concepts," or in Piaget's terminology, *schemes,* accord well with our current experiences. **Schemes** are mental patterns or systems that describe the ways people think about the world. Infants, for example, use sucking, grasping, and listening schemes to solve problems and discover more about their environment. Schemes can be simplistic such as a toddler's scheme for buttoning or unbuttoning, or they can be terribly sophisticated such as a philosopher's moral scheme about the purpose of life.

Schemes then are the building blocks of thinking. At each successive stage of cognitive development, an individual's schemes not only incorporate those of the previous level but become more sophisticated and complex. This gradual transformation of schemes becomes the propelling force that moves children from one stage of cognitive development to the next and subsequently defines major cognitive stages of development and their substages.

schemes
Mental patterns or systems that describe the way people think about the world.

organization
The innate process of synthesizing or consolidating existing information.

adaptation
The process of adjusting our schemes and experiences to each other to maintain a state of equilibrium.

assimilation
The process of taking in new information and fitting it into an already existing notion about objects and the world. In this sense, to assimilate is to use what we already know how to do to do something new.

accommodation
Adding a new scheme or modifying an old one.

Organization and Adaptation

To Piaget (1976), two innate processes form the core of intelligence: organization and adaptation. As we acquire an abundance of new schemes, **organization** is the innate process of synthesizing or consolidating our existing information. As such, young children may organize their thoughts by classifying information. So, for example, information about dogs, cats, and horses is organized into an "animal" classification. Similarly, you may organize the information you learned in related courses, such as psychology and sociology, by linking one idea with another or integrating your knowledge.

However, as we continue to acquire new experiences, our existing schemes become inadequate; if we are going to function more effectively, we have to adapt. **Adaptation** is the process of adjusting our schemes and experiences to each other to maintain a state of equilibrium. For the infant, this may mean modifying her kicking scheme. When a 3-month old baby girl accidentally kicks a mobile hanging over her crib, the mobile will move and momentarily catch her attention. Initially, she will not connect her kicking with the gyrating mobile. But over time, she will randomly kick the mobile repeatedly, and eventually (usually by the time she is 5 months old) she will come to understand the relationship between her kicking and the movement of the mobile. On a more sophisticated level, if you are used to driving a car with an automatic transmission and you buy a car with a stick shift, you will have to adjust your driving scheme to successfully drive your new car. Adaptation consists of two complimentary processes: assimilation and accommodation.

Assimilation and Accommodation Through the interplay between assimilation and accommodation, according to Piaget, more and more complex schemes will be formed, combined with each other, and organized into patterns. This process makes infants increasingly capable of dealing with the complexities of their environment, or increasingly capable of "intelligent behavior."

With **assimilation**, individuals incorporate new experiences that are consistent with their existing schemes. An infant, for example, will tightly curl her fingers around any object placed in the palm of her hand. However, when she is given a bottle to hold, the tightly curled fingers do not work. The child then experiences a state of disequilibrium and must realize that her existing grasping scheme is not adequate. This state of disequilibrium, or unsatisfactory interaction, propels her to learn, and subsequently modify or add, new schemes—a process known as **accommodation**. She now adjusts or modifies her grasping scheme by spreading her fingers around the object so that she can successfully hold her bottle. It is through assimilation and accommodation that we build an increasingly more sophisticated understanding of the world; these processes continue throughout our entire life.

Understanding Their World

The cognitive system Piaget envisaged is an extremely active one, in which the child plays an active role in the construction of its own knowledge rather than passively copying information exactly as it is presented to

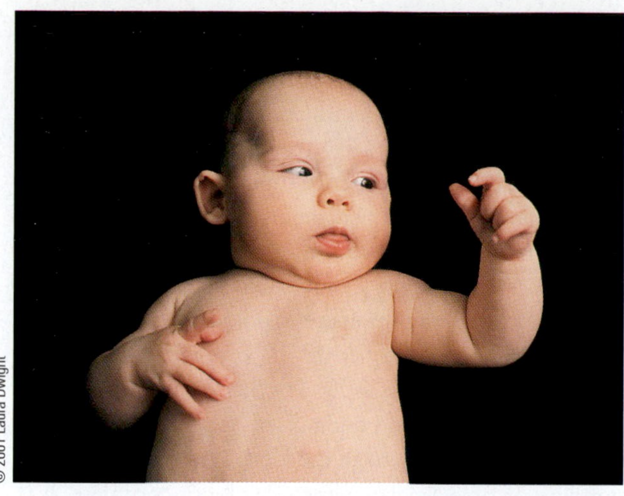

Piaget believed infants played an active role in *constructing* their knowledge about their world.

the senses. Children do not merely incorporate the already developed knowledge of the world into their schemes but reconstrue and reinterpret the environment to make it fit in with their own existing mental framework. To Piaget, children are cognitively active and inventive; they are always trying to construct a more coherent understanding of events by continually integrating what they know and making sense out of discrepant experiences. The view that cognitive development takes place as the child actively constructs a system of knowledge during the course of interaction with the environment is a pivotal Piagetian contribution in explaining children's cognitive development.

Piaget makes us aware of the rhythm inherent in the process of cognitive growth. Beginning with the refinement of reflexes in the infancy period and continuing throughout the entire cycle of development to the adolescent's abstract reasoning, we see how children's minds seek to understand and explain at all levels. When cognitive equilibrium is established in one area, the restless individual begins to explore in another.

We can follow the progressive advancements of sensorimotor thinkers by looking at Piaget's substages of the sensorimotor period.

Substages of Sensorimotor Thinking

The **sensorimotor period** consists of six stages because so much change occurs in children's thinking skills in the first two years of life. As the infant navigates these stages, behavior becomes more intentional and, therefore, more intelligent:

- **Substage 1:** *Reflexive Stage (Birth to 1 Month)* The baby spends her time practicing and repeating such reflexes as grasping, sucking, gazing, and listening. Note that even these basic types of adaptations are not evoked merely by direct external stimulation; infants are active, not passive, creatures and often initiate reflexive activity.
- **Substage 2:** *Primary Circular Reactions (1 to 4 months)* Infants can now put together two separate actions—fist waving and sucking—to form a new behavior pattern, or scheme, of bringing the fist to the mouth to be sucked. Infants now engage in nonintentional, spontaneous actions that center about their bodies (thus these actions are termed "primary"), and they are repeated (circular) until the adaptation becomes strengthened and established.
- **Substage 3:** *Secondary Circular Reactions (4 to 8 months)* In the third stage, the child turns from movements centered on himself and now responds to things in the external environment. A more complicated "circular reaction" occurs when the baby accidentally produces a change in the environment and then seeks to maintain it. He may bump a rattle, and when it makes a noise, he moves around and explores until he bumps it again.

> Observation 95: Lucienne, at 4 months, is lying in her bassinet. I hang a doll over her feet which immediately sets in motion the scheme of (shaking). . . . But her feet reach the doll right away and give it a violent movement which Lucienne surveys with delight. Afterward she looks at her motionless foot for a second, then recommences. There is no visual control of the foot, for the movements are the same when Lucienne only looks at the doll or when I place the doll over her head. On the other hand, the tactile control of the foot is apparent; after the first shakes, Lucienne makes slow foot movements as though to grasp and explore. For instance, when she tries to kick the doll and misses her aim, she begins again very slowly until she succeeds (without seeing her feet). In the same way I cover Lucienne's face or distract her attention for a moment in another direction; she nevertheless continues to hit the doll and control its movements. (Piaget, 1952)

Here Lucienne is intentionally adapting to repeat a response that she finds new and interesting. Already, she is becoming a curious little explorer who repeats actions that please her until she has mastered them.

sensorimotor period (from birth to age 2) Period during which children solve problems using senses and motor activities; they are action thinkers—meaning they think and do at the same time.

- **Substage 4:** *Combination of Secondary Schemes (8 to 12 months)*
  For the first time, infants' behavior is truly intentional in nature, and they begin to solve simple problems. For example, if Laurent wants a toy and an object is in his way, he is able to take directed action if the needed response is already in his repertoire of sensorimotor schemes. In this case, Laurent may combine the schemes of reaching and grasping to obtain the toy. He has begun to comprehend cause and effect; he recognizes that certain acts will bring about predictable results. To Piaget, this is the beginning of practical intelligence.
- **Substage 5:** *Tertiary Circular Reactions (12 to 18 months)*
  The fifth stage is marked by the emergence of what Piaget called *directed groping,* in which the child begins to experiment to see what will happen. No longer does he simply repeat movements to produce a desired result. Now he begins to vary his movements as if to observe how the results will differ. Piaget describes his little son Laurent breaking off one piece of bread at a time and dropping it on the floor, watching with great interest to see where it would fall. Most of us would probably take the bread away in annoyance, but Piaget waited quietly, noting the child's absorbed attention. Like a serious young Galileo, the little boy dropped the bread from various positions and watched it land in different places on the floor. Piaget considered this behavior experimental.
- **Substage 6:** *Beginning of Representation (18 to 24 months)*
  In the sixth and last stage of sensorimotor behavior, the child begins to do his groping mentally rather than physically. As Piaget put it, the child's physical or motor action is "interiorized"; the child thinks about how he would do something without actually doing it until he reaches a satisfactory solution. Piaget called this "the invention of new means" and believed it develops along with symbolic representation. The child at this stage is making the transition from physical to mental operations, or thought, and can represent actions in a symbolic way without actually performing them.

Thus, in six stages Piaget showed us how the infant develops from a biological organism into a social one. He traced the growth of cognition from the first primitive reflex to the complex and varied combinations of behavior soon to be telescoped in thought. Development always spirals upward. The various behavior patterns are repeated until they are mastered; then, propelled by the hierarchic movement of growth, they occur again in new and more complicated forms.

object permanence Over six substages in the first two years of life, children realize that objects continue to exist even though they are out of sight.

Object Permanence

According to Piaget, infants gradually come to realize that objects in their environment continue to exist even when they cannot see them (Piaget, 1973). This is known as **object permanence**. In the earliest stages of development of object permanence, children do not respond to an object once it is removed from sight. For example, if you show a 7-month-old your car keys, he will stare at them and prepare to snatch them from you. If, however, you quickly cover the keys with a cloth, he simply stops and looks away. Try this with a sophisticated 9-month-old, and undaunted he will tear the cloth off and triumphantly seize the keys. But, the understanding of object permanence is still not complete. It is fully achieved when children are able to retrieve objects after they have been hidden. These transformations do not take place over a weekend Piaget maintained; rather, the process is a gradual one developing over the first two years of life (see Table 6.1).

Infants' sensorimotor development thus proceeds from responding reflexively to the immediate world to understanding the properties of the surrounding world. Sensory and motor experiences lead to an awareness of spatial relationships and the development of the concept of permanence of objects. In this unfolding process, the early activities in sensing and manipulating objects in the environment allow the infant to gain increased knowledge of and organization of the environment.

Criticisms of Piaget's Theory

Recent findings on children's cognitive development, many of them recorded by Renee Baillargeon and Elizabeth Spelke, depart drastically from Piaget's theory in two major ways: First, they suggest that young infants know a lot more about the physical properties of objects than Piaget's theory allowed (Needham, Baillargeon, & Kaufman, 1997). Second, according to Piaget, action is a main tool to gain knowledge; recent research tells us, however, that young infants display considerable mental sophistication long before they can reach and manipulate objects (Spelke & Hermer, 1996).

One of the most heavily researched areas of Piaget's theory is when object permanence appears and how it can be tested. Piaget argued that infants' understanding of objects develops slowly over six stages of infancy, so that, for instance, during the first three stages (until around 9 months) the expression "out of sight, out of mind" literally depicts the infant's understanding. Infants assume that objects cease to exist when they

TABLE 6.1

Object Permanence

Substage	Age	Principal Characteristics
1	Birth–1 month	Infants do not know that objects exist even when they do not see them.
2	1–4 months	Infants prolong images by staring at where they were last seen. If the mother's face suddenly appears in infants' field of vision, then disappears, infants will continue to stare at the place where the face was last.
3	4–8 months	Infants search for partially covered objects.
4	8–12 months	Infants search for completely covered objects but only where they were first hidden. If an object is hidden under blanket A, children will find it. If, before their eyes, you take that object from under blanket A and hide it under blanket B, they continue to look for it under blanket A.
5	12–18 months	Infants search after visible displacements. If you move an object behind screen A, then behind screen B, and finally behind screen C, children will follow these visible displacements and look for the object behind screen C.
6	18–24 months	Infants search after hidden displacements. If you put a penny in your hand, put your hand under the blanket and leave the penny there, children, seeing that the penny is no longer in your hand, will look under the blanket.

cease to be visible and exist again when they reappear, he theorized. The main evidence Piaget used in drawing this conclusion was infants' failure to search manually for hidden objects, and all of Piaget's tests of object permanence involved infant's reaching for objects.

For example, in his classic object permanence task, infants, usually in the age range of 8 to 12 months, are shown a toy that is then hidden (perhaps under a cover) either to their right or left in what is called location A. The infant is then allowed to reach for and retrieve the object. After she retrieves the toy from location A, it is then, in full view of the infant, hidden in an identical manner, but this time in a new location on her other side, called location B. When the infant is again allowed to search for the toy, she will search at A, not B! The A-not-B error occurs, according to Piaget, because infants do not attribute a continuous existence to the object. However, more recently developed tests seem to show otherwise. Current research seems to bear out that infants do have mental representations of objects or events independent of perceptual cues (Baillargeon, 1994; 2000; Goubet & Clifton, 1998). They have difficulty in the classic hidden object task because of their inability to coordinate or guide their actions not because of a failure to represent the existence of hidden objects. They may not be able to control their eye movements, to reach, or to pick up the object.

Baillargeon suggests that there is a lag between infant's understanding and acting in the world. It is possible, she argues, for an infant to know that a hidden object continues to exist behind another, occluding object, while being unable to plan and execute an action sequence, such as reaching, to retrieve the object. Her basic design for exploring infants' physical knowledge is to present them with possible and impossible events. The impossible events violate some physical principle relating to understanding support, gravity, continuity of motion, and so on. Figure 6.1 displays an example of continuity of motion.

That infants will look longer at novel than at familiar events has been well documented in research. To Baillargeon, this suggested one alternative method for investigating young infants' beliefs about objects. In this design, the infant first *habituates* (becomes accustomed to and begins to look away) to the movement of a hinged screen through a 180-degree arc. Next, a box is placed in the path of the screen. The child is then shown the two "possible" and "impossible" events. In each case, young infants look significantly longer at the impossible events, indicating, in this example, that children as young as 4½ months are aware that the box does exist even though they cannot see it behind the screen. Baillargeon's research suggests that when tests are designed so that the very young infant does not have to depend on his searching abilities or motivation to search, he probably has some understanding that hidden objects continue to exist. This understanding comes months earlier than Piaget had thought (Lutz & Sternberg, 1999). In support of Baillargeon, Ayesha Ahmed and Ted Ruffman (2000) report from their research that when infants are not allowed to search and when looking is the dependent measure, greater looking at the toy at location B occurs. This clearly indicates, according to the authors, that the infant has some memory of the object's location.

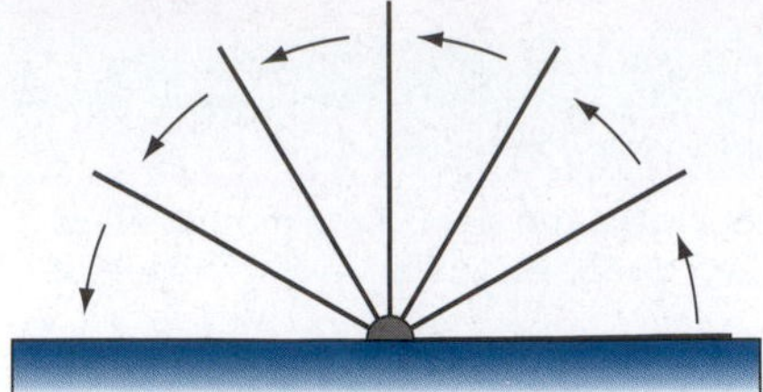

Test event

Possible event

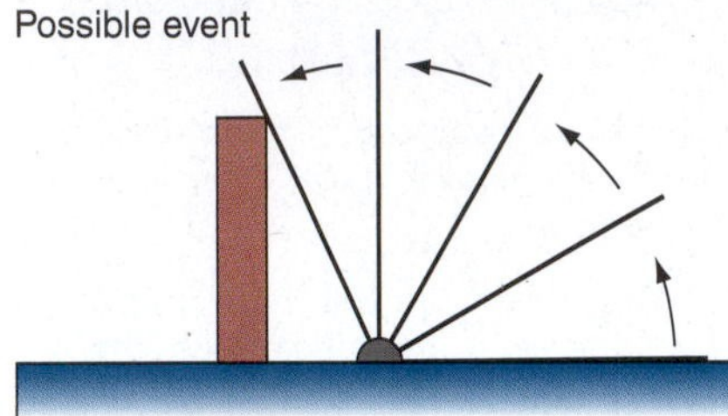

Impossible event

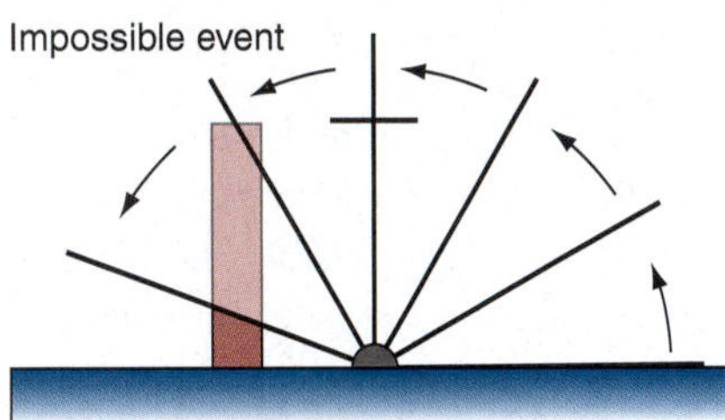

FIGURE 6.1 ***Design for Studying Infants' Understanding of Barrier***

Infants first become habituated to a screen that rotates through a 180-degree arc, in the manner of a drawbridge. Next, a large box is placed behind the screen. In the "possible" event, the screen stops when it encounters the box; in the "impossible" event, the screen stops after rotating through the top 80 percent of the space occupied by the box.

From "How Do Infants Learn about the Physical World?" (pp. 193–212), by R. Baillargeon, 2000, in D. Muir & A. Slater (Eds.), *Human Development.* Malden, MA: Blackwell.

Renee Baillargeon and her colleagues (Baillargeon, 1994; Patenaude & Baillargeon, 1996) also questioned whether the only knowledge infants have is what things look and sound like and how to move themselves around and manipulate objects. Her research has shown that infants can understand language, engage in symbolic activity, and conceptually reason about their environment. One way in which infants demonstrate conceptual and symbolic thinking is by gesturing to refer to something else. An infant, for example, is capable of gesturing at the sight of a familiar toy in a new location. To illustrate, the baby sees a fuzzy rabbit toy that she is accustomed to kicking in her crib. When she sees the rabbit across the room, she will make a brief, abbreviated kicking motion. Her findings have led Baillargeon to the belief that Piaget's theory of sensorimotor development needs to be substantially modified.

According to some critics, Piaget ignored the role that extrinsic motivation, instruction, and culture play in learning. They argue that Piaget's notion that we are all personally and internally motivated to make sense out of what we encounter to achieve a state of mental equilibrium is rather idealistic. For example, some children (particularly older children) may be motivated to learn because they may receive money for all the A's they get on their report card. Relatedly, some college students may be motivated to understand so they can do well in a course, maintain their GPA or their scholarship to school, or get into graduate school. But, Piaget ignored this external type of motivation.

Piaget also tended to underestimate the role of adults and family members in fostering cognitive development. As noted in Chapter 1, sociocultural theorist Lev Vygotsky (1962) made us aware of the importance of social interactions between children and more experienced adults and parents in mastering more complex tasks. Piaget also ignored the role that culture plays in learning. Vygotsky helped us to recognize the culturally specific nature of children's cognitive development—that children learn skills that are valued by their culture and that will enable them to successfully adapt as adults to their specific society. (Vygotsky's views on cognition are covered more in depth in Chapter 9.)

Looking Beyond the Challenges

The core theoretical assumption of Piaget's theory is that children are active thinkers, constantly trying to construct more advanced understandings of the world. The awareness of this innate drive to create more advanced understandings that Piaget gave to us is a remarkable vision. Similarly, as John Flavell (1996) noted, Piaget helped us to accept the idea that children's cognitive behavior is intrinsically (generated within the child) rather than extrinsically motivated (generated by reward). Although social and other reinforcements may influence children's curiosity and cognitive explorations to some degree, basically children think and learn because they are built that way. Piaget's descriptions give us a highly memorable and at least fairly true picture of how children at different ages think: the action-oriented sensorimotor thinker; the qualitative thought of the preschooler; the quantitative thought of the school-age child; and the more abstract thinking of the adolescent.

APPLICATIONS:

A Piagetian Approach to Fostering the Infant's Cognitive Competence

Piaget altered the way we view children. No longer do we view children as "imperfect" grownups. Rather, we see them as constructive cognitive beings busy forming their own thoughts about their world. It is quite clear that infants, from the opening days or weeks of life, have cognitive skills that will enable them to acquire vast amounts of information about their world, which in turn, will enable them to develop still more complex skills. It is also apparent that infants actively participate in discovering their environment generated from their own need for mental activity. Caregivers enter into the process of children's development by selecting and shaping environments in which children develop.

One of Piaget's last books, *The Grasp of Consciousness* (1976), dealt with how young children come to understand their world. In it, Piaget argued that young children learn primarily through physical knowledge. To Piaget, then, it is only through *active experimentation* with objects that children can begin to understand the operations of their acts. He advised that they be given opportunities to play with such materials as pegs, clay beads, or blocks. Piaget's advice underscores the fact that children do not necessarily require fancy toys or expensive educational aids, but rather, they learn best from ordinary materials found around the house. (See First Person.)

Just what can young children learn through randomly playing with blocks and pegs? As children experiment with blocks or pegs, they use their senses to learn about physical properties such as shape, size, length, and height. As the child builds her castle out of blocks, she learns that large blocks support smaller ones to make her castle. She learns that clay can be flattened to look like a cookie or rolled to resemble a sausage. She learns that it feels sticky and can be rolled smooth. She learns that there are different colors of beads. Through active participation and sensory exploration, she gains physical knowledge about these materials.

Logical Knowledge

From these beginnings, as children get older, they also gain in **logical knowledge**—the development of concepts such as relationships of objects through size, shape, and color; the development of numbers and quantity such as less, more, and equal; and notions about space and time. As the child plays with blocks, he learns that blocks can be plastic or wood. He develops a scheme or mental picture of blocks as things that have particular qualities. He also learns that he can arrange these blocks according to shape, that he can line them up from small to big, and that he has a few or a great many blocks. He may also learn that three small blocks equal one large block as he experiments by building many different projects. Thus, he begins to explore the concept of measurement.

The Importance of Play

Experimenting and playing are important during the first two years of life. As children play, for example, they may learn that they can sort across classification by putting all red blocks together even if they are of

Piaget believed that children learn best when they play with ordinary household objects such as pots and pans.

FIRSTPERSON

Everyday Learning

My son Grant is 13 months old. It is so amazing to me just to watch him explore his newly found walking world. Ordinary household objects hold a special fascination for Grant. He beams with delight at the noise he creates from banging on pots and pans with a wooden spoon. He spends long periods of time filling an empty container with blocks, and when full, he dumps them out and starts filling the container again. He will carefully build a tower of three blocks—then knock them down. His favorite word is "whazzat?" as he points to pictures in his books and objects around the house. Mirrors are magical to him; he loves looking at his handsome face and giggles at his reflection when I plunk a funny hat on his head. His curiosity seems endless in his examination of objects as he grabs, twists, smells, tastes, and throws them. His favorite game is bringing me a toy and shortly afterward demanding it back; this game of giving and taking goes on endlessly. Shortly before his naptime, he'll grab his favorite blanket and curl up on the floor. No wonder he's tired; he's done so much and learned so much about his exciting world. After naptime, he'll venture forth on brand new adventures. How exciting everyday learning is for him—how resourceful and creative young children are.

—*Abigail Baur*

different sizes or shapes or all round blocks together even if they are red, blue, or green. Piaget stressed that children only learn when they are biologically able to form a new scheme. A child who is not ready to classify blocks by shape or color, then, may group them in a haphazard fashion; a child who is ready to classify will group them by shape and color.

logical knowledge The development of concepts such as relationships of objects through size, shape, and color; the development of numbers and quantity such as less, more, equal; and notions about space and time.

information-processing theory A branch of cognitive psychology that is interested in studying the nature of information that children pick up and the series of stages they pass through as they absorb and transform this information.

Active Manipulation

Piaget felt strongly that young children should be given every opportunity to manipulate objects. He argued that children may begin to count in a rote fashion, but the physical correspondence of objects on a one-to-one basis can only be learned through active manipulation of the objects that are to be counted. Active manipulation games such as counting on fingers or reciting nursery rhymes of "This Little Piggy" on their toes help children see the items to be counted. Later, they can visualize the number and begin to understand that numbers are symbols.

Piaget stressed that adults need to look at play and active manipulation of play objects in the child's environment in a more serious manner. Children prosper when adults recognize the importance of what may seem like random, and perhaps meaningless, play activities to the learning process.

Concept Checks

1. Simone is 14 months old, and she purposely explores new possibilities with objects; she is in the ____________ substage of sensorimotor development.
2. Efrain is 5 months old and is receiving his first tablespoon of solid food. Initially, he sucks the spoon, but on the third mouthful, he opens his mouth wide. Efrain has just ____________ his sucking scheme.
3. Piaget's theory has been criticized primarily because
   a. his timing of stages appears to be incorrect.
   b. cross-cultural research has not supported his findings.
   c. infants and toddlers know more than he believed.
4. Piaget would advise adults to let children
   a. freely explore and manipulate ordinary objects found in their environment.
   b. exercise their new schemes with daily instruction from caregivers.
   c. enroll in preschool as soon as possible.

Information-Processing Views of Cognition

Before Beginning . . .

After reading this section, you will be able to

- describe the structure of memory.
- grasp the concepts of habituation and dishabituation.
- discuss infants' memory skills.
- recognize the problems associated with overstimulating infants.

Information-processing theorists define *intelligence* as the ability to solve problems and adapt effectively to the environment, and as such, they are interested in studying the series of stages through which children pass as they absorb and transform information. The information-processing method refers to the *processes* by which children take in, analyze, store, and retrieve various types of things they have perceived or that have happened to them—*information*. Information-processing theorists maintain that intelligent infants are those who encode information more rapidly than others, store material more durably, and retrieve it with greater efficiency. Given the vast amount of learning that infants acquire in the first two years of life, it is apparent that they must have efficient but elementary means by which to process information.

Unlike Piaget, information-processing theorists do not believe cognitive development occurs in discrete stages. Instead, they see the operations of the mind as continuous from infancy into adulthood. In particular, they are interested in studying how information is coded, stored, and retrieved in memory.

The Structure of Memory

According to the information-processing model, memory consists of three phases: the sensory register, short-term memory, and long-term memory. The **sensory register** permits the effect of a stimulus to persist briefly after the stimulus itself has been removed. It is a type of a primitive photographic memory, in that it will record faithfully but decay quickly. When information from the sensory register is selectively attended to and perceptually interpreted it passes into our *short-term memory*.

Our **short-term memory** (**STM**) is temporary, active, and conscious; it is our attention span or working memory. Information in the short term is either forgotten (not processed), or it is passed into our *long-term memory*. **Long-term memory** (**LTM**) is the repository of our more permanent knowledge and skills. Basically, it includes all things that have been coded in memory that are not being currently used. Memory sequencing is depicted in Figure 6.2. According to information-processing theorists, these three aspects of the mind are present in infants but, as the child matures, she becomes more proficient in all areas.

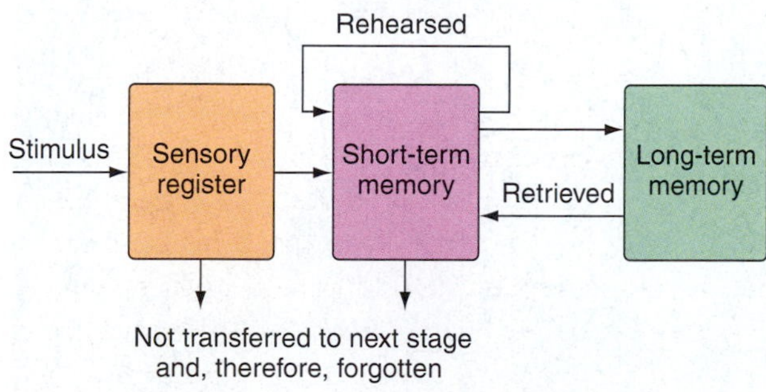

FIGURE 6.2 *Steps in Information Processing*

This information-processing chart shows the steps in memory sequencing: (1) information is initially processed in the sensory register (taking information from our senses); (2) it is then transferred to short-term memory (our momentary awareness), (3) where it is either forgotten or processed into our long-term memory (our permanent storehouse of information).

From *Memory*, by E. Loftus, 1980, Reading, MA: Addison-Wesley.

Habituation and Dishabituation

When I was in graduate school, my apartment was approximately 15 feet from the Illinois Central Railroad Line (an apartment that left a lot to be desired). On my first night in this apartment, a freight train came through at 3:00 A.M. Awakened from a sound sleep, I jerked to wakefulness, with owl-eyes, and lay very still. To my dismay, I discovered that this would be a nightly phenomenon! Amazingly enough, however, after about three evenings I did not even hear the train. In principle, this experience describes one of the most commonly used paradigms in information-processing research—**habituation**, defined as a decrease in response to an unchanging stimulus.

One way to assess infants' memory abilities and discover their growing sophistication in memory processes is through habituation designs. The process is quite simple; rather than using roaring freight trains, however, information-processing theorists use a novel stimulus such as a picture, odor, or flashing light to get the infant's attention. The infant's increased attention is called an *orienting response,* which can be measured physiologically because his heart rate slows down, his eyes widen and pupils dilate, and he exhibits increased muscle tension. But, if the stimulus is presented over and over again, the infant's attention to it decreases. This change, too, is reflected in changes in his heart rate, pupils, and muscle tension. Now suppose that once the baby has habituated to one stimulus, another stimulus is introduced. His attention will again be aroused, this time in response to the new stimulus. The recovery of attention to the novel stimulus is called **dishabituation**.

Habituation is believed to be a basic form of learning in infants that is a primitive memory process. Through the processes of habituation and dishabituation, we know that infants remember something they have seen or heard before when they cease to respond to the old and familiar stimulus and spark to attention when a new one is introduced. When, through repetition, the stimulus becomes familiar, a "match" occurs with the internal model and the orienting response decreases. The orienting response is reactivated upon the presentation of a novel stimulus for which an internal model has not been formed. For several reasons, then, habituation is seen as a measure of infant intelligence as well as later intellectual functioning (as noted in Table 6.2).

Similarly, recognition memory has been used with a visual preference procedure as a measure of infants' intellectual ability. Visual recognition of a previously presented stimulus is among the basic information

sensory register
A part of the memory sequence that picks up sights and sounds and allows them to persist for a brief period of time after they have been removed.

short-term memory (STM)
The temporary, active, conscious memory; our attention span or working memory.

long-term memory (LTM)
According to information-processing theory, this is our permanent storehouse of information

habituation
The gradual decrease of attention paid to a repeated stimulus.

dishabituation
The recovery of attention to a novel stimulus.

TABLE 6.2

Habituation

1. Habituation to visual stimuli is thought to involve information processing, attention, and memory, all of which are implicated in intelligence. 2. Habituation is characterized by interage differences, with older infants taking less time to reach the same criterion of habituation than younger ones. 3. Infants habituated to one stimulus later distinguish a novel stimulus by comparing it with their internal representation of the familiar stimulus.	4. Infants who habituate in shorter times ("short lookers") process stimuli more rapidly than infants who take longer to habituate ("long lookers"). 5. Simpler stimuli provoke more rapid habituation than do more complex stimuli in infants of a given age. 6. Infants "at risk" for cognitive delay or handicap habituate less efficiently than "normal" matched controls.

From "Stability of Mental Development from Infancy to Later Childhood: Three 'Waves' of Research," by M. H. Bornstein, A. Slater, E. Brown, E. Roberts, & J. Barrett, 1997, in G. Bremner, A. Slater, & G. Butterworth (Eds.), *Infant Development: Recent Advances* (pp. 191–195). East Sussex, UK: Psychology Press. Used by permission.

processes that seem to be present from early in life (Nelson & Collins, 1991). Visual and auditory recognition capabilities in infants have been well documented. A baby, for example, will stare longer at a toy she has not seen before; she recognizes the new toy as different from what she has seen before (Hood, Murray, King, & Hooper, 1996). These findings show that infants can discriminate between the two stimuli (the strange new toy and the old toy), as well as use their memory to recall the old toy (Slater, Brown, Mattock, & Bornstein, 1996).

The Infant's Memory Skills

Information-processing theorists also point out that 3-month-old infants can retain and retrieve information over relatively long periods of time (Adler, Gerhardstein, & Rovee-Collier, 1998; Borowsky & Rovee-Collier, 1990; Rovee-Collier, 1996; Rovee-Collier & Gerhardstein, 1997). In a characteristic experiment, Carolyn Rovee-Collier places a baby in a crib underneath an attractive mobile. She ties a ribbon to the infant's ankle, which is connected to a mobile. The infant quickly learns that when she kicks her feet, the mobile moves; soon she makes repeated kicks, controlling the dancing movement of the mobile overhead.

What happens, however, when the infant is hooked up to the apparatus days later? When she is allowed to see the mobile before being hooked up to the apparatus, even 6 to 8 days later, she immediately starts to kick to create the exciting movement of the mobile. If she is not shown the mobile first, however, she does not kick; this indicates significantly impaired retrieval of the memory. Thus, by 3 months infants appear to encode information about the physical setting of an event, and this information is an important source for remembering the event, particularly after longer intervals of time. According to Rovee-Collier, even by 3 months, the infant's memory is incredibly detailed.

Early Imitation

One of Piaget's students inadvertently discovered that if she stuck out her tongue at a 2-month-old infant, the baby responded by sticking its tongue out at her. This was most perplexing to Piaget because he believed that this act of imitation should not occur before the infant was 8 months old. Piaget thought about this as he puffed on his pipe—then apparently dismissed his student's findings.

Decades later, Andrew Meltzoff (1988, 1996) found that young infants can match gestures after seeing adults display certain facial expressions. Infants between 12 and 21 days old can imitate both facial and manual gestures. And, according to Meltzoff, who has conducted numerous studies of the imitative abilities of infants, this behavior cannot be explained in terms of either conditioning or some innate mechanism (Meltzoff & Moore, 1999). Further, Meltzoff believes that this is not just a random act, because infants match gestures *only* after seeing an adult do them.

By the age of 3 months, infants can rapidly learn to activate a mobile tied to their ankle with ribbon by kicking their legs. When shown the mobile as much as a week later, the infants will begin kicking their legs in memory of their previous experience.

Meltzoff also found that infants were capable of **deferred imitation**—a form of representation. When infants, for example, see the experimenter stick out his tongue, they immediately imitate it *and* they imitate it again if brought back to the laboratory the next day (Barnat, Klein, & Meltzoff, 1996; Meltzoff & Moore, 1999). Such imitation implies that human infants can equate their own unseen behaviors with gestures that they see others perform and suggests a link between perception and the production of a body movement.

Evaluation of Information-Processing Theory

Information-processing theorists focus intently on specific cognitive processes and view cognitive development as the acquisition of problem-solving strategies in many different domains. The specificity of the information-processing approach can be viewed as a strength and a weakness. On the negative side, the theory has not led to a general model that provides us with a comprehensive picture of children's cognitive development. On the positive side, because of its focus on task demands for specificity, clarity, and fine-grained analysis in the account of behavior, information-processing theory presents us with specific predictions about children's problem-solving abilities and makes us more sensitive to the diversities found in children's thinking and abilities. Information-processing theory also makes us aware of the importance of stimulating infants through exposing them to various stimuli.

APPLICATIONS:

The Perils of Overstimulation

Most of us are aware of the importance of enhancing infant's cognitive development through stimulation; few, however, may be aware of the perils of overstimulation. Overstimulation occurs when our senses are bombarded, and we move into "overload." For example, I can spend perhaps an hour in a shopping mall. After that, my tolerance level drops and my annoyance level rises as the throngs of people, noises, lack of fresh air, and smells wafting from the food court take their toll. Babies can get overstimulated and annoyed, too. Consider, for example, the interaction styles of these two mothers:

> Mother and child are playing a delightful game of pat-a-cake; the infant turns away and sucks her thumb. The mother stops playing and watches her infant. Within a few seconds the child turns back and looks at mother with an inviting smile; the mother moves closer and says, "So, you want to play another game." The game continues. After a short while the baby again turns away and stares without expression. Mother again waits. Soon the young infant turns back, and they greet each other with smiles.
>
> Now, imagine a similar situation; only this time when the young child looks away, the mother gently turns the child's face to hers and continues the game. The infant, however, does not interact and again turns away. The mother brings back the infant's line of vision, while clicking her tongue to gain his attention. The child begins to fuss and suck his thumb.

Relational Styles

Which relational style is better? The first mother's is better because her and her child's communications are in sync with each other. Why is that important? The

© Myrleen Ferguson Cate/PhotoEdit

When infants look away, they are telling their caregivers that they do not want to talk right now. When they are ready to resume the "conversation," they once again look at their caregivers.

deferred imitation The imitation of actions that have occurred at an earlier time.

way we relate to infants establishes (or fails to establish) affective communication relationships. Good interaction is characterized by mutually coordinated states and results in positive emotions between mother and child. By contrast, the second mother's interactions are poor because they are characterized by miscoordinated interactions and negative emotions. When the infant turns away it means that he has had enough and needs to calm down; it is his way of escaping by becoming perceptually unavailable. It is important that caregivers respond contingently to their infant's cues; when the child looks away, adults should wait until the child is ready to begin communicating again.

Overstimulating Infants

Adults tend to overstimulate infants quite often. It has been observed in spontaneous play situations that when mothers overstimulate their infants, the infant attempts to withdraw by decreasing its gaze time and communicative efforts (Mangelsdorf, Gunnar, Kestenbaum, Lang, & Andreas, 1990). "Overstimulation" means that the mothers continued to initiate interactions through talking, smiling, and touching their infants, even when the infant had turned away. Looking away is one of infants' earliest devices for regulating interactions with others. Some studies have reported, however, that whereas mothers interact up to 90 percent of the time, infants look in response only 30 percent of the time (Field, 1995).

Optimal Interactions

Excessive or minimal caregiver activity results in nonoptimal interaction (Ramey, Breitmayer, Goldman, & Wakeley, 1996). Adults may severely overload children with signals as they try to engage their infants in playful encounters. The child who is overloaded turns away and may cry. If this overstimulation continues, the parent–child relationship may be seriously damaged. The fact that overstimulation may be damaging is often forgotten. Therefore, caregivers need to engage in contingent stimulation, or stimulation dependent on the cues from the infant.

Optimal Responding

psychometric approach Concerned with quantifying individual differences in children's intelligence.

Another important caregiver behavior is responding to the infant's needs in an immediate and appropriate fashion. By responding in this fashion, the infant develops a sense of trust in his environment and learns that she has influence over what happens in that environment, which is vital to future cognitive achievements (Webster-Stratton, 1992). Waiting several minutes before responding to the child does not allow the infant to connect his or her behavior with the parent's response. When infants are responded to within a short period of time after demonstrating a cue or need for the caregiver, they learn their behaviors are important and that they can affect the people and things in their environment. In cases where the infant is unable to give clear cues or respond to the parent, the infant is not in a position to change. Therefore, it becomes the adult's responsibility to recognize this and adapt his or her own behaviors so that the interaction becomes positive and flows smoothly.

Concept Checks

1. Our perception of a passing automobile would be temporarily stored in our ________ ________.
2. We know that infants remember something they have seen or heard before when they ________ to the old and familiar stimulus and spark to attention when a new one is introduced.
3. Overstimulation occurs when
   a. infants are perceptually unavailable.
   b. caregivers continue to interact when the infant has looked away.
   c. adrenalin is pumped into their system.

Psychometric Assessment

Before Beginning . . .

After reading this section, you will be able to

- describe infant assessment procedures.
- discuss early intervention programs for at-risk infants.

The **psychometric approach** is another way of looking at infants' cognitive abilities. Unlike Piaget and the information-processing theorists, who are interested in finding out how thinking changes over time, psychometric theorists are interested in studying how infants and children differ in their thinking skills and how such differences can be measured. These theorists generally define *intelligence* as information a child has at a given point in time. They are interested in *quantifying* intelligence, which usually means producing a number, an IQ (intelligence quotient), to describe a child's current level of intelligence.

Testing procedures performed on infants focus on assessing developmental norms and not on "cognitive abilities" as later tests of intelligence will do. Unlike tests given to older children or adults, however, these psychometric indices do not assign an intelligence quotient or number, and they do not measure abstract and verbal abilities. The prime purpose of these early infant assessment procedures, such as Gesell's Developmental Quotient assessment, is to appraise the infant's developmental maturation as compared with other infants.

Gesell's Developmental Quotient

Arnold Gesell (1925) and his associates at the Yale University Clinic of Child Development revolutionized infant assessment by developing a *normative approach* to assessing infant development. They developed a measure that was used as a clinical tool to help sort out potentially "normal" babies from "abnormal" ones. This was useful to adoption agencies who had large numbers of infants waiting for placement. Gesell schedules were designed primarily for the purpose of determining the integrity and functional maturity of the nervous system between 1 month and 6 years of age. Gesell identified norms of infant behavior in four developmental domains:

1. Motor (gross and fine motor skills)
2. Language (infant's communication whether vocal or facial)
3. Social (cooperation during play)
4. Adaptive (problem-solving abilities)

(Sample test items from each of the developmental domains appear in Table 6.3.) The scores from the four areas of performance are combined and calculated to obtain an overall developmental score, called a *developmental quotient* (DQ). The DQ was originally conceptualized as analogous to IQ, but in fact the DQ measures very different behaviors.

TABLE 6.3

Sample Items from the Gesell Developmental Scales

	Age	Behavior
Motor Schedule	4 weeks	Rolls partway to side
	12 weeks	Lifts foot while standing
	36 weeks	Leans forward in sitting position and re-erects
Language	16 weeks	Laughs aloud
	36 weeks	Imitates sound
Personal–Social	8 weeks	Eyes follow moving person
	20 weeks	Smiles at mirror image
Adaptive	12 weeks	Follows dangling ring 180 degrees
	44 weeks	Points out pellets through the glass bottle

From *The Mental Growth of the Preschool Child,* by A. Gesell, 1925, New York: Macmillan.

Bayley's Scales of Infant Development

While Gesell was working on the East Coast, Nancy Bayley (1933) was investigating the development and modification of patterns of infant behavior on the West Coast. Like Gesell, Bayley focused on normative behavior and, in 1933, used the findings of the Longitudinal Berkeley Growth Study of Infant Development to publish the first version of the Bayley Scales of Infant Development. She subsequently revised her initial scale, and the BSID-II became the best-known and most widely used test of infant development.

The Bayley Scales consist of three major subscales that can be used independently or in combination for assessment purposes:

1. *The Mental Scale:* including measures of language, object permanence, problem-solving skills, imitation, and visual and auditory attention
2. *The Motor Scale:* which measures gross and fine motor items, such as sitting, walking, grasping objects, and eye-hand coordination
3. *The Infant Behavior Record:* assesses state of arousal, sensitivity to test materials, motor control, activity level, and social responsiveness (Bayley, 1993)

Table 6.4 presents sample items from the BSID-II. If infants do well on these tests, does that mean they will do well on later tests of ability? In other words, will smart infants become smart children? (See Child Development Issues.)

TABLE 6.4

Sample Items from the Bayley Scales of Infant Development

Age	Mental Scale Item	Motor Scale Item
7 months	Cooperates in games	Pulls to standing position
11 months	Rings bell purposely	Throws ball
14–16 months	Names one picture	Grasps pencil at the midline
23–25 months	Matches four colors	Walks forward on a line
32–34 months	Compares sizes	Walks upstairs alternating feet

From *Bayley Scales of Infant Development* (2nd ed.), by N. Bayley, 1993, San Antonio, TX: Psychological Foundation.

APPLICATIONS:

Early Intervention Programs for At-Risk Infants and Toddlers

We have made some quantum leaps forward in our knowledge about behavioral genetics (see Chapter 4) and brain development (see Chapter 5). One of the major findings from both these fields of research underscores that the environment has its greatest potential to influence IQ during the early developmental years. We also know that children who grow up in poverty and are often exposed to impoverished environments are at increased risk for lower cognitive performance, which often equates to later school failure (Zigler & Styfco, 1998). Infants and toddlers from disadvantaged environments tend to encounter sterile learning environments; they are restricted in their movement and freedom; their diet is poor; their home environment is more disorganized and unpredictable; and their mothers tend to spend little time interacting with their children (Rickel & Becker, 1997). All of these disadvantages hamper the infant's intellectual development; subsequently, federally mandated special programs for socially and economically disadvantaged children were inaugurated to target children between the ages of 2 and 5 years. One such program was Head Start.

Head Start, which began in the late 1960s, is designed to help young children from impoverished environments improve their academic skills and performance. How successful is this program? Children who attend Head Start are more likely to complete high school and less likely to repeat a grade or be placed in special education classes. They progress in school, stay in the mainstream, and satisfy teacher's requirements better than peers who do not attend (Zigler & Styfco, 1998). Thus, children who participate in Head Start programs may be at a more global advantage in school.

However, the results of several research projects do not cite lasting increases in IQ for Head Start participants. For example, most researchers have concluded that while children in the program initially show an increase of 10 to 15 IQ points, when they enter formal education, their IQs drop and continue to drop, so that later there are no measurable effects of the Head Start experience (Ramey & Ramey, 1998). Fortunately, current research has uncovered important variables that lead to continuous benefits for children in intervention programs. One such factor is intervention during the infancy years (Wolfe & Brandt, 1998).

Early Intervention

An ambitious idea for breaking the cycle of disadvantage began with Craig Ramey. His idea was to start children in an enrichment program in early infancy—beginning as young as 6 weeks. His enrichment program is called the Abecedarian Project, which means "learning fundamentals, like ABCs." In their research, Craig Ramey and Sharon Ramey (1998) demonstrated that infants and toddlers living in impoverished environments responded very favorably to intensive, early academic intervention. They showed that infants' scores on intelligence tests increased by 15 to 30 percent as a result of participating in early intervention enrichment programs.

Intense Intervention

Interventions that continue longer afford greater benefits to children than those that do not last as long (Walkins, & Bunce, 1996). Programs that are more intensive (greater number of home visits per week; number of hours per day, days per week, and weeks per year) produce larger positive effects than do less intensive interventions. Further, children and parents who participate the most actively and regularly are the ones who show the greatest developmental progress (Ramey & Ramey, 1998). Thus, new findings indicate a strong relation between intensity of *early* educational intervention and continuous benefits into later childhood. To date, however, there are no compelling data to support the notion of an absolute critical period such that educational intervention provided after a certain age cannot be beneficial.

Extended Intervention

According to Arthur Reynolds and Judy Temple (1998), better classroom performance is seen in children when intervention programs are extended from infancy to the primary grades (first to third) for the following reasons: first, longer duration of intervention programs may be necessary to promote greater and longer-lasting changes in academic and social outcomes. Many economically disadvantaged children need more time to gain all the benefits the program has to provide. Moreover, because the rate and negative consequences of poverty are growing, existing programs may require expansion to be effective.

Second, developmental research overwhelmingly indicates that academic success correlates highly with the child experiencing a stable and predictable learning environment from infancy onward (Cole & Cole, 1993; Ramey & Ramey, 1998). By giving children and their

Child Development Issues

Do Smart Infants Become Smart Children?

Developmental psychology is as much interested in stability of development as it is in change. Is there some continuity of development? The interest in stability has focused on the ability (or not) to predict later IQ from measures taken in infancy. Earlier research suggested that the correlation between infant intelligence scores and preschool intelligence measures is quite low.

One reason for this lack of predictability between infancy and later childhood may lie in the types of tests that are used in the infancy and post-infancy periods. Intelligence tests for infants are designed for use with children who have not developed language. They test attending to objects, visual following, and simple motor tasks. Later tests, even so-called nonverbal tests, assume that the subject understands language. Thus the aspects of intelligence tested during infancy (sensorimotor) are not the same aspects of intelligence tested during later childhood (verbal). For example, the Bayley Scales tap sensory and motor capacities, such as reaching, grasping, and orienting, that bear little conceptual relation to measures included in traditional psychometric tests of intelligence administered in childhood. This lack of consistency between infancy and later childhood measurements may be explained by differences in tests rather than differences in ability (Brody, 1997).

The problem is to find some aspect or aspects of intelligence that are present in both infants and older children and that can be measured in both. Infant research into attention and information processing has shown that individual differences in infancy can predict later IQ.

Research findings indicate that smart babies show relatively greater amounts of looking at novel stimuli or reciprocally lesser amounts of looking at familiar stimuli (Thompson & Fagan, 1991) and prefer novel stimuli (Fagan, 1997).

As an example, when a baby initially responds to a picture of a dog with attention and visual activity, this shows that she is looking at the picture. After the picture of the dog has been presented repeatedly, the baby spends less time looking (habituation). If the now-familiar picture of the dog is taken away and then brought back again, the baby will scan it briefly (dishabituation) and will habituate once more. Now, if a new picture is introduced, a picture of a tree, the baby will scan vigorously because it represents a novel and new stimulus.

These behaviors are generally interpreted as more efficient styles of information processing in infancy and are related to better intellectual performance in childhood (Bornstein, Slater, Brown, Roberts, & Barrett, 1997; Lang, Simons, & Balaban, 1997). Thus, evidence is emerging that part of the intellect that involves the seeking, finding, learning, and solving of novel problems may be an important part of intelligence that is stable across the remainder of the life span.

A number of infant capabilities then are thought to indicate later intelligence:

- Habituating rapidly
- Showing short durations of attention to repeated or unchanging stimuli
- Demonstrating a strong preference for novel stimuli
- Inhibiting responses to uninformative and familiar stimulation
- Turning their attention away from it toward more informative stimuli Bornstein, 1996; Sigman, Cohen, & Beckwith, 2000)

Search Online

Explore InfoTrac College Edition, your online library. Go to **http://www.infotrac-college.com/wadsworth** and use the passcode that came on the card with your book. Try these search terms: age and intelligence, intelligence levels, intellect.

parents the opportunity to enroll in programs for up to five or six consecutive years, the stability of the school learning environment may enhance school performance and social competence.

Third, the transition to formal schooling in kindergarten and first grade is a sensitive if not "critical" period in children's scholastic development. The provision of additional educational and social support services to children and families during this key transition would promote better adjustment.

Family Factors

The most constructive early intervention programs are those that have actively involved parents (Gray & Wandersman, 1990). Decades ago, Urie Bronfenbrenner made us aware of the importance of parental involvement by noting that "the family seems to be the most effective and economical system for fostering and sustaining the child's cognitive development. Without family involvement, intervention is likely to be unsuccessful and what few effects are achieved are likely to disappear once the intervention is discontinued" (1974, p. 300). Current research verifies this.

When studying economically disadvantaged high-risk children from birth through age 5, it has been found that combining daily center-based intervention with weekly parent-oriented home visits results in significant cognitive gains for the children. When parents did not receive home visits, there were not measurable benefits on children's cognitive or social performance (Wasik, Ramey, Bryant, & Sparling, 1990).

Family education is another factor that tends to enhance at-risk infants' future performance. When families are provided with general family support, including helping parents learn specific knowledge and skills related to positive infant development, in later years, school performance improves and tends to be stable (Wasik, Ramey, Bryant, & Sparling, 1990). Home visits and family education then are two other effective components in helping at risk infants.

Concept Checks

1. Assessment scales measure the infant's
   a. cognitive competencies.
   b. motor control, social responsiveness, and activity level.
   c. ability to solve perceptual problems.
2. One of the key variables in determining the success of intervention programs for at-risk infants is
   a. to start intervention programs one year before the child enters kindergarten.
   b. to actively involve parents.
   c. to have highly trained professional caregivers.

ethnolinguistics The study of the relationship between language and culture.

Language Development

Before Beginning . . .

After reading this section, you will be able to

- discuss theories of language development.
- recognize the progressive development of language skills.
- characterize features of effective communication with infants.

By definition, infants do not talk; in fact, the latin *infans* means "incapable of speech."

> What do you mean babies don't talk! Those searching eyes, those furrowed eyebrows, those hands stretching out to us, those furiously kicking feet, the sighs, the grunts. What more proof do you need?

Thousands of times before infants learn to talk, they participate in these shared rhythms of "speech" and movement. They have laid down the rhythmic forms of language even before they start to babble. The acquisition of *language,* that uniquely human ability, begins, it seems, with the micromotions of a baby just a few hours old. Language is the most complex skill that children acquire. Unlike calculus, abstract painting, chess, or many other very difficult skills, no animal or machine has ever been able to "do" language like people do (Wang & Baron, 1997).

Language in Its Cultural Setting

The 6000 plus different languages throughout the world may astound us by their great variety and complexity. However, any human language is a means of transmitting information and sharing with others both cultural and individual experiences. The study of the relationship between language and culture is the province of **ethnolinguistics**, which is concerned with every aspect of the structure and use of language that has anything to do with culture.

Ethnolinguists have found that while language is flexible and adaptable, once a terminology is established, it tends to perpetuate itself and to reflect the social structure of a culture's perceptions and concerns (Haviland, 1999). For example, English is richly endowed with words having to do with war; we often speak of "*conquering* space," "*fighting* poverty," "*battling* the *war* against drug abuse," "making a *killing* in the stock market" or "*bombing* out on an exam." Similarly, anthropologists have noted that the language of the Nuer, a nomadic people of southern Sudan, is rich in words (more than 400 words) that have to do with cattle. An observer of these two cultures would learn about the importance of warfare to one culture and cattle to the other simply from what these cultures have found necessary to name and to talk about. Thus, by studying other languages, we can get a glimpse into the social structure of a culture and what individuals in that culture deem important (Woolfson, 1972).

Language is also a source of national pride. Some countries have attempted to proclaim their linguistic national pride by purging their vocabularies of "foreign" terms. France, for example, is attempting to purge their French language from such Americanisms as *le hamburger*. Linguistic nationalism is also apparent in Israel's campaign to revive Hebrew as its first language. As a result of the hard work of many Native Americans from various tribes across the United States, Congress, in 1990, passed the Native American Languages Act, which encouraged tribes to use their native languages.

Language enables people in every culture to share their experiences, concerns, and beliefs in the past, present, and future by communicating these to the next generation. Ethnolinguists make us aware that language tends to reflect a culture's beliefs; it is a source of national pride and self-identity; and it heightens certain perceptions in a society and dims others. Language, then, is a by-product and a vehicle for the transmission of culture.

Language: A Rule-Governed System

Language is *an ordered system of rules* that people comprehend in speaking, listening, and writing. Children tend to learn language in a very methodic, rule-governed way. The rules children simply "know" rather than learn are known as **implicit rules**. For example, look at these two sentences:

1. The boy aggravates his father.
2. The aggravates boy his father.

Sentence 2 is obviously wrong. Because the words are out of order, it makes little sense. You notice this right away, even though you may not be able to explain why; you know it *implicitly*. You know that it is wrong because you never say sentences like 2. A collection of these implicit rules is termed a **grammar of language**. Not until children attend school and study grammar do they learn **explicit rules**—rules that help them to learn (among other things) the eight parts of speech and then to arrange these words into a grammatically correct sentence.

Within a short period of time and with almost no direct instruction children will analyze language completely. A child's mind is somehow "set" in a predetermined way to process the types of structures that characterize human language. This is not to say that the grammatical system is innately known but that the child has innate means of processing information, and when these capacities are applied to the speech she hears, she succeeds in constructing the grammar of her native language.

The three main branches of grammar relate to phonological, semantic, and syntactic development. The **phonology** branch of grammar studies how children go about learning the rules for combining basic sound patterns, or **phonemes**. Table 6.5 lists the phonemes of American English. It is from these 34 basic sounds that all words in the English language are formed. No language uses more than about 50 phonemes.

Peter Eimas (Eimas, 1999; Eimas, Sigueland, Jusczyk, & Vigorito, 1971) concluded from his research that infants as young as 1 month old are able to make fine discriminations between speech sounds, which implies that perception of speech sounds may well be part of infants' biological makeup. In his experiment, 1-month-old infants activated a recording of the "bah" sound whenever they sucked on a nipple. At first, they sucked diligently, but as they habituated, sucking

language
An ordered system of rules that people comprehend in speaking, listening, and writing.

implicit rules
Language rules that are innately known.

grammar of language
The study of the three branches of language development: phonology, semantics, and syntactics.

explicit rules
Rules of grammar that are taught; such as identifying the eight parts of speech.

phonology
The study of the meaning of sounds that compose the English language.

phonemes
The smallest units of sound in a spoken language.

TABLE 6.5

Common Phonemes of the English Language

Consonant Phonemes		
p (pass)	th (this)	n (no)
b (but)	s (so)	ng (ring)
t (to)	z (zero, boys)	l (love)
d (do)	sh (should)	w (wish)
k (kiss, calm)	z (azure)	wh (when)
g (go)	ch (church)	y (yes)
f (for)	j (Jim)	r (run)
v (value)	m (more)	h (how)
th (thing)		
Vowel Phonemes		
i (bit)	e (bet)	ae (map)
i (children)	ov (above)	o (not)
u (put)	o (boat)	u (law)

decreased. At this point, Eimas changed the sound from "bah" to "pah." Upon hearing the new sound, the infants immediately began sucking harder. Eimas and his colleagues concluded that the newborns could discriminate between the very similar sounds of *p* and *b*.

A study of Kenyan infants at 2 months of age supported Eimas' work (Streeter, 1976). The infants were all from Kenyan homes in which only Kikuyu, a Bantu language, was spoken. This study also measured nonnutritive sucking to establish habituation. The Kenyan infants also distinguished the speech sounds.

Infants also have the ability to discriminate between and produce a vast number of phonemes, including those that are not a part of their native language. For example, Japanese babies can tell the difference between *r* and *l* sounds—a distinction that is difficult for many Japanese adults. Similarly, babies in English-speaking homes can distinguish between certain Hindu and Czech phonemes that their parents cannot discriminate (Kuhn, 1993). When it comes to phoneme discrimination, infants are "universal citizens." This helps explain why any baby, regardless of ethnicity or country of origin, will grow up to speak the language of its adopted nation. The ability to discriminate and produce foreign speech sounds, however, begins to wane as early as 6 months (Kuhn, 1994). By this age, babies in English-speaking homes have already lost some of their ability, still present at 4 months, to discriminate certain German or Swedish vowels. By 10 or 12 months, the infant loses her ability to discriminate foreign consonants—like *r*'s and *l*'s for Japanese babies or Hindi consonants for infants from English-speaking homes. Because certain sounds not indigenous to their native tongue are generally not reinforced, they are dropped from the child's repertoire.

Phoneme perception is thus another example of "use it or lose it" in the developing brain. This phenomenon is demonstrated by the Northern Ute Tribe. Like many Native Americans, these people had experienced a decline in fluency in their native tongue as they interacted more and more intensively with people who only spoke English. As adults sought employment off the reservation, traded in non-Indian communities, and were exposed to television, English began to replace their native Ute language. Infant Ute children were spoken to in English. Soon, the Ute language had almost disappeared—with only a handful of elders in the tribe speaking in their native language (Leap, 1987). Language, however, is more than a collection of words; it is a cultural phenomenon and represents a socially embedded communication system. Language often represents a sense of identity and self-worth; so, in the late 1980s the Ute tribe established a program that resulted in language projects to teach adults and children the Ute language to reestablish its prominence as the tribally sanctioned language.

syntax
A branch of linguistics that studies the way words come together to form sentences.

semantics
A branch of linguistics that studies the meaning of words and sentences.

morphemes
When phonemes are combined, they form meaningful structures known as words.

The **syntactic** branch studies the way words come together to form sentences. Initially, children hypothesize very general rules about sentence structure; gradually, they narrow them by adding more precise rules, which apply to a more restricted set of sentences. Children continually revise and refine the rules of their internal grammar, learning increasingly detailed subrules, until they achieve a set of rules that enables them to create the full array of complex, adult sentences. The **semantics** branch studies the meaning of words, or *morphemes*. When phonemes are combined so that they express meaning, they are called **morphemes**. Not all morphemes are words; some are word fragments. For example, the prefixes (pre-, re-, ex-, con-), the suffixes (-tion, -est, -ic, -ly), and the verb tense markers (-ing, -ed) are also morphemes.

Theories of Language

But, how do children go about learning the "elements of language," or the phonological, syntactic, and semantic rules that make communication possible? In short, how do children learn to speak? There are three basic perspectives on this question: the behaviorists, the nativists, and the social interactionists. The behaviorists maintain that language is learned entirely from experience. The nativists assert that environment plays a limited role in the acquisition of language; instead, children are born with an innate capacity to acquire language. The social interactionists conceptualize language development in terms of both environmental and biological factors.

The Behaviorists

Little Henry, lying in his crib, is contentedly babbling away in what sounds like a language from some remote country. He blurts out a sound that resembles "mama." Mother, near at hand and unable to suppress her joy, picks Henry up and hugs and kisses him. "You said 'mama!'" she gasps with delight. Just to make sure Henry doesn't forget, she repeats "mama" a few dozen times, interspersing the repetitions with more kisses and hugs. If surprised little Henry responds with a meaningless babble, he does not receive such a positive response from his mother.

Learning theorists, particularly B. F. Skinner (1972), believe that language occurs through the action of the environment shaping the individual's behavior. In particular, learning a language comes about through reinforcement as well as by imitation. Although babies are born with the tendency to babble, these early sounds are gradually shaped into meaningful language by the way in which those around them respond to the sounds babies make. Sounds that are not reinforced eventually are extinguished. Thus, children come to use language by operant conditioning and imitation. Skinner's theory may be able to explain how children in France learn French and children from Poland learn Polish, but how does Skinner's theory explain some of the universals in language development around the world? All children, for example, learn to speak with surprisingly similar sequencing; children, in mastering their language, progress from single words to two-word communiques and finally to telegraphic speech and beyond. How would Skinner's theory explain children's "invented" words or sentences like, "No, me no want to go home!" when they have never heard these types of sentences (at least we hope not)?

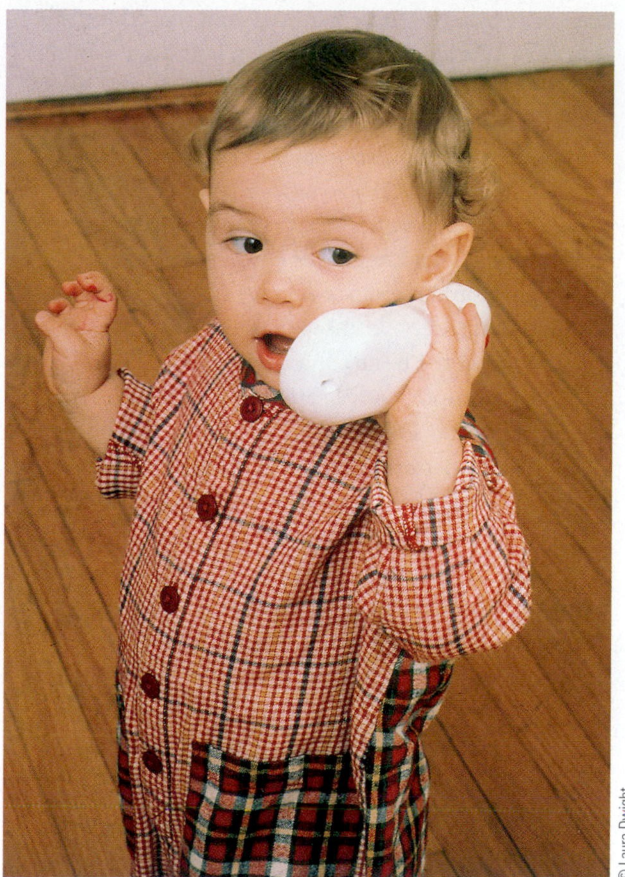

© Laura Dwight

Consistent with Chomsky's theory, children all over the world learn to speak with surprisingly similar sequencing.

Thought CHALLENGE

Virtually all children acquire a language, and they do so in strikingly similar ways. The fact that children all over the world follow the same implicit rules tells us what about language development?

Nativistic Theory

If you answered the Thought Challenge by saying something like "If language acquisition is simply a matter of environment shaping the child's language," as Skinner maintains, "the resulting shapes and sequences and processes leading to language would be far more diverse than they in fact are." Noam Chomsky (1968, 1986) would applaud your thinking.

Chomsky discusses several universals in language development that appear to underscore some kind of innate component to language development:

1. The onset of language regularly occurs between the second and third years of life.
2. Language emerges before it is of any immediate use to children.
3. Early vocalizations, such as cooing and babbling, do not represent practice or learning requirements for later language acquisition.

It is interesting to note that children all over the world learn language in a remarkably similar way. Although there are differences between languages, children, worldwide, follow identical stages—one-word, two-word, telegraphic (multiple-word sentences), and then sentences that are more complex—and all this is done in the first four years of life. Similarly, all languages are composed of the same parts of speech (nouns, verbs, adverbs, adjectives, and so on) whose order and agreement are specified by rules.

Chomsky also believes that language development is primarily a matter of maturation and that the environment is of little importance. Language is innate, an aspect of children's genetic makeup. Universal principles allow children to develop grammar as rapidly as they do. The only environmental factor necessary for the child to learn to speak is exposure to some language. Therefore, he does not rule out environmental "fine tuning" for communicative development.

But, Chomsky maintains, knowledge of language rules—rules of how words are combined into meaningful phrases and sentences (syntax)—is biologically based. Every human being is born with a highly specialized innate capacity to acquire language, which he calls a **language acquisition device (LAD)**. Every child is born with this universal linguistic structure, which guides his or her efforts to grasp underlying rules of grammar. The brain's language acquisition device allows a young child to deduce the basic rule system without being taught just by listening to language. Children discover abstract regularities in the speech

language acquisition device (LAD) According to Chomsky, this refers to an innate capacity to acquire language. It is a universal linguistic structure found in the brain.

they hear, analyze these patterns, and reproduce the results of this analysis in their own language. Chomsky does help us to understand the fact that all children proceed through the same stages of language acquisition despite great differences in their vocabulary or native language. LAD also accounts for children's commonly made errors in forming plurals ("feets"), past tense ("goed"), and negatives ("no go bed").

Where in the brain would we find the language acquisition device? We know that there are special language areas in the brain: Broca's area, which enables us to produce sounds, and Wernicke's area, which enables us to understand sounds. Wernicke's area is believed to recognize the pattern of auditory signals. We also know that for each different signal (that is, for every different word), a distinct set of neurons is activated (see Figure 6.3). Thus, when the child hears the word *cup,* auditory pathways transmit the signal to Wernicke's area, where neurons that correspond to the sound "kup" become activated. These neurons then activate other neurons that store a visual picture of a cup and still other neurons that store concepts about how cups are used. Thus, the child's knowledge (auditory, visual, and conceptual) about "cup" is stored in a neural network that encompasses many brain regions, not in a single central processing unit. The existence of LAD, however, has not been empirically verified (or disproved, for that matter).

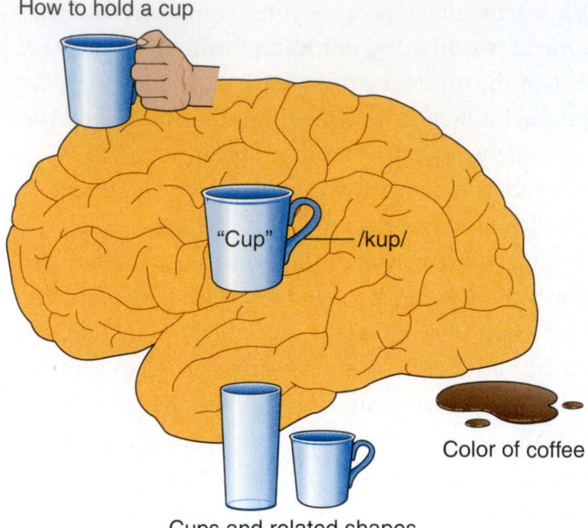

FIGURE 6.3 ***Processing the Word "Cup"***

For each different signal (for every different word) a distinct set of neurons is activated.

Social Interactionist

The social interactionists attempt to establish a compromise between these two extremes (Bates, 1995; Slobin, 1971; 1988). This perspective assumes that biological factors influence the course of language acquisition but that interaction between children and adults is also absolutely necessary if language skills are to develop. Innate mechanisms alone cannot explain the child's mastery of language, and the mastery involves more than conditioning and imitation.

The social interactionists would agree with Chomsky that there is a special, innate capacity for language in humans. Special features of the brain and articulatory apparatus make it clear that language capacity has a distinct biological foundation. Species-specific behavior and distinct neural and anatomical structures are good evidence for the special evolution of these capacities, preserved in the genetic code, which make us mature into speaking creatures. The uniquely human biological foundations of language thus support the theoretical and empirical arguments for inborn language capacities in human beings.

Dan Slobin (1985), however, explores and questions the nature of this innate language ability. Is it some sort of advanced knowledge that is activated by language exposure? Is it processing abilities? Slobin suggests that children's special capacity for acquiring language may be special processing strategies or operating principles that enable them to figure out how language works. "A child is not born with a set of linguistic categories but with some sort of process mechanisms —a set of procedures and inference rules, if you will— that he uses to process linguistic data. The linguistic universals, then, are the result of an innate cognitive competence" (Slobin, 1971, p. 114).

The Infant's First Communications

Theorists may disagree about how language develops, but they do agree language development predominates in the infancy and toddlerhood period as young babies progress from a few gurgling syllables to somewhat sophisticated conversationalists. Patterns of language development follow *prelinguistic* and *linguistic* stages. Before infants speak their first intelligible words, they are called **prelinguistic**. They communicate to us initially through their crying, cooing, and babbling. The **linguistic** period begins when children utter their first words, followed by the two-word stage, and then simple sentences known as telegraphic speech.

prelinguistics Communication that precedes intelligible words; crying, cooing, and babbling.

linguistics Begins when children utter their first words, followed by the two-word stage, and then simple sentences.

Recognizing different speech sounds is the beginning of understanding a language and learning to use it. Almost from the moment of birth a baby pays special attention to the sounds of speech—a skill basic to learning to talk. Infants have receptive abilities, enabling them to hear sounds, discriminate among different sounds, and interpret them. Young infants turn their heads toward the sound of someone talking more than toward any other sound. By the end of their first month, infants discriminate the human voice from other sounds and can be quieted by soft, high-pitched, calm speech.

Infants tend to find language sounds especially interesting. Newborns consistently show distinctive overt reactions (visual fixation, increased motor activity) when hearing complex auditory stimuli such as speech sounds, whereas they show little overt response to other sounds such as pure tones that contain no speech sounds (Roberts, 1997).

Cooing

Children typically do not say their first words until approximately 10 to 12 months of age, but these words are preceded by a history of vocalization. By 2 months, infants have developed the musculature to produce certain sounds basic to language. At 3 to 4 months most infants' vocalizing consists of open vowel sounds; they say "aaa," "ooo." This is known as **cooing**. Babies everywhere cry and coo alike. The appearance of cooing is related to physical and sensory changes that take place around 6 or 8 weeks, including increased visual attention and greater control of the tongue.

All infants increase and diversify their vocalizations during these months, but there are marked differences in the number of different sounds they make and the richness of their use. Highly stimulated infants are far more vocal than less stimulated ones. The baby's surroundings play an important role in influencing these early vocalizations. Babies will vocalize more when they are touched and when their sounds are greeted by a response that enables them to interact with people around them.

Babbling

Nothing sounds cuter or more innocent than a baby chattering away in long strings of varied sounds. Their earnestness makes you think that they are speaking some authentic foreign language. It is obvious that infants take pleasure in the sounds of their own voices. As babies gain increased control of the tongue and mouth, they begin, by the fifth or sixth month, to combine them into a series of sounds resembling language, which we call **babbling**.

The babbling sounds of infants from all language backgrounds are remarkably similar. The babbling of an infant learning English cannot be distinguished from that of an infant learning Russian, Chinese, or Spanish (Nakazima, 1992). Babbling sounds become differentiated beginning at around 6 months when infants begin taking on the characteristics of the language that surrounds them. One cross-cultural study showed that 10-month-olds babble in distinctive ways; the babbling of those in the study reflected French, Chinese, or Arabic consonants (De Boysson-Bardies, 1989). The same appears to be true for establishing dialects. A child who grows up in Boston, for example, will thus store a prototype for the sound "a" that is more open and throaty than a child in the Midwest, who will pronounce this phoneme in a more nasal and closed manner. Infants in the early months of life acquire a great deal of information about the phonetic properties of their native language simply by listening to adults speak. However, after as little as 15 minutes of "training" by a female speaker, infants, no matter what their native tongue, will modify their vowel pronunciation to match the vowels presented to them (Kuhn & Meltzoff, 1996).

At 7 months the infant's babble becomes enriched by two-syllable "words." The syllables are quite distinct; they are not lifted subjectively out of a blur of sound, but can be written down phonetically, as they are uttered, with a high degree of agreement between one listener and another. The infant says words like "mimi," "ippi," "aja," and so forth. By late infancy, babbling begins to take on the intonations and rhythms of the baby's native tongue.

By 8 months, most infants have learned to listen to and try to join conversations that are not directly aimed at them. If the mother and the father are talking, and the infant is sitting between them, his head will turn from one adult to the other and back again, as if closely watching a tennis match. Soon children learn how to interrupt; they develop a shout for attention (Rubin & Fisher, 1982). Similarly, their comprehension becomes more visible. When the father says, "ball," the baby will look at the ball.

Toward the end of the eighth month, and in the ninth, the repetitive babbling syllables are strung together into long, drawn-out phrases of four or more syllables, such as "loo-loo-loo-loo." Sometimes infants repeat a sound over and over again; sometimes they add more variety—"ahdee-dah-dah."

cooing
Vocalizations infants make at 3 to 4 months, consisting of long, open vowel sounds.

babbling
By the fifth or sixth month, infants combine various sounds, including consonants and vowels.

By 12 months, English-speaking babies can produce most vowels and about half of all the consonants. It takes a few more years before children can master the more difficult consonants. That is why a 4-year-old may say, "I dink I want my lellow bwanky" (I think I want my yellow blanket).

Receptive Language

The meaning the infant attaches to what other people say is called **receptive speech**. Babies usually understand more words than they can say at all stages of language development. It is, however, impossible to gauge just how many words babies actually understand; it has been estimated that their comprehension may exceed expression by a factor as high as 100 to 1. Although some babies are slow in starting to talk, comprehension appears to be equal between late-talkers and early ones (Nelson, 1996).

Previous studies have estimated that the onset of comprehension of words begins around 9 months or later. These estimates, however, were based on the infant's responses to names of relatively immobile, familiar objects. Comprehension of names referring to salient, animated figures (such as Mother or Father) appears to begin earlier. Ruth Tincoff and Peter Jusczyk (2000) tested this possibility on 6-month-olds. The infants were shown side-by-side videos of their parents while listening to the words *mommy* and *daddy*. In this situation, the infants looked significantly more at the video of the named parent. A second experiment revealed that infants did not associate these words with men and women who were not their parents. When, for example the infants were shown videos of unfamiliar parents they did not adjust their looking patterns in response to "Mommy" and "Daddy."

After infants begin to say their first words, they demonstrate their comprehension of words by being able to follow simple directions and commands. Toward the end of the second year, 2-year-olds can usually understand and carry out two or three related requests combined in a single utterance.

receptive speech The meaning infants attach to what others say.

gestures Nonverbal means of conveying messages that are conventional in form and universally recognized.

Gestures

Some researchers have suggested that gestures are related to the acquisition of first words (Wellman, 1993). Toward the end of the first year a considerable expansion takes place in the range of devices the infant has for communicating with others. In particular, even before they speak words, children begin to use **gestures**—nonverbal means of conveying messages that are conventional in form and universally recognized.

One of the earliest examples is pointing. Pointing gestures can be seen in 3- to 5-month-old infants, but at that age it is merely a spontaneous display of interest or attention. Up to about 9 months of age there is no indication that infants understand the meaning of the gesture; when another person points they are unable to follow the target of the pointing finger and instead look at the finger itself. Thereafter, they begin to follow correctly but only under "easy" conditions—that is, when the finger and the target are near each other in the same part of their visual field. Infants' own use of pointing as a means of indicating something of interest also emerges around this time. It is noteworthy that pointing appears in the same form in all cultures—with arm and index finger extended—with no suggestion that it is in any way learned or imitated (Wellman, 1993).

Initially, however, the gesture takes the form of "pointing-for-self"—the infant points to the target but without checking whether the other person is following the gesture. "Pointing-for-others" as an indication of the child's desire to share the object with another person emerges later. By looking from object to person and back again infants show that they can now integrate the two objects of interest into the same activity, thus providing yet another demonstration of the important role the development of this ability plays in social interchange. Shortly after "pointing for others," the young child speaks her first words (Clark, 2001).

First Words

First words mark the transition from prelinguistic to linguistic development. As noted, children understand more language than they can speak but productive speech (what they actually produce, or say) is limited to single words at a time. The first words produced by infants are often nouns and references to things that move, things that can be acted upon, or objects of particular interest or familiarity (car, dog). These styles of communication have been labeled *referential*. Children who communicate referentially show a predominance of common nouns; in contrast, children who communicate expressively show a preference for personal–social words, proper names, and routine social phrases (Mohanty & Perregaux, 2000).

Cross-cultural research has shown that cultural variables affect the nature of children's speech. The referential style is related to a higher proportion of adult contact with the infant and a lower proportion of peer contact (Hampson & Nelson, 1993). For example, in samples of infants from the United States and Korea, first words tend to be composed of object names or nouns (Au, Dapretto, & Song, 1994); with infants from Kenya—who tend to have multiple caregivers, many of whom are young girls—expressive languages styles were found. (Nelson, Hampson, & Shaw, 1993). Other characteristics of the infant's first words are highlighted in Table 6.6.

Yet, children's one-word utterances carry more meaning than might be expected from their brevity, and the term **holophrastic** speech has been used to describe the notion that children's words sometimes serve as entire sentences. For example, if the child says "cookie," it is taken to mean that the child is expressing "I want a cookie." The problem in interpreting meaning is that parents are attempting to read the mind of the child who is providing them with only the barest of clues, a single word; thus, misinterpretations are common and most frustrating to the young linguist.

We all so readily accept that speech begins with single words that we seldom stop to ask ourselves why infants should choose to begin in this way. Why does their speech not begin with the phrases that they hear repeated quite often, such as "night-night" or "upsadaisy"? If they are going to begin with single words, why do they choose certain words? We do not know the answer. Some speculate that infants may be able to store in their memories only a single word at this stage, not a word sequence. Perhaps, they subjectively perceive certain isolated words or the first, last, or most stressed words of a sentence. These words may stand out from what is otherwise still a blur of talk. These "topic" words may be repeated more often. They learn the word *bottle* because the bottle is important to them, and because whatever parents say about the bottle, that word is the one consistent sound in a vast complexity of other sounds they often hear: "Do you want your *bottle*?" "Here's your *bottle* of juice." "Let's get your *bottle* and have a nap." Moreover, some words may be used by some children because they are easy to pronounce—"mama," for example.

Lois Bloom (1993) has observed that the words children use are more than just labels for things. Observations of infants suggest that these first words have a more complex communicative purpose. Infants do not simply state, "Dog" as if to say, "That is a dog." Sometimes they use the word as an emphatic "Dog!" expressing surprise, annoyance, or delight at the dog's arrival. They use the word as a question, too. "Dog?" they ask, perhaps looking at an animal, perhaps hearing a noise outside. Children are able to separate the different functions that are indicated by a word by applying their semantic knowledge of stress and pitch.

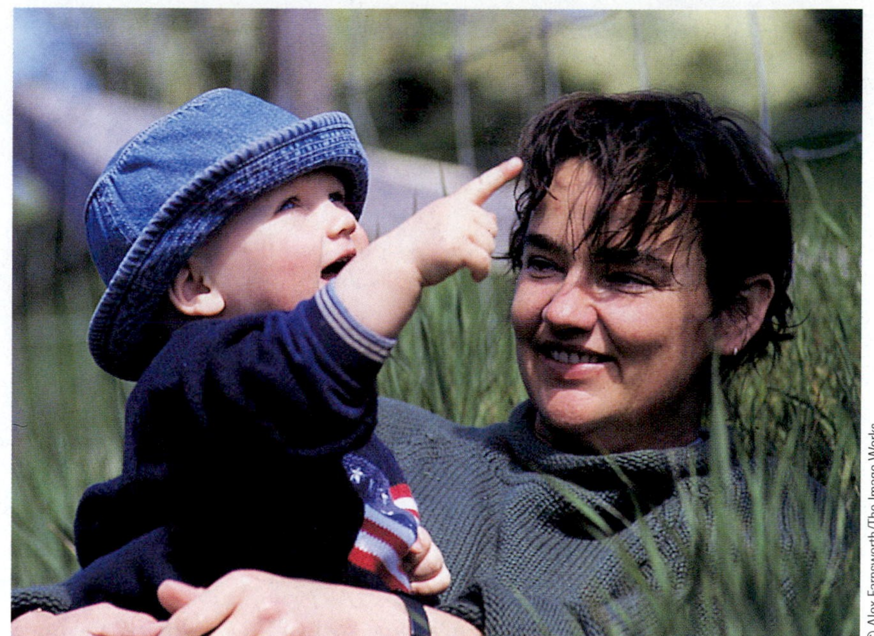

When infants "point for others," first words are not far behind.

Most infants will say three words by the end of their 12th month, whether these are standard, approximations, or self-words. They will say four or five words clearly by their 15th month and six or seven by their 17th month. During the next three years, children will acquire over 1800 words. Most agree that new words come very slowly at the beginning, so that the child may acquire only one to three words a month between 11 and 15 months (Bloom, Margulis, Tinker, & Fujita, 1996). These are age approximations, and when infants speak their first words varies. However, there are some signs to look for that should alert caregivers to seek a professional evaluation if the infant is not communicating in some fashion by 12 months of age (see Table 6.7).

holophrastic The notion that children's words sometimes serve as entire sentences.

Most researchers agree that vocabulary explosion occurs during the 18th month (Waxman & Kosowski, 1990), but it can be as early as 12 or as late as 24 months.

TABLE 6.6

Characteristics of First Words

First words tend to	
▪ be single-syllable words such as "go" or "no."	▪ begin with consonants, such as *s, b, d, t, m,* or *n,* followed by a variety of vowel sounds.
▪ be reduplicated (repeated) monosyllables such as "ma-ma" or "bye-bye."	▪ appear one at a time.
▪ end with *ie* or *y* (birdie, doggie).	▪ refer to objects or events familiar to the child.

From *Infant Development* (p. 203), by C. W. Snow, 1989, Englewood Cliffs, NJ: Prentice-Hall.

TABLE 6.7

Seven Warning Signs of Delayed Language Development in Infants

1. Is "too good"—sleeps all the time 2. Makes habitually poor eye contact with parents 3. Consistently fails to respond to voices or other sounds 4. Has noticeable asymmetry of limb movements (right and left sides of the body should appear equally strong and active during the first year)	5. Exhibits noticeable delay in many or all of the commonly accepted milestones for motor development 6. Displays noticeable delay in social responsiveness (doesn't participate in pat-a-cake, peek-a-boo, bye-bye) 7. Is abnormally overresponsive to physical stimuli, such as noises, lights, touch

From *Your Child's Growing Mind,* by J. M. Healey, 1994, New York: Doubleday.

A 20-month old, for example, may speak as few as 3 words or more than 500, with the median at 169 (Pinker, 1995). It does not take long for children to catch up, once a child begins adding 200 words a month to her vocabulary (see Table 6.8). Not surprisingly, the toddler's vocabulary explosion is associated with a growth spurt in brain development (Marchman, 1990).

When babies begin to speak, they also develop gestures, facial expressions such as smiling and laughing, and variations of anger that aid in the communication process (Bates, O'Connell, & Shore, 1987). These gestural components of language are often referred to as body language. In English, at least 90 percent of emotional information is transmitted not by the words spoken but by body language and tone of voice (Haviland, 1999). Body language signs are transmitted by adults and also tend to be culture bound (Dresser, 1996).

Children, cross-culturally, are socialized by their families to communicate in culturally appropriate ways (Mohanty, Panda, & Misra, 1999). For example, many toddlers in the United States are familiar with the crooked index finger and its backward motion, which means "come here." In other countries, toddlers learn that this gesture has negative connotations. In Yugoslavia and Malaysia, it is used to call animals—not people; in Indonesia, Japan, and Australia, the gesture is used to beckon an "inferior" person. When used between persons of equal status, it becomes an act of hostility. The influence of culture on body language can be further demonstrated in the gestural expressions for "yes" and "no." In North America, one nods his head for "yes" or shakes it for "no." The people of Sri Lanka, also will nod to answer "yes" to a factual question, but if they are asked to do something, a slow sideways movement of the head means "yes." Body gestures such as these, which vary cross-culturally, have to be learned through cultural imitation.

TABLE 6.8

How the Infant's Vocabulary Grows

Age (Months)	Number of Words	Gain
8	0	
10	1	1
12	3	2
15	19	16
18	22	3
21	118	96
24	272	154

From *Infant Development,* by C. W. Snow, 1989, Englewood Cliffs, NJ: Prentice-Hall.

parentese
A simplistic way of speaking to young children, using shorter sentences, emphasis on certain words, and repetition.

Caregiver Speech

Caregivers' language styles when talking with children differ from those they use with adults. Adults do not complain to children about the difficulties in obtaining a bank loan. Or if they do, they do not expect them to understand. They do not expect them to follow long explanations, so they frequently check to make sure that the children understand them.

Parentese involves communications that include fewer words per utterance, more repetitions and expansion, better articulation, and decreased structural complexity (Hoff-Ginsberg, 1990). Parentese also includes exaggerated intonation, fewer pronouns, higher pitch, slower tempo, and fewer endings (for example, plurals or possessives). Parentese is child-directed speech; it is not "baby talk." Baby talk is a muddled pronunciation that turns a sentence such as "Is she the cutest baby in the world?" to "Uz seeda cooest wiwo baby inna wowud?" When adults enunciate clearly, they give their young children a clear and cleaner model of speech.

Mothers speak to young children in short, simple sentences; the average sentence length is four words, compared with eight- or nine-word sentences used when communicating with adults (Phillips, 1973). In addition, when communicating with children, caregivers tend to talk in the "here and now," usually about whatever is directly in front of the child's eyes. Do fathers' speech display the same modifications and characteristics as mothers'? Yes and no. Fathers do adjust their speech similar to mothers by using shorter phrases and repeating sounds. But, in contrast to mothers, fathers tend to use fewer repetitions and expansions of child utterances and more imperatives and directives—"Come, here, Molly, and get your toy car."

Is infant-directed speech found in other cultures? Again, yes and no. Cross-cultural data have shown that although adults everywhere speak to children differently than they speak to older children and adults, the particular form of caregiver speech involving simplified grammar and vocabulary is not universal (Cole, 1999). Other features such as distinctive pitch and intonation, however, do appear to be worldwide. Moreover, in some societies children are rarely spoken to before the age of 1 year; in other countries, such as Japan, mothers tend to interact with their infants through nonverbal gestures (rocking, holding) rather than through verbal communication (Toda, Fogel, & Kawai, 1990).

What is the significance of these modifications in adult speech? Is it at least plausible that simplification is an aid to learning language? The most general feature of parental speech—simple, short sentences—is that it increases the probability of children following the adult's request "Bring me the green block." (Tomasello & Merriman, 1995). Children may not respond at all if the input is too complex (Jackendoff, 1994). Infant-directed speech is thought to serve other purposes as well, such as eliciting the infant's attention, modulating the infant's arousal, and facilitating language comprehension (Bornstein, 1995; 1996). With regard to eliciting attention, infants respond more to their own mothers' voice when she is speaking "parentese" than when she is using adult-directed speech (Cooper, Abraham, Berman, & Staska, 1997; Papousek, Bornstein, Nuzzo, Papousek, & Symmes, 1990).

Parentese, involving simple grammar and short sentences, does not occur universally.

APPLICATIONS:

The Growth of Shared Understandings

What role can adults play in promoting their infant's or toddler's language development? For speech to develop, children must receive warm emotional and physical contact with the caregiver. It is in this way that children are motivated to coo, babble, and finally make the transition to meaningful speech. The reasons, then, that children learn to speak are social. They are ultimately tied up with their attachment to the parents and the pleasure and affection infants get from them.

Communication, then, is so much more than just talking. It is about the infant and the caregiver building an intimate relationship that will become the prototype for the infant's relationships with others. When the caregiver enters the infant's world of vision, he brightens, looks her in the eye, smiles, and makes those wonderfully pleasant cooing sounds. Soon the infant realizes that he has an impact on his parents. He makes some sounds and his father responds in turn; he reaches out to his mother, and she reaches back. Research has confirmed and extended the idea that pleasure and affectionate relations are vital in early speech development (Gottfried, Gottfried, & Bathurst, 1995; Reddy, Hay, Murray, & Trevarthen, 1997). Moreover, because many adults and older children express their pleasures at a baby's communication by smiling at, stroking, or talking to the baby, we can presume that these positive personal responses to vocalization have an important effect on children's progress. Early babbling and later sound making almost always occur when infants are pleased. When they are angry or distressed, they do not "talk" (just like you perhaps). It certainly seems that the precursors of language are related to pleasant emotions, not to unpleasant ones.

Interacting with Others

A child who hears no language learns no language (Werker, Lloyd, Pegg, & Polka, 1996). Most infants coo and babble, but deaf infants cease babbling after six months, whereas hearing infants continue. A child does not learn language, however, by simply hearing it spoken. A boy with normal hearing but with deaf parents who communicated by the sign language was exposed to television every day, so that he could learn English. Because the child was asthmatic and was confined to his home, he interacted only with people at home, where his family and visitors communicated in sign language. By age 3, he was fluent in sign language

Cultural Variations

The Language We Speak: The Message We Give

The way we communicate with young infants is related to specific cultural beliefs. In the United States, individuals tend to think talking is important and that infants can understand speech; thus, we talk a lot to our infants. Adults tend to be more lively and animated when interacting with infants, and this is reflected in similar types of behavior that infants display. In contrast, Japanese mothers tend to soothe and stroke their infants rather than verbally communicate with them; this interactive style is reflected in the behavior of their infants who tend to be more quiet and passive than American infants (Azuma, 1998). These patterns of communication then tend to promote the types of behaviors desired in each of these countries. American mothers desire open, expressive, assertive, and self-directed behavior; Japanese mothers covet quiet, calm, and less-assertive behaviors.

© Iven DeVore/Anthro Photo

Among the Gusii of Kenya, there is very little if any verbal interaction between mothers and infants. The Gusii believe that infants are unable to comprehend speech until they are about 2 years old (Richman, Miller, & LeVine, 1992). What little interaction there is between mothers and infants tends to be slow, unchanging, and devoid of affect. Bouts of play and talk are extremely brief; in fact, the mother's most common response to her baby's gaze or vocalizing is to look away. Similarly, there is little verbal interaction between infants and mothers among the !Kung, a hunting and gathering society of the Kalahari Desert in southern Africa. In societies, such as the !Kung and Gusii, mortality is high and babies may not even be named until they are sure that they will survive. Communication does not begin until their survival is assured—around the age of 2 (Serpell, 1989). Infants in these countries tend to be less verbal and more passive as well.

In Uganda, mothers talk and smile to infants more than is true in many other cultures, trying to coax a happy smile in return. It seems the natural way to play with babies. The social skills both expressed and trained in such interaction, however, are talents needed for personal advancement in the relatively mobile Baaganda social order. Today, as has traditionally been the case in this group, personal skills are powerful means to gaining status and material resources.

Certain words in various languages have different connotations that also may convey messages about social roles. In the English language, we do not have a pronoun that applies to both sexes.

but neither understood nor spoke English. It appears that to learn a language, a child must also be able to interact with real people in that language (Barton & Tomasello, 1991). To effectively interact with others, the infant must be able to hear human speech.

Thus, mere exposure to television does not result in normal acquisition of language, apparently because it provides no social interaction. A responsive partner is a necessary condition, then, for the emergence of intentional communication skills (Wilcox, 1993). Although social interaction is important in the acquisition of language, children's vocabularies do increase when viewing television (Rice, Huston, Truglio, & Wright, 1990). Young children who viewed animated programs that introduced unfamiliar words in a story context learned two new words after two viewings.

Subsequently, for years, "he" was the proper pronoun to use. What kinds of messages were given as a result of rarely using the female pronoun "she"? It must have had some impact because today, many writers are careful to avoid the sexist use of only masculine pronouns. Other languages have words that carry clearly sexist meanings. For example, in the Japanese language, *zo* refers to a male speaker. However, this word carries the connotation of "strength and forcefulness" (Ochs, 1990). *Wa* refers to a female speaker, and this word connotes "weakness and hesitancy."

The language we use may also show respect depending on whether the formal or informal version is used. Using formal language is an acknowledgment of power and respect. When speaking to someone who is an "equal" or a friend, the more comfortable informal mode of communication is used. These linguistic differentiations underscore the importance of social relationships within a culture. Thus, it appears that children are learning much more than how to communicate; they are learning about the beliefs of their culture as well. They are learning about their society's values, relationships, behaviors, and the roles they play in that society.

© Owen Franken/Corbis

Children do not learn how to speak by watching television; they must interact with others.

Considering the Infant Capable of Speech

One of the most important ways in which caregivers can promote effective communication is by considering the child capable of communication and behaving as though the child, from the very beginning, is a partner in the communications exchange (Bates, Marchman, Thal, Fenson, Dale, Reznick, Reilly, & Hartung, 1994). As Roger Brown urges:

> Believe that your child can understand more than he can say, and seek, above all, to communicate. To understand and be understood. To keep your minds on the same target. . . . There is no set of rules of how to talk to a child that can even approach what you unconsciously know. If you concentrate on communicating, everything else will follow. (1987, p. 28)

Adults need to be sensitive to their children's linguistic attempts by responding with an act that is meaningful and relevant in the context of the ongoing situation (Baumwell, Tamis-LeMonda, & Bornstein, 1997). One way of developing a sensitivity to children's communications is by really trying to listen to what the child is saying. Linguistically enriched infants later on enjoy excellent relationships with peers and adults and often become intellectual and social leaders (Sigman, Cohen, & Beckwith, 1997). Further, less vocal and responsive caregivers have children who tend to have overall lower scores on IQ tests.

Imitation

It is commonly believed that imitation plays an important role in children's language development. It is one characteristic of children's speech that most everyone notices. This imitation typically assumes the form of telegraphic speech. For example, the adult may say, "There is a big truck," and the child responds, "Big truck." This has been called "imitation with reduction," and it is theorized as important to learning proper grammar (Brown & Bellugi, 1964).

Teaching a child proper grammar via imitation, however, may be quite difficult:

Child: Nobody don't like me.
Adult: No, say "nobody likes me."
Child: Nobody don't like me. (Eight repetitions of this dialogue)
Adult: No, now listen carefully; say, "Nobody likes me."
Child: Oh! Nobody don't likes me. (McNeill, 1970, pp. 106–107)

Finally, the child partially corrects his utterance. So, it is possible to teach language through imitation, but in this case, at least, the process hardly seems very efficient. The major importance of imitation to communications development might be in learning the individual sounds and words of language (Masur, 2000).

These methods have been shown to be effective ways of helping children to learn to communicate. But will the way we speak to children, the words we use, and the connotations of these words encompass broader lessons, such as promoting the type of behavior, social roles, and values a culture desires? (See Cultural Variations: The Language We Speak.)

Concept Checks

1. Failure to explain children's use of words they have never heard before would be a criticism against ________________ theory.
2. Children can detect differences in sounds and discriminate among different sounds
   a. almost from birth.
   b. by 6 months.
   c. by 2 years.
3. One of the best ways that caregivers can promote language development in children is through
   a. imitation.
   b. labeling objects.
   c. being sensitive to the infant's linguistic attempts.

Reviewing Key Points

Piaget's Sensorimotor Thinker

- Piaget viewed children as being intrinsically active and thus responsible, to a large extent, for their own development. When children are confronted with something new, they try to take in or modify the stimuli; when they acquire a new way of doing things, they revise their existing schemes to accommodate the new stimuli.
- Piaget described the intelligence of human infants as sensorimotor in nature, in that infants, through the first two years of life, understand the world mostly in terms of their actions upon it. A major accomplishment of the sensorimotor period is the development of object permanence, the knowledge that an object has an existence independent of one's perceptions of or actions on that object.
- Piaget emphasized that during the sensorimotor period infants and toddlers should be given ample opportunities to freely manipulate and actively explore toy objects. In this way, children learn a great deal about color, classification, measurement, space, and so forth. Active manipulation and play are not the meaningless, random activities that some adults may think they are.

Information-Processing Views of Cognition

- Information-processing theorists believe that infants are capable of retaining and retrieving information over relatively long periods of time. In addition, infants display recognition by attending more to a previously seen stimulus than to a familiar one; that is, they recognize it as different from something they have seen before.
- The way we relate to infants establishes (or fails to establish) affective communication relationships. Good interaction is characterized by mutually coordinated states and results in positive affect between mother and child.

Psychometric Assessment

- These theorists are interested in assessing children's maturational level as compared with other children of the same age.
- During infancy, the Gesell Scales and the Bayley Scales are two types of assessment procedures that measure the child's abilities in motor, social, adaptive, and language areas.

Language Development

- Three principal theories of language acquisition were presented. The behaviorist theory, associated with B. F. Skinner, stresses the importance of the environment in language learning. Children learn to say certain words because they are reinforced (operant condition). The nativist theory, associated with Chomsky, asserts that children learn language via a language acquisition device in the brain. This device allows children to deduce basic rules of language of the grammar of language just by listening to language without being taught. The social interactionist theory, associated with Slobin and others, proposes that every child possesses a basic language-making capacity made up of a set of fundamental information-processing strategies and sees the child as an active participant in deciphering the operating principles or rules of language acquisition.
- Infants communicate in the prelinguistic stage of language development by cooing and babbling. Cooing (producing open vowel sounds) begins around 3 months of age and babbling (combining a series of sounds) begins around the fifth or sixth month. The linguistic stage, when children produce their first words, begins at 1 year of age.
- Providing experiences in which the child verbally interacts with others is important to the infant's language development. Similarly, when children are happy, they tend to communicate more. There is also evidence that the infant's language development is enhanced through parentese, imitation, and contingent responding.

Answers to Concept Checks

Piaget's Sensorimotor Thinker

1. fifth 2. accommodated 3. c 4. a

Information-Processing Views on Cognition

1. sensory register 2. habituate 3. b

Psychometric Assessment

1. b 2. b

Language Development

1. Skinner 2. a 3. c

Key Terms

accommodation
adaptation
assimilation
babbling
cooing
deferred imitation
dishabituation
equilibrium
ethnolinguistics
explicit rules
gestures
grammar of language
habituation
holophrastic
implicit rules
information-processing theory
intelligence
language
language acquisition device (LAD)
linguistics
logical knowledge
long-term memory
morphemes
object permanence
organization
parentese
phonemes
phonology
prelinguistics
psychometric approach
receptive speech
schemes
semantics
sensorimotor period
sensory register
short-term memory
syntax

InfoTrac College Edition

For additional readings, explore InfoTrac College Edition, your online library. Go to **http://www.infotrac-college.com/wadsworth** and use the passcode that came on the card with your book. Try these search terms: language acquisition, speech development.

Child Development CD-ROM

Go to the Wadsworth Child Development CD-ROM for further study of the concepts in this chapter. The CD-ROM also includes quizzes and additional activities to expand your learning experience.

CHAPTER SEVEN

Socioemotional Development: *Infancy and Toddlerhood*

CHAPTER OUTLINE

Attachment Relations
- The Developmental Progression of Attachment
- Assessing Attachment Relations
- Strange Situation Attachment Classifications
- Developmental Significance of Attachment
- The Mother's Contributions to the Attachment Process
- The Father's Contributions to the Attachment Process
- Applications: Fostering Strong Attachment Relations

Understanding Others and Self
- How Infants Learn About Their Social World
- Gender-Based Socialization of Infants
- The Emerging Self
- Applications: Developing a Sense of Self

Emotional Development
- Emergence of Emotional Displays
- Social Referencing
- Imitating Others' Emotions
- Autism
- Patterns of Emotionality: Temperament
- Applications: Recognizing and Accepting the Infant's Temperament

Family Influences
- Maternal Employment
- The Effects of Child Care on Attachment
- Overall Effects of Maternal Employment
- Fathers in Dual-Wage Families
- Applications: Generative Fathering

Reviewing Key Points

Jason, age 12 months, and his mother enter a room equipped with lots of interesting toys. Mother takes a seat and puts Jason on the floor. For a minute or two, he remains stationary and then crawls to a toy not far from the chair, picks it up and stands. Although his attention is directed at the toy, he frequently glances back at his mother. A stranger enters and Jason turns and notices her. He drops the toy, drops to the floor (being able to crawl faster than walk), and scurries toward his mother. Mother extends her arms and Jason leaps into her lap, clinging to her and peering warily at the stranger. When the stranger leaves, Jason smiles in relief and begins to explore the room and the toys again.

Sitting on the other side of a one-way mirror, observing Jason and his mother, is Mary Ainsworth. She is interested in studying **attachment**—the strong physical and emotional bond between infants and their principal caregivers—and finding the answer to the question "What factors are related to the strength and security of infant attachment?"

Ainsworth began her research decades ago; since that time, hundreds of scholars have conducted numerous studies on this topic. Because of this extensive research, we can say with confidence that secure attachment relations are vital to the infant's future adjustment. In fact, the quality of the infant–mother relationship is considered one of the major cornerstones of children's socioemotional development. Because attachment is so critical to the infant's growth, it is important not only to understand this process but to enhance it.

This chapter is about social development. During the first two years of life, infants make major strides in acquiring knowledge about their social world. Behaviors such as fear of strangers, separation anxiety, formation of specific attachments, and the onset of communications skills are all reflections of this. The infancy period also ushers in the emergence of discrete emotional states such as happiness, anger, and fear. Patterns of emotionality, known as temperament, are also explored. Numerous developmental psychologists have discussed the importance of caregivers attending to and respecting each child's temperament.

We will also investigate maternal employment. Today, the majority of mothers work outside the home. This was not true in the 1950s; an excerpt from a 1950s home economics textbook states:

- Show your husband you are concerned with his needs by having his dinner ready when he comes home after a long day at the office. Plan the meal the night before to ensure that it will be ready on time.
- Take 15 minutes before he arrives home to look special for him. Put a pretty ribbon in your hair.
- Greet him at the door looking refreshed when he comes home.
- Keep the children quiet and allow your husband to relax.
- Make him the focus of your evening. Do not complain about your day.

Advice for the "good wife" today might be, "Take 15 minutes to collapse at the kitchen table while you try to get up the energy to boil the water for macaroni and cheese." What are the effects on infants and toddlers of mothers' working outside the home? Does it affect the mother–child bond? Do parents engage in 50–50 sharing of household tasks and child-rearing activities in dual-wage families? Our concluding segment relates the current research findings on these important questions.

attachment
A strong physical and emotional bond between the infant and the principal caregiver.

Attachment Relations

Before Beginning . . .

After reading this section, you will be able to

- explain the basic premises of Ainsworth's attachment theory.
- identify attachment classifications and how they are assessed.
- discuss the developmental significance of attachment.
- understand the role that mothers, fathers, and infants play in the attachment process.
- discuss ways to enhance attachment relations.

The Developmental Progression of Attachment

> The infant, just a month old, begins to squirm and make small humming sounds as she lies in her bassinet. The baby's actions attract her mother's attention and bring her to the infant's side. Mother picks up her infant. Crunched in her little fetal position, she nestles against her mother and tucks her head close to her mother's face. Each is content as the mother rocks and soothes the baby.

According to Sigmund Freud, the mother's caring and stroking plays only a secondary role in contributing to building attachment relations. To Freud (1938), the infant becomes attached to her mother because she is the provider of food. Harry and Margaret Harlow and Stephen Suomi (1971), however, found that an infant monkeys' urge to seek bodily contact with their mother was much stronger than their urge to satisfy their hunger. Given a chance to cling to a terry cloth form shaped like a monkey mother and a wire-mesh monkey "mother" that provided milk, infant monkeys overwhelmingly preferred to cling to the former. Such experiments indicate that mothers may not be the first "love object" just because they provide food.

The ethological theory of attachment, promoted by the work of the British psychoanalyst John Bowlby (1969) and in this country by Mary Ainsworth (1973), emphasized the biological usefulness of attachment in human beings, a species in which the young have a long period of dependency. Under these circumstances, survival requires the development of behavioral patterns that keep the young in contact with or close to a protector. Bowlby and Ainsworth proposed that the infant's attachment to the mother has its origin in these behavioral patterns.

Bowlby identifies several kinds of infant behavior that give rise to infant–mother proximity and contact. Some of these are apparent at once in the newborn; others emerge later as the infant matures. The behaviors include such things as signaling—crying, smiling, and vocalizing—which attract the mother; active sucking, clinging, and embracing initiated by the infant; and crawling and walking—which enable the infant to follow and approach the mother, thereby staying close to her. Feeding, then, plays only a partial role in seeking and maintaining the contacts that give rise to attachment, according to this theory.

Bowlby and Ainsworth were the first to distinguish four phases of the development of attachment: indiscriminate sociability, attachments in the making, clear-cut attachments, and goal-coordinated partnerships.

Phase 1: Indiscriminate Sociability

During their first two months of life, infants signal their caregivers by crying, smiling, cooing, and gazing, which promotes contact from caregivers. Newborns are attracted to all social objects, but they begin to prefer humans to inanimate objects. During this period, however, infants do not form specific attachments. Anyone's warm arms and cuddles are welcome.

Phase 2: Attachments in the Making

From 2 to 7 months, infants make a clear distinction between familiar and unfamiliar figures, smiling and vocalizing more to familiar figures than to strangers. Mother enters the baby's room and is greeted by a big toothless grin from her wide-awake baby. These preferences for familiar individuals reinforce the caregiver's affection. During this stage, the infant tolerates only temporary separations from parents.

Phase 3: Clear-Cut Attachments

From 7 to 24 months, preferences for specific people become much stronger due to the infant's ability to represent persons mentally (Piaget's fourth stage of sensorimotor development). Now the toddler has the added skill of being able to crawl and walk, which enables him to establish physical proximity to his mother. The child may be playing with blocks in the room adjacent to the kitchen when he quickly scrambles to the kitchen to peek at his mother. A quick look gives him security, and he can now go back to his important block-building task.

Although infants show preferences for familiar adults, they show no preference for the mother over the father. However, some studies have shown that when both parents are present in very stressful situations, year-old infants intensify their attachment behavior toward their mothers. In a relaxed home atmosphere, however, the babies connected to their fathers as much as their mothers, and their fathers soothed them as often as did their mothers. Infants, however, are learning about the "division of labor" when it comes to mothers' and fathers' interaction.

Little Caitlin's dad buries his head in her tummy and makes a funny sound; he picks her up to play the tickle game. Mother picks up Caitlin and cuddles her; holding her close, she softly sings a song.

Although Caitlin responds positively to both her mother and father, her most positive and intensive responses occur when playing with her father (Belsky, 1996). If the father–infant bond were simply a replica of the mother–infant relationship, it would have little developmental significance. But it is not. Fathers interact with their infants in a qualitatively different way. Infants, then, come to distinguish their parents not merely by their appearance but also by differences in their caretaking behaviors.

Finally, the child's increasing verbal skills allow her greater involvement with parents and others. Strong indications of clear-cut attachment are the child's fear of strangers and unwillingness to tolerate even brief periods of separating from the principal caregiver, which is known as **separation anxiety**.

Phase 4: Goal-Coordinated Partnerships

Ainsworth (1973) labels the fourth phase in the development of attachment, from 24 months onward, as the *goal-directed partnership phase*. During this phase, children begin to understand caregivers' goals, feelings, and points of view and are able to adjust their behaviors accordingly. Children also become attached to more than one person, including older brothers and sisters, grandparents, and regular baby-sitters. The Child Development Issues section examines whether there is a particular time, a **critical period**, when attachment relations are best established.

separation anxiety The distress that infants show when their mother leaves the room.

critical period Denotes a particular interval of time in which the development of attachment behaviors must take place; after this time, it is extremely difficult if not impossible for bonding to take place.

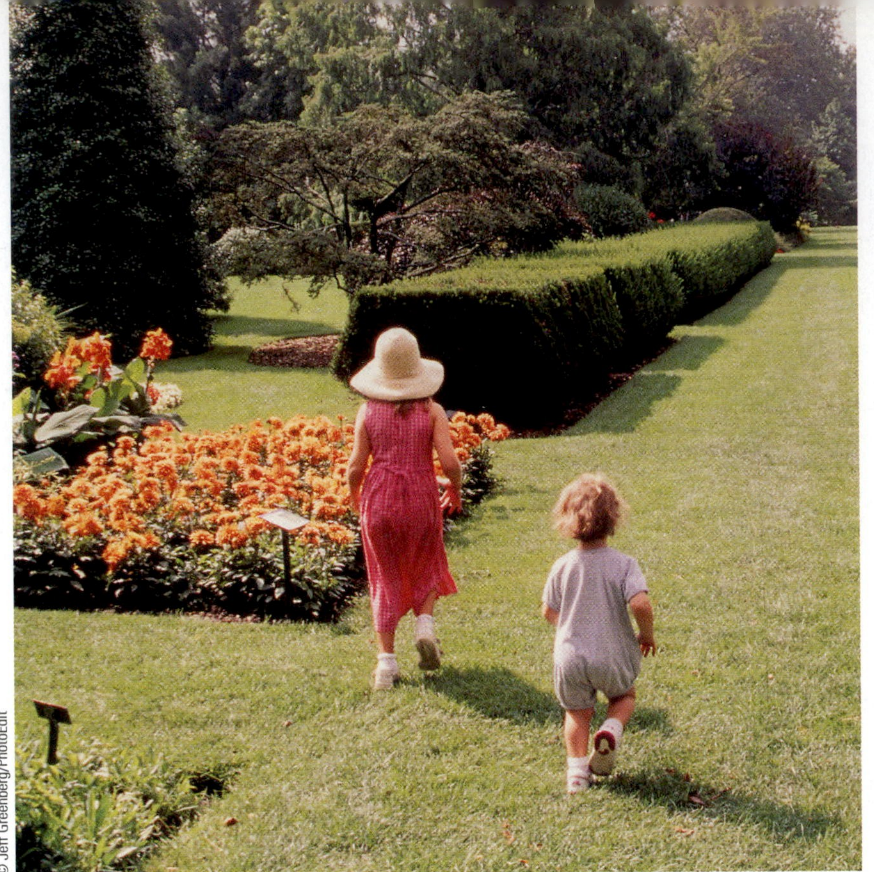

© Jeff Greenberg/PhotoEdit

In the final phase of attachment, toddlers become attached to more than just one person and begin to show strong bonds for others such as siblings.

Assessing Attachment Relations

Mary Ainsworth (1973) pioneered the empirical study of individual differences in infant's quality of attachment to their caregivers. She based her attachment theory on three premises:

1. Over the course of infants' first year of life, they develop an emotional tie with the person who provides their primary care.
2. The quality of this relationship is significantly influenced by the nature of interactions between caregivers and infants.
3. The attachment relationship infants develop with caregivers provides them with a set of expectations (caregivers' availability and predictability) of social interactions that children carry forward and that is likely to influence their subsequent socioemotional functioning and development.

She advanced the proposition that it is caregivers' consistent perceptions and accurate interpretations of as well as contingent and appropriate responses to infants' signals that are thought to nurture the development of strong attachment relations. To assess the child's quality of attachment with his or her mother, Ainsworth used the Strange Situation test.

The Strange Situation

The Strange Situation test is a structured observation involving a mother and an infant (usually between the ages of 12 and 18 months) entering a small room. The mother interests the infant in some toys and allows it to explore or play freely. This is followed by a series of 3-minute periods of separations and reunions. First, an unfamiliar adult enters the room, talks to the mother, and interacts with the infant. Then, the mother leaves the room, often resulting in a distressed infant. The eight episodes in the Strange Situation test are summarized in Table 7.1.

Strange Situation test A series of eight separation and reunion episodes to which infants are exposed to determine the quality of their attachments.

TABLE 7.1

Strange Situation Episodes

Episodes	Participants	Duration	Behavior Highlighted
1	Mother, baby, experimenter	30 seconds	Introduction
2	Mother, baby	3 minutes	Exploration of strange environment with the mother present
3	Stranger, mother, baby	3 minutes	Response to the stranger with the mother present
4	Stranger, baby separation	3 minutes	Response with the stranger present
5	Mother, baby	Variable	Response to reunion with the mother
6	Baby	3 minutes	Response to separation when left alone
7	Stranger, baby	3 minutes	Response to continuing separation and to the stranger after being left alone
8	Mother, baby	Variable	Response to second reunion with the mother

Child Development Issues

Is There a Critical Period for Establishing Attachment Relations?

Anyone who has read an introductory psychology book has probably seen a picture of one of the most discussed examples of imprinting: a set of little goslings walking in single file behind a large, stooping, elderly scientist named Konrad Lorenz (1965). Goslings imprint (bond) with the first thing they see moving as they are hatching out of their shells, and Lorenz made sure that he was their first visual target. The goslings bonded with Lorenz; they followed him everywhere and were dependent on him for food. Lorenz noted that goslings would not imprint on any other creature—even their own mother—after the second day. (In later research, Lorenz found that the goslings could form other attachments and that the critical period was more flexible than he had first thought.)

Nevertheless, his first results were translated into the notion of "critical periods." A critical period denotes a particular interval of time in which certain physical and psychological growth (in this discussion, the development of attachment behaviors) must take place. After this time, so the theory goes, it is extremely difficult if not impossible for bonding to take place.

Projecting from Lorenz's work, the notion developed that the first few minutes or hours of life are crucial in the development of attachment. For the first 45 to 60 minutes of the newborn's life, she is in a quiet alert state. In this state, the infant's eyes are wide open and she is able to respond to her environment. She can see, has visual preferences, and will turn her head toward sounds. After this hour, the exhausted newborn sleeps for 3 to 4 hours.

Because the opening moments of the child's life were trumpeted as being crucial to building attachment relations, women were advised to avoid medication during delivery so they could be alert for this important moment of bonding. Fathers received the message to be there in the delivery room so they, too, could develop attachment relations with their child. It has become "standard" hospital procedure to put the newborn baby on the mother's abdomen with the message that this is the time for attachment to take place. Advice to new parents, projected from Lorenz's chicks and applied to children, is perhaps, responsible for generating a great deal of guilt for the father who was away on a business trip, for the mother who had a cesarean section, for children who were born prematurely, and for many who, after entering the world, were whisked off to be wrapped in blankets and checked by the attending physician.

Critical periods are relativistic rather than deterministic; that is, the length of time defining a critical period is flexible—certainly more than a brief exposure to specific stimulation is necessary. Babies do develop best when, in their earliest contacts with their caregivers, they are given loving, responsive care. And, clearly, if an infant stays too long in circumstances that do not allow her to become attached to some specific individual, her ability to become involved in intimate relationships may be permanently impaired (Colins, 1996). This emphasis on early attachment, however, may create an expectation on the part of many parents that if they do not have this experience they have somehow failed and will never be fine parents (Mukhamedrakhimov, 1996).

For all those who cannot have these early experiences with their infants, it is important to emphasize that the parent–infant relationship is a complex system with many possible routes to the same outcomes. Its success or failure does not hinge on a few brief moments in time. Early and extended contact are important, but in many cases, overrated.

Search Online

Explore InfoTrac College Edition, your online library. Go to **http://www.infotrac-college.com/wadsworth** and use the passcode that came on the card with your book. Try these search terms: attachment behavior in children, attachment behavior, attachment bonds.

The Strange Situation test is designed to assess infants' attachment using three criteria:

1. How well the infant can use the mother as a *secure base* for exploration
2. How the infant reacts to strangers
3. How the infant reacts to separation from and reunion with the mother

secure base
The use of the familiar caregiver for emotional support and as a base from which the infant confidently explores the environment.

securely attached attachment relations
An infant–caregiver bond in which the child welcomes contact with a close companion and uses this person as a secure base from which to explore the environment.

attachment Q-sort
An alternative method of assessing attachment security that is based on observations of the child's attachment-related behaviors at home; it can be used with preschool children.

anxious-avoidant attachment relations
The quality of insecure attachment that characterizes infants who are usually not distressed by parental separation and who avoid the parent when she returns.

anxious-resistant attachment relations
An insecure infant–caregiver bond, characterized by strong separation protest and a tendency of the child to remain near but resist contact initiated by the caregiver, particularly after separation.

The **secure base** is the caregiver, used by the infant for emotional support, allowing her to confidently explore the environment. Ainsworth considered attachment to be interrelated with separation anxiety, fear or wariness of strangers, and exploration of the environment. In assessing the overall quality of the infant–mother attachment relationship, she utilized a configuration of infant behaviors. It is not so much the infant's crying on separation or even willingness to approach a stranger that reliably indexes differences in the security of the infant–mother attachment relationship but rather the behavior that the toddler directs or fails to direct to the mother on reunion following separation. These behaviors include the extent to which the toddler seeks proximity to the mother; strives to maintain contact with the mother; directs anger or resistant behavior toward the mother; and ignores or otherwise avoids the mother's bid for interaction. On the basis of the behaviors exhibited by the infants, they are classified as *securely attached* or *insecurely attached*.

Attachment Q-Sort

The Strange Situation test is not a reliable index of attachment relations after the age of 2. By this time children become quite accustomed to and less anxious about separations from their mothers and encounters with strangers. Thus, researchers needed to have an additional standardized means of assessing attachment after infancy. One such tool is the attachment Q-sort (Waters & Deane, 1985). In this assessment procedure, an observer (a parent or a trained observer) sorts a set of 90 descriptors of attachment-related behaviors—"Child looks to mother when wary" "Child smiles and greets mother"—into categories "most like" and "least like" the child's behavior at home. Next, the observer or parent's Q-sort is compared with an infant who is securely attached. Based on this comparison, toddlers are given a score for the security of their attachments to their mothers.

Strange Situation Attachment Classifications

Securely Attached Infants (Type B)

Securely attached children may be friendly with the stranger and even seek comfort from her when their mother is absent, but they clearly prefer their mother to the stranger. These children tend to become visibly upset when their mother leaves; welcome her return with a warm greeting; and then return to exploring and playing. Jason, in the opening vignette, would be considered securely attached.

According to attachment theorists, the quality of attachment is the cumulative product of caregivers' responses to infants' signals for proximity and contact. Securely attached children have caregivers who responded sensitively (promptly and appropriately) to their needs as infants (Ainsworth, Blehar, Waters, & Wall, 1978). Sensitive caregivers are able to perceive and accurately interpret their infants' communications and are more responsive to their infants' needs.

Sensitive caregivers hold their babies more tenderly and carefully and exhibit greater sensitivity in initiating and terminating feeding. They are tuned in to their infants' signals. The underlying characteristic related to infant security appears to be the caregivers' ability to establish an atmosphere of harmony between themselves and their babies (Rauh, Ziegenhain, Mueller, & Wijnroks, 2000). Approximately 65 percent of infants in the United States are classified as securely attached. As you can see in Figure 7.1, secure attachments are the most common around the world.

Insecurely Attached Infants

Insecurely attached infants may display one of three attachment relations: anxious-avoidant, anxious-resistant, or disorganized–disoriented. Characteristics of the infant's Strange Situation behavior for the securely attached and all three insecurely attached classifications are summarized in Table 7.2 on page 234.

Anxious-Avoidant Attachments (Type A)

Lymont looked up when the stranger entered. He was holding a rattle and greeted her with a smile. He walked toward her with his arm outstretched as if he intended to give her the rattle but then turned, sat down near the other toys, and resumed independent play. He glanced up when his mother passed by on her way out the room. He appeared to be content to play throughout his mother's 3-minute absence. When his mother returned, he looked up with a neutral expression and then turned back to the toys.

Babies, like Lymont, who display **anxious-avoidant attachments**, show conspicuous avoidance of proximity to or interaction with the mother in the reunion episodes. When the mother and child are left alone in the room, these infants are indifferent to where their mothers are sitting. They rarely react with outward displays of distress when left with a stranger. They may or may not cry when their mother leaves. If they do become distressed, strangers are as likely to be effective in comforting them as their own mothers. When their mother returns, the infant may turn away instead of seeking closeness and comfort. The infant may even ignore her when she tries to gain his attention. These infants are sociable with strangers but may avoid or ignore them in much the same way as they do their mothers (Jacobvitz, Hazen, & Riggs, 1997). An anxious-avoidant child expects the caregiver to push him away if he seeks comfort or protection, so he tries to live without love or support from other people. About 20 percent of U.S. babies show this response.

Mothers of infants with anxious-avoidant attachment tend to be highly insensitive to their babies' signals. These mothers display the highest and lowest levels, respectively, of reciprocal interaction and involvement (Isabella & Belsky, 1991). The evidence suggests that anxious-avoidant attachment has its origins in intrusive and overly responsive caregiving.

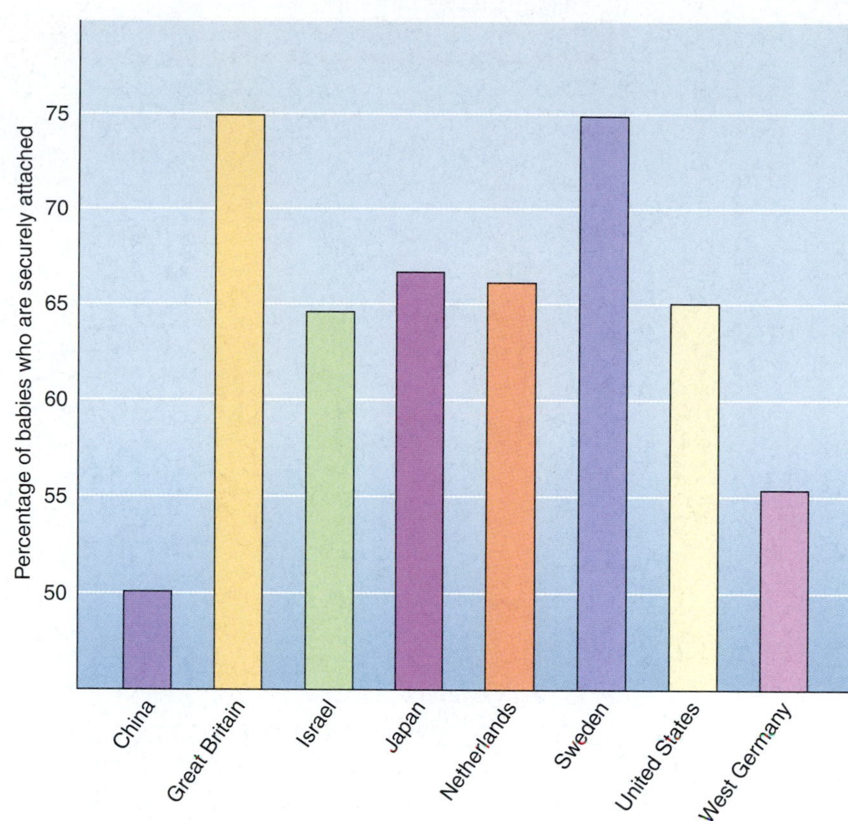

FIGURE 7.1 *Secure Attachment Percentages Around the World*

The percentages of infants that could be classified as securely attached varies across countries; Great Britain and Sweden have the highest percentages (75%) and China has the lowest percentage (50%).

From "Cross-Cultural Patterns of Attachment: A Meta-Analysis of the Strange Situation," by M. van IJzendoorn & P. M. Kroonenbert, 1988, in *Child Development, 59,* 147–156. Used by permission.

Anxious-Resistant Attachments (Type C)

The mother's second departure prompted immediate protest from Linda. She cried angrily at the door and then threw herself onto the floor and kicked and thrashed in classic tantrum style. Twenty seconds after the mother's exit, the stranger came in and picked up Linda. She screamed, pushed, kicked, and struggled hard against being held. Linda's mother re-entered. Linda went right to her mother and pulled on her skirt. The mother bent down and picked her up. Still crying, Linda pushed away as if she wanted to get down. The mother set her down. Linda screamed, clung to her leg again, and then hit her.

When entering the playroom, **anxious-resistant** infants stay close to their mother. They appear to be tense and anxious even when she is present. Before separation, these infants appear to be unusually angry or unusually passive. They appear upset when their mother leaves and, yet, are not comforted by her return. They may cry and lift up their arms signaling that they want to be held; but, once they are picked up they squirm or remain frigid. These children express very little joy in the course of face-to-face interactions with their mothers. They explore very little before their mother leaves, and they do not resume play after she returns (Schuengel, Van IJzendoorn, Bakermans-Kranenburg, & Blom, 1997). About 10 percent of infants are classified as anxious-resistant.

John Bowlby (1989) wrote later in his life that the anxious-resistant child is uncertain whether the caregiver will be available or helpful when called upon. The child therefore tends to be clingy and almost always anxious about separation; her anxiety about

Thought CHALLENGE

Some parents are very pleased to have babies who seem to be so independent. Others would find the baby's relative unresponsivenss disappointing. How would you interpret Lymont's behavior?

TABLE 7.2

Ainsworth's Classification of Attachment

Classification	Behavior
Secure	Uses caregiver as a secure base for exploration Actively seeks contact or interaction at reunion Shows little or no resistance to contact or interaction If distressed, seeks and maintains contact and is soothed by caregiver's conduct
Anxious-resistant	Appears ambivalent about the caregiver Seeks proximity or contact, or resists release Shows open resistance to contact or interaction Tends to be very distressed during separations Shows little or no avoidance Shows generally maladaptive behavior
Anxious-avoidant	Shows little or no active resistance to interaction Often shows little or no distress during separations Often is affiliative toward strangers Displays little or no proximity-seeking to caregiver Displays little affective-sharing with caregiver Does not use caregiver as a secure base for exploration
Disorganized–disoriented	Displays disordered sequences of behavior (for example, approach, then dazed avoidance) Displays simultaneous contradictory behaviors (for example, marked gaze aversion during approach or contact) Displays inappropriate, stereotypical, repetitive gestures or motions Displays freezing or stilling behaviors Shows open fear of the caregiver (usually very brief) Directs attachment behavior toward the stranger when the caregiver returns Displays high avoidance and high resistance in the same episode Is depressed, dazed, or disoriented or shows affectless facial expressions

access to her attachment figure often prevents her from directing her energy and attention toward exploration and play.

Anxious-resistant relations tend to originate from depressed levels of maternal involvement and responsiveness (Rosenblum, Mazet, & Benony, 1997). These mothers' responses to their babies' cues are dependent on the changing moods of the mother. Anxious-avoidant and anxious-resistant attachment organizational patterns by infants are believed to develop as a defensive response to insensitive (rejecting or unpredictable but not frightening) caregiving behavior.

Disorganized–Disoriented Attachments (Type D)

Travis first approached his mother upon her return but then showed a dazed avoidance. He seemed to "freeze" as he remained immobile for several minutes. Suddenly, he cried out and approached his mother. She picked him up, but Travis took great care not to look at her.

disorganized–disoriented attachment relations The quality of insecure attachment that characterizes infants who respond in a confused, contradictory fashion when reunited with their caregiver.

Disorganized–disoriented attachment relations are a curious combination of resistant and avoidant patterns that reflect the infant's confusion about whether to approach or avoid the mother. These infants may toddle to the door upon hearing their mother enter and then turn to run to the opposite side of the room upon her entrance. These babies show unpredictable alterations in their behavior with their mother. At times, they happily approach her as a securely attached infant would, and, at times, they avoid her. Thus, their attachment is considered disorganized (Main & Morgan, 1996). Further, they often appear confused as to how to respond; thus, the term *disoriented* is used to describe them. More often than not, their behavior at reunion is characterized as dazed, freezing, or stilling upon seeing the mother (Main & Hesse, 1990). If the mother picks them up, they look away when being held or approach her with a flat, depressed gaze.

Mothers of disorganized–disoriented infants often have not resolved their own experiences of trauma, loss, and unresolved mourning due to divorce, separation, or death (Lyons-Ruth, Repacholi, McLeod, & Silva, 1991). Some of these mothers also have ongoing drug or alcohol use, which interferes with their parenting interaction (Rodning, Beckwith, & Howard, 1991). In these situations, the mother may withdraw from her infant as though the baby were the source of her alarm or she may lapse into dissociated or trancelike states, greatly taxing the infant's organizing capacities and producing anxious attachment.

These infants perceive their mothers as both frightening and as a source of reassurance (McKenna, 1999), producing strong conflicting motivations for the child. Thus, disorganized, proximity-seeking, mixed with avoidance, behavior may be the result of the infant's attempt to balance these conflicting tendencies (Carlson, 1998). Mother is the only source of safety; yet, at the same time, she is a source of alarm. About 5 to 10 percent of infants display this type of attachment behavior.

Nonattachment

What about infants who do not develop attachment relations with their caregivers or who develop attachment disorders? **Nonattachment** is the failure to form an enduring bond to a specific individual. Such a disorder is likely to develop only when the infant has no opportunity to form an enduring bond because no major caregiver stays involved in the child's life.

Children who were placed in residential care before they were 4 months old and stayed there until they were at least 4½ years old were studied in England (Tizard & Rees, 1975). These children received good physical care, rich cognitive stimulation, and opportunities for exercise and play but did not encounter close, enduring caregiver–child relationships. By the time these children were 2 years old, they had had an average of 24 different nurses who had taken care of them for at least one week. One child had had 45 different nurses. By age 4½, the children had had an average of 50 different caregivers. According to the staff, by that age, 18 of the 26 children did not care deeply about anyone. These children are likely to show disruptive, attention-seeking behavior for years, perhaps throughout childhood. The critical period may be shorter than 4½ years. Thus, parents play a crucial role in helping their infants develop a secure relation with them.

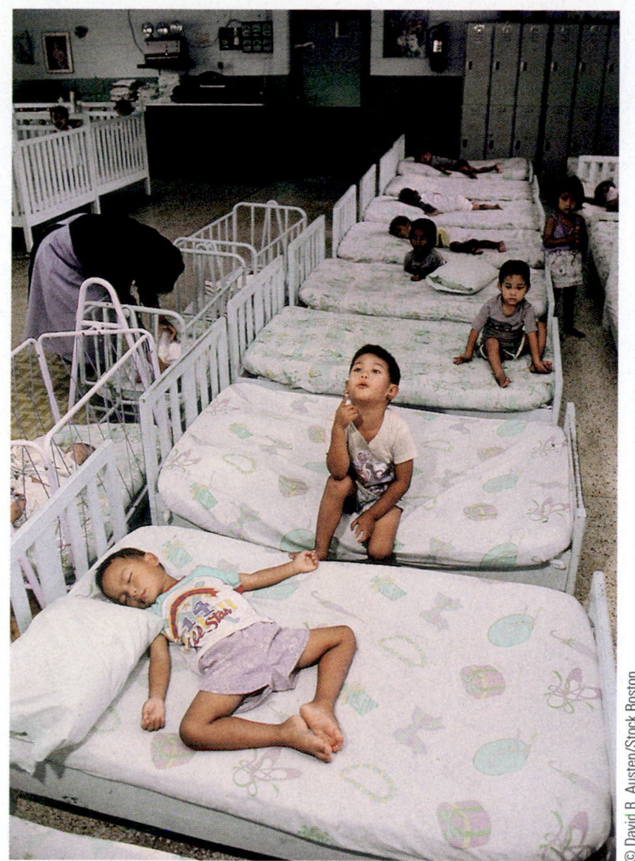

Research suggests that children who have no opportunity to form a first attachment in their first four years may have difficulty ever forming deep personal bonds.

Developmental Significance of Attachment

Crucial to Survival

Returning to Bowlby's theory (1980), he argued that affectional ties between children and their caregivers have a biological basis, which is best understood in an evolutionary context. According to Bowlby then, attachment between the caregiver and the infant is, first and foremost, crucial to the *infant's survival*. For example, René Spitz (1945) observed infants in institutions. Although these infants were physically taken care of—that is, diapered and fed—they did not have affectionate interactions with their caregivers. This was crucial to the bonding process. In these extreme kinds of conditions, where the infants were not held, touched, or caressed, many failed to develop, sickened, and even died. More recent research appears to support Bowlby's theory (Rutter, 1995).

Because children's survival may depend on the affectionate care they receive from adults, the development of attachment would seem to be a necessary, universal biological requirement to be found in all cultures. The first important cross-cultural confirmation came from Ainsworth (1967) in Uganda. Ainsworth was struck by the fact that children in Uganda exhibited patterns of attachment-related behaviors similar to children from the United States (distress during brief separation from their mothers, fear of strangers, and the use of the mother as a secure base from which to explore).

nonattachment The failure of the infant–caregiver bond to form.

© Mary Kate Denny/PhotoEdit

Worldwide, children show distress during brief separations from their mothers.

Social and Cognitive Skills

Attachment also works to help children develop essential social and cognitive skills. Their many differences notwithstanding, most of the major theorists approve of Freud's (1938) dictum that "the mother–infant relationship is unique, without parallel, established unalterably as the prototype of all later love relations" (p. 45). All of children's later choices in the realms of friendship and love follow on the basis of memory traces left behind by these prototypes. Ainsworth (1973) concurs, writing that children who do not form bonding ties as infants may suffer from a lifelong inability to "establish and maintain deep significant interpersonal relations" (p. 53).

internal working model A mental model that infants build as a result of their experience with their caregivers that they use to guide their behavior in other relationships.

Bowlby (1980) suggests that infants and young children develop an **internal working model** of themselves and others. This is more than the learning of roles; children internalize the very nature of relationships themselves. Thus, in experiencing sensitive caregiving, the securely attached child not only learns to expect care but also that when a person is in need, another responds empathically. The internal working model that is formed during the early childhood years serves as the basis for the construction of subsequent relationships (Howes, Hamilton, & Philipsen, 1998).

There is also a vital link between quality of children's attachment to caregivers and developmental outcomes in social areas (Meins, 1997; Youngblade, Thurling, Tapia, Ruiz, & Reed, 2001). Children who develop a secure attachment relationship with their caregivers during infancy are, during later childhood, more socially active, are sought after by other children, exhibit more leadership qualities, and are more sympathetic to other children than are same-age children who have not developed a secure attachment relationship with their caregivers (Weinfield, Ogawa, & Sroufe, 1997).

Children labeled securely attached as infants tend to be "more satisfied, more resourceful, more able to be occupied when alone, have better relationships with people and are more capable of age adequate behavior" (Brody & Axelrod, 1978, p. 243). Young children with secure attachments to their mothers play more harmoniously with peers than insecurely attached toddlers (Colin, 1996). Securely attached children are less likely to fight and more likely to share with others (Belsky, Campbell, Cohn, & Moore, 1996). Children with secure attachment histories tend to have many friends, more often select as partners other children with secure attachment histories, and experience deeper friendships (Beach, 1998).

Insecurely attached children tend to be less competent, less sympathetic in interaction with their peers, more fearful of strangers, and more prone to behavioral problems, including social withdrawal and being more dependent on adults. Infants classified as insecure have been rated by preschool teachers as less empathic, less compliant, less cooperative, and as exhibiting more negative affect and less self-control than securely attached age-mates (Egeland & Erickson, 1993). Researchers in other countries are also interested in studying individual differences in attachment relations (see Cultural Variations).

The Mother's Contributions to the Attachment Process

Maternal characteristics that have been identified as antecedents of secure attachment during the child's first year include sensitivity, cooperation, acceptance, accessibility, sociability, and displays of positive affect (Calkins & Fox, 1992). Parental sensitivity is a crucial factor leading to the development of a secure relationship (NICHD—Early Child Care Research Network, 1997). Sensitivity relates to the ability of the mother to respond appropriately and promptly to the signals of the infant.

Caressing, encouragement, and even affectively neutral stimulation are generally perceived as subjectively pleasurable by the child and engage her in the type of affective sharing, enjoyment of communication, and physical contact that are considered typical in interactions of secure mother–infant dyads (Izard, Haynes, Chisholm, & Baak, 1991). Insensitive, hostile, and rejecting environments are perceived as aversive, with indifferent care provoking the highest irritation in infants (Ahnert, Meischner, & Schmidt, 2000).

Sensitivity also implies a *synchrony*, or an appropriate fit between caregivers' and infants' behavior. Synchrony derives from the parent's sensitive responsiveness to the infant and fosters a state of social harmony between the two. Conversely, insecure attachments are thought to develop as a function of mothers' insensitivity—that is, inconsistent or negligent perceptions, interpretation, and responses to infants' signals. Maternal intrusiveness, unresponsiveness, and inconsistency characterize interaction of insecure dyads (Pedlow, Sanson, Prior, & Oberklaid, 1993).

Courtesy of Karen Owens

A crucial factor that affects the father's attachment relation with his newborn is the emotional quality of his experience in participating in the birth of his child.

The Father's Contribution to the Attachment Process

To date, father–infant relations have not received extensive attention in attachment research (Cowan, 1997). The fact that fathers are infrequently studied gives the impression that they are not important in what is considered a central domain of children's development. The lack of research may also imply that it is not necessary to the child's adjustment to form attachment relations with fathers or that children do not form attachments to fathers—all of which are untrue.

Attending the Child's Birth

The view of fathers' potential role in childbirth has evolved in the United States from one of an unnecessary source of *infection* to an essential source of *affection* for both the mother and the newborn. Since the early 1980s, the concept of fathers' attending the birth of their children has gained wide acceptance, and popular beliefs assume that birth attendance plays a significant role in the development of the father–child attachment. No conclusive evidence, however, has been reported that strongly suggests secure attachment relations are a result of fathers' attending their child's birth (Lamb, 1997). Studies reporting positive findings for birth-attending versus nonattending fathers, however, slightly outnumber studies finding no group differences.

One crucial variable that may affect the father's attachment relations with his newborn is the emotional quality of the birth experience (Parke, 1996). According to the Parke study, fathers who attended the birth *and* experienced positive involvement and emotions during delivery received higher attachment scores when the child was 6 months old than a control group of fathers who did not attend the birth or who did attend the birth but experienced negative emotions. Although many fathers reported their pleasure and excitement at being present at the birth, which had a positive effect on attachment relations, at the same time, many found birth shocking and overwhelming emotionally, which appeared to have a negative impact on attachment relations (Pettit, Brown, Mize, & Lindsey, 1998). The

Cultural Variations

Attachment Relations

In the United States, secure attachment appears to depend on attentive, contingent caregiving, but its association with moment-by-moment interaction probably does not apply to certain other cultures. When we take a look at cross-cultural research, although the majority of infants, worldwide, are classified as securely attached, certain insecure attachment relations appear more common.

GERMANY

For example, a study of middle-class German families measured attachment classifications in two German cities—one in the north (a region known for its restrained emotional style) and one in the south (where a more open emotional style is encouraged). The results revealed that only 30 percent of children from northern Germany showed a secure attachment style, as opposed to 58 percent from the south (Grossmann, Fremmer-Bombik, & Rudolph, 1988). The authors suggest that the difference in attachment styles relate to the mothers' interaction patterns, which reflect the "cultural tone" between the two regions. Another study of urban, middle-class German families showed considerably more infant *avoidant* attachment classification ratings (Schoelmerich & van Aken, 1996). Perhaps, this is related to the type of parenting style observed in these German mothers, who tended to encourage independent behaviors and discourage clinging, close contact. These German mothers expressed concerns about "spoiling" their infants, and as a result, responded to them less. Even though mothers in Germany may follow the cultural norm of aloofness, many of their babies still become securely attached (Wartner, Grossmann, Fremmer-Bombik, & Suess, 1994).

JAPAN

Children and the mothering role have traditionally been valued very highly in Japan. This cultural tradition encourages the development and continuation of very close ties between the mother and the child throughout life. According to these norms, children are expected to rely on their mothers for help and emotional support in a wide variety of situations throughout childhood. In fact, caregivers in Japan rarely separate from their infants. It is not a common practice to leave infants with substitute caregivers, so infants spend very little time away from their mothers (Vereijken, Riksen-Walraven, & Van Lieshout, 1997). Some Japanese mothers would not consent to participate in the Strange Situation test (Yamamoto & Wallhagen, 1997) because they were unwilling to subject their babies to being alone in an unfamiliar place or to so much stress. The Japanese infants who participated in the Strange Situation assessment for one study did tend to experience intense separation and stranger anxieties (Yamamoto & Wallhagen, 1997). This may help to explain why an unusually high *resistant* response was found in Japanese infants studied. The following table illustrates the cultural differences in the responses exhibited by the U.S. and Japanese babies who were exposed to the Strange Situation assessment.

ISRAEL

Children in Israeli kibbutzim are reared in groups and apart from their nuclear families. For the first six months, most infants do not leave the kibbutz infants' house. (Oppenheim, 1998). For the first six weeks after having a baby, the mother usually does not work so she can frequently feed the baby at the kibbutz. After six weeks, the mother gradually returns to her regular work but still visits the kibbutz frequently until the child is weaned at 6 to 8 months. After six months, the child is taken to the parents' room for evening visits. Otherwise, the care of the infant is entirely entrusted to the *metapelet* (a Hebrew term for the workers with infants and small children).

As a result, attachment and emotional involvement with parents tends to be much less intense for kibbutz infants than in the United States (Freedman, 1997). However, infants raised in a kibbutz frequently develop strong attachments to their peer groups and very real emotional ties to the kibbutz and its members. These ties are notably stronger than those commonly exhibited by U.S. children in relation to their playmates and community.

It was customary that when infants at the kibbutz became fussy during the night, their needs went unattended mainly because each kibbutz dormitory had only two caregivers (Mesch & Manor, 1998). When comparing attachment classifications of infants who were cared for in the home at night and those who remained in the kibbutz, the former had higher secure attach-

U.S. and Japanese 12-Month-Olds Strange Situation Assessments

Episode	Behavior	Percent Showing Behavior U.S.	Japan
First reunion	Baby cried when mother returned	42	37
	Baby stopped crying within 15 seconds	Most	45
	Baby showed some initial avoidance	30	32
	Mother went to her chair directly	41	41
	Mother held baby	34	52
	Mother held baby over 120 seconds	7	20
Baby alone	Baby cried at some time in 15 seconds	78	100
	Episode was curtailed	53	90
	Baby cried immediately when mother left	45	93
	Baby was crying at end of episode	58	91
	Baby engaged in exploration	62	9
Second reunion	Baby achieved contact within 15 seconds	78	100
	Baby showed some avoidance	47	17
	Baby was crying at start of episode	53	79
	Mother held baby	89	100
	Holding failed to soothe baby	9	33
	Baby was in contact over 120 seconds	24	51
	Baby manipulated toys	82	44

From "Are the Key Assumptions of the 'Strange Situation' Procedure Universal? A View from Japanese Research," by K. Takahashi, 1990, in *Human Development, 30,* 23–30. Reprinted by permission of S. Karger, AG, Basel, Switzerland.

ment relations with their parents and the latter had higher *anxious-resistant* classifications (Sagi, van IJzendoorn, Aviezer, Donnell, & Mayseless, 1994).

Abraham Sagi and his colleagues (Sagi, van IJzendoorn, Scharf, & Joels, 1997) suggested that kibbutz babies who remained at the kibbutz at night developed anxious-resistant relations because of the inconsistency and unpredictability of responsiveness from their assigned caregiver. As a result of his research demonstrating the importance of attachment and the needs of the infant, however, only 1 percent of Israeli infants now spend the entire night in communal dormitories (Aviezer, van IJzendoorn, Sagi, & Schuengel, 1994; Oppenheim, 1998).

In cross-cultural research on attachment, the variation within countries may be as large as that between countries. A well-known example arises from the work done in Germany. The avoidant pattern characterized some German infants, but other researchers have found that the secure pattern characterized the German infants they studied. Thus, one must be wary of ascribing results to an entire country. Further, significant differences in infant care practices can arise between groups living within the same area. Therefore, we cannot assume cultural homogeneity even within a particular area, let alone an entire country. Detailed analyses of the cultures under study then is required to determine the normative life courses of members that shape the everyday interactions of child–caregiver relationships.

Thought CHALLENGE

From the cross-cultural variations in attachment relations, what can be concluded about the Strange Situation as a universal assessment of attachment?

positive or negative emotions fathers experience during the birth experience, then, can act as a powerful catalyst for future nurturing behavior or lack thereof.

Fathers' presence at delivery may also have an indirect positive effect in terms of providing his support for the mother during labor and delivery. When fathers are present, mothers often relax more, experience less pain, and hence need less medication and have shorter labors. In addition, the father's presence may be seen positively by the mother as an indicator of his acceptance of and interest in the child. This foundation may deepen parental closeness and their joint interest in the child and the father's sense of competence around the child.

On-the-Job Training

Michael Lamb (1997), after reviewing the research on parental caretaking in Western cultures, concludes that neither mothers nor fathers are "natural" caretakers. Rather, both parents learn "on the job." In this light, Ross D. Parke (1996) believes that the father must have an extensive early exposure to the infant in the hospital or at home where the parent–infant bond is initially formed. He maintains that there is a lot of learning that goes on between mother and child in the first few weeks of life from which the father is often excluded. The father must be included so that he will not only have the interest in and a feeling of closeness to his child, but also so that he can develop the kinds of skills that the mother develops.

APPLICATIONS:

Fostering Strong Attachment Relations

Because early attachments are so important for babies, we want to do all we can to encourage their formation.

Support and Sensitivity

Support, sensitivity, adaptability, a sense of being effective, emotional outlook, and physical contact are all factors that impact the formation of parent–infant attachments. Scholars tell us that when parents support each other, they make positive contributions to themselves, to their marriage, and indirectly to their babies, who flourish in this type of happy marital atmosphere (Scarr, 1998). Parental sensitivity is another important ingredient in fostering secure attachment relations between infants and caregivers. Sensitivity reflects parents' accuracy in reading children's signals and responding to them in a timely manner; it also determines how rewarding the parents' reactions will be to the infant.

Thought CHALLENGE

Are mothers more naturally attuned to caring for infants than fathers? Why or why not?

Several personality traits appear to be especially relevant in producing sensitive parents. *Child-centeredness*—putting the infant's needs before the caregiver's own needs—creates a sensitive adult. The baby becomes the caregiver's top priority. This is not to say that caregivers become martyrs and totally neglect their own needs; but, for awhile, the baby's needs come first. In contrast, *self-centeredness*—putting one's own needs before the infant's—compromises attachment relations. Aspects of caregiving that promote secure mother–infant attachment relations are illustrated in Table 7.3.

Adaptability

In the first few months of life, in particular, it may be rather difficult to "read" infants' signals correctly. Parents who are able to tolerate this ambiguity are likely to be more adaptable. Persistence will undoubtedly affect how long parents attempt to soothe the distressed infant and how patient they are in trying alternative strategies.

Feelings of Effectiveness

Feelings of effectiveness may also be important in determining attachment relations. When parents think of themselves as competent in their role, they are more likely to foster secure attachment relations. The amount of time that parents have available to be with their children and the quality of their interactions have an important bearing on attachment as well. Each parent can aid the other in trying to make sure that both of them have time to effectively interact with their children.

Parent's Emotional Outlook

The parent's, in particular the mother's, emotional outlook is related to forming close and securely attached bonds with their infants. It has been found, for example, that depressed mothers (who have feelings of sadness, hopelessness, irritability) are more likely to express less positive emotion toward their infants and to respond less frequently and less meaningfully to their infants' bids for attention. Depression seems to interfere with mothers' ability to relate to their children in ways that promote secure attachment (Kessler, McGonagle, Zhao, Nelson, Hughes, Eshleman, Wittchen, & Kendler, 1994).

TABLE 7.3

Maternal Behaviors That Promote Secure Attachment Relations

Behaviors	Description
Sensitive	Mother responds promptly and appropriately to her infants proximity-seeking behaviors
Positive attitude	Mother expresses positive emotions toward and affection for her infant
Stimulation	Mother frequently directs actions toward her infant
Support	Mother attends closely to and provides emotional support for her infant's activities
Synchrony	Mother engages in smooth, reciprocal interactions with her infant
Mutuality	Mother and her infant engage in coordinated communication and play

Physical Contact

The amount of physical contact with the infant does appear to promote attachment. When a group of mother–infant pairs who received soft baby carriers that afforded more physical contact were compared with mother–infant pairs who received infant seats that afforded less physical contact, the former group of infants had higher secure attachment ratings than the latter group (Anisfeld, Casper, Nozyce, & Cunningham, 1990). In addition, the actual physical presence or proximity of the infant made the mother more aware of and thus more responsive to her infant's needs and states.

Assisting Insensitive Caregivers

Receiving training and help may be vital for parents of avoidant, resistant, and disorganized infants. Fortunately, there are some ways to assist at-risk parents in becoming more sensitive. When families with insecurely attached infants, for example, receive a coordinated set of medical and social services, and parental training in sensitively responding to their children, these infants, who were previously classified as insecure, moved to a secure-attachment classification. Children whose families did not receive these services continued to be classified as insecure (Jacobson & Frye, 1991; Lyons-Ruth, Zeanah, & Benoit, 1996). Intervention studies, then, clearly indicate that caregiving sensitively can be fostered, which in turn, promotes secure attachment relations.

Conditions associated with being reclassified from insecurely to securely attached also include the presence of a supportive family member; a less stressful, chaotic lifestyle; and developmentally oriented home visits (Lyons-Ruth, Connell, Grunebaum, & Botein, 1990). Workers in extended visiting programs who have gone into high-risk homes to promote appropriate parenting skills have had success in establishing secure attachments between mothers and infants. The important implication here is that the quality of attachment can change even when early attachment is poor or nonexistent. The causal link between children's better social adjustment appears to be related to the greater parental nurturance brought about through parents' receiving support and training (van IJzendoorn, Juffer, & Duyvesteyn, 1995). Strengthening the mother–child bond leads to better emotional development and long-term behavioral differences.

Concept Checks

1. One of the key behaviors in establishing secure attachment relations is
   a. for the mother to be an affectionate and sensitive caregiver.
   b. for infants to show responsiveness to the caregiver's behavior.
   c. for the principal caregiver to provide appropriately stimulating environments.
2. Twelve-month-old Katrina shows wariness when a stranger enters during the Strange Situation test but is soon comforted by her mother and joins her in playing cooperative games. Katrina would be classified as ______________ ______________.
3. The quality of a child's attachment to a caregiver has been related to developmental outcome in the following area(s):
   a. Social development
   b. Physical development
   c. Both a and b
5. Two caregiver behaviors that promote secure attachment relations are ____________ and ____________.

Understanding Others and Self

Before Beginning . . .

After reading this section, you will be able to

- describe the acquisition of social knowledge during the infancy period.
- understand gender-related responses to and treatment of infants.
- delineate the stage sequence in developing an awareness of "self."
- discuss how an infant's sense of self can be enhanced.

Social cognition deals with children's knowledge and thinking about psychological events—those that occur in themselves as well as in others. Social cognition research on knowledge of others focuses on children's conceptions of social relationships. It explores issues such as concepts of friendship, fairness, and authority. Research on the knowledge of self has centered on the development of children's notions of themselves as distinct from others and on the growth of their self-concept and self-esteem. Developmental social cognition, then, has to do with the way in which knowledge of others and self develops.

How Infants Learn About Their Social World

Friendship contributes to the child's social development in two important ways, according to Harry Stack Sullivan (1953): It broadens the child's understanding of social reality by providing new possibilities for social exchange, and it expands the child's self-understanding by providing a sense of mutuality with others. Children begin to develop a real sensitivity to what matters to the other person.

Although you would not say that infants have friends in the usual sense of the term, it is interesting to note that play between familiar babies (those who have had regular contact with each other) is more interactive and their social behaviors more synchronized than between unfamiliar infants (Hock & Lutz, 1998). These babies, however, have not chosen each other, and "friendship" overtures may be in the eye of the adult rather than in the activities of the babies.

social cognition When infants possess thoughts and feelings about their own and other people's motives and behaviors.

Initially, 2- to 3-month-old infants respond to each other's presence with diffuse arousal (general excitement) as opposed to discrete social actions such as smiling. By 6 months of age, discrete social actions such as smiling or vocalizing while looking at another infant or reaching out to touch the infant can be discerned (Oatley & Jenkins, 1996). Furthermore, over the course of an interaction between 6-month-old infants, mutual regulation can be observed. Infants, for example, are reliably likely to start to fuss or cry if the other infant does so (Reddy, Hay, Murray, & Trevarthen, 1997).

Over the next six months of life, gestures of pointing, showing, and offering toys come to be directed to other infants as well as to adult companions (Franco & Butterworth, 1996). Indeed, by 12 months of age, the interactions of infants with other infants show sequences of both cooperative and conflictual exchange that are virtually identical to the interactions of much older children.

Gender-Based Socialization of Infants

Colored-coded blankets and identification bracelets are generally provided by the hospital nursery, with pink identifying girls and blue boys. Gifts are selected for newborns depending on their sex; girls receive pastel outfits, often with ruffles, whereas boys are given tiny jeans and bright, bold-colored

Infants were once labeled "socially blind," but this does not appear to be the case.

outfits. So that other people can readily identify their infants' sex, parents habitually dress them in gender-appropriate clothes and style their hair in stereotypical ways.

Newborns enter a world in which there are well-developed belief systems with associated expectations, hopes, and desires on the part of their parents and others. Perhaps, the most well-documented issue concerns the beliefs that parents hold in connection with the sex of the child. From conception on, the baby elicits stereotypical gender-related responses and treatment because of its sex. Characteristics that are perceived as more masculine (for example, big, sturdy, hungry, curious, vigorous, irritated) are more often attributed to the baby if it is believed to be a boy. Feminine attributes (for example, pretty, cute, little, fine-featured, cuddly) are used to describe the baby if it is believed to be a girl. Moreover, caregivers tend to respond differently toward their sons and daughters during infancy. They tend to respond more quickly to a crying girl than a crying boy, offer "masculine" toys for boys and "feminine" toys for girls, and encourage more motor activities for boys and "nurturance play" for girls. Parental belief systems tend to translate into parental actions, which, in turn, are reflected in children's behavior (Goodnow, 1995).

The Emerging Self

During infancy, the child's major task, in terms of self-development, is to learn to differentiate self from others and come to see "self" as an active, independent, causal agent. With the passage of time, children show increasing signs of being able to distinguish between people and things and between themselves and others. They acquire an increased awareness of their personal identity and resources. Children notice that things from the outside world act on them, and they, in turn, act on and influence objects and people in their environment.

Stages of Self-Awareness

Another important milestone during the infancy period is the organization and emergence of a sense of self—an awareness that the self exists as a separate being. Margaret Mahler (1968) suggests that infants are born with no sense of identity. Their sense of self is totally fused with that of their caregivers, and it is only in the course of development that children develop a sense of their own boundaries and identities. She proposes that infant self-awareness develops in a sequence of stages. In early infancy, the infant and the environment are merged, and the infant is unable to distinguish between the "me" and the "not me." With advances in motor, cognitive, affective, and social development, the infant gradually begins to differentiate between the self and others until, somewhere between 18 and 24 months, children recognize that they are distinct from primary caregivers.

APPLICATIONS:

Developing a Sense of Self

Learning that one is a separate, causal agent is related to the child's age or developmental status. In fact, some researchers feel that age is the single most important determinant of self-awareness. Given that self-recognition is both a social and a cognitive skill, differences in self-awareness may be related to these factors. For example, mentally retarded children are nearly 3 years old before they can recognize themselves in mirrors. This delay in self-recognition indicates that self-awareness may be closely linked to the child's level of cognitive development. Differential social experiences also may affect the acquisition of self-knowledge in human beings.

Social Expectancies

Age and cognitive and social factors play a role in the development of self-awareness, but several experiential and cognitive achievements also contribute to the emergence of self. Infants become aware that events occur as a direct result of their own actions. For example, the infant strikes at the mobile hanging over the crib and gradually learns that the action of striking the object causes it to swing back and forth.

In addition, social stimuli, especially by caregivers, provide extensive feedback and form the basis for the development of self-awareness. Feedback given by adults provides for infants' generalized expectancies about control of their world. When infants cry and their caregivers respond by picking them up and cuddling them, gradually, children learn that crying brings their caregivers. Such expectancies also help infants differentiate their actions from those of others. The consistency, timing, and quality of the caregiver's responsiveness to the infant's cues create powerful expectancies for the infant about his or her control of and competence in the social environment.

Children's conceptions of self begin to emerge in late infancy and early childhood through the affirmation of others. Children increase their competence under the care of loving, capable, and nurturing adults. The ability to trust is rooted in the child's sense of being loved and valued in a world that has constancy and permanence. As infants approach toddlerhood, they experience the satisfaction of mastering the art of walking successfully or solving a problem with a new toy. The development of a sense of autonomy is an important facilitator of positive feelings about self, influenced greatly by the central adults in the life of the child. Adults then have unique opportunities to reinforce the ways in which children learn about themselves by providing opportunities for self-discovery and consistently accepting the individuality of each child.

Concept Checks

1. Infants make great strides in their acquisition of social knowledge. Cite two of the four behaviors that exemplify this: ______________ and ______________.
2. Caregivers differ in their treatment of baby boys and girls by
   a. responding quicker to a crying boy than to a crying girl.
   b. perceiving boys as capable and girls as nurturing.
   c. encouraging more motor activities in baby girls.
3. ***True or False:*** Toddlers struggle with their desire for independence yet fear losing their mother altogether if they are too independent.
4. Caregivers help infants develop a sense of self as a separate and causal agent when they
   a. play affectionately with the infant.
   b. provide extensive feedback to the infant.
   c. provide social experiences with other infants.

Emotional Development

Before Beginning . . .

After reading this section, you will be able to

- understand the emergence of emotions during infancy.
- define *social referencing.*
- understand autism and the diagnostic criteria of autism.
- delineate temperamental clusters.
- recognize the importance of respecting individual temperamental styles.

Emergence of Emotional Displays

Young infants can discriminate the emotional expressions of others. We know this because infants look more at facial expressions of joy than anger (Ludemann, 1991). More significantly, infants appreciate the emotional content of different maternal emotional expressions. Infants as young as 10 weeks, for example, will react to maternal facial and vocal displays of anger with anger (Tronick, 1989). Further, infants of very intrusive mothers have the most negative affect; whereas, infants of very positive mothers express the most positive affect (Cohn & Tronick, 1989; Tronick, 1989). Similarly, infants' affective expressions are strongly related to maternal reports of their own affect (Kochanska, Coy, Tjebkes, & Husarek, 1998). Infants whose mothers report more anger express more anger; whereas infants of mothers who report more sadness express more distress.

One of the most dramatic early changes in emotional behavior occurs when a baby is 3 or 4 months old. To the U.S. caregiver, the baby begins to seem more "like a real person." The third month, it is occasionally said, makes the first two worthwhile. The baby becomes not only less incessantly demanding—often sleeping through the night, for example, and fussing less, but also more reliably rewarding. Many U.S. parents find a qualitative change in the baby's social responsiveness and expressiveness that brings real joy. A similar reaction by Kipsigis mothers in rural Kenya may be reflected in the fact that at this time they cease referring to their babies as "monkeys" and begin referring to them as "children" (Harkness & Super, 1995).

There was a parallel change at 3 months in the behavior of both Kipsigis and U.S. mothers: they were more likely to be found holding their babies than they were in the previous month. The kinds of mutual, flowing social play that are salient at this time looked very similar in the two groups. Kipsigis mothers and their 4-month-old infants smiled and looked at each other with about the same frequency as did mother–infant pairs in Boston (Harkness & Super, 1995).

Smiling

Smiling is certainly a central feature of the changes in the baby's behavior. The frequency of smiling in normal infants rises dramatically in the third and fourth months in infants from cultures as varied as the kibbutz settlement in Israel to Bedouin families in the Negev Desert. The frequency of smiling by these

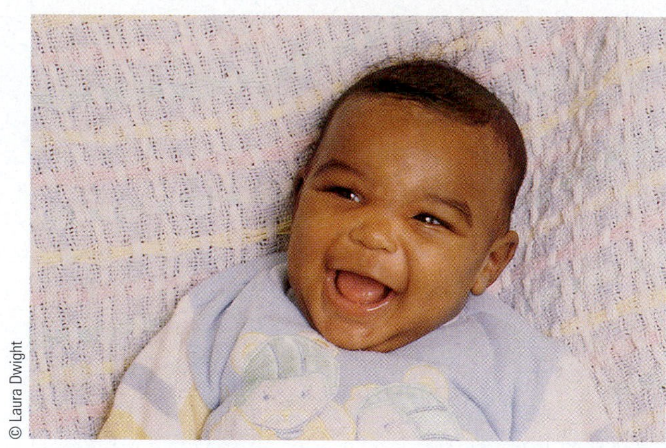

© Laura Dwight

Infants, cross-culturally, begin social smiling at around 3 months of age.

babies, as observed in the course of a normal day, rises in a similar manner despite substantial differences in the social context of care. Further, in normal interactions, specific facial expressions are related to specific behaviors (Weinberg, 1989). In 6-month-olds, for example, facial expressions of joy are more likely to occur when the infant is looking at the mother, positively vocalizing, and using gestural signals, whereas facial expressions of sadness occur when the infant is looking away and fussing, but not crying. These abilities demonstrate the organized quality of the infants' emotions.

Distress and Anxiety

Infant distress in response to being left by the mother appears at around 7 or 8 months; this rate is similar around the world. In experiments conducted in the urban United States, urban Guatemala, the Kalahari Desert of Botswana, and Israeli kibbutzim, before they were 7 or 8 months old infants generally did not cry when their mother left. After this age, however, some infants became more and more distressed; this phenomenon, often referred to as separation anxiety, reached a peak sometime after their first birthday (Aviezer, van IJzendoorn, Sagi, & Schuengel, 1994). Between the ages of 2 and 3 years, children generally become less fearful when their parents leave (Muris, Merckelbach, van Brakel, Mayer, & van Dongen, 1998).

The intensity of separation anxiety is influenced by many factors. Young children are more likely to cry when left in an unfamiliar place, such as at a new babysitter's house. In addition, seeing their mother leave through an unfamiliar exit rather than a familiar one produces a more intensive response (leaving via the patio door rather than the front door). Being left with someone familiar (Aunt Lynne) produces less anxiety than being left with an unfamiliar person. Developmental experts note that children adjust better to parents' leaving when they say good-bye and give them a hug before leaving (Wille, 1998). It is generally not a good idea for the parent to just disappear without saying good-bye to children to avoid hearing their cries. Separation anxiety is only temporary, but the anxiety produced by a parent vanishing without a word may not be.

Not only do children become unhappy when their mother or father leaves, they often get upset when a strange person approaches. Many babies show a pronounced fear of unfamiliar people, or **stranger anxiety**. Stranger anxiety begins somewhere around 6 months, reaches a peak at 8 to 10 months, and generally disappears around 15 months. This is not a universal characteristic of infancy; its presence or absence is determined by a complex set of factors. Why are some children afraid of strangers and others are not? It is speculated that youngsters who have been exposed to only a very limited variety of caregivers are more likely to show stranger anxiety (Fine & Grun, 1998). Children who have been exposed to a diversity of people are less likely to show stranger anxiety.

Social Referencing

I have noticed something countless times—and perhaps, if you are a dog owner, you have noticed it too: For a few minutes each time we walk our dog, he is allowed off the leash and is free to run down the bike path. He dashes ahead of us, stops to capture what must be deliciously wonderful smells, pauses, and turns to look to see if we are coming. Once he catches sight of us, reassured, he is off again.

Young children engage in this "reassurance—refueling" behavior as well. But, by the end of the first year and early in the second, infants also become capable of discerning the emotional meaning underlying an adult's facial and vocal expressions and incorporate this meaning into their interpretation of the adult's behavior, which is known as **social referencing** (Thompson, 1999). That is a pretty demanding skill because to do this, infants must have some basic understanding of the meaning of emotional expressions. They must not only detect and discriminate facial or vocal expressions, but they must be aware of a connection between an event and another's expression. Further, for social referencing to occur, an infant must perceive the caregiver's message as information about an event, not as an invitation for social interaction.

stranger anxiety A wary or fretful reaction that infants often display when approached by an unfamiliar person.

social referencing Relying on a trusted person's emotional reaction to decide how to respond in an ambiguous situation.

To study social referencing, interesting events with ambiguous consequences have been set up and mothers have been instructed to respond to the event with a designated expression. When children are presented with a set of novel, mobile toys and their mothers pose different expressions, the infants respond in different ways (Reddy, Hay, Murray, & Trevarthen, 1997). For example, if the infant is across the room and the mother is sitting by the toys and poses a happy expression, the infant comes closer. When the mother poses a fearful expression, however, the infant moves farther away.

Social referencing then appears to be an important process by which infants gain information about how to deal with ambiguous events. It also seems to have unexpectedly powerful consequences in regulating behavior. It is not yet clear by what process the emotional expressions of others affect the child. One possibility is that such expressions serve as mere *cues*—conditioned stimuli associated in the past with certain outcomes. Moreover, a positive message from the caregiver, for example, might lead to a positive evaluation of an event or object; or it could engender a more positive mood in the infant, resulting in friendlier or less fearful responses. Another possibility is that emotional expressions create a similar emotional state in children and produce their behavioral consequences through an empathic process unmediated by past social learning. Unfortunately, no one has been able to establish if the infant's response to its mother or father is a demonstration of understanding or merely an imitative or reflexive act.

Babies keep a watchful eye on their caregivers to see how they should interpret unusual events.

Imitating Others' Emotions

Newborns tend to imitate facial changes associated with emotions (Walden & Field, 1990). Although imitation of another's emotional reactions does not necessarily imply the internal experiencing of the other's emotion, it is possible that such imitation is a manifestation of emotional contagion. Even if the infant's imitation does not involve any emotional component, it may reflect the infants' attempt to understand the other's emotional state.

autism A condition in which children are unable to interact with others normally, their language development is retarded, and their behavior is often compulsive and ritualistic.

When a 10-week-old infant's responses to her mother's happy, sad, and angry expressions were recorded during a play session, the infant showed some imitative responses to her mother's happy expressions (Rothbart & Bates, 1997). Interestingly, infants will frequently match their mothers' angry expressions, while showing only chance levels of facial movements associated with joy and a decrease of interest expressions when anger is presented to them. Infants can discriminate joy, anger, and sadness; they can match joy and anger; and they can both inhibit specific behaviors or show imitative responses to their mothers' facial expressions. As the mothers also accompanied their facial expressions with vocal expressions, however, it was possible that the infants were responding to auditory information for emotion as well. It is unclear whether both auditory information and visual information are necessary for imitation to occur, or whether either one will suffice. Unfortunately, some infants not only appear to be unresponsive to the emotional expressions of others, they are also unable to relate emotionally to others.

Autism

Some children seem to lack the ability to interact in emotionally meaningful ways with others; these children have been diagnosed as **autistic**. Infantile autism was first described as a syndrome (a group of behavioral characteristics that describe a particular disorder) by Leo Kanner (1943). In his first paper, Kanner discussed 11 autistic children, 8 boys and 3 girls (a sex distribution fairly typical of the child population seen in clinics and hospitals). It is a rare disorder affecting about 2 to 4 infants per 10,000 (Serra, Jackson, van Geert, & Minderaa, 1998). The American Psychiatric Association's *Diagnosis and Statistical Manual of Mental Disorders* (American Psychiatric Association, 1994), better known as DSM-IV, lists broad categories of disorders. It classifies infantile autism as a *pervasive developmental disorder,*

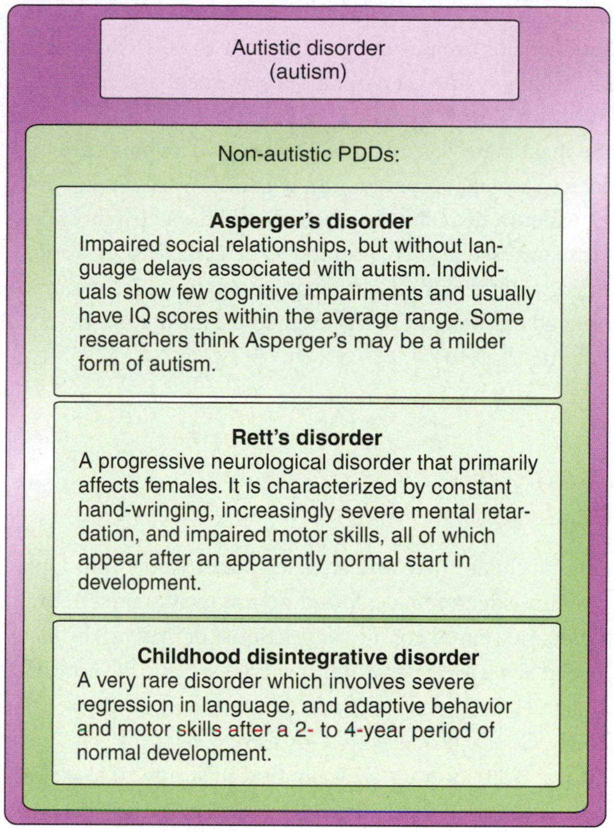

Autistic disorder
(autism)

Non-autistic PDDs:

Asperger's disorder
Impaired social relationships, but without language delays associated with autism. Individuals show few cognitive impairments and usually have IQ scores within the average range. Some researchers think Asperger's may be a milder form of autism.

Rett's disorder
A progressive neurological disorder that primarily affects females. It is characterized by constant hand-wringing, increasingly severe mental retardation, and impaired motor skills, all of which appear after an apparently normal start in development.

Childhood disintegrative disorder
A very rare disorder which involves severe regression in language, and adaptive behavior and motor skills after a 2- to 4-year period of normal development.

FIGURE 7.2 ***The Pervasive Developmental Disorders: Autistic Spectrum Disorders***

Autistic disorder is considered a pervasive developmental disorder. *Pervasive* means that these problems are not relatively minor (as in learning disabilities); they significantly affect individuals throughout their lives.

From *The World of the Autistic Child,* by B. Siegel, 1966. © by Oxford University Press, Inc. Used by permission of the publisher.

meaning that it significantly impacts the individuals' development throughout their lives. The other types of pervasive developmental disorders—Asperger's disorder, Rett's disorder, and childhood disintegrative disorder—are highlighted in Figure 7.2.

There is general agreement that children with a pervasive developmental disorder can be identified because of delays in their daily functioning. What is not so easily agreed on, however, is how we should define specific subdivisions of the general category of pervasive developmental disorders. Most specialists agree that autism should remain a separate category. There is less agreement, however, on whether Asperger's disorder, Rett's disorder, and childhood disintegrative disorder are distinctly different conditions. Some believe that they are different points on an autistic continuum; others believe that there are important differences, and that the disorders should be considered separately.

Characteristics of Autistic Children

> Ben was initially evaluated when he was 3 years old, because his parents noticed that he was not talking. His birth, the first to his young parents, was much anticipated and uncomplicated. However, he was fussy and not cuddly as an infant. His grandparents attributed this to his parents' inexperience. At his second birthday, Ben was still not speaking and avoided eye contact. Rather than play with toys, he lined them up in rows and twirled them. He was hyperactive and had frequent temper tantrums that included head banging. He could not make his needs known, and his parents were exhausted from caring for him. Ben also stopped eating most table foods and limited his intake to peanut butter sandwiches. This was the final straw; his parents sought help.

Ben has many of the classic features often described as autistic: he seems to have a language delay, possible cognitive challenges, trouble with joint attention, requesting behaviors, poor emphatic response, and doesn't engage in pretend play (Landa & Goldberg, 2001). Characteristics of autistic children are reviewed in Table 7.4.

TABLE 7.4 ***Characteristics of Autistic Children***

Characteristic	Description
Socioemotional impairments	Socioemotional impairments are reflected in the autistic child's extreme isolation and an inability to relate to people in ordinary ways. Some children fail to form emotional attachments to significant people in their environment. (Lincoln, Courchesne, Allen, Hanson, & Ene, 1998)
Need for sameness	Another impairment is a pathological need for sameness. The need for environmental sameness can be expressed in wanting to wear the same article of clothing or in having the same type of food at each meal. (Szatmari, 1998; Wing, 1990)
Noncommunicative speech	Autistic children suffer from language impairments, which include either mutism or noncommunicative speech. Almost half of the population of autistic children never acquire functional language. (Pomeroy, 1998)
Sensory dysfunction	They tend not to respond to the sights and sounds in their environment. Because of this lack of response to external stimuli, or irregularity in their response to sensory stimuli (exhibiting extreme sensitivity or underresponsiveness to touch, light, sound, pain), they often are misdiagnosed as deaf or blind.

Causes of Autism

No single etiological factor is known to be responsible for this disorder. A number of etiological theories, however, have been advanced. Initially, autism was thought to be entirely environmental in origin (a cold, austere mother). Empirical research, however, has produced no evidence that autistic children have been rejected by emotionally distant mothers. In fact, the once popular notion that parents are the primary causative factors in autism has been dismissed. There are studies suggesting that the cause of the disorder is probably unrelated to the psychological characteristics of the parents (Haussler, 1999). Parents of autistic children, for example, are very similar to other parents in displaying normal personality characteristics, marital adjustment, and family interactions (Greenspan, Wieder, & Simons, 1998).

Annemarie Haussler (1999) reports from her research that attitudes of parents about the causes and treatment of autism vary cross-culturally. She found that her sample of U.S. and Danish parents tended to believe in genetic or organic explanations for the disorder and placed high value on parental involvement and partnership with a professional in treating their children. One of the main concerns of these parents is in helping the child achieve social competency. In contrast, German parents, Haussler notes, tended to believe additional psychosocial factors caused autism, seemed to be considerably dissatisfied with the parent–professional relationship, and prioritized emotional growth over social adaptation as treatment goals.

TABLE 7.5

Questions Rated "Mostly True" by Parents of Autistic Children

Age (Months)	Behavior
Birth–6 months	Does your infant seem unusually interested in moving objects (compared, for example, to his interest in looking at faces)?
6–12 months	Does your baby sometimes stare or tune out, making it hard to get his attention? Some babies show they want "up" by reaching, others cry or fuss; would you say your baby is the type to cry or fuss and not reach up when he wants "up"?
12–18 months	Does your baby ever seem bored or uninterested in conversations around him? Have you noticed that your baby can be very alert to some sounds and not to others? Does your baby either ignore toys most of the time, or almost all the time play with 1 or 2 things? Have you ever suspected that your child might have hearing difficulties? Do you wonder if your baby knows his name? Does your baby strongly prefer or strongly dislike particular foods?
18–24 months	Does your baby seem uninterested in learning to talk? When you're trying to get your baby's attention, do you ever feel that your baby will avoid looking right at you? Does your baby ever seem to be talking in his own language? Does your baby avoid playing with dolls and stuffed animals, or even seem to dislike them? Does your baby have a hard time getting used to playing with new toys, or playing new games, even though he may enjoy it when he gets used to it? Has your baby not yet begun to show what he wants, either by using words, pointing, or making a noise?

From *The World of the Autistic Child* (pp. 107–108), by B. Siegel, 1996. © 1996 by Oxford University Press. Used by permission of the publisher.

Diagnosis, Prognosis, and Intervention

Autistic children are an extremely heterogeneous population. Investigators have found no uniquely shared neural deficit, no shared cognitive functional deficit, no distinct shared behavioral pattern, no shared specific life course, and no shared response to drug treatment (Le Couteur, Bailey, Goode, Robertson, Gottesman, Schmidt, & Rutter, 1993). Studies typically find that only 10 to 40 percent of sampled individuals diagnosed as autistic exhibit the general characteristics relating to the language disorder; however, they differ in specific behaviors. One child may be mute, whereas another exhibits *echolalic*—parrotlike and meaningless—speech (Charman, Swettenham, Baron-Cohen, Cox, Baird, & Drew, 1998).

Even the autistic aloofness in emotional and social functioning, which is identified as the hallmark of the syndrome and is used as a diagnostic feature in all systems of diagnosis, is quite variable and may change with increasing age and in different environments. Thus, the label autism does little to communicate the specific characteristics or abilities of any individual child. These factors may contribute to the relatively low reliability in diagnosing a given child as autistic. There are some telltale signs that may be used by caregivers in diagnosing autism in infants. Questions rated "mostly true" by 50 percent or more of parents of children with autism are noted in Table 7.5.

Prognosis is always tentative. Speech, IQ scores, and severity of disturbance are the most potent predictors of future development (Hagerman & Silverman, 1991). Children who have not developed communicative speech by age 5, who are untestable or have an IQ score below 60, and who are evaluated as being severely handicapped, have a poor prognosis. Even those who achieve communicative speech and have average IQ scores stand only a 50–50 chance of making an adequate social adjustment as adults (Schopler & Mesibov, 1998).

Perhaps the most frequent intervention prescribed for children with autism, particularly young children, is speech and language therapy (Greenspan, Wieder, & Simons, 1998). This is not surprising, considering that difficulty with communication is a central feature of autism, and language ability is positively associated with later adjustment. In speakers and nonspeakers alike, idiosyncratic and even self-injurious behaviors may be understood as efforts to communicate, and intervention may focus on replacing such behaviors with appropriate alternatives. For instance, a child who appears to use aberrant behavior to obtain attention or disagree may be taught how to get physical contact by asking or signing or may learn to protest undesirable proposals by shaking his or her head rather than inflicting harm on self or others (Schopler & Mesilov, 1998). Similarly, erratic flapping or jumping may be replaced by pointing and looking as a means of securing desirable objects.

Patterns of Emotionality: Temperament

Viewing children in a hospital nursery just moments after birth, one can see their amazing individuality; some infants are squirmy and restless, whereas others are passive and calm. Each newborn appears to have his or her own emotional style of behaving, or **temperament**. From the very beginning, parents may notice differences in each of their offspring's behavior. The firstborn child of Rosa and Javier was quiet and passive and quickly established sleeping and eating routines. Their second-born was more difficult, cried more often, and "demanded" much more attention. According to geneticist Robert Plomin, "Every parent thinks that environment is important in determining their child's behavior, until they have their second child." Temperament is largely a product of the genes the infant inherits and plays an important role in children's developing distinctive personalities.

When parents fail to recognize the child's individuality, problems may occur. The playwright Tennessee Williams, for example, was a quiet, placid infant. As he grew older, he preferred more insular activities—writing poetry, reading, and listening to music. Unfortunately for Tennessee Williams, his father never did accept his son's quiet nature. He wanted his son to be a football player and was constantly coercing him to engage in rough and tumble sports. Tennessee Williams could never be what his father wanted him to be, and he anguished about it all his life. What is your temperamental style?

© Spencer Grant/PhotoEdit

If you were an "adventurous" spirit as a small child, chances are that, temperamentally, you probably are still drawn to new and exciting experiences.

- Were you an active child who bounced off the walls, opened closed doors, and pulled things out of drawers? Or were you content to sit on your mother's lap, play with her hair between your fingers, and watch the world go by?
- Were you the kind of child who was upset by change? Did the arrival of a new baby sitter cause screaming and foot stomping or curiosity and a desire to show off your pretty dress? Did a novel situation feel like a treat or an adventure?
- Did you find yourself happy one minute and sad the next? Did some days seem far better than others for no real reason? Did your moods swing back and forth, or were you generally calm and on an even keel?

These questions describe three measurable aspects of temperament: activity level, reactivity, and mood (Hamer & Copeland, 1998). These traits are expressed very early in life, are not learned from parents, and cannot be easily controlled through willpower. What kind of temperament do you have? (To analyze your temperamental style, see the Self-Insight section.) An active and inquisitive toddler does not learn to be that way; he just

temperament Stable individual differences in quality and intensity of emotional reaction.

Analyzing Your Own Temperament

To assess your own temperament, rate each of the items using the following scale:

Not at all characteristic of me	Somewhat uncharacteristic of me	Neither characteristic nor uncharacteristic of me	Somewhat characteristic of me	Very characteristic of me
1	2	3	4	5

_____ 1. I like to be with people.

_____ 2. I usually seem to be in a hurry.

_____ 3. I am easily frightened.

_____ 4. I frequently get distressed.

_____ 5. I always have many projects going at the same time.

_____ 6. I am something of a loner.

_____ 7. I like to keep busy all the time.

_____ 8. I am known as hot-blooded and quick-tempered.

_____ 9. I often feel frustrated.

_____ 10. My life is fast-paced.

_____ 11. Everyday events make me troubled and fretful.

_____ 12. I often feel insecure.

_____ 13. There are many things that annoy me.

_____ 14. When I get scared, I panic.

_____ 15. I prefer working with others rather than alone.

_____ 16. I get emotionally upset easily.

_____ 17. I often feel as if I'm bursting with energy.

_____ 18. It takes a lot to make me mad.

_____ 19. I have fewer fears than most people.

_____ 20. I find people more stimulating than anything else.

The survey measures three components of temperament: activity (a person's level of energy output); emotionality (intensity of emotional reactions); and sociability (tendency to affiliate and interact with others).

ACTIVITY ITEMS 2, 5, 7, 10, 17 (Scores of 13.4 for women and 12.8 for men indicate average scores. Higher scores indicate a preference for more activity; lower scores indicate the reverse.)

SOCIABILITY ITEMS 1, 6, 12, 15, 20 (Scores of 15.2 for women and 14.6 for men indicate average scores. Higher scores indicate more outgoingness; lower scores indicate more introverted sociability.)

EMOTIONALITY ITEMS Distress: 4, 11, 16 (average scores: 10.0 for women; 9.7 for men); Fearfulness: 3, 14, 19 (average scores: 10.6 for women; 8.9 for men); Anger: 8, 13, 18 (average scores: 10.2 for women; 10.8 for men)

Being aware of your temperamental style will help you as parents to acknowledge similarities (goodness-of-fit) and differences (poorness-of-fit) in your temperament and your child's. If temperamental patterns differ, it is important for parents to accept and not try to change the child's temperament if optimal development for your child is to occur.

From *Temperament: Early Developing Personality Traits,* by A. H. Buss & R. Plomin, 1984, Hillsdale, NJ: Erlbaum.

is. This is not to say that temperament comes fully formed in a new baby. Instead, the baby is born with the potential to acquire a temperament in response to the environment.

Temperament and emotions are not the same thing (Thompson, 1999). Emotions are shaped by our experiences; they can be enduring or brief and change considerably over the developmental years. For example, in infancy we can observe the extremes of emotional arousal, from raucous crying to exuberant delight, unregulated by the infant and uncontrollable except through the sensitive intervention of caregivers. As children grow, they develop more control over their emotions, and their range of emotions branches to include far more than distress and delight.

In contrast, temperament refers to individual differences in tendencies to express the primary emotions (Goldsmith & Campos, 1990). It is the apparently innate inclination toward a consistent style of emotional response in many different situations; it is not just a matter of personality but something more basic that has to do with rhythms, gestures, and *emotions.* Temperament then refers to an early or stable pattern of emotional response, or the child's intensity of emotional response, and appears to have a strong genetic basis. Most researchers agree that temperament includes individual behavioral differences in affective expressiveness, motor activity, and stimulus sensitivity (Braungart, Plomin, DeFries, & Fulker, 1992).

Individual differences in temperament are produced in part by biology; but, genes alone are not responsible for making some individuals gregarious car salespeople and others shy computer programmers. To this extent, temperament is learned—but, not in the same way as memorizing a math formula (Loken, 2001). Temperament is learned through our emotional memory. If a baby is frightened by a new face, chemical reactions in the brain make the baby feel anxious and afraid. However, one scary viewing of the witch in *The Wizard of Oz* is not going to permanently scar a child; it takes many reactions to build the emotional pathways in the brain. Later in life, it would not be terribly surprising to find that the extremely shy baby, now an adult, just hates to meet new people. We naturally do things that make the brain feel good, and that feeling is stored in our emotional memory found in our limbic system.

We go on to perpetuate these good feelings by creating experiences that make us feel comfortable. This is why some people will come to prefer going to a museum alone, and some individuals will prefer attending a rock concert with large numbers of people. Temperament is not easy to change; it tends to endure as the person matures (Hamer & Copeland, 1998). If you were an adventurous child, you still probably enjoy doing new things. If you were a sad child, most likely there still are days when you do not want to get out of bed.

Temperamental Clusters

We have identified several dimensions of temperament (see Table 7.6), and they can be categorized into three temperamental clusters—*easy, difficult,* and *slow-to-warm-up* temperaments (Thomas, Chess, & Birch, 1968). Children with **easy temperaments** are characterized by high rhythmicity (predictable regularity in behavior); they are usually positive in mood, low or mild in the intensity of their reactions, and take positive approaches to new situations. The child with a **difficult temperament** is characterized by the opposite pattern of behaving. These children are moody and intense, react negatively to new people and situations, exhibit frequent expressions of negative moods, sleep poorly, and cry often and loudly (Chess, 1997). For a number of years, it was believed that these children were at risk for adjustment problems. Children with **slow-to-warm-up temperaments** adapt slowly to new situations, are reluctant to participate in activities, and are negative in their moods. Unlike children with difficult temperaments, they are reluctant to express themselves.

The view that temperament is present at birth, rigidly stable across time, and invariant across situations is no longer accepted (Wachs, 1992). Results tend to support a view of temperament as a tendency to display certain behavioral patterns; however, these tendencies are modulated by situations, occasions, and other dispositions (Goldsmith & Campos, 1990). For example, individual caregivers' characteristics may modulate relations between child temperament and parent behavior. To illustrate, experienced mothers are less upset by cries of infants with difficult temperaments than are less experienced mothers. Similarly, parents' beliefs about their ability to cope with their infant's behavior also have been reported as moderating parental reactivity to infant difficultness (Chess & Thomas, 1996). The child's gender also may modulate relations between child temperament and caregiver behavior. For example, mothers tend to be less tolerant of difficult behavior from daughters than from sons.

Degree of Fit

The impact of temperament on a child's development depends on whether her behavioral repertoire provides a goodness- or poorness-of-fit with her environment. In other words, the influence temperament has in shaping healthy or unhealthy development and functioning is impacted by the simultaneous effects of temperament and environment. **Goodness-of-fit** occurs when the demands and expectations of the environment are consonant with the individual's capacities and characteristics (Teti & Teti, 1996). When this is so, healthy psychological development and functioning is likely. **Poorness-of-fit**, on the other hand, results when the individual does not have the capacities or characteristics to cope adequately with environmental demands and expectations. In other words, there is a discrepancy between the child's actual temperament and others' (usually the parents') (Kochanska, De Vet, Goldman, Murray, & Putnam, 1994). When this is so, excessive stress is likely to occur, and the child becomes at high risk for behavior problem development.

Thus, goodness-of-fit indicates that the meaning of temperament lies not in the child's possession of particular attributes per se but rather in the extent to which the attributes coincide with cultural demands on behavioral style. The stability of temperamental characteristics is not inevitable but rather a function of interaction effects between temperamental characteristics and the attitudes

easy temperament Temperament in which the child quickly establishes regular routines in infancy, is generally cheerful, and adapts to new experiences.

difficult temperament Temperament in which the child is irregular in its biological functions, is irritable, and often responds intensely and negatively to new situations or tries to withdraw from them.

slow-to-warm-up temperament Descriptive of babies who are low in activity level and their responses are typically mild; they tend to withdraw from new situations.

goodness-of-fit Development is likely to be optimized when parents' child-rearing practices are sensitively adapted to the child's temperamental characteristics.

poorness-of-fit Development is not likely to be optimized when parents' child-rearing practices are not sensitively adapted to the child's temperamental characteristics.

TABLE 7.6

Dimensions of Temperament

Characteristics	Rating	2 Months	6 Months	1 Year	2 Years
Activity level	High	Moves during diaper change	Bounces; crawls after people	Eats rapidly; walks quickly	Climbs furniture; explores actively
	Low	Moves little during sleep	Plays alone quietly	Goes to sleep easily; eats slowly	Likes quiet play; listens to music
Rhythmicity	Regular	Regular feeding and sleep patterns	Consistent food intake; goes to sleep and awakes same time each day	Naps after lunch; regular bowel movements	Always snacks in the afternoon and before bedtime
	Irregular	Awakes at different time each day	Food intake varies, as does sleep pattern	Wakes at different times; no pattern in bowel movements	Nap times change daily; problems with toilet training
Distractibility	Distractible	Will not stop crying during diapering	Cries until fed	Is not comforted by a toy or a game	Throws tantrum if not given desired toy
	Not distractible	Stops crying during diapering	Stops crying if the mother talks or sings; quiets if given a toy	Is comforted by a toy or a game during diapering	Ceases tantrums when given a toy
Approach or withdrawal	Positive	Smiles	Smiles and expresses joy and pleasure with strangers	Approaches strangers easily	Sleeps well first time at grandparents' home
	Negative	Cries at appearance of strangers; rejects first cereal	Wary of strangers	Stiffens when picked up	Avoids new children
Adaptability	Adaptable	Enjoys bathing	Did dislike new faces but now accepts them	Was afraid of toy animals, now likes to play with them	Obeys quickly
	Not adaptable	Startled by sudden noises	Fusses and is uncooperative during dressing	Keeps rejecting new foods	Cries each time hair is cut

From *The Dynamics of Psychological Development,* by A. Thomas & S. Chess, 1980, New York: Brunner/Mazel. Reprinted by permission of Taylor & Francis.

Thought CHALLENGE

Eddie is a shy child who is quite uncomfortable around others. You are more of an outgoing parent. How can you change Eddie's behavior so he is more like you? Should you? Can you?

of individual's within various cultures. Among a sample of Puerto Ricans, for example, arhythmicity, characterized by negative mood and high-intensity reactions, tended to be highly regarded (Wachs, 1992). The parents believed that children, particularly boys, who exhibit these behaviors will grow up to be leaders in their community. Because these temperaments were perhaps encouraged and reinforced, it is likely that the children of those sampled will exhibit these patterns of behavior and do so for a considerable period of time. Similarly, among the Masai in East Africa, infants with difficult temperaments were more likely to survive a serious drought than infants with easy temperaments (DeVries, 1984). Within this culture, infants who were fussy and irritable were more likely to be preferred and fed by caregivers, based on the belief that these infants would survive. A similar pattern has also been shown in caregiver preferences for infants with difficult temperaments in areas of endemic high-infant mortality in Brazil (Wachs & King, 1995).

Thus, children who have a "difficult" temperament are not necessarily at an elevated risk for later childhood problems. Temperament affects development only in interaction with environmental and cultural forces. If the fit between early infant behavior and cultural/parental values and expectations is a good one, infants are likely to experience optimal development. By contrast, if the parents' values and expectations do not coincide with the infant's temperamental style, the child's development may not be optimal.

APPLICATIONS:

Recognizing and Accepting the Infant's Temperament

An important factor contributing to goodness- or poorness-of-fit may be the caregivers' subjective perceptions, because how adults perceive children is likely to play a role in how they actually interact with children. *Recognizing* children's individual temperamental styles and *accepting* them is an important task for caregivers if

TABLE 7.7

Difficult Temperament Traits

Temperamental Trait	Characteristic Behavior	Possible Alternatives
High-activity level	Restless, very active; may be impulsive and reckless	Anticipate high-activity situations. Use safety precautions if necessary. Practice distraction techniques. Provide opportunities to burn off energy and cool down.
Irregular behavior	Unpredictable patterns of eating and sleeping	Identify patterns and adhere to them as much as possible. Do not force her to eat or sleep when she is not ready. Require her to follow routines like coming to the table or going to bed without forcing her to eat or sleep.
Poor adaptability	Difficulty with changes and transitions; takes a long time to adapt and adjust	Establish daily consistent and predictable routines. Prepare him for changes in advance. Try multiple brief exposures.
High intensity	Expresses emotions in extremes; yells rather than talks	Learn to be tolerant. Model more appropriate responses, give general feedback, and provide alternative responses.
Negative mood	Fussy, complains a lot; appears very serious or displays little pleasure in words and actions	Understand that mood is a major part of temperament. It is not your fault. Adjust expectations or demands that intensify the mood.
Stubborn behavior	Strong-willed; refuses to be budged; has prolonged tantrums	Anticipate and avoid high-risk situations. Be firm but gentle.
Inattention	Does not listen; has difficulty concentrating	Keep tasks, instructions, and explanations short and simple. Remove distractions. Get her attention, and address her by name. Use eye contact. Repeat, clarify, and review.

optimal development is to occur for children. Although parents may want their son to be a rough and tumble football player, they need to recognize that their quiet, slow-to-warm-up son may be more suited as a violinist than as a linebacker for the Chicago Bears. In contrast, quiet and reserved parents of a highly active and curious child might have difficulty accepting their child's "unregulated" behavior, whereas a less active and more inhibited child might fit comfortably into their home environment. Lack of fit can lead to parental attributions of poor motivation or ill will to the child and can maintain conflictual and angry interactions—although it need not, if the parents accept and acknowledge the child as he or she is. Acceptance of a child's temperament helps to assure a goodness-of-fit and optimal development for the child.

Sensitivity and Flexibility

The adaptable, easy to soothe, or sociable child may elicit warm and responsive treatment from others, whereas the irritable, demanding, or withdrawing child may elicit irritation and withdrawal of contact or stimulation. However, if caregivers can be warm and responsive to the more difficult child, the child's expression of negative emotionality generally decreases (Hinde, 1989). Other caregiving factors for working with a difficult child are highlighted in Table 7.7. Any universal prescription for good caregiving, other than parental sensitivity and flexibility, is difficult because what may work for one child may not be effective with another child. Some babies, for example, dislike being cuddled and resist adults' attempts at close physical contact. Tactile soothing is not comforting to these children. Caregivers, then, need to recognize this and substitute other forms of contact—in this case, more active forms such as play or distraction with toys are more effective than cuddling.

Adapting to the Child's Temperamental Signals

Similarly, depending on temperamental styles, some children may be highly sensitive to punishment, whereas others may be so strongly driven to engage in a forbidden behavior that punishment is inconsequential to them. Caregivers can be more effective disciplinarians by adapting to these temperamental signals from children. Some children need extra encouragement; others will need help with limits and controls on their behavior (Rothbart & Ahadi, 1994). Although children are remarkably adaptable, they are not infinitely malleable. Therefore, the happiest families are those in which each member acts with consideration and respect for the unique and individual temperament of every other family member.

To many parents concerned by their offspring's shyness, brashness, or other untoward tendencies, Jerome Kagan (1997) offers a few pragmatic insights gleaned from his research. First, because children are born with different temperaments, caregivers should not assume they are mishandling a baby who is neither pleased nor pleasing. Second, a child's disposition while not completely changeable is malleable. Caregivers, advises Kagan, should acknowledge that some things are harder for the child to control. Finally, he reminds us that in a complex society like ours, each temperamental type can find its adaptive niche.

Concept Checks

Matching

1. Social referencing
2. Goodness-of-fit
3. Temperament
4. Autism
5. Easy temperament
6. Difficult temperament

a. establishes routines readily
b. using affective expressions of others as cues
c. shyness of parent; child is slow to warm up
d. moody and intense
e. emotionally aloof
f. patterns of emotional response

Family Influences

Before Beginning . . .

After reading this section, you will be able to

- understand infant attachment in relation to maternal employment and nonmaternal care.
- characterize the role of fathers in dual-wage families.
- explain generative fathering.

Before we discuss dual-wage families, we need to make the point that all mothers work. The labels "at-home mothers" and "working mothers" are not meant to imply that mothers who choose to remain at home do not work. The labels are meant to differentiate between mothers who are full-time homemakers and mothers who are homemakers that also engage in employment outside the home.

Maternal Employment

Another change in family life that has far-reaching social implications is the increase in the number of women who are working outside the home. This change is largely due to economic necessity and changes in attitudes about women's roles. The rate of working mothers has steadily increased among women of all ages and in many countries worldwide.

Cross-Cultural Rates and Views of Maternal Employment

In the United States, the current rate of maternal employment for two-parent families with school-age children is 73 percent (Hoffman, 2000). This rate increases modestly each year. In the early 1970s, mothers typically waited until their children were in school to return to paid employment, In contrast, today, the fastest growing subgroup of employed mothers is mothers with children under age 1. One out of two infants under age 1 has a working mother; among college-educated mothers, the figures are even higher—68 percent of them return to work before the infant is 1 year old (Zigler & Finn-Stevenson, 1999). Employment figures for U.S. single mothers are even higher: 84 percent of single mothers of school-age children and 70 percent of the single mothers of children under the age of 6 years are employed outside the home (Scarr, 1998).

U.S. mothers who returned to work within one year after the birth of their first child tended to be highly educated mothers engaged in professional occupations who earned high incomes; the money they brought in averaged about 40 percent of their total household income (Pascual, Haynes, Galperin, & Bornstein, 1995). Although a smaller percentage (approximately 17%) of women from Great Britain returned to work within the first year of their infant's life, these women also were better educated and had high status occupations (Brannen, 1992). In contrast, research on a sample of mothers from Argentina revealed that better educated women with higher status occupations were the most likely not to return to work (Pascual, Haynes, Galperin, & Bornstein, 1995).

Women from Russia have always worked (Broschart, 1992). Nearly all (97%) Russian women in the prime child-rearing years, ages 25 to 44, are in the labor force (Tudge, Hogan, Snezhkova, Kulakova, & Etz, 2000). Despite Russia's emphasis on the importance of mothers working; Russian mothers occupy a distinctly inferior position to men in the labor market. Many typically female jobs in Russia are much worse in quality than in other countries because most of the unskilled physical jobs in urban areas and agricultural jobs in rural areas have been assigned to women. Currently, because of the severe economic trouble in

Russia, women are in a weak position to press for employment rights.

The potential impact of this trend on young children is enormous, as families have to rely on out-of-home care for their children, increasingly relegating the rearing of their children to people who are nonrelatives. Because maternal employment necessitates the need for nonparental child care, there is concern that this will interfere with the attachment relationship between the infant and the mother.

The Effects of Child Care on Attachment

The U.S. Department of Labor informs us that 25 percent of infants with working mothers are cared for by parents; 27 percent by relatives; 26 percent by family day care center caregivers, 16 percent by child-care center employees, and 7 percent by sitters in the home. Ethnicity influences the type of child care received during the child's first three years of life. For example, Latinos and African Americans have a higher rate of family-member care in conjunction with other types of child care, including nonrelative and center care (Averett, Gennetian, & Peters, 2000). Latinos, however, tend to rely on fathers and African Americans have a higher rate of grandmothers caring for young children. These children are generally cared for in their own homes.

Care by family members should not be confused with *family day care*. In this type of child-care arrangement, the child is cared for by a nonfamily member, day-care provider in her home. The caregiver may care only for one child and her own or she may run a program for a small group of children. A *child-care center* is group care that takes place outside a home setting and offers group care in a school-like setting. A child-care center may be privately run or run by a larger corporation, such as a church, synagogue, community center, university, or business.

Child-Care Controversy

Because of the importance of attachment and possible deleterious effects of insecure attachment, studies have looked at the impact of maternal employment and nonmaternal care on infant attachment. The results, however, have been unclear. The controversy among researchers pertains to whether extensive nonmaternal care is a risk factor for insecure attachment. Some investigators find higher rates of insecurely attached infants among those mothers who are employed and whose infants are in full-time child care. Jay Belsky (1998), for example, suggests that infants in full-time child care are more likely than infants in part-time child care and infants who remain at home to have insecure-attachment bonds. Belsky suggests a strong and reliable association exists between extensive nonmaternal care in the first year of life and an elevated risk of insecure infant–mother attachment.

This position is not without its critics and has provoked a number of rebuttals. Alison Clarke-Stewart (1992) points out a number of problems with the conclusion that nonmaternal care results in heightened risk of insecure attachment and concludes that there is insufficient evidence to support these claims. Clarke-Stewart, using a meta-analysis of studies that employed the Strange Situation test as an index for attachment classification, reveals there is only a slightly higher "risk" of insecure attachment for some infants in child care (36 percent of children in full-time child care were rated as insecure compared with 29 percent of children who were not in full-time child care). Clarke-Stewart, however, questions the use of the Strange Situation test as an appropriate procedure for measuring the quality of attachment between infants and working mothers. These infants are more used to the absence of their mother and as a result, the short separations during the SST might not be stressful to them. Current research is now focusing on the variables that may explain variations in attachment classifications.

Overall Effects of Maternal Employment

Studies of the effects of maternal employment must take into account factors such as the age of the child, ethnicity, family structure, socioeconomic class, circumstances leading to work, and the mother's attitude toward work and the family. However, the most frequently supported conclusion documented by U.S. research since 1960 is that, taken by itself, the fact that a mother works outside the home has no universally predictable negative effects (Gottfried, Gottfried, & Bathurst, 1995; Greenstein, 1993). In a recently conducted study involving 10 cities in the United States, it was found that infants in alternative forms of care were no less securely attached to their mothers than infants who stayed at home (NICHD—Early Child Care Research Network, 1997). The researchers further concluded that the mother's sensitivity to her infant has much more to do with attachment security than whether or not the infant is in some form of alternative care.

Thought CHALLENGE

As women's roles become more like men's, should men's roles become more like women's?

Moreover, the mother's working outside the home does not appear to lead to psychological maladjustment, poor self-esteem, immature social behavior, behavioral adjustment, or cognitive insufficiency across infancy, childhood, adolescence, or adulthood (Gottfried, Gottfried, & Bathurst, 1995; Scarr, 1998; Stifter, Coulehan, & Fish, 1993). Part- versus full-time employment status also fails to result in any differential effects for children's development or parenting (Greenstein, 1995).

These results have been verified cross-culturally as well. In the Netherlands, for example, approximately 30 percent of women work in outside employment. Most working mothers of children between the ages of 0 and 4 years use some kind of nonmaternal care facilities outside their extended families. However, many also depend on private solutions such as baby-sitters, because most facilities allow for only a very restricted period of care per day per week. The conclusion of studies done on samples of Dutch infants and working mothers is that full-time employment and quality of attachment do not appear to be related (Clerkx & van IJzendoorn, 1992; van Dam & van IJzendoorn, 1990). These studies further indicate that infants of full-time working mothers tend to develop secure attachment relations with professional caregivers. Marinus IJzendoorn points out that the U.S. debate does not take into account that working outside the home does not necessarily imply the disruption of every attachment relationship the child has developed. A child, indeed, needs secure attachment, but this is not generally restricted to just one figure (Clerkx & van IJzendoorn, 1992).

For infants, the overwhelming impression of attachment studies is that maternal employment and full-time infant child care may not be such robust variables that they can be related to child outcomes. Thus, mother's employment and subsequent full-time infant child care may operate through other factors that affect parental behavior and subsequently, the parent–child relationship (Booth, 2001).

Other Factors That Influence Attachment Relations

Many researchers believe it is not maternal employment per se that may affect child development (Gatmon, 1999; Hoffman, 2000), but rather, how a mother's employment affects her relationship with her child and how that relationship, in turn, influences the child's development. Rarely is there a direct link between the mother's work status and the child's development. However, there is evidence that other factors may mediate the effects of the mother's working (Caruso, 1996). The quality of the mother–infant relationship, for example, has a stronger influence on child development than maternal employment status (Lerner & Galambos, 1991). Other important mediating factors are the mother's well-being (Hoffman, 2000); role strain (Etaugh & Folger, 1998); level of family stress and mother's feelings of guilt (Elvin-Nowak, 1999); family support (Yuen-Tsang, 1999); and maternal role satisfaction.

These factors are applicable to cultures outside the United States as well. For example, in a sample of mothers in Hong Kong, role satisfaction, whether mothers were employed or not, correlated highly with positive child development outcomes (Shek, 1998). Relatedly, women in Sweden who are exposed to cultural contexts that support women's work as manifested in social policy in support of working parents and division of labor in the home, reported less guilt about working and experienced less role strain than a sample of mothers from the United States (Gatmon, 1999). Both these factors contribute to promoting positive attachment relations. Further explanation of variables that may mediate the effects of the mother's working and full-time child care are highlighted in Table 7.8.

One still must be cautious about making a definitive conclusion about full-time child care and attachment relations. At this point in time, those who conclude that existing research provides no basis for concern are as guilty of reaching premature conclusions from this evidence as those who argue that infant care is a cause for grave concern. Whether early child care is hazardous to children's development is really not the issue. Maternal employment is a reality, thus discussing whether infants should be in full-time child care is superfluous. It is important to know how to make their experiences there and at home supportive of their development and their parents' peace of mind.

Fathers in Dual-Wage Families

According to Michael Lamb (Lamb, 1998; Lamb & Oppenheim, 1989), U.S. fathers tend to spend about 20 to 25 percent as much time as mothers do in "engagement" (direct, one-to-one interaction) with their children. They are accessible to their children (available whether or not interaction is actually taking place) about one-third as much of the time as mothers are. Perhaps the biggest discrepancy between paternal and maternal involvement is with *responsibility*, defined as providing appropriate care at all times. Fathers, reports Lamb, tend to help out when "it is convenient." Further, they

TABLE 7.8

Variables Influencing the Attachment Relationship between Mothers and Infants

Variable	Impact
Role strain	When mothers feel they are successfully managing work and home responsibilities, they experience less role strain and attachment relationships between the mother and the infant are strong. However, if mothers feel they cannot effectively manage their competing roles, role strain occurs and this may adversely affect the mother–infant attachment relationship.
Mother's guilt	Mothers' feelings of guilt may also impact attachment relationships (Bretherton, 1996). Some working women strongly believe that their working will have a negative impact on their children, and subsequently they carry around a lot of guilty feelings.
Maternal separation anxiety	Maternal separation anxiety is an unpleasant emotional state reflecting a mother's apprehensions about leaving her child. A mother's expressions of maternal separation anxiety include feelings of sadness, worry, or uneasiness about being away from her child. The degree to which the mother experiences anxiety about separation from her child has implications for attachment relationships between the mother and the infant (Hock & Lutz, 1998).
Role satisfaction	Mothers' satisfaction with employment and parenting roles has emerged as a significant factor in attachment relationships. The mother's satisfaction with her role, whether employed or not, is more important to her infant's attachment and development than her employment status. Simply put, when the mother is happy; the children are happy.

appear to be actively involved with their children only if it does not jeopardize their paramount role as a breadwinner (LaRossa & Reitzes, 1996).

Mothers' employment has tripled over the past 30 years; however, during this time, relatively few men have significantly increased their contributions to household and child-rearing work (Dollahite, Hawkins, & Brotherson, 1997). Research evidence is consistent in the finding that fathers, in general, do far less parenting work than mothers and that most men view their parenting involvement as discretionary (Dienhart & Daly, 1997). For example, fathers spend, on average, 2 hours each weekday and 6.5 hours on weekends in direct engagement with their children (Griswold, 1997). National data suggest that fathers spend about 27 hours a week with their children compared to their wives' reports of 37 hours a week (Dollahite & Hawkins, 1998).

Direct and Indirect Child Care Involvement

When fathers talk about what they do for their families beyond breadwinning, they usually focus on direct child care: watching the kids, playing with them, disciplining them, and teaching them skills (Baydar, Greek, & Gritz, 1999). Usually left in the background are the indirect domestic tasks associated with running a household and physically maintaining the children. Mundane and repetitive tasks like cooking children's meals, washing their clothes, and cleaning up after them are as much a part of child care as more direct activities, but they are less important to most men and are likely to be ignored.

What Determines Fathers' Involvement?

Paternal attitudes, motivation, and skills are important determinants of fathers' involvement. One of the most consistent predictors of fathers' involvement is their motivation, or the extent to which they want to be involved (Jordan, 1990). Many expectant and recent first-time fathers want to be involved parents, but they do not believe they have the knowledge, skills, or support to do so, and thus, remain uninvolved. They feel alone in their experience and without resources to enact the parental role as they would have chosen it ideally (Furstenberg, 1998). Another factor is the father's educational level. Among samples of African American, Latino, and European American fathers, Rebekah Coley and Lindsay Chase-Lansdale (1999) reported that as the level of the father's education increased, the likelihood that fathers would be highly involved with their children also increased.

Differences in Mothers' and Fathers' Interactions with Children

Mothers and fathers differ in their responsibility of management of family tasks. Throughout childhood, mothers are more likely to assume the managerial role than are fathers. Mothers, for example, are more likely to take the child to the doctor, arrange for child care, direct the child to have a bath, and initiate and arrange children's access to playmates (Ladd, Profilet, & Hart,

1992). Fathers appear to be less likely than mothers to perform these supervisory roles:

> In most families, husbands notice less about what needs to be done, wait to be asked to do various chores and require explicit directions if they are to complete the tasks successfully . . . most couples continue to characterize husbands contributions to housework or child care as 'helping' their wives. (Coltrane, 1995, p. 175)

Fathers as Playmates

Fathers participate less than mothers in caregiving but spend a greater percentage of time in play activities than mothers do. Dads engage in rough and tumble types of play, whereas mothers tend to be more verbal when playing with their children; this pattern continues after infancy and toddlerhood as well. Physical play between the father and his children is highest when children are 2 years old; between 2 and 10 years, the physical interaction gradually decreases (Marsiglio, 1993). A study of fathers in Japan found that their playtime with their children commonly came in the form of "chatting" with them primarily at breakfast and to a lesser extent at the evening meal (see Figure 7.3). These tended to be the only times available for fathers to play or interact with their children due to their long six-day workweeks. Subsequently, the fathers' participation as playmates or indeed in any form of father–child interaction or involvement in domestic chores was significantly less than that of fathers studied in the United States (Ishii-Kuntz, 1995).

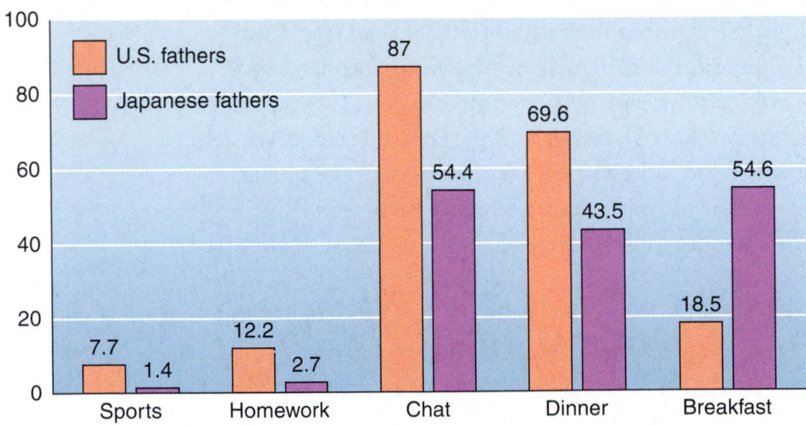

FIGURE 7.3 *Fathers and Everyday Activities in the United States and Japan*

In a sample of U.S. and Japanese fathers, the U.S. fathers spent more time interacting with their children at dinnertime; the Japanese fathers, because many work late into the night, interacted with their children during breakfast.

From "Paternal Involvement and Perception toward Fathers' Role: A Comparison between Japan and the United States" (pp. 102–118), by M. Ishii-Kuntz, 1995, in W. Marsiglio (Ed.), *Fatherhood: Contemporary Theory, Research, and Social Policy*, Thousand Oaks, CA: Sage.

It is interesting to note that when fathers are studied within a cross-cultural context (Hwang, 1997), those who have a great deal of contact with their young children are no more likely than mothers to participate in vigorous play. Relying on vigorous play as a way of engaging children is now thought to be a means of establishing an attachment relationship by caregivers who have less consistent involvement with the child (Hewlett, 1991). For example, among the Aka Pygmy of Central Africa, it was the aunts who were the caretakers most likely to be observed in vigorous play with infants. Some have suggested that the rough and tumble play characteristics of much U.S. fathering behavior would lessen or disappear if these fathers were to increase their direct interaction with their children (Silverstein, 1996).

APPLICATIONS:

Generative Fathering

Fathers' role as the sole provider often gave them the privilege "to be taken care of" in the family rather than "to give care." Now that mothers in Western industrialized countries have become co-providers, it is apparent that their husbands share responsibility for household management and child care. However, one of the most significant impediments to equality for women in the *public* world is the failure of men to assume equal responsibility in the *private* world of the family (Silverstein, 1996). (Of course, there are exceptions, as you will read about in the First Person box.) The clear majority of mothers now work, but the corresponding entrance of men into meaningful roles within the family has not yet occurred (Palkovitz, 1998).

Some fathers are still entrenched in the norms of the traditional masculinity in the following ways: (1) Fathers are often bothered by participating in nontraditional child-care tasks; (2) they are more involved in personal direct child-care activities than domestic work associated with child rearing (such as cooking and cleaning); (3) they rarely cite as favorite tasks those related to the affective dimension of child care (nurturing and comforting); and (4) they seem quite satisfied with their paternal roles in child care.

Society's Role

Society could do much more to help the transition of the father in dual-career families toward a more equal parenting role. In the United States, work and family life are seen by many as separate rather than as interdependent and overlapping worlds. As such, the structures of the workplace are steeped in traditional values and often ignore family life. Many U.S. employers, for example, lag far behind in making family leave policies that accommodate involved fathers. Current occupational arrangements still mean that the vast majority of fathers have less opportunity for interaction with their infants and children than mothers. The average father's parental leave of absence after the birth of a child is five days. Seventy-one percent of fathers take five or fewer days; 91 percent take at least some leave—usually vacation days (Hyde, Essex, & Horton, 1993). Fathers take care of their children more when they have flexible or alternating work schedules, but this is not a reality for most U.S. fathers.

In the United States, the family-leave policy guarantees up to twelve weeks of unpaid leave per year to any worker who is employed for at least twenty-five hours per week at a company with more than fifty employees. Most industrialized countries have more generous policies than those found in the United States. In fact, when it comes to public subsidies for child care, maternity leave, and parental leave, the United States usually appears at the bottom of the list of industrialized countries. As was discussed in Chapter 2, Sweden has the most advanced family leave policy (Gatmon, 1999). Fathers in Sweden receive two weeks paid leave at the time of childbirth. In addition, the mother and father can take a fully protected leave, with full insurance benefits, for six months. If both parents choose to continue to work, they are guaranteed access to high-quality child care for their child. In France, a working parent is entitled to 90 percent reimbursement for four months after childbirth through a social security system. In Germany, a parent can take a leave of absence from work for three months while receiving 100 percent of his or her salary!

In addition to job constraints, a major reason for men's lack of equal parenting is that many still do not see an identity for fathers beyond that of a good provider. Many experts believe this needs to change (Garbarino, 1993; Lamb, 1998; Parke, 1996): "Until our culture includes nurturing and attachment as highly valued qualities in male gender-identity formation and defines child care as central to fathering, the achievement of equality within the confines of heterosexual marriage will remain elusive" (Silverstein, 1991, p. 1030). Common definitions of the father's role are still steeped in past traditions—that of fathers as family founders, breadwinners, protectors of wife and children, and models for character development and behavior. If a father spends too much time at home, he is considered lazy, unmasculine, and unsuccessful—not a very good example for his children.

FIRSTPERSON

Chris, A "Stay-at-Home" Dad

Things to do for Tuesday:

Put out trash	Take Maggie to preschool 1:45
Vacuum	Mow lawn
Prepare dinner	Grocery shopping
Get gas	Write/mail Maggie's birthday invitations

I don't believe I was brought up to be especially proficient at raising children, nor am I naturally inclined to be that way. I was born in the early 1960s into a "traditional" household. My father worked, and my mother stayed home with the kids. I was raised to think that the man made the money and the woman had and cared for the children.

My wife and I were married eight years before our daughter was born. We waited because we are both ambitious, career-conscious individuals, and we thought there wasn't time for a baby. There wasn't. Then Maggie came along. We both continued to work—six days a week—and our daughter was in day care nine hours per day, five days per week. By the time she was 2, our family was fractured. Then, when my wife received a promotion, we made our decision that I would be the stay-at-home parent.

It has been a tremendous change for me. For the previous thirteen years my career had been an enormous part of my life. I abruptly went from working sixty hours per week to not working at all. Not working, that is, by my old standards. My family and friends were not very supportive either. My father didn't care for the arrangement one bit. Every time we would speak, he would lecture me about going back to work. My brothers and male friends also couldn't understand how I could survive outside the workplace for long. It all made me feel somewhat inferior. Men are often evaluated based on their career and income level. Now, I had no career and I wasn't earning any money. Don't misunderstand me, there are many positive aspects to raising children (we now have a one-month old son). To watch my kids grow, learn and experience things for the first time and to have fun is simply wonderful. And knowing my children love me and need me is priceless.

—***Chris Hambleton***

There is not much evidence that fathers have been fully integrated into the family system (Russell & Radojevic, 1992). This may be due, in part, to many people's curiously ambivalent attitude about who a father really is and what his role in the family is. In contrast, mothers have always had a clearly defined role as a parent. Perhaps, then, it is not an accident that Mother's Day received national recognition for 58 years before Father's Day was even thought of. Nor is it accidental that Mother's Day is the busiest day of the year for phone calls (Mintz, 1998).

© Dorothy Littell Greco/Stock Boston

In part, generative fathering involves fathers communicating and demonstrating their love and affection for their children.

Reinventing Fatherhood

Generative fathering refers to fathering that meets the needs of the next generation across time and context (Hawkins & Dollahite, 1997). This means fathers need to become involved parents. As James Garbarino (1993) points out, in years past, the nurturing and available mother made traditional fatherhood work—at least passably well—in the lives of children. But the many changes in the roles, opportunities, and interests of women have altered this balance in ways that call us to reinvent fatherhood. In 1924, most children took for granted that their mothers were available to them. Only 38 percent of the children stated that the most important thing about a mother is that she spends time with her kids. By 1977, this figure had risen sharply to 62 percent. Based on current trends, in this millennium one can speculate with confidence that this percentage will rise much higher.

Thought CHALLENGE

Does the ideology of the workplace perpetuate the myth that family life must accommodate men's commitment to employment rather than the needs of men and women who both rear children and are employed?

If in the past we could sustain a culture in which fathers were distant, preoccupied, and authoritarian because mothers "made up the difference," today we cannot. To develop a new kind of father, a new kind of man must be encouraged. What does generative fathering mean? It means developing new roles for fathers that better reflect the needs of children in this modern era of changed roles for mothers. This means restoring fathers to the lives of the many children who live without them. Generative fathering will require men to know their children, change their diapers, kiss their hurts, spoon in the applesauce, throw and catch balls, read them stories, and hear their confidences. It will require men to communicate their love clearly and unconditionally. While it is becoming clear that fathers play an important role in children's lives, it is also becoming clear that fathering is good for men (Parke, 1995).

generative fathering
Refers to fathering that meets the needs of the next generation with fathers becoming sensitive, nurturing, and involved parents.

When fathers assume responsibility for children, they develop sensitivities that have been assumed to be the sole province of mothers (Lamb, 1997). In addition, children with involved fathers thrive intellectually and emotionally and develop more balanced gender expectations (Biller, 1993). When men enthusiastically enter a relationship with their children predicated on unconditional love, this is a profound experience for most men—one that enables them to "open up" to various expressive qualities (Amato, 1998; Strauss, 2001).

50–50 Parenting

Will you and your partner engage in the equal sharing of caregiving roles? Both mothers *and* fathers (and each partner in same-sex unions) are assumed to be capable of providing human, financial, and social resources to the family and the children. These goals, however, cannot be achieved without role-sharing marriages and changes in the workplace. Table 7.9 provides an opportunity for you to assess your beliefs about 50–50 parenting.

Concept Checks

1. Which of the following women is most likely to create the best climate for her child's development?
   a. Janice, who wants to work but stays at home because her husband thinks she should
   b. Dawn, who values her position in the world of work
   c. Alicia, who never worked before and now must for economic reasons
2. The general consensus from research is that the mother's working and full-time child care for the infant
   a. lead to insecure attachment relations.
   b. appear not to relate to each other.
   c. are problematic, and thus, mothers should stay home with their infants.
3. Which of the following statements is true?
   a. Mothers enjoy doing chores by themselves; domesticity is their "domain."
   b. In two-paycheck families, fathers engage in managerial tasks for their children.
   c. Fathers tend to help out when it is convenient for them.

TABLE 7.9

50–50 Parenting

Below are 15 sample items from Kimball's (1988) 50–50 parenting test. Check the column on the right to indicate whether you believe the mother, father, or both should do the following chores.

	Mother	Father	Both
1. Who should change the baby's diapers most of the time?	_____	_____	_____
2. Who should take off from work to care for the child?	_____	_____	_____
3. Who should get out of bed at night when the child wakes up?	_____	_____	_____
4. Which parent should be contacted when the child becomes sick at school or day care?	_____	_____	_____
5. Who should stay home from work with a sick child?	_____	_____	_____
6. Who should go to parent/teacher conferences?	_____	_____	_____
7. Who should check to make sure that homework is completed?	_____	_____	_____
8. Who should prepare the child's lunch?	_____	_____	_____
9. Who should make dental and medical appointments for your child and take the child to them?	_____	_____	_____
10. Who should cook dinner?	_____	_____	_____
11. Who should take care of the bedtime routine?	_____	_____	_____
12. Who should shop for the family's food?	_____	_____	_____
13. Who should clean up around the house?	_____	_____	_____
14. With whom does your child spend the most time?	_____	_____	_____
15. Who does your child see as the boss of the family?	_____	_____	_____

Although no test can provide a precise measure of equal parenting, your answers will indicate basic styles of parenting. If you have checked "Mother" most often that is a strong indication that you believe mothers should be carrying the heaviest—and stereotypical—part of the family work. If you checked "Both," then you are on your way to an equitable sharing of the work—and the rewards of 50–50 parenting.

From *50–50 Parenting,* by G. Kimball, 1988, Lexington, MA: Lexington Books. Reprinted by permission of Equality Press.

Reviewing Key Points

Attachment Relations

- Attachment refers to the strong physical and emotional bond that exists between infants and their principal caregivers. Infants develop best when in their earliest contacts with their caregivers they are given loving, responsive care.
- The Strange Situation test is a structured observation involving a mother and her infant that is used to assess their attachment relationship. The attachment Q-Sort is an assessment procedure in which an observer sorts through a set of descriptors of attachment-related behaviors and compares this Q-sort with infants who have been labeled securely attached.
- Four attachment classifications have been identified:
  1. Securely attached infants welcome their mothers' return and can use her as a secure base from which to explore the environment. Mothers of securely attached infants are sensitive and reliable in meeting their infants' needs.
  2. Anxious-avoidant attachment behavior characterizes infants who are indifferent to their mothers, sometimes seeking attention and then avoiding. Mothers of these infants tend to be highly insensitive to their infants' signals.
  3. Anxious-resistant infants appear to be unusually angry or unusually passive. They explore very little before their mother leaves, and they do not resume play after she returns. Mothers of these infants sometimes respond to their infants' needs and at other times they do not.
  4. Disorganized–disoriented attachment relations are a curious combination of resistant and avoidant patterns. Mothers of these infants tend to withdraw from their infants and become a source of alarm or fear.
- Attachment is related to children's very survival, to their emotional well-being, and to their social competence later in childhood. Infants, according to Bowlby, develop an internal working model of self and others based on their relationship with their principal caregivers.

- Mothers contribute to the child's attachments by being sensitive to the infant's signals and responding in a loving and consistent manner.
- Fathers who experience positive affect as a result of attending the child's birth may develop stronger attachment relations than fathers who do not attend their child's birth or who do attend but experience negative affect.
- Attachment relations can be fostered when parents are sensitive and adaptable, feel competent and effective in their roles, and maintain close physical proximity (cuddling, stroking infant).

Understanding Others and Self

- Children make great strides in understanding others. Fear of strangers, first "friendships," and the onset of communications skills are all reflections of this. Young infants, by 6 months of age, respond to other infants with smiling and vocalizing. Over the next six months, gestures of pointing, showing, and offering toys come to be directed at other infants as well.
- During infancy, children receive some strong messages in gender-role socialization on what it means to be a boy and what it means to be a girl. Infant boys are perceived as more masculine, sturdy, and curious than infant girls; infant girls are described as pretty or cute, fine-featured, and delicate.
- An important developmental task, in terms of self-development, is for infants to establish a strong sense of self as a separate and causal agent. Margaret Mahler charted the emergence of a sense of self over a series of stages.
- Developing a separate sense of self is enhanced when parents respond contingently to their children's needs, helping children establish a cause–effect connection between their behaviors and the behavior of others.

Emotional Development

- Young infants are able to react to human facial and vocal displays, imitate emotional expressions, and engage in affective communication with their parents. At about age 1, children use social referencing, which involves using the affective expressions of others to evaluate an external event. Social referencing appears to be an important source by which infants gain information about how to deal with ambiguous events. It also seems to have expectedly powerful consequences in regulating behavior.
- Autism is a pervasive developmental disorder. Autistic children fail to display warm, affectionate behavior toward other people. Language is meaningless—if they learn to talk at all. The prognosis for these children is poor; roughly two-thirds of all autistic children remain institutionalized for life. Adults can foster development in autistic children by promoting a less stressful environment, eliminating maladaptive behaviors such as tantrums and self-injurious behavior, and aiding in their language development.
- Temperament refers to the infant's consistent way of emotional responding. Three types of temperament were identified: easy, difficult, and slow-to-warm up. It is not necessarily having a difficult temperament that causes adjustment problems but, rather, whether there is a goodness- or poorness-of-fit with the child's environment. Children make more effective adjustments when their temperament matches the demands of their environment.
- Caregivers need to recognize and accept their infant's temperament. Temperament can be modified, but it is difficult to change completely. Helping children develop self-regulatory behaviors enhances their emotional development.

Family Influences

- The norm in modern U.S. society is mothers working outside the home. A significant recent change in maternal employment rates has been the increased numbers of mothers working with infants under age 1. A controversy exists as to whether extensive nonmaternal care in the first year of life can lead to insecure attachment relations. Mediating variables such as role strain, mother's guilt, and maternal separation anxiety may have a stronger effect on attachment relationships between mothers and infants than full-time child care.
- Maternal employment has tripled over the past thirty years, but during this time, relatively few fathers have increased their contributions to household and child-rearing work. Fathers' involvement generally includes direct child care such as watching the kids, playing with them, and teaching them skills.
- Generative fathering refers to fathers meeting the needs of the next generation of children across time and context. This translates into fathers assuming more responsibility for their children not just as playmates or baby-sitters but becoming involved in every aspect of their lives. Experts advise that both mothers and fathers are capable of providing loving and caring resources; financial resources, and family and community benefits that aid children's adjustment.

Answers to Concept Checks

Attachment Relations

1. a 2. securely attached 3. a
5. sensitivity; timely responding

Understanding Others and Self

1. forming attachment relations; onset of communication, anxiety, stranger anxiety
2. b 3. true 4. b

Emotional Development

1. b 2. c 3. f 4. e 5. a 6. d

Family Influences

1. b 2. b 3. c

Key Terms

anxious-avoidant attachment relations
anxious-resistant attachment relations
attachment
attachment Q-sort
autism
critical period
difficult temperament
disorganized–disoriented attachment relations
easy temperament
generative fathering
goodness-of-fit
internal working model
nonattachment
poorness-of-fit
secure base
securely attached attachment relations
separation anxiety
slow-to-warm-up temperament
social cognition
social referencing
stranger anxiety
Strange Situation test
temperament

InfoTrac College Edition

For additional readings, explore InfoTrac College Edition, your online library. Go to **http://www.infotrac-college.com/wadsworth** and use the passcode that came on the card with your book. Try these search terms: attachment behavior in children, temperament in children, autism, children of working mothers.

Child Development CD-ROM

Go to the Wadsworth Child Development CD-ROM for further study of the concepts in this chapter. The CD-ROM also includes quizzes and additional activities to expand your learning experience.

Let me introduce you to
K. Alison Clarke-Stewart

Alison Clarke-Stewart is a professor in the Department of Psychology and Social Behavior, School of Social Ecology, University of California, Irvine. Her work was first introduced to you in Chapter 7 when the controversial topic of the effects of infant child care on attachment relations was addressed. Her book *Children at Home and in Day Care* highlights the results of her longitudinal research in this area. In Chapter 13, we revisit her research as she discusses how divorce and different custody arrangements impact children's developmental outcomes. Her work is of special interest to me because of her integrative approach of bridging research and applications. Dr. Clarke-Stewart's research has immediate and practical implications as well as being informative about basic processes of development. In her introductory comments, she examines a recent interest of hers—disciplining practices.

Courtesy Alison Clarke-Stewart

PART 4

Developmental Contexts: Early Childhood

Child Rearing in Early Childhood

by K. Alison Clarke-Stewart, Professor, Department of Psychology and Social Behavior, School of Social Ecology, University of California, Irvine

Ideas about how to rear young children are in the news every day—in newspapers, in magazines, on television. Early childhood is a period when concerns about how to rear children are of particular interest because their experiences during this time affect whether children grow up to be intelligent or dull, fearful or self-assured, and articulate or tongue-tied. Parents and concerned adults are hungry for scientific information they can use to guide them in caring for children: How and how much should they stimulate their child's mental development? How many hours should they let their child watch television? How early should they enroll their child in preschool? How strictly should they punish their child?

Perhaps you think that this intense concern about how to rear children during the years of early childhood is new—a product of our heightened consciousness about child development. It is not new. The Pilgrims who landed at Plymouth Rock and the other colonists who followed them in the 1600s believed that careful child rearing was the key to survival and success in the New World. Unlike today's parents, however, they were not interested in promoting their children's psychological well-being; they were not motivated to have their children like them; they were not concerned about making their children intelligent and articulate. But despite these differences, these parents were concerned about doing the "right" thing in educating and disciplining their children—just as parents are today.

Throughout our history, few child-rearing issues have been as contentious as that of corporal punishment. Should children be spanked? In the 1600s, as pointed out in Chapter 1, under a Puritan ethic, discipline was harsh. During the 1700s, parents became more loving and permissive, but religious leaders in the 1800s advocated a return to more repressive and punitive treatment of young children. As we continue through history, the pendulum has vacillated from one extreme to the other. It continues to do so even today with psychologists and parents holding very different views on this issue.

In a recent survey, only 15 percent of psychologists approved of corporal punishment, but 68 percent of U.S. parents claimed that a good hard spanking is sometimes necessary and that spanking helps young children be better people when they grow up. There is more of a consensus about spanking in Sweden, Finland, Austria, Norway, and Cyprus—in these countries corporal punishment has been outlawed.

Disagreements about the benefits and risks of physical punishment are a lasting legacy of our U.S. child-rearing history. There are still strong disagreements about the best way to discipline children. If you take a walk down the "parenting" aisle at your local bookstore or listen to a radio or television talk show on the subject, you will see that experts differ widely in their advice about how strict parents should be—from "unconditional acceptance" to "firm limits" to "tough love." The debate is never ending. This issue of whether to hit or spank children if they misbehave will be with us into the foreseeable future, and you will have to confront this issue when you have your own children. As you read about young children's development in the next three chapters, and guidance strategies and the effects of punishment in particular, think about your views on discipline and how you, as caregivers and concerned adults, plan to guide children through these important years.

PART OUTLINE

Chapter Eight
Physical Development: Early Childhood

Chapter Nine
Cognitive Development: Early Childhood

Chapter Ten
Socioemotional Development: Early Childhood

CHAPTER EIGHT

Physical Development: *Early Childhood*

CHAPTER OUTLINE

Physical Transformations
- The Developing Brain
- The Nature of Physical Growth
- Applications: Factors Affecting Growth

Motor Development
- Movement and the Young Child
- Perceptual Development
- Gross and Fine Motor Skills
- Assessing Children's Gross and Fine Motor Development
- Applications: Enhancing Children's Motor Development

Health Factors in Early Childhood
- Safety Concerns
- Illness and Infectious Diseases
- Nutrition
- Applications: Meeting the Preschooler's Nutritional Needs

Health-Related Issues
- Sleep Patterns
- Bed-Wetting
- Sexuality
- Applications: Sex Education for Preschoolers

Reviewing Key Points

There was a big (at least I remember it as such) field not far from our house—it seemed to go on forever. I guess I was about 5, pretending that I was an explorer and this was some kind of untamed, unconquered area. The grass was almost as tall as we were and many interesting creatures—frogs, caterpillars, earthworms—dwelled therein. I often think of these days as a very special time—for very special imaginations.

In the section from London that I am from our play yards consisted of things that most people would call junk—things like tires, old wooden chairs, crates, and things of this sort. But, it really was brilliant fun for young kids. I think I was about 6 and my friends and I built a fort out of all the stuff that we could find, and this became our club-house. It was our place—no adults were allowed. I remember this time as a wonderful time in my life.

We may not be able to remember more than a handful of particular experiences from our early preschool years, but emotional impressions of that time probably have left a vivid impact on us. The years from 2 to 6 are appropriately called the "play years." To this extent, we often look back at this part of our lives as magical, carefree, and unencumbered—when perhaps our greatest challenges were learning the fine art of simultaneously steering, peddling, and balancing on our two-wheel bikes. Early childhood is a time when children master such great feats as printing their names or hopping on one foot and boastfully demonstrate these skills to others with a pride commensurate to discovering the theory of relativity. Weekend mornings may have been spent watching our favorite cartoons, wearing our favorite pajamas, and eating our favorite cereal (or did you just do that last Saturday?).

Young children exhibit tremendous growth, progressing from the toddlers' initial forays away from their parents to becoming "self-sufficient and independent" first-graders. Erik Erikson (1963) rightly characterizes early childhood as a time when children, upon reaching their second birthday, take their first decisive steps toward their eventual "Emancipation Proclamation." Erikson portrays autonomy as the chief developmental challenge of the preschool years. Initially, the 2-year-old's struggle for independence is heralded by the classic imperatives "No" and "Me do it." As children approach the age of about 5, they begin to establish a sense of initiative in which creativity and fantasy in play allow them to "do" many things they cannot yet perform in reality. The initiative stage is a time when children say, "I can make things happen and use my newly developed skills," and the early childhood years bring quantum leaps in newly developed skills.

Surveying physical development in the early childhood years is the objective of this chapter. The physical achievements of preschoolers are made possible, in part, by the continuing growth of the brain's structural complexity. Learning about the developing brain in early childhood is where our chapter begins. We also examine the nature of physical growth during the early childhood years. Physically, the protruding stomachs, chubby cheeks, and double chins (all those endearing things that grandparents love) disappear.

With their more streamlined bodies, preschoolers demonstrate growing sophistications in motor areas. They become more agile and movements become more controlled. Gross motor development (large muscles for running and peddling tricycles and bicycles) and fine motor development (small muscles such as finger dexterity for coloring and cutting) improve rapidly. Young children seem to delight in exercising these marvelous skills by performing some hair-raising stunts on any apparatus suitable for climbing, much to the chagrin of concerned adults. Our final sections discuss health factors, such as safety concerns, illnesses and infectious diseases, and nutrition, and health-related issues, such as sleep patterns, bed-wetting, and sexuality.

myelination
The slow buildup of fatty sheaths around axons in the brain, which enables neurons to conduct messages at faster rates and allows actions and thoughts to be automatic.

cerebellum
The part of the brain that allows growing coordination and advanced motor skills.

Physical Transformations

Before Beginning . . .

After reading this section, you will be able to

- trace the continuing growth of the brain's structural complexity and to understand how this connects with the corresponding development of new motor skills.
- describe the physical changes in height, weight, and proportions that occur during early childhood.
- identify the factors that affect children's growth.

The Developing Brain

Mack is 2½; it's hard to believe that just over a year ago, he learned to walk. Today, he rarely stands still except when having to examine a perplexing problem, such as where his tennis ball rolled. Mack is an imaginative and energetic child—as are most children in early childhood.

Many of Mack's new achievements go hand in hand with the progressive maturation of the brain. **Myelination**—the slow buildup of fatty sheaths around axons—enables neurons to conduct messages at faster rates and allows Mack's actions and thoughts to become faster, less deliberate, and more automatic (Diamond & Hopson, 1998). Myelination in the neurons that compose the cerebral cortex (which goes on until about age 10) allows these neurons to conduct information more efficiently and Mack to focus his attention for longer periods of time and remember things more effectively (Bell, 1998). Selective pruning (the brain's way of eliminating excess or weak contact points—see Chapter 5) in the visual and prefrontal cortex continues, thus, streamlining the brain's communication system. Correspondingly, we see a sharpening of Mack's language skills, problem-solving abilities, and overall intelligence (Nolte, 1998).

Brain maturation also enabled Mack to progress from a stiff, wobbly walk at the age of 14 months, and will allow him to develop fluid, heel-to-toe movement when he is 6 years old. Growing coordination and more advanced motor skills can also be attributed to the continuing maturation in the **cerebellum** (Nolte, 1998), which is responsible for coordinating and integrating motor activity such as learning to ride a tricycle. The young child's explosion of synapses or contact points between nerve cell branches produces a high density of synapses in the visual cortex by age 4

(Dowling, 1998). The **visual cortex** is involved directly in vision but also in visual thoughts and images. It is speculated that the preschooler's powerful imagination at this age could stem, in part, from the density of synapses in this region (Woods & Rosenstein, 1998).

"Super-Charged" Brains

Neurons require a great deal of oxygen and glucose; in fact, they cannot survive without them even for a short period of time. The brain (even though it only represents 2 percent of our total body size) "demands" 25 percent of the body's oxygen all the time whether you are running a quarter mile, studying for a difficult exam, or even sleeping. The brain's need for oxygen is so acute that when a part of the brain is active, blood flow rapidly increases in that region. Harry Chugani's (1996) measurements of brain cell metabolism in 3- and 4-year-olds show that their brains are burning glucose at twice the rate of an adult's brain. The preschoolers' "super-charged" brains may be responsible for their boundless energy—incessant running, playing, and general chattering—which are indeed common to children during early childhood. Further, this high metabolic rate supporting the preschooler's overpopulation of synapses, underlies, according to Chugani, the almost effortless learning in young children.

During early childhood, the rapid rate of glucose metabolism in the brain may be responsible for children's high energy levels.

Language Development

Kurt Fischer and Samuel Rose (1998) report that there is a spurt in head size around the age of 4, which appears to coincide with certain other observed changes. Brain wave measurements by an electroencephalogram (EEG) show a dramatic upsurge of activity between ages 3 and 4 in two major language regions: Broca's area and Wernicke's area. **Broca's area**, our verbal speech center is located in the frontal lobe, close to the region of the primary motor area involved in initiating face, tongue, and jaw movements. The other language area is found in the temporal lobe and is known as **Wernicke's area**, implicated in understanding expressive speech. This part of the brain sits between the primary auditory and visual areas and is concerned primarily with the comprehension of speech and reading and writing. The increase in activity found in Broca's area between ages 3 and 4 is reflected in the preschooler's increased vocabulary—from about 900 words at age 3 and mushrooming to 2500 to 3000 words before age 5. Growing sophistication of Wernicke's area is responsible for preschoolers' developing skills in understanding speech.

Vivid Imaginations

Fischer (Fischer & Rose, 1996) notes that the preschooler also experiences a new level of abstract thought based on what he calls *representational mapping*. Characteristic of this new level of abstract thinking is the young child's penchant for imagination and fantasy.

> Young Natasha sits at the table with her dolls; they are having a tea party. She pours pretend tea for her pretend guests and engages in animated conversation with all her party goers. One of her dolls spills her tea and is not acting very nice; Natasha admonishes her for it.

This sort of play, emerging around the age of 4, requires "theory of mind" skills; that is, Natasha has developed an awareness not only of her own mind but that others also have minds with memories, wishes, and secrets. Although no one is exactly sure which growing brain regions and connections account for this new awareness of others' thoughts, there is a big growth spurt around 4 or 5 years in the region of the brain that is responsible for enabling the right and left hemispheres to function as a single unit.

visual cortex
The part of the brain that controls vision, visual thoughts, and images.

Broca's area
Our verbal speech center; located in the fontal lobe of the brain.

Wernicke's area
A language area located in the temporal lobe of the brain; it assists with understanding expressive speech.

Hemispheric Cross Talk

The part of the brain responsible for "cross talk" between the two hemispheres is the **corpus callosum**. Over two hundred million neurons are found in this band of fibers, enabling the brain to function as a single unit. If you had no corpus callosum, your left hemisphere could only talk about the information from the right side of your body, and your right hemisphere could only react to information from the left side. Because of the corpus callosum, each hemisphere receives information from both sides of the body.

The two hemispheres of the brain are not mirror images of one another. In many humans, the left hemisphere, which is responsible for language, reading, writing, math calculations, and complex voluntary movements, is dominant. The right hemisphere is more concerned with complex visual, auditory, and tactile pattern recognition. Spatial senses, intuition, singing, and music making are primarily right hemispheric functions in most individuals. Although the right hemisphere cannot control speech or writing, it is crucial for understanding the emotional context of speech. For example, if the right hemisphere is temporarily out of condition (lightly shocked) leaving only the left hemisphere in charge, a person would sound much like a robot when speaking. We would not understand inflections, body language, gestures, or sarcasm. These appear to reside in the right hemisphere. Take the inventory in Figure 8.1 to test your brain dominance.

corpus callosum
The part of the brain responsible for cross talk between the two hemispheres.

lateralization
The process by which brain functions become specialized either in the left or the right hemisphere.

© Elizabeth Crews

Whether children are left-handed or right-handed is determined by both heredity and the environment.

Lateralization

The division of labor between the right and left hemispheres is known as **lateralization**. During early childhood, the brain continues to lateralize, or specialize in cognitive functions. To illustrate, the left hemisphere of the brain shows a dramatic growth spurt between the ages of 3 and 6, which parallels a dramatic increase in the child's vocabulary and complexity of language (Reeve, 1998). Further, due to lateralization, one side of the brain becomes the dominant hemisphere. For most of us, this will be the left hemisphere.

Because the right side of the brain controls the left side of the body and the left side of the brain controls the right side of the body, children's dominant cerebral hemisphere is apparent in their *handedness*. Most children are right-handed, indicating a dominant left hemisphere. Handedness may also be a product of both heredity and environment. Environmental influences, such as the way the fetus lies in the uterus may influence handedness (Springer & Deutsch, 1998). If the child is turned toward the left, this may promote greater control of the right side of the body. Genetic factors may also play a role in handedness (Rothi & Heilman, 1997); 42 percent of all children with left-handed parents are left-handed (Dowling, 1998). Data also suggest that these inherited preferences are molded by a culture in which right-handedness is preferred; thus, we find a decrease in left-handedness in older children and adolescents.

Leg preference is not usually as marked as hand preference. At times, children will be seen to kick and otherwise engage in learned motor skills with one foot, and, yet, when given general directions to hop on or stand on one foot, they may evidence a preference for the other foot. Lack of perfect correspondence between leg use in various tasks is reflected in the findings of several studies (Dowling, 1998). About 94 percent of children have a clear preference for their right foot. Leg preferences, like hand preferences, appear to be determined by heredity but are later modeled by subtle social and cultural pressures.

The Nature of Physical Growth

At 2½, Mack still has a short-legged, rounded, sturdy appearance, but as he progresses through early childhood his arms and legs will grow longer; he will lose his baby fat; his stomach will become flat; and he will grow proportionally thinner as he grows taller.

Essentially, young children gradually take on a more adultlike appearance. Although their muscles have grown in size and strength, they are still immature in function compared with those in middle childhood and adolescence. Children, during this stage also experience changes in height and weight, minigrowth spurts, and changes in their proportions.

Height and Weight

The rapid increases in body size so apparent in infancy now, in early childhood, begin to taper off into a slow growth pattern. If growth continued at the astounding rate of infancy, little Mack would now be the size of an adult. Ninety percent of Mack's height, like all children,

FIGURE 8.1 *Right and Left Brain Dominance: The Wagner Preference Inventory*

Instructions: Read the statements carefully. There are 12 groups of 4 statements each. Place an "X" in the parentheses in front of each item you select. Mark *one item* only under each of the 12 numbered items. Choose the activity you *prefer* even though it does not necessarily mean that you have the *ability* to do it. If you are undecided, make a decision anyway by guessing.

1. ( ) a. Major in logic
   ( ) b. Write a letter
   ( ) c. Fix things at home
   ( ) d. Major in art
2. ( ) a. Be a movie critic
   ( ) b. Learn new words
   ( ) c. Improve your skills in a game
   ( ) d. Create a new toy
3. ( ) a. Improve your strategy in a game
   ( ) b. Remember people's names
   ( ) c. Engage in sports
   ( ) d. Play an instrument by ear
4. ( ) a. Review a book
   ( ) b. Write for a magazine
   ( ) c. Build new shelves at home
   ( ) d. Draw a landscape or seascape
5. ( ) a. Analyze market trends
   ( ) b. Write a movie script
   ( ) c. Do carpentry work
   ( ) d. Imagine a new play
6. ( ) a. Analyze management practices
   ( ) b. Locate words in a dictionary
   ( ) c. Put jigsaw puzzles together
   ( ) d. Paint in oil
7. ( ) a. Be in charge of computer programming
   ( ) b. Study word origins and meaning
   ( ) c. Putter in the yard
   ( ) d. Invent a new gadget
8. ( ) a. Analyze production costs
   ( ) b. Describe a new product in words
   ( ) c. Sell a new product on the market
   ( ) d. Draw a picture of a new product
9. ( ) a. Explain the logic of a theory
   ( ) b. Be a copy writer for ads
   ( ) c. Work with wood and clay
   ( ) d. Invent a story
10. ( ) a. Be a comparison shopper
    ( ) b. Read about famous men and women
    ( ) c. Run a traffic control tower
    ( ) d. Mold with clay and putty
11. ( ) a. Analyze your budget
    ( ) b. Study literature
    ( ) c. Visualize and re-arrange furniture
    ( ) d. Be an artist
12. ( ) a. Plan a trip and make a budget
    ( ) b. Write a novel
    ( ) c. Build a house or shack
    ( ) d. Make crafts your hobby

Quadrant analysis

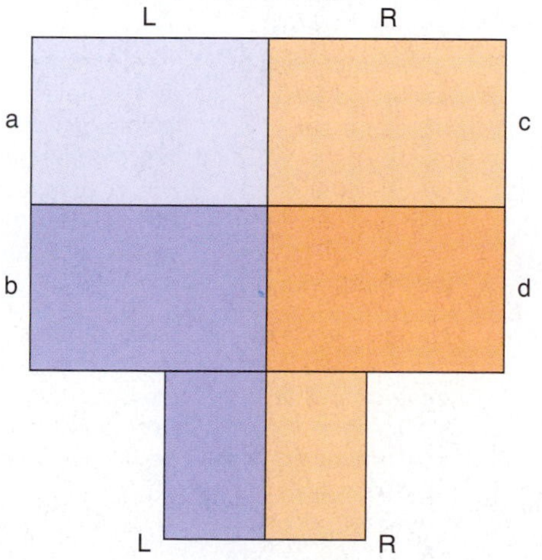

L R

a c

b d

L R

To ascertain your score: Write down the number of times you chose "a" in the box labeled "a"; do the same for "b," "c," and "d." Add the total number of times you chose "a" or "b," and write the number in the box marked L. Add your "c" and "d" answers, and write that total in the box labeled *R.* A difference between the two boxes of at least 3 points indicates that the higher-scoring hemisphere is dominant. Thus, for example, 8/4 is left-dominant; 3/9 is right-dominant, and 6/6, 5/7, and 7/5 indicate hemispheric balance.

From "A Refined Neurobehavioral Inventory of Hemispheric Preference," by R. F. Wagner & K. A. Wells, 1985, in *Journal of Clinical Psychology, 41,* 672–673. Reprinted by permission of John Wiley & Sons, Inc.

is determined by heredity (Plomin, 1998). Two tall parents are more likely to have tall children—although this is not always the case. Similarly, growth patterns are genetically determined. Monozygotic twins reared together, for example, are very similar in their patterns of growth. Similarly, if the parents were early maturers as children, the odds increase that their offspring will also mature at a faster rate.

Despite preschoolers' slower growth pattern, their weight more than doubles during the early childhood years, from roughly 25 to 65 pounds, which is about one-third to one-half of their adult weight (DiGirolamo, Geis, & Walker, 1998). Inches and pounds tell us children are growing; however, the best measure of establishing a child's level of physical maturation is to X ray the child's wrist or hand. The X ray shows the number of bones and the extent of their ossification (skeletal age). X rays tell the maturity of the child's skeleton and show how fully the immature central cartilage cells have broken down and hardened into bone.

Minigrowth Spurts

Growth is slow in early childhood, but often it is not steady. Increases in height often come in spurts during the early childhood years. These spurts are then followed by periods in which little or no growth occurs. Growth spurts are accompanied by increases in appetite, just as periods of little growth are accompanied by a decreased interest in food. Boys and girls in early childhood develop at almost the same rate (Tanner, 1998). When children enter kindergarten, however, the average boy is both heavier and taller than the average girl. But the differences are quite small and both sexes are able to perform gross and fine motor skills with equal efficiency. As muscles continue to grow and strengthen, boys will develop more muscles per pound of body weight and bone. Girls have more fatty tissue. Increasing muscle strength for both boys and girls makes them more agile and coordinated than their toddler counterparts.

Changing Proportions

As young children grow, their proportions change. Their heads grow more slowly than the toddler's, but their faces grow more rapidly and their jaws widen. The more linear look of the young child is a result of growth occurring primarily in the legs and trunk. Legs become longer in proportion to total body length. Whereas the legs make up about 34 percent of total body length at the age of 2, by the age of 5, it is 44 percent (Tanner, 1998). The child's leaner look is also the result of the spine straightening and the torso increasing in length. By 5½ years of age, the body fat layer is half as thick as it was at 9 months (Tanner, 1990). The body systems slow down and stabilize during early childhood. As one can see in Table 8.1, the child's metabolic rate, heart rate, respiration rate, and blood pressure all are slower than in infancy.

TABLE 8.1

Changing Proportions

	Eyes	Ears	Immune System	Cardiovascular System	Neurological System	Musculoskeletal System
2 Years	Still bumps into things but depth perception is improving	Eustachian tube still short and soft; frequent ear infections caused by allergies and colds that lead to buildup of fluids in the ear	Can manufacture all the antibodies that adults can but has fewer antibodies because has not yet encountered all the infections that adults have	Essentially mature; heart rate remains between 80 and 125 beats per minute, with an average of 105. Blood pressure is usually 100/60	Brain has reached 90% of adult size; still a great deal of neurological development taking place because the brain continues its maturation during the preschool years	System with the greatest development because the child is an active toddler; steady improvement in quality of motor activity; becoming less awkward and jerky
6 Years	Essentially normal vision but tends to be somewhat far-sighted	Ear infections still occur but less frequently	Immune system continues to develop, so infections are less severe than earlier	Heart continues to grow in size and efficiency; pulse rate 75 to 120, blood pressure 100/60	Nervous system continues to develop but at a slower rate; sensory and motor functions are being refined	Loses tummy; stomach muscles are becoming stronger; flat feet become arched

APPLICATIONS:

Factors Affecting Growth

There are laws of sequence and of maturation that account for the general similarities and basic trends of children's physical development, but no two children (with the partial exception of identical twins) grow in exactly the same way. Each child has a tempo and a style of growth that are as characteristic of individuality as is his or her personality. Differences in size are quite apparent. The next time you pass a park or a child-center playground, just notice the vast differences in height and weight among the children; one 5-year-old child, for example, may weigh 60 pounds and be 48 inches in height, whereas another is 42 inches tall and just over 40 pounds. Children's unique patterns of development are influenced by both environmental factors such as nutrition and genetic variables.

Environmental Factors

The environment plays a role, albeit a less dominant one, in height. A poor diet may impede the child from achieving his maximum height. One monozygotic twin, for example, may be significantly smaller than the other because of an illness. Social class has an impact on maximum height as well. Children from disadvantaged classes tend to be smaller than children from middle or upper classes. This is not the case in Sweden, however. There are no differences found in height among different socioeconomic classes, and this is attributed to the government food programs that provide all children with nutritious food. Nutrition, then, is one of the key environmental factors influencing a child's height. The importance of nutrition during the preschool years is covered later in this chapter.

Deprivation dwarfism is a growth-related disorder that appears to be caused by environmental factors. It usually appears between the ages of 2 and 15 and generally stems from emotional deprivation and lack of affection, which appear to interfere with the production of the growth hormone. Even though children suffering from this disorder appear to be receiving adequate nutrition and physical care, they often lack a loving, caring, affectionate adult in their lives. Their small stature and dramatically reduced rates of growth, for example, may be caused by excessively stressful family environments, such as a depressed caregiver in an unhappy marriage, a divorced parent, or family economic hardships. The prognosis for these children, however, is quite positive. If the family situations responsible for this disorder are corrected, or if the child is removed from this environment, his or her growth hormone levels return to normal (Brockington, 1996). However, if the emotional neglect that underlies deprivation dwarfism persists for several years, affected children may display a long-term smaller-than-normal stature.

Genetic Factors

Our genetic inheritance also influences the body's production of hormones that influence children's height. The most critical of the endocrine (hormone-secreting) glands is the pituitary gland, which is responsible for secreting two important hormones related to growth. The first hormone is known as the **growth hormone** (**GH**), which stimulates the rapid growth and development of body cells. Tiny amounts of the growth hormone are secreted several times a day and about 60 to 90 minutes after the child falls asleep. So, there is some truth to the old parental adage, "Lots of sleep will help you grow big and strong." Children who lack this hormone, will, as adults be correctly proportioned but will fail to grow much beyond 4 feet in height. If treated early enough, children can achieve their normal height by receiving expensive injections of GH.

The second hormone secreted by the pituitary gland is the **thyroid-stimulating hormone** (**TSH**). TSH is secreted by another endocrine gland, the thyroid gland, a double-lobed mass on either side of the windpipe. It secretes a hormone known as *thyroxin*, which is responsible for normal development of neurons in the brain and is necessary for GH to have its greatest impact on body growth. Young children with such a thyroxin deficiency must receive this hormone at once. If not, they will be mentally retarded. When older, the thyroxin-deficient child will grow at a below-average rate.

Concept Checks

1. Continuing myelination of the visual cortex is reflected in the preschooler's vivid ________________.
2. The proportionally thinner look of preschoolers can be attributed to the growth of legs as well as the result of __________ growth and the ________________ straightening.
3. The rapid growth and development of body cells is stimulated by the __________ ________________.

deprivation dwarfism
A growth-related disorder that appears to be caused by environmental factors.

growth hormone (GH)
A pituitary hormone that affects all body tissues, except the central nervous system and the genitals.

thyroid-stimulating hormone (TSH)
A pituitary hormone that stimulates the thyroid gland to release its hormone thyroxin, which is necessary for normal brain development and body growth.

Motor Development

Before Beginning . . .

After reading this section, you will be able to

- understand body-build proportions and body image and how they relate to motor skills.
- characterize how body/spatial awareness, temporal awareness, and visual perceptual maturity develop.
- trace the development of gross and fine motor development.
- discuss how young children's motor development can be enhanced.

Growth changes influence motor performance to a marked degree. As the head becomes relatively smaller, the child's performance in balance tasks is undoubtedly facilitated. As legs get longer, children become able to engage in a larger variety of accurate locomotor activities. And as shoulders widen and arms lengthen, children become able to throw with greater mechanical efficiency.

Movement and the Young Child

Movement is at the very center of young children's lives, and vigorous physical activity enables them to experience the joy of efficient movement as well as the health benefits of movement. Differences in body-build proportions are apparent during early childhood, and body build is related to motor proficiency even in young children.

Body-Build Proportions

Perhaps you have noticed that most stocky parents tend to have stocky children; thin parents have thin children; and long-legged parents have long-legged children. This resemblance relates in part to genetics as the findings of a study involving Danish parents and their adopted children showed (Stunkard, Sorensen, Hanis, Teasdale, Chakraborty, Schull, & Schulinger, 1986). Adopted children's body structure and weight correlated significantly with their genetic parents and showed little relationship to their adoptive parents.

Ethnic groups also differ in body structure. Although there are often even greater variations among individuals in an ethnic group, researchers have found a few normative tendencies. For example, according to Gregory Payne and Judith Rink (1997), African American children tend to have longer legs and narrower hips, and their average height tends to be greater than the norm for their European American counterparts. In addition, the normative height for Japanese American and Chinese American children tends to be shorter than normative heights for African American and European American children. As a result of different body shapes, these children may excel at different types of sports. For example, African Americans often excel at running and jumping activities and Japanese American and Chinese American children tend to perform better at sports such as wrestling, gymnastics, and weight lifting—activities that require more upper body strength (Tanner, 1998).

Sex differences are also significant in regard to growth. Generally, girls mature more rapidly, as reflected in their longer legs and arms, although boys are about 4 percent heavier than girls during early childhood. Girls tend to be slightly shorter and lighter than boys. Boys are better at throwing a ball, jumping, and going up and down ladders; girls are more coordinated and can balance and hop better than boys (Allen & Marotz, 1999). Girls tend to have more mature fine motor skills than boys; thus, they do better than boys at tasks such as writing, drawing, and cutting (Gallahue, 1993; Gallahue & Ozmun, 1998). There appears to be little difference in strength between boys and girls until the age of 6, when boys generally become stronger than girls (Galahue & Ozmun, 1998).

Body Image

The development of the child's awareness of her body, its parts, its movement capabilities, and its relationships to environmental supports probably begins shortly after birth. In the preschool years, however, it reaches new levels of sophistication. *Body image* is a rather global term; here, however, it is defined as encompassing all the child's movement capabilities as well as the sensory impressions created by these movements. It includes the child's abilities to draw a human figure, identify body parts, and discriminate between left and right.

Drawing a Human Figure A frequently used clinical tool to assess body image development (also used as an assessment of children's intelligence) involves requiring the child to draw a picture of a person. Figure drawings by children reveal that initially the child perceives the face and some of its parts, primarily the eyes. Later in development, children begin to gain an awareness of the limbs and their placement, revealed in drawings that include a Charlie Brown–type head from which the arms and legs directly protrude in the form of sticks. With further development, children include some indication of a trunk, and final development of the body image is reflected in the inclusion of legs, arms, hands with more details, and limbs that are two-dimensional as opposed to the early "spaghetti-like" stick versions. From an analysis of children's drawings of human figures, one then gets a glimpse into the evolvement of their body image.

Identifying Body Parts Others have taken a different approach to evaluating the child's awareness of his body and its parts. This second type of evaluation utilizes the child's verbal responses to various directions as a means of evaluating body awareness. Here the child is generally asked to point to various body parts (neck, nose, hands) of a picture. Awareness of the parts of the face, the arms and hands, and eyes and eyebrows is found in 80 percent of 5-year-olds (Hendrick, 1996). Body parts such as elbows, palms of hands, and ring fingers are usually not correctly labeled until the age of 6.

Perception of Left and Right "Raise your right hand." Can you remember that when you were 5 or 6 this was a very difficult task? Can you remember your confusion about left and right? Most children under the age of 6 are bewildered when asked about left and right directives. It is not until about the age of 7 that children show less confusion. But, even then, when they are asked to raise their right hand, for example, they often have created some clever tricks to assist them. Some children, for example, may have a mole on their left leg, and this becomes their fail-safe way to always know the difference between right and left. Other children, when asked how they know left–right discriminations will say, "This is my right hand; I use it to eat with." It takes children a little longer to recognize left–right discriminations in other people. When an examiner, for example, asks a child seated opposite of her to correctly identify her left and right hands, it is not until age 8 that the majority of children can successfully project themselves into the reference system of the examiner. The developmental stages of awareness of the names of various body parts and of their left–right dimensions are highlighted in Table 8.2.

TABLE 8.2

Body Perception by Children

Age	Perceptions Formed
2–3 years	Becomes aware of front, back, side, head, and feet and can locate objects relative to these body reference points; begins to gain awareness of more body parts (thumb, hand, feet, and so on); learns parts of face
4 years	Becomes aware that there are two sides of the body and knows their names but not their location; gains more detailed awareness of body parts; can name little and first fingers
5 years	Knows that there is a left and right side of the body but is usually confused about their location; can locate self relative to objects and objects relative to self; trunk appears in figure drawings
6 years	Begins to distinguish left and right body parts and to locate body relative to the left and right of things and objects relative to the left and right of the body; becomes aware of ring finger and can name it

Perceptual Development

Another aspect of motor development that becomes obvious during the preschool period is *perceptual-motor development*. **Perceptual-motor movements** are a combination of what the child sees or perceives through her senses and the body movements that respond to those perceptions. Young children are continually developing a greater *body/spatial awareness*, which translates into their getting better about avoiding objects and furniture when they are on the move. By age 4 or 5, they can run through an area and miss all the obstacles, clear evidence that they are better aware of their bodies and the space surrounding them. They also develop *temporal*, or *time awareness*, evidenced by their sense of the proper sequence of their daily routines, such as eating breakfast, lunch, and then dinner.

Visual-perceptual maturity increases during the early childhood years as well. As visual maturity increases, children's eye muscles mature adequately enough to allow them to scan from left to right and focus on a series of words—important prerequisites for learning to read. Their continuing visual maturity is evidenced in other abilities as well. For example, 2-year-old children are as likely to look at figures and pictures upside down as in the correct position. Children 3 to 4 years old can distinguish vertical lines from horizontal lines, and 6-year-olds generally evidence little difficulty in dealing with discriminations involving vertical, horizontal, and oblique lines (Allen & Marotz, 1999).

perceptual-motor movements A combination of what the child sees or perceives through her senses and the body movements that respond to those perceptions.

Moreover, children can often identify forms and objects that are inverted and otherwise removed from the usual upright orientation better than adults (Allen & Marotz, 1999). However, their ability to discriminate between *b* and *d*, *p* and *q*, and other asymmetrical numbers and letters often is faulty until the age of 7. Letter and number reversals are common in children of 5 and 6 years; about 60 percent of all 5-year-olds reverse letters and numbers (Diamond & Hopson, 1998). By the age of 7, however, only about 12 percent of children evidence reversals of numbers and letters (Sternberg & Williams, 1998). Five- and 6-year-olds can reverse numbers and letters in a variety of ways. Thus the left–right dimensions of the space field seem more difficult to organize than the up–down dimensions. Some have speculated that the ability to make correct left–right orientations in space is somehow dependent on and influenced by the child's ability to make left–right discriminations about her own body parts (Diamond & Hopson, 1998). The young child's growing perceptual skills are highlighted in Table 8.3.

At times two-digit numbers may be reversed: 10 may be written as 01 and 20 may be written as 02. Further, a lack of rhythm may be seen as a child reverses the order in which he writes two-digit numbers yet puts them in the correct order. For example, the child may write the 5 before writing the 1, but he still writes the number 15 correctly.

Gross and Fine Motor Skills

Around the age of 4 or 5, children seem to conquer gravity, evidenced by their penchant for hopping and jumping. They also gain increased control over their musculature (stability). They are now able to explore the movement potential of their bodies as they move through space. Further, as coordination increases, children are now able to make controlled and precise contact with objects in their environment (Assaiante, 1998).

Gross Motor Development

Large muscle development continues to have an edge over small muscle development; as such, children generally become more skillful in activities that involve **gross motor** movements as opposed to those that require fine motor movements. During the early childhood years, children begin to show proficiency in running, jumping, hopping, skipping, and galloping.

Running The child of 18 months often has a somewhat hurried walk that resembles a run. This is not a genuine run, however, because the child's leg power and balance do not permit him to leave the ground with both feet at the same time. Between the ages of 2 and 3, he will evidence a true run but will generally lack the ability to start and stop efficiently. By the ages of 4½ to 5, however, the child's running ability will

gross motor development
Behavior that involves the movement of the entire body or major parts of the body (large muscles controlling arms and legs, for example).

TABLE 8.3

The Young Child's Growing Perceptual Skills

Age	Perceptual Skill
2 years	Eye–hand movements are better coordinated; puts objects together and takes them apart; names objects in picture books; may pretend to pick something off the page and taste or smell it
3 years	Likes to look at books and may pretend to "read" to others or explain pictures; points with a fair degree of accuracy to correct pictures when given sound-alike words: *keys–cheese, fish–dish, mouse–mouth;* places 8 to 10 pegs in pegboard, or 6 round and 6 square blocks in formboard; attempts to draw; imperfectly copies circles, squares, and some letters
4 years	Stacks at least five graduated cubes from largest to smallest; builds a pyramid of six blocks; indicates if paired words sound the same or different: *sheet–feet, ball–wall*; near end of year, names 18 to 20 uppercase letters and writes several; prints own name; recognizes some printed words (especially those that have a special meaning for the child)
5 years	Forms rectangle from two triangular cuts; builds steps with set of small blocks; understands concept of *same* shape, *same* size; understands the concepts of smallest and shortest; places objects in order from shortest to tallest and smallest to largest
6 years	Attention span increases; works at tasks for longer periods of time, though concentrated effort is not always consistent; understands concepts, such as simple time markers (today, tomorrow, yesterday) or uncomplicated concepts of motion (cars go faster than bicycles); recognizes some words by sight; attempts to sound out words (some children may be reading well by this time)

From *Developmental Profiles*, by K. E. Allen & L. R. Marotz, 1999, Albany, NY: Delmar Publishers. Reprinted by permission of the publisher.

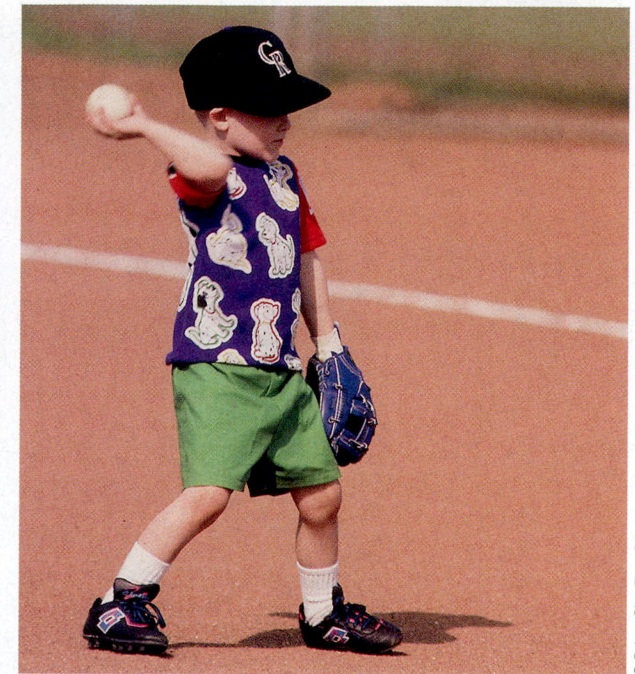

© Felicia Martinez/PhotoEdit

© Robert Ginn/PhotoEdit

Girls generally have more advanced fine motor development, whereas boys tend to do better at activities requiring gross motor skills.

increase markedly, and a good reciprocal arm action will be seen in the running pattern.

Jumping As with their first attempts at running, young children remain in contact with the ground with one foot when they first try to jump. They will usually be seen at around 18 months of age to simply step off low objects. Shortly afterward, the child will step off with one foot and remain momentarily suspended in the air. At about age 2, jumping over barriers will occur. By the age of 4, many children are considered to be skillful jumpers. Five-year-olds can broad jump a distance of almost 3 feet using a two-foot take-off.

Hopping, Skipping, Galloping One-foot hopping, skipping, and galloping are other variations of locomotor abilities evidenced by children as they pass from early childhood to the school years. These tasks may be sex-linked: boys may prefer to gallop, feeling that skipping is too feminine for them to attempt. On the other hand, girls sometimes skip well but have not experimented with the more forceful-appearing masculine activity of galloping (Gallahue & Ozmun, 1998). Between 3 and 4 years, most children can hop from one to three steps on their preferred foot if no precision (hopping into squares), rhythm (alternate hopping from foot to foot), or distance is required of them. It is not until age 5 that children master these hopping skills, which require more endurance, balance, and strength. Skills in skipping and galloping are not generally achieved until children are about 6 years old. Table 8.4 summarizes these motor achievements.

Balance Balance is a rather common measure of the general integrity of the nervous system. It generally reflects the efficiency and the integration of the muscular system (particularly the reflexes that enable children to unconsciously adjust their posture to the upright), the visual system, and the child's sense of equilibrium. Children gain the ability to walk lines with reasonable accuracy at a remarkably early age. The ability to walk a reasonably straight pathway is achieved by most 3-year-olds. It is not until nearly 4 years of age, however, that children are able to walk a circular line. Five-year-olds are able to balance on one foot—even with their arms folded.

Ball Skills Proficiencies in ball throwing, ball catching, and ball kicking are influenced to a marked degree by cultural expectations. One of the first things athletically oriented caregivers may do is place a ball in the hands of their young children. In many cultures around the world, soccer is an extremely popular sport. As such, various foot–eye coordinations are valued by these parents and taught to their children. Thus, success and failure at ball skills are predictable to a

TABLE 8.4

Motor Skills Development in Early Childhood

Motor Pattern	Skill Characteristics 2–3 Years	4 Years	5–6 Years
Walking/running	Run is smoother; stride is more even; cannot turn or stop quickly; can take walking and running steps on toes	Run improves in form and power; greater control, stopping, starting, and turning; in general, greater mobility than at age 3	Has adult manner of running; can use this effectively in games; runs 35-yard dash in less than 10 seconds
Jumping	Can jump down from 8-inch elevation; 42% can jump well	Jumps down from 25-inch height with feet together; 72% skilled in jumping; can do standing broad jump of 8–10 inches	Makes running broad jump of 28–35 inches; 80% have mastered the skill of jumping
Climbing	Ascends stairway unaided, alternating feet; ascends small ladder, alternating feet	Descends long stairway by alternating feet, if supported; descends small ladder, alternating feet	Descends long stairway or large ladder, alternating feet; further increase in overall proficiency
Throwing	Throws approximately 3 feet, using two-hand throw; throws without losing balance, body remains fixed during throwing	Distance of throw increases; 20% are proficient throwers; begins to assume adult stance in throwing	Introduction of weight transfer; right-foot-step-forward-throw; 74% are proficient in throwing
Catching	Catches large ball with arms extended forward stiffly; makes little or no adjustment of arms to receive ball	Catches large ball with arms flexed at elbows; 29% are proficient in catching	Catches small ball using hands more than arms; 56% are proficient in catching

From *Understanding Motor Development: Infants, Children, Adolescents, and Adults,* by D. L. Gallahue & J. C. Ozmun, 1998, Boston: McGraw-Hill. Reprinted by permission of the McGraw-Hill Companies.

remarkable degree by the amount of social esteem these skills engender.

During early childhood the child's throwing efficiency improves as she begins to incorporate first a weight shift in her throwing and, later, a step with the foot opposite to that of the throwing arm. The body remains facing the direction of the throw, and there is either little or no weight shift. By the middle of the third year the child will usually engage in some body rotation accompanying the arm movement but without any marked weight shift. By the ages of 5 and 6, the child will be seen to take a step and make a pronounced weight shift as she releases the ball. Improved speed and accuracy will result from these refinements in the throwing pattern.

Catching, in early childhood, is merely the passive acceptance of an object. Initially, young children, around 3 years old, will stand with their arms held straight and stiff in front of their bodies. In the second advancement of catching skills, we can observe a 4-year-old, with a stance similar to a 3-year-old, but now the child will open his hands to receive the ball. Finally, at around age 5 to 5½, children will flex their arms and elbows permitting them to "give" when the ball arrives. Greater levels of overall body coordination and dexterity and general body awareness contribute to the development and refinement of motor skills.

fine motor development Behavior that depends primarily on small muscles that control fingers and hands.

Fine Motor Development

Two- and 3-year-olds have the ability to pick up tiny interesting objects between their thumb and forefinger because of **fine motor development**. They can build a rather tall tower of blocks and put together a simple puzzle—albeit sometimes rather clumsily, trying to fit a puzzle piece in the wrong section. Four-year-old's fine motor skills continue to become more sophisticated as they now can copy designs such as pluses and squares. They can draw a person with three parts, such as a head, arms, and legs. Five- and 6-year-olds can use crayons appropriately, reproduce letters, and copy short words.

Most young children are enthusiastic artists. Just give a child a pencil or crayon and some paper and she will occupy herself for relatively long periods of time. Young children's drawings may look like meaningless scribbles to some, but to the child they are works of art, to the caregiver they are to be treasured, and to Rhoda Kellogg, they are fascinating objects of study. Kellogg (1967) is one of the several scholars interested in this facet of children's perceptual-motor behavior

FIGURE 8.2 *Five Drawings of the Human Figure*

These drawings were made by the same boy within a one-week period.

From *Analyzing Children's Art,* by R. Kellogg & S. O'Dell, 1969, Palo Alto, CA: National Press Books. Used by permission.

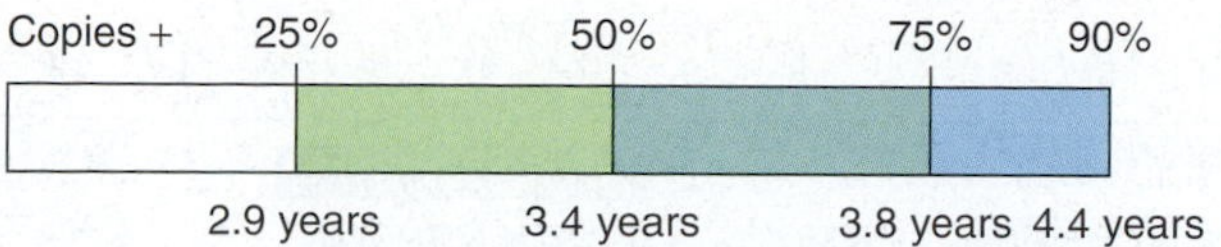

FIGURE 8.3 *Age Distribution of Children Performing a Test Item*

The Denver Developmental Screening Test (revised) identifies the percentile rating of the child being examined with respect to other children's particular developmental achievement. Twenty-five percent of children can copy a plus sign at 2.9 years; 50 percent at 3.4 years; 75 percent at 3.8 years; and 90 percent at 4.4 years.

From "The Denver II: A Major Revision and Restandardization of the Denver Developmental Screening Test, by W. K. Frankenburg, 1992, in *Pediatrics, 89,* 91–97. Used by permission.

and she has studied over a million drawings and paintings over a period of many decades.

Around the age of 3, scribbles turn into placement patterns, in which the child places patterns within a spaced border. Around the age of 4, young children delight in drawing circles, squares or rectangles, crosses, and so forth. The design stage ushers in new artistic talents. The 4-year-old mixes two shapes; for example, she places an X within a circle. Finally, around the age of 5, children enter the pictorial stage, in which their artistic renderings are now meaningful and recognizable representations of objects (Kellogg, 1967).

During the last stage of artistic development, children engage in drawing actual pictures—often of other people. As noted earlier, various forms of the draw-a-person test are utilized to assess a wide range of subtle and obvious attributes in children including body image, intelligence, and social competency. Kellogg, however, expresses concern about this because of the rather tenuous nature of children's artistic renderings. She states that one-third of the large number of children she has sampled drew such different people on different days that ratings of their intelligence by an expert differed by 50 percent from drawing to drawing that were produced by the same child. Kellogg suggests that any ratings of a child's mental state from inspection of his or her drawings should be carried out only after examining a large number of drawings from the child (see Figure 8.2).

Assessing Children's Gross and Fine Motor Development

How does one know if children's motor development is developing normally? One assessment procedure, known as the *Denver II Developmental Screening Test* (DDST) (Frankenburg, 1992; Frankenburg & Dodds, 1967), is designed to detect developmental normalcy or delays in development in gross and fine motor development as well as in personal-social and language development.

For example, Figure 8.3 illustrates the item "copies +" under fine motor behavior. The left end of the bar designates the age (2.9 years) at which 25 percent of the children can copy a plus mark; the hatchmark at the top of the bar, the age (3.4 years) at which 50 percent of the children can copy this design; the left end of the dotted area the age (3.8 years) when 75 percent of the children perform this well; and the right end of the bar the age (4.4 years) at which 90 percent of the children can copy the plus sign. Detecting developmental delays during the early childhood years is important, as early diagnosis of developmental delays increases the opportunities for effective therapy. How adults can assess if children are developing normally in these four areas of development is displayed in Figure 8.4.

APPLICATIONS:

Enhancing Children's Motor Development

Can we teach young children to develop motor skills at a faster rate? Can we teach them to become skilled athletes? Or, do motor skills simply unfold as a part of nature's grand plan? *Maturation* refers to qualitative changes that enable one to progress to higher levels of function. Maturation, when viewed from a biological perspective, is primarily innate; that is, it is genetically determined and resistant to external or environmental influences. *Experience* refers to factors within the environment that may alter the appearance of various developmental characteristics through the process of learning. A child's experiences may affect the rate of onset of certain patterns of behavior.

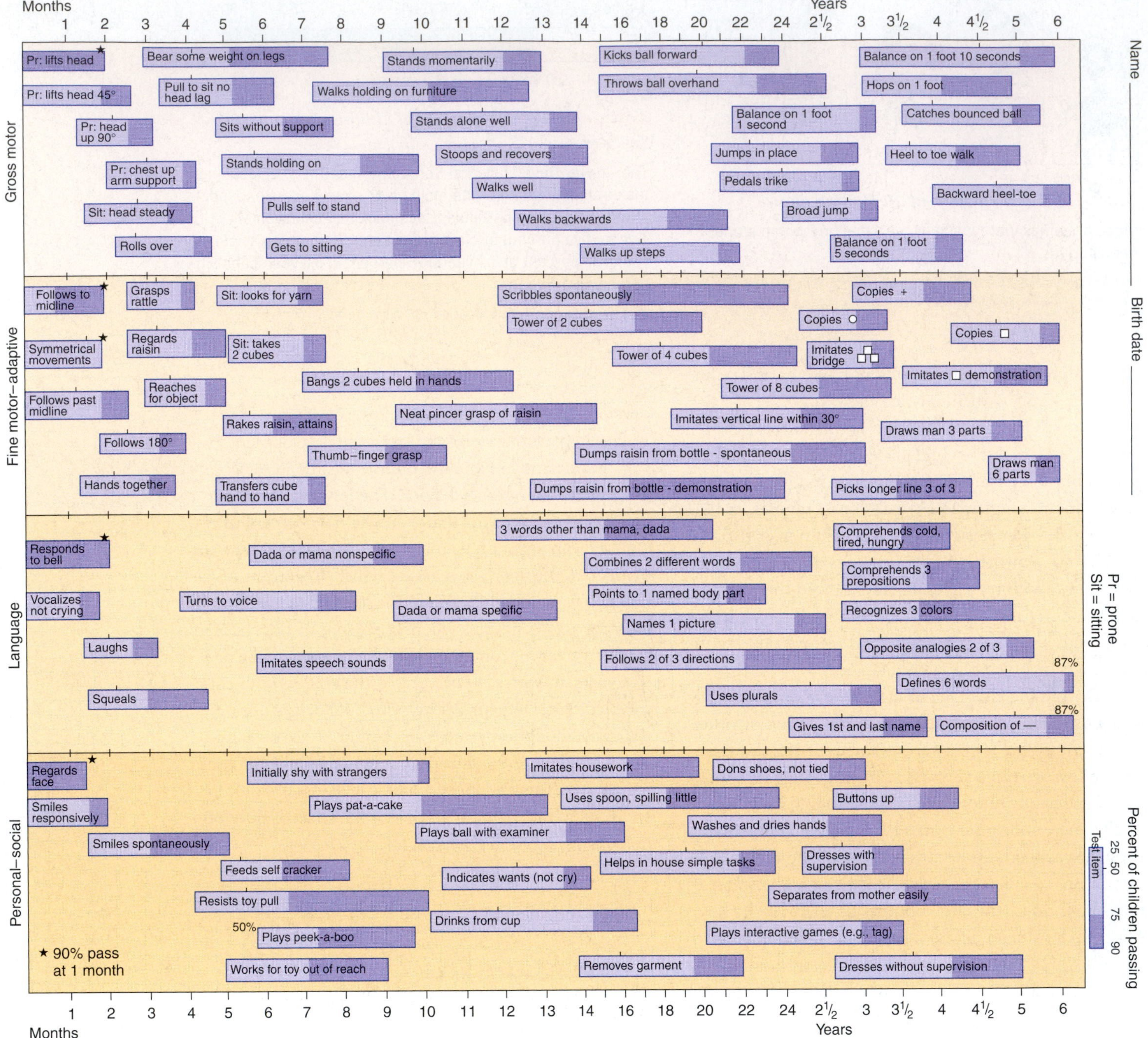

FIGURE 8.4 *The Denver Developmental Screening Inventory*

To assess if a child is developing at a normal rate, draw a line from the child's age at the top of the scale to the bottom. The child should be able to perform all the tasks the line passes through at the 90th percentile. Two "failures" in each domain indicate that the child would profit from a formal assessment by a professional.

From "The Denver II: A Major Revision and Restandardization of the Denver Developmental Screening Test, by W. K. Frankenburg, 1992, in *Pediatrics, 89,* 91–97. Used by permission.

Complex Motor Skills

Although maturation underlies general motor development, experience is a vital component in mastering complex motor skills, such as ball throwing, catching, and balance. If children are restricted from engaging in more complex motor activities, they tend to lag behind in abilities compared with those who have received more specialized training. Studies also indicate that instruction of more complex physical skills can make a difference in what children are able to do. For example, in a representative study, college students majoring in physical education worked with Head Start children, teaching them throwing, catching, and balancing skills (Ignico, 1991). After all the children were assessed as performing at the same level of motor competency, half of them (Group A) worked with the physical education majors for one hour once a week, and half (Group B) received no training in these skills. At the end of 10 weeks, the children were retested, and the results clearly demonstrated that Group A children significantly outperformed Group B children in their motor abilities for the skills taught. When we consider the contributions to the foundations these skills lay for development of even more complex motor activities as children grow, the value of providing carefully planned motor opportunities becomes clear.

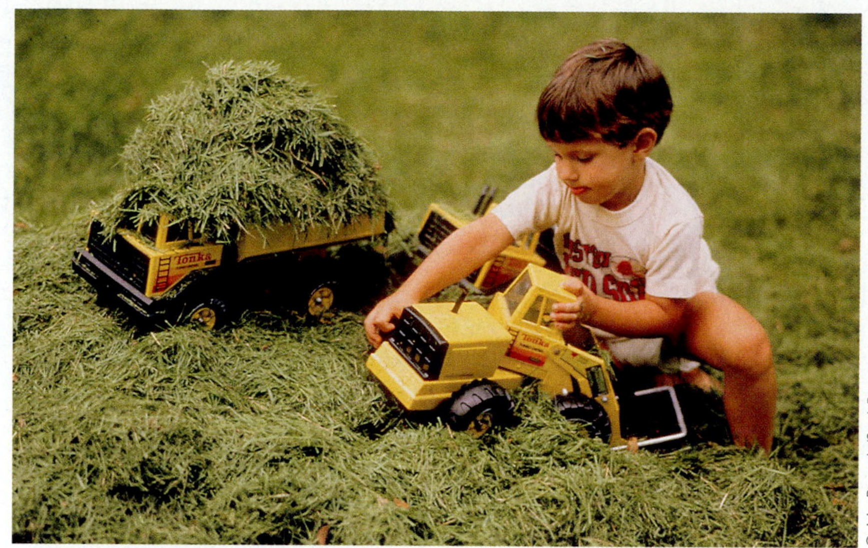

© John Dewaele/Stock Boston

In general, children should be exposed to a large assortment of big, sturdy, durable toys that provide opportunities for many kinds of physical activity.

A Variety of Motor Activities

David Gallahue and John Ozmun (1998) also advise that personalized, developmentally appropriate instruction is essential if children are to attain mature skill levels in a variety of fundamental movement tasks. This instruction needs to be coupled with sufficient time for practice in movement skill learning and the use of positive reinforcement techniques to continually encourage the young learner. Gallahue and Ozmun, however, do not advise adults to immediately enroll preschoolers in specialized motor skill programs—such as the Tiger Woods golf camp for preschoolers.

They do recommend, however, that young children be exposed to a variety of motor activities that are fun and challenging. Galloping to music, balancing on a balance beam, unpressured swimming, tumbling, or dancing lessons are recommended. Target games that promote eye–hand coordination, such as beanbag toss, ring toss, low hoop, and basketball toys, are also recommended. Providing wagons or large trucks that can be loaded, pushed, and sat on are also effective means of promoting young children's motor development. Equipment good for crawling through, climbing up, and hanging from should be included. Children need things they can lift and shove around to test their strength.

These activities stress large muscle involvement, but children can also profit from fine muscle activities as well. Manipulative toys that foster small muscle development and eye–hand coordination include large, interlocking blocks and large beads for stringing. Activities such as sewing and working with pegboards, puzzles, beads, and put-together materials are important as well. Manipulating art materials such as pencils, brushes, scissors, and crayons can also foster fine motor development. Fine muscle activities should be of reasonably short duration (Hendrick, 1996). It is difficult for young children to hold still for very long, much less sit and concentrate on a fine muscle task that requires considerable self-control. For this reason, several activities should be available at the same time, and children should always be free to get up, move around, and shift to more or less taxing experiences as they feel the need.

The process of movement skill development is age related but not age dependent. Movement skill acquisition is highly individualized because of the unique hereditary and experiential background of each child. Therefore, it is inappropriate to classify movement activities solely by age or by grade level. Care should be taken, however, to select movement experiences based on the ability levels of the "real" children being taught, not the mythical "average" children presented in many books. The emphasis of skill development should always be on fun.

Thought CHALLENGE

Are there any repercussions from young children not being able to perform more complex motor skills as well as their same-age counterparts?

Concept Checks

1. In general, boys are better at ____________, than girls; girls, however, outperform boys at ________.
2. Temporal awareness perceptual skills refer to young children's
   a. depth perception.
   b. sense of time.
   c. body / spatial awareness.
3. Large muscle activities refer to ______________ development; an example would be ______________.
4. Which statement best summarizes the role of maturation and learning and motor development?
   a. Basic and complex motor skills are a product of maturation and experience.
   b. Developmentally appropriate instruction is essential to learning basic motor skills.
   c. Basic motor skills simply unfold.

Health Factors in Early Childhood

Before Beginning . . .

After reading this section, you will be able to

- discuss common infectious illnesses and immunizations needed during early childhood.
- describe the nutritional needs of young children.
- identify how children's nutritional needs can be met.

Health promotion refers to the many behaviors and attitudes that strengthen a child's own resources for well-being. A child, for example, who eats a healthy diet generally has greater resistance to disease and will recover from illness or injury more quickly than a child who does not. Certainly, nutrition is an important part of promoting health; however, promoting health also means recognizing illness, helping to prevent the spread of disease, and avoiding preventable accidents.

Safety Concerns

Each year thousands of children die from accidental injuries (Morrongiello & Dawber, 1998). Today, unintentional injuries are the leading cause of death in children over age 1, and most of these deaths are preventable. Most of these deaths are due to car accidents, drownings, severe burns, or gun violence. Accidents leave many more children with lifelong impairments.

Automobile accidents are responsible for more deaths than any other cause. Most car accident fatalities and injuries can be avoided. Car seats and seat belts continue to be the primary defense against occupant injuries. Children who weigh more than 40 pounds should wear an adult seat belt; children who weigh less than 40 pounds should be secured in car seats. Studies show that if children were securely buckled in their seats, the number of child fatalities would decline by an astounding 70 to 85 percent, and serious injuries would decrease by 50 to 60 percent (Public Health Service, 1999). However, failure to use child restraints or to use restraints properly continues to be the cause of many injuries each year.

Drownings rank slightly behind motor vehicle accidents as the leading cause of death among young children (Public Health Service, 1999). Burns are also a leading cause of death among children, with most fatalities occurring in home fires. Even more often, deaths in fires are caused by smoke inhalation. Children need to be taught about the dangers of stoves and microwaves and how to use them properly when they are able to do so. All children should be taught to stop, drop, and roll if their clothing catches fire and to crawl low to get out during a fire.

Other common causes of fatal injuries during early childhood include poisoning, falls, and suffocations. Lead poisoning is a serious threat to children because it accumulates in the body and eventually causes damage to the brain, sickness, and even death (Tesman & Hills, 1994). Children pick it up accidentally from many sources but mainly from licking lead-based paint. Mechanical suffocation, another common cause of death, occurs when oxy-

Lead poisoning is seen by health experts as the most hazardous threat to young children's health.

gen cannot get to the child's lungs because an object (such as a pillow or plastic bag) is covering the mouth and nose or there is pressure on the throat or chest. Mechanical suffocation can also occur when a child is trapped in an airtight enclosed space such as a refrigerator or other large appliance.

Some safety measures include teaching young children how to swim. Swimming instruction and floatation devices, however, are not substitutes for careful adult supervision. Good supervision by certified water instructors coupled with teaching and enforcing water safety rules will prevent many drownings. Caregivers can also provide safe environments at home by making sure that space heaters and fans are well out of the reach of children; buying clothes and cloth toys made of flame-retardant fabric; taking locks off of discarded appliances; and removing all poisonous products from children's reach.

Colds and flu account for approximately 75 percent of infectious illnesses in early childhood.

Illness and Infectious Diseases

Although illness can strike at any age, certain diseases and health problems are more common in young children than in adults. These may range from scarlet fever to mild colds. Children get more diseases than adults because their immune systems are still immature and do not provide complete protection. Similarly, other infections, such as earaches, are more common because of children's immature physical structures.

All infectious illnesses follow a similar pattern: once the child has become infected, an *incubation period* follows during which the "pathogenic microbes" or germs multiply inside the body without giving any outer signs that the child is infected. Incubation periods can range from hours to weeks, depending on the disease. During the second stage, known as the *prodromal stage*, children start to show nonspecific signs of illness. For example, just before a cold hits you may say, "I'm beginning to feel terrible; I think I'm coming down with something." In this stage, children (like you) may be irritable and restless, complain their head hurts, or have a low-grade fever. The *acute stage* follows, in which the child is definitely sick and shows symptoms typical of the illness. This is the stage in which the physician can diagnose the illness. Finally, comes the *recovery stage* when symptoms begin to disappear and health gradually returns.

Diseases such as the common cold, influenza, strep throat, and chicken pox are spread through tiny droplets of respiratory secretions. As children talk, sing, cough, or sneeze, millions of these tiny droplets are airborne and other people breathe them in. When these droplets contain disease-causing bacteria or viruses, other people become infected. Upper respiratory infections, or colds, account for 60 to 75 percent of all infectious illnesses in children (Public Health Service, 1999). Some diseases are spread by direct contact. An uninfected person must touch an infected person or object to contract conjunctivitis (pinkeye), head lice, and ringworm. These diseases, while not life threatening, must be treated and controlled for good health.

Immunizations

Shots are never a favorite part of childhood; however, they are necessary to prevent such infectious diseases as polio, diphtheria, pertussis (whooping cough), hepatitis B, mumps, measles, rubella (German measles), tetanus (lockjaw), and Haemophilus influenzae type b (Hib). Without the proper vaccinations, children can still contract these illnesses. Immunizations for these illnesses stimulate the body to make antibodies that provide protection against the particular disease, but the period of immunity varies. The variability depends on the vaccine, the age of the person being immunized, and other factors.

Unfortunately, about 30 percent of all families in the United States have poor access to medical care, mainly because they are economically disadvantaged. Young children from these families are substantially less healthy than those from more advantaged families. For example, young children from low-income families contract 25 to 50 percent more minor illnesses than do young children in general (American Academy of

Child Development Issues

> Life is grim and hard and the child simply has to find that out. He does, too; he learns it and learns it and learns it. The average person may know all that, but find little time to dwell upon the social and psychological forces that make children of poverty so very different before they have had one day of school. (Coles, 1971)

Does Poverty Influence Child Development Outcome?

Some 12 to 14 million U.S. children live in homes in which the family income is below the poverty level (Brooks-Gunn, Britto, & Brady, 1999). It is estimated that one out of four children under the age of 6 lives in poverty. Poverty rates among U.S. children are one-third higher than they were two decades ago and 1.5 to 4 times as high as the rates for children in Canada and Western Europe (Duncan, Yeung, Brooks-Gunn, & Smith, 1998).

Income poverty refers to caregivers not having enough money to meet the basic needs for food, clothing, and shelter. Children enter (or avoid) poverty by virtue of their family's economic circumstances. Although there are government programs to help these families, poor children still do not fare as well as children from more advantaged families. How does living in poverty-stricken families influence children? What are the consequences for children growing up poor? The most common long-term consequences include dropping out of school, welfare dependency, and adult unemployment. For young children, the immediate effects of poverty are numerous:

- *Physical health:* Poor children are more likely to experience diminished physical health and poor health care (Zigler & Finn-Stevenson, 1999). In the 1998 National Health Interview Survey, parents reported that poor children were only two-thirds as likely to be in fair or good health as nonpoor children. Children born to poor mothers are more likely to be infants with a low birth weight; this is significantly associated with lower levels of intelligence and of math and reading achievement (Shiono, 1995).
- *Cognitive abilities:* Poor children score between 6 and 13 points lower on various standardized tests of IQ, verbal ability, and achievement (Smith, Brooks-Gunn, & Klebanov, 1997). These differences are very large from an educational perspective and are present even after controlling for maternal age, marital status, education, and ethnicity. Further, children living below the poverty threshold are 1.3 times as likely as nonpoor children to experience learning disabilities and developmental delays (Korenman, Miller, & Sjaastad, 1995).
- *School achievement outcomes:* The long-term effects of poverty negatively impact high school graduation and years of schooling obtained (Haveman & Wolfe, 1994; Ludwig, Ladd, & Duncan, 2001). Educational attainment is well recognized as a powerful predictor of experiences in later life. In general, the studies suggest that a 10 percent increase in family income is

Pediatrics, 1999). Moreover, the health care system provides less help to poor families than it does to more well-off ones. In the United States, medical services for the poor are paid through Medicaid, a federally sponsored insurance program. It will pay up to a certain point for taking a child with an earache to a general practitioner. Doctors who want to charge more are free to do so, but this often becomes too expensive for low-income families. The result is that low-income parents have fewer doctors and clinics to choose from than do more advantaged families.

Nutrition

What children eat has a far-reaching effect on their physical growth and development, and children being raised in poverty-stricken environments are particularly vulnerable (see Child Development Issues). It is important that children's diets provide the nutrients they need. Children's nutritional status is a product of the nutrients they take in compared with the nutrients they require, which, of course, depends largely on diet.

associated with a 0.2 percent to 2 percent increase in the number of school years completed (Haveman & Wolfe, 1995).

- *Emotional and behavioral outcomes:* Poor children suffer from emotional and behavioral problems more frequently than do nonpoor children. Emotional outcomes are often grouped along two dimensions: externalizing behaviors, including aggression, fighting, and acting out, and internalizing behaviors, such as anxiety, social withdrawal, and depression. Several researchers have reported that children in poor families have more internalizing and externalizing problems than nonpoor children (Brooks-Gunn & Duncan, 2001; Chase-Lansdale & Brooks-Gunn, 1995).

The broad range of effects of income poverty on children is clear—family income appears to be strongly related to children's measured ability and achievement-related outcomes. Further, the timing of poverty is also important. Low income during the preschool and early school years exhibits the strongest correlation with low achievement rates and low high school completion, as compared with low income during the middle childhood and adolescent years (Duncan, Yeung, Brooks-Gunn, & Smith, 1998). Poverty often means living in unsafe neighborhoods, which can be frightening (see the First Person box).

There are effective ways of helping children from low-income families, and nutrition programs are a good beginning because of their beneficial effects on both physical and cognitive outcomes. Similarly, because the home environment is important to children's early cognitive development, children will also profit from programs that focus on working with parents and how they can provide instruction, materials, and effective learning experiences for their children. Because of the greater impact of poverty during the early childhood years, it is especially important that efforts be made to eliminate deep and persistent poverty during a child's early years (McCourt, 2000).

Identifying protective factors that lead to resiliency among the poor has also been studied (Egeland, Carlson, & Sroufe, 1993; Nettles & Pleck, 1993). Both internal factors (for example, the ability to elicit positive responses from others, easy temperament, and perceptions of personal control over life outcomes) and external factors (for example, a strong social support network beyond the family, positive academic experiences, and good role models) have been identified as protective factors. Given the knowledge on risk and protective factors that has been gained through research, intervention programs designed to help provide or set in motion critical protective factors should be adequately funded and implemented (Erika Bolig, John Borkowski, and Jay Brandenberger, 1999).

Search Online

Explore InfoTrac College Edition, your online library. Go to **http://www.infotrac-college.com/wadsworth** and use the passcode that came on the card with your book. Try these search terms: poverty and development, poverty and child development, resilience in children.

Energy Needs

Young children do not need as many calories per body weight as they did during the infancy period. According to Recommended Dietary Allowances (RDAs), there are three ways in which one can measure the child's daily calorie needs. *Age-related* measures start with a base of 1000 calories and add 100 calories for each year of age. Thus, a 5-year-old needs 1500 calories per day. According to *weight methods*, children between the ages of 2 and 6 require 41 calories per pound. A 5-year-old who weighs 40 pounds needs 1640 calories a day. If *height measures* are used as a base, the RDAs translate into 41 calories per inch; thus, a 5-year-old who is 43 inches tall would need 1760 calories per day. Whichever method is used, it is important to remember that energy needs vary from child to child and should be linked to the child's level of activity. Young children need energy as much for their level of activity as for their growth. The more active the child, the greater the child's energy level.

FIRSTPERSON

Breaking Away from Poverty

I had many fears living on North Magnolin Street. It was a bad neighborhood with many children in gangs. At any time of day or night you could hear gunshots, and I was afraid for me and my son Hugo. Our apartment was small, but I tried hard to keep it clean and respectable. I tried to keep the door to my home clean. I would have to scrub it every day because many children would write things on the doors and all down the hallway. Across the street from where I live was an apartment full of kids living there. Some of the kids would come out of the apartment, approach a car, and give them something. Then they would run back to the apartment house. At first, I wondered what they were doing. I was later told they were selling drugs.

Some of these boys were very nice to me and protected me from my abusive husband and his brother. They chased them to their car and broke the rear and side windows as they were leaving. They told them not to come back. I was divorced from my husband four months after my second son, Fernando, was born. My husband didn't show up for the court date and lost custody of his two sons. I think that my sons now believe that he abandoned them and didn't care about them.

When Fernando was 11 he refused to go to school. He was difficult. Fernando was sent to juvenile home because he had gotten caught with a gun. He was with the wrong kind of kids. This is when I knew that somehow I had to find a nicer place to live. I found a new apartment with no scribbling and in a nice neighborhood. I found a job as a packer in a factory. The hours are very long, but I have the responsibility of taking care of my children as they grow up. Here, in our new home and new town far from Magnolin Street, I feel safe and my sons can go out or to school and Fernando is no longer getting into trouble.

—***Catalina Salgado***

Nutrient Needs

As with daily calorie requirements, the specific nutrient needs of young children are different for 3-year-olds than for 6-year-olds. In particular, 5- and 6-year-olds need more protein; more vitamins A, C, and K; and more magnesium and iodine than 3-year-olds (Duyff, Giarratano, & Zuzich, 1995). Young children need protein for growth and maintenance of body tissues. This requirement can be met by drinking 2 or 3 ounces of milk and eating 2 ounces of meat daily. Carbohydrates provide the body with energy and are essential to a healthy diet.

Fats also provide the body with energy and are important in growth and development. Most Americans, including young children, have plenty of fat in their diets. Each gram of fat yields 9 calories—more than twice the 4-calorie intake of protein or carbohydrate. Fats can be found in butter, vegetable oils, meat, and dairy products.

Satisfying the RDAs for most vitamins is not difficult because the amount of vitamins required is small, and each vitamin can be found in many different foods. Vegetables, fruits, and grain products are good sources of vitamins. Minerals are substances that help regulate body processes. Minerals contribute to skeletal and dental structures, blood, muscle, and other body tissues. They also help to regulate a wide variety of metabolic processes, including maintaining the chemical balance of body fluids. Compared with carbohydrates, fats, and proteins, children need relatively small amounts of minerals. Major minerals needed by children are phosphorus, magnesium, sodium, chloride, potassium, and calcium.

Every cell in the child's body uses nutrients that come from the food he or she eats. If a child does not get enough of a particular nutrient or group of nutrients, a deficiency disease may develop. With nutrients such as the B vitamins, folic acid, and mineral zinc, deficiency interferes with growth. Other nutritional deficiencies disturb processes such as blood clotting (vitamin K) or water balance (potassium). Six kinds of nutrients—carbohydrates, fats, proteins, vitamins, minerals, and water—are necessary for good health.

Restricting Certain Foods

Processed sugar should be limited not only because it is a nutritionally empty source of calories but also because it is a major factor in causing dental decay and cavities. Bacteria in the mouth feed on sugar as well as starches, forming a substance that destroys the tooth enamel and creates a cavity.

The connection between too much salt in the diet and high blood pressure, or hypertension, even in young children has been verified in research (Duyff, Giarratano, & Zuzich, 1995). Reducing the amount of salt used in cooking and making sure that the prepared foods served are low in sodium is recommended. Similarly, fats are a dietary concern because a diet too high in fats has been linked to obesity, cardiovascular disease, and some cancers. Thus, foods that have a high saturated fat content, such as hot dogs, luncheon meats, and ice cream, should be served sparingly to children.

Nutritional Deficiencies and Allergies

A nutritional deficiency known as **pica** has been extensively documented in the pediatric literature, as it appears to be a common problem both in the United States and in other cultures. Pica is defined as a pattern of eating nonfood (paper, paint, plaster, string, rags, leaves, and so forth). In the United States, however, pica is more commonly seen in young children with severe or profound mental retardation. A similar phenomenon, involving the eating of clay or soil, however, is an ordinary, often sanctioned activity in many cultures worldwide. These culturally determined forms of pica are not considered a mental disorder. Both here and in other cultures, children exhibiting pica, particularly young children, are at risk for accidental poisoning.

About 10 to 20 percent of U.S. children are believed to show pica as a symptom at some point in their lives. Childhood pica is often described as an ordinary part of exploratory learning or a reflection of a young child's inability to differentiate food from inedible objects. It usually starts at about 2 years and resolves by age 6. Ingestion of lead-containing paint, plaster, and earth can lead to toxic encephalopathy in severe cases, fatigue and weight loss in moderate cases, and learning impairments in mild cases. Approximately 80 percent of severely lead-poisoned children have pica (Allen & Marotz, 1999).

Some conditions can have a variety of causes, including nutritional deficiencies, and **anemia** is such a condition. Children with anemia do not have enough hemoglobin, or red blood cells, to carry oxygen from the lungs to all parts of the body. Hemoglobin is the substance that actually carries the oxygen throughout the body. It can be difficult to detect anemia as some children show few outward signs of the problem. A simple blood test, however, can measure the volume of red blood cells to detect anemia. The most common cause for anemia in childhood is insufficient iron in the diet.

Some young children show **food allergies**. In these instances, the body's immune system reacts to a food substance as if it were an attacking organism. The food is an *allergen*, which is any substance that causes an allergic reaction. The symptoms of food allergies are diverse and range widely in their seriousness. Digestive system responses to food allergies include vomiting, diarrhea, and abdominal pain. Other symptoms may include runny nose, hives, and rashes. Although food allergies may aggravate hyperactive behavior, they do not necessarily cause hyperactivity (Whaley & Wong, 1991). Some children "outgrow" their allergies as they mature, while others develop food allergies only during certain stages of development. Food allergies tend to be inherited, and the most common allergens include cow's milk, eggs, wheat, corn, soy, peanuts, chocolate, citrus fruits, strawberries, fish, and shellfish.

APPLICATIONS:

Meeting the Preschooler's Nutritional Needs

The quest for independence is pervasive during early childhood, and this applies to children's eating habits as well. Because children in early childhood grow at a slow and steady rate (interspersed with growth spurts), their appetite often becomes sporadic. One day they may eat three healthy meals, the next day they may only want jello. Temperament enters into eating patterns as well. The quiet child may play quietly for fairly long periods of time and will obviously expend less energy and eat less than the more active child who is more rambunctious and consequently may have a more hearty appetite.

Variety

Children's tastes in food are highly influenced by the foods they encounter in their environment. Mexican children, for example, may delight in eating hot, peppery foods and thrive on a diet rich in whole grains and beans. Children from the Caribbean may eat many dishes of rice and beans. In Ghana, a special dish relished by many preschoolers is a casserole containing yams, eggs, and palm oil. Dutch children eat sweet, round white breads called *boller* on special occasions. In Iceland, thin pancakes called *ponnukokur* are served with strawberry jam to the delight of many young children. In Japan, *osekihan*, a dish of red beans and rice is a favorite. Navajo youngsters often love mutton and sheepherder's bread. The lesson here is that serving children a variety of foods will help them to develop broader tastes and preferences in foods.

Further, research seems to show that the key to helping children develop tastes for unfamiliar foods is

pica
A pattern of eating nonfood (paper, paint, plaster), which can be seen in young children and individuals with profound or severe mental retardation.

anemia
A nutritional deficiency in which the body lacks sufficient hemoglobin, or red blood cells, to carry oxygen from lungs to all parts of the body.

food allergies
Condition in which the body's immune system reacts to a food substance as if it were an attacking system.

through frequent exposure (Duyff, Giarratano, & Zuzich, 1995). Preschoolers are developing their eating patterns and food preferences, which tend to be quite stable into adulthood (Hakim-Larson, Voelker, Thomas, & Reinstein, 1997). For this reason, it is recommended that young children be exposed to as many new foods as possible (without too much direct pressure from caregivers to eat it).

Snacks and Eating Healthy Foods

Most young children cannot eat enough at mealtimes to provide them with their daily nutrient and caloric needs. And most young children are hungry within three hours of having a meal. Snacks then are an important part of a well-balanced diet. Foods eaten at snack time should provide nutrients that may be missing from other meals. Sugary snacks should be avoided. Many preschoolers, however, are influenced by the preponderance of sugared snacks that are advertised on television. Nancy Signorielli and Jessica Staples (1997) have found there is a positive relation between television watching and the expression of preferences for more unhealthy foods. The more time that preschoolers spent watching television, the more likely they were to prefer less nutritious foods.

Creating a Positive Eating Environment

A calm and pleasant environment at mealtimes is conducive to eating well. Similarly, it has long been recommended that children be encouraged to eat the foods being offered but not forced to do so. The quickest way to teach a child to hate a food is to make her eat it all. Caregivers should avoid using sweets as a reward. "You can have dessert, as soon as you eat your peas." These kinds of comments give special preference for sweet foods and undervalue the nutritious ones. Children should also be allowed to serve themselves; they know how hungry they are.

Thought CHALLENGE

Some children are very cosmopolitan eaters (they will try anything); others are finicky. These patterns are often observed very early in life. Is genetics the reason?

Concept Checks

1. One of the most disheartening facts about injury and death during early childhood is that
   a. there is little parents can do to reduce the likelihood of such an event.
   b. fatal injuries are due to parental neglect
   c. most accidental injuries and deaths could have been prevented.
2. ***True or False:*** Diseases such as polio, whooping cough, and measles are no longer a threat to children; thus immunizations are not necessary.
3. When children do not have enough hemoglobin or red blood cells, to carry oxygen from the lungs to all parts of the body, this condition is known as ________________.
4. Phillip is from the Virgin Islands, and his favorite meal is rice and beans. From what we know about culture and ethnic food preferences, we can conclude that tastes for certain foods are
   a. genetic.
   b. trained by the foods children encounter.
   c. highly influenced by the peer culture.

Health-Related Issues

Before Beginning . . .

After reading this section, you will be able to

- discuss sleep patterns and sleep concerns.
- understand nocturnal enuresis.
- discuss sexuality in early childhood.
- characterize effective components of early childhood sex education.

Sleeping Patterns

As noted in Chapter 5, infants should gradually learn to perfect their own patterns of self-comforting to get to sleep or go back to sleep if they wake up at night. Thumb-sucking, stroking a blanket bed, and rocking are among the ways that a baby calms himself. By the age of 2, most children who have perfected these self-comforting patterns are able to get back to sleep by themselves. In early childhood, however, it is not uncommon to see children exhibiting a whole new self-comforting pattern—that of talking out loud to themselves. These rambling (they sometimes go on for 45 minutes) monologues (to stuffed animals or even the wall) help children to calm down and get ready for sleep as they methodically trace the day's meaningful events or random thoughts that pop into their heads.

Children may talk in their sleep as well. In fact, most people talk in their sleep more than they realize. We cannot remember sleep talking ourselves because usually no one else is awake to hear us. But, perhaps, you have heard your roommate talk in his or her sleep. These "conversations" may consist of a simple guttural grunt or a more complex string of utterances. They sometimes pause between words giving the impression that they are holding actual conversations. Sleep talking in children (and college students) is not related to any mental or emotional disorder and thus it is nothing to worry about.

Other sleep concerns may relate to nightmares and night terrors. The 3- to 4-year-old may begin to have **nightmares**, which are frightening to both the child and the parents. Generally, nightmares occur during deep sleep and may be accompanied by out-of-control crying and thrashing. The calm presence of a parent coming in to gently arouse the child may be enough. The child sees the parent, is comforted, and settles back down again. Nightmares usually appear on the nights that follow a tough and stressful day. Children generally remember the content of their nightmares and will awaken from them quite readily. The occurrence of bad dreams is believed to be due to the fact that the preschooler has a lot of imagination and is more likely to worry. In contrast, **night terrors** are very intense nightmares from which the child does not easily awaken and does not recall. Night terrors result in extreme panic, including a heart rate three times the normal rate. They are fairly common in young children and less common in adults. If the episodes are very bad, caregivers can seek out a sleep expert.

Many parents report that by early childhood their children are sleeping through the night. Actually, these "good sleepers" wake up as many times during the night as "bad sleepers"; however, the good sleepers manage to soothe themselves back to sleep without disturbing their parents. Sometimes, however, children do call out for their parents or climb quietly into their parents' bed. When children are anxious and fearful, they need to be comforted by their parents. Most developmental experts agree that cuddling, some talk about what is bothering him, and a little reassurance are usually enough to enable the child to relax and go back to sleep.

Bed-Wetting

Most children stay dry at night by age 3 or 4. By the time a child is 5 or 6 years old, **nocturnal enuresis**, or bed-wetting, is perceived as a problem. Because of societal pressures, bed-wetting becomes a problem for many children, especially boys. If it continues, the child cannot visit others overnight. He dares not to admit to himself or anyone else that he has this problem. Parents become desperate about such a failure, which they see as their own. Whether hushed up or treated as a reason for punishment, bed-wetting can make the child feel hopeless and helpless. He may say he does not care and may develop all kinds of strategies for hiding his failure each morning.

Causes

Children wet the bed for a great variety of reasons. Some do it to get attention and service, some want to remain a baby, some feel entitled to do whatever they want, and some want to punish their parents. However, almost all children continue wetting the bed once they have lost confidence in their ability to control this function. Reasons may also be physiological, such as an immature bladder that empties frequently, or too-deep sleep (the result of an immature signaling system), and immature sleep patterns (their arousal patterns in light, or REM, sleep are not well developed enough to alert them to get out of bed and stay dry). In some cases, parents and physicians may need to investigate reasons and institute measures. A

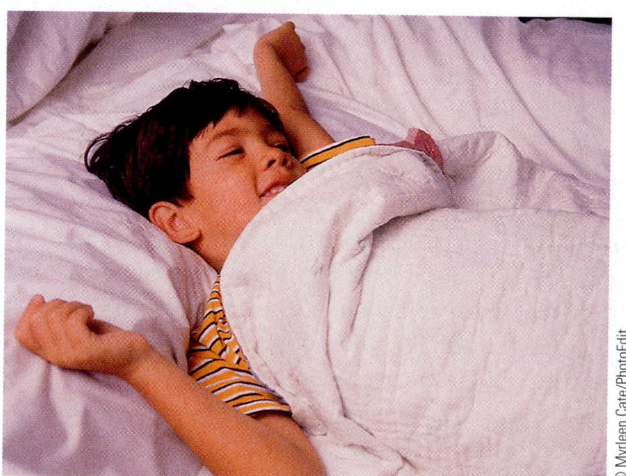

Staying dry at night should become the child's goal, not the caregiver's.

nightmares Frightening dreams that usually occur toward the early morning hours.

night terrors Less common and more intense than nightmares and characterized by a sudden arousal from sleep; accompanied by physiological changes (rapid heart beat; crying); the child usually does not remember dream content.

nocturnal enuresis Repeated bed-wetting during the night.

child's need for autonomy and need for control, however, should not become lost. When this occurs, children see themselves as failures, who are immature, guilty, and hopeless. The damage to their self-image will be greater than the bed-wetting itself.

It is generally advised that the less fuss caregivers make, the sooner the child will regain his control. Some experts suggest that logical consequences be instituted. The logical consequence in this situation is for the child to put his dirty linen in a container to soak, and, if he is older, wash it himself. Under these circumstances, he will realize it is up to him to manage his functions. However he does this, he will not receive special attention, pity, or punishment. Parents should avoid giving the child a lot of liquids before going to bed. In addition, with the child's permission, they may wake him up when they go to bed and tell him to go to the bathroom.

Sexuality

Another health-related issue in early childhood relates to sexuality. All of us are sexual beings, and we have been learning "formally and informally" about sexuality all our lives. Questions and concerns are likely to arise about sexuality throughout the child's developmental years. During the early childhood years, activities such as exploratory sex play and masturbation may be two activities that are natural for children but may be particularly problematic to adults.

Exploratory Sex Play and Masturbation

Around the age of 2 to 3, children may become interested in exploring the differences between boys and girls—a curiosity that is not only normal but healthy. Part of their sexual experimentations relate to children's attempts to firmly establish their gender identity—"I am a boy." "I am a girl." Subsequently, sex role play may ensue to help reinforce their ideas of who they are. Little boys, for example, may play with their penises and girls may even insert things into their vaginas (Bybee, 1998). Children may also be interested in exploring the bodies of other children.

We do not become sexual creatures all at once and childhood experiences, such as sex play, make their contributions in our continuing sexual development. In fact, about half of all adults report having engaged in some sort of sex play as young children, and the actual number may exceed that. That children's involvement in sex activity is not rare may come as a surprise to some.

Three-year-old Jacob and his friend Dominick were found by Jacob's father in the closet. Both boys had pulled their pants down and were touching each others' genitals. The father was most distraught: "I didn't say anything to the boys other than to put their pants on and to go outside and play. But, I watch them constantly and I never let them play together alone."

Although most experts would approve of the father's verbal actions of not making a big deal out of this behavior, they would not approve of his "watchful eye" actions. Clearly, the father is sending a message that this type of behavior is bad and unhealthy as he hovers over his child's every move. The overreaction of adults in these types of situations may actually serve as the catalyst for the development of unhealthy views of sexuality (Bybee, 1998).

Young children also learn sexual information through touching their own bodies. Some children know that touching a penis or clitoris is pleasurable in a way that touching an elbow or knee is not. As a matter of fact, it is not at all unusual for little boys to clutch their scrotums for pleasure and for reassurance. Young children tell us that they know something about their bodies that they enjoy very much. Again, as with sex play, the more matter of fact and nonchalant the adult can be about young children masturbating, the better for everyone. If the child withdraws to masturbate to tease you and others, or masturbates in public, these may be signs of tension in the child's life. If the child masturbates excessively, the child may be under too much pressure from parents. In situations like these, caregivers may need to lighten up on other pressures such as mealtime behavior, toilet training, and so forth.

Proper Names for Body Parts

Young children are curious about everything and delighted to have information. One of the first kinds of sexual information caregivers can teach young children is the names of their body parts. When adults begin identifying eyes, ears, legs, and arms, they can incorporate penis, nipples, testicle, vagina, and anus. Although adults would not think of finding a substitute name for neck or nose, many do substitute other names for sexual organs and body parts. All young children need to know the proper names for body parts; thus, it is not advisable to use babyish euphemisms. Conversations while dressing or bathing offer good opportunities for labeling and discussing body parts. Two-year-olds are satisfied with names. As children become more verbal, they begin to show interest in what these body parts do. By approximately 4 years, children should know what sexual organs do (penis is for urinating and helping make babies).

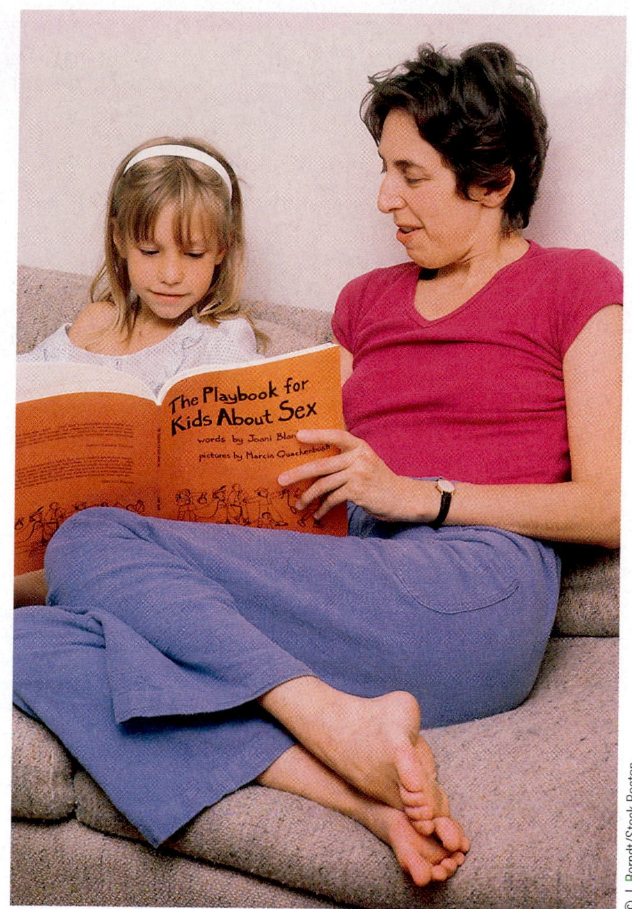

Sex education should begin during the preschool years.

Respecting Their Bodies

Along with this information, young children need to be taught about inappropriate or bad touching. If children have already learned about breasts, vaginas, penises, testicles, and anuses, caregivers can refer to these organs as private parts. Just as caregivers matter-of-factly warn children about looking both ways before crossing a street, caregivers must warn children about protecting themselves. By the time the child is 4, he or she should know these rules:

1. No one has a right to touch your private parts.
2. No one has a right to make you touch their private parts.
3. Being asked to touch another's private parts or having someone touch yours is not a secret you can keep. You must tell your parents if that happens, even if you have promised not to tell or even if you are told something awful will happen to you if you do tell. You must tell.

APPLICATIONS:

Sex Education for Preschoolers

Preschoolers are aware of the anatomical differences between boys and girls and may show a heightened curiosity about their sexuality. Yet, some parents do little to convey information about sex-related matters to young children. Some adults may have hesitant attitudes because they lacked a "formal" sex education from their parents, or, perhaps, it was crudely done. Some may feel uncomfortable about talking about sex with children. Because of this heritage, some adults may avoid helping children in this phase of their development. Developing a sense of comfortableness about sexuality is an important prerequisite to becoming more effective in talking with children about sexuality and sexual issues. (The Self-Insight section provides you with an inventory that will enable you to evaluate your present level of comfort with sexuality.)

Parents as Role Models

Some of the most important lessons children learn about sex are "caught not taught." One of the most potent ways then for young children to learn about sexual matters is by observing their parents, who hopefully serve as models of what love is all about: trust, commitment, companionship, dedication to

Thought CHALLENGE

Why do most parents find it difficult to talk to their children about sexual matters?

Sexuality Comfort Inventory

Please indicate the extent to which the following statements apply to you *in your personal life.*

Section A: For the following statements, please place a check under the response that most closely reflects your opinion.

	Strongly Disagree	Disagree Somewhat	Neutral	Agree Somewhat	Strongly Agree
1. I believe that sex, in general, is positive and adds zest to living.	_____	_____	_____	_____	_____
2. I have a foundation of support for my values, knowledge, and beliefs about sexuality.	_____	_____	_____	_____	_____
3. I am tolerant of sexual beliefs and lifestyles that are different from my own.	_____	_____	_____	_____	_____
4. People have a right to diverse expressions of sexuality if they are non-exploitative.	_____	_____	_____	_____	_____
5. It is OK for a person to choose not to explore his/her sexuality.	_____	_____	_____	_____	_____
6. I consider sexuality to be an integral part of the total human personality.	_____	_____	_____	_____	_____
7. In my opinion, sexuality is an acceptable topic for everyday conversations.	_____	_____	_____	_____	_____
8. Sexuality is a topic worthy of academic study.	_____	_____	_____	_____	_____
9. I view the topic of sexuality as an important part of the school curriculum.	_____	_____	_____	_____	_____

Section B: For the following statements, please circle the number on the continuum that most closely reflects the way you feel about your own sexuality.

10. Basically, the way I feel about my sexuality is: In turmoil 1 2 3 4 5 6 7 At peace

11. The way I feel about my own sexual standards and behavior is: Anxious 1 2 3 4 5 6 7 Secure

spouse and family. Parents who show affection toward each other are teaching their children to associate sexuality with comfort and happiness. The importance of parental modeling behaviors and attitudes has been stressed in the academic literature (Casper, Cuffaro, Schultz, & Silin, 1996). Parents, as the child's first sexuality educators, play a vital role in demonstrating that sex and love develop from a commitment to and caring for each other.

Learning about the Facts of Life

The information that adults present to children should be given at a level that they can understand.

12. When confronted with sexual values different from my own ideal: Offended 1 2 3 4 5 6 7 Tolerant

13. In general, the way I feel when discussing sexual topics with others is: Uncomfortable 1 2 3 4 5 6 7 Comfortable

Section C: For the following statements, please indicate how often you exhibit or experience the described behavior *in your personal life.*

	Almost Never	Seldom	Sometimes	Often	Almost Always
14. I am open with others regarding my personal sexual experiences.	____	____	____	____	____
15. I can discuss sexual topics with ease.	____	____	____	____	____
16. I tend to avoid rather than explore sexual issues.	____	____	____	____	____
17. I avail myself of opportunities to increase my knowledge of sexuality.	____	____	____	____	____
18. I avail myself of opportunities to increase my comfort with sexuality.	____	____	____	____	____

SCORING THE SEXUALITY COMFORT INVENTORY

Section A: Moving from left to right, "strongly disagree" to "strongly agree," assign each column a number from "1 to 5." Then tally the number of checks you have in each column and multiply that number by the corresponding number you have assigned to that column. Then add up your final score from each column. (Note: Missing responses should be counted as a neutral score of "3.")

Section B: Total the numbers you circled. (Note: Missing scores should be counted as a neutral score of "4.")

Section C: Follow the same procedure given for *Section A*, except for number 16. For number 16 only, reverse the assigned numbers "1 to 5" to score "5 to 1."

Total all three sections for your composite score. The highest score possible is 93; the lowest is 18. High scores reflect high comfort with sexuality and low scores reflect low comfort with sexuality. It would seem to follow that the lower your comfort level, the less comfortable you will be talking with children. Now that you have a general idea of how comfortable you are with sexuality, you can begin to work on the areas where you are least comfortable (Hedgepeth & Helmich, 1996).

Adults need to be attuned to teachable moments; giving the child too much information at one time, or offering information that a child may not be ready for, will probably be ignored. When children ask questions, it is suggested that adults begin by asking what the child knows. In this way, adults are able to gauge what kind of information (or misinformation) children have and what they are curious about knowing. When is the best time to begin a child's sex education? Most experts say that sex education should begin in early childhood. In Sweden, with lessons in sex education beginning in preschool and continuing through high school, teachers work in cooperation with parents in helping children learn more about

Cultural Variations

Sex Education

Some cultures, such as Sweden, far surpass the United States in transmission of sex-related knowledge and attitudes. Sex education in the United States is controversial, and attitudes toward it have been characterized as generally reticent; the Swedes, however, generally accept sex as a basic part of life and candidly disseminate information about sex.

Controversy in the United States centers on who should teach sex education, what should be taught, and when it should be taught. Some believe that sex education is the responsibility of parents and should be taught in the home; others deem it is better to have it taught in the schools by professional, knowledgeable teachers. There are debates about whether sexual education should just reflect biological factors or whether it should incorporate spiritual, moral, or pleasure aspects as well. Finally, some believe that sex education should make its debut in middle school, whereas others believe earlier training is advisable. In Sweden, it is believed that sex education is a shared responsibility between parents and school; all aspects of sex—including biological and moral information—should be taught; and the best time to begin is in early childhood.

In Sweden, sex education programs begin in preschool and extend through secondary school (Miettinen, 1999). And there are several good reasons for beginning sex education in the early childhood years. By beginning early, children accept adults (both teachers and parents) as natural resources for sex education. Correct knowledge of sex at an early age helps prevent anxiety and equips growing children with a healthy and positive attitude toward their bodies and their adult sex roles. Moreover, preschoolers wonder about many things, including death, God, and where babies come from, and this is the time when questions about all these matters begin. If young children can ask questions about sex as they need, then sexuality becomes a normal and natural part of their lives.

When children are not properly informed about sex, they depend on information (more often misinformation) received from their friends when they are older. As one adult expressed it, "Everything I ever learned about sex was during summer camp when I was 9 years old." Unfortunately, adults cannot control what children hear, when they hear it, and how they interpret it. In today's society, then, it is vital that children learn correct information about sex before they hear it from friends or make assumptions based upon television and media portrayals of sex. Further, studies today show that sexual activity in the United States is starting at a much earlier age. Approximately 30 percent of our ninth-graders have engaged in sexual intercourse. Thus, it seems clear that we need to prepare our children well in advance of the time at which they may begin to become sexually active. The success of Sweden's early and thorough dissemination of material is reflected by the teenage preg-

nancy rate, which is less than half that of the United States (Watkins & Dahlin, 1997).

Although the Swedish Board of Education provides a handbook on sex instruction for teachers from preschool to secondary school, the first principle of Sweden's program is to provide an atmosphere in which informal sex education becomes a normal part of the educational curricula. Sex education then does not take place in a vacuum. It is not accomplished through one single event, or a string of isolated, unrelated events. As such, when questions arise about sex-related matters or natural yet pertinent events come up, time is taken to discuss them and learn. While I was observing a third-grade class in Stockholm, for example, one young boy announced as he entered the class that there was a new baby girl in his home, which resulted in an impromptu sex-education discussion/lesson.

All young people should receive an exemplary sex education. Ideally, educating children about sex can have its greatest effect through the cooperative efforts of both home and school. And Sweden, with its emphasis on sexual enlightenment and guidance for all ages and its formal and informal approach to helping children learn about sexuality, stands at the forefront of successful school programs.

this important aspect of their development (see Cultural Variations).

The key to sex education is listening as well as talking. Children need to hear that sexuality is a normal part of life. They should know that if they have questions their parents are there to answer them. At every age, questions change and the answers given by the parents should be tailored to the child's understanding. If a 4-year-old asks about AIDS, for example, telling her that it is a very serious illness and reassuring her that she or her parents will not get it is appropriate. At around age 7, children are able to understand more complex information about how AIDS is transmitted and prevented.

Well-Rounded Sexuality

Scholars suggest that both parents discuss sexual matters with their children (Watkins & Dahlin, 1997). The old-fashioned way was for mothers to discuss sex with their daughters and fathers to do so with their sons. By conducting discussions together, children get a more well-rounded view of sexuality. Discussing sex in early childhood gives parents an opportunity to establish a pattern of relaxed, open communication with their children that will continue into later periods of childhood. Equally important, it gives parents the time to communicate that sex is strongly related to love, responsibility, and commitment.

Concept Checks

1. ***True or False:*** Nightmares generally occur when young children have had a very stressful day.
2. Generally, sound advice for dealing with bed-wetting is to
   a. follow a logical consequence approach.
   b. show special attention and pity to the child to help his or her self-esteem.
   c. ignore it and it will go away.
3. Masturbation in young children is considered
   a. a sign of tension and stress.
   b. defiance against their parents.
   c. normal and healthy.
4. Sex education for young children should
   a. start early with telling children the facts of life commensurate with age and level of understanding.
   b. begin in early adolescence when children are older and more capable of understanding.
   c. be left to professional teachers who have more information than do parents.

Reviewing Key Points

Physical Transformations

- Many of young children's "new skills" are a result of the growing complexity of the brain. Increased myelination in the frontal lobes, visual and motor cortex, and corpus callosum and dendrite branching are responsible in part for sharpening of motor skills, problem solving, and overall intelligence in early childhood.
- Children in early childhood lose their babyish appearance by developing long legs and flat stomachs. Growth during the preschool years is slow and steady interspersed with minigrowth spurts. Increasing muscle strength enables children to become more agile and coordinated.
- Nutrition is a key factor in children's growth and development exemplified by the fact that children from poor families with inadequate diets are shorter than children from more advantaged families who receive proper nutritional care.
- Two hormones affecting children's growth are the growth hormone (GH), which stimulates the rapid growth and development of body cells, and thyroid-stimulating hormone (TSH), which is responsible for achieving optimal height. Deprivation dwarfism is a growth-related disorder that interferes with the production of the growth hormone. It is believed to be caused by children being exposed to an impoverished affective environment.

Motor Development

- Body build is basically genetically determined as exemplified in different body structures found in various cultures and ethnic groups. There appear to be sex differences as well with girls being slightly shorter and lighter than boys. Differences in strength appear at around the age of 6, with boys becoming stronger than girls. Body image is the child's awareness of her body, its parts, and its movement capacities. Assessing children's body image skills generally involves analyzing a child's drawing of a person, knowledge of body parts, and left–right discriminations.
- Gross motor skills involving the large muscles in arms and legs develop before fine motor skills involving small muscles in hands and fingers. As such, children are more adept at activities such as running and jumping before they are able to color, cut, and paste.
- The Denver II Developmental Screening Test is designed to detect developmental normalcy in gross and fine motor development as well as personal–social and language development. Early diagnosis of developmental delays increase opportunities for effective therapy.
- Genetics play a role in motor development, but the child's environment must supply practice with motor activities for children to develop appropriate skills. Although basic motor skills appear to be more related to maturation, more complex motor skills are advanced through skill training. The emphasis of skill-training programs should be on fun and the use of positive reinforcement and be age related.

Health Factors in Early Childhood

- Unintentional injuries are injuries that could have been foreseen and possibly prevented. Many injuries can be prevented by providing a developmentally appropriate environment, being aware of possible hazards in the environment, working to eliminate or minimize them, providing alert adult supervision, and teaching children about safety.
- Infectious illnesses follow a similar pattern: incubation period, prodromal stage, and acute stage. Infections transmitted by respiratory droplets include the common cold, influenza, strep throat, chicken pox, and Hib disease. Infections transmitted by direct contact include head lice, conjunctivitis, and ringworm. Immunization prevents children from becoming ill with certain diseases.
- Age-, weight-, and height-related measures can be used to determine a young child's daily calorie needs. A child's energy needs are also linked to his or her level of activity. Sugar, fat, and salt should be offered sparingly to young children. Preschoolers should have at least four servings each day of bread, cereal, rice, and pasta. They should have two servings a day of fruits and meats or meat alternates and three servings a day of vegetables and milk or milk products.
- Pica, an eating problem in which children eat nonnutritive substances, such as dirt or paint, can seriously affect their health. A common nutritional deficiency in children in the United States is iron-deficiency anemia.
- Meals and snacks for preschoolers should contain a variety of foods. Encouraging new foods and relaxed, stress-free meals are important as eating

patterns are established in early childhood. New foods should be introduced one at a time and served with familiar foods.

Health-Related Issues

- Children's sleeping patterns are regular. Nightmares (an unpleasant dream from which the child is awakened rather easily and quite often can tell adults about the dream) and night terrors (less common, in which the child is in an extreme anxiety state, does not remember the dream, and is hard to awaken and calm) may occur during early childhood.
- Nocturnal enuresis may be caused by psychological factors (stress, for example) or physical factors (immature bladder). Developmental experts advise that this should be considered the child's problem, and adults should avoid bringing undue attention to the problem.
- Preschoolers are curious about many things, including their own bodies and where babies come from. A consistently reported finding is that sex education should begin during the preschool years.
- During early childhood, children learn a great deal about sexuality from their parents who serve as role models. In this sense, sex education is "caught not taught" by parents who communicate to the child through their actions a sense of love and commitment. It is generally advised that adults ask children what they know and then they can fill in missing information and correct the child's misinformation.

Answers to Concept Checks

Physical Transformations

1. imagination
2. torso; spine
3. growth hormone

Motor Development

1. throwing, jumping, going up and down ladders; writing cutting, and drawing
2. b
3. gross motor; riding a bike
4. a

Health Factors in Early Childhood

1. c
2. false
3. anemia
4. b

Health-Related Issues

1. true
2. a
3. c
4. a

Key Terms

anemia
Broca's area
cerebellum
corpus callosum
deprivation dwarfism
fine motor development
food allergies
gross motor development
growth hormone (GH)
lateralization
myelination
nightmares
night terrors
nocturnal enuresis
perceptual-motor movements
pica
thyroid-stimulating hormone
visual cortex
Wernicke's area

InfoTrac College Edition

For additional readings, explore InfoTrac College Edition, your online library. Go to **http://www.infotrac-college.com/wadsworth** and use the passcode that came on the card with your book. Try these search terms: child nutrition, child health, nightmares and night terrors, enuresis.

Child Development CD-ROM

Go to the Wadsworth Child Development CD-ROM for further study of the concepts in this chapter. The CD-ROM also includes quizzes and additional activities to expand your learning]experience.

CHAPTER NINE

Cognitive Development: *Early Childhood*

CHAPTER OUTLINE

The Young Child's Thinking Skills
- Piaget's Preoperational Thinker
- Vygotsky's Sociocultural Theory
- Information-Processing Theory
- The Young Child's Theory of Mind
- Applications: Supporting the Child's Developing Theory of Mind

Language Development
- The New "Second Word"
- Multiple-Word Utterances
- Speech and Hearing Problems
- Applications: Learning a Second Language

Early Education
- Child Care
- School Readiness
- Reading Readiness
- Learning and Television and Videos
- Applications: Helping Children Make a Successful Adjustment to School

Reviewing Key Points

On making cookies:

3-year-old: Well, you bake them and eat them.

4-year-old: Add three cups of butter, two lumps of sugar, and one cup of flour. Knead it up. Get it in a pan. Bake it. Set it up to 30. Take it out and it will be cookies.

On making pork chops:

6-year-old: You need some chops that are enough to fill up your pan, fresh salt, fresh pepper, fresh flour, and one ball of salad lettuce. Put chops in the bag and shake them for an hour, and the flour too. Put them in a skillet on the biggest black circle on the roof of your stove. Cook them for plenty of time. Fringe up the lettuce in little heaps in all bowls. Add fresh salt and pepper to chops on stove. But stoves really is dangerous and you shouldn't go near one till you get married.

As children progress through the early childhood period, their thinking, as exemplified in these young children's recipes, becomes more sophisticated and organized. The 3-year-old describes two major actions for making cookies;

the 4-year-old adds several more dimensions; and the 6-year-old shares a special recipe for making pork chops along with precautions about dangerous stoves. What is noteworthy is that the change in children's thinking as they get older is not one of generality but of elaboration. During the preschool years, children are constantly expanding their knowledge about their physical and social world—a process that persists throughout adulthood.

Cognitively, preschoolers learn increasingly to represent their world mentally by means of memories, imagery, language, or symbols. They move from the action-oriented thinking predominant in the infancy period to thinking based on mental representation. Their imaginations soar as one can see in their pretend play of bringing a bottle to a crying doll or making car sounds as they push a block of wood across the floor.

Young children, curious little individuals that they are, constantly pursue a clearer understanding of their world, with asking "why" as their chief *modus operandi*. The ability to think—to generate ideas, to fantasize, to understand cause and effect, to solve problems—progressively matures during early childhood. In this chapter, we first look at the ideas of Piaget, Vygotsky, and information-processing theorists. Their theories concerning young children's thinking help illuminate the preschool years in all their cognitive complexity.

The qualitative changes we observe in preschooler's thinking skills are signaled by several achievements; one is clearly language development, which dominates this period. The child from 2 to 6 years of age learns, on average, an astounding five to nine words every day. With this new arsenal of ever-increasing vocabulary words, language continually becomes more sophisticated and complex, as you will discover in reading the next section of this chapter.

Many concerned parents and educators share a commitment to the child's academic future, and, to many educational scholars, becoming a good reader enters heavily into the academic success equation. There are few more attractive icons than the image of a parent sharing a picture book with a young preschooler. Shared book reading speaks of love, the importance of the family unit, and to educational commitment. It is, to use a phrase from Jerome Kagan (1996), a very "pleasing idea." But as you shall see in the concluding section, in addition to reading readiness, there are many other important ingredients that need to come together for children to be "school ready."

preoperational stage
Ages 2 to 7; thinking is perception bound—that is, children focus on what strikes them first perceptually and error accordingly.

The Young Child's Thinking Skills

Before Beginning . . .

After reading this section, you will be able to

- characterize the nature of Piaget's concept of preoperational thinking skills, with particular emphasis on representational skills.
- grasp the main components of the theories of Fischer and Case.
- see the learning implications of Vygotsky's theory.
- understand the changing nature of children's memory skills.
- analyze children's "theory of mind" abilities.

Piaget's Preoperational Thinker

The roots of our knowledge about children's cognitive development during the preschool years continue to be influenced by Jean Piaget's theory. Recall from Chapters 1 and 6 that Piaget believed children's cognitive development is characterized by abrupt shifts in thinking at each stage of cognitive development: sensorimotor (birth to 2 years); preoperational (2 to 7 years); concrete operational (7 to 11 years); and formal (11+ years). During the **preoperational stage**, a child evolves from functioning primarily in a sensorimotor mode, where her thinking is through actions, into functioning increasingly in a conceptual and representation mode. This means that the child becomes able increasingly to represent events in her mind and becomes less dependent on her direct actions for solving problems.

Preoperational thinking is *perception bound*. That is, preschoolers tend to organize their thinking around the perceptual appearance of things (Piaget, 1970). Do you remember, as a preschooler, that you were infinitely richer when you were holding six pennies rather than one measly dime? If it *looks* like there is more money, then you must have more money. A single, isolated cognition of this sort is the hallmark of the preoperational child's thinking.

The genius of Piaget is never more apparent than in his analysis of young children's ways of thinking. Piaget tried to understand not only what children were saying but why they were saying it. After interviewing hundreds of children at the Maison des Petits in

Geneva, he discovered many things about preoperational thinkers (Piaget, 1952), including impediments to thinking and the importance of representation in children's thinking.

Impediments to Logical Thinking

"Preoperational" does not suggest an incomplete stage of development. When Piaget used the term **operation**, he meant an action or mental representation carried out through logical thinking. Preoperational thinkers, then, are *prelogical thinkers*. The main impediments to logical thinking are perceptual centration, irreversibility, egocentrism, animism, and transductive reasoning.

Perceptual Centration

> Rosio, here are two tall glasses and one short glass. I want you to fill the second tall glass with this dark liquid, so that it has the same amount of liquid as the one in the first tall glass. (Rosio does so and is happy that there is the same amount in both tall glasses.) I am going to pour the liquid in this tall glass into the short glass (see Figure 9.1). Now, is there the same amount of liquid in the short glass as in the other short glass? Rosio, focusing on the volume level line, answers, "No, there is more liquid in the tall glass."

Piaget's beaker problem is a good example of **perceptual centration**, the tendency to attend to only one attribute of what one observes and to ignore others. Preoperational thinkers seem unable to "explore" all aspects of the stimulus; they tend to center their attention on what strikes them first and most vividly. As a result of not being able to take in multiple dimensions, such as the size and shape of the beakers, they tend to make perceptual errors. For example, Rosio's perceptual attention is drawn to the volume level line of the liquid in the beaker experiment. He then says that the tall glass contains more because the liquid level is higher; another child may say that the short glass contains more because it is wider.

Kurt Fischer and his colleagues (Fischer & Farrar, 1988; Rose & Fischer, 1998) note that a critical change in reasoning occurs between the ages of 6 and 7. At this age, children begin to be able to focus on more than one critical dimension in a problem-solving situation. These thinking changes can be illustrated by asking 5-year-old Leontyne "If you had 5 dogs and 2 cats, would you have more dogs or more animals?" Leontyne, as well as most 5-year-olds, will say "more dogs," because she cannot simultaneously view an object as both a dog and an animal. In contrast, 6-year-old Nicolas will answer the same class-inclusion question by saying "more animals," demonstrating that he can simultaneously view an object as a dog and an animal. Thus, children under 6 are more limited in the maximum number of dimensions they can represent. In contrast, 6-year-olds can solve this problem because they can form representations involving multiple dimensions.

Irreversibility The second impediment to logical thinking is **irreversibility**, an inability to reverse an operation. Referring back to the beaker problem, young children cannot mentally pour the water from the tall, thin glass back into the short, shallow glass. Relatedly, they do not understand the logic behind simple mathematic subtraction (reversal) problems such as $4 + 5 = 9; 9 - 5 = 4$.

Egocentrism and Animism According to Piaget, preoperational children are quite **egocentric** in their thinking; they are self-centered cognitively. They look

First, you show a preschool child two tall glasses with exactly the same amount of water in each.

Then the child watches you pour the water from one of the glasses into a third, wide glass.

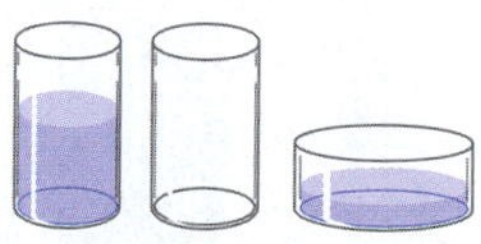

Finally, you ask the child, "Is there more water in the wide glass than in the (remaining) tall glass, or less, or just as much?"

A child who lacks reversibility (is non-conserving) in thinking about liquids says either, "The tall glass has more," or "The wide glass has more." She is fooled by its appearance.

FIGURE 9.1 *Piaget's Conservation of Liquid Problem*

operations To Piaget, mental representations carried out through logical thinking.

perceptual centration The tendency to attend to only one attribute of what one observes and to ignore others.

irreversibility An impediment to logical thinking that is the inability to reverse an operation cognitively.

egocentrism The tendency for young children to view the world from their own perspective while failing to recognize that others may have different points of view.

at the world from their own perspective and fail to realize that there are other perspectives. This egocentrism reveals itself in how young children act, think, and feel. This is delightfully demonstrated in a 4-year-old's telephone conversation with his grandfather:

> Grandfather: How old will you be?
> John: Dis many. (Holding up four fingers)
> Grandfather: Huh?
> John: Dis many. (Again holding up four fingers)
> Grandfather: How many is 'at?
> John: Four.
> John: I'm gonna change ears, okay?
> Grandfather: Okay.
> John: I'm back. I had ta change ears.
> Grandfather: Okay. Was one of your ears gettin' tired?
> John: Yeah. This one (points to his left ear). (Warren & Tate, 1992, pp. 259–260)

Piaget's demonstration of egocentrism involves a problem known as the three-mountain task, shown in Figure 9.2 (Piaget & Inhelder, 1969). In this experiment, the child first walks around the model of the mountains in order to become familiar with what the mountains look like from different perspectives. The child then stands on one side of the table on which the mountains are placed. A doll is placed at various positions around the three mountains and the child is asked to tell the experimenter how the mountains would appear to the doll at each position. From a collection of photos, children tend to choose the picture that reflects their own perspective rather than the doll's.

FIGURE 9.2 ***Piaget's Three Mountains Problem***

According to Piaget's findings, children in the preoperational stage cannot easily assume another person's perspective. Often, they respond that someone viewing the mountain from a different spot would see exactly what they see.

animistic thinking According to Piaget, the tendency of young children to assume that nonliving objects like the sun or the wind have thoughts, motives, or feelings.

From this experiment and similar experiments, Piaget (1928) concluded several things about egocentric thought in early childhood. Preschoolers, for example, think that natural events serve their own needs: "It's dark because I want to go to sleep." They are the *raison d'être* of the universe. The egocentrism of these young children leads them to assume that everyone thinks as they do and that the whole world shares their feelings and desires.

I recently visited the child-care center at a college and observed a group of 4-year-olds who were making up a new game with their own rules. Malcolm asked, "Do you want to play?"

"Sure."

Shortly after I was situated in their little circle, Malcolm rather impatiently said, "Go ahead, it's your turn." Apparently, no explanation of the rules or even what game they were playing would be forthcoming—and why should there be when young children think that everyone knows what they know.

This sense of oneness with the world leads naturally to their assumptions of magic omnipotence. The world is not only created for them, but they can control it. The sun and the moon must follow them when they go for a walk; they can make it snow by frantically dancing around in circles. They do not feel that they need to justify their own statements.

Piaget also asserted that younger preoperational children engage in **animistic thinking**; that is, they assume that inanimate objects such as the sun or the wind have the properties of living things. In particular, these objects have motives, feelings, and intentions that affect their behavior. This way of thinking is illustrated in an excerpt from Piaget's (1969) interview with Kenn, age 7:

> Interviewer: Is water alive?
> Kenn: Yes.
> Interviewer: Why?
> Kenn: It moves.
> Interviewer: Is fire alive?
> Kenn: Yes. It gives light.
> Interviewer: Is the sun alive?
> Kenn: Yes. It gives light.

When Kenn is asked if a candle is alive, he responds, "Yes and no." It is alive when it is giving light, but it is not alive when it is not giving light. For a preschooler, something appears to be alive if it displays any type of action.

Transductive Reasoning

> A recent hurricane produced a massive power failure that blacked out most of upstate New York. The *New York Times* reported a story about a 5-year-old boy who ran his tricycle into an electric pole at the exact moment of the power failure. The little boy saw the lights go out and believed that he caused the blackout. He was fully expecting to be punished for having broken the power system.

This example nicely captures the "logically illogical" thinking of preoperational thinkers. Piaget labels this type of thinking as **transductive reasoning**, in which the child reasons from one particular instance to another, linking two events that occur close together in a cause-and-effect fashion (Ginsburg & Opper, 1988). Preoperational thinkers are capable of rudimentary cause-and-effect understanding, but their grasp of this concept is elementary.

Representation

All too often, children's preoperational thinking is described in terms of a dreary litany of their wrong answers to concrete-operational tests. There are, however, numerous cognitive accomplishments during this period along with other cognitive features that are destined for development during early childhood, and these need to be highlighted as well. Clearly, one such preoperational skill is **representation**—the ability to represent objects mentally. Several kinds of representation are apparent in children: deferred imitation, symbolic play, and spoken language. Each is a form of representation in the sense that something other than objects and events is used to represent objects and events.

Deferred Imitation With the ability to represent objects and events mentally comes deferred imitation, the ability to repeat the behavior of a model that is no longer present. A well-known example of deferred imitation involves a Piaget's (1952) description of his daughter Jacqueline when she was 2:

> Jacqueline had a visit from a little boy . . . whom she used to see from time to time, and who, in the course of the afternoon, got into a terrible temper. He screamed as he tried to get out of a playpen and pushed it backward, stamping his feet. Jacqueline stood watching him in amazement, never having witnessed such a scene before. The next day, she herself screamed in her playpen and tried to move it, stamping her foot lightly several times in succession. (p. 63)

Jacqueline's internalization of the boy's behavior was quite apparent because she produced the event quite accurately a day later.

Symbolic Play Mental representation also ushers in the beginnings of **symbolic**, or pretend, **play**—a form of self-expression with only self as the intended audience. Symbolic play comes from separating behaviors and objects from their actual use and using them for play. For instance, a child eats dinner at dinnertime, in the kitchen, and usually when hungry. However, when pretending to eat dinner, a child can do so at another time and another place.

Spoken Language The single most evident development during the preoperational period is the development of spoken language. According to Piaget, during the sensorimotor period the child had to carry out actions to "think"; movement produced thought. With the development of spoken language, thinking can occur, in part, through representations of actions rather than actions alone. The ability to use words and to understand their symbolic meanings gives children's surroundings a whole new meaning and significance. Moreover, it enables children to engage in socialized verbal interchange with others. Table 9.1 summarizes the characteristics of a preschooler's preoperational thought.

Evaluating Piaget's Theory

New research findings do not support Piaget's portrayal of young children as being as animistic, intuitive, illogical, or egocentric as he suggested (Bird-David, 1999; Guthrie, 2000). In conducting his research on animism, Piaget often asked children if objects such as the sun, moon, stones, or water could feel pain or heat. Children most often responded that stones would not feel pain "because they are hard," but they could feel heat from fire "because they would get burnt." However, current findings suggest that young children's decisions about what is alive and what is not reflect a general uncertainty about the precise properties of many objects rather than judgment of animateness (Flavell, Green,

Thought **CHALLENGE**
How will knowing these typical features of young children's thinking enable adults to work more effectively with them?

transductive reasoning Preoperational thinkers' tendency to reason from one particular instance to another particular instance.

representation The understanding that an object in a model stands for a corresponding object in a real-life setting.

symbolic play Pretend play; substituting imaginary situations for real ones.

TABLE 9.1

Characteristics of Preschoolers' Preoperational Thinking

Thinking Patterns	Description	Example
Perception-bound thinking	Preschoolers solve problems based on what first strikes them vividly and perceptually.	When a mother cuts her child's meat into small pieces, the child comments, "Now you have given me much more to eat."
Perceptual centration	Preoperational thinkers can only perceive and thus reason about one dimension of a situation at a time.	In the beaker problem, children notice the volume level line of the liquid but do not take into consideration the size and shape of the beakers.
Egocentrism	Preschoolers believe that others think, feel, and perceive the same as they do.	The preschooler is drawing a picture in the den and asks her mother, who is in the kitchen, if she likes her drawing. The child is unable to realize that her mother cannot see her drawing.
Animism	Preschoolers believe inanimate objects have feelings.	The child announces that her doll is sleepy and needs to go to bed.
Transductive reasoning	Preschoolers reason from event to event rather than in a more logical fashion.	Teacher: Why does it get dark at night? Child: So we can go to sleep.

& Flavell, 1998). Thus, when Piaget questioned children about objects with which they had minimal experience, such as the sun and the moon, they might have become confused because of their unfamiliarity with the objects. Research suggests that this is the case. For example, when 3-, 4-, and 5-year-olds were asked whether more familiar animate objects (such as, a rabbit or a little girl) and inanimate objects (windup toy and a pile of colored blocks) could feel pain, or runaway from a fire, or if they were alive, only 3-year-olds showed a "general uncertainty about the precise properties of many objects, regardless of object type" (Bullock, 1985, p. 224). Ninety-four percent of the 4-year-olds and 98 percent of the 5-year-olds answered correctly. Other researchers have reached similar conclusions (Gelman, 1998). Research has failed to find any significant degree of animism in young children (Bullock & Lutkenhaus, 1990).

Piaget's pioneering work also ignored possible cultural variables that can play a crucial role in the development of animistic thinking. Some investigators of animism within non-Western cultures found that children drew sharp distinctions among the various denotations and connotations of the concept of being "alive." In a classic study of the Hopi Indians, Wayne Dennis (1943) found that children believe such things as rivers, fire, and wind are "alive" but not in the sense in which people are alive. The Hopi language, in fact, possesses specific words that sharply distinguish this difference in meaning. In addition, Gustave Jahoda (1958, 2000), working in West Africa, found no instances of attributing life or consciousness to inanimate objects by children.

Similarly, more recent research finds children to be less egocentric than Piaget concluded. When Piaget's three-mountain experiment was changed to include familiar items and children were given the chance to report what the doll saw by methods other than selecting a picture, even 4-year-olds passed the test with flying colors. To illustrate, when the mountains contained a lake with a boat, a house, and a cow, and children were asked to rotate an actual model of the mountains rather than pick a picture out of a collection of photos, they had little difficulty imagining what things look like from another person's perspective (Newcombe & Huttenlocher, 2000).

Further, Margaret Donaldson (1996) found that preschoolers can take the perspective of others if the problems presented to them are meaningful and understandable. Studies of children's emotional development also reveal that many preschoolers display empathy and awareness of how other people feel. It seems fair to conclude that young children have the capacity to be nonegocentric, depending upon the demands of the situation. When the task is made easier, enabling young children to express their understanding, they are able to imagine spatial perspectives other than their own.

Challenges to Piaget's Theory

In commenting on his scientific contributions, Piaget (1976) remarked that he laid down only a rough sketch of human development and that research would certainly identify the parts missing from the sketch, the parts that needed to be modified, and the parts that needed to be discarded. That task has been taken over by the neo-Piagetian theorists. Basically, they have challenged Piaget's claim that clearly defined *cognitive structures* associated with distinct stages play a major role in determining children's problem-solving abilities.

According to Piaget, similar understandings tend to be acquired at about the same age across a wide variety of learning tasks because they are based on the same underlying cognitive structures. If Piaget were correct, neo-Piagetian theorists argue, we should find a consistency in a child's performance on a variety of tasks at each of the four stages of cognitive development (see Chapter 1 for a summary table of these stages). There is, however, a good deal of evidence of uneven performance on different tasks and even on the same task in all stages.

For example, children generally achieve an understanding of one type of transformation, such as liquids, before they understand another, such as mass. While they are able to solve the beaker problem (the amount of liquid is the same in the tall and short beakers), they cannot successfully solve the clay problem. In this problem, children first identify that the two round balls of clay are of equal size and weight. When one of these balls is flattened, children insist that the round one now weighs more. Because these problems require the same logical operations, children, according to Piaget's theory, should be able to perform both of these tasks. However, there appears to be little correspondence between the level of understanding exhibited by children at one level and the developmental level they display at another level. To address these inconsistencies in children's thinking, Robbie Case and Kurt Fischer have studied children's cognitive development from a more domain-, task-, and context-specific perspective.

Kurt Fischer (1980, 1994), agrees that cognitive development is an action-based, self-regulating, and constructive process. In contrast to Piaget, Fischer argues that there is no "generalized competence" or cognitive structure, and cognitive development must be described for each skill and in each different context (Rose & Fischer, 1998). For example, when a child helps to set the table by counting out four forks and placing each by a plate, she is exhibiting a *specific numerical skill* that she has constructed *in a particular context*. This skill will undoubtedly contribute to her developing a more general and abstract set of mathematical skills, but it does not, in itself, imply a generalized cognitive structure as Piaget would maintain. It is only after time that children will eventually coordinate several context-specific skills into a general logical principle.

Fischer's theory also emphasizes how environmental support, such as a helpful parent, influences cognitive development. For example, if the child is engaging in dramatic play pretending to be a doctor, the parent may show the child an object such as a stethoscope and explain how it works or demonstrate how to "bandage" a wound thus providing environmental support. In contrast, if merely silently leaving the objects in front of the child, this would represent a low level of environmental support. Fischer has found that children who receive high levels of environmental support function at higher levels of cognitive competence.

Robbie Case (1985, 1996), like Piaget, maintains that children's thinking unfolds in a stagelike fashion. However, this stagelike progression is not due to limiting cognitive structures as Piaget maintained. The reason for this process, in Case's view, is that children's thinking is subject to what he calls "a limited executive processing space" (Case, 1999), his term for active, temporary, conscious memory. **Executive processing space** refers to the maximum number of schemes children can activate at any one time. According to Case, the functional capacity of this executive processing space increases as children move from laborious execution of a skill to execution that is smooth and without deliberation.

For example, remember when you were just learning how to drive? There were a lot of things for you to remember, and, you had to constantly and perhaps laboriously think about what you were doing. Thinking back, could you imagine talking on a cell phone while you were taking your driver's license road test? Now, however, you can drive on an internalized, almost automatic pilot. Case contends that as each operation is executed more efficiently, executive processing space is freed for additional operations. This constraint on executive processing space guarantees that children's cognitive development will proceed at a relatively slow pace through identifiable stages.

executive processing space Refers to the maximum number of schemes children can activate at any one time.

Vygotsky's Sociocultural Theory

Lev Vygotsky, a contemporary of Piaget, criticized the lack of cultural influences on children's cognitive development in Piaget's theory and made this a central aspect of his theory (Vygotsky, 1978). Recall from Chapter 1 that Vygotsky's *sociocultural theory* stresses that all cognitive activities reflect the cultural context in which the child lives. He argues that each culture provides its children with the tools that will enable them to make an optimal adjustment to their culture. For example, cognitive skills of how to track and kill a lion may be important for children in South Africa who are living in nomadic tribes, whereas computer skills may be important for children living in the urban United States.

Social Interactions

Vygotsky maintains that children's cognitive skills and competencies result from interaction between them and more knowledgeable and mature members of society, such as caregivers. Although he sees children as active, constructive beings, he views their development as a socially mediated process. Parents play a large part in children's "apprenticeship in thinking." As part of this apprenticeship, parents give children formal (explicit teaching of rules) and informal (modeling other family members) instruction and support in helping them acquire cognitive skills.

Language and Thought

egocentric speech Piaget's term for self-talk in children; it plays no functional role in cognitive development and disappears at the end of the preoperational stage.

private speech Vygotsky's term for children's self-talk; a precursor to inner speech.

inner speech Self-guiding and self-directing speech; an important cognitive tool for intellectual growth according to Vygotsky's thinking.

Piaget (1955) suggested that the rudiments of intelligence evolve before language develops; that is, cognitive development comes first, which in turn, makes language development possible. To Piaget, then, language was not the cause of intellectual advancement but merely a tool used in operational thinking. As such, Piaget argued that language is a reflection of cognition and not independent from cognition or a shaper of it.

Vygotsky (1962) disagreed with Piaget. He believed that language ability affects almost every aspect of the child's thought. To him, language is a potent instrument in structuring thought and regulating cognitive behavior. Therefore, thinking would not be possible without language. Vygotsky emphasized that when children are young, speech does not involve thought (babbling), and thought does not involve speech (reaching, grasping). However, at some point in the maturational cycle (generally around age 2), speech and thought combine forces. When this occurs, they begin to mutually influence one another: thought takes on some verbal characteristics and speech becomes rational as the expressive outlets for thought. As Vygotsky (1962) wrote, "Speech begins to serve intellect and thoughts begin to be spoken" (p. 43). Whereas Piaget felt that language was not necessary for thinking, Vygotsky saw it as constantly interacting with thought.

Egocentric versus Private Speech

> Four-year-old Darin is playing in his sandbox making sandcastles. During his sand play, Darin talks and mumbles to himself. "I got a new shovel for my birthday. A red one. I can make a bigger castle . . . Got to get some more water. . . ."

To Piaget (1962), this **egocentric speech** is nothing more than an example of children's general egocentrism during the preoperational stage. According to Piaget, egocentric speech plays no functional role in cognitive development but is merely symptomatic of ongoing mental activity, and it disappears at the end of the preoperational period of thinking.

Vygotsky rejected Piaget's notions that egocentric speech was mere childish ramblings serving no cognitive or communicative function. He accorded a great deal of significance to the ongoing monologues, and labeled them **private speech**. To Vygotsky, private speech is exceedingly important because it is the precursor for **inner speech**—a self-guiding and self-directing type of speech we use when we talk to ourselves, especially when we are trying to solve problems. It is an important cognitive tool for intellectual growth. Once children internalize speech, they have much more powerful and well-integrated sets of tools for thinking and problem solving. In fact, Vygotsky defined thinking as "inner speech." Vygotsky maintained that this self-directed speech does not disappear around the age of 7. Even adults use inner speech to regulate and guide further learning, particularly when they are not quite sure about what they are doing. Ever try to assemble something that came in 20 pieces with triple that number of washers and bolts and an instruction pamphlet written in Sanskrit?

Older children and adolescents may profit by using inner speech. It appears to help them focus on their work and improve academic performance and skill acquisition (Kronk, 1994). Adolescents who make more evaluative comments, generate more explanations, and "talk" their way through problem-solving situations are better problem solvers than those who

Jean Piaget and Lev Vygotsky differed in their views on the role that language plays in children's thinking.

do not engage in such inner speech dialogues (Chi, deLeeuw, Chiu, & La Vancher, 1994).

Researchers concur that private speech serves a self-regulating function (Kohlberg, Yaeger, & Hjertholm, 1999); forms the foundation for complex cognitive skills such as sustaining attention and memorizing information (Mang, 1998); and facilitates task performance (Chi et al., 1994). They also agree that children and adults produce a greater amount of private speech as their task increases in difficulty (Mang, 1998).

Symbolic Play

For Piaget, symbolic play, substituting imaginary situations for real ones, as in playing house or Spiderman®, is primarily an assimilative activity—meaning that, in play, children modify reality to fit their existing schemes and desires. In Piaget's view, symbolic play does not facilitate development but is used to consolidate existing schemes. For Vygotsky, however, symbolic play is a precursor to symbolization, and he considered it to be a leading factor in development. Vygotsky argued that children's symbolic play provides them with an important mental model support system that allows them to think and act in complex ways. Moreover, language is also enriched by symbolic play as children express their points of view, persuade others, and resolve conflicts. In addition, symbolic play supports the emergence and refinement of a number of cognitive competencies, such as memory. In an illustrative study, 4-year-old children were asked to remember a set of toys (Newman, 1990). One group of children was allowed only to name and touch the toys; the other group was allowed to play with the toys. Children participating in the play condition produced significantly greater recall.

Vygotsky's Zone of Proximal Development

Vygotsky's theory has had considerable impact in education. His notion that finely tuned and coordinated adult support assists children in completing actions that they will later come to accomplish independently holds special relevance for the education of children. Vygotsky's theory placed considerable emphasis on children's potential for intellectual growth rather than their intellectual abilities at a particular point in time. To understand how potential intellectual development occurs, Vygotsky

Thought CHALLENGE

What are some of the negative consequences of adults continuing to complete tasks for children once they have "mastered" a task?

proposed the notion of the **zone of proximal development**. The "zone" refers to the difference between the developmental level a child has reached and the level the child is potentially capable of reaching under the tutoring of a more skilled adult or peer. According to Vygotsky, working within a child's zone—that is, by giving her adult or peer assistance—allows her to respond to her environment in more complex and competent ways and to achieve more than she might by herself.

One form of instruction inspired by Vygotskian thinking is known as **scaffolding**, in which adults provide assistance just *slightly beyond* the child's current competence, stimulating the child to reach to a new level. To give the support (or scaffold) necessary for the child to accomplish a task, the adult or teacher may define the activity, demonstrate support skills, or provide direct guidance. Thus, scaffolding is an instructional process that always involves social interaction.

Scaffolding has been demonstrated in a variety of studies employing a number of different learning tasks. One representative study describes how scaffolding works. Five-year-old children were attempting to build a pyramid out of interlocking wooden blocks for the first time (Rogoff, 1998). Throughout the learning process, the tutor taught the children by verbal scaffolding (verbal suggestions) and physical scaffolding (demonstrating how the blocks linked together). She constantly adjusted the task to make it manageable and provide assistance when needed. As the children became more skilled, the tutor reduced the amount of support, so that eventually the children could execute the task independently.

According to Vygotsky, children learn skills through modeling and verbal instruction from more skillful and knowledgeable adults.

zone of proximal development Range of various kinds of support and assistance provided by a more skilled adult who helps children to carry out activities they currently are unable to complete but will later be able to accomplish independently.

scaffolding Temporary assistance provided by one person to a lesser-skilled person when learning a new task.

Similar scaffolding models are used in Japan, in which children work in groups, called *han* (see Chapter 2) with more capable children helping those in need of cognitive assistance. Teachers also use the scaffolding model, particularly in science education, by defining the central issue, reviewing possible alternatives, and encouraging students to develop innovative ways of getting more information (Kobayashi, 1994).

Thus, in helping children reach a higher level of performance, Vygotsky would advise adults to work within children's "zone." Adults can help children learn best when they teach them skills that they are capable of learning and apply just the right amount of assistance. Working outside the zone can occur in two directions, both of which impede learning. First, the adult can provide too much assistance. If, for example, the child is learning to put a puzzle together, and the adult does too much (puts the puzzle together for the child), the puzzle is completed, but the child has not learned any skills as to how to complete a puzzle. In contrast, if the adult does too little (does not provide the child with helpful hints on solving the puzzle), the task remains incomplete, and again, the child has not learned anything.

Thus, Vygotsky would recommend that adults provide support and assistance when the child is learning something new. Assistance begins by explaining the task (We are going to learn how to put a puzzle together by taking the pieces out and putting them back in their right place). Next, the adult directs the child's attention to the important objects and events (Here is the second part of the red triangle; can you find the first part in the puzzle?). As the adult and child interact, further suggestions and guidance are offered to the child.

The types of guided participation vary cross-culturally. In comparing a sample of U.S. mothers of preschool children from Salt Lake City with a sample of Mayan mothers from San Pedro, Guatemala, some striking differences in the skills taught and how scaffolding is carried out were apparent (Rogoff, Mistry, Goncu, & Mosier, 1993). The U.S. mothers taught their children how to count and label objects—skills that prepared the child for school. The Mayan mothers taught their children how to do various chores—skills that prepared them for future work in the village. The U.S. mothers engaged in more verbal scaffolding; the Mayan mothers used more nonverbal communications such as gestures and modeled the behavior they wanted their children to emulate.

Despite differences in scaffolding procedures, the adult's goal should always be to gradually transfer responsibility for the task to the child. As children become more capable at the task, adults need to reduce their assistance to enable children to perform the task independently. This type of structuring a task and transferring responsibility to children helps them become independent learners and also increases their chances for academic success when they enter learning situations outside the home (Llyod & Fernyhough, 1999).

Comparing Piaget and Vygotsky

Piaget and Vygotsky both agreed that the children play an active role in constructing their knowledge of the world, but there are a number of differences between their theories. One of the key differences is that Piaget believed his stages of cognitive development to be universal—that children everywhere progress through his stages of cognitive development at approximately the same ages relatively independent of the particular culture in which they live. In contrast, Vygotsky stressed that cognitive development can only be understood in terms of the child's particular social and cultural experiences. Culture determines the kinds of experiences children have, the language they use, the way they solve problems, and the types of problems they can solve.

Moreover, Piaget focused on children's individual construction of knowledge; learning is a product of independent discovery. Like lone, little scientists, young children create new knowledge when old information becomes inadequate to handle the new experiences they encounter. They then strive to bring about a state of cognitive balance or equilibrium that compels them to learn. Vygotsky focused on learning as a product of social interactions and assisted discovery. It is through interacting with more sophisticated adults and peers and receiving their guidance and assistance that children learn and solve more complex problems.

Piaget stressed that language was a representation system—speech simply represents existing schemes of what the child already knows. He further characterized the speech of preoperational thinkers as egocentric—rather meaningless, self-mutterings that end as children approach the concrete operational period of thinking. Language plays a critical role in Vygotsky's scheme of things. To him, language is without doubt the single greatest binding force of all cultures and the means by which knowledge is transferred from one individual to another and from one generation to another. He also accords children's private speech more prominence. Private speech does not disappear but rather becomes internalized inner speech, which plays a critical role in memory and thought. Other important differences are highlighted in Table 9.2.

TABLE 9.2

Comparing and Contrasting Piaget's and Vygotsky's Theories

Issue	Piaget	Vygotsky
Application of theory	Developmental universals: All children (worldwide) progress through the same stages at approximately the same ages.	Cultural specificity: What children learn and how they learn depends on their social, cultural, and historical experiences.
Discovery and learning	Each child learns new knowledge to achieve a state of cognitive equilibrium. Piaget also focused on independent discovery.	Learning is a product of social interactions; children need to interact with more sophisticated adults and peers. Through their assistance, children develop more sophisticated cognitive skills and abilities.
View of learners	Learners are active in manipulating objects and ideas.	Learners are active in social contexts and interactions.
Research methods	He devised tasks that aid assessment at different stages of cognitive development.	He rarely used standardized tasks to assess children's thinking; he often used observation to assess their thinking in context.
Language and thought	Language is a representational system that represents existing schemes; it is nonessential to thought.	Language is essential in guiding cognitive development.
Speech	Young children engage in egocentric speech with no intent to communicate; it has no impact on cognition. It ends around age 7.	Young children engage in private speech, a self-directed instructional tool that aids thinking. It does not end; it becomes internalized in the form of inner speech, which is essential to thought.
Stages of development	A stage theorist, he believed cognitive development proceeds through stages that result in abrupt shifts in cognitive development.	Cognitive development quantitatively improves as adults work with children in their zone of proximal development.

Evaluating Vygotsky

Vygotsky's sociocultural theory makes us aware that children's behavior is so strongly influenced by the cultural context in which they live that "universal" descriptions of development cannot be presented. As such, he has increased our appreciation of the importance of culture and has deepened our understanding of the diversity found in children's development. Children in different cultures acquire different cognitive and behavioral tools that will enable them to achieve maturational success in their culture. To understand development, then, we must understand the values and beliefs of a particular culture and how particular patterns of behaving and thinking fit into the child's cultural context.

One weakness of his theory is that Vygotsky overlooked developmental processes that are not primarily social, such as the role of biological factors in guiding children's development. Vygotsky was not an extreme environmentalist; he did discuss the importance of maturation but did not explain it precisely. Further, with his emphasis on social transmission of cultural tools, he slighted children's active and curious potential to master learning skills on their own—effectively characterized by a 3-year-old's insistence "Me do it myself!" Perhaps due to his untimely death at the age of 37, Vygotsky did not develop an elaborative description of how children's thinking changes across childhood. Vygotsky's work, however, has generated a significant amount of research, and because of the current interest in his theory, no doubt will continue to do so in the future.

Information-Processing Theory

Information-processing theorists agree with Vygotsky that cognitive skills develop over time, but their theory takes quite a different view of and approach to studying cognitive development. Like Vygotsky, information-processing theorists have abandoned Piaget's concept of cognitive stages. Taking their inspirations from modern technology, they believe that cognitive development is a more complex, multifaceted process than Piaget suggested in his stage theory. They contend that children may gradually acquire skills in many different content areas such as spatial and moral reasoning, mathematics, and verbal skills. Development may occur in small, orderly steps, but, there is no assumption of consistency across the stages as Piaget suggested. To explain the inconsistency in reasoning and problem-solving abilities among children, information-processing theorists look for changes that take place in children's memory systems.

Short-Term Memory

Short-term memory (STM) is the child's central processing unit where information from the immediate environment and his arsenal of old information are combined. Changes in short-term memory are apparent. As children progress through early childhood, they are progressively able to hold more material in short-term memory. For example, if you asked a 3-year-old child to repeat the four digits 5, 9, 20, 25, she might have some trouble. A 5-year-old, however, would find this an easy task (Gelman, 1998). Similarly, younger children find it very hard to perform a secondary task, such as tapping a finger on the table, while performing a primary task, such as counting a set of objects. The majority of information-processing psychologists (but not all) have taken these findings to mean that short-term memory develops with age, making older, school-age children able to deal with more simultaneous information than preschool children. With greater age, children need not just tap or count, they can do both.

Long-Term Memory

Does long-term memory—our permanent storehouse of information—even exist during early childhood? After all, most of us can recall very little of what happened to us before the age of 5. Determining whether long-term memory actually exists therefore presents a challenging test of whether information-processing views have relevance to early childhood. In spite of everyday forgetfulness and early childhood amnesia, it turns out that certain kinds of long-term memory do occur even in early childhood.

Two-year-olds can often remember the locations of novel objects seen only once, many months earlier—for example, the drawer where a rarely visited grandparent kept a deck of cards on a previous visit. By the age of 3, many children can verbally recall events that occurred up to 18 months in the past (Hudson, 1990). When the experience is a repeated one, such as a bedtime routine, however, the particulars of specific occasions quickly become clouded with a general memory of the routine—in this example, a bedtime "script."

Processing information from short-term memory to long-term memory also improves as young children gradually discover that they can take deliberate actions to help them remember things. Techniques that improve memory are called memory strategies; these generally refer to voluntary, purposeful plans adopted to enhance performance and are subject to conscious evaluation. Two of the most investigated memory strategies are **rehearsal**, in which children repeat the target information, and **retrieval**, the process of accessing information and entering it into consciousness.

© Lawrence Migdale/Stock Boston

Four-year-olds can remember and verbally recount many details of unusual experiences—like a visit to Disney World—experienced a full year earlier.

Rehearsal A large part of all the changes that take place in children's intellectual processes during their development can be described as changes in the memory strategies they carry around with them. There is now abundant evidence that young children are less likely than older children to use rehearsal, in which they repeat material silently or out loud, and as a result they hold verbal material in short-term memory less effectively than older children.

The use of external memory aids, such as rehearsal, seems to come naturally to most of us—so much so that we may take it for granted that we have always used them. But, in fact, we have not. A 6-year-old is shown a set of pictures and is told that when the pictures are covered, she will be asked, after a 15-second delay, to recall as many pictures as she can. Then, we test a 10-year-old who is shown a set of pictures and asked to remember them after a 15-second delay.

The majority of the older children will engage in spontaneous rehearsal (verbally repeating the types of pictures they saw). The younger children (ages 2 to 5 years), however, do not rehearse (Flavell, Green, & Flavell, 1997). The older children rehearse more and recall more than the younger children. John Flavell concludes that the major difference between the memory of young and older children is not in basic mechanisms, but in learned strategies, such as rehearsal. Thus, rehearsal appears to be a powerful memory strategy that increases with age.

Retrieval Another skill that progressively improves as children get older is being able to pull information from long-term memory; this is known as retrieval. The term refers to the resourceful moves a child may make when actively trying to recover things from memory storage. Development here consists of an increasing ability to search memory intelligently, efficiently, flexibly, systematically, and selectively in whatever manner the specific retrieval problems at hand require. Young children have much to learn about what retrieval cues are and about how to use them effectively. In fact, young children seriously overestimate their ability to recall information, and many firmly believe that they can remember or relocate an object without retrieval cues. Thus, they have not acquired detailed knowledge about exactly how retrieval cues can help them remember.

There are two common forms of retrieval: recognition and recall. For **recognition**, the task is usually easy, with the original stimulus prompting the retrieval of the memory representation (an example would be your taking a multiple-choice exam). Recall is not that simple. In **recall**, the familiar something is not initially present in conscious thought or perception (an example would be your taking an essay exam). Rather, recall is the term used for the very process of retrieving a representation of it from memory.

In general, children have excellent recognition memory but poor recall memory (Hintzman, Caulton, & Levitin, 1998). Marion Perlmutter (1980) performed a series of classic studies to test children's recall and recognition skills. In the recognition tests, 2- and 4-year-old children were shown 18 unrelated objects; they were then presented with 36 items, including the 18 objects presented earlier and 18 new objects. As can be seen in Figure 9.3, children of both ages were quite accurate in their recognition.

rehearsal
A memory strategy that involves repeating the words or information to be remembered either aloud or mentally.

retrieval
A class of strategies aimed at getting information out of long-term memory.

recognition
A type of memory that involves noticing whether a stimulus is identical or similar to one previously experienced.

recall
A type of memory that involves remembering a stimulus that is not present.

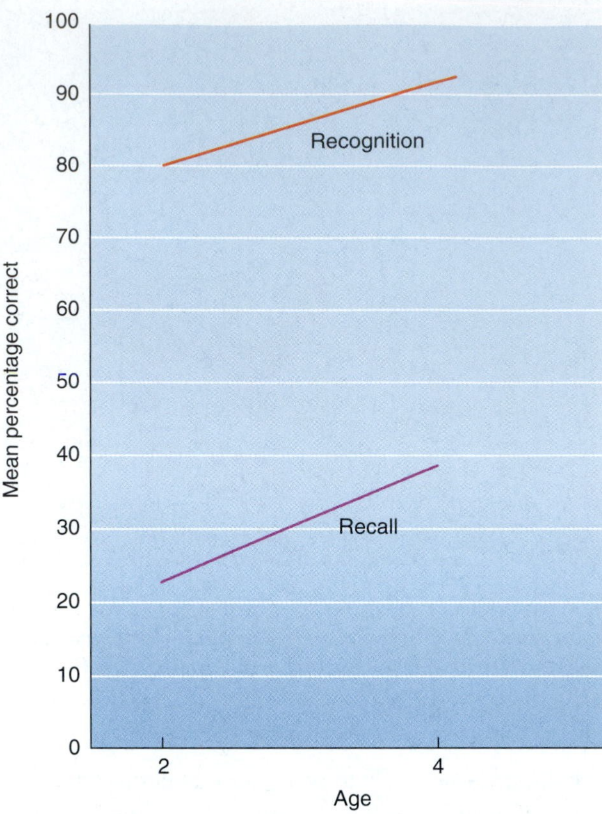

FIGURE 9.3 ***Recognition and Recall for 2- and 4-Year-Olds***

Two- and 4-year-old children's recognition memory abilities (ability to tell whether an object is the same as the one they saw before) are far superior to their ability to recall information (child generates an image of a previously seen object that is not presently visible).

From *Children's Memory: New Directions in Child Development*, by M. Perlmutter, Ed., 1980, San Francisco: Jossey-Bass.

In testing recall, children were shown nine unrelated objects from the recognition task. Each item was shown and named, and the children were told as an added incentive that they could keep all the objects that they could successfully recall. Despite this tempting reward, recall, as can be seen from Figure 9.3, was quite poor. Perhaps this is because recall unlike recognition requires more active rehearsal strategies and a more thorough search in memory to retrieve the right cues, which young children find difficult (Hudson & Sheffield, 1998).

Metamemory

metamemory Knowledge of memory skills or of when it is most appropriate to use these strategies.

One factor that influences children's strategic functioning is **metamemory**, knowledge of memory skills or of when it is most appropriate to use these strategies. Young thinkers fail to use rehearsal, and that limits their abilities to recall information. Interestingly, in studies, they are generally quite capable of rehearsing and can do so with only minimal instruction and demonstration by an adult. Once induced to rehearse, their recall increases to the level of that of spontaneous rehearsers. When subsequently given the option on later trials of rehearsing or not rehearsing, however, more than half of the young children abandoned the strategy and reverted to their original preexperimental status as nonrehearsers. If young children are quite capable of utilizing memory strategies such as rehearsal, why do they fail to do so spontaneously?

John Flavell and his colleagues (Flavell, Green, & Flavell, 1997) suggest that children fail to utilize these strategies, such as rehearsal, because they do not possess metamemory. Young children often do not know "what to do" when they have to remember something and thus cannot employ effective strategies. Older children, however, are more aware of how memory works (Siegal, 1997); for example, they know that saying things out loud, writing things down, and grouping similar items all help them remember (Lyon & Flavell, 1993). More so than younger children, they use these strategies in memory tasks.

This is not to say that young children do not have some rudimentary knowledge of how memory works. Even 2-year-olds, for example, can exploit cues as sources of knowledge about the location of a hidden object (Marzolf & DeLoache, 1997). When children watch while a small Snoopy toy is hidden and are told they can retrieve the toy after a prescribed delay interval, they tend to visually rehearse. From time to time, they look at the place where the toy is hidden and then nod their heads affirmatively. Some children walk over to the hiding place.

Young children are also aware of some factors that affect memory functioning. For example, 3-year-olds know that more items are harder to remember than a few and that distracting noise interferes with remembering. By age 5, most children also understand that memory is facilitated by drawn or written reminders, increasing age, help from others, longer study time, a short time between encoding and recall, and external cues (Wellman & Gelman, 1992). Thus, young children are beginning to understand the utility of various cues for recall. They also understand that a child who is motivated (likes the activity) or is in a quiet rather than a noisy room is more able to write numbers and listen to his mother's instructions. Young children do engage in simple visual and behavioral strategies, and these strategies correlate positively with memory performance. Children who produce more memory strategies tend to achieve higher retrieval scores (DeLoache & Brown, 1997).

The Young Child's Theory of Mind

Another major focus of cognitive processes in preschoolers is how they develop **theory of mind**—their ideas about mental activities. As they develop a theory of mind, children are able increasingly to construe people's outward behaviors in terms of underlying mental states such as beliefs and desires (Astington & Gopnik, 1988; Joseph, 1998; Wellman 1990). A preschooler's theory of mind also includes guiding assumptions about how desires and beliefs influence human action. Piaget believed that children have little appreciation of mental life until the ages of 6 or 7. In his view, the thoughts of other people do not exist for preschoolers: "We may say that up to the age of 7, introspection seems to be completely absent, and that from 7–8 until 11–12 there is a consistent effort on the part of thought to become more and more conscious of itself" (Piaget, 1928/1976, p. 143).

Recent investigations call into question Piaget's assertion that the ability to think about other people's mental states does not start to develop until a child is 6 or 7 (Astington, 1993; Brainerd, Stein, & Reyna, 1998; Lagattuta, Wellman, & Flavell, 1997; Taylor, 1996). Current researchers maintain that theory of mind becomes relatively sophisticated even before children enter school.

Scholars further indicate that young preschoolers and even toddlers operate with a rudimentary appreciation of people's mental lives that allows them, for example, to understand that people may be influenced by their particular experiences and that individual desires motivate and explain behaviors (Estes, 1998). Even 2- and 3-year-old children have some knowledge that others are thinking and feelings beings, which becomes more sophisticated and coherent with age. Consider this discussion between a mother and her 3-year-old son:

Child: Why is Billy (a baby brother) crying?
Mother: Because he is tired but just can't get to sleep.
Child: Does that hurt?
Mother: Yes, I suppose it does.
Child: But going to sleep doesn't hurt me.
Mother: You cried when you were a baby and were tired.
Child: Does Billy have pain?
Mother: Well, being tired is a sort of pain.
Child: There (patting the baby), you go to sleep and the pain will stop.

This conversation contains a number of references to feeling states such as fatigue, pain, and distress. There is further evidence that by the age of 4, children's earlier awareness of the connections between people's mental states, experiences, and behaviors expands to include an understanding of mental states as subjective representations of the world that are independent and do not necessarily correspond with reality. Much of the evidence for preschoolers' theory of mind comes from research about children's capacity for false beliefs and their belief-dependent emotions.

False Belief

False beliefs are measured by the preschooler's ability to attribute to another individual a belief that differs both from reality and from what she knows to be true. An example is the "Sallie–Anne" task—a story about two girls playing together (see Figure 9.4). Sally places a marble in a basket and then leaves the room, whereupon Anne moves the marble to another location. Sally returns and looks for the marble. The child being tested is then asked, "Where will Sally look?" Nearly all 3-year-olds will state that she will look in the new location where they themselves know the marble has been put; they cannot attribute a false belief to Sally and use that to predict her action. Thus, 3-year-olds do not understand that a person acts on the basis of what he or she believes to be true rather than what they themselves know to be true. These children say where the marble actually is even though the seeker has no way of knowing the marble has been removed.

Thus, until about 4 years of age children go on the assumption that there is only one world out there—that is, the one that accords with their own experience—and that other people will therefore act in the way they would. The most consistent finding in this research is that children around the age of 4 or 5 (but *not* younger) recognize that the target person, who has been systematically kept in ignorance, will, as a consequence, end up holding to some false belief.

Cross-cultural evidence also indicates that the ability to think about other people's mental states comes into being during the fourth year of life (Astington & Olson, 1995). For example, children living in the Baka community, a hunter–gatherer society in West Africa,

theory of mind Ideas about mental states like thoughts, beliefs, or dreams, and the relations among those states.

false belief The ability to attribute to another individual a belief that differs both from reality and from what is known to be true.

also change in their understanding of other people's false beliefs between the ages of 4 and 5 (Avis & Harris, 1991).

Other cross-cultural studies indicate that children's understanding of the mind appears to develop universally, as recently shown on a sample of children from Australia, New Guinea, Cameroon, and Great Britain (Vinden, 1999). In this design, children were shown a piece of fruit by a secondary experimenter. The primary experimenter then asked the children to hide the fruit from the secondary experimenter. To test their understanding of the secondary's false belief about where the fruit was located, the children were asked a series of false belief questions. The results indicated that these children understood false belief by 4 years of age. Further support of understanding false belief comes from research by Twila Tardif and Henry Wellman (2000). In sampling Mandarin- and Cantonese-speaking children from Hong Kong their data show that a pattern of theory-of-mind development is similar to the results found in previous research.

These studies demonstrate that, around the age of 4 or 5, children realize that what is in our mind is only a representation of reality and therefore not necessarily an accurate image, and that a representation which the child knows to be false may nevertheless and quite justifiably be considered as true by another person (Astington, 1998; Hala, Chandler, & Fritz, 1991). These new abilities do not just appear out of the blue; they depend on various precursors evident at earlier ages. Table 9.3 summarizes the prior developments necessary for the acquisition of a theory of mind.

This is Sally. Sally has a basket.
This is Anne. Anne has a box.
Sally has a marble. She puts the marble into her basket.
Sally goes out for a walk.
Anne takes the marble out of the basket and puts it into the box.
Now Sally comes back. She wants to play with her marble. Where will Sally look for her marble?

FIGURE 9.4 ***Theory-of-Mind Task***

This sequence of events is used when testing children's knowledge of false beliefs.

TABLE 9.3

Prior Developments for Acquisition of a Theory of Mind

- *Self-awareness.* This refers to the child's recognition of its own mental states. This is evident at quite an early age and can be seen in children's comments about their feelings and desires. Such an ability represents a basic prerequisite for the understanding of mental operations generally.
- *The capacity for pretense.* From the second year on, children are able to engage in make-believe play, including pretend play with dolls, which the child endows with various mental states. A powerful imagination—a prerequisite for being able to work out how other people function—is thus already at work.
- *The ability to distinguish reality from pretense.* Pretend play may involve children projecting their feelings onto dolls. Their ability to see that others are not just extensions of their desires is a later and more sophisticated development. Only when this appears will children no longer confuse the mental states imputed to other people with their own mental states. There is evidence that this does not become reliably established until the fourth year; only then can children imagine another person's beliefs and feelings as something apart from their own.

From "Theory of Mind, Humpty Dumpty, and the Icebox," by J. W. Astington, 1998, in *Human Development, 41,* 30–39. Used by permission.

Can Younger Children Understand False Beliefs?

In the basic form of these experiments, children 3 and under fail to understand false beliefs, but children 4 and over do. Some scholars share a sense of unease with all the claims to this effect. As Michael Chandler and Chris LaLonde (1996) point out, 4- and 5-year-olds regularly pass various measures of false belief understandings, but there is a good deal of room for real disagreement over whether still younger subjects legitimately fail them. For example, 3-year-olds may not understand the test questions. In responding to the question "Where will Sally look for the marble?" 3-year-olds, in their impatience, often end up answering quite different questions about where Sally "will eventually look" or about where Sally "should look" for the marble.

Varying the conditions of the task, such as making the tasks more personally relevant, can sometimes make even younger preschoolers understand false belief. Some researchers have demonstrated that when story protagonists are represented as having a real "need to know," 3-year-olds are quite skillful in understanding false belief (Hala, 1991; Winner & Sullivan, 1993). So disagreements about the precise age when children become capable of insight into mental states do exist. What is clear is that somewhere in the 3- to 5-year-old range children acquire understanding of how various end results, such as actions and emotions, are produced and that the ability to mentally represent other people's psychological states lies at the heart of this development (Ziv & Frye, 2001).

Belief-Dependent Emotions

Most theory-of-mind research has examined belief-dependent actions (such as Sally's search for her marble), but the same concepts can be applied to the development of children's insight into belief-dependent emotions such as surprise. People experience surprise when something occurs that they had not believed would occur; to gain understanding of such an emotional state children must learn that surprise rests on an individual's prior belief. By telling children stories about individuals who had various prior expectations and encountered various outcomes and then asking each child about that individual's reaction, it has been found that signs of rudimentary understanding occur at around age 3 (Wellman & Banerjee, 1991). However, by age 4 or 5, considerable improvement takes place and children become increasingly accurate and consistent in their judgments.

Despite recent controversy over the age of understanding false belief, theory-of-mind research draws our attention to the fact that quite early in development children construe not only themselves but also other people as thinking and feeling beings. The "theory" they develop is not a conscious one; it is rather an intuitive grasp about human action—a practical knowledge that develops gradually but has its beginnings in the preschool years.

Cultural Variations in Theories of Mind

Angeline Lillard (1998) and others (Astington & Olson, 1995; Vinden, 1996; Wellman, 1998) note that culture influences theories of mind. There are some similarities or universals in the early years because children everywhere will have certain common experiences and arrive at a core set of conclusions (Harris, 1995). Eventually, however, the child's theory of mind will reflect culture-specific ideas. The social practices, materials, and symbolic tools of each culture support, direct, or stifle different thoughts and feelings about the mind.

For example, an important aspect of children's theory of mind relates to their thoughts on behavioral intentions. It is apparent that one child's thoughts regarding intention may differ from that of another child reared in a different cultural context. For example, individuals in the United States usually consider themselves responsible for their own behavior but not that of others (Hamilton & Sanders, 1992). In contrast, in Japan even preschoolers feel responsible for the actions of others (Lewis, 1995). Moreover, other cultures may simply avoid talking about behavioral intentions and other aspects of the mind. According to the LeVines (R. LeVine, 1984; S. LeVine, 1979), the Gusii of Kenya prefer to discuss overt behavior, avoid talking about aspects of the mind, and rarely comment on reasons for actions, even their own. Similarly, a study of Samoans revealed that the cultural norm was that minds are unknowable and thus not relevant (Ochs, 1988). Clearly, there appear to be meaningful cultural variations in the extent of responsibility for one's actions and in ideas about how the mind is conceptualized, and this variability will influence children's theory-of-mind beliefs.

APPLICATIONS:

Supporting the Child's Developing Theory of Mind

When children have developed a theory of mind—an understanding that others have feelings and desires and beliefs—they are likely to engage in more positive interactions with others (Happe & Frith, 1996). Because constructive social relations play an important role in children's overall adjustment, a key goal for caregivers is to support this development. Researchers believe that understanding other minds comes with biological maturation and the accompanied increases in cognitive ability, but studies also suggest that parents and teachers can support the development of their understanding of others (Youngblade & Dunn, 1995). Angeline Lillard (1998) suggests that engaging children in pretend play and having conversations about mental states enhances the development of children's social understanding.

Encouraging Pretend Play with Others

Piaget would be one of the first to endorse the view that interactions with peers promote social understanding. As young children interact with others, they are exposed to others' representations of their pretend world. In these pretend-world situations, children must negotiate and accommodate others' representations. Moreover, in pretend play, children often pretend to be other people, which enables them to take on others' views of the world. Lillard (1998) suggests that caregivers should encourage pretend play with peers, by doing so they can boost children over the edge to understand how others mentally represent their worlds.

Talking to Children About Minds

Research suggests that by age 3, discussions of what other people are thinking may be helpful in promoting theory-of-mind understandings (Lillard, Zeljo, & Harlan, 1998). Thus, talking with young children about minds and mental states of others may help them to understand others' feelings, beliefs, and desires. Studies suggest that discussing mental states with children from storybooks or real-life encounters is associated with better performance on theory-of-mind tasks (Dunn, Brown, & Beardsall, 1991). Many children's books focus on the character's feelings and changes in feelings, and by reading such books and discussing the character's feelings, caregivers assist in promoting children's understanding of how other people think and feel (Lillard, 1998).

Talking about different viewpoints may also help children understand that people have beliefs about the world, that their beliefs may be different from those of others, and that beliefs may change when a person acquires new information. Studies found that both African American and Japanese parents engaged in more emotion talk than did European American parents (Blake, 1994). For example, Japanese families talked more to their children about others' emotions, engaging in what could be seen as intensive "empathy training" (Azuma, 1994). Instead of telling children to eat their dinner so they would grow up big and strong, Japanese parents were more apt to emphasize that a poor farmer had worked hard to grow the food and that the child would hurt the farmer's feelings if she did not eat her dinner. These types of adult conversation with children about mental states help them to learn to be good at making inferences about the mental states of others.

Concept Checks

1. The preoperational child's ability for inner, symbolic operations includes
   a. planning for and tracing the sequences involved in a future action.
   b. picturing objects and events mentally and symbolic play.
   c. assigning a purpose for all objects.
2. Hyun-woo, who is 4, wants to watch Disney's *101 Dalmatians* movie and listen to *Sesame Street* tapes at the same time. Hyun-woo's request suggests that she has not yet developed
   a. selective attention.
   b. long-term memory.
   c metamemory.
3. ***True or False:*** Case, like Fischer, moves away from the notion of general cognitive structures and, instead, focuses on specific concepts that pertain only to a particular area or areas.
4. The ability to think about other's mental states is known as ______________, and it becomes relatively sophisticated at approximately age ______________.
5. A temporary aid provided by one person to encourage, support, and assist a less skilled person is known as ______________________.

Language Development

Before Beginning . . .

After reading this section, you will be able to

- discuss language achievements during the early childhood period.
- understand common language problems.
- analyze the possible merits of learning a second language.

Language held a prominent place in Vygotsky's theory of cognitive development. As children's language becomes internalized and more sophisticated, they are capable of performing more complex cognitive tasks. From ages 2 to 6, children learn, on average, an astounding five to nine words every day (Goodman, McDonough, & Brown, 1998). With this new arsenal of ever-increasing vocabulary words, language and cognition become more sophisticated and complex. We will look at how their language expansion unfolds as well as the speech and hearing difficulties that some children develop.

The New "Second Word"

Around age 2, children begin making two-word utterances. In this stage, children put together nouns with main verbs and principal adjectives (Goodman, McDonough, & Brown, 1998). They use their new "second word" to amplify what they used to communicate with one word by intonation and inflection only. Earlier they might have watched the family cat depart through the backyard and said, "Cat!" in tones of shock. Now they say, "Cat gone!" When two-word sentences first begin to appear, they are primarily of the following forms: subject and noun ("Mommy go"), verb and object ("Read it"), and verb or noun and location ("Bring home") (Clark, 1998).

Two-word phrases allow the child to communicate more accurately. In one-word communications, after consuming a biscuit, the child might say "bikkit," indicating he wants more. The mother might misunderstand, thinking he is merely commenting on the biscuit. When, however, he says "more bikkit," he is less likely to be misunderstood and get his "bikkit" more quickly.

Some sounds and words are very difficult for young children to say. The development of the sound system is a long process; it is generally not completed until age 7 (Medvescek, 1994). At age 4, for example, children are still learning consonants such as *s* (as in ship), *v* and *z*. Even though they can produce a large range of sounds, this does not mean they will be able to use the sound in combination with other sounds. Three- and 4-year-olds, to illustrate, have trouble with words like *macaroni* or *ravioli*. They also have trouble with double consonants such as *st, dr,* and *sm*. Children often drop the first consonant; thus, "steak" becomes "take," for example.

Children produce two or three words in succession and intend to express certain relations between ideas. They demonstrate that they have already learned the basic rules of grammar and syntax in their language. They invariably get the sequence of words right in the context of what they are trying to say; for example, if Estella saw a cat bite a dog, she might say, "Cat bite dog" or "Cat bite." It is this kind of discrimination with respect to order that shows that the child has in mind not only certain animals, persons, things, qualities, and actions but definite structural relationships among them. As the child is now able to express a primitive sense of property, certain objects and spaces seem to be assigned to particular family members. Children's possessives always omit the possessive inflection, and they come out simply with "Daddy chair" or "Mommy dress" (Brown, 1996).

Multiple-Word Utterances

By the age of 3½, most children have learned the essential elements of language and use them creatively. They continue further learning of the sound system, gaining better understanding of the grammar of language, vocabulary growth, and more sophisticated conversational skills. There is no three-word stage in child language. Early **telegraphic speech** is characterized by multiple-word utterances. These communications are short, simple sentences made up primarily of content words, which are rich in semantic content, usually nouns and verbs. However, the sentences lack function words, tense endings on verbs, and plural endings on nouns: "Daddy go bye-bye car"; "Me want this story."

As the telegraphic speech stage progresses, function words are gradually added to sentences. Why do children typically omit low-information words and include high-information words, such as nouns and verbs? Children's memory span is too short to include more than just high-information words, and their vocabulary is too limited to copy adult kinds of sentences.

telegraphic speech
Early utterances by young children that leave out words not essential for communicating meaning.

Children's Expanding Knowledge of Language

As children's knowledge of words expands, they begin to understand and appreciate relational contrasts. Words that specify relations between people, objects, and events occur quite early in child language, although young children do not fully appreciate the meaning of many of these terms. The word *more*, for example, is often one of the child's first words. Generally, it is a request for some kind of a repetition ("more tickle"). Yet it is not until they are 3½ that children use this relational term in its full comparative sense to specify relations (She has more than I do). Understanding less does not occur until 4½ or 5. Relational words such as *big/little* are usually the first spatial adjectives to appear followed by *short/tall* and *in/on* (Gelman, 1998). Children hear these adjectives more than others and generally pay more attention to heights and lengths than to widths and thicknesses.

Children continue to make some grammatical errors. For example, they frequently misinterpret passive constructions such as, "The boy was hit by the girl." They more readily understand the active version, "The girl hit the boy" (Lempert, 1989). Children younger than 5 or 6 tend to interpret passive constructions as if they were active sentences. One exception to this rule is passive sentences that make little sense. For example, even a 3-year-old will correctly interpret "The candy was eaten by the girl," because it is nonsense to assume that the candy was the agent doing the eating.

Most young children begin to learn that objects can be categorized at multiple levels (Au, 1990). For instance, they may know that their pet is an animal as well as a dog and that their toy train is a toy as well as a train. There is some evidence that even 2- and 3-year-olds can learn a new subordinate label such as *terrier* and *mutt* for an object that they already have a basic label for such as *dog*.

Rule Systems

Roger Brown (1973, 1977, 1988) has examined the telegraphic phase of language development and identified a series of stages that describe different rule systems. Brown does not assign particular ages to these stages of syntactic development but believes that children's mean length utterance (MLU), the number of words used in a sentence, is a more useful benchmark of children's syntactic sophistication than their age.

Brown noticed several types of errors that children make in forming the past tense of verbs and pluralizing nouns; these occur when children's MLU is 4 to 5 words. When forming the past tense of verbs, children learn the *ed* rule and then how to apply that rule. Initially, they may use irregular verb forms such as *came, saw, went,* but once they have formulated a rule for saying verbs in the past tense they add the *ed* sound to all past tense verbs so that they say "goed" and "comed" as well as "jumped" and "laughed." They use this form even after they have heard the correct usage and after they have used correct forms. Once again, the child proves to be a sensible linguist by learning the *ed* tense that exhibits the least variation in form.

When plurals begin to appear regularly, the child forms them according to the most general rule: add the *s* or *z* sound to the end of the word to make it plural. However, at this point, children overgeneralize the rule, resulting in words such as *mans, foots* or *feets, sheeps,* and *gooses.* The grammatical mistakes the child makes are both logical (in the sense that they are wrong but logical deductions) and consistent from child to child.

Jean Berko Gleason (Berko, 1958; Berko Gleason, 1997) invented a production test known as the "wug test" to see whether children have mastered the English rules for making plurals. In one case, they are shown a funny birdlike creature and told: "This is a wug. Now there's another one. There are two . . . ?" If they correctly answer "wugs," one can be sure that they know how to make plurals because they could never have heard that word from anyone else.

Studying the way children use negative forms in a sentence is another way to analyze their syntactic structures. Children acquire negative structures in a systematic orderly rule-governed way. Initially, the child makes a sentence negative by simply attaching *No* or *Not* to the beginning of a declarative statement ("No, singing song"; "No, sun shining"). Negative words do not appear inside the sentence. In the next stage, children incorporate into their grammars more complex rules that generate sentences, including the negatives *no, not, can't,* and *don't* after the subject ("I don't want it"; "He not little he big"). Sometimes they go overboard: "No, I don't not have none." In the third stage of acquiring negatives, many more details are incorporated into their use. The main thing they still need to learn is how to use pronouns: "I didn't see something"; "I don't want somebody to wake me up."

Promoting Language Development

Adults can also help promote language development through the use of *expansions* and *recastings.*

Child: More joos.
Father: You want more juice, do you?
Child: Ummm. (Takes drink) Good.
Father: Tastes good, doesn't it? Especially after playing awhile.

Expansions involve adults reformulating the child's communications to reflect the complexity of the child's statement ("You want more juice, do you?"). **Recasting** involves correcting language features used by the child into an appropriate form ("Tastes good, doesn't it?"). In the dialogue, the father provides support for a more elaborate dialogue than the child alone could sustain and thereby creates a zone of proximal development—reminiscent of Vygotsky's theory. Caregivers of preschoolers who frequently extend, elaborate, and recast the children's comments and questions have preschoolers who make especially rapid language progress (Farrar, 1990).

Speech and Hearing Problems

There may be several reasons why a child is slow to begin speaking; reasons range from birth order, to personal style, to poor hearing. Children with older siblings tend to talk less. Basically, the younger child may just have to grunt and point and the obliging older sibling becomes the interpreter, "What? You want a cookie? Okay, here's your cookie." For some children, the coordination needed to vocalize speech sounds and syllables may be slow to develop. Poor hearing, sometimes caused by chronic ear infections, is a common culprit. If it remains undetected, children can miss out on a critical period of language development. If the child is not using two-word phases by the time he or she is 2 to 2½, it is generally a good idea to see your pediatrician (Edwards, 1995). The doctor may recommend hearing-and-language-assessment testing.

If the parent or pediatrician suspects that a hearing problem may exist, an otolaryngologist (ear and throat specialist) should be consulted. Some symptoms that may indicate a hearing problem are reflected in the child's language skills. For example, 2-year-olds usually engage in two-word communications. Even if the child is not combining words, rich and appropriate gestural speech means that actual speech will follow. If these signposts are not evident, a child should be evaluated for auditory impairment (Edwards, 1995).

Other symptoms of speech and hearing problems include no intelligible speech by age 2; high-pitched or nasal quality to utterances; dull look as the child tries to speak; no rhythm of communication, or turn-taking; evident overload or inattention when the child is spoken to or looked at; and incessant repetition of adult speech, in which the child parrots exactly what adults say (Edwards, 1995). Problems with *articulation* (producing sounds correctly), difficulties with pitch or loudness, or the quality of the voice, as in hoarseness or shrillness, are other indications of speech and hearing problems. If parents notice these problems, they should consult an expert. The earlier that repair of a defect or speech therapy is started, the better this will be for the child's overall development.

Impediments to Language Development

Problems that interfere with speech development include the frequency in the fluency of speech, or stuttering. *Stuttering* or *stammering* (also called **dysfluency**) is a disorder of communication in which sounds or whole words are repeated as the child speaks, interrupting the flow of his communication. Sometimes these children make sounds that are prolonged, or their speech may actually stop momentarily. Stuttering first becomes apparent during the preschool years, when children first learn to speak. About 90 percent of children between the ages of 18 months and 4 years have some degree of "normal dysfluency." Perhaps these fluency problems occur because the child's thought processes move much more rapidly than his ability to put those ideas into words. Without undue attention from parents or stress from the environment, this stuttering disappears on its own.

Only when stuttering becomes more severe or is combined with other speech problems, such as the child becomes extremely self-conscious and fearful of communication or she develops new facial grimaces or tics, should parents seek help. The prognosis for children who stutter is excellent. About 80 percent outgrow their stuttering by adolescence (Mallard, 1998). In a small number of individuals, however, it persists into adulthood, and they require continuous support and intervention.

expansion Rephrasing a child's communications in correct grammatical form.

recasting Rephrasing something the child said to reflect the complexity of speech.

dysfluency A disorder of communication in which sounds or whole words are repeated as the child speaks, interrupting the flow of his communication; stammering or stuttering.

APPLICATIONS:

Learning a Second Language

With all these linguistic feats, is this also a good time to teach children a second language? Before answering this question, let us examine a few myths surrounding *bilingualism* in children. The first misconception is that young children acquire language more easily than adults. This idea originated with the assumption that children are biologically programmed to acquire languages. Early acquisition of a second language, although not harmful to young children's language development, is not a piece of cake for them. A second related misconception is that the younger the child, the more quickly a second language is acquired. In fact, adults may learn a foreign language quicker than children. Children who receive natural exposure to a second language, however, are likely to eventually achieve higher levels of second language proficiency than adults (Mayo, Florentine, & Buss, 1997).

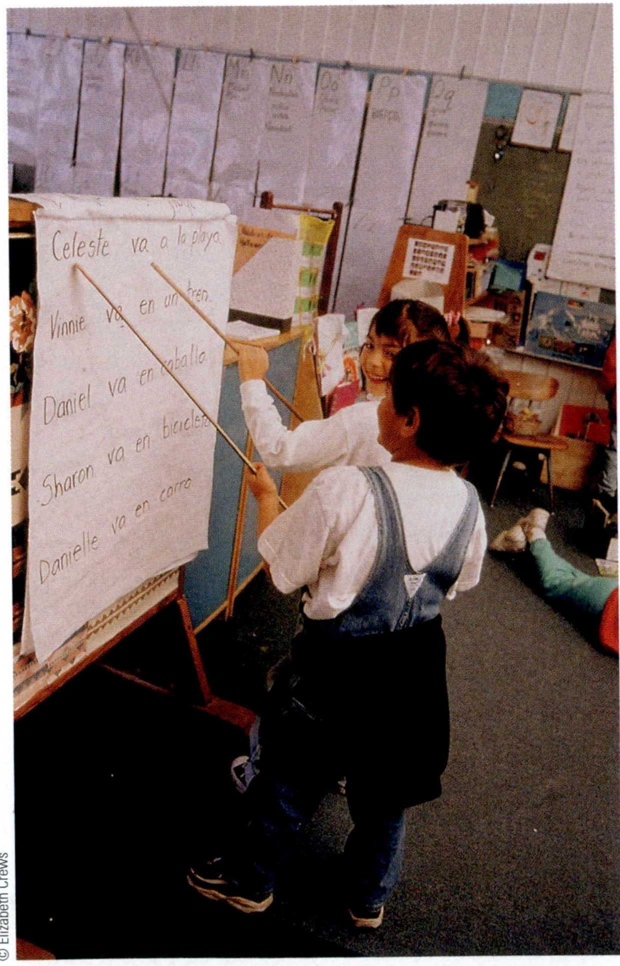

© Elizabeth Crews

Children who learn a second language during their preschool years are able to speak it later on with an appropriate accent.

Phoneme Flexibility

However, a wonderful advantage that young children have over adults when learning a second language is their great flexibility in pronouncing many word sounds known as phonemes (Rodriguez, 2000). Children learning a second language are more likely than adults to develop a more appropriate accent (Birdsong, 1999). After several semesters of studying French as an adult, I never really mastered the true Parisian sounds. Brain research tells us that the window of opportunity for learning a language and being able to speak it as the natives do is from birth to age 10 (Chugani & Phelps, 1996). After that, the perceptual map of the first language constrains the learning of a second language.

Does learning a second language mean the child will have difficultly speaking both languages? Elena Nicoladis and Giovannie Secco (2000) point out that initially young children may show "gaps" in speaking two languages. For example, Felicity's mother speaks to her in Spanish and her father communicates with her in English; Felicity responds with sentences that contain some Spanish words and some English words. Rather than this showing confusion, Nicoladis and Secco argue that 90 percent of word-mixing is accounted for by the child's vocabulary gaps in one language or the other. Parents often make creative use of the child's limited linguistic resources, and they actually substitute words in their sentences (either using Spanish or English words) that are in the child's productive vocabulary. As the child's linguistic resources become more sophisticated word-mixing disappears.

Does learning a second language mean that the child will lose the first? No. Adam Winsler and his colleagues (Winsler, Diaz, Espinosa, & Rodriguez, 1999) studied a sample of Spanish-speaking, Mexican American children who attended a bilingual (Spanish/English) preschool. These children were compared with children who remained at home learning only Spanish. No evidence of Spanish proficiency loss for children attending bilingual preschool was found. In fact, the children attending bilingual preschool showed significant and parallel gains in Spanish language development as well!

In studying the acquisition of an ancestral language and ethnic affinity, Alison Imbens-Bailey (2000) reported on a sample of 8- to 15-year-old Armenian children living in the United States. In comparing Armenian children who learned their native language as young children with Armenian children who did not learn to speak Armenian, Imbens-Baily noted differences in their attitudes toward their bicultural background. The bilingual children demonstrated closer affinity with their ethnic background and toward their community.

Bilingual Preschools

There appear to be other positive effects of bilingual education in preschool. In a sample of preschoolers in Singapore, the National Institute of Education sponsored a one-year preschool program in which young Asian children learned English as a second language (Gan & Chong, 1998). Language lessons were integrated with music activities and punctuated with high-interactive teacher–student activities. Data show that the children in the project, motivated by this language-rich environment, made gains not only in learning English but also noticeable progress in musical and social skills during the year. Early bilingual programs also seem to promote early phoneme awareness, and this tends to have a positive impact on later reading and spelling skills (Carlisle, Beeman, Davis, & Spharim, 1999; Stuart, 1999). This type of preschool bilingual program in other countries such as Japan (Kanno, 1998) and France (Thorn & Gathercole, 1999) demonstrate similar positive results.

I was in a long line at the information center in Lausanne, Switzerland, and was absolutely amazed by the clerk answering the questions of the people in line ahead of me. She spoke German, French, Japanese, and perfect English. How impressive. She told me that she spoke about six different languages and commented that learning one language helps you learn others more easily; research supports her statement. Bilingual children are better language learners because they develop superior metalinguistic skills and sensitivity to other languages, develop an awareness of languages and the rules for their use, have greater sensitivity to intonational cues, and successfully utilize these cues to perceive the intonation-appropriate meaning of sentences (Bild & Swain, 1989; Cenoz & Valencia, 1994).

Many countries have programs for teaching language other than the "official" language of the country. Singapore, for example, is a multilingual country, and for the past two decades the official policy has extended the mother tongue notion to include Chinese, Malay, and Tamil languages for the main ethnic groups. In addition, children learn English as well. In the United States, however, rather than having a pluralistic goal of promoting bilingual communication, we tend to promote monolingualism or limited bilingualism. Vygotsky, however, saw the importance of bilingualism; he argued that "the capacity to express the same thought or experience in different languages enables a bilingual child to see his language as one particular system among many, to view its phenomena under more general categories and this leads to an awareness and sensitivity into the societies of others" (1962, p. 110).

Thus, bilingualism is an interesting phenomenon because it involves changes in the individual's attitudes and identities with respect to languages and other cultures. Sharing of languages, then, also involves sharing of cultures. With the large-scale migrations and language contact, the role of bilingual education is an important issue. In the minds of many, education can no longer follow a traditional monolingual framework. Young children also can learn a second language at home with some effective guidelines offered by linguistic researchers.

Making It an Enjoyable Adventure

Children should not be pressured into learning a second language; this should be a fun learning activity for them (Agnihotri & Khanna, 1997). Children should be given opportunities to practice both their native and newly taught language. It's helpful to plan and incorporate opportunities for conversation such as dramatic play, storytime, puppetry, and social experiences such as field trips, cooking, and other activities. Learning words with the accompaniment of musical instruments also helps children to master another language (Gan & Chong, 1998). It is suggested that adults avoid rigid didactic grammatical approaches with young children (Gopaul-McNicol & Thomas-Presswood, 1998).

Concept Checks

1. Short sentences consisting mainly of content words are called
   a. holophrastic sentences.
   b. structural speech.
   c. telegraphic speech.
2. Evidence of a speech or hearing problem may be
   a. no legible speech by 2 years of age.
   b. not using plural words.
   c. not being able to pronounce word sounds such as *st*.
3. Teaching children a second language during early childhood causes them
   a. to forget their native language.
   b. to develop a more appropriate accent.
   c. a great deal of confusion; it is better to wait until they are 10 years old.

Early Education

Before Beginning . . .

After reading this section, you will be able to

- understand the factors that are most critical to quality preschool child care.
- understand the possible factors that contribute to school readiness.
- examine whether some children should postpone school entry for one year.
- understand the possible factors that contribute to reading readiness.
- analyze the impact that television and videos have on learning.
- identify factors that help children make a successful transition to school.

Child Care

Terms used for care of children provided by people other than their mother include a variety of titles but generally fall into two categories: *family care* and *center care.* Even when children are cared for by their own fathers it is known as *other relative care.* Different terms relate to the age of the child (infant, toddler, preschooler) and the setting (home versus center).

Family Care

Family care is the name given to an arrangement in which the child is cared for by a family day care provider in her home. The caregiver may care for only one child and her own, or she may run a program for a small group of children. Parents who desire a homelike environment and a small number of children with one caregiver tend to choose family care. This arrangement offers the least expensive form of child care. In this situation, the provider is running a business, and the parent is the consumer.

Most states require that the family child care homes be licensed, certified, registered, or otherwise approved. Regulations include the maximum number of children, by age, who may be cared for, as well as health and safety standards. Some states go further by regulating the activities provided for the children, equipment, nutrition, discipline, and so forth. Unfortunately, it has been estimated that approximately 80 percent of family-care homes operate outside of the scrutiny of the states (Keats, 1997); thus, this form of care is largely unregulated. Advantages and disadvantages of this care system are highlighted in Table 9.4.

Center Care

Center care is group care that takes place outside the home. Day care is probably the most frequently used

TABLE 9.4

Advantages and Disadvantages of Family Care

Advantages	Disadvantages
The child may be more comfortable in a home setting than in a center.	If the provider or her child is sick and she does not have backup care, the parent may be stuck.
If the caregiver has unusual work hours, the family care provider may offer care that can begin early, include breakfast, and go on late to include dinner.	If the child is sick, the parent may not be able to take her to the family care home.
If there are regulations governing family care, the parent can use a provider who has met licensing requirements.	If there are no licensing requirements where the parent lives, the parent needs to evaluate the safety and quality of the care provided.
If the parent has an older child in school, the family care provider may be able to pick her up and provide care for the afterschool hours and days when school is closed.	The provider may change the hours or days of care she can offer, and these may not fit the parent's need.
In some areas, family care is less expensive than center care.	The provider may not have the skills and materials necessary to offer the child a variety of age-appropriate activities.
	If the provider does not have her own yard and is caring for a group of children, it may be difficult for her to take them out to a park or playground.

family care
An arrangement in which the child is cared for by a family child care provider in her home.

center care
Group care that takes place outside a home setting and offers care in a school-like setting.

term, although child care workers prefer the term child care—"we take care of children, not days."

Infant and Toddler Day Care Approximately 68 percent of mothers with infants and toddlers work outside the home and therefore many need specialized care. Infant and toddler day care are often regulated more stringently than centers serving the needs of older children. For example, the ratio of caregivers to infants is generally smaller—one adult for every three or four infants. Activities include maintaining physical routines (eating and sleeping) and a mixture of supervised play involving projects which stimulate language and social development.

Preschools Preschools generally serve the needs of an "older clientele"—3- to 5-year-olds. These centers vary in style and philosophy. Some programs have a more academic curriculum and a schoollike environment. Others place more emphasis on children's social development and focus on helping children learn to get along with others. Sometimes preschools provide preventative services, such as Head Start, a federally sponsored program of early education designed to give extra help in learning to disadvantaged children considered at-risk for later academic success (see Chapter 6). Other centers, such as the Montessori schools, are considered supplementary programs. Today there are Montessori schools in 52 countries on six continents, and their number continues to expand worldwide. Maria Montessori (1870–1952), a medical doctor and pioneer in education, emphasized that children play an active role in their learning; thus these schools tend to encourage children to explore and actively pursue their innate self-interests (Montessori, 1948). Despite stylistic and philosophic variations in center care, each must strive to meet the developmental needs of preschoolers highlighted in Table 9.5.

Day-Care Centers A day-care center may be privately run or run by a larger corporation, such as a church, synagogue, community center, university, or business. Parents may choose this setting because they perceive this age group as increasingly peer oriented and find the more explicit educational components offered by center care more appealing. Day-care centers can offer a wider array of materials and play spaces than a home. These centers are licensed by the state; thus, parents know that the program must meet certain minimum standards. Are these minimal standards enough? Quality and costs for day care are highly variable in the United States; this is not the case in Sweden, however, as Ann-Katrin Svennson notes in First Person. Table 9.6 provides possible advantages and disadvantages of center care.

TABLE 9.5

Meeting the Preschooler's Developmental Needs

Educational Component	Need
Environment	Children want to "see what there is to see," and caregivers at the child-care center should encourage their innate curiosities, while still providing them with comfort when they need emotional refueling.
Activities	Young children enjoy pillows to sit on, corners to play in, and exciting toys. There should also be a balance between activities that exercise their large muscles and "calming" activities such as listening to music or having a story read to them.
Communication	We see an explosion of vocabulary in toddlerhood, and caregivers should encourage communication skills by talking with toddlers and listening carefully to them. Naming objects for the child, playing with words, and singing songs are also important for the child at this stage.
Emotional support	Preschoolers should also be encouraged to do things by themselves. They may want to hold their own juice cup or put on their shoes. Sometimes these attempts at independence result in frustration when the children spill their juice or cannot master putting on their shoes. In these situations, a good caregiver assists, reassures, and helps by offering a new and different task that the child can succeed at by himself or herself.
More structured activities	Older 3- and 5-year-olds are ready for more structured materials—puzzles, blocks, crayons, paint, and glue. These materials help children develop the skills they need later for reading, writing, and math.

FIRSTPERSON

Child Care in Sweden

We have a very fine care center for children at Jonkoping University. I have been the director for our care center for several years, and I have noticed some interesting changes. The one that strikes me first is that the number of children attending our center has increased, even though the number of mothers working in Sweden has been rather constant for the past five years. More and more mothers who do not choose to work still choose to send their children to child-care centers. They want their children to learn skills that will help them do better once they attend the systematized school program at age 5. Our daily schedules have changed as a result. We have more "lessons" than ever before—lessons in printing, drawing shapes, and reading. But, reading is not a formal lesson. We try to have interesting and colorful picture books on many tables so that children will want to look at the books, and we encourage them to "read" these books to us by telling stories as they look at the pictures.

There has also been a big increase in the number of very young children, infants, attending child care on a full-time basis. Opinions in other countries vary on whether infants should be in extended child-care situations. In Italy, for example, it is strongly believed that infants should remain at home with their mothers. In the United States, I think the opinion is quite mixed. In Sweden, however, we believe that child care is not harmful and quite positive for the very young child. Full-time infant care is quite common here and very rare in Italy.

My work in child care has taken me to many countries. I am quite amazed at the cost of child care in other parts of the world. In Lausanne, Switzerland, the cost can be prohibitive. Middle-class parents can expect to pay about SFr 134 or $100 (U.S.) a day. These fees translate into about one-quarter of their total monthly income. This is not the case in Sweden. Although some things have changed in child care in Sweden, cost and quality of child care has not. For example, for one child to be at a child-care facility for 39 hours a week, the parents would pay $202 (U.S.) a month, regardless of the age of the child. Our child-care centers are of the highest quality in regard to staff training and stability, caregiver–child ratios (1:4), and educational and material environment. Our smallest student gets the best of care.

—*Ann-Katrin Svensson, Ph.D.*

TABLE 9.6

Advantages and Disadvantages of Center Care

Advantages	Disadvantages
Center care is usually regulated and inspected to set minimum standards for health, safety, and group size.	Centers have specific hours that may not match the parents' hours.
Centers often have on their staffs directors and teachers who have studied child development.	The child will probably have to conform to a schedule for meals, snacks, and naps that may be difficult for him or her.
The child will be with other children at a center.	If the child is sick, the parent cannot take him to the center, and the parent will have to find alternative care.
The center will provide care even if the child's teacher is absent.	If the group is large and there are not enough teachers, the child may not get the individual attention she needs.
Centers offer greater variety in the materials and activities they have available.	Most centers close for certain holidays and vacations—some for the entire summer—during which the parents will have to make other arrangements.
Most centers include outdoor play as part of their daily schedule.	In some areas center care, particularly for infants and toddlers, is very expensive.
It is unlikely that a center will close without a fair amount of advance notice to parents.	

Quality Care

The demands for quality outside care for children are continuously increasing, not only in the United States but around the world (see Cultural Variations). But, just what is quality care? Several criteria determine the quality of the child care (see Table 9.7 on page 326), but an often overlooked factor (and one that is exceedingly important) is the child-care provider. Studies quite consistently show that the child-care provider's behaviors in the child-care or preschool setting predict the performance and development of children. Children whose teachers talk to them more are advanced in communication and language skills, and they score higher on intelligence tests (Erwin & Kontos, 1998). Children whose caregivers are stimulating, educational, and respectful and who offer them "intellectually valuable" experiences, especially language mastery experiences, have more advanced social and intellectual skills. Children tend to become more socially competent if teachers encourage their self-direction and independence, cooperation and knowledge, and self-expression and social interaction (Clarke-Stewart, Gruber, & Fitzgerald, 1994).

Quality day-care centers have well-trained, stable caregivers. Many researchers demonstrate a link

Cultural Variations

Child Care

Increasing demands for child-care centers are found in many countries throughout the Western world as a result of a tremendous growth in the number of children attending child care. In France, for example, nearly 25 percent of children under the age of 2 and 80 percent of the 3- and 4-year-olds are in group-care settings (Pierrehumbert, Ramstein, Karmaniola, & Halfon, 1996). In Switzerland, about 90 percent of children go to nursery school, and in urban regions the figure rises to nearly 100 percent. Even in countries such as Holland, where child care outside the home is relatively rare (with only 2.5 percent of children under 4 years attending child care), the demand for child-care facilities is rising so rapidly that plans have been made to increase the number by nine times the current number by the year 2002 (Duindam & Spruijt, 1998).

Some countries, such as the United States, Canada, and Great Britain, are simply not able to meet current demands. These three countries rank in the bottom third of all Western countries with respect to supply and demand (Lamb, 1999). Although is it often difficult to determine accurately the true demand for child-care services, there are waiting lists for parents who want access to child care in countries such as Belgium, Germany, and Italy (Corsaro & Emiliani, 1992).

Why are we seeing such an increase in the numbers of children attending child care? Certainly, the rising number of women working in paid labor is a factor, but it appears to be only part of the cause. In France, for instance, demand for child-care facilities is increasing faster than female employment (Pierrehumbert et al., 1996). Further, another observed phenomenon is that well-off social classes are choosing increasingly more often to send their children to child-care facilities. To illustrate, in Sweden (Wessels, Lamb, Hwang, & Broberg, 1997), the higher the social status of parents, the earlier they tend to have their children attend child-care facilities. In French-speaking Switzerland, the social composition of customers of child-care centers has changed radically, with fewer children of working-class families and more children attending from the more well-to-do classes (Pierrehumbert et al., 1996). Educational services are a major reason they enroll their children in preschool.

As a result of this new kind of customer, we are also witnessing a change in the purpose of children attending child care; no longer viewed as some kind of custodial service, it has evolved into a sought-after provider of educational and social services. William Corsaro and Francesca Emiliani (1992) note that in Italy the *asilo nido* (child-care center) mainly existed, until recently, as a necessity for working mothers rather than an educational service. Today, however, the *asilo nido* is seen as the first stage of schooling, and learning skills are stressed to help young children become "good pupils" in school. As in Italy, the purpose of sending children to child care in the United States, Germany, and France is to help prepare them for the academic world.

Although academic goals may be a primary reason for sending children to child care in some countries, this is not the case in Japan and China. In Asian countries, it is believed that social skills and social relations with the teacher must precede school-based learning. Therefore, a variety of social skills have to come first before one can focus fruitfully on the intellectual development of the child. In almost every Japanese and Chinese child-care setting, the greatest attention is first given to building the teacher–child and child–peer relationships; only after this can one effectively promote cognitive development (Yi Qing, 1999).

between the level of education and/or training that a caregiver has received and her behavior with children in her care. Child-care providers who have more training in child development are generally more knowledgeable, interactive, helpful, talkative, playful, positive, affectionate, and involved. Caregivers with fewer than 2 or 3 years of experience too often just go along with children and do not initiate educational activities. Caregivers with more professional child-care experience are likely to be more stimulating, responsive, accepting, and positive (Clarke-Stewart et al., 1994).

TABLE 9.7

Characteristics of High-Quality Child Care

Characteristic	Criteria
Health and safety	Adult supervision is constant; no children are left unattended; the setting is reasonably clean and the procedures for preparing food and diapering children are sanitary; meals are nutritious and served at appropriate intervals.
Physical setting	The indoor environment is clean and well-lighted; outdoor play areas are fenced, spacious, and free of hazards and include age-appropriate toys (slides, swings).
Child-caregiver ratio	There are no more than 3 infants or 4 to 6 toddlers per caregiver.
Toys/Activities	Toys and activities are age-appropriate; infants and toddlers are always supervised, even in free play indoors; enough materials are available so that children do not have to compete for them.
Family links	Parents are always welcome, and caregivers confer freely with them about their child's behavior.
Licensing	The child-care setting is licensed by the state and (ideally) accredited by the National Family Day Care Program or the National Academy of Early Childhood Programs.

From *Finding the Best Care for Your Infant and Toddler,* by L. L. Dittman, 2000, [Brochure], Washington, DC: National Association for the Education of Young Children. Used by permission.

Another factor that influences the quality of care that providers offer is the length of time they have been in the particular child-care or preschool setting. In stable settings, the caregiver has more opportunity to get to know the children. Finally, the degree of the caregiver's commitment to or emotional investment in children is another important characteristic. Child-care providers who are less committed or emotionally invested are likely to keep an emotional distance from the children they care for, which in turn, decreases the likelihood that the children will form a positive relationship with them. Clearly, the research shows that the child-care provider plays a crucial role in determining the quality of the child's experience in nonparental care.

Thought **CHALLENGE**

Should parents be responsible for their children's school readiness, or should it be a public responsibility with communities offering universal early care and educational services to children?

Kindergarten

In the United States age 5 is a culturally mandated turning point; it signals a shift in the setting for child development from the family and other small, intimate groups such as child care to a larger, less intimate public context: kindergarten. Although some states do not require children to attend kindergarten, for those who do, the first day is generally a time of excitement for most children. As they wait to enter the world of academia for the very first time, some children look eager and confident; some look a bit more fearful and timid; some wait quietly while holding their mothers' hands, and some dash around playing tag—an exuberant burst of energy perhaps before settling into their desks inside the classroom.

Are all these children ready to successfully participate in kindergarten? Does attending preschool help prepare children for this all-important day? What role do parents play in assisting their children to make a satisfactory adjustment to school? For many adults "school readiness" equates to "reading readiness."

School Readiness

Unfortunately, *school readiness* is a term that is nearly as widely misunderstood as it is frequently used. *Readiness* actually involves a number of factors, such as

- *Specific skills* Has the child acquired the simpler skills that enable him or her to learn higher or more complex skills taught in the formal school setting?
- *Health and nutritional status* Does the child's health status enable him or her to both attend school and be able to concentrate in class?
- *Social competence* Does the child have sufficient social skills (sharing and taking turns, for example) to enable him or her to get along with other children?
- *Psychological preparedness* Can the child effectively adapt to and cope with school requirements, such as listening and following directions?

Schools require certain skills to be "mastered" before children are deemed ready for their first systematic educational experience (either kindergarten or first grade). What are some behaviors or skills that you believe are important for the preschooler to learn—not only in academic areas but socially and emotionally? Caregivers differ in the types of expectations that they encourage in children, the age at which they expect a given skill to be acquired, and the level of proficiency they want their children to achieve (Kessler & Graham, 2001).

Further, systematic patterns of variations in parental expectations can be found cross-culturally. Research on a large sample of U.S. and Japanese mothers found that the U.S. mothers in San Francisco expected earlier achievement of social skills with peers and verbal communication in their preschoolers; Japanese mothers, in contrast, expected earlier development of emotional control, compliance with authority, and courtesy (Hess, Kashiwagi, Azuma, Price, &

Child Development Expectations

On the following sample of items, place a check mark in the column that reflects when you expect children to master this skill.

	Before 3 years	Between 3 and 4	After 5 years
1. Sympathetic to feelings of children	____	____	____
2. Comes or answers when called	____	____	____
3. Withstands disappointment without crying	____	____	____
4. Is able to count to 20	____	____	____
5. Shares toys with other children	____	____	____
6. Is able to follow simple directions	____	____	____
7. Gets over anger by himself or herself	____	____	____
8. Recognizes four colors	____	____	____
9. Resolves disagreements without fighting	____	____	____
10. Stops misbehaving when told	____	____	____
11. Stays focused for short periods of time	____	____	____
12. Knows the letters of the alphabet	____	____	____
13. Waits for turn in game	____	____	____
14. Does tasks when told	____	____	____
15. Entertains himself or herself	____	____	____
16. Knows home address	____	____	____

SCORING: 1 point for every response in After 5 years
2 points for every response in Between 3 and 4
3 points for every response in Before 3 years

Higher scores correspond to expecting a behavior to occur at younger ages, which generally equates to your attaching more importance to this behavior. The questionnaire is grouped into four clusters: *Social Competency* items—1, 5, 9, and 13 reflect expected positive peer interactions; *Psychological Preparedness* items—2, 6, 10, and 14 represent orientation toward adaptation to and coping with school requirements; *Independence* items—3, 7, 11, and 15 reflect the child's ability to do things for himself or herself; and *Specific Skill* items—4, 8, 12, and 16 represent learning skills that are often required before entering kindergarten. All four clusters are important to children's readiness for school, so clusters receiving low scores may need more adult attention.

From "Maternal Expectations of Mastery of Developmental Tasks in Japan and the United States," by R. D. Hess, K. Kashiwagi, H. Azuma, G. G. Price, & W. P. Dickinson, 1980, in *International Journal of Psychology, 15,* 259–271. Used by permission.

Dickinson, 1980). Research on samples of mothers in Israel revealed that they expected earlier cognitive development in their infants (Ninio, 1979). High cognitive expectations were also apparent among samples of Vietnamese, Haitian, & French-Canadian parents in Montreal, Canada (Pomerleau, Malcuit, & Sabatier, 1991). Parents' developmental expectations would appear to reflect cultural values as well as beliefs, and they should logically be associated with cultural differences in socialization practices.

What is your *timetable of expectations* for a preschooler? Analysis of your timetables and associated ideas provides a highly feasible way of exploring your notions about the skills that are important in helping to make young children "school ready." (Self-Insight presents a questionnaire, *Child Development Expectations,* designed to reflect your expectations for various school-readiness behaviors and skills—expectations which are then translated into socialization practices.)

Determining Children's School Readiness

In the United States and other Western cultures, age is one of the biggest factors that determine whether or not a child is ready for school (May & Kundert, 1997). Age, in and of itself, however, does not appear to constitute an accurate determinant of school readiness (Morrison, Griffith, & Alberts, 1997). Arbitrary age cutoffs (child turns 5 before December 1) may not be the most satisfactory way of determining kindergarten entry age (Wilgosh, Meyer, & Mueller, 1995). Children who are relatively young when entering first grade make as much progress as older children (Morrison, Griffith, & Alberts, 1997). Other background variables such as social class, parental education, and child-care experience may be more influential than the child's chronological age (Morrison, Griffith, & Alberts, 1997) in determining children's school readiness.

Quick assessment procedures or readiness tests administered by school personnel also are employed as the gatekeepers in granting or denying school entry. These procedures, however, often are problematic in terms of their reliability and validity (Brent, May, & Kundert, 1996; Shepard, 1997). Experts recommend that several indices be used in addition to age or skill-assessment procedures. A currently promising one is assessing the child's basic nervous system processes (functional mobility and strength), which appear to correlate highly with school readiness (Makarenko, Chaichenko, & Bogutskaya, 1999). Moreover, input from parents, teachers, administrators, and health personnel should be utilized when assessing the child's school readiness status. Age, however, continues to be the deciding factor in determining a child's readiness for school.

Delayed Entry

Claudia and Eduardo have a dilemma. Their son Mauro, who is turning 5 in late November, will just make the cutoff age for entering kindergarten in the fall. He seems ready, but they are not sure. After all, he would be one of the youngest children there. Should they let him go?

At one time, parents were not given this choice; if their child was turning 5 by December 1, in most states, he or she had to enter kindergarten. But in recent years, parents have had the option of holding children back a year to make them one of the oldest in the class, in the hope of giving them an academic boost. The recommended alternatives include staying home another year before kindergarten, spending an extra year in "developmental kindergarten," or attending a pre–first-grade class after a year in kindergarten (Buntaine & Costenbader, 1997).

The benefits claimed for allowing children an extra year to grow are largely based on Arnold Gesell's (1972) theory, which predicts that developmentally immature children who are given an extra, maturational year, "the gift of time," will experience fewer learning problems and demonstrate superior academic achievement when compared with their matched counterparts who do not have the benefit of this additional readiness year (May & Kundert, 1997). The academic literature, however, does not back up this claim (Gredler, 1997; Shepard, 1997). At this time, the educational effectiveness of delayed entry or "developmental" kindergarten and first-grade programs for developmentally immature children is not supported by research. The preponderance of studies shows essentially no difference academically between retained children and matched "unready" children who go directly to first grade (Ziegler, 1998).

Better Alternatives

A serious developmental problem in the United States and in many other countries is that some children are not ready when they enter kindergarten or first grade. This has led to high rates of repeating grades, lower overall academic achievement, and dropping out of school. Some schools have identified up to 62 percent of children entering their kindergarten classes as unready (Brent, May, & Kundert, 1996); others say about 35 percent of their students are unready (Ziegler, 1998). Further, parents are increasingly, voluntarily delaying elementary school entry for their children (Meisels, 1996). Clearly, it is certainly important to identify and intervene with children who might not succeed in school, but the philosophical idea that they need more time to mature is questionable. The efficacy of school readiness practices has not been demonstrated and the outcomes of an additional year of kindergarten or first grade in terms of improving academic performance are questionable (May, Kundert, Nikoloff, Welch, Garrett, & Brent, 1994).

The effectiveness of transitional programs for developmentally immature children is not supported by research. A better approach, suggested by Roberta Buntaine and Virginia Costenbader (1997), is simply to have children who are not developmentally ready for kindergarten or first grade attend a program the year *before* kindergarten rather than the year *after* kindergarten or first grade. In this way, perhaps the "early failure syndrome" seen in some children who have been delayed in "developmental" transitional programs can be avoided.

It is further suggested that kindergarten programs, which are often run like academic boot camps, need to be modified (Gredler, 1997). As more and more children attend preschool (more than 50 percent nationally) and watch educational television shows such as *Sesame Street,* there is pressure on kindergarten teachers to implement uniform, academic programs to prepare children for first grade. Thus, expectations are being raised about what children should already know when they come to school. At the same time, first-grade teachers, feeling pressure from higher-grade colleagues or basic-skills mandates, are increasingly reluctant to accept children into first grade who are not already reading. More demanding classrooms may be a factor in promoting school phobia for children (see Child Development Issues).

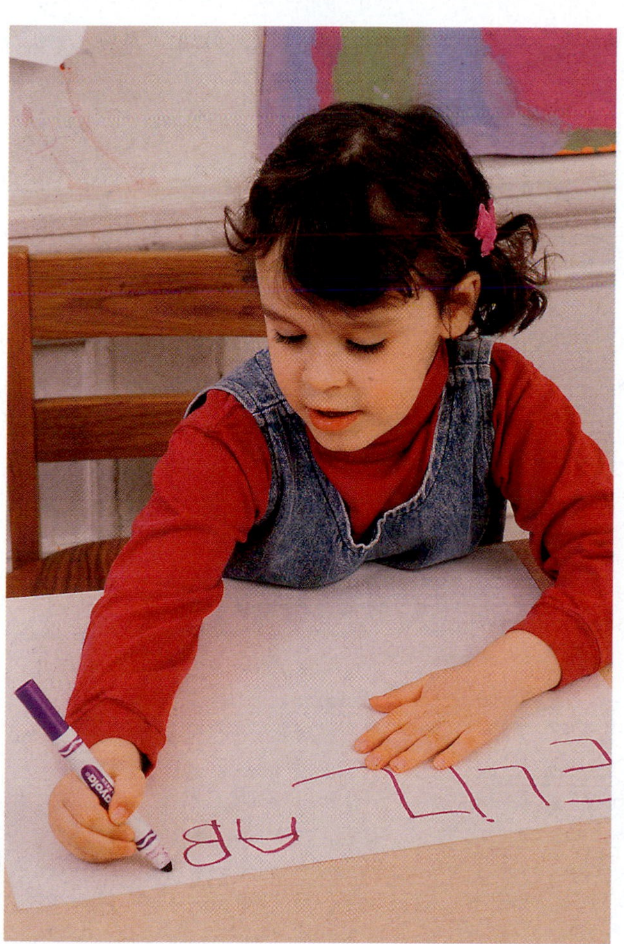

© Laura Dwight

Children once were taught to print their names in kindergarten; now, it is a prerequisite for entering kindergarten.

Rethinking Today's Kindergarten Curriculum

Despite the knowledge of child development research, which maintains that 5-year-olds learn from concrete, hands-on experiences, many teachers are providing fewer opportunities for this type of learning. Lorrie Shepard (1997) notes, for example, that in some kindergartens, children receive red marks on their coloring assignments when they fail to stay within the lines, in contrast to the more developmentally appropriate practice of having children draw their own pictures. Many educators have questioned whether the academically focused kindergarten curriculum has demonstrated its superiority in a way that justifies the retentions that are often a byproduct of its requirements (Ziegler, 1998) and are calling for a more developmentally appropriate, less-academic approach to kindergarten (Gredler, 1997; Nason, 1991).

Reading Readiness

One of the most important skills that children need to master is reading; almost all school subjects make demands on the child's ability to read. Formal reading instruction begins in first grade and if a child is not reading well at the end of first grade, the odds are significantly high that he or she will continue on this poor-reader trajectory in the grades that follow (Juel, 1998). The child's overall academic performance will suffer as well (Baydar, Brooks-Gunn, & Furstenberg, 1993). How can concerned adults help young children prepare for reading success?

Developing an Early Love for Reading

Children's first introduction to the world of reading usually comes through exposing them to all kinds of attractively illustrated printed matter, such as picture books and magazines that capture their interest. Library visits, parents' own print exposure, and reading to children are all related to children's reading success (Senechal, LeFevre, Hudson, & Lawson, 1996). An early love for reading is a key prerequisite in predicting a lifetime of literacy experience (Cunningham & Stanovich, 1998). Further, the more children read, the better their reading skills and the richer their vocabulary.

Thought CHALLENGE

In your opinion, what should be the primary goals achieved in the kindergarten setting?

Child Development Issues

School Phobia: What Is It and What Can Be Done About It?

Austin no longer wanted to go to kindergarten. He said he felt scared there. Probably he was worried that while he was gone something might happen to me. He didn't want me out of his sight at home. He would play upstairs in his room as long as I was nearby. But, if I went downstairs, he would stop what he was doing and follow me. If I went outside, he insisted on coming. He was like a shadow. Before he started school, he had been quite independent.

Entering the formal school setting can be quite stressful for some children; being away from home causes a great deal of anxiety. Such children, in their attempt to relieve this anxiety, try with dogged determination to keep from going to school (Elliott, 1999). This perplexing and challenging problem is known as school phobia or school refusal. School phobia is the irrational dread of some aspect of the school situation, accompanied by symptoms of anxiety or panic when attendance is imminent. The most common ages for school refusal are 5 to 12 years. It affects between 5 to 10 percent of American children in its milder form and about 1 percent of them in its severest form (Evans, 2000).

Usually, these school-avoiding children experience discomfort or become upset when they even think about facing another day at school; most do not know exactly why they feel this way. They just know they feel better and more comfortable when they are home. Their anxiety-related symptoms may be vague and unexplainable or, in some cases, take on particular complaints of headaches or stomachaches. More clear-cut symptoms like vomiting, fever, or weight loss (which may have a physical basis) are uncommon. Whatever the symptoms, they occur on school days but rarely on weekends. Often doctors cannot detect any true illness.

Often these symptoms are young children's way of communicating their emotional struggle because of issues like:

- Separating from their mother
- Worrying about parents getting hurt (killed or kidnapped)
- Being picked on or teased by the other children
- Thinking about younger siblings at home who are getting all of their mother's attention

Older school-age children may experience school refusal because of "generalized" fears such as:

- Taking quizzes and tests
- Talking in front of class
- Doing poorly in a particular subject
- Fear of failure
- Not getting along with classmates
- A perceived "meanness" of the teacher
- Being humiliated or embarrassed

At home, parents may observe further reluctance to venture away from home. The child, for example, may not want to go on overnight stays at friends' houses or go to summer camp. In the classroom, these children may cry often, spend excessive time in the nurse's office, or withdraw from participating with their classmates.

To allay these fears and worries, these children find comfort in clinging to their parents and demanding constant attention. Parents then may unwittingly reinforce the child's behavior by catering to their whims and coddling and pampering them, which, according to experts, only worsens the problem (King, Ollendick, Tonge, Heyne, Pritchard, Rollings, Young, & Myerson, 1998). Instead, parents need to acknowledge the child's concerns, but, in a caring way, set firm rules about school attendance (Kearney & Roblek, 1998). Scholars agree that missed days from school take their toll on children's educational progress; chronic absenteeism holds many children back (Hansen, Sanders, Massaro, & Last, 1998). For these reasons, it is often suggested that it is better to err on the side of sending the child to school. Generally, once children begin to attend school regularly, their physical symptoms tend to disappear (King et al., 1998).

As a first step, the management of school phobia involves an examination by a doctor who can rule out physical illness. The next step for younger children may involve helping them deal with separation anxiety. Desensitization, a common anxiety treatment, often helps children grow accustomed to separating from their mother and to grow more accustomed to the school setting. With this treatment, an adult stays with the child in the classroom for periods of time that gradually decrease in duration and frequency. Or, the child, on day 1, may attend for a favorite activity or lesson time and then go home; on day 2, he or she attends for a half day; on day 3, the child attends the entire day. Throughout, children are helped to realize that extended separations from their mother hurt neither them nor their mothers. For older children, pinpointing their fears and helping them overcome them helps to resolve school refusal issues. For example, if the child fears failure in a particular class, receiving additional help from a tutor may solve the problem. If the child fears the class bully, coping-skills training helps children avert the bully's tactics.

Finally, overcoming school phobia requires a team effort. By selectively targeting and overcoming fears and eliciting help from parents, pediatricians, and school staff, most phobias about attending school can be conquered.

Search Online

Explore InfoTrac College Edition, your online library. Go to **http://www.infotrac-college.com/wadsworth** and use the passcode that came on the card with your book. Try these search terms: school phobia, fear of school, school anxiety.

Shared Reading

> Mayra reads to her preschooler every night. She mentions that her purpose for reading to her child is to "prepare him for school." Mayra is the active one, eliciting little input from her child. Louisa also takes time to read to her child. Her objective is to open up the exciting world of books to her preschooler. Louisa actively draws her child into the story by asking for input. "Why did Pooh lose the honey? Where should he go and look for it?"

Mayra's reading style does not further her child's reading success; Louisa's shared-reading style does (Durkin, 1990). Adults who read to their children to "enchant them with the world of books" and those who frequently ask for input from the child about the story have children who become successful readers. Grover Whitehurst and his colleagues (Whitehurst, Arnold, Epstein, Angell, Smith, & Fischel, 1994; Whitehurst & Lonigan, 1998) point out that this type of shared reading, called *dialogic reading,* can produce substantial changes in preschool children's language skills. During typical reading styles, such as Mayra's, the adult reads and the child listens passively. In dialogic reading the child learns to become the storyteller. The adult assumes the role of an active listener, asking questions, adding information, and prompting the child to increase the sophistication of descriptions of the material in the picture book. A child's responses to the book are encouraged through praise and repetition, and more sophisticated responses are encouraged by expansions of the child's utterances and by more challenging questions from the adult reading partner (Cooney, 2001).

Emergent Writing Skills

Engaging in "writing" activities helps promote reading skills as well (Cunningham & Stanovich, 1998). Behaviors such as pretending to write and learning to write letters are examples of emergent writing skills. Many adults have had the experience of seeing a young child scribble some indecipherable marks on paper and then ask an adult to read what it says. The child is indicating that he or she knows print has meaning without yet knowing how to write. These "writing" activities need to be encouraged. For many children in the late preschool period, letters come to stand for the different syllables in words, and from this stage children finally begin to use letters to represent the individual sounds,

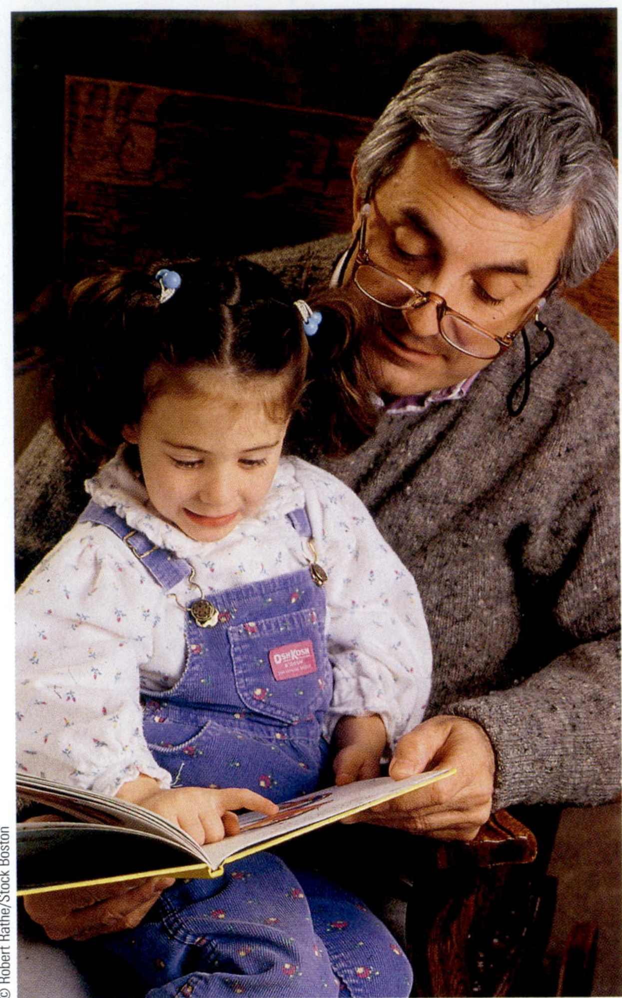

© Robert Rathe/Stock Boston

Shared reading enables the child to be an active participant in the reading process, and this leads to more sophisticated language skills and reading success.

or *phonemes*, in words. In the English language, phonemes are the hard and soft consonant sounds and the long and short vowel sounds.

Knowledge of Letters

Knowledge of the alphabet at entry into school is one of the strongest single predictors of reading success (Adams, 1990). A number of studies indicate that letter knowledge significantly influences the acquisition of phonological sensitivity skills (Bowey, 1994; Johnston, Anderson, & Holligan, 1996). Sensitivity to phonemes, individual letter sounds, is one of the strongest predictors of later reading achievement. Adults can help the young child develop phonological sensitivity skills by drawing attention to the alphabet letters and the sounds they produce. Children who develop skills such as detecting syllables, rhymes, or phonemes learn to read at a faster and easier rate (Wagner & Torgesen, 1997), and this relation is present even after variability in reading skills due to intelligence, receptive vocabulary, memory skills, and social class is accounted for (Bryant, MacLean, Bradley, & Crossland, 1990).

Learning and Television and Videos

Clearly, reading preparedness equates to reading success and, in turn, academic success. What about the roles of television and videos? Do they enhance children's academic success? Television is a familiar companion to children. Most families have a television set (98 percent), and several households (52 percent) have more than one (Dorr & Rabin, 1995). Clearly, young children spend a great deal of time watching television. The average U.S. preschooler watches an average of 3 hours of television and videos a day (Huston & Wright, 1996). Averages tell only part of the story; variations among individuals are extremely high. For example, the range of total hours viewed in one week is from 0 to 75 hours (Berry & Asamen, 1993).

Establishing Patterns

The total time children spend watching television and videos is stable; this pattern is established in early childhood (Troseth & DeLoache, 1998). The amount of television and video viewing found at ages 3 to 5 is generally the same amount as at ages 5 to 7 (Asamen & Berry, 1998). Three-year-olds who watch 2 to 3 hours of television a day also watch the same number of hours of television a day when they are 5 years old (Huston, Wright, Rice, Kerkman, & St. Peters, 1990). These consistencies may reflect the influence of family environments in which adults and older siblings have stable habits of television and video use to which children are exposed early in life. Whatever the reason, the finding is important because the acquisition of television- and video-viewing patterns established in early childhood appears to have long-term implications.

Similarly, the types of shows that children watch also show a pattern of stability. For example, children who tend to watch humorous cartoons watch comedy shows at a later age. Many children prefer adventure programs and continue to prefer these types of shows when they are older. There does, however, tend to be a difference in the type of television viewing that young boys and girls prefer both in the United States and other countries as well. Patti Valkenburg and Sabine

Janssen (1999), for example, collected data from Dutch and U.S. first- through fourth-graders and found that boys in both samples attached more value to action and violence in children's programming, whereas girls in both samples attached more value to family and romance in children's programming.

Because watching television is usually defined as presence in the room with the television on, it can signify active, concentrated attention or passive, shallow exposure. However, videotapes of home viewing show that children between the ages of 3 and 7 attend visually to the television 50 to 70 percent of the time that they are in the room (Van Evra, 1998). Attention tends to peak at 80 percent in later childhood (ages 10 to 12).

Educational Advantages

Such educational television shows as *Sesame Street, Barney & Friends,* and *The Electric Company* can develop readiness skills in preschoolers (Singer & Singer, 1998). The results of a two-year longitudinal study offers solid evidence for the positive linguistic impact of *Sesame Street* on young children, particularly 3- to 5-year-olds (Rice, Huston, Truglio, & Wright, 1990). Such skills, however, may be limited to specially programmed and lower-level skills such as alphabet naming, matching forms, and naming numbers. Language comprehension may be facilitated by television and videos because the language used is similar to parentese; that is, it includes short sentence structures, recasting of key information, and emphasis on important words (Van Evra, 1998).

Other critics have hypothesized that the production techniques of programs such as *Sesame Street* engender hyperactivity, short attention spans, and lack of interest in slower paced, less visually appealing classroom work. Is your past viewing of *Sesame Street* responsible for your preference for action-packed movies? Can this explain why you are constantly flipping television channels with your remote control? Research, however, does not seem to support the claim that production techniques involving fast pacing and relatively high action levels produce hyperactivity (Jason & Hanaway, 1997).

Parent–child verbal interaction while watching television and videos is clearly important. For example, parents contribute to their children's linguistic processing when they watch television with their young children, take turns asking questions, and label and comment on the content, thus providing a rich combination of television/video dialogue, their own language, and comments about language and television events.

The Downside of Television

The primary problem of television lies not so much in the behavior it produces as the behavior it prevents: family interaction—the talks, the games, the family festivities, and arguments through which much of the child's learning takes place and his or her character is formed. When young children are watching television with their parents, the nature of interaction between family members is "parallel" rather than interactive. Parents and children talk less, they are less active, and children pay less attention to their parents when watching television (Bryant, 1990; Kubey & Csikszentmihalyi, 1990).

Some maintain that there is a trend toward restricting the content and amount of children's television and video viewing (Desmond, Singer, & Singer, 1990). However, restriction seems rather rare; most parents "never" or only "occasionally" engage in restrictive practices (Dorr, 1993).

APPLICATIONS:

Helping Children Make a Successful Adjustment to School

Entry into the formal school setting of kindergarten or elementary school introduces several systematic changes into children's social worlds—formal evaluations of their competence begin, ability grouping begins with their assignments to reading groups, and peers begin to play a more prominent role in their lives. Each of these changes affects children's adjustment to school. Children's *social adjustment,* however, appears to have a profound impact on their making a successful transition to school, including perceptions of school (liking or disliking), involvement in school (increased or avoidance of participation), and performance (doing well or not doing well) (Birch & Ladd, 1998).

Social Adjustment

Social adjustment refers to the child being accepted by peers, engaging in prosocial behaviors toward others, and developing positive feelings toward classmates. Research shows that poor peer relationships are a significant predictor of both short-term school adjustment as well as long-term school adaptation and retention (Ladd, Kochenderfer, & Coleman, 1997). Short-term consequences involve children not doing well academically; long-term consequences pertain to higher incidences of dropping out of school (Birch & Ladd, 1997; Kantrowitz & Wingert, 1994).

Fostering Friendships

Parents play an important role in fostering positive peer adjustment. In a careful examination of the relationships between parent–child interactions prior to school entrance and children's social adaptation in kindergarten, Joan Barth and Ross Parke (1993) observed parent–child physical play interactions prior to children entering school. Parent–child physical interactions were used because such physical play is an emotionally arousing activity that requires skillful and coordinated interaction between parents and children for play to succeed. Both mother–child and father–child interactions predict subsequent school social adaptation (Ladd & Kochenderfer, 1998).

First, the amount of time that the parent and children were engaged in sustained-play interaction was a significant predictor of school adjustment. For mothers, play engagement prior to the child entering school was associated with more considerate and less-dependent behavior and more favorable school attitudes by children during kindergarten. Low play engagement was associated with loneliness immediately after school began and hostile classroom behavior at the end of the school semester.

For father–child dyads, play engagement was associated with more favorable home behaviors both prior to the onset of school and at school. These results deserve special attention because play engagement seems to be positively linked to children's emotional skills and to other peer acceptance measures (Parke, MacDonald, Burks, Bhavnagri, Barth, & Beitel, 1989).

Getting along with others plays a paramount role in children's academic success in school.

Second, the style of interaction is an important correlate of children's social adjustment. Children who are highly directive with their mothers and unwilling to accept her input are more hostile and less considerate in the classroom. In addition, these children experience higher levels of loneliness after the initial onset of school and greater dependency on the teacher at the end of the first school semester. Dyads with a controlling mother and an uncooperative, resistant child are related to dependence and hostility at the end of the semester. Similarly, father–child dyads characterized by this control–resist pattern are associated with school loneliness and home behavioral problems.

In another related study (Cowan, Cowan, Schulz, & Heming, 1994), parents were evaluated during the preschool period and kindergarten when children's academic competence and social relationships with peers were evaluated. Ineffective parenting, characterized by low warmth and structuring, in the preschool period predicted low academic achievement and shy, withdrawn behaviors in kindergarten. In addition, low warmth in the preschool period was related to aggressive ways of behaving toward peers in the kindergarten setting. Taken together, these studies show that controlling and directive parenting styles and noncompliant demanding child behaviors are negatively related to social adjustment in school settings and peer sociometric assessments. Most important, these data suggest that earlier observed parent–child interaction patterns have value in predicting subsequent social adjustment in school and peer contexts.

Evidence reveals that children whose parents tend to foster contact with peers at home and in the community during preschool tend to have higher levels of social adjustment when they enter new kindergarten classrooms (Ladd & Kochenderfer, 1998). Moreover, higher levels of adjustment are found for children whose parents supervised their peer contacts in indirect, noninterfering ways. Further, enrolling the child in a good preschool a few days a week may be another way to help foster children's social readiness for school. Even if children stay home and do not attend preschool, however, they also need quality time with peers (Ladd & Coleman, 1997). Parents might, for example, arrange for children to attend preschool and develop neighborhood friendships with age-mates prior to the time they enter grade school. Although scholars have always emphasized quality time with parents, recent research is beginning to recognize the importance of quality time with peers.

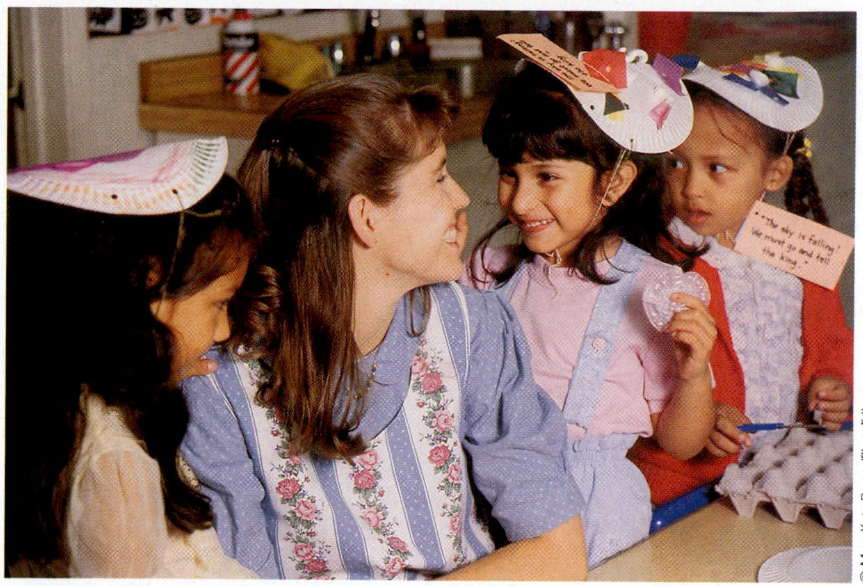

A positive teacher–child relationship in the early years of school facilitates the child's adjustment to and success in school.

Teacher Relationships

Teacher–child relationships also play an important role in children's adjustment outcomes in kindergarten and first grade (Pianta, Nimetz, & Bennett, 1997). Both the teacher's perception of the student and the student's perception of the teacher are important dimensions of the teacher–student relationships. Beyond the quality of children's ties with peers, supportive relationships with teachers appear to facilitate adjustment and success in the school setting. Further, conflictual or stressful teacher–child relationships seem to interfere with successful adaptation in school contexts.

> Alexis has been in kindergarten for four months. In this particular kindergarten class, a child receives a yellow card to warn them to "settle down"; they receive a blue card as a warning that he or she will be sent to the principal's office; three blue cards within a week sends a child to the principal's office. Alexis has been sent to the principal three times already for various behaviors such as not having her homework assignment, talking out of turn, and not listening. The teacher notes that she is constantly having to "discipline" Alexis.

Three qualitatively distinct aspects of the teacher–child relationship are related to young children's school adjustment: closeness, dependency, and conflict (Birch & Ladd, 1997). *Closeness* involves the degree of warmth and open communication that exists between a teacher and a child. *Dependency* refers to possessive and "clingy" child behaviors that are indicative of an overreliance on the teacher as a source of support. *Conflict* in the teacher–child relationship functions as a stressor for children in the school environment and may impair their successful adjustment to school.

Specifically, children who have a positive teacher–child relationship—relationships that are relatively close, nondependent, and nonconflictual—perform better academically than children with less close, more dependent, or more conflictual relationships with their teachers. Children who share a close relationship with the teacher may perceive the school environment as a supportive one, and this may promote positive attitudes toward school.

Three child behaviors that play a central role in the formation and maintenance of teacher–child relationships are moving "against" others, moving "away" from others, and moving "toward" others (Ladd, Kochenderfer, & Coleman, 1997). Children who move against others tend to exhibit asocial behaviors such as defiance and aggression toward teachers. Moving away from others signifies a reluctance or lack of interest on the child's part in relating to teachers; the child tends to display fearful and anxious behaviors. Moving toward others constitutes an interaction style that is engaging, cooperative, and helpful to teachers.

These behavioral orientations may be useful indicators of early risk for teacher–child relationship difficulties. As such, it is important that teachers recognize the significance of supportive teacher–child relationships in children's early school adjustment (Furman, 1998).

Early Intervention

Some other potentially useful strategies for adults and educators interested in preventing children's school adjustment problems follow from this research. Prior to kindergarten entrance, it may be useful to identify children who are prone to exhibiting maladaptive behavioral dispositions and involve them in interventions designed to promote prosocial, adaptive behaviors. For example, it may be beneficial to help children learn how to inhibit aggressive acts and pursue more extensive positive contacts with others. Gains in these skills may better enable children to form positive relationships with teachers as well as to make new friends and achieve higher levels of peer acceptance when they enter grade-school classrooms.

Concept Checks

1. Cite two factors that will promote school readiness in children:

   ____

   ____

2. Cite two factors that will promote reading readiness in children:

   ____

   ____

3. Your advice to Claudia and Eduardo's dilemma about their son Mauro, who will turn 5 in November, would be to
   a. delay his school entry for one year giving him the "gift of time."
   b. delay his school entry because age is the most influential criteria in succeeding in kindergarten.
   c. have him attend a one-year program before starting kindergarten.
4. Which child is likely to make the most satisfactory adjustment to school?
   a. Peter, who tends to move "against" others
   b. Sam, who tends to move "away" from others
   c. Mimi, who tends to move "toward" others

Reviewing Key Points

The Young Child's Thinking Skills

- Preoperational thinking in children is so organized that they "overattend" in the attention they pay to the appearance of things; as such they are "perceptual" thinkers. Piaget described the thought of preoperational children as intuitive, egocentric, and illogical.
- Neo-Piagetian theories such as Robbie Case's focus on children's working memory, known as executive processing space. The functional capacity of working memory depends on the automaticity with which operations are executed. As working memory increases, it becomes easier to acquire more elaborate structures. This increases the problem-solving strategies available to children.
- Vygotsky focuses on how culture (values, beliefs, customs, and skills of a social group) is transmitted to children. He maintains that children's skills and competencies result from interaction between them and more knowledgeable and mature members of society, such as parents. To this end, parents play a large part in children's "apprenticeship in thinking."
- As information processors, preschoolers are less likely to rehearse (repeat material silently or out loud) than older children. Young children can be "taught" to rehearse with only minimal instruction; however, when given the option on later trials, most children revert to their nonrehearsal status. Young children have excellent recognition but poor recall skills.
- Young children's theory of mind suggests that they are increasingly able to construe people's outward behaviors in terms of underlying mental states such as beliefs and desires. Sometime between the ages of 3 and 5, children are able to understand false beliefs, which refers to their ability to understand that another individual holds a belief that differs both from reality and from what they themselves know to be true.
- According to Vygotsky, to help children achieve a high level of performance parents need to work within children's zone of proximal development. Adults can help children learn best when they teach them skills they are capable of learning and apply just the right amount of guidance and assistance.

Language Development

- At about the age of 2, children enter the two-word stage of language development. Some sounds (*st, sm*) are still difficult for them to pronounce. Between 3 and 4 years, most children enter the telegraphic stage, in which they use short, simple sentences made up primarily of content words.
- Speech and hearing problems need to be attended to promptly before developmental delays occur. Expansions and recastings help to promote language development.
- Early childhood may be a good time to learn a second language mainly because young children are able to pronounce phonemes in other languages more successfully than when they are older. Learning a second language should be a fun experience for young children and not just consist of regimented drills.

Early Education

- For many preschoolers, family care and center child care represent the child's first exposure to informal "learning" settings outside the home. To maximize children's cognitive growth in these settings, certain criteria for quality of the setting are important. Attending quality preschool programs, with warm and empathic caregivers who communicate frequently with them helps children learn vital social and academic skills that will help them to succeed in school both socially and academically.

- Reading readiness can be fostered by helping children develop a love for reading, engaging in shared reading (dialogic reading), encouraging emergent writing skills, and helping them learn the alphabet and its phonetic sounds.
- Watching television may help children acquire certain language and cognitive skills, however, television-viewing patterns, both the amount children watch and the types of television shows they watch, are established in early childhood.
- Social readiness is extremely important in helping children make a successful transition from preschool to the formal school setting. Children will do better in school if they learn how to get along with others. Similarly, children do better in school when their relationships with teachers are positive. Parents can help children develop social skills directly through teaching them how to share, for example, and indirectly by arranging for them to attend preschool and play with neighborhood friends. Teachers can help promote social skills by helping children maintain old friends and form new ones. Teachers also need to be aware of the impact their relationship with children has on their academic progress.

Answers to Concept Checks

The Young Child's Thinking Skills

1. b
2. c
3. true
4. theory of mind; 4
5. scaffolding

Language Development

1. c
2. a
3. b

Early Education

1. health and nutritional status, social competence, and psychological preparedness
2. develop a love for reading; read to the child; engage in writing activities; learn alphabet letters
3. c
4. c

Key Terms

animistic thinking
center care
dysfluency
egocentric speech
egocentrism
executive processing space
expansion
false belief
family care
inner speech
irreversibility
metamemory
operations
perceptual centration
preoperational stage
private speech
recall
recasting
recognition
rehearsal
representation
retrieval
scaffolding
symbolic play
telegraphic speech
theory of mind
transductive reasoning
zone of proximal development

InfoTrac College Edition

For additional readings, explore InfoTrac College Edition, your online library. Go to **http://www.infotrac-college.com/wadsworth** and use the passcode that came on the card with your book. Try these search terms: early childhood education, second language acquisition, school-age child care.

Child Development CD-ROM

Go to the Wadsworth Child Development CD-ROM for further study of the concepts in this chapter. The CD-ROM also includes quizzes and additional activities to expand your learning experience.

CHAPTER TEN

Socioemotional Development: *Early Childhood*

CHAPTER OUTLINE

Social Understandings
- The Young Child's World of Play
- Preschool Friendships
- Understanding Self
- Gender Roles
- Applications: Socializing Children into Gender Equality

Emotional Development
- Culture and Emotion
- Emotional Understandings in Early Childhood
- Common Emotions: Fear and Anger
- Applications: Helping Young Children Deal Effectively with Anger

Family Influences in Early Childhood
- Parents as Guidance Engineers
- Guidance Strategies
- When Punishment Goes Awry: Child Abuse
- Applications: Helping Abused Children

Reviewing Key Points

ho are you?"

My name is Khisha. I am this many (holds up 2 fingers). I have 14 freckles.

I'm Michael. I am in first grade. I am strong and can ride my bike lots of places. I can print well and the teacher likes me.

"What is a friend?"

A friend is someone who likes you and you like her. You play together and have fun. But when you fight, she is no longer your friend.

Drew is my friend. We play video games after school, make forts in the backyard, and go to Scouts together.

The best term to describe the socioemotional development of children during early childhood is expansion. **Expansion** describes young children's broadening sense of who they are. Initially, 2-year-olds categorize themselves in terms of two or three self-defining traits—their gender, names, and perhaps age—but by age 6, they not only have developed a relatively large array of self-categorizations across many different areas (physical, social, cognitive, for example) but have formed self-evaluations (good, bad, neutral) of these traits.

Expansion describes their social existence as well. Initially, preschoolers' social world centers around their family and other caring adults, but now their social horizons broaden as they venture forth to meet other children in settings outside the home. Neighborhood friends and preschool classmates become the chief way in which children learn firsthand about sharing and aggression. Friendships evolve from quick and fleeting relationships into those that have a more solid and enduring basis. As children's interest in friends and activities outside the home progresses, we witness the lessening in intensity of their exclusive focus on their mothers.

Our first look at socioemotional development during the early childhood years makes us aware that the preschooler's world is one of expanding understandings of self and others: learning what it means to be a boy or a girl, experiencing a broader range of emotions, and searching for independence and individuality. As expansive as their social world becomes—as daring, invincible, and independent as they behave—these "grown-up" behaviors are often closely followed by the "baby-ness" in all preschoolers. As one mother notes in reflecting on her children's early childhood years:

> They seem to feel invincible and capable of mastering anything yet always need guidance. They are brave little souls—spending their first night in a big bed, yet needing assurance, witnessed by their middle-of-the-night visits because there's a dragon in their room. Paradoxically, they are constantly showing acts of daring followed shortly by cuddling close. They venture off—saying good-bye and walking away on their first day of kindergarten; yet, they remain close—"Read *Winnie the Pooh* again tonight, okay Mom?"

The preschool years also represent a time when caregivers begin in earnest to socialize children to behave in socially competent and appropriate ways. What are some effective guidance strategies? Is punishment a good technique for helping children learn to behave in proper ways? What about when punishment goes awry as in the case of child abuse? How are physically, emotionally, and sexually abused children affected by these inhumane actions? Research findings offer some intriguing answers to these questions, as you will see in the chapter's final section.

Social Understandings

expansion
Describes young children's broadening sense of who they are as they enter middle childhood.

Before Beginning . . .

After reading this section, you will be able to

- identify the types and understand the functions of children's play.
- examine the nature of children's first friendships.
- characterize the development of self-systems in early childhood.
- describe the development of gender roles.
- see the implications of gender-role equality.

The Young Child's World of Play

> The afternoon sun warms the muddy banks of the Kuskokwim River as several 6-year-old Eskimo girls sit quietly talking and working their dull, flat knives into the mud in front of them. They carefully prepare smooth mud palettes, which will be used for telling stories. This spot on the riverbank has been a favorite storyknifing place of the girls for years. It is well away from the foot and bicycle traffic that connects the houses to the church, school, post office, and grocery store. After their palettes are ready, the young girls begin their storytelling. Each storyteller illustrates her tale by drawing symbols in the mud, which are erased and replaced with new symbols as the story unfolds. When one storyteller finishes, another begins, until they tire of the play or it is time to go home for dinner. (DeMarrais, Nelson, & Baker, 1994)

From the very first days of a child's development, his or her activities take on a meaning of their own in a unique cultural system. To understand play, then, it is essential to examine specific social and cultural contexts in which it takes place. Play not only reflects children's culture but provides them opportunities to learn about their culture. Historically, the Eskimo culture has relied on cooperation among its members to survive in extremely harsh environmental conditions.

Through closely knit kinship systems, Yup'ik Eskimo communities are able to maintain this cooperation. Storyknifing, pictorially telling stories in the mud, was common among villagers in southeastern Alaska. It provided a forum for young children to learn cultural knowledge about group cooperation and consensus, kinship patterns, gender roles, and community norms and values. It was also a way children learned and practiced the skills necessary in the society in which they lived. Play is a universal part of early childhood. Do you remember when you were a child with nothing to do but play for hours and hours each day? Do you remember the excitement of that first climb to the top of the monkey bars, your first successful ride on a two-wheeler, or your first swim all the way across a pool? Our early childhood play experiences may seem meaningless to us now, but they are anything but that.

During early childhood, most of children's social exchanges, like the storyknifing of the Eskimo girls, occur in the setting of play, which generally involves engaging in a nonserious activity for the sheer satisfaction it brings. Most children spend countless hours at play reveling in being silly and gleeful and in just plain having fun. Play is more important, however, than just being silly or having fun. Most theorists, researchers, and educators adhere to the belief that play leads to growth in a variety of developmental domains. During early childhood, many of a child's attempts to gain effective control of the environment and autonomy occur in the context of social interaction with peers (Crews, 2000).

Play facilitates the development of competence and autonomy and helps children achieve a balance between independence and dependence (Haight & Miller, 1993). Through active involvement with the environment, play stimulates creativity and cognitive growth (Bjorklund & Brown, 1998). Moreover, play facilitates language development; during play, children are stimulated to use language to ask questions, talk about their experiences, solve problems, tell stories, and direct activities.

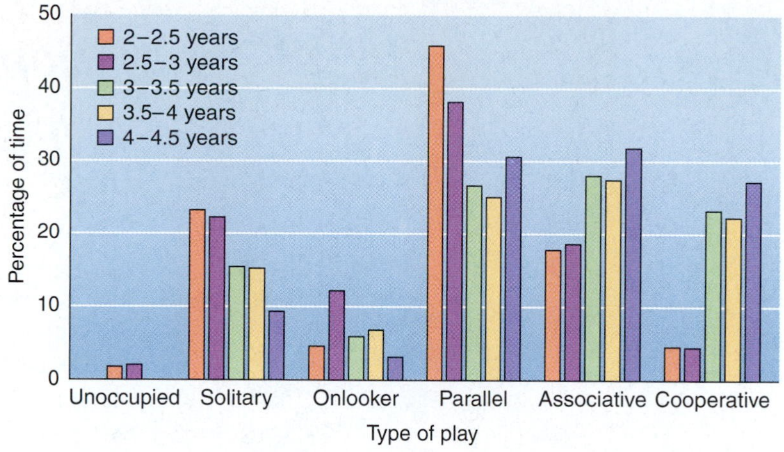

FIGURE 10.1 ***Children's Frequency and Type of Play***

Parten defined six types of play children engage in between the ages of 2 to 4½ years: (1) unoccupied, during which the child wanders about, observing things of momentary interest but does not become involved in any activity; (2) solitary, during which the child plays alone with no direct involvement with other children; (3) onlooker, during which the child observes others play without entering into their activities; (4) parallel, during which the child plays alongside other children; (5) associative, during which the child engages in common activities and talks with other children about them; and (6) cooperative, during which the child plays with a group of children to make something or achieve a goal.

From "Social Participation Among Preschool Children," by M. Parten, 1932, *Journal of Abnormal and Social Psychology, 27,* 243–269.

Social Levels of Play

Mildred Parten (1932) studied children in child-care situations and patiently observed the types of play in which they engaged. She defined six types of play and assessed how often children between the ages of 2 and 4 engaged in each type (see Figure 10.1).

Parten ordered the six play types according to their complexity, beginning with the simplest form of play, **nonsocial activity**, which encompasses the first three types—*unoccupied, solitary,* and *onlooker* play. The other three forms are parallel, associative, and cooperative play.

> Gavin, one of a class of preschoolers, seemingly wanders aimlessly around the room, frequently stopping and observing the other children at play but does not play with them. Sandra plays alone with different toys; even though other children are nearby, she does not get involved them. Tony watches others play without actually entering into their activities. Yet, he is clearly engaged by what is happening and is within speaking distance of the other children.

These types of play reflect unoccupied, solitary, and onlooker play, respectively. Across the room, Sonia and Portia play with the same toys. In **parallel play**, children are aware of each other's presence but do not share toys, talk, or interact except in very minimal ways. In contrast, we may observe other children engaging in a common activity and talking about it with each other. These children, however, do not assign tasks or roles to particular individuals and are not very clear about their goals. This play, common among 4-year-olds, is **associative play**.

Children in early childhood also engage in **cooperative play**, in which they consciously form groups to make something. One or two members organize and direct the activity with others assuming different roles and responsibilities. Four-year-olds spend 51 percent of their free-activity time in cooperative play (Vandenberg, 1998).

In all of Parten's levels of social play, toys are the prime currency of social exchange (Kavanaugh & Engel, 1998). For young children, play materials seem so important that when all objects are removed from the room they take off their shoes to create toys! Young children's sociability seems to revolve around doing some things together, and object-centered contacts are the initial basis of their sustained social interactions.

nonsocial activity The simplest form of play, which is reflected in *onlooker, unoccupied,* and *solitary* play.

parallel play Playing near other children with similar toys but not trying to interact with them.

associative play A form of play when children engage in true social participation; they interact by exchanging toys and commenting on each other's activities.

cooperative play A more sophisticated type of play, in which children work toward a common goal with the same product.

Cultural Variations

© Clave Bryant/PhotoEdit

Play

Walking along the rocky shore, a large group of children discover a rotting old rowboat. They decide that this will be a great place to hide all the treasures they have collected that morning—some shells and rocks mainly. As they hide their cache between the planks of the boat, there is no "captain"; all the children are of equal rank.

A small group of boys play in a nearby field. One young boy, after a hard-won battle, is declared "King of the Hill." He becomes the leader and tells the others what to do. He captures as many children as he can to be on his side to help him defend the hill and his role as the leader.

These brief comparisons highlight some of the differences Mary Martini (1994) found between play among U.S. and Polynesian children from the Marquesas Islands in the South Pacific. The U.S. children tended to be led by one or two dominant children who "bossed" the others around. The Polynesian children, however, were extremely sensitive to relative status and avoided play that required bosses who set rules, decided on scripts, enforced rules, or distributed roles. They preferred play activities that did not require influencing others or individual competition. They rejected leaders or bosses who told them what to do.

The Polynesian children played rather far away from the village and had little contact with adults in the course of their play activities. They did not seek out adults to help them resolve conflicts or to structure their play. In

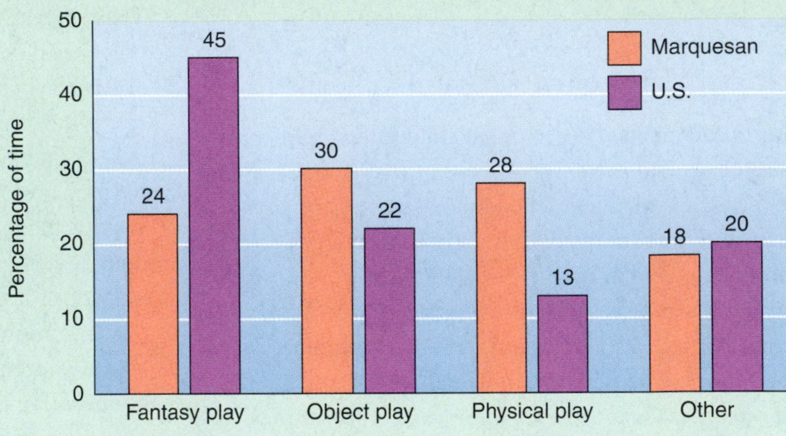

Cross-culturally, object play between parent and child differs. In the United States, for example, parents tend to follow their children's initiatives and become engaged in their activities. This is consistent with the value placed on egalitarianism in the United States. They also tend to engage their children in functionally oriented object play (for example, "Let's see how many blocks we can stack on top of this one"). In non-Western cultures, such as Japan, toys generally serve to mediate social interaction (for example, the mother shows the child how to cuddle the doll) (Tamis-LeMonda, Bornstein, Cyphers, Toda, & Ogino, 1992). Research by Catherine Tamis-LeMonda and her colleagues suggests that the values of encouraging independent activity with objects by U.S. parents and the importance of interpersonal connectedness among the Japanese are manifested in their contrast, young U.S. children played close to home and their parents were likely to know their whereabouts even when they were engaged in unsupervised play. Relatedly, the U.S. parents scheduled eating and resting times, and quite often were seen in roles of negotiator, attempting to solve young children's conflicts. The Polynesian children played in large groups of children; the U.S. children stuck to a few playmates. Fewer playmates made it easier for the parents to coordinate plans, set up play, and perform their role as mediators from time to time.

All the children, however, spent much of their play time in similar types of play that were reminiscent of Parten's play categories.

© Joe Carini/Bear Productions/Pacific Stock

Although children in both cultures engaged in pretend play, the U.S. children did so with twice the frequency of the Polynesian children. The types of pretend play differed between the two groups as well. The Polynesian children's pretend play often included "ship" play (sailing off to unknown lands), in which they docked, loaded, and unloaded the ship. They also fought off invaders and saved drowning shipmates. They prepared and "ate" feasts made out of mud. Like the U.S. children, the Polynesian children engaged in physical play where they ran up and down the boat ramp, chased waves, swung on rope swings, swam in the stream, and ran, galloped, and jumped just for the fun of it. Object play for Polynesian children did not consist of computerized, battery-operated toys but was more likely to involve gathering lemons, picking up leaves, sorting rocks, and pounding them to make different sounds. The Polynesian parents rarely bought toys, which to any U.S. parent who has been caught up in a toy-buying frenzy may seem quite appealing.

object-play organization. Other cross-cultural play differences are highlighted in Cultural Variations.

As children get older, they will engage in more interactive and cooperative play. Although play types do emerge in the order Parten suggested, those that appear later do not replace earlier forms. Rather, all types of play are observable during these early childhood years (Creasey, Jarvis, & Berk, 1998).

Cognitive Levels of Play

Cognitive theorists (Piaget, 1962; Smilansky, 1968) have identified four major types of play that loosely parallel Piaget's stages of cognitive development: functional play, constructive play, pretend play, and games with rules.

During the sensorimotor period, infants engage in functional play, which often involves using their own bodies in play—for example, kicking a mobile. During the preoperational period, between ages 2 to 6, children often engage in constructive play, which involves manipulating objects to build something such as constructing a tower of blocks. **Pretend play**, in which children substitute make-believe, imaginary, and dramatic situations for real ones, is also common to this period. During the beginning of the concrete operational period, at about age 6 or 7, children begin to play games with rules. Play becomes more formal and rule governed.

Pretend Play Pretend play begins as soon as a child can symbolize or mentally represent objects.

> "Shhh, dolly napping. Oh, no, she waked up. Now, I have to give her breakfast." Two-year-old Melinda takes a cup and fills it with imaginary milk and gives her doll a drink.

This simple pretend play is, in actuality, tremendously empowering. Melinda is beginning to think abstractly, which enables her to experiment with ideas in her mind without actually having to carry out the acts. Most young children, with no prodding from adults, automatically move into this magical word of make-believe.

Cross-culturally, when comparing children from Argentina and the United States and their mothers' play interactions, girls in both cultures tended to engage in more pretend play than boys, and boys tended to engage in more exploratory play than girls (Bornstein, Haynes, Pascual, Painter, & Galperin, 1999). Further, mothers of boys in both cultures engaged in more exploratory play with boys and more symbolic play with girls—perhaps encouraging these variations in play.

In industrialized cultures, such as the United States, pretend play serves primarily to encourage creativity (Saracho & Spodek, 1998); in nonindustrialized cultures, such as Baoule, Africa, it serves to maintain traditional values (Segall, Dasen, Berry, & Poortinga, 1999). For example, children in the United States tended to engage in pretend play that involved numerous roles (doctor, astronaut, or cowboy), including fictional ones, such as Superman® and Spiderman®, that were highly unlikely to have any real correspondence with future adult activities. Learning a large number of potential roles and to deal with unexpected novelty probably stimulates flexibility, an important characteristic in societies undergoing rapid change. In Baoule, girls played domestic scenes in which they imitated the work that they will, before long, perform in reality. This included pretend play in which they prepared a meal or a medicinal treatment or pretended to fetch water and wash clothes. Meanwhile, the boys imitated their fathers' agricultural jobs and mimicked their ritual dances; they also engaged in pretend play involving occupations that were accessible to them, such as driving a truck.

pretend play
Play in which children take on imaginary roles, like Mommy and baby. Also known as symbolic or pretend play.

Preschool Friendships

Through the media of play, children expand their social relationships with others. An important milestone in early childhood is establishing good peer relationships (Pianta, 1999). The quality of their peer relationships is a major indicator of their social and emotional development, mental health, and general adaptation (Howes, 1998).

Peers and Attachment Relations

Peer relationships appear to be clearly linked with children's early relationship history with their caregivers (Sroufe, Carlson, Levy, & Egeland, 1999). Children with histories of secure attachment tend to become friends with one another. They relate better to teachers, are rated by teachers as the most competent, and are well suited to activities that go on in the school setting. Teachers describe them as attentive, flexible, sociable, compliant, and self-reliant.

In contrast, children with insecure attachment histories adapt much more poorly. Children who displayed the insecure/ambivalent pattern in infancy tend to be described as dependent, whiny, and contentious as preschoolers. Alternately, they may emphasize their dependence with extreme coyness (for example, whispering) and feigned helplessness. Children who displayed avoidant attachment patterns in infancy tend to be described as aggressive, noncompliant, and inattentive by their teachers. Their peer relationships often find them bullying others, especially if paired with another child with a history of insecurity (Sroufe, Egeland, & Carlson, 1999). These findings clearly indicate the importance of helping caregivers develop secure attachment relations with their infants (see Chapter 7) to help young children get off on the right socially competent foot. They also speak to the importance of identifying children who may be at risk for developing poor peer relations and helping them learn more prosocial ways of interacting with others.

Children's Understandings of Friendships

As early as age 2, children begin to develop preferences for particular peers and seek them out as play partners (Monsour, 1997). In fact, researchers suggest that at least two types of peer relationships emerge during the preschool years: friendship and peer acceptance. Friendship refers to a dyadic relationship, and peer acceptance denotes the degree to which an individual child is liked and/or disliked by the members of his or her social group. Some scholars give a slight edge to the importance of friends over peer acceptance in terms of children's overall adjustment (Hartup, 1998; Ladd & Kochenderfer, 1998).

Robert Selman (1980) has studied children's friendships and has given us a great deal of information about how their understanding of interpersonal relationships changes over time. He suggests that children's development of social ideas depends on systematic developmental shifts in their role-taking skills. Selman defines developmental change in interpersonal understanding as an orderly progression through a series of five hierarchically organized stages or levels. Table 10.1 lists the five stages; each stage will be discussed in more detail in its appropriate age-related chapter.

TABLE 10.1

Selman's Stages of Perspective Taking

Level	Age (years, approximate)	Description	Example
Level 0 Undifferentiated perspective taking	3–6	Children recognize that "self" and "other" can have different thoughts and feelings, but they frequently confuse the two.	The child predicts that Holly (herself) will save the kitten because she does not want it to get hurt and believes that Holly's father will feel just as she does about her climbing the tree: "Happy, he likes kittens."
Level 1 Social-informational	4–9	Children understand that people may have different perspectives because they have access to different information.	When asked how "Holly's father" will react when he finds out she climbed the tree, the child responds, "If he didn't know anything about the kitten, he would be angry. But if 'Holly' shows him the kitten, he might change his mind."
Level 2 Self-reflective	7–12	Children can "step into another person's shoes" and view their own thoughts, feelings, and behavior from the other person's perspective. They also recognize that others can do the same.	When asked whether Holly thinks she will be punished, the child says, "No, Holly knows that her father will understand why she climbed the tree." This response assumes that Holly's point of view is influenced by her father's being able to "step into her shoes" and understand why she saved the kitten.
Level 3 Third-party perspective taking	10–15	Children can step outside a two-person situation and imagine how the self and others are viewed by a third, impartial party.	When asked whether Holly should be punished, the child says, "No, because Holly thought it was important to save the kitten." But she also knows that her father told her not to climb the tree. So she thinks she should not be punished only if she can get her father to understand why she had to climb the tree. This response steps outside the immediate situation to view both Holly's and her father's perspectives simultaneously.
Level 4 Societal perspective taking	14–adult	Individuals understand that third-party perspective taking can be influenced by one or more value systems of larger societal values.	When asked if Holly should be punished, the individual responds, "No, the value of the humane treatment of animals justifies Holly's action. Her father's appreciation of this value will lead him not to punish her."

From *The Growth of Interpersonal Understanding,* by R. Selman, 1980, New York: Academic Press. Reprinted by permission of the publisher.

The first stage, level 0, is known as *undifferentiated perspective taking.* Selman tells us that during this stage, young children's definitions of friends give no indication of a lasting relationship. These children are unable to define friendship beyond the momentary or repeated incidents of interaction between two persons who come together to play. Even though these friendships are not associated with well-articulated expectations, they can be quite intense but may be short-lived. Adults sometimes express surprise at the number of and frequency of changes among their children's young friends. It is not uncommon for children to announce that someone they just met and talked with briefly is a friend. It is also not uncommon for young children to drop friends of long standing because they have had a fight.

According to Selman, young children's friends are people who are nice; those who are mean are not friends. Trust in a friend is knowing that he or she can play with the child's toys without breaking them. Previous research has indicated that preschoolers' descriptions about friends lack any psychological statements pertaining to inner states and emotions. However, Rebecca Eder (1990), after asking 3½- and 5½-year-old children about their best friends, reports that these children did have a rudimentary understanding of the internal states and emotions of others. For example, when asking a 3½-year-old to tell about a friend's day at school, the child responded, "He didn't feel very good. He was naughty today and got a time out." Children frequently justified their responses by referring to a belief or attitude, "I don't feel that good with grown-ups 'cause I don't like grown-ups."

Preschoolers are considered to be friends based on their familiarity with each other, consistency of social interaction between the partners, and/or the presence of particular behaviors within the dyad, such as mutual display of positive affect, sharing, and play (Howes, Hamilton, & Philipsen, 1998). In short, there is an "affective tie" between the youngsters characterized by mutual preference, mutual enjoyment, and the ability to engage in skillful interaction. Preschoolers are able to name their "best" friends and can also articulate their reasons for liking them (for example, common activities, general play). The characteristics of preschoolers who are accepted by others and tend to have many friends are summarized in Table 10.2.

Friendships during early childhood are based on where one lives and with whom one is playing at the moment.

Imaginary Friends

Many children in early childhood also develop imaginary friends. Having imaginary playmates is a sign of children's developing imagination as well as their privacy needs. Because firstborn children have greater opportunities to explore and fantasize, they are more likely to have invisible pals (Friedberg & Taylor, 1997).

Imaginary friends can serve a very positive purpose. They give children a safe way to find out who they want to be. A child can dominate these friends, control them, and be bad or good safely because of them. Through them, he can identify with children who are overwhelming to him. He can safely become another child. He can also identify with each of his parents in the safe guise of these imaginary friends.

Sometimes adults, who find these creative explorations quite new, become worried and question whether the child knows the difference between fantasy and reality, or if he or she will use the "bad" friend to explain away a misdeed. Current research suggests that neither is likely to happen (Friedberg & Taylor, 1997). Moreover, most 3-, 4-, and 5-year-olds have not developed the capacity to distinguish between reality and fanciful thinking. This issue is generally tackled when children are around 7 years old.

Children, like parents, need time to be by themselves. However, there is cause for concern if the child has no friends—other than her imaginary ones—and would rather stay by herself than play with others. In contrast, children who have imaginary friends and are actively involved in playing with other children are not cause for concern.

TABLE 10.2

Behaviors Associated with Peer Acceptance

▪ Sympathetic toward peers' distress ▪ Confident of his or her own ability ▪ Other children seek his or her company ▪ Peer leader ▪ Expressive of positive emotions ▪ Communicates messages clearly ▪ Helpful to peers ▪ Suggests activities ▪ Creative use of materials ▪ Does not hit peers ▪ Is considerate and thoughtful of other children	▪ Is admired and sought out by other children ▪ Shows concern for moral issues (for example, fairness, reciprocity) ▪ Uses and responds to reason ▪ Tends to give, lend, and share ▪ Is resourceful in initiating activities ▪ Can recoup or recover after stressful experiences ▪ Is verbally fluent, can express ideas well

From "Social Competence, Social Support, and Attachment: Demarcation of Construct Domains, Measurement, and Paths of Influence for Preschool Children Attending Head Start," by K. K. Bost, B. E. Vaugh, W. M. Washington, K. L. Cielinski, & M. R. Bradbard, 1998, *Child Development, 69,* 192–218. Reprinted by permission of the publisher.

Understanding Self

Of all the social concepts, the self is the most basic. Self-systems play a key role because they determine how children construe reality and what experiences they seek out to fit in with their self-images. Thus, to understand the nature of child development in general and of any given individual in particular the self—self-concept and self-esteem—must be taken into account.

Self-Concept: Children's Descriptions of Themselves

Self-concept refers to how children describe themselves and is generally viewed as one's awareness of personal characteristics, attributes, and limitations, and the ways in which these qualities are both like and unlike those of others. Tommy, for example, may describe himself by saying, "I am a boy. I am 5 years old. I have red, curly hair." Young children's concepts are simple affairs. Children may think of themselves as big or small or strong or weak and not make any finer discriminations. As children get older, their self-conceptions become more differentiated, consistent, abstract, and comparative (see Table 10.3).

Children in early childhood are particularly attuned to physical features (Gergen, 1996). They do not differentiate the outward, observable aspects of the person from the inward, covert aspects (Bullock & Lutkenhaus, 1990). A person is how he or she looks and behaves. In particular, children focus on physical features associated with sex and age (Bullock & Lutkenhaus, 1990). They find it especially easy to tell themselves apart from opposite-sex children and from older persons. The young child generally attends to the overt, exterior, and public aspects when categorizing the self rather than to underlying qualities or feelings (Marsh, Craven, & Debus, 1998). For example, children between the ages of 2 and 3 are likely to organize their self-concepts around physical features and motor performance ("I have big feet; I can run fast").

Children between the ages of 3 and 5 tend to categorize themselves in terms of bodily activity.

TABLE 10.3

Developmental Changes in Self-Esteem

Younger Children	Older Children	Description of Change
Simple	Differentiated	Younger children form global concepts; older children make finer distinctions and allow for circumstances
Inconsistent	Consistent	Younger children are more likely to change their self-evaluation; older children appreciate the stability of the self-concept
Concrete	Abstract	Younger children focus on external, visible, physical aspects; older children focus on internal, invisible, psychological aspects
Absolute	Comparative	Younger children focus on self without reference to others; older children describe themselves in comparison with others
Public self	Private self	Younger children do not distinguish between private feelings and public behavior; older children consider the private self as the "true" self

From "The Personal Self in Social Context: Barriers to Authenticity (pp. 81–105)," by S. Harter, in R. D. Ashmore & L. J. Jussim (Eds.), *Self and Identity: Fundamental Issues. Rutgers Series on Self and Social Identity,* New York: Oxford University Press.

self-concept The acquisition of categories that define the self; how children describe themselves.

They say things like, "I play baseball"; "I walk to school" (Kemple, David, & Wang, 1996). Moreover, young children do not differentiate themselves from their physical surroundings; they are what they own and where they live.

Self-Esteem: Children's Value of Themselves

Self-esteem is essentially a social structure; it arises in social experiences. Whereas the self-concept is how one describes herself or himself without passing personal judgment or making comparisons with others, self-esteem is the value that one attaches to his or her unique characteristics, attributes, and limitations. Self-esteem represents the evaluative and effective component of one's self-concept; it refers to the qualitative judgments and feelings attached to the descriptions one assigns to self. Tommy, for example, may evaluate his self-conception "I have red, curly hair" as being a wonderful attribute, one that is very negative, or somewhere in between.

self-esteem How individuals evaluate their conceptions of self.

The origin of self-esteem lies in the complex interrelationships between children and others who compose their environment. As such, self-esteem initially reflects the responses and appraisals of others. Children come to evaluate themselves from the "reflected appraisals" of others. These self-representations then are strongly influenced by how children believe they are regarded by others, particularly parents (Cordell, 1999).

Young children do not use social comparisons to evaluate themselves; they are egocentric in orientation and preoccupied with their own point of view rather than that of others. Moreover, they live within a limited social environment that does not yet foster appreciation of social standards. Children younger than age 7 base their self-evaluations on the "absolute standard" of whether or not they complete the tasks. Children older than age 7, however, begin to compare their performances against those of others and base their self-evaluations on such social comparisons (Pomerantz & Ruble, 1997).

As they develop greater cognitive sophistication (increased memory skills, appreciation of past, present and future; ability to take others' perspectives), social comparison becomes possible. Moreover, with the lessening of egocentrism and the development of perspective-taking skills, children have the ability to imagine what others think of them (Marshall, 1994). One might explain this phenomenon as indicating that these children have reached the Piagetian stage of reciprocity and cooperation; they are obliged to take the viewpoint of others into account and as a result they become more self-conscious.

Children's self-evaluations are not stable or enduring. One moment a child may evaluate her capabilities in a positive way; she may say "I am smart," because she can tell you how old she is. Tomorrow, she may evaluate herself as "not smart" because she cannot tell you when her birthday is. Young children's self-esteem relates to that which they observe about themselves and requires no probing or sophisticated analysis on their part. Self-esteem consists of two components: feeling loved and worthy and being competent.

The Loved and Worthy Component of Self-Esteem

Parents provide the atmosphere in which most children have their first experience as social beings and are considered significant sources in the development of children's self-esteem. The home has a unique power because it is the first institution to make a powerful impression upon the child. Because it remains the child's chief environment for so long, its "design for living" tends to become part of the child before the world outside has any consistent chance to exert an influence. The process by which an awareness of children's own attributes is translated into self-esteem is diagrammed in Figure 10.2.

Children evaluate and value themselves in congruence with the general reactions others have toward them. The conditions in the affective interpersonal environment that cause children to know success or failure, triumph or humiliation, or acceptance or rejection are important determinants of their self-esteem. From chil-

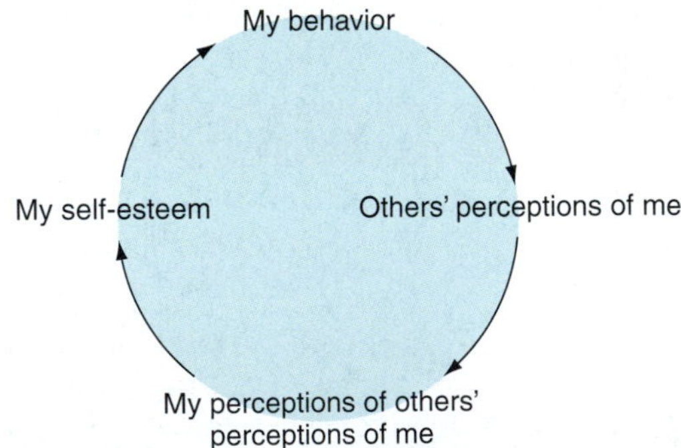

FIGURE 10.2 *The Origins of Self-Esteem*

Initially, the process by which children's awareness of their own attributes is translated into self-esteem logically begins with "Others' Perceptions of Me." Young children's self-esteem is gradually abstracted from the ways other people have reacted to them.

From *Raising Your Child's Inner Self-Esteem,* by K. Owens, 1995, New York: Plenum Press.

dren's experiences and the quality of those experiences with the significant others in their environment, they mentally begin to construct evaluations of themselves.

Charles Cooley (1909) labeled this outer component of self-esteem as the "looking-glass" self. Parents become the social mirrors into which children look for information that comes to define the self. This reflective, passive component of self-esteem derives from feeling loved and worthy.

The Competency Component of Self-Esteem

Evaluative feedback from others is a powerful determinant of self-esteem, but it is not the only factor. William James (1890/1950) noted that self-perceived *competencies* in areas that are valued by the person, the active component of self-esteem, provide an important basis for self-esteem. Cooley (1909) and George H. Mead (1934) also described this active, inner source of self-esteem, which is based on children's actual skills, behaviors, and competencies. Inner self-esteem results from being able to act effectively and master one's environment (Bandura, 1997). This component of self-esteem is earned through one's own competent actions and is labeled **competency self-esteem** (Owens, 1997). Thus, there are two sources of self-esteem—an outer component based on feeling loved and worthy and an inner source derived from children's demonstrated proficiencies. Adults who want their children to have high self-esteem, then, have two socialization goals: (1) helping children feel loved and worthy *and* (2) helping them develop competent skills and behaviors (Owens, 1996).

Feeling Worthy and Being Competent Initially, young children's judgments of how capable, significant, and worthy they are tend to align with others' general reactions toward them. Thus, the first component of the self-system is established in the infant and young child through the affirmation of others. Children increase their feelings of worthiness under the care of loving, capable, and nurturing adults who provide them with firm but fair rules and treat them with respect (Coopersmith, 1967). As children progress through early childhood, however, competency self-esteem takes on greater importance and must be incorporated into children's self-pictures. Children need to move from "I am special because I am me" to "I am special because I am competent and capable."

The emphasis of caregiving efforts now shifts from giving children self-esteem by providing an accepting environment to helping children *earn* self-esteem through building their skills. Teaching children the skills that will enable them to do well in school, get along with other children, and act in kind and decent ways toward themselves and others leads to competency self-esteem (Owens, 1997). Further, caregivers enhance young children's self-esteem when they help them identify their own competent behavior by labeling it. For example, when the child finishes a project adults can comment, "You are the kind of person who finishes what she starts." As adults begin to look for strengths in children, they will find many more. This labeling gives children an exceptionally good basis from which to develop their individual talents and skills and translates into healthy, competency-based self-esteem.

Children's self-esteem has two important components: feeling loved and worthy, and acting in competent ways.

Gender Roles

"I would like to take your picture with 1-year-old Brian," the teacher tells her preschoolers. Little girls are told to act "like Mommy" and little boys to act "like Daddy." The children have their pictures taken separately. One little girl, acting like Mommy, moves close to the infant and touches the baby. In contrast, when a little boy is asked to play the role of the father, he actually moves farther away from the baby! Girls smile more than boys. When preschoolers are asked "Who's smarter—your mother or your father?" Dad receives the laurels. When asked, "What would you rather be a boy or a girl?" The majority of 3-year-olds, both boys and girls, respond "a boy." When preschoolers are asked, who owns a

competency self-esteem
Feelings of worthiness based on demonstrated competencies, behaviors, and skills.

Thought CHALLENGE
How can the Oedipal complex be proven or disproven?

big store, talks loudly, and makes rules, they respond, "Father." When asked who is fussy, weak, and talkative, they respond, "Mother." (They think the former category of traits is better.)

Consider these findings:

- By late infancy, children can already distinguish faces by gender.
- By age 2, children verbally label themselves and others as male or female.
- Gender stereotyping in children's choice of toys is found by age 2 or 3.
- Around age 3 or 4, children begin to develop some rigid stereotypes as to what occupations (doctor or nurse) and what activities (car repair or cooking) are "right" for males and females.
- From about age 3, children prefer to play with same-sex peers.
- By age 5, they associate certain personality traits with males and others with females (toughness; gentleness).

Whereas sex is biological, gender is psycho-sociocultural. Gender refers to the meanings attached to being male or female, as reflected in social statuses, roles, and attitudes regarding the sexes. How children develop such conceptions has been a matter of much theoretical debate. The study of gender-role development takes form in multiple theories on the subject as well as discussions of whether engendering children is based on differential treatment.

Theories of Gender-Role Development

Freud in his psychoanalytic theory is generally credited with developing the first detailed view of the child's gender-role development. Other views include social learning, cognitive, gender schema, and biological theories.

defensive identification Little boys, out of fear of castration anxiety, repress a desire to possess their mother and identify with their father.

anaclitic identification Little girls, fearing their mother's resentment and loss of love, resolve anxiety by identifying with her.

Psychoanalytic Theory: Sigmund Freud According to Freud's (1973) theoretical speculations, during boys' early years, the development of gender roles or adoption of "appropriate" gender-type behavior centers on the resolution of the Oedipal complex and their identification with their fathers. Anna Freud (1974), Freud's daughter, maintained that girls experience an Electra complex, the female counterpart of the Oedipal complex. Sigmund Freud (1973) insisted, however, that it is only in the male child that we find the fateful combination of love for one parent and simultaneous hate for the other as a rival. Freud was a stage theorist (see Chapter 1) and believed that children pass through five psychosexual stages of development, with the first three stages being the most influential.

In the third stage, the phallic stage, 3- to 6-year-old boys become aware of their genitals. This awareness leads to sexual fantasies toward the opposite-sex parent. Although these sexual desires take place at the unconscious level, the child does feel an inner conflict and anxiety. To relieve this anxiety, little boys pattern their behavior after their fathers. The process of identifying with the parent of the same sex forms the basis for appropriate gender-role behavior, with the parent also becoming the model for values that will become part of the child's adult personality. Incorporating Anna Freud's view, the Electra complex contends that girls first desire their fathers but later disband this notion and begin to identify with their mothers. Why do children give up their desire for the opposite-sex parent? The process proceeds differently for boys than for girls. A boy views his father as a competitor, and he fears his powerful father will retaliate by castrating him. After all, the boy assumes, this is why little girls do not have penises. Out of fear and "castration anxiety," the little boy then represses his desire to possess his mother and at the same time begins to identify with his father. Freud referred to this as **defensive identification**. For the boy, it has the effect of making him more similar to his father, and the child expects that this similarity should decrease the possibility of his father's harming him.

Little girls, when they discover that they do not possess the noticeable, external genitals of the male, blame their mothers for this loss. In Freud's view, the little girl wants to have a penis and is greatly disturbed by her lack of such an impressive organ. She gradually turns away from her mother as an object of her sexual affection and begins to prefer her father who has the organ she is missing. Her love for her father is mixed with envy because he possesses something she does not have. This is known as penis envy; it is the feminine counterpart of the boy's castration anxiety. The little girl, however, failing to supplant her mother and fearing her mother's resentment and loss of her love, resolves the anxiety she feels by once more identifying with her mother. This is known as **anaclitic identification**.

By identifying with the same-sex parent, children incorporate the parent's standards and characteristics into their own personalities. Boys who successfully identify with their fathers develop "masculine" behavior, whereas girls who successfully identify with their mothers show "feminine" behavior. Although, according to Freud, a portion of identification is direct and self-conscious, much of children's behavioral patterns is acquired unconsciously.

The development of gender roles, according to Freud, arises out of children's recognition of their own genitals. Freud saw **gender identity**, the realization of one's sex, as being intrinsically tied to the genitals: "I have a penis" means "I am a boy." "I do not have a penis" means "I am a girl." Freud, however, fails to explain how children learn to see the genitals as the dichotomizing feature by which they distinguish all people and categorize self. Why not bigger muscles or shorter hair? Moreover, Freud's theory does not explain how blind children have stable gender identities, even though they cannot see genital differences.

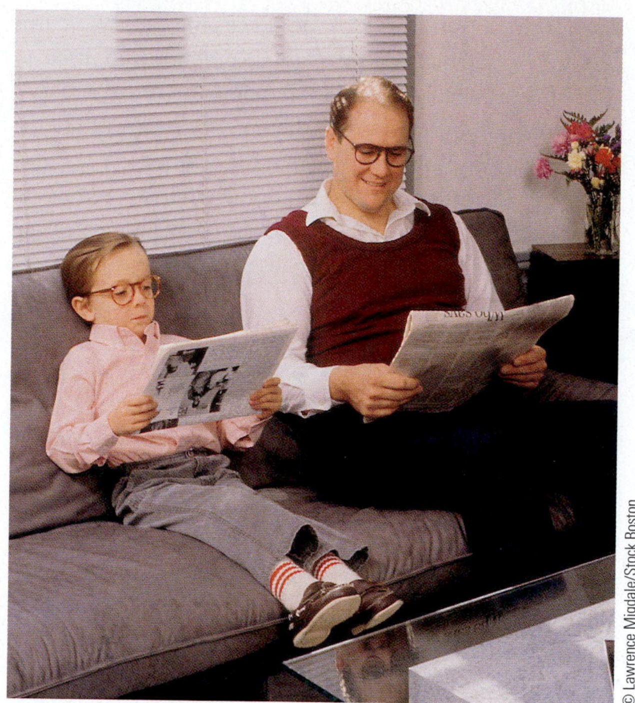
© Lawrence Migdale/Stock Boston

Bandura believed that children learn their respective gender roles by imitating same-sex models.

Social Learning Theories Social learning theorists assume that no particular kind of knowledge about gender is required for the acquisition of gender-typed preferences (Bandura, 1997). Instead, they emphasize that gender behaviors are acquired, maintained, and changed primarily through the learning process. This view focuses particularly on learning by identification, or **imitation** (a term most frequently used by social learning theorists), as well as reinforcement and punishment. Social learning theorists maintain that from the beginning of life, parents and other caregivers treat boys and girls differently. Little girls are rewarded for certain behaviors and punished for other behaviors, and these are not the same set of behaviors for which little boys are rewarded or punished. Children are also believed to choose to imitate models of the same sex. By and large, social learning theory depicts the child as a somewhat passive recipient of culturally transmitted information.

It is through observing and imitating parents that children first begin to flesh out the behavior categories outlined by a gender identity. When the child does imitate the behavior of the same-sex parent, the reinforcement outcome (reward, neutral, punishment) influences the probability the child will repeat the performance. For example, a young son and daughter observe their mother putting on lipstick. When the little girl tries this, adults may comment, "How cute," whereas the son is told disapprovingly, "Boys don't wear lipstick." Gradually, from this differential reinforcement from parents, teachers, peers, and others, children learn what they can or cannot do.

Thus, according to the social learning theory, in a "typical" family, the girl would be reinforced for imitating the behavior of the mother and a boy for imitating the masculine acts of the father. These behaviors, learned from their respective parents, are most often appropriate to the child's sex and are the ones most likely to be rewarded. Males are generally rewarded for aggressive, independent behaviors, and females are rewarded for nurturing, passive behaviors. According to this framework, children learn appropriate gender roles through observation of the rewards and punishments received by models. It is in this way that they learn to engage in the stereotypical behaviors rewarded in North American culture.

Some social learning theorists emphasize the importance of learning that takes place without explicit reinforcement or punishment, portraying observational, or **vicarious, reinforcement** as a crucial process in gender-role development. If children see someone punished after engaging in a particular activity, or there is no particular result, it is less likely that they will imitate that behavior than if they see the person being rewarded. When a little boy sees a classmate ridiculed for behaving like a "sissy," or when a little girl observes another little girl commended for her "neat" picture, these actions vicariously reinforce the child's understanding of appropriate gender-role behavior.

There is not nearly the exclusive identification with the same-sex parent in social learning theory that is emphasized in psychoanalytical theory. Rather, children

gender identity
Correct labeling of self and others as males and females.

imitation
According to social learning theory, children learn gender roles by observing and imitating others of the same sex.

vicarious reinforcement
Indirect reinforcement; children observe others being reinforced and then emulate that behavior with the anticipation that they, too, will receive reinforcement and praise.

learn from various models. Social learning theory focuses on learning particularly through observation and imitation of others rather than emphasizing the unconscious psychodynamics of Freudian theory. The major problem with social learning theory is that the majority of the related experiments have been conducted in a laboratory situation under controlled conditions. Very little research has been based on naturalistic observations in real-life settings.

Cognitive Theory Psychoanalytical and social learning theories argue that children first focus on the same-sex parent, either on a psychodynamic or a reward-probability basis, and then acquire behavior appropriate to their own sex. Lawrence Kohlberg (1966) states that "the child's gender-role concepts are the result of the child's active structuring of his own experience; they are not passive products of social training" (p. 85). Cognitive developmental theory places the identification with the same-sex parent at a much later stage in the process of gender-role learning. Kohlberg was one of the first people to postulate a cognitive basis for gender identification. He proposed that children's understanding of gender follows Piaget's model of cognitive development; children do not have a mature notion of gender until the advent of concrete operational thinking, beginning at about age 7. Kohlberg (1978) argues that the development of gender roles takes place in a three-stage sequential pattern, which is summarized in Table 10.4.

First, around the age of 1½ to 2, the child establishes gender identity, the realization of one's sex. Around age 3 to 4, the child can correctly label the sex of others and realizes that gender is permanent. This is called **gender stability**. However, certain situations cause some confusion. Many young children believe that a change in external features can result in a change in gender. If a female is wearing a man's suit and hat, for example, they may label her as a male. At about 6 to 7, children recognize that gender is invariant over time and situations; Kohlberg refers to this as **gender consistency**, or **constancy**. At this point, children understand that gender does not change regardless of changes in appearance, clothing, or activities. This leads them to seek out same-sex models to observe and imitate. The sure knowledge that one's gender is unchangeable, Kohlberg believed, has a tremendous influence on the development of gender roles.

One criticism of Kohlberg's theory is his contention that it is only when children develop gender constancy, at around age 7, that they will identify with the parent of their own sex and seek out, from all available sources, the behavior and attitudes that go along with that gender. Research does not seem to support this contention.

Gender Schema Theory In response, Carol Martin and Charles Halverson (1981) have proposed a theory that derives from information-processing approaches to cognitive development and features social learning and cognitive theories. They suggest that children's motivation to behave in gender-appropriate ways derives from their *gender schemas.* A **gender schema** is a pattern of beliefs and stereotypes about gender that children use to organize information about gender-related characteristics, experiences, and expectations. Schemas develop gradually from observation. Gender is a salient characteristic in children's worlds, relating both to themselves and to others. It is thus used to organize information in a place that may be used by older and more knowledgeable children.

Martin and Halverson (1987) suggest that sex stereotypes serve as schemata to organize and structure social information. Young children form concepts of maleness and femaleness by age 2 or 3 and thus readily incorporate stereotyped views of play activities, roles, and behaviors that are appropriate to

gender stability
Understanding that a person's sex remains constant throughout life.

gender consistency/constancy
The realization that biological sex is invariant despite superficial changes in appearance.

gender schema
A pattern of beliefs and stereotypes about gender that children use to organize information about gender-related characteristics, experiences, and expectations.

TABLE 10.4

Kohlberg's Sequential Understanding of Gender

Step	Age	Types of Questions Asked	Characteristics
Identity	1½–2	Are you a boy or a girl?	The child correctly identifies self and others as male or female.
Stability	3–4	Will you be a Mummy or a Daddy when you grow up?	The child understands people retain the same gender throughout life.
Constancy	6–7	If a boy puts on a dress, will he be a girl?	The child is aware gender is not dependent on changes in appearance (for example, hair, clothes).

From "A Cognitive-Developmental Analysis of Children's Sex-Role Concepts and Attitudes (pp. 82–173)," by L. Kohlberg, 1966, in E. E. Maccoby (Ed.), *The Development of Sex Differences,* Palo Alto, CA: Stanford University Press. Reprinted by permission of the publisher.

their gender. A friend of mine, for example, related that her 3-year-old son met her older daughter's ballet instructor after a recital. On their way home, the mother commented to her son about what a talented and nice person the instructor was. Her 3-year-old's response was, "He acts like a girl."

Sex stereotypes function at two levels. The first level is an overall "in-group/out-group" schema, which consists of general information children need to categorize objects, behaviors, and roles as being masculine or feminine. Second, there is an "own sex" schema, a narrower, more detailed version of the first, consisting of information children have about objects, behavior, traits, and roles that characterize their own sex. Once gender schemata are formed, they help children "structure" experiences by providing an organization for processing social information.

The overall schema guides behavior by giving information at the level of labels: "This is appropriate/inappropriate behavior for girls." "This is appropriate/inappropriate behavior for boys." Boys should play with trucks; girls should not (Martin, Wood, & Little, 1990). Girls should play with dolls; boys should not. Thus, young children can identify their gender and reliably place themselves in the appropriate gender-related category (in-group) and not in the other (out-group).

© Tony Freeman/PhotoEdit

According to the gender schema theory, children learn gender roles by organizing social information into categories: "This is appropriate for me." "This is inappropriate for me."

Biological Theory Of the major theories detailing how children learn gender-role behaviors, only the biological theory stresses genetic and hormonal influences. It is difficult, however, to determine the extent to which a child's learning of gender-role behavior may be influenced by underlying biological predispositions, because from the moment of birth, the child's maleness or femaleness is constantly being shaped by environmental experiences. Biological theorists, although recognizing that environment is implicated in the development of gender roles, stress that the genetic makeup of the individual and the influence of hormones cannot be overlooked when studying gender-role development.

When androgens, for example, are present during the prenatal period, the pituitary will function at puberty to cause a regular production of testosterone and sperm. When androgens are absent during the prenatal period, the pituitary will function at puberty to cause high levels of cyclical hormonal activity, which result in ovulation and menstruation. It is believed that sex hormones in the developing embryo, in addition to controlling the growth of genitalia and directing pituitary activity at puberty, also throw a neural switch in the brain toward "male" and "female" behavior.

Prenatal hormones, it is believed, affect certain areas of the brain and may influence the ease with which certain behaviors are acquired. Prenatal exposure to androgen, for example, may predispose the individual to engage in more vigorous kinds of activities. Such a predisposition may increase sensitivity to certain stimuli such as large muscle movements, making them more rewarding and thus more likely to occur. This "ease of learning" model (Hamburg & Lunde, 1966) attempts to account for gender differences as a result of the impact of androgens on the prenatal organization of cortical and subcortical pathways in the brain. Simply stated, there are behavior patterns that are easier for males to learn and others that are easier for females to learn. A higher concentration of androgen in the system means that it takes *less* stimulation to evoke children's responses as far as aggressive activity is concerned and *more* stimulation to evoke children's nurturing behavior. It is most probable, however, that gender-role behavior is influenced by both biological and environmental factors (Plomin, 1998).

Engendering Children

In recent years, research efforts have focused primarily on the issue of whether adults treat boys and girls differently—particularly in ways that would lead to gender-based differences in behavior. A common question guiding this research is, "Do mothers and fathers

Thought CHALLENGE

Are young children's "appropriate/inappropriate" scripts still structured along stereotypical lines?

differ in their reactions to children?" Perhaps this question is too simplistic. Any statement comparing the roles of the mother and father needs to specify the age of the children being considered. Most studies show parents treat males and females differently, particularly among younger children (Lytton & Romney, 1992).

Between 1½ and 3 years of age, children begin to show pronounced gender-typed behavior (Jacklin, 1989). Their behavior is largely based on parental beliefs of what is gender-appropriate behavior (Bem, 1998). An extensive literature has documented differential socialization practices based on the sex of the child (Honig, 1991; Stattin & Klackenberg-Larsson, 1991).

Fathers If your 6-year-old son wanted to bring a doll to show-and-tell at school tomorrow, would you let him? When I ask this question, the general consensus among my female college students is that they do not see anything wrong with that because the child is so young. Their only reservation is that he might get teased by the other children. However, the majority of male college students respond, "What is a boy doing with a doll!" Most men answer, rather emphatically, that they would not let their son go to school with a doll (and further maintained that no son of theirs would have a doll).

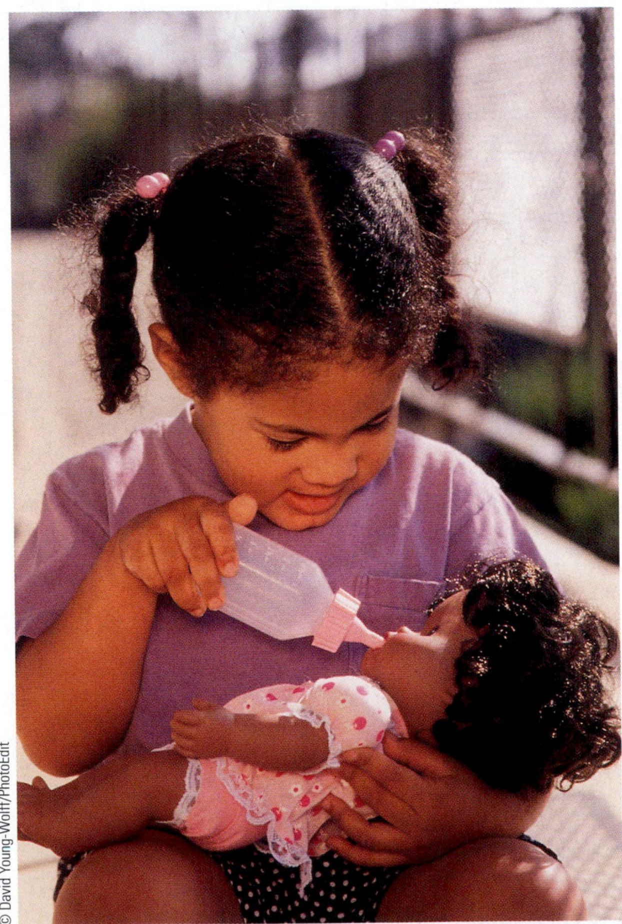

During the early childhood period, children rapidly acquire knowledge about their culture's gender-typing of behaviors, activities, and occupations.

Some studies have found that fathers are more likely to make gender-based differentiations between their children; this is even true among fathers who believe in nonsexist child rearing (Lamb, 1998; Russell, 1999). Fathers tend to act *instrumentally* with their sons and *expressively* with their daughters. Instrumental behavior is competency-focused and achievement oriented; expressive behavior encourages nurturing and caring behaviors. Differential treatments of sons and daughters can be observed in types of play. Fathers tend to play physically with their sons and encourage more involvement in sports activities than with their daughters (Lytton & Romney, 1992). Although fathers encourage cognitive growth in both sons and daughters, they focus their direct teaching on sons. Fathers tend to set higher standards for their sons than their daughters and place greater emphasis on achievement (Fagot & Hagan, 1991; Lamb, 1998). With their daughters, fathers focus more on interpersonal aspects of the teaching situation, such as encouraging and supporting them.

Young children, particularly boys, learn their gender lessons quite early. Children as young as 2 to 2½ years of age already have accrued a great deal of knowledge about appropriate gender roles (Burnham & Harris, 1992). Such knowledge increases significantly and rapidly throughout the early childhood years, and, before beginning elementary school, children have considerable knowledge of the gender typing of toys, clothing, household objects, activities, and occupations (Bussey, & Bandura, 1992).

When preschoolers were offered an opportunity to play with a tool set or a dish set, a high frequency of boys reported that they would not play with the dish set because their fathers would think this was "bad" (Raag & Rackliff, 1998). Fathers tend to think their sons should show an ability to hold their own in a man's world—a reaction to perceived gender-role demands the world will place on their sons—and thus to reward stereotypical behavior.

Rewarding Stereotypical Behaviors Activity, independence, and assertiveness are rewarded in boys; passivity, cooperation, and compliance are rewarded in girls by parents, teachers, and other adult models. Adults react more positively to "adult-oriented independent behavior," such as acting in self-assertive ways, when exhibited by boys and more negatively when girls exhibit these same kinds of behavior (Fagot, 1998).

Adults tend to associate physical ability or athletic skill as the most appropriate characteristics for boys, together with getting dirty, being rough, and taking interest in cars, trucks, and tools. Traits considered appropriate for girls are being gentle, taking interest in clothes and makeup, and not being rough. Parents are more protective of their daughter's well-being, encourage their dependency, and keep them close to the family.

Boys are allowed to play outside more, are allowed to go farther away from home, and are supervised less than girls. Girls are more highly chaperoned; they are encouraged to bring a friend home to play. Parents also make greater use of explanation with girls. The patterns of interaction that mothers develop with girls encourage a person-oriented rather than a thing-oriented approach. Thus, young children receive some fairly clear information from adults upon which to build bipolar gender behavior. By the time they are 4 or 5 years old, children hold highly gender-based occupational aspirations as well as play interests (Hofstede, 1998). The data cited thus far on direct influences of social agents in a child's life suggest genuine differences in the treatment of boys and girls. Is the differential treatment of boys and girls simply a unilateral tendency on the part of parents and other social agents? This question is addressed in Child Development Issues: Who's Socializing Whom?

Child Development Issues

Who's Socializing Whom?

Parents, teachers, other children, and television are all socializing influences that clearly play a part in making children aware that gender differences matter and that they are expected to conform to stereotypical behavior. But, children are not passive recipients of information. The fact that adults treat children differentially according to their sex does not mean that any behavioral differences in the children are the effects of such treatment; they may, on the contrary, be its cause.

As most parents will testify, young boys are more active and disruptive than girls. Boys are more likely to show greater resistance to control and are less likely to be responsive to adult directives, both at home and at school, thereby more frequently eliciting critical, negative reactions from adult caregivers.

Parents may treat their sons and daughters differently partly in response to the children's behavior (Snow, Jacklin, & Maccoby, 1983). In an experiment, fathers and their sons and/or daughters are observed in a "waiting room" (with a one-way mirror). The room has several tempting but potentially disaster-producing objects: a vase with flowers, a plastic pitcher filled with water, and ashtrays filled with cigarettes. There are also some toys (dolls, trucks, a vacuum cleaner, and a shovel) placed on a shelf that is low enough for the children to see but too high for them to reach.

Fathers are significantly more likely to use physical and verbal prohibitions with their sons than with their daughters. It is also the case, however, that boys are more likely than girls to touch these tempting objects. The father–daughter interactions tend to include more holding and proximity than father–son interactions. The close physical nature of father–daughter interactions actually prevents the girls from being as mischievous as the boys. Girls appear more content when being held; boys are fussier and do not like being confined. When the fathers offer the toys to their children, girls play longer with them. The boys' attention span is shorter, and after a short period of time, the boys are ready to explore the room once again.

From this research, it seems that it may not simply be fathers who display gender-based behaviors toward their children, but rather, that boys and girls differ in the behavior they exhibit in the presence of their fathers. This may play an integral role in the socialization practices used by fathers.

Search Online

Explore InfoTrac College Edition, your online library. Go to **http://www.infotrac-college.com/wadsworth** and use the passcode that came on the card with your book. Try these search terms: socialization, parents and socialization, socializing children.

Physical Environments In examining the physical environment of boys and girls, Andrée Pomerleau (Pomerleau, Bolduc, Malcuit, & Cossette, 1990) reports that parents still encourage gender-typed behavior through their selection of the quantity and types of toys, the colors and types of clothing, and the colors and motifs of children's rooms. Parents provide boys with more sports toys, equipment tools, and large and small vehicles. Girls are provided with dolls, fictional characters, toys, children's furniture, and other toys for manipulation. They wear pink and multicolored clothes. Boys wear blue, red, and white clothing. These differential environments have an effect on the development of dichotomous abilities and preferential activities for boys and girls.

Toys have properties that elicit particular types of behavior in children. Thus, play with gender-typed toys may be the source of some observed behavioral sex differences. For instance, masculine toys, such as trucks and adventure figures, promote motor activities. Yvonne Caldera and her colleagues (Caldera, Huston, & O'Brien, 1989; Caldera & Sciaraffa, 1998) found that sex-stereotyped toys have clear effects on the nature of the parent-child interaction. Masculine toys (trucks, cars) were associated with relatively low levels of questions and teaching and low proximity between parents and children. Further, parents tended to make animated sounds (beeps and whistles) rather than statements that conveyed or elicited information from the child. Play with feminine toys (dolls) elicited physical proximity and more verbal interactions in the form of comments and questions. These patterns of interaction were evident for both boys and for girls and both fathers and mothers.

Even when parents provide their children with both same-sex and cross-sex toys, they may defeat their attempts toward a nonsexist upbringing of their children by the way in which they then interact with their children and use those toys. Caldera found that neither mothers nor fathers actively encouraged play with same-sex toys or discouraged play with cross-sex toys. Both mothers and fathers, however, showed more enthusiasm for playing with same-sex toys and especially when playing with a child of the same sex as themselves. Thus, not only did they encourage gender-stereotyping behavior but they also modeled such behavior to their children. Other socialization areas in which adults adopt different interaction styles to boys and girls are summarized in Table 10.5.

APPLICATIONS:

Socializing Children into Gender Equality

The most important insight from research on gender-role socialization is that because boys and girls are treated differently and put into different learning environments, they develop different needs, wants, desires, and skills; in short, they become different kinds of people. Although the specific social and psychological processes through which gender socialization occurs are the subject of much debate, the basic underlying model is that of the self-fulfilling prophecy (Bem, 1998). Because people think boys and girls are supposed to be different, they treat them differently and give them different opportunities for development.

TABLE 10.5

Socialization Areas and Differential Interaction Styles

Socialization Area	Findings
Toy selection	Adults encourage children to choose sex-typed toys.
Play style	Adults encourage boys to and discourage girls from engaging in vigorous, active play.
Dependence	Girls' help-seeking is responded to more favorably than boys'.
Aggression	More attention is paid to aggression and assertion by boys than by girls.
Emotions	Verbal and behavioral expression of emotion is tolerated more in girls.
Control	More verbal and physical prohibitions are given to males.
Task assignment	Boys are given "male" household tasks, and girls are given "female" household tasks.

This differential treatment promotes certain behaviors and self-images that re-create preconceived cultural stereotypes about gender.

Early Childhood Messages from Parents and Preschool Teachers

At first, adults tend to invest children with different gender characteristics based on stereotypical gender class expectations. Adults, for example, may perpetuate stereotypical gender roles through the types of comments they make to children. A father may laughingly say to his son, "Come on, you're throwing like a girl!" When you were a child, you may have received "conventional" messages, such as those described in Table 10.6, from parents, teachers, and other adults. Later, as a result of stereotypical socialization practices, children themselves take up the gauntlet and actively enact stereotyped gender roles as they begin to incorporate their own "appropriate" gender schemas. To be considered competent members of society, boys and girls soon learn how to fit in as appropriately engendered individuals (Coltrane, 1998). Recognition of these often-used phrases and the gender-stereotyped messages they convey may help adults avoid using them.

TABLE 10.6

Messages from Parents and Preschool Teachers

Read the descriptions of the two columns. Then read each statement and mark "Yes" or "No" in Column A and Column B.

	Column A I remember hearing something like this when I was a child.		Column B I might say something like this to my own child.	
Statements Made to Girls				
Sugar and spice and everything nice—that's what little girls are made of.	___ yes	___ no	___ yes	___ no
Mind your manners.	___ yes	___ no	___ yes	___ no
Don't get your dress dirty.	___ yes	___ no	___ yes	___ no
Little girls don't climb trees.	___ yes	___ no	___ yes	___ no
You're Daddy's little girl.	___ yes	___ no	___ yes	___ no
Girls are crybabies.	___ yes	___ no	___ yes	___ no
Be kind to others.	___ yes	___ no	___ yes	___ no
Be polite.	___ yes	___ no	___ yes	___ no
Statements Made to Boys				
Big boys don't cry.	___ yes	___ no	___ yes	___ no
Take it like a man.	___ yes	___ no	___ yes	___ no
You throw like a girl.	___ yes	___ no	___ yes	___ no
Men don't belong in the kitchen.	___ yes	___ no	___ yes	___ no
Never admit defeat.	___ yes	___ no	___ yes	___ no
Boys will be boys.	___ yes	___ no	___ yes	___ no
Only the strong survive.	___ yes	___ no	___ yes	___ no
Stand up and prove how tough you are.	___ yes	___ no	___ yes	___ no
Boys who give others hugs are weird.	___ yes	___ no	___ yes	___ no
Don't act like a sissy.	___ yes	___ no	___ yes	___ no

From Catalyst, 2000. Used by permission.

Differing Emotional Worlds

Developmental scholars suggest building more egalitarian ways of behaving into boys and girls (Bem, 1998). For example, independence tends to be encouraged in boys and emotional sensitivity in girls, but independence can be encouraged in girls when they are given opportunities to explore, take risks, and engage in active play. Expressive characteristics in males may be enhanced if social agents encourage boys to express their emotions more freely. Girls are given much more freedom in expressing emotional kinds of behavior, but boys, as though their tear ducts automatically stop functioning at the age of 6, are given strong messages to suppress feelings. It does seem ironic that little boys are socialized to be nonemotional, yet later, as men, often find themselves criticized by mothers, girlfriends, sisters, and wives for being insensitive and noncaring. The message many little boys receive is that showing feelings is a mark of weakness and must be suppressed. Males profit when socialization practices allow them to express their feelings (Bem, 1993). As males very likely will continue to display higher levels of aggression due to hormonal differences, they may need greater reinforcement of gentleness than girls.

Exposure to the "Less Traditional"

Children's books are still very stereotypical in their depictions of males and females; consequently, caregivers need to search for literature that is less biased (Bem, 1995). Moreover, exposing children to "less traditional" models in the workplace—female executives, male nurses—may help young children to open up new thoughts on what they may want to be when they grow up. Finally, parents can be role models by sharing household tasks equally rather than modeling "mother chores"—cleaning, cooking, and washing—and "father chores"—mowing the lawn and taking out the garbage (Gottman, 1998).

Concept Checks

1. ***True or False:*** Play is important because it is one of the major ways in which children learn about social relationships and develop their social skills.
2. Preschoolers consider others as friends based on their familiarity, consistency of social interaction, and mutual __________ ______________.
3. The rapid growth of self-concepts during early childhood results from
   a. the emergence of representational thought.
   b. reinforcement from caregivers.
   c. a positive resolution of one's self-identity.
4. Which theorist is likely to say, "I believe that gender roles are learned by reinforcement and imitation of adults"?
   a. Kohlberg
   b. Freud
   c. Bandura
5. As a nonsexist parent, you have decided that you will raise your boy to be more ______________ and your girl to be more ______________.

Emotional Development

Before Beginning . . .

After reading this section, you will be able to

- understand cultural variations in the expression of emotions.
- characterize emotional understandings in early childhood.
- examine the discrete emotional states of fear and anger.
- note possible ways of helping children deal effectively with anger.

Culture and Emotion

After distributing questionnaires to missionaries in different parts of the world, asking whether their observations led them to conclude that people in those faraway cultures expressed emotion in similar ways, Charles Darwin (1872/1998) concluded from their responses that emotional states were universal. Darwin's claims appeared to be based on faulty reports and rather imprecise definitions of emotional states (Ekman, 1973); however, his work did lead to a number of questions about culture and emotions. Is there universality in classifying emotions? Are emotions expressed in the same way throughout the world? Do people react the same way to emotional situations? Can facial expressions be interpreted the same universally?

Classifying Emotions

In the United States, research focuses on several basic emotions: happiness, sadness, anger, fear, surprise, disgust, and contempt. Cross-cultural research suggests that there are innumerable ways in which different cultures view emotional states. Tahitians, for example, often equate sadness with illness (Levy, 1984). Tahitians, in fact, have no word equivalent to "sadness"; they have a vocabulary for "grief" or "lamentation" but not for a generalized sadness (Barr-Zisowitz, 2000). Tahitians who have moved away from the village where they grew up are not supposed to visit there more than a few days or they will become, not sad, but ill. In contrast, the Toraja of Indonesia, associate illness with anger (Hollan, 1996).

Cross-cultural research also points to culture-specific emotional states. The Hindu Newar, in Nepal, have one such emotion known as *lajja* (pronounced lud-já), a combination of shyness, shame, and embarrassment. Sensitivity to lajja makes one a moral and civilized person. It is associated with physical signs, like blushing, but also with psychological traits such as pride and loyalty (Menon & Shweder, 1994; Parish, 1991). Lacking lajja is equated with lacking social sense or integrity.

In some cultures, such as China, anger violates the "rational" worldview (Mesguita, Frijda, & Scherer, 2000). Aggression only makes things more unpleasant and does no good, so the rational attitude is simple resignation and acceptance, and subsequently anger is an unrecognized emotion. These examples seem to be not just a difference in emphasis but truly a difference in conceptualization of basic emotions.

Expression of Emotions

> "Good Morning, Mrs. Polska. How are you today?"
> "Not so good. My back has been acting up again and I can't seem to get rid of this horrible cold."
>
> "Good Morning, Mrs. White. How are you today?"
> "Great, wonderful, fantastic!"

Whereas the Polish culture emphasizes honesty and spontaneity of expression, U.S. culture values politeness, control, and what the Polish might view as a false sense of cheerfulness (Goddard & Wierzbicka, 1997). Accordingly, Poles respond to "How are you?" with a frank listing of their ailments and difficulties, whereas people in the United States, despite perhaps feeling miserable, respond with "Just great." How many times have you said that you were feeling "fine" even though you were experiencing a thoroughly rotten day?

Differences in cultural expressions of emotions begin early in life with adults socializing children into emotional worlds that are consonant with their culture. For example, a study found that Japanese and U.S. infants received very different messages about emotional expressiveness. Japanese mothers spent more time rocking and carrying their babies, whereas U.S. mothers looked at and chatted with their babies (Camras, Oster, Campos, Miyake, & Bradshaw, 1992). This type of socialization may explain the fact that U.S. babies appear to be more active and emotionally expressive than Japanese babies.

Further, Japanese mothers talked with their preschoolers about emotional experiences and emotional states (for example, what it is like to experience sadness; other occasions during which they felt sad), and U.S. mothers talked about emotions in a problem-solving fashion (how to deal effectively with sadness; what to do to not feel so sad) (Chen & Miyake, 1986). The Japanese mothers were more controlling of their children's free play than the U.S. mothers and had higher expectations for emotional control and etiquette for their children. The U.S. mothers tended to value freedom in emotional expression more highly. Subsequently, outward expressions of anger or being upset were less common in the Japanese children studied.

David Ho (1996) also found some differences between U.S. and Chinese mothers. The Chinese mothers were reported to be very indulgent and lenient toward their young children, who they considered not yet capable of "understanding." At the same time, the Chinese mothers did not seem to value or encourage the expression of positive emotions as much as the U.S. mothers.

How to Act

Culture also plays an important role in specifying socially prescribed ways to communicate and act in emotional situations. In Nepal, for example, many young children are socialized to mask negative emotions (Cole & Tamang, 1998). Similar processes are found in other cultures such as China and Australia as well (Chen & Sanson, 1997). In all these cultures, children involved in a peer or family conflict situation are often taught not to express anger or negative emotions. In contrast, many U.S. children are taught that emotions that are not expressed are "bottled up" and may cause "inner explosions."

Facial Expressions

Numerous studies have suggested that there is a universality in facial expressions of emotion (Ekman, 1998; Izard, 1977; Russell, 1994). Across cultures, people judge facial expressions of emotion with high levels

© Myrleen Cate/PhotoEdit

Children in some Asian cultures are often taught not to express anger or other negative emotions.

of accuracy, typically between 60 and 80 percent, that exceed chance. Moreover, studies have documented the universality of facial, postural, and vocal expressions of emotion cross-culturally (Ekman, 1973). For example, in studying a sample of 5- and 12-month old Japanese and U.S. infants, similar facial and vocal expressions of anger were observed in response to a nonpainful arm restraint (Camras, Oster, Joseph, Campos, Capose, Kazuo, Wang, & Meng, 1997).

The notion that emotions are biologically based and that they are culturally formed are not incongruent. Emotions are biologically based and universal, but the type of events attended to, the appraisal of these events, and the relevant ways of behaving may vary as a function of culture (Hess & Kirouac, 2000; Mesquita, Frijda, & Scherer, 1997). Once largely ignored, the study of culture and emotions is now at the center of the emergent field of affective science. Cross-cultural differences and similarities in emotional states, expression, and response can shed light on the origins of groups' differences in adult emotional behavior as well as on the processes involved in emotional development across cultures.

self-conscious emotions Emotions such as embarrassment, empathy, pride, shame, and envy emerge when children become self-aware of a standard of behavior against which the self can evaluate its own action.

Emotional Understandings in Early Childhood

Children reveal considerable emotional growth during the preschool years. Between 2 and 4, they produce increasingly appropriate facial expressions when provided with a verbal label. They also become progressively sophisticated in talking about emotions between ages 2 and 3 (Barrett, 1997). Approximately 60 to 90 percent of 2-year-olds recognize the four basic emotional terms (happy, sad, mad, and scared), whereas 83 to 97 percent use them in their own speech by age 3. Similar age trends are seen in identifying emotional expressions (Jenkins, Oatley, & Stein, 1998).

Between 3 and 4, they begin to be able to determine what emotions are appropriate to particular situations (Izard & Ackerman, 2000). Children's emotional experiences become increasingly more clearly defined through their interactions with their social environment. The expansion of children's emotional communications parallels the heightened displays of feelings that appear during the late toddler and early preschool period (Kopp, 1989). Temper tantrums are common and negativism and resistance to adults seem to peak.

Children's recognition and labeling of the basic emotions of joy, sadness, anger, and fear develop earlier than emotions such as contempt and shame. It is not until the middle of the second year that the secondary emotions are observed (Lewis, 2000). These emotions are sometimes called **self-conscious emotions**, because their emergence is dependent on the development of self-awareness. Self-conscious emotions include embarrassment, empathy, pride, shame, and envy. For these emotions to be felt, the child must not only be self-aware of but must understand a standard of behavior against which the self can evaluate its own action.

Distinguishing among negative emotions, especially correctly identifying anger and fear, is most difficult for children ages 2 to 3 (Denham & Couchoud, 1990). Inferring emotions from facial expressions becomes more differentiated during the early childhood years, coming to include anger and surprise (Walden & Field, 1990), excitement and disgust (Bortolotti, D'Elia, & Whissell, 1993), and calm and sleepy. Interestingly, young children can more accurately infer the causes of negative emotions than positive ones.

Young children find it more difficult, however, to combine various cues concerning another's emotional state. For example, their ability to infer emotions by resolving discrepant information from these cues is limited. When personal cues, such as facial expressions or behaviors, conflict with situational cues (child frowning at a birthday party), young children prefer personal cues when labeling an emotion (Barrett & Nelson-Goens, 1997). With increasing age, children's emotional understanding deepens; their lexicon of emotional terms expands, and they make more complex differentiations of the emotions appropriate to different situations (Russell, 1990). Two common emotions experienced during early childhood are fear and anger.

Common Emotions: Fear and Anger

Imagine that you are a volunteer for an experiment being conducted by your school. You are in the lab, wired to an electroencephalograph (EEG) that will measure your heart rate, blood pressure, face and hand temperature, skin conductance, and muscle tension. You have not the foggiest notion what the researchers are trying to find out, but you are in a good mood and willing to go along with the experiment. After a few minutes, you feel an intermittent shock in your little finger, coming from the wire that is attached to it. It is noticeable, and you call the experimenter over. The wires are checked and he presses a button on the EEG machine. Suddenly, sparks start flying, and the experimenter shouts, "There is a dangerous high-voltage short circuit!" Wouldn't you be frightened? Eventually, the wire is fixed and things get back to normal.

After about 15 minutes, the polygraph operator enters. You can immediately see that this guy is arrogant. He criticizes you for moving, tells you your reaction has threatened the outcome of the experiment, and comments on how useless you are. Before you can say anything about his rudeness, he leaves the room. Wouldn't you be angered by this treatment? You did not know it, but you have just been measured for your physiological responses while you were afraid and then angry.

Two powerful hormones secreted during an emotional state are responsible for the physiological changes that occur when we experience emotions. *Adrenaline* produces an increase in heart rate (in strong anger or fear, the heart rate may increase as much as 40 to 60 beats per minute), secretion of sweat glands, constriction of blood vessels, and the shutting off of digestion. (That is why, when you are excited, scared, or wildly in love you do not want to eat.) *Noradrenaline* causes a decrease in heart rate, secretion of the salivary glands, and dilation of blood vessels; it constricts the pupils of the eyes and facilitates digestion. These dramatic changes in body functions when experiencing various emotions suggest that virtually all of the neurophysiological systems and subsystems of the body are involved in emotional states. What do we know about children's experiences with fear and anger?

Children's Fears Fears come in all sizes, shapes, and intensities. Children's responses to fear vary from being mildly timid to being wide-eyed and paralyzed with terror. Not all children's fears are bad—some fears provide a safeguard against harm and disaster. Children's fears help them to be aware of possible dangers. Some fears are reasonable and justifiable within the limits of our experience; other fears are unreasonable. The fear of walking across a bridge that looks decrepit and decayed is reasonable; fear of walking across a bridge that is solidly constructed is unreasonable. Fears can mobilize the body for action. Whether the action is purposeful or not depends on many factors; intensity of fear is one. Fear, unlike anger, has probably been the subject of scientific investigation more frequently than any other fundamental emotion.

What causes fear in children? The tendency to be afraid may be increased by a weakened condition due to illness or being tired. Lack of familiarity, competition, or loss of affection may cause fear as well as circumstances that belittle children, humiliate them, or make them feel guilty, worthless, or reprehensible (Smedley, 1999). Also, because they are dependent on their parents, they may be troubled by any sign of fear or weakness their parents may show.

Sudden, intense stimuli confronting a child will produce a fear reaction. The cause of fear may be either the presence of something threatening or the absence of something that provides safety and security. The causes of fear are influenced by their contexts, by individual differences in temperament, and by experience or person–environment interactions. The threshold of fear, like that of any other emotion, is influenced by biologically based individual differences, idiosyncratic experiences, and the total sociocultural context of the occasion (Levine, Stein, & Liwag, 1999). Being alone, strangeness, sudden approach, sudden change of stimuli, and pain are conditions that tend to increase the probability of fear. Finally, the causes of fear are, in part, a function of age or maturation.

Younger children experience a greater number of fears than children in middle childhood (Gullone & King, 1993). Younger children tend to fear animals, the dark—especially being alone in the dark—imaginary creatures, separation from parents, sudden intense stimuli, and loud noises (Bowlby, 1973; Spence & McCathie, 1993). Fear reactions are generally limited to situations that threaten their immediate physical security, for example, being separated from their mother (Ohman, 2000).

Thought CHALLENGE

Many children's fears parallel the fears of their parents, particularly their mother's. Does this seem to be true in analyzing your fears and those of your parents?

Four situations that are likely to arouse fear in the first five years of life are noise and situations associated with noise; sudden change of illumination; sudden, unexpected movement; the approach of an object; and heights. Similarly, strange people and familiar people in strange guise, strange objects, and strange places produce fear.

Anger Whereas the study of some emotions such as distress and fear has been widespread, the study of anger has not. It does seem paradoxical that anger research has been so minimal because several researchers have reported that anger seems to occur more frequently among children than fear, jealousy, and other emotions (Fabes & Eisenberg, 1992; Smedley, 1999). Yet, early in life children are indoctrinated against expressing anger (El-Sheikh & Cummings, 1997). The result is that some children are overloaded with anger. However, experiencing anger in moderate and resolute form is not only normal but essential.

Anger is an arousal state that is primarily socially instigated, often under conditions of threat or frustration. Early anger reactions may be caused by objection to routine physical habits (dressing and eating), disagreement with peers over possession of toys, loss of possessions, minor physical discomfort, changes in routine toilet training, arrival of a second baby, and conflict with parents over authority. Conflict over possession is the most common cause of anger (Fabes & Eisenberg, 1992).

In younger children, responses to anger frequently involve venting (particularly for boys) or active resistance whereby children attempt to defend themselves in nonaggressive ways (particularly for girls) (Fabes & Eisenberg, 1992). For example, children may display anger by shoving a child who has grabbed a toy, or they may throw tantrums when their mother turns off the television because it is time for bed.

Research findings suggest that cross-cultural differences in expressing discrete emotional states begin quite early and are reflective of cultural beliefs and values. In a representative study, Carolyn Zahn-Waxler and her colleagues ((Zahn-Waxler, Friedman, Cole, & Mizuta, 1996) asked 4- and 5-year-old Japanese and U.S. children to respond to various hypothetical vignettes. Stories included having one's tower of blocks knocked down, having to stop playing and go to bed, and being hit. After each story, children were shown pictures of four different emotions (happy, sad, angry, afraid) and asked to choose the one facial display that best showed how he or she felt. In the second part of the study, children were again told stories reflecting various dilemmas and conflicts but were now asked, with the use of miniature figures of playmates, how they would respond. Young Japanese children were more apt to display feelings of sadness and fear and to respond with more prosocial behavior (sharing, cooperation) to the interpersonal conflict situations. The U.S. children tended to respond more aggressively and assertively and expressed emotions that often accompany these behaviors.

As noted in Chapter 2, socialization patterns are consistent with these differences in emotional responding in each of these cultures. Japanese mothers' childrearing practices are consistent with promoting concern for others, interdependency, harmony, and subtle expression of emotions. In contrast, Western guidance strategies are commonly characterized as valuing independence, self-actualization, assertiveness, and open expression of emotions.

As children get older there is a shift from wholehearted and violent reactions to more subdued, controlled responses. Four-year-olds in the United States, for example, were exposed to hypothetical situations involving eating something they disliked, receiving a disappointing birthday present, or being in a boring place (Zeman, Penza, Shipman, & Young, 1997). The children most often reported that they would feel angry in these situations and that they would respond by expressing their anger verbally. By the time children reach school age, many have learned to control overt reactions of anger (Lemerise & Dodge, 2000). An older child's response may take the form of sulking, staring, swearing, and the old silent treatment (Kochanska, Murray, & Harlan, 2000).

APPLICATIONS:

Helping Children Deal Effectively with Anger

Three-year-old Katrina stomps down the stairs and enters the kitchen. Her mother takes one look at the angry scowl on her face and promptly says, "Listen, young lady. I don't want to see that angry expression on your face. It's a beautiful day and you should be happy. Now march upstairs and when you come down again, I want to see a smile on your face!"

What is Katrina learning as a result of her mother's comments? When adults view anger as something bad or they refuse to recognize children's anger, children fail to learn how to deal effectively with angry feelings. What adults are teaching them is to hide, cover up, disguise, or deny the existence of these feelings (Renk, Phares, & Epps, 1999). When children are continually told that it is wrong or bad to display angry feelings or perhaps are punished for their fits of anger, they may become obsessed with feelings of guilt and fear (Saarni, 1999). Because their angry feelings have been bottled up inside, some children may become overwhelmed by them.

Most of us may not like being angry, but we cannot ignore it in ourselves or refuse to recognize it in children. To keep children's angry feelings from erupting into harmful actions, these feelings need to be acknowledged so that they can learn to deal effectively with them. Those who have grown up being unafraid of angry feelings; those who are aware of their angry feelings and see them as being natural emotions; and those who feel they can control angry feelings rather than being at their mercy are the ones who can apply their energies to change the cause of anger and engage in planned and effective action (Mayne & Ambrose, 1999).

© Elizabeth Crews

By understanding that angry feelings are a natural and necessary part of life, adults can help children learn how to control anger.

Distinguishing Between Angry Feelings and Angry Acts

Experts advise that adults need to make a distinction between children's angry feelings and angry acts (Brondolo, DiGiuseppe, & Tafrate, 1997). Children often have angry feelings and cannot control them, but they must learn to control angry acts. They should be free to express their feelings, but they must learn to refrain from engaging in violent behavioral actions. Expressing angry feelings can help them learn to cope with them so they do not become too much for them or for adults to handle. Adults can acknowledge a child's angry feelings, "I know you are angry with Danny for breaking your toy," and assure him that this feeling is normal. Firm limits, however, need to be set upon the angry impulses of physical expression of anger; the child needs to internalize (incorporate) these limits: "But I cannot allow you to hit him." The child must learn that certain actions are not permitted. Children need to be inhibited in actions such as hitting other children or parents, being cruel to animals, and destroying property.

Learning Self-Control

Learning self-control can help children deal more effectively with anger (Mayne & Ambrose, 1999). Self-control is the ability to regulate and control one's own actions in age-appropriate ways. It also involves the ability to make the better choice in situations. Self-control is the act of purposely motivating oneself to do or not to do some action. It also involves delaying gratification, resisting temptation, and making decisions reflectively (with some prethought) not reflexively (in an impulsive manner).

Adults play an important role in helping children develop self-regulation skills. Young children are able to develop self-control when they are provided with clear, consistent, and appropriate limits. When appropriate and clear limits have been consistently carried out, young children are able to modulate their reactions; begin to comply with simple parental requests; and anticipate the need to inhibit certain acts (for example, not touching a dangerous object). Self-control then implies inhibition of inappropriate behavior or the ability to delay gratification.

Delaying Gratification

During the 1970s, Walter Mischel and Ebbe Ebbesen (1970) conducted "the marshmallow challenge" experiment. Four-year-olds were chosen because at this age important developments in self-control seem to unfold. The preschoolers were given one marshmallow but were told that if they could wait and not eat that marshmallow until the adult returned from an errand (the adult returns after a maximum of 20 minutes) that they could have two marshmallows. However, the children were free to end the delay any time by ringing a bell. If they rang the bell, the adult returned immediately. But, if they rang the bell, they got the less preferred reward (one marshmallow rather than two).

Oh, what a struggle it was. The children looked away from the lone marshmallow and gazed at other objects in the room to keep their minds off the tempting treat; some put their heads down and tried to sleep; some fidgeted and gave commands to themselves, "Don't eat the marshmallow." Some children kept their minds on the two-marshmallow reward rather than focusing on quickly eating the less-preferred one marshmallow reward. Some children used techniques such as singing and making up games. All these techniques enabled these children to convert the waiting situation into a more pleasant nonwaiting one. Some children were able to delay their gratification and others, within seconds of the experimenter leaving the room, rang the bell as they gulped down the treasure in one gigantic swallow.

Twelve years later these children were tested during high school (Shoda, Mischel, & Peake, 1990). Those who resisted temptation at age 4, were now, at age 16, more socially competent, more self-assertive, and more organized under pressure. They exhibited more self-control than those preschoolers who were unable to resist temptation. The children who gave in to temptation early on were more likely to be lonely, easily frustrated, and stubborn. They buckled under stress and shied away from challenges. The ability to delay gratification in the service of a goal appears, then, to be an important skill in promoting anger control.

Concept Checks

1. Cross-cultural differences in emotional expression suggest that
   a. Japanese children are more emotionally expressive than U.S. children.
   b. Japanese children are expected to display more emotional maturity in expressing their feelings.
   c. U.S. parents consider young children not yet capable of understanding emotions and allow freer expression of emotions than do Japanese parents.
2. ***True or False:*** Most 2-year-olds can recognize the four basic emotional terms (happy, sad, mad, and scared), but they have difficulty expressing these emotions.
3. If your heart rate increases, the palms of your hands are sweaty, and your blood vessels are constricted, this is due to the secretion of the hormone known as ________________.
4. In working with a child who frequently shows anger responses, the best advice would be to help her
   a. internalize these inappropriate behaviors.
   b. acquire greater control over her anger impulses.
   c. learn the difference between angry feelings and angry acts.

Family Influences in Early Childhood

Before Beginning . . .

After reading this section, you will be able to

- define discipline and discuss its objectives.
- identify Baumrind's parenting styles and discuss how each style affects children.
- discuss effective guidance strategies.
- note the distinction between discipline and punishment and discuss short- and long-term effects of punishment.
- discuss the various forms of child abuse.

Bringing up children is not merely a matter of what parents do; it is also a matter of how they think about their task. Adults do have preconceptions and do form theories about the nature of children, the forces responsible for their development, and their own role in this process. Caregiver belief systems play a major part in determining socialization practices (see Figure 10.3), which in turn influence children's behavioral development as well as the belief systems that they come to develop (Ruble & Goodnow, 1998).

Do you believe that parents should own all the power and relegate very little to children? Do you believe that parents and children should share power? (The Self-Insight box provides a questionnaire to help you gain a further understanding of your beliefs.)

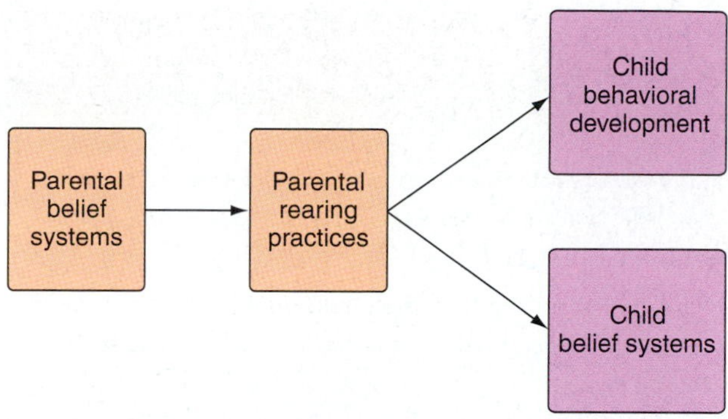

FIGURE 10.3 ***The Relationship of Parental Belief Systems to Rearing Practices and Children's Development***

A caregiver's beliefs are often translated into parental child-rearing practices that directly impact on the child's developmental outcome and the child's belief systems.

From "Social Development in Childhood and Adulthood (pp. 741–787), by D. N. Ruble & J. J. Goodnow, 1998, in D. T. Gilbert & S. T. Fiske (Eds.), *The Handbook of Social Psychology,* Boston: McGraw-Hill. Used by permission.

Parents as Guidance Engineers

Socialization is an adult-initiated process by which developing children, through insight, training, and imitation, acquire the habits and values congruent with adaptation to their culture (Baumrind, 1989). A major part of children's socialization involves helping them to develop social controls, or to adopt society's rules of behavior. In this sense, adults monitor children's acts, offering approval or withholding it, to help shape children's future acts. Although socialization does occur in the child's first year, the onset of socialization pressure generally comes in the second year (McCord, 1997).

Socially approved ways of behaving, however, vary according to one's cultural milieu. According to Corsaro (1997), Italian mothers, for example, see development in children as being natural and inevitable and as not requiring adult intervention. As a consequence, they are less likely to be concerned with playing an active disciplining role. Italian mothers, however, do see their role as one of providing protection and warmth and view folding the child into the family (*la famiglia*) as a principal parenting task. The Argentinean mother might see her role as the primary disciplinarian but be most fearful of making mistakes that could cause her child future unhappiness. Thus, she might be reflective, self-critical, self-questioning, and perhaps, too indulgent. On the other hand, a widely held Israeli tenet is that child-rearing responsibilities are to be shared with extended family and others in the community; they are not the sole obligation of the biological parents (Bornstein et al., 1998).

In the United States, mothers as well as fathers are expected to play an active role in socializing children to behave in socially competent ways, which usually means helping them to establish meaningful and sustained relationships with others, to work cooperatively with others, and to play an active part in the social order. Through the use of various guidance strategies (reinforcement, disciplining and punishing techniques, establishment of rules and regulations), parents seek to refine children's behavior in culturally approved ways. These strategies are impacted by the age of the child and differences in parenting styles.

Disciplining Across the Ages

The term **discipline** comes from the word *disciple,* meaning "one who gives instruction." Discipline goes beyond the confines of short-term, immediate behavioral gains; it influences children's future behavior. The process of child rearing and discipline undergoes important changes as children develop. During each phase of children's development, adult concerns and subsequent actions focus on different problems. Concerns in the infancy period center on irritability, illness, and sleeplessness. Concerns during early childhood focus on toilet training, disobedience, inability to play cooperatively with others, delayed verbal skills, bedtime routines, controlling temper tantrums, fighting with siblings or other children, eating and table manners, getting dressed by themselves, and attention seeking. Parents attempt to protect the child from dangers ("Don't talk to strangers"); infection ("Don't eat dirt"); cleanliness ("Wash your hands"); and etiquette ("Say 'thank you' "). Some of these issues carry over into school age with, for example, fighting and children's reactions to discipline.

In middle childhood, parents tend to be concerned about standards of performance, encouraging children to entertain themselves, their children's relationships with peers, being kept informed of where they are, dealing with problems at school, and their children's achievement. During adolescence, parents continue to be concerned about their children's social and academic performances, along with dating, sexual activities, and drugs.

At different ages, parents' disciplining techniques are apt to reflect their inferences about their children's

discipline
Comes from the word *disciple,* meaning "one who gives instruction." Discipline goes beyond the confines of short-term, immediate behavioral gains; it influences children's future behavior.

Assessing Parenting Styles: What Would You Do If Your Child Did This?

INSTRUCTIONS: Select the response that describes how you might discipline the child in each of the following situations (Eastman, 1994):

1. Your 3-year-old son has been cranky all day. After a horrible tantrum, as you are putting him down for a nap, he bites you.
   a. I would bite him back, saying, "See what it feels like."
   b. I would let it pass and rock him to sleep.
   c. I would worry about what might be bothering him and call someone for advice.
   d. I would say, "Biting is not okay. After you have a nice sleep, we will talk about why you are so angry."
2. Your preteen has been avoiding chores. Every request turns into an angry tirade. She promises to have her room cleaned by the time you get home from work. You come home, and her room is messier than ever.
   a. I would yell in frustration and tell her that she is grounded.
   b. I would give her another chance when she explains that she just had s-o-o-o much to do.
   c. I would give lecture #99 about why she must learn to do her fair share around the house.
   d. I would tell her that, as we had previously agreed, she will receive no phone calls or watch television until the room is clean.
3. Your son had a fight on the playground. When a teacher tried to break up the fight, your son slugged the teacher.
   a. I would spank him.
   b. I would believe him when he says the other kid started it and that the teacher has a reputation for being rough and must be exaggerating.
   c. I would worry about his low self-esteem and that he might be getting a bad reputation.
   d. I would let him know that regardless of the cause of his anger, nothing justifies hitting and violence.
4. A friend was over to play and broke your daughter's special music box. Your daughter proudly told you how she refrained from hitting her friend. Later, you learn that your daughter has been spreading vicious rumors about the other girl.
   a. I would order her to go to school and tell everyone she lied or that she will be punished.
   b. I would understand that she must have been very hurt and try to console her.
   c. I would worry that her reputation might be ruined if she admitted she was spreading rumors.
   d. I would let my daughter know that it is up to her to decide how she will make amends to her friend, but that, until she does, she will have to do one hour of extra chores each day.

ANSWERS: If you have answered mostly a's, you may be an authoritarian parent (you own all the power). It may be helpful to learn more cooperative ways of disciplining children. If you answered mostly b's, you may be an indulgent parent (child owns all the power). It may be helpful to learn to be less of an appeaser and more authoritative. If you answered mostly c's, you may be an indecisive parent (you can't make decisions). It may be helpful to learn more authoritative disciplining methods. If you answered mostly d's, you may be an authoritative parent (power appropriately shared by parent and child), and, as you shall see, this is the most effective parenting style.

competence and responsibility for misconduct. When parents think misdeeds reflect an absence of competence, they prefer calm induction more and power assertion less.

Adults certainly recognize that enormous advances in social skills occur across age and therefore, generally, believe that older children are more responsible. Studies suggest, at least in some respects, that the transfer of power from parent to child occurs slowly with the major shift to genuine autonomy beginning to occur at about age 12. Adults tend to give children more responsibility for their behavior as they get older by replacing directive techniques such as forcing compliance and repetition of commands with less directive approaches involving reasoning and explanation (Honig & Chung, 1989).

The importance of the parent fitting the discipline strategy used to the child's developmental level has been stressed by a number of child developmentalists (Crockenberg, Jackson, & Langrock, 1996).

Parenting Styles

Over the years, researchers have examined many different kinds of parent disciplining styles. One prominent researcher, Diana Baumrind (1971, 1989), has characterized two aspects of parents' behavior toward children: parental responsiveness and parental demandingness. **Responsiveness** refers to the degree to which parents respond to children's needs in an accepting, supportive manner. **Demandingness** refers to the extent to which parents expect and demand mature, responsible behavior from children.

Because responsiveness and demandingness are more or less independent of each other, it is possible to look at various combinations of these two dimensions. A parent who is very responsive but not at all demanding is considered **indulgent**, whereas one who is equally responsive but also very demanding is labeled **authoritative**. Parents who are very demanding but not responsive are **authoritarian**; parents who are neither demanding nor responsive are considered **indifferent** (see Figure 10.4).

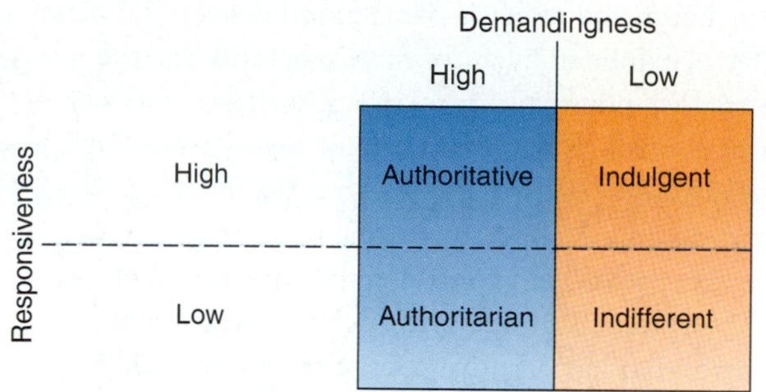

FIGURE 10.4 *A Scheme for Classifying Parenting Types*

Authoritative parents display high levels of control, clarity of communication, and high demandingness for mature behavior and nurturance; authoritarian parents also show high levels of control and maturity demands but are low on clarity of communication and nurturance; indulgent parents are low on control and maturity demands but high on nurturance; indifferent parents display low levels of control and demandingness.

From "Socialization, Personality, and Social Development," by E. E. Maccoby & J. A. Martin, 1983, in E. M. Hetherington (Ed.), *Handbook of Child Psychology* (Vol. IV, p. 39). New York: Wiley. Used by permission.

Authoritative Parents

> "Let's discuss some of the pros and cons of having a sleepover."
>
> "Tell me how you feel about the matter."

The categorization proposed by Baumrind provides a useful way of summarizing and examining some of the relations between parenting practices and children's psychosocial development. The authoritative parent expects mature behavior from the child. These parents exhibit a high level of demandingness and a high level of responsiveness to their children. Such parents encourage children to be independent but still place limits, demands, and controls on their actions.

Children who are most responsible and mature tend to have parents who establish consistent standards of behavior, negotiate with their children concerning those standards, use explanations, and have warm relationships with their children. Generally speaking, children raised in authoritative households are more psychosocially competent than children raised in authoritarian, indulgent, or indifferent homes. Children from authoritative homes show greater social responsibility (achievement orientation, friendliness toward peers, cooperativeness toward adults) and independence (social dominance, nonconforming behavior, purposeful).

Authoritarian Parents

> "As long as you live in this house, you'll do as you're told."
>
> "You'll do it because I said so."

Authoritarian parents exhibit high levels of demandingness and low levels of responsiveness to their children. Rules in these homes are not discussed in advance or arrived at by any consensus or bargaining process. They are decided upon by the parents. These parents attach strong value to the maintenance of their authority and suppress any efforts by their children to challenge it.

Authoritarian parenting styles may increase conformity and obedience in the short term, but the children are at risk for developing more external styles where they lack internal controls on their own behavior and are more concerned about getting caught than about doing what is right for its own sake. Children with external controls are also more likely to blame others when things go wrong and are less likely to take responsibility for their own decisions and behavior. This type of parenting can also lead to rebellion and a complete breakdown of parent–child relationships. Parents are likely to believe that the answer to this problem is to become more and more controlling. The more strict and rigid these parents become, the lower the chances are that their children will do what their parents want.

responsiveness Refers to the degree to which parents respond to children's needs in an accepting, supportive manner.

demandingness Refers to the extent to which parents expect and demand mature, responsible behavior from children.

indulgent parenting styles Parents are minimally controlling but affectionate; low levels of demandingness and high levels of responsiveness.

authoritative parenting styles Parents exhibit a high level of demandingness and a high level of responsiveness.

authoritarian parenting styles Parents exhibit high levels of demandingness and low levels of responsiveness.

indifferent parenting styles Parents are low on demandingness and low on responsiveness.

Baumrind makes a distinction between the firm control exhibited by authoritative parents and the restrictive, punitive control of authoritarian parents. Firm control "is not a measure of restrictiveness, punitive attitudes, or intrusiveness, but is a measure of strict discipline" (1971, p. 6). She notes that "it is not the exercise of firm control per se, however, but the arbitrary, harsh, and nonfunctional exercise of firm control that has negative consequences for child behavior" (Baumrind, 1989, p. 139).

Indulgent Parents

"What do you want to do, dear?"

"Whatever you decide is fine with me."

Whereas authoritarian parents make all the decisions, indulgent parents are minimally controlling but affectionate. These parents do not feel in control and do not exert control. Indulgent parents behave in an accepting, benign, and somewhat more passive way in matters of discipline. They place relatively few demands on the child's behavior, giving the child a high degree of freedom to act as he or she wishes. Indulgent parents are more likely to believe that control is an infringement on the child's freedom that may interfere with the child's healthy development. Instead of actively shaping their child's behavior, indulgent parents are more likely to view themselves as resources that the child may or may not use.

Impulsive behavior in children is associated with little or no parental control. In addition, these children tend to be immature, dependent, regressive, the least self-reliant, spoiled, and the poorest in self-control. These parents may be well intentioned, and they try to spare their children from unpleasant experiences, but in reality, they are infantilizing these children. Overindulged children do not learn how to subordinate their desires and needs to others, and appear to be unhappy. The discontent, impatience, and joylessness that characterize these children shows to what extent spoiling has succeeded in making life easier for them (Dreikurs & Soltz, 1995).

Indifferent Parents

"I don't have time to talk now, maybe later."

"It makes no difference to me one way or the other."

Indifferent parents are neither demanding nor responsive. Indifferent parents try to do whatever is necessary to minimize the time and energy they must devote to interacting with their child. In extreme cases, indifferent parents may be neglectful. They know little about their child's activities and whereabouts, show little interest in their child's experiences at school or with friends, rarely converse with their child, and rarely consider their child's opinion when making decisions. Rather than raising their child according to a set of beliefs about what is good for the child's development, indifferent parents are "parent-centered"—structuring their home life primarily around their own needs and interests. Children raised by indifferent parents are often impulsive and more likely to be involved in delinquent behavior and in precocious experiments with sex, drugs, and alcohol. In general, the effects of indifference tend to be slightly worse among boys than girls. A summary of parenting styles is found in Table 10.7.

TABLE 10.7

Parenting Styles

Parenting Style	Description	Children's Behavior
Authoritarian	High levels of demandingness; low levels of responsiveness; rules decided upon by parents; suppresses children's efforts to challenge authority; highly restrictive; imposes absolute standards	Likely to display dependent behavior; fail to initiate activities; lack internal controls over own behavior
Indulgent	Parents are minimally controlling but affectionate; behave in an accepting and passive way; place relatively few demands on children	Children likely to be impulsive, immature; the least self-reliant; and spoiled
Indifferent	Parents are neither demanding nor responsive; may be neglectful; home is structured in a "parent-centered" way	Children are likely to be impulsive; more likely to be involved in delinquent acts
Authoritative	High levels of demandingness; high levels of responsiveness; expect mature behavior from child; encourage independence, but place limits on their actions	Children likely to be the most responsible; more prosocial; academically competent

From "Rearing Competent Children (pp. 349–375)," by D. Baumrind, in W. Damon (Ed.), *Child Development: Today and Tomorrow*, San Francisco: Jossey-Bass. Used by permission.

Guidance Strategies

Aside from the research experts in the field, children often have interesting insights as to effective guidelines for disciplining. (Their thoughts are highlighted in the First Person box.) The "other" experts focus on reinforcement, consistency, and punishment.

Reinforcement

From the very beginning, parents often train their children in the Skinnerian fashion of rewarding or reinforcing them for certain kinds of behavior. To illustrate, in the United States it is quite common for young children to receive positive attention when they begin to share with others. Negative behaviors are sometimes ignored or punished. Parents generally reward children when they behave in socially approved ways (sharing with others) and show disapproval when their behavior is socially unacceptable (kicking Stanley in the shins and grabbing his truck). In other countries, such as Pakistan, samples of parents reported that they tended to ignore the positive and focus on the negative through punishment (Sahibzada, 1992).

Which method is most effective? Findings from the samples of Pakistani mothers who punished their children to eliminate misbehavior revealed that they tended to have more aggressive, acting-out children than those from a U.S. sample (Sahibzada, 1992). Whether physical discipline leads to aggressive, acting-out behavior, however, remains unclear. Some researchers see a direct line between physical punishment and negative, aggressive behavior (Huesmann, 1997); and some do not (Baumrind, 1997). Still, other scholars argue that the link between physical punishment and aggressive behavior may be culturally specific (Deater-Deckard, Dodge, Bates, & Pettit, 1996). Among European American children, physical discipline does appear to lead to higher rates of aggression. However, the use of physical discipline does not appear to lead to higher rates of externalizing problems in African American children (Hopkins, 1998).

FIRSTPERSON

The Best Disciplinarian Ever!

K: Zach when you misbehave, what would you want your parents to do to discipline you?

Z: I don't know. They sometimes yell at me.

K: Do you like that?

Z: No.

K: Should they send you to your room?

Z: Yes.

K: Do you like that?

Z: No.

K: Should they just let you do anything you want?

Z: Yes, that's good.

—Kelly Favela and 5-year-old Zach

I would say, be like my grandma, she doesn't yell, she just gives hugs.

—Beeta Mozdzimski, age 6

I would not like to be grounded. If I did not eat my dinner, I would not get dessert. If I did not do my homework, I would have to eat vegetables.

—Daniel Orsini, age 8

I think I would not spank my child because I heard stories about kids' parents who spank them and they are afraid of them.

—Taylor Milne, age 8

Don't give so many rules. My parents have so many rules and I forget them. Just have two or maybe three, like do your homework and go to bed on time.

—Rick Larsen, age 10

The perfect disciplinarian is one who listens before they yell. Someone who tries to understand the situation before administering punishment. To understand that everyone makes mistakes and give us a second chance.

—Kenji Wallace, age 16

Consistency

Another important element in the socialization of children is consistency in disciplining (Sherrill, O'Leary, Albertson-Kelly, & Kendziora, 1996). Most parents know that if they follow through with predictable and reliable actions toward their children's behavior, the results will be effective. Most parents are also aware that this, at times, is difficult to do. There are times when various family situations, interruptions, and diversions prevent adults from following through. If, however, parents make threats ("No television for a week!"), they should follow through. If they do not, children learn very quickly not to believe in their parents' authority. The use of idle threats is associated with high levels of disobedience. In addition, if children encounter wide fluctuations in the type of discipline they encounter (parents are tyrants one day and Mr. and Mrs. Milquetoast the next), or if some behaviors are punished one day and overlooked the next, they soon learn not to comply with parental requests.

Similarly, there should be a consistency in the number and type of rules. Consistent enforcement of rules is related to high levels of voluntary compliance by children. Adults can become more consistent by not creating too many rules and demands. If adults have numerous rules, there are numerous areas of behavior that they have to monitor, and they are liable to slip up and forget their own rules. Moreover, adult rules and requests need to be clearly stated and easy to remember and must deal with behaviors that can be regulated.

Punishment

> My child has been getting into a lot of trouble at school lately. He's disruptive and picks fights. I've told him, if I ever hear from a teacher that he's caused another fight he's really going to get it.
>
> I was hit as a child. I was wild and disobedient, and if my parents hadn't spanked me, there's no telling how I would have turned out; I'm okay now, so I don't see how spanking could hurt my child.

Physical punishment often involves slaps on the hand or leg, spanking on the buttocks, pinching, shaking, hitting on the buttocks with a belt or paddle, and slapping in the face. Murray Straus and Julie Stewart (1999) report that the overall prevalence rate (the percentage of parents using any of these types of punishment during the previous year) reached a peak of 94 percent at ages 3 and 4 years. Severity was greatest for children ages 5 to 12 and was more prevalent among African American and low socioeconomic status parents in the South. Most punishment was directed at boys by mothers. Carla Bradley (1998) also examined the types of disciplinary methods used by African American parents. Her data on African American mothers showed that they preferred to use nonphysical forms of discipline—a more authoritative approach to discipline. This refutes the opinions of some social scientists who have asserted that African American parents engage in very little give-and-take dialogue with their children. When physical punishment was used by the parents, it involved a child who directly challenged the authority of the parent.

Adults who use punishment do not realize that punishment is retaliatory—not corrective. A child, however, who is hit sees the punishing authority as trying to impose his or her will by brute force. In these situations, most children try to find ways of defeating the punishment because they resent the action and refuse to accept it. Punishment and discipline are not synonymous. Discipline influences children's future behavior. Punishment, on the other hand, is causing children to pay some kind of price that is more painful than the forbidden behavior or activity in which they are engaging. Adults may erroneously think that punishment works and that its effects are long term (Brenner & Fox, 1998).

Clearly, the immediate effects of punishment account for its popularity, but, as research points out, although it has an immediate effect in reducing a tendency to behave in a certain way, in the long run its effects are temporary and impermanent (Day, Peterson, & McCracken, 1998). Moreover, when punishment is consistently used, the punishing agent must be present for it to be effective. For example, in an experiment, children of mothers who resorted to power-assertive disciplining techniques such as punishment worked well on a task while the mother was present but did not continue to do so when she left (Spieker, Larson, Lewis, Keller, & Gilchrist, 1999). Here, punishment worked only when the mother is present. However, children whose mothers explained the importance of the task and did not resort to punishment worked persistently on the task in her absence (Deater-Deckard & Dodge, 1997).

Moreover, temporary control may be obtained at a rather high price. Although there are many ways that children can learn to respond to punishment, in general, they try to avoid contact with the punishing agent, which gives the parent less opportunity to socialize the child. When children are physically punished for inappropriate behavior, they are hurt from the experience, frustrated at not being understood, resentful that no one will help, helpless to retaliate directly, and fearful of further punishment. The result of all this is further negative feelings (Straus & McCord, 1998) and poorer social relationships with peers (Tencer, 2001).

Deviant behavior (negativism for its own sake) is associated with parental control strategies that are highly power-assertive, such as parental anger, harshness, and criticisms, and excessive control characterized in particular by physical punishment (Gough & Reavey, 1997). The most effective strategies appear to combine firm control and guidance for eliciting compliance (Chang, 2001). When control is combined with guidance, it provides the child with clear information about what the parent wants, but at the same time it invites power sharing. These techniques are reminiscent of Baumrind's authoritative pattern of parenting: Authoritative parents exert firm parental control, but they also listen to what their children have to say and can be influenced by them.

Punishment does not teach a child self-discipline. Fear of punishment may restrain children from doing wrong, but it does not make them want to do right. Disregarding this simple fact is the great error into which parents and educators fall when they rely on these negative means of correction. The only effective discipline is self-discipline, motivated by the child's inner desire to act meritoriously to do well in his or her own eyes. Good behavior is based on values that children have internalized because they love, admire, and want to emulate their parents. It is not much of a conscience that tells children not to do wrong because they might be punished.

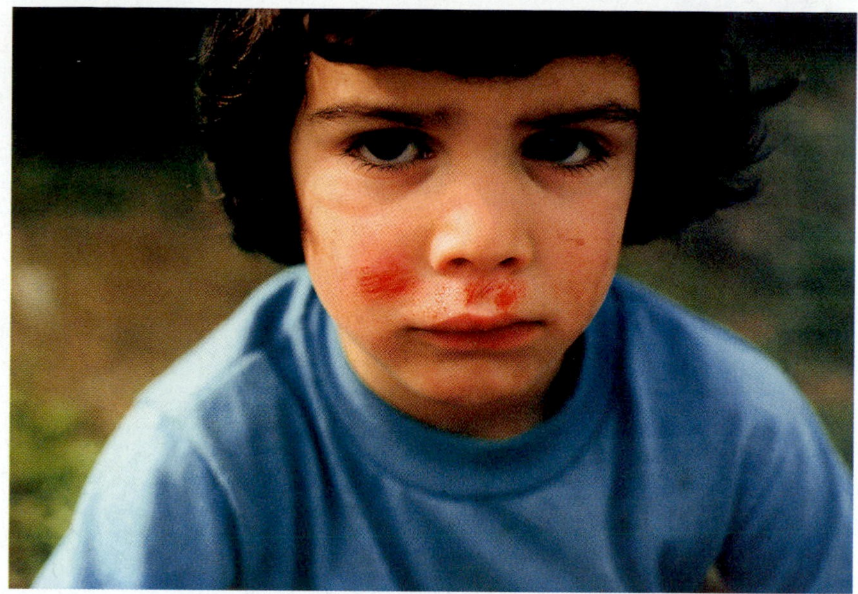

© Robert Eckert/Stock Boston

Child abuse can take many forms; physical, sexual, and emotional abuse are all forms of child maltreatment.

When Punishment Goes Awry: Child Abuse

Our strong repugnance to the stories of child abuse can be attributed to the compassion of most adults, who seek to protect the young. Researchers and policy makers have recognized the extent and severity of violence toward children. Despite the flurry of research, however, there is still disagreement about its development, the consequences for victims, and the most effective avenues for intervention. We will look at the types of abuse, characteristics of abusive parents, the effects of abuse on children.

Types of Abuse

Physical child abuse involves *acts of commission* by the parent, characterized by overt physical violence, beating, or excessive punishment (Barth, 1998). The use of physical punishment against children seems to reflect a mixture of positive belief in force as a tool for shaping behavior, lack of effective alternatives to force, and emotional tension in the parent. Young children are more at risk for physical abuse than are older children; over half of the reported cases occur to children under 4 years of age, with children under 2 at the greatest risk. Physical abuse typically involves minor bruises or burns, but about 3 percent of the reports describe life-threatening assaults resulting in broken bones, fractured skulls, and serious burns.

Child **neglect** involves maltreatment due to *acts of omission,* when the parent fails to meet a child's physical, nutritional, medical, emotional, and other needs (Friedman, Sandler, Hernandez, & Wolfe, 1991). Emotional abuse has been defined as the parents' failure to encourage normal development by assurance of love and acceptance. It involves verbal put-downs, labeling, humiliation, and unrealistic expectations. Physical neglect includes inadequate provision of food, clothing, or personal hygiene also compounded by a delay in or refusal to seek health care. Inadequate supervision—which has been called the "silent killer" because it results in a substantial number of deaths—is most typical of neglect.

Sexual abuse in families, or incest, involves dependent, developmentally immature children and adolescents in sexual activities they do not fully comprehend that violate the social taboos of family roles. Three-quarters of sexual abuse reports involve fondling or exposure, with genital contact and penetration claimed about one-quarter of the time (Barth, 1998).

Although the most publicized form of child abuse may now be sexual abuse, it is far less commonly reported to public child welfare authorities than either physical abuse or neglect. Nearly three times as many parents are reported for child neglect (including failure to supervise, parental abandonment, parental incapacity) as for sexual abuse, with the number of physical abuse reports falling in between (Barth, 1998). About 55 percent of child abuse reports are on white children, about 25 percent on African American children, and about 10 percent on Latino children, with the remainder on children of other backgrounds (Barth, 1998). Pacific Islander and Filipino Americans reported the least incidence of sexual child abuse; although cultural factors such as shame and denial common within these cultural groups may reduce reporting (Okamura, Heras, & Wong-Kerberg, 1995).

Table 10.8 provides a detailed list of the four categories of child abuse just discussed: physical, emotional, sexual, and neglect.

physical abuse
Characterized by overt physical violence to the child.

neglect
The failure of the caregiver to properly provide an atmosphere in which the child has responsible safeguards for physical health, safety, and general well-being.

sexual abuse
The involvement of a developmentally immature child or adolescent and an adult in sexual activities that violate social mores.

TABLE 10.8

Categories of Child Abuse

Physical Abuse	Emotional Abuse	Neglect	Sexual Abuse
▪ Minor ▪ Serious (such as bone fractures or head injuries) ▪ Premeditated/sadistic ▪ Burns and scalds ▪ Bites ▪ Repeated abuse resulting from lack of control ▪ Punishment with implements ▪ Genital/anal area injuries	▪ Rejection ▪ Lack of praise and encouragement ▪ Lack of comfort and love ▪ Lack of attachment ▪ Lack of proper stimulation (such as fun and play) ▪ Lack of continuity of care (frequent moves) ▪ Lack of appropriate handling (such as age-inappropriate expectations) ▪ Serious overprotection ▪ Inappropriate nonphysical punishment (such as locking in bedrooms)	▪ Abandonment or desertion ▪ Leaving alone ▪ Malnourishment, lack of food, inappropriate food, or erratic feeding ▪ Lack of warmth ▪ Lack of adequate clothing ▪ Unhygienic home conditions ▪ Lack of protection or exposure to dangers (including moral danger or lack of supervision appropriate to the child's age) ▪ Persistent failure to attend school ▪ Nonorganic failure to thrive	▪ Inappropriate fondling ▪ Mutual masturbation ▪ Digital penetration ▪ Oral/genital contact ▪ Anal or vaginal intercourse ▪ Exploitation for pornography ▪ Exposure to pornography

Characteristics of Abusing Parents

Parents who physically abuse children often display deficient social skills, low social desirability, high anxiety, and lack of receptiveness and support-seeking behavior (Gilbert, 1997). Abusive families tend to score higher on certain child-rearing factors, such as authoritarian control and lack of encouragement of autonomy, and family climate factors, such as conflict and lack of cohesion (Trickett, Aber, Carlson, & Cicchetti, 1991). Abusive parents tend to be controlling, interfering, and either covertly or overtly hostile (Barnett, Manly, & Cicchetti, 1993).

Abusive parents interpret certain age-appropriate behavior in children as "willful disobedience" or intentional misbehavior when the children's actions do not conform to their commands (Azar & Bober, 1999). Moreover, abusive parents tend to interpret noncompliant behavior as an indication of the child's "bad" disposition, often using such descriptors as "stubborn," "unloving," and "spoiled" as explanations of contrary behavior. When abusive mothers respond to vignettes in which their child behaves in ways that might be considered provoking, they respond more frequently than do nonabusive mothers that they would administer greater levels of punishment in these situations but also that their child is misbehaving to annoy them (Wolfe, Wekerle, Reitzel-Jaffe, & Lefebvre, 1998).

Thought CHALLENGE

When would you consider it appropriate to intervene if you witnessed a child being spanked in public?

Neglecting mothers are unresponsive in that they tend neither to initiate interaction nor to respond to their infants' initiatives. Infants of abusive mothers tend to be difficult, and infants of neglecting mothers tend to be quite passive.

In the case of sexual abuse, some mothers condone their daughter's sexual role with her father. Such women may have a history of emotional deprivation and be ill-equipped to protect their daughters. It appears that relatively few women actually take assertive action to protect their daughters once they find out (Coleman, 1997).

Child abuse occurs across different social classes, ethnic groups, and genders. Nonetheless, the public's perception is that ethnic-minority group children are more often the victims of child abuse and neglect. Ethnicity appears to be insignificant as a predictor of child abuse (Ferrrari, 1999). Poverty and young motherhood, however, compound the risk of all types of child maltreatment (Lee & Goerge, 1999). Another moderating effect is the parent's history of childhood maltreatment; however there are sex differences. Although a history of childhood maltreatment was predictive of a mother's current use of physical and verbal punishment with her child, a history of child maltreatment in fathers predicted less use of physical punishment, greater use of reasoning, and greater use of nurturing behaviors (Ferrari, 1999).

Effects of Abuse and Neglect on Children

Child abuse is characterized by most experts as producing problematic behavior patterns in children (Simons, Whitbeck, Conger, & Chyi-In, 1991). These include antisocial aggression, troubled peer relationships, impaired social cognitions, lack of empathy, and depression (Azar,

Breton, & Miller, 1998). As a group, abused children of all ages have been found to have a variety of psychological difficulties in comparison to nonabused children. Depression and low self-esteem have been linked to adverse child experiences (Gilbreath & Cicchetti, 1990).

Effects of Incest on the Child

According to research by Beth Molnar (2001), sexually abused children are depressed and withdrawn. They often engage in fantasy and babylike behavior. Also, they often have poor relationships with other children and are unwilling to participate in physical activities. At times, the sexually abused child engages in delinquent acts or runs away from home. Short-term effects of incest include regression to earlier behaviors, such as thumb sucking, eating disorders, sleep disorders, bed-wetting, tics, or excessive fears. Although 49 percent of abused subjects show no evident sign of emotional or mental trauma on pediatric examination (Caffaro-Rouget, Long, & Van Santen, 1989), the longer the duration of abuse, the greater the likelihood of negative effects in the form of emotional and behavioral trauma and school problems in the victims. Table 10.9 summarizes the symptoms useful for recognizing a sexually abused child.

It is difficult to disentangle the effects of sexual abuse from those of the disturbed environment in which it occurs. In general, the closer the relationship between the aggressor and victim, the more damaging the abuse. Other considerations include the age and developmental status of the child, the use of force, the degree of shame or guilt the child feels, and the reaction of the parents.

TABLE 10.9

Symptoms of Sexual Abuse
▪ Child seems to be afraid of a particular person or place and being left alone with that individual.
▪ Child overreacts to a question about being touched.
▪ Child suddenly seems more aware of and preoccupied with sexual conduct, words, and parts of the body.
▪ Child's behavior changes dramatically in any number of ways: Younger children may regress to bed-wetting or soiling their underwear. Eating habits might change. The child may relate to peers differently, either by withdrawing or by becoming more aggressive. The child might act up in school, motivation and concentration may suffer, and grades may fall. Child may appear fearful, frequently crying and clinging to his/her parent(s), or alternatively, may avoid normal family intimacy completely.
▪ Child has unreasonable anxiety over a doctor's physical examination.
▪ Child has inexplicable physical complaints, such as headaches, stomachaches, or genital itching or pain.
▪ Child draws unusually frightening or sad pictures using a lot of black and red colors.
▪ Child masturbates excessively and tries to get other children to perform sexual acts.

Caffero-Rouget, A., Long, R., & Van Santen, V. (1989). The impact of sexual abuse on victims' adjustment. *Annals of Sex Research, 2,* 29–47.

APPLICATIONS:

Helping Abused Children

Unfortunately, most families who are reported for suspected child abuse do not receive any ongoing services. There are simply not enough staff to provide services to all children at risk. Nationally, less than half of the estimated one million abused and neglected children receive some welfare services in their homes (Azar, 1998). Despite this general paucity of in-home service, certain types of in-home services, such as home visits from a social worker and some practical services to repair dangerous aspects of the home situation, are increasingly available for some children.

Leaving children in abusive environments while those environments are rehabilitated, however, can be dangerous for children. The risk of subsequent harm may not be neutralized despite careful planning and routine surveillance. Although many children can be safely protected at home, every year scores and perhaps hundreds of physically abused and neglected children die while receiving in-home child welfare services in response to a child abuse report (Azar, Breton, & Miller, 1998).

Foster Care

In some situations, children are removed from the home and placed in foster care. Although placement of a child in foster care occurs following fewer than half of substantiated child abuse reports, nearly a quarter of a million children enter foster care each year in the United States (Barth, 2001). The length of time that children will stay in foster care varies considerably across the states—the median length of time in Texas is 9 months compared with 34 months in Illinois. A reasonable national estimate is 18 to 20 months. Studies consistently indicate that abused children who have been in family foster care function better than those abused children who remain at home (Orme & Buehler, 2001).

Supportive Relationships

Kerry Bolger, Carlotte Patterson, and Janis Kupersmidt (1998) have found that maltreatment by parents is associated with impaired social competence in children and corresponding negative feelings about the self. There is also evidence of high mobility among abusive families, and abused children appear to show poorer school attendance (Eckenrode, Laird, & Doris, 1993). Thus, abused children may have an unstable connection with the neighborhood and school, both of which are critical contexts in children's development. Therefore, children who have been maltreated and who are also disliked by peers may miss out on opportunities to learn social skills. As a result, they may suffer cascading effects of negative social relationships.

As such, helping maltreated children develop social skills has beneficial results. Peer contact is a prominent source of support and provides a backdrop against which many social skills are mastered. Sandra Azar and Sharon Bober (1999) note from their research that supportive relationships outside the family buffer the child from some of the effects of maltreatment. Having a positive relationship with a best friend moderates the effect of maltreatment on self-esteem. These findings suggest that maltreated children may be especially in need of, and able to benefit from, peer-based intervention strategies to improve their personal and social adjustment. Learning to act in socially competent ways that will enable them to have special friends may help to restore their feelings of companionship, trust, and feelings of personal worth.

Concept Checks

1. "Do as I say, because I say so!" and "Children should be seen and not heard" would most likely be said by which type of parent?
   a. Authoritative
   b. Authoritarian
   c. Indulgent
2. A child who goes along with anything that others do and is highly dependent probably had what type of caregiver discipline?
   a. Autocratic
   b. Physical punishment
   c. Authoritative
3. Parents who resort to looking for negative behavior and punishing children for it, tend to have
   a. more aggressive children.
   b. more prosocial children.
   c. more dependent children.
4. ***True or False:*** Parents must earn the respect of their children by the way they act.

Reviewing Key Points

Social Understandings

- Children's conceptions of self focus on physical features, things that distinguish them from others, and action statements. Self-esteem, the evaluative component of the self-system, consists of two sources: outer sources (based on the evaluations of significant others) and inner sources (based on our personal assessments of our competencies).
- The first component of the self-system involves children feeling loved and worthy, and children experience this when parents are warm, loving, and respectful. The second component of self involves helping children develop actual skills and competencies in physical, social, moral, and academic areas, which leads to competency self-esteem—an overlooked but critical component of self-esteem.
- Children's understanding of others grows more sophisticated. Children's friendships, however, are rather fleeting and are based on who one is playing with at the moment. Parents, particularly fathers, play important roles in socializing children to act in typically feminine and masculine ways.
- Freud's theory of gender-role development stresses that identification with the same-sex parent is crucial to the development of masculine and feminine ways of behaving. For social learning theorists, the source of gender-role acquisition is found in cultural factors; children will imitate the models in their particular society and emulate their behavior. Information-processing theorists argue that gender-role behavior is learned by forming schemata about behaviors that are "appropriate/inappropriate" for me and my gender. Biological theory stresses genetic and hormonal influences in the development of masculine and feminine ways of behaving.
- More equalitarian gender roles can be fostered if adults encourage more instrumental behavior in girls and more expressive behavior in boys. Introducing them to nonstereotypical books to read, meeting nonstereotypical males and females, and exploring different occupational pursuits are some of the ways in which adults can engender children along less traditional and bipolar lines.

Emotional Development

- Children in different cultures are often socialized in different ways, which is reflected in their expressions of emotion. For example, U.S. mothers talk more with their children and encourage positive emotions, and their children tend to display these emotional characteristics. Japanese mothers cuddle their children more rather than talking to them. Japanese children tend to be less active and talkative than their U.S. counterparts.

- Emotionally, secondary emotions (pride, shame, embarrassment) appear during the early childhood period. Preschoolers experience fear because of lack of familiarity, encountering a sudden, intense stimulus, competition, and loss of affection. Anger is caused when children are blocked from achieving a goal.
- Children can be helped to deal more effectively with anger when adults help them to distinguish between angry feelings and angry acts and allow them to express the former but not the latter. Children manage angry feelings more effectively when they learn self-control and how to delay gratification. With cognitive advancements, such as representational thinking and the development of more sophisticated memory skills, children learn how to monitor their behavior in accordance with social rules.

Family Influences in Early Childhood

- Social pressures begin in earnest during the second year of life in most cultures around the world. Although there are no hard and fast rules for effective discipline, some guidelines were offered such as the use of inductive reasoning, avoiding harsh, physical punishment, having the discipline fit the misbehavior, being authoritative, being in control, and showing warmth.
- Parenting styles are authoritative (high demandingness/high responsiveness); authoritarian (high demandingness/low responsiveness); indulgent (low demandingness/high responsiveness); and indifferent (low demandingness/low responsiveness). Through the use of various disciplining techniques, punishment, and establishing rules and regulations, parents play an important role in socializing children to behave in socially approved ways.
- Physical abuse is characterized by overt physical violence to the child. Neglect is defined as the failure of the caregiver to properly provide an atmosphere in which the child has responsible safeguards for physical health, safety, and general well-being. Sexual abuse, or incest, is the involvement of a developmentally immature child or adolescent and his or her parent in sexual activities that violate the social mores of family roles.
- Leaving children in abusive environments can be dangerous for them and for this reason foster care is often recommended. Abused children also profit from developing social skills, because many lack social competence and harbor negative feelings toward others. A supportive relationship outside the family may also buffer the child from the ill-effects of maltreatment.

Answers to Concept Checks

Social Understandings

1. true 2. display of affect 3. a 4. c
5. emotionally expressive; independent

Emotional Development

1. b 2. true 3. adrenaline 4. c

Family Influences in Early Childhood

1. b 2. b 3. a 4. true

Key Terms

anaclitic identification
associative play
authoritarian parenting styles
authoritative parenting styles
competency self-esteem
cooperative play
defensive identification
demandingness
discipline
expansion
gender consistency/constancy
gender identity
gender schema
gender stability
imitation
indifferent parenting styles
indulgent parenting styles
neglect
nonsocial activity
parallel play
physical abuse
pretend play responsiveness
self-concept
self-conscious emotions
self-esteem
sexual abuse
vicarious reinforcement

InfoTrac College Edition

For additional readings, explore InfoTrac College Edition, your online library. Go to **http://www.infotrac-college.com/wadsworth** and use the passcode that came on the card with your book. Try these search terms: children's emotions, discipline of children, child abuse.

Child Development CD-ROM

Go to to the Wadsworth Child Development CD-ROM for further study of the concepts in this chapter. The CD-ROM also includes quizzes and additional activities to expand your learning experience.

Let me introduce you to James Garbarino

One of the topics of concern to us in Part Five is children's peer status. Most children get along with others, but some children are mercilessly picked on and rejected by their classmates. A small percentage of these children react toward others in exceedingly harmful and sometimes lethal ways. Who is responsible? Parents? Society? and What can we do to help these children? Violence among our youths is one of Dr. Garbarino's concerns.

Courtesy of James Garbarino

As a professor of Human Development at Cornell University, James Garbarino has been involved in efforts to understand the social environments in which many of today's youths reside, and he believes many socially toxic factors lead not only to rejection and violence but to other problems we observe in our young children today. His research has culminated in a particularly poignant work, entitled *Raising Children in a Socially Toxic Environment.*

PART 5

Developmental Contexts

Middle Childhood

Raising Children in a Socially Toxic Environment

by James Garbarino, Professor of Human Development, Cornell University

When children do not get along with others, when they become harmful to themselves, who is responsible? I think the concept of "social toxicity" is an important vehicle for approaching many of the problems children and society face today. What I mean by the term socially toxic environment *is that the social world of families, the social context in which they evolve and function, can become poisonous to development. I offer this term as a parallel to the environmental movement's analysis of physical toxicity as a threat to human well-being and survival. The nature of physical toxicity is now well known and is a matter for public policy and private concern. For example, we know that air quality is a major problem in many places, so much so that in some cities, just breathing "normally" is a threat to your health, and cancer rates reflect that physical toxicity.*

But what are the social equivalents to lead and smoke in the air, PCBs in the water, and pesticides in the food chain? I think some social equivalents include violence, racism, and community inequality. Beyond these dramatic issues are more, many more, that are subtle yet equally serious. High on the list is the departure of adults from the lives of kids. The lack of adult supervision and time spent doing constructive, cooperative activities are important toxic aspects of the social environment today, and these forces compound the effects of other negative influences in kids' social environments. Kids "home alone" are more vulnerable to every cultural poison they encounter than are children backed up by adults. These are the forces that contaminate the environment of children and youths. These are the elements of social toxicity.

Although every child is vulnerable to toxicity in the social environment, high-risk children living in high-risk families are the most vulnerable. These are the children who already have accumulated the most developmental risk factors: poverty, racism, abuse, neglect, absent parents, or parents incapacitated by drugs, alcohol, or mental illness. It is as if these children are "psychological asthmatics" living in an ever more polluted environment.

In the last 10 years, some communities have improved the quality of their physical environment as enhanced public and professional awareness has led to changes. In the matter of recognizing social toxicity, however, we lag far behind. We need a direct social equivalent to Silent Spring, *Rachel Carson's landmark analysis of physical toxicity. Her book, first published in 1953, called attention to the problem and stimulated reforms, which led to public action to ban DDT and counter many of the physical environment's most severe manifestations of physical toxicity. Like the physical environment, we need to counter the severe manifestations of social toxicity. We need to recognize, understand, and take active steps in reversing social toxicity. As we improve the quality of children's environments, we improve the quality of their lives and ours.*

PART OUTLINE

Chapter Eleven
Physical Development: Middle Childhood

Chapter Twelve
Cognitive Development: Middle Childhood

Chapter Thirteen
Socioemotional Development: Middle Childhood

CHAPTER ELEVEN

Physical Development: *Middle Childhood*

CHAPTER OUTLINE

How the Body Changes
- Height and Weight
- Skeletal and Muscular Growth
- Vision and Hearing
- Perceptual Development
- Brain Development
- Applications: Exercising Growing Intelligences

Motor Development
- Basic Skills Expanded and Refined
- Motor Fitness
- Play
- Applications: Physical Fitness

Health in Middle Childhood
- Illnesses, Injuries, and Accidents
- Death
- Precursors for Undereating Disorders
- Obesity
- Applications: Helping Obese Children

Stress
- Is This a Stressful Situation or Not?
- Common Childhood Stressors
- Daily Hassles
- Stress and Illness
- Applications: Stress Management

Reviewing Key Points

Olga is 10 years old. At 140 pounds and 5′1″, she is overweight. Her mother, a well-meaning but overbearing and demanding woman, nagged Olga incessantly about her appearance. Her friends were no kinder. After several weeks on a strict diet, Olga noticed she was losing weight. She felt a control and mastery that she had never known before. It wasn't long before she received compliments from her mother and her friends. Olga was satisfied with eating a few carrot and celery sticks a day—and that was all. (Barlow & Durand, 1999)

That was Olga at 10 years old; she is now 12 and weighs 75 pounds. If you can look past her sunken eyes and pasty skin, you can see that she was once an attractive girl. Now, she looks emaciated. Olga suffers from an eating disorder known as anorexia nervosa. Although this may seem to be a very young age for such a complicated problem, signs of developing undereating disorders for some young girls, like Olga, are apparent during the elementary school years. We will address undereating disorders, and at the other end of the spectrum—overeating.

Children are not too young to experience eating disorders or stress—another topic of interest in this chapter. A growing number of school-age children take tranquilizers, presumably to handle overwhelming stress. Does that seem surprising and a bit shocking to you? What is stress and how can we help children manage the stressors in their lives.

First we will examine how the body changes during these middle childhood years. As we explore physical development during the school-age years, it will become apparent that changes in height and weight are slow and gradual; body proportional changes are less striking; and brain development is less dramatic than in preceding stages.

However, expanded and refined motor development enables these children to make striking gains in athletic skills. The school-age years represent a significant time when children grow from physical immaturity to the threshold of adultlike appearances; develop from a state of clumsiness and awkwardness to become proficient in games and sports; and shift from undefined interests to multiple accomplishments that may well open doors to future proficiencies. Our second section focuses on the impact of motor developments during the middle childhood years.

In other ways, a child's elementary school years are quieter than the preceding preschool years and the adolescent years to come. Even in the psychological domain, Freud did not envision any libidinal hang-ups in middle childhood. In his psychosexual scheme of things, the "latency" period was a more-or-less carefree time in terms of any sexual fixations.

In revisiting Erik Erikson's psychosocial stages, we find that school-age children (ages 6 to 12) are now entering the stage of industry and accomplishment. These children are ready for larger worlds of thought and action. They begin to derive joy and satisfaction from producing and demonstrating their abilities in ways that will prove they are growing up, such as riding bikes to friends' houses and working with other children on school projects. In Erikson's scheme, the challenge to those guiding these children is to provide opportunities that will bring positive feelings of accomplishment and maintain a balance between independence and cooperation.

How the Body Changes

Before Beginning ...

After reading this section, you will be able to

- understand the physical changes that occur during ages 6 to 12.
- trace the growth of the skeletal and muscular systems.
- see the role of brain development in the total development of the child.
- identify and help to exercise schoolchildren's multiple intelligences.

The steady physical development that occurred during the preschool years continues during middle childhood. As noted in Chapter 4, the fastest rate of growth occurs prenatally when in approximately nine months two cells multiply into trillions. If this rate were to continue to age 20, adults would be 20 feet tall and weigh several tons. So, fortunately, during middle childhood, height and weight changes are slower and less spectacular than in utero. This period of slow growth gives the child time to get used to his or her body and is an important factor in the typically dramatic improvement seen in coordination and motor control during the middle childhood years. The gradual change in size and the close relationship maintained between bone and tissue development may also be important factors in increased levels of motor skill functioning.

Some pretty amazing things, however, do happen to the body during the middle childhood years, such as the changing of body proportion and profile and the acquisition of motor skills. Most children have a slimmer appearance than they did during the preschool years, due to shifts in the accumulation and location of body fat (DiGirolamo, Geis, & Walker, 1998). As a youngster's entire body size increases, the amount of body fat stays relatively stable, giving children a thinner look. Also, during this stage of life children's legs are longer in proportion to their bodies.

Height and Weight

"Don't have time for breakfast, Mom; I'm late for band practice." Travis grabs his lunch and in a flash, he is out the door and racing down the street on his bike. A few houses away, he comes to a rolling stop and shouts to his friend, Ling, "Come on, we'll be late." Ling tucks his trumpet into the basket of his bike and peddles furiously to catch up to Travis.

Children in middle childhood seem to always be in a hurry, but the growth of their bodies slips into a more leisurely developmental pace. On average, the steady growth of middle childhood results in an increase in height of a little over 2 inches a year in both boys and girls.

By age 11, the average girl will reach 90 percent of her adult height and half of her adult weight. Boys, on the other hand, reach only 80 percent of their adult height by age 11. Weight gain averages about 6.5 pounds a year. But these are only averages. A number of factors, including how close the child is to puberty, will determine when and how much the child grows. Puberty often begins earlier than adults may think. For example, breast budding in girls—their first sign of puberty—starts at age 10 on average, with some girls starting as early as 8 and others not until 13.

At age 11, Travis is taller than Ling and seems to be growing quite fast this fall, evidenced by his mother's having to "constantly" buy him new clothes. Many children in middle childhood, like Travis, often experience clear growth spurts, but these are usually followed by periods in which they grow very little. In general, there tends to be a period of a slightly increased growth rate between ages 6 and 8 (Walco, 1997). Some children grow as much as three times faster during a particular season of the year compared with their "slow" seasons (Tanner, 1998). These individual differences in timing—along with hereditary factors—are largely responsible for the wide variations in size among youngsters of the same age.

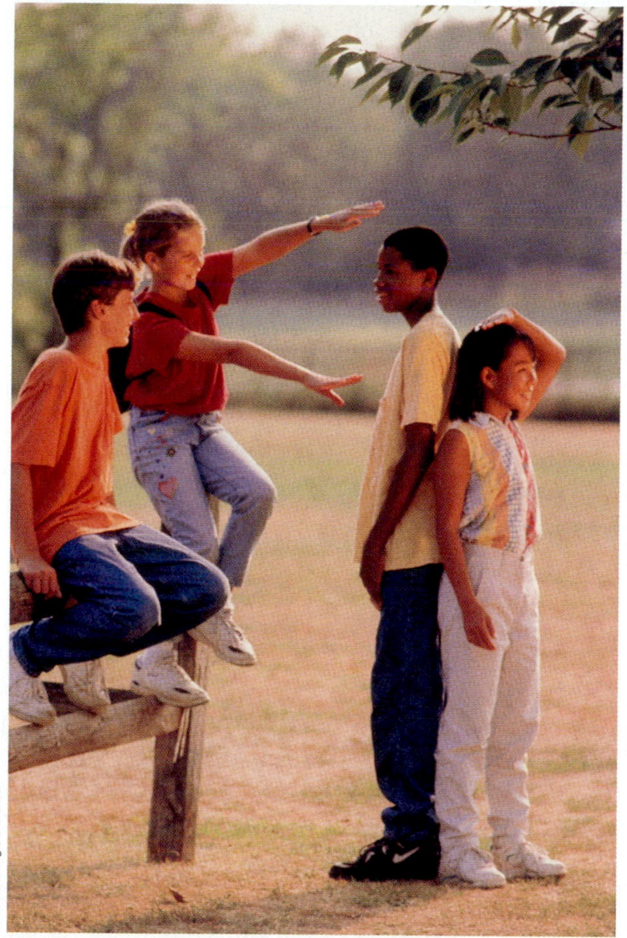

Although growth is slow and steady during middle childhood, children do experience minigrowth spurts followed by slow-growth periods.

This does not mean that all children in the same family will have the same ultimate size, but the total growth pattern of siblings is apt to be more alike than that of unrelated children. Race and climate are two factors that are difficult to separate from the total growth picture. Japanese American children, like Ling, who was born and reared in California, are taller and heavier than cousins born and reared in Japan (Lee, 1999). The California-reared Japanese children are also more advanced in skeletal development. These differences are generally attributed to better food, climate, and exercise.

As Travis, Ling, and their classmates enter the classroom, vast differences in height among the children are immediately apparent. Some children are 4 or 5 inches taller than others. Although boys and girls are generally of similar height during middle childhood, that changes with the beginning of puberty. Differences in growth patterns, however, are minimal during the middle years. Both boys and girls have greater trunk growth, but boys tend to have longer legs, arms, and standing heights during middle childhood. Likewise, girls tend to have greater hip widths and thigh sizes during this period. There is relatively little difference in physique or weight exhibited until the onset of the preadolescent period. Therefore, in most cases, girls and boys should be able to participate together in physical and motor activities.

Many structures in the body, such as the skeleton, muscles, liver, spleen, kidneys, and face, follow the normal curve in growth. Others, such as the brain and skull, reproductive organs, tonsil lymphoid tissue, intestines, and subcutaneous fat, do not. Each system and organ reaches maturity at its own time, resulting in uneven growth patterns.

During middle childhood, the nose grows considerably, the shoulder line becomes squarer, and the abdomen becomes flat. There are no marked sex differences in body proportions. Perhaps the most outstanding physical change during middle childhood is the changing proportion of the child's head to his or her body. At age 5, the child's head attains 91 percent of its mature size, whereas the body height is less than 75 percent of its adult size. The surface area of the child's head at age 5 accounts for 13 percent of her total body surface, whereas that of an adult accounts for 8 percent (Tanner, 1998).

Skeletal and Muscular Growth

Skeletal age confirms that girls are maturationally ahead of boys throughout childhood. At birth, girls are already four weeks ahead of boys in skeletal age, and at age 12, they are almost two years ahead. Skeletal maturity, which is typically measured by an X ray of the hand and wrist, may predict the approximate age at which puberty will be achieved. Skeletal age is estimated by the percentage of cartilage that has been replaced by bone. Children's bones, however, have proportionately more water and proteinlike materials and fewer minerals than those of adults. The blood supply to these growing structures is greater, and the ligaments are less firmly attached, with larger spaces between the bones at the joints. These characteristics make a child more susceptible to bone infections carried by the bloodstream, less resistant to extreme pressures and muscle pull, and more flexible in movement than an adult (Walco, 1997).

The developmental maturity of girls is not just confined to bones. Girls' teeth also erupt earlier. Moreover, girls perform almost all basic motor skills earlier than boys, including creeping, sitting, talking, toileting, dressing, and writing. Given these facts, it should not be surprising to find out that in cultural communities around the world parents generally expect young girls to show more mature, responsible social behavior than boys of the same age (Lee, 1999).

Beginning at age 5 or 6 there is a rapid increase in muscle growth, which accounts for the major portion of the weight gain during middle childhood (Tanner, 1998). No new muscle fibers develop after birth, but those that are present grow in length and breadth and are accompanied by changes in composition. Both exercise and general state of health affect muscular development and status; illness or lack of use diminishes muscle tone and causes fatigue to occur more easily.

The extreme physical flexibility of children in this growth period is due to muscle growth and the fact that their ligaments are not firmly attached to bones. However, if flexibility is not maintained through practice (climbing on jungle gyms or trees, acrobatics, hanging from monkey bars), it will diminish. Flexing their new muscular strength becomes a common part of middle childhood; these children always seem to be engaging in some sort of rigorous activity.

The heart muscle grows more slowly in these years and is smaller in relation to the body than at any other period of life. This fact contributes to the danger of highly competitive sports for school-age children. With maturity, the heartbeat slows down, and the blood pressure rises. The heart continues to increase in size until around the age of 20. The most common cause of heart disease in children is rheumatic fever, believed to be the result of a streptococcal infection. The potential damage to the heart is in the form of scarred valves or adhesion of the valve leaflets that affect the blood supply. Because of the greater work demanded of the muscle due to leaking or obstructed valves, the heart enlarges. Later, it develops irregularities in rhythm. Surgery is now able to remedy some of the damage and allow persons to live moderately active lives under medical care.

myopia
Nearsightedness.

Vision and Hearing

There is disagreement concerning the age at which 20/20 vision is normally achieved, but it is after age 7 that the eyeball reaches its full weight and several years later before full development is complete. Binocular vision is well developed for many children by age 6, but large print is still recommended for children throughout the elementary school years. **Myopia**, or nearsightedness, is common during the early years of middle childhood. Visual irregularities such as cross-eye or an eye that turns in or out should be treated (DiGirolamo, Geis, & Walker, 1998). No child will outgrow eye conditions of this type. Corrective lenses or surgery may be the recommended treatment.

Hearing acuity is thought to increase between ages 3 and 13. Ear infections are less likely to occur now than during preschool years. Because the eustachian tube (a narrow tube that equalizes air pressure on both sides of the eardrum) lengthens, narrows, and becomes more slanted, it is more difficult for disease organisms to invade.

Perceptual Development

Although this period of development is typified by slow but steady increases in height and weight, great organizational progress is made in the sensory and motor systems. The sensorimotor apparatus is working in ever-greater harmony so that by the end of this period children can perform numerous sophisticated skills. Being able to strike a pitched ball, for example, improves with age and practice due to improved visual acuity, tracking abilities, reaction and movement time, and sensorimotor integration. A key to maximum development during this time is experience and practice. Failure to have the opportunity for practice, instruction, and encouragement will prevent many children from developing more sophisticated motor abilities. Table 11.1 summarizes the physical and motor developmental milestones of middle childhood.

Brain Development

In keeping with the rest of the body systems, brain growth during middle childhood is slow and steady. Between ages 2½ and 10, the brain grows only another 15 percent, reaching 90 percent of its adult weight. (Growth spurts during the 11th and 15th years then complete the brain's weight.) Although brain enlargement slows down during the middle childhood years, its structure continues to become more elaborate. Without its continuing development, the physical and sensory achievements (along with motor, social, and emotional advancements) during middle childhood would not be possible. The cerebral cortex continues to grow more neural extensions (dendrites); well-used circuits and connections between neural branches (synapses) become more stabilized, and the brain continues to become more selective in its pruning process of eliminating underused neural networks (Huttenlocher, 1998).

The Brain's Pruning Process

Measurements of brain cell activity based on the cell's use of glucose support the idea that a dramatic pruning of weak or unused connections occurs during the school-age years (Mueller, Rothermel, Behen, Muzik, Mangner, & Chugani, 1998). This is particularly apparent in the visual region of the cerebral cortex. The elimination of weak connections leads to more streamlined communication between neurons in the visual cortex, which contributes, for example, to the child's increasing eye–hand coordination skills. This dramatic pruning of weak or unused connections continues throughout adolescence.

Harry Chugani (1996) notes that the child's brain shows a large increase in metabolic activity at around age 2 and continues to burn at a high rate until ages 8 to 10. After that time, glucose declines steadily until, at ages 16 to 18, it reaches its steady adult level. Chugani reasons that this high burning of cellular fuel is needed to support the huge forests of branching neurons, each with their 10,000 branches synapsing on 50,000 others. Only when the unused connections have been "weeded out" and the cells have smaller "forests" to encompass

TABLE 11.1

Physical and Motor Developmental Characteristics

- Growth is slow, especially from age 8 to the end of this period. There is a slow but steady pace of increments, unlike the more rapid gains in height and weight during the preschool years.
- The body begins to lengthen, with an annual gain in height of only 2 to 3 inches and an annual gain in weight of only 3 to 6 pounds.
- Boys and girls range from about 44 to 60 inches in height and 44 to 90 pounds in weight.
- The cephalocaudal (head to toe) and proximodistal (center to periphery) principles of development, in which the large muscles of the body are considerably more developed than the small muscles, are quite apparent.
- Girls are generally about a year ahead of boys in physiological development.
- Reaction time is slow, causing difficulty with eye–hand and eye–foot coordination at the beginning of this period. By the end, they are generally well established.
- Both boys and girls are full of energy but often possess low endurance levels and tire easily.
- The visual–perceptual mechanisms are fully established by the end of this period.
- Children are often nearsighted (myopic) during this period.
- Basic skills necessary for successful play become well developed

Pruning processes in the brain, particularly in the visual cortex, continue during middle childhood, which may account for increasing eye–hand coordination.

Child Development Issues

How Adaptable Is the Human Brain?

An 8-month-old baby, with electrodes taped to his head to register brain activity, listens to speech sounds "da . . . da . . . ba. . . ." Interestingly, his left hemisphere shows a great deal of activity. When the infant listens to nonspeech sounds, the right hemisphere becomes more active. At this young age, we already see some specialization of neurons. Some neurons are already dedicated to processing certain types of experiences. But, the infant's young brain is still immature and many neurons are unspecialized. For this reason, the brain displays a great deal of *plasticity*, which refers to recovery of function after damage to the brain.

If, for example, damage occurs to the language center of the brain, Broca's area, during the early years, uncommitted neurons (those that are not already engaged in a particular function), will "take over" language functions, and the child will develop normal speech. If an adult suffers from the same damage to the language center from a stroke, for example, achieving the same degree of rich language complexity as before the stroke is doubtful. As we get older, more and more neurons are already involved in specialized functions and cannot take over for neurons damaged in other parts of the brain. Thus, damage to the brain results in less effect on behavior when that injury occurs in infancy and early childhood than during mature years (Ramey & Ramey, 1998).

Although the power of adaptive plasticity of the brain may be greatest during the developmental years up to ages 8 or 9 (Mueller, Rothermel, Behen, Muzik, Mangner, & Chugani, 1998), there is room for modification in the brain after that time. The fact that adults are continually learning new and complex tasks shows that modifiability exists in the mature brain. Recovery from damage, however, involves a number of factors. An important factor involved in the brain's plasticity, for example, is the redundancy of neural connections. Neurons have many pathways by which they can communicate with other neurons—actually more than they need to carry on normal functions. If some of these communicative pathways are damaged, connections not previously used may take over and thus behavior will be spared.

Sprouting is another factor involved in restoring brain function; newly sprouting fibers will "rearrange" neural circuits. After damage to a set of axons, the cells that had received input from them react to the loss by secreting chemicals that will stimulate nerve growth. These chemicals induce nearby uninjured axons to form new branches

and support does the fuel-burning slow. With pruning and lessened activity, comments Chugani, some of the brain's plasticity disappears (see Child Development Issues). This is reflected in its slowly fading ability to recover from brain surgery or other brain traumas without major deficits.

Growth Spurts

As pointed out in Chapter 5, emerging mental and physical capacities coincide with brain growth spurts. The brain growth spurt that occurs at 2 years, for example, enables the young child to pretend her doll is walking across the table as she says, "My doll walking." Similarly, a brain growth spurt that occurs at age 7 enables the child to combine several ideas in her head at the same time. She can carry on make-believe conversations between two dolls. Another brain growth spurt that occurs at age 11 coincides with the child's being able to think abstractly. She understands, for example, abstract concepts such as "horizon" and "democracy."

Robert Thatcher's (1998) research also contributes to our understanding of how the growing brain is connected to the evolution of new abilities during the middle childhood period. Thatcher believes that the growth spurts in the brain follow a cyclical pattern that occurs every five years. Based on brain wave patterns, growth spurts begin in the left hemisphere, move to the center, and then the right hemisphere. Kurt Fischer (1997) agrees that there are brain growth cycles, as demonstrated in EEG readings of the electrical pat-

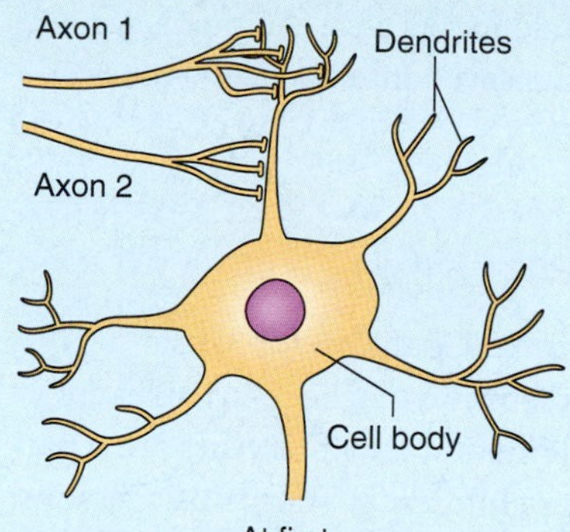

At first

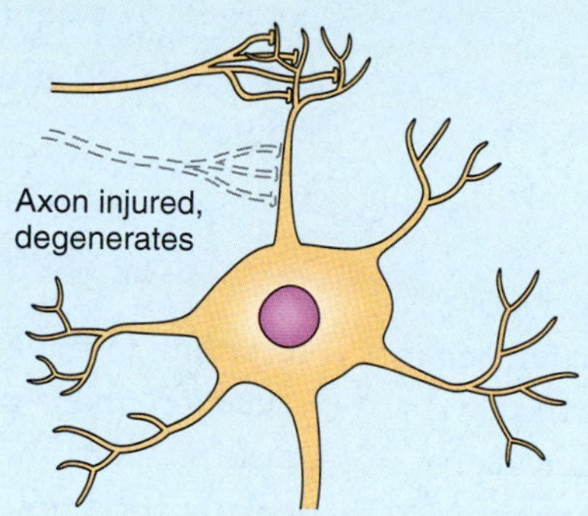

Loss of an axon

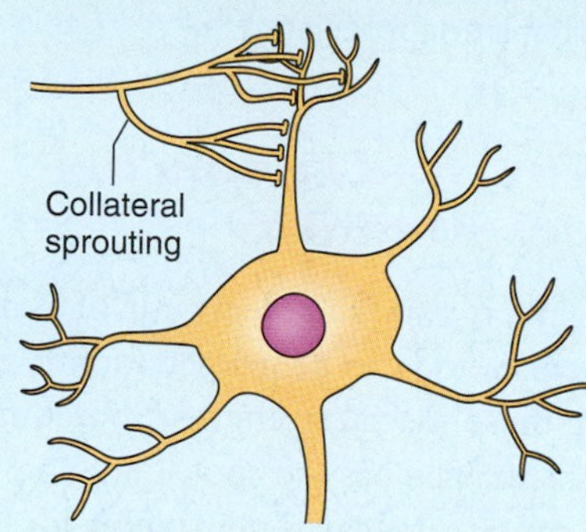

Sprouting to fill vacant synapses

that attach to the vacant synapses. Gradually, over several months, the sprouts fill in most of the vacated synapses. Over the next several months, the surviving axons sprout enough to restore almost completely normal input (Fritschy & Grzanna, 1992) and regular functioning is again attained.

Moreover, some researchers believe that recovery from cerebral damage essentially represents a recovery from *diaschisis*, from the Greek term meaning to *shock throughout* (Perani, Vallar, Paulesu, Alberoni, & Fazio, 1993). Immediately after damage occurs to the brain, and often for long periods of time, the neurons near to and distant from the injury site decrease in their response function. This decreased responsivity is believed to be caused by an inhibitory mechanism in the brain. With time, this inhibitory process is reduced, and normal functioning is again attained. Further, much of the recovery that takes place after brain damage is learned; the individual with brain damage makes better use of unimpaired abilities. For example, one who has lost vision in all but the center of the visual field may learn to move his or her head back and forth to compensate for the loss in peripheral vision.

Search Online

Explore InfoTrac College Edition, your online library. Go to **http://www.infotrac-college.com/wadsworth** and use the passcode that came on the card with your book. Try these search terms: brain plasticity, brain development, early brain development.

terns in a child's developing brain. Fischer points out that at around the age of 7, there is an increased coordination between the EEG activity in the frontal lobes and the EEG activity in other parts of the brain. This suggests that maturation plays a significant role in the newfound thinking abilities of the school-age child. Children, for example, are now more capable of controlling their behavior (known as inhibitory control). Further, as the control pathways develop in the frontal lobes, they are increasingly able to pay attention to one thing selectively, to stay focused on the task, and to keep irrelevant details from intruding (Samago-Sprouse, 1999). Emerging mental and physical capacities coincide with brain growth, but their emergence is also dependent on environmental support in the form of exercising and strengthening individual capabilities.

APPLICATIONS:

Exercising Growing Intelligences

Howard Gardner's **theory of multiple intelligences** (1983, 1997) appeals to our common sense observations about individual capabilities or intelligence. To Gardner, intelligence is not merely confined to abstract reasoning abilities but, rather, includes a number of different capacities. Each of us, for example, knows the world through capacities for language, logic and mathematics, spatial representation, music, movement, understanding others, and understanding ourselves (see Table 11.2). Recently, Gardner proposed an eighth type of intelligence—the capacity to understand and appreciate

theory of multiple intelligences Howard Gardner's theory that dismisses the idea of general intelligence and proposes eight independent intelligences.

nature (Gardner, 1999). Many parents and educators agree with Gardner, noting that traditional IQ tests, which mainly focus on verbal and math ability, leave a whole other spectrum of mental strengths untested and perhaps unappreciated.

Noticing and Enhancing Special Strengths

Every child is good in at least one of Gardner's listed intelligences and can be praised for and encouraged to develop these special strengths. Sometimes the child's strengths may be easy to spot. Ling does exceedingly well in music. He learns new pieces for his trumpet with relative ease. His teacher often comments that he has an "ear for music." Travis, however, must work harder in practicing on his saxophone and appears not to be as gifted as Ling in music. Travis, however, even as a small boy, was very agile. He could run well at an early age. He learned how to catch and throw easily; in fact, his sports skills are quite exceptional. Some children may demonstrate a mixture of capabilities, such as being able to understand others as well as themselves very well. Some children may require exposure to many different opportunities and experiences before their strengths are apparent. Gardner's theory not only helps us to see intelligence from a broader perspective but enables parents and educators to develop strategies for enriching brain development by discovering and enhancing the child's talents. As a case in point, we will look at one of Gardner's seven intelligences—musical abilities.

Musical Abilities

According to the National Coalition for Music Education, made up of music teachers, artists, and music retailers, the elementary school years are a particularly good time for children to start music lessons either with private teachers or through the school music program. The organization recommends starting children on piano lessons at ages 5 to 8. The ease of learning to play string, wind, and percussion instruments depends on the child's size and ability to concentrate, but it is suggested that children should start no later than age 10 or 11.

Are these timetables self-serving in that they come from the music industry? The answer appears to be "no" based on recent research on brain development (Demorest & Serlin, 1997; Miller & Clausen, 1997).

TABLE 11.2

Gardner's Multiple Intelligences

Intelligence	Description	Occupation
Linguistic	Sensitivity to the sounds, rhythms, and meanings of words and the different functions of language	Poet, journalist
Logico-mathematical	Sensitivity to, and capacity to detect, logical or numerical patterns; ability to handle long chains of logical reasoning	Mathematician, scientist
Musical	Ability to produce and appreciate pitch, rhythm, melody, and aesthetic-sounding tones; understanding of the forms of musical expressiveness	Violinist, composer
Spatial	Ability to perceive the visual–spatial world accurately, to perform changes on those perceptions, and to re-create aspects of visual experience in the absence of relevant stimuli	Sculptor, navigator
Bodily-kinesthetic	Ability to use the body skillfully for expressive as well as goal-directed purposes; ability to handle objects skillfully	Dancer, athlete
Interpersonal	Ability to detect and respond appropriately to the moods, temperaments, motivations, and intentions of others	Therapist, salesperson
Intrapersonal	Ability to discriminate complex inner feelings and to use them to guide one's own behavior; knowledge of one's own strengths, weaknesses, desires, and intelligences	Persons with accurate self-knowledge

From *Frames of Mind: The Theory of Multiple Intelligences*, by H. Gardner, 1983, New York: Basic Books.

The ability to identify and hear an A-sharp or a B-flat or any particular note simply by hearing it is called perfect pitch, and the part of the brain responsible for this talent resides in the left hemisphere in a region called the planum temporale (which is also involved in speech). In musicians with perfect pitch, the planum temporale is twice as large as in either nonmusicians or musicians lacking perfect pitch. Ninety-five percent of musicians with perfect pitch started music lessons before the age of 7. According to this research, early music training is associated with more growth in this particular brain region and with it a skill that is vital to playing an instrument well.

Moreover, stringed instrument players have a larger area of the cerebral cortex that is more devoted to moving and sensing fingers of the left hand (which play the notes) than to the right hand (which moves the bow) (Miltner, Braun, Arnold, Witte, & Taub, 1999). Nonmusicians have no such variation. The differential is greatest for string players who started playing their instruments before age 13.

So, is there a critical period for developing musical abilities? Many say "yes" (Chugani, 1996). Although far more proof exists for a language critical period than for a musical window, the general implications are similar: the elementary school years are an ideal time for children to learn to sing or play an instrument. Even among children with an average musical intelligence quotient, practice can help perfect these skills. When experience with music is stimulating and fun, it can help to open doors to future music appreciation (Gardner, Hatch, & Torff, 1997).

Concept Checks

1. The wide variations in size that we see in middle childhood are more than likely due to
   a. growth spurts.
   b. nutritional factors.
   c. participation in sports.
2. The physical flexibility of children during the elementary school years is related to
   a. developing new muscle fibers.
   b. the fact that their ligaments are not firmly attached to their bones.
   c. the shortening of ligaments.
3. As EEG patterns in the frontal lobes become more coordinated, children are now able to
   a. reason abstractly.
   b. think about more than one thing at a time.
   c. engage in more sustained attention.
4. Howard Gardner's theory of multiple intelligences emphasizes that
   a. learning opportunities can help children develop intellectual strengths.
   b. intelligence is best measured by the existing IQ tests.
   c. smart individuals have superior logico-mathematic skills.

Motor Development

Before Beginning ...

After reading this section, you will be able to

- examine the basic motor fitness skills.
- trace the components involved in being physically fit.

Basic Skills Expanded and Refined

Movement in middle childhood becomes more controlled, more efficient, and increasingly complex. By the end of middle childhood, children move with considerable agility; they become quite proficient at balancing, locomotion, and manipulative abilities. Motor development in middle childhood is summarized in Table 11.3. Children can discriminate left from right in their own bodies by age 7. Handedness is well established and fine muscle ability improves steadily until age 12. By age 12, children have developed about 90 percent of their potential mobility and speed of reaction. Balance, speed, strength, and coordination seem to improve with time and practice. Physical action is important in helping children master skills such as batting a ball or balancing on a beam.

Motor Fitness

Heredity plays a role in determining one's motor ability, and environment determines to what extent any individual will achieve his or her genetic possibilities. Maturation must precede learning; before skilled movements can be learned, the muscular mechanism must be sufficiently matured to allow such learning. Voluntary muscles are controlled by nerves and nerve centers. Until these have sufficiently developed, coordinated action of a voluntary type will be impossible. Such development occurs gradually throughout the

TABLE 11.3

Motor Development in Middle Childhood

Age	Selected Behaviors
6	Girls are superior in movement accuracy; boys are superior in forceful, complex acts.
	Girls can throw a small ball 19 feet; boys 34 feet.
	Children can throw with proper weight shift and step.
	Children can jump vertically 7 inches.
	Children can paste paper toys and sew crudely if the needle is threaded.
	Both can skip.
7	Children can balance on one foot without looking.
	Children can walk a 2-inch-wide balance beam.
	Children can hop and jump accurately into small squares.
	Children can execute accurate jumping-jack exercises.
	Girls can perform a standing long jump 41 inches; boys 43 inches.
	Children can use a table knife for cutting meat.
8	Children have 12-pound grip strength.
	The number of games children participate in is greatest at this age.
	Children can engage in alternate rhythmic hopping in different patterns.
	Girls can throw a small ball 40 feet; boys 59 feet.
	Children can engage in routine household tasks.
	Children repeat physical performances to master them.
9	Girls can jump vertically 8–9 inches; boys 10 inches.
	Boys can run 16½ feet per second.
	Boys can throw a small ball 70 feet; girls 41 feet.
	Children's perceptual-motor coordination becomes smoother.
10–12	Children can judge and intercept pathways of small balls thrown from a distance.
	Girls can run at 17 feet per second.
	Boys can do a standing broad jump of 5 feet; girls 4½ feet.
	Children can do a standing high jump of 3 feet.
	Children can make useful articles or do easy repair work.

balance The ability to maintain the equilibrium of one's body when it is placed in various positions, and it is basic to all movement.

coordination Skills that require considerable amounts of visual input integrated with motor output.

childhood years. Training a child prior to the time he or she is maturationally able to learn may produce temporary gains, but the long-term effects may be more damaging than enhancing.

An example might be found in bike riding. Children who are encouraged to attempt perfection of this skill prior to the time their muscles, coordination, and sense of balance have developed to a sufficient degree may experience failure and suffer enough physical injuries to hinder their normal progress even when they are maturationally ready for this feat.

Children's motor fitness is intricately interrelated with movement acquisition. One depends in large part on the other: Without adequate motor fitness, a child's level of skill acquisition will be limited, and without adequate skill acquisition, the level of motor fitness attainment will be impeded. The components of motor fitness—coordination, balance, speed, agility, and power—are summarized in Table 11.4. An observational visit to Travis' and Ling's fifth-grade gym class reveals school-age children's abilities in each of these areas.

Coordination

The children, in a circle formation, play with a volleyball-size, light rubber ball. Some deftly bounce, catch, throw, and kick the ball; some awkwardly, in a Charlie Brown–like manner, kick the ball and miss it entirely; and the other children are average in these skills. Bouncing, catching, throwing, kicking, and trapping are skills that all require considerable amounts of visual input integrated with motor output—a skill known as **coordination**. The more complicated the movement tasks, the greater the level of coordination necessary for efficient performance. Coordinated behavior requires the child to perform specific movements in a series quickly and accurately. Movement must be synchronous, rhythmical, and properly sequenced to be coordinated. Eye–hand and eye–foot coordination are characterized by integrating visual information with limb action. These skills are necessary, for example, in playing tennis; movements must be visually controlled and precise to project, make contact with, or receive the tennis ball.

Balance

Over in the corner of the gym is the balance beam and Gesila, the star of the class. Standing on one foot, in an arabesque fashion, she does a swivel turn. **Balance** is the ability to maintain the equilibrium of one's body when it is placed in various positions, and it is basic to all movement. Balance is influenced by visual, tactile–kinesthetic, and vestibular stimulation (fluid contained in the inner ear). Static balance refers to the ability of the body to maintain equilibrium in a stationary position, such as balancing on one foot or standing on a balance beam. Vision plays an important role in balance with young children. Six-year-olds, for example, cannot balance on one foot with their eyes closed. (Use of the eyes enables the child to focus on a reference point to maintain bal-

TABLE 11.4

Motor Fitness Components

Motor Fitness Components	Common Tests	Synthesis of Findings
Coordination	Cable jump	Year-by-year improvement with age in gross body coordination; boys outperform girls from age 6 in eye–hand and eye–foot coordination
Balance	Beam walk	Year-by-year improvement with girls often outperforming boys, especially in dynamic balance activities, until about age 8; abilities similar thereafter
Speed	20-yard dash; 30-yard dash	Year-by-year improvement with age; boys and girls similar until age 6 or 7, at which time boys make more rapid improvements; boys outperform girls at all age levels
Agility	Shuttle run; side straddle	Year-by-year improvement with age; girls begin to level off after age 13, whereas boys continue to improve
Power	Vertical jump; standing long jump; distance throw	Year-by-year improvement with age; boys outperform girls at all age levels

ance.) By age 7, however, children are able to maintain balance with their eyes closed, and static balancing ability continues to improve with age. Dynamic balance refers to the ability to maintain equilibrium when moving from point to point. Balance beam walking tests are used most often as measures of dynamic balance in children.

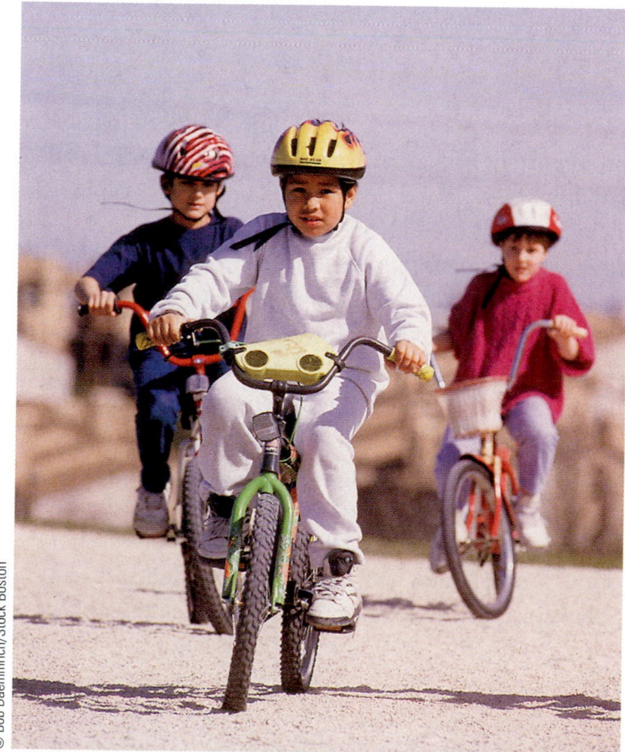

© Bob Daemmrich/Stock Boston

Before a child is ready to learn a skill, such as riding a bike, muscles, coordination, and the child's sense of balance need to be maturationally ready.

Speed

One of the first things that the gym teacher does when each class enters is to have them run around the gym a few times to expend some of their pent-up energy from sitting in class. Boys and girls appear to be similar in running speed skills at ages 6 and 7, but boys outperform girls from ages 8 onward. For example, in using the 50-yard sprint run as a measure, both boys and girls make annual incremental improvements with males slightly outperforming females at all ages. **Speed** is the ability to cover a short distance in as brief a time as possible. Speed is influenced by reaction time (the amount of elapsed time from the signal "go" to the first movements of the body) as well as movement time (the time elapsed from the initial movement to the completion of the activity). Reaction time is about twice as long in 5-year-olds as it is in adults for an identical task (Cratty, 1986). These developmental differences are probably due to neurological maturation, variations in the ability to process information, as well as to environmental and task considerations.

Agility

Girls are generally more *agile* than boys. **Agility** is the ability to change the direction of the body rapidly and accurately. With agility, one can make quick and accurate shifts in body position during movement. Agility is one of the greatest contributors to motor skills. It is extremely important in most sports and in dancing. It is largely dependent on the looseness of the joints and the abilities of the muscles to stretch and relax. Scores from the 30-foot run are typically used as a measure of agility.

speed
The ability to cover a short distance in as brief a time as possible.

agility
The ability to change the direction of the body rapidly and accurately.

Annual incremental improvements are seen throughout childhood with an edge given to boys at all ages.

Power

Power is the ability to perform a maximum effort in as short a period as possible. This combination of strength and speed is exhibited in children's activities that require jumping, striking, throwing for distance, and other maximum efforts. Boys outperform girls at all ages but, particularly, after puberty. After puberty boys become stronger, with larger muscles, hearts, and lungs; a greater number of red blood cells; and greater oxygen-carrying capacity in the blood. The gap that begins to widen after age 10 increases in magnitude throughout adolescence.

power
The ability to perform a maximum effort in as short a period as possible.

The Importance of Motor Skills

The achievement of the developmental task of perfecting the skills necessary for sports and games is one index of a child's physical development. In addition to the value placed on motor skills in the United States, there are a number of other reasons why it is important for school-age children to develop motor abilities:

- They allow the child to enter into peer-group projects, whether these are hide and seek, ice-skating, modeling with clay, hiking, or waterskiing.
- Practice of such skills contributes to all aspects of the child's total development: social, emotional, physical, and mental.
- Children also derive many hours of self-entertainment through the practice and refinement of motor abilities, whether the activity is tree climbing, skating, or (for some) piano lessons.
- Physical skills carry with them prestige value, which contributes to heightened self-image. (Roopnarine, Lasker, Sacks, & Stores, 1998)

Lack of "everyday" motor ability that affords movement and enjoyment may cause children to be excluded from activities and possibly hinder other aspects of their development. Not every child must be a superstar athlete, but every child needs the opportunity to engage in activities from bike riding to kite flying. (See First Person.)

FIRSTPERSON

Being Physically Fit

Over the years of my being a physical education teacher and coach, I have seen changes in children's sports and game activities. Just a decade ago, one could observe children engaging in spontaneous games: softball, touch football, four square, and dodge ball. These activities were mostly unorganized, but usually vigorous and always fun. Today, athletics has become "serious work." Now, children engage in youth athletic programs—which are highly structured; focus on skill-related parts of fitness such as power, speed, reaction time; and tend to be goal-oriented such as producing a good quarterback, pitcher, or goalie. These programs emphasize the practice and perfection of task-specific skills. You will see children standing in lines that are 8 to 12 deep just waiting for their turn to practice kicking or dribbling a soccer ball. The big picture of health, fun, and overall body fitness seems to be fading away. Parents are often spectators or sometimes become involved by coaching the child so that he or she can master the task-related skills needed to do well in a particular sport.

As an educator and coach, I try to tell the parents of my students that if they value physical activity for the sheer pleasure and fun of it, their children will also. When parents are physically involved with their children by taking walks in the forest preserves, going on family bike rides, playing a game of catch, or just engaging in a game of tag, it communicates several messages to children. It tells them that physical activity is fun and "overall" fitness is important. Parents who value being physically active will have children who have positive feelings regarding overall fitness. Most important, these children are more likely to remain active and experience the joy of being physically active throughout their lives.

—*Josephine Gerardi*

Play

Play, which monopolizes preschoolers' time, still plays an important role in the lives of elementary school-age children. Now, however, play becomes more skill-based as increases in strength and coordination permit children to enjoy activities that were formerly beyond their abilities, such as catching a ball, climbing a tree, or riding a bike. The benefit of play, however, does not diminish. Play not only fosters development of the body and skills using it, it can also serve therapeutic purposes as a tension and emotion outlet. It is also educational in terms of teaching children to follow rules, make decisions, solve problems, and practice democratic operations. Children's schedules filled with homework, household duties and routines, and formal commitments, such as Scouts or music, also need to allow for free-time play.

Games and Sports

Games and sports become the dominant forms of play during the school-age years. Games are ways of behaving in play that tend to conform to patterns that are generally experienced and shared by several individuals. A game pattern is emphasized by the elements of organization or structure that bring about a definite and often repeated end. Early elementary school children enjoy games with rules such as checkers and Monopoly. Do children in other cultures show interest in similar types of games? Cultural Variations takes a look at patterns of play around the world.

By age 10, team sports become popular as do clubs like Boy Scouts, Girl Scouts, 4-H, and Campfire Girls. Sports or athletic games involve and demand more specialized skills of players than do other games. Our sports heritage, like games, has deep roots in the past. Though the pattern and organization of a sport may have changed from its past, the skills of accuracy, speed, strength, and agility still prevail in sports today. Specific skills may be more closely related to one sport than to another; however, muscular coordination and emotional stability are prerequisites for enjoyment and mastery.

Play during middle childhood becomes more organized and structured.

Contributions of Games and Sports What are some of the positive things that you remember from your participation in games and sports? Becoming part of a team? Working for the good of the team? Learning cooperation? Are children receiving the positive lessons that they should be learning from engaging in organized sports? Many are, but a great number of young sport participants are not.

> Okay, men, we've got a really tough game ahead of us today. Remember we're here to win! Hernandez, look sharp today. I don't want to have to bench you again. Rickard, keep your eye on the ball and don't let me catch you picking daisies in right field. Strandberg, you'll pitch today. Okay, men, are you ready to play?

The "men" are 8 years old. Is this "win at all costs" a philosophy that is prevalent today? Many coaches emphasize that sports should be fun and character building, but some coaches and parents often send a different message. For example, in assessing boys' thoughts about the purpose of sports, Sally White and her colleagues (White, Duda, & Keller, 1998) report that middle and high school boys indicate that the function of sport participation is to increase status and popularity, to teach deceptive behaviors and superiority, to increase their competitiveness, and to win. According to many sports experts, we need to find ways for children to discover sports for the joy of sports—to enter the game so that playing is winning. According to Ronald Kamm (1998), many adults would benefit from a better understanding of the development and psychological needs of children involved in organized sports during middle childhood.

It's not about winning and it's not about competition, points out Kamm. Rather, youth sports should be seen as opportunities to teach not only physical skills and playing strategies but also psychological skills and coping strategies that have applicability throughout life. Kamm points out that adults' changing their attitudes may reduce some of the pressure to win that occurs on the playing field and in the home.

"Please, Mrs. Enright, if I let you pinch-hit for Tommy, all the mothers will want to pinch-hit."

Cultural Variations

Games and Sports Around the World

The ancient Greeks demonstrated their love for activity through the Olympic Games. Today, that tradition is captured by the young children of Greece who participate in their own Olympiclike games: wrestling and running, throwing spears at targets, and gymnastics. The Greeks still believe that the development and discipline of the body should be the main purpose in life.

Quiet games and games of nature are common to the Native Americans of the United States. North American Indian games may be generally divided into two groups: games of chance (guessing games) and games of dexterity. As with the Greeks, physical skill is an important part of the games that Native American children play (Roopnarine & Johnson, 1998).

Similarly, the resourcefulness of the children of Africa is evident in their game patterns and in their play equipment. The children run races, pretend they are galloping horses, and have contests of balancing. A game of "traders," in which they make clay imitations of articles used in trade by their elders and play a game of trading the articles, is also popular with many African children (Bloch & Adler, 1998). Stones, sticks, small twigs, colored beads, and cloth often constitute their play equipment.

There is less strenuous activity in the majority of games that children play in Africa; this is true of the Far East as well. This may be due in part to the influence of climate and in part to the philosophy of leisurely living. In Malaysia, children do not spend as much time in "free play" as children do in the United States. Mainly because from the time the children are big enough (around age 5 or 6), they are required to help in the

© Keren Su/Stock Boston

In some countries, such as China, children spend less time playing than U.S. children because they are often required to help with chores around the house.

APPLICATIONS:

Physical Fitness

Middle childhood is a time of energetic motor activity—of play, games, and sports. Or is it? Think back to when you were in the fourth or fifth grade. How did you spend your time after school? Were you constantly in motion—riding your bike, swimming, shooting hoops? Or, did you dash home from school, grab a can of pop and a bag of powdered donuts, and watch television or play video games? How physically fit were you? How many sit-ups and chin-ups could you do? Could you walk or run a mile in under 10 minutes? How are today's children spending their free time? How physically fit are they? The answers to these questions are not as optimistic as we might want to believe.

Grade schoolers spend about 10 hours per night sleeping, and of their 14 remaining hours, only 4⅓ are spent in school classes. They spend about 3 additional hours eating, doing homework, talking to parents, visiting relatives, doing chores, engaging in personal activities, and going to religious services or events. The remaining 6 hours per day, then, are the child's free time. Sociological studies show that for children under age 8 parents determine to a large extent how a child spends much of that free time, and that child care and organized activities account for most afterschool free time (Lee & Zane, 1999).

Afterschool Free Time

How do older children spend their time? Older children, ages 9 to 12, spend a significant amount of their home, particularly with the care of smaller children. Whereas U.S. girls may play with dolls, Malaysian girls are playing with their baby brothers or sisters (Roopnarine, Lu, & Ahmeduzzaman, 1989).

Norwegian children do not enjoy the freedom of year-round play as the children in the United States do because of their long winters. They know little about outdoor games and sports such as football, golf, hockey, or tennis, but they are experts in their national sports— skating and skiing. Swedish boys and girls play many games that are similar to those enjoyed by U.S. children. The outstanding characteristic of all the Swedish play activities is that there is no evidence of roughness. The players enter into the game with the desire to share the fun with others and thus gain a great deal of pleasure in a simple and natural way.

The more than twenty Latin American countries cover a vast land area and are peopled by millions, yet they have fewer games than other continental or societal groups. One reason for the scarcity of games is that the Latins have through the years developed rhythmic patterns that combine song, dance, and gamelike activities, instead of game patterns as such. Fiestas are a combination of religion, fasting, feasting, and game contests. The children seldom do more than look on—only men participate. Most of children's "play time" is spent in activities that will lead into an occupation—wood carving for example. In Mexico, for example, the children make puppets, and puppet shows are a frequent sight there (Roopnarine, Lasker, Sacks, & Stores, 1998).

Swedish children are experts in their national sports—skiing and skating.

Games are ways of behaving in play that tend to conform to patterns that are generally experienced and shared by several individuals. Games are today's play heritage of the past. Although some changes in form, name, and materials of traditional games have evolved through the centuries, an analysis of the worldwide game patterns reveals a thread of consistent similarity in play and games. The universal interest of children in play and games helps to open gateways for knowledge and understanding of other peoples.

free time watching television or playing video games (Funk, 2001). Between these ages, time spent playing declines sharply, whereas watching television continues to climb to an average of 2 to 3 hours everyday after school (Larson, Gillman, & Richards, 1997). It may seem that our parks and playgrounds are filled with children, but many U.S. children are much too sedentary, and physical fitness skills may suffer as a result (Tuckman, 1999). This appears to be true cross-culturally as well.

Children's play in Japan has changed enormously. This is partly due to technological growth and to the deluge of information provided by television. Japanese children are spending more time viewing television and performing other sedentary indoor activities than ever before (Takeuchi, 1994). Although the total number of hours children engage in play has barely changed in the past 20 years, changes are evident in the content of children's play. The number of hours of outdoor play has decreased from 3.2 hours to 1.8 hours. Furthermore, television watching and video/computer activities have increased.

During free time, 75 percent of Japanese children watch television, 64 percent spend their time reading comics, and only 42 percent engage in outdoor activities. Presently, traditional forms of group play, such as hide-and-seek, blind man's bluff (or tag), rope skipping, and playing house, that have been recorded during different periods in Japanese history have virtually vanished. Figure 11.1 shows the hours children, ages 10 to 15, from various nations spend in play after school hours.

Japan is not alone. According to Patricia Greenfield (1998) by age 18, the average child in the United States will have spent more of his or her life watching

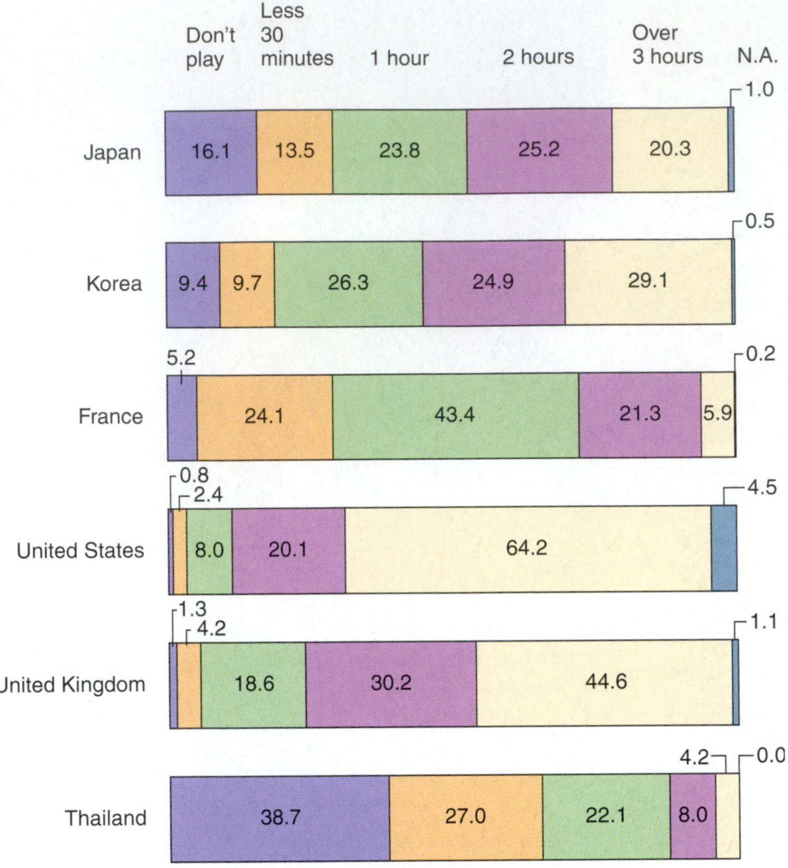

FIGURE 11.1 ***Time Spent Playing After School (Ages 10 to 15)***

Rapid growth in technology and the loss of play space has partially contributed to decreasing amounts of children's outdoor active play.

From "Children's Play in Japan (pp. 51–72)," by M. Takeuchi, 1994, in J. L. Roopnarine, J. E. Johnson, & F. H. Hooper (Eds.), *Children's Play in Diverse Cultures.* Albany, NY: State University of New York. Reprinted by permission.

In Japan, the total number of hours children engage in unstructured outdoor play has declined significantly. The number of hours children spend in sedentary activities, such as television viewing and computer time, is increasing.

television than any other single activity but sleep. African American and Hispanic children watch more television that European American children, regardless of socioeconomic levels (Ward & Greenfield, 1998). This excludes the time spent watching videos at home or movies in theaters.

An amazingly low 36 percent of children participate in daily physical education at school (Overbay & Purath, 1997). Because of budgetary constraints, this figure may decline further. As a result, today's children are less fit than they should be. The results of the President's Council on Physical Fitness are also very discouraging. In the 6- to 12-year-old category, only 64 percent of boys and 50 percent of girls could run or walk a mile in less than 10 minutes (Payne & Rink, 1997). In that same age group, just 50 percent of boys and 30 percent of girls could perform more than a single chin-up. Boys performed better than girls in terms of mean times for both the half-mile and the mile walk/run at all ages.

Furthermore, a higher percentage of boys tend to remain more active than girls (Taylor, Beech, & Cummings, 1998). For example, a recent longitudinal study on a large and diverse sample of African American girls (Ransdell & Wells, 1998) found that a high percentage engaged in sports activities between the ages of 6 and 12 years. However, they became quite sedentary during the high school years, and as adults, only 8 percent engaged in moderate to vigorous physical activities for at least 30 minutes most days of the week.

Physical fitness of children should be of great concern to all, not just the physical education teacher, coach, and physician. Many elementary school children are not sufficiently active in their daily lives and are physically unfit. Physically inactive children turn into physically inactive adults (Telama, Yang, Laakso, & Viikari, 1997).

Cardiovascular Endurance

Physical fitness is essential to normal growth and development; as such, all children will profit from engaging in activities that promote their health and fitness, particularly in ways that will strengthen their cardiovascular system. Aerobic activity can make the heart pump more efficiently, thus reducing the incidence of high blood pressure. Even though most cardiovascular diseases are thought to be illnesses of adulthood, fatty deposits have been detected in the arteries of children as young as age 3, and high blood pressure exists in about 5 percent of children (Overbay & Purath, 1997). At least three times a week, school-age children need to exercise continuously for 20 to 30 minutes at a heart rate above their resting level.

Improving Large Muscle Strength and Endurance

As children's muscles become stronger, they will be able to exercise aerobically for longer periods of time, as well as protect themselves from injuries—strong muscles provide better support for the joints. Modified sit-ups (knees bent, feet on the ground) can build up abdominal muscles, increase lung capacity, and protect against back injuries. For upper body strength, children can perform modified pull-ups (keeping the arms flexed while hanging from a horizontal bar) and modified push-ups (positioning the knees on the ground while extending the arms at the elbow).

Increase Flexibility

Stretching exercises (touching toes in a standing position) are the best way to help children maintain or improve flexibility. For complete physical fitness, children need to be able to twist and bend their bodies through the full range of normal motions. When children are flexible, they are more agile, can move faster, and have a decreased chance of sprains or strains.

Concept Checks

1. Matching

___ 1. coordination	a. 30-foot run
___ 2. balance	b. hopping for accuracy
___ 3. strength	c. 20-yard dash
___ 4. agility	d. standing long jump
___ 5. speed	e. beam walk

2. Modified sit-ups will improve
   a. cardiovascular health.
   b. large muscle strength.
   c. flexibility.

Health in Middle Childhood

Before Beginning ...

After reading this section, you will be able to

- identify the common illnesses, injuries, and accidents that occur during middle childhood.
- recognize the precursors to undereating disorders.
- understand the causes and consequences of obesity.
- see how obese children can be helped.

Illnesses, Injuries, and Accidents

Children in middle childhood generally enjoy good health, and their accident rates are lower than in the early childhood years and in the adolescent period. But, they may still contract the standard childhood illnesses such as chicken pox, measles, and mumps along with periodic colds and influenza. In this section, we will look at common illnesses, injuries, and accidents that children in middle childhood face.

Illnesses

Respiratory and digestive upsets are the most frequent types of illnesses in middle childhood (see Figure 11.2). The most common illnesses in middle childhood are **acute illnesses**—a term applied to diseases that have a definite beginning and end. The standard childhood illnesses (already noted), colds, and gastrointestinal flu are acute illnesses that develop from viruses. Antibiotic drugs can treat bacterial diseases, but unfortunately there are no medications that will effectively treat viral diseases. Children must let these viral illnesses run their course and allow their natural immunities to rid the body of the virus.

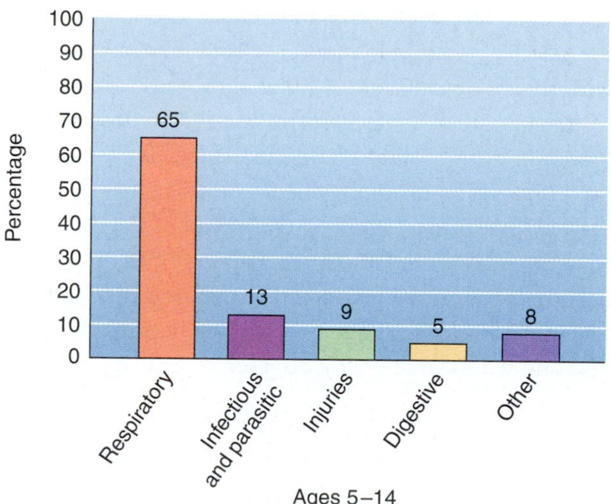

FIGURE 11.2 *Frequency of Occurrence of Various Types of Illness in Middle Childhood*

From Chart B, "Problems of Youth (p. 18)" Legislative Reference Service, U.S. Government Printing Office, Washington, DC, 1994.

Thought CHALLENGE

Describe a physically fit child. Do your friends agree with your description?

acute illnesses
Illnesses having a sudden onset and a strong possibility of ending quickly.

A small percentage of school-age children (approximately 5 to 10 percent) develop **chronic illnesses**. These are illnesses that may persist for many months without the child showing any significant improvement. One of the most common chronic conditions is asthma—a persistent congestion in the lungs. On average, school children get sick about half as often as preschoolers do, but this appears to vary with gender and ethnicity. Girls appear to get sick with both acute and chronic illnesses more often than boys; in fact, they get sick about as often as preschoolers. African American children seem to be healthier than their European American counterparts (Johnson, 1995).

However, some African American children do suffer from **sickle-cell disease**—an inherited disorder. Sickle-cell disease occurs in 1 out of every 500 live African American births. It is accompanied by severe anemia, and markedly reduces life expectancy; the child does not usually live beyond the third decade. Sickle-cell disease is not curable, and early recognition of the condition is vital to proper care of the affected child. The child with sickle-cell disease has to visit the doctor and the hospital regularly. In addition, the sufferer must receive special medications and guard other illnesses such as colds, pneumonia, and intestinal upsets. Although the condition does not affect intelligence, children with the disorder are frequently absent from school because of illness and sometimes fall behind their age group as a result.

Why is this disease particularly prevalent among African Americans? The sickle gene, producing elongated instead of round blood cells, is believed to have arisen by spontaneous mutation in Africa thousands of years ago. This trait seems to enhance one's resistance to malaria, resulting in natural selection for persons with the sickle-cell trait. A small percentage of people of Italian, Greek, Near Eastern, and Indian descent have also been found to have the sickle-cell trait.

Prevention through genetic counseling is currently the only method of avoiding the spread of the disorder to later generations. When two carriers of the trait become parents, the probability is that one child in four will inherit sickle-cell disease, two will become carriers, and one will be free of the disease.

chronic illnesses
Illnesses having a gradual onset and long duration.

sickle-cell disease
An inherited disorder that affects predominantly African Americans; it is accompanied by severe anemia and markedly reduces life expectancy.

Injuries

Although physical activity generally has positive effects on the growth of children, it may have some negative effects if carried to the extreme. It is clear that the dangers of overusing a muscle can result in physical injuries. Strenuous activity carried out over an extended period of time may result in injury to the child's muscle and bone tissue. "Swimmer's shoulder," "tennis elbow," "runner's knees," and stress fractures are but a few of the ailments plaguing children who have exceeded their developmental limits. Subsequently, exercise and activity programs for children need to be supervised carefully. The potential benefits to the growth process (both physically and psychologically) are great, but individual limitations must be accommodated.

Accidents

Some 19 million boys and girls are injured in accidents annually, the majority occurring in or near the home. The leading cause of accidental death in the 6-to-12-age group is from motor vehicles. Drowning is the second leading cause among boys with fires and explosions the leading causes among girls. Tragic numbers of children are injured or killed each year because of poisoning or explosions resulting from experimenting with or mistaking as harmless common household products, such as furniture polish, iodine, bleach, cleaning compounds, aerosol sprays, and medicine. Figure 11.3 identifies other causes of death in middle childhood.

Death

Human death is a universal and recurring event. Every culture has its own values, ideas, beliefs, and practices concerning it. An individual learns the orientations of his culture toward death, and thus when faced with bereavement, one factor involved is his or her conception of the meaning of death. In this connection many, if not most, societies throughout the world do not regard the event of death as being an inevitable fact of life; rather, it is often construed as being the result of an accident, negligence, or malice on the part of magicians or sorcerers (Aiken, 2001). Similarly, the cultural orientation of many peoples toward death is that it represents a gain for the deceased—an improvement in his prospects and status—and that mourning for his loss of life is inappropriate. These are in marked contrast to the prevailing beliefs in the United States, where death is viewed as inevitable, mourning is deemed appropriate, and the fate of the deceased may not be clear (Silverman, 2000).

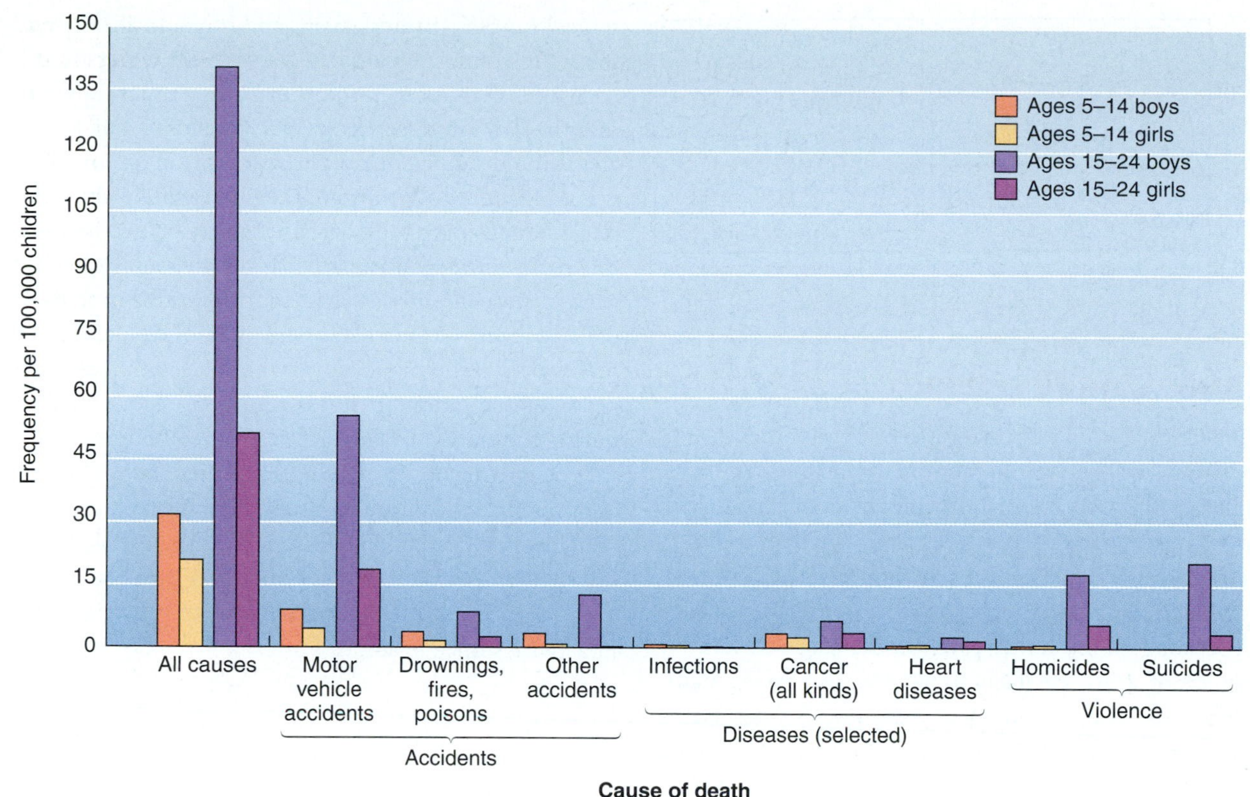

FIGURE 11.3 ***Selected Causes of Death in Childhood and Youth***

From *Statistical Abstract of the United States, 1994,* by United States Department of Commerce, 1995, Washington, DC: U.S. Government Printing Office.

The culture into which a child is born also determines to a considerable degree his or her beliefs and feelings about death. Within Native American societies, death is generally viewed as part of a natural process. The understanding of death in Native American societies emphasizes the significance of living one day at a time, with purpose, grateful for life's blessings, in the knowledge that it could all end abruptly. This way of relating to death is typified in the Lakota battle cry "It's a good day to die!" (Halfe, 1989).

The traditional African attitude toward death is essentially positive because it is comprehensively integrated into the totality of life (Ajayi, 1993). In the Western world, life and death are generally conceived of as opposites; in the African tradition, the opposite of death is birth. Birth is the one event that links every human being with all those who have gone before and with all those who will come after. Rebirth is seen as a by-product of death. This basically optimistic attitude can be found in the festive sounds of trumpets and drums played at African funerals.

Like the Africans, Mexicans celebrate death. Throughout Mexico, every year in November a national fiesta—*el Dia de los Muertos*, the Day of the Dead—is held to honor the dead. The fiesta is a unique occasion for communion between the living and the dead. Bread in the shape of human bones is eaten; sugar-candy skulls and tissue-paper skeletons poke fun at death but also celebrate the renascence of life. Mourners are cautioned against shedding too many tears, because excessive grief may make the pathway traveled by the dead too slippery.

Death in the United States is rarely seen in such an optimistic light. Adults often wonder how to explain death to children. We often fear it, face it with dread, and communicate this to children. Children often discover death—a pet turtle dies—and examine its phenomena long before they understand its significance. A certain degree of maturation has to be reached be there is any realization of its finality. The experien loss is complex and will vary with background and maturity. Children vary in their understanding of death, how they experience the stages of grief, and how they react to their grief.

Understanding Death

Children vary in individual rates of development—not only physically but also emotionally and cognitively. Thus, with respect to a child's understanding of death, as with other human traits, developmental levels do not correspond neatly to chronological age. However, in applying Erikson's model to death, we find that, depending on the child's psychosocial stage, certain aspects of death are likely to be more important than others. For example, in infancy, the sudden loss of a parent may temporarily impede the infant's developing a sense of trust. The preschooler's fantasies of a parent's death may be accompanied by feelings of guilt. The child in middle childhood may temporarily experience a sense of inferiority and lack of industry. The adolescent's response to death may trigger anxieties concerning whether death can block the realization of his or her own dreams and goals.

Young children often equate death with immobility (Worden, Davies, & McCown, 1999). A child playing some variation of a shooting game may yell, "I just shot you, you're dead—You can't get up." If you are playing dead, you lie still until you're "undead." So, after lying still for a few minutes, the child who was shot gets up and the game resumes. Young children also observe this phenomenon when watching cartoons—the character is shot dead in one frame and a few frames later is alive and well. They do not understand the *permanence* of death until around age 8 (Mahon, Goldberg, & Washington, 1999). They comprehend the *universality* of death—that all people will eventually die—a bit later on. Finally, they understand that death means *nonfunctionality*—an irreversible state of lifelessness in which everything ceases to function when someone dies (Potts, Farrell, & O'Toole, 1999).

Stages of Grief

John Bowlby (1981) in working with bereaved children observed that most children go through three stages of grief—protest, pain, and hope. In the *protest stage*, the youngster cannot believe that the person is dead and tries to get him or her back. Bowlby advises that the child in this stage of grief needs to talk a lot about the dead person and how important he or she was to the child. With time, the child will be able to put the memory of the deceased into perspective and move on. The second stage of grief, the *pain stage*, is a time of despair and disorganization. By this time the child realizes that the person is gone forever, and as reality sets in, he may be overwhelmed with feelings of anger and guilt, loneliness, and depression. Finally, during the third *hope stage* of grief, the child realizes that no matter how much he loved the person, he can continue life without him, and he begins to reorganize his life. The child begins to find the feeling of hope. As the pain eases, the good days begin to outnumber the bad and the child begins to get involved in activities once again.

Common Reactions to Grief

How do children faced with death express their grief? Many children who are experiencing grief may develop physical symptoms like exhaustion. Common exhaustive reactions may be loss of appetite and lethargy. Children may become quite dependent. In the early days after a death, a number of children may feel as though this is happening to someone else, that they are watching a movie with themselves in it. The child may still be able to function—go to school or talk with friends—but there is a feeling that he or she is going about the routine of life without thinking and filled with a sense of unreality (Saldinger, Cain, Kalter, & Lohnes, 1999).

Children may also become fearful—afraid that some other devastating thing is going to happen, afraid of being alone at night, afraid of the future. Some children may show a preoccupation with the person who died (Nolen-Hoeksema & Larson, 1999). Everything reminds the child of that person. To identify with the dead person, the child may occasionally start imitating the dead person's actions or the way he talked. Hyperactivity is another common symptom of grief. These children hop from one thing to another aimlessly, searching for something to do.

The importance of allowing bereaved children the opportunity to be involved and mourn the loss of a loved one has been supported by a number of scholars (Potts, Farrell, & O'Toole, 1999; Saldinger, Cain,

Kalter, & Lohnes, 1999). Children need the opportunity to discuss their thoughts and express their feelings. Adults need to express their thoughts and feelings as well. Young children are especially sensitive to adults' nonverbal attitudes. If adults are reserved, fearful, and reticent, children pick up on these feelings (DeSpelder & Strickland, 1999). Therefore, it is recommended that adults be open, honest, and warm with children; by doing so they are letting children know that showing emotion is okay.

Precursors for Undereating Behaviors

Another health concern during middle childhood relates to undereating disorders. Undereating disorders, such as anorexia nervosa and bulimia, were once thought to have their onset in the early adolescent period. Current research, however, has made us aware that there are several precursors that occur during middle childhood that are red flags for later development of these types of eating disorders. **Anorexia nervosa** is a condition in which girls and, rarely, boys starve themselves until they lose 15 to 25 percent of their body weight; **bulimia nervosa** is characterized by binge eating and subsequent purging of food through vomiting.

These disorders are discussed in more depth in Chapter 14; our purpose here is to highlight the behaviors that may indicate which children are at risk for developing these disorders. An obsession with thinness, a negative body image, low self-esteem and depression, early dieting, and parental pressure for children to be thin are all factors that may signal risks for eating disorders.

Obsession with Thinness

One of the key symptoms of girls who are at risk for developing eating problems is their obsession with thinness (Veron-Guidry, Williamson, & Netemeyer, 1997). Early concern about being overweight is the most powerful predictive factor of later undereating disorders. It was found in a sample of 9- and 10-year-old girls, for example, that a strong drive for thinness is associated with being at risk for developing an eating disorder such as anorexia (Striegel-Moore, Schreiber, Pike, & Wilfley, 1995). During the junior high school years, children of different ethnic groups use varying means of losing or controlling weight to overcome their strong drive for thinness. European American and Hispanic girls report greater use of diuretics and African American girls report higher rates of vomiting (Story, French, Resnick, & Blum, 1995).

Negative Body Image

Body image views and concerns appear before puberty, and a negative body image may be a precursor to developing eating disorders (Sands, Tricker, Sherman, & Armatas, 1997). Girls at risk for eating disorders also tend to have mothers who show dissatisfaction with their own bodies (Stice, Agras, & Hammer, 1999). Body dissatisfaction has shown up in a number of cross-cultural studies. For example, Swedish girls who have a negative body image are significantly more likely to develop full-blown eating disorders during adolescence than girls who had more positive images of their bodies (Edlund, Halvarsson, Gebre-Medhin, & Sjoeden, 1999).

Native American girls are more likely to be satisfied with their bodies and thus run a lower risk for eating disorders. Similarly, higher rates of body satisfaction, lower perceptions of being overweight, and less dieting are found among African Americans. Among both males and females, high socioeconomic status is associated with greater body satisfaction and lower rates of pathological weight control for all ethnic groups (Gruber, Anderson, Ponton, & DiClemente, 1995).

Other findings illustrate the influence of culture on the perceptions of ideal body size and corresponding behaviors. Jeanine Cogan and her colleagues (Cogan, Bhalla, Sefa-Dedeh, & Rothblum, 1996) investigated cross-cultural trends in attitudes toward thinness in a sample of students from Ghana and the United States. The subjects completed questionnaires about their weight, frequency of dieting and restrained eating, the degree to which their weight interfered with social activities, perceptions of ideal bodies, disordered eating, and stereotypes of thin and heavy peoples. Subjects in Ghana more often rated larger body sizes as ideal for both sexes and assumed these to be held as ideals in society more so than students in the United States, who were more likely to have dieted than Ghanaian subjects. Additionally, U.S. females scored higher on restraint, eating-disorder behavior, and the experience of weight as social interferences.

anorexia nervosa
A condition in which girls starve themselves until they lose 15 to 25 percent of their body weight.

bulimia nervosa
A condition characterized by alternating between binge eating and purging.

Low Self-Esteem and Depression

Low self-esteem and depression have also been isolated as significant risk factors for eating disorder symptoms in preadolescent girls (Hartley, 1998). Links between food and mood factors are well documented as risk factors for later eating disorders.

Early Dieting

Dieting at early ages is seen as a precursor for developing eating disorders (Shapiro, Newcomb, & Loeb, 1997). Children may be dieting earlier than most of us may suspect. A particularly startling finding comes from a study on 7-year-old girls in Sweden (Edlund, Halvarsson, & Sjoeden, 1996). Twenty-two percent of these children reported they had tried to lose weight; 20 percent admitted that they ate less with the purpose of losing weight; and 28 percent reported wanting to be thinner! One-quarter of the 7-year-old girls reported concerns regarding their body weight and that they have made attempts to lose weight. In the United States, 9- and 10-year-old girls have also reported dieting and are quite serious about their dieting intentions (Edmunds & Hill, 1999). Social contact with boys is suggested as a factor in the increase in dieting and weight consciousness observed in middle childhood (Lask & Bryant-Waugh, 1999).

Parental Pressure and Parental Relationships

Parental pressure for thinness is associated with high risk for eating disorders (Shisslak, Crago, McKnight, Estes, Gray, & Parnaby, 1998). Direct parental commands to children on watching weight, especially by the mother, seem to be a powerful influence in fostering eating disorders (Smolak, Levine, & Schermer, 1999). Parents who rate their daughters as less attractive than other girls also appear to have daughters with a higher risk for eating disorders (Hill & Franklin, 1998).

Theresa Spinello (1998) in focusing on the antecedents of adolescent eating disorders noted from her research that a significant percentage (88%) of her adolescent subjects with anorexia or bulimia had experienced some form of parental trauma (maternal unavailability, rejection) during middle childhood that disrupted the secure attachment process between mother and daughter. Spinello proposes that the rupture of the early mother–daughter relationship creates early emotional dysregulation, fosters a deep insecurity, and alters neurochemical functions in the brain, making the individual more vulnerable to undereating disorders.

Present research, then, makes us aware of the symptoms to look for in preadolescent girls who may be at risk for developing eating disorders. It is suggested that from elementary school upward this vulnerable group should be the target of specific health education (Dixey, 1998). Although teachers should not be expected to tackle clinical cases of eating disorders, there is much more that can be achieved in school to promote positive body image together with teaching children about food and eating (Lask & Bryant-Waugh, 1999). Increasing nutritional knowledge and developing positive attitudes toward their bodies are seen as two primary factors in preventing eating disorders (Huon, Roncolato, Ritchie, & Braganza, 1997).

obesity
A child who weighs more than 20 percent of what is considered to be normal for his or her height and weight.

Obesity

Whereas a scarcity of research on undereating problems during the school age years exists, there is an abundance of research on overeating—particularly the study of **obesity**. An obese child is one who weighs more than 20 percent of what is considered to be normal for the child's height and weight. There appears to be some continuity between being overweight as a child and being overweight as an adult. Over 40 percent of the children who are obese at age 7, for example, become obese adults (Vogt, 1999).

Middle childhood also represents a time when children may overeat to the point of becoming an overweight or obese child. Juvenile obesity is a serious, increasingly prevalent problem in technologically developed countries. Almost one-quarter of U.S. children are now obese, a dramatic increase of over 20 percent in the past decade (Bar-Or et al., 1998). Studies among Latino children consistently find that Mexican American children are overweight. This ethnic difference between Mexican Americans and non-Hispanic whites is greater in girls/women than in boys/men (Allan, 1998). African American girls also have a higher prevalence of obesity than do either African American boys or European American children (Hopp & Herring, 1999).

Health professionals often attribute the weight problem of African American and Latino girls to three major risk factors, which they term the "triple threat": gender, ethnicity, and poverty (Allan, 1998). Ethnicity and class play powerful but often neglected roles in girls' weight and in the perceptions and attitudes that accompany it. Studies have also found that obesity is six times more common among disadvantaged girls than among girls from more affluent families (Magnus, 1991). Ethnic differences probably are not due to genetic differences or differences in calorie intake between African American, Latino, and European girls (Williams, 1992). Rather, it is thought that differences in physical exercise may be an important contributor to obesity among African American girls (Cook, Nies, & Hepworth, 2000) and Latino girls (Mueller, Joos, Hanis, Zavaleta, Eichner, & Schull, 1994). It has also been suggested that, among Latino girls, poor eating patterns—eating foods high in fat and cholesterol—contribute to the risk of their becoming overweight (Juarabe, 1996).

In some societies, however, obesity is considered a good thing. For example, in Nepal 10- to 12-year-olds express a positive preference toward peers who are overweight (Harper, 1997). Nepalese children's attitudes imply that body size is associated with wealth, power, and food availability. However, this finding departs from the results of all Western findings. In the United States, overeating is seen as a significant problem in physical development. There is some evidence that children view obesity as a handicap worse than facial or body disfigurement (Wisnicwski & Marcus, 1999).

Causes of Obesity

What causes obesity? Heredity and environment both play a role. **Set point** is the weight maintained when no effort is made to gain or lose weight, and that is determined by the genes we inherit and the environment. Environment can affect the child's set point. Lack of exercise, for example, can raise the body's set point for weight. Heredity determines our body type, including the distribution of fat. Further, genes may have a direct effect on the metabolic rate (how quickly we burn food calories into energy) and energy expenditure (Vogt, 1999). The environment also determines the amount of physical activity in which we engage (inactive people are likely to burn fewer calories), the types of food we eat, and the quantity of food we consume. Contrary to what we may think, normal-weight children show higher food preferences for sweets, meat, and cereals than obese children (Perl, Mandic, Primorac, Klapec, & Perl, 1998); thus, metabolic rate and energy expenditure may be more important factors in obesity than the types of food children eat.

"Emotional" eating is more common in obese African American and European children (Epstein, Saelens, Myers, & Vito, 1997). Once obesity is a fact of life, the child is often unable to develop socially because of ostracism or ridicule by peers. To compensate for this failure children may turn to food as a solace, thereby compounding the problem.

Another important environmental factor that plays a contributing role to becoming overweight is television (Drucker, Hammer, Agras, & Bryson, 1999). In fact, the prevalence of obesity increases 2 percent for each increase of one hour in the amount of television children watch (Kolata, 1995). Nancy Signorielli and Margaret Lears (1992) found, in testing a sample of fourth and fifth graders, that there is also a significant relationship between watching television and having poor eating habits. Heavy television watchers are more likely than light television watchers to eat less nutritious foods and have unhealthy conceptions about food and the principles of nutrition. Further, African American children are more than twice as likely as white children to engage in weight-gain-related eating practices such as eating with television and eating while doing homework (Bar-Or et al., 1998).

Children are receiving lots of information about food and nutrition through the myriad commercials generously sprinkled throughout television programming. In analyzing the type of commercials found in children's programs, 68.5 percent of the commercial messages are for food, of which 25 percent are for cereal, 25 percent for candy and sweets, 8 percent for snacks and other foods, and 10 percent for fast-food eating places (Ward, Levinson, & Wackman, 1992). Another detailed survey of the diets of children under age 13 in the Bogalusa Heart Study (Nicklas, Webber, Jonson, Srinivasan, & Berenson, 1995) shows overall consumption of foods high in saturated fat, sucrose and sodium, with snack foods high in fat, salt, and sugar accounting for approximately one-third of children's total calorie intake. It appears, then, that children are receiving unhealthy messages from television, which may then translate into their eating foods high in fat and refined carbohydrates (Bull, 1992).

set point
The weight the child maintains when no effort is made to gain or lose weight.

Thought CHALLENGE

Why do many children have such a negative view of obesity?

APPLICATIONS:

Helping Obese Children

Because our society places such a stigma on fatness, and because the child's general health may suffer as a result of his or her obesity, every effort should be made to help the overweight child. There is also evidence that peers view obesity more negatively than physical handicaps, and it is reasonable to infer that ridicule and social isolation contribute significantly to the obese child's problems. In a related study, African American and European American girls described their weight-related stigmatization experiences and their responses to these experiences (Neumark-Sztainer, Story, & Faibisch, 1998). Out of a sample of 50 girls, all but 2 described experiences of direct, intentional name-calling and teasing by their peers. They also received hurtful comments and behaviors by family members that were viewed as less intentional, but hurtful. Responses to these experiences included ignoring or attempting to ignore hurtful experiences, feeling hurt, and getting mad. Further, obese children themselves report more negative physical self-perceptions than their nonobese peers and score lower on feelings of self-worth (Braet, Mervielde, & Vandereycken, 1997).

The first step in helping the overweight child is to determine the cause of his or her problems. A thorough medical examination may be most helpful in this determination. Even children with physical symptoms predisposing them to obesity, such as underactive thyroid glands, can control their weight through diet. Further, the family, exercise programs, and school intervention programs can all help the obese child.

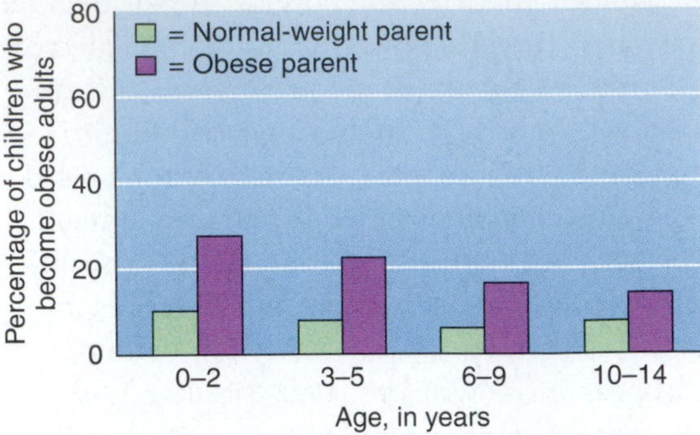

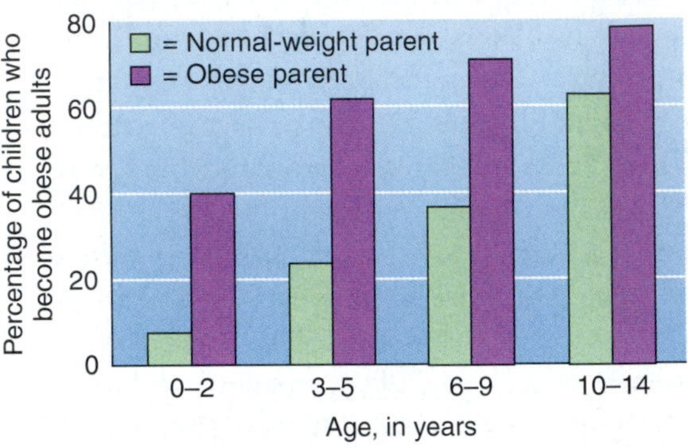

FIGURE 11.4 ***Obese Parents–Obese Children***

From "Predicting Obesity in Young Adulthood from Childhood and Parental Obesity," by R. C. Whitaker, J. A. Wright, M. S. Pepe, K. D. Seidel, & W. H. Dietz, 1997, *New England Journal of Medicine, 337,* 869–873.

Family Factors

Many obese children have obese parents. As you can see in Figure 11.4, the chance of a child becoming obese is increased when he or she has an obese parent. Similarly, mothers who derive much pleasure and satisfaction from preparing delicious things for the family to eat and insisting that the child eat a good amount of what she prepares can promote obesity. Reeducation of parent and child concerning nutrition and food selection may be the key to solving the problem. Research also suggests that parents play a major role in monitoring what children eat and act as models for healthy eating behaviors. However, the fact that children are increasingly eating meals without parents suggests that parents may be allowing children to assert too much independence in this area (Fitzgibbon, Stolley, & Kirschenbaum, 1995).

Exercise Programs

An exercise program might be helpful if the overweight condition is being intensified by inactivity (Locuy, 1999). Obesity begins in childhood and fat children typically become fat teenagers and fat adults. For this reason, children need to be helped to overcome obstacles to health as early as possible. Summer camps for obese children that work on targeting children's self-esteem, body image, nutrition, and exercise appear to be beneficial to the child and to the family (Tonkin, 1997). Because obesity is related to the child's level of inactivity (Jiang, Xia, Hui, & Cheng, 1997), *decreasing children's sedentary activities* is a good starting point. As we have seen, many youngsters spend large amounts of their time in front of television sets and consume large quantities of food while doing so. Therefore, caregivers can monitor not only the number of hours children spend engaging in television viewing and playing video games but the types of foods they are munching on while doing so (Signorielli & Lears, 1992).

Encouraging overweight children to engage in sports activities to use up food energy is another effective way to help them control their weight. This may be difficult to do, because it appears that obese children prefer sedentary activities over high physical activities (Epstein, Saelens, Myers, & Vito, 1997). However, placing emphasis on having fun while engaging in sports activities, rather than competition and winning, may help the obese child to become a more active participant in sports and sports-related activities.

School Prevention Programs

School prevention programs implemented in the middle school years have the potential to help build good eating habits, especially if parents are also encouraged to participate in these programs (Graber & Brooks-Gunn, 1996). Intervention programs generally target such topics as normal development during puberty and the growth spurt; what to expect at puberty in terms of normal weight gain as well as nutritional ways of eating. Because obese children tend to be "emotional eaters," eating more when they are emotionally upset or stressed, helping them learn alternate ways to deal with stress is also a way that school programs can help obese children (Schmidt, 1998).

Concept Checks

1. Acute illnesses refer to those that
   a. are terminal.
   b. have a definite beginning and end.
   c. are inherited.
2. A child experiences loneliness and depression during which stage of grief?
   a. Stage 1: Protest
   b. Stage 2: Pain
   c. Stage 3: Hope
3. Two factors that appear to be linked to undereating disorders are ____________ and ____________.
4. An important environmental factor that leads to obesity is ________________.
5. ***True or False:*** Placing emphasis on increasing activity and involving parents in nutrition programs are crucial for short-term weight loss in obese children.

Stress

Before Beginning ...

After reading this section, you will be able to

- define stress and stressors.
- identify common childhood stressors.
- see the association between stress and illness.
- note effective stress management techniques.

Stress is a feeling of high emotional tension that children, of all age levels, experience when they encounter an event or situation that is perceived by them as a threat to their existence and well-being. Too much stress can affect children in physical ways, such as an upset stomach, headaches, and nervousness. These environmental forces or events, called **stressors**, make individuals feel that they lack adequate coping strategies. Stressors can be physical, such as walking on a long hot road, or psychological, such as having a teacher that the child does not like. Stress has three components: the *reaction* to an *event* and the *perception* of the event. Children may interpret the events and situations in their lives as good, bad, neutral, terrible, or great. These interpretations, then, relate to how much stress the child experiences (Wheaton, 1999). (See Self-Insight.)

Is This a Stressful Situation or Not?

It is the first day of junior high. Naomi is quite "stressed out." There are lots of new faces, new teachers, and new classes. It all seems terribly frightening. Tom, however, looks forward to being able to take a computer class with all the state-of-the-art equipment that he is eager to learn about.

It is the "same" situation—the first day of school—but Naomi and Tom perceive it quite differently. A child's perception or appraisal of life events, then, strongly influences his or her response (Lazarus, 1993). It works something like this: "The individual

stress
A feeling of high emotional tension that children experience when they encounter an event or situation that is perceived by them as a threat to their well-being.

stressors
Environmental forces or events that make children feel they lack adequate coping strategies.

Self-Insight

Stress Test

INSTRUCTIONS Rate each item from 1 (almost always) to 5 (never), according to how much of the time each statement applies to you.

_____ 1. I eat at least one hot, balanced meal a day.
_____ 2. I get seven to eight hours sleep at least four nights a week.
_____ 3. I give and receive affection regularly.
_____ 4. I have at least one relative within 50 miles on whom I can rely.
_____ 5. I exercise to the point of perspiration at least twice a week.
_____ 6. I do not smoke.
_____ 7. I take fewer than five alcoholic drinks a week.
_____ 8. I am the appropriate weight for my height.
_____ 9. I have an income adequate to meet basic expenses.
_____ 10. I get strength from my religious beliefs.
_____ 11. I regularly attend club or social activities.
_____ 12. I have a network of friends to confide in about personal matters.
_____ 13. I am in good health (including eyesight, hearing, teeth).
_____ 14. I am able to speak openly about my feelings when I am angry or worried.
_____ 15. I have regular conversations with people I live with about domestic problems (chores, money, and daily living issues).
_____ 16. I do something for fun at least once a week.
_____ 17. I am able to organize my time effectively.
_____ 18. I drink fewer than three cups of coffee (or tea or cola drinks) a day.
_____ 19. I take quiet time for myself during the day.
_____ 20. I feel relaxed most of the time.

To obtain your total score, add the numbers you have placed in front of the 20 items, and subtract 20. Any number over 30 indicates vulnerability to stress. A total score between 50 and 75 suggests serious vulnerability and a score of over 75 means extreme vulnerability. After scoring the stress inventory, you might then want to fill out the Stress and Illness Chart. Check those items that you experience on a regular basis. Students who receive high scores on the stress test tend to check more items.

From *Vulnerability Scale*, by L. H. Miller & A. D. Smith, 1987, Brookline, MA: Biobehavioral Associates.

engages in cognitive appraisal of an event, interprets it as threatening or nonthreatening in terms of his or her capacity to deal with it, and only when a disparity is found to exist between the demand of the situation and the individual's ability to meet that demand is the stress-induced response, with its marked emotional component activated" (Garmezy & Rutter, 1983, p. 47).

As such, if a child's primary appraisal of a particular life event (first day of school) is negative (Naomi's perception), she will interpret this event as threatening ("It is too noisy; I don't know these kids; I can't deal with this"). Naomi then experiences stress because there is a disparity between the event and her belief that she is able to meet that demand. In contrast, if the child's primary appraisal is positive (Tom's perception), he will interpret this event as nonthreatening in terms of his or her capacity to deal with it ("Cool! I'll get to experiment with computers") and will not experience stress. So, it is not necessarily what children experience that causes stress but the way in which they view the event and their reaction to it.

A hypothetical story involving two sons whose father was an alcoholic further illustrates this point. One of the sons followed in his father's footsteps, the other never drank. When the sons were asked about their drinking habits each replied, "With an ole man like that, what do you expect!" One of the more salient points that we can conclude from stress research is that it may not be what children face but how they interpret what they face that really matters.

Pinpointing stressful events in children's lives is difficult. It cannot simply be said that negative events

Stress and Illness Chart

Physical	
Appetite change	Pounding heart
Headaches	Accident prone
Tension	Teeth grinding
Fatigue	Rash
Insomnia	Restlessness
Weight change	Foot-tapping
Colds	Finger-drumming
Muscle aches	Increased alcohol, drug, tobacco use
Digestive upsets	
Emotional	
Anxiety	"No one cares"
Frustration	Depression
The "blues"	Nervous laugh
Mood swings	Worrying
Bad temper	Easily discouraged
Nightmares	Little joy
Crying spells	Irritability

produce stress in children, for what we may tend to think of as negative events or situations may not be perceived that way by the child. It is possible, for example, that divorce, not making the team, or moving could be viewed by the child as positive. (Not making the team, for example, may mean that a child won't have to suffer the nightly harassments from his father for a poor performance in the game.) Therefore, it is important to keep in mind that children's perceptions of events determine whether situations are considered stressful or not.

Common Childhood Stressors

The most common stressors for school-age boys and girls are *school related* (failing a test, being scolded by the teacher, receiving a poor report card); *family related* (parents might break up, sibling issues, parents arguing); and *social relationships* (betrayal, rejection, being picked on). Other stressors in middle childhood pertain to *appearance* (too fat/too skinny, not looking good enough, too short/tall); *health* (going to doctor or dentist, death of family members); and *little things* (worry about others' feelings, making mistakes). The more children worry about these matters; the more stress they experience. As can be seen in Figure 11.5, African American boys and European American, African American, and Hispanic American girls report the highest number of worries and experience a greater amount of stress. European American and Hispanic American males report fewer worries and experience less stress (Silverman, La Greca, & Wasserstein, 1995).

Hans Selye (1956/1976) lists several common childhood stressors. *Change*, such as moving to a new location, may produce stress. It may not just be moving that produces stress but the fact that the child has

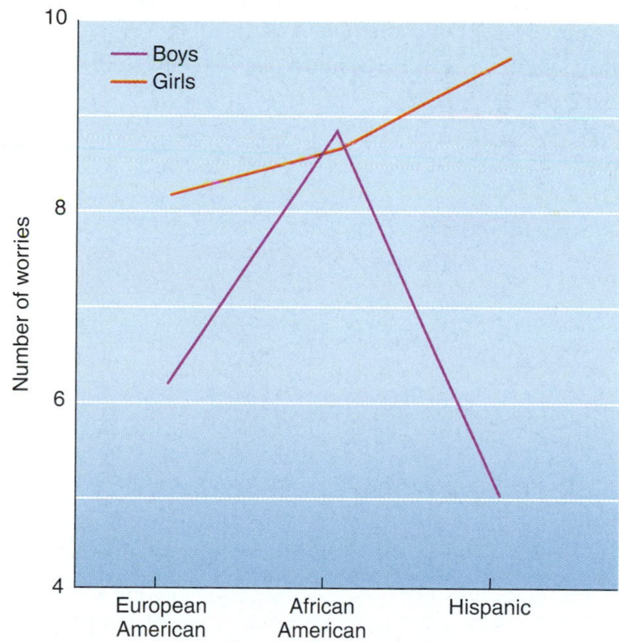

FIGURE 11.5 ***Interaction of Gender and Ethnicity in Terms of Children's Worries and Related Stress***

African American males and European American, African American, and Hispanic American girls report the greatest number of worries and higher levels of stress.

From "What Do Children Worry About? Worries and Their Relation to Anxiety," by W. K. Silverman, A. M. Greca, & S. Wasserstein, 1995, *Child Development, 66,* 671–686. Used by permission.

no control over the situation. Dad's new job means a new place to live, and the child must simply go along with the parent's decision. Relocation can also mean attending a new school and having to make new friends. This can produce stress in some children. *School* may also produce stress in children. Lack of ability to read is a major stressor for children. School is also a place where test anxiety is learned. In a typical school day, the child experiences a great deal of stress in terms of academics, sports, peer relations, and teacher interactions. Other common stressors for school-age children are found in Table 11.5.

How many stressors can children handle? When children with just one stressor in their lives are studied, they do not appear any different from children with no presumed stress in their lives. When stressors increase to two, however, the risk of stress increases four times (Work, Parker, & Cowen, 1990). If a child has zero or one stressor in his or her life, then the chance of psychological problems is about 1 percent. If the child has two stressors, then the chance of psychological problems increases to 5 percent. If a child has four stressors, the chances of psychological problems increase to 20 percent (see Figure 11.6). One conclusion from this research is that whatever can be done to alleviate stress in children should be done.

Daily Hassles

You have been working at your computer for some time making the final important adjustments for your absolutely brilliant research paper. Becoming so absorbed in your task, you forget to periodically save your material. A mini-brownout occurs, and you lose all your changes. Your parents call and announce that they will be coming to see you next weekend. You have to change your prescheduled plans. These daily stressors have been called hassles (Scott & Melin, 1998). **Daily hassles** are the unexpected, irritating, frustrating, distressing demands that to some extent characterize everyday transactions with the environment. School-age children experience hassles as well. Common hassles for them include school-related pressures (grades, teachers, exams), peer relations (argument with friends), and family relations (conflict over homework) (Spencer, Dupree, Swanson, & Cunningham, 1998).

Interestingly, daily hassles have a stronger association with adaptive outcome than major stressors. For example, daily hassles play a prominent role in a wide range of physical and emotional disorders (Rowlinson & Felner, 1998). In addition to their association with children's self-reported indexes of physical and affective problems, negative hassles are also

TABLE 11.5

Common Childhood Stressors

Stressor	Description
Peer relations	Children have many relationships to juggle in the course of their day. Further, they may feel intensely about these relations—running the gamut of love, hate, anger, and envy.
Climate	Children react to changes in the weather. Teachers have reported that schools are louder on rainy days, children are uncontrollable on gray and gloomy days, and more work is completed on sunny days.
Crowding	Children feel stress when they do not have any private space for themselves. As with adults, children need to be away from the crowd from time to time.
Boredom	"I have nothing to do. I am bored." Is there a child who has never said that? Schools can be tedious and boring. Being at home with no one to play with is boring. Children do experience their share of boredom.
Urbanization	With increasing urbanization, it may be more difficult for children to find a place to fly a kite or ride a bike.
Anxiety or uncertainty	The uncertainty of the future in a nuclear age, unsettled racial and religious issues, a family struggling economically may all be potential stressors to children.
Family situation	Of course, the child's family may be a major stressor. Arguing parents, divorce, loss or separation from parents, rejection by parents, and verbal and physical abuse are all major stressors.

daily hassles
The irritating and frustrating demands that occur on a day-to-day basis.

predictive of other adjustment problems, including negative parent and teacher behavior ratings, decreasing grades, and increasing absences from school.

Consistent with these findings, Bruce Compas and his colleagues (Compas, Howell, Phares, Williams, & Ledoux, 1989) found that daily hassles are more closely associated with psychological distress than are major life events. The results do not imply that major stressors and daily hassles are totally unrelated because clearly the occurrence of a negative major stressor (doing poorly in school) can lead to an increase in daily hassles (arguments with parents).

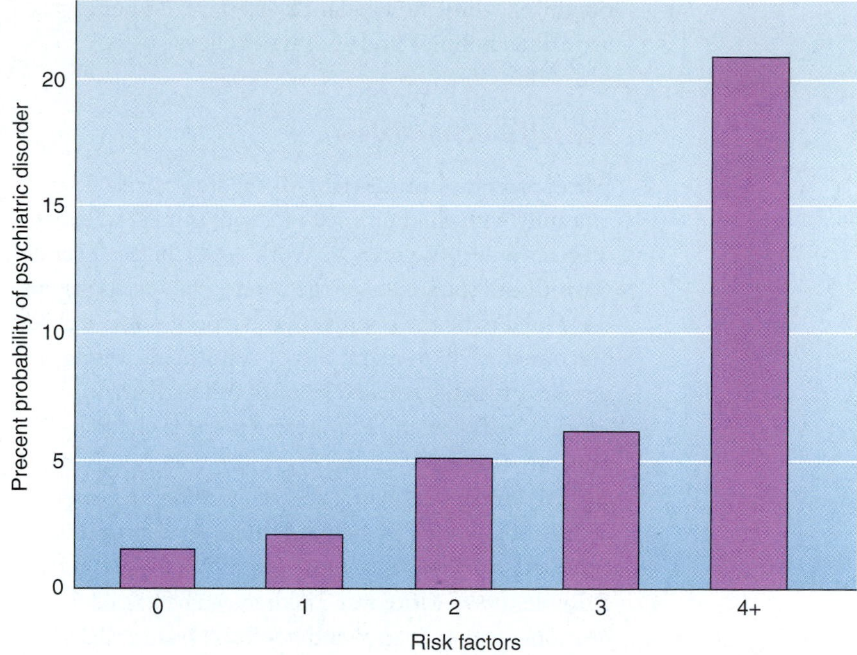

FIGURE 11.6 *Combinations of Stress Factors*

As the number of stressors in a child's life increases, his or her chances for developing psychological problems become greater.

From "The Impact of Life Stressors on Childhood Adjustment: Multiple Perspectives," by W. C. Work, G. R. Parker, & E. L. Cowen, *Journal of Community Psychology, 18,* 73–78. Used by permission.

Stress and Illness

Unremitting stress can cause our immune systems to function less effectively. When children (and adults) are under a great deal of stress, they are far more likely to catch an illness that, in peak condition, they could usually resist. The illness is due neither to the germ nor to the stress but to the combined effect of both (Rutter, 1996). For example, you may be sitting in class next to a person with a cold. If you are not under a great deal of stress, you will not be as susceptible to catching the cold. If, however, you are under a great deal of stress, your immune system is not working effectively, and the odds are greater that you will catch the cold. To further demonstrate how stress affects us physically, ask a few students in your class who scored high on the stress test how many check marks they had in the stress and illness chart under physical symptoms and compare that with the number of check marks noted by low-stress people. More than likely, the high-stress people had significantly more check marks under the physical category.

APPLICATIONS: Stress Management

Coping involves the child's efforts to manage (that is, master, tolerate, reduce, minimize) environmental demands and conflicts that tax or exceed his or her resources (Lazarus, 1993). The ways in which children cope with stress may be even more important to overall moral and social functioning and health/illness than the frequency and severity of episodes of stress themselves.

Hans Selye's Advice

A pioneer in the study of stress, Hans Selye (1976) has identified four ways in which children can learn to cope with stress: First, they can *remove the stressor*. A child who is stressed by the fifth-grade bully who is always beating him up may learn the "art of self-defense" and thus remove the stress of being victimized. Second, they can *refuse to allow neutral situations to become stressors*. A child who has a book report to write can plan ahead by deciding what steps need to be completed on a daily basis to get the paper completed on time. In this way, the child can keep a neutral event neutral and avoid the hysteria of having to write the report in two days (This works for college students as well . . .). Third, children can *deal directly with the stress*. A child can try to manipulate or alter his or her relationship to the stressful situation. The boy being victimized by the bully can think of different routes to and from school so the bully is unable to find him. And, finally, children can *find ways of relaxing* to ease the tension of stress. Children can ride bikes, climb trees, dance, exercise, and engage in various hobbies and sports to relieve stress.

Family Variables

Warm parental attitudes toward children correlate significantly with children's self-rated adjustment to stress (Fagen, Cowen, Wyman, & Work, 1996). In fact, overall warmth and soundness of the parent–child relationships was found to be the strongest predictor of positive child outcomes on child self-ratings of adjustment among samples of highly stressed second- and sixth-grade African American and European American children (Magnus, Cowen, Wyman, Fagen, & Work, 1999). It is also recommended that parents can strengthen children's coping skills by helping them develop their self-confidence and learn to delay gratification (Altschuler & Ruble, 1989). Moreover, children can be helped to be more open to change and novelty (Lohaus, Klein-Hessling, & Shebar, 1997). They can be encouraged to engage in as many different types of activities as possible. Other family variables that will enable children to cope with stress are highlighted in Table 11.6.

Controlling the Environment

Children are better able to cope with stress when they feel that they have some control over their lives. To this end, adults can praise children for trying; give them tasks or chores that are commensurate with their abilities; and, whenever possible, allow them some choice in family decisions. As Selye (1980, p. 143) said, "Though internal and external factors influence or even determine some responses, we do have control over ourselves. It is the exercise of this control, or lack of it, that can decide whether we are made or broken by the stress of life." We can further learn how to help children cope with stress by observing the habits of "stress resistant" or resilient children.

Developing Resiliency

Faced with life stresses, many children develop psychological difficulties, whereas others function well. Children in the latter group have been labeled resilient or "stress resistant." In adverse situations, **resilient children** defy expectation by developing into well-

resilient children Children able to bounce back from those unwanted curves life sometimes throws us; they are positive in mood and adaptive to change.

TABLE 11.6

Factors Influencing Children's Susceptibility to Stress

Factor	Description
Family harmony	Children from conflict-free families are less likely to be harmed by stress than children from conflict-filled families.
Close attachments	Supportive relationships protect children; even one good relationship with a parent can buffer the child against the adverse effects of an unsatisfactory relationship with the other parent.
Parental caregiving styles	Styles such as the authoritative one, which foster children's self-esteem, provide them the confidence to face up to adversity.
Availability of substitute caregivers	The beneficial influence of alternate figures such as grandparents is an insurance against the loss of support from parents.
Separation	Children leading a stable, predictable existence develop more means to deal with life's problems.
Number and spacing of children in the family	When children do not have to compete to an inordinate degree for parental attention they are more likely to develop personal resources for coping with stress.
Parental psychopathology	Children whose parents are psychologically unavailable because of mental illness or addiction may be less secure and more vulnerable.
Poverty	The large number of stresses associated with poverty makes children more susceptible to any problematic experience.

From *Social Development*, H. R. Schaffer, 1998, Malden, MA: Blackwell. Used by permission.

adapted individuals (Luthar, 1991). Behaviors that are closely related to resiliency are *positive mood* and *adaptability to change* (Carson & Bittner, 1994). Further, these children have been labeled *proactive* (take charge of their lives) rather than reactive (wait for others to do things for them). These children appear to operate under the conviction that they are distinct human beings. They are not made to feel that their destiny is tied to that of their parents—or, indeed, to anyone else. Resilient children are highly resourceful in finding and creating environments conducive to their personal development (Masten, Hubbard, Gest, Tellegen, Garmezy, & Ramirez, 1999).

Suniya Luthar (1991) recommends that adults can help the school-age child become more resilient by helping them deal with rejection. Rejection should not be accepted too readily by children (or adults) as indications of their personal failings. Resilient individuals have a remarkable ability to override repeated rejections without shaking their beliefs in themselves and their abilities. The novelist William Saroyan accumulated over a thousand rejections before he had his first literary piece published. Gertrude Stein submitted poems to editors for over 20 years before one was finally accepted (how invincible is that!). The works of noted poet e. e. cummings, who only wrote in lowercase letters, was rejected by over fifteen publishers. His mother finally published his work with the dedication "WITH NO THANKS TO" and then she proceeded to list the publishers who had rejected her son's poems. Rejections are common, of course, in other fields as well. Both Columbia and Decca records rejected the Beatles, and Jerry Seinfeld's pilot for television was so badly reviewed by the television powers that the show was only scheduled for four episodes after his first show ran.

Children are bound to experience social failure or rejection at one time or another throughout childhood, and therefore learning to deal with rejection or social failure is important. How children view their social setbacks plays an important role in helping them to deal with rejection (Joseph, 1994). Children who are able to deal with rejection tend to blame their failure on external factors. A child not selected to play a game at recess time, for example, might say, "They didn't feel like playing with me today." Less resilient children tend to blame their failures or setbacks on internal factors. In the same recess situation, this child might say, "Nobody likes me" or "I'm not good at making friends." Therefore, when difficult situations arise, children need to be encouraged to look at external factors and to believe in the power of effort so they will try again to improve strategies and engage in more positive actions (Werner, 1995).

Parents can tilt the balance from vulnerability to resiliency by helping children develop a special hobby or interest (Donegan-Johnson, 1992). Almost all resilient children have hobbies and special interests that bring solace to them when negative things occur in their lives.

We also know that resilient children, at some point in their lives, were required to carry out a socially desirable task to prevent others in their family, neighborhood, or community from experiencing distress or discomfort (Joseph, 1994). Such acts of required helpfulness lead to enduring and positive changes in the young helpers. The nurturing behavior of children who were victims of the Holocaust is a good case in point. Despite the wretched, life-threatening situation, the victims were kind, caring, and helpful to others. Thus, helping others less fortunate is an effective way for children to develop resiliency.

Concept Checks

1. Stress is the *reaction* to an *event* and the *perception* of an event, which means that
   a. all children have similar stressors.
   b. children interpret events as bad or neutral.
   c. stress is in the eye of the beholder.
2. You find that your car needs new brakes, this type of unexpected event is known as a ________________ ________________.
3. ***True or False:*** Stress causes our immune system to function less effectively, therefore making us more susceptible to illness.
4. ***True or False:*** "Stress resistant," or resilient, children are proactive rather than reactive.

Reviewing Key Points

How the Body Changes

- Growth slows to about 2½ to 3 inches a year. Children take on a slimmer appearance as legs and trunks grow. Individual differences in timing of growth and hereditary factors are largely responsible for wide variations in size among youngsters of the same age.
- Girls are maturationally ahead of boys, which is confirmed by their skeletal age. Skeletal age is estimated by the percentage of cartilage replaced by bone. At age 5 or 6, there is a rapid increase in muscle growth, which accounts for the major portion of weight gain during middle childhood. Both exercise and general state of health affect muscular development and status.
- Binocular vision is well developed by age 6; there is a tendency, however, toward nearsightedness during the early years of middle childhood. Hearing acuity increases and ear infections are less likely to occur because of the lengthening and narrowing of the ear's eustachian tube.
- The brain reaches 90 percent of its adult weight. The cerebral cortex continues to grow more neural extensions and well-used circuits become more stabilized. Dramatic pruning, eliminating unused neural networks, reaches its peak during middle childhood. Increased EEG patterns between the frontal lobes and other parts of the brain contribute in part to increased thinking abilities and attention spans.
- Howard Gardner's theory of multiple intelligences makes us aware that each of us knows the world in different ways and has special talents and strengths that encompass more than just logico-mathematical reasoning intelligence skills. One kind of intelligence, of the eight that Gardner identifies, is music abilities. According to brain research, a good time to foster children's singing and instrument playing abilities is during the elementary school years.

Motor Development

- Maturation must precede learning of motor skills. Children's motor fitness is influenced by coordination, balance, speed, agility, and power skills and abilities. The achievement of the motor fitness necessary for sports and games is one index of children's physical development.
- Exercise and sports are associated with increased self-esteem, improved physical fitness, and social competence for children. Competitive sports should not emphasize winning at all costs.
- A significant percentage of today's youths are deemed physically unfit—many children are unable to pass the President's Physical Fitness test consisting of chin-ups, sit-ups, and running or walking a mile in under 10 minutes. Part of the physical fitness problem with today's youths is linked to watching television and engaging in similar sedentary activities at the expense of outdoor exercise and play.

Health in Middle Childhood

- Children suffer from fewer illnesses during middle childhood than they did as preschoolers. Acute illnesses, those with a definite beginning, middle, and end, such as colds and flu, account for a large percentage of illness and loss of school time. African American children are generally healthier than their European American counterparts; however, some inherit sickle-cell anemia. Another common illness of elementary school children is asthma—a persistent congestion in the lungs.
- Physical activity may have some negative effects if carried to the extreme. Sports injuries such as "tennis elbow" and "runner's knee" occur when children exceed their developmental limits. Car accidents are the leading cause of death during middle childhood followed by drownings and poisonings.
- Children's first association with death is immobility—if you are dead you cannot move. Young elementary school children have little understanding of the permanence of death. It is not until around the age of 8 that children understand that people cannot become "undead." The universality of death and that dying results in nonfunctionality are understood a few years later.
- Precursors to later eating disorders such as anorexia nervosa and bulimia nervosa include obsession for thinness, body dissatisfaction, low self-esteem and depression, dieting at early ages, and parental pressure for thinness.
- Obesity is a health problem that is increasing in school-age children and has been linked to their sedentary life and watching too much television while snacking on snack foods. Proper exercise and rigorous activity need to be a part of children's lives.

- Careful monitoring of what and how much children eat by parents; an exercise program; encouragement to participate in sports for fun; and school intervention programs that involve parents and focus on exercise and nutrition are all recommended for obese children. This results in short- and long-term weight loss.

Stress

- Stress is the perception of threat to physical or psychological well-being and the individual's reactions to that stress.
- Some of the common stressors occurring during middle childhood are change, school, and peer relations. The chance of psychological problems increases as children encounter more and more stress.
- If a stressor continues unabated for a long period of time, children's adaptation energy is depleted, causing their immune systems to function less effectively. Subsequently, they are more susceptible to catching various illnesses that in peak condition they could have resisted.
- Children can learn to cope more effectively with stress when caregivers encourage them to be open to change, help them feel more in control of themselves in various situations, and develop their resiliency in stress situations.

Answers to Concept Checks

How the Body Changes

1. a 2. b 3. c 4. a

Motor Development

1. a. hopping for accuracy
   b. beam walk
   c. standing long jump
   d. 30-foot run
   e. 20-yard dash
2. b

Health in Middle Childhood

1. b 2. b
3. negative body image; obsession with thinness; early dieting; parental pressure
4. television 5. true

Stress

1. c 2. daily hassles 3. true 4. true

Key Terms

acute illnesses
agility
anorexia nervosa
balance
bulimia nervosa
chronic illnesses
coordination
daily hassles
myopia
obesity
power
resilient children
set point
sickle-cell disease
speed
stress
stressors
theory of multiple intelligences

InfoTrac College Edition

For additional readings, explore InfoTrac College Edition, your online library. Go to **http://www.infotrac-college.com/wadsworth** and use the passcode that came on the card with your book. Try these search terms: physical fitness for children, obese children, childhood stress.

Child Development CD-ROM

Go to the Wadsworth Child Development CD-ROM for further study of the concepts in this chapter. The CD-ROM also includes quizzes and additional activities to expand your learning experience.

CHAPTER TWELVE

Cognitive Development: *Middle Childhood*

CHAPTER OUTLINE

The School Child's Thinking Skills
- Piaget's Concrete Operational Thinker
- Information-Processing Skills
- Creativity
- Applications: On Academic Success

Technology, Culture, and Achievement
- The Impact of Video Games
- Education and Technology
- The Hidden Curriculum
- Culture, Ethnicity, and Achievement
- Applications: Multicultural Education

Children with Special Learning Needs
- Mentally Challenged Children
- Gifted and Talented Children
- Children with Learning Disabilities
- Attention Deficit Hyperactivity Disorder
- Applications: Helping Children with Learning Difficulties

Refinements in Language Development
- Understanding Sarcasm
- Pragmatics of Language
- Children's Sense of Humor
- Applications: The Gift of Laughter

Reviewing Key Points

Two boys are overheard at the top of the Empire State Building. Both boys look down at the sidewalk and exclaim simultaneously, "Look at the people. They're tiny ants!" (younger boy). "Look at the people. They look like tiny ants!" (older boy).

The conversation between these 4- and 7-year-olds may not seem particularly earthshaking to you, but to Piaget, it would be. This simple exchange of words, Piaget would excitedly inform us, actually demonstrates a shift away from the preoperational world of "perceptual illusions" to the concrete operational world of logical thinking. Whether the younger boy actually believes the people have become tiny ants is not clear. What is known is that the older boy voices a perspective based on his own perceptions: "They *look* like tiny ants." His statement is as much about his looking at his perception as it is about looking at the people. Because middle childhood, which begins at about age 6 or 7, ushers in logical thinking, it is universally regarded as "the age of reason." Many societies around the world begin to formally educate their children at age 6 or 7, which according to the information-processing theorists is the best time, because logical thinking results in more sophisticated organization and memory skills.

The logical thinking of concrete thinkers, however, reveals a rather "black and white" thinking. Their thinking is tied to immediate settings and reflects a binomial "right/wrong" way of viewing things. Some children, however, seem to be driven toward a divergent way of thinking that more prone to concentrate or center his attention exclusively on some single feature or limited portion of the stimulus array that is particularly interesting to him (*centration*), thereby neglecting other task-relevant features. **Decentration** in school-age children allows them to focus on several aspects of the problem all at once and relate them.

Class Inclusion

The child's knowledge that a superordinate class (flowers) is always larger than any of its subordinate classes (tulips, daffodils), known as **class inclusion**, is considered a concrete operational thought. The child is able to reason simultaneously about the part and the whole. If a child is given five daffodils and three tulips and asked whether there are more daffodils or more flowers, the child who has mastered class inclusion will respond, "Flowers." Most children are 10 before they can successfully solve class-inclusion problems of this kind.

Robert Siegler (1997) thought that the way experimenters phrase class-inclusion problems might preclude children from answering them correctly. When the questions were rephrased deleting the words *more* and *less*, even preoperational thinkers did well on class-inclusion problems. When the children in his study were shown three M&Ms® and two jelly beans and asked, "Do you want to eat the M&Ms® or the candy?" most children showed some understanding of class inclusion by gulping down all the candy.

decentration
The ability to focus on several dimensions of a problem at once and relate them.

class inclusion
The child's knowledge that a superordinate class (flowers) is always larger than any of its subordinate classes (tulips, daffodils).

conservation
The understanding that a quantity remains the same despite its appearance.

horizontal decalage
Asynchronous development within a Piagetian stage; for example, gradual understanding of conservation beginning with number and later volume.

attention
The amount and type of information to which one attends.

Conservation

Children in the concrete stage of operations understand that quantity is the same despite a change in its appearance. This skill, **conservation**, enables concrete thinkers to easily solve the following problem. A child is presented with two boards covered with a green cloth, several barns, and a cow. Initially, the child is asked to indicate which cow has more grass to eat when the barns are solidly packed in one corner on both boards. The child answers, "The same." Then, the barns are randomly distributed on one board and again the child is asked if the cows have the same amount of grass to eat. The child with conservation skills will answer, "The same," because he or she realizes that the amount of grass to eat remains the same if the only change is in the arrangement of the barns.

Although most children acquire conservation skills in about the same sequence, the ages at which these abilities appear can vary (see Figure 12.1). There is evidence of asynchronous development of conservation skills. Children master the number of things around 6 or 7, followed by conservation of substance and length (age 7 or 8), area and weight (age 9 or 10), and finally volume (age 12). Further, children who are slower in developing simple conservation skills are slower in developing more complex conservation skills such as weight and volume. Piaget recognized these inconsistencies and used the term **horizontal decalage** to describe when the same structure is applied to contents of different difficulty, for example, when conservation is applied to quantity before weight and to weight before volume.

Information-Processing Skills

The viewpoints of Piaget and information-processing theorists are quite different. Unlike Piaget's theory, which is derived from one man's astute observations of children, the information-processing approach is the accumulation of the work of many investigators. Information-processing theorists draw heavily on Piaget's description of development, while refining it (by describing more stages and substages), but most of them reject the use of general cognitive structures such as those favored by Piaget (Segall, Dasen, Berry, & Poortinga, 1999). Rather, they see the child's mind as a diverse collection of individual processes that do not necessarily follow the same patterns of thinking. Information-processing theory may thus be more sensitive to diversities found in children's thinking and abilities.

In this approach, the human mind is conceived of as a complex cognitive system, analogous to a digital computer. Its primary objective is to provide an explicit, detailed understanding of what the subject's cognitive system actually does when dealing with a task or problem. Information-processing theorists are interested in studying the nature of information that children pick up from the vast amount of stimuli that bombard their senses and the series of stages through which they pass, absorb, and transform this information. According to information-processing theorists, cognition subsumes a large number of individual processes such as attention, perception, and memory strategies.

Attention

Although individuals are information-gathering creatures, it is evident that under normal circumstances they are highly selective in their **attention**—the amount

Type of conservation	Basic principles	Child sees step 1	Child sees step 2	Child asked
Number (ages 6–7)	The number of units remains the same even though they are reorganized in space.	A B	A B	Which row has more beads? Pre-cons: "row B" Cons: "same"
Substance (ages 7–8)	The amount of clay remains the same, regardless of the shape it assumes.	A B Two clay balls same size	A B One ball is flattened out	Are the clay balls the same? Pre-cons: "B is bigger" Cons: "same"
Length (ages 7–8)	The length of a line from one end to the other remains unchanged, regardless of how it is arranged in space or changed in shape.	A B	A B	Which stick is longer? Pre-cons: "stick B" Cons: "same"
Area (ages 8–9)	The total amount of surface covered by a set of plane figures remains unchanged, regardless of the position of the figures.	A	B	Which picture has more surface area? Pre-cons: "B" Cons: "same"
Weight (ages 9–10)	The heaviness of the object remains unchanged, regardless of the shape it assumes.	A Units placed on top of each other	B Units placed side by side	Which weighs more? Pre-cons: "A" Cons: "same"
Volume (ages 12–13—formal)	The volume of the water is changed if something is added to it, regardless of the way it appears.	A B Two balls of clay placed in two beakers containing equal amounts of water; child sees water level rise equally in both beakers.	A B Clay ball B is molded into a different shape and held above the beaker.	When clay ball B is placed in a beaker, will the water level be higher, lower, or the same as in A? Pre-cons: "lower, because the ball flattened out" Cons: "same, nothing has changed"

FIGURE 12.1 *Conservation Tasks*

and type of information to which they attend. One important aspect of attention is *selectivity*, which refers to the ability to screen out distractions and concentrate on a particular stimulus while ignoring others. Young children are somewhat less able to control their attentional processes as well. For example, if young children are asked to look at the pair of houses as shown in Figure 12.2 and tell you if they are the same or different, they tend to be more distractible and less flexible in discerning what is relevant information than are children in middle childhood (Gelman & Kit-Fong, 1998).

Younger children will say "same" or "different" after viewing only about half the windows in the two houses, and their visual exploration of the houses is unsystematic. They become distracted on the way to the solution, and sometimes even forget the problem. Therefore, they are not very successful on this task.

Older children, around the age of 8, fare much better on the house comparison task. First, they methodically view all the windows in the two houses before responding; they then attend to only those aspects of the house that are relevant to their task. The improvement with age in children's ability to attend to relevant stimuli and to explore systematically appears to be related to a developmental increase in their ability to follow instructions and to allocate attention in accordance with task demands (Ruff, 1998).

Older children are more flexible than younger children in modifying their attention in accordance with the task requirement. For example, preschoolers and 9- and 10-year-olds were presented with a card containing 12 doors arranged in two rows. Behind each door was either a picture of an animal or a household object. A logo of a cage (indicating an

FIGURE 12.2 *House Comparison Task*

Are these houses the same or different? Younger children's visual exploration is unsystematic; school-age children tend to scan more systematically and are able to focus on relevant stimuli.

Older children, 9 to 11 years, demonstrate superior attentional skills, such as modifying attention in accordance with a task requirement.

animal) or a house (indicating a household object) revealed what type of picture was behind each door. The children were asked to remember what type of animal was behind each door and were given a study period in which they could open any doors they wished. Preschoolers opened all the doors and not surprisingly did not remember the types of animals they found. The 9- and 10-year olds, however, opened only those doors with the cage logo and remembered the animals they found (Trudge & Rogoff, 1999).

Perception

As with attention, we see age-related improvements in perceptual processes. **Perception** is the process by which children extract meaningful information from physical stimuli. For example, young children need to have a lot of information presented before they are able to interpret perceptually an object or event; in contrast, older children can recognize events with incomplete information. In Figure 12.3, an older child is more likely to recognize the stimulus in drawing A as a chair than is a younger child. The younger child needs to see more of the chair (drawing B) to recognize it as such.

perception
The process by which children extract meaningful information from physical stimuli.

Perception also becomes more differentiated as children get older. Practice or prior experiences teach children which features or patterns of features are distinctive and critical for identification. For example, if we presented young children with four letters, *b, d, p,* and *q*, they might think that the line and the loop are distinctive features. Because these two characteristics are irrelevant to this discrimination, the four letters would not be distinguished. With more experience, the loop's position (at the top or the bottom of the line) and the left–right orientation of the loop are noted and the four letters become distinguishable. Perceptual processes do not function in isolation from other thought processes. Perceptions are stored in memory, where information is recalled to help interpret incoming perceptions. Thus, memory strategies become important as the next process in thinking.

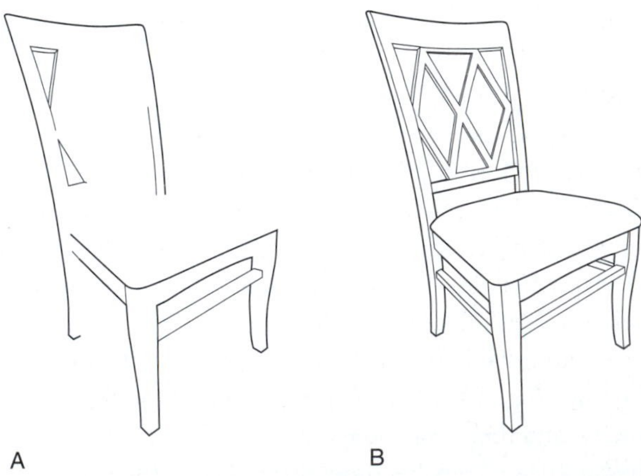

FIGURE 12.3 *Partially completed Drawings of a Chair*

Memory Strategies

Children between the ages of 6 and 12 are better information processors than younger children because of changes in short-term memory, where information is temporarily stored, and long-term memory, the permanent storehouse of information. The changes in short-term memory involve more sophisticated rehearsal strategies and more efficient memory skills (Jansen & van der Maas, 1997). Children in early middle childhood (ages 6 to 8), for example, are less likely to use rehearsal strategies or to use them effectively than children in older middle childhood (ages 9 to 12) (Cox, Ornstein, Naus, Maxfield, & Zimler, 1989). Older children are more likely to construct larger chunks of information by using a cumulative rehearsal strategy. For example, if the series "yard, cat, man, dog" is presented to a younger child, a typical rehearsal pattern after the presentation of dog would be to say the word over and over again "dog, dog, dog." Ten- and 12-year-olds, however, would combine the newly presented word with those that preceded it. They would say "yard, cat, man, dog."

What exactly do school-age children understand about memory? Five-year-old Alek and 8-year-old Mayra are asked, "How do you remember things?"

Alek: If you want to remember something in your mind, you have to say it over and over, or two times.

Mayra: If I have a lot of things to remember, I say things out loud and I write things down. I even made up a song once to remember things for a test in school.

Children ages 7 to 8 show an apparent qualitative shift in the way they speak about their own memories, particularly events in their lives. Between the ages of 6 and 7, memory processes increase in sophistication, enabling children to report the same number and quality of details as adults do (Flavell, Miller, & Miller, 1993). Jeri Janowsky and Ruth Carper (1996) propose that changes in the brain occurring between these ages may account for these more sophisticated memory shifts. In particular, they point out that a reorganization of the frontal lobes (which are, among other things, responsible for attention, planning, abstract thinking, and memory) that occurs during this period leads to more sophisticated memory skills. This continued development of the frontal lobes enables children to access and flexibly recombine information in memory to include the context of events as well as their metamemory about the events in their lives. The frontal lobes, then, may help facilitate the elaboration of memory performance witnessed toward the beginning of middle childhood (Samango-Sprouse, 1999).

Without ample retrieval cues, children 5 and younger report fewer details of events than do older children. For example, when asked about the events surrounding a fire drill, younger children will not recall contextual information such as who was with them at the time or what time of day the event occurred. Yet, if they are asked about an event and the context surrounding an event, younger children can recall or recognize facts that they do not spontaneously recall. Although recall is commonly improved with retrieval cues and contextual support, it is possible that this information is especially inaccessible or unusable in young children.

Creativity

One aspect of intelligence that has not received much attention from the cognitive literature is **creativity**, the ability to think about something in a new way and generate new responses and unique solutions. J. P. Guilford (1967), a psychologist, gave impetus to the scientific study of the process of creating by contrasting two types of thought: convergent and divergent. **Convergent thinking** involves trying to find the correct solution to a problem. For example, what is the missing number in the following series: 1, 2, 5, 10, . . . , 37? To solve this problem, we need to know the problem's various data and to understand their logical connections. This question has only one solution, and it can be found only when we find the rule operating in the series. Intelligence tests tend to measure convergent thinking.

In contrast, **divergent thinking** generates multiple solutions to a problem by expanding upon a basic idea or concept. It assumes that a question can have several equally good answers. In such a case, one plays with different ideas and possibilities and chooses the ones that seem most appropriate. The composer working on a symphony, an author writing a novel, and a mathematician building a theory all approach their work primarily through divergent thinking mental processes.

Creative children have the ability to look beyond the obvious to see relationships in unusual and new ways; they are not prisoners of habitual ways of thinking. They seem to ask persistently, "What if?" Creativity not only demands divergent thinking processes, it

creativity The ability to think about something in unusual ways, generate many responses, and come up with unique solutions.

convergent thinking Produces one correct answer and is characteristic of the kind of thinking on IQ tests or standardized tests.

divergent thinking Produces many answers to the same question and is characteristic of creative thinking.

also, and as importantly, involves the ability to translate ideas into a given medium such as writing or drawing. This further requires strenuous effort and perseverance. Creative individuals often work hard and steadily at realizing their ideas and using all their abilities (Lubart, 1999).

Creativity Across Cultures

Creativity from a Western perspective is often defined as the ability to produce work that is novel and appropriate, and an important feature of Western creativity seems to be its relationship to an observable product (Ochse, 1998). In contrast, Eastern conceptions of creativity focus less on innovative products and more on a state of personal fulfillment or the expression of an inner essence (Kuo, 1996). Creativity is related to meditation because it helps one to see the true nature of one's self, an object, or an event. In Hinduism, for example, creativity is seen as spiritual or religious expression rather than as an innovative solution to a problem: To create is to imitate the spiritual—to make traditional truths come alive (Bedi, 2000).

Despite cross-cultural variations in defining creativity, a number of common parameters are used to judge creativity. From such diverse cities as Dhaka City, the capital of Bangladesh (Khanam & Sen, 1998) to Shanghai, China (He, Zha, & Xie, 1997), the richness of thought or number of relevant ideas a child has, use of original or divergent thinking, and degree of flexible thinking employed are consistently used to assess creativity.

A sample of U.S. and Chinese teachers tended to agree on the behaviors that describe creative children: imaginative, always questioning, quick in responding, and active (Chan & Chan, 1999). The study also suggested that Chinese teachers regarded some characteristics of creative students as less desirable than U.S. teachers—always questioning, for example.

Culture-based norms encourage creativity in some situations but discourage it in others. Colligan (1983) analyzed the development of musical creativity in the Samoan, Balinese, Japanese, and Omaha Indian cultures, drawing upon the anthropological evidence available with respect to fostering musical innovativeness among them. In both the Samoan and Balinese culture, the dancers were encouraged to recognize the individual (as a person in Samoa, and as a member of the group in Bali); hence in these cultures, they tended to develop unique individual styles within the basic framework of their society's art (Gaines & Price-Williams, 1990). The Japanese and Omaha Indian cultures, in contrast, had no cultural norm supporting innovation and originality; instead, there was great pressure to maintain the form and style of the music. Hence, these cultures have continued to live with an unchanged form of music. Any variation is not considered creative but highly incorrect and disrespectful to their elders. Not all cultures value or nurture creativity.

Todd Lubart (1999) suggests that individualistic cultures that value independence and self-reliance, such as in the United States, tend to nurture creativity and place a great deal of importance on developing it. Lubart argues that collectivist cultures, such as China, which place more emphasis on obedience, cooperation, and duty, tend not to foster creative endeavors or regard it that highly.

Tests of Creativity

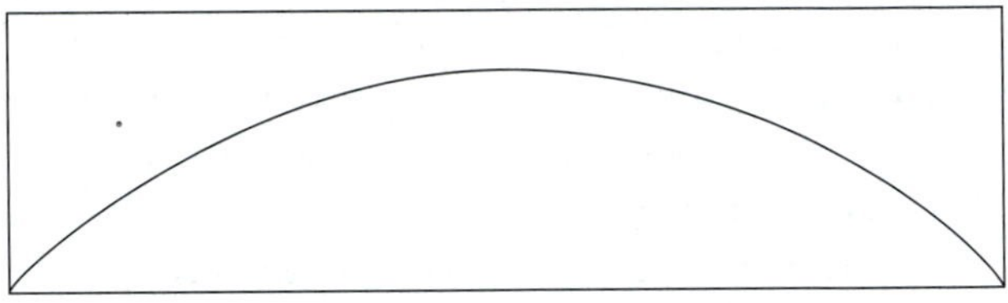

Give your best and most creative responses to what you see in this design. To assess creativity in children, various tests to measure fluency, elaboration, and originality have been constructed (Getzels & Jackson, 1962; Torrance, 1962). For example, in the test just presented, children look at somewhat nebulous designs and describe what they see. A rather convergent response to this example might be "a sunset." A more divergent response would be, "Well, you can't see the fisherman on the left but he is holding his fishing rod. All you can see is his line. On the other end, is a huge fish."

In some tests of creativity, children are asked various questions and encouraged to give as many responses as they can. One example of a question taken from these types of tests is, "What are the possible uses of a cardboard box?" Table 12.1 lists the answers given by two school-age children.

In other creativity tests, children are presented with various kinds of pictures of rather common scenes and asked to tell a story about what is happening in each picture. One picture is of a man sitting in an airplane. In the following stories, it is rather obvious that one child's response diverges from the expected, is more original and novel, and thus is considered more creative.

TABLE 12.1

Creativity in a Cardboard Box

"What can be done with a cardboard box?"

David	Sara
Put papers in it	Put things in it
Put flowers in it	A base for a table lamp
Put buttons in it	A baby's cot
Keep books in it	An ashtray for heavy smokers
Put food in it	A rain hat
A drawer	Use for making a bonfire
A toy for a child	Use for basketball practice
Serve food in it	Make into a picture with gouache paints
Dog kennel	Upside down—a chair for a thin kid
Draw on it	For sailing on a pond for a few seconds
Make two holes for a mask	Garbage pail
Base for a tree	Topographical map with projections
Burn it	Hide TV screen when programs are bad
Painting box	Keep lists of fulfilled promises (you need a very small box)

Although Sara and David gave the same number of responses, there are qualitative differences between their lists. Sara has higher scores on flexibility, elaboration, and originality; thus, on the basis of this test, she can be considered more creative than David.

From S. Ziv, *Personality and Sense of Humor,* 1984, New York: Springer. Reprinted by permission of Springer Publishing Co.

Child 1 responds:

Mr. Smith is on his way home from a successful business trip. He is very happy, and he is thinking about his wonderful family and how glad he will be to see them again. He can picture it, about an hour from now, his plane landing at the airport and Mrs. Smith and their three children all there welcoming him home again.

Child 2 relates:

This man is flying back from Reno where he just won a divorce from his wife. He couldn't stand to live with her anymore, he told the judge, because she wore so much moisturizing cream on her face at night that her head would skid across the pillow and hit him in the head. He is now contemplating a new skidproof face cream.

Creativity in children is fostered when:

- their unusual questions are treated with respect.
- they are provided opportunities for self-initiated learning and given credit for it.
- they are shown that their ideas have value.
- they are provided with periods of nonevaluated practice or learning. (Gerrard, Poteat, & Ironsmith, 1996)

Thought **CHALLENGE**

A businessman orders 20,000 pairs of shoes from Taiwan. On delivery, he discovers that he has received 20,000 left shoes. In the meantime, the factory in Taiwan has gone bankrupt. What can he do?

APPLICATIONS:

On Academic Success

The cognitive theories discussed in this section carry some clear implications for helping children succeed academically. Helping children believe in the power of effort, develop an internal locus of control, and achieve more success than failure are all key to academic success.

Believing in the Power of Effort

I know some college kids who don't do well in their classes. Do you think this means they are not smart?

Do you think that if a person can't solve a math problem in 10 minutes, the problem is probably too hard for him or her to do?

Did you answer "No" to these questions? If so, you probably have an *incremental* view of intelligence. An incremental view of intelligence emphasizes that intelligence is a trait that is malleable and dependent on effort. Did you answer "Yes" to these questions? Then you may have an *entity* view of intelligence. An entity view of intelligence emphasizes that intelligence is a fixed trait that cannot be changed.

Children (and adults) with an entity view of intelligence achieve less and are at risk for not trying very hard when faced with challenges (Heyman & Dweck, 1998). Although they agree that people can learn new things, they do not feel that how smart you are is something that can be changed. In contrast, individuals with an incremental view of intelligence believe that effort, in the form of persistence and hard work, is the key component of intelligence, and subsequently they are more likely to achieve academic success.

Young children tend to have an incremental view of intelligence. To illustrate, a young child is presented with the following scenario:

> Two children, Billy and Bobby, both received A's on the test. Billy studied very hard and Bobby didn't study at all. Who is the smarter child?"

The young child will insist that the child who achieves a high performance outcome coupled with effort is smarter than the one with the same performance outcome who exerts less efffort (Nichols, 1979).

These are important findings in that children's views on intelligence affect how well they do in the academic setting (Heyman & Dweck, 1998). For example, preschool through second-grade children explain high self-perceptions of academic competence by citing their engagement in activities that foster skill development ("I practice a lot"). Further, younger children do not differentiate ability from effort; that is, they do not have a concept of ability as a stable trait that limits the effectiveness of effort. Thus, effort is an isolated construct that explains most if not all of a child's academic competence. If a child in the early years of schooling performs well academically, it is likely that she or he will attribute academic competence to the level of effort expended. Younger children also tend to attribute nonmastery of a task to a lack of effort rather than ability. As such, young children's persistence on academic tasks does not decline as a consequence of failure.

However, beginning around the age of 8 or 9, we do see a decline in academic performance as a result of failure (Cain & Dweck, 1995; Miller, 1995). Why is this so? By this time, children no longer conceive of intelligence as a repertoire of skills that can be endlessly expanded through their efforts. They have come to learn to see intelligence as a global, stable entity whose adequacy is judged by their performance. Intelligence is thought of as fixed and unalterable—something you inherit (Stevenson, 1998). Subsequently, children tend to conceive of ability as a stable trait, unaffected by effort (Bryant, 1998). Thus, in our earlier scenario, older children infer from identical performance outcomes that effortless "A" Bobby must be the smarter.

internal locus of control
When children perceive a causal relationship between their personal actions in an academic setting and the resultant outcomes.

Older children also infer low ability when they receive parental or teacher praise on an easy task that required a great deal of effort on their part (Stipek, Recchia, & McClintic, 1992). Thus, studies indicate that the debilitating effect of failure is associated with the development of a concept of ability as a stable trait. When children associate ability with effort, their motivation levels and academic performance exceed those who associate ability as a stable trait (Stevenson, 1998).

An adult's praise for ability ("Wonderful work, Emil, you're so smart") is commonly considered to have beneficial effects on academic performance. Contrary to this popular belief, Claudia Mueller and Carol Dweck (1998) have demonstrated that praise for intelligence has more negative consequences for students' achievement motivation than praise for effort. In their study, fifth graders who were praised for ability were found to care more about performance goals (getting a good grade) relative to learning goals (a desire to understand). After failure, these children also displayed less task persistence, less task enjoyment, more low-ability attributions, and worse task performance. Finally, children praised for ability were likely to describe intelligence as a fixed trait. Children who were praised for their effort and hard work ("You continued to work on this math problem until it was solved; good work"), however, were found to care more about learning goals, displayed more task persistence, enjoyed learning tasks more, and believed that intelligence could be improved through hard work.

These findings suggest that adults should use techniques that encourage children to attribute their failures to factors over which they have some control, such as effort, before self-defeating attributions occur (Gopnik & Wellman, 1994). When parents and teachers are instructed to give children explanations that attribute the child's task failures to lack of effort rather than ability, his or her levels of achievement increase (Heckhausen & Dweck, 1998).

Developing an Inner Locus of Control

Another factor that affects children's learning and performance is their belief about the outcomes they might experience on academic tasks, which tends to guide their subsequent behavior in that and analogous situations. Individuals tend to attribute achievement outcomes to either internal or external causes. Students with an **internal locus of control** believe that they exercise more control over events and outcomes affecting them and, thereby, achieve better than do students with an external locus of control (Eccles, Wigfield, & Schiefele, 1997; Mukhopadhyay

& Dash, 1999). If you do not do well on an exam, are you more likely to say, "Everyone in that class does poorly; the tests are impossible" or "I guess I'll have to study harder." (Self-Insight presents the Norwicki-Strickland Locus of Control Scale [Norwicki & Strickland, 1973], an instrument designed to measure the degree to which individuals have an internal versus an external locus of control.)

Children with an internal locus of control know that they are responsible for the caliber of work they are doing in school. Children who report that they control their outcomes in the academic setting are rated by teachers as more engaged in school activities and achieve higher grades than are those with less understanding of control (Skinner, Zimmer-Gembeck, & Connell, 1998). In gifted children, their internal control actually may serve to fortify the pursuit of their talents. The importance of the internal locus of control also has been found cross-culturally in samples of children from Germany, Japan, and Russia (Karasaw, Little, Miyashita, & Mashima, 1997). African American and European American gifted children were found to have a higher internal locus of control than their nongifted counterparts (McLaughlin & Saccuzzo, 1997).

Children with an **external locus of control** believe events in their lives are beyond their control and usually achieve less. These children often believe they lack the ability to do the task ("I can't do this, because I am no good at it"). If they achieve success in a certain task, they often attribute it to luck or some external circumstance over which they have little or no control.

Children who are praised for their effort and hard work tend to be intrinsically motivated.

More Academic Success Than Failure

A few semesters ago, I visited a third-grade classroom. Upon entering, my attention was immediately drawn to a wire draped above the blackboard spanning the entire width of the classroom. Hanging from the wire were evenly spaced cards containing the numbers 2 through 9. Each child had a racing car on which his or her first name was printed in dark, bold letters. This was a motivational strategy for the children, who were learning their multiplication tables. Racing cars were scattered in various positions, mainly hovering between 4s and 5s; however, there were three cars that had not crossed the starting line. How did these children feel? Every morning for the past several weeks, they had entered the classroom and could not help but focus on their three cars that had made no progress.

Children who experience failure are particularly likely to develop unwarrantedly low expectations for success on academic tasks (Eccles, Wigfield, & Schiefele, 1997). They are likely to develop expectations, or **levels of aspiration**, that are consistent with their past performances. Children exposed to frequent failure either set goals for learning that are so low they can attain them effortlessly, or they set ridiculously unobtainable goals. (Failing on an extremely difficult task has more face-saving potential then failing on an easy task.) Low evaluations of their competence can result in children repeating ineffective strategies and giving up when they encounter difficulties in tasks. When children experience failure, their expectations of themselves as achievers are lowered, and they are not inspired to work to their fullest abilities.

Moreover, when children are exposed to frequent failures, they may develop a feeling of **learned helplessness**. These children tend to feel they are unable to handle certain tasks; they perceive themselves as unable to surmount failure (Witkowski, 1997). They often put themselves down when they fail, yet when they succeed they are likely to say it is just luck. Children view failure experiences as indicative of their ability, and as more failure experiences occur this "lack of ability" feeling is continually reinforced. They may resort to cheating or to

external locus of control
When children believe that they do not exercise control over events and outcomes affecting their academic achievement.

levels of aspiration
Expectations and goals set by children in the academic setting.

learned helplessness
When children are exposed to repeated failure, they develop a feeling that they are unable to handle tasks presented to them and perceive themselves as unable to surmount failure.

Self-Insight

Do You Have an Internal Locus of Control?

Answer "Yes" or "No" to the following questions.

1. Do you believe that most problems will solve themselves if you just don't fool with them?
2. Are some adults just born lucky?
3. Most of the time do you feel that getting good grades means a great deal to you?
4. Are you often blamed for things that just aren't your fault?
5. Do you believe that if somebody studies hard enough he or she can pass any subject?
6. Do you feel that most of the time it doesn't pay to try hard because things never turn out right anyway?
7. Do you feel that cheering more than luck helps a team to win?
8. Do you believe that your parents should allow you to make most of your own decisions?
9. Do you feel that when you do something wrong there's very little you can do to make it right?
10. If you found a four-leaf clover do you believe that it might bring you good luck?
11. Do you often feel that whether you do your homework has much to do with what kinds of grades you get?
12. Have you ever had a good luck charm?
13. Do you believe that whether or not people like you depends on how you act?
14. Most of the time do you find it useless to try to get your own way at home?
15. Do you feel that when good things happen they happen because of hard work?
16. Do you feel that it's easy to get friends to do what you want them to?
17. Do you usually feel that it's almost useless to try in school because most other students are just plain smarter than you are?
18. Are you the kind of person who believes that planning ahead makes things turn out better?
19. Most of the time, do you feel that you have little to say about what your family decides to do and when?
20. Do you think it's better to be smart than to be lucky?

The following answers are indicative of an external locus of control attitude.

1. Yes	4. Yes	7. No	10. Yes	13. No	16. No	19. Yes
2. Yes	5. No	8. No	11. No	14. Yes	17. Yes	20. No
3. No	6. Yes	9. Yes	12. Yes	15. No	18. No	

Individuals who have eight or more answers that agree with the key have an external locus of control. They tend to believe that they have little control over what happens to them. These people tend to think that their successes and failures are due to lack of luck, fate, or some other circumstances beyond their control. If you have fewer than eight answers that agree with the key, you have an internal locus of control. These individuals tend to think that they are responsible for their successes or failures. They sense that their own efforts and activities influence success and failure and the events that happen to them.

From "Generalized Expectancies for Internal Versus External Control of Reinforcement," by J. B. Rotter, 1966, in *Psychological Monographs: General and Applied, 80,* 1–28. Washington, DC: American Psychological Association.

failure-avoidance strategies (low effort or procrastination, because failure without effort is viewed as "failure with honor"), or they may attempt to gain self-esteem through acting out in class, thereby earning "admiration" or at least attention from their peers (Bryant, 1998; Covington, 1985). By their actions, these children are increasing the likelihood that they will continue to fail.

Children, then, need to experience more academic success than failure. Helping children master the academic tasks at hand may be accomplished through additional help with a tutor, which will enable them to learn the necessary academic skills needed for academic success. Other steps adults can take to prevent children from acquiring a sense of learned helplessness include avoiding frequent criticisms and focusing on the positive (this paper is neatly written) rather than the negative (look how many misspelled words you have) (Heyman & Dweck, 1998). Helping children view tasks as an avenue for learning rather than as tests of their ability also prevents feelings of learned helplessness. Encouraging children to engage in activities simply for pleasure leads to greater self-determination and higher academic achievement (Gottfried, Fleming, & Gottfried, 1998).

Concept Checks

1. Recently, Josephine has come to understand that when you cut a piece of pie in half, you still have the same amount of pie. According to Piaget, Josephine
   a. will understand this for pieces of pie and nothing else.
   b. is demonstrating the principle of conservation.
   c. must be 5 years old.
2. Information-processing theory regards changes in cognition to be the result of
   a. experience.
   b. the development of more sophisticated structures.
   c. improved memory strategies.
3. Which of the following questions requires divergent thinking?
   a. How many dimes can you get for $10?
   b. How do you interpret the book *Moby Dick*?
   c. What is wrong with the car?
4. Ralph is very upset about the score he received on his history test and says, "The teacher has it in for me—she just never asks the right questions!" We would characterize Ralph as having
   a. an external locus of control.
   b. a minor learning disability.
   c. an internal locus of control.

Technology, Culture, and Achievement

Before Beginning ...

After reading this section, you will be able to

- examine the effects of video games on aggression, social and cognitive development, and educational achievement.
- evaluate the possible educational benefits of computers in the classroom.
- analyze teacher behaviors that tend to perpetuate stereotypical behaviors in boys and girls.
- see implications for narrowing gender gaps in math, science, and technology skills.
- discuss the possible causes of differing achievement levels among those from Asian cultures, European Americans, and African Americans.

The changing technological landscape has allowed us to make the transition from the Industrial Age to the Information Age. Computers continue to further edge their way into children's lives. According to the National Center for Education Statistics, U.S. parents, in the year 2000, spent $424 million on educational CD-ROMs for their children, and 95 percent of schools and 63 percent of all classrooms had Internet access. Computers have not only infiltrated homes and schools, they have captured children's attention and begun to consume much of their free time—most often in the form of video game play.

The Impact of Video Games

A highly intelligent friend of mine related that she had tried playing one of her son's video games but found it a visual maze of confusion. Her son had tried to explain the game to her, adding, "Gosh, Mom, it's *so* obvious. *Anyone* can see how to play this game." Does playing video games program the brain differently? If so, many children get a lot of brain reprogramming.

In the United States, 7- to 12-year-old European American boys report that playing video games consumes most of their free time, followed by watching television, and playing sports (Harrell, Gansky, & Bradley, 1997). African American boys, however, report more vigorous activities, such as playing sports. In other countries, watching television still monopolizes most of children's free time. In Japan, for example, school-age children report spending 45 percent of their time watching television, followed by computer and video time (Suzuki, Hashimoto, & Ishii, 1997).

Although there are a number of instructional video games, by far, the most popular games are the highly graphic, aggressive form, such as Mortal Kombat®. Around the world, boys tend to find war games and more violent videos appealing (Goldstein, 1998; Wiegman & van Schie, 1998; Yi & Lee, 1997). What impact do violent and nonviolent video games have on children's aggression, sociability, cognitive skills, and educational achievement?

© PhotoEdit

Will playing violent video games produce aggressive behavior in children?

Video Games and Aggression

A number of studies of children and adolescents report little or no evidence that games increase aggressive behavior in players—even on a short-term basis (Dietz, 1998; Funk, Flores, Buchman, & Germann, 1999). But, no research question is ever that easily resolved and there are studies that do show aggressive side effects from playing violent games. In many video games, players must shoot or harm their symbolic opponents to win, and it has been found in some studies that children who play aggressive video games subsequently become more aggressive in their social play (Griffiths, 1997). They also tend to see others' behavior as more hostile (Kirsh, 1998).

Video Games and Sociability

Do video games reinforce social isolationism, or do they encourage sharing, excitement, and social collaboration? Gerard Bonnafont (1992) reports that parent and child communication may be disrupted as a result of video game play. This may occur because parents often do not understand video games, exclude themselves from the video game culture, and subsequently are unable to talk to their children about or play the games with them (Jason & Hanaway, 1997). Studies have also found that prosocial behaviors that benefit others may become inhibited in those who play violent video games (Jones & Selby, 1997).

Video Games and Cognitive Skills

Playing video games also may increase hand–eye coordination and spatial skills. Three important spatial skills are affected: (1) *spatial relations ability* (the capacity to rapidly transform objects in the mind, as is required when one "mentally rotates" an object about its center); (2) *spatial visualization* (the ability to deal with complex visual problems that require imagining the relative movements, as in folding and unfolding flat patterns); and (3) *perceptual speed* (rapid encoding and comparison of visual forms). Video games tend to enhance all three spatial skills (Subrahmanyam & Greenfield, 1998).

Video Games and Educational Achievement

Most researchers report that there is no relationship between playing video games at home and lower academic achievement (Fletcher-Flinn & Suddendorf, 1996). However, there is a relationship between lower academic achievement and playing video games at arcades (Lin & Lepper, 1987). Parental involvement and monitoring of children's school performance plays a dynamic role in school achievement, and it may be that lack of parental monitoring that is typical of arcade play that may also cause the decrease in academic performance. Further, arcade play may be more prevalent with children from lower socioeconomic classes (SES), and a lower SES is associated with poor academic achievement.

Education and Technology

If you close your eyes and imagine a classroom, chances are you will picture an adult standing at the front of a room that contains 30 or more students sitting in straight rows of desks. The students may be listening to the teacher talk, raising their hands to participate in a class discussion, or working quietly and independently on some written exercise. Closely allied with this scene are assumptions about basic school organization: textbooks, courses of study set by some central curriculum office, grade levels, bell schedules, and testing.

Now, consider this learning environment. The children return from the library, where they have been researching back copies of newspapers for information about hurricanes. They join their group of students, who are on-line with the computer. The computer is linked with the university and can access satellite images of weather information from the National Weather Service. The children are tracking the progress of a tropical depression in the Caribbean. Educational technology software is transforming today's classroom. But do students genuinely benefit from these digital technologies? And are there conditions that maximize the educational benefits these technologies provide to students?

The Image Works

There appears to be a positive association between computer use and academic achievement.

Educational Technology Software

The use of technology in the classroom continues to increase. It is found in a wide assortment of educational materials: computer-assisted instruction, simulation, word processing, hypertext and hypermedia, and the Internet.

Computer-Assisted Instruction (CAI) **Computer-assisted instruction** is learning in which students use the computer and instructional programs in fairly controlled conditions to master a typical school subject matter. CAI often relies on drill-and-practice and tutorial software.

Drill-and-practice programs focus on providing intensive work on specific academic skills. Because most are based on Skinner's operant conditioning, they emphasize stimulus, response, and reward. Most programs give students a number of problems, offer direct feedback on whether their answer is correct, and dispense a reward for a correct answer. Rewards can range from verbal prompts ("Great job!") to playing a game. Critics claim that these programs are boring and encourage rote learning, not thinking.

Tutorials attempt to mimic a competent and ever-patient tutor. Students work through a linear setup in which they begin with the first frame and work through subsequent frames in a given sequence. Incorrect responses prompt supplementary material that attempts to reteach that particular information. Tutorials offer more sophisticated self-paced teaching and "coach" students rather than simply giving them the answer.

Simulations **Simulations** combine content and problem-solving by immersing students in experiences that would be difficult to duplicate in real life. For example, students may construct a new planet and control its ecosystem, design a car, or travel through the human circulatory system. System thinking models are a new form of simulation that mimics behavior of a complex system, letting students explore the mutual interactivity of component parts and processes. Teachers using the basic software have developed curriculum materials for osmosis, chemical reactions, earthquakes, and immunology (Mandinach & Kline, 1996).

Word Processing In its most common usage, **word processing** amounts to using the computer as a sophisticated typewriter, adding the flexibility of revising and editing into the learning process. Word processors are one of the most prevalent computer educational applications.

Hypertext and Hypermedia **Hypertext**—which consists of written material—and **hypermedia**—a more general term for a mixture of sound, graphics, and text—describe nonlinear programs. In these programs, users choose the order in which they want to view, read, and hear the elements of a presentation. This flexibility, called *linking*, is attained by inserting links or "buttons" into the program, which the viewer can click to move from one display to another. The buttons are often contained in key words highlighted in the text or in prompts such as "Click here to see. . . ."

The use of hypermedia puts the student in charge of developing a project and constructing both knowledge

computer-assisted instruction Learning in which students use the computer and instructional programs in fairly controlled conditions to master a typical school subject matter.

simulations Models that combine content and problem-solving, immersing students in experiences that would be difficult to duplicate in real life.

word processing Using the computer as a sophisticated typewriter, adding the flexibility of revising and editing into the learning process.

hypertext/hypermedia Hypertext—which consists of written material—and hypermedia—a more general term for a mixture of sound, graphics, and text—describe nonlinear programs.

and problem-solving strategies, making it one of the applications that may drastically change education as we know it (MacGregor, 1999). For example, for a report on France, using hypermedia, one high school student wrote about French history, drew illustrations, recorded herself singing the "Marseillaise," took her "readers" through a visual tour of relevant paintings in world museums, added an animated street scene, and worked in a quiz on irregular French verbs (Healy, 1998, p. 58).

The Internet The Internet offers two basic educational uses: (1) finding information by either searching documents "published" on the web or receiving information through e-mail and (2) sending information or messages, again through "publishing" on a structured Web page or an on-line information source or through informal correspondence. Both uses have advantages and both have problems. The most commonly cited problems are that the information presented has no citations, and no authority "fact-checks" it. Second, the Internet is poorly organized; in searching for a particular subject, students may have to go to several web sites to find it. Further, the Internet is dominated by those organizations with the means to purchase advertising links that can subtly guide consumers toward their products or idea. The student who, for example, is doing research on the Nile River may be sent to an advertising page of a travel company.

Benefits: Hype or Hope?

Do students really benefit from this plethora of digital instruction technologies? Some evidence suggests that children who use computers on a regular and frequent basis tend to get better grades than their non–computer-using counterparts (Rocheleau, 1996). However, social class may also enter into this equation, because having personal computers is still associated with higher socioeconomic levels, and a higher socioeconomic status is associated with better academic achievement. Other studies indicate that children's dynamic representation of space (Greenfield, Brannon, & Lohr, 1994); memory skills (Greenfield, Camaioni, Ercolani, Weiss, Lauber, & Perucchini, 1994), and attentional skills (Greenfield, deWinstanley, Kilpatrick, & Kaye, 1994) benefited from computer experience. Computer usage appears to enhance information-processing skills, promote collaboration, and stimulate higher-level idea generation in students.

Computer programs that encourage active problem solving and discovery promote inductive reasoning and process-oriented thinking, which may enhance academic achievement. In this sense, computers may facilitate the type of thinking that leads children to acquire the skills to discover new information. Static thinking—fact-oriented, memorization-related, and "know what information"—is an inferior way of learning compared with fact-finding, information-processing, and "know how to find information" ways of thinking. Computers may promote the latter, more effective, way of processing information (Greenfield, 1999).

Research tells us that, contrary to the common image of a sullen and lonely child hunched over a keyboard for long hours at a stretch, computers actually increase social contact among peers (Bonnafont, 1992). They produce a forum for collaborative learning and researchers see them as a powerful catalyst for peer collaboration (Glissov, Siann, & Durndell, 1994). Ann Katrin Svensson (2000) found that there were twice as many interactions between children in front of the computer as there were with other schoolwork activities. Computers function to organize social activity. It is possible, for example, to dial into an adventure computer game on the Internet and develop its narrative partly through interacting with other individuals who are simultaneously logged in and taking part.

Further, Gavriel Salomon's (1993) research suggests that word-processing programs prompt higher-level idea generation and the use of more sophisticated revision practices. However, other studies have shown that although students wrote longer papers when using word processors, the quality or the complexity of their writing was not enhanced (Bangert-Drowns, 1993).

Conditions for Successful Outcomes

Researchers have noted various conditions that support more successful learning outcomes when technology is employed (Bond, 2000). One important factor is teacher training; teachers need to be able to use and teach students to use computers for discovery not just drill-and-practice activities. Further, teachers need to receive appropriate technical support. Computer learning is enhanced when it is combined with personal guidance throughout the learning process—both from active, enthusiastic, and knowledgeable teachers and explicit metacognitive prompts that allow students to plan, monitor, and evaluate learning in the software itself.

Among the many contributions to ideas about learning made by Lev Vygotsky is the idea that the tools we use shape what and how we learn and how we come to understand our world. Instruction supported with computers, along with multimedia software—simulations, word processing, hypertext and hypermedia, the Internet, and other forms yet to be created—have tremendous implications for our underlying perspectives on how children learn.

In the traditional school setting (such as the classroom we pictured at the start of this section), learning is viewed as *knowledge instruction*. In this type of setting, knowledge is transferred from one who is knowledgeable to one who is not. Teacher work is perceived as direct instruction. With the effective use of digital technologies, however, the emphasis shifts to *knowledge construction*. In this setting, digital technologies are used to promote critical thinking, problem solving, decision making, and exploration. Teacher work is construed as facilitating students' abilities to integrate ideas and experiences. The two approaches to learning are not incompatible but, rather, should be viewed as positions on a continuum of possible learning strategies. When combining instruction and construction, we are creating learning environments that enhance the learning process as well as children's understanding of the world.

The Hidden Curriculum

The children are seated in a circle, and the teacher asks them questions about the story she just read. All hands wave frantically, "I know. I know." She calls on Malcolm. Later on during a science lesson, she encourages Matt to experiment with his project further. When she hands back papers, she tells Tim that the content of his paper is wonderful but that his work needs to be neater. When Sally asks a question about the homework for tomorrow, the teacher gets up and goes over to talk with her. While talking with her, Rick interrupts, and the teacher acknowledges his question, taking her attention away from Sally.

Seemingly innocuous events? Or, are teachers sending strong but subtle messages to children that will determine their achievement levels and behavior? Research done in the classroom documenting behaviors, attitudes, and expectancies of teachers supports the theory of a "hidden curriculum" (Steele, 1997). The literature suggests that our educational systems still support a policy of training boys for individualistic behavior and girls for socially conforming behavior, and thus is perpetuating stereotypical behavior (American Association of University Women, 1999). This hidden curriculum begins with teachers showing a preference for one gender.

Which Gender Do Teachers Prefer?

Research suggests that, in general, female teachers prefer male students to female students (Thorne, 2001). Some teachers say that males are more honest, more willing to exchange their ideas, more willing to try new things, and in general, are easier to talk with. The one trait they do identify as admirable in girls is that they are rule-abiding and, thus, do not present disciplinary problems. Stereotyping girls as orderly, conforming, and dependent tends to work against them, because it discourages active, assertive learning styles that tend to further students academically in the long run.

Attention and Individual Instruction Although teachers cite girls as being more hardworking than boys, boys have the most interactions of all kinds with their teachers. In particular, teachers prefer high-achieving boys and will interact at a higher level and encourage continued responses from them. Teachers tend to pay more attention to these boys and give them twice as much individual instruction on tasks as they give girls (Orenstein, 1994). High-achieving boys receive more praise than high-achieving girls at the elementary and high school level (Sadker & Sadker, 1994). In fact, boys for whom the teacher has high expectations have the most favorable interactions with their teachers; boys for whom teachers have low expectations are criticized the most, whereas girls of all achievement levels are treated similarly to one another.

Also, boys are rewarded more for academic achievement. Ninety percent of the praise for boys' schoolwork is directed at the intellectual content and quality of their work; 80 percent of praise for girls' work is directed toward form and neatness. Relatedly, girls are recognized and reinforced for their physical appearance (hairstyles, clothing), presumably denigrating their intellectual capabilities. As a consequence, teachers may facilitate less achievement in girls. Teachers prefer the dependent girl—the one who is attentive in class, does extra credit assignments, follows directions, is compliant and quiet, stays close to the teacher, and obeys rules. Girls are given more reprimands for calling out the answer. This all can stifle achievement. Thus, the submissive kind of achieving girls and the high-achieving outspoken boys are preferred, and their behavior is rewarded by their teachers.

Mathematics and Science

The "hidden curriculum" encourages boys to be more autonomous, to find out things for themselves, and to develop their own abilities and resources. Conversely, it encourages girls to be more dependent, to wait to hear answers rather than discover them, and to rely on the teacher for guidance. These gender differences in behavior appear to have their greatest impact on academic performances in math and science. To date, boys continue to outnumber and outperform girls in math and science classes. Beginning in the fourth grade (see Figure 12.4) boys earn higher scores in math and science on the National Assessment of Educational Progress, a nationally representative exam of student knowledge in specific subject areas (Campbell, 1997). The gender gap increases in later grades. How can this lingering disparity in math and science scores be explained? Differences in expectations for boys and girls and variations across ethnic groups are examined.

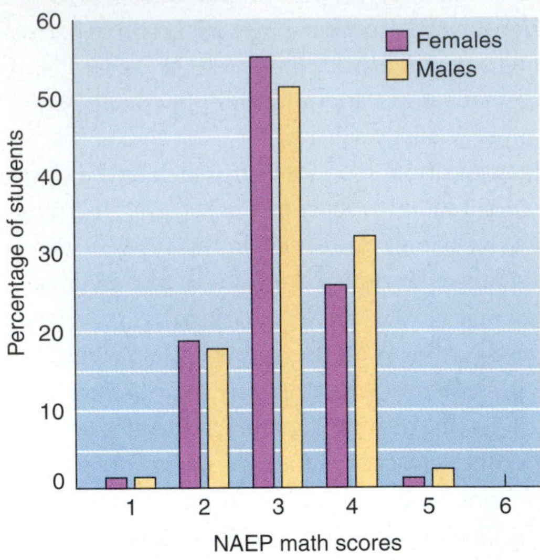

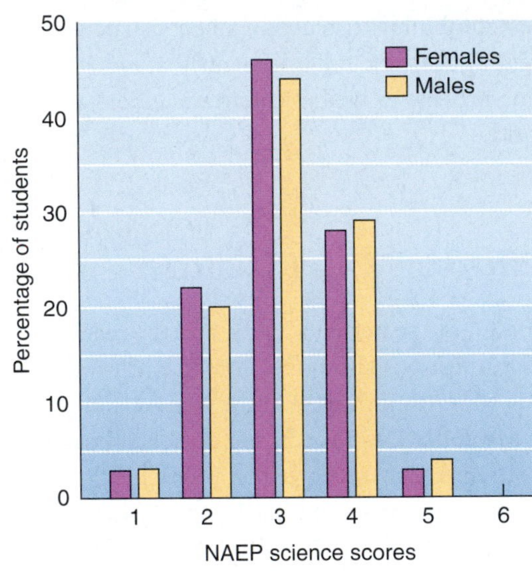

FIGURE 12.4 ***Math and Science Scores of Fourth-Grade Students***

From *NAEP 1996 Trends in Academic Progress,* by J. R. Campbell, 1997, Washington, DC: U.S. Department of Education, National Center for Education Statistics.

Expectations One factor that accounts for gender differences in math and science is differing expectations for the two genders. Sally Reis and Carolyn Callahan (1996) found that male teachers, in particular, tended to stereotype girls and their talents, often expressing doubts about their capabilities to succeed in higher-level math and science courses. Such critical judgments of their abilities could deter many girls from persevering in these courses. It has also been observed that teachers, in general, do stereotype their students in the area of mathematics, attributing characteristics such as volunteering answers, enjoying mathematics, and working independently to males—not females (Reis & Gavin, 1998).

Parental expectations may play a role in determining mathematics and science grades. Parents, for example, tend to think their sons will do better in math than their daughters and this apparently causes sons to see themselves as better in mathematics than daughters (Wren, 1999). Moreover, boys may be given more encouragement to develop mathematical skills, because many adults believe that boys will need mathematics training more than girls, and as a result perform better on tests of mathematical knowledge (Stevenson & Lee, 1990).

Children also show gender role inflexibility. During the middle school years, children also become more stereotypical in their interests and achievement-related behavior. Girls often develop the opinion that their math abilities are lower and their language abilities are higher than boys—even when standardized tests reveal similar abilities (Eccles & Bryan, 1994). Girls also may become less assertive in classroom activities, such as science demonstrations and equipment use. They tend to experience a decreased interest in math and science and a change in career orientation, with an increased interest in marriage and children and a narrowing of career interests to those careers most com-

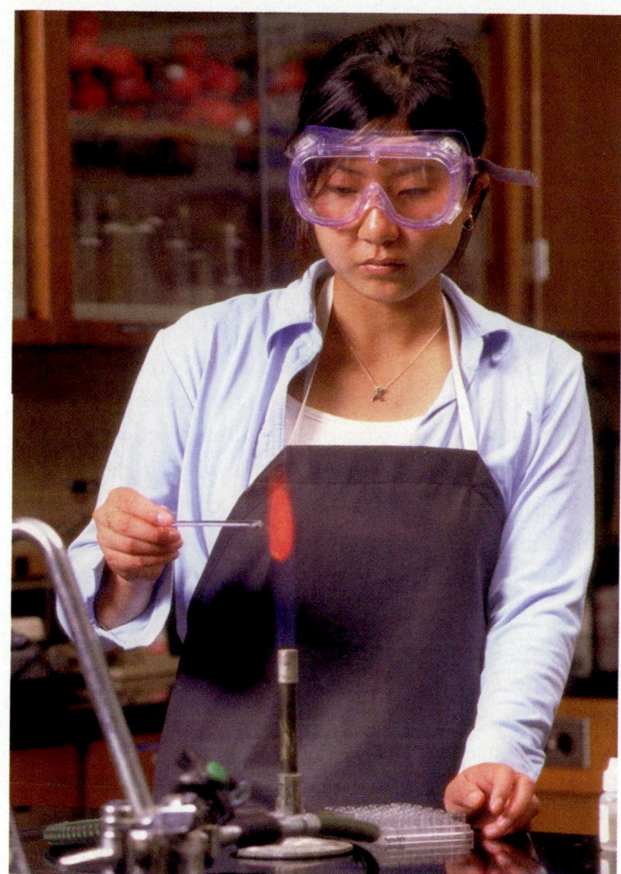
© Jonathan Nourok/PhotoEdit

Boys tend to demean girls' comments through jokes, which may undermine girls' achievement, particularly in mathematics and science.

monly occupied by women. Whereas girls' confidence in their academic abilities is declining, boys are starting to feel more confident in theirs (Bush & Simmons, 1987). Peggy Orenstein (1994) observed, for example, that it is socially acceptable for boys to ridicule girls and their ideas—particularly in mathematics and science courses. Boys tended to demean and devalue girls' comments through asides, jokes, and putdowns. As important as adult validation is, children need validation from peers as well (Maher & Tetreault, 1994; Weis & Fine, 1993).

Ethnic Differences Is this gender disparity in math and science performance found across all ethnic groups? The results from several studies suggest that Asian American girls performed as well as boys in math and science (Cross, 1991; Stevenson, 1998). These girls tended to receive more parental encouragement and less negative peer pressure about preparing for math and science careers. African American girls were the most underrepresented group in math and science courses (Cross, 1991). The Cross (1991) study found that African American girls tended to have relatively high levels of performance anxiety and little confidence in their personal abilities, and they tended to attribute their successes to luck rather than to their own efforts and abilities.

Bridging Gender Gaps in the Classroom

Bridging these gaps becomes an important task as jobs in the 21st century leave no room for individuals who fall behind in math and science and fail to keep up with the ever-expanding world of technology. It has been estimated that 65 percent of all jobs in this new millennium will require more than just a passing knowledge of math, science, and technical skills (American Association of University Women, 1999).

Girls achieve higher math and science grades when their parents are more liberal and egalitarian in their treatment of their sons and daughters (Fagot & Leinbach, 1995). When parents expect and encourage their daughters to do well in mathematics, there are no sex differences in mathematics ability at all grade levels through high school (American Association of University Women, 1999). Thus, raising our expectations, encouraging girls to take more math and science courses, helping teachers become aware of the gender biases they may have, particularly in math and science areas, and training prospective teachers against gender bias are important variables that will help to bridge the math and science gender gap between boys and girls.

Students, both boys and girls, need encouragement, validation, and support for expressing their opinions, from parents, teachers, and classmates. As important as teacher validation is, children need validation from peers as well. A major challenge in this regard is to create an atmosphere in which male students will seriously listen to the opinions of female students. As we have seen, beginning at an early age, boys either ignore or devalue what girls have to say. All children's voices need to be heard; and perhaps, cooperative learning, often in small groups, may provide the context in which children will be listened to and understood (Maher & Tetreault, 1994; Weis & Fine, 1993). Being aware of this hidden curriculum may help adults engage in more egalitarian behavior and thus encourage independent, exploratory activities and problem-solving skills in boys and girls.

Culture, Ethnicity, and Achievement

Asian and Asian American children tend to outperform European American children. Their overall academic performance is superior and they tend to excel in subjects such as mathematics and science.

Students from Asian Cultures

The relative academic standing of students from Asian cultures in cross-cultural comparisons has been impressive. These students typically receive higher scores in mathematics and science than students in other countries, including Canada (Kwok & Lytton, 1993), the Netherlands (Picke, 1991), Great Britain, Australia (Rosenthal & Feldman, (1991), and the United States (Ginsberg, Choi, Lopez, Netley, & Chao-Yuan, 1997).

Harold Stevenson and his colleagues (Stevenson, 1998; Stevenson & Lee, 1997) have done extensive cross-cultural research on children from the United States and Asian countries. One representative study was conducted in 120 classrooms in Taipei (Taiwan) and in the Minneapolis metropolitan area. Kindergartners and first and fifth graders from representative schools in these cities were given a test of mathematics that required computation and problem solving. The distribution of mathematics scores obtained by the students appears in Figure 12.5, which summarizes the results for over 5000 participants. Only one U.S. child received a mathematics score that ranked among the top 100 students.

What factors may account for differences in achievement levels of these various ethnic groups? Is IQ a factor? Interestingly, IQ test scores are going up everywhere in the world (Neisser, 1998). Recent cross-cultural findings from samples of children from the United States, Great Britain, the Netherlands, Israel, and Belgium revealed IQ gains ranging from 18 to 22 points over the previous generation (Flynn, 1998). It is as if some unseen hand is propelling scores upward at a rate of about 6 IQ points per decade. What are the causes of these IQ gains? Patricia Greenfield (1998) and Ulric Neisser (1998) suggest such things as video games and computers as possible causes. Richard Lynn (1998) argues that nutrition is a key factor responsible for the secular increase in IQ. Wendy Williams (1998) suggests that better schools and increased test sophistication on the part of students account for these massive gains.

Perhaps the most consistent advocate for an interpretation of Asian academic success in terms of IQ differences is Richard Lynn (1982, 1989, 1997), an Irish psychologist who argues for genetically determined differences in intelligence and also for the possibility that children from Asian cultures have some genetic predisposition for working hard for long-term goals.

On the other side of the equation, Harold Stevenson and his colleagues argue that there is no clear evidence that IQ scores on samples of Japanese, Taiwanese, and European American children differed significantly. Stevenson bases this conclusion on studies in which IQ tests measured general knowledge of common, everyday phenomena, such as why we need to put stamps on letters when we mail them, why people cannot live under water, what is needed for a plant to grow, and so forth. Answers to these questions are not necessarily taught in school but presumably depend on information children have acquired from their everyday experiences. According to Stevenson, tests of general knowledge correlate at a high level with overall IQ scores and are thought to be one of the most reliable indicators of cognitive ability. The performances of the Taipei and U.S. children were very similar. Moreover, Stevenson maintains that Asian cultures tend to view children's academic success as being extremely important. The cultural emphasis on academic success, more so than IQ, may help to explain the superior performances of Asian children.

Chin is 7 years old and lives in Tokyo. Even though he is quite young, his goals are clear—to do well in school. Traditionally, Japanese families teach children the importance—indeed, the moral imperative—of repaying one's parents for their sacrifices by succeeding academically (Shweder, 1999). Behind children's striving for academic success and beyond any effort to seek recognition for themselves, then, is the image of the larger value their success will have for their family and society. The consequences of failure, as well as of success, are magnified by children's identities through their families and the larger society. Just as success enhances the family's status, the consequences of poor performance include not only loss of status and prestige for the child but a far more critical loss of family face.

Various research findings also indicate other factors that contribute to Asian and Asian American children's academic success, namely: (1) time spent and effort expended, (2) a more egalitarian educational philosophy, (3) a more academically demanding classroom, and (4) teachers.

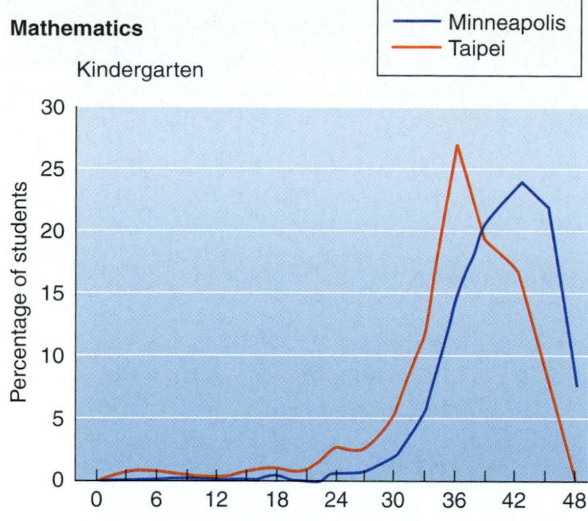

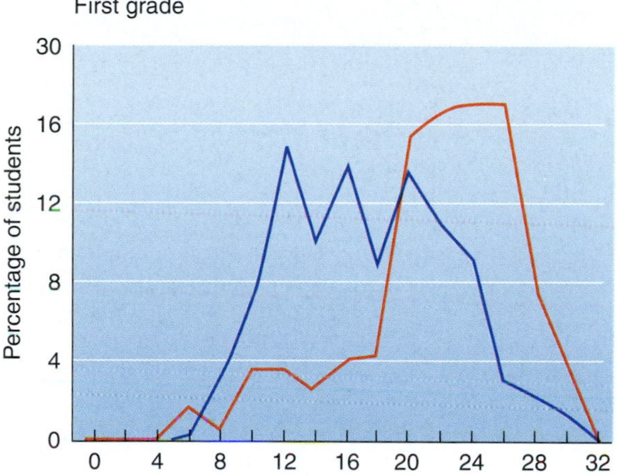

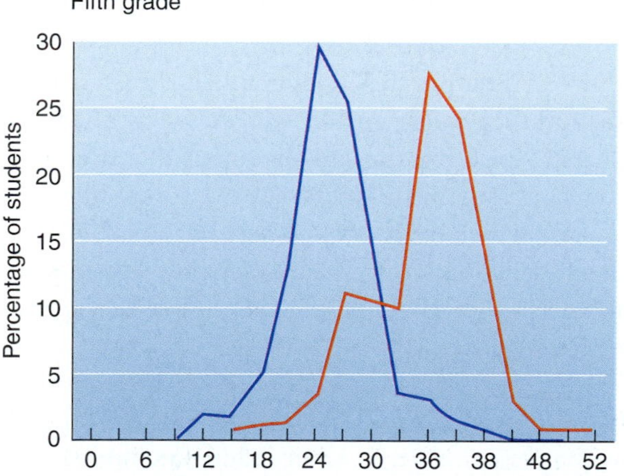

FIGURE 12.5 ***Mathematics Scores in Taipei and Minneapolis***

Samples of children from Taipei, Taiwan, show more impressive achievement scores on standard mathematic tests than a sample of children from Minneapolis.

From "The Academic Achievement of Chinese Students," by H. W. Stevenson & S. Lee, 1996, in M. H. Bond, *The Handbook of Chinese Psychology* (pp. 124–142). New York: Oxford University Press. Reprinted by permission.

Time Spent and Effort Expended The achievement levels of the Taipei children, according to Stevenson (1998), appeared to be attributable in part to the great amounts of time they spent on their studies. Students in Taipei compared with students in Minneapolis, for example, were at school longer each day (an average of 9.2 hours versus 7.3) and each week (50 versus 36 hours). When the amounts of afterschool time they spent studying, taking lessons, and reading for pleasure were summed, the Taipei students averaged 25.5 hours a week and the U.S. students 15 hours. In Taipei, 36 percent of students were enrolled in afterschool academic classes compared with 3 percent in Minneapolis. The Taipei students attended school 240 days a year compared with 180 days in the United States. The idea of a longer school day as an impetus to increase achievement levels of U.S. students has captured the interest of educators in several states, but would this be effective? (See Child Development Issues.)

Effort, rather than innate endowment, was also seen as a major reason for the Taipei students' academic success. Parents and teachers of these children assumed that they would be more willing to work hard if they and other adults pointed to the virtues of hard work and effort. These parents attempted to reinforce the importance of effort by helping their young children with their schoolwork on average about 7 hours per week.

A More Egalitarian Philosophy In Asian cultures, it is generally assumed that all children possess the necessary capacity for advancement to higher levels of development, including advancement in school. Tracking does not exist in Japanese and Chinese elementary schools, and children are never separated into different classrooms according to their presumed levels of intellectual ability (Ginsberg, Choi, Lopez, Netley, & Chao-Yuan, 1997). Teachers, parents, and children hold the sincere belief that everyone is capable of mastering the curriculum, and that academic success is within the grasp of all children if they apply themselves wholeheartedly to their schoolwork (Stevenson & Lee, 1990). Some children, however, do progress more rapidly than others; but "the slow bird," says an ancient Chinese proverb, "must start out early" and try harder. Often brighter students spend time with slower students when they need help.

This egalitarian view of human development is a residual of Confucian precepts, which emphasize

Child Development Issues

Will Extending the School Year Lead to Growth in Academic Achievement?

During the last decade, national and international studies have documented the shortcomings of U.S. students' achievements in such core subject areas as reading, mathematics, and science (International Association for the Evaluation of Educational Achievement, 1998; Stevenson, Chen, & Lee, 1993). Some educational experts have suggested that lengthening the school year would reverse U.S. children's achievement decline (U.S. Department of Education, 1999). Some educators' claim that year-round school promotes continual learning, reduces memory loss by shortening summer vacation, and makes more efficient use of school facilities (National Association for Year-Round Education, 1996). Currently, about 500 school districts in 41 states have a year-round educational program.

The findings of Julie Frazier and Frederick Morrison (1998) indicate that an increase of 30 instructional days in early elementary school can have a significant impact on mathematics and reading achievement. Extended schooling is particularly beneficial for low-income children, because they suffer the worst math- and reading-achievement declines when school is not in session. If extended-year schooling helps low-income children, what does it do for middle-income children? Instead of simply maintaining achievement levels during school vacations, extended-year schooling also promotes significant gains in middle-income children's math and reading achievements.

Overall, although improving U.S. education will require changes in many areas, these findings do raise the possibility that providing additional instruction time by extending the school year represents a promising educational reform.

Search Online

Explore InfoTrac College Edition, your online library. Go to **http://www.infotrac-college.com/wadsworth** and use the passcode that came on the card with your book. Try these search terms: school year, longer school year, summer schools.

© Charles Gupton/Stock Boston

In Japan, parents, teachers, and students believe that academic success is within the grasp of all children.

hard work. But, are these children being pushed too hard? Are they overly anxious and stressed? There appears to be very little support for the idea that children in Asian countries are slaves to an oppressive, regimented system that values learning at all costs (Azuma, 1998; Chan, 1996). It is actually U.S. students who indicate more frequent feelings of school-related stress.

Higher Parental Expectations Despite the outstanding performance of Asian children in international competitions, surprisingly few parents express high degrees of satisfaction with their children's academic achievement. In contrast, parents in the United States appear to have rather low educational expectations for their children, and this may be working against their children's academic achievement. Cross-national differences are even more dramatic when only the "very satisfied" mothers are considered. Less than

5 percent of the Japanese mothers, but over 40 percent of the U.S. mothers, said they were very satisfied with their child's performance (Stevenson, Chen, & Lee, 1993). The Japanese mothers also were more likely than the U.S. mothers to adopt successively higher criteria for their children's academic performance as their children became older. Perhaps then, low U.S. parental expectations prevented their children from achieving at higher levels and high parental expectations were an impetus to the Japanese students' success.

Teachers Shinn Ying Lee (1998) gives glowing marks to teachers in China and Japan. Teachers from these countries are characterized as being thoughtful, relaxed, and nonauthoritarian. Moreover, they frequently rely on students as sources of information. Lessons are oriented toward problem solving rather than rote mastery of facts and procedures and utilize many different types of representational materials. The role assumed by the teacher is that of a knowledgeable guide rather than as prime dispenser of information and arbiter of what is correct. There is frequent verbal interaction in the classroom as the teacher attempts to stimulate students to produce, explain, and evaluate solutions to problems. Although the number of children in classes is significantly greater than the number in U.S. classes, Japanese, Chinese, and Taiwanese students receive much more instruction from their teachers than U.S. students. In Taiwan, for example, the teacher is the leader of the child's activity 90 percent of the time, as opposed to 74 percent in Japan, and an astonishing 51 percent of the time in the United States (see Figure 12.6). (Cultural Variations discusses how these effective teaching techniques stimulate learning and achievement.)

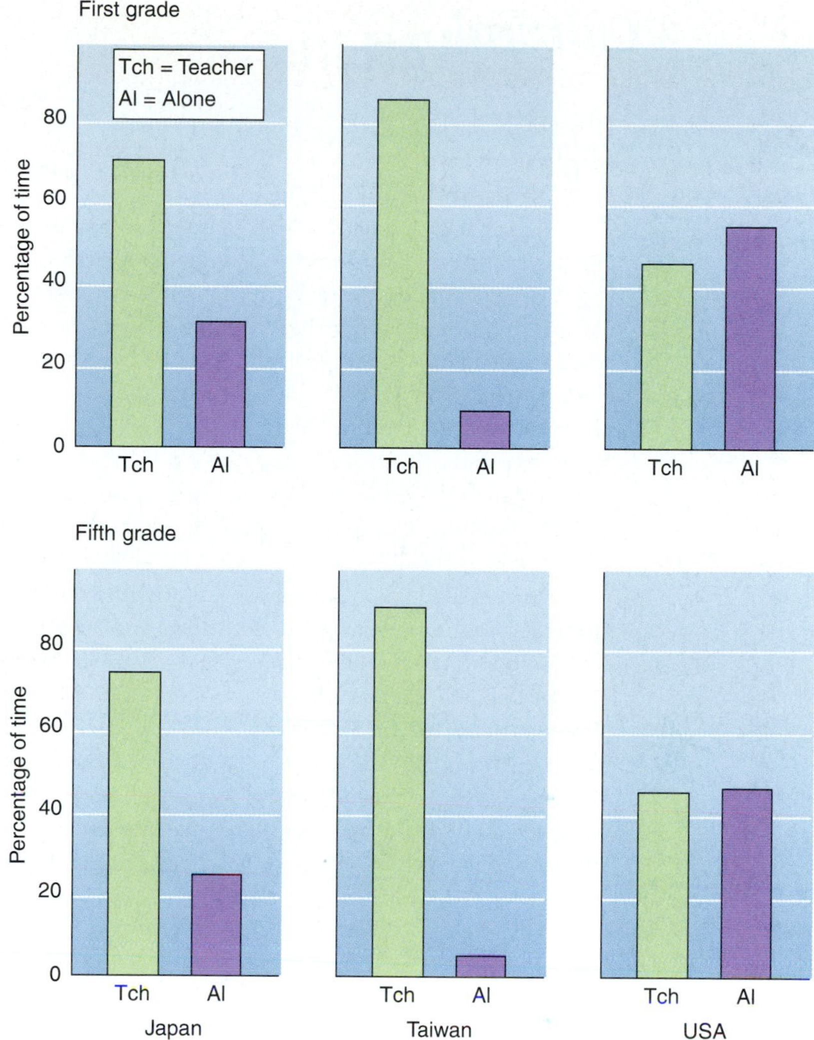

FIGURE 12.6 ***Percentage of Time Students Spent in Activity Led by Teacher and Alone***

Teachers' leadership and involvement with their students in the classroom is higher in Taiwan than in Japan or the United States.

From "How Asian Teachers Polish Each Lesson to Perfection," by J. W. Stigler & H. W. Stevenson, 1999, in *Child Growth and Development*, 69. From *American Education*, 1991, Spring. Reprinted by permission.

African Americans and Latinos

In general, students from Asian cultures outperform European Americans, and European American students outperform African American, Latino, and Native American students (Ginsberg, Choi, Lopez, Netley, & Chao-Yuan, 1997). The origins of these achievement level differences are unclear. John Ogbu (1997, 2000; Ogbu & Simons, 1998) argues that academic achievement levels can be attributed in large measure to whether students are from a "voluntary" or "involuntary" minority status. Ogbu classifies Asian American children as voluntary minorities and African American, Native Americans, and Latinos as involuntary minorities.

Voluntary minorities are those who have more or less willingly moved to the United States mainly because they expect better opportunities in terms of better jobs or more political/religious freedom than they had in their homelands. Voluntary minorities are likely to see themselves as part of the "American Dream" of achieving and becoming part of the mainstream culture. Some examples of voluntary minorities in the United States are immigrants from the Caribbean (Jamaica, Trinidad, the Dominican Republic), Mexico, Cuba, China, and India.

Involuntary minorities are peoples who have been conquered, colonized, or enslaved. Unlike voluntary minorities, involuntary minorities have been

Cultural Variations

Meet Miss Ying

The teacher walks in carrying a large paper bag full of clinking glass. Entering the classroom with a large paper bag is highly unusual, and by the time she has placed the bag on her desk the students are regarding her with rapt attention. What's in the bag? She begins to pull items out of the bag, placing them, one-by-one, on her desk. She removes a picture, a vase, and a bottle of beer. She soon has six containers lined up on her desk. "I wonder which one would hold the most water?" Interest is high and guesses from the children follow.

The students soon agree that to find out how much each container holds they will need to fill the containers with something. The teacher finds some buckets and sends several children out to fill them with water. When they return, the teacher asks, "Now what do we do?" Again there is a discussion, and after several minutes the children decide that they will need to use a smaller container to measure how much water fits into each of the larger containers. They decide on a drinking cup.

At this point the teacher divides the class into their groups (*han*) and gives each group one of the containers and a drinking cup. Each group fills its container and counts how many cups of water it holds. As each group reports, the teacher draws a bar representing the amount, in cups, the container holds. Finally, the teacher returns to the question she posed at the beginning of the lesson: Which container holds the most water? She reviews how they were able to solve the problem and points out that the answer is now contained in the bar graph on the board. She then arranges the containers on the table in order according to how much they hold and writes a rank order on each container from 1 to 6. No definitions of ordinate and abscissa and no discussion of how to make a bar graph preceded the example; these all became obvious in the course of the lesson and only at the end did the teacher mention the terms that describe the horizontal and vertical axes of the graph they had made (Stigler & Stevenson, 1999).

made to be a part of the U.S. society against their will. To illustrate, Africans were brought to the United States as slaves and, even after emancipation and desegregation, were perceived as inferior based on their ethnicity. As a result of military conflicts over land and territory between American Indians and European Americans, Native Americans were removed and transferred to reservations; Hispanics also were incorporated through conquest and displacement. John Ogbu (1992) argues that if your ancestors had been brought here as slaves or you had had your native land taken from you, then you would probably resist the values of the mainstream cultures, including being socialized or educated into those same values. The resistance to learning that characterizes the behavior of some involuntary minorities can be attributed in large measure to the discriminatory treatment they receive from society in general and from school in particular—all of which leads to lower levels of achievement (Lytton & Pyryt, 1998; Ogbu & Simons, 1998; Suzuki & Valencia, 1997). Children of involuntary minority groups may have few incentives for academic achievement and be adversely impacted by negative stereotypes of their groups.

Few Incentives for Academic Achievement

Children of involuntary minority groups may not consider the classroom a relevant domain for achievement. Incentives outside the classroom may gradually assume a greater value for these children, with a resulting decline in motivation for academic achievement. As such, many minority students may find it difficult to see the relationship between their efforts and the rewards that are available to them in U.S. society (Flynn, 1999). Many have become disillusioned and do not believe that continued diligence and devotion to their schoolwork will eventually enable them to advance their social and economic status. Perceived barriers imposed by a society that perpetuates inequality along ethnicity and class lines communicates to involuntary minority youngsters that there is little relationship between their efforts and eventual outcomes.

To illustrate, one study has shown that minorities distrust the schools, because these institutions do not deliver what they promise to their children (Ogbu, 1988). As a community, for example, minorities may experience a "job ceiling" regardless of their level of educational attainment. Ogbu (1997) argues that even though youths from involuntary minority groups may know that those with more education achieve greater occupational success in mainstream America, they still may reject the emphasis on academic achievement on two grounds: (1) they perceive that they must "act white" to achieve in this arena, and (2) many individuals in their own families are not perceived to be generously rewarded by their achievement efforts.

Negative Minority Stereotypes A further impediment to the achievement of students from involuntary minority groups is negative stereotyping. As we observe a classroom lesson in progress, from our observational point of view, everything may look the same in Mrs. Damascus' fifth-grade class. The teacher is the same; the textbooks are the same; and she appears to treat her students the same. But, is it possible that the children could experience the classroom differently? Could a Latino child perceive things differently from a European American child? How children perceive themselves in the classroom may be influenced by societal stereotypes that their peers hold. Drawings are a useful way to get children to represent some important notions they have about their particular ethnic perceptions.

If you asked a group of school-age children to draw a picture of a scientist, what would they draw? In examining cultural impressions of a scientist, 5- to 9-year-olds tended to include several standard indicators such as a white lab coat, eyeglasses, symbols of knowledge (books) and research (laboratory equipment), and even captions such as "Eureka!" (Chambers, 1993). A few girls depicted the person as a female; otherwise, males were drawn predominantly. Relatedly, in another study, a group of 8- to 12-year-olds rendered their artistic conceptions of a "smart person." Unequivocally, the artists' conceptions (blacks and whites, boys and girls) were of an adult male—most often white (see Figure 12.7) (Raty & Snellman, 1997). The results of both these studies suggest that elementary school-age children embrace discriminatory ideas of intelligence in our culture.

In related findings, Sandra Graham and her colleagues (Graham, 1997; Graham, Taylor, & Hudley, 1998) asked a mixed-ethnic sample of sixth, seventh, and eighth graders to nominate peers that they admired, respected, and wanted to be like. By identifying the peers, the researchers hoped to learn something about the characteristics that the students admired. African American, Latino, and European American girls consistently chose high-achieving female classmates of their own ethnicity. Those nominated were also seen as students who worked hard in school and followed the rules.

In contrast, the data depicted a more complex picture of achievement values among boys. Whereas European American boys valued male, high-achieving, same ethnicity classmates, African American and Latino males nominated low-achieving males (see Figure 12.8). Boys across all ethnic groups were remarkably consistent in nominating low-achieving minorities as not trying hard and as disobeying school rules. Other studies with multiethnic samples also found that African American and Latino boys valued academic success less than European American boys (Goodenow & Grady, 1995; Steele, 1997).

Paul Wachtel (1999) argues that a pivotal factor in lower achievement levels among African American students can be attributed to the impact of years of injustice on their confidence, attitudes, and opportunities to develop educational and occupational skills. Ethnic bias may be a factor as well. Charles Richman and his colleagues (Richman, Bovelsky, Kroovand, Vacca, & West, 1997) found that student teachers estimated the

FIGURE 12.7 ***Example of Drawing of an Intelligent Person***

U.S. children from all ethnic groups tend to draw an "intelligent person" as white, wearing glasses, and carrying a briefcase.

From "Children's Images of an Intelligent Person," by H. Raty & L. Snellman, 1997, in *Journal of Social Behavior and Personality, 12,* 773–781. Used by permission.

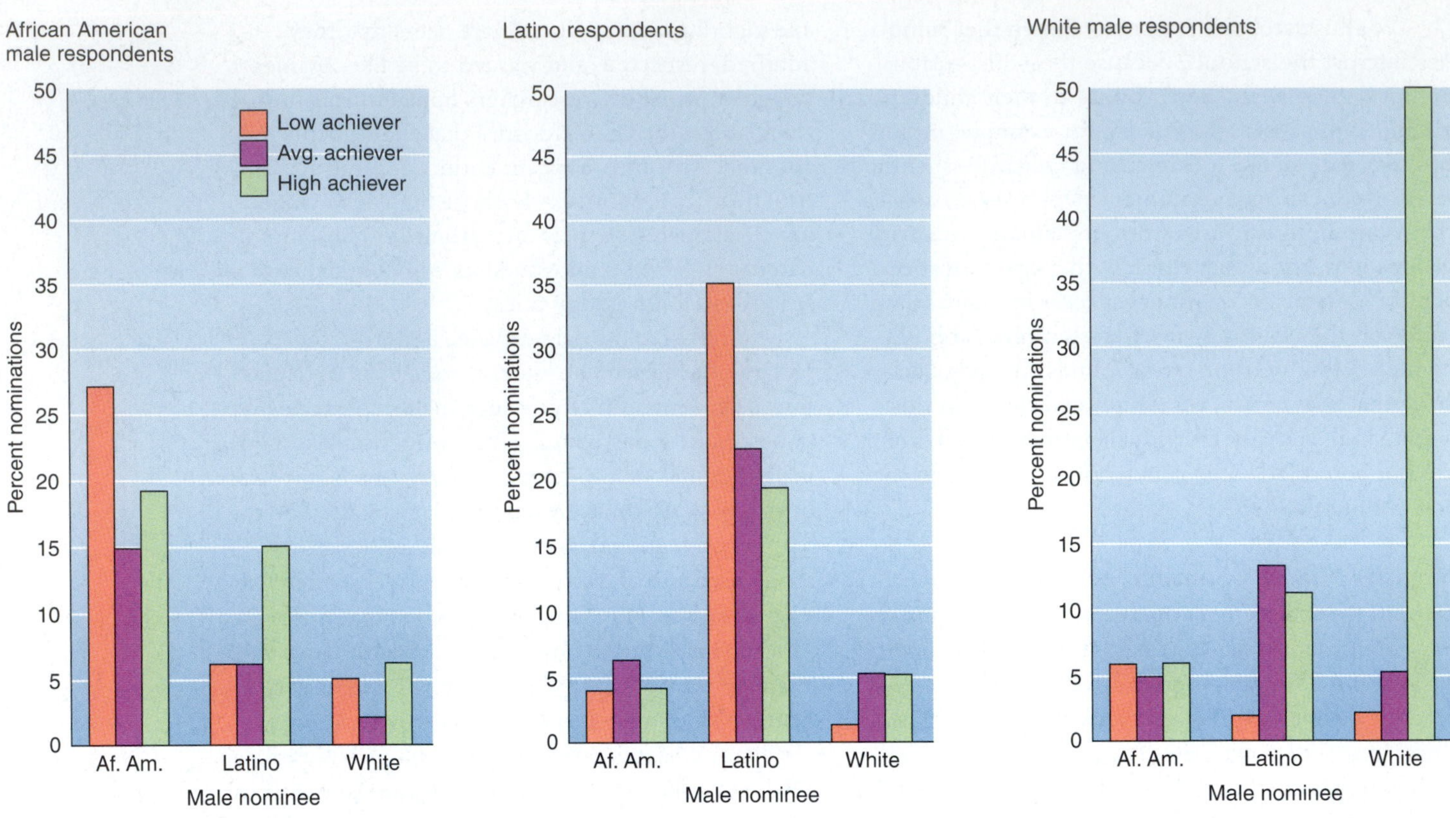

FIGURE 12.8 ***Peers Who Are Admired and Academically Respected***

In self-reports, European American respondents chose high-achieving white males as the most valued type of student, whereas African American and Latino males chose low-achieving males of their own ethnicity.

From "Exploring Achievement Values Among Ethnic Minority Early Adolescents," by S. Graham, A. Z. Taylor, & C. Hudley, 1998, in *Journal of Educational Psychology, 90,* 616.

GPA and IQs of African American children as being significantly lower than those of European American schoolchildren. According to the authors, these student–teacher attitudes were then translated into their evaluations of these students; they concluded that "old-fashioned racism" remains a fundamental problem affecting African Americans' achievement levels.

In addition, society often has lower expectations for academic success for minority males (Gibbs & Huang, 1998). As one African American parent notes, "I think low expectations are a major problem. From the beginning, society thinks that black children should achieve less. They put my child in a lower class, and then they have some idea that since you are black all you can do is run or do sports. This is nonsense. These are problems that we have to deal with in the black community." Thus, if society, in general, and parents and teachers, in particular, view minority children as less capable and hold lower expectations for these children, it follows that they may be less academically effective than European American children (Gibbs & Huang, 1998).

How do these negative stereotypes affect minority students? Claude Steele (1997) suggests that negative stereotypes about minorities hamper their academic achievement. To illustrate, John Ogbu (1986) reports an interesting fact: Among the castelike minorities in industrial and nonindustrial nations throughout the world (for example, the Maoris of New Zealand, the Baraku of Japan, the Harijans of India, the Oriental Jews of Israel, and the West Indians of Great Britain), lower academic achievement levels exist between them and the nonstigmatized members of their society just as they do between minorities and European Americans in the United States. What these groups share is a castelike status that, through negative stereotypes, stigmatizes their intellectual abilities.

All of these factors: low expectations on the part of others; inaccurate, rigid, exaggerated stereotypes; racism, prejudice, discrimination, and segregation exert a powerful and negative effect on academic achievement (Coll, Lamberty, Jenkins, McAdoo, Crnic, Wasik, & Garcia, 1998; Madon, Jussim, Keiper, Eccles, Smith, & Palumbo, 1998) often leading to chronic disengagement from school among African Americans and Latinos (Major, Spencer, Schmader, Wolfe, & Crocker, 1998).

APPLICATIONS: Multicultural Education

A fundamental problem for educators is that many involuntary minorities do not trust "white" institutions such as schools. As a result of discrimination and racism, many involuntary minorities have developed an oppositional identity to white mainstream society that makes them reluctant to cross cultural boundaries or adopt what they consider to be "white ways" of talking, thinking, and behaving because they fear doing so will displace their own minority identity and alienate them from their peers and family. The net result is ambivalence about the usefulness of school as a vehicle to success in life.

To help involuntary minority students succeed in school, the problem of the mistrust of schools and the fear of being seen as acting white (and the subsequent lack of effort) must be recognized and addressed. Culturally responsive instruction that fosters cultural pride, is culturally sensitive, teaches children how to accommodate without assimilating, builds trust, and utilizes role models of the same ethnicity may help to alleviate these problems.

Focusing on Success

Research on minority children and families has tended to focus on problems. Few studies have focused on factors related to the success of minority children. This central question of what factors distinguish African American and Latino children who are doing well in the cognitive and behavioral domains from those who are not has not been researched extensively. However, research findings do suggest that

Building positive ethnic identity helps children achieve academic success in the classroom.

minority children who are successful in school are more likely to come from homes and schools in which their cultural pride is fostered—not smothered (Baharudin & Luster, 1998; Garrison, Roy, & Azar, 1999).

In addition, successful minority children experience relatively supportive home environments; come from small families that have income levels above the poverty line; and have educated mothers who have high scores on intelligence and self-esteem measures. Other competence-promoting family processes are noted in Table 12.2. Clearly, however, more research on successful minority children is needed; in particular, more attention needs to be directed toward understanding the processes—activities, roles, relationships—in the family, school, and community that contribute to success in the academic setting (Hrabowki, Maton, & Greif, 1998).

Cultural Sensitivity

At my school, Lincoln Middle School in California, making us into Americans did not mean scrubbing away what made us originally foreign. The teachers called us as our parents did, or as close as they could pronounce our names in Spanish. No one was ever scolded or punished for speaking in his native tongue on the playground. Sometimes, we would talk to our class about Hispanic customs.

TABLE 12.2

Summary of Factors Associated with Academic and Psychosocial Competence

■ Caregiving support ■ Harmonious, engaged-family interactions with low levels of conflict ■ Firm parental control coupled with affectionate parent–child relationships ■ Religious affiliations ■ Parental monitoring of children's whereabouts	■ Continually high parental expectations ■ Open, consistent, and strong communication ■ Positive ethnic identification ■ Drawing upon community resources ■ Parental—particularly mother's—involvement with the child's school

> Miss Hopley herself had a way of expressing excitement when we talked about our families in Mexico. It made me proud. It was easy for me to feel that becoming a proud American, as Miss Hopley said, does not mean feeling afraid of being a Mexican.

Culturally responsive instruction in the classroom shows minority students that the teacher recognizes and honors their cultural and personal experiences and will help make school a less alien place. Teachers can learn about the students' cultures through observation of children's behavior in the classroom, asking them questions about their cultural practices and preferences, talking with parents about their cultural practices and preferences, and doing research on various ethnic groups with children in school.

Accommodation Without Assimilation

If involuntary minority students adopt "white" academic attitudes and behaviors, they may experience isolation from other black students, resulting in high psychological costs (Ogbu, 1992). An alternate model—accommodation without assimilation—roughly translates to "when in Rome, do as the Romans do, without becoming Romans." The essence of this model is that students recognize and accept the fact that they can participate in two cultural or language frames of reference for different purposes without losing their own cultural and language identity or undermining their loyalty to the minority community.

For African American students, for example, speaking standard English is a major characteristic of "acting white." Thus, as Ogbu (2000) suggests, acknowledging the validity of the use of black English in appropriate contexts can help students acquire standard English without seeing it as threatening their own language and ethnic identity. Students can be taught that different ways of speaking are considered appropriate in different situations. In school and in other formal situations standard English is expected and rewarded, whereas at home and out of school their own language is appropriate. Rather than trying to replace students' dialects with standard English, teachers need to encourage the use of code switching by showing them that appropriateness to the situation determines language use.

Building Trust

Many involuntary minority students come to school with an ambivalence about the value of education and about conforming to the demands of a "white" institution, so building trust needs to be the first priority of teachers (Ladson-Billings, 1994). Although it may not be an easy task to change the student's trust in "the system" as a whole, individual teachers can foster a trusting relationship between themselves and their students.

Role Models

Role models play an important part in student motivation to succeed in school. Role models provide students with an adult to admire and emulate. For many involuntary minorities, academically and economically successful role models are particularly important because they come from communities where, due to poverty and discrimination, there are not enough successful role models. Students need to be exposed through mentoring programs and other ways to members of their own groups who are academically and professionally successful and who retain their minority identity. Successful minorities who are seen as having abandoned their cultural identity to succeed in the "white world" will not be very useful role models (Ogbu & Simons, 1998).

As John Ogbu (1998) points out, it is not realistic to expect mainstream culture (schools, businesses, and professions) to change much. Thus, readjustments on the part of the less powerful are necessary. Inequalities must be corrected. Academic success for minorities,

TABLE 12.3

School-Wise Strategies

Strategy	Description
Optimistic teacher–student relationships	The prevailing stereotypes make it plausible for minority students to worry that people in their school environment will doubt their abilities. Thus, one wise strategy, suitable for all students, is to discredit this assumption through positive teacher expectations.
Challenge over remediation	Giving challenging work to students conveys respect for their potential and thus shows them that they are not regarded through the lens of an ability-demeaning stereotype.
Stressing the expandability of intelligence	The threat of negative-ability stereotypes is that one could confirm or be seen as having a fixed limitation inherent to one's group. Stressing the incremental view of the nature of intelligence—its expandability in response to experience, effort, and training—should help to deflect this implication of the stereotype.
Exposure to role models	Exposure to minorities who have been successful will help to carry the message that stereotype threats are not insurmountable barriers.

From "A Threat in the Air," by C. M. Steele, 1997, in *American Psychologist, 52,* 613–629.

however, does not just involve preparing children for school, it involves preparing schools for children as well (see Table 12.3).

Concept Checks

1. ***True or False:*** There is a positive association between computer use and academic achievement with heavy users of computers getting better grades.
2. Cite two reasons why Asian Americans tend to excel academically.
   a. ______________________________
   b. ______________________________
3. Part of the reason why girls do not do as well in math as their male counterparts is that
   a. boys have better spatial skills than girls.
   b. teachers and parents have low expectations of girls' mathematic abilities.
   c. girls do not like mathematics.
4. Miss Jacobs, a fifth-grade teacher, pays a great deal of attention to this student and often gives this student high praise for academic content. This student most likely is
   a. an Asian American female.
   b. an African American high-achieving male.
   c. a European American low-achieving male.

Children with Special Learning Needs

Before Beginning ...

After reading this section, you will be able to

- identify the strengths of mentally challenged children.
- note the possible characteristics of gifted and talented children.
- examine the symptoms of children with learning disabilities.
- discuss the characteristics of children with attention deficit hyperactivity disorder.
- recognize techniques for helping children with learning difficulties.

Mentally Challenged Children

Figure 12.9 shows the IQ ranges and the theoretical distributions of IQ scores. Below-average performances are on the left side of the curve and represent **mentally challenged children**. Mental retardation, or mentally challenged, is a label that describes a child's position in relation to other children on the basis of

mentally challenged children A label that describes a child's position in relation to other children on the basis of some standard of performance—usually an IQ test. The most common form of mental retardation is Down syndrome, in which the child's IQ is between 20 and 80.

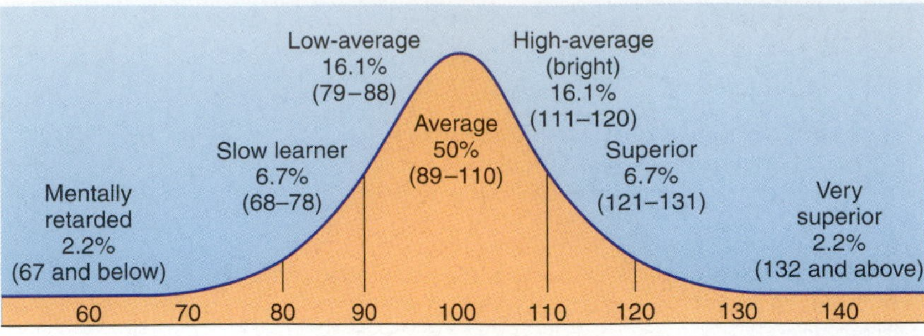

FIGURE 12.9 *The Bell Curve*

some standard or standards of performance—usually an IQ test. Children with Down syndrome, for example, usually have an IQ between 20 and 80; 45 to 55 is the average range. Down syndrome is the most common cause of mental retardation. The behavior of a Down syndrome baby is similar to that of any other baby during the first 6 months of life, but after this the child's rate of developmental advancement slows down (Drews, Yeargin-Allsopp, Decoufle, & Murphy, 1995). Although continuing to make developmental progress, the mentally challenged child does so at a slower pace.

Causes of Down Syndrome

Individuals with Down syndrome usually have 47 chromosomes instead of 46. The extra chromosome is responsible for the syndrome. All the chromosomes of a Down syndrome child are in pairs except the 21st pair—represented in triplicate and known as Trisomy 21. This extra chromosome affects many aspects of development, the most salient of which is a decreased rate of intellectual development. Chromosomal abnormalities represent the single most important class of genetic causes of mental retardation.

Assisting Mentally Challenged Children

Although having a mentally challenged child presents many challenges, the joys in raising these children counteract the challenges. Further, raising these children in loving and caring homes enables them to advance much further than those who do not receive this care. Those who work with these children are often constantly surprised by their self-help skills and general intellectual abilities.

gifted children Those who are generally in the top 3 to 5 percent of their class academically and have an IQ of 125 or above.

How family members cope is largely determined by how they perceive the mentally challenged child and their family situation. Families who have a positive perception of their child and his or her abilities make a much better adjustment and are able to take pleasure and pride in the special individual they are raising. If parents and others see mentally challenged children as hopeless and fear for their future, the children will do the same. If, however, they see their children as capable and able to meet the demands of life, their children will do the same (Hyche, Bakeman, & Adamson, 1992).

Gifted and Talented Children

At the age of 12 months, the British scientist and cousin of Charles Darwin, Sir Francis Galton (1822–1911), knew the alphabet. He could sign his name before age 3. His reading at the age of 5 was intelligent and not mechanical, as demonstrated by his ability to offer quotations that would fit a given situation. By 6, Galton had become thoroughly conversant with the Greek classical works the *Iliad* and the *Odyssey* (Galton, 1869/1978).

Identifying the Gifted Child

No doubt, Galton was a genius and his above-average performances would surely place his IQ on the right side of the curve in Figure 12.9. Children in this category are often described as **gifted children**—those who are generally in the top 3 to 5 percent of their class academically and have an IQ of 125 or above. (Some school districts use a cutoff of 125 to determine who gets into the gifted program, whereas others choose 145.) Three out of 100 children have IQs of 130, 1 out of 1000 has an IQ of 150, 1 out of 10,000 an IQ of 160, and 1 out of 100,000 an IQ of 168 or more (Runco, 1997).

Standardized testing and IQ tests with specific cutoff scores are not the only tools for identifying academically gifted students. A "multiple criteria approach" is now used to gather as much information as possible about the child from a variety of sources. Schools are likely to use group intelligence tests, individual IQ texts, standard achievement tests, and teacher nominations to identify gifted children.

None of these measures, however, is infallible. Because there is so much more to children than an IQ, many potentially academically gifted children may miss being identified by group or individual IQ tests. Similarly, with standard achievement tests, designed to measure knowledge of proficiency in something learned or taught, one's potential is not being measured. Finally, teachers may rely on such factors as how the children are dressed or their verbal skills in identifying gifted students and overlook creative divergent thinkers. Thus, the identification of gifted children requires the use of formal and informal measures obtained from many sources in a wide variety of settings (Subhi, 1997).

The saying "all children are gifted," may be true to a certain extent, but true giftedness is recognized by people other than parents and doting grandparents. Further, giftedness does not just apply to academically gifted children but to talents in other areas as well. Special talents are to be found in many domains: The composer Igor Stravinsky had special musical talents that were keenly sensitive to pitch, melody, rhythm, and tone; Pablo Picasso had spatial talents enabling him to perceive the world in unique ways and to re-create or transform aspects of that world; Albert Einstein had logico-mathematical skills, and his genius lay in his intelligence of numbers and the ability to handle chains of reasoning; and Mother Teresa had interpersonal gifts that gave her special abilities to understand people and be compassionate toward their plights.

Insight skills form particularly important criteria for identifying intellectual giftedness (Sternberg & Williams, 1995). Significant and exceptional intellectual accomplishments, such as major scientific discoveries, new and important inventions, and new and significant understandings of major literary, philosophical, and similar works almost always involve major intellectual insights. These thinkers' gifts seem to lie in their insightfulness and abilities to think in a nonentrenched manner rather than in their IQ-like abilities or their mere abilities to process information rapidly. Moreover, gifted children are generally superior in applying their intellectual skills to novel kinds of tasks and situations in general. Although precocious academic skills do not necessarily single out the gifted child, it is estimated that many gifted children read before coming to school (Young & Fouts, 1993). In most instances, the parents have provided little formal instruction other than pointing out the letters of the alphabet (Feldman & Piirto, 1995). Basic arithmetic skills also appear early. Many gifted children seem to possess remarkable memories. Gifted preschoolers are very curious creatures and ask endless questions; they appear almost driven to explore their environment. Gifted children usually read above grade level and have good memories and large vocabularies, long attention spans, and complex ideas. They are well-informed and curious, learn easily, understand relationships, and develop cognitive skills earlier than their peers (Walker, 1991).

Some gifted children exhibit early signs of their special talents; others do not. For neurologists, mathematicians, and to some extent sculptors, there are few early signs of children's extreme potential (Ackerman, 1997). However, swimmers, tennis players, pianists, and artists tend to have a special inclination toward their particular field before the age of 5 (Milbrath & Houston, 1998).

Encouraging Talented Children

Most adults do their best to bring forth and nurture the abilities and interests of talented and gifted children. Children with outstanding talent demand special efforts not only from parents but from teachers and society as well. What seems necessary in encouraging gifted children is a commitment to identify their talents early and to help systematically develop their talents (Dai, Moon, & Feldhusen, 1998). Although families of talented children cope with their children's giftedness

Some gifted children show early signs of their special gifts.

TABLE 12.4

Nurturing the Gifted Child

1. Provide a private place for creative work to be done. 2. Provide materials (for example, musical instruments, sketchbooks). 3. Encourage and display the child's creative work and avoid overevaluating it. 4. Do your own creative work and let the child see you doing it. 5. Value the creative work of others, attend museums, theater, and movies and talk about books and events.	6. Pay attention to what your family background, your family mythology, and your family system are teaching the child. 7. Avoid emphasizing sex-role stereotypes. 8. Provide private lessons and special classes. 9. Emphasize that talent is only a small part of creative production and that discipline and practice are important. 10. Enjoy your child.

From "Parenting Talented Children" (pp. 285–304), by D. H. Feldman & J. Piirto, 1995, in M. H. Bornstein (Ed.), *Handbook on Parenting.* Hillsdale, NJ: Erlbaum.

in various ways, a number of studies agree that a responsive set of adults and a family system that values achievement in the child's target domain are critical catalysts (Feldman & Goldsmith, 1991; Feldman & Piirto, 1995). Children become exceptional, then, through nature and nurture.

Adults are further advised to encourage children to be well-rounded, kind, and friendly (Robinson & Clinkenbeard, 1998). Adults should not overemphasize or continually label the child as "the gifted one" (Ackerman, 1997). When they do this, children have a tendency to form less favorable images of themselves; become more prone to stress, anxiety, and depression; develop social problems; and become conceited and less liked by their peers (Walker, 1991). Table 12.4 lists other ways in which adults can provide optimal environments for nurturing the creative talents of gifted children.

Children with Learning Disabilities

Jeff arrives home from a frustrating day in second grade, where he has struggled unsuccessfully to understand "borrowing." He bursts into tears as he crashes through the back door. His mother is shocked by his sudden explosion and rushes to put an arm around him. Jeff shakes her off and says, "There is something wrong with me. I can't do anything right. No matter how hard I try, I just can't. Why can't I be like the other kids?" Mother wishes she could answer his question. Jeff has had a complete physical. Everything, including vision and hearing, is fine. He has no physical handicaps, his IQ is 115, and the home environment is excellent.

learning disability
Refers to a specific disorder in language, perception, reading, spelling, writing, or mathematical reasoning.

Jeff cannot remember the alphabet. Julio's written work is riddled with spelling errors. Jason reverses letters and numbers, and his handwriting is almost unreadable. When Montgomery reads a paragraph in class he skips entire lines. All these children have a **learning disability**, which refers to a specific disorder in one or more of these areas: problems with language (technically know as *aphasia*); perception and reading (known as *dyslexia*); spelling and writing (*dysgraphia*); and mathematical reasoning or computation (*dyscalculia*). Dyslexia is by far the most common form of learning disability, accounting for approximately 80 percent of all learning-disabled children (Flynn & Rabar, 1994; Roush, 1995). Thus, *learning disabilities* is a generic term that refers to a heterogenous group of disorders manifested by significant difficulties in the acquisition and use of listening, speaking, reading, writing, reasoning, or mathematical abilities.

A few generalizations can be made from this definition. The learning disabilities concept provides a canopy coverage for all those children who are not performing as expected. The child with learning disabilities is affected in different areas of function not in a generalized inability to learn. There is generally a significant discrepancy between the child's estimated intellectual potential (in the average or above-average range) and their actual level of performance. These children are achieving considerably less than the composite of their IQ, age, and educational opportunity (Drake, 1997). Children who are severely brain damaged (mentally retarded, cerebral palsy) are not categorized as learning disabled. What are the characteristics and causes of learning disabilities? How can children with learning disabilities be helped?

Characteristics of Children with Learning Disabilities

Children with learning disabilities display difficulty in abstract thinking, have poor organizational skills, are unable to pick out significant information, have difficulty with concepts of right and left and time relationships, and have trouble getting their ideas on paper. These children generally lack good judgment. They make snap judgments, reach conclusions that do not follow from the facts, and fail to use problem-solving skills.

Causes

There are a number of complex and diverse causes of learning disabilities. Some forms of dyslexia may have a genetic basis. Parents of children with dyslexia, for example, may be dyslexic as well (Reeve & Kauffman, 1988). Further, children with dyslexia show chromosomal irregularities on chromosome 6 (Cardon, Smith, Fulker, Kimberling, Pennington, & Defries, 1994). Various forms of subtle brain damage have also been linked to learning disabilities. For example, it appears that children with delayed language or reading skills are unable to distinguish certain sounds such as "ga" or "da," suggesting that the child's brain simply does not register the difference between these sounds (Krause, McGee, Carrell, Zecker, Nicol, & Koch, 1996). Problems in learning are extremely diverse as are their probable causes; undoubtedly learning disorders are influenced by both biological, genetic, and psychosocial influences.

Helping Children with Learning Disabilities

Educational efforts for children with learning disabilities generally involve educational intervention. For example, they are taught visual, auditory, and perceptual skills that will enable them to solve problems more effectively. Further, educational intervention programs focus on improving the child's cognitive competence by improving their listening, comprehension, and memory skills. Finally, specific skills are targeted that will enable these children to compensate for specific problems that they may have in particular areas such as reading, mathematics, or written expression. For example, children with reading problems are taught how to re-read certain material and ask questions about what they read. Children with learning disabilities are not a homogeneous group; each child has his or her own developmental stage, personality structure, and needs. As Ann Marie Higgins, a learning disabilities professional, notes in the First Person insert, children's individual needs must be viewed and a program worked out that best meets these needs.

FIRSTPERSON

Working with Learning Disabled Children

Working with the learning disabled population has always fascinated me. It is rewarding and motivating to help someone understand that they can accomplish goals and that they are not stupid or ignorant. It is a wonderful feeling to see someone's face light up and say, "Oh, now that you did it that way, I get it" or "Is that all I have to do to get that answer?" Many learning disabled students are frustrated because they have had several years of school failure and they want to give up. Understanding, patience, creative teaching, and using a variety of learning tools can help these students feel the happiness of success.

I believe that one of the best things we can do to reflect what these children are all about is to change the label from "Learning Disability" to "Learning Different." A difference in how these children learn is what I have witnessed in the many years that I have taught them. One memorable experience helps to bring this point home. One of my students, a fifth-grade boy with severe visual-comprehension problems could not answer any questions about what he read. He could, however, comprehend things that he heard on television or on the radio. He was also a gifted singer and dancer. The class play that year was *The Wizard of Oz*. More than anything, he wanted to be in the play. After his audition, the director spoke with me and commented about his great voice and dancing abilities. She wanted to give him one of the leads but was afraid that he couldn't handle the script. I knew how important this was to the boy and told the director that somehow I would make it work. We put the entire script on a cassette. He learned not only his part but the entire cast's lines. He would even prompt fellow cast members during rehearsals. As the Tin Man, he stole the show on opening night. It was a very moving experience for me, knowing that no one in the audience was aware of his severe learning disability. They just saw a very talented entertainer in front of them.

A label such as "learning disabilities" carries negative connotations; a label such as "learning different" conveys children's potential for learning and academic success as long as they are taught in the manner in which they learn best. It helps teachers and parents focus on the child's strengths, and in turn, the child will also.

—Ann Marie Higgins

Attention Deficit Hyperactivity Disorder

attention deficit hyperactivity disorder A learning disability characterized by impulsivity, lack of attention, and hyperactivity.

hyperactivity A constant high level of activity in situations where it is clearly inappropriate coupled with an inability to inhibit activity on demand.

Danny, a handsome 9-year-old, has a great deal of energy and loves to play most sports. Academically his work is adequate, although his teacher reports that his performance is diminishing and she believes he would do better if he paid more attention in class. Danny rarely spends more than a few minutes on a task without some interruption. He gets up out of his seat, rifles through his desk, or constantly asks questions. His peers are frustrated with him because he is equally impulsive during his interactions with them. He never finishes a game, and in sports, he tries to play all the positions simultaneously.

TABLE 12.5

Diagnostic Criteria for ADHD

I. Symptoms of inattention
   1. Often fails to give attention to detail or makes careless mistakes
   2. Often has difficulty sustaining attention
   3. Often does not seem to listen
   4. Often does not follow through on instructions and fails to finish tasks
   5. Often has difficulty organizing tasks and activities
   6. Often avoids or dislikes tasks that require sustained mental alertness
   7. Often loses things
   8. Often is easily distracted
   9. Often is forgetful

II. Symptoms of hyperactivity/impulsivity
   1. Often fidgets or squirms
   2. Often leaves seat when remaining seated is expected
   3. Often runs about or climbs excessively in inappropriate situations
   4. Often has difficulty engaging in activities quietly
   5. Often talks excessively
   6. Often blurts out answers before questions have been completed
   7. Often has difficulty waiting turn
   8. Often interrupts or intrudes on others

III. At least 6 of 9 from category I or category II or both

IV. Additional criteria: Symptoms are
   1. Present for at least six months
   2. Of a degree that is maladaptive and inconsistent with development level
   3. Present before age 7
   4. Present in more than one setting
   5. Not due to pervasive developmental disorder, a psychotic disorder, or another mental disorder

From *Diagnostic and Statistical Manual of Mental Disorders* (4th ed., pp. 83–85), 1994, American Psychiatric Association, 1994 APA. Used by permission of the publisher.

Attention deficit hyperactivity disorder is a learning disability that consists of two clusters of symptoms: (1) inattention and (2) hyperactivity and impulsivity. **Hyperactivity** is a constant high level of activity in situations where it is clearly inappropriate coupled with an inability to inhibit activity on demand (Towell, 1997). Because of their inattention, hyperactivity, and impulsivity, these children's academic performance tends to suffer, especially as they progress in school. They do not listen to others, may lose school assignments, and make careless mistakes. They are always fidgeting, have trouble sitting for any length of time, blurt out answers before questions have been completed, and have trouble waiting their turn. Indeed, in hyperactive children, something is always moving. They are incessantly pulling, twisting, bending, and manipulating. They never appear to run out of energy. They seem compelled to react to all stimuli and are unable to respond only to appropriate stimuli. They appear to be distracted by sights, sounds, or ideas that are interesting and significant for them but irrelevant to the main objective of the moment (Greenspan, Wieder, & Simons, 1998).

Either the first (inattention) or the second (hyperactivity and impulsivity) cluster must be present for someone to be diagnosed with ADHD. Table 12.5 provides the diagnostic criteria for children with ADHD.

Children with ADHD tend to exhibit these symptoms in many different settings, but the intensity of the symptoms varies across settings. Symptoms can vary with environmental structure, sensory stimulation, and the emotional state of the child, as well as with physiological factors such as general alertness, hunger, and sleep deprivation (Colin, 2000). Most children experience more environmental pressure at school than at home, and the "overflow" into hyperactivity and impulsivity is particularly clear in the classroom (Hales, 1996).

Causes and Prevalence

ADHD research has been plagued with controversy; however, researchers do say with great certainty that this disorder is biological and inherited (Landau & McAninch, 1993). Suspicions that a diet high in sugar might cause hyperactivity have been dismissed. But the influence of genes is unmistakable. It is estimated that

40 percent of ADHD kids have a parent who has the trait and 35 percent have a sibling with the problem; if the sibling is an identical twin, the chances rise to 80 to 92 percent (Wallis, 1994).

The number of students diagnosed and treated for attention deficit hyperactivity disorder has increased dramatically, by some estimates doubling between 1990 and 1995 (Young, Young, & Ford, 1997). Given the prevalence of this disorder, approximately 1 in every 20 students will have ADHD (Vallano & Slomka, 1998). The estimated male to female ratio is 9 to 1 (American Psychiatry Association, 1994; Sandberg, 1996). Approximately 85 to 90 percent of ADHD children are taking stimulant medication to control their behavior. The use of Ritalin (or its generic equivalent, methylphenidate) has more than quadrupled; from 1996 to 2001, prescriptions rose more than 390 percent (Klin, Volkmar, Sparrow, & Cicchetti, 1996). Approximately 9.4 million prescriptions were written for Ritalin in 1998 up 6.1 million from 1993. This means that as many as five million children are taking the drug (Widener, 1998).

The child with ADHD exhibits inattentiveness, impulsivity, and hyperactivity.

ADHD and Ethnicity

ADHD is the most common behavioral disorder in U.S. children. However, of the thousands of articles on ADHD, only 16 were identified that dealt with ADHD in African American and Latino youths (Samuel, Curtis, Thornell, George, Taylor, Brone, Biederman, & Faraone, 1997). A handful of studies have shown that ADHD was identifiable in cultures as diverse as Taiwan (Li, Copeland, & Martin, 1995) and Sharjah, Arabia (Bu-Haroon, Eapen, & Brener, 1999). The limited cross-cultural and ethnic studies do concur on one point—the disorder is more prevalent in boys than girls (Bu-Haroon et al., 1999; Keogh, Gallimore, & Weisner, 1997).

APPLICATIONS:

Helping Children with ADHD

Stimulant drugs remain the best-known therapy for ADHD. Typically, the goal of biological treatments is to reduce the children's impulsivity and hyperactivity and to improve their attentional skills. Though Ritalin is the most popular choice, some children do better with Dexedrine or Cylert or even certain antidepressants. About 70 percent of children respond to the stimulants. Surprisingly, these uppers, in the correct dosage, make children slow down. Ritalin, for example, appears to reinforce the brain's ability to focus attention during problem-solving tasks (Mattay, Berman, Ostrem, Esposito, Van-Horn, Bigelow, & Weinberger, 1996). Although the use of stimulant medication remains controversial, most clinicians recommend them temporarily, in combination with psychosocial interventions, to help improve children's social and academic skills.

Drugs, along with behavior modification, appear to be very effective treatment methods. Behavior modification teaches parents how to help their child gain more control over his impulsive and restless energy. Response cost strategies, which are typically directed at limiting impulsive responding and enhancing selective attention and task maintenance behaviors, have been helpful (Vallano & Slomka, 1998). The child is taught how to internalize a self-guidance script, much like learning to talk to himself and advise the appropriate behavior—"Don't blurt out an answer; wait until the teacher calls on you." Other strategies involve self-monitoring skills, which are designed to reduce impulsivity. These include training in strategies that foster self-evaluation, for example, by helping the child recognize instances of on-task (paying attention) and off-task behavior (interrupting) and choosing to engage in the former not the latter.

Behavior Beyond Their Control

Mavis Donahue (1997) advises adults to remember that so much of the irregular and often irritating impulsive behavior that these children exhibit is beyond their control. Recognizing that the child is not merely being rebellious and uncooperative helps produce positive changes in attitude toward him. Further, one can expect great variability in the child's day-to-day performance. A bit of knowledge or skill apparently mastered one day may be completely strange to the child the following day.

Environmental Management

Environmental management of sensory stimulation is beneficial to ADHD children (Hales, 1996). Thus, it is suggested that the child's environment should be as free from too much stimulation as is reasonably possible. At home, this may mean using soft, neutral colors on the child's bedroom walls rather than wallpaper with a busy design. Parents also need to establish a quiet place in the home for the child. Toys should be kept in the closet when not in use, and only one friend should visit at a time. Supermarkets and malls should be avoided (Hales, 1996). When asking the child to do something, the adult needs to give the child short, simple directives. To teach the child a new activity, break it into simple, sequenced steps. The child may need to go over and over these steps until the actions become a habit.

Hyperactive children pay too much attention to too many things (Evans & Docking, 1996). They are overwhelmed with stimuli, such as the number of words, numbers, or problems found on one page of printed material so, their worksheets need to be clear and simple. Similarly, the environment should be simplified and structured in such a way as to produce a predictable, regimented, consistent everyday life pattern for the child. Such routinization becomes a stabilizing influence for the child (Palumbo, 1996).

Sequencing Activities

At home, scholars advise establishing a definite sequence of activities starting when the child wakes up in the morning. It is also suggested that adults provide some definite warning as a signal to get ready to move to the next activity. The child may then be adequately prepared for any change in routine or for new experiences. Children can be taught the fine art of being organized by establishing a predictable schedule of activities, learning to use a date book, and assigning a location for possessions at school and at home (Blum & Mercugliano, 1997). Praise, most agree, is vitally important.

Understanding Inconsistent Behavior

It may be easy for parents and teachers to conclude that some children with ADHD who have average or above-average intelligence are simply lazy and could do better academically if they just tried harder (Weisz & Tomkins, 1996). Consequently, these children may be continually pressured by increasingly irritated and exasperated adults to improve a situation that they are unable to change. As a result, emotional or behavioral problems may compound the child's already existing learning disability. When adults try to understand and accept this inconsistent behavior, children sense this and it does much to relieve their anxiety and insecurity.

Looking Beyond

Finally, adults need to look for the special talents in children with learning disabilities. The sculptor Rodin, and Harvey Cushing, the famous brain surgeon, had dyslexia. Thomas Edison never did learn to spell, and his grammar and syntax were appalling. Woodrow Wilson was 13 before he learned to read. Albert Einstein failed the entrance examination for college. Abbott Lowell, president of Harvard from 1909 to 1931, was hyperactive, had no visual memory, and spelled the way he heard words. And finally, William James, psychologist and philosopher, could seldom recall a single letter of the alphabet.

Concept Checks

1. Down syndrome
   a. may be related to family variables.
   b. indicates anoxia at birth.
   c. indicates a biological abnormality.
2. An important criterion for being identified as someone with intellectual giftedness is
   a. the ability to process information rapidly.
   b. applying intellectual skills to novel situations.
   c. physical precocity.
3. The most common type of learning disability is ____________________.
4. You are a professor of special education. What would be one thing you would want your students to understand about children with attention deficit hyperactivity disorder? Why is that important?

Refinements in Language Development

Before Beginning ...

After reading this section, you will be able to

- discuss the refinements that occur in language development during the school-age years.
- examine improvements in the pragmatics of children's language.
- understand the positive effects of laughter.

By age 7, what amazing little linguists children have become. Their language is so well established that there are few deviations from the adult norms. Those deviations tend to be more in style than in grammatical capabilities. By middle childhood, children have mastered the syntax of their language and have a rather extensive vocabulary. They pluralize nouns, specify verb tenses, include prepositions like *on* and *in*, and inject the articles *a* and *the*. Six-year-olds know about 10,000 words, but, by the end of middle childhood, their vocabulary will expand to over 40,000 words. These children seem to be in love with words—rhyming words, using words in an unusual way to form a secret code, and impressing others with their big words are exciting for them.

The process of language refinement continues until the age of 10 and probably considerably longer for most children. Learning about grammar continues until adolescence in two areas: comprehension of increasingly complex grammatical structures using conjunctions (although, since, unless) and comprehension of structures in which some sentence elements are embedded, such as, "The lady who came to sing was funny" (Bates & Elman, 1996). The normal child's use of these constructions may begin at an early age, but he or she may not have full control until age 10 to 12.

Moreover, the child uses such words as *because, so,* and *but* to signal subordinate clauses. This kind of language use is indicative of the presence of complex syntactic rules, and it is not fully developed until adolescence although its beginnings can be seen in 3-year-olds. Despite these tremendous advances over a few short years, children in middle childhood do have some language limitations. For example, they take all statements literally and tend not to understand figures of speech. If we say something like, "The cat's got her tongue." the child may think that the cat is literally holding the child's tongue.

Understanding Sarcasm

Children do not always understand sarcasm (Dews, Winner, Kaplan, & Rosenblatt, 1996). A remark that may be obvious sarcasm to you may not be so obvious for the younger school-age child. Some studies (Winner, Kaplan, & Rosenblatt, 1989) show that by the age of 8, children are able to understand the intended meaning in sarcastic utterances in some instances. A complete understanding of sarcasm actually requires a couple of complex ideas. First, children have to understand that the speaker did not intend what was said literally but rather intended to convey a meaning quite different (often opposite to his literal meaning). Children also need to be able to interpret contextual and intonational cues.

Children, even in middle childhood, tend to rely more heavily on intonation than context to help them infer the intent of the speaker (Shwe, 1999). This may account for their less than 100 percent accuracy in identifying sarcastic speech (Capelli, Nakagawa, & Madden, 1990). Adults tend to use both cues. For example, you and your roommate oversleep and are late for class; you arrive at class and find that you will be taking a pop quiz. Further, after class a friend informs you that he could not get you tickets for a concert. Your roommate then turns to you and says, "This is turning out to be a great day." This is a contextual cue. The second important cue is intonational, in which someone making a sarcastic remark uses a characteristically mocking tone.

Pragmatics of Language

In middle childhood, children become increasingly aware of the pragmatics of language, or the rules specifying when to say what and to whom to communicate effectively. They become more adept at varying their way of talking to teachers, peers, and parents. They display a greater use of gestures, pauses, and facial expressions. In addition, they are more adept at adapting information to fit the listener's needs and adopting the listener's point of view, if the situation warrants it. Pragmatic abilities and social editing skills evolve rather gradually over the course of childhood as new social contexts are encountered. With this increase in communication skills, and more advanced abilities to process information, children in middle childhood also develop a rather sophisticated sense of humor.

Children's Sense of Humor

> Professor of physics Dr. Max Wiebe and his wife are sitting at home. He's working on lecture notes and she's reading Hegel. She remarks, "God, it's cold in here!" He replies, "Dear, when we're alone, you can call me Max."

Although we all seem to recognize a sense of humor when we see it, no one seems to agree on how to define it. Does a sense of humor characterize one who laughs a great deal? One who is witty? One who is easily amused? Perhaps a sense of humor is best described as a smiling attitude toward life. However we define it, humor is one of the greatest gifts we have. Children's laughter offers a window into their heads and their hearts. Most of us love to hear children's laughter for its joy, but we also are intrigued by what they think is funny. Younger children, for example 2-year-olds, think it is funny when they call something by its wrong name. They find great mirth in pointing to a dog and calling it a "cat." Young school-age children overrely on appearance; a picture of an elephant in a tree is very amusing. Children in late middle childhood become capable of understanding more abstract and implied incongruities and not just those that can be immediately perceived (Bergen, 1998).

During middle childhood, children become capable of understanding verbal humor based on the double meaning of a word, which not only involves knowing both meanings of that word but also the ability to keep one meaning in mind while shifting to the other. They begin to use puns. They also discover ambiguity in words, which is linked to being able to enjoy riddles and jokes that are based on double meanings.

APPLICATIONS:

The Gift of Laughter

> "Okay! I've had enough! Tomorrow I'm not going to school anymore, and I'll give you two good reasons: The kids hit me and the teachers are nasty to me."
>
> "I'm sorry, but tomorrow you will go back to school, and I'll give you two good reasons: You're 48 years old, and you're the principal."

Some of you may be laughing or at least smiling. If you are not laughing, you undoubtedly will laugh at jokes of another sort. For example, the following is a direct quote from a church bulletin:

> Thursday at 8 P.M. there will be a meeting of the Little Mother's Club. All those wishing to become Little Mothers will please meet the minister in his study.

Jokes such as these provoke different reactions: "That's funny." "It's infantile." "I fail to find it amusing." Humor is a matter of perspective and perception, and the best way to judge the degree of a person's enjoyment is to examine his or her laughter. Most children, however, appear to be laughing all the time. Just listen to children playing around your home or at the playground. You will hear almost nonstop laughter punctuated with shrieks of delight. Some adults laugh frequently as well—although not as frequently as children; and others laugh rarely.

Development of Laughter

Infants' first laugh occurs around the age of 4 months and is connected mainly with tickling. A fun game of "peek-a-boo" can arouse laughter in an 8-month-old. Unsuitable behavior on the part of an adult (such as drinking from the baby's bottle or walking on all fours) will cause laughter in a 1-year-old. Laughter and smiling in kindergarteners are associated with enjoyable experiences, and they accompany the main social activity of children—play.

Children in early middle childhood find incongruity extremely funny—a picture of a horse walking away leaving human footprints behind is a real side-splitter to young children. As children's mastery of language becomes more sophisticated, they experience instant mirth when another child uses words in an incorrect fashion. Aggressive humor occurs in middle childhood as well. For children, sources of frustration—parents, teachers, siblings, and other children—become the brunt of many jokes. Aggressive humor takes on many forms, from direct and insulting attacks to a clever, gentle play on words. It is often directed at expressing hostility toward those whose position enables them to dictate what children can and cannot do. All of these sources of humor are quite different from adults', which prompted Freud (1916) to comment that children do not have a sense of humor.

Humor Is More Than a Laughing Matter

Functions of humor seem remarkably similar across the world and in many situations. In a wide variety of cultures, people use humor to foster relationships, exert social control, release frustration, and, returning to Freud, approach the subject of sex in a socially acceptable way (Du Pre, 1998). Sexual humor becomes very much a part of children's jokes in late middle childhood (Veatch, 1998).

Humor is created and enjoyed because it allows us to express all these fundamental needs (aggressive, sexual, social, intellectual) in socially acceptable and pleasurable ways. But laughter appears, for the most part, to have a positive, physical effect on our systems—a cathartic, almost releasing effect (Rothbart, 1996). Just writing this section has put me in happy spirits—at least more so than discussing phenotypes and genotypes with you. Darwin (1809–1882) stated that laughter derives from the excitement of pleasure and affects our physical systems in positive ways: "Circulation becomes more rapid; the eyes are bright, and color of the face rises. The brain is being stimulated by the increased flow of blood, and increases our mental powers" (1872/1965, p. 32).

Laughter makes us feel better physically (Martin, 1998). Laughter actually stimulates the production of catecholamines, which stimulate the production in the brain of endorphins, the body's natural pain-reducing enzyme. Humor may also serve as a coping mechanism when we have to deal with the pressures and frustrations of everyday life. It was found that when taking blood samples from participants every 10 minutes (a stressful situation), cortisol levels dropped significantly among those subjects watching a funny video but not among the no-video control group (Berk, Tan, Fry, Napier, Lee, Hubbard, Lewis, & Eby, 1989). The hormone cortisol is typically secreted by the body during stress, and excessive amounts are believed to suppress immune functions. Thus, laughter may be capable of counteracting the negative effects of classical stress. Moreover, subjects who report having a healthy sense of humor also list fewer health problems than subjects reporting a poor sense of humor (Carroll & Shmidt, 1992).

Humor also has an intellectual function, exemplified by the phrase "learned with laughter is learned well." In the educational setting, laughter may lead to better retention of educational material, or, at the very least, arouse the attention of students who are beginning to fade away. Further, varied forms of humor may uniquely impact teacher–student rapport.

The desire to laugh as well as to transmit humor is an important characteristic in each of us; you are not only a social being but a pleasure-seeking one as well. Individuals with a good sense of humor are quick to laugh in commonplace situations, tend to judge themselves by less harsh and rigid standards, enjoy a more stable and positive sense of self, and can more effectively deal with life's frustrations (Kuiper & Martin, 1993).

Concept Checks

1. ***True or False:*** Although vocabulary increases during middle childhood, more words are learned during the preschool period.
2. Children in late middle childhood would most likely tell jokes that are ______________ in nature.
3. One of the positive functions of laughter is that it
   a. actually aids in stimulating the production of endorphins (pain-reducing enzymes).
   b. does not seem to be an aid in remembering educational material.
   c. is innate and necessary for our survival.

Thought **CHALLENGE**

Sexual expression has become more liberal in our society. Consequently, has the need to look for roundabout and hidden means of sexual expression in the form of sexual humor gradually weakened?

Reviewing Key Points

The School Child's Thinking Skills

- To Piaget, concrete operational thinkers are conservers; that is, they realize that quantity remains the same despite perceptual transformations. Concrete thinkers are able to classify objects and know that a superordinate class is always larger than any of its subordinate classes. Their thinking becomes decentered and they are capable of reversing thought.
- There is a developmental trend toward deliberate use of memory strategies during middle childhood. Compared to early childhood, school-age children engage in more active systematic rehearsal, process information more deeply, organize it more richly, and store more relevant features in long-term memory.
- Effort (the time and energy expended on studying); an internal locus of control (an individual's sense that his or her own efforts and activities influence success); and more success than failure are three factors that have an important influence on children's academic success.

Technology, Culture, and Achievement

- A preference for playing violent video games appears to be linked with aggressive behavior. Prosocial behavior diminishes as a result of playing violent video games. Violent games aside, computers and less aggressive video games can positively impact on spatial abilities, perceptual speed, and eye–hand coordination.
- Girls may be treated differently from boys, which may perpetuate stereotypical behaviors of being dependent, nonassertive, and not doing well in mathematics and science. Teachers tend to prefer high-achieving males, have higher expectations for their success in mathematics and science, praise boys for content, and encourage them in more risk-taking.
- To bridge the gender gap, it is recommended that parents and teachers encourage girls to take math, science, and technology courses; have higher expectations for their success in these areas; and help teachers become aware of possible gender biases.
- Involuntary minority children's generally lower achievement in the academic setting may be related to stress and insufficient incentives provided by the educational system and society to achieve. Higher levels of success among children from Asian cultures are attributed to time spent and effort expended, high parental expectations, a more egalitarian educational philosophy, and effective teaching.

Children with Special Learning Needs

- Children with IQs of 80 or lower are categorized as mentally challenged. The most common form of mental retardation is Down syndrome. The syndrome is most often caused by a condition known as Trisomy 21. Mentally challenged children can be helped to be more productive in society, when adults teach them life skills and treat them with respect.
- Gifted children, those who have an IQ of 125 or higher, are divergent thinkers, have special insight skills, and are superior in dealing with novel kinds of tasks and situations in general. Children are not just gifted academically but may be talented in other areas as well—the arts, sports, and interpersonal gifts. Children become exceptional through nature and nurture.
- Children with learning disabilities are affected in different areas of function, not in a generalized inability to learn. The most common form of learning disability is a reading difficulty known as dyslexia. The chief characteristics of children with attention deficit hyperactivity disorder are constant motion, impulsivity, and inattention.
- Children with learning difficulties can be helped by controlling the level of stimulation in the environment, sequencing their activities, recognizing that their behavior is beyond their control and is inconsistent, and establishing routines.

Refinements in Language Development

- Vocabulary increases are more rapid in middle childhood than they were in the preceding preschool period. By the end of this period, children know about 40,000 words. Children pluralize nouns, specify verb tenses, include prepositions, inject articles, use conjunctions, and subordinate clauses. Their speech matches adult norms in terms of grammatical capabilities.
- Children in early middle childhood have a hard time understanding sarcasm. They tend to take all statements literally. Their sense of humor centers on incongruities and double meanings of words.
- Children in middle childhood are perfecting their sense of humor. Humor is enjoyed because it allows children (and adults) to express fundamental needs such as aggression, sexual, social, and intellectual. Laughter has both physical and psychological benefits.

Answers to Concept Checks

The School Child's Thinking Skills

1. b 2. c 3. b 4. a

Technology, Culture, and Achievement

1. true
2. time spent, effort expended; high parental expectations, more egalitarian classroom, teachers
3. b
4. b

Children with Special Learning Needs

1. a
2. b
3. dyslexia
4. A number of responses may be offered, such as characteristics (impulsivity, hyperactivity, inattention); effective teaching strategies (behavior modification); or understanding their behavior is beyond their control. The important point is understanding why knowing this information will help adults work more effectively with ADHD children.

Refinements in Language Development

1. false 2. sexual 3. a

Key Terms

attention
attention deficit hyperactivity disorder
classification
class inclusion
computer-assisted instruction (CAI)
concrete operational thinker
conservation
convergent thinking
creativity
decentration
divergent thinking
external locus of control
gifted children
horizontal decalage
hyperactivity
hypertext/hypermedia
internal locus of control
learned helplessness
learning disability
levels of aspiration
mentally challenged children
perception
reversibility
simulations
word processing

InfoTrac College Edition

For additional readings, explore InfoTrac College Edition, your online library. Go to **http://www.infotrac-college.com/wadsworth** and use the passcode that came on the card with your book. Try these search terms: computers and children, hidden curriculum, mentally disabled children, attention deficit hyperactivity disorder.

Child Development CD-ROM

Go to the Wadsworth Child Development CD-ROM for further study of the concepts in this chapter. The CD-ROM also includes quizzes and additional activities to expand your learning experience.

CHAPTER THIRTEEN

Socioemotional Development: *Middle Childhood*

CHAPTER OUTLINE

Understanding Self and Others
- Changes in Self-Systems
- Friendships
- Group Acceptance: Popular Children
- Group Difficulties: Neglected Children
- Group Difficulties: Rejected Children
- Stability of Peer Adjustment
- Consequences of Peer Relationships
- Applications: Helping Children with Peer Difficulties

Moral Development
- What Is Morality?
- Piaget's Theory of Moral Development
- Kohlberg's Theory of Moral Reasoning
- Applications: Promoting Morally Competent Behavior in Children

Family Influences in Middle Childhood
- When Parents Divorce
- Single-Parent Families
- Blended Families
- Applications: Helping Children Adjust in Single-Parent and Blended Families

Reviewing Key Points

Do not tell a white lie unless necessary.

Do not hurt anyone in any way.

Do not hit anyone except Ronny.

Do not tell a black lie.

Do not use words worse than "brat."

Do not curse at all.

Do not make faces except at Ronny.

Do not be selfish.

Do not make a pig of yourself.

Do not tattle except on Ronny.

Do not be a sneak.

Do not destroy other people's property, except Ronny's.

Do not be grumpy, except to Ronny.

Do not answer back, except to Ronny. (A secret club of third-graders. *New Yorker*, September, 1954)

Membership in a group is structured within a hierarchy, ranging from those accorded the highest status to those, like Ronny, at the bottom of the popularity poll. To determine a child's status in the peer group, sociometric assessment procedures, such as the peer nomination method, are frequently used. These measures rely on children's perceptions of others and can identify children's "rankings" within the peer group.

The children in Mrs. Cattell's third-grade class write their responses to the following questions:

Name three people you would like to	*Name three people you would* not *like to*
invite to your birthday party.	invite to your birthday party.
sit next to.	sit next to.
work on a book report with.	work on a book report with.

No one named Ronny as their most liked classmate and 15 out of 23 children cited him as their least-liked classmate. Is this a cause for concern? How important is group acceptance? An impressive number of studies say "very important." So important, that at any age level, a feeling of belonging is essential to functioning effectively. Interpersonal relations play such an important role in children's lives that they may be regarded as a barometer of their level of adjustment to life in general. Children who are liked by others do better in school, have more positive feelings about themselves, are happier, and exhibit higher levels of adjustment.

An equally impressive number of studies conclude that there are strong connections between poor peer relations and maladjustment. The strongest associations between peer difficulty and adjustment are found in the prediction of early school withdrawal, delinquency, and mental health problems. These are some compelling reasons for understanding friendship systems in middle childhood, the focus of the opening section of this chapter.

We then turn to moral development in middle childhood. Piaget's and Kohlberg's theories offer insights into how children think about rules and proper "moral" ways of behaving. Kohlberg, in particular, studied the moral justifications given by children for acting in certain ways when encountering various moral dilemmas. Who do you think is more influential in promoting higher levels of moral reasoning—parents or peers? Piaget's and Kohlberg's answers to this question may surprise some of you.

Our concluding section examines divorce, single-parenting, and blended families and the factors that facilitate children's positive adjustment in each of these family situations. Families today represent a number of different family structures. No longer do first-time marriages with a father, a mother, children and a dog named Spot predominate. Half of all marriages end in divorce. However, the popular image that all family members will experience divorce in a similar fashion, and that the experience is always negative, is not correct.

Understanding Self and Others

Before Beginning . . .

After reading this section, you will be able to

- characterize changes in children's self-systems.
- discuss children's conceptions of friendship during middle childhood.
- analyze the characteristics, causes, and consequences of peer acceptance and peer difficulties.
- note the possible ways of helping socially incompetent children.

Changes in Self-Systems

During middle childhood, children's self-concept increases from superficial descriptions to a multidimensional view of themselves. Physical qualities, motor skills, sex type, and age are the hallmarks of young children's self-descriptions. By middle childhood, children are capable of distinguishing among various domains of competency, such as academic achievement, athletic prowess, peer popularity, physical appearance, and behavioral conduct. They also have a better understanding of personality traits as internal dispositions that are manifested in diverse behavior. Older children begin to perceive themselves as persons with complex personalities (Harter, Waters, & Whitesell, 1998). Consider, for example, the following self-descriptions reported by Eddie, age 5, and Lisa, age 9.

> My name is Eddie. I am 5 years old. I live in a white house with my mom and dad and one sister. I have dark brown hair and brown eyes. I can count to 50. I like coloring. I am happy not sad. I go horseback riding every Wednesday and I am very good. I have lots of toys. I like milk to drink and lemonade. I like meat to eat and potatoes as well as meat. I am very strong. Want to see my muscles?
>
> I am Lisa, and I am a 9-year-old African American. I am a quick worker but am sometimes lazy. I am good but often mischievous and naughty. My behavior is sometimes silly, sometimes serious. I am smart in English—I got an A on my report card in English. I don't like math—other kids do better than I do. Other kids like me, so I guess I am popular and that's important to me.

The self-attributes of the younger child are based on concrete, observable behavior (brown eyes and hair; can count to 50). Particular skills are emphasized (good equestrian; strong), which often spill over into actual demonstrations (want to see my muscles). The young child also defines self in terms of preferences (I like to color; I like milk and lemonade) and possessions (I have lots of toys). The young child's self-descriptions often translate into characteristics that can be observed by others.

The older child, in contrast, is more likely to use generalizations in describing self such as "mischievous," "smart," and "popular." Similarly, the older child often provides justification for these self-labels (smart because I got an A in English). Also indicative of children in middle childhood is that one's relationships with peers (I am popular and that's important to me) and ethnicity (I am an African American) become salient dimensions in self-descriptions. According to many researchers, ethnic identity is part of a positive self-concept that consciously anchors children to a particular ethnic group (Dasgupta, 1998). Central to this identity is a sense of belonging, as well as a commitment to the group's values, beliefs, behaviors, and customs.

Another developmental shift can be seen in the way older children experience conflicting behaviors or emotions. Lisa, for example, can be silly and serious (two opposing self-affects) and smart and yet have difficulty with math (opposite attributes). These changes tend to occur between the ages of 7 and 8 (Harter, 1996). Before the age of 7, children are unable to describe the self in terms of conflicting behaviors or traits; for example, Eddie is just happy and not capable of experiencing opposite attitudes or behaviors (Eder & Mangelsdorf, 1997).

Comparing Self to Others

In middle childhood, children spontaneously and more thoughtfully compare their capabilities and attributes with those of their peers ("smarter than most kids in my class"; "faster than Jimmy") to determine how well they measure up (Thompson, 1999). Because few children excel in all aspects, social comparison fosters a more differentiated awareness of personal strengths and weaknesses.

Not until age 9, however, is the information provided about other children used consistently and systematically (with remarks such as "I must be pretty good because I beat all the others"). According to Diane Ruble and Jacqueline Goodnow (1998), children under the age of 7 use social comparison information only to judge appearance and action, whereas older children are capable of evaluating competence and ability and will therefore make a point of seeking out any comparative data that throw light on their own status.

Social Self-Conceptions

Social self-conceptions make their appearance during the school-age years. Social self-descriptive terms identify a child in terms of family and peer relationships ("I have a mother who works"; "I am quite popular with other kids"). These are frequently mentioned qualities in middle childhood and may be extended to the child's feelings of belongingness to particular groups and organizations such as a school, a gang, or a church. As can be see in Figure 13.1, the importance of physical and activity characteristics to children decreases rapidly in importance during middle childhood. Up to early adolescence (ages 11–13), the most significance is attributed to social characteristics. Interpersonal relationships are perceived as constituting the core of self—a finding that helps to explain why children in late middle childhood become so distressed when such relationships are damaged or terminated.

Developmental Shifts in Self-Esteem

A final developmental shift involves the manner in which self-esteem manifests. Susan Harter (1996) suggests from her research findings that it is not until

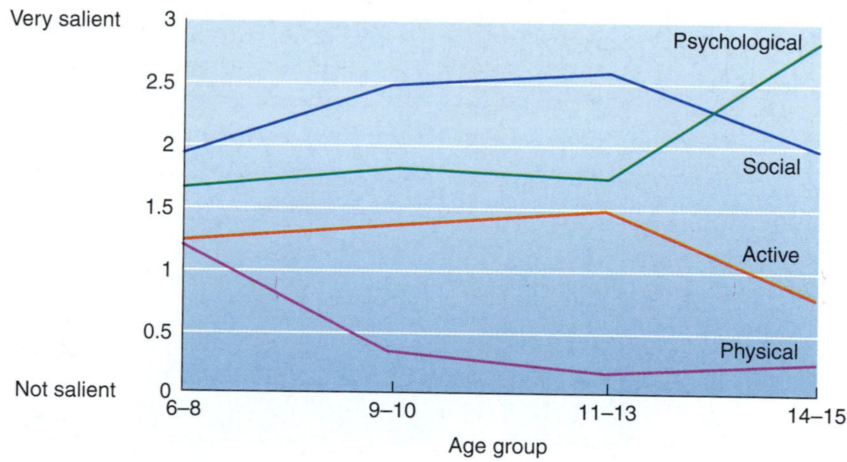

FIGURE 13.1 *Average Salience Scores for Four Sets of Self-Descriptive Characteristics at Different Age Levels*

As children get older, psychological and social traits play an increasingly important role in evaluating their self-esteem.

From "Judgments About Personal Identity in Childhood and Adolescence," by D. Hart, S. Fegley, Y. H. Chan, D. Mulvey, & L. Fischer, 1993, in *Social Development, 2,* 66–81.

© Myrleen Cate/PhotoEdit

Social self-comparisons become part of the self-system in middle childhood: "I am popular with other kids."

around the age of 8 that children develop a concept of their overall worth as a person. It is also around this time that children begin to solidify their self-pictures and to resist any changes that disturb their self-system; they move to an evaluation of "me" in terms of stable personality traits (Harter, Waters, & Whitesell, 1998). Once children's self-esteem begins to jell, they tend to behave in accordance with their preconceived impressions of themselves. Their behavior must always be consistent with their self-evaluations (Baumeister, 2001).

Consistency of Self Any value entering the self-system that is inconsistent with individuals' evaluation of themselves will not be assimilated (Bandura, 1997). If a child's evaluation is that he is a poor speller, for example, and he receives a good grade on his spelling test, he may resort to a number of things to "reject" this information, because it is inconsistent with that particular self-evaluation. He may say that the words on this test were so easy that anybody could have gotten a good grade or that he was just lucky this time.

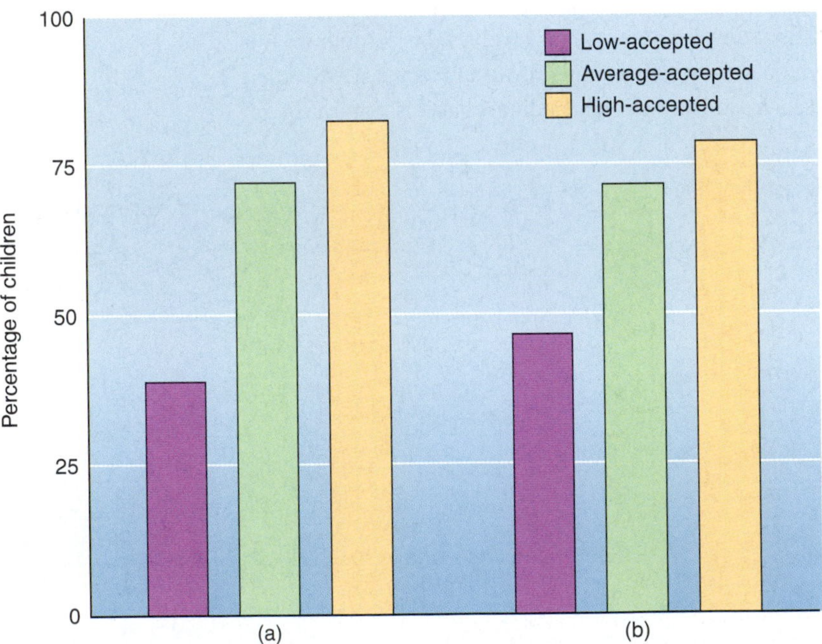

FIGURE 13.2 ***Perceptions of High-, Average-, and Low-Accepted Children Who Have a Best Friend***

(a) From "Friendship and Friendship Quality in Middle Childhood: Links with Peer Group Acceptance and Feelings of Loneliness and Social Dissatisfactions," by J. G. Parker & S. R. Asher, 1993, in *Developmental Psychology, 29*, 611–621. (b) From "The Relationship Between Children's Social Goals, Social Strategies, and Friendship Adjustment," by A. J. Rose, 1995. Unpublished master's thesis. Urbana, IL: University of Illinois, Urbana-Champaign.

Friendships

Peer status plays a key role in forming positive or negative concepts of self. **Peer acceptance** refers to a child's inclusion in the group as a whole; **friendship** refers to the establishment of a particular dyadic relationship between two children characterized by strong mutual liking, a mutually expressed preference for one another, and a sense of shared history. Researchers suggest that friendships and peer acceptance are sufficiently independent to make them of separate interest (Parker & Asher, 1993). There are children who are well accepted yet lack best friends in school, and conversely there are some poorly accepted children who do have close friends. Figure 13.2a shows the relationship between acceptance and friendship for a sample of children in third through fifth grades. Figure 13.2b shows this same relation for a sample of fourth- and fifth-grade students. Both studies make clear the particular independence of the two dimensions.

The Benefits of Friendship

"Me and Diana can count on trusting one another. Yesterday, me and Diana talked about how our parents got a divorce. We share our deepest, darkest secrets; talk about boys; and go shopping."

"Me and Alexis act like we're cousins. We play a lot together. She comes over to my house a lot. Alexis comes and talks with me when I'm sad. She says we are best friends. I help her with homework. She helps me with my homework. And we play a lot together."

TABLE 13.1

Functions of Friendship
1. Friendships are contexts in which children can acquire or elaborate basic social skills like communication and cooperation.
2. They provide children with self-knowledge as well as knowledge about other people and about the world.
3. They give children emotional support in the face of stress.
4. They are forerunners of subsequent relationships (romantic, marital, and parental) in that they provide experience in handling intimacy and mutual regulation. (Hartup, 1998)

These quotes from fifth-grade girls suggest the richness and complexity of friendships. Some of the benefits parallel those of group acceptance or inclusion but are experienced in a more intensive form. Friendships can be beneficial when children are cooperative, their friends are prosocial, and each member of the dyad socializes the other in prosocial directions. Other benefits of friendship are summarized in Table 13.1. Friendships can also be a source of frustration because of the inevitability of conflict between friends (Meyer, Park, Grenot-Scheyer, Schwartz, & Harry, 1998). Friendships can be harmful when children are antisocial and aggressive and behave in maladaptive ways (Haselager, Hartup, van Lieshout, & Riksen-Walraven, 1998).

Conversely, lack of friendship can lead to some rather lonely consequences (see Table 13.2). For some children, friendlessness may be a temporary state. In these situations, children may experience feelings of loneliness, but it is unlikely that lasting emotional problems will result from temporary states of friendlessness (Schaffer, 1998).

Defining Who Friends Are

Between the ages of 6 and 8, children define friends as those individuals who share their worldly goods, act nice, and are fun to be with (Selman, 1980). The relationship is seen as momentary and transient with little individuality associated with a friend; that is, "all friends are the same." The child focuses on specific acts performed by the friend that meet the child's wishes. Friends are important because they perform something children want done ("You need a friend because you want to play games"). A close friend is one who is known better than others. Knowing someone better means knowing his or her likes or dislikes, which children feel is necessary before making friends.

TABLE 13.2

Conditions Associated with Friendlessness	
Children without friends are more likely to ▪ Have emotional problems ▪ Lag behind other children in perspective-taking skills ▪ Be less altruistic	▪ Have deficiencies in such social skills as group entry, cooperative play, and conflict management ▪ Be generally less sociable ▪ Show poorer school adjustment ▪ Make fewer educational gains

Between the ages of 8 and 10, friends are defined as people who help one another, either spontaneously or in response to an expression of need. The two most central features of this level are trust and reliability. In this stage, the child can take a relativistic perspective and see that each party has a set of likes and dislikes that need to be coordinated. Conflicts occur between parties rather than being caused by one person. Both parties must engage in resolution. The basic limitation, however, is that the child still feels that the solution to the problem should be self-serving. Friends are important because everyone needs a companion. Trust implies someone you can tell a secret to and it will be safely stored away.

Between the ages of 10 and 12, children are able to simultaneously consider the viewpoints of both the participants in a conflict. They are aware of their own unique feelings but also recognize that others may have unique feelings.

> "Do girls of your age have any interest in boys?"
> Kyra: No, not really. We don't like boys. They're basically annoying.
>
> "Do boys of your age have any interest in girls?"
> Seth: No. Other guys would say, "You're friends with a *girl!*" Girls are okay; sometimes they can be nice, but mostly they're dorks.

Cross-sex friendships are relatively rare in middle childhood; in most studies they account for about 5 percent of the friendships. The sex of a friend is a very important consideration for children; more so than ethnicity (Graham, Cohen, Zbikowski, & Secrist, 1998).

Throughout the early and middle elementary school grades, same-sex friends remain constant, but mixed ethnic friendships increase (Graham & Cohen, 1997). However, African American and Latino children tend to be more accepting of European American children than the reverse. Cross-ethnic evaluations, however, tend to be generally quite positive. Even when children develop cross-ethnic friendships, myriad barriers obstruct those relationships and social supports (Townsend, 1998). Specifically, these children have

peer acceptance Refers to a child's inclusion in the group as a whole.

friendship Refers to the establishment of a particular dyadic relationship between two children characterized by strong mutual liking.

© Mary Kate Denny/PhotoEdit

Same-sex friends remain constant during middle childhood, and interracial friendships increase.

reported difficulty in maintaining those friendships in settings outside of school. Distance, lack of organized extracurricular activities, and self-perceived social skills deficits are included among barriers in nurturing cross-ethnic friendships in nonschool settings (DuBois & Hirsch, 1993).

In describing the most important characteristics of good friends, Latinos emphasize relational support, Asian Americans emphasize a caring, positive exchange of ideas, African Americans emphasize respect and acceptance, and European American children emphasize recognizing the others' needs (Garcia & Rivera, 1999). Boys and girls from all ethnic groups, however, choose loyalty as another major element in friendships. Friends are expected to stick up for and be loyal to each other (Azmitia, Kamprath, & Linnet, 1998).

Describing One's Friends

Consider the difference between the following two children's accounts of friends:

> (7-year-old): He is very tall. He has dark brown hair; he goes to our school. I don't think he has any brothers or sisters. He is in our class. Today, he has on a dark orange sweater and jeans and tennis shoes.
>
> (12-year-old): Nate is even shyer than I am when near strangers and yet is very talkative with people he knows and likes. He always seems good-tempered and I have never seen him in a bad temper. He tends to degrade other people's achievements and, yet, never praises his own. He does not seem to voice his opinions to anyone. He easily gets nervous.

Several differences immediately become apparent. First, the younger child's account is briefer and less differentiated. It is also stated in absolute terms, lacking the comparative statements ("even shyer than I am") contained in the second child's description. The older child is able to make allowance for different circumstances (for example, shy with strangers but talkative with well-known people); in addition, this boy introduces gradations ("tends to") into his judgments and acknowledges uncertainty ("seems to"). Above all, however, personal qualities are almost wholly absent from the younger child's account: the individual is described in terms of physical appearance and clothes rather than the psychological attributes on which the older boy focuses. We see here the same developmental trend that was noted in children's self-descriptions—that is, the trend that proceeds from a primarily concrete to an increasingly abstract descriptive style. The developmental trends of social cognition are summarized in Table 13.3.

Making and Keeping Friends

Does it take special skills to make and keep friends? Steve Asher (Asher, Parker, & Walker, 1998) suggests that there are certain social tasks that are unique to making and keeping friends. The first task is maintaining the "spirit of equality" of friendship. In friendships, children must participate as equals and be able to maintain reciprocity and balance in the relationship. The second task is helping a friend when the friend is in need. The third task involves being a reliable partner to a friend. Children need to be available for their friends consistently rather than sporadically. Children also need to learn how to amicably solve a problem when a conflict of interests occurs (a friend wants to talk about a problem when the other friend has homework to complete). The last task involves managing a friendship in the larger social context of the classroom and peer group. This means being able to coordinate multiple friendships and deal with issues such as exclusivity and jealousy. Managing best friends may be more difficult for girls than for boys because girls, significantly more than boys, tend to structure their friendships around triads (Azmitia, Kamprath, & Linnet, 1998).

> See, what happened is that I was best friends with Jacqueline and Marilyn for a very long time, and then all of a sudden they started ganging up on me. I couldn't do anything about it, even after I decided that talking to them about it wouldn't

TABLE 13.3

Three Developmental Stages of Social Cognition

Stage	Description
1	Up to the age of about 7, children describe others in terms of external characteristics—their looks, their actions, their possessions, and where they live. If they do refer to psychological aspects, they use global terms such as nice or good; however, these are employed egocentrically ("nice to me") and refer to here-and-now behavior, with no indication that they may represent lasting dispositions.
2	From age 7 or 8, children show a marked increase in the use of trait terms (shy, anxious, clever) in their accounts of other people. They continue to describe visible features but now assume that behind the external facade there are psychological qualities that transcend here-and-now behavior. Traits, however, are merely listed; they are not integrated into an overall personality organization, and allowance for different circumstances remains rare.
3	In late middle childhood/early adolescence, qualifying terms, such as "sometime" or "quite," appear; judgments are made relative to situation and circumstances; and there are attempts to resolve contradictions within the context of the individual's total personality. Increasingly, people are also assessed in comparative terms, whether in relation to other individuals or to some general standard adhered to by society. (Selman, 1980)

> make them stop. They even told everyone that I was a terrible, mean person; and they didn't talk to me anymore.

Why are girls so often cruel to their best friends? Sociologists have suggested that girls' experience with "lack of power" often turns one girl against her best friend (Morley, 1992; Skevington & Baker, 1989). They suggest that girls often feel powerless and helpless in many arenas of their lives, and when they do encounter a situation, such as convincing others to freeze out their friend, they exercise their power. Friendship, then, is an arena in which girls feel that not only do they not have to compete with boys, but that even when they do, they wield more power.

It is not that boys do not engage in physical aggression or derogate their friends in public. Boys' retaliation, however, tends to last only a few days, and then they are back to being best friends (Azmitia, Kamprath, & Linnet, 1998).

Group Acceptance: Popular Children

> Everybody in sixth grade wants to be friends with Gabe, even though he makes fun of most of them all the time. But they still all want to pick him on their team and have him be friends with them because he's a good athlete, even though he brags a lot about it. He's popular.

> It's just that she has a lot of money, so it's like that's why she has the prettiest clothes, and, you know, the prettiest hair. And she thinks that she's the prettiest girl in the whole school—just because she's blond and all the boys like her.

Who are the **popular children**? What determines a child's status in the popularity poll? What determines a child's acceptance or rejection? There are modest but statistically significant relationships between prosocial behavior (helping, sharing) and peer acceptance and between antisocial behavior and peer rejection.

Characteristics of Popular Children

Social competence appears to be related to a similar set of behaviors. During the early school years, popular children tend to display a high degree of social competence, such as seeking out peers and initiating and sustaining positive interactions with them; forming ties or relationships with peers; achieving positive or rewarding qualities within these relationships; and avoiding debilitating peer-related emotional states such as loneliness, anxiety, or wariness (Ladd & Le Sieur, 1995). Social popularity and peer acceptance in later elementary grades is related to athletic or extracurricular competencies for boys and attractiveness for girls (Hartup, 1996, 1998). Popular children are leaders, trendsetters, and socially outgoing; and the other children often follow their rules and norms (Bukowki, Newcomb, & Hartup, 1998).

Cross-culturally, varying characteristics positively correlated with peer acceptance. Xinyin Chen and his colleagues provide one example in their comparative study of peer relationships in Canada and China (Chen,

popular children Often engage in prosocial behavior, are seldom aggressive, and are able to pick up on the emotions of others and how their behavior is affecting other children.

social competence Refers to a set of skills that collectively result in successful social functioning with peers.

Rubin, & Sun, 1992). In their Shanghai sample, they found that shyness (as opposed to social boldness) in 8- to 10-year-old children was associated with higher peer acceptance and positive teacher ratings of social competence. This was opposite to the relationship generally found in European and North American settings. At age 12, however, the relationships in their Chinese sample reversed in part; shyness-sensitivity became associated with peer rejection (Chen, Rubin, & Li, 1995), consistent with findings in Western samples. The authors explain that earlier ratings were consistent with the value in Chinese culture placed on the soft-spoken, well-mannered, school-achieving child, whereas the later similarity across samples may reflect the rise in the influence of peers among that age group.

Group Difficulties: Neglected Children

neglected children Children who receive little attention from their peers but are not necessarily disliked by their peers.

Unpopular children fall into two very different categories: rejected and neglected children. The former are actively disliked; the latter may not be popular but they are not disliked. As can be seen in Table 13.4, the three main groups of the children—popular, neglected, rejected—are characterized by distinct behavioral profiles.

TABLE 13.4

Behavioral Profiles of Popular, Rejected, and Neglected Children

Child	Behavioral Profile
Popular	Positive, happy dispositions Physically attractive Lots of dyadic interaction Willing to share Able to sustain an interaction Seen as good leaders Little aggression
Rejected	Much disruptive behavior Argumentative and antisocial Extremely active Talkative Frequent attempts at social approaches Little cooperative play, unwilling to share Much solitary play Inappropriate behavior
Neglected	Shy Rarely aggressive, withdraws in the face of others' aggression Little antisocial behavior Not assertive Lots of solitary activity Avoid dyadic interaction, spend more time with larger groups

© Will Hart/PhotoEdit

Children who are leaders in the United States often display assertiveness toward others. In many other cultures, such as the Japanese and Chinese, however, leaders are those who display sensitivity toward others.

Neglected children, who seldom interact, garner very little in the way of liking or disliking in the peer group; they are simply "overlooked" by their peers. They receive few peer nominations of any kind, and thus, the defining characteristic of this group appears to be lack of "noticeability." Neglected children tend to display less aggression (Sanson, Pedlow, Cann, & Prior, 1996) and engage in more solitary play (Coie, 1990). They tend to receive fewer social overtures from peers than more sociable children. Neglected children tend to exhibit more egocentric speech and direct more of their utterances to imaginary companions or inanimate objects (Rubin, LeMare, & Lollis, 1990). They are less mature, less assertive, and more compliant or deferential. Neglected children are more likely to report feeling lonely and socially dissatisfied than the other groups of children. They report the least companionship from best friends and also report the lowest perceived social competence. Neglected children tend to display a generally negative pattern of self-perception, including low efficacy and low social expectations. They are often characterized as shy and withdrawn.

Shy children exhibit *overcontrol*—they are more likely to socially withdraw from others. Shy children are outwardly submissive, never show signs of anger, have few friends, and appear lost in a nonreal world. Not all shy children are "disturbed," and headed for disaster, however (Asendorpf, 1998). In fact, in some cultures, shyness is a sign of social competence as noted in Cultural Variations.

Neglected children are often shy children and are generally overlooked by the other children.

Causes for Withdrawal

Some researchers believe that shyness is not something that children are born with, but rather, that it is a learned phenomenon. Some of the factors that may cause shyness in children are difficulties in school; unfavorable comparisons with older siblings, relatives, or peers; loss of usual social supports that result from frequent family moves out of the neighborhood or from sudden changes in social bonding due to divorce, death, or going to a new school; and lack of experience in social settings. Table 13.5 highlights other factors that may contribute to children developing shy behavior.

Other researchers conclude that biological factors predispose children to display either shy or inhibited behaviors (Kagan, 1997; Kagan, Snidman, & Arcus, 1998). Robert Plomin (1998) asserts that heredity plays a larger role in shyness than in other personality traits. Shy children tend to experience an unusually intensive physical response to mental stress, indicating that their sympathetic nervous system is aroused. For example, when young children were exposed to specific social situations—such as episodes of free play, stranger modeling of doll activities, a talking robot, or brief separation from their mother—extremely shy children had significantly higher heart rate variations than uninhibited children. Further, these very shy children, under stressful situations, tended to have high levels of the hormone cortisol, which may produce changes in the amygdala—the brain structure implicated in emotions such as fear—intensifying their fearfulness (Schmidt, Fox, Rubin, & Sternberg, 1997). Higher levels of cortisol triggered a state of heightened bodily arousal to cope with the challenging situation. This arousal state was reflected in a number of measurable changes, including increased blood pressure, muscle tone, and pupil dilation (Balaban, Snidman, & Kagan, 1997).

shy children Nonassertive, they tend to be uncomfortable around strangers; they prefer solitary activities.

TABLE 13.5

Causes for Shyness

Cause	Description
Physical factors	Some forms of shyness are motivated by physical weaknesses. Frail children with poor physical stamina may resist attempts to push them into active participation with others. In such cases, shyness is a defense mechanism; it helps them avoid strenuous activities that they feel unable to undertake. Sometimes physical factors, such as braces or being overweight, can cause feelings of shyness.
Overemphasis on competition	Shyness in the United States may be a result of cultural norms that overemphasize competition, individual success, and personal responsibility. Adults may encourage shyness in children by adhering to these traditional values of individual achievement, aspiration, and social approval as the primary measures of self-worth. These pressures for individual achievement may be greater for firstborn children.
Fears	Some shy children may be overwhelmed by all kinds of fears: school, failure, or rejection from their peers, and a general fear of the future.
Emulating shy parents	A common reason for shyness in children is that they are simply copying their parents' shyness. Children with shy mothers tend to be more shy than children with more sociable mothers. (Chung & Doh, 1998)

Cultural Meanings of Social Behavior

Culture imparts meanings to social behavior; determines how adults and children perceive, evaluate, and react to the behavior; and eventually regulates and directs the developmental processes of social behavior (Chen, Hastings, Rubin, Chen, Cen, & Stewart, 1998). To this end, there are some interesting discrepancies in the cultural meaning of social behavior.

What types of social behaviors are valued in the United States? Most of us are likely to describe well-liked children as outgoing, self-assertive, and friendly. As such, we encourage our children to be assertive and independent in challenging situations. In contrast, shy and withdrawn behaviors signal relationship difficulties and are regarded as reflecting internal fearfulness and a lack of self-confidence and are not encouraged by caregivers (Rubin, Coplan, Nelson, Cheah, & Lagace-Seguin, 1999).

Behaviors, however, that may be highly valued in Western cultures may not be likewise evaluated in others. In China, Indonesia, Thailand, and Korea, for example, shyness is positively valued and considered adaptive. Behaviorally inhibited children are called *Guai Hai Zi* in Mandarin, which means "good" and "well-behaved" (Chen, Rubin, & Sun, 1992). These children are the recipients of their caregivers' positive values and emotions. Inhibited behavior is considered to reflect social maturity and understanding; and thus, the sensitive, shy, cautious, and behaviorally restrained children are the most popular, and, according to parents, teachers, and peers, shy-sensitive children are the most well-adjusted and competent children (Chen, Rubin, Li, & Li, 1999). Moreover, the extent to which inhibited behavior is exhibited by children varies across countries as well. Children in China, for example, tended to be more cooperative and less likely to engage in conflict than were U.S. children (Attili, Vermigli, & Schneider, 1997).

Psychological meanings vary across cultures in other behaviors as well. A study found a preference for power, assertiveness, directedness, and aggressiveness in the Israeli culture (Krispen, Sternberg, & Lamb, 1992). Relatedly, in southern Italy, aggressive behavior in children was seen as increasingly accepted as a means to negotiate interpersonal exchanges (Casiglia, LoCoco, & Zappulla, 1998). A "jolly friend" was profiled as sociable, exuberant, and ready to make friends; a "leader", however, was described as aggressive, engaged in disputes, and was generally oppositional to the actions of others. Relatedly, Italian preschoolers engaged in significantly more disputes than the young children studied in the United States (Corsaro & Rizzo, 1990). Both Israeli and Italian children tended to associate aggressiveness with sociability and leadership. Aggression was not seen as a developmental risk as it is here in the United States; on the contrary, it might be considered a resource in positive social relationships.

The implications of these findings are that social traits, such as shyness or aggression, may be reflected in the social behavior of children according to their cultural desirability. Both behavioral inhibition in East Asia and aggressive behavior in Italy and Israel were more prevalent in these cultures than in the West. Further, behaviors regarded as adaptive or maladaptive varied from culture to culture and consequently, behaviors that might predict rejection in some cultures might predict peer acceptance in others.

Group Difficulties: Rejected Children

rejected children Actively disliked by their peers. Some rejected children are aggressive and some are nonaggressive.

One day a fourth-grade teacher intercepted a note that was being passed up and down the rows in class. The note read, "If you hate Graham, sign here." The note was about to reach Graham's desk, and all the children had signed! Approximately 10 to 15 percent of children, like Graham, have serious peer relationship problems at school (Asher & Rose, 1997). **Rejected children** tend to be conceited, disruptive, and silly. Additional attributes of the low-acceptance child are anxiety, excessive emotional dependence on adults, uncertainty, bitterness and sarcasm toward others, withdrawal or aggression, and social indifference. Further, rejected children are likely to be low achievers in school and to experience learning difficulties (Asher, Parker, & Walker, 1998).

Perhaps the group of children that causes the greatest concern are those who exhibit high amounts of aggression (French, 1990). These **rejected-aggressive children** display a greater number of adjustment problems—evidenced by high levels of anxiety and behavioral and academic difficulties—than any other peer-status group (Rubin, Coplan, Nelson, Cheah, & Lagace-Seguin, 1999). Rejected-aggressive children exhibit *undercontrol*—they are more argumentative, disruptive, inattentive, and imperceptive and less prosocial (Bierman, Smoot, & Aumiller, 1993). Undercontrol is one of the major reasons for treatment referral during middle childhood (Farrington, 1991). Why do some children develop these annoying ways of behaving that alienate them from other children?

Factors Leading to Aggressive Behavior

Aggression is defined here as a sequence of behaviors with the intent of bringing injury to the person toward whom it is directed (Segall, Dasen, Berry, & Poortinga, 1999). Aggression differs from assertiveness, with which it is often confused. Assertiveness does not necessarily inflict harm, whereas aggression always produces harm —whether psychological or physical. Several factors may lead to aggressive ways of behaving toward others, including those associated with the family, the child, the family and the child, peers, and television.

Family Factors Unfortunately, rejected-aggressive children report the least supportive relationships with their fathers of any group (Stromshak, Bierman, Coie, & Dodge, 1998). They tend to report receiving less love and affection from their fathers than popular, average, and neglected children. Their reports of relationships with mothers and teachers do not appear to differ from the other children (Hickman & Morales, 2001). This finding fits well with other data showing tighter linkages between father–child relationships and peer acceptance than between mother–child relationships and peer acceptance (Coie, Terry, Lenox, Lochman, & Hyman, 1998).

Child Factors Several children are watching a video; at one point in the film one child brushes against or bumps into another child. Russ says, "Did you see that? Did you see how he smashed into the kid? Man, if that had been me, I'd have socked him one." In contrast, popular children watching the same video provide more benign interpretations of the incident (one child accidentally bumped into another) and subsequently more prosocial behavior responses ("I'd ignore it and go on playing"). Rejected children have deficits in understanding the perspectives, feelings, and intentions of others (Dodge, Coie, Pettit, & Price, 1990; Quiggle, Garber, Panak, & Dodge, 1992). They tend to *overperceive* others' aggression and *underperceive* their own (Lochman & Dodge, 1998). Further, these children are much more likely to attribute hostility to the provocative act of a peer than are nonaggressive children and are therefore more likely to respond with retaliatory aggression.

Moreover, these children are less able to recognize the inadequacy of certain potential responses than are nonaggressive children and expect more positive outcomes and fewer negative outcomes for responding with aggression. They also expect less guilt and less parental disapproval for their aggression than nonaggressive children (Dodge et al., 1990). Further, rejected-aggressive children are more likely than more popular peers to think that unfriendly strategies (for example, commanding a peer) will succeed in getting what they want.

© Richard Hutchings/PhotoEdit

Both caregiver and child contribute to the child's aggressive behavior: parents engage in more threats and physical punishment, and children tend to be more oppositional and inattentive.

Thought **CHALLENGE**

Was there a "Graham"—a child who was the sole target of ridicule and rejection in your school? This appears to be more common than most of us think. Who was the "scapegoat" in your school, and why was he or she picked on?

rejected-aggressive children
Actively disliked by peers; they are argumentative, disruptive, inattentive, and unsociable. These children are most at-risk for pathological problems.

Family and Child Factors Both the parent and the child can contribute to problematic relationships. Rejected children tend to display oppositional, hyperactive, and inattentive behavior, and parents tend to become more coercive in attempting to control such behavior. Parents tend to engage in more threats, scolding, and hitting, and children tend to engage in more yelling, hitting, and defiance. Moreover, aggressive children are less responsive to social reinforcement and social punishment, such as threats and scolding (Minde, 1992). Both mothers and fathers are much more likely to initiate conflict—that is, to launch unprovoked attacks—with their aggressive children than are parents of nonaggressive children. Rejected-aggressive children, however, are more likely to *counterattack* than nonaggressive children. Aggressive exchanges continue for a longer time and more frequently in aggressive families than in normal families; they also tend to escalate in intensity.

The fact that both parents and children play influential roles in the development of aggression can be seen cross-culturally as well. For example in China, parents of sampled rejected-aggressive children were found lacking in warmth and tended to be authoritarian; similarly, the children tended to be combative and defied authority (Chen & Rubin, 1993). The great virtue of these studies is that they nicely demonstrated the interactive nature of parent and child in the development of rejected-aggressive behavior.

Peer Factors Not only do peer social networks play a supportive role in the development of aggression in adolescence, it is also true during middle childhood (Cairns, Mahoney, Xie, & Cadwallader, 1999). Aggressive

Child Development Issues

Does Viewing Media Violence Increase a Child's Aggression?

Mark and Sam are playing a video game. Like many video games, the player is obliterated if he fails to choose a correct and predetermined strategy. There are no compromises, there are sexual stereotypes, and there is little portrayal of any realistic consequences of violence (Funk & Buckman, 1996). Many television programs contain violent content as well. If children watch 2 to 4 hours of television a day, by the time they finish elementary school, they will have seen 8000 murders and 100,000 other violent acts (Donnerstein, Slaby, & Eron, 1994). Cable television further adds to the level of violence.

In the United States, the most violent country in the industrialized world, violence has reached epidemic proportions (Osofsky, 1997). Whereas adult violence has actually decreased, the level of violence among juveniles is increasing. Homicide is the second leading cause of death among all 15- to 24-year-olds and is now the third leading cause of death among elementary schoolchildren ages 5 to 14 (Herbert, 1996). Most researchers agree that there is a strong association between viewing violence and behaving aggressively, but there is considerable disagreement about the nature and direction and duration of that relation.

TELEVISION LEADS TO VIOLENCE

Brandon Centerwall (1995) asserts that televised violence leads to an increase in a child's aggression, with numerous studies to back him up. Researchers have shown a positive relation between exposure to television violence and aggressive behavior, and exposure seems not only to increase violence but to decrease prosocial behavior as well (Stoff, Breiling, & Maser, 1997). One representative study examined children's viewing habits, aggression, aggressive and fear fantasies, and self-rated and peer-rated measures of aggression (Viemero & Paajanen, 1990). For boys, there was a significant positive relationship between aggression and watching aggression on television. The authors conclude that the more children watch television, the more they fantasize about the programs and replay the scenes they saw, which then leads to explicit aggressive behavior. Children imitate what they see and, unfortunately, in our country through television, movies, and videos, children see violence. They often learn that violence is an accepted way of solving conflicts, and many children receive little opportunity to learn about alternative ways to settle disputes (Murray, 1997).

Boys and girls may differ in displaying aggressive and violent children tend to hang around with other aggressive children; this is true cross-culturally as well (Sun, 1995). Children will imitate aggressive behavior in peer models more often than passive behavior (Bagwell, Newcomb, & Bukowski, 1998). Further, nonaggressive children may learn to become aggressive in a peer setting. To illustrate, a child who is constantly the victim of physical attacks from others, may, to avoid being picked on, lash out at others in an aggressive fashion. In some peer cultures, greater status is given to highly aggressive children and antisocial actions may be more highly valued. In these situations, children may be reinforced for their aggressions, which may then increase in frequency (Dodge & Schwartz, 1998). When less status is given to highly aggressive children, these behaviors decrease in frequency.

Television The effects of television violence and aggressive ways of behaving have received intensive investigation in the scientific literature. Startling statistics have been reported for the number of violent incidents on television to which children are exposed. Primetime programs, for example, average 8 to 12 violent acts an hour (Lamson, 1995). That works out to be 1845 violent acts in 18 hours of viewing, an average of 100 an hour or one every 36 seconds. During their television viewing time, children between the ages of 5 and 15, on average, will have witnessed some 18,000 violent acts. (These violent acts average 1 per minute in standard television cartoons.) How does viewing aggression or violence on television affect children? Does it lead to aggressive and violent behavior? Child Development Issues explores the answer to the question, "Does viewing media violence increase a child's aggression?"

behavior because boys are more exposed to viewing violence. Boys prefer aggressive video games and more violent programming than girls. Girls enjoy violence less, approve of it less, and see it as less realistic (Levine, 1995). Boys seem more drawn to violent shows and are more agitated by them, whereas girls are more often repelled by them and saddened.

According to Judith Page Van Evra (1998), there are three major effects of viewing violence: (1) *direct effects:* children who watch a lot of violence on television become more aggressive and/or develop favorable attitudes and values about the use of aggression to solve conflicts; (2) *desensitization:* children who watch a lot of violence become less sensitive to violence in the real world around them; and (3) *mean world syndrome:* children who watch a lot of violence on television may begin to believe that the world is a mean and dangerous place.

TELEVISION DOES NOT LEAD TO VIOLENCE

Brian Siano (1994) contends that factors other than television are more influential on a child's tendency toward aggressive, violent actions. One important factor, Siano maintains, is the style of parenting to which children are exposed. Children of nurturing, involved parents are less likely to be affected by the violence they see in the media than those with rejecting parents. Further, Siano discusses how the media has turned correlational results (watching lots of violent programming is a correlate of behaving aggressively) into causal relations (watching violent programming causes aggression); correlation does not necessarily indicate causation. Siano contends that a further problem contaminating research is the numerous definitions of "violence" used. Some maintain that the zany actions of cartoon characters (defective ACME catapults in the Road Runner; or Bugs Bunny bopping Elmer Fudd with a carrot stick) are acts of violence. Others see violence as being more serious and involving clear-cut intent to hurt or kill. The main point, however, is that studies lack a concise definition of the very factor they are studying, which makes for rather sloppy science in Siano's view.

Who's right? For children to be "safe," should violence in the media be eliminated? Or is censorship of all violence too high a price to pay for the influence of media violence?

Search Online

Explore InfoTrac College Edition, your online library. Go to **http://www.infotrac-college.com/wadsworth** and use the passcode that came on the card with your book. Try these search terms: violence in mass media, violent television, aggression and development.

Stability of Peer Adjustment

Do popular children retain their positive status? Does a shy child remain that way? Do rejected children continue to be the target of taunts by their classmates as they get older? There is a modest degree of stability of social status for popular and shy children over the years (Eisenberg, Shepard, Fabes, Murphy, & Guthrie, 1998). For rejected children, however, findings support high stability for social status (Coie, 1990). About 30 to 50 percent of children who are rejected by peers during the middle childhood years are still being rejected when assessments are made five years later (Asher & Rose, 1997). One plausible explanation for the stability of rejection is that children acquire reputations that operate as biases against them as they move from one grade level to the next in school. How children view the behavior of peers is strongly affected by the reputation of the child being viewed.

The stability of being rejected, however, is not simply due to the fact that the composition of the child's peer groups remains the same over time (Parke, O'Neil, Spitzer, Isley, Welsh, Wang, Lee, Strand, & Cupp, 1997). Even when children are placed into entirely new groups of previously unfamiliar peers, the degree to which children are accepted versus rejected is quite stable. For example, when unfamiliar boys of differing social status are brought together in play groups once a week for six weeks, within three weeks their social status in these new groups is similar to their social status in the classrooms. Boys who are rejected in school are similarly actively shunned by their peers in their new settings. This important finding indicates that even when reputational biases are not a factor, rejection is a fairly stable phenomenon (Zakriski, Jacobs, & Coie, 1997).

Consequences of Peer Relationships

What consequences result from difficulties in peer relationships in school? Low acceptance and lack of friends means that children will miss out on positive opportunities for inclusion, companionship and recreation, emotional support, and help and guidance.

Shy and neglected children, however, are more likely than rejected children to improve their status over time (Coie & Dodge, 1988). Children who are neglected by peers at one point in time in one context may not commonly be neglected at other times in other contexts. Furthermore, even though neglected children receive few best-friend nominations, they are as well liked by peers, on a rating scale measure, as average-status children (Hecht, Inderbitzen, & Bukowski, 1998). Together, these data concerning neglected versus rejected children suggest that it is having few friends in class and being widely disliked by the peer group that lead to behavior adjustment problems.

Research seems to bear out the theory that rejected children present a more serious problem than neglected children. Children who are rejected in preadolescence tend to have more adjustment problems in adolescence, as measured by encounters with the police, truancy, dropping out of school, or being held back or suspended in school (Kupersmidt & Coie, 1990).

Children who are actively disliked or rejected by their peers also seem to be at a heightened risk for a wide range of mental health difficulties (Kupersmidt & Coie, 1990). Although much more needs to be learned, the most clearly identified risk factors for psychopathology, delinquency, and substance abuse are (1) antisocial, rebellious, and defiant behavior, (2) poor peer relations, (3) poor academic skills, and (4) low self-esteem (Guralnick & Groom, 1990). Rejected-aggressive children present a greater risk of disorders than other rejected children (Rubin, LeMare, & Lollis, 1990). Rejected children report feeling significantly more lonely than children in other peer status classifications. Children's reports of loneliness may be implicit calls for help. In admitting loneliness, children are saying that they are unhappy with their social situation.

APPLICATIONS:

Helping Children with Peer Difficulties

Children with peer difficulties can learn to relate to others in socially competent ways, and the sooner they receive help, the easier it is to modify their behavior. Accordingly, the early school years may be particularly important as entry points for the prevention or amelioration of social problems (Rubin et al., 1999). When children do not receive help in overcoming their peer difficulties, they often develop considerable frustration and alienation. They often cling to unproductive and unskilled ways of reaching out to others. If they lack social acceptance, their lowered social status causes them to feel inadequate, helpless, and alone.

Much of the anxiety and stress children feel is produced because they feel they do not belong. In fact, it is impossible to find one study to refute the statement that children's general emotional adjustment is related to their general acceptance by others. Data consistently show that the degree of children's emotional adjustment is associated with their degree of social acceptance throughout their formative years (Asher & Coie, 1990; Parker & Asher, 1993).

Relatedly, scholars point out that it is a mistake to dismiss social incompetence as one of those things that the child will grow out of (Hartup, 1998; Stromshak, Bierman, Coie, & Dodge, 1998). Social skills are a requisite for normal adjustment. Problems in this area require adult attention to the same degree as does academic difficulty. If a child cannot connect with neighborhood children or school peers, there is no basis for expecting miraculous change in a new social setting. Outside changes will not alter the child within, and old patterns cannot help but be repeated. For these reasons, it is important for concerned adults to help these children develop socially competent ways of behaving.

Working with Neglected Children

Shy children who are uncomfortable and miserable because of their shyness, and children who have no friends whatsoever, need to be helped to feel more secure and to join in social activities (Ladd & Kochenderfer, 1998). It is recommended, however, that they not be pushed or forced into something they feel uncomfortable doing. Jerome Kagan (1997) asserts that shy children's anxieties increase under pressure. To aid shy children, adults need to avoid overprotectiveness, and encourage risk-taking.

Overprotectiveness Overprotectiveness is associated with children developing clinging, dependent personalities, which further increases their social timidity and withdrawal. Overprotective adults are those who tend to restrict children's behavior and actively encourage dependency. They fail to encourage children in risk-taking and active exploration in unfamiliar situations (Hinde, Tamplin, & Barret, 1993).

Adults should not try to anticipate shy children's every need, fight their every battle, and suffer their every pain. In doing so, caregivers are robbing children of the freedom to develop their own emotional strength. According to Kagan, overprotection backfires; shy children profit when they are encouraged to develop skills that will enable them to actively explore and develop their independence.

Getting to Know Others Many shy individuals comment that they are shy around strangers, but once they get to know people they are not shy or socially awkward around them; research bears this out. Shy children tend to act in socially competent ways when they are in the company of children they know (Asendorpf, 1993). In light of this, adults can help children adjust to group situations by making sure that they know some of the children before they enter the group. In these situations, shy children experience less disturbing and less uncomfortable feelings when interacting socially (Shotton, 1998). It is particularly helpful to choose children that are close in temperament to the shy child. Not only will knowing some children help shy children to become less inhibited in school settings, but it will also give them an opportunity for more equal companionship (Eisenberg et al., 1998).

Helping Rejected-Aggressive Children

Rejected-aggressive children can be aided by altering their expectations of rejection, helping them to not view others' acts as hostile, moderating the effects of television violence, and not using physical punishment to discipline them.

Altering Expectations of Rejection

> "Do you want to go the park and play after school today?" Robert asks John on the playground. "Sorry, I'm busy after school." Robert storms off.
>
> "Do you want to go skating with me on Saturday?" Malcolm asks Jim. "No, I can't on Saturday." "How about on Sunday?" "Yeah, that'll be okay."

What are the psychological processes underlying the distinct reactions of Robert and Malcolm's social rejection? Kenneth Dodge would attribute their responses to their differing *perceptions of intentionality* underlying the event. Thus, Robert's reaction results from perceiving the rejection as motivated by negative or hostile intent. Each of these children is carrying around a different internal or working model of relationships that incorporates different expectations about acceptance and rejection. Dodge and his colleagues (Deater-Deckard, Dodge, & Bates, 1998; Valente & Dodge, 1997) hypothesize that rejected children differ from nonrejected children by more readily attributing hostile intent to others; this attribution then morally justifies aggressive retaliation. Negative behavior, then, is motivated in part by children's

© Spencer Grant/PhotoEdit

Co-viewing is an effective way of ameliorating the effects of violence on television.

expectations of rejection. These children have been labeled *rejection sensitive.*

Over time negative behavior by rejection-sensitive children increases, evidenced by their exhibiting high levels of disruptive, oppositional, and conflictual behavior. Further, they tend to disengage from school, with resulting increases in absences, suspensions, and declining grades (Downey, Lebolt, Rincon, & Freitas, 1998). Expectations of rejection, however, can be altered. For example, Dodge has found that when peer-rejected children are helped to see positive intentions in others, they in turn act in more prosocial ways toward others. Thus, an important way of helping rejection-sensitive children, according to Dodge, is to alter their expectations of rejection.

Making Less Hostile Attributions Second, research has consistently shown that rejected children process social cues in ways that contribute to their behavioral difficulties. Thus, helping aggressive children to make less hostile attributions for others' ambiguous behavior will help to lower their aggression levels (Hudley & Graham, 1995; Underwood, 1997). The problem may not be the situation itself but the child's *interpretation* of that situation. Different individuals may perceive the same stimulus as either hostile or benign: highly aggressive boys are likely to attribute hostile intent to another child who, say, knocks down some toys; nonaggressive boys, on the other hand, tend to see the same incident as accidental. The former are therefore more likely to retaliate aggressively, provoking further hostility and dislike from the other children. This in turn will make the aggressive child all the more ready to behave aggressively on future occasions (Zakriski, Jacobs, & Coie, 1997). A vicious circle is thus set up. Adults can foster more positive and neutral attributions by discussing social situations that may occur in the child's life and how he or she can perceive and deal with these situations in positive ways (see Figure 13.3).

Tom makes a derogatory remark about Mike's mother.

Happening +	Attribution =	Feeling	Reaction
Tom calls Mike's mom a bad name.	How mean; I'll get him for that.	Mike feels out-of-control anger.	Mike hits Tom.
Tom calls Mike's mom a bad name.	He doesn't even know my mother.	Mike feels mild anger.	Tom walks away.

FIGURE 13.3 ***Learning to Make Less Hostile Attributions***

Moderating the Effects of Television Violence

Whatever the final outcome of research on the relationship between viewing violent television content and aggressive behavior, no one has argued that heavy viewing of violence is desirable or that it enhances children's development. Further, there is virtually no evidence to support the contention that viewing violence leads to a decrease in aggressive behavior by draining off a child's aggressive tendencies in fantasy. Research to date does indicate strongly that reducing levels of viewing of such violent programming is a worthy aim. Options include voluntary reductions of violence by networks, regulatory controls, enforced rating systems, and technological devices for television sets, such as the V-chip that flags programs that exceed a chosen level of violence, language, or sexually explicit content, and screens them out.

Another effective way of ameliorating the effects of violence on television is parental co-viewing. In these situations, adults can enhance children's understanding of television content by offering comments about what they are watching during and after viewing a program (Wright, Peters, & Huston, 1990). This basic intervention involves talking about how violence is faked and what would happen if they actually did some of those things. If parents watch with their children, they can provide other views to supplement, alter, modify, or refute information that their children are receiving. Direct parental communication and discussion help to shape the child's perception of families in the real world, which are then used to assess the realism of the television world (Austin, Roberts, & Nass, 1990). It is best when parents watch television with their children, talk about programs with them, and help their children relate the television content to their own lives.

Avoiding Physical Punishment

My son is very aggressive
He's always hitting other children
I don't understand why. . . .
I hit him every time he does it.

Unfortunately, when children behave aggressively, their behavior is often met with counteraggressive behavior by adults. In this situation, neither party reduces tension and neither learns to understand the other or solve the problem. The more adults deal with children in negative ways, the more aggressive children become. No amount of punishment seems effective with these children (Pettit, Bates, & Dodge, 1997).

Aggressive children usually have had their share of punishment; and experts advise that they do not need any more (Patterson, DeBaryshe, & Ramsey, 1989). Rather, they need firm help in controlling and channeling their aggressive tendencies. They need to realize that there are other ways to solve their problems than by bulldozing their way through life. When children behave aggressively in an abusive way, they must be shown that they are using their strength in misguided ways.

One of the best ways for adults to help aggressive children is to make it abundantly clear that aggression is frowned on, to stop it when it occurs, but not to punish children physically for that aggression. Although physical punishment may stop a particular form of aggression temporarily, it appears to generate a great deal of hostility in children, which leads to further aggressive outbursts at another time and place. The most peaceful setting is the one in which adults will not tolerate aggression, especially toward themselves. Settings in which children frequently show angry, aggressive outbursts are likely to be when adults have a relatively tolerant attitude toward aggression, or where they administer severe punishment for it, or both.

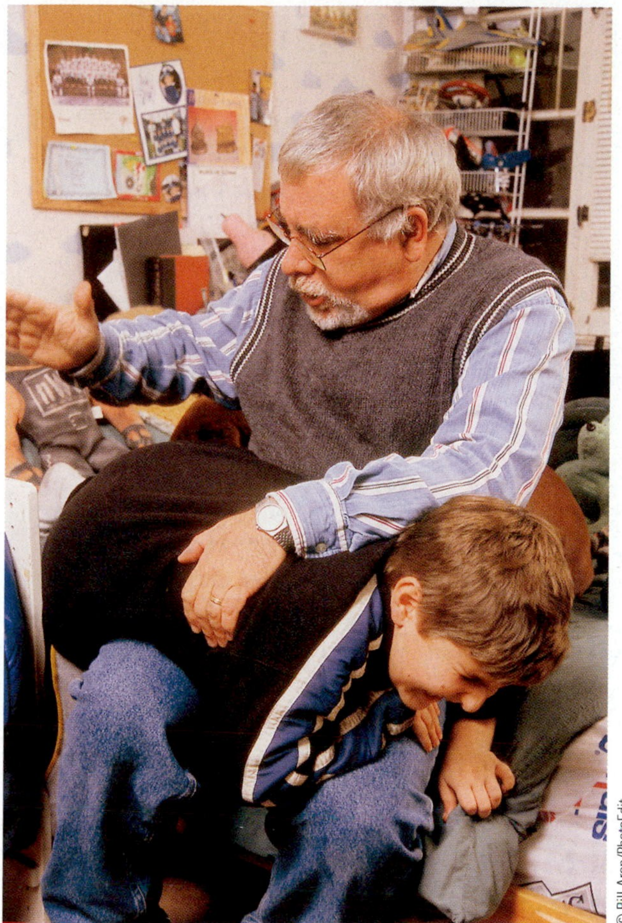
© Bill Aron/PhotoEdit

Children disciplined by adults with punitive tactics are more likely to use these same tactics in dealing with other children.

Concept Checks

1. In terms of children's developing self-systems, which statement best captures their use of social comparisons? Children in middle childhood
   a. use comparisons to judge their appearance and action.
   b. are more likely to compare themselves to evaluate their competence and ability.
   c. do not use social comparisons in evaluating self.
2. Children between the ages of 8 and 10 are likely to describe friends as
   a. performing something that they want done ("You need a friend to play games with").
   b. someone who has the same set of likes and dislikes ("We both love to play video games").
   c. all being "the same."
3. Which of the following children causes the greatest concern in terms of short- and long-term consequences?
   a. Maury who receives few social overtures from peers
   b. Jacob who tries to remain inconspicuous
   c. Kevin who is annoying and disruptive
4. In enhancing rejected children's status, it is recommended that
   a. their expectations of rejection be altered.
   b. they socialize with shy children to curb their aggression.
   c. their rejection sensitivity be increased.

Moral Development

Before Beginning . . .

After reading this section, you will be able to

- outline the major tenets of Piaget's theory of moral development.
- delineate Kohlberg's stages of moral reasoning.
- understand the influence of peers on children's moral development.
- discuss factors that promote morally competent behavior.

What Is Morality?

A simplistic definition of morality is to know right from wrong behavior and engage in the former. But, who or what determines what is right or wrong conduct? The "right" way to behave, by and large, is determined by one's level of moral development. Morality develops in a sequential pattern; that is, the growth of moral reasoning follows certain stages of development.

Piaget's Theory of Moral Development

Piaget (1965) was interested in studying children's *conceptions about rules* and the role that *intent* plays in children's thinking about moral transgressions. In studying children of different ages, Piaget was able to trace the transformations in these two aspects of children's moral development as they reached greater levels of cognitive maturity. Piaget played games with children to learn more about their understanding of rules. While engaging in a game of marbles, for example, he would ask children questions such as, "Where do these rules come from?" "Must everyone obey a rule?" "Can these rules be changed?" To study children's thinking about moral transgressions, he would tell them pairs of stories, each of which was about a child causing some undesirable outcome. In one story, however, the child was intentionally naughty, whereas in the other the undesirable outcome was purely accidental. The following is an example:

moral realism
When children adopt inflexible moral codes based on adult rules.

moral relativism
Cognitively more mature stage of moral reasoning characterized by an understanding that morality depends on mutual respect rather than on unquestioned obedience to authority.

> A little boy who is called John is in his room. He is called to dinner. He goes into the dining room. But behind the door there was a chair, and on the chair there was a tray with 15 cups on it. John couldn't have known that there was all this behind the door. He goes in, the door knocks against the tray, bang go the 15 cups and they all get broken.
>
> Once there was a little boy named Henry. One day when his mother was out he tried to get some jam out of the cupboard. He climbed up onto a chair and stretched out his arm. But the jam was too high up and he couldn't reach it and have any. But while he was trying to get it he knocked over a cup. The cup fell down and broke. (Piaget, 1965, p. 122)

The child was then asked to say whether John or Henry was the naughtier one and to explain the reasons for the choice made. From his work with children, Piaget proposed that there are two broad stages of moral development: *moral realism* and *moral relativism.*

Moral Realism

Moral realism is characterized by the naive assumption on the part of children that rules are external, absolute, and unchanging. Children in the moral realism stage tend to judge behavior in absolute terms; behavior is totally right or totally wrong. Moreover, the young child feels that everyone sees and judges the morality of people and behavior exactly the same way he or she does. Further, children see themselves as inferior to adults and, from a mixture of fear, affection, and admiration, they adopt their parents' moral beliefs unquestioningly. In the process, they adopt an inflexible moral code based on obedience. Morality at this stage is essentially conformity to social prescriptions. These children would regard John as the naughtier of the two children because he broke 15 cups, whereas Henry only broke 1. Around the age of 10, this absolute view gives way to a more relative one, as children become capable of moral relativism or autonomous morality.

Moral Relativism

The shift from moral realism to **moral relativism** occurs primarily as a result of changes in cognitive ability as well as the child's broadened social experience. As children become members of a group, their moral judgments may become less absolute and authoritarian and more dependent on the needs and desires of the group; when that occurs moral relativism replaces moral realism.

Around ages 10 to 11, children alter rules to fit unusual situations and may invent new rules to cover special circumstances. Rules are decisions made by the children who play the games; they can be changed at will as long as everyone agrees. A higher level of moral reasoning, noted Piaget, enables children to view rules as changeable; they are no longer seen as sacred laws laid down by adults. But, does flexibility in rule making necessarily reflect a higher level of moral reasoning? In a classic study, the understanding of rules of 6- to 18-year-old children from seven Native American cultures (Navajo, Papago, Sioux, Zuni, Zia, and two groups of Hopi) were examined (Havighurst & Neugarten, 1955). The majority of these children saw rules as unchangeable—particularly with regard to the traditional games. To change a rule would show disrespect for the ancestors. In fact, as children became older, the more convinced they became that game rules must not be changed. One simply cannot assume that this unchangeable-rule thinking reflects a lower level of moral reasoning, because as in the samples of Native American youths, cultural values may explain attitudes toward rules (Eckensberger & Zimba, 1997). Children who use moral realism reasoning are no longer controlled by egocentrism; thus, they can more easily consider and appreciate the viewpoint and feelings of a peer, which leads to genuine cooperation. Children learn that cooperative social arrangements can lead to mutually valued goals. In addition, they show a thorough mastery of the rules of a game, often delighting in a legalistic fascination with the rules. For these older children, rules are products of lawful convention and mutual respect among peers; they are not imposed by an external authority.

In addition, children gradually lose their sense of objective responsibility (focusing on the obvious concrete aspects of a situation) and begin to place more emphasis on subjective intentions (the individual's motives and the circumstances of the situation). Their notions of justice now include consideration of intention. To illustrate, in the example given previously, breaking 15 cups accidentally is not as bad as breaking one to take some forbidden jam. The child who did not mean to break the cups is now excused, whereas the one who deliberately disobeyed is guilty. As children grow older, they feel that the punishment should fit the crime so that the wrongdoer will better appreciate the consequences of his or her act. In the moral relativism stage, children are aware that things are neither all bad nor all good but a mixture of both. As children come to notice the more subtle cues of intention, they may more regularly take intentions into account. This Piagetian three-stage progression—from premoral period to moral realism to moral relativism—is summarized in Table 13.6.

TABLE 13.6

Piagetian Stages of Moral Reasoning

Stage	Age Range (Years)	Characteristics
Premoral	Up to 4	No understanding of rules or of the bases of right and wrong.
Moral realism (heteronomous morality)	4 to 9 or 10	Actions judged by material outcome. Rules emanate from authority; can't be changed. Wrong is whatever adults forbid.
Moral relativism (autonomous morality)	From 9 or 10	Actions judged according to intentions. Rules made by people; can be changed by mutual agreement. Wrong is transgression of moral principles.

Progressing from Moral Realism to Moral Relativism

Piaget concluded from all the various findings of his research that up to age 4, children are still in a **premoral period**. At this time, they have little conception of what a rule is and what purpose it serves. When playing marbles, for instance, children do so initially in an uncoordinated way and subsequently make up their own rules. Ideas about right and wrong are still arbitrary; the choice of wrongdoing when presented with pairs of stories such as the cups stories tends to be random. After the age of 4 or 5, however, children's ideas become much more systematic. They then enter the stage of moral realism—so called because judgments tend to be based on the real or objective damage done.

Progressing from moral realism to moral relativism involves passing through three periods during the elementary school years. Within the first period, typically found in children up to age 7, justice is whatever has been prescribed by adult authority and it means abiding strictly by these adult-formulated rules. Over time, this conception is gradually altered so that by the ages of 8 to 11, children believe in justice as equality. Justice now means treating everyone alike—reciprocity and equality among peers. At the higher and final level of morality that appears around age 11 or 12, "purely equalitarian justice is tempered by considerations of equity" (Piaget, 1965, p. 315).

Morality, according to Piaget (1965), is constructed by the child out of social experience, shaped by the cognitive understanding of which the child is capable at particular points of development. Children and adults in each morality stage have a somewhat different conception of what good behavior is and how they can best fulfill their moral ideal. Each successive stage is said to build upon the previous stage. A later stage is "higher" than an earlier one because it can more adequately organize the multiplicity of facts, interests, and possibilities life holds in store. Moreover, higher stages of moral reasoning are superior to lower stages because they show greater understanding about society and thus are more socially adaptive. Piaget was not only interested in how children's moral reasoning develops but also in how and why their thinking changes over time.

premoral period The first of Piaget's three-stage moral development periods; during this time, children (up to age 4) have little conception of what a rule is and what purpose it serves.

TABLE 13.7

The Heinz Dilemma

In Europe, a woman was near death from a special kind of cancer. There was one drug that doctors thought might save her. It was a form of radium that a druggist in the same town had recently discovered. The drug was expensive to make, but the druggist was charging $2,000 or 10 times the cost of the drug, for a small (possibly life-saving) dose. Heinz, the sick woman's husband, borrowed all the money he could, about $1,000 or half of what he needed. He told the druggist that his wife was dying and asked him to sell the drug cheaper or to let him pay later. The druggist replied, "No, I discovered the drug, and I'm going to make money from it." Heinz then became desperate and broke into the store to steal the drug for his wife.

Should Heinz have done that?

Although Piaget's theory has been extremely influential, it has been criticized as well. For example, the stories presented in his moral dilemmas tend to be long and complex—perhaps too long and complex for young children. His theory has also been criticized because, according to other investigators (Kochanska & Thompson, 1998), children do not necessarily belong to either one stage or another but may give situation-specific responses. Perhaps Piaget's theory—with only three stages and one transition from moral realism to moral relativism—is just too simplistic. Subsequently, others have tried to remedy these deficiencies.

Kohlberg's Theory of Moral Reasoning

Lawrence Kohlberg's (1978, 1981) approach to moral development is an elaboration of Piaget's with respect to both theory and method. Like Piaget, Kohlberg's original position is based on the responses of 7- to 17-year-old boys to brief stories depicting moral dilemmas. Typically, children have been asked to resolve moral dilemmas in which a story protagonist can assist another at a cost to the self. Table 13.7 presents one of Kohlberg's dilemmas, the story of Heinz.

preconventional moral reasoning Involves avoiding punishment or gaining a fair exchange.

conventional moral reasoning Consists of mutual social expectations and following rules to maintain law and order.

postconventional moral reasoning Involves knowing that rules are not always applicable because of extenuating circumstances and following one's individual conscience for the good of humanity.

Unlike Piaget, what matters in Kohlberg's model is not the nature of the solution a child offers to a moral dilemma; one choice is no better than another. Instead, the basis on which the child reasons in making a decision is deemed important. Kohlberg and his colleagues asked children to decide what an individual ought to do in a certain situation. The children had to decide and justify a course of action for the individual and define his or her rights and obligations. Kohlberg's interest focused on the quality of their judgments as indicated by the justifications they gave for their replies. By analyzing the child's responses to a number of dilemmas, his or her predominant stage orientation can be assessed.

Levels of Moral Reasoning

Kohlberg used Piaget's set of general cognitive growth stages as a foundation for erecting a six-stage hierarchy of moral judgments that refined Piaget's original conception of heteronomous and autonomous morality. Table 13.8 describes the three levels and six stages proposed by Kohlberg. The stages advance from the earliest levels, indicative of the thinking processes of young children, to the higher levels, which can be achieved by individuals who are more mature intellectually. Kohlberg (1976) suggests that moral judgments progress through these unvarying series of stages (see Figure 13.4). Although interactions with peers provide its impetus, the progression is irreversible and not all people reach the highest stages of moral development. The notion implies that moral judgments across different moral domains will show an underlying unity. Kohlberg assesses moral development by having trained coders examine a child's justifications for his or her decisions on a series of morally tough calls. Should Heinz break into a drugstore to obtain expensive medicine that would improve his wife's illness? By evaluating not the decision itself, but the justifications behind it, Kohlberg has assumed that all moral decisions are equally amenable to justification.

The stages are arranged in ascending order of complexity, each representing a more stable and logically powerful framework for resolving conflicts than the one before (Kohlberg, 1978). Each stage in the sequence is progressively more differentiated and integrated. With development, each new stage employs cognitive thinking that is more elaborate and sophisticated. Development, then, is essentially a change from global, diffuse, and confused thinking to systematic, articulate, and hierarchical thinking.

Kohlberg (1971) maintains that as children grow older, more of their judgments are made at higher levels of reasoning. **Preconventional moral reasoning** involves avoiding punishment or gaining a fair exchange. **Conventional moral reasoning** consists of mutual social expectations and following rules to maintain law and order. **Postconventional moral reasoning** involves knowing that rules are not always applicable because of extenuating circumstances and following one's individual conscience for the good of humanity.

Preconventional Moral Reasoning In the first level, preconventional moral reasoning, children are responsive to cultural rules and labels of good and bad, right or wrong. Children interpret these labels in terms of either the physical or the hedonistic consequences of action (punishment, reward, exchange of favors) or in

TABLE 13.8

Kohlberg's Stages of Moral Reasoning

	Stage	Description	Response
Level 1 Preconventional morality	1: Punishment and obedience orientation	What is right is whatever others permit; what is wrong is what others punish. There is no conception of rules. The seriousness of a violation depends on the magnitude of the consequence.	"He should steal the drug because if he lets his wife die he will get into trouble."
	2: Individualism and instrumental orientation; rewards	Rules are followed only when it is in the child's immediate interest. Right is what gains rewards or when there is an equal exchange ("You scratch my back and I'll scratch yours").	"You may not get much of a jail sentence if you steal the drug, but your wife will probably die before you get out so it won't do you much good."
Level 2 Conventional Morality	3: Mutual interpersonal expectations, relationships, and conformity; approval	"Being good" means living up to other people's expectations, having good intentions, and showing concern about others. Trust, loyalty, respect, and gratitude are valued.	"No one will think you're bad if you steal the drug, but your family will think you're inhuman if you don't."
	4: Social system and conscience; law and order	"Right" is a matter of fulfilling the actual duties to which you have agreed. Social rules and conventions are upheld except where they conflict with other social duties. Contributing to society is good.	"It's natural for Heinz to want to save his wife, but it's still always wrong to steal."
Level 3 Postconventional morality	5: Social contract or utility and individual rights	People hold a variety of values and opinions, and although rules are relative to the group these should be upheld because they are part of the social contract. Rules that are imposed are unjust and can be challenged. Some values, such as life and liberty, are nonrelative and must be upheld regardless of majority opinion.	"You can't have everyone stealing when they get desperate. The ends may be good, but the ends don't justify the means."
	6: Universal ethical principles	Self-chosen ethical principles determine what is right. In a conflict between law and such principles, it is right to follow one's conscience. The principles are abstract moral guidelines organized into a coherent value system.	"If you don't steal the drug and let your wife die you will always condemn yourself for it afterward. You will not have lived up to your own standards of conscience."

Thought **CHALLENGE**

Two brothers want to get $1,000 each before they sneak out of town. One gets the money by stealing it, and the other by feigning illness and begging an elderly man to "lend" him $1,000 for an operation. Which of the brothers did the worse thing, and why is that worse than the other brother's action?

terms of the physical power of those who enunciate the rules and labels. In stage 1 (punishment/obedience), children under the age of 7 avoid breaking rules that are backed by punishment. Actions are judged in terms of their physical consequences. Thus, the motivating force behind children's moral reasoning is the avoidance of punishment from authority figures.

According to Kohlberg (1976), children during the ages of 7 to 11 reason at stage 2. The overriding concern is looking out for one's own self-interests. What is right is what satisfies the child's needs. Children tend not to consider the needs of the other person unless they think it will benefit them to do so. Elements of fairness and reciprocity are present, but they are always interpreted in a physical, pragmatic way. Reciprocity is a matter of "you scratch my back and I'll scratch yours," not of loyalty, gratitude, or justice. The other stages are presented in Table 13.8.

Evaluating Kohlberg's Theory

One criticism of Kohlberg's model is that it is culturally biased. Kohlberg's theory does not appear to be applicable to cultures outside a constitutional democracy. Cross-cultural findings indicate, for example, that Kohlberg's model of moral development may not incorporate the concerns and experiences of non-Western people (Ji, 1997). To illustrate, the Confucian principle of *jen* (love,

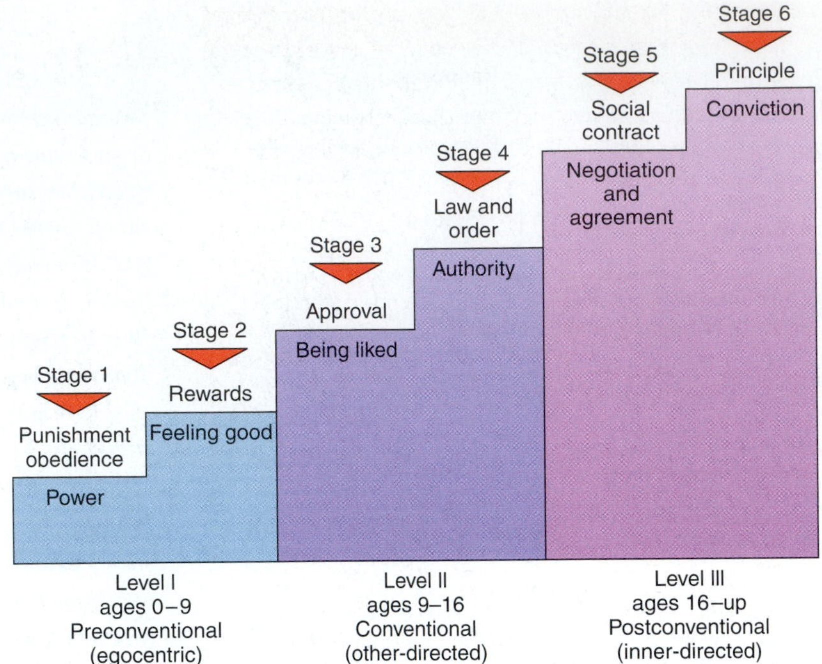

FIGURE 13.4 ***Kohlberg's Theory of Moral Reasoning***

In Kohlberg's stagelike progression theory of moral reasoning, shifts in children's and adults' moral reasoning occur as they progress from one stage to another.

benevolence, human-heartedness, perfect virtue) and expressions of parental obedience and family interdependence, for example, are not included in his stages of moral reasoning (Okonkwo, 1997). Similarly, the principle of respect for all life as a moral principle, which leads to the principle of nonviolence (*ahimsa*) in Hinduism, is overlooked in Kohlberg's scheme (Eckensberger & Zimba, 1997).

Kohlberg (1971) also asserted that the moral reasoning of some cultures is more "adequate" than that of others. To Kohlberg, "more adequate" equates to a higher stage of moral reasoning. Why is it important for his stage theory that "higher" stages be considered morally "better" (rather than simply later in the developmental sequence)? To Kohlberg (and to Piaget) higher stages of moral development represented more mature and complex moral reasoning strategies and thus provided better equilibrium between the individual and the social environment. For any culture, however, there may be a stage of moral reasoning that best corresponds to their principles of social organization. For example, stage 3 (approval) may generally represent the best framework for individuals living in a homogeneous culture—a small rural community in western Kenya, for example—composed of people who share moral values and respect authority out of a personal belief in the leader's personal goodness. Thus, Kohlberg's claim that "higher moral reasoning is more adequate reasoning" is drastically limited.

Moreover, he made some very bold claims about a subject's consistency in moral judgment across situations. Kohlberg believed that each stage must be traversed in order, that order is never reversed, and that no stage can be skipped. In general, empirical studies of moral reasoning have confirmed that people do apply the perspectives of the first five stages in their responses to hypothetical moral dilemmas. However, there remains a question about whether stage 6 might perhaps be an ideal condition that is never actually achieved in practice.

Kohlberg's theory has been called sexist because he places women at a lower level of moral reasoning (stage 3, approval) than he does men (stage 4, law and order). Carol Gilligan (1993) argues that the reasoning exhibited by women in response to moral dilemmas is not adequately assessed in Kohlberg's model. Gilligan's views are discussed in Chapter 16.

APPLICATIONS:

Promoting Morally Competent Behavior in Children

Children's level of moral reasoning is an important factor in determining how they will act in certain situations involving moral conduct. Higher levels of moral reasoning are superior to lower levels because children show a greater understanding about society and thus are more socially adaptive. How do children develop from a lower level of morality based on parental constraint to a higher one based on mutual cooperation? How can adults facilitate the development of moral reasoning in children? Family factors, peer factors, and learning to develop empathy seem to hold the key.

Family Factors

Family factors that impact the development of children's moral reasoning include their discussion styles, their level of democratic parenting, and how they facilitate prosocial behaviors.

Discussion Styles Parental discussion styles are predictive of children's moral reasoning (Walker & Taylor, 1991). The parental discussion style that predicts the greatest moral development in children includes behaviors such as eliciting the child's opinion, asking clarifying questions, paraphrasing, and checking for understanding. Informative discussion styles, in which parents directly challenge the child, critique the child's position, and lecture, are associated with low levels of moral reasoning in children. Parental practices that promote children's autonomy and independent thinking, particularly in a supportive atmosphere, are associated with high-level moral reasoning in children (Eisenberg & Murphy, 1995).

Democratic Parenting Children who exhibit higher levels of moral reasoning have parents who are verbal, rational people who encourage warm, close relations with their children (Janssen, Janssen, & Gerris, 1992). The parents tend to promote a democratic style of family life, with a fair consideration of everyone's point of view. A democratic home requires more freedom of choice for the child and more time for the parent to discuss, when necessary, the choices made and to evaluate the consequences with the child. By living in accordance with the same basic rules that are expected of the child, and by allowing the child a reasonable role in decision making, parents can be an example of reciprocal morality. Giving children opportunities to participate in decision making promotes a higher level of moral reasoning.

There is also a relationship between children's levels of moral reasoning and various disciplining techniques. Power-assertive techniques (physical force, deprivation of material objects or privileges) are associated with lower levels of moral reasoning; induction (explaining the possible consequence of the child's behavior) is associated with higher levels. Love withdrawal (ignoring child, threatening to leave child, explicitly stating dislike for child) is rather ambiguous, perhaps because the anxiety it induces can operate in two ways. It can lead a child to conform to please the parent and maintain emotional harmony or to refuse to conform to annoy the parent. In either case, it is not a good method (Piaget, 1965).

Developing Prosocial Behaviors Concerned adults often spend much time attempting to ensure that children become generous, helping, and caring individuals. In our society these are **prosocial behaviors** that bring credit to the adult and the child alike. Although there are individual differences in prosocial abilities among children and some may be attributed to innate factors, adults undoubtedly account for some of the variation. John and Beatrice Whiting (1975) illustrated in their classical study how socialization practices are linked to the development of prosocial behavior. When children, from early childhood on, are given chores that are considered necessary for the common good of the family, and the children are aware of how the family depends on them for these chores, they are more prosocial. Age-appropriate chores such as helping make the meals, being in charge of feeding the pets, and taking care of siblings help children to learn that they are making an important and genuine contribution to the welfare of the family, and, in turn, this feeling promotes prosocial behavior.

In a multicultural study sampling children from Kenya, Belize, Nepal, and Samoa, findings again confirmed that the children who engaged in domestic and subsistence-related tasks displayed more prosocial behavior (Munroe, Munroe, & Shimmin, 1984). Children, who were engaged with younger children, for example, often extended the behaviors they employed with them to other social situations, such as offering assistance or affection to others.

Peer Factors

Piaget insisted that interaction with peers rather than with adults enables children to progress from moral realism to moral relativism. When playing with other children of the same age, children frequently get involved in conflicts about how games should be played and what rules should be followed. As everyone has equal status there is considerable pressure on children to compromise, thereby acknowledging that others can also have a valid point of view even though it may differ from their own.

Interpersonal conflict gives rise to cognitive conflict, which Piaget saw as the vehicle for all developmental progress. Children need to resolve in their own minds the discrepancies between their own and others' ideas and do so by accepting that rules are merely social contracts dependent on mutual consent and not on some all-powerful authority. It is in these peer situations that children's moral reasoning is enhanced.

Both Piaget and Kohlberg relegated parents to a minimal and nonspecific role as agents in their children's moral development. They believed that the best way to enhance children's moral development is to expose them to "equals," such as peers, who are reasoning at a slightly higher level of moral reasoning. Such experiences challenge children's current ways of thinking, reveal their inadequacy, and thereby stimulate development toward a higher stage of moral reasoning.

According to Piaget, moral development cannot take place under heteronomous conditions—that is, when parent–child relations are one-sided and authoritarian, with adults over children. Piaget believed that children cannot develop a true sense of justice when adults are strong and demanding and children feel weak and inferior. In these kinds of situations, children

prosocial behaviors
Generous, helping, and caring behaviors that promote a society's values.

© Myrleen Ferguson/PhotoEdit

Piaget believed that peer interaction rather than adult directives enables children to develop more sophisticated moral reasoning strategies.

know what they are supposed to do and not do, but the rationale for conformity is often not understood and there is no sense of working out some arrangement for mutual benefit. Hence, interaction with adults short-circuits the process of building a deeper understanding of cooperative arrangements.

As children get older, however, and attain a relative equality with adults and older children, they gain the confidence to participate with peers in decisions about applying and changing rules on the basis of reciprocity. The mutual give and take, which occurs among peers who have equal status, fosters a reciprocity of cooperation in which each child has the freedom to enter into cooperative agreements and each must be satisfied with the agreement for it to be effective. Peer-group experiences help move children away from moral realism, in which rules are seen as external, constraining forces arbitrarily imposed by powerful adult authority figures, and toward the notion of morality based on principles of cooperation and mutual consent (Buzzelli, 1992). Morality, then, develops from acquisition of autonomy, emerging from the need to get along with others.

Developing a Sense of Empathy

empathy
A largely involuntary response to the emotional cues from other people or their situations.

Laying a foundation for acting in morally responsible ways requires developing a sense of empathy (Eisenberg, 2000). **Empathy** is frequently defined as a largely involuntary response to the emotional cues from other people or their situations. It is not simply to understand the feelings of others but to act on that understanding through thoughts and deeds to benefit the other. Before children can develop empathic ways of responding to others, they need to have developed an awareness that people may have responses to a situation that differ from their own (Eisenberg, 2000). When children come to understand that they and others have separate and different feelings, they can imagine the others' emotional state in the immediate context of the situation. Empathic behavior takes on many forms, including sharing, helping, and comforting others in distress.

If adults want children to be empathic, they must be empathic to children—that is, to understand their child's experiences from his or her perspective rather than their own (see Self-Insight: How Empathic Are You?"). Empathic understanding enables adults to respond more accurately to the child's individual needs, wishes, and feelings, and for children to do this for their parents and others as well.

Children can gain a sense of empathy through being assigned chores upon which the family depends. Parents then need to point out how the child is helping out the whole family. Similarly, reinforcing empathic behaviors demonstrated by the child fosters empathy. Teaching empathy, however, is more a matter of reinforcing a certain perspective on good deeds. For example, when the child does something nice for a friend, instead of saying, "Oh, what a good little boy you are to share the toy with Jimmy," ask the child to connect his sharing the toy with how good he has made Jimmy feel. Playing games such as imagining what it is like to be in certain situations (a child looking for his lost puppy; not being invited to a party) and what children can do or say to make the person feel better help children gain a stronger sense of empathy (Shaffer, 1998).

Concept Checks

1. Piaget's stage of moral relativism is characterized by
   a. the child's idea that everyone sees and judges behavior exactly as he or she does.
   b. an awareness that things are neither all good nor all bad but a mixture of both.
   c. congruence of moral judgment and action.
2. According to Kohlberg, moral reasoning
   a. is strongly influenced by one's cultural expectations and values.
   b. changes from global, confused thinking to systematic and hierarchical thinking.
   c. is not possible until around age 12 when egocentrism decreases.

How Empathic Are You?

One of the best ways in which parents can assist their children to develop morally conscious behavior is to help them develop a sense of empathy. Empathy is a complex concept that includes both the ability to assume the perspective of another and react in an emotionally helpful and compassionate way.

Circle the appropriate number in each of the following items.

1. Before criticizing somebody, I try to imagine how I would feel if I were in his or her place.
Does not describe me very well 0 1 2 3 4 Describes me very well

2. If I'm sure I'm right about something, I don't waste much time listening to other people's arguments.
Does not describe me very well 0 1 2 3 4 Describes me very well

3. I sometimes try to understand my friends better by imagining how things look from their perspective.
Does not describe me very well 0 1 2 3 4 Describes me very well

4. I believe that there are two sides to every question and try to look at them both.
Does not describe me very well 0 1 2 3 4 Describes me very well

5. I sometimes find it difficult to see things from the "other guy's" point of view.
Does not describe me very well 0 1 2 3 4 Describes me very well

6. I try to look at everybody's side of a disagreement before I make a decision.
Does not describe me very well 0 1 2 3 4 Describes me very well

7. When I'm upset at someone, I usually try to "put myself in his shoes" for a while.
Does not describe me very well 0 1 2 3 4 Describes me very well

8. When I see someone being taken advantage of, I feel kind of protective toward him.
Does not describe me very well 0 1 2 3 4 Describes me very well

9. When I see someone being treated unfairly, I sometimes don't feel very much pity for him.
Does not describe me very well 0 1 2 3 4 Describes me very well

10. I often have tender, concerned feelings for people less fortunate than me.
Does not describe me very well 0 1 2 3 4 Describes me very well

11. I would describe myself as a pretty softhearted person.
Does not describe me very well 0 1 2 3 4 Describes me very well

12. Sometimes I don't feel very sorry for other people when they have problems.
Does not describe me very well 0 1 2 3 4 Describes me very well

13. Other people's misfortunes do not usually disturb me a great deal.
Does not describe me very well 0 1 2 3 4 Describes me very well

14. I am often quite touched by things that I see happen.
Does not describe me very well 0 1 2 3 4 Describes me very well

Questions 1 through 7 compose the "perspective taking" scale and reflect an ability to shift perspectives or to step "outside the self" when dealing with other people. Reverse the scores on 2 and 5, and then add the scores on questions 1 through 7. Scores between 16 and 17 indicate empathic perspective-taking abilities.

Questions 8 through 14 reflect the "empathic concern" scale and assess the degree to which you experience feelings of warmth, compassion, and concern for another. Reverse items 9, 12, and 13, and then add the scores on questions 8 through 14. Scores between 19 and 20 indicate empathic concern for others.

From "A Multidimensional Approach to Individual Differences in Empathy," by M. H. Davis, 1980, in *Catalog of Selected Documents in Psychology, 10*(4), 85.

3. ***True or False:*** Both Piaget and Kohlberg agree that it is interaction with peers rather than with adults that enables children to progress to higher levels of moral reasoning.
4. Before children can develop a sense of empathy, they
   a. need to have developed an awareness that people may have responses to a situation that differ from their own.
   b. must understand their parents' value system.
   c. must know which explicit cues to look for in other children.

Family Influences in Middle Childhood

Before Beginning ...

After reading this section, you will be able to

- examine the variables that affect children's adjustment to divorce.
- identify adjustment variables in single-parent families.
- understand the dynamics of blended family systems.
- explain factors that facilitate children's development in single-parent and blended families.

Where have all the nuclear families gone? *Diversity* in family structures is the norm among contemporary families; today, less than 20 percent of all families are composed of first-time marriages with two opposite-sex adults and their children (Mason, Skolnick, & Sugarman, 1998). The structure of the family in the United States has changed dramatically over the last 30 years witnessed by a significant decline of two-parent families in first marriages and a complementary increase in the number of single-parent households and stepfamilies due to divorce (Hetherington, Bridges, & Insabella, 2000).

The annual divorce rate in the United States doubled between 1960 and 1996, and comparable rates of increase are evident in many other developed countries, including Denmark, France, Germany, Great Britain, Sweden, and Switzerland (Lamb, Hwang, Ketterlinus, & Fracasso, 1999). Canada has long held the distinction of having one of the lowest rates of divorce among industrialized nations. However, in Canada today, a marriage still cannot be terminated because the relationship has stagnated or because one or both partners want a change unless there is a one-year separation with the idea that the marriage is over (McKenry & Price, 1995). In the United States 60 percent of all divorces involve children; in Great Britain the figure is nearly 75 percent.

Findings also indicate that African American women have higher divorce risks than their European American counterparts and African American marriages disintegrate sooner after first marriage than European American marriages (Kposowa, 1998). The rate of divorce among Latinos varies considerably by subgroup. Mexican Americans and Cubans have more stability in marriage than European Americans; however, Puerto Rican marriages have divorce rates similar to African Americans (Sanchez-Ayendez, 1998). Asian Americans exceed European Americans in terms of marital stability; the divorce rate among Asian Americans is estimated to be less than half the overall rate in the United States (Min, 1998). Although the divorce rate has been interpreted as a rejection of the institution of marriage, 75 percent of men and 66 percent of women eventually will remarry, suggesting that although people are rejecting specific marital partners, most are not rejecting marriage itself (Cherlin & Furstenberg, 1994).

When Parents Divorce

Divorce is an experience that can be very different in various kinds of families; its effect will vary for fathers, mothers, and children, and the event is not always experienced as a negative (Stewart, Copeland, Chester, Malley, & Barenbaum, 1997). For example, studies on African American divorced couples showed a more positive adjustment to divorce than European Americans (Kitson & Holmes, 1992). It is suggested that positive adjustment on the part of parents and children is due to strong extended family resources, greater acceptance of alternative child-rearing structures, and fewer perceived barriers to divorce. Current research has taken a more positive approach in studying the effects of divorce on children and highlighting the important factors that will help children make a healthy adjustment to divorce.

Children's Developmental Status

Short-term reactions of children to the separation of their parents vary as a function of their age (Bray & Berger, 1993). Infants and toddlers up to 2 years may show their distress by failing to form secure attachments (Cowan, Cowan, Schulz, & Heming, 1994). Preschool children are most likely to worry about their own contribution to their parent's departure, to believe that the separation is temporary, and to be confused by a parent assuring the child of his or her love, yet, moving away. Preschool children show intense separation anxiety and fear abandonment by both parents, which leads to regression and self-blaming (Wallerstein & Corbin, 1999). Elementary school children react with anxiety, depression, worry, loyalty conflicts, guilt, and anger at one (or both) parents for deciding to divorce. Although initially anxious and upset about the divorce, adolescents appear to be least affected by parental separation and divorce. This may reflect their relative maturity and the availability of emotional support from peers and group activities. Adolescents can see positive outcomes of the divorce in terms of their own increased sense of self-reliance and responsibility and positive personality changes for parents (Summers, Forehand, Armistead, & Tannenbaum, 1998). The most vulnerable children, at all developmental ages, are those who are involved in legal battles between their divorcing parents on custody issues and visitation rights (Zigler & Finn-Stevenson, 1999).

Quality of the Ex-Spouse Relationship

In addition to children's age at the time of divorce, another prominent factor influencing children's adjustment is whether the parents engage in cooperative behavior or in combative interchanges, such as quarrels, sarcasm, demeaning the other parent, or physical abuse. Several researchers have noted that this is one of the major variables affecting child development outcomes (Crockenberg & Forgays, 1996; Davis & Cummings, 1998; Eddy, Heyman, & Weiss, 1991).

Unfortunately, conflict between parents often precedes the divorce and survives the legal divorce by many years. It is not uncommon for open parental discord to continue even 10 years after the dissolution of the parents' marriage (Fauber, Forehand, Thomas, & Wierson, 1990). Current evidence suggests that interparental conflict, whether in intact families or in divorced families, and no matter what the ethnic group, is the most salient factor in creating childhood behavior problems. For example, in a study of European and African American preschoolers whose parents were either to be divorced or already divorced, ex-spouse conflict equated to higher rates of preschool-age behavior problems for both groups of children (Shaw, Winslow, & Flanagan, 1999).

The existence of a negative relationship between ongoing parental conflict and childhood adjustment has been well documented. High levels of interparental conflict have been shown to be related to increases in the behavior problems of toddlers (Cowan, Cowan, Schulz, & Heming, 1994), school-age children (Fincham & Linfield, 1997), and young adolescents (Harold, Fincham, Osborne, & Conger, 1997). Children in the high-parental-conflict group report significantly higher levels of adjustment difficulties. The nature of these difficulties included academic problems, internalizing problems (high anxiety, withdrawal), and externalizing problems (conduct disorders) (Harold, Fincham, Osborne, & Conger, 1997). Other long-term effects on the child include poorer parent–child relationships, lower psychological well-being, and more violence in their own relationships (McNeal & Amato, 1998).

Conflict occurs to some extent in all marriages, yet most children do not develop emotional or behavioral problems; in fact, observing their parents resolve disagreements may even be beneficial for children (Grych & Fincham, 1999). However, there are some conditions under which marital conflict is likely to be harmful for children. Children's interpretation of the conflict is one factor (Flyr & Wild, 2001). When children evaluate parental discord as an event that threatens their own security, they are likely to be adversely affected. Similarly, when children believe that they are responsible for the parental discord, it will significantly affect their behavior.

What follows from research on parental conflict is that if the marriage is characterized by strife and strain, then it might be better for the children if the parents do divorce. Children in harmonious, one-parent households function better than those in nondivorced families characterized by marital discord. Research results, then, support the possibility that marital dissolution following high conflict may actually improve the emotional well-being of children relative to high conflict family status (Jekielek, 1998).

Gender Matters

One of the most consistent findings in earlier research is that boys are more negatively affected by divorce than girls. Girls tend to recover faster from the divorce of their parents. More recent research has found that gender effects depend on the age of the child at the time of divorce, the time of assessment, and measures used in assessment (Hetherington & Stanley-Hagen, 1995). Using these multiple indices, gender differences have been found in the adjustment of younger, but rarely in older, children.

Why should young boys find adjustment to divorce more difficult than girls? It appears that boys more than girls are exposed to conflict between the parents, and this parental discord is related to their being more aggressive, impulsive, and full of misguided energy (Morrison &

Cherlin, 1995). Further, assessments used in analyzing children's adjustment to divorce often measure acting out, externalizing behaviors which tend to be the modus operandi of boys more than girls. Also, father–son relations appear to be more vulnerable to marital distress than father–daughter relations (Osborne & Fincham, 1996) particularly if unhappy fathers withdraw from the marriage and the child.

Single-Parent Families

Historically, Italy has had a strong antidivorce tradition, with Italian families characterized by the stability of both their nuclear and their extended family relationships. Consistent with the tradition of family stability, Italy has one of the smallest proportions of single parents due to divorce of any European nation (Sabbadini, 1995). Like Italy, divorce in rural areas in Nigeria is low because it is considered a "bad thing" and, thus, single parenting is quite uncommon (Amoateng & Heaton, 1989). In India, under Islamic law, after the divorce, the husband is obligated to pay his wife maintenance only during the *iddat* (3 months following the divorce) (Pathak & Rajan, 1989). Therefore, if a woman is not able to maintain herself after divorce, it becomes the responsibility of her children, parents, or other relatives.

Thought CHALLENGE

What responsibility, if any, does society bear for protecting the millions of children who have suffered from their father's economic abandonment?

In the United States, it is often heard that children raised in single-parent homes are "at risk," which means that they are more likely to have developmental difficulties than other children. However, the degree of variability within single-parent homes—economic resources, stressors, personal well-being, and the quality of family relations, for example—makes this an overly broad generalization. The data show that single families differ by gender, age, ethnicity, and education, and that resources (such as income) and stressors (such as residential instability) determine whether the children of single parents are at risk (Amato, 2000). Other factors if present are associated with high risk for adjustment problems: an ongoing pattern of stress, isolations experienced by the family, and minimal social supports—all of which exact a toll on a single parent's abilities and resources and subsequently children's adjustment. Research indicates that one of the major reasons children from single-parent families may be at risk relates to economic factors.

Economic Variables

Of the many life changes that may occur after divorce, those of greatest concern stem from increased financial hardship. Almost half of the mothers with primary custody experience a 50 percent drop in income in the year following divorce (Grych & Fincham, 1999). African American women and European American women whose predivorce income is below the median suffer particularly large losses. Approximately 40 percent of these women live below the poverty line after divorce. The greater the financial hardship following a family breakup, the harder are the adjustments for all family members and the more adjustment problems shown by children (Cohen, 1993). Similarly, parents who are preoccupied with family finances will find it harder to be attentive and responsive to their children. Children who suffer minimal loss of material resources and who are able to maintain predivorce routines generally do not show impairment in their cognitive, emotional, and social functioning (Wallerstein, 1998).

The overwhelming body of scholarly research and governmental and other policy studies shows that fathers' contributions to the economic support of their children are much reduced after marital dissolution. Approximately three-fourths of single mothers have child support agreements; however, of these women, only about half receive the full amounts ordered in the agreements (Clarke-Stewart, Vandell, McCartney, Owen, & Booth, 2000). One-fourth receive no payment and the other one-fourth receive irregular payments in amounts less than those ordered. Further, it is common when a father remarries to give priority to the family with whom he resides and to share his financial and emotional resources first with them and secondarily with the children of his first marriage (Wallerstein, 1998).

Moreover, economic variables appear to play an important role in determining children's social and academic achievement. When children from one-parent and two-parent homes in similar economic circumstances are compared, little difference is found in children's school performance and their social adjustment (Jarrett, 1995). Thus, living with one parent may not necessarily be the most important factor that affects a child's development but rather the economic difficulties encountered by single parents (Amato & Rezac, 1994).

Blended Families

Almost half of all new marriages are remarriages (U.S. Bureau of the Census, 1999). Each year in the United States about one-half million children are involved in a remarriage, adding to the 7 million stepchildren under 18 (Grych & Fincham, 1999). About 10 percent of children at any given point are living with a stepparent as well as one of their biological parents. Because mothers most frequently have custody of children, stepparent families are usually stepfather families. Approximately 82 percent of remarried households are stepfather families (Hetherington & Stanley-Hagen, 1995).

The average age of children at the time of parental remarriage is 2 to 5 years for about one-third of the children in remarriage. Divorces, unfortunately, are more frequent in remarriages and occur at a rate of 10 percent higher than in first marriages (Hetherington, Bridges, & Isabella, 2000). Half of all divorces occur within 5.5 years. Consequently, one may conclude that many adults and their children will encounter a series of changes in family structure within a brief period of time. By the time a child reaches the teen years, for example, he or she could have been part of an original, first-marriage family, then spent time in a single-parent household, resided in a stepfather family, and finally lived again in a single-parent household. Thus, many children are exposed to a series of marital transitions and household organizations following their parents' initial separation and divorce.

TABLE 13.9

Challenges Confronting Stepparents

- Competition with ex-spouse in relationship with children
- Criticism from spouse and relatives about performance as a parent
- Problem of how to discipline but also maintain love of stepchildren
- Financial strain of raising children in possibly two separate families
- Negative stereotypes about stepparents
- Developing trusting, intimate relationship with stepchildren
- Dealing with complex structure of blended families and its impact on communication channels, stress, and interpersonal relationships
- A lack of institutionalized guidelines about normative behavior in stepfamilies
- A lack of research and reading material available on similar but also different challenges for parents and stepparents

Problems Encountered in Blended Families

Because of many challenges, second marriages frequently falter. The most common reason for this is that the demands of parenting allow too little time for the couple to get to know each other. As a result, parents tend to view the marriage as less cohesive, more problematic, and more stressful than do parents in first marriages. Other challenges that confront stepparents are summarized in Table 13.9.

Discipline is a thorny issue. Some children resent having a stepfather or stepmother telling them what to do. Both remarried mothers and fathers report poor family communication, less effective problem resolution, less consistency in setting rules, less effective discipline, and less family cohesion in the early months of remarriage (Bray, 1990). Experiences with hostile children may be so negative that they offset any pleasures that the couple may find in each other's company, swinging the balance against continuing the relationship. Causes of conflict often center around the children, their behavior, how to respond to them, and money spent on them.

Sometimes it is hard for children to adapt to the new situation, which may make life difficult for the parents. For example, children may have a special bond with the solo parent following the marital dissolution and feel betrayed when he or she remarries. If the parent marries too soon, the child may not have had enough time to adjust to the divorce before having to adjust to the remarriage. Some children continue to harbor hopes that their "real" parents will get back together; a new marriage obviously undermines this possibility.

Boys Fare Better

Whereas boys, particularly younger ones, experience more pervasive problems in postdivorce adjustment, girls have more problems adjusting to remarriage. Preadolescent boys in families with stepfathers are more likely than girls to show improvement on measures of adjustment; girls, in contrast (who often have close relationships with their custodial mothers and considerable independence) may find stepfathers disruptive and constraining, and view them as intruders or competitors for their mothers' attention. Even two years into the remarriage, girls often still show unhappiness; mothers have less control over them and conflict with daughters increases. Daughters may become demanding, hostile, and coercive to both their mother and the stepfather (Taylor, 1997).

Boys tend to show more pervasive effects from divorce than girls except in postdivorce families in which a stepparent is present (Zaslow, 1989). Within six months of the remarriage, boys show increased intellectual performance, their vocabulary increases, and their arithmetic skills improve (Taylor, 1997). Boys benefit from remarriage, but most of the benefit comes from an improved relationship with the custodial parent and not from the new relationship with the stepparent (Hetherington & Clingempeel, 1992).

APPLICATIONS:

Helping Children Adjust in Single-Parent and Blended Families

Single-Parent Families

According to Judith Wallerstein (1998), there are two major protective psychological factors that help children adjust successfully in single-parent family systems: (1) a reasonably harmonious parental relationship in which parents support and help each other through the rigors of parenting and (2) ongoing economic support.

Harmonious Relationship Between Ex-Spouses

The significance of continuing interparental conflict for children's adjustment to divorce, and the frequency with which conflict occurs between ex-spouses, suggests that attempts to help parents learn to resolve disagreements constructively may be one of the most powerful interventions for children. Court-mandated programs attempt to educate parents about the effects of conflict on children and teach them basic conflict resolution skills. Although this kind of program may be brief, it does appear to be helpful for raising parental awareness and improving problem solving in some couples (Grych & Fincham, 1993). When parents continue to engage in bitter battles, children, at all age levels, feel unable to master the resulting stress and psychic pain. The ability of parents to handle differences in their relationship through appropriate conflict management and communication skills is vital to children's adjustment and well-being (see First Person).

Continuing Financial Support from the Father

Single mothers and single fathers have similar as well as different hurdles to overcome. Mothers, more than fathers, experience economic disadvantages, and it is this factor, rather than the absence of the father, that contributes to children's adjustment difficulties (Cohen, 1993). In addition, single mothers generally report being less happy than single fathers, which is generally attributed to economic factors. Men, typically, do not lose economic support after a divorce. Experts suggest that if the mother does not have to incessantly worry about financial matters, she, in turn, is able to more effectively parent her children (Wallerstein, 1998). A dollar of child support makes a much greater impact on children's well-being than a dollar of income impacts on fathers' well-being. Noncustodial fathers can help to alleviate mothers' economic disadvantages and help them to devote more of their energies to meeting their children's needs when they continue to support their children financially.

Within the well-functioning family, these protective aspects of family life come together to provide an environment that is conducive to the healthy development of child and adult alike. A healthy environment is one that continuously changes to support the ever-changing needs of all family members. "Indeed, the mark of a healthy family is its capacity to bend, to adapt to the many changes in the adults and the continuous changes in the growing child as well as the social surroundings" (Wallerstein, 1998, p. 73).

Blended Families

The success of blended families can be tied to how well the stepparent accepts the role of supporting the biological parent, the biological parent's willingness to be the disciplinarian, how effectively the couple plans for the way daily practical problems will be addressed, and the nurturing of parent–child relationships.

Supporting the Biological Parent Stepparents often quickly discover that they have been issued a limited license to parent. Some accept and even appreciate the limits, draw back, and disengage. Others feel rejected and insist on trying to extend their mandate. The best strategy, according to Hetherington (1993), is for the stepparent not to make an active attempt to initiate, shape, and control children's behavior but rather to be supportive of the biological parent. Later, the stepparent may become more authoritative. Stepparents who are authoritative in their parenting style appear to have fewer negative encounters with their stepchildren, and their relationships improve over time. In contrast, stepparents who use permissive or authoritarian styles have stepchildren who exhibit negative behavior that continues over time.

Biological Parent as the Disciplinarian The biological parent should be in charge of setting and enforcing limits and in carrying out negative sanctions for his or her own children. When the biological parent is not able to do so, it is helpful if he or she makes it clear to the children that the stepparent is in charge and needs to be obeyed. Stepparents report higher marital satisfaction if they are not expected to either bond with or discipline their stepchildren immediately (Amato & Booth, 1996). It is particularly important in blended families for the biological parent and the stepparent to present a united front, at least in the initial stages of parenting. When a stepparent requests or presents an unpopular decision, stepchildren are likely to use this as a wedge between the parents, and this becomes a constant source of friction—"She's unfair; she's always picking on me." "He doesn't care about me; I'm not his real son." By being united, parents can insulate themselves from these attempts to separate them.

Advanced Planning Terry Arendell (1997) notes that in reconstituted families, as soon as possible the parents need to plan how they will handle everyday practical problems, ranging from major issues such as finances to more minor concerns such as what to call the stepparent. Advanced planning helps to avoid misunderstanding. The more preliminary planning that is done, the smoother the transition will be. It is also helpful to schedule weekly family meetings to talk about the previous week and any problems or misunderstandings that may have occurred. Leadership for these meetings should be rotated among all family members.

Nurturing Parent–Child Relationships Similarly, relationships between parents and children need to be nurtured. But, in an instantaneous family, these relationships have to be discovered and developed, which takes time, finesse, and patience (Hetherington, Bridges, & Insabella, 2000). Love is not essential but respect and concern for one another is. Good relationships between stepparents and stepchildren are a result of perseverance, self-sacrifice, and hard work. Although family activities can help to establish relationships between stepparents and stepchildren, it is also important to have individual time away from other family members (Anderson & Greene, 1999). For this reason, a private and individual space, no matter how small, should be created in the home for each family member.

New stepfamilies may need several years to develop a smooth, acceptable life (Anderson & Greene, 1999). Although there may be a temporary period of disruption and an increase in conflict and negativity between parents and children immediately following the remarriage, research findings suggest that these aversive interactions diminish over time (Duran-Aydintug, 1998). Generally two years after the remarriage, few differences are found between the relationships of nondivorced parents and their children and the relationship of remarried parents. Successful blended families, once they have established rules, have an organized family life, have agreed upon major and minor issues through careful planning, and can concentrate on developing relationships that will contribute to the growth of the parents and their children.

Closing on a very positive note, one of the most interesting conclusions of several researchers (Chan, Raboy, & Patterson, 1998; Hetherington, Bridges, & Insabella, 2000; Weinraub & Gringlas, 1995) is that *children's well-being is more a function of parenting and relationship processes within the family* (cohesion, warmth, respect, love) *than it is of household composition and family structure* (single-parent and blended families). Thus, the assumption that only two-parent families can raise healthy children is not supported by current research. The overriding conclusion is that children's outcomes appear to be unrelated to family structure.

FIRSTPERSON

Single Parenting after Divorce

After 13 years of marriage, the unthinkable happened . . . my husband wanted a divorce. That "traditional" family I always imagined having would no longer be a reality. My greatest fear about the impending divorce was not the end of my marriage but the reality that I would have to parent our 6-year-old son alone. I was scared! How would I find the time to work, be a mother and father, housekeeper, landscaper, teacher, and cook? Would the divorce have a negative effect on my son, and would I be able to offset those negatives by being a good parent?

Fortunately, my ex-husband and I have a very amicable relationship and that not only helped my son to adjust but also keeps us both involved in his life. I believe we have a very unique relationship that helps make my single-parenting job much easier than most in the same situation. I also realize that in our case, we are better parents apart than we would have been together. We parent differently, but I realize now that neither of us does it wrong. As long as we put our differences aside and keep the goal of maintaining a good, healthy environment for our son, parenting alone is not so difficult and hopefully will prove positive for our son.

Don't get me wrong. It is not always a positive experience or easy especially when you consider the emotions involved when a relationship ends. During difficult days I still feel very alone in my parenting. I'll never forget the time my son told me he hated me and maybe should just go live with his dad! My feelings were hurt. But, I had to remind myself that he was upset, and, of course, didn't really mean what he was saying. Days are long; we leave the house at 7:30 A.M. and don't return until 6:00 P.M. Once home, there is that dreaded homework and chores to do. But, no matter how many chores or time spent on homework, we spend time together as well. I have not experienced another relationship since my divorce; I often wonder where I would find the time. I believe I have adjusted well to my new role as a single parent and assume, when the time comes, I will make the necessary adjustment into the role of single Mom—with a date.

—***Joanna Werling***

Concept Checks

1. The most critical aspect of family function that determines children's adjustment to divorce is ______________ ______________.
2. Social adjustment and academic achievement of children from one-parent and two-parent families
   a. varies with ethnic groups.
   b. is the same when one controls for social support and economic status.
   c. is inevitably better for children from intact homes.
3. Which of the following statements is true about children in blended families?
   a. Girls make a better adjustment.
   b. Boys fare better in blended families.
   c. Boys and girls do equally well.
4. The best family systems are those in which the parents
   a. remain married, even if they don't get along.
   b. and children have a respectful and warm relationship regardless of family structure.
   c. are child-centered and consider the child's needs rather than their own.

Reviewing Key Points

Understanding Self and Others

- In middle childhood, children see themselves as distinct from others because they think and feel differently from others. They feel more in control of their thoughts and actions. Middle childhood is a time when the self-concept is expanding to incorporate new dimensions of self in myriad domains and from many sources (peers, teachers, other authority figures). But, it is also a time for solidifying self-esteem. Once children have achieved various stable self-evaluations, they tend to process information received from their environment in congruence with their self-evaluations.
- Children between the ages of 6 and 8 define friends as those who share their worldly goods, act nice, and are fun to be with. Children ages 8 to 10 describe friends as those who help one another and are reliable and trustworthy. They understand that their own perspective may not be the only valid one and begin to evaluate themselves in terms of how others view them. At ages 10 to 12, children are able to simultaneously consider the viewpoints of both participants in a conflict.
- Children's peer status is an important determinant of their later adjustment. Popular children are sociocentric and attuned to other children's feelings. Rejected-aggressive children are egocentric, aggressive, and quarrelsome. Neglected children seldom interact with others and engage in more solitary play. It appears that rejected-aggressive children are more at risk for future developmental problems than neglected children.
- Neglected children can be assisted in overcoming their "overlooked" status, by making sure they know some of the children in a group before entering that group and encouraging them in risk taking and adventures in independence. Overprotection and encouraging dependency backfire and cause these children to become clingy and nonassertive. Rejected-aggressive children can be helped by working to change their attributional perspectives, helping them become less rejection-sensitive; training them to make more accurate attributions to others' responses toward them, and avoiding physical punishment.

Moral Development

- Piaget suggested that moral development involves two successive stages: heteronomous (moral realism) and autonomous (moral relativism). According to Piaget, children during the stage of moral realism (middle or late childhood) generally accord unilateral respect for authorities, such as parents and teachers, and for the rules they make. Children operating at the autonomous perspective tend to base their moral judgments on mutual respect among peers or equals and regard for the rules that guide their actions.
- Kohlberg elaborated and refined Piaget's theory, erecting three levels and six stages of moral development. Kohlberg suggests that moral development proceeds unvaryingly through these stages with each succeeding stage reflecting a higher stage of moral reasoning. Preconventional moral thinking is dominated by avoiding punishment or gaining a fair exchange. Conventional morality consists of mutual expectations and beliefs in rules and justice. Postconventional moral reasoning involves individual rights (which are often based on extenuating circumstances) and following one's individual conscience for the good of humanity.
- It is suggested, based on both Piaget's and Kohlberg's theories, that children need exposure to other children and the conflicts that naturally arise among them to further their levels of reasoning.

- Adults can help children become morally conscious individuals by being effective role models, using inductive disciplining techniques, living in accordance with the same basic rules expected of the child; being firm but fair; and engaging children in family discussions in which they have a voice in the decision making. Prosocial behaviors may be fostered when chores are assigned to children that give them a sense of helping the entire family.

Family Influences in Middle Childhood

- Several factors affect whether children make a healthy adjustment to their parents' divorce: children's developmental status, the quality of the ex-spouse's relationship, custody arrangements, the quality of the parent–child relationship, children's gender, and social support systems available to the family. Boys are more negatively affected by divorce than girls, as exemplified in their aggressive, acting-out, noncompliant behaviors, and girls are more negatively affected by remarriage, demonstrated by their antagonistic behavior toward their mother and stepfather.
- The majority of single-parent homes are headed by mothers. The absence of a father is not believed to be the salient factor in producing adjustment problems in children. Rather, economic deprivation appears to play a more important role in determining children's social and academic achievement. When socioeconomic status is controlled, there is very little difference between children from two-parent and single-parent homes in terms of children's academic performance and social standings with peers.
- The divorce rate is higher for blended families than it is for first marriages. Most husbands and wives feel that they did not have adequate time to get to know each other because the logistics of running the house and managing the children took precedence. Discipline seems to be a tricky problem area for parents. Younger children may be easier to manage than older children who have more sophisticated cognitive skills and thus can more effectively sabotage the disciplinary efforts of their new stepparent.
- Factors that enhance children's development in single-parent families include establishing a reasonably harmonious relationship with the ex-spouse, sensitivity and commitment to the children and continued financial support from the noncustodial father; supporting the biological parent; having the biological parent as the disciplinarian; engaging in advanced planning, establishing a strong husband–wife bond, and nurturing parent–child relationships are some of the factors that promote successful blended family systems.

Answers to Concept Checks

Understanding Self and Others
1. b 2. b 3. c 4. a

Moral Development
1. b 2. b 3. true 4. a

Family Influences in Middle Childhood
1. spousal relationships 2. b 3. b 4. b

Key Terms

conventional moral reasoning
empathy
friendship
moral realism
moral relativism
neglected children
peer acceptance
popular children
postconventional moral reasoning
preconventional moral reasoning
premoral period
prosocial behaviors
rejected-aggressive children
rejected children
shy children
social competence

InfoTrac College Edition

For additional readings, explore InfoTrac College Edition, your online library. Go to **http://www.infotrac-college.com/wadsworth** and use the passcode that came on the card with your book. Try these search terms: moral education, divorce and children.

Child Development CD-ROM

Go to the Wadsworth Child Development CD-ROM for further study of the concepts in this chapter. The CD-ROM also includes quizzes and additional activities to expand your learning experience.

Let me introduce you to *Jeanne Brooks-Gunn*

Dr. Brooks-Gunn is a professor of Child Development and Education at Columbia University's Teachers College. Her special interests involve applying her research findings to social policies and interventions that will improve the lives of children—particularly at-risk children being raised in impoverished environments. Her research interests also include adolescents. In Part Six, we explore this transitional time when physical and sexual metamorphoses transform children into young adults. Dr. Brooks-Gunn's work has been pivotal in contributing to our understanding of the physical, cognitive, and social changes that occur during the years of 13 to 19. One of her key works, *The Encyclopedia of Adolescence*, not only discusses the prominent milestones that occur during these developmental years but addresses common concerns and questions. One question, "Is adolescence a period characterized by 'storm and stress'?" has been asked over time by such notables as Socrates, Freud, and G. Stanley Hall, the father of adolescent psychology. Setting the stage for our exploration into adolescence, Dr. Brooks-Gunn brings us an up-to-date reply.

PART 6

Developmental Contexts: *Adolescence*

How Stormy and Stressful Are Adolescent Transitions?

by Jeanne Brooks-Gunn, Professor of Child Development and Education, Columbia University Teachers College

The question of how stormy and stressful adolescent transitions are never seems to go out of style. Socrates may have been the first to raise the issue when he stated that adolescents "are ready to contradict their parents, monopolize the conversation in company, eat gluttonously, and tyrannize their teachers." Why do so many view adolescence as a particularly rough transitional time? Perhaps, adults generalize from the few adolescents who do have tumultuous experiences to all youths. It may be a more argumentative time and given a certain rate of negative events and flare-ups, social cognitive theorists may overestimate their probability of occurrence. Or perhaps adults, when they remember their own adolescent experiences, tend to highlight the feelings of uncertainty that accompany the rapid and numerous challenges that adolescence heralds and reinterpret these as overwhelmingly negative.

However, somewhat surprising to many researchers, the majority of youths do not report their adolescent experiences as being crisis laden—a point discussed further in Chapter 14. Some factors, how-

ever, may cause some adolescents to experience this period as more stressful. Pubertal events such as breast development and menarche (for girls), pubic hair development (boys and girls), and spermarche (boys) are salient events that contribute to stress in some adolescents—particularly those who are maturing more slowly than their age-mates. The stress and anxiety of late maturers often takes the form of wanting to be like everyone else. We have also found that children whose parents tease them about puberty have less positive experiences. A mother, for example, making some joking remark about her daughter's Triple-A cup bra causes her daughter not only humiliation but stress as well.

Another line of research has shown some links between the rapid hormonal increases of early puberty and more negative moods and behavior. The effects seem to be significant, yet small. At the same time, the social events of early adolescence are more predictive of negative behavior. Events such as moving to middle school and encountering new teachers and new students are viewed as stressful by many youths. Suggestions are being made for how middle schools might be designed to be more "youth-friendly."

Another path taken by many researchers is to examine, in great detail, interactions between parents and youths. What are the disagreements that actually occur, and how are they resolved? What is the contribution of parent and of adolescent to these conflicts? When is conflict growth enhancing, and when is it destructive? These issues are covered further in Chapter 15. In understanding the transition from childhood to adolescence, current research is focusing on how institutions, parents, and concerned adults can support youths who do experience storm and stress to help them successfully negotiate this stage of betwixt and between.

PART OUTLINE

Chapter 14
Physical Development: Adolescence

Chapter 15
Cognitive Development: Adolescence

Chapter 16
Socioemotional Development: Adolescence

AIR
AIR

CHAPTER FOURTEEN

Physical Development: *Adolescence*

CHAPTER OUTLINE

Physical Transformations
- Defining Adolescence
- Pubertal Changes
- Early- and Late-Maturing Males and Females
- The Ideal Male and Female Physiques
- Adolescents and Nutrition
- Eating Disorders
- Applications: Helping Anorectic and Bulimic Adolescents

Sexuality Issues
- Physical Attractiveness
- Dating and Intimacy
- Sexual Awakenings
- Sexually Active Teenagers
- Sexually Transmitted Diseases
- Teenage Pregnancy
- Applications: Helping Teenage Parents

Health-Related Issues
- Youths and Violence
- Drugs
- Why Do Teenagers Use Drugs?
- Treatment
- Applications: Should Adults "Buzz Off" or "Butt In"?

Reviewing Key Points

Holding up a picture of Super Model Ulma, Jane asks her friend, "Do you think I look at all like her?" Sarah glances up, looks at the picture and then her friend, "Yeah, maybe . . . if you didn't have freckles." Sarah studies the picture a bit more intensely. "Gee, she's really thin. Look how skinny her arms are!" Jane glances off and imagines how she would look in the model's ideal body and then glances back in the mirror at what seems to her a very chubby reflection. Jane worries about being too fat.

Collectively, the adolescent's doctrine seems to be the following: Worry if your nose is too fat. Worry if your nose is too long. Worry that your ears stick out. Worry that your eyes are too close together. If you are a boy, worry that your voice will never change. Worry that you'll never be able to grow a mustache. Worry that you are too short. If you are a girl, worry that your breasts are too small or too large or that your hips are too wide or too narrow. Worry about people liking you. Worry that you are just too unattractive.

Oh, the perils of puberty. Teenagers worry, and puberty provides a whole series of matters to worry about. Teenagers often conceive of a physical ideal or a standard of physical development and are disturbed because they do not measure up. To this end, many teens are rather unhappy about the pace of the physical changes in their body; they are too slow or too fast. Moreover, many believe that Mother Nature has unfairly failed to endow them with the features they need to be the "perfect teen." For most teenagers, physical appearance becomes part of their self-identities.

Our purpose here is to capture not just the biological and physical nature of the changes that occur during adolescence but to understand the interwoven psychological consequences those transformations entail.

Adolescence has come to represent the developmental bridge between middle childhood and adulthood. Physical, social, and cognitive changes set this period apart from each of these two stages of life. Physically, over a period of about four years, the child is transformed into an adult; this process is known as **puberty**. It is a biological change, a multifaceted process, that occurs over time and consists of a series of interdependent events. Puberty includes the growth spurt, which adds inches to height and pounds to body weight. It also involves sexual maturity, which propels children into mature reproductive status. Psychologically, these physical and sexual transformations have a different impact for early and late maturers; such timing strongly influences whether or not teenagers feel comfortable with the appearance of their bodies.

Like Jane, in the opening vignette, many teenagers, particularly girls, see themselves with "chubby reflections." In their quest for thinness, they may begin dieting. For some teenagers, undereating may develop into serious eating disorders such as anorexia nervosa and bulimia nervosa. How do these teenagers get on this track of out-of-control weight loss, and how can they be helped?

Our next section discusses sexuality issues, which encompass dating, intimacy, and sexual awakenings. Many positives arise in each of these sexual progressions, but the negatives—sexually transmitted diseases and teenage pregnancy—represent serious repercussions of sexuality during adolescence that cannot be overlooked. In our concluding section, we will look at other health-related issues arising during adolescence such as violence against others and drug use.

Adolescents also ponder broader identity issues, such as who they are and what they will become. According to Erik Erikson, adolescence is a time of seeking one's ego identity. It is a time when adolescents seek to establish continuity with the past and to mentally work out various and sometimes fragmentary idealizations and identifications to ultimately form a coherent unity in character. Thus, identity not only extends backward, building on earlier childhood experiences, but is projected forward in the form of establishment of goals, aims, and anticipated career and lifestyle. In later adolescence, the sense of intimacy, or ability to be intimate with those of the opposite sex, normally emerges. To this end, many adolescents want to look "perfect" and be admired by others.

puberty
Biological developments that transform individuals from a state of physical immaturity to one in which they are mature and capable of reproduction.

adolescence
Begins with the biological changes of puberty and ends with the assumption of adult work and family roles.

Physical Transformations

Before Beginning . . .

After reading this section, you will be able to

- understand the physical and sexual changes that accompany puberty.
- identify the psychological consequences of early and late maturation.
- delineate the symptoms and causes of anorexia nervosa and bulimia nervosa.
- identify ways of helping adolescents with undereating disorders.

Defining Adolescence

Adolescence begins with the biological changes of puberty and ends with the assumption of adult work and family roles. Although the specific ages for these changes may differ from person to person, adolescence is typically a long period with distinct phases. *Early adolescence* is characterized by puberty and related changes and usually occurs between the ages of 10 and 13. *Middle adolescence,* characterized by resolving identity issues, includes the ages of 14 to 16. *Late adolescence* marks the transition into adulthood and is thought of as the ages of 17 to 20.

Adolescence is a time of transition—not just in terms of physical and sexual transformations that are the topics of interest to us in this chapter—but, as we shall see in the next two chapters, adolescence involves changes in cognitive and socioemotional areas as well. Cognitive capacity increases throughout childhood and continues to develop into adolescence. In general, young people develop increased capacity to think in terms of ideas and abstract, formal thinking. Increasingly, adolescents also develop a sense of self in all aspects of functioning. Social development moves increasingly in the direction of intimacy with peers, including romantic partners.

Although each individual adds his or her own special twist of individuality to adolescent development, there are some common milestones characterizing adolescence that are interwoven throughout various cultures and ethnic groups. These include issues of dependence versus independence, changes in the parent–adolescent relationship, exploration, more need for privacy, and idealization of others.

Dependence Versus Independence

Adolescence is a time for emerging independence. Adolescents strive for a sense of emancipation from the nuclear family and often feel that they must loosen themselves from the caretaking hold of parents. To this end, teenagers spend increasingly more time with peers. The goal of adolescence was once thought to be *detachment* of the adolescent from the family in the service of independence. Current theory and research discards this orientation, concluding that the key challenge of adolescent development is to separate from the family while *connecting* with it in new ways (Petersen, 1998).

The Parent–Adolescent Relationship

Today's adolescents are continually questioning the legitimacy of parental jurisdiction over particular issues, such as friends, grades, dress, and curfew. Although conflict does tend to escalate from early to middle adolescence, less than 10 percent of families endure serious relationship difficulties characterized by chronic levels of conflict and repeated arguments over serious issues during adolescence.

Exploration

Adolescence is characterized as a period of experimentation with sexuality, drug use, general disobedience, and other opportunities seen as temptations. Today, the consequences of experimenting sexually and with drugs may lead to unwanted pregnancies and sexually transmitted diseases and drug abuse, respectively.

Needs for Privacy

Teenagers today, in their quest for independence, commonly develop privacy needs. The closed bedroom door, secret telephone conversations, diaries, and music blasting through earphones are but a few examples of the adolescent's need for privacy. Family get-togethers often become begrudgingly tolerated affairs.

Idealization

Crushes and hero worship are two of the hallmarks of adolescence. A crush on a teacher or the longing to be a superstar quarterback or a rock star may help the young adolescent to take the appropriate steps toward developing personal career goals and achieving them.

Adolescence is the last phase before a child becomes fully grown and takes his or her place in the adult world. Gradually between the ages of 13 and 19 (and often beyond) adolescents spend their time passing through these milestones of adolescence before they can move on into adulthood. In this sense, adolescence then refers to the psychological alterations that take place during this phase of development; *puberty* is used to describe the physical changes that accompany it.

Thought **CHALLENGE**

Why are adolescents so concerned about the appearance of secondary sex characteristics during puberty? What societal influences promote such concerns?

Pubertal Changes

Biological change is the hallmark of the transition from childhood to early adolescence and is the one universal aspect of the adolescent experience found in all primate species, in all cultures, throughout history. Within a few years, the child is, in physical appearance, transformed into an adult. The slow steady growth of middle childhood gives way to a rate of development that is more rapid than at any other time of life except during fetal development in utero. The onset of adolescence is usually associated with puberty, a period of rapid biological and sexual changes. These physical advancements directly influence biological systems and functions but also the adolescent's social and emotional development. Many adolescents feel awkward and unfamiliar with their changing physical appearances. Changes at puberty include those related to accelerated physical growth—known as the growth spurt—the development of male or female sexual characteristics, sleep needs, and the parent–adolescent relationship.

The Growth Spurt

The **growth hormone** is produced throughout life in varying amounts and is directly related to gradual increases in body size and weight over the childhood years. During adolescence, the system is flooded with this hormone, causing an acceleration of growth known as the **growth spurt** (Nicholas, Lancer, & Silva, 1997). There is a fairly regular order in which the dimensions accelerate; leg length as a rule reaches its peak first, followed a few months later by shoulder width, and a year later by trunk length. Most of the spurt in height is due to trunk growth rather than leg growth (Tanner, 1998).

In girls, the growth spurt begins about age 10, reaches its peak about 11¾ years, and decreases at age 13, with slow continual growth for several additional years. Boys begin their growth spurt later than girls,

growth hormones Produced throughout life in varying amounts; it is directly related to gradual increases in body size and weight over the childhood years. During adolescence, the system is flooded with this hormone, causing an acceleration of growth known as the growth spurt.

growth spurt The rapid growth in height during adolescence, triggered by the so-called growth hormone.

around age 12½, reaching a peak at 14, and declining at age 15½. Girls reach 98 percent of their adult height at 16¼ years; boys reach 98 percent of their adult height at 17¾ years (Tanner, 1998). The growth in height results from the final stages of bone maturation. The muscles, too, lengthen and strengthen. A similar spurt in growth at adolescence can be shown for weight, muscle size, head and face growth, and especially for reproductive organs. In fact, "every muscular and skeletal dimension of the body seems to take part in the adolescent's growth spurt" (Tanner, 1962, p. 10).

hormones
Hormones literally mean "to set in motion." The sex hormones, testosterone in males, and estrogen in females, are responsible for sexual maturation.

gonadotrophic hormones
In males, these hormones stimulate the testes and adrenal glands to manufacture the hormone testosterone, which brings about the manufacture of sperm. In females, these hormones stimulate the ovaries to manufacture the hormones estrogen and progesterone, which trigger numerous physical events, including the release of mature ova from the ovaries; this eventually allows for reproduction.

gonads
Primary sex organs; the ovaries in females and the testes in males.

testosterone
A hormone associated in boys with the development of secondary sex characteristics.

estrogen
Female hormone responsible for sexual maturation during puberty.

secondary sex characteristics
The anatomical and physiological signs that outwardly distinguish males from females. They make their appearance as the primary sexual organs are maturing.

menarche
A girl's first menstrual period.

Sexual Maturity

Puberty involves a complex series of hormonal changes. **Hormones** are powerful and highly specialized chemical substances that interact with cells. The entire process of maturing sexually begins when hormones of the hypothalamus gland trigger hormones from the pituitary gland. The anterior pituitary, which lies just beneath the base of the brain in approximately the geometric center of the head, secretes **gonadotrophic hormones**. These hormones stimulate the **gonads**, the ovaries in the female and the testes in the male, which in turn secrete their own hormones. When the testis is stimulated by the gonadotrophic hormones, it secretes **testosterone**; when the ovary is stimulated, it secretes **estrogens**, female hormones of which the chief one is estradiol (see Figure 14.1).

Testosterone in boys is responsible for **secondary sex characteristics**, such as the growth of the testes, penis, and first pubic hair; the capacity for ejaculation, the growth spurt, voice changes, beard development, and completion of pubic hair. The first sign of puberty in boys is the increase in the rate of growth of the testes and scrotum (see Table 14.1). Approximately a year later, there is an acceleration in the growth of the penis and, in the following year, the beginning of the growth spurt in height. Body hair and facial hair usually make their first appearance about two years after the beginning of pubic hair growth. The most obvious aspect of development is perhaps the lowering of the voice, which occurs late in puberty. The larynx enlarges and the vocal cords double in length. This lengthening of the vocal cords results in a drop in pitch of about an octave.

In girls, estrogen causes the beginning of breast development, the first pubic hair, the widening of hips, a growth spurt, **menarche** (first menstruation), and the completion of breast and pubic hair growth. The sequence of these developments is quite similar, although there is great variation in the age at which each starts. Girls' first external sign of puberty is elevation

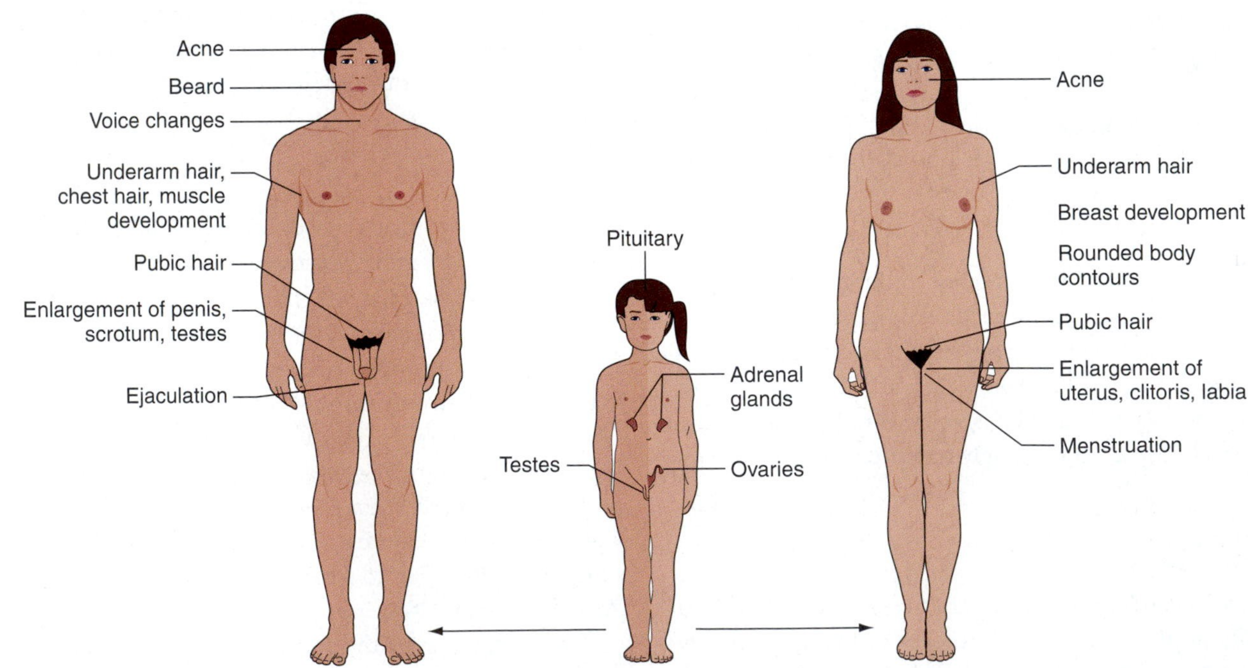

FIGURE 14.1 *Hormonal Changes During Puberty*

Androgen hormones in males and estrogen hormones in females contribute to the development of secondary sex characteristics.

TABLE 14.1

Age and Appearance of Sexual Characteristics During Puberty

Age (Years)	Boys	Girls
9–10		Growth of bony pelvis; budding of nipples; growth spurt begins
10–11	First growth of testes and scrotum	Budding of breasts; pubic hair
11–12	Activity of prostate gland producing semen; growth of penis	Changes in lining of vagina; growth of external and internal genitalia; breast development; peak of growth spurt
12–13	Pubic hair; height spurt begins; spermarche (first ejaculation) occurs	Pigmentation of nipples; breasts fill out; menarche (12.4 years; range: 9 to 17 years)
13–14	Rapid growth of testes and penis; peak of growth spurt	Auxiliary hair (under arms)
14–15	Light hair growth above upper lip; voice change	Earliest normal pregnancies
15–16	Mature spermatoza	Acne
16–17	Facial and body hair; acne	

of the breasts. Growth of the uterus and vagina occurs simultaneously with breast development. The labia and clitoris also enlarge. Menarche almost invariably occurs after the growth spurt has begun to slow. In the United States, girls achieve menarche at a mean age of 12.4 years, with 5 percent beginning at 11 to 11.5 years, 25 percent at 12 to 12.5 years, and 60 percent by age 13 (Graber & Brooks-Gunn, 1998).

The findings of Marcia Herman-Giddens and her colleagues (Herman-Giddens, Slora, Wasserman, Bourdony, Bhapkar, Koch, & Hesemeier, 1997) indicate ethnic differences in menarche as well as the onset of puberty. They report, for example, that African American girls exhibit secondary sex characteristics earlier than European American girls. The average age of onset of breast development in African American and European American girls is 8.87 years and 9.96 years, respectively. Menarche occurs at an average of 11.6 years in African American girls and 12.4 years in European American girls.

Whereas menarche signals sexual maturity for girls, **spermarche** is the first sign of puberty in boys. Around the age of 12 or 13, boys experience the enlargement of the testes that manufacture sperm and shortly thereafter are likely to experience their first ejaculation of **semen**—a sticky fluid produced by the prostate gland, which provides the medium for sperm to live after ejaculation. When the testes and prostate gland begin producing seminal fluid, pressure builds up and the fluid is discharged more or less periodically, usually at night. Thus, most boys have their first ejaculation as nocturnal emissions, or "wet dreams," during sleep.

The Secular Trend During the past hundred years there has been a striking tendency for children to become larger at all ages. This is known as the **secular trend**. Most of the trend toward greater size in children reflects a more rapid maturation. This trend

spermarche
Around the age of 12 or 13, boys experience their first ejaculation of semen.

semen
The sticky fluid that men ejaculate, containing sperm, which is capable of fertilizing eggs and making a woman pregnant.

secular trend
A trend toward earlier maturation, in which children at all ages are growing larger than those from earlier generations.

Some findings indicate ethnic differences in menarche as well as the onset of puberty.

toward earlier maturation is best shown in statistics on age at menarche. In 1880, for example, the average age at which girls had their first menstrual period in well-nourished industrialized countries was 15 to 17 years; now median menarcheal ages are between 12½ and 13½ years. By contrast, among the Bantu in the South African Transkei, where children's living conditions have not improved, the median menarcheal age is about 15½ years. One hundred years ago, males reached their adult height at ages 23 to 25 and the average female at ages 19 to 20 years. Today, maximum adult height for males is reached between 18 and 20 years and 13 to 14 years for females.

The causes of the secular trend are probably multiple. Clearly, the rate of maturation and the age of the onset of puberty are dependent on a complex interaction of genetic and environmental factors. The improvement of health care and overall living conditions and control of infectious diseases can account for some of these changes. A major environmental factor, however, appears to be better nutrition. Most of these physical advancements are probably due to more protein and calories operating during the whole of the growth period from conception onward (Tanner, 1998). Thus, hormonal changes may be occurring at more rapid rates because children in our culture are better nourished. The tendency of succeeding generations to achieve physical maturation and greater height and weight at earlier ages, however, appears to be leveling off in industrialized nations (Tanner, 1998). Many Third World countries, however, are now experiencing their own secular trends.

Sleep

Do these physical and hormonal changes impact sleep, which critically influences the adolescent's ability to think, behave, and feel during the daytime hours? According to researchers, parents, and teenagers, it appears that they are not getting enough sleep (Carskadon, 1990). Moreover, a significant percentage of teenagers want more sleep.

Part of the reason for not getting enough sleep has to do with changes in adolescent sleeping patterns. Teenagers, for example, tend to stay up late; indeed, they report *enjoying* staying up late. Approximately 90 percent of surveyed 10th and 12th graders report going to bed later than midnight on weekends (Carskadon & Mancuso, 1998). Survey and field studies show that adolescents usually obtain much less sleep than school-age children, averaging from 10 hours during middle childhood to less than 7.5 hours by age 16 (Allen, 1992). The most obvious explanation for adolescent sleep deprivation appears to result from a combination of early school start times, late afternoon/evening jobs and activities, academic and social pressures, biological changes that take place during puberty, and a physiological sleep requirement that does not decrease with puberty (Wolfson & Carskadon, 1998). As a result, adolescents go to bed late, have difficulty waking up in the morning, and struggle to stay alert and to function successfully during the daytime.

Relatedly, students with short total sleep time report increased levels of depressed mood, daytime sleepiness, and problematic sleep behaviors in comparison to longer sleepers (Morrison, McGee, & Stanton, 1992). Amy Wolfson and Mary Carskadon (1998) suggest that if adolescents had the opportunity to obtain more sleep each night, they would experience fewer fluctuations in their daily moods and fewer behavioral difficulties. More sleep, then, may be a simplistic solution to teenagers' moodiness and sleepiness. Unfortunately, however, the magnitude of sleepiness in adolescence has been largely overlooked because it is so widespread that it almost seems to be a normal part of adolescence (Manber, Pardee, Bootzin, Kuo, Rider, Rider, & Bergstrom, 1995).

Parent–Adolescent Relationships

The physical changes that take place during puberty may have an impact on the parent–adolescent relationship (Buchanan, Eccles, & Becker, 1992). As a result of hormonal changes (and, perhaps, teenagers' sleeping patterns), adolescents may be irritable, negative, and prone to breaking rules, causing some friction with their parents. And, reciprocally, parents often react to these behaviors by becoming overly intrusive and monitoring behavior too closely, causing further conflict. Similarly, as children mature physically, parents may begin to believe they can expect more mature behavior from their adolescent, more than the adolescent may be capable of (Freedman-Doan, Arbreton, Harold, & Eccles, 1993); this may also be a source of dissension between parent and teenager. Expectations for maturity may be stronger in the teenager who is physically maturing at an earlier age (early-maturing adolescent) as opposed to one who is developing more slowly (late-maturing adolescent).

Early- and Late-Maturing Males and Females

The psychological consequence of early or late physical maturation is one factor that appears to relate to the adolescent's comfort with and acceptance of his or her body image. This may be truer for girls because the changes they undergo are more dramatic. Some teenagers are painfully shy and often frustrated because they are not as well developed as their peers. Others may be overly self-conscious because they are more well-developed than their peers.

Early-maturing individuals tend to have a more intensive adolescent growth spurt than do late-maturing individuals who have a more uniform increment of growth spread over a longer time period. James Tanner suggests that "in early maturers, the whole process goes more quickly, and also more intensely, so that a great total result is achieved despite the small amount of time taken" (1978, p. 94).

Early Maturation: A Plus for Boys

Early-maturing males are large for their age, more muscular, and better coordinated than late-maturing males, so they enjoy a considerable athletic advantage. They also enjoy considerable social advantages in relation to peers. Early-maturing males tend to have a more positive self-image. Adults tend to rate early-maturing males as more physically attractive, more masculine, and more relaxed than late-maturing males. However, adults tend to expect more adult behavior and responsibility of early-maturing males. Thus, early-maturing males may have less time to enjoy the freedom that comes with childhood. Another disadvantage is that early-maturing males may be more likely to get involved in problem or deviant activities.

Late-maturing males may suffer socially induced inferiority because of their delayed growth and development (Hayward, Killen, Wilson, & Hammer, 1997). At age 15, the late-maturing male may be 8 inches shorter and 30 pounds lighter than his early-maturing counterpart. Accompanying this size difference are marked differences in body build, strength, motor performance, and coordination. Because late-maturing males tend to be shorter and physically weaker, they are less apt to be outstanding athletes.

Late-maturing males are seen by their peers as more childish; they are less popular and less likely to take on leadership positions. On personality measures, late-maturing males exhibit stronger feelings of inadequacy, higher needs for autonomy, more negative conceptions of self, less control, and less self-assurance.

Early Maturation: Not a Plus for Girls

Whereas early maturation tends to be a plus for boys, this is generally not so for girls. This negative effect may have its greatest impact during the elementary school years (Ge, Conger, & Elder, 1996). A physically mature fifth or sixth grader, for example, is at some disadvantage because she is out of phase with the majority of her classmates. Early-maturing girls often find themselves towering over others, and many assume a slouching posture to conceal their height. Their advanced breast development seems to violate others' expectations of petiteness and femininity. Because girls mature about two years earlier than boys, the early-maturing girl is not only more physically advanced than her female age-mates but far more advanced than all her male classmates as well. By eighth or ninth grade, however, the early-maturing female comes into her own socially. She now begins to look more like a grown-up woman, is envied by the other girls, begins to attract the attention of older boys, and may start dating. The girl, however, may find herself emotionally unequipped to deal with sophisticated social activities and sexual enticements (Brooks-Gunn, 1991).

Late-maturing girls have a different set of problems. Unlike their early-maturing counterparts, these girls find themselves in a childish state both physically and in sexual maturation. This may result not only in problems with peer relations and self-esteem but also in difficulty with being treated like a child by parents and other adults. Although these concerns may seem trivial to some, they are very real and disturbing to the child who desperately wants to be grown up but whose body is just not cooperating.

Most teenagers tend to worry that they are not physically normal. In early adolescence when most adolescents want more than anything else to be like everyone else, the early- and late-maturing adolescents may feel that they are the least alike among their contemporaries. Whereas adults are aware that every teenager is growing and changing at his or her own pace and that adolescents come in all sizes and shapes, young adolescents know no such thing. Perhaps the critical issue then in understanding how early and late maturation affects adolescents is the degree to which they are out of step with their peers. Thus, we might expect disadvantages to be associated with the very early maturing or a very late maturing girl or boy.

Thought CHALLENGE

Females appear to be highly pressured by (and attuned to) media advertising portraying the ideal female body as thin. Are males targeted and attuned to similar types of media messages? What sort of pressures, if any, impact boys to develop a lean and muscular physique?

The Ideal Masculine and Feminine Physiques

Another factor that affects adolescents' comfort with their body image is physical attractiveness. Most adolescents desire to be physically attractive, to have the "ideal body." In our culture "the ideal" most often means tall and muscular for boys and tall and slender for girls.

The Male Physique

Adolescents favor a muscular build for boys. To get bigger muscles, boys may inject themselves with steroids. Today, an estimated 10 percent of high school students —overwhelmingly adolescent boys—either take or have taken steroids (O'Malley, Johnson, & Bachman, 1999). Many teenage boys say they take steroids not so much for improved athletic performance as for cosmetic purposes—to make themselves more muscular (Yarnold, 1998). **Anabolic steroids** come in many chemical structures, but essentially they are forms of testosterone, the chief male hormone. Some steroids may be taken orally in tablet form, but injection is actually preferred because it lessens the harmful effects on the liver.

The potentially severe side effects of long-term use of steroids and practices such as "stacking" (taking 2 or 3 types of steroids simultaneously) are the possibility of liver dysfunction, cancer, and damage to the reproductive system. Short-term effects are hair loss, severe acne, and high blood pressure as well as shrunken testicles and low sperm production. (Women users may develop masculine characteristics such as growth of facial hair and male pattern baldness; these effects tend to be irreversible.) Steroids may have a profound effect on behavior. Increased aggressiveness, known as "roid rages," often leads to violent, destructive behavior. Recovering steroid users can become extremely depressed when they try to give up the drug; in some cases, this has led to suicide.

anabolic steroids Strength enhancers that come in many chemical structures; the prime one is testosterone. They are used to increase muscle mass but carry potentially negative side effects such as liver infection and damage to the reproductive system.

The Female Physique

The importance of physical attractiveness in Western society is undeniable. Unfortunately, many teenage girls are not happy with their body image (Ephron, 2000). Perhaps, this is so because girls tend to be pressured into thinking that they have to be thin. Researchers consistently point out that body image dissatisfaction is significantly related to dieting (Strong & Huon, 1998). Subsequently, new diets proliferate for that segment of the population that wants to lose a few extra pounds. Over 70 percent of girls 15 years and older have been found to desire weight loss or engage in dieting (Sanders, Kapphahn, & Steiner, 1998). About 30 to 40 percent of 12- and 13-year-old girls also admit to concerns about weight.

Adolescents and Nutrition

Countless books, articles, and advertisements in teen magazines describe diets that claim to melt away pounds, promote good health, and give you radiant skin—all things that many young teenage girls appear to desire. Among the magic diet schemes are eating no carbohydrates, eating no meat, drinking massive quantities of water, and consuming large doses of various vitamins. Most of these diets are short-lived. However, some diets have withstood the test of time and have become acceptable, healthy ways to eat. The vegetarian diet is an example of what many claimed to be just a fad; millions of people, however, are vegetarians, and the diet continues to grow in popularity in developed countries. A vegetarian diet can be a nutritious way to eat, for adults, but may be hazardous to an adolescent's health because it lacks sufficient amounts of vitamin B12 (found only in animal proteins), calcium, zinc, iron, riboflavin, and possibly vitamin D—all of which are necessary for proper growth and development during the adolescent years.

Many adolescents, however, insist on becoming vegetarians; for these adolescents, nutritionists recommend that their diet be carefully planned to meet all the body's needs for vitamins, minerals, and protein. Because vegetarians do not eat red meat, there is a particular concern that they will not consume amino acids in the right proportions (Kenyon & Barker, 1998). The key to a sensible vegetarian diet, therefore, is to combine foods to form high-quality protein. In addition, milk, dairy products, and eggs can be mixed in or eaten along with any food from these four groups to enhance the protein in the vegetable source.

Food Patterns and Development

Nutritionists have long been aware of the effect that food has upon the physical well-being and growth of individuals. For example, consider the dietary customs of and their effect on two African tribes (Jessor, Turbin, & Costa, 1998). The Masai live largely on meat, milk, and various tree barks used for teas. The Akikuyu diet consists mainly of cereals, plants, legumes, and green leaves. In comparing the adolescents of these two tribes, the Masai male in late adolescence is, on average, 5 inches taller and 23 pounds heavier than the Akikuyu male, and his muscular strength is 50 percent greater. Diseases fostered by poor nutrition also are more prevalent among the Akikuyu. In contrast, despite the abundance of food sources in the United States, the diets of some U.S. adolescents may be worse than that of the Akikuyu.

© Mary Kate Denny/PhotoEdit

Adolescents are the poorest eaters of any age group.

Snacks or "Pigging Out"

Teenagers, in fact, are the poorest eaters of any age group (Rockett, Breitenbach, Frazier, Witschi, Wolf, Field, & Colditz, 1997). Most often they skip breakfast (sleeping a few minutes later is significantly more important than taking time for breakfast); frequently eat at fast-food restaurants; and snack on favorites such as ice cream, pizza, hamburgers, fries, and soft drinks. Although adults may recommend baked foods over fried or milk and juice over soft drinks, teenagers will not change their eating habits unless they see some real advantage in doing so. They must see the connection between the way they look and feel and what they eat before they will make some alterations.

Eating Disorders

For many teenagers, their customary ways of eating gradually improve to include more sensible eating habits. For some adolescents, however, eating patterns without some kind of helpful intervention may develop into lifelong patterns of poor nutrition and, in particular, inadequate amounts of food.

The Quest for the Ideal Body

Good feelings about our physical selves are important for achieving a sense of comfort with one's body image. Adolescents' general appearance reflects their feelings about themselves. Observations of the following can be indicators of the adolescent's feelings about his or her body image:

- Cleanliness and grooming
- Clothes in good repair and coordinated according to the current style
- Erect posture
- Making eye contact as opposed to looking away
- Hesitancy to undress for an examination

In response to attempts to have an "ideal body," eating disorders may develop during adolescence. Eating disorders are found in both Eastern and Western societies (Kam & Lee, 1998). The same cluster of symptoms seems to be found cross-culturally in girls with eating disorders: fear of gaining weight and becoming fat and distorted body image (Osone, 1997). Table 14.2 highlights the warning signs of teenagers who are at risk for eating disorders. These symptoms may appear in late middle childhood (see Chapter 11).

TABLE 14.2

Warning Signs of Anorexia and Bulimia Nervosa

Anorexia Nervosa	Bulimia Nervosa
Overidentification with a doctor-prescribed weight-control program	Eating binges
Obsession with dieting and talk of food	Irregular weight loss
Social isolation accompanying slimness	Long periods in the bathroom after meals
Sudden increased involvement in athletics	Prolonged/extreme exercise
Exaggerated concern with achieving high grades	Emotional instability and impulsivity
Failure to consume food	Loss of tooth enamel
Denial of hunger	Depression and mood swings
Obsessed with exercise	Throat, esophageal, and stomach problems

Anorexia Nervosa

Mary is a 16-year-old European American female. She is 5 feet 6 and weighs 106 pounds. She has been a vegetarian for about six months, claiming that she is trying to eat healthier food. Her diet consists of a very limited variety of foods. She does not use diuretics or laxatives, and she does not overexercise.

Individuals with anorexia nervosa use two different means of achieving thinness. The first group, who rely on strict dieting, are known as *restricters*. They suffer from the eating disorder known as **anorexia nervosa**. It is characterized by self-induced starvation (intake of 300 to 600 calories a day), fear of fatness, amenorrhea (absence of menstruation) in girls, and diminished sexual drive in boys.

The second group alternates between dieting and binge eating followed by self-induced vomiting or purging, excessive exercise, or use of diuretics or laxatives. This eating disorder is known as **bulimia nervosa**. The central psychopathologic feature of both these disorders is an extreme fear of fatness (Bon De Matte, 1998).

Estimates of the incidence of anorexia nervosa in the United States range from 1 to 3 percent of the female teenage population (Stice & Agras, 1998). Roughly 1 out of every 250 adolescent girls struggles with anorexia nervosa, which may vary from a single episode followed by weight and psychological recovery to an unremitting course, resulting in death (Jeammet & Corcos, 1998). The common age of onset is between 13 and 22 (Levenkron, 1992). Disturbingly, the incidence of anorexia nervosa has increased in the past 30 years both in the United States and Western Europe (Goreczny & Hersen, 1999).

Anorexic females tend to be conforming, reliable, insecure, socially obsessed, and inflexible in their thinking (Katzman & Lee, 1998). Typically, they go on a diet during their early teenage years to lose 5 to 20 pounds. Many of these individuals come from a family of upper or middle income socioeconomic status. Exhibiting *obsessional thinking* about food and liquid intake, they are likely to have feelings of inferiority about their personality and appearance. Obsessive-compulsive behavior often develops after the onset of anorexia nervosa (Barker & O'Neil, 1999). An obsession with cleanliness, an increase in house cleaning activities, and a more compulsive approach to studying are commonly found in these girls. They tend to show a disinterest in sexuality or fear physical and emotional intimacy.

They develop delusional thinking, especially with regard to body size and quantities of food ingested. They often experience paranoid fears of criticism from others, especially with respect to being seen as "too fat." Their anxiety is alleviated only by weight loss and fasting. They generally tend to deny their emaciated appearance, viewing others who are substantially heavier as thinner than themselves. Such individuals have a history of high achievement at school and are compliant and cooperative both in school and at home. They are often considered "model children" without associated behavioral abnormalities (Sokol & Gray, 1998).

anorexia nervosa Characterized by an extreme fear of fatness; more common in females; it is characterized by self-induced starvation (intake of 300 to 600 calories a day).

bulimia nervosa An eating disorder in which the individual (usually female) alternates between dieting and binge eating followed by self-induced vomiting or purging.

Bulimia Nervosa

Laura (16): I would always buy things in the same order. First, I would get the bagels; then I'd stop for the doughnuts, then down the ice cream aisle, and finally, I'd get a bag of M & Ms®. I would bring everything home and into my bedroom, turn on the TV, and eat everything in the same order in which I had bought it. I would feel great for a while, eating in control, until I got to the M & Ms®. By then, I would be so stuffed I could hardly move. Then I would begin to panic and eat the M & Ms®, rapidly, to get rid of them. I was afraid that if I left them, I'd eat them the next day, and of course, I needed to begin my diet the next day.

Bulimia occurs in approximately 25 to 33 percent of girls and 5 percent of males in the United States (Heffernan, 1998). Bulimia is an eating disorder that occurs when an individual has repeatedly lost control of the impulse to binge and engages in the rapid ingestion of a large quantity of food, followed by attempts to avoid weight gain through purging. An anorectic eating pattern between binges is common. Some individuals starve all day only to eat for hours at night. Their preferred foods are usually high in sugar and carbohydrates. Some individuals alternate overeating with extended fasting, but most relieve it by purging. The typical person suffering from bulimia is a European American female who begins overeating at about 18 and purging by vomiting a year later (Heffernan, 1998).

Individuals with bulimia tend to be extroverted and sociable but unstable. They tend to have problems with impulse control such as stealing and substance abuse. While socially more skillful than girls with anorexia nervosa, girls with bulimia nervosa tend to have relationships that are brief, superficial, and troubled. Their families tend to be more unstable than those of restricters; there is more discord, maternal and paternal depression, impulsivity, and substance abuse. Bruce Etringer and his colleagues (Etringer,

Altmaier, & Bowers, 1998) report that bulimic females have a lower self-appraised problem-solving ability, a lower sense of personal efficacy in successful performance of life tasks, and a tendency to attribute positive events to external, global factors. Bulimic females are characterized by a high degree of social dependency on men and low levels of social support from men.

In sum, girls with anorexia nervosa tend to be reticent, introverted, constricted, and socially obsessed, whereas those with bulimia nervosa are characterized as relatively more social, impulsive, and emotionally unstable. Further, females with anorexia nervosa tend to be more self-regulating and less demonstrative in their emotional behavior, more socially conscientious and conforming, and more inhibited interpersonally (Pryor & Wiederman, 1998). Girls with anorexia appear to be serious, rule-conscious individuals who are concerned with doing the right things. Such individuals keep tight rein on their emotions and prefer to live in a very orderly, predictable fashion. Some researchers state the obsessive-compulsive traits are the most salient features of adolescents with anorexia (Pryor & Wiederman, 1998). They tend to be "people pleasers" who typically apply their compulsive style to schoolwork and consequently earn good grades.

Adolescents with bulimia nervosa tend to exhibit greater sociability, forcefulness, and emotional sensitivity than those with anorexia nervosa. The one commonality between these two disorders is body dissatisfaction (Rosenblum & Lewis, 1999). Body dissatisfaction may emerge in middle childhood. Girls increase in their body dissatisfaction as they get older, whereas boys tend to decrease in their body dissatisfaction. The differences between the two disorders are summarized in Table 14.3.

TABLE 14.3

Differences Between Anorexia Nervosa and Bulimia Nervosa

	Anorexia Nervosa	Bulimia Nervosa
Prevalence	0.5–1.0%	1–3%
Characteristics	85% of average expected body weight Restriction of calorie intake; overly controlled behavior; amenorrhea	Often within normal weight range Repeated episodes of of binge eating followed by inappropriate behaviors (self-induced vomiting, laxatives, diuretics, or enemas)
Medical complications	Lethargy; cold intolerance; hypotension; anemia; lanugo (fine body hair)	Electrolyte abnormalities; gum disease; arrhythmias
Psychological characteristics	Depression; obsessive-compulsive features; rigid, controlling personalities	Mood changes; anxiety disturbances; more likely to have substance abuse or dependence
Treatment	Weight gain; nutritional restoration; antidepressants	Cognitive therapy; antidepressants
Course or outcome	Highly variable; mortality six times that of the general population	Chronic or intermittent; long-term outcome unknown

From "Anorexia Nervosa" (pp. 350–357), by M. A. Sokol & N. S. Gray, 1998, in E. A. Blechman & K. D. Kelly (Eds.), *Behavioral Medicine and Women: A Comprehensive Handbook.* New York: Guilford Press. Used by permission.

Causes of Eating Disorders

Many experts on eating disorders believe that what drives so many young people into this self-punishing and life-threatening pattern of semistarvation or purging is societal pressure to be thin. For many young women looking "good"—being thin—is more important than being healthy.

Social–Cultural Factors Evidence is increasingly clear that it is this glorification of slenderness in magazines, in movies, and on television that propels many young girls to develop undereating disorders (Brownell & Fairburn, 1995). Standards of beauty, however, are never static. In the 1950s, beauty equaled voluptuousness, with Marilyn Monroe as the leading Hollywood queen. Today, teenagers tend to think full-body figures are "gross" and that the thin, "waif" look is desirable. Because beauty pageants are a tradition through which society defines its ideal of beauty, Sharon Rubinstein and Benjamin Caballero (2000) used data on weight and height of the winners of the Miss America Pageant from 1922 to 1999 to determine weight changes. Results showed that over the years, a significant decline in body mass index has taken place, with an increasing number of the later winners falling into the range of undernutrition.

European American males prefer thin females; African American males, however, are not as attracted to thin females. This may contribute to the somewhat lower incidence of eating disorders in African American women (Greenberg & LaPorte, 1996). African American girls may have beauty standards that differ from the mainstream culture; they may not view the attainment of extreme thinness as a way to convey beauty and are more likely to endorse a slightly larger body ideal. These differing beauty standards may provide some degree of protection against the development of eating disorders. However, the importance of social factors in developing eating pathology is illustrated in the fact that those African American girls who report being exposed to social pressure (for example, peer pressure) are as likely as European American girls to feel dissatisfied with their weight and to try to lose weight by dieting (Schreiber, Robins, Striegel-Moore, Obarzanek, Morrison, & Wright, 1996).

Cross-culturally, Jeanine Cogan and her colleagues (Cogan, Bhalla, Sefa-Dedeh, & Rothblum, 1996) investigated trends in attitudes toward thinness and the corresponding dieting behaviors in a sample of subjects from Ghana, Africa, and the United States. In Ghana, the subjects rated larger body sizes as ideal for both sexes and assumed these to be held as ideals in society more so than subjects in the United States, who were more likely to rate thin models as ideals. In addition, U.S. subjects were more likely to have dieted than Ghanian subjects. Additionally, U.S. females scored higher on restraint and eating-disorder behavior than Ghanian females. These findings illustrate the influence of culture on the perceptions of ideal body size and behaviors. The efforts of some people to maintain this thin look and their subsequent abhorrence of "fatness," however, can have some very negative effects.

Family Factors Family factors, such as overprotectiveness, rigidity, masking unconscious hostilities, parental preoccupation with appearance and success, and poor conflict resolution between parent and adolescent, also appear to impact teenage eating disorders (Clark & Harned, 2001). It has been maintained by others that these eating disorders represent a struggle for a self-respecting identity that takes the form of willful starvation (Jones, Lee, & Vigfusdottir, 2001). The mother–daughter relationship has been described as being riddled with guilt, anger, and overprotectiveness (by both toward each other) and characterized by mutual clinging that is devoid of trust. Fathers of these daughters are often described as nondemonstrative.

Girls suffering from anorexia are often characterized as being fearful of growing up and assuming adult responsibility. Failure to accept a more adult-looking body (that is, to be more separate from their parents) leads them to diet as a means of gaining control over fears of inadequacy and rejection by others. Cynthia Bulik and her colleagues (Gendall, Sullivan, Joyce, Fear, & Bulik, 1997; Sullivan, Bulik, & Kendler, 1998) in studying the family environment and psychiatric histories of 35 bulimic women reveal that 12 of the 35 subjects had been sexually abused. Females with bulimia from families in which sexual abuse occurred were more likely than bulimic subjects with no personal or family history of sexual abuse to have a personal history of dependence (Ritenbaugh, Shissiak, Teufel, & Leonard-Green, 1998).

APPLICATIONS: Helping Anorectic and Bulimic Teenagers

Obtaining effective treatment is essential in anorexia nervosa and bulimia nervosa because these illnesses rarely are cured spontaneously, and intervention improves prognosis. Treatment has two immediate goals: nutritional rehabilitation (restoring normal body weight and metabolic balance) and restoring normal eating patterns. Longer-term goals are aimed at relapse prevention.

Approximately 40 percent of teenagers with anorexia totally recover, 30 percent improve considerably, and 20 percent remain unimproved or seriously impaired by depression (Muuss & Porton, 1998). Early onset (before the age of 16) is associated with a favorable prognosis; having had the disorder for a long period of time, pronounced family difficulties, and poor vocational adjustment are associated with poor outcome.

Family Therapy

It is possible that eating disorders have a single discrete cause, but it is more likely that complex chains interact to precipitate these illnesses. Subsequently, a multifaceted treatment endeavor with medical management and behavioral, individual, and family therapy is necessary to treat anorexia and bulimia nervosa (Charpentier, 1998). In treating these disorders, there must be simultaneous improvement in weight and eating abnormalities, along with fundamental therapeutic attempts to uncover the underlying psychological conflicts. Most experts agree that strict attempts at getting these patients to eat their way out of the hospital are not successful unless one deals with the underlying causes of the pathology as well (Goreczny & Hersen, 1999).

Hospitalization

A higher proportion of girls with anorexia than bulimia are hospitalized. A major focus of treatment is the gradual identification by patients of uncomfortable mood states that trigger unconscious anxiety into abnormal weight control or an abnormal eating pattern. All patients need to be reassured while being treated that they will not be allowed to gain too much weight (Barker & O'Neil, 1999). Otherwise, they may return to their rituals to bring about relief from unresolved fears. Families of these patients need to be involved in therapy as well (Wood, Flower, & Black, 1998).

Hospitalization is less likely with those suffering from bulimia but may be necessary because of fluid and electrolyte imbalance, severe depression, the threat of suicide, or resistance to intensive outpatient treatment (Mash & Barkley, 1998). Inpatient treatment involves monitoring intake and purging behaviors and some combination of supportive, behavioral, group, individual, and family therapies. Other ways in which adults can help adolescents with anorexia and bulimia are discussed in Table 14.4.

Concept Checks

1. Puberty involves a complex series of hormonal changes with ____________ as the principal male hormone and ____________ as the principal female hormone.
2. Two causes of the secular trend appear to be ____________ and ____________.
3. Which of the following individuals is most pleased about the way he or she looks?
   a. Laurence, an early-maturing male
   b. Lydia, an early-maturing female
   c. Tyrone, a late-maturing male
4. ***True or False:*** Adolescents may eat snacks and fast foods, but these types of diets actually are good for them because they have all the essential minerals and proteins.
5. Cassandra tends to be conforming, perfectionistic, and inflexible. She seems to be obsessed with how many calories she eats per day. These are symptoms of an eating disorder known as ____________ ____________.
6. As a counselor working with teenage girls with eating disorders, state two things you would recommend to their concerned parents.
   a. ____________
   b. ____________

TABLE 14.4

Helping Adolescents with Anorexia Nervosa and Bulimia Nervosa
1. Demand less decision making from the anorectic or bulimic adolescent.
2. Avoid letting adolescents buy food and prepare meals for the family. When they cook the evening meal, through the preparation of the food, they believe that they have satiated their appetites for food.
3. Develop a parent–adolescent relationship on personal issues other than food or weight.
4. Do not demand weight gain or berate the adolescent for having an eating disorder.
5. Avoid statements such as, "Your illness is ruining the whole family." "I can't take much more of this behavior from you." These statements put the adolescent in charge of the family's well-being and are received by her as dependent remarks, which further throws her deeper into weight loss and illness.
6. Try to avoid abandoning statements such as, "Help me to help you." "What can I do for you?" These statements request that the adolescent take charge of the family's behavior toward her. Because she does not know the answer to these questions, she feels like more of a failure.
7. Do not demand that she eat with you, but do not allow her eating problem to dominate the family's eating schedule or use of the kitchen.

Sexuality Issues

Before Beginning ...

After reading this section, you will be able to

- examine the role of physical attractiveness in choosing dates and how attractiveness affects our perceptions and actions.
- discuss petting and masturbation, early sexual actions.
- explore teenage sexual attitudes and behaviors.
- delineate the types, causes, and symptoms of sexually transmitted diseases.
- discuss how teenage pregnancy affects adolescent mothers, fathers, and their infants.
- understand how teenage parents can be helped.

Most females (and males) want to be considered sexually attractive. Attraction to others begins around the age of 10. For most teenagers, dating begins between ages 13 and 16, and teenagers tend to base their first dating choices on the physical attractiveness of the individual.

Physical Attractiveness

One of the key criteria in determining attractiveness in the United States is the individual's body weight—particularly for girls. For example, in one experiment, adolescents were given information about the person's physical appearance (nice smile, great hair, and so on) (Regan, 1996). The only thing that varied was weight, with males and females either being normal weight or overweight. The female adolescents felt that a male's dateability was unaffected by his weight. However, overweight females were not considered attractive or a desirable date by males. These results clearly indicate that being overweight is a more stigmatizing experience for females than for males. Teenage boys generally do emphasize physical attractiveness more than teenage girls for dating, sexual intercourse, and a serious relationship (Lundy, Tan, & Cunningham, 1998).

There is amazing cross-cultural verification that boys (and men) tend to rate attractiveness as the key variable in mate selection (Buss, 1989). In this study, over 10,000 respondents (ranging in age from early adolescence to middle-age adults) in 37 cultures drawn from 33 countries completed a questionnaire dealing with factors in choosing a mate. In all 37 cultures, males rated good looks as extremely important. In contrast, in 36 of the 37 cultures, females rated financial prospects as more important than good looks!

We also tend to choose friends that are attractive to us. Although a number of personal characteristics such as sociability and similarities in values and interests enter into friendship choices, one of the most salient is attractiveness (Aboud & Mendelson, 1998). Attractive individuals are also more popular with their peers. In fact, attractiveness is a stronger predictor of positive friendships and peer acceptance than is sociability (Hanna, 1998).

Physical attractiveness also appears to impact perceptions about personality characteristics. When we see an attractive person—someone we have never met—we do tend to associate various social traits (mostly positive) with that person (Adams, 1991). Attractive people are generally seen as more likable and interesting than those who are unattractive. They are also judged as more competent and intelligent. Further, this social-stereotyping process can actually evolve into social reality. It works something like this: Due to our being favorably biased in our reactions to good-looking people, we actually engage in positive social interactions with them. As a result, the individual internalizes the "desirable" social message and begins to manifest it in positive social behaviors. When the individual shows the very behaviors we have expected him or her to have (based on our stereotypical impressions), we have a confirmation of our stereotype.

"Beauty Is Good" Hypothesis

The research on physical attractiveness and its social and psychological impact is quite extensive. From very early in life we tend to prefer attractive individuals. Two-month-old infants preferred to look at attractive faces (spent a longer time gazing at them) when paired with faces judged by adults to be unattractive (Slater, Von der Schulenburg, Brown, Badenoch, Butterworth, Parsons, & Samuels, 1998). Attractive adolescents are more likely than unattractive adolescents to be judged as possessing better character and to be seen as more poised. They are viewed as more self-confident, kind, flexible, and sexually responsive and are perceived as having greater control over their destiny (Adams, 1991).

Attractive adolescents also tend to be viewed as having greater credibility and are more effective in persuading others. Other evidence indicates that teachers are also influenced by these adolescents' attractiveness as it relates to their academic competence (Chia, Allred, Grossnickle, & Lee, 1998). In this investigation, the role of physical attractiveness was examined in predicting teachers' expectations and their judgment of academic abilities. As predicted, teachers held higher expectations of performance for attractive individuals, and these teenagers actually received higher grades in comparison to their less attractive student colleagues.

As adolescents enter the workforce, attractiveness also seems to have a bearing on their employability. We do not mind if coaches insist on tall basketball players or if dentists hire dental assistants with straight teeth, but for most occupations, it seems unfair for employers to discriminate. However, employers do appear to discriminate in favor of attractive candidates (Cesare, 1996). Further, attractive job-seekers are judged as having better employee potential than unattractive applicants. Moreover, when they are hired and under evaluation, attractive adolescents are judged to have higher task performance than unattractive peers (even though the performance of the attractive teens was actually poorer than the unattractive adolescents). Evidence seems to support the theory that a perception-based mechanism operates around a "beauty is good" principle.

As adolescents get older, they tend to broaden their conceptions of physical attractiveness and focus on social sophistication and personality. This is later followed by a focus on deeper psychological traits when choosing their dates (Berndt & Perry, 1990). Open communication and mutual dependency become the typical goal of social dating in middle and late adolescence (Sanderson & Cantor, 1995).

Dating and Intimacy

One major purpose of dating in early adolescence is to have fun and to get out and do things. Dating is also associated with gaining or improving one's status with peers. It provides a means of personal growth as males and females learn to know, understand, and get along with different types of people. Through dating, adolescents learn cooperation, consideration, responsibility, and matters of etiquette. It can also be a boost to an adolescent's self-esteem.

> Sidney works up the courage to ask a pretty girl from his French class to a school dance. To his amazement, she accepts and says she was hoping he would ask her. When they show up together, his status among his peers rises as does his self-esteem.

Dating can also help teenagers discover who they are, especially with regard to gender identity. A series of dating relationships allows adolescents to try out different masculine and feminine personas. Do girls like a boy who acts in a macho manner or one who reveals his vulnerability? Do boys like a girl who acts dependent and emotional or can she show herself to be strong-willed and self-reliant?

The first stage of dating involves group dating, in which several boys and girls meet at prearranged places. There may or may not be couples involved at these encounters. The second stage consists of individual dating. About 30 percent of adolescents at any one time are "going steady" (McDonald & McKinney, 1994). Corresponding with dating, we see the beginning of overt expressions of sexuality in males and females.

Courtesy of Karen Owens

In early adolescence, group dating is common. During middle and late adolescence, individual dating with corresponding expressions of intimacy begins.

Sexual Awakenings

Members of both sexes have daydreams involving sex. Young women and men may build mental scenes in which they are engaging in various sexual pleasures. Some may be very curious about sex and read about it in various types of books and magazines. Adolescents are filled with questions, ranging from whether their sexual urges are normal to how to receive pleasure from sex or how to achieve an orgasm. Apparently, college students may have similar interests and questions. One professor who reviewed this text mentioned that one semester a perplexingly large number of students at his university registered for organic biology. In checking the undergraduate catalog, the error was discovered. The course was listed as "orgasm biology."

Many young couples engage in a variety of mutually sexually stimulating acts lumped together as *petting* activities. **Petting** involves kissing and perhaps genital stimulation but does not involve sexual intercourse. The actions may start with relatively mild things such as holding hands, draping an arm over shoulders, clasping a waist, or exchanging kisses. Further along, the sequence of petting actions that make up sexual behavior generally follows a pattern of lip to tongue kissing, to petting above the waist to petting below the waist with clothes on, to genital touching. For some young people, petting is a sort of game in which the sensations are the prize. For others, the purpose may be exploration to satisfy curiosities. For still others, it is a context in which the boy seeks to induce his companion to go just a bit further than she intends.

Wide variations of sexual behavior exist within different cultures (see Cultural Variations). In China, for example, the Communist government has outlawed pornography and has taken a very firm stand on purposefully eliminating "decadent" Western sexual behaviors (Wehrfritz, 1996). In the Middle East, it is said that Muhammad gave sexual desire in 10 parts: 9 parts to women and 1 to men. The custom of women wearing veils, female circumcision, and segregation of the sexes until marriage is considered to be necessary to contain the power of female sexuality (Dolto, 1998).

Some cultures approve of adolescents' being sexually active. For example, among the Trobriand Islanders of Melanesia, bachelor houses are maintained where adolescent males are expected to engage in sexual experiences with a number of different partners. The children of the Marquesas Islands in French Polynesia often sleep with their parents and frequently

Thought **CHALLENGE**

What are some potentially negative psychological consequences of dating for males? for females?

petting
A variety of mutually sexually stimulating acts that do not involve intercourse.

Cultural Variations

Sexuality

Geert Hofstede's (1998) research shows that even sexual behavior is culturally constructed and that the position of a country on a masculine or feminine dimension impacts on the sexual views and behavior of its people. Hofstede describes feminine countries, such as Sweden, as those in which partners are less dependent on each other; women take an active role during sexual intercourse; parenthood is positively valued; and the well-being of children plays an important role in the parents' ways of arranging their lives. These are not highly valued in masculine countries, such as Brazil. Abortion, contraception, and masturbation are more taboo in masculine countries than in feminine countries.

Further, the timing and pattern of when sexual intercourse emerges is a result of cultural background. For example, African American adolescents are more likely to proceed directly from kissing to sexual intercourse and do so at earlier ages (Benda & Corwyn, 1998). Approximately half of African American males have intercourse by the time they are 15 years, slightly earlier than Latino males at 16½ and European American males at 17 years. Females, however, present a slightly different picture with half of African American females having intercourse by age 17, European Americans at age 17½, and Latinas at almost 18 years. A nationwide survey indicates that 73.4 percent of African American high school seniors have experienced sexual intercourse compared with 57.6 percent of Latinos, and 48.9 percent of European Americans (Centers for Disease Control, 1997). The results of this study also revealed that African American youths tend to have their initial experiences with intercourse at an earlier age than either Latinos or European Americans. For example, 24.2 percent of African American respondents reportedly had had sexual intercourse before age 13 as compared to 8.8 percent of Latinos and 5.7 percent of European Americans. Moreover, African Americans are also more likely to have intercourse because their peers are sexually active (Eyre & Millstein, 1999).

Although many adolescents engage in premarital sexual intercourse, males are twice as likely as females to have intercourse. Gender stereotypes appear to account for these differences. Males are expected to surrender to their sexual desires, and adolescence for males is considered a time of sexual exploration and self-definition. In contrast, female adolescents' sexual desires are constrained, and the expression of their sexuality is viewed as wrong, immoral, and fraught with danger. These stereotypes are beginning to fade, and relatedly, the differences between males and females experiencing intercourse has been narrowing (Feldman, Turner, & Araujo, 1999).

Economic status appears to be more highly related to intercourse than ethnicity (Stephens & Willert, 2001). Recent studies indicate that African American adolescents raised in more affluent homes are significantly more likely to abstain from sexual intercourse than their poorer counterparts (Leadbeater & Way, 1996; Murry-McBride, 1996). Poverty is a strong predictor of sexual activity among adolescents (Brewster, 1994). Adolescent pregnancy continues to affect the United States to a greater degree than any other industrialized nation in the world. Even with similar rates of adolescent intercourse, England, France, and Canada have less than half the incidence of adolescent pregnancy found in the United States (Langfield & Pasley, 1997). The rate of adolescent pregnancy in the United States is three times higher than that noted for Sweden and nine times higher than that noted for the Netherlands (Alan Guttmacher Institute, 1994). Despite the similarity of these countries' economic and cultural norms, the United States continues to experience more teenage pregnancy. What we know is that teens in these countries report about the same level of sexual intercourse. However, U.S. teens are less effective in preventing pregnancy (for example, poorer use of contraception) and have less access to abortion. Further, many of these other countries have a policy supporting the inclusion of sex education in the school curriculum. Sex education also impacts abstinence (Hofstede, 1998). No such policy exists in the United States.

observe adult sexual activity (Crooks & Baur, 1999). Some societies, however, are very limiting and sexual intercourse is not sanctioned until marriage. The United States tends to be more on the restrictive end of the continuum. Variation can also be seen within various ethnic groups within the United States. Asian Americans, for example, are less likely to engage in premarital sex than are Latinos, African Americans, and European Americans (Cochran, Mays, & Leung, 1991; Feldman, Turner, & Araujo, 1999).

One outlet for sexual urges may be through *masturbation*, which reaches its highest intensity during adolescence. **Masturbation** involves self-stimulation that produces erotic arousal—whether or not arousal proceeds to the point of climax or orgasm. It used to be thought that masturbation was evil and would lead to insanity, impotency, or to some kind of detriment to later sex life. Today, health, medical, and psychiatric authorities believe that masturbation is a normal part of growing up and clearly does not have harmful physical and mental effects. Perhaps the only ill effect from masturbation comes not from the act itself but from the guilt, fear, or anxiety that comes when the adolescent believes he or she is doing something wrong. Although feelings of discomfort and guilt resulting from cultural and religious beliefs about masturbation have decreased, adolescents still find the subject embarrassing.

For males, adolescence is commonly characterized by the onset of overt sexual activity, with masturbation being the most common way of having an orgasm. More males than females masturbate (see Figure 14.2) (Elliott & Brantley, 1997). Various reasons are given for this, but the most prevalent one appears that it is not due to a biologically weaker sex drive in females but to the emphasis on sexual chastity during the socialization of girls. One might be tempted to conclude that masturbation occurs most commonly among adolescents lacking other outlets. Interestingly, however, current evidence suggests that masturbation is about three times as frequent among those engaged in sexual intercourse or petting to orgasm than among the sexually inexperienced.

Can one masturbate too much? We can look at this question in the same sense as watching too much television. These activities themselves are not bad but when they become all-consuming activities, they may suggest the presence of problems that the individual is unable to handle. For example, an adolescent who masturbates to the exclusion of normal friendships and social activities has a problem—not with masturbation—but with social relationships.

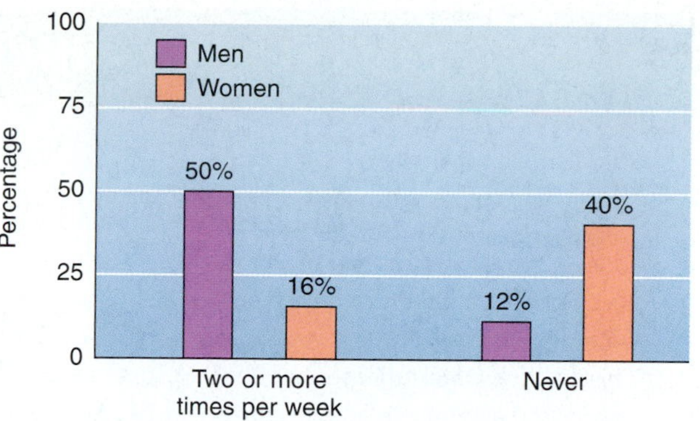

FIGURE 14.2 ***Two Thousand College Students Answer "How Often Do You Masturbate?" (Percentages given only for far ends of the continuum)***

From *Sex on Campus*, by L. Elliott & C. Brantley, 1997, New York: Random House. Used by permission.

Sexually Active Teenagers

Interest in dating and first loves can represent an exciting time for many adolescents. The young couple must cope with special challenges, however, in the expression of their sexuality. One of the problems that besets some adolescents during this period centers on becoming sexually active. Adolescent sexual behavior generally does not begin with intercourse, nor does it necessarily begin in adolescence. During late childhood and early adolescence, for example, sexual behaviors include fantasies and masturbation. Later, sexual behaviors extend to another person. Although few adolescents claim sex was forced or even pressured, nearly half wish that they had waited longer before having sex, particularly girls. Most subjects are going steady when they first have sex or are dating and "know each other well." Three-quarters have their first sexual encounters at home or at a friend's house (Millstein & Halpern-Felsher, 1998).

Couples engage in premarital intercourse for a variety of reasons, ranging from physical enjoyment, expressing love, maintaining a relationship, proving independence from parents, controlling one's partner, to affirming their sexual identity (Hogan, Hao, & Parish, 1990).

Many teens do not consciously plan to become sexually active, and they often do not foresee their first sexual experience. As such, it frequently is not experienced as a decision but rather as something that "happens." Although most teenagers have *knowledge* about risks, such as sexually transmitted diseases and pregnancy, it appears to do little to deter them from having unprotected sex. Is this risk-taking behavior a general characteristic of the adolescent years? (See Child Development Issues.)

masturbation Self-stimulation that produces erotic arousal.

Child Development Issues

Is Risk-Taking Part of Being an Adolescent?

Risk-taking is considered by many to be very much a part of what it means to be a teenager; this has been true throughout history. The Greek philosopher Plato proposed a minimum age for drinking, commenting that "fire should not be poured on fire." French philosopher Rene Rousseau compared adolescents to lions, claiming they are simply "ungovernable." Plato and Rousseau seemed to be implying by their statements that all risk-taking behaviors are negative. Some risk-taking behaviors, however, such as exploration, are essential for growth and healthy adolescent development (Millstein & Igra, 1995).

Risk-taking behaviors today may range from "normative risks" (looking for parties, playing pranks, engaging in sporting feats) to "high-risk" activities (wild driving, drug use, early sexual intimacy) that can produce grave consequences. By no means do all teenagers engage in high-risk behaviors that are a danger to self or others, but teenagers are more likely than at any other developmental period to engage in some risky behavior of the more normative type (Arnett, 1999).

	Normative Risk (%)	Deviant Risk (%)
Group 1	50	3
Group 2	35	0
Group 3	25	0
Group 4	40	8
Group 5	22	48

From *The Culture of Adolescent Risk-Taking* (p. 151), by C. Lightfoot, New York: Guilford Press.

As such, the topic of risk-taking has harnessed the energy of a number of theorists and researchers in an attempt to analyze why it occurs. David Elkind (1978) suggests that adolescent egocentrism in the form of the "personal fable" accounts, in part at least, for a variety of perplexing behaviors exhibited by the young teenager. For example, an adolescent may "know" that even though serious catastrophes may happen to others, they will never happen to him; he will never get seriously ill, be injured, or die. It is, in part, a belief that their lives are unique; they are safe from harm.

Relatedly, adolescent egocentrism, according to Jean Piaget (1965; Inhelder & Piaget, 1958), is expressed in the "idealistic crisis" or "crisis of juvenile originality," in which adolescents believe they are invested with unlimited possibilities and must push these possibilities to their very limit. Vygotsky (1994) commented that while play is most significant during the preschool years, at other ages, most notably adolescence, it becomes a most serious pastime.

Joy Dryfoos' (1997) analysis of the data concurs with Vygotsky's comments. Approximately one-third of all teenagers are at extremely high risk because they "do it all," one-third are involved in several high-risk behaviors, and one-third are at a relatively low risk. Who are the high-risk teenagers? In looking at the broader picture, adolescent risk-taking is higher in individualistic countries (United States, France, Germany, for example) than in collectivist ones (China, India) (Arnett, 1999). Perhaps one factor lowering risk behavior in collectivist countries is tighter parental control. Lower levels of parental monitoring tend to lead to higher levels of adolescent risk-taking (Ary, Duncan, Duncan, & Hops, 1999).

Ethnicity is also associated with risk-taking. In examining three cate-

Thought CHALLENGE

As globalization increases individualism, will adolescent risky behavior increase?

Parental influences on sexual behavior are believed to be strong, although there is not much research on this topic. Adolescents who rate perceived communication with their parents as poor are more likely to initiate sex early (Chase-Lansdale & Brooks-Gunn, 1994). Close relationships with parents as well as feelings of connectedness and supportiveness seem to be associated with later onset of intercourse (Binghma, Miller, & Adams, 1990).

> I felt sure I was the only one left in my crowd who had not had sex. I mainly just wanted to get it over with and be able to say, like everyone else, that I had done it. Otherwise, it was like I was an outsider or a baby or something. At first I felt guilty and bad for the girl. But I did it mostly because everybody was doing it or said they were and I didn't want to be out of it.

Perceptions about what one's peers are doing or what is normative in one's peer group are strongly associated with sexual behavior (DiBlasio & Benda, 1992). Teenagers who are not doing well in school and gories of risk-taking—antisocial behavior, sexual behavior, and substance abuse—in a sample of ninth- and twelfth-grade Native Americans, African Americans, and European Americans from the Minnesota public schools, Enid Gruber (Gruber, DiClemente, & Anderson, 1996) reports that the Native American adolescents have a significantly higher prevalence in all three risk behaviors. Adolescents' personal characteristics also affect their risk-taking behavior. Adolescents, regardless of ethnicity, who are high on "sensation seeking" measures are more likely to engage in risky behavior (Zuckerman, 1994).

There is also a relationship between peer groups and risk-taking. Cynthia Lightfoot (1997) examined risk-taking based on extensive interviews with 41 16- to 18-year-olds (see figure). Lightfoot reports, based on sociometric data, that popular adolescents and leaders (Groups 1 and 4) are most active in normative risks and relatively few deviant categories; adolescents who do well in school and those that are considered shy (Groups 2 and 3) engage in less risk-taking and show a complete absence of deviant categories. Group 5 adolescents, those who are not doing well in school and are disengaged from their parents, school, and community, distinguish themselves from all other groups by their marked propensity for deviant risk-taking.

For teenagers who engage in high-risk behaviors that lead to injury, infection, addiction, incarceration, and death, obvious intervention is needed such as broad-based school, community, health clinic, and home programs. As with most complex behaviors, "reasons why" are multiple, as should be the preventive measures designed to help these teens. It needs to be underscored, however, that not all risk-taking behavior is bad. For the majority of adolescents, there are some positive effects of normative risk-taking. For example, risk-taking behaviors appear to play a strategic role in achieving social status; friends are often impressed by those who attempt the extraordinary. Normative risk-taking also provides challenge and pleasure. Adolescents are in the process of forging identities in fellowship with their peers, and risks and adventures have a privileged role to play in this process. Normative risk-taking provides a natural and perhaps essential part of adolescents' quest for learning about themselves and life.

© David Young-Wolff/PhotoEdit

Search Online

Explore InfoTrac College Edition, your online library. Go to **http://www.infotrac-college.com/wadsworth** and use the passcode that came on the card with your book. Try these search terms: adolescent risk-taking, risk-taking, adolescent sexual behavior.

have lower educational aspirations are more likely to have sex during adolescence than those faring better in school.

Sexual Attitudes

There appear to be gender differences in adolescents' sexual attitudes and behavior in the United States and cross-culturally. In exploring gender differences in sexual attitudes on a sample of Swiss females and males (ages 15 to 20), Florence Moreau-Gruet and her colleagues (Moreau-Gruet, Ferron, Jeannin, & Dubois-Arber, 1996) found that a higher proportion of girls reported having a close emotional relationship with their partner when they first had sex. Males, however, often expected sex in the absence of emotional closeness. Laurie Cohen's and Lance Shotland's (1996) research on a sample of U.S. adolescents support these findings as well.

For females, love relationships appear to provide an almost universal context for their first sexual experience, whereas for males the reward is often intrinsic to the act itself or perhaps, for the recognition of the achievement by self and others (Mebert & Leonard, 2001). A significant percentage of males, for example, talk about their sexual experiences with friends (Brooks-Gunn, Duncan, Klebanov, & Sealand, 1993). In contrast, most females engage in sexual relations to maintain an enduring relationship.

Jaqueline De Gaston and her colleagues (De Gaston, Weed, & Jensen, 1996) surveyed seventh and eighth graders about their sexual activities. The researchers report that girls more than boys were likely to believe that sexual urges can be controlled and were less likely than males to engage in sex. The girls also indicated a stronger commitment to abstinence and viewed sexual activity as more detrimental to future goal attainment. They viewed parents as less approving but were more likely to discuss sex and dating practices with them. Females perceived less peer pressure for sex and more support for waiting. Females also saw teen parenthood as more of a problem than did males.

Sexual Behaviors

Sexual gender is a biological given at birth, but determination of *sexual identity* is a complex psychological process that takes place over many years. Heterosexuality, homosexuality, transsexuality, bisexuality, and asexuality are childhood possibilities that become crystallized in adolescence with the emergence of sexual impulses and sexual maturation. Unfortunately, there is a lot we still do not understand about the development of sexual identity and much to be learned about homosexuality.

Homosexuality Homosexual youths appear to go through various stages in forming a homosexual identity: sensitization, identity confusion, identity assumption, and commitment (Troiden, 1989). In the *sensitization* stage, beginning before puberty, the individual has homosexual feelings or experiences without understanding the implications for self-identity. We have learned through retrospective research that some gay males recalled being aware of gay feelings as early as late middle childhood and early adolescence but did not label themselves as such until late adolescence or early twenties (D'Augelli & Hershberger, 1993).

Thought CHALLENGE

What do you think the impact would be if sexual orientation were absolutely proven to be biological?

In the *identity confusion* stage, which usually occurs during adolescence, the individual realizes that he or she may be homosexual. This may cause some anxiety or discomfort. Because their sexual identity is still developing, teenagers are often particularly disturbed by anything sexual that may appear "out of the ordinary." Unusual sexual habits or choices may seem particularly frightening to adolescents and feelings of bisexuality (which are quite normal in all of us) or homosexuality are often especially uncomfortable. This is why adolescents are often homophobic, making the fate of a homosexual teenager particularly painful.

In the *identity assumption* stage, the individual comes out as a homosexual. Disclosure is dependent on a number of variables, including access to a homosexual community that can support and encourage the adolescent's identity and supportive, understanding parents and friends. The individual first attempts to come out to the homosexual community and then attempts to come out to the heterosexual community, if any, follow. Various studies have reported that between 6 to 11 percent of adolescent girls and 11 to 14 percent of boys who have disclosed their sexual identity report experiencing same-sex contact between peers (Crooks & Baur, 1999). Same-sex contact with the intent of sexual arousal, however, does not necessarily reflect a lifelong sexual orientation. Many homosexual individuals do not act on their sexual feelings until adulthood.

In the *commitment* stage, the individual adopts a homosexual lifestyle and develops a comfort with his or her sexual identity. African American and Latino lesbian, bisexual, and gay adolescents often have a more difficult time experiencing a sense of self-contentment (Greene, 1994). Minority adolescents who embrace both their ethnicity and sexual identities may feel that neither identity is capable of validating the values, behaviors, and self-concepts invoked by the other. Consequently, they may feel forced to choose a primary identification or to alternate identities or, more commonly to hide their homosexual identity. Openly gay and lesbian youths, for example, often "exclude themselves from cultural activities in order to avoid shaming the family in front of friends" (Tremble, Schneider, & Appathurai, 1989, p. 261). To live as an individual within two minority identities is best summarized by a gay Chinese adolescent: "I am a double minority. Caucasian gays don't like gay Chinese, and the Chinese don't like the gays. It would be easier to be white. It would be easier to be straight. It's hard to be both" (p. 263).

Is homosexuality an inborn trait coded in our brain, metabolism, or genes? Is it learned through early experiences? Or is it the result of family dynamics? Is it a choice or a destiny? In trying to establish possible causes for sexual orientation, investigators have focused on the role that prenatal hormones may play in contributing to homosexuality (Money & Lehne, 1999). Research findings have demonstrated, for example, that hormonal levels in animals can masculinize fetal females and demasculinize fetal males. This results in other-sex social and mating behavior when the animals mature (Zuger, 1989). There is a sensitive period during human gestation in which the developing human fetus is especially sensitive to levels of sex hormones, and imbalances during this period could contribute to homosexuality (Meyer-Bahlburg, Ehrhardt, Rosen, Gruen, Veridiano, Vann, & Neuwalder, 1995).

Another line of investigation has centered on structural differences in the brains, particularly the hypothalamus, of homosexual and heterosexual men (Swaab & Gofman, 1995). In evolutionary terms the hypothalamus is an ancient structure involved in a number of important functions such as eating and drinking, temperature regulation, hormone regulation, and sex. Different regions in the hypothalamus play a role in the generation of "male-typical" and "female-typical" sexual behavior. The region that helps produce male-typical behavior is toward the front and female-typical behavior is further back. In homosexual men, the front region of the hypothalamus is half as large as it is in heterosexual men. Researchers caution, however, that the differences in observed brain structures do not provide direct evidence that they cause sexual orientation (Byne, 1996).

There also appears to be a strong link between adult homosexuality and gender nonconformity as a child. Gender nonconformity concerns the extent to which an individual conforms to stereotypical characteristics of masculinity or femininity during childhood. Researchers have found that male and female homosexual adults are more likely than heterosexual adults to have experienced gender nonconformity during childhood (Bailey & Zucker, 1995).

What can we conclude from these research findings? At this point in time, we can only conclude that an individual's sexual orientation is most likely determined by multiple factors, including genetic, hormonal, and environmental influences. Almost certainly, however, biological vulnerability interacts in complex ways with various environmental contributions (Diamond, 1995). Many researchers realize, however, that different weights need to be given to different factors in different homosexual lives (Greene, 1994).

Researchers may disagree about the causes of homosexuality, but they do agree that the type of relationships homosexual adolescents have with their parents has a strong impact on their overall adjustment. Despite the fact that during the coming-out process many homosexual youths experience stigmatization and disapproval from peers, those from highly supportive families exhibit greater feelings of security, higher self-esteem, and a more positive attitude about their sexual orientation (Beaty, 1999; Greene, 1994). Conversely, the effects of a low-support or no-support family environment hamper the adolescent's adjustment. Although mothers tend to be generally closer and more supportive than fathers, relationships with both parents appear to be important, independent predictors of how well homosexual youths adjust (Floyd, Stein, Harter, Allison, & Nye, 1999).

Sexually Transmitted Diseases

With so many sexually active teenagers, **sexually transmitted diseases** (STDs) are of concern. STDs refer to any disease that can be transmitted through sexual contact. These diseases are significantly associated with high-risk sexual activities, particularly those that involve unprotected sexual intercourse, intercourse with multiple partners, and sex in exchange for drugs—all major predictors of these diseases (see Table 14.5).

National data on the prevalence of **gonorrhea** among sexually active adolescents show that those between the ages of 10 and 19 had the highest rates of infection, approximately 3500 cases per 100,000 (Coverdale & Gruenbaum, 1998). Similar data regarding **syphilis** reveal that the highest rates occur among adolescents, despite the impression that sexually transmitted diseases are a problem particularly endemic to the adult population (McLanahan & Sandefur, 1994).

sexually transmitted diseases
Any disease that can be transmitted through sexual contact.

gonorrhea
Sexually transmitted disease contracted through vaginal, anal, and oral intercourse; in women symptoms are burning when urinating, menstrual irregularities; pelvic pain; and yellow-green discharge from vagina; in men, a pus-like discharge from the urethra or pain during urination. Oral antibiotics are used for treatment.

syphilis
Sexually transmitted disease contracted through vaginal, anal, and oral intercourse and kissing; symptoms are sores and ulcers and, 3 to 6 weeks later, body rashes, fatigue, and sore throat; if untreated with antibiotics, death may result.

TABLE 14.5

Facts and Myths About Sexually Transmitted Diseases

Identify the following statements as Fact or Myth.

_____1. A person can only get one STD at a time.
_____2. Once you have gotten an STD, you cannot get the same disease again.
_____3. It is possible to get an STD even if you do not have sexual intercourse.
_____4. You cannot get an STD from a toilet, sharing food, or someone's cough or sneeze.
_____5. A virgin cannot get an STD; the first time is always safe.
_____6. You can always tell someone with a sexually transmitted disease—they look unhealthy.

Answers

1. Myth: Getting one type of STD provides no immunity against getting another STD.
2. Myth: STDs are not like measles; some of them can be cured, and some of them cannot, but only one of them—hepatitis B—gives you immunity.
3. Fact: Sexual intercourse is the most likely way to contract an STD; however, some STDs can be transmitted through kissing. Other risky activities are oral and anal sex.
4. Fact: STDs are passed on by intimate contact; they are not like the flu or a cold.
5. Myth: Anyone who has been exposed to a sexually transmitted disease is at risk.
6. Myth: Looking healthy has very little to do with STDs and how they are transmitted.

From *Straight Talk About Sexually Transmitted Diseases,* by M. Brodman, J. Thacker, & R. Kranz, 1998, New York: Facts on File, Inc. ©1993 by Rachel Kranz. Reprinted by permission of the publisher.

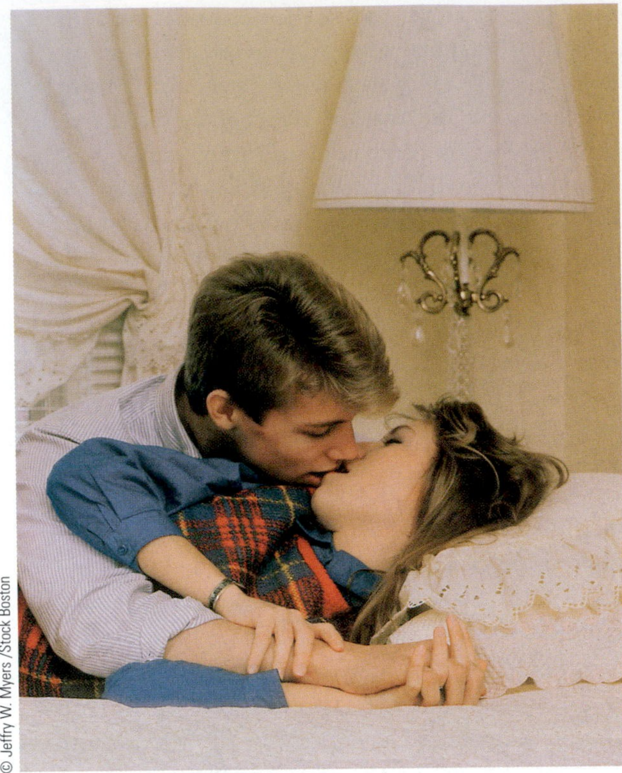

It is estimated that individuals between 15 and 19 years account for 25 percent of STD cases reported annually.

Common symptoms, how these diseases are spread, diagnosis, and treatment of common sexually transmitted diseases are summarized in Table 14.6.

African American adolescents have higher rates of sexually transmitted diseases, with rates for gonorrhea and syphilis substantially higher than their European American counterparts. The average age-adjusted gonorrhea rate in black males ages 15 to 19 is approximately five times greater than that of white males, and that of black females in the same age group is approximately tenfold that of white females (LoConte, O'Leary, & Labouvie, 1997).

human immunodeficiency virus (HIV) HIV infections weaken the body's ability to fight disease and lead to acquired immune deficiency syndrome (AIDS). Symptoms may include weight loss, lack of appetite, diarrhea, night sweats, fever, whitish coating of yeast on tongue and purplish growths on skin.

Adolescent AIDS

Because of the high number of sexually active teens, the threat of their contracting AIDS is of major concern. Different subgroups of adolescents represent varying degrees of risk. Because of the sexual and drug experimentation that is common in this age group, adolescents are at high risk for **human immunodeficiency virus** (HIV)—the virus that can give a person AIDS (see Table 14.7 on page 514.) The two groups at highest risk for HIV infection are male homosexual adolescents and adolescent runaways who live on the street. Among 18- to 24-year-olds, 79 percent report having contracted AIDS through homosexual activity (Orlandi & Dalton, 1998).

Because the symptoms of AIDS may not appear for up to 8 to 10 years after initial infection with HIV, these young adults may have been infected as younger adolescents (Centers for Disease Control, 1997). There are no reliable statistics on the rate of infection in adolescents who live on the streets. This group, however, is potentially at high risk because many survive by engaging in prostitution and often use intravenous drugs.

Knowledge About Contracting AIDS High school and college students are reasonably well informed about AIDS (Hoffman, 1999). They are aware of the recommended precautions for avoiding HIV infection and fearful that the virus may spread within the student population. Data also show, however, that students are reluctant to change their sexual behavior unless the threat of infection is personalized (Miner, 1998). Similar data, generated from a sample of high school students, show that 96 percent of them know how AIDS is contracted; yet, one-third of these teenagers continue to engage in risky sexual behavior (Curran, 1998). For example, high school and college students report that they are "more selective" in choosing sexual partners. Their "selectiveness," however, is questionable. For example, some look for signs such as blisters or other physical manifestations, and if the partner does not "look" like he or she has the disease, they believe they are safe (Quirk, Rhodes, & Stimson, 1998).

Adolescent knowledge about AIDS indicates that they are generally unaware of the risk (Sigelman, Maddock, Epstein, & Carpenter, 1993). Only 15 percent of sexually active adolescents have changed their behavior to avoid contracting AIDS. Of those who have changed their behavior, only 20 percent have adopted methods that are effective. Of sexually active adolescents, only 47 percent of females and 25 percent of males report using condoms (Murphy, Rotheram-Borus, & Reid, 1998). Although adolescents may cognitively recognize the value of using condoms, they may not acknowledge a personal susceptibility to AIDS that necessitates the use of condoms (Richardson, 1998).

For younger children who need to understand what HIV is and how it is transmitted, clear informational materials can be quite effective. However, for teenagers, just supplying information about AIDS appears to be insufficient. The research evidence suggests that a substantial proportion of adolescents engage in

TABLE 14.6

Symptoms, Diagnosis, and Treatment of Common Sexually Transmitted Diseases			
STD	**Symptoms**	**How It Is Spread**	**Treatments**
Syphilis: A spirochete that can remain in the body for life	Syphilis has several phases that may overlap one another: (1) painless sores or ulcers; (2) (three to six weeks later) body rashes on hands and feet, mild fever, fatigue, sore throat, and patchy hair loss; (3) serious damage to heart, brain, or other organs; death may result	Vaginal, anal, oral intercourse; kissing; during pregnancy	Antibiotics are successful for both partners. The damage caused in later phases cannot be undone.
Gonorrhea: A bacterium that can cause sterility, arthritis, and heart problems	Women: Frequent, often burning urination; menstrual irregularities; pelvic pain; green or yellow-green discharge from the vagina Men: A puslike discharge from the urethra or pain during urination	Vaginal, anal, oral intercourse	Both partners can be successfully treated with oral antibiotics. Often, people with gonorrhea also have chlamydia. They must be treated for both diseases.
Hepatitis B virus: It is the only sexually transmitted infection that is preventable with vaccination	Extreme fatigue, headache, nausea, vomiting, lack of appetite, tenderness in the lower abdomen	In semen, saliva, blood, feces, and urine; by intimate and sexual contact, including kissing, vaginal, oral, anal sex; using unclean needles to inject drugs	None; in most cases, the infection clears within four to eight weeks of rest.
Herpes: Herpes simplex virus-1 and herpes simplex virus-2	Cold sores and fever blisters. Itchy sores appearing on the vagina, cervix, penis, mouth, anus, buttocks; pain and discomfort around the infected area of sores	Touching, sexual intimacy (including kissing); vaginal, anal, and oral intercourse	No cure; symptoms can be relieved and the number of occurrences reduced with drugs such as valacyclovir and acyclovir.
Chlamydia: A bacterium that enters the body, latches onto a cell, then moves inside to reproduce	Men: Painful urination, watery discharge from penis, pain in testicles Women: Heavier vaginal discharge, inflammation of pelvis	Vaginal and anal intercourse	Antibiotics
Human Papillomavirus (HPV): sexually transmitted virus	May not show worst effects until years after first infection; genital warts	Vaginal and anal intercourse	Ointment is spread over infected areas.

high-risk behavior such as unprotected sexual intercourse even though they are well aware that this is a primary route of disease transmission. The alarming high rate of pregnancy and the fear of AIDS have opened up the debate over what to do about the precocious sexual activity of young people. It has been suggested that if we want to lower the risk of adolescent AIDS priority must be given to improving condom use among sexually active teens (Bailey & Piercy, 1997). Improving condom use may also help in preventing another unwanted consequence of sexual intercourse—teenage pregnancy.

Teenage Pregnancy

The average age at which females become sexually active in the United States is 16. Over one million of these sexually active teens become pregnant each year and about a half million give birth (Mauldon, 1998). Longitudinal data suggest that the proportion of adolescents who are sexually active is increasing for all ages from 15 to 19, with the greatest increase observed for 16-year-old European American females (Hardy, 1998). Moreover, data indicate that adolescents below the age of 14 show the greatest increase in rate of initiation of sexual activity relative to other ages (Chase-Lansdale & Brooks-Gunn, 1994).

Most sexually active teenagers do not plan on having a child (Crane, 1991). However, even if pregnant teenagers did not plan to become pregnant, as their pregnancy progresses, motivational processes are certainly involved in decisions about pregnancy outcome (whether to keep the baby, have an abortion, place the baby for adoption). Two-thirds of pregnant teens carry their pregnancy to term, and 96 percent will decide to keep their babies—only 4 percent will give up their child for adoption (Lerner & Galambos, 1998). The strongest motivation for keeping the child is stimulation and fun, followed

TABLE 14.7

Human Immunodeficiency Virus (HIV)

Factor	Description
Common symptoms	Possibly no symptoms for approximately 8 to 10 years Constant or rapid unexplained weight loss, diarrhea, lack of appetite Fatigue, persistent fevers, night sweats, dry cough Light-headedness, headaches, mental disorders A thick, whitish coating of yeast on the tongue or mouth Purplish growths on skin
How HIV is spread	Anal, vaginal, and oral intercourse Sharing contaminated needles for injecting drugs Transfusion of contaminated blood products Childbirth
Diagnosis	Blood tests detect HIV antibodies
Treatment	No cure or vaccine AIDS cocktail: combines several different anti-HIV drugs that attack HIV in different ways; most effective method so far to treat HIV infection; not a cure and drug resistance remains a concern; severe side effects (nausea and diarrhea, painful kidney stones) Many AIDS-related conditions such as pneumonia, cancers, and a variety of infections that take advantage of weakened immune systems; can be managed to some extent with a variety of treatments. Fatal: at this time, no one has recovered from AIDS

by achievement and creativity, love and affection, power and influence, expansion of self, adult status and social identity, and security in old age (Furstenberg, 1991).

Teenage Mothers

Having a child as an adolescent can have negative implications for all aspects of the young mother's life, including her financial, social, educational, physical, occupational, psychological, and developmental well-being (MacPhee, Fritz, & Miller-Heyl, 2001). Experientially, the teenage mother has had fewer years to observe parenting and other adult roles. Emotionally, she is more egocentric about her own needs than are older parents, who are more likely to have been sharing a marital/mate relationship for a few years. Teenagers are less ready for their pregnancies than are older women and, as a result, they view childbirth less positively than older women (Roosa, Lein, Reinholtz, & Angelini, 1997). Most teenage mothers do not understand the time and energy demands of children. They often have unrealistic expectations about both the mothering role and infant behavior. The child mother may have wanted a child, but when the child has problems and the teenager sees how difficult it is to parent, she may wish that she had not had the child (Culp, Culp, Osofsky, & Osofsky, 1991).

Teenage mothers are often faced with educational and economic instability, which may be further compounded because adolescent mothers are prone to having more offspring over their reproductive careers than are their sexually abstaining teenage peers. In addition, teenage mothers experience family pressures, and if they marry, considerable marital disruption. Separation and/or divorce is two to three times as likely among adolescents as among women who are 20 years or older (Furstenberg, Hughes, & Brooks-Gunn, 1992).

Another risk for the adolescent mother is the probability of an uncompleted education. Eight out of 10 girls who give birth at age 17 or less do not complete high school (Baydar, Brooks-Gunn, & Senior, 1995). Teenage mothers are more likely to drop out of high school, even when compared with women of similar socioeconomic backgrounds and academic aptitude who postpone child rearing.

Other risks include a death rate resulting from pregnancy and childbirth that are 60 percent higher for

Adolescents should not be parents, but many are.

teenage mothers under 15 than for females in their early 20s (Carey, McCane-Sanford, & Davidson, 1991). One risk has to do with medical complications (Mauldon, 1998). When teenage mothers receive good prenatal care, they can have a healthy pregnancy, but more often than not they do not receive good prenatal care.

Teenage Fathers

There are very few studies of teenage fathers and a number of myths surrounding them (see Table 14.8). Premarital pregnancy and childbearing are apparently considered to be female problems. For example, the father has no right to decide on an abortion or to have the baby—this decision is solely up to the female at present. Teenage fathers are generally less well educated, have lower academic abilities, start sex at earlier ages, and engage in more crime than do other young men (Lerman, 1993). Socially, people tend to look at the male as the bad guy, the one who caused this whole problem. Some fathers, however, do view the problem of pregnancy as a dual responsibility. The fact remains, however, that teenagers need to develop some foresight into the consequences of their sexual activities.

Not all teen pregnancies, however, are fathered by teenage boys. In fact, an astonishing 74 percent of teenage pregnancies in the United States are fathered by men older than 18 (Alan Guttmacher Institute, 1994). The younger the mother, the greater the partner age gap tends to be (Males, 1993). For example, among mothers 11 to 12 years of age, the fathers of their children were on average 9.8 years older; among mothers 13 to 14 years of age, the fathers averaged 4.6 years older; and among those mothers 15 to 19 years, the fathers averaged 3.7 years older. However, statements from health agencies continue to portray teenage pregnancies as resulting from intercourse between adolescent partners. The reality that most babies born to adolescent mothers are fathered by older men has particular relevance for prevention; intervention must do more to target the behavior of older men if decreases in teenage pregnancy are to be realized.

Infants of Teenage Parents

Studies show that low birth weight babies are two to six times as common in adolescent mothers (Coley & Chase-Lansdale, 1998). Eighty-five percent of low birth weight infants are premature, and 15 percent are small for gestational age. Stillbirths are twice as frequent in adolescent pregnancies. Infants born to adolescent mothers are two to three times more likely to die within the first year of life than children born to women 20 to 30 years of age. Furthermore, infants born to these young mothers seem to experience long-term developmental problems. One report shows that 12 percent of children born to young mothers (under the age of 16) score less than 70 on

TABLE 14.8

Myths and Reality of the Teenage Father

Myth	Description	Reality
The Stud	He is a worldly, wise, villainous "stud" who knows more about sex and sexuality than most teenage boys.	Although adolescent fathers become sexually active earlier and have more varied sexual experiences than adolescent mothers, most young fathers are as uninformed about sex and sexuality as young mothers.
Macho	He feels psychologically inadequate, has no inner control, and unlike other boys his age has a psychological need to prove his masculinity.	Adolescent fathers are psychologically and intellectually more alike than different from their nonfather contemporaries.
Mr. Cool	He usually has a fleeting, casual relationship with the young mother and has few emotional feelings about the pregnancy.	Contemporary research indicates that adolescent males do experience emotional feelings about their impending fatherhood.
Phantom Father	He is absent and rarely involved in the support and rearing of his children.	Most studies on adolescent fatherhood reveal that young fathers want to become deeply involved with their children.
Big Spender	He completes school and enters a high-paying job, leaving his partner and offspring to fend for themselves.	As adults, adolescent fathers generally have truncated education, remain in lower-paying jobs, and have lower incomes than men who become fathers in adulthood. (Hawkins & Dollahite, 1997, pp. 109–110)

intelligence tests at age 4, versus 2 percent of children in the general population (Brooks-Gunn & Paikoff, 1992). Many studies in the research literature document the fact that infants of adolescent mothers are more prone to be the victims of child abuse and neglect (Osofsky, 1998; Washington, 1992).

APPLICATIONS:

Helping Teenage Parents

Keeping and raising the child without adequate support from family is probably beyond what one can reasonably expect of most girls under the age of 16. Their emotional immaturity and inability to deal with frustration (often extreme frustration) may cause them undue hardship. Nor does it seem that marriage is the answer: Teenage fathers are more likely to be emotionally immature. Many are not through with school and therefore their job opportunities are limited. Furthermore, marriage does not protect them from both unhappiness and many practical problems. It appears to be a no-win situation all the way around. The most reasonable policy is one of prevention.

There are, however, some alternatives for pregnant adolescents—one of which is abortion. Teens who decide to abort are more educationally ambitious, are more likely to be good students, are more likely to be from higher socioeconomic backgrounds, are from less religious families, have mothers and peers who have more positive attitudes toward abortion, and are less likely to have friends or relatives who are teenage single parents. Many teenagers, however, are rather far along in the pregnancy (beyond the first trimester) when they discover they are pregnant. Also, on the negative side, a young female is more likely to suffer damage to the cervix during the abortion procedure, because the cervix is small and inelastic.

Adoption is another recourse. Relative to those who choose to have and parent the child, adoption appears to be a positive choice with more favorable social outcomes for the mother and child (Namerow, Kaimuss, & Cushman, 1997). For those teenage mothers who decide to keep their child, role-sharing family systems seem to work best.

role-sharing families
Families of teenage mothers where each member shares in the responsibilities of raising the infant.

Role-Sharing Families

Teenage motherhood affects several members of the family, not just the teenage mother. Because young mothers are likely to spend a few years living with their family, the study of family systems is critical. Families that incorporate the teenage mother and her infant into the family do so in three ways: role blocking, role binding, and role sharing (Smith, 1983). In *role-blocking* families, the teenage mother does not assume the mothering role. She either willingly abdicates or a family member takes over. These family dynamics prevent her growth in the mother role. In *role-binding* families, all tasks and responsibilities of "Mother" are delegated to the teenage mother and she performs them alone. This is the "You made your bed, and you'll lie in it" attitude.

In **role sharing**, the family shares in responsibilities, enabling the teenage mother to grow in other roles as well as the mother role. The family, through a role-sharing process, commits itself to a new system. The pregnancy, and later, the infant are accepted by the family without stigmatization. Other studies have shown that when grandparents and relatives act as supplemental rather than substitute parents, adolescent mothers and their children fare better (Azzarto, 1997).

Social Support

Another influence on family functioning and therefore on the teenage mother is availability of social support. Several scholars have noted that social support is important in dealing effectively with pregnancy and/or parenting (Azzarto, 1997). Support from parents is a particularly salient fact in fostering coping and adaptation skills in adolescent mothers and their children. For example, a woman in her 30s remembers her mother's response to her pregnancy:

> My mother discovered that I might be pregnant when she overheard me talking to a friend on the phone. Her immediate reaction was to take me for a pregnancy test. On the way, she discussed alternatives to going away to college if I were pregnant. Though I knew she was terribly disappointed, not once did she say any words of judgment. Her conversation was both practical and sympathetic. I will never forget this. I want to try to be as understanding, loving, and forgiving with my own children.

The adolescent mother not only needs emotional support in the form of empathy, caring, love, and trust but also physical support (direct help for financial support); information support (information about pregnancy, delivery, parenting); and appraisal support (feedback from the important persons in her social network that is necessary for self-evaluation). Mothers who receive support from family and friends in all these areas demonstrate more knowledge about babies, report greater satisfaction with mothering, develop more responsive attitudes toward their babies, and experience less depression (Langfield & Pasley, 1997).

Preventive Measures

Many experts say that sex education helps prevent unwanted pregnancies (Brooks-Gunn & Chase-Lansdale, 1995). Sex education in many studies, however, has been finitely defined. It is more than just one parent–child talk about the facts of life (see Chapter 8), a sixth-grade course in physical development, or a lecture on contraception and family planning. From infancy on, parents influence a child's attitudes toward sex in hundreds of ways. A loving, accepting family system, for example, is conducive to development of sex attitudes that will allow children to make future decisions regarding their own sexuality.

Although girls may talk to their mothers about sex-related topics, both females and males indicate that they see sex education as an important need. In examining the social and family issues facing contemporary adolescents, they rank sex education third in importance preceded by coping with problems and managing family relations (Strom, Oguinick, & Singer, 1995). Marsha Harman and James Johnson (1995) found that Asian American, African American, and European American adolescents all indicated that friends were the most frequent source of information regarding sex; that they wanted themselves, as parents, to be the primary sex educators for their children; and that they believed that children should be informed about sexual matters early in childhood. An obvious conclusion from these studies is that teenagers need more sex information, education, and guidance.

However, researchers have found that teen reports of whether parent–teen communication has taken place show relatively little correspondence to parental reports of such communication. In one study, 75 percent of mothers reported teaching their children something about sex, but only 33 percent of the children reported that this was the case (Jaccard, 1995; Jaccard, Dittus, & Gordon, 1998). It appears that parents tend to overestimate the amount of time they spend on sex education with their teenagers.

James Jaccard (1995) has pointed out five effective communication patterns when discussing sex-related issues with teenagers:

1. The *extent* of the communication is important (frequency and depth). Sex education is an ongoing activity, not one brief chat at one point in time.
2. The *style* or manner in which information is communicated is important. A relaxed, open manner of communication is best.
3. The *content* of the information that is communicated is important. Sometimes it is better to ask teenagers what they "know" first and then expand and, perhaps, correct any misinformation.
4. The *timing* of communication is a factor. Jaccard recommends the earlier the better.
5. The *general family environment* has an impact. The overall quality of the relationship between parent and teenager is important.

Commitment

Further, a loving, accepting family system is conducive to development of attitudes that will allow children and adolescents to make future decisions about their own sexuality. It is in this context that something like prevention of pregnancy in lovemaking fits into the natural course of learning. In this type of environment, young people learn to understand that sexual conduct with another person involves a deep, emotional commitment; respect; and concern for the other's welfare. In addition, classes combined with school-based clinics offering contraceptives or information about birth control have been effective in delaying sex and lowering birth rates. No study has shown that teaching adolescents about birth control encourages them to have sex.

Concept Checks

1. Neldreka is an attractive female; next, we are likely to associate positive ______ ______ with her.
2. Who is the least likely to masturbate?
   a. Males who are actively engaged in sexual intercourse
   b. Females who are sexually inexperienced
   c. Females who are sexually active
3. ***True or False:*** Most teenagers who engage in premarital sexual intercourse do not plan their first sexual experience.
4. A sexually transmitted disease that is spread by kissing is
   a. AIDS.
   b. gonorrhea.
   c. hepatitis B virus.

5. Teenage mothers often face ____________ and ____________ instability.
6. This teenage mother comes from a family in which her parents have said, "You made your bed, and you'll lie in it." This type of family is labeled as
   a. role sharing.
   b. role binding.
   c. role blocking.

Health-Related Issues

Before Beginning ...

After reading this section, you will be able to

- identify the variables that contribute to youth violence.
- describe the types of drugs most commonly used by adolescents.
- analyze why teenagers use drugs.
- understand effective treatments for teenagers who abuse drugs.
- characterize the influence of peers on subsequent use of drugs.

Youths and Violence

Six o'clock news anchor: A sniper fired 57 rounds on the playground at the Kingston Elementary School in Los Angeles today, killing two students and a passerby and injuring 14 children. Scores of children were pinned on the playground under gunfire. Some ran screaming across the yard; others hid behind trees. The bullets pierced school doors and shattered school windows.

Community Violence

Murders, drive-by shootings, shootouts with police, battles between gangs—these seem to be the now standard events reported on the nightly news. For some children, in some communities, such experiences as victim or witness are not rare. On Chicago's south side, 26 percent of African American youths ages 7 to 15 reported witnessing a stabbing; 30 percent had witnessed a shooting (Bell & Jenkins, 1993). Nearly 75 percent of a sample of 1000 elementary and high school students in the Washington, DC area reported witnessing at least one robbery, stabbing, shooting, or murder (Richters & Martinez, 1993).

Children also experience community violence indirectly through knowing others who have been assaulted. In the Bell and Jenkins (1993) study, over 50 percent of the children reported knowing someone who had been robbed, 29 percent knew someone who had been shot, and 26 percent knew someone who had been stabbed.

Various research findings suggest that children exposed to violence in the community often develop serious psychological problems (Horn & Trickett, 1999). Symptoms tend to be the type that characterize post-traumatic stress disorder: free-floating anxieties, depression, sleep disturbances, psychosomatic complaints, repetitive nightmares, and fears of recurrence (Dulmus & Wodarski, 2000). Internalizing problems (depression) appear to be more likely in children who witness violence, and externalizing problems (aggression, conduct disorder) are more common in those victimized by violence (Shahinfar, Fox, & Leavitt, 2000).

Violence committed in the home is likely to be more traumatic to children than the same acts of violence involving nonfamily members (Daniels, 2001). Witnessing a fight between two neighbors is likely to be emotionally quite different from the experience of seeing a fight between one's mother and father. When children are exposed to family violence, their symptoms are likely to be more chronic, less controllable, and more damaging to the continuing relationships on which the child's development must be based (Margolin, 1999). In contrast, home environments unsullied by violence provide a safe haven for children and thus mitigate the effects of violence they may experience in the community outside the home (Overstreet & Braun, 2000). In addition, the presence of a mother in the home and male support figures appear to reduce symptoms in children exposed to or victimized by community violence.

In neighborhoods in which violence is common, the percentages of children who report witnessing violence and being a victim of it increase with the children's age; the older they are, the more likely they are to have witnessed violence. Relatedly, the longer they reside in such neighborhoods, the more likely they are to be repeatedly exposed to violence (Hill & Madhere, 1995). This chronic exposure to community violence may also lead to teenagers' attempting to solve their own problems through violence.

Violent Youths

> Judonne and Jermaine face each other in the concrete courtyard of their inner-city housing project. They had argued about a girl. Now a crowd gathers as Jermaine flicks insults at Judonne. Suddenly, Judonne pulls out a gun and shoots Jermaine three times in the chest. The dead boy is 15. The shooter is 14. They had been best friends. (Bender, Leone, Szumski, Wekesser, Biskup, & Cozic, 1992)

The most prominent pattern of noneconomically motivated violence is fighting with peers, and more and more teenagers are solving their problems through violence. The victims and assailants are getting increasingly younger and the fatal disputes are becoming more trivial. Disagreements that were once settled by angry words or fistfights now end up as gun battles—senseless violence. Some of these killings are crimes of premeditated violence motivated by greed, lust, or a desire for revenge. Others are crimes of passion arising from impulsive overresponses to provocation or some explosive drive within the killer.

Every year at least 1000 and often more than 1500 U.S. youngsters under the age of 18 intentionally take the lives of others and are arrested for murder or manslaughter (Heide, 1999). Homicides committed by children and adolescents generate a great deal of media attention. Although these are heinous crimes, they are not as frequent as you might think. People younger than 18 constitute roughly one-quarter of the total population in the United States. Yet, annually for the past decade or so, consistently fewer than 11 percent of all individuals arrested in the United States for murder or intentional manslaughter have been under the age of 18. This equates to approximately 5 teenagers in every 100,000 being arrested for intentionally killing someone.

The homicide rate for younger adolescents is even lower. The vast majority (85 percent) of adolescents who kill are 15 and older; fewer than 1 percent of those arrested for murder or non-negligent manslaughter are under the age of 15. Only a handful of those arrested for these homicide crimes have been younger than 10 years old. However, arrest data undoubtedly underestimate the number of very young children who kill because at least some of these youngsters are probably never formally arrested. In most jurisdictions, children under the age of 7 years are automatically deemed incapable of criminal conduct. Still, there is little doubt that extremely few homicides are committed by children under the age of 10.

Concern about the growing level of violence among young people is not limited to the United States. Youth violence occurs in all parts of the world. One of the most widely publicized and worst examples occurred in England in 1993 when two 11-year-old boys abducted a 2-year-old from a shopping mall outside of London. The boys dragged the young boy away from the mall and stoned him to death along a railway track. One of the boys reportedly was "laughing his head off" as the child was being killed (*Ashland Daily Tidings*, 1993, p. 14). International studies confirm, however, that teenage crime in the United States is far more serious than similar problems anywhere else in the world. The homicide rate in the United States for the 15- to 24-year-old age group is five times that of our nearest competitor (Canada). How did our nation get to this point?

Factors in Teen Violence

Ethnicity is a variable that factors in youth violence. African American youths are vastly overrepresented among teenagers arrested for murder and non-negligent manslaughter. One-half of the adolescents arrested for these homicides are black. Hispanic youths are similarly overrepresented, accounting for almost one-quarter of all youth arrests for homicide crimes (Grunbaum, Basen-Engquist, & Pandey, 1998). Although minorities have the highest arrest rate, studies reveal that these arrests significantly underestimate crimes committed by whites who are never caught. Further, when poverty is controlled for in studies looking at ethnicity and homicide, the ethnic differences diminish; homicide is not so much linked to ethnicity as it is to economic differences.

Gender is also a factor in youth homicide with boys being much more likely to commit these crimes than girls. At all ages under 18, the vast majority of those arrested for murder or non-negligent manslaughter are boys. This is the most consistent and documented cross-cultural finding concerning youth homicide.

Philadelphia, New York, Chicago, Detroit, Washington, DC—we have become accustomed to crimes by teens in the nation's largest cities, but, mid-sized cities and suburbs now realize that they are no longer safe from the violent crimes that larger cities have long had to live with. Even small towns and rural areas across the nation have had to react to the growth of teen violence in their own backyards.

Causes

"It's the breakdown of the American family that is causing these violent crimes!" "It's easy access to guns that are the culprit!" "Violence on TV and video games causes kids to commit these homicides!" Many seem to think that one factor causes youth violence; the debate over the ultimate cause of teen violence continues with relatively little consensus. Most violent behavior probably results from some complex mixture of genetic and environmental factors. Environmentally, violence has been linked with child maltreatment, changes in the family structure, the absence of role models, the saturation of violence in society, easy access to weapons, youths' increasing abuse of drugs and alcohol, and the rising number of children raised in poverty (Heide, 1999). Leonard D. Eron (1997) lists massive exposure to violent television programs as a factor in the creation of antisocial adolescents, noting that males growing up in homes that lack nonviolent male role models are the most vulnerable to television's violence-promoting messages.

Youth gangs are often cited as a key cause for youth violence (Thornberry, 1998). Increasingly, large numbers of adolescents are turning to gangs for the sense of belonging that their families no longer provide. Violence plays an important part in some gangs as members seek to protect their territory, prove their masculinity, and consolidate their unity against other gangs and nongang members. Gangs are much more violent today than in years past, and one reason is the easy access to lethal weapons that gang members have.

> If you have a gun, you have power. That's the way it is. Guns are just part of growing up these days. . . . You fire a gun and you can just *hear* the power. (Hull, 1993)

Many adolescents are growing up in a milieu where violence is an ordinary fact of life. Exposure to violence, day in and day out, may make adolescents insensitive, or perhaps immune, to violence and death. Many observers feel that the ready availability of guns is the single most important factor in today's spread of teen violence. There are over 250 million guns in the nation—nearly one weapon for every man, woman, and child. Illegal drug commerce and use is also a major factor in violent crime. The correlation between drug use and crime is often very strong (Heide, 1999).

Available data shed some light on the characteristics of adolescents who kill. The first type is the "good" kid who seemingly "out of the blue" commits a very violent crime. Rather than coming from a caring, nurturing family with positive role models, however, these children generally have had a history of being rejected and/or abused by their parents (Eisikovits, Winstok, & Enosh, 1998). Over the years, their lack of social skills and isolation from others causes them to be rejected by their classmates as well. Anger and hostility then begin to build up until one day rage overcomes them, hurling them out of control and into violence.

The second type is the career offender, who regularly breaks the law and is occasionally violent (Huizinga & Jakob-Chien, 1998). Rather than quietly accepting their fate, these kids tend to lash out violently when frustrated. They have little control over their anger; are filled with feelings of suspicion, fear, rage; and often carry a knife or a gun.

© Michael Newman/PhotoEdit

Gangs are primarily composed of adolescent males, although there is evidence of increasing numbers of female gangs.

Solutions

Take guns away!

Get rid of violence on television and in video games!

Help parents learn to deal with their angry children!

Make our criminal system more strict for these youth offenders! Sanctions should be swift and sure. Young criminals should know that this is what they can expect!

Violent youths need rehabilitation, not harsh punishment. Imprisoning them only exposes them to physical and sexual abuse and turns them into hardened criminals!

All these proposed solutions are real issues. Because we have not always dealt with this level of violence in our towns and cities, and because a similar level of violence does not exist in most European and even Canadian cities we assume that there must be solutions. To this end some experts have recommended proposals, from subsidized quality child care to job training programs, to help ameliorate violence. Prevention, however, may be the real issue that must be addressed to counter youth violence. Most experts agree that society must be as willing to devote enormous resources to the search for cures of violent youth crime as it does for the cures for diseases such as cancer. The fact does remain, however, that youth crimes would not be lethal without guns, and, similarly, teenagers might not be so apt to pull the trigger without the use of drugs.

Drugs

In France, wine is considered a food rather than an alcoholic beverage. Parents teach their children how to drink wine with meals, airline pilots drink it on the job, and any 6-year-old may buy wine at the store. No meal is complete without wine—it "cleans the blood" and "builds strong bodies." Italians similarly praise wine. Germans, as well as others, hail beer as a boon to nursing mothers. There are dozens of medicines in China to cure varying aches and pains; in the United States, however, we would call these medicines liqueurs. In the Andes of South America, Aymara Indians have produced coca for centuries. These leaves are chewed in a way that relieves cold, hunger, and thirst, yet cause no psychic disturbances. Tourists in the Netherlands are often surprised at decals in the windows of coffee shops that signal easy availability of marijuana. That these substances can have such different uses and meanings in a single culture demonstrates that something very different from biochemistry and physiology must be involved. As counterintuitive as it may first appear, it is commonplace that people who have the easiest access to a given substance are more likely to use it but not abuse it (Klee, 1997). The United States, however, has the highest rate of illicit drug use of any industrial nation (Inciardi, McBride, & Surratt, 1998), and a major problem facing many of our teenagers is drug and alcohol abuse.

The National Commission on Marijuana and Drug Abuse defines a **drug** as any substance, other than food, that by its chemical nature affects the structure or function of the living organism. **Drug abuse** is using a drug(s) to such an extent that everyday functioning is impaired.

Issues surrounding teenage drug use include the types of drugs they use, the prevalence, the progression of drug use, why they use drugs, and treatment for drug abusers.

Types of Drugs

Drugs are classified according to the type of effect they have on the human body. Four major types of drugs can be distinguished: depressants, hallucinogens, opiates, and stimulants.

Depressants Central nervous system **depressants** (downers) depress or slow down the activity of the central nervous system. Examples are alcohol, inhalants (anesthetics and solvents), tranquilizers (Librium and Valium), and sedatives (barbiturates, Quaaludes, and PCP). The most commonly used drug in this category is alcohol. The circulatory system distributes alcohol throughout the body, where it contacts every major organ. Long-term effects include liver disease, pancreatitis, cardiovascular disorders, and brain damage.

© Tony Freeman/PhotoEdit

The most widely abused drug of all is alcohol, which has been implicated in almost every form of violent crime.

drug Any substance, other than food, that by its chemical nature affects the structure or function of the living organism.

drug abuse Using a drug(s) to such an extent that everyday functioning is impaired.

depressants Drugs that slow down the activity of the central nervous system; examples include alcohol, inhalants, tranquilizers, and sedatives. Also known as downers.

Most depressants interact with specific receptors in the brain cells. Alcohol, however, influences a number of different receptor systems in the brain. It appears to have a particularly potent effect on the gamma-aminobutyric acid (GABA) system. Alcohol seems to increase the production of the neurotransmitter GABA, which interferes with effective firing of neurons. Because the GABA system seems to act on our feelings of anxiety, alcohol's anti-anxiety properties may result from its interaction with the GABA system.

Drinking and driving is the leading cause of death among young people, and the number of teenagers who drink is increasing. By the time adolescents reach the 12th grade, over 92 percent have at least tried alcohol (Vik & Brown, 1998). Five percent of high school seniors are daily drinkers, and 37.5 percent have on at least one occasion in the past month drunk heavily—more than five drinks in a row (Tucker, 1998). As graphically displayed in Figure 14.3, it appears that more youngsters are drinking to get high rather than to show their "adult status" as they did a few years ago (Chen & Kandel, 1998). One reason that was once frequently given for the increase in the use of alcohol was that it was easy to get and not too expensive (compared with other drugs). This is no longer true; hard drugs are getting very inexpensive and the delivery system for the drug world is better than the one for Federal Express®.

hallucinogens
Mind-distorting drugs that create altered perceptions; they include marijuana and lysergic acid diethylamide (LSD).

opiates
Drugs that have an analgesic effect and are used to relieve physical and mental pain; most are derived from the opium poppy (morphine, codeine, heroin).

Hallucinogens **Hallucinogens** are mind-distorters. Marijuana, mescaline, and lysergic acid diethylamide (LSD) are the most commonly used hallucinogens. Hallucinogens have an analgesic effect. They are used to relieve physical and mental pain, reduce frequency of coughing, stop diarrhea, and induce sleep or stupor. Most hallucinogens are derived from the opium poppy (morphine, codeine, heroin) but can also be produced synthetically (methadone). All drugs are psychoactive in that they affect the central nervous system in such a way as to produce alterations in subjective feeling states.

Marijuana is most commonly used in the 10- to 15-year-old range. The older the adolescent, the more likely it is that he or she has tried marijuana—6 percent of the 12- to 13-year-olds have used marijuana, 22 percent of the 14 to 15 age group, 39 percent of those 16 to 17, and 53 percent of the 18- to 24-year-old group (National Institute on Drug Abuse, 1997). Generally, marijuana tends to break down inhibitions; its usual effect is giggling and laughter and a distorted sense of time and space. For numerous adolescents the subtle change from uptight behavior to a state of relaxed drifting has been attributed to the use of significant amounts of marijuana. Impairments of memory, concentration, motivation, and relationships with others are common outcomes of long-term use (Roffman & Barnhart, 1987).

Marijuana produces an active resin known as tetrahydrocannabinol (THC) that is capable of effecting hallucinatory states within the user. The brain makes its own version of THC, a neurochemical called *anandamide* after the Sanskrit word, *ananda*, which means bliss. Because work in this area is so new, scientists are only beginning to explore how this neurochemical affects the brain and this behavior.

We are only beginning to understand how LSD affects the brain and behavior. We do know that LSD is chemically similar to certain neurotransmitters, such as serotonin, acetylcholine, and norepinephrine. However, the mechanisms responsible for the hallucinations and other perceptual changes remain unknown.

Opiates The major effect of **opiates** is to temporarily produce analgesia (reduce pain) and euphoria. Heroin, opium, codeine, and morphine are included in this group. Opiates induce euphoria, drowsiness, and slowed breathing. The brain actually produces two natural painkillers, or opioids—enkephalins and endorphins—and opiates activate this system.

The life of an opiate addict is bleak. In a 24-year follow-up study of more than 500 addicts in California (Hser, Anglin, & Powers, 1993), 27.7 percent had died, and their mean age at death was only 40. About half the deaths were the results of homicide, suicide, or accident, and one-third were from overdoses. Because these drugs are usually injected intravenously, users are at increased risk for AIDS through the use of contami-

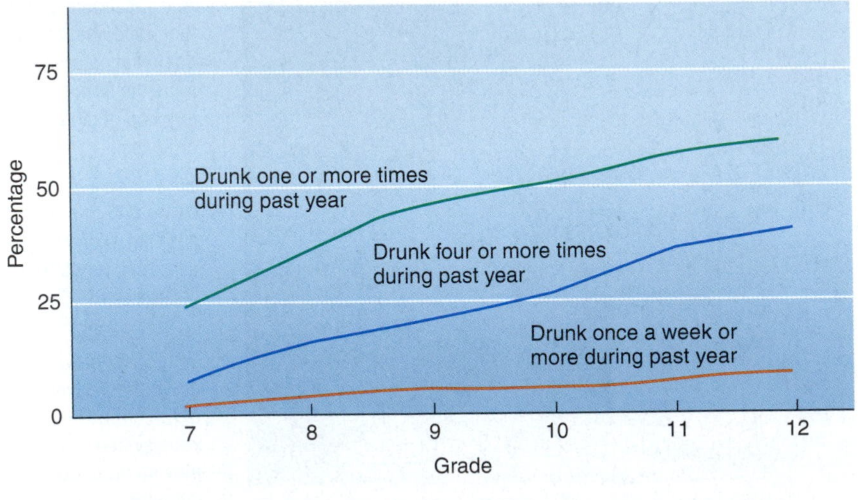

FIGURE 14.3 ***Percentage of Teenage Drinkers Who Report Getting Drunk by Frequency and School Grade***

From "Characteristics of Alcoholic Families and Adolescent Substance," by A. Orenstein & A. Ullman, 1996, in *Journal of Alcohol and Drug Education, 42*(3), 86–101. Used by permission.

nated needles. Opium use, in particular heroin, was popular in the mid-1970s and has since been replaced by cocaine and its derivatives as the drug of choice.

Stimulants **Stimulants** (uppers) are used to stimulate activity, suppress the appetite, and ameliorate emotional depression. They include legal drugs, such as caffeine and nicotine, as well as legal and illegal amphetamines and the illegal methadrine and cocaine.

Because of availability, experimental use of tobacco products has the widest prevalence during early adolescence (Killen, 1998; Murray, Swan, Johnson, & Bewley, 1993). Even among preadolescents, we are seeing a substantial portion of children experiment with puffing cigarettes by age 9, and in a new and disturbing trend, a small but significant portion (13 percent of third-grade boys) use smokeless tobacco (West & Michell, 1999). Teenagers continue to smoke despite the health hazards of increasing heart rate, shortness of breath, constriction of blood vessels, irritation of the throat, and deposits of foreign matter into sensitive lungs.

Peer groups are crucially important in influencing whether teenagers start smoking (West & Michell, 1999), especially with Native American and African American girls (Alexander, Allen, Crawford, & McCormick, 1999). European American and Hispanic girls describe their parents and family members as more instrumental in their first smoking experience. Further, girls are also more likely than boys to continue smoking once they have begun. Perhaps this is so because girls may believe that smoking helps them lose weight or, at best, maintain their current weight. On the average, smokers do weigh 5 to 7 pounds less than nonsmokers. But averages disguise the range of individual differences; there are as many fat smokers and there are thin nonsmokers. Smoking stimulates the metabolism, so calories are burned at a faster rate; but, as it should be pointed out to girls, so does exercise and without the very negative side effects of smoking (Douthitt, 1998).

Friends, the wider peer group, and society in general are important factors relating to smoking behavior (West & Michell, 1999). Advertising and smoking in movies, which portray it as cool and sexy, are culprits and play an influential role in promoting this habit among children and teenagers. Evidence also indicates an intergenerational transmission, teens are more likely to smoke if their parents smoke (Chassin, Pressen, Rose, & Sherman, 1998). Today, tobacco smoking *supersedes* alcohol use and marijuana smoking; that is, cigarette use plays an important role in the subsequent involvement with alcohol and marijuana use rather than the other way around (West & Michell, 1999).

Smoking, then, has very dangerous implications in terms of "graduating" to the use of other drugs. Further, most teenagers are aware that smoking has other devastating consequences such as cancer. But, for most adolescents, the repercussions of smoking are a long way off—something that happens when you are "old." Adolescents are not interested in this distant future. An effective way of addressing smoking then may not be to discuss the grim facts of cancer and heart disease but, rather, to address issues closer to their hearts—namely, their looks and popularity. Smoking causes bad breath, yellow teeth, gum disease, hacking coughs, and stained fingers. Further, recent surveys show that many teenagers do not want to date, much less kiss, someone who smokes (West & Michell, 1999).

There is now indication that the use of crack cocaine has increased dramatically among high school populations. Crack is easily manufactured by cooking down ordinary powdered cocaine with bicarbonate of soda. Small pieces of the resulting solid are then smoked, usually in a special pipe known as a waterpipe. The euphoric effect occurs within approximately 5 to 10 seconds and is far more intense than that associated with inhaling ordinary cocaine. Cocaine stimulates the central nervous system. Its immediate effects include dilated pupils and elevated blood pressure, heart rate, respiratory rate, and body temperature. The euphoric state seems to come primarily from the effect cocaine has on the dopamine system (the sites in the brain that seem to be involved in the experience of pleasure). The stimulation of the dopamine neurons causes the high associated with cocaine use. Cocaine is extremely addictive; its use can cause death by disrupting the brain's control of the heart and respiration.

Prevalence Rates and Overall Drug Use

From the small, solid world of middle childhood, adolescents enter a world of confusions and uncertainties—a world that begs for experimentation. Teens experiment in areas of sexuality, general disobedience, drug use, and other opportunities seen as "temptations." The consequences of experimenting with drugs, many experts note, is drug abuse. Are teenagers using alcohol and drugs to excess? Is it a serious social problem that is out of hand?

Alcohol, nicotine (tobacco), marijuana, and cocaine are the drugs most frequently used by young people. The statistics on regular drug use by adolescents are alcohol, 37.2 percent; smoking, 35 percent; marijuana, 16.7 percent, and cocaine, 6.5 percent; sedatives and other drugs

stimulants
Drugs that stimulate activity, suppress the appetite, and ameliorate emotional depression: examples include caffeine, nicotine, methadrine, and cocaine; also known as uppers.

FIRSTPERSON

Making Money the Wrong Way

There was a group of five of us; we had been friends for a long time. In our junior year in high school we were very popular with females, mainly because of playing basketball. Anyway, it was senior year now and one of my friends didn't make the basketball team. So, during the basketball season I didn't see much of him. Eventually, basketball season was over and now it was his time to "shine." One day after school I saw him and he was driving a very expensive new car and was wearing very fine clothes. Attention from the kids at school was focused back to him. Now we all spent more time together. Now this is where I stood. Two of my other friends received scholarships (I did not) and were going to college in the fall, and two of my friends were drug dealers.

That summer I had a job but didn't make very much. My mother and sister plus me were going to pay for college, but I felt bad about my Mom and sister laying out cash for me. I began to sell drugs. At first I made about $700 a week, which soon turned into making $2000 a week. I kept telling myself, I am selling drugs so that I can pay for my college tuition and that helped to ease my conscience. I kept telling myself this is a good cause. So it was easier to sell drugs. I didn't stand on street corners, no run-ins with the police, and no one really knew what I was doing. I was now making $3000 a week and kept saying it was for school but I was getting scared. When I was around other drug dealers, I felt I wasn't doing anything wrong. When I was around my friends who didn't sell drugs, I didn't want to sell drugs anymore. Then I got caught. Because my record is clean, I am serving time in a work-release program and paying fines. I am so motivated right now that I have a second chance. I want to finish college and make something of myself and feel good about myself again.

—*Vincent*

with cocaine use are the fastest-growing drug problem in the United States (McCaul, 1998). Not only do teenagers get involved in taking the drug, but (as "Vincent" explains in the First Person insert) some get involved in selling the drug as well. Most alarming is the recent availability of cocaine in a cheap but potent form called crack or rock. Crack is a purified form of cocaine that is smoked.

African American youths report lower rates of usage than white youths of cigarettes, alcohol, cocaine, and amphetamines; marijuana use is not statistically different for the two groups (O'Malley, Johnston, & Bachman, 1999). African American females report the lowest rates of illicit drug use among European American and Latino American youths (Reardon, Brennan, & Buka, 2001). Use of alcohol is virtually identical in African American and European American males.

Progression of Drug Use

Table 14.9 shows the progression of drug abuse. The first stage produces pleasurable feelings. In the second "seeking" stage, negative feelings occur as a result of the adolescent's problems. As teenage users go through the drug use progression, the bad feelings grow. They use more drugs, they have more problems, they feel worse, and therefore, the drug use becomes increasingly urgent to cope with those bad feelings. Most adolescent users should stop, considering the painful feelings they encounter in stage 3. But, they don't. And, they continue to use drugs to help them feel good enough to go through life (Newton, 1995).

Why Do Teenagers Use Drugs?

Early adolescence has been noted to be a period in which experimentation with various substances, such as tobacco and alcohol, occurs (Bettes, Dusenbury, Kerner,

TABLE 14.9

Progression of Drug Abuse

Stage	Drugs	When	Behavior	Feelings
1. Learning	Alcohol, pot	Occasional	None	Pleasure
2. Seeking	Pot/alcohol, hash, pills	Regular weekends, weeknights	Mood swings	Pleasure/minor pain
3. Preoccupied	Pot/alcohol; hash, pills, LSD, cocaine	Regular weekdays	Openly a drug user	Euphoria/pain
4. Using to function	Shooting up, crack	Everyday	Burnout; suicidal	Pain

From *Adolescence: Guiding Youth Through the Perilous Journey,* by M. Newton, 1995, Newbury Park, CA: Sage. Used by permission.

James-Ortiz, & Botvin, 1990). Consequently, a great deal of research has been conducted examining factors that influence substance-use initiation in this age group. Two general classes of variables have been identified as critical in substance-use initiation in early adolescence: social factors, such as peer and parental influence, and personality factors. Most use of drugs occurs as a result of social influences, whereas abuse of drugs is more strongly tied to internal psychological processes such as too much stress and anxiety (Winters, Latimer, & Stinchfield, 1999). When stress gets to be too great, drugs for many adolescents and young adults become the answer. (See the Self-Insight section to determine how you cope with stress.)

Treatment

There is no definitive treatment for either substance misuse or chemical dependency, yet there are multiple treatment philosophies and procedures. Finding the most appropriate treatment for a specific child or adolescent is a difficult task. The publication *Adolescent Drug Abuse: Analysis of Treatment Research* (Rahdert & Grabowski, 1988) suggests that dividing substance-abusing patients into homogeneous subgroups with common treatment problems allows better and more cost-efficient treatment. The publication identifies four general types of care: outpatient, inpatient, aftercare, and residential therapeutic communities.

General Types of Care

Most young substance abusers are treated as outpatients. **Outpatient treatment** is a generic mixture of resources available in a particular community, such as hotlines, drug and alcohol counseling and information centers, specialized staff in emergency rooms, halfway houses, self-help groups, and community mental health centers. **Inpatient treatment** involves a structured, time-limited stay in a treatment center. Treatment stresses an ongoing commitment to an Alcoholic Anonymous–like 12-step recovery program with considerable emphasis on educating the youth and the family about chemical dependency and the goal of exploring and developing alternatives to chemical use. **Aftercare** is follow-up intensive, partial-day programs, weekly meetings, or both.

The need for aftercare is critical because the adolescent faces the greatest temptations in maintaining abstinence once returned to the home environment (Bailey, 1998). Residential treatment is generally indicated for substance-abusing youths with additional psychiatric behavior (generally antisocial or family problems) and for those who have been unsuccessful following an inpatient stay.

Family Therapy

According to a growing body of research, family therapy appears to be a viable treatment alternative for families that have substance-abusing adolescents (Lewis, Piercy, Sprenkle, & Trepper, 1990). In contrast, if adolescents are treated individually (without their families) and their family systems have not changed, the adolescents may return home to play out the same roles that earlier fostered their addictive behaviors. Furthermore, family system approaches view an adolescent's addiction as possibly serving a functional role in the psychosocial dynamics of the family. For example, an adolescent may use drugs to gain his or her parents' attention and to get them to stop fighting. Robert Lewis and his colleagues (Lewis et al., 1990) found that in treating drug-abusing teenagers family-focused drug interventions are significantly more effective than individual therapy in decreasing drug dependence.

APPLICATIONS:

Should Adults "Buzz Off" or "Butt In"?

I would never have taken acid if it wasn't offered or if the kid hadn't said, "It's such a good time." If the kid had said, "We don't know what's in this and it might be dangerous, it could mess up your mind," I don't think I would have taken it. When I took the Quaaludes, everyone else was taking them, so I did it too. It was the same thing with cigarettes, I started because everybody else was smoking them. It wasn't just one or two people using drugs. It was everybody I know. I'd go to a party and the whole place would be an ashtray and everyone was doing drugs. (Norman & Harris, 1981)

Potent Peers

Peers have a dominant influence on adolescents' subsequent use of drugs. Several studies have suggested that peer influence on substance use is four times more potent than parental influence (McCord, 1990). But, there are some important caveats to add. Teenagers are not willing to self-destruct as are lemmings. The

outpatient treatment
A generic mixture of resources available in a particular community, such as hotlines, drug and alcohol counseling and information centers, specialized staff in emergency rooms, halfway houses, self-help groups, and community mental health centers.

inpatient treatment
A structured, time-limited stay in a treatment center.

aftercare
Follow-up intensive, partial-day programs, weekly meetings, or both.

Self-Insight

Coping with Stress

Identify the most important problem you were faced with last year. Then, using the scale below, indicate how often you used each of the following strategies to deal with it.

Not at all	A little	Occasionally	Fairly often
0	1	2	3

____ 1. Took things a day at a time.
____ 2. Got away from things for a while.
____ 3. Tried to find out more about the situation.
____ 4. Tried to reduce tension by drinking more.
____ 5. Talked with a professional person (e.g., doctor, lawyer, clergy).
____ 6. Made a promise to myself that things would be different next time.
____ 7. Prepared for the worst.
____ 8. Let my feelings out somehow.
____ 9. Took it out on other people when I felt angry or depressed.
____ 10. Prayed for guidance and/or strength.
____ 11. Accepted it; nothing could be done.
____ 12. Talked with spouse or another relative about the problem.
____ 13. Talked with a friend about the problem.
____ 14. Tried to reduce tension by taking more tranquilizing drugs.
____ 15. Told myself things that helped me feel better.
____ 16. Kept my feelings to myself.
____ 17. Bargained or compromised to get something positive from the situation.
____ 18. Tried to reduce tension by exercising more.
____ 19. Tried to reduce tension by smoking more.
____ 20. Tried to see the positive side of the situation.
____ 21. Considered several alternatives for handling the problem.
____ 22. Made a plan of action and followed it.
____ 23. Went over the situation in my mind to try to understand it.
____ 24. Tried to reduce tension by eating more.
____ 25. Got busy with other things to keep my mind off the problem.
____ 26. Drew on my past experiences.
____ 27. Avoided being with people in general.
____ 28. I knew what had to be done and tried harder to make things work.
____ 29. Tried to step back from the situation and be more objective.
____ 30. Refused to believe that it happened.
____ 31. Sought help from persons or groups with similar experiences.
____ 32. Tried not to act too hastily or follow my first hunch.

Holahan and Moos suggest that there are three types of strategies for coping with stress:

1. Active-cognitive effort: constructing thoughts to help with the problems
2. Active-behavioral effort: active efforts to change the situation
3. Avoidance: trying to keep the problem out of awareness

The score for each set of coping strategies is the sum of the scores for the items indicative of each of these strategies:
Active-cognitive: 1, 6, 7, 10, 11, 15, 20, 21, 23, 26, and 29
Active-behavioral: 2, 3, 5, 8, 12, 13, 17, 18, 22, 25, 28, 31, and 32
Avoidance: 4, 9, 14, 16, 19, 24, 27, and 30

The higher the score, the more often you use this as a coping strategy. Those who use active-cognitive and active-behavioral tend to be less anxious and less stressed. Those who use avoidance tend to be more anxious and may resort to more drug use as a form of escapism.

From "Personal and Contextual Determinants of Coping Strategies," by C. Holahan & R. Moos, 1987, in *Journal of Personality and Social Psychology, 52,* 946–955.

fact is that adolescents, like adults, tend to choose friends whose attitudes and values are similar to their own—friends who see them as they want to be seen. A young person who strongly opposes drugs does not befriend "druggies" nor does a young person who dislikes school and gets poor grades hang around with the top students in the class (Berndt, Hawkins, & Jiao, 1999). Peer pressure is not one-directional but, rather, circular. For example, the adolescent who is doing poorly in school tends to make friends with classmates in similar academic situations. Thus, they can reassure one another that school does not matter, or make fun of their achieving counterparts, or act out in class (if they attend). Their attitudes and behavior ensure that they will fail. The same mutual reinforcement occurs among other cliques in high school.

Vulnerability to Peer Pressure

Adolescents may differ in their vulnerability to succumb to peer pressure. When peers do play a prominent role in influencing drug use, is there anything adults can do? Based on her current research, Karen Bogenschneider and her colleagues (Bogenschneider, Wu, Raffaelli, & Tsay, 1998) point out that parents play a critical role in their teenagers' lives and are influential in helping them abstain from drug use. Whereas some researchers in the field believe that adults and peers operate primarily in isolation from each other and that adults are not highly influential in preventing drug abuse (Cooper & Cooper, 1992), others suggest differently (Bogenschneider et al., 1998).

Parental Closeness

Parental closeness, for example, has been shown to discourage drug use (Kandel & Andrews, 1987). Adolescents who have warm, affectionate relationships with their parents are less likely to agree to something they do not want to do than are adolescents whose relationships with their parents are cool and distant. One reason is that teenagers who have a good relationship with their parents also tend to be higher in self-esteem and assertiveness and have a strong sense of identity. All these factors enable adolescents to withstand the pressures of peers and to avoid situations that will jeopardize themselves for the momentary approval of a transient peer group. Peer pressure is powerful but more so when relations between the parent and the child are poor.

Ethnicity and Culture

Some research has suggested that friends' substance use may be less influential for African American than for European American adolescents (Urberg, Degirmencioclu, & Pilgrim, 1997). The lack of friend influence on adolescent substance use with African Americans suggests that prevention programs should be culturally geared toward intended participants. Programs that have been successful with European Americans with their emphasis on resisting peer pressure will not necessarily be effective with African Americans.

The strong link between parental closeness and authoritative parenting and substance use suggests that programs focused on changing parenting styles may be beneficial. Again, we find cross-cultural variations. Whereas authoritative parenting is associated with less substance use in European American and African American adolescents, this does not appear to be the case for Chinese Americans (Pilgrim, Luo, Urberg, & Fang, 1999). Parents of Chinese heritage exert a great deal of control over their adolescent offspring and authoritarian parenting deters drug use for Chinese American adolescents (Pilgrim, 1998).

"Butting In"

Other studies reveal that parents who fail to grant increasing decision-making opportunities or to relax power have adolescents who become extremely peer-oriented at the expense of heeding parental rules (Fuligni & Eccles, 1993). If rules are too extreme, they may backfire and encourage the behavior they intend to discourage. On the other extreme, permissive parental attitudes and values about adolescent alcohol use are a strong predictor of adolescent substance use (Duncan, Duncan, & Hops, 1998). Results suggest that a more mutual and interactive parent–adolescent relationship works best.

"Butting in," then, when it comes to peer relationships, means that adults should:

- be responsive and available to adolescents.
- spend time with their adolescents.
- be responsive to adolescents in ways such as being available when needed.
- engage in give-and-take discussions.
- monitor the adolescent's whereabouts.

All these factors are directly related to lowering the adolescent's chance of substance use as well as being indirectly related to the adolescent's choice of non-drug-using friends (Bogenschneider et al., 1998).

Concept Checks

1. The key variable in youth violence is _______________.
2. These drugs create altered perceptions and are commonly known as mind distorters:
   a. Depressants
   b. Amphetamines
   c. Hallucinogens
3. ***True or False:*** Most teenagers use drugs because of social influences.
4. A structured, time-limited stay in a treatment center is known as _______________.
5. ***True or False:*** The best advice for adults is to "bug off" and not try to influence an adolescent's choice of friends even if they are setting the wrong example.

Reviewing Key Points

Physical Transformations

- Puberty signals the onset of adolescence, a time of sexual maturity and physical growth. Gonadotrophic hormones stimulate the gonads (ovaries in females, testes in males). When the testes in males are stimulated, they secrete the hormone testosterone, which causes the growth of testes, the penis, and pubic hair, as well as the growth spurt and voice changes. Estrogen, the female hormone, causes breast development, growth of pubic hair, widening of hips, the growth spurt, and menarche.
- Although the progression of events leading to sexual maturity in males and females is similar for all adolescents, there is a tremendous variation in the age at which it starts. Puberty also signals the beginning of the growth spurt, for girls, around ages 10 to 12 and for boys, around age 13.
- Adolescents often idealize the body and decide theirs does not measure up. The ideal male physique is one that is tall and muscular. To get bigger muscles, boys may use anabolic steroids composed mainly of testosterone. To gain their ideal physique, girls may diet. Almost all teenagers have poor eating habits. To get teenagers to engage in nutritious eating patterns, they must see a connection between a good diet and some positive personal gains (better skin, more energy) before they will make alterations. The ideal body to some females is to be tall and thin. In their desire to become thin, some girls develop anorexia or bulimia nervosa—eating disorders with potentially dire consequences.
- Adults can help the anorectic and bulimic teenager by demanding less decision making; not allowing them to buy or prepare food; developing a relationship independent of food or weight; not demanding weight gain; not demeaning the adolescent for having this disorder; and avoiding statements such as "Let me help you." "I can't take this behavior from you anymore."

Sexuality Issues

- Initially, teenagers tend to choose dating partners based on their physical attractiveness. Whereas weight does not appear to be a deciding factor in choosing desirable male dates, it does impact on the dateability of females. Physical attractiveness is influential in other ways: we tend to attribute more positive social attributes to attractive individuals and interact with them in more affirmative ways. Teachers and employers appear to be guilty of this as well.
- Among adolescents who date regularly, vast numbers are sexually active, which can present problems such as contracting sexually transmitted diseases such as AIDS. Teenagers are informed about how people can contract AIDS, but they are not altering their sexual behavior. Priority should be given to improving contraceptive use among sexually active teenagers.
- Unwanted pregnancies may also be an outcome of adolescents' increased sexuality. Teenage parents are at a higher risk for physiological problems during labor and delivery, and their infants are also at a higher risk for certain anomalies. Psychologically, teenage mothers are not prepared for raising a child and frequently are ill-informed about their infant's needs and developmental milestones.
- The best situation for teenage mothers is to have parents and family members who share the role of caring for the infant as opposed to letting the teen mother do it all herself or taking sole responsibility for the infant themselves. By sharing responsibilities, the teenage mother can grow in other roles in addition to her parenting one. Further, adolescent mothers and their children fare better when they receive social support in terms of emotional, physical, information, and appraisal support from the family, community, and concerned agencies.

Health-Related Issues

- Although youth violence may not be as prevalent as the media leads us to believe, it is disconcerting that senseless crimes of kids killing kids exists at all. Several variables have been implicated in these crimes of homicide: guns, drugs, the breakdown of the family structure, a court system that is too lenient, gangs, and exposure to violence. One factor that appears to be a common thread woven throughout all these variables is poverty.

- Drugs are classified according to the type of effect they have on the human body. Four major drug types have been distinguished: depressants (alcohol); hallucinogens (marijuana, LSD); opiates (heroin, morphine); and stimulants (caffeine, nicotine, cocaine).
- Perhaps because of availability, peer pressure, and a desire to lose or maintain current weight, smoking among European American adolescents is increasing. Rather than discussing the grim consequences of smoking, an effective way to deter smoking might be to target areas that "hit home" such as factors affecting attractiveness and popularity.
- The number of adolescents drinking alcohol is increasing, and it is occurring at earlier ages. Over 5 percent of young children between grades 7 and 12 report getting drunk at least once a week. Like alcohol, marijuana use among the young is increasing as well. Marijuana is capable of effecting hallucinatory states within the user. The use of crack cocaine has also dramatically increased among high school populations.
- The profile of the adolescent at risk for substance abuse includes low self-esteem, psychological distress, poor family relationships, and a tendency to take risks. Although there are not definitive treatments for either substance misuse or chemical dependency, there are multiple offerings: inpatient treatment, outpatient treatment, halfway houses, and community mental health centers. Helping children with drug abuse problems involves outpatient, inpatient, aftercare, and residential therapeutic communities. A growing body of research indicates that family therapy is a viable treatment alternative for families that have a substance-abusing adolescent.
- Peers play an important role in influencing drug behavior, but so do parents. When relationships are close between parent and adolescent, young teens are less influenced by peers who go against parental standards and ideals.

Answers to Concept Checks

Physical Transformations

1. testosterone; estrogen
2. genetic; improved health care and overall living conditions; control of infectious diseases; better nutrition
3. Laurence, an early-maturing male
4. false
5. anorexia nervosa
6. see Table 14.4

Sexuality Issues

1. social traits 2. b 3. true 4. c
5. educational and economic 6. b

Health-Related Issues

1. poverty 2. c
3. true. Most use of drugs occurs as a result of social influences, whereas abuse of drugs is more strongly tied to internal psychological processes such as too much stress and anxiety
4. inpatient treatment
5. false

Key Terms

adolescence
aftercare
anabolic steroids
anorexia nervosa
bulimia nervosa
depressants
drug
drug abuse
estrogen
gonadotrophic hormones
gonads
gonorrhea
growth hormone
growth spurt
hallucinogens
hormones
human immunodeficiency virus (HIV)
inpatient treatment
masturbation
menarche
outpatient treatment
petting
puberty
role-sharing families
secondary sex characteristics
secular trend
semen
sexually transmitted diseases (STDs)
spermarche
stimulants
syphilis
testosterone

InfoTrac College Edition

For additional readings, explore InfoTrac College Edition, your online library. Go to **http://www.infotrac-college.com/wadsworth** and use the passcode that came on the card with your book. Try these search terms: eating disorders, adolescent sexuality, adolescence, drug abuse.

Child Development CD-ROM

Go to the Wadsworth Child Development CD-ROM for further study of the concepts in this chapter. The CD-ROM also includes quizzes and additional activities to expand your learning experience.

CHAPTER FIFTEEN

Cognitive Development: *Adolescence*

CHAPTER OUTLINE

The Adolescent's Thinking Skills
- Piaget's Formal Operational Thinker
- The Adolescent's Information-Processing Skills
- A Psychometric Look at Intelligence
- Applications: Possible Solutions to Underachievement

Possible Outcomes of the Adolescent's New Thinking Skills
- Imaginary Audience
- Personal Fable
- Idealism
- Argumentativeness
- Applications: Managing Argumentativeness

Adolescents and School
- Curriculum: Rigor or Relevance?
- Occupational Role Development
- Adolescent Employment
- Dropping Out of School
- Applications: Helping Potential High School Dropouts

Language Development
- Refined Understandings of Language
- Communication Patterns
- Typical Ways of Responding
- Applications: Communicating with Adolescents

Reviewing Key Points

Twenty Questions

8-year-old Danisha:

Is it a cat?

Is it George Washington?

Is it green?

Is it my friend Kareem?

13-year-old Natasha:

Is it alive?

Is it male?

Did he live within the last 100 years?

Equally dramatic as the physical changes discussed in Chapter 14 are the cognitive changes that take place in adolescence. Young people not only begin to look more like adults, they begin to think like adults. In the Twenty Questions game, concrete thinkers like Danisha are more likely to guess in very limited ways without using any system or plan. Adolescents, however, ask categorical, systematic questions that progressively limit the possibilities and allow them to strategically gain information from negative answers.

The adolescent's use of this sort of thinking is not limited to games; we see it in the types of arguments they employ with their peers and adults and the types of problem-solving abilities they display in school. As such, adolescent's thinking is not limited to the immediate environment; they now have the mental abilities to grasp abstract concepts, hypothetical situations, possibilities, and formal logic. As you shall see, our understanding of the way thinking develops during adolescence continues to be shaped in the context of Piagetian and information-processing theories. Our opening section in this chapter also explores cognitive development from a psychometric—testing and quantifying intelligence—perspective.

But, cognitive development during adolescence involves so much more than just learning about their logical, abstract reasoning abilities and the psychometric domain of test-taking. Adolescents' new mental equipment allows them to think in more expansive, idealistic ways—what Erikson called idealism. They become infinitely expansive thinkers—visionaries, idealists, and even harsh social critics—particularly over environmental issues, animal rights, and adults over the age of 30. As teenagers flex their new intellectual muscles with a passion, they may become argumentative.

Schools for adolescents, including junior high and senior high schools, function primarily to socialize young people to meet the expectations of the dominant culture and to select and train individuals for productive adult roles in our society. As our society continues to become more complex, the tasks of meeting students' expanding academic needs—most notably in the area of technology, and nonacademic skills, such as learning to effectively manage their own affairs and preparing for future life plans—have shifted to the schools. Can schools meet these varied responsibilities? Our third section analyzes adolescents and school, with particular emphasis on students' curriculum needs, occupational training, employment, and dropping out of school.

Finally, we look at language development in adolescence. More specifically, we will examine the most important aspect of language development—communicating effectively with others.

Mother: How was your day?
Son: Okay.
Mother: Learn anything new at school today?
Son: Nope.
Mother: Are you going out tonight?
Son: Yep.
Mother: Where are you going?
Son: John's.
Mother: When will you be back?
Son: Later.

"It's nice to know," reflects this mother of a teenage son, "that my son and I are still able to communicate."

formal operational thinking
Thinking that is more hypothetical, future oriented; adolescents can think abstractly.

The Adolescent's Thinking Skills

Before Beginning ...

After reading this section, you will be able to

- list the cognitive accomplishments of the formal operational thinker.
- explain the information-processing skills of adolescents.
- identify gifted children, overachievers, and underachievers.
- understand how underachievers can be helped.

Adolescence is a time of transitions, and thinking patterns during this period involve great changes as well. Thinking during adolescence is marked by movement from the realm of reality to the realm of possibility. Continuing brain development, increasing brain weight, and refinement of the synaptic connections in the corpus callosum (which connects and coordinates the two hemispheres of the brain) make many of the adolescent's newly acquired cognitive skills possible. In addition, myelination (coating of the axons with myelin) continues, with particular concentration of the brain cells in the prefrontal cortex and related temporal and parietal areas. These systems are involved with executive functions of the brain: language, planning, verbal fluency, and attention.

Further, there appear to be three peaks of brain maturation during adolescence: one at age 12, one at 15, and one at 18½ (Diamond & Hopson, 1998). These coincide with the development of what Piaget called formal operational thinking processes, or logical reasoning. As the brain changes in its capability, the individual begins to formulate ideas and theories involving numbering, ordering, causality, abstract reasoning, and spatial awareness. All of these propel the adolescent from the concrete thinker's black-and-white world of facts to the adolescent's world of more muted shades of gray, in the abstract world of ideas.

Piaget's Formal Operational Thinker

Just as development from preoperational to concrete operational thinking is marked by movement from fantasy to reality, development from concrete operational thinking to **formal operational thinking** is marked by movement from reality to possibility.

Thinking is more hypothetical, multidimensional, and future oriented. Formal operational thinkers are no longer exclusively preoccupied with systematizing and organizing what comes to their senses. At the formal level, concrete props and points of reference are no longer needed. The adolescent can imagine all that might be, from the very obvious to the very subtle. This rebalancing and qualitatively different way of thinking unhinges the concrete world—the actual becomes one instance of the infinite array of the possible.

Contrasts Between Middle Childhood and Adolescent Cognition

Formal operational thinking differs from concrete operational thinking in several important ways: formal thinkers engage in prepositional thought, use relativistic thinking, emphasize the possible versus the real, use combinatorial analysis skills, and employ scientific reasoning in approaching conceptual problems.

Propositional Thinking

> An experimenter and a subject face one another across a table strewn with poker chips of various solid colors. The experimenter explains that he is going to say things about the chips and that the subject is to indicate whether the experimenter's statements are true, false, or uncertain ("can't tell"). He then conceals a chip in his hand and says, "*Either* the chip in my hand is green *or* it is not green," or alternatively, "The chip in my hand is green *and* it is not green." On other trials, he holds up either a green chip or a red chip so that the subject can see it and then makes exactly the same statements. (Osherson & Markman, 1975)

Children in middle childhood are very likely to try to assess the true value of these two assertions solely on the basis of visual evidence. They focus on the concrete, empirical evidence concerning poker chips *themselves* rather than on the nonempirical, purely logical properties of the experimenter's *statements* about the poker chips. Consequently, they say they "can't tell" on the trials in which the chip is hidden from view. When it is visible, both statements are judged to be true if the chip is green and false if it is red. If the color (green) mentioned in the statement matches the color of the visible chip, the statement is said to be true; if there is a mismatch, it is judged false; and if the chip cannot be seen, its truth status is uncertain.

Whereas concrete thinkers can only evaluate the logic of statements by cross-referencing them against actual evidence, adolescents, using propositional thinking, can evaluate the logic of statements without referring to concrete evidence in the real world. They understand that "either-or" statements are always true and "and" statements are false (regardless of the poker chip's color). Thus, they appear to have a better intuition than the younger subjects do of the distinction between abstract, purely logical relations and empirical relations. These new cognitive capabilities hint at some of the other important changes in the nature and quality of thought during the adolescent years.

Relativistic Thinking To the concrete thinker, absolute right answers exist for everything and are known by an authority. The formal thinker recognizes the subjective construction of knowledge and the possibility of differences in the interpretation of the same facts. Thus, thought is relative. This change is fueled by the developing ability to take the perspective of another, not only in terms of seeing what the other sees but also in thinking about what the other thinks about. Initially, differences of perspective or dualistic thinking is attributed to prejudice, bias, distortion of the real facts, or the individual's subjective interests. In the case of two discrepant interpretations, one must be wrong.

Gradually, the relativistic thinker begins to see that reasonable, valid differences in the interpretation of facts exist and that these stem from different points of view, values systems, or interpretations. As children get older, they come to believe that there is not always a single, ascertainable truth in any given case, and that knowledge may be inherently subjective and relative. The costs associated with relativistic thinking may lie in promoting wholesale uncertainties that begin to call into radical question the prospect of any kind of trustworthy knowledge. This shift from realism to relativism is the business of adolescents rather than school-age children. This is not to suggest that concrete thinkers are unaware of the relativity of what knowledge different people hold. However, what is novel to the adolescent period is the potentially more disruptive recognition of the relativity of what knowledge is held to be.

Real Versus Possible Piaget argued that adolescents tend to differ from children in the way they conceive of the relation between the real and the possible. Elementary school children's characteristic approach to many conceptual problems is to burrow right into the problem data as quickly as possible. Subsequently, their problem-solving techniques are characterized as earthbound, concrete, and practical-minded. The child generally begins with reality and moves reluctantly, if at all, to possibility. Adolescents are more likely to begin with possibility and only subsequently proceed to reality. They may examine the problem situation carefully to try to determine all the possible solutions or states of affairs and then systematically try to discover which of these is, in fact, the real one in the present case. Beginning with the possible and proceeding to "reality" enables the adolescent to engage in what Piaget termed combinatorial analysis reasoning and hypothetico-deductive—hallmarks of formal operational thinking.

Combinatorial Analysis

The ability to separate the effects of several variables in an experimental situation through the method of holding all the factors constant except one is presented by Piaget as another clear sign of the presence of the formal operational system. The formal operational thinker subjects all the variables to **combinatorial analysis**, a method that ensures that all possible combinations of all possible values of all possible variables inherent in a problem will be exhaustively inventoried. Formal operational thinkers hold all but one variable constant and test one variable at a time as compared with concrete operational thinkers who haphazardly test variables in a random order.

combinatorial analysis
Refers to being able to organize an array of all possible combinations inherent in a problem.

hypothetico-deductive reasoning
Involves identifying all the various alternative hypotheses by moving from the specific to the general, followed by deducing a conclusion.

The capacity to think using combinatorial analysis is best illustrated by the problem of the colorless liquids. The subject is exposed to five colorless, odorless bottles of liquid. The bottles, labeled 1, 2, 3, 4, and *g*, contain diluted sulfuric acid, water, oxygenated water, thiosulfate, and potassium iodide. The subject does not know the chemical elements in the flasks. While the subject is watching, the contents of three of these containers are mixed, resulting in a yellowish liquid. Adding the contents of a fourth container returns the liquid to its original colorless state. The subject's problem is first to reproduce the yellow, using any combination of the bottles and then return the liquid to its colorless state.

The approaches of concrete operational children are characterized by two forms of behaviors: First, they systematically add *g* to all the liquids because this is what they saw the experimenter do. Second, they appear to attribute the color to only one of the elements. This reveals the difference between a noncombinatorial and a combinatorial structure of thought; the adolescent, or formal operational thinker, shows understanding that the color results from the *combinations* of elements. The final phase occurs when the adolescent establishes that the color is due to a combination of 1, 3, and *g*, and then experiments with 2 and 4 to verify which one will bleach out the color. This systematic structuring of formal thought provides the adolescent with the necessary tools for separating out the variables that might be causal by holding one factor constant to determine the causal action of another.

Hypothetico-Deductive Reasoning

Bärbel Inhelder and Jean Piaget (1958), in assessing scientific reasoning, used a series of tasks, one of which is the pendulum problem:

> I want you to look at this apparatus (see Figure 15.1). Each piece of string can be tied to the center of a stick. If I tie one of the weights to the other end of the string, the string swings freely back and forth. Sometimes the string swings more rapidly than at other times. Let me demonstrate this to you. I will attach string s_1 to the stick, with weight w_3 suspended from its other end. I will repeat the same procedure with string s_3 and weight w_1. Notice that the string swings more rapidly in the former case than in the latter. The experimenter then asks, "What exactly is it that makes the string swing more rapidly on some occasions than on others?"

Being able to start with the general or possible and move to the specific or reality is an important factor; it sets the stage for new thought capacities. In **hypothetico-deductive reasoning** formal thinkers are able to reason from the general to the specific; that is, when faced with a problem, they begin with a general hypothesis or theory of all possible factors that may affect the outcome and deduce a specific hypothesis about what might happen. Only then do they proceed to test it.

In the pendulum problem, for example, adolescents, like scientists, begin by formulating hypotheses about what specific factors might possibly influence the speed of the string's oscillations. They try to envision all the possible relations revealed in the data: length of string, weight of swinging object, height

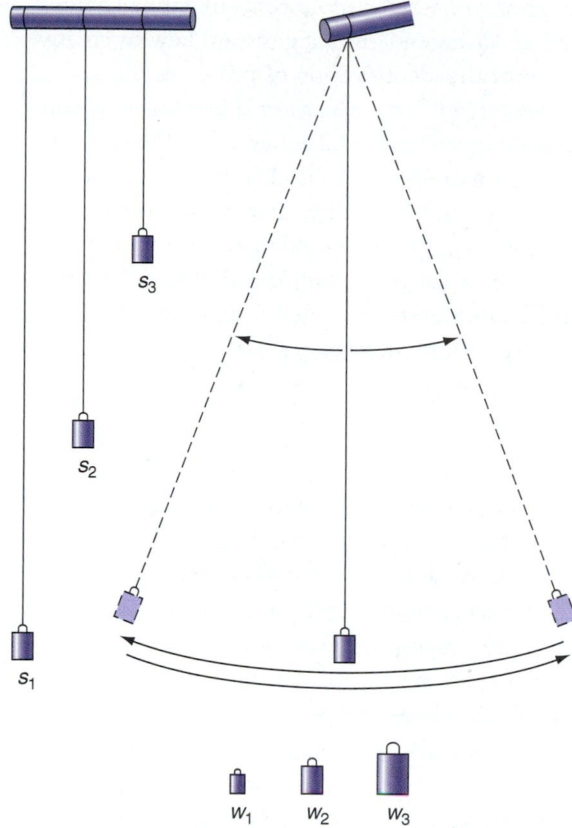

FIGURE 15.1 ***The Pendulum Problem***

The pendulum consists of three strings of different lengths ($s_1 < s_2 < s_3$) and three pieces of metal of different weights ($w_1 < w_2 < w_3$).

from which the weight is dropped, and the push given to the object. The fact that they can generate correct tests and recognize their necessity indicates that they have used formal reasoning. In their attempt to find out which of these relations holds true, they start with the variable that they believe will have the greatest potential for influencing oscillation. Then, they carefully test all the variables before finishing.

The capacity to reason in terms of verbally stated hypotheses and no longer merely in terms of concrete objects and their manipulation, to reason hypothetically and deduce the consequences that the hypotheses necessarily imply, is a formal operation reasoning process. If you think that you have just heard a description of scientific reasoning, you are absolutely right. It is called hypothetico-deductive reasoning because of its heavy trade in hypotheses and logical deductions from hypotheses, and it contrasts sharply with the much more nontheoretical and nonspeculative reasoning of concrete operational thinkers.

On a more pragmatic level, hypothetico-deductive reasoning enables the adolescent to engage in systematic planning for the future. Even the young child can "plan" to become a doctor, but it is only at the level of formal reasoning that this plan becomes a system of possibilities that extends into the future and is realized in an ordered pattern of actual events. The shift in focus from observing what is concretely present to contemplating possibilities, it is suggested, contributes to adolescents' increased focus on their own future and possible identities.

Further, hypothetico-deductive reasoning changes the nature of discussion: a fruitful and constructive discussion means that by using hypotheses the adolescent can adopt the point of view of the adversary (although not necessarily believing it) and draw the logical consequences it implies. In this way, the adolescent can judge its value after having verified the consequences. Individuals capable of hypothetico-deductive reasoning, by this very fact, will interest themselves in problems that go beyond their immediate field of experience—hence, their capacity to understand and even construct theories and to participate in society and the ideologies of adults. (As you shall see later in the chapter, this is often accompanied by a desire to change society.)

Newly developed cognitive skills allow adolescents to engage in systematic planning for their future.

Do We All Attain Formal Operational Thinking?

Cross-cultural studies demonstrate that cognitive development through concrete operations is universal (Durbin, Darling, Steinberg, & Brown, 1993). Formal operational thinking, however, appears to only be partially attained by most and fully attained only by some. Although many adolescents may have the capacity for formal operational thinking, whether they actually use it depends on their experience and their education—particularly, the extent of the math and science courses they have taken (Smith, Cowie, & Blades, 1998).

There is considerable evidence that not all adults use formal operational thinking. Only 40 to 60 percent of adults from Western cultures are successful at formal tasks, and it is an even lower percentage for underdeveloped countries (Durbin et al., 1993). Thus, cross-cultural research has not demonstrated the universal development of formal thinking. However, according to the cross-cultural perspective, the Piagetian procedures for assessing formal operational thinking across all cultures may be inappropriate. In Piaget's seminal work, a series of classic physics-type problems were used to assess formal reasoning: balance scales, pendulums, projections of shadows, falling bodies, and so on. The intellectual attributes assessed by these tests are designed for discovering the ideal scientist—one that has the ability to engage in purely abstract thought, to reason both inductively and deductively, to consider all possible outcomes, and to recognize and admit when the evidence is insufficient to reach any conclusion.

Researchers more sensitive to a cultural-context approach need to identify and analyze when formal operational thinking is required and, thus, how it is likely to be manifested. Systematic thinking dealing with specialized modes of thinking such as mathematics and science is only likely to appear in cultures where it is most demanded. As such, researchers can expect variability in this kind of thinking across different cultural contexts.

Problem-Finding Thinkers

Although not all adolescents attain formal operational thinking during early adolescence, there is evidence that some older adolescents may go beyond formal operations. This phase has been called *problem finding* in contrast to the problem solving that typically characterizes formal operations. Thus, the self-directed thinking of some older adolescents might be characterized as "divergent" (moving toward new or creative solutions or the identification of problems) rather than "convergent" (moving toward known or accepted solutions to problems) (Gallagher, 1997). This second phase of formal operations is identified by the quality of the questions asked rather than arrival at known conclusions. The problem-finding thinker is able to rethink or reorganize existing knowledge and then to ask important questions or define totally new problems (Klaczynski, Fauth, & Swanger, 1998).

Postformal Thinking

Piaget hypothesized that no new mental capabilities emerge after formal operational thought, and that intellectual development consists solely of an increase in depth of understanding. One critique of Piaget's theory is that it does not capture the cognitive development that may occur after the formal operational stage is reached. Might there be a period or stage beyond formal operations? Some scholars suggest that the formal operational stage is not the concluding stage of cognitive development (Mcbride, 1999). With this recognition, researchers turned to look for a model of development that might outline systematic and positive cognitive elaboration that occurred beyond formal operations.

Postformal theories build upon Piagetian theory with expectations that postformal stages evolve from formal operations. In post–formal operational thinking, the adult is expected to bring certain wisdom to the tasks of everyday life and look for a "best" answer, not necessarily the most logically correct answer. Older adults tend to look for "workable" answers, whereas younger adults often look for logical answers to a variety of posed everyday problems (Klaczynski et al., 1998). The content of thought, then, is free to vary and improve after the formal operational period, which helps to explain, in part, some of the classical differences between adolescent thought and adult thought.

The Adolescent's Information-Processing Skills

Piaget believed that stages are universal for all children and are determined primarily by internal maturational functions. In contrast, information-processing theorists, such as Robert Siegler, suggest that abstract reasoning is strongly influenced by children's particular environmental situations and often needs to be directly taught.

Robert Siegler

Unlike Piaget, Robert Siegler's (1997; Siegler & Chen, 1998) theory is not a stage theory; Siegler (2001) views the process of cognitive change as arising from the accumulation of specific knowledge and strategies. He believes that much of cognitive growth can be usefully characterized as the sequential acquisition of increasingly powerful rules for solving problems. He begins by predicting the different problem-solving rules that children of different developmental levels might use. These hypotheses about the developmental ordering or sequence of rules are based, in part at least, on prior research findings by Piaget.

Siegler's model of cognitive development portrays children as qualitative information processors and as *rule governed.* Typically, a rule refers to a mental procedure whose operation affects performance on many problems within a task domain. The concept of rule provides a tool for describing change and continuity in cognitive organization. Changes in performance are typically explained in terms of modifications, additions, or deletions of particular rules. Siegler formulated his precise description of the rules that children develop at different ages by using a balance beam and asking children how it operates.

Siegler used the balance beam problem—a Piagetian formal operational task—to assess children's understanding of rules. Children are shown a balance beam with four pegs at equal intervals on either side of the fulcrum, along with a stack of doughnut-shaped weights that can be slipped onto the pegs. The child's task is to predict how the beam will behave if the weights are arranged in various quantities and at various distances along the beam. Siegler proposed that children develop one of four possible strategies or rules based on the information of the number of weights and the distance of the weights from the fulcrum.

- *Rule 1:* Children, typically preschoolers, using this rule attend to only the number of weights on each side of the fulcrum. If they are the same, the children predict balance; otherwise, they predict that the side with the greater number of weights will go down.
- *Rule 2:* Some children first apply rule 1, but if the weights are equal, they predict that the side with the weights farther from the fulcrum is heavier. The side with the weights that are a greater distance from the fulcrum will go down. Children using rule 2 are more advanced in that they consider the distance of the weights from the fulcrum.
- *Rule 3:* Some children consider both weight and distance but do not fully understand the relationship between the two (for example, if one side has fewer weights but they are farther from the fulcrum, children become confused and guess what will happen).
- *Rule 4:* Some children attend to both weight and distance and understand the relationship between the two. This rule represents mature knowledge of the task because it includes torque calculation; children using it always make the correct prediction.

Siegler then constructed six types of problems that would differentiate children at the different levels of sophistication. Thus, it is possible to determine which, if any, of these rule models accurately characterizes children's knowledge about the balance scale by examining correct answers and errors on these six types of problems:

1. Balance problems: The same configuration of weights on pegs on each side of fulcrum
2. Weight problems: Unequal amounts of weight equidistant from the fulcrum
3. Distance problems: Equal amounts of weight at different distances from the fulcrum
4. Conflict-weight problems: One side with more weight, the other side with its weight farther from the fulcrum, and the side with more weight going down
5. Conflict-distance problems: One side with more weight, the other side with more distance, and the side with more distance going down
6. Conflict-balance problems: The usual conflict between weight and distance cues and the two sides balancing

Children who use different rules produce different response patterns on these problems. Those using rule 1 predict correctly on balance, weight, and conflict-weight problems but never predict correctly on the other three problem types. Children using rule 2 behave similarly except that they also solve distance problems. Those adopting rule 3 invariably are correct on all three types of nonconflict problems and perform at a chance level on the three types of conflict problems. Those using rule 4 solve all problems.

Siegler has been quite successful in his efforts to predict and find orderly developmental sequences of rule acquisitions in several problem areas, most notably in his work with the scale-balance problem involving the concept of torque. In addition, he, and other information-processing researchers have shown that older minds develop more efficient attention strategies and thus increasingly sophisticated information-processing systems. In a number of ways Siegler's theory has accounted for phenomena that were not adequately explained by Piaget. For instance, as noted in Chapter 12, the fact that children conceive of the conservation of substance, quantity, weight, and mass at different ages rather than simultaneously casts in question the existence of a single qualitatively distinct mode of concrete operational thinking covering the entire range of the elementary school years. Piaget's term *horizontal decalage* (the gradual mastery of concepts within a stage) describes but does not explain such inconsistencies. Siegler's notion, however, explains some of the inconsistencies—namely, that children may focus on separate factors (dimensions such as height, width, weight, mass), each of which may develop at a different time.

Changes in Information-Processing Skills

Cognitive development during adolescence also involves a change of orientation relative to time. First, adolescents exhibit an increased speed of information processing (Kail, 1996), which, combined with greater awareness and control of an increased knowledge base (Keating, 1990), produces a more efficient form of thinking than existed during childhood. Second, adolescent thought becomes more complex as teens begin to consider longer term implications and possibilities rather than the here-and-now focus that is more characteristic of concrete thinkers (Kail, 1996).

Third, an adolescent can process more information than a younger child. Being able to retain more information is related to two developments: structural capacity and functional capacity. Adolescents' cognitive ability, or *structural capacity*, is greater than that of school-age children. They can handle more information at any one time and thus are able to have more efficient short- and long-term memories. *Functional capacity* refers to making effective use of existing mental abilities, and adolescents do this more competently than school-age children by making judicious use of attentional and mnemonic aids. Like skilled athletes, skilled information-processing adolescents deploy their resources in efficient, "cost-effective" fashions.

metacognition Monitoring and evaluating one's current memory capabilities.

Metacognition

A group of preschool and junior high children were asked to study a small set of items until they were sure they could recall them all. The older children studied them for a while, judged that they were ready (and they usually were), and then went on to recall every single item correctly. The younger children studied them for a while, judged that they were ready (and they usually were not), and they failed to recall some of the items.

As noted in Chapter 9, **metacognition** (or metamemory) involves the child's ability to monitor and evaluate one's current memory capabilities, and it is one of the many developmental advances that continue to improve during adolescence. The adolescent's own awareness and consideration of his or her cognitive processes and strategies, or "cognition about cognition," plays an important role in many types of new adolescent cognitive activities, including oral persuasion and comprehension, reading comprehension, writing, perception, memory, and problem solving.

Metacognitive knowledge and beliefs are those accumulated through experience and stored in long-term memory; they concern the human mind and its doings. Some of this stored knowledge is more *declarative* ("knowing that") than *procedural* ("knowing how"). For example, declarative knowledge may be recognizing that you have a rather poor memory. Your procedural knowledge might consist of how and when to supplement that poor memory by the use of a "list of things to do" and other external memory aids. Further, adolescents sense when one area of study might need more attention than another to be recalled or understood and therefore allocate more time and attention to that material. It is for these reasons that adolescents display superior memory skills compared with concrete operational thinkers (Wo, Shen, & Lin, 1997).

Knowledge Base: Novices and Experts

Another factor that contributes to adolescents' improved memory is that they know more things than children in middle childhood. Thus, another important information-processing trend in adolescence is the acquisition of a great deal of knowledge and skill in many specific areas or domains. In the course of years of learning and experience teenagers gradually change from being novices to being experts (or near experts) in a wide variety of domains. In recent years, several investigators have postulated that, to a large extent, age differences in what children know, or their **knowledge base**, is responsible for corresponding differences in memory performance.

Basically, when children are very knowledgeable about a particular subject, they process information from that domain rapidly and display advanced levels of memory performance. Developmental changes in knowledge lead to developmental changes in what is stored and retrieved. For example, people who are very knowledgeable about chess can remember chessboard arrangements better than those who are less knowledgeable about chess (Keating, 1990).

It may not seem a very big deal that cognitive development consists largely of the accumulation of knowledge; for that matter, I cannot imagine my grandmother being exactly bowled over by the idea either. However, as Michelene Chi (1997) points out, this rather trite-sounding piece of wisdom deserves our serious attention. Information-processing theorists are trying to build up, through careful, detailed research, a precise picture of exactly what the acquisition of expertise in a domain does to and for our thinking. They are trying to discover everything that the acquisition of domain-specific knowledge does to the nature of our problem-solving and other information-processing activities in that domain. Much of the research in this area has examined cognitive differences between adult novices and experts in the domain of elementary physics, a richly structured area of knowledge. Chi, for example, has recently summarized some important differences between novices and experts in physics. She begins by making a rough distinction between novices and experts.

For the novice, mass may only be represented as related to the concepts of weight and density. In contrast, the expert's mental representation of mass may include acceleration, force, and other related concepts. This means that each of the expert's concepts is closely connected in long-term memory with many other concepts. As a consequence, there are multiple routes from each concept to every other concept in the expert's stored conceptual network; we might say that each concept is cross-referenced in the expert's mental dictionary of physics concepts. This greater density of interconnected links means that the probability is higher of any one concept evoking other, related concepts. Thinking of one concept is more likely, in the expert's case, to cue the retrieval from memory of related concepts and concept features.

What children know (memory in the wider sense) greatly influences what they learn and remember (memory in the strict sense).

A Psychometric Look at Intelligence

There is little doubt that you have taken some type of standardized test by this point in your academic career. So questions, such as the following, may look pretty familiar to many of you.

Canoe is to ocean liner as glider is to:
a. kite b. airplane c. balloon d. car

What is the following word when it is unscrambled?
HCPRAATEU

From middle school to medical school, children are given a myriad of assessment tests. Standardized

knowledge base
What children know; their background of information.

Thought CHALLENGE *Would the reaction be different if females were in the SAT driver's seat, and males watched as their college choices were dominated by high-scoring young women?*

test scores from high schools around the country are analyzed and thus provide a national picture of U.S. adolescents. Achievement and IQ tests are used to try to help measure children's abilities and identify their potential for success in given areas.

Achievement Tests

One achievement test is the Preliminary Scholastic Assessment Test, or PSAT. The PSAT is generally taken in October of students' junior year in high school, and the results of the test are used to select winners of the prestigious National Merit Scholarships. Further, many states and colleges also use PSAT scores to award scholarships of their own. The PSAT serves as an early indicator of the winners and losers in the great SAT contest soon to follow (the PSAT is similar to the SAT, with both math and verbal questions, but it is much shorter). The "losers" appear to be girls; boys score so much higher than girls on the PSAT that two out of three Merit semifinalists are male. The Educational Testing Service, creators of the PSAT, knows this and in an attempt to ameliorate the imbalance, gives twice the weight to verbal performance, traditionally an area of female strength. This effort still does not result in equal male and female performance (see Figure 15.2) (Cole, Martin, Peeke, Seroczynski, & Fier, 1999).

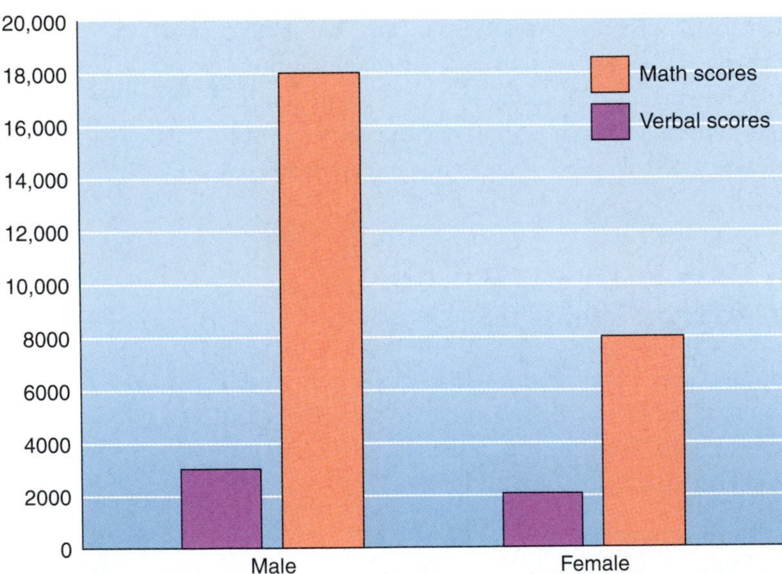

FIGURE 15.2 ***Number of Males and Females Scoring in the Top Categories on the PSAT***

Whereas 18,000 boys score in the highest PSAT categories, only 8000 girls do.

From *Failing at Fairness*, by M. Sadker & D. Sadker, 1994, New York: Charles Scribner's Sons. Reprinted by permission of Scribner, a Division of Simon & Schuster.

Students' high school records are gradually playing a less important role in college admissions decisions as high school transcripts and grade point averages become increasingly difficult to interpret and compare. College admissions officers rely more upon the results of college entrance examinations in comparing applicants, and a large number of colleges are using the Scholastic Assessment Test (SAT). On this critical exam, boys typically receive scores that are 50 to 60 points higher on the math section. The fact that boys also surpass girls on the verbal section is less well known. Actually, males' verbal SAT scores add another 8 to 12 points to their overall testing lead. This gender gap is so predictable that it has become an accepted feature of the educational landscape. Few people talk about the SAT gender gap; fewer still get angry or upset about it.

Each year one million students take the American College Test (ACT). This test is described not as an aptitude measure but as an assessment of academic achievement. It evaluates students in four areas: English, mathematics, the natural sciences, and reading. To create questions directly measuring what students learn in school, ACT test makers analyze textbooks and interview teachers. Because girls attain better grades in classwork, many expect that they will achieve similar success on the ACT. They do not.

Unlike the SAT and the ACT exams, which develop academic pictures of only the college-bound, the National Assessment offers information on a sample of all students during elementary, middle, and senior high school. It is through this and other national tests that we learn how well girls begin their school careers and what happens with each year's promotion to a new grade. Girls begin school outperforming boys on almost every measure.

Most of us are aware of their verbal advantage and their reading and writing skills. Fewer realize that in these early years girls also surpass boys on math and social studies tests; in fact, they surpass boys on every standardized test in every academic area except science, where boys hold a slight advantage (LeFore & Warren, 1997). Girls' test scores continue their downward slide through the rest of their education. Females are the only group in the United States to begin school testing ahead in elementary school and leave having fallen behind in high school. Why does this happen? Are our schools responsible for this decline in girls' academic performances? (See Child Development Issues for a discussion of this issue.)

IQ Tests

How smart are you? Mensa, an organization of intellectually superior adults, requires that its members have at least an IQ of 132 on the Stanford-Binet or a score of 130 on the Wechsler scales. (Self-Insight provides the How Smart Are You? Scale, which will let you know if you are Mensa material.) Who is smarter—males or females? Adolescents have some very definite opinions about who is smarter. In the United States and Great Britain, males tend to think males are smarter (British adolescents are more likely to give higher estimates of IQ differences between males and females). Adolescents from Singapore and Hawaii, however, see the sexes as more equal in IQ and estimate few sex differences (Furham, Fong, & Martin, 1999). Psychologists agree (Lynn, 1997).

In quantifying intelligence, based on the results of an IQ test, children are assigned a number, or IQ. A critical question, however, is, "What do scores on IQ tests predict? Clearly, the individual's intellectual level is related to his or her school success. A variety of investigations indicate that the correlation between intelligence and academic achievement, as measured by some external test, ranges from .50 to about .70, which is a strong correlation (Sternberg & Williams, 1998). This is hardly surprising because IQ tests have always been validated by school success. Questions that seemed to identify good students were considered good test questions, and those that did not were dropped.

Are IQ tests useful, however, for predicting anything else—for example, success in later life? Apparently not. Scores on IQ tests show remarkably little relation to performance in most adult roles. People with higher scores do a little better in most jobs than people with lower scores, and they earn somewhat more money, but the differences are surprisingly small (Neisser, Boodoo, Bouchard, Boykin, Brody, Ceci, Halpern, Loehlin, Perloff, Sternberg, & Urbina, 1998).

Thus, the usefulness of IQ tests may lie in giving us a fairly accurate picture of the scholastic potential of a child. They do not, however, measure the great number of abilities that might be included under intelligence. Because they are relatively good predictors of success in school, IQ tests may be a beneficial tool in identifying children who may have learning deficits and as such require special attention.

Most societies, however, do rank their children in terms of their "potential abilities," and IQ tests often serve this purpose. In the United States, children who receive an IQ score that places them in the top 3 to 5 percent are labeled "gifted." Yet, some teenagers may not achieve IQ scores in the top 3 to 5 percent on the bell curve but still achieve very high grades. These individuals are generally labeled *overachievers*.

Overachievers

Overachievers are a salient reminder that intelligence is not the only determinant of school achievement. Indeed, among some students, intelligence may be far less important than other factors, including motivation, interest, work habits, and personality characteristics. **Overachievers** are those whose academic performance (in English, science, mathematics, and social science)

© Jose Galvez/PhotoEdit

IQ tests do not measure a great number of abilities such as creativity, motivation, persistence, and adaptability.

overachievers Those whose academic performance (in English, science, mathematics, and social science) exceeds what would have been anticipated statistically on the basis of their IQs.

Child Development Issues

Are Girls Getting Shortchanged in School?

Consider these facts:

- In the early grades, girls are ahead of or equal to boys on almost every standardized measure of achievement and psychological well-being. By the time they graduate from high school, they have fallen behind.
- In high school, girls score lower on the SAT and ACT tests, which are critical for college admission. The greatest gender gap is in the crucial areas of science and math.
- The gap does not narrow in college. Women score lower on all sections of the Graduate Record Exam, which is necessary to enter many graduate programs.
- Women also trail on most tests needed to enter professional schools: the GMAT for business school, the LSAT for law school, and the MCAT for medical school.

Whereas girls score less than boys on standardized tests that measure achievement, they earn higher report card grades. Is there any favoritism in the way teachers evaluate and grade boys and girls? Here's what one 17-year-old senior reports:

> In my organic chemistry class, the girls are definitely graded easier than boys. Last week the teacher returned a lab report with low grades, and some girls were upset and practically in tears. He let them go back and redo it again, and they got the points back. I would never have been able to get those points back from my organic chemistry teacher. I think that teachers will bend and cater to the sensitivities of females.

Another senior, Ben, tells us a similar story:

> I was working on a problem in calculus and I asked the teacher for help. He said, "You can handle this. Figure it out yourself." Then a girl asked for help on the same problem. The teacher went over to her desk, took her pencil, set up the problem for her; started the computations, and let her do the last step. And I was still sitting there trying to figure it out. I was really burned. She got a better grade than I did.

exceeds what would have been anticipated statistically on the basis of their IQs. Overachievers demonstrate significantly better work habits, greater interest in schoolwork generally, more persistence in carrying out assignments, and they tend to be more grade-conscious. They also emerge as being more responsible, conscientious, and are more likely to plan than "normal" achievers.

Overachievers are characterized by:

1. Positive self-value (optimism, self-confidence, self-acceptance, high self-esteem)
2. Acceptance of authority (conformity to expectations of teachers and parents)
3. Positive interpersonal relations (interest in and responsiveness to the feelings of others)
4. Little independence–dependence conflict (freedom to make choices, initiate activities, and lead, although within a generally conforming context)
5. An academic orientation (orderly study habits, high motivation for academic achievement, interest in academic values and subject matter)
6. Realistic goal orientation (a drive to organize and plan their lives, basic seriousness of purpose, ability to delay short-term pleasures for longer term goals, efficiency and energy)
7. Better control over anxiety (direction of inner tensions into organized task-related activities) (Sharma, 1998)

Girls may receive higher grades than boys but if these situations exemplify most classroom grading procedures, the grades girls receive carry a very heavy price tag. Teacher favoritism or doing the work for a student obviously results in girls' learning less. Further, after taking the SAT, for example, girls may wonder if their excellent school grades were just given to them for hard work rather than real intelligence. Or perhaps their higher grades were only the teacher's "thank you" for their being quiet and cooperative in the classroom. Moreover, many girls reject the validity of grades and believe that test scores are the true measure of their intelligence.

Why are girls the only group to start school ahead and leave behind? Some experts believe that a critical factor is the negative effect that co-educational classrooms have on girls. In co-educational classes, for example, girls act more like spectators than educational players. They often defer to the males; wait until they are called on to give an answer; and are interrupted frequently by their male counterparts. We see a totally different picture in single-sex or all-female classrooms. Girls in single-sex schools have higher self-esteem, are more interested in nontraditional subjects such as science and math, are less likely to stereotype jobs and careers, are more intellectually curious, ask many questions, are serious about their studies, and achieve more (McEwen, Knipe, & Gallagher, 1997; Sadker & Sadker, 1994; Streitmatter, 1994).

At the turn of the 20th century, G. Stanley Hall (1904) extolled the single-sex school. His ideal girls' school was to be dedicated to girl's learning domestic skills, good manners, religion, and the arts. Hall's ideal school is not the ideal school at the turn of the 21st century. Schools for girls in this millennium have entirely different goals, such as the development of intellectual growth, academic curiosity, independence, and experimentation. Proponents of these types of single-sex schools see the by-products of their curriculum in their female graduates who display traits of self-confidence, leadership, assertiveness, self-efficacy, and more ambitious educational and occupational horizons (LeFore & Warren, 1997).

Search Online

Explore InfoTrac College Edition, your online library. Go to **http://www.infotrac-college.com/wadsworth** and use the passcode that came on the card with your book. Try these search terms: gender and school, girls school, boys school.

Underachievers

June asked her sixth-grade son, "Have you finished your math homework?" Michael answered, "Yes, I have." When June looked over his assignment, he had written "I don't know" after each problem.

Individuals whose performance falls below their measured IQ levels are called **underachievers**. A discrepancy between the adolescent's actual performance and his or her predicted performance (measured potential) always draws considerable attention. Underachievers are individuals who perform markedly below their capacities to learn. Although underachieving children have superior ability and have scored roughly in the top quarter on measured academic ability, their grades are significantly below their high measured aptitudes or potential for academic achievement. Approximately two boys are designated as underachievers for every girl, but this may be partly because boys generally get poorer grades than girls. Approximately 16 percent of students, at any age at which grades and ability measures are available, are labeled as underachievers. Both parents and teachers, however, tend to complain about underachievement with the beginning of adolescence and the beginning of more intensive homework assignments.

How do the different types of underachievers vary? What are their personal characteristics? What are the parental factors that impact underachievers? What do we know about the causes of underachievement?

underachievers Individuals whose performance falls below expected IQ levels.

Self-Insight

How Smart Are You?

The following twenty questions represent what you may encounter on an intelligence test, although we tried to make them a little more amusing than the average IQ-type question. Take the twenty questions and mark your answers carefully. Time yourself very carefully and work as quickly as you can.

Time Started: ________

1. The day before two days after the day before tomorrow is SATURDAY. What day is it today?
2. What comes next, most logically, in the following sequence?
   SAIBLCVDEERFAGNHNIIJVKELRMSNAOR
   a. PY b. BQ c. RR d. BR
3. What is one twentieth of one half of one tenth of 10,000?
4. What is the following scrambled word?
   NNREAIVARYS
5. In the following examples, each set of symbols stands for a word. Study all three words given and the symbol equivalent and translate the fourth line into a word.

6. Which of the sentences given below means approximately the same as: "beauty is only skin deep"?
   a. Some actresses are made up by the studios so that you cannot tell what they really look like.
   b. Don't judge a book by its cover.
   c. Some people have prettier appearances than others
   d. Good looks don't matter that much.
7. Which of the figures shown below the line of drawings best continues the sequence?

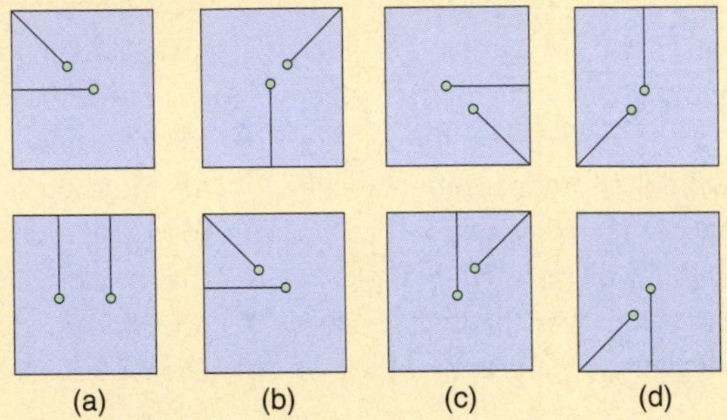

8. Canoe is to ocean liner as glider is to:
   a. kite b. airplane c. balloon d. car
9. Everyone at the Mensa party contest won prizes. Tom won more than Sally; Ann won less than Jane; Jane won less than Sally but more than Walter. Walter won fewer prizes than Ann. Who won the most prizes?
10. There is one five-letter word which can be inserted in each of the two blanks below. When you have put in the right word, you will have four new words, two on each line. (Example: Place WORK on the line between HAND ___ PLACE, giving HANDWORK and WORKPLACE.)
    BOAT ___ WORK
    DOG ___ HOLD
11. Tom, Jim, Peter, Susan, and Jane all took the Mensa test. Jane scored higher than Tom, Jim scored lower than Peter but higher than Susan, and Peter scored lower than Tom. All of them are eligible to join Mensa, but who had the highest score?
12. If it were two hours later, it would be half as long until midnight as it would be if it were an hour later. What time is it now?

13. Pear is to apple as potato is to:
    a. banana b. radish c. strawberry d. lettuce
14. Continue the following number series below with the group of numbers which best continues the series.
    11039587796??
    a. 11 5 b. 10 5 c. 10 4 d. 11 6
15. Which of the following is least like the others?
    a. poem b. novel c. painting d. statue
    e. flower
16. What is the following word when it is unscrambled?
    HCPRAATEU
17. What is the number that is one half of one quarter of one tenth of four hundred?
18. Which of the sentences given below means approximately the same as the proverb: "Don't count your chickens until they are hatched"?
    a. Some eggs have double yolks so you can't really count eggs and chickens.
    b. You can't walk around the henhouse to count the eggs because it will disturb the hens and they won't lay eggs.
    c. It is not really sensible to rely on something that has not yet happened and may not ever happen.
    d. Since eggs break so easily, you may not be accurate in your count of future chickens.
19. The *same* four-letter word can be placed on the blank lines below to make two new words from each of those shown. Put in the correct four-letter word to make four new words from those shown below.
    (Example: HAND could be placed between BACK ____ WORK to make BACKHAND AND HANDWORK.)
    HEAD ____ MARK
    DREAM ____ FALL
20. Which of the figures shown below the line of drawings best completes the series?

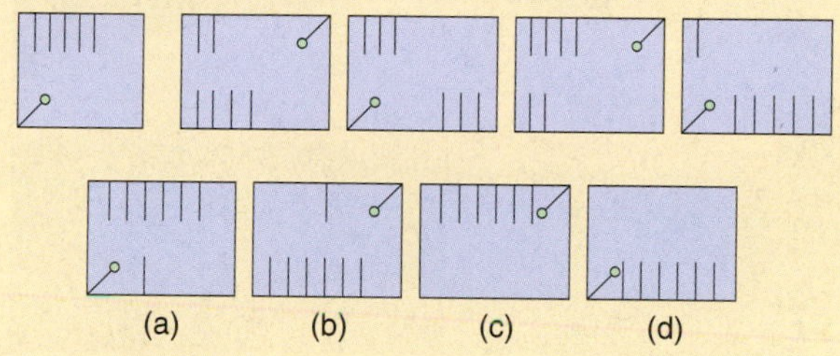

Time finished: ________

Mensa Key

1. Friday
2. a. P Y. The alternate letters starting with S spell "silver anniversary," and this sequences completes the phrase "silver anniversary."
3. 25
4. ANNIVERSARY
5. MENSA
6. b
7. b
8. b
9. Tom
10. HOUSE
11. Jane
12. 9 P.M.
13. b. Both grow in the ground.
14. a. Alternate numbers go up by 2 and down by 1, starting with 1 and 10.
15. The only one that is not an artistic work made by man is e.
16. PARACHUTE
17. 5
18. c
19. LAND
20. c. The number of lines goes down opposite the stick and up on the side with the stick and the stick alternates from lower left to top right.

Score one point for each correct answer. Add 5 points if you finished in less than 20 minutes, and 3 points if you finished in less than 30 minutes. Scores range from 0 to 25. On the basis of the scores of some Mensa members who took the test, Salny (1988) provides the following interpretation of scores:

25	You're an excellent Mensa candidate.
20–24	You can almost surely pass the Mensa supervised test.
14–19	A very good candidate for Mensa.
10–13	A fair candidate.
Below 10	Everyone has an off day!

From *The Mensa book of words, word games, puzzles, and oddities* (pp. 145–149), by Dr. Abbie F. Salny. Copyright © 1988 by Abbie F. Salny. Reprinted by permission.

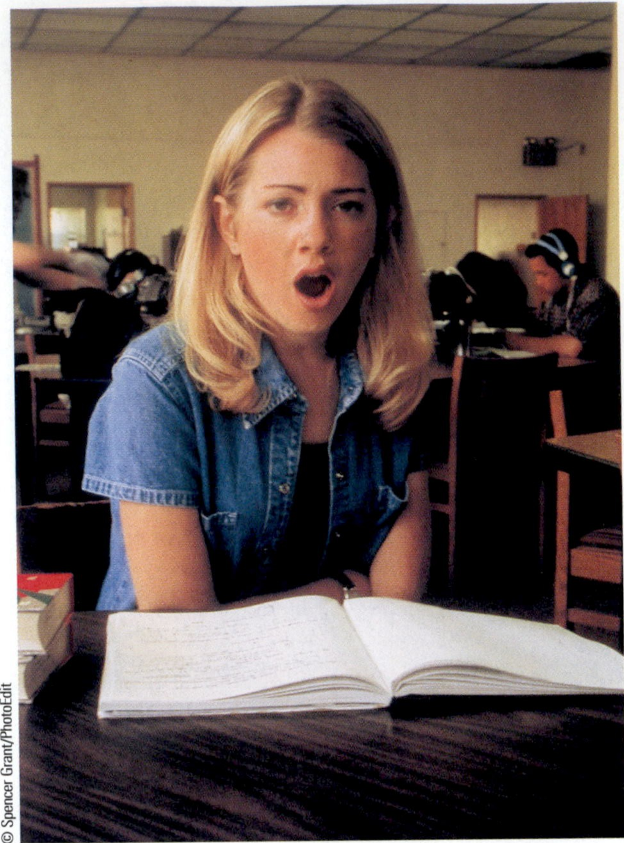

© Spencer Grant/PhotoEdit

Underachievers could do better in school, based on their standardized test performance, but do not or will not.

Types of Underachievers

> Twelve-year-old Melissa is often described as a lovely child. She has a winning personality, and it is hard for anyone to stay angry with her for long. All Melissa has to do is grin sheepishly and look out from her big, brown eyes, and everyone is instantly charmed. Test scores indicate that Melissa has an extremely high level of intelligence. She has a keen wit, good sense of humor, and likes to read poetry. You'd never guess that her report card is a mess. Melissa is an underachiever.

Some underachievers, like Melissa, are disinterested and bored and do not try or participate; these students have been labeled as *withdrawn underachievers.* They are not a problem because of what they do but, basically, because of what they do not do. They have a more pronounced tendency toward passivity; their overt behavior is submissive and docile. This seemingly docile nature makes the underachiever easy to be with. These underachievers generally follow a path of non-resistance: they do not rebel at given assignments; they usually follow school regulations; and generally are quiet, but nonparticipating, members of the classroom.

Some underachievers are described as *aggressive underachievers.* These children tend to be disruptive, talkative, rebellious, and hostile. However, they tend not to express their inner aggressive feelings and anger openly; they are unable to express direct hostility and therefore use indirect means. They fear what may happen to them if they openly express their anger. Therefore, their aggressive tendencies are stored up and resentments are expressed secretly and deviously. They seek hidden and passive ways to express their inner anger such as through the development of an educational problem.

Personal Characteristics Both withdrawn and aggressive underachievers have a low capacity to function under pressure and are easily frustrated, and frustrating incidents occur with high frequency because they are unconsciously geared to look for trouble. They start several projects but complete few. They stay with a project or an assignment until things get tough, then quit. They may dash off any response to school assignments and call them done, or they will give up in the middle of a task when things are not going well. Underachievers lack persistence, especially in the face of challenge.

Parental Characteristics Parents of underachievers seem to be of two general types: One type is indifferent, disinterested, and distant, with neutral to negative attitudes toward education. They also may be authoritarian, restrictive, and rejecting, or they may be extremely permissive or lax, granting the child extraordinary freedom as if he or she were an adult. The second kind of parent is preoccupied with achievement, directly or indirectly setting high standards and pressuring the adolescent to achieve. They may be overindulgent, oversolicitous, overprotective, and too helpful. Although they are well-meaning and may have other children who achieve very well, such parents can give children the impression that they are loved only if they achieve and that they are not capable of going it alone without the parent to guide them and prevent them from failing. Table 15.1 highlights the differences between parents of underachievers and parents of achieving students.

Causes Although many theories and explanations of underachievement have been offered, none has been widely accepted or empirically tested. On the surface, many underachievers are simply disinterested in school, because they come from home environments that do not value education and/or attend a school system that permits them to fall by the wayside (Fordham & Ogbu, 1998). Some are predominantly shy and lack the self-confidence, persistence, and resilience that are necessary to conquer challenges. Others are rebellious, aggressively or passively getting back at their parents who want them to achieve at levels they may perceive as personally unattainable.

APPLICATIONS:

Possible Solutions to Underachievement

It is often assumed that adolescents' achievement level (or the desire to achieve) is more heavily influenced by their peer group than by their parents. Data, however, suggest the opposite (Hebert, 1998; Sage & Kindermann, 1999). Parents are more influential when it comes to motivating them to do well in school. Although peer influence may predominate in some current customs and tastes, parental influence is likely to be predominant in more fundamental areas such as educational achievement. What kinds of parents have academically motivated children? Parents who place high value on autonomy and independence, and on competence and achievement; tend to be democratic; encourage active give-and-take interaction with their teenagers; and who themselves show active curiosity and interest in learning.

TABLE 15.1

Differences Between Families of High Achievers and Underachievers

High Achievers	Underachievers
Family members share in recreational activities, decision making, exchange of confidences, and ideas	Parents are more rejecting, authoritarian, and less involved with their children
Encourage child to achieve but are less insistent on achievement	Typical parents of underachievers feel their own status depends on their child's accomplishments; they demand achievement
Positive family attitudes toward school, education, teachers, and intellectual activities	Parents are either uninvolved and uninterested in child's intellectual pursuits or excessively controlling
Children feel more daily belongingness and identity with parent	Relationship between parent and child is poor and psychologically distant
Home environment more emotionally supportive; greater harmony between parents	Greater emotional tension exhibited in home environment
Freer, more involved communication	Achievement sole topic of conversation; focuses on failures and inadequacies
Achiever will feel the pain of a particular and single instance when he/she fails something	The underachiever experiences a complete loss of confidence and security when he/she fails something
Achiever able to make conflict-free identification with his/her achievement-oriented parents	Parental identification holds much more conflict and fear
Parents are more sure of themselves and their capabilities	Parents are less secure about their intellectual abilities
Parents show greater independence in their social and intellectual activities	Parents show greater dependency in their social and intellectual activities

Parental Involvement

High levels of *parental involvement* are associated with the adolescent's academic competence. Three types of parental involvement are identified (Grolnick & Slowiaczek, 1994): *Cognitive/intellectual* involvement involves exposing children to cognitively stimulating activities and materials such as books and current events. In *personal* involvement, parents indicate to children that they care about school and enjoy interactions with children around school. The third category is parental *behavior.* Parents, for example, can be involved in skill-building activities, guiding their children with their homework, or attending school activities such as parent–teacher conferences and open houses. Students whose parents attend school functions earn higher grades than those of parents who do not.

As can be seen in Figure 15.3, parental involvement may help the child feel more competent and have more control over academic achievement outcomes, which can lead to higher levels of effort and engagement in schoolwork and more positive academic outcomes (Connell, Spencer, & Aber, 1996). Conversely, low parental involvement can precipitate low attendance and low test scores and grades.

Giving Attention Beyond Academics

Adolescent's academic achievement is enhanced when adults establish a positive relationship with them and focus their attention on more than just academics

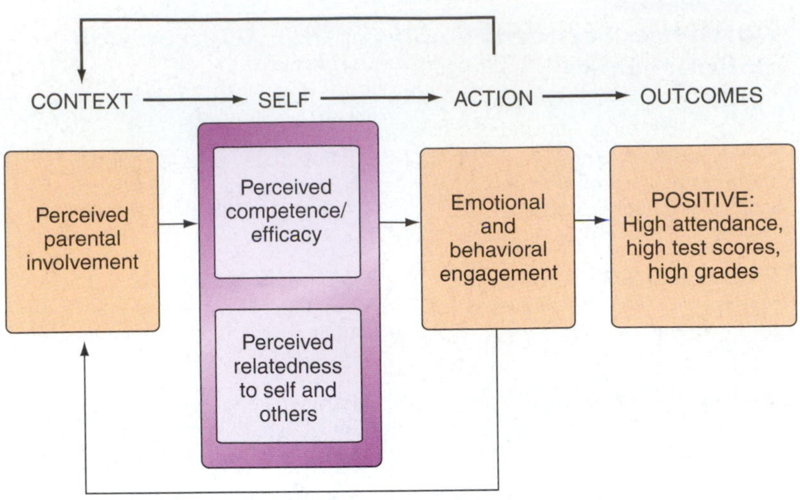

FIGURE 15.3 ***Parental Involvement and Subsequent Achievement Outcomes***

Parental involvement appears to be a pivotal factor in enhancing children's academic success in terms of promoting high attendance, test scores, and grades.

From "Educational Risk and Resilience in African-American Youth: Context, Self, Action in School," by J. P. Connell, M. G. Spencer, & J. Aber, 1996, in *Child Development, 65,* 493–506. Used by permission.

(King, 1998). Sometimes adults exert too much pressure and are too preoccupied with the child's achievement to the exclusion of all other characteristics of the child—strengths in social or physical domains, for example. Relatedly, caregivers also need to foster an appropriate "academic distance" between themselves and the child. Parents need to be cautious about being too helpful, too concerned lest the child fail, always showing the child how to do it better, and never allowing the child to go off on his or her own without guidance and a safety net (Peterson & Colangelo, 1996). Although these parents are well-meaning, they are providing too much and the adolescent is providing too little.

Until the adolescent recognizes that he or she is an underachiever, it will be very difficult to persuade the child to change. Adults can help adolescents avoid a sad, wasteful, and futile academic adventure by challenging and inspiring them, not nagging, compelling, or forcing (Holland, 1998).

© Bob Daemmrich/Stock Boston

Caregivers who are actively involved in their child's education have children who are more likely to succeed in that setting.

Seeing the "Separateness" of Their Lives

Children may find more pleasure in their unconscious motive of frustrating their parents than in achievement. Research findings suggest that it is best to let the adolescent assume the responsibilities for his or her academic successes and failures (Holland, 1998). This is not accomplished by an increased pressure to achieve or indifference to their achievements. For example, in examining differing parenting styles in three cultures (China, Australia, and the United States), academic achievement was positively related to parental academic authoritativeness and negatively related to academic authoritarianism (Leung, Lau, & Lam, 1998). The authors suggest that adults should try to value the child's academic accomplishments but not directly pressure the child to attain them. These children need to see the separateness of their own lives, and that may inspire them to do well for their own sakes.

Concept Checks

1. An adolescent who has developed formal operational thinking solves the pendulum problem by
   a. developing a hypothesis, followed by random testing of various variables.
   b. centering on the most likely variable and testing it randomly.
   c. envisioning all possible factors and testing each systematically.
2. ____________ highlights the adolescent's own awareness of his or her cognitive processes and strategies.
3. Danisha tends to be submissive and docile in the classroom even though she is extremely bright. Her teacher has labeled her as a ____________ ____________.
4. ***True or False:*** One of the key ways in which adults can help underachieving adolescents is by challenging and inspiring them.

Possible Outcomes of the Adolescent's New Thinking Skills

Before Beginning . . .

After reading this section, you will be able to

- understand adolescent egocentrism.
- explain adolescent idealism.
- understand why argumentativeness may increase during the adolescent years.
- recognize how to manage argumentativeness in adolescents.

People just don't understand me because I am not like everyone else.

That will never happen to me.

I'm in control; I can handle it.

Oh, this is terrible; how can I face anybody with this huge zit on my cheek!

No one understands what I am going through, least of all my parents.

Abstract thinking is apparent during adolescence. It is seen in adolescents' increased *introspection* (thinking about their own thoughts and feelings); *self-consciousness* (thinking about what others think about them); and *intellectualization* (turning relatively simple and concrete matters into complex and abstract ones). These patterns of thinking, exemplified in the preceding comments by teenagers, are all forms of egocentrism, which can lead to periods of self-absorption during the adolescent years.

Imaginary Audience

Concern over negative social evaluation during early adolescence helps explain why some adolescents construct an **imaginary audience**. These adolescents may mistakenly perceive (1) an attentive audience (2) that is focused on them uniquely and (3) is critical in nature. David Elkind (1967, 1998) suggests that hypersensitivity to social evaluation or perception that the self is like an actor on stage occurs because changes in physical growth and cognitive growth intensify adolescents' thoughts about themselves. Because they fail to differentiate between what others are thinking and their own thoughts, adolescents imagine that others are as interested in their appearance and behavior as they are. It is this belief that others are preoccupied with their appearance and behavior that constitutes the egocentrism of adolescence. Because teenagers are totally focused on the transformations they are undergoing—in their bodies, in their thinking, and in their feelings and emotions—wherever they go, they feel like they are on stage. Everyone around them, they believe, is as aware of and concerned about their appearance and behavior as they are.

However, teenagers are not the only ones who maintain imaginary audience fantasies; to a certain extent we all do. Some adults play to an imaginary audience in choosing the kind of car they drive. An adult wearing glasses for the first time may think that the new glasses are the focus of others' abiding attention. The difference between adolescents and adults, however, is that in early adolescence these "logical lapses" are much more common and pervasive.

In the young teenager's life the imaginary audience is everywhere: A teenager laments over which sweater to wear to a rock concert, so he will look good (presumably to the other thousands attending the concert). A young girl with a dime-sized spot of spaghetti sauce on her blouse is convinced that "everyone will see this ghastly spill." Moreover, how else can we explain the change in the behavior of a 10-year-old who hates baths to one, at age 14, who now spends great lengths of time bathing and combing his hair? Although adolescents are often self-critical, they are frequently self-admiring too. A good deal of adolescent loudness or faddish dress is probably provoked, according to Elkind, by a failure to differentiate between what the person believes to be attractive and what others admire. It is for this reason that the young person frequently fails to understand why adults disapprove of the way he or she dresses and behaves.

Personal Fable

Adolescent egocentrism can also be seen in another type of social thinking—the **personal fable**, or feeling that one is unique and omnipotent. The personal fable is an overdifferentiation of the self from others (Elkind, 1978). Failing to see similarities in the experiences of self and others, young adolescents are left with exaggerated feelings of personal uniqueness. The feeling that one is the center of attention can also lead to feelings of exaggerated self-importance. The adolescent sees herself as unique and special; social rules and natural laws apply to others but not to her. She is invulnerable and invincible. An example is the teenage girl who after receiving a phone call from her mother

imaginary audience Hypersensitivity to social evaluation or perception that the self is like an actor on stage.

personal fable An overdifferentiation of self from others in which the adolescent fails to see similarities in the experiences of self and others, leaving him or her with an exaggerated feeling of personal uniqueness.

informing her that her boyfriend will be calling back at 9 o'clock races home, dangerously ignoring the speed limit to make it home on time. She only thinks about receiving this important call and is relatively unmindful of her reckless driving.

Personal fable is also reflected in the adolescent's feeling that no one can possibly understand her joys, trials, and tribulations. A teenage girl may become pregnant because, in part at least, her personal fable convinces her that pregnancy will happen to others but never to her and so she does not need to take precautions. Or a teenage girl may be convinced that no one understands the love she has for her boyfriend and only confides these feelings to her diary. Such diaries are also written for posterity in the conviction that the young person's experiences, crushes, and frustrations are of universal significance and importance.

Imaginary audience and personal fable are often associated with new experiences, such as the transition into middle or high school (Vartanian & Powlishta, 1996). Females show higher levels of both than do males (Rycek, Stuhr, McDermott, Benker, & Schwartz, 1998). Concerns with the imaginary audience and personal fable, however, begin to diminish as teenagers grow older and their experiences and expanding social relationships help them to become more "other" focused. Erikson (1959) called this "intimacy." Once young people see themselves in a more realistic light as a function of having adjusted their imaginary audience to the real one, they can establish true rather than self-interested interpersonal relations. In the process, they discover that others have feelings similar to their own and have suffered and been enraptured in the same way.

To illustrate, when older teens are given this scenario, "You've been looking forward to going to this party for over a month. Once you arrive, after an hour-long drive, you notice a big grease spot on your slacks or skirt. Do you stay or return home?" On a rather consistent basis 16- and 17-year-olds answer, "No one will really care; they are my friends so I would stay." Young teens, 13- and 14-year-olds, answer that they would go home, or, if they stayed, they would stay in a dark corner so no one would notice the stain (Elkind & Bowen, 1979). Ultimately, the best cure for the teenager's center-stage syndrome is developing close friendships, sharing intimate thoughts, and discovering that other people can be as self-conscious as they are.

The term "center stage syndrome" nicely sums up the adolescent assumption that everyone around them is concerned with the same thing they are concerned with—namely, themselves.

Idealism

> Hi. My name is Cindy and I am 16 years old. I am trying to make the world a better place. I love animals and actively work for their rights. They are defenseless and powerless. If animals are to talk, I must be their voice.

Moving to the world of the possible opens up the world of the ideal. Adolescents can now imagine a world of peace and harmony. Their critical attitudes toward parents derive in part from their ability to imagine ideal parents against whom their parents generally suffer by comparison. Parents then may bear the brunt of the adolescent's criticism. "Mom, let's go shopping for some clothes for you so you don't look like a homeless person." "Dad, everyone is going to some place special for spring break, why is it that we can never afford to do *anything* neat like all my other friends?" In early adolescence, not only is the grass greener in the other person's yard but, as Elkind informs us, their house is bigger and their parents are much better as well. For some teenagers, the obedient school-age child is transformed into a less respectful, less obedient, always questioning, and more critical adolescent. The value and importance of this process of measuring parents and others against abstract standards gradually subsides in later adolescence when teenagers are able to see that all people are "flawed" to some extent but still worthy of love and respect.

Although teenagers are usually very vocal in expressing their ideals, they often fail to carry out the actions that would seem to follow logically from their professed ideals. Cindy, our animal rights advocate, for example, has to be constantly prodded at home to feed her own dog. Some teenagers will participate in a walk for a cleaner environment but leave the path strewn with food wrappers and pop cans. As such, adolescents can appear extraordinarily hypocritical. They expound lofty principles one minute, violate those same principles the next, and become indignant if an adult points out the discrepancy between their words and deeds.

This apparent hypocrisy is not a result of moral weakness but rather intellectual immaturity (Elkind, 1967). Teenagers simply do not recognize the difference between expressing an ideal and working toward it. They become intoxicated with the discovery of abstract ideals and principles for behavior, and they simply cannot be bothered with practical details. If their lofty goals are not realized once they are expressed, then the fault lies with "others." They are unaware of the connection between theory and practice. With time, teenagers do come to recognize the hard work involved in bringing an ideal to fruition.

Moreover, young adolescents often get carried away with their newfound abilities to grasp complexities and may overlook the obvious and simple. As such, there is often a gap between thought and experience. Teenagers do not have much experience in applying their advanced knowledge to the mundane, practical realities of everyday life. Consequently, they can be intellectually astute one day and childish the next.

Argumentativeness

> The children now love luxury; they have bad manners, contempt for authority, and show disrespect for their elders. They no longer rise when elders enter the room. They contradict their parents, chatter before company, and are tyrants over their teachers. (Braude, 1957)

The Greek philosopher Socrates (469–399 B.C.) made this comment about adolescents thousands of years ago—and, yet, it has a familiar ring to us today. Is adolescence a time of warring parents and confrontational, unapproachable teens? Many adults believe that teenagers are about as likely to get along with them or to talk with them about their concerns as they are to play Beethoven CDs at a low volume.

However, for the most part, the same issues that parents once debated with their parents lie at the root of today's conflicts with their own teenagers. Many families soon realize that not all parent–adolescent conflict is bad; some of it is a healthy part of the process of differentiation between the parent and the adolescent. This healthy process occurs cross-culturally. Not surprisingly, parent–adolescent conflicts are more likely to occur with the same-sex parent.

The Roots of Conflict

In most studies it has been shown that the majority of arguments between parents and their adolescents are about normal, everyday, mundane family matters such as schoolwork, social life and friends, home chores, disobedience, and disagreements with siblings (Montemayor, 1998). Some issues appear to be "arguments for the sake of arguing"—a sort of practice time in which teenagers exercise their new cognitive abilities to state their case and argue in their defense. Interestingly, today's adolescents tend to have the same kinds of disagreements with their parents that their parents once

© David Young-Wolff/PhotoEdit

During adolescence, parents demand more responsibility and teenagers demand more freedom, such as choosing the kind of clothes they will wear.

Thought CHALLENGE

What were some of your values as a young adolescent? Have the values of today's adolescents changed?

had with their own parents. The issues remain the same, but when adolescents become parents their perspectives on the issues change.

Some argumentative discussions involve more "philosophical" issues pertaining to values, religion, and politics. Adolescence seems to be a time when teenagers examine their values—a time of pondering, "What do I want out of life?" Teenagers may wonder about which values are most important: self-fulfillment and self-expression or personal wealth and material possessions. Some may profess a commitment to the welfare of others and want to take an active interest in correcting societal problems such as homelessness, world hunger, or child abuse. Adolescence may also be a time when teenagers change their religious beliefs or experience a reawakening of their religious values. Teenagers may also begin to think seriously about the nature of society, politics, forms of government, laws, and social control. The absence of overt conflict about these issues is quite remarkable given the great differences that generally exist in the attitudes of adults and youths about these topics. Arguing over these issues helps adolescents develop their own positions on issues and their own identity as a person separate from the family.

Another common source of family conflict pertains to issues of freedom and control. David Elkind has interpreted this type of parent–adolescent conflict as a stage in adolescent self-differentiation. His theory of interpersonal relations highlights how tensions between control and autonomy set the stage for conflicts. During socialization, parents demand that the adolescent fulfill certain responsibilities (relative neatness, good relationships with friends, responsible behavior, fulfillment of home duties). The adolescent, in turn, insists on more freedoms in areas such as later hours, use of the family car, friendship choices, and individual dress.

Parents and adolescents tend to perceive their conflict levels and the content differently. Parents, for example, report higher levels of conflict than do adolescents. This appears to be especially true for conflict over chores and appearance. Adolescents, however, report higher conflict rates with parents over substance abuse.

Conflict Is Not Always Bad

From early to middle adolescence, there is a simultaneous increase in both the rate and the emotional intensity of conflict between adolescents and parents (Laursen, Coy, & Collins, 1998). Conflict rates then decrease. Conflict, however, is not always bad; in fact, it is viewed by some as a normal and essential factor in adolescent development and, within limits, beneficial. Adolescence is a time for realignment and redefinition of family ties (Muuss & Porton, 1998). Adolescents slowly begin the process of detaching from their families, and parent–adolescent conflict is seen as both a normal outgrowth of detachment and a necessary stimulus to that process. Some researchers, for example, have found that conflict, within a supportive environment, leads to character development in adolescents (von der Lippe, 1998). If conflicts are not excessive, disagreements with parents enable adolescents to form and argue for their own ideas and opinions. However, a high degree of conflict between parents and their adolescents is not related to psychological growth but is predictive of a variety of adolescent problems such as running away from home, dropping out of school, and marrying earlier than their counterparts who report calmer relations with their parents (Sampson & Laub, 1998).

Physical, social, and cognitive adolescent transformations appear to be responsible, in part, for more confrontational exchanges between adolescents and their parents. Jeanne Brooks-Gunn and Roberta Paikoff (1997) note that decreased sharing of experiences and increased parent–child conflict directly coincide with puberty changes. Cognitive changes may result in more confrontational interactions with parents, as adolescents increasingly question and debate parental rules and expectations. Although confrontations do occur prior to adolescence, increases in sophistication and complexity of thought allow adolescents to demonstrate more adultlike reasoning, making such interchanges potentially more prolonged and more challenging to parents.

The popular stereotype often portrayed by the media of the adolescent's family as a crucible of intrafamiliar tension and hostility has not been confirmed in most empirical studies of adolescents and their parents (Brooks-Gunn & Paikoff, 1997). The majority of adolescents speak favorably of their parents and value their relationships with them.

Cross-Cultural Parent–Adolescent Conflicts

European American families tend to place considerable emphasis on individual autonomy during adolescence, and parent–child conflict and emotional distancing are considered to play an important function in the development of adolescents' independence. But what about families in which individual autonomy is not traditionally seen as an important task of adolescent development? Does conflict occur in these families as well?

Andrew Fuligni (1998) assessed the rates of parent–child conflict in three immigrant groups that traditionally place a different emphasis on autonomy—Mexican, Chinese, and Filipino American families in comparison with that in European American families. The immigrant families tended to emphasize the importance of parent–child hierarchies and the obligations of children to their families. As can be seen in Figure 15.4, despite holding different beliefs about parental authority and individual autonomy, adolescents from all four cultural backgrounds reported similar levels of conflict with their parents.

Gender-Based Parent–Adolescent Conflicts

Mothers appear to have more conflict with their adolescent daughters than do fathers (Holmbeck, Paikoff, & Brooks-Gunn, 1995). In particular, studies have shown that conflict tends to be highest between mothers and early-maturing girls. Fathers are more involved with and sensitive to their adolescent sons than their adolescent daughters. In dual-wage families, however, fathers are more involved in conflict with both sons and daughters. Perhaps this is because these fathers are more obligated to be involved with their children, so boys and girls may be treated more similarly.

APPLICATIONS:

Managing Argumentativeness

Most adults do not want adolescents to become unquestioning and compliant individuals. Parents do not want their teenagers, for example, to go along with their friends to spray paint the walls of the school. Educators do not want their students to just obediently memorize, never ask questions, and never disagree. On the contrary, most adults want teenagers to develop such qualities as curiosity, inquisitiveness, self-assertiveness, and independence. Despite these desires, parental stress and anxiety are highest in early adolescence, and, presumably, this is due to conflicts that arise over various issues during this time of development.

These conflicts appear to be influenced by adolescents who use parents versus their peers as a safe sounding board for arguments, the strength of early parent–child relationships, parents' sensitivity to the adolescent's needs, and parenting styles.

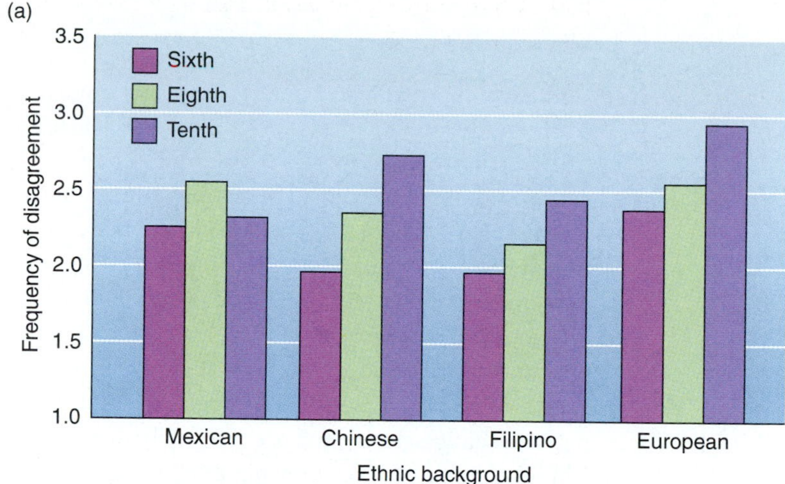

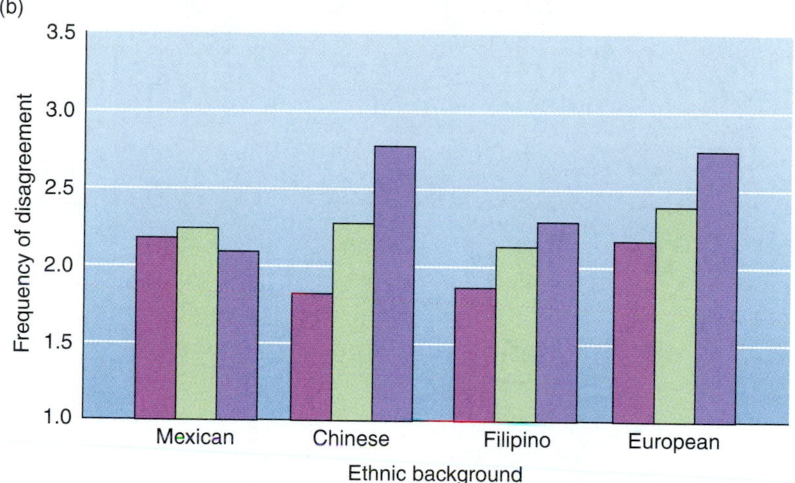

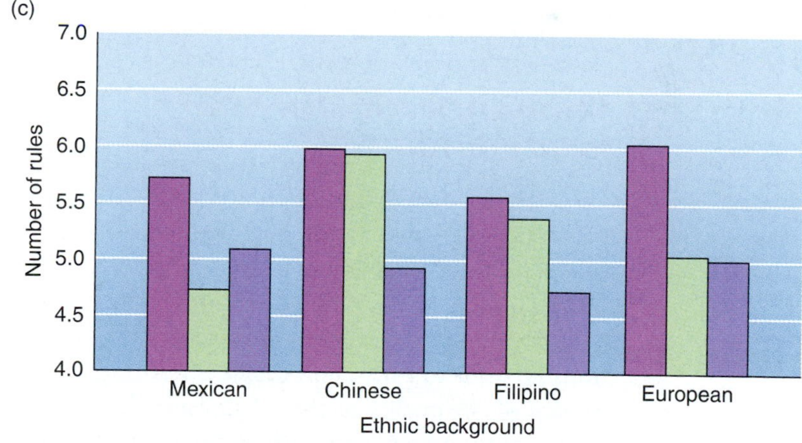

FIGURE 15.4 ***Adolescents' willingness to openly disagree with (a) mothers and (b) fathers and (c) their endorsement of parental authority, by grade and ethnicity.***

U.S. adolescents from Mexican, Chinese, Filipino, and European American backgrounds reported similar levels of conflict with their parents. The study looked at the number of rules parents made (for example, "You must be home by 10 P.M.") and the frequency of parent–adolescent disagreements.

From "Authority, Autonomy, and Parent–Adolescent Conflict and Cohesion: A Study of Adolescents from Mexican, Chinese, Filipino, and European Backgrounds," by A. J. Fuligni, 1998, in *Developmental Psychology, 34,* 782–792.

Conflicts with Parents Versus Peers

Conflict can provide an impetus for growth and communication, and this is best fostered in close relationships that consist of frequent, interdependent, mutually rewarding interactions (Bukowski, Newcomb, & Hartup, 1998). The closer the relationship, the more opportunities for expressing disagreement and dissatisfaction. Of all adolescent relationships, the closest ones typically are with parents and close friends (Laursen & Bukowski, 1997). Adolescents recognize that close relationships with parents change slowly and are not easily disrupted. The likelihood of a relationship in close families being irreparably damaged as a result of arguing is minimal. Teenagers perceive most conflicts with their parents as rather benign events with little or no negative impact (Shulman, Laursen, Kalman, & Karpovsky, 1997).

However, teenagers tend to perceive other relationships such as with close peers as being more fluid and more easily dissolved. As such, they more carefully manage most disagreements with close friends to ensure amiable outcomes. In conflicts with peers, adolescents prefer forms of resolution such as negotiating whereas power assertion prevails in parental conflict. Adolescents use parents as sounding boards that will enable them to learn lessons they can apply to peers and other adults in different situations (Laursen & Bukowski, 1997).

Strong Affective Parental Relationships

Researchers agree that it is extremely rare that a young person who was not defiant as a child will, suddenly, become an argumentative adolescent (Montemayor, 1998). This underscores the fact that the affective quality of the parent–adolescent relationship prior to early adolescence is a strong determinant of the quality of the relationship during adolescence. Adolescents with warm, caring relationships with their parents tend to argue less with them (Brickle, 1997). Adolescents thrive developmentally when their home environment is characterized by warm parental relationships in which teens are permitted to express their opinions and assert their individuality in conjunction with parents' setting expectations of mature behavior and enforcing reasonable rules and standards.

Sensitivity to the Adolescent's Needs

This is not to say that disagreements between caring parents and adolescents never occur. Some adolescents have communication traits of argumentativeness, assertiveness, and verbal aggressiveness, and they tend to argue more (Brickle, 1997). Endless and sometimes tiresome debates can occur simply as a result of the adolescent's maturing intellectually. Adolescents can now recognize flaws in the adults' arguments and inconsistencies in their principles, and they delight in noticing and pointing these out. Unreasonable and unfair requests are responded to with arguments and sometimes defiance. Consider, for example, the following: The parents have made plans to do something after dinner and they are running late. It is the parents' turn to do the dishes, but because of their lateness, they may say, "We'll forget about the dishes tonight and do them tomorrow." But, if it is the adolescent's turn to do the dishes and he is running late for a commitment, a lecture is generally forthcoming about how he has to become a responsible person and the dishes have to be done right now—no matter what! Even well-meaning adults can sometimes be too insensitive to their adolescent's needs (Stern, 1999).

Parenting Styles

> Lately, my mother and I haven't been getting along that much. It really irritates me that I have so many rules to follow. My grades are not permitted to slip under a 3.5 GPA; I have an early curfew; and she is constantly criticizing me for the clothes that I wear. I work part-time and pay for my own clothes and stuff, but she still nags me about responsibility. All I want is more freedom and my mother won't grant it to me. She won't let go and still treats me like a child. All I want is a little trust and a little more freedom. Every teenager wants more freedom—and every parent still treats us like babies.

It is interesting to note that cross-cultural research shows that in the United States authoritarian parenting, in which parents own the power, predominates during adolescence, and in other countries such as Denmark and Germany, authoritative parenting, in which the parents share power with their children, is more common during the adolescent years (Kandel & Lesser, 1969;

Karr & Wesley, 1966). Further, U.S. parents tend to be more authoritarian when children are younger (presumably to help them acquire self-discipline at an early age). Danish and German parents are also described as being less permissive and providing less explanation for rules (authoritarian) when children are young. As children become older in both these countries, the number of rules decrease and the proportion of adequate freedom increases; and interestingly, parents report less argumentative and more compliant behavior.

U.S. parents, however, move increasingly toward greater restrictiveness during adolescence. U.S. adolescents, at age 18, are still subject to more rules than Danish children are at age 14. Could U.S. parents be doing things backward? Findings do indicate that intense parent–adolescent conflicts result from parental rigidity in response to the adolescent's assertion of freedom of choice in a personal area (Smetana, 1996). The exertion of parental authority is resisted by the adolescent primarily in cases where the parent is interpreted as attempting to control actions the adolescent views as within the personal sphere. These types of tumult are also evident in Hong Kong families. These findings suggest that adolescents must enjoy increasing independence from parental domination if they are eventually to assume adult responsibilities, and thus it is recommended that there be more flexibility and fewer rules as children get older—not the other way around.

Concept Checks

1. An adolescent who remarks "Nothing can happen to me" is expressing a __________ ________________.
2. Daria is a member of several organizations that are dedicated to creating an ideal world; her lofty view of what the world should be like is often called ________________.
3. A general conclusion about argumentativeness in adolescence is that
   a. adolescents from different ethnic groups experience conflict with their parents.
   b. conflict between parents and adolescents only occurs in homes with uncaring parents.
   c. conflict almost always leads to negative parent–adolescent relationships.
4. Evidence from cross-cultural research implies that during adolescence, parents need to practice
   a. more authoritarian parenting.
   b. more authoritative parenting.
   c. more indulgent parenting.

Adolescents and School

Before Beginning ...

After reading this section, you will be able to

- examine the curriculum dilemmas of middle schools and high schools.
- think about the role of occupational role development in high school curricula.
- evaluate adolescent employment.
- understand why adolescents drop out of school.
- note the possible measures for dropout prevention.

To prepare students for life after high school, researchers and critics have called for more effective experience-based educational opportunities, including vocational training. The problem of deciding on and preparing for a vocation represents one of the major developmental tasks of adolescence. To this end, educators have noted that students need to learn more about vocational possibilities.

Curriculum: Rigor or Relevance?

Are high schools adequately preparing students for their post–high school occupational and academic roles? What kind of curriculum is best suited for teenagers in this new millennium? If you were asked to make a list of what you think high school students need to know to function as competent, responsible, and satisfied adults, which of your items should be the responsibility of high school? Should high school curricula be limited to traditional academic subjects, or should schools play a broader role in preparing young people for adulthood, by providing instruction more directly pertinent to work, family, leisure, and citizenship? Or, should students receive instruction primarily in "core" subjects such as math, science, English, and history? Should students take courses in general education, or in subjects such as art, health, sex education, and personal finance? Which courses should be required? Which courses should be electives? These are pretty tough questions to answer and, more than likely, other classmates may not agree with the answers you have suggested for these questions.

Schools seem to follow a cyclical pattern which, at times, has sounded the cry for a more rigorous and focused curriculum with emphasis on "basic" classes

Cultural Variations

Occupational Training

Many experts in the United States voice concerns about the lack of a coherent and challenging curriculum for high schoolers who do not plan to attend college (Orfield, 1997). These students are often referred to as "the forgotten ones." Some recommend that an integral part of the education curriculum for these students should be "occupational role development," modeled after Germany's programs (Steinberg, Dornbusch, & Brown, 1998). Students would receive information about skills required for various jobs, job market demands, and whether or not the individual's interests and capabilities are compatible with certain lines of work. Despite the importance of vocational adjustment for U.S. adolescents, they typically have only a vague idea of the nature of the many different kinds of jobs available in the society. They do not know which ones they would be able to do successfully and enjoy.

Perhaps an answer to the curriculum dilemma is to look cross-culturally at countries who have provided various curricula that appear to meet the needs of non–college-attending students. Countries differ in how they organize the transition from high school. In Japan, there are tight linkages between high school and employment (Rosenbaum & Kariya, 1989). Major employers come to the high schools to recruit students, and teachers recommend which students are qualified for the position and the firm (Stevenson, Kochanek, & Schneider, 1998). Because many adolescents spend their entire work career with a single company, schools have active apprenticeship training programs. The adolescent's first employer has an important influence on their later career opportunities.

Germany is recognized worldwide for its successful system of preparing its youths to enter the world of work (Weymann, 1999). Secondary education is stratified into different educational tracks organized around different types of schools. These schools offer different diplomas that are tightly linked to later educational and labor market opportunities. All students attend school full time until they are 16; school, however, is still compulsory until the age of 18. Those who will be attending college enter *gymnasium* and spend their last two years taking college preparatory classes. The gymnasium provides students with preparation for taking the examinations for the *Abitur,* a certificate required for admission to university. Students in the *Realschule* earn a certificate that permits them to go from secondary school to training programs for white collar positions in banking, telecommunications, government, and the service industry (Reitzle, Vondracek, & Silbereisen, 1998). Finally, students in the *Hauptschule* earn occupational certificates through apprenticeship programs that qualify them for specific manual and skilled occupations. In contrast to Japan and Germany, the United States has relatively weak institutional ties between high schools and the worlds of work and college.

Thought CHALLENGE

It is said that high schools reflect the needs of society. What kind of curriculum should be offered in our schools for current students to function effectively in the new millennium?

(English, mathematics, science, social studies). The pendulum then swings away from the emphasis on "essentials" to stressing the need for more practical subject areas that have real-world relevance to students. Why can't we seem to make up our mind? Why can't we decide on the content of the high school curriculum and keep it that way? Part of the reason is that high schools, like any other social institution, are embedded in the broader society. As such, the sort of preparation high school students get reflects the needs of society. As society changes so does the type of preparation young people receive to develop into competent adults (Cornbleth, 1998). Are U.S. high schools currently preparing students to meet their future academic or occupational endeavors? Do other countries do a better job? (See Cultural Variations.)

Where Do High School Students Go Next?

Two decades ago, less than 50 percent of high school seniors enrolled full time in college after high school. Currently, the percentage of seniors going directly to college full time is 58 percent (Stevenson, Kochanek, & Schneider, 1998). High school seniors who go to college full time are increasingly drawn from those who score in the highest quartile on reading and mathematics tests. Not only do high school seniors attend college in greater numbers, but they also are more persistent. For example, 80 percent of high school seniors who entered college directly after high school are still enrolled full time two years later.

Today, there is also a decline in the percentage of high school seniors who go directly to work. Even though today's high school graduates have improved academic skills compared with high school graduates a decade ago, employers claim they lack the skills and abilities required for entry-level positions. Some argue that there have been fundamental changes in what is required of workers and that schools have not kept up with these changes.

© Michael Newman/PhotoEdit

Certain occupational environments are well suited to individuals with certain personalities, and others are not.

Occupational Role Development

A number of theories have been proposed about adolescent vocational development. One of the most influential is John Holland's (1987) model. Holland postulates that for optimal vocation development, it is essential to achieve a good match between an individual's attributes and the characteristics of his or her chosen career. He views the accomplishment of such a match as the first step toward an enduring, often life-long career commitment. After years of extensive analysis of jobs and people who select them, Holland determined that career choices can be viewed as a reflection of basic personality styles.

A successful career choice, in Holland's model, entails the matching of a particular personality type—a given set of interests and personality characteristics—with a vocation that allows the expression of these traits. Through completing a series of questions in a standardized personality inventory, an individual can determine which of six basic personality dimensions (summarized in Table 15.2) is characteristic of himself or herself and then examine directories in which occupations have been classified according to the same topology.

Among the developmental tasks described by Erik Erikson (1968) none is more far reaching in its implications for adult life than the choice of one's future vocation. Some educational experts believe that our high schools could do more in this area than they are currently doing (Lange, 1998). They further contend that vocational development does not take place in a vacuum, and for this reason working in outside employment during high school may have vocational benefits for young people. It is often pointed out, for example, that schools do not teach students how to find employment, fill out a job application, behave during a job interview, or perform responsibly on the job—skills working adolescents learn (Blyth, Simmons, & Carlton-Ford, 1998).

TABLE 15.2

Holland's Basic Personality Factors

Personality	Description
Realistic	Individuals who are realistic prefer practical jobs—often requiring physical labor and motor coordination rather than interpersonal skills. A construction worker probably has realistic interests.
Investigative	Individuals who are investigative are oriented toward thinking rather than acting. They are often interested in work situations in which they can use conceptual and theoretical skills. Scientists are often investigative.
Social	Individuals who are social enjoy being involved in interpersonal situations and social interaction. They are often interested in work situations in which they can help other people. Counseling is a good example.
Conventional	Individuals who are conventional like structured job environments and prefer to subordinate their own personal needs to the needs of others. They often seek work situations where they can work under the direction of supervisors. Office clerks are typically conventional.
Enterprising	Individuals who are enterprising are often verbally skilled and interested in supervising and directing other people. A sales manager for a large corporation is likely to be enterprising.
Artistic	Individuals who are artistic show strong needs for artistic self-expression and prefer tasks that are unstructured and that emphasize physical skills or interpersonal interaction. Artists, musicians, and actors have artistic interests.

From "Current Status of Holland's Theory of Careers: Another Perspective," by J. Holland, 1987, in *Career Development Quarterly, 36,* 24–30.

Thought CHALLENGE

Does finishing high school and receiving a core education still appear to be the best means of preparing for full-time work?

Adolescent Employment

In our society, adolescents spend a considerable amount of time providing labor for adults. Approximately 80 percent of high school youths have held or are holding part-time positions (Skorikov & Vondracek, 1997). About 17 percent of U.S. high school students tend to work at fast-food restaurants and about 10 percent work in offices as clerical assistants (Kelloway & Harvey, 1999). The remainder tend to work in retail stores as cashiers and sales clerks. Few of these jobs permit independent decision making or allow for the use of skills being taught in school. Moreover, adolescents rarely receive any type of instruction from their supervisors at work.

In the United States, most adolescents begin working in a part-time job when they are 16 or 17 years old (Finch, Mortimer, & Rhy, 1997). Working students may acquire "survival skills," such as balancing a checkbook, planning a personal budget, having more knowledge about consumer and financial matters, and knowing how credit cards work than do students without work experience, but are there other possible benefits from working during the high school years? Which of the following benefits do you believe are true?

Students who work part time in high school learn to:

- be more reliable.
- manage finances.
- be more dependable.
- develop social responsibility (cooperate with and take responsibility for others).
- develop more mature work orientations (complete work tasks and take pride in what they are doing).
- budget their earnings.
- save for important long-term goals such as college tuition.
- become more personally responsible.
- develop positive attitudes about work.

Research findings suggest that none of these statements is true. Most adults, however, assume that having a job is good for adolescents. Work, they believe, builds positive attitudes toward work. In fact, many teens develop a rather cynical attitude toward work—"Anyone who works harder than he or she has to is just plain weird" (Mortimer & Johnson, 1998). Does working promote responsibility, self-discipline, and a positive work ethic? Not necessarily. Many teenagers are more inclined to think in rather unethical ways—"It's okay to take stuff from work; that's one way to make up for the poor wages they pay us" (Bidwell, Schneider, & Borman, 1998). Paid employment gives adolescents experience in the "real world of working," but most jobs held by teenagers are dull, monotonous, stressful, mundane, dreary, repetitive, not intellectually stimulating, and hold little chance for advancement or development (Frone, 1999).

Further, teenagers who work do not have any advantages over nonworkers with respect to work orientation or self-esteem. The suspected positive outcomes, such as lower rates of dysfunctional behavior, better school performance, or enhanced psychosocial well-being have not been found (Steinberg, Dornbusch, & Brown, 1998). What are the effects of teenagers' working on their earnings, stress, and school achievements?

Working and Money Management

Few adolescents engaged in outside employment exercise a great deal of judgment when it comes to managing money. Most youths who work spend their earnings in self-indulgent ways, such as buying expensive clothing and personal entertainment. They see earnings as a means to achieve a higher standard of living for themselves. A fair proportion is spent on drugs and alcohol (Steinberg et al., 1998). Parents appear to appreciate no longer having to pay for their teenager's extra, "personal" items. Teenagers' sense of social obligation may be enhanced if a certain portion of their money is saved for some worthwhile cause such as advanced schooling. Some youths, however, do put money aside for education. U.S. data show that by the time working teenagers are in the 10th grade, approximately 30 percent of them report saving their earnings for long-range goals, primarily for their future education (Shanahan, Elder, Burchinal, & Conger, 1996). Most teenagers, however, are not working for necessities but for luxuries (Lowe & Krahn, 1999).

Working and Stress

Further, long work hours (in excess of 15 to 20 hours) during the school year appear to be associated with increases in psychological distress and somatic complaints, higher rates of drug and alcohol use, higher rates of delinquency, and greater autonomy from parental control (Skorikov & Vondracek, 1997). The kinds of jobs available to teenagers often expose them to heat, dirt, noise, and time pressures; their work schedules interfere with other activities they enjoy; and they may have to deal with irate customers and bosses who never listen to their suggestions and opinions—all of which lead to stress.

The most energy-depleting activities are those that individuals must engage in even though they find them of little or no value or interest. In contrast, activities that inspire intrinsic motivation and high levels of effort may be energy-enhancing. Whether any particular job is energizing or enervating depends on the individual's subjective perception. But, as noted, most teenagers find the types of work they do useless for enhancing skills and abilities needed for future employment, generally lacking in variety and challenge, and nonstimulating (usually repeating the same simple activities again and again). Thus, under these conditions most teenagers' jobs are energy-depleting and thus stressful (Schoenhals, Tienda, & Schneider, 1998).

Working and School Achievement

Studies on part-time employment and student achievement suggest that employment in excess of 20 hours per week during the school year may adversely affect high school students' school performance and investment in school, especially among those who begin working when they are sophomores or juniors (Mael, Morath, & McLellan, 1997). Adolescents, for example, who work 20 hours a week have lower GPAs and more school absences than other teenagers who work less or do not work (Lenarduzzi & McLaughlin, 1996). Adolescents who work at moderate intensity (1–20 hours per week) have higher GPAs than both non-workers and students who work more hours per week (Mortimer, Finch, Scongryeol, Shanahan, & Call, 1996). Other studies have found that students who work only a minimal number of hours on weekends have the highest GPAs (Worley, 1995).

Working Less Than 20 Hours a Week

Adolescents who work less than 20 hours per week have more positive outcomes. They are more likely to grow in self-reliance (Steinberg, Greenberger, Garduque, Ruggiero, & Vaux, 1992). They tend to develop a more mature "work orientation" and the ability to complete work tasks and take pride in doing so. Part-time work may also aid adolescents in their transition from school to the world of work. What is learned at work—even so-called menial work—is not inconsequential.

Many adolescents, for example, report that their work experience helped them acquire experiences that would make them "better" adult workers, such as how to find a job, how to keep a job, accepting responsibility, learning to deal with customers and clients, being on time, and following directions (Mortimer & Johnson, 1998). Exposure to different work environments may encourage adolescents to think about future occupational goals, recognize the importance of getting a good education, and reflect on issues for future vocational development—"What kind of job would I like to have in the future?" "What am I good at?"

Thus, adolescent employment is not all bad. Some adolescents give their wages to their families and save for the future. Others help their families indirectly. The general consensus of research is that moderate involvement in the workplace (less than 15 to 20 hours a week) is usually harmless and sometimes beneficial.

Unemployment

Although teenage employment has become commonplace in the contemporary United States, a small number of young people who want to work are nevertheless unable to find jobs. Approximately 90 percent of our youths are either in school, working, or both. Only 5 percent are out of school, unemployed, and looking for full-time work. Most studies show that unemployment during adolescence results primarily from a combination of economic and social factors rather than from a lack of motivation on the part of unemployed individuals. Minority youths are more likely to experience unemployment than white youths. Unemployment is more common among teenagers who come from low-income families and live in areas that have high overall unemployment rates and where competition for available employment is severe. Youth unemployment is a problem mostly because it is associated with higher rates of crime, drug abuse, and violence. The majority of unemployed youths are high school dropouts.

Thought **CHALLENGE**
Are 16- and 17-year-olds who commit to 20-hour workweeks missing out on important socialization and learning experiences that occur in other settings?

Dropping Out of School

Jake cannot keep up academically. He is of average intelligence but often finds much of the curriculum puzzling and irrelevant to his needs. This causes Jake to feel that school is a frustrating and unrewarding experience. He does not participate in any of the school activities and just prefers to hang out with his friends who have dropped out of school. Although he "gets along" with his teachers, he feels that he is not very important to them. In fact, Jake notes, most of his teachers don't even know who he is! Jake has decided to drop out of school. In this way he can escape from the burdens of a wasted high school existence.

Failures in keeping up academically or finding relevance and challenge in the school curriculum are two important factors that make continuance in school frustrating and unrewarding (Steighner, 2001). Each year dropouts tend to fall further behind in their academic skills and in the grades they receive. The typical dropout, even though of average IQ, is two years behind in reading and mathematics by the time he or she reaches the seventh grade, and a majority of the dropout's grades are below average. Also, dropouts are likely to have failed one or more school years. For many lower-class youths (among whom the largest numbers of dropouts are found), school is an unrewarding experience academically as well as socially. Often they do not share the values of their largely middle-class teachers; they do not participate to the same degree as other adolescents in the social life and activities of the school; and they are likely to feel inadequate or resentful when confronted with the social and academic demands of the school.

Reasons for dropping out of school vary by ethnicity and gender. European American dropouts cite alienation from school more often than either African Americans or Hispanics of both sexes (Jordan, Lara, & McPartland, 1996). African American males report being suspended or expelled from school more than the other groups. Hispanic and African American females cite family-related reasons more often. The overwhelming majority of dropouts, however, do have plans for resuming their education (White & Kaufman, 1997). Male and female European American dropouts plan to take equivalency tests; Hispanic adolescents favor attending alternative high schools; and African American adolescents plan to return to a regular high school to earn their diplomas (Beauvais, Chavez, Oetting, & Deffenbacher, 1996).

Statistics indicate that the current rate of youths who leave high school without a degree or diploma is 35 percent (Edmondson & White, 1998), but the rates vary profoundly according to social class, ethnicity, and gender. None of the students from the highest social class drop out, whereas 71.4 percent of the lowest social class do. It is reported that 13.9 percent of white males, 12.8 percent of white females, 19.4 percent of African American males, 20 percent of African American females, 31.5 percent of Hispanic males, and 34.2 percent of Hispanic females drop out of school (U.S. Bureau of Census, 1997). Native American students seem to leave school at rates substantially higher than youths in the general population. A number of studies report dropout rates ranging from 15 to 60 percent; comparable rates in the general population range from 5 to 35 percent.

Native American dropout rates at the high school level are roughly double those of other minority groups (Allen & Mitchell, 1998). A variety of contradictory views exist on who the dropouts are. Some researchers and educators portray these individuals as helpless and inadequate, hopeless individuals. However, many dropouts are above-average intellectually and are keenly aware of the ethnic/class/gender discrimination in school (Stevenson, Maton, & Teti, 1998). Students most vulnerable to dropping out of school have high levels of aggressive behavior and low levels of academic performance (Fordham & Ogbu, 1998). Over 80 percent of the boys and 47 percent of the girls who fit this statistical cluster drop out before completing grade 12.

What Happens to These Dropouts?

Dropouts are likely to encounter higher unemployment rates, more personality problems, lower aspiration levels, and a higher incidence of delinquency after they leave high school. However, these problems are at least as likely (and probably more likely) to reflect the kinds of problems that led to them dropping out in the first place.

Further, a high school diploma does not reverse the effects of ethnic/class/gender discriminations. African American and Latino youths, particularly females, face bleak employment and income prospects whether they hold a high school diploma or not. It is a false assumption that a high school diploma is the path to equal opportunity. African American teens with high school diplomas suffer 54 percent unemployment.

Perhaps, we need to see dropouts as individuals who are aware of the ethnic/class/gender discrimination both in school and out of school in the market force. This is not to say that these individuals do not need a high school diploma, but rather, dropping out of high school needs to be recognized not as aberrant and not as giving up. Often it voices a critique of educational and economic systems promising opportunity and mobility and delivering neither.

APPLICATIONS:

Helping Potential High School Dropouts

The greatest challenge is not to keep a young person in a school situation that is unrewarding and irrelevant; the challenge lies in improving these conditions. To this end, some common themes in research have shown that strong emphasis on vocational training and community-vocational experiences; intensive programs with low teacher–student ratios; individualized counseling; and multiple motivational approaches help the potential dropout to see school as more rewarding and relevant. Special programs also seem to create a special atmosphere among administrators, teachers, and students. Other important factors that help students stay in school include enabling them to feel that they have some control over what happens to them in school (Tucker, Harris, Brady, & Herman, 1996); adult involvement, particularly parents; and extracurricular activities.

Being in Control

Students who drop out tend to report that they have a less positive teacher–student relationship than persistent students and that their teachers are controlling toward them (Fordham & Ogbu, 1998). Adult practices that are overly controlling—for example, telling the adolescent what to do and how to do it, with little respect for his or her own choices and orientations—undermine the student's self-determined motivation. These students, relative to persistent students, report that they participate much less in the decision-making process at school, that they are told to improve more often, and that they are disciplined much more (Dohn, 1992). They have lower perceptions of school competence (Horowitz, 1992) and autonomy than persistent students. Finally, students who drop out are more likely to be pursuing their schooling because of parental pressure rather than their own wishes or goals.

Low expectations and perceptions of the potential dropout's ability from parents and other critical social agents in the school system undermine the student's perceptions of his or her own competence and autonomy. Those perceptions then further diminish their self-determined motivation. Low levels of self-determined motivation lead them to develop intentions to drop out of school, and these intentions are later acted on when it is possible to do so (Vallerand, Fortier, & Guay, 1997).

Factors that lead to successful school achievement are helping students develop a sense of being in control within the academic domain, achieving more positive and less controlling relationships with teachers, and becoming more autonomous in decision making (Ellickson, Bui, Bell, & McGuigan, 1998; Trusty, Watts, & Erdman, 1997). Coming to class and school on time, being prepared for and participating in classwork, expending the effort needed to complete assignments in school and homework, and avoiding being disruptive in class are behaviors to be reinforced. By doing so, students are apt to develop a more self-determined motivational profile.

Adult Involvement

Another factor that appears to act as a deterrent to dropping out of school is involvement from school personnel and parents. Personal and academic support provided by adults may be especially important to students at risk. Research has demonstrated that family support is a key factor in promoting achievement among students at risk. Parents who make continuous attempts to create emotionally supportive home environments and provide reassurance when youngsters encounter failure have academically successful children. In these family situations, school performance is encouraged as being an important activity and, more important, as being accomplished through regular practice and work. Parents in these homes accept responsibility for assisting their children in acquiring learning strategies as well as a general fund of knowledge. When parents talk with their teenagers about school, courses, activities, things studied in class, and grades, their children are less likely to harbor thoughts of leaving school (Trusty et al., 1997).

Extracurricular Activities

Participation in school activities may lead students to acquire new skills (organization, planning, time-management, and so on), to develop or strengthen particular attitudes (discipline, motivation), or to receive social rewards that influence personality characteristics. Extracurricular activities can serve as protective mechanisms that improve a student's chances of school success in spite of being a member of a high-risk group (Finn & Rock, 1997).

Organized sports, special-interest academic pursuits, vocational clubs, supervised student government, and newspaper and yearbook committees are examples of the various types of school activities that can raise an individual's status within the school and extend her or his social affiliations in the school community

© Michael Newman/PhotoEdit

Being involved in extracurricular activities decreases the adolescent's chances of dropping out of school.

(Csikszentmihalyi, Rathunde, & Whalen, 1993). The impact is to render school a more meaningful and attractive experience for students who have experienced few successes in academic subjects. In terms of reducing the dropout rate, the least competent students benefit most from extracurricular involvement (Mahoney & Cairns, 1997).

The picture that emerges from research is that dropping out of school is not so much a decision that is made during the adolescent years but rather is the culmination of a long process. For the dropout, this process is characterized by a history of repeated academic and social failure and increasing alienation from school. Given the high dropout rates and the enormous resultant social and financial consequences, it would be worthwhile to invest in prevention programs that systematically identify students at early ages and provide them with the motivation, skills, and successes they need (Stone, 2001).

Concept Checks

1. John Holland suggests that it is essential for optimal vocational development to achieve a good match between the individual's ______________ and occupational ____________.
2. The most positive aspect of adolescents' part-time employment is ________________; in contrast, __________ describes its most negative impact.
3. ***True or False:*** Most dropouts fall behind in their academic skills and the grades they receive.
4. Potential help for dropouts may come from establishing
   a. good relationships between the adolescent's parents and school.
   b. a way to help give them a feeling of control over their behavior.
   c. rules against disruptive behavior and disobeying school rules.

Language Development

Before Beginning ...

After reading this section, you will be able to

- examine language achievements during the adolescent period.
- recognize communications that close the door to further communication.
- describe effective ways of communicating with others.

Refined Understandings of Language

Although language acquisition is basically complete by the beginning of adolescence, important refinements continue. There is greater precision in speaking, more sophistication in writing, and better comprehension in reading. Beginning around age 13, children no longer focus on the literal meanings of metaphors, parables, and proverbs. For example, in interpreting the proverb, "People in glass houses shouldn't throw stones," a 5-year-old might comment, "Because it breaks the glass"; a 7-year-old might relate, "You know people don't live in glass houses"; and a 9-year-old might say, "If you buy a glass house, expect to have a window broken." However, a 13-year-old might say, "If you hurt people, you may get hurt yourself." Thirteen-year-olds are able to understand that words can have symbolic meaning beyond their reference to physical objects.

Adolescents continue to increase their vocabulary and refine their understandings of word meanings as well. Their definitions are more abstract, and they often include the superordinate category to which the object belongs. An adolescent, for example, might define a chair as a piece of furniture on which people sit. A younger child will indicate that a chair is for sitting but would not mention the class of things—furniture—to which it belongs.

Julio uses clear, concise, logic statements when he is debating for the school debate team; after school he meets with some friends and laughingly informs them of an incident that occurred during gym class and the awesome job he did for the debate team.

Varying one's language style according to the situation begins early but continues to undergo refinements throughout childhood and adolescence (Nippold, 2000). Learning the purposes and ways in which words and sentences are used in conversation is known as **pragmatics**. Knowledge about the pragmatics of language can range from taking turns in conversations to using more formal or polite language in appropriate situations (conversing with a teacher, for example) and less formal and casual language with friends. Conversing with friends may also involve using slang words and body and facial expressions.

Nonverbal Behaviors

A lot can be communicated even when nothing is said; nonverbal behaviors—gestures, postures, facial expressions, and even the distance between you and the other person—send a message. For example, if you are interacting with someone who stands far away from you, farther than you think is normal, is this communicating something to you? What would happen if you tried to move closer and the person moved farther away? You might get the impression that this person did not really want to talk with you.

What about talking with a person from another culture? If you are unfamiliar with the language you can look up key words, but there is not a dictionary for the silent, nonverbal languages of the world. Meanings of words can change considerably, depending on the accompanied nonverbal behaviors. In Japan, *hai* in most dictionaries means "yes." But the word does not necessarily mean yes when accompanied by various gestures. *Hai* accompanied by a head nod means "I am listening." Without eye contact, *hai* means "no."

Eye contact, or lack of it, sends a powerful nonverbal message. If you are talking with someone whose eyes are diverted from yours, you probably think they are not interested in your conversation. In Arabic cultures, however, eye gazing is done much more frequently. In fact, Arabs tend to think Americans tend to gaze too little. Even within the United States, there are differences in gaze and visual behavior between different ethnic groups. African Americans, for example, tend to gaze less directly than do European Americans when interacting with someone (Fehr, 1981).

Gestures convey messages as well. Some cultures (Italians, for example) tend to be very expressive in their gestures when speaking—often using large arm movements. Other cultures (Japanese, Thai) tend to be much more reserved, using gestures as illustrators. To more "reserved" cultures, arm and hand gestures may be quite threatening. Each culture has a different set of gestures and meanings. When we point with our index finger toward our head, it generally means "I'm smart." In some parts of the world, however, it means "I'm stupid." Just as verbal languages differ from culture to culture, so do nonverbal languages. Often, we are so accustomed to sending and receiving nonverbal messages, we often do so automatically and sometimes unconsciously. Because nonverbal language makes a tremendous impact on our verbal message, it is important to recognize its valuable role in the communication process.

Communication Patterns

My mom and I always try our best to talk, and I talk with her more than with my father. I do not feel comfortable talking about certain things with him because he is my dad. My dad works a lot and the only quality time we can spend together is if we watch a football game or fix stuff around the house. I don't necessarily enjoy doing things he likes to do but I get to spend time with him so I deal with it.

In comparing gender differences in communication patterns, adolescents talk more with their mothers than with their fathers. Adolescents tend to see their mothers as both initiating more discussions with them and recognizing and accepting their opinions more so than fathers. They describe their communications as more open, despite the fact they report more conflict with mothers than with fathers. The higher level of conflict with mothers is likely to be related to the fact that the adolescent tends to have more frequent and more meaningful communications with mothers than with fathers (Herman & McHale, 1993).

This also has been found in samples of European American, African American, and Latino adolescents (O'Sullivan, Jaramillo, Moreau, & Meyer-Bahlburg, 1999) and across other cultures, such as in China (Shek, 2000). Adolescents also tend to discuss a wider range of topics with their mothers than their fathers. Daughters report stronger relationships with mothers than with fathers; mothers are seen as being more open, understanding,

pragmatics Learning the purposes and ways in which words and sentences are used in conversation.

and accepting. Fathers are more likely to impose authority, and as a result adolescents tend to limit self-disclosure to fathers. For example, in a sample of U.S. and Chinese children from Hong Kong, China, fathers were perceived to be less responsive and to demonstrate less concern; subsequently, adolescents were less likely to communicate with their fathers (Shek, 2000; Socha & Diggs, 1999).

Daughters more than sons communicate more frequently with their mothers about sexual attitudes and relationships (O'Sullivan et al., 1999). They tend to discuss their interests, their relationships with others, sexual problems, and general problems with mothers more so than with fathers. The amount of communication about sexual matters, however, is quite limited, especially with sons. Many adolescents report that they would like to have better sex-related communications with their parents, and many parents report that they want to be active resource agents for sex education. However, many parents report that they do not know how. It seems apparent that we need more resources in helping adolescents and parents open up to one another on this important topic.

Typical Ways of Responding

The most important aspect of language is communication, an interaction between two or more people that involves an exchange of information. When communication problems exist, adults sometimes remark that teenagers just "clam up and don't say anything anymore." Adolescents may remark, "Parents boss too much. My mom is always telling me what to do. Sometimes I want to plug up my ears when she opens her mouth." (Many do.) Most scholars agree, however, that good communication skills between adults and children should begin when children are young. The earlier effective communication strategies can be applied, the better adult relationships with children will be.

Many adolescents and their parents report good communication patterns (as Marilyn and Michelle relate in the First Person segment). Other adolescents, however, experience problems communicating with their parents—particularly parents who criticize them for being disobedient, breaking family rules, not being ambitious enough, and being messy and sloppy. The greater the level of parental criticism, the lower the communication level and the personal relationship. When communications consist mainly of criticisms, a vicious cycle is perpetuated: criticisms lead to low self-esteem in adolescents, which leads to more negative behavior and subsequently more criticism from parents. Criticism is just one way in which adults' responses can close the door to further communication.

Thomas Gordon (1970) points out typical ways in which adults respond to adolescents and the subsequent feelings they arouse in them. Often adults simply *order or command:* "As long as you live in this house, you will do as you are told to do." Many adults *moralize or preach:* "When I was your age, my parents didn't help me with my homework. It was up to me to finish it." They *judge and criticize:* "You are such a messy kid; your room looks like the city dump." They *advise and give solutions:* "Listen to me; I know what's best. If I were you I would spend more time studying." These kinds of communications close the door to effective communication. They communicate unacceptance of the individual, produce fear of the adult's power, cause feelings of guilt, and make the adolescent feel inadequate and inferior.

Solution-Type Messages

The typical ways of responding are often used to send what Gordon (1970) calls a "solution-type message" to the adolescent. For example, adults may not wait for the adolescent to initiate appropriate behavior; they simply blurt out what the adolescent must, ought, or should do. How would you respond in the following situation? Suppose you are up for a promotion and your boss is coming over for dinner. During dinner, he happens to put his feet on the rungs of one of your new dining room chairs and scrapes them back and forth as he carries on his conversation. Most of us would not say to him "Get your feet off my chair this minute!" This sounds ridiculous in a situation involving another adult, because most people treat other adults with more respectful communications. Most likely (if you say anything at all) you might send some message, such as, "I am really worried that my new chair might get scratched by your feet."

The Put-Down Message

Similarly, adults tend to send "put-down" messages: "You lose everything; you're so irresponsible." "John, you are never prepared for your math work; why don't you wake up!" It seems that most adults do not use these put-downs to intentionally wound adolescents and destroy their self-esteem; the statements are made with the hopeful expectation that they will somehow change the adolescent for the better. However, if adults could really understand just how devastating these comments can be, they would use some other form of verbal message in an attempt to change negative behavior.

Adults can use a number of techniques to increase their effectiveness as communicators with children and adolescents (as well as with other adults). Being a good listener, engaging in active listening, and sending "I" messages are important techniques that will help to establish a positive relationship between adult and adolescent and open the door to further communication.

APPLICATIONS:

Communicating with Adolescents

One of the most effective and constructive ways of responding to adolescents is to offer them an invitation to say more and to share their own judgments, ideas, and feelings by giving responses that reflect their thoughts—a technique known as **active listening**. The listener restates, in his or her own words, the emotional feelings behind the message the speaker has just sent. It involves paraphrasing the speaker's emotional message, not parroting his or her words. If the message is simply repeated verbatim, there is still a great chance that the listener might be misunderstanding what has been said. Simply feeding back a person's emotions often helps the adolescent sort out and solve the problem.

For example, in responding to the adolescent who has just discussed a boring work situation, one might say, "When you talk about all the petty tasks your boss gives you, I hear you saying that you're hurt and disappointed that she hasn't given you more responsibility." These comments are phrased tentatively, not dogmatically. Adults are sharing an interpretation and allowing the speaker to decide whether or not it is correct. Active listening is a great way to get through the layers of hidden meanings.

Active listening is not meant to be used in all situations. Sometimes adolescents are just looking for information and not trying to work out their feelings. At times like this, active listening would be out of place. In addition, active listening takes a great deal of time. Therefore, if adults are in a hurry and do not have time to listen, it is wise to avoid starting a conversation that cannot be finished.

FIRSTPERSON

A Mother and a Daughter on Communication

Parent-child communication occurs in different ways; one obvious way is through talking with each other. Other types of communication such as body language, facial expressions, and even eating habits can all communicate something between people who are close to each other. I feel my daughter Michelle and I have fairly good communication on all these levels. If she is quiet, has a pouting expression on her face, or doesn't want to eat some of her favorite foods, I know something is wrong. She doesn't tell me everything; I wouldn't want her to. There are some things that she needs to work out for herself. When she doesn't want to talk, I wait until she is ready. Sometimes, a trip to McDonald's helps to cheer her up and helps her to discuss her current problem. Do we get angry at each other and sometimes engage in "heated" discussions? Yes, we do. But, even when arguing, communication is about respect and a willingness to listen.

—*Marilyn Graves*

My mother and I seem to mesh well together. I can still remember coming home from grade school and the first thing my mother would say was, "How was your day?" And I would pour out every little detail. We both heard horrible stories about some teens rebelling against their parents and how bad these years could be when parents and teens don't talk to each other. Although my mother and I never discussed this, we both made it very clear that we were not going to allow those types of things to happen to us. Because our communication bridge was built early on, I knew she would be there for me. Now don't get me wrong, we have our little tiffs, and we certainly do not agree about everything, but I feel comfortable in confiding with my mom. I know she cares, and she never lets a day go by without asking, "How was your day?" and just as when I was little, I tend to confide in her.

—*Michelle Graves*

I Messages

Adults, when communicating with teenagers, often send "you" messages, which imply sending a judgment. "You are always picking on your younger brother." "You are being inconsiderate when you blast your stereo like that." A more constructive approach is to rephrase these sentences to begin with an "I" plus a description of the speaker's feelings. "I get upset with all this fighting." "I cannot think straight when the music is being played so loudly." Adults simply say how the adolescent's behavior is making them feel. In this way the adult is taking responsibility for and acknowledging ownership of their thoughts, opinions, and feelings. The message focuses on the adult, not on the adolescent.

active listening Involves paraphrasing the often unspoken emotions that often accompany the speaker's verbal message.

Concept Checks

1. *True or False:* Adolescents tend to have more positive communications with their mothers and argue less with them.
2. A typically ineffective way to communicate with others is to
   a. advise and give solutions.
   b. ask questions.
   c. show empathy.
3. Active listening involves reflecting the speaker's ________________ in a nonjudgmental way.

Reviewing Key Points

The Adolescent's Thinking Skills

- In the cognitive realm, adolescents enter Piaget's formal operational thinking stage. Adolescents in this stage can now reason abstractly, hypothetically, and inferentially. Two new structures in their thinking are combinatorial analysis and hypothetico-deductive reasoning. Combinatorial analysis allows the formal thinker to hold one variable constant while testing combinations of variables in an attempt to separate the effects of several variables in an experimental situation. Hypothetico-deductive reasoning is a "scientific method" in which adolescents begin with a general hypothesis of all possible factors that may affect the outcome and deduce a specific hypothesis about what might happen and then test it.
- Robert Siegler proposed that children will develop one of four possible rules, which they will use when attempting to solve various balance-scale problems.
- Metacognition (knowledge about how memory works) and a knowledge base (what adolescents know) are responsible for differences in adolescents' memory performance. With a good knowledge base, "experts" as compared with "novices" tend to process information from that domain rapidly and display advanced levels of memory performance.
- Psychometric researchers are interested in quantifying intelligence. Achievement or assessment tests (SAT and ACT) are given in the last two years of high school and often determine college placement. Boys perform significantly better on both the math and verbal portions of these tests. Based on the results of IQ tests, adolescents are often labeled as an overachiever or an underachiever.
- Some of the factors that will help underachievers succeed in the school setting involve parental expectations (parents valuing education and achievement); parental involvement; giving the child attention that goes beyond just school and academics; providing an academic environment in which the child feels responsible for the caliber of work he or she is doing in school; and helping the underachiever see the "separateness" of his or her life.

Possible Outcomes of the Adolescent's New Thinking Skills

- Adolescents often fail to differentiate between what others are thinking and their own thoughts, they imagine that others are as wrapped up in their concerns over behavior and appearance as they are. Adolescent egocentrism may also take the form of personal fable, in which teenagers typically feel that they are invincible and invulnerable. They also tend to feel very unique ("No one could possibly understand how I feel"). By learning to take the perspective of others and forming intimate relationships with others, imaginary audiences and personal fables begin to decline in later adolescent years.
- Idealism is another consequence of the adolescent's new thinking skills. Adolescents can now imagine an ideal world and ideal parents in which reality has a way of never measuring up. Although it may seem that the adolescent is hypocritical, saying one thing one minute and violating those same principles the next, most experts agree that this is a case of intellectual immaturity not hypocrisy.
- Early adolescence seems to be a period of bickering and seemingly constant confrontations. Actually, warm, pleasant relationships are more prevalent in most parent–adolescent relationships than arguments. The roots of most conflicts are over mundane, everyday issues, such as friends, schoolwork, and dress. Elkind believes that the cause of most conflicts between parents and adolescents involve real or imagined violations related to responsibility and freedom.
- Conflict is not always necessarily negative; it can provide for growth and communication. This is best fostered in families in which parents and adolescents have a warm and caring relationship. Homes in which parents expect mature behavior, set and enforce reasonable rules, encourage the adolescent to express his or her ideas and feelings; are sensitive to the adolescent's needs; and limit confrontations to those issues that really matter tend to have less contentious teenagers.

Adolescents and School

- Deciding which curriculum can best meet the academic and nonacademic needs of high school students is difficult. For "forgotten" non–college-attending students, vocational training is often an important means for them to be able to successfully adapt to society as an adult.
- Schools today often lack a coherent and challenging curriculum for those who will enter the working world upon graduation. Holland points out that it is crucial to prepare students for the job market by receiving information about market demands, what kinds of skills are required for certain jobs, and knowledge about individual personality skills that will match the characteristics of his or her chosen career.
- Teenagers spend a considerable amount of time working in outside paid employment during high school. Despite what adults may believe, working in excess of 20 hours of week may cause adolescents to experience high amounts of stress and suffer from poor academic achievement. Most youths who work spend their earnings in self-indulgent ways on luxuries not necessities. A small number of teenagers want to work but are unable to find employment; the majority of unemployed youths are high school dropouts.
- An alarming number of adolescents drop out of high school each year. It is suggested that helping these at-risk students to develop a sense of control within the academic domain, achieve more positive relations with teachers, become more autonomous in decision making, and become involved in extracurricular activities are deterrents to dropping out of school.

Language Development

- The most important aspect of language is communication. Adolescence is a time when many adults complain of a breakdown in communication. It has been suggested that breakdowns in communication may occur because adults, when communicating with teenagers, often ask too many questions, use "you" messages or send "put-down" messages—all of which close the door to further communication.
- Using active listening, reflecting the adolescent's feelings in a nonjudgmental and nonaccusative manner, and using "I" messages are effective ways to open the door to further communication.

Answers to Concept Checks

The Adolescent's Thinking Skills

1. c
2. metacognition
3. withdrawn underachiever
4. true

Possible Outcomes of the Adolescent's New Thinking Skills

1. personal fable 2. idealism 3. a 4. b

Adolescents and School

1. attributes; characteristics
2. they acquire survival skills; developing a cynical attitude toward work or thinking in unethical ways
3. true 4. b

Language Development

1. false 2. a 3. feelings

Key Terms

active listening
combinatorial analysis
formal operational thinking
hypothetico-deductive reasoning
imaginary audience
knowledge base
metacognition
overachievers
personal fable
pragmatics
underachievers

InfoTrac College Edition

For additional readings, explore InfoTrac College Edition, your online library. Go to **http://www.infotrac-college.com/wadsworth** and use the passcode that came on the card with your book. Try these search terms: high school dropouts, adolescence communication.

Child Development CD-ROM

Go to the Wadsworth Child Development CD-ROM for further study of the concepts in this chapter. The CD-ROM also includes quizzes and additional activities to expand your learning experience.

CHAPTER SIXTEEN

Socioemotional Development: *Adolescence*

CHAPTER OUTLINE

Understanding Self and Others
- Self-Understandings
- Friendships in Adolescence
- Identity Issues
- Gender Roles in Adolescence
- Applications: Rewriting Gender Scripts

Emotional Concerns in Adolescence
- Juvenile Delinquency
- Teenage Suicide
- Applications: Warning Signs of a Potentially Suicidal Teenager

Moral Development
- Moral Reasoning in Adolescence
- Moral Feelings: Guilt
- Morality and Peers
- Applications: Morality and the Power of Parents

Family Influences During Adolescence
- Emotionality
- Emotional Separateness from Parents
- Emotional Connectedness to Peers and Parents
- Applications: Fostering the Adolescent's Emancipation Proclamation

Reviewing Key Points

My son, who is 13, has started going to dance parties. Only minutes ago he was this little boy whose idea of looking really sharp was to have all the Kool-Aid stains on his He-Man T-shirt be the same flavor; now, suddenly, he's spending more time per day on his hair than it took to paint the Sistine Chapel. And he's going to parties where the boys dance with actual girls. Fifteen minutes before it was time to leave for Robby's first party, he strode impatiently up to me, wearing new duds. My wife and I arrived at the dance-party home . . . where the kids were dancing. We tried to watch Robby, but he gestured violently at us to leave, which I can understand. Two hours later, when we came back to pick him up, the kids were slow-dancing. By peering through a window from another room, we could catch glimpses of couples swaying together. My son was in there somewhere. But not my little boy. (Dave Barry, syndicated columnist)

As we venture into the socioemotional world of adolescence, it will become apparent that the teenage years represent more than just a shift from the "Kool-Aid stained shirts" of middle childhood to the "slow-dancing" of the young teenager. The individual moves toward advancements in self-knowledge, intimacy with friends, developing a sense of identity, and, for a period of time, intensification of stereotypical gender roles. These topics form our opening discussion of adolescence.

The period of adolescence often can best be described by the opening lines of Charles Dickens' *A Tale of Two Cities:* "It was the best of times, it was the worst of times. . . ." Paradoxically, adolescence is a time of excitement and anxiety, of discovery and bewilderment, of happiness and troubles. To many adolescents it is the best of times—pizza and burgers, high school dances, first loves, learning to drive a car. To some it is the worst of times—depression and alienation—which, for a tragic few, can lead to juvenile delinquency and suicide. These latter topics are discussed in the second section of this chapter. Fortunately, most teenagers are happy with their lives, and most "get it together" without getting into trouble.

We will then turn to moral development during adolescence. Sixty-seven percent of U.S. high school and college students report cheating on exams. Further, most report they do not feel guilty about doing so. Does this surprise you? What types of experiences produce guilt in adolescents? What types of values do adolescents have? Are they unduly influenced by peers? Do adolescents struggle with peer-approved versus parent-approved values?

Separating emotionally from parents becomes an important task during adolescence. This means being able to make decisions and stand by the consequences of those decisions. Changes in social roles and personal capabilities transform relationships in the adolescent's family, and by the end of adolescence individuals are far more emotionally independent from their parents than they were as children. But, even though teenagers need space and separation from parents, they still need to have their dependency needs met as well. *Get out of my life, but first could you drive me and Cheryl to the mall?* is the title of Tom Wolfe's best-selling book, and it nicely captures the teenager's vacillation between needs for independence and dependency.

Understanding Self and Others

Before Beginning . . .

After reading this section, you will be able to

- note the changes that occur in self-systems during adolescence.
- describe the adolescent's changing conceptions of friendship.
- analyze identity issues confronting teenagers.
- think about gender-role transitions during adolescence.
- note possible ways of promoting androgynous behavior in adolescents.

Self-Understandings

The emergence of formal operational thinking (see Chapter 15) substantially affects the adolescent's self-concept and self-esteem (Petersen, Compas, Brooks-Gunn, Stemmler, Ey, & Grant, 1993). During the adolescent period there are several dramatic changes in how the self is construed—changes that reflect, in part, a rapid growth in cognitive capacities.

Self-Concept

In early adolescence, the adolescent begins to view self-defining traits as stable across time and in various situations (Harter, Waters, & Whitesell, 1998). The belief in such enduring personality traits enables young adolescents for the first time to remove the self from the immediate present and to establish links between their past, present, and future selves (Damon, 1998). Whereas younger children invariably describe themselves in terms of the immediate present, adolescents describe themselves in terms of their past and future. As one example, the adolescent might say, "I use to be sort of a class clown, but now I feel more serious about doing well in school so I can get into college."

Adolescents begin to describe themselves more in terms of psychological traits (their feelings, personality traits, and their relations with others), reflecting on an inner world of thoughts and feelings (Bandura, 1997). Thus, with increasing age, an individual's self-concept becomes more introspective. Adolescents no longer describe themselves in terms of specific acts and qualities but of abstractions and general evaluations. They also engage in more self-reflection. The advent of formal operational thought is, in the view of many theorists, a prerequisite for this ability to think about one's thinking and to reflect on internal events, a skill that does not become fully developed until adolescence (Montemayor, Adams, & Gullotta, 1990).

In addition to the increased use of abstract psychological terms, the descriptions of early and late adolescents are more likely than those of younger children to include explanations for and qualifications of the self-descriptions and descriptions of others (Harter, Stocker, & Robinson, 1996). For example, in describing a friend, an adolescent might say, "He's not very smart, but then again, he doesn't study." Such descriptions are indicative of both a greater ability to organize one's thoughts and a greater recognition of the multidimensional nature of personality.

Further, adolescents are capable of acknowledging that the self can be characterized by traits and qualities that are opposites, for example, that one can be smart in one thing and not good at something else, "I'm great in English, but math is hard for me." Moreover, the use of the number of these paired oppositions increases dramatically between the seventh and ninth grades (Harter, 1993).

Self-Esteem

Do you have above average leadership ability? How well do you get along with others? In a national survey of U.S. college students (Myers, 1987), 70 percent thought they were above average in leadership ability and 0 percent thought they were below average with respect to their ability to get along with others. What percentage of the population at your college or university has higher intellectual abilities than you do? When this question was asked of U.S. and Japanese students, U.S. students assumed that only 30 percent of people on average had higher intellectual abilities than they did (Markus & Kitayama, 1991). The Japanese, however, thought that 50 percent of the students were better than they. Here in the United States, we tend to think that positive self-esteem is a powerful predictor of behavior and try to enhance individual feelings of self. (As early as age 4, U.S. children think they are better than most people.) Across cultures, the form of self varies. In Japan, self-effacement is emphasized, not self-enhancement (Crocker, Luhtanen, Blaine, & Broadnax, 1994). It is culturally incorrect to think one is too great or too competent. It is apparent also that within cultures and ethnic groups self-esteem may vary, particularly along gender lines.

Gender Differences Teenage boys tend to evaluate themselves differently from their female counterparts. Both, however, tend to define themselves along stereotypical gender-role lines (Friedrichsen, 1998). Herbert Marsh in samples of European American subjects (Hattie & Marsh, 1996; Marsh, 1989) found that sex differences in self-esteem are consistent with sex stereotypes. Boys have higher self-esteem in achievement and leadership; girls have higher self-esteem in congeniality and sociability. Boys tend to evaluate themselves as more self-sufficient and achievement oriented; girls perceive themselves as more sociable and help-seeking. Girls also had higher self-esteem as it related to competence in spelling, penmanship, neatness, reading, and music (Eccles, Wigfield, Harold, & Blumenfeld, 1993). Marsh and his colleagues (Hattie & Marsh, 1996; Marsh, 1989) reported that boys had higher self-esteem in math, and girls had higher self-esteem as it related to verbal skills. No significant differences for general ability and confidence, however, were noted.

Hispanic girls tended to view themselves along similar stereotypical lines; they saw themselves as more "feminine" than did European American girls in terms of submissiveness and dependence (Vasquez-Nuttall, Romero-Garcia, & De Leon, 1987). In contrast, African American girls were twice as likely as European American girls to describe themselves along less stereotypical and more androgynous lines (Binion, 1990). They tended to describe themselves with strong, active, instrumental traits as well as strong nurturant and expressive traits.

Cross-ethnic gender differences are apparent in the family domain and are also consistent with stereotypical conceptions of males and females (Farruggia, Dmitrieva, & Tally, 2001). Females tend to emphasize relationship, connection, and expressive function within the family context as compared with males' preference for agency and autonomy (Eccles, Midgley, Wigfield, Buchanan, Reuman, Flanagan, & MacIver, 1993). Moreover, the establishment of independence seems to be more easily achieved by males than by females (Olver, Aries, & Batgos, 1990). Adolescent females tend to experience greater increases in anxiety and self-doubt when faced with choices, along with lack of separation/individuation from the family and stereotypical cultural expectations (Ollech & McCarthy, 1997).

These self-evaluational differences in male and female adolescents appear to continue into adulthood. Self-esteem for adult women, for example, is characterized as being embedded in relationships and the emotional responses of others, whereas self-esteem for adult men is characterized as having more distinct boundaries between self and others (Izard & Ackerman, 1998). Women come to experience themselves as less autonomous than men. For men, seeing oneself as a separate and distinct person is an important aspect of their self-esteem. Females, however, tend to define themselves through others. A female comes to know herself as she is known—as a daughter, a wife, a mother. Consequently, females often defer to the wishes of others, take on the interests and orientations of others, and experience greater difficulty than men in knowing their own needs or what they genuinely want (Izard & Ackerman, 1998). Women's identity is anchored more deeply in relationships (Kernis,1993). As such, women are more in need of affirmation from others, and their assessment of their abilities is more vulnerable to criticism by others.

Explaining Sex Differences in Self-Esteem Some provocative arguments have been put forward in an attempt to explain these sex differences in self-esteem. Some maintain that it has its origins in the mother–child relationship (Ollech & McCarthy, 1997). There is more distancing and separateness between mother and son, for example, than between mother and daughter. As a result, boys are pushed out and encouraged to separate and individuate (Owens, 1997). Separation from the mother and assertion of independence are crucial for the development of masculinity. Girls, however, are encouraged to remain in a matrix of emotional connectedness. Rose Olver and her colleagues (Olver, Aries, & Batgos, 1990) reported from their studies that mothers were more highly involved and intrusive in their relationships with their daughters' lives, at all ages from infancy to adulthood, than in their sons' lives.

Reorganization of Self-Esteem During middle childhood, ages 7 to 11, girls' identification with feminine characteristics declines. Girls during this age period tend to be strong, self-confident, and outspoken. They trust their feelings and their knowledge and are not afraid to say what they think. They play sports, music, or games with little concern about the activity's gender-stereotyped "appropriateness" (Brown & Gilligan, 1992; Dorney, 1995). Adolescence, however, represents critical challenges to the development of self—perhaps more for girls than for boys.

> Tess, as a preadolescent girl, was active in all kinds of activities. Her personality was characterized by courage, competency, and energy. Her interests encompassed many areas—sports, nature, books, people, and music. Tess is now 14 years old. She seems to have lost her assertive, energetic personality and has become more deferential and self-critical. She's sensitive, slow to trust, and elusive. She also seems to have lost some of her resiliency, optimism, and spirit of adventure.

Some researchers have noted that because of cognitive, physical, and social changes during adolescence, a considerable amount of reorganization and reorientation of self-esteem takes place (Blyth & Traeger, 1991). They identify early adolescence as an apparently disturbing period in terms of self-esteem (Harter, Waters, Whitesell, & Kastelic, 1998; Roeser & Eccles, 1998). Disturbance refers to any change in a direction presumed to be uncomfortable for the adolescent. Findings, however, on the effects of early adolescent transitions and self-esteem are mixed.

Some studies report that the self-esteem of boys and girls decreases significantly across the transition to middle school (Wigfield, Eccles, Mac Iver, Reuman, & Midgley, 1991). Other researchers, however, report that boys' and girls' self-esteem either changes little or increases slightly across the transition (McDougall & Hymel, 1998). Most available evidence, however, suggests that the adolescent's self-esteem becomes less stable and more negative in early adolescence (roughly the middle school years) compared with earlier and later periods (Leary & Downs, 1995), with European American females experiencing a greater decrease in self-esteem than females in other ethnic groups (Block & Robins, 1993).

Studies on African American girls have found they do not exhibit lower levels of self-esteem during adolescence. In fact, a significant number of African American girls report higher levels of self-esteem when compared with Native American, Asian American, European American girls (Akan & Grilo, 1995; Dukes & Martinez, 1994), and Latinas (Rotheram-Borus, Dopkins, Sabate, & Lightfoot, 1996). Studies have also found that African American girls, compared with European American girls, have more positive physical and social images (Doswell, Millor, Thompson, & Braxter, 1998). Various studies have also found that African American girls' self-esteem is not significantly different from that of African American boys (Denmark, 1999; Mwamwenda, 1991).

Although African American and Hispanic American girls appear to have higher levels of self-esteem than European American girls, they do tend to experience a drop in self-esteem during the middle school/high school years according to a study by the American Association of University Women. The results of this longitudinal study indicated that among elementary school girls, 55 percent of European American girls, 65 percent of African American girls, and 68 percent of Hispanic American girls reported being "happy as I am" (AAUW, 1992). But by the end of middle school, agreement with the statement came from only 22 percent of the European American girls, 30 percent of the Hispanic American girls (the biggest percentage drop), and 58 percent of the African American girls (the lowest percentage drop). Further research is needed to determine why Latinas experience the biggest drop, after starting with the highest levels of self-esteem.

Cross-culturally, it has been reported in samples of girls in Nepal, the Philippines, and Australia that although adolescent girls seem to be less satisfied with being girls than boys are with being boys, and boys perceive themselves to be more competent than girls, that girls' dissatisfaction does not seem to manifest itself in lower levels of self-esteem (van Dongen-Melman, Koot, & Verhulst, 1993; Watkins & Akande, 1992).

Are there particular variables that make some girls more vulnerable to self-esteem reorganization? What is the specific impact of pubertal development, environmental change, and social behaviors on self-esteem? Girls who demonstrate the lowest self-esteem appear to be the ones who experience change in three major areas earlier than their peers. Girls who reach *puberty earlier*, those who embark early on the new social behavior of *dating*, and those who experience a major environmental change by *moving into a middle school setting* are a particularly vulnerable group (Harter, 1999). The pattern of environmental change, early development, and dating, although a disadvantage for girls, appears to be an advantage for boys. The boys who are maturing faster, dating earlier, and entering middle school demonstrate higher self-esteem than their later maturing, nondating, non–school-changing counterparts.

Why is it that boys and girls react quite differently to the transition into early adolescence in terms of their self-esteem? It may be that the sexes develop different value systems at this age. Girls, as noted earlier, have a tendency to value sociability or popularity and appearance. For example, when girls were asked to rank popularity, competency, and independence, they ranked popularity first, whereas the boys rated competency as most important (Harter, 1999). Others' opinions may assume a greater importance for girls.

Girls who place a higher value on popularity than boys may feel more vulnerable in middle school (Harter, Stocker, & Robinson, 1996). Also, placing value on one's appearance or looks may place girls' self-pictures in jeopardy, particularly because physical changes are more dramatic in girls than in boys (who are becoming more muscular looking). David DuBois and his colleagues (DuBois, Tevendale, Burk-Braxton, Swenson, & Hardesty, 2000) found that a positive "body image" (being thin and tall) was the strongest unique predictor of overall feelings of self-worth in a sample of European American teenage girls. African American girls tend to view a healthy body size as more physically attractive (Root, 1990).

There are some factors that tend to buffer the effects of lower self-esteem for adolescent girls. Multiple studies have found that authoritative parents, those who maintain high expectations for their children in the context of a close and affectionate relationship, tend to have adolescents with higher self-esteem (Harter, 1999). Several investigations have reported findings that the influence of perceived positive regard from parents on self-esteem helps adolescent girls in a number of different areas, including self-esteem (Baumrind, 1991). Further findings indicate that the influence of positive regard from parent to adolescent is stronger among African American girls than European American girls (Sanders-Thompson, 1999). Given the importance of the family within the Latino culture (Vega, 1995), it might be expected that similar results would characterize Latinas. In addition, positive appraisals from teachers have a significant and positive impact on adolescent girls' self-esteem across ethnic groups (Carlson, Uppal, & Prosser, 2000).

Fortunately, for most adolescents, disturbances in self-esteem usually result in nothing more serious than relative transient emotional discomfort. Self-esteem rises during late adolescence as many of the psychological and social transitions of early adolescence are accommodated and as teenagers look increasingly to young adulthood with goals and plans that they are working to achieve (Thompson, 1999).

Thought **CHALLENGE**

How might imaginary audience and personal fable (Chapter 15) affect the self-esteem of young girls?

Friendships in Adolescence

Socially, adolescents begin to compare their own views with those of society at large, and they realize that the social system in which they operate is a product of the shared views of the members of society. Friendships are seen as open relationship systems subject to change, flexibility, and growth. Trust is knowing that each partner helps the other and allows the other to develop independent relations. True close friends attend to each other's deeper psychological needs (Selman, 1980).

During adolescence, friendship changes from being defined as a concrete, behavioral, surface relationship of playing together to giving goods to a more abstract and mutually gratifying relationship of caring for one another, sharing one's thoughts and feelings, and comforting one another (Buhrmester, 1998). Friendships no longer need to be so exclusive, as pairs of friends accept each other's need to establish relationships with other people. Whereas younger children tend to express their feelings toward others in vague, global, and nonspecific ways ("nice," "kind," "good," "bad"), with increasing age, descriptions become more precise and differentiated ("cheerful," "generous," "considerate of others"). There is a greater emotional investment with peers during adolescence evidenced, perhaps, by the increase in the amount of time that is spent with friends. Adolescents spend approximately 16 percent of their time socializing and the majority of this time is spent with their friends (Larson & Richards, 1994).

clique
A small and exclusive group of individuals with similar interests.

crowd
A larger, more interpersonal, peer group consisting of 10 to 20 members who share common interests in social activities.

Cliques and Crowds

Adolescent peer groups range in size from the two-person friendships popular among early adolescent girls to the increasingly larger groups more popular in middle or late adolescence. One variety of peer groups is the small and exclusive **clique** made up of individuals with similar interests. It usually consists of four or six persons of the same sex and provides companionship and security. Cliques also tend to adopt the same images, such as dress style, to highlight the uniqueness of its members (Arthur, 1999). Often it is difficult to enter an existing clique, particularly if one is from a different culture. (See Wen Yu Su, from Taiwan, in the First Person box.)

Some research suggests that many African American and European American teenagers attending ethnically diverse schools become less accepting of one another during adolescence (Jackson, 1998) and tend to form cliques within their own ethnic group. In contrast, Jill Hamm's research (1992, 1993, 1998) indicates that more than three-fourths of Asian American and Latino adolescents in ethnically diverse high schools reported at least one cross-ethnic friend. Roughly one-half of African American and European American adolescents reported one or more friendships with peers of other ethnic groups. Contact with mixed-ethnic friends, however, is more likely to take place outside the school setting (Clark & Ayers, 1991). A dominant theme in cross-ethnic friendships is that they tend to revolve around interest- or ability-based similarities and participation in sports (Way, 2001). To adolescents of all ethnic groups, a strong component of friendship is the desire to be considered on the basis of individual characteristics rather than on the basis of their ethnicity. An estimated 70 to 80 percent of adolescents belong to cliques (Asher, Parker, & Walker, 1998). A larger, more interpersonal peer group is the **crowd**, which generally consists of 10 to 20 members who share common interests in social activities. Unlike cliques, which tend to be unisex, crowds are heterosexual. Groups of cliques generally compose the crowd.

As can be seen in Figure 16.1, in late childhood, boys and girls generally participate in small, same-sex cliques (Meyer, Park, Grenot-Scheyer, Schwartz, & Harry, 1998). As they move into the early adolescent years, the same-sex cliques begin to interact with each other. Gradually, the leaders and high-status members form further cliques based on heterosexual relationships. Eventually, the newly created heterosexual cliques interact with each other in large crowd activities, too—at dances and athletic events, for example. In late adolescence, the crowd begins to dissolve as couples develop more serious relationships.

FIRSTPERSON

Cliques and Friendships

苏 文 宇

Su, Wen Yu

See the "picture"? This is how I write my name in Taiwanese. The first name was given by my dad's father, my grandfather. *Wen* means knowledge. *Yu* means universe. It is a great name. I like it. In Taiwan we have little time for friends. I spent all day in school. I got up at 5:30 and got to school at 7:00 A.M. We would then clean a part of the school building. I would go to class from 7:40 to 5:30. I would see my friends in class but we would not talk so we could get a good report from the teacher. I did not fear teachers, but I was afraid that they would say bad things to my parents if I was not quiet and learning. We also have lots of homework and spend most weekends doing our assignments. On Sunday afternoons, though, my friends and I would play video games.

My first day at high school in America was very hard. I didn't know where to go, my English was still not very good, and I didn't know any people. American teenagers have lots of fun. They have much more free time to see movies and eat pizza. It was hard to make friends so I didn't like weekends because there was nothing to do. Americans spend much time with small numbers of friends. These small groups are for different purposes—some are for athletes, some for smart kids—and it's hard to become a part of them. I joined a chess club, and now I have my own small group of friends. My friends here think I am now a real American, but I still eat Taiwanese food.

—*Wen Yu Su*

Changing Conceptions of Friendship

An important aspect of peer relationships is the development of friendships. Some adolescent friendships offer intimacy and mutual support within two-person cliques; others are more autonomous in nature and provide similar benefits through meaningful relationships with more than one significant other (Selman, 1980). Further, there are various types of friends, including *acquaintances* whom an individual sees periodically; *companions* who share common interests through regular interaction; and *intimates,* or best friends, whose opinions and support are valued. It also appears that it is important for adolescents to be able to claim at least one best friend (Parker & Asher, 1993). Friendship conceptions undergo a great deal of change; the major changes are summarized in Table 16.1.

Intimacy

Duane Buhrmester (1998) reports that the ability to establish close, intimate friendships becomes increasingly important during early adolescence. Intimacy is often equated with the depth and breadth of self-disclosure as well as feelings of being understood, validated, and cared for. Adolescents who have friendships that are rated by both self and friend as companionate, disclosing, and satisfying tend to be more competent, more sociable, less hostile, less anxious or depressed and have higher self-esteem than peers involved in less intimate friendships (van Lieshout, Cillessen, &

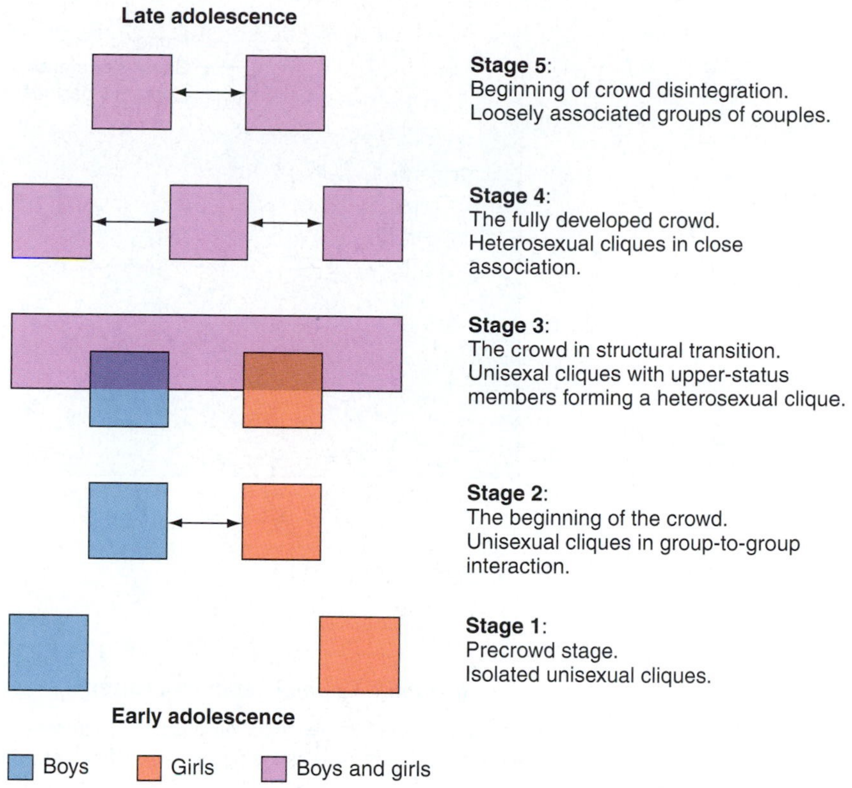

Late adolescence

Stage 5: Beginning of crowd disintegration. Loosely associated groups of couples.

Stage 4: The fully developed crowd. Heterosexual cliques in close association.

Stage 3: The crowd in structural transition. Unisexal cliques with upper-status members forming a heterosexual clique.

Stage 2: The beginning of the crowd. Unisexual cliques in group-to-group interaction.

Stage 1: Precrowd stage. Isolated unisexual cliques.

Early adolescence

Boys Girls Boys and girls

FIGURE 16.1 ***Stages of Group Formations in Adolescence***

From "The Social Structure of Urban Adolescent Peer Groups," by D. C. Dunphy, 1963, in *Sociometry, 26,* 236. Used by permission of the American Sociological Association.

TABLE 16.1

Changing Conceptions of Friendships

Concept	Description
Forming deeper relationships	Adolescents move from defining friendships in a rather superficial way, as concrete, behavioral, surface relationships, to more abstract, internal dispositional relationships of caring for one another, sharing one's thoughts and feelings, and comforting one another.
More intimate relationships	Adolescents view their friendships as intimate and supportive relationships more often than do younger children.
Sharing	Adolescents compete less and share more equally with friends than younger children.
Mutually satisfying relationships	With increasing age, adolescents shift from a self-centered orientation of the friend satisfying one's wants and needs to mutually satisfying relationships.
Enduring relationships	Adolescents change from momentary or transient relationships to those that endure over time and despite occasional conflict.
Spending more time	Adolescents are more involved with friends than are children and spend more time with them. The impact of friends may be greater in adolescence than in childhood.
Loyalty	Early adolescents regard loyalty or faithfulness as more critical in friendships than do younger children.

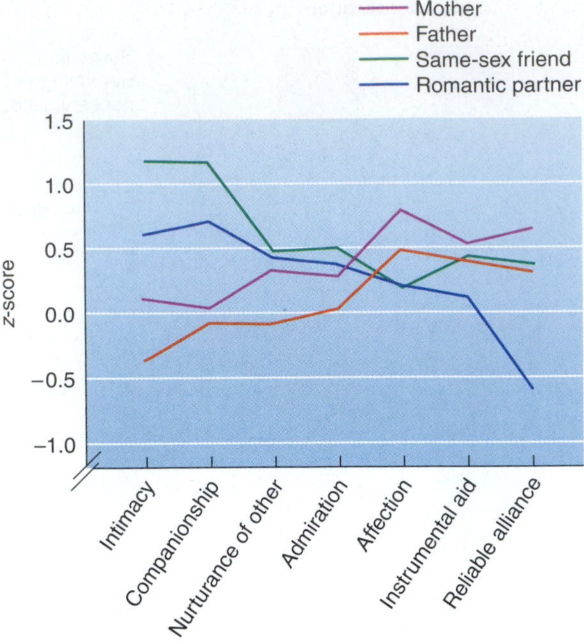

FIGURE 16.2 ***Intimacy Among Friends and Parents***

The breadth and depth of adolescents' disclosures or intimacy with others is highest with a romantic partner or a same-sex friend.

From "Friends and Lovers: The Role of Peer Relationships in Adolescent Romantic Relationships" (pp. 133–154), by W. Furman, 1999, in W. A. Collins & B. Laursen (Eds.), *Relationships as Developmental Contexts. The Minnesota Symposia on Child Psychology.* Mahwah, NJ: Erlbaum. Used by permission.

Thought **CHALLENGE**

Why is it important for boys to express their intimacy to friends in verbal ways?

Haselager, 1999). Adolescents tend to be more intimate with a same-sex friend or a romantic partner than they are with their parents (see Figure 16.2).

> The friend world is probably either the most important or second most important next to the family world. Friends are important because I can talk and share things that I wouldn't normally with my family. I can tell them things and they would see both sides of the story unlike when I tell my parents, and they usually just talk of their point of view. Friends seem to see things more clearly because they can relate to it more; whereas the parents see things how it was when they were a certain age. . . . (Phelan, Davidson, & Yu, 1996)

Boys and girls choose different styles of friendship. Consider these separate conversations between two adolescent boys and two teenage girls at poolside. The boys' conversation went something like, "Let's do the 4-3-1 sequence." After checking their timers, they dove in, leaving behind a large splash as they did the butterfly stroke across the pool. The girls, however, talked about their high school prom and discussing what they were going to wear. Boys and men tend to get together to do things, like compete; and girls and women tend to get together to bond through emotional sharing with their friends. This is not to say that girls do not engage in physical activities with friends, or that boys do not adopt emotional intimacy patterns with friends.

For the most part, however, findings indicate that friends as a source of social support is more common among girls, and they are more capable of forming intimate relationships than are boys (Furman, 1999). Other researchers suggest, however, that only boys who are highly stereotypically masculine are significantly lower than girls in intimacy (Jones & Dembo, 1998). Sex differences, however, may be merely a matter of style: Girls express their intimacy with friends by talking about personal matters, and boys express their intimacy in nonverbal ways (Newcomb, Bukowski, & Bagwell, 1999). However, scattered evidence suggests that boys' friendships are less intimate because they trust their friends less than girls do (Berndt, 1994). More boys than girls say that friends might tease them if they talk about something clumsy or foolish that they did. More girls than boys say that they share intimate information with friends because their friends listen and understand them (Azmitia, Kamprath, & Linnet, 1998).

Boys who are less stereotypical in their gender-role behavior tend to report intimacy levels with friends that are as high as those reported by girls.

Identity Issues

"What do I want out of life?" "What kinds of roles and responsibilities will I assume as an adult?"

In addition to establishing one's self within various social groups or cliques, adolescents, according to Erikson (1968), engage in an active search to try to achieve a new understanding of self, and in doing so they begin a process of forging an occupational, religious, political, and sexual identity. This search has been referred to as the **identity crisis**—a sense of confusion about who one is and what one wants out of life and the ensuing effort to "discover" or "find" one's self. An important task is for adolescents to bring together all the things they have learned about themselves as students, sons, daughters, friends, workers, and so on and begin to develop a sense of what they are and where they are going—an identity.

Development of an inner sameness and continuity of the personality is a major task of adolescence. Only when adolescents can imagine themselves in a definite, reasonably attainable role that is acceptable to them and their social environment do they feel they are unique as individuals. Establishment of a sense of identity is not a static endpoint but rather continues to evolve and change direction over the life course.

For most adolescents, the development of identity is a gradual, cumulative, and relatively peaceful process that begins in early adolescence and continues into young adulthood. Most adolescents are able to "find themselves" without losing the values and standards they acquired in childhood. In early adolescence the search for identity often leads to overidentification with peers and conformity. For a time, the adolescent may become a stereotypical teenager. The youth culture provides a ready-made identity that sets the new adolescent apart from his former identity as a child and from his identification with his parents.

If early adolescence is a time for identifying with the crowd, middle adolescence is a time for distinguishing one's self from the crowd. The quest for identity now takes the form of exploration and experimentation. The teenager tries on a variety of different political attitudes, religious persuasions, occupational commitments, and romantic involvements. In late adolescence, the search becomes more introspective—"Who am I really?" What do I want out of life? How can I achieve these goals?"

The current emphasis on identity has been stimulated by Erikson whose description of this stage has inspired a diverse and rich body of research. Notable among those who have expanded Erikson's theory is James Marcia, who defined identity status as four distinct phases.

Identity Statuses

Marcia's (1988) interviews with adolescents reveal four possible identity statuses. An individual's position on these tasks can be described along two dimensions: commitment and crisis. *Commitment* refers to a stable investment in one's beliefs with supportive activity, and *crisis* refers to the examination of alternatives with an intention to establish a firm commitment. The four identity phases, as shown in Figure 16.3, are derived from combinations of these two dimensions. They are identity foreclosure, moratorium, identity achiever, and identity diffusion.

identity crisis A sense of confusion about who one is and what one wants out of life and the ensuing effort to "discover" or "find" one's self.

identity foreclosure An identity status characterizing adolescents who have not actively questioned alternatives but have made a commitment.

Identity Foreclosure **Identity foreclosure** status exists when individuals have made a commitment before actively questioning the alternatives. This commitment is typically an extension of the values or expectations of significant others, which the adolescent accepts without consideration of alternatives. The teenager accepts without active exploration that he will be a tax accountant like his father. Hence, foreclosed commitments may be

	No crisis experienced	Crisis experienced
No commitment made	Diffusion status The person has not yet thought about or resolved identity issues and has failed to chart directions in life. *Example:* "I haven't really thought much about religion, and I guess I don't know what I believe in exactly."	Moratorium status The individual is currently experiencing an identity crisis and is actively raising questions and seeking answers. *Example:* "I'm in the middle of evaluating my beliefs and hope that I'll be able to figure out what's right for me. I like many of the answers provided by my Catholic upbringing, but I've also become skeptical about some teachings and have been looking into Unitarianism to see if it might help me answer my questions."
Commitment made	Foreclosure status The individual seems to know who he or she is but has latched onto an identity prematurely, without much thought (for example, by uncritically becoming what parents or other authority figures suggest he or she should). *Example:* "My parents are Baptists and I'm a Baptist; it's just the way I grew up."	Identity achievement status Individual has resolved his or her identity crises and made commitments to particular goals, beliefs, and values. *Example:* "I really did some soul-searching about my religion and other religions too and finally know what I believe and what I don't."

FIGURE 16.3 *Adolescent Identity Statuses*

From *Life-Span Human Development* (p. 280), by C. K. Sigelman & D. R. Shaffer, 1995, Pacific Grove, CA: Brooks/Cole.

labeled premature and deemed developmentally unsophisticated. The foreclosed group have a strong commitment to obedience, strong leadership, and respect for authority; and, according to Marcia, their self-esteem is the most vulnerable of all groups.

Moratorium The **moratorium** adolescent is actively involved in a process of exploration and experimentation with value systems, beliefs, and vocational and sex roles. Unable to make a permanent commitment, they are probers and critics who tend to challenge authority and question the system. Moratorium status exists when adolescents are in the process of selecting among alternatives, actively seeking information, and looking to make a decision. They are in crisis. The moratorium status is seen as an antecedent to the most sophisticated decision-making mode, identity achievement.

Identity Achievers **Identity achievers** refer to those adolescents who experience an optimal sense of identity. The most obvious outcomes of achieving a sense of identity are feeling at home in one's body, a sense of knowing where one is going and an inner assuredness of anticipated recognition from those who count. If an adolescent is to function satisfactorily as an adult, a conception of "my way of life" or a sense of personal identity must be achieved. Recognition of continuity and sameness in one's personality, even when in different situations and when reacted to by different individuals, leads to identity. Identity achievers are the healthiest of the four status groups in terms of general adjustment and relationship with peers and authority figures. They exhibit high levels of internal control and self-esteem and low levels of anxiety (Muuss, 1998).

moratorium
An identity status in which adolescents are in the process of selecting alternatives, actively seeking information and looking to make a decision.

identity achievers
An identity status that characterizes adolescents who questioned alternatives and made a decision; these adolescents experience an optimal sense of identity.

identity diffusion
An identity status that indicates that these adolescents have made no commitment nor are they attempting to arrive at a commitment about their lives.

Identity Diffusion

> "Who are you?" said the caterpillar.
>
> Alice replied rather shyly, ". . . I . . . I hardly know, sir, just at present—at least I knew who I was when I got up this morning, but I must have changed several times since then." (Carroll, 1865/1995)

Alice's comment from Lewis Carroll's *Alice in Wonderland* provides a most fitting illustration of **identity diffusion**. The hallmark characteristic of a person in the least sophisticated identity status, diffusion, is the lack of goal orientation, direction, and commitment. The individual may mention some vague interest in a future career but demonstrates no real understanding of the advantages and disadvantages of a particular occupation. Personal goals are subject to frequent change. An individual's self-identity must be fairly consistent, or the personality will be fragmented and the individual will suffer from identity diffusion. Individuals in this status have made no commitment nor are they attempting to arrive at a commitment in a given content area. According to Erikson, failure to accept one's self, crystallize one's goals, receive recognition from those who count, and experiment with various roles may lead to delayed commitment, to prolonged adolescence, negative identity, or adjustment problems of varying degrees of severity.

The identity diffusion status is characterized by the absence of any commitment to a system of values, by a reluctance to accept explanations, and by a tendency to challenge authority. Adolescents experiencing identity diffusion appear unable to find a direction in life or to define any goals, either educational or vocational. They may be avoiding making such long-term decisions out of fear or from psychosocial inability to explore and make decisions (Lucente, 1996).

The loss of a sense of identity is often expressed in a scornful and snobbish hostility toward the roles offered as proper and desirable in one's family or immediate community. Any aspect of the required role, or all of it—be it masculinity or femininity, nationality, or class membership—can become the main focus of the young person's acid disdain (Erikson, 1968, p. 173). An adolescent boy, for example, whose parents have constantly stressed how important it is for him to do well in school so that he will be admitted to a prestigious college, may deliberately do poorly in school or quit school entirely.

Does society contribute to identity diffusion? Adolescents are clearly given mixed messages as to when adult status is earned. We tend to tantalize youths with hints of adult status, then undermine or limit this adult-status role. As a case in point, voting and legal signatory rites are granted at 18, but the ability to borrow money from a bank on one's signature usually is not granted until the age of 23. These mixed messages keep adolescents in a limbo zone—they are not children but neither are they adults. Would a "rite of passage" transition ritual that clearly delineates "now you're an adult" help to establish a firmer sense of adult identity status? (See Child Development Issues.)

Identity Statuses and Parental Relationships

Identity status affects adolescents' relationships with their parents. Adolescents in the identity foreclosure status have the closest relationships with parents while those in the identity diffusion status tend to be more distant from their families. These individuals see their parents as indifferent to them, not understanding them, and rejecting them. Conflict is more characteristic of the families of adolescents in the moratorium and identity achievement groups. These young people are often highly critical of their parents. Tensions between adolescents and their parents seem to focus on the young person's attempts at individuation.

Research findings have left little doubt about the importance of these statuses. For instance, adolescents in the achieved and moratorium identity statuses are more cognitively mature (Boyes & Chandler, 1992), score higher on measures of internal locus of control and career planning and exploration (Wallace, Serafica, & Osipow, 1994), and hold more philosophical and analytical attitudes (Read, Adams, & Dobson, 1985) than other adolescents. By contrast, youths identified as having foreclosed and diffused identity statuses tend to hold more traditional masculine or feminine attitudes, experience more social anxiety, and display fewer prosocial behaviors and cognitions than moratorium and achieved adolescents (Adams, Ryan, Hoffman, Dobson, & Nielson, 1985). Do these results apply to all ethnic groups?

Identity Differences: Ethnic Groups

Black adolescents who have immigrated from the West Indies appear to have significant flexibility in forming their identities (Fordham, 1993). They are able to claim an ethnic identity, achieve an optimal sense of identity, and maintain a position of solidarity with their ethnically similar peers. In contrast, research based on Marcia's (1988) identity status model done on a sample of African Americans and Latinos shows that many adolescents in these ethnic groups score higher in foreclosure than do European American adolescents (Phinney, 1998). European American adolescents tend to score significantly lower than the minority adolescents on foreclosure in both interpersonal and ideological components of identity. Factors that interfere with the identity formation of minority youths are, most notably, value conflicts that exist between cultures, the lack of identity-achieved adult role models, and the lack of culture-focused specific guidance from the family (Spencer, & Markstrom-Adams, 1990). A strong ethnic identity and acceptance of their ethnicity, however, appears to assist adolescents in developing a positive sense of identity (Phinney & Rosenthal, 1992). Thus, adolescents' ethnicity can have an important influence on the development of their identity in terms of affecting their sense of self-acceptance and belonging in a world that often determines inclusion and exclusion on the basis of skin color (McGoldrick & Giordano, 1996).

Before definitive conclusions about minority identity statuses can be drawn, however, some important methodological problems need to be addressed. In previous studies, for example, confounding variables such as socioeconomic status and family constellation patterns have not been controlled. To obtain a true picture of whether the high level of foreclosure of minority groups can be attributed to ethnicity, or some other factor, it will be important for future studies to match European American and minority subjects on both these variables.

Further, all models of identity development suggest that the identity process begins with a questioning period or moratorium. For many minorities, however, this period begins not with questioning but with an internalization of the negative views of their own group that are held by the majority (Ogbu, 1997). Minority individuals may express, for example, "I believe that the white man is superior intellectually" and "Sometimes I wish I belonged to the white race." In this phase of development, minority adolescents tend to show preference for dominant cultural values over those of their own culture. Thus, this first stage of minority identity development might be compared with Marcia's identity foreclosure, in that individuals take on without question the values and attitudes to which they have been exposed. This period is then followed by a time of experimentation and inquiry, involving an effort to better understand themselves and their people (Ogbu, 1997). John Ogbu notes that the assessment procedures on the identity status of minorities may have taken place during this initial acceptance of a negative view of their own group and, thus, may reflect a transitory time, not a permanent or stable reflection of their identity status.

Promoting a Sense of Identity

Successful identity achievement is important because this allows young adults to develop mature relations with others, so that they can convey love and emotional security to them. If the identity crisis is not successfully resolved, the adolescent is faced with a sense

Child Development Issues

Rites of Passage: Are They a Necessary Step to Fostering Adult Identity Status?

Adolescence in the United States is a period when young individuals make their gradual trek toward adulthood. Many cultures, however, have no concept of adolescence as a distinct phase of development. Young individuals relinquish their child status to that of adult via rites-of-passage ceremonies.

Rites of passage are cross-cultural phenomena that have existed throughout human history. These rituals mark the end of childhood and announce that the child is now an adult. Among the Okiek, a tribal people of Kenya, both boys and girls, between the ages of 14 and 16, participate in a similar ceremony, though they are initiated separately. The initiates are first ceremonially circumcised or excised. After this, they live in seclusion from adults of the opposite sex for 4 to 24 weeks. At the end of the period the initiates, often dressed in new clothes and given new names, are returned to the community with great fanfare in their new status as adults.

Festa das Mocas Novas is an initiation into womanhood traditionally performed by the Tukuna people of the Northwest Amazon in South America. It begins with the onset of menstruation, and over the next 4 to 12 weeks, the girl remains in seclusion. She is put under the care of female relatives or of older women who teach her how she should treat her husband, her duties toward her mother-in-law, and whatever else the particular society thinks a young woman should know. For the climax of the rite, the initiate emerges from her seclusion and is led out by her family to join in the festivities and celebration of her adult status.

Cassandra Delaney (1995) notes that all rites of passage involve these basic elements:

1. A separation from society
2. Preparation or instruction from an elder
3. A transition (in the case of adolescence, from child to adult)
4. A welcoming back into society, acknowledging the adolescent's changed status

Puberty rites function generally to provide intensive instruction in adult sex roles, instill cultural loyalty, regulate and publicize the attainment of adult status, and enhance the mate value of the initiate (Weisfeld, 1997). But, what are some negative repercussions of this single, swift transition from child to adult? Further, we may ask, do adolescents in our culture suffer negative consequences as a result of not having a "child-to-adult" type of ceremony?

Whereas rites of passage are traditional in non-Western cultures, there is really nothing in our culture that corresponds to these formalized ceremonies marking the definitive end of childhood and the clear beginning of adulthood. Some adolescents do participate in *bar mitzvah* and *ba mitzvah* ceremonies; however, although the child is recognized as a "mature" religious member of the synagogue, adults do not see the child as an adult outside the religious

of identity diffusion and an inability to cope with the demands of adulthood. Identity achievers have the highest self-esteem, followed by those in the moratorium status, followed by foreclosure, and last, identity diffusion (Swanson, Spencer, & Petersen, 1998). The adolescent's self-identity, then, is crucial in the development of an integrated personality.

Three ingredients that appear necessary to consolidate an optimal sense of personal identity are (1) adolescents must carry forward from middle childhood an inner confidence about their competence and ability to master new tasks; (2) they must have ample opportunity to experiment with new roles both in fantasy and practice; and (3) they must get support in this effort from parents and adults (Erikson, 1968).

These tasks are more easily fulfilled when parents adopt an inductive, democratic style of discipline; allow adolescents to make their own decisions; and organize and adopt appropriate plans. Further, in these types of democratic home situations, adoles-

realm. In the traditional sense, then, this passage does not signal "adult status." Some decades ago, graduation from high school was viewed as a rite-of-passage ceremony. This is no longer true today, nor is graduation from college always hailed as a ceremonial signal that you are now an adult.

© Alan Oddie/PhotoEdit

In fact, some have argued that pubertal rites of passage may offer some structure during the adolescent period and other general advantages. If that is the case, there are some questions worth thinking about:

- Is it possible that our omission of any rite of passage is responsible for the lack of direction some U.S. youths experience and the apprehension with which they contemplate the future?
- Does the lack of a clear entry into adulthood and celebration of adult status foster identity confusion and interfere with the development of a stable adult personality?
- Do adolescents in the United States seek to supplement the rite of passage by seeking adult-status recognition through peers by engaging in experiences afforded by drugs, alcohol, and early sexual intercourse?

Some have suggested (Delaney, 1995) that our society needs to provide some kind of formalized structure in which adolescents are more fully prepared for their adult status and provided with a clear acknowledgement of their changed status from that of an adolescent to that of an adult. Do you agree?

Search Online

Explore InfoTrac College Edition, your online library. Go to **http://www.infotrac-college.com/wadsworth** and use the passcode that came on the card with your book. Try these search terms: puberty psychological aspects, puberty rites, adult transition.

cents are more apt to seek guidance and advice from their parents. Subsequently, adolescents strongly identify with their parents and, in turn, are more likely to internalize their parents' rules and values.

Relatedly, the strength young people find in adults at this time—their willingness to let teenagers experience life, consistency in correcting adolescents' excesses, and the guidance they give adolescents—helps determine whether adolescents eventually make sense out of their necessary inner confusion (Clinchy & Norem, 1998). By encouraging adolescents to express their own opinions and ideas, allowing them to take an active role in decision making in the family context, tolerating their assertiveness, and allowing them to consider various alternative solutions to a problem, adults help adolescents achieve identity formation during the late high school years.

The journey toward self-identity is not an easy one; small progressions may be followed by regressions. There will be times when adolescents vacillate

© Dwayne Newton/PhotoEdit

In supportive families, adolescents develop strong identities because they are able to develop independence and autonomy, and they are given more possibilities to experiment with new roles.

between the world of their childhood and the world of adulthood. Adolescents at times enjoy the safety and protection of home; at other times, they want to be free-spirited and independent.

Gender Roles in Adolescence

As children approach the middle school years, they engage in more "sex-appropriate" behavior and demonstrate polarization of their gender-role stereotypes: boys may become "Macho-Macho" men and girls may act like Scarlett O'Haras. This reorganization of gender identity and gender conceptions occurs around age 11 or 12—the threshold of adolescence (Richards & Larson, 1989). The increased flexibility of early childhood diminishes, and both boys and girls adopt more rigid conceptions of gender roles, a process described as **gender intensification** (Basow & Rubin, 1999). Gender intensification appears to apply to European American, African American, and Latino adolescents. For example, *Etiqueta* describes the "proper" gender role for Latinas, and in early adolescence, patience, nurturance, and passivity were common behaviors observed on a sample of Latinas from Rio de Janeiro, Brazil (Barker & Loewenstein, 1997). This stage is viewed as temporary and allows time for the organization of gender roles to occur. In later adolescence, we see a transcendence of gender-role stereotypes. Rigidity in gender roles, then, diminishes throughout adolescence.

gender intensification hypothesis
During early adolescence, individuals hold very rigid gender-role conceptions and behaviors.

Stereotypical Gender Roles

Girls in early adolescence, however, tend to become more self-conscious, and their competencies in the academic and social domain become more stereotyped. For example, they begin to excel in verbal skills and to invest more time in forming intimate friendships. Male adolescents show more independent behaviors, become involved in sports as participants and spectators, and display less emotional ways of responding (Galambos, Almeida, & Petersen, 1990). Because these masculine and feminine behaviors, preferences, and interests appear to be socially valued, it is not surprising that there is an escalation of "gender intensity" during early adolescence.

The best-known study of valuing gender stereotypes comes from a cross-cultural investigation involving almost 3000 individuals from over 30 countries (Williams & Best, 1994). As part of this project, students were asked to indicate whether, in their culture, each adjective was more frequently associated with men, with women, or not differentially associated by gender. The degree of consensus these adjectives received in describing males and females is amazing. In fact, Marshall Segall and his colleagues (Segall, Dasen, Berry, & Poortinga, 1999) contend that this degree of consensus was so large that it may be appropriate to suggest that the stereotypes are universal psychologically.

In the Segall study, across all countries, dominance, autonomy, aggression, exhibition, and achievement were associated with men, whereas nurturance, deference, and abasement were associated with women. In all countries, the male stereotype items were described as "more active and stronger" than the female stereotype items. The male stereotype was judged more positively in some countries (for example, Japan, South Africa, Nigeria), whereas the female stereotype was more favorably viewed in others (for example, Italy, Peru, Australia). (See Table 16.2 for more gender-associated adjectives.)

One of the most interesting of the findings relates to gender-role ideology. Ideally, what traits should men and women exhibit? European countries (the Netherlands, Germany, Finland, England) were the most "modern," believing in androgynous ways of behaving. African and Asian countries (Nigeria, Pakistan, India, Japan, Malaysia) were the most "traditional," and the United States was in the middle—generally preferring more feminine girls and more masculine boys.

In contrast, another cross-cultural study shows that in comparing Swedish and U.S. girls, Swedish girls tended to behave in more "liberated," instrumental ways (Intons-Peterson, 1988). The Swedish subjects tended to display behaviors such as ambitious, hard-working, willing to take a stand, self-reliant, and independent. In comparison, the U.S. girls acted in more expressive ways—compassionate, caring, eager to soothe hurt feelings. Similarly, Norwegian adolescent girls and boys have been found not to differ significantly on masculinity measures (Vikan & Claussen, 1994). As noted in Chapter 2, Sweden has actively pursued a governmental policy of equal opportunities for men and women. Norway's governmental practices resemble Sweden's; the United States has followed a less programmatic course. Differences in socialization practices in preparation for adult roles may explain why the U.S. adolescents were more gender stereotyped than were the Swedish and Norwegian adolescents.

TABLE 16.2

The 100 Items of the Pancultural Adjective Checklist

Male-Associated Adjectives		Female-Associated Adjectives	
Active	Loud	Affected	Modest
Adventurous	Obnoxious	Affectionate	Nervous
Aggressive	Opinionated	Appreciative	Patient
Arrogant	Opportunistic	Cautious	Pleasant
Autocratic	Pleasure-seeking	Changeable	Prudish
Bossy	Precise	Charming	Self-pitying
Capable	Progressive	Complaining	Sensitive
Conceited	Rational	Confused	Sexy
Confident	Realistic	Curious	Shy
Courageous	Reckless	Dependent	Softhearted
Cruel	Resourceful	Dreamy	Sophisticated
Cynical	Rigid	Emotional	Submissive
Determined	Robust	Excitable	Suggestible
Disorderly	Serious	Fault-finding	Superstitious
Enterprising	Sharp-witted	Fearful	Talkative
Greedy	Show-off	Fickle	Timid
Hardheaded	Steady	Foolish	Touchy
Humorous	Stern	Forgiving	Unambitious
Indifferent	Stingy	Frivolous	Understanding
Individualistic	Stolid	Fussy	Unintelligent
Initiative	Tough	Gentle	Unstable
Interests wide	Unfriendly	Imaginative	Warm
Inventive	Unscrupulous	Kind	Weak
Lazy	Witty	Mild	Worrying

From *Cross-Cultural Views of Men and Women. Psychology and Culture* (p. 193), by J. E. Williams & D. L. Best, 1994, in W. J. Lonner & R. S. Malpass (Eds.), *Psychology and Culture*. Needham, MA: Allyn & Bacon. Reprinted by permission.

APPLICATIONS:

Rewriting Gender Scripts

Do "feminine" girls and "masculine" boys feel better about themselves? Are they happier, healthier, and more well-adjusted? Or, would they be better off being somewhat androgynous, as some psychologists suggest? **Androgyny** is defined as the ability to behave in ways traditionally associated with both sexes. A male or female, for example, can be nurturant to a child, assertive on the athletic field, and sympathetic with a friend. How androgynous are you? (See Self-Insight.)

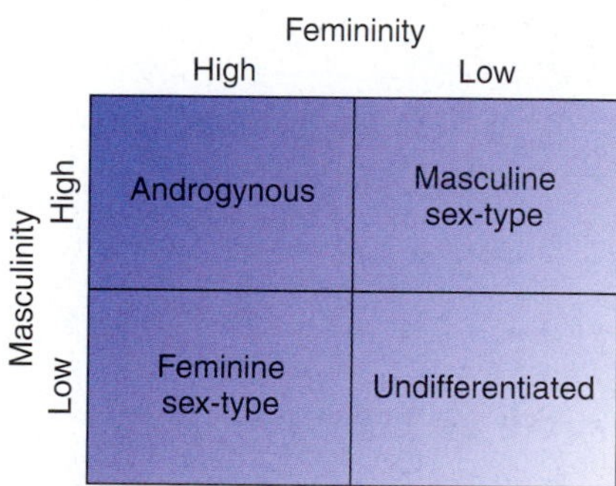

FIGURE 16.4 ***Dimensions of Masculinity and Femininity***

Androgynous individuals are high in both masculinity and femininity traits; masculine sex-types are high in masculinity and low in femininity traits; feminine sex-types are low in masculinity and high in femininity traits; undifferentiated are low in masculinity and low in femininity traits.

From *Life-Span Human Development* (p. 322), by C. K. Sigelman & D. R. Shaffer, 1995, Pacific Grove, CA: Brooks/Cole.

Sandra Bem (1981) introduced the concept of androgyny. Prior to her work, masculinity and femininity were seen as polar opposites. Being masculine meant being unfeminine and being feminine meant being unmasculine. Bem, however, believed that masculinity and femininity are different dimensions of personality rather than merely extremes of one dimension. In her conceptualization, a person can be either high or low on both masculinity and femininity (see Figure 16.4).

Androgynous Individuals

> It is pure folly that men and women do not unite to follow the same pursuits with all their energies. . . . (Plato, *Laws*, Book 7, Section 804)

According to Bem (1998), the combination of masculine and feminine characteristics is deemed to have desirable implications for an individual's behavior

androgyny Being able to behave in ways traditionally associated with both sexes as the situation warrants.

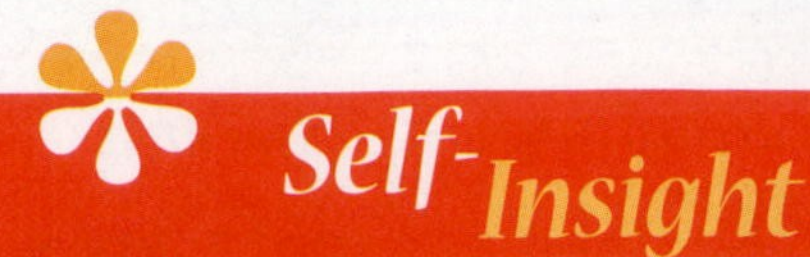

How Androgynous Are You?

	True	False
1. I like to be with people who assume a protective attitude with me.	_____	_____
2. I try to control others rather than permitting them to control me.	_____	_____
3. Adventures where I am on my own are a little frightening to me.	_____	_____
4. People like to tell me their troubles because they know I will try to do everything I can to help them.	_____	_____
5. I feel confident when directing the activities of others.	_____	_____
6. I get little satisfaction from serving others.	_____	_____
7. I am usually the first to offer a helping hand when it is needed.	_____	_____
8. If I have a problem I like to work it out alone.	_____	_____
9. I prefer not being dependent on anyone for assistance.	_____	_____
10. When I am with someone else, I do most of the decision making.	_____	_____

	True	False
11. I am quite independent of the people I know.	_____	_____
12. If I were in politics, I would probably be seen as one of the leaders of the party.	_____	_____
13. I am quite good at keeping others in line.	_____	_____
14. To love and be loved is of greatest importance to me.	_____	_____
15. I avoid some hobbies and sports because of their dangerous nature.	_____	_____
16. One of the things that spurs me on to do my best is the realization that I will be praised for my work.	_____	_____
17. I feel incapable of handling many situations.	_____	_____
18. People's tears tend to irritate me more than to arouse my sympathy.	_____	_____
19. I usually try to share my problems with someone who can help me.	_____	_____
20. I dislike people who are always asking me for advice.	_____	_____

Give yourself one point every time your answer agrees with the following key. Count your masculine and feminine points separately. The scale contains separate masculinity and femininity subscales, which are scored as follows:

Masculine
2. T 3. F 5. T 8. T 10. T 12. T 13. T 15. F 17. F 19. F

Feminine
1. T 4. T 6. F 7. T 9. F 11. F 14. T 16. T 18. F 20. F

What was your ratio of feminine to masculine scores? An equal amount indicates that you are an androgynous person. Or, did you score significantly more on one subscale, indicating distinctly masculine or feminine ways of behaving?

From *The PRF Andro Scale User's Manual*, by J. Berzins, M. Welling, & R. Wetter, 1975. Unpublished manuscript, University of Kentucky. Used by permission.

regardless of sex. Androgynous adolescents are more likely to develop a firm self-confidence and a broad range of adaptive qualities that transcend narrowly defined gender-role stereotypes. Androgynous youths have a wider range of capabilities and, depending on what the situation requires, can show assertiveness and warmth and be equally effective in many situations. These individuals are not constrained by their gender roles and are freer to respond effectively in a variety of situations and thus make a more successful adaptation to life. This appears to be true for youths in non-Western cultures as well (Shimonaka, Nakazato, Kawaai, & Sato, 1997).

Bem's (1998) work suggests that androgynous adolescents have personality characteristics that make them more adaptable to changing social conditions and situations. Androgynous males and females are capable of changing their behavior to suit the situation and thus are psychologically more adaptive and healthy (Stake, 1997). Kim Shifren (Shifren & Bauserman, 1996) reports on her sample from different ethnic backgrounds (Latin Americans, Asian Americans, and African Americans)

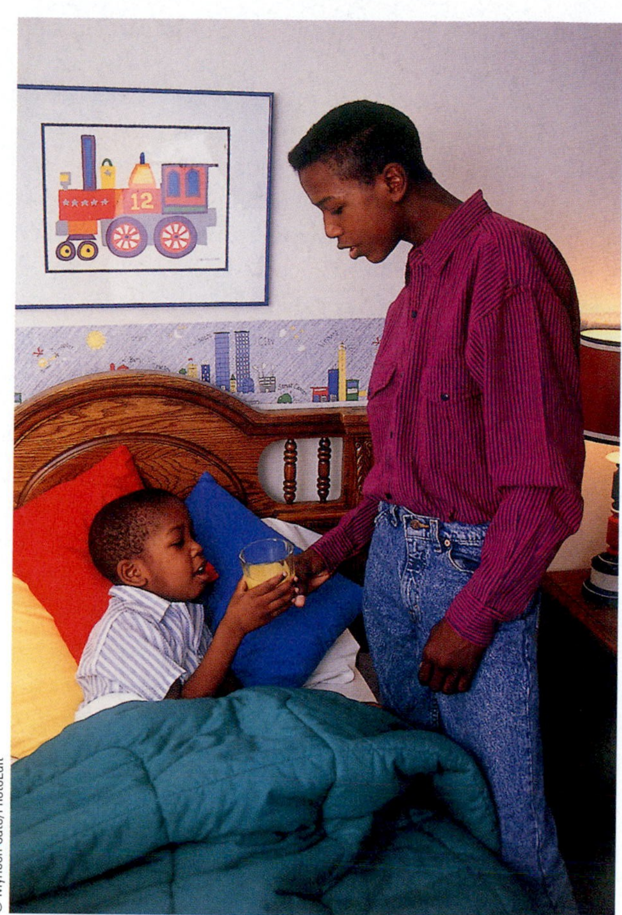

Androgyny is the ability to behave in "masculine" and "feminine" ways as the situation warrants.

that androgynous individuals report significantly better mental health than other individuals, providing further support for the androgyny model.

In contrast, other researchers note that it is the masculine traits that have been found to contribute more to heightened self-esteem than feminine traits (Sigelman & Shaffer, 1995). It is not necessarily individuals that display androgynous ways of behaving that exhibit higher self-esteem or better adjustment, but rather, in both males and females, positive self-esteem is linked to masculine traits, such as being independent, assertive, and self-confident. Males as well as females who receive high scores on masculinity scales also receive high scores on self-esteem scales and show the highest levels of self-acceptance and overall high peer acceptance (Shaffer, 1996). Thus, the evidence about androgyny leading to better adjustment is mixed.

These findings also suggest that it is easier for girls to behave, at times, in masculine ways during adolescence than it is for boys to act occasionally in feminine ways. Androgynous males may be more likely to be criticized, but, as adults, their flexibility and multiple interests and attitudes may also enable them to more successfully adapt to their surroundings (Bem, 1995). There may be a deeper message from these studies as well—perhaps our culture values masculine traits more highly than feminine traits.

Although rigid sex typing may facilitate the organization of gender roles, current research suggests that transcendence in gender roles is more desirable (Bem, 1995; Polce-Lynch et al., 1998). In our society an adult needs to be independent, assertive, and self-reliant as well as nurturant, sensitive, and concerned about the welfare of others. An androgynous person is one who combines all these traits depending on the situation. It appears, however, that *instrumental behaviors* (competence-directed, achievement-oriented) are inhibited in many women and *expressive behaviors* (nurturant, empathic) are restrained in many men (Polce-Lynch et al., 1998). Bem (1995) advises that adolescent males should learn to mitigate instrumental behaviors with expressive behaviors, and adolescent females should do the reverse. Socializing agents such as parents and educators can foster and help maintain expressive and instrumental behavior in boys and girls.

Androgynous Females

Bem notes that perhaps the reason that we are slow to see educationally and occupationally liberated women and emotionally liberated men is that parents and other influential agents in the child's world have a hard time overcoming their own socialization histories, and they continue to reinforce children's traditional masculine and feminine ways of behaving. According to traditional models, boys should be aggressive and nonemotional, are expected to do well in such subjects as mathematics, and are socialized to behave in this manner. Girls should be passive, nurturant, and sensitive. Bem (1995) maintains that we need to remove the burden of these stereotypes and allow individuals to feel free to express the best traits of men and women.

Daughters need to be taught by adults that roles labeled by society as masculine will not compromise their sense of themselves as women (Jackson & Tein, 1998). As Bem notes, the social definition of femininity needs to be broadened to include achievement and self-assertion. Exposure to nontraditional models, such as a strong, intelligent, competent female friend, boss, or mother, is another influential factor in promoting androgynous behavior in females (Gilligan, 1998). Daughters of working women, for example, conceive

© Spencer Grant/PhotoEdit

It may be more acceptable for girls to engage in "masculine" ways of behaving than for boys to engage in more nurturing kinds of behavior, which is typically considered to be more "feminine."

of the ideal woman in our society as being independent and active—adjectives traditionally associated with men.

Positive reinforcement from family, teachers, and counselors for achieving in the academic domain is perhaps the most significant factor in producing androgynous females (Wulff & Steitz, 1997). Androgynous women describe themselves as coming from high-achieving, academically oriented families. These women report having fathers who pushed and rewarded achievement or assertiveness and mothers who encouraged them to be able to support themselves and advance in school. Daughters who identify with an affectionate and competent father tend to be more assertive and competent than daughters who do not (Witt, 1997).

Athletics for girls may be another opportunity to challenge traditional gender expectations. In an investigation of 10th-grade girls, Susan Shaw, Douglas Kleiber, and Linda Caldwell (1995) found that girls' participation in sports was associated with psychological maturity, positive identity development, and androgynous gender-role behavior (being nurturing as well as independent and assertive). Other research supports the finding that girls who engage in athletics tend to be androgynous and to have more active-instrumental personality traits than do female nonathletes (Butcher, 1989). In addition, athletics may provide girls with a buffer against negative feelings toward their body image; girls may learn to appreciate the body for what it can do rather than what they must do to change it (Miller & Levy, 1996).

Androgynous Males

Across cultures men may shed tears on appropriate occasions. Male soldiers, for example, may weep over their fallen comrades. Perhaps we feel that being a soldier is sufficient validation of one's manhood to make weeping permissible. However, only under certain circumstances are boys and men generally allowed to be "emotionally expressive." Girls are given much more freedom to express emotional behavior, but boys are given strong messages to "take it like a man . . . big boys don't cry" (Polce-Lynch et al., 1998).

As a result of not expressing their feelings, male relationships may be rather superficial. Rarely does a male confide his innermost feelings to another person. As a result, many men do not receive the maximum benefits from friendships. Bem (1995) advises that males need to be socialized to express their innermost feelings. She further suggests that boys should not have to walk such a rigid tightrope to conform to masculine roles. Adults, as we have seen, put much more emphasis on their sons' conformity to masculine roles than on their daughters' femininity. Inappropriate behavior for girls does not appear to carry with it the social stigma that inappropriate behavior for boys does.

One factor that stands out as an overwhelming influence in producing androgynous males is the impact of key women in men's lives. Sensitivity toward gender-role equality appears to be influenced by exposure to competent, professional women, be it early in life with exposure to a mother figure or relative or in adolescence with a girlfriend (Barker & Loewenstein, 1997).

Boys should not just be reared to be nurturant and sensitive and girls should not just be reared to be superstar athletes. However, both society and the individuals who compose it will certainly benefit if individuals are free to develop androgynous traits. In helping adolescents to adapt successfully to a variety of situations, giving both girls and boys equal opportunities to develop nurturing and expressive traits along with fostering their academic achievement and independence is critical (Brannon, 2001).

Concept Checks

1. Adolescent males have higher self-esteem in ________________; girls have higher self-esteem in ________________.
2. Two important ways in which conceptions of friendship change involve ________________ and ________________.
3. John, despite his parents' wishes to attend college, has left home to join a commune. John is most likely in the identity status known as
   a. moratorium.
   b. identity confusion.
   c. identity diffusion.
4. Androgynous individuals are those who exhibit
   a. high levels of masculine and feminine traits.
   b. sex-atypical characteristics.
   c. a blend of masculinity and femininity as the situation requires.
5. To raise androgynous males, we need to
   a. expose them to competent, professional men.
   b. promote instrumental behaviors.
   c. broaden our definition of masculinity to include nurturing and caring behavior.

Emotional Concerns in Adolescence

Before Beginning ...

After reading this section, you will be able to

- identify factors that lead to juvenile delinquency.
- understand suicide ideation in adolescence.
- recognize the warning signs of adolescent suicide.

Every day, adolescents are faced with choices that involve doing the right thing versus engaging in unethical or illegal behaviors. Adolescents' ability to resist wrongdoing reflects socialization, which stresses the importance of subordinating individual impulses to the requirements of conventional authority or law. Although the majority of teenagers, even under duress, show a reasonable degree of adherence to moral principles, others may yield to temptation or to group pressure to engage in illegal behavior.

Juvenile Delinquency

Juvenile delinquent refers to a young person, under the age of 18, who has been apprehended and convicted for transgression of established laws. Juvenile delinquency presents a serious moral concern to society. More than 1.4 million juveniles are arrested each year for crimes such as vandalism, drug abuse, or running away, and almost 900,000 for crimes such as larceny-theft, robbery, or forcible rape (Brezina, 1998). Individuals under the age of 18 account for 17 percent of all crimes. Offenses committed by males are more apt to involve burglary, auto theft, aggravated assault, and other aggressive behaviors. Girls, however, are more likely to commit such offenses as running away from home or illicit sexual behavior.

juvenile delinquent Refers to a young person, under the age of 18, who has been apprehended and convicted for transgression of established laws.

Factors Contributing to Juvenile Delinquency

Researchers have extensively studied the variables that appear to predict the occurrence of juvenile delinquency. Although juvenile delinquency is a result of a

© Shelley Gazin/Corbis

Boys have a higher recorded delinquency incidence than do girls; however, an increasing number of females are being arrested for a widening range of offenses.

Thought CHALLENGE *Why are there significantly more male juvenile delinquents?*

number of complex factors with no single factor explaining its occurrence, high incidences of lying and stealing at an early age, poor relationships with parents, high marital discord in the family setting, dislike for school, and truancy are some of the more frequently cited factors.

Family Factors There is a long history of empirical studies that have identified family variables as consistent factors for early forms of antisocial behavior and later delinquency. A disproportionate number of juvenile delinquents come from large families in which there is poor parental supervision and poor parental behavior. Adolescents' feelings of alienation have been linked to juvenile delinquency, and these feelings appear to have their origins in the family (Loeber, Farrington, Stouthamer-Loeber, & Van Kammen, 1998). Alienation is defined as adolescents' sense of separation from work, themselves, or significant others. Families characterized by disorganization and disintegration generated by external forces such as economic and social pressures, and families in which the child is rejected, abused, and neglected, nurture an environment that is conducive to the growth of alienation. Adolescents who are raised in such unstable environments frequently respond by exhibiting antisocial behaviors such as rebelling or withdrawing from society.

Peers Many who engage in juvenile delinquent acts as adolescents were not very popular in the early and middle elementary school grades (Barrett & Ferguson, 2001). These children are often described by their peers as aggressive, unfriendly, and troublesome. The association between antisocial behavior and rejection by the conventional peer group has been well documented. Antisocial behavior and peer group rejection are important preludes to deviant peer group membership. Gerald Patterson (1982) explains how earlier social experiences contribute to children's gradually selecting deviant peer relationships by the time they reach adolescence.

The first stage underlying child antisocial behavior begins with maladaptive parent–child interaction patterns with parents providing primary attention to their child's negative and antisocial behavior. The second stage is failure in school and not being accepted by the conventional peer group. Poor performance in school results in being put in slower classes. Delinquent adolescents' poor performance in school is not due to lack of intelligence—they generally have IQs in the normal range. The one outstanding trait of juvenile delinquent adolescents, however, is that they are "educationally retarded." In other words, these adolescents have a tendency, from an early age on, to repeat grades, hate school, want to leave school, be truant, and frequently misbehave in the classroom. Further, antisocial behavior may be molded and shaped, according to Patterson (1982), as a result of rejection by normal peers and constant exposure to peers with similar behavior, social, and academic profiles. Figure 16.5 displays the developmental progression from poor parenting, to rejection by peers and school failure, to commitment to the deviant peer group, followed by delinquency.

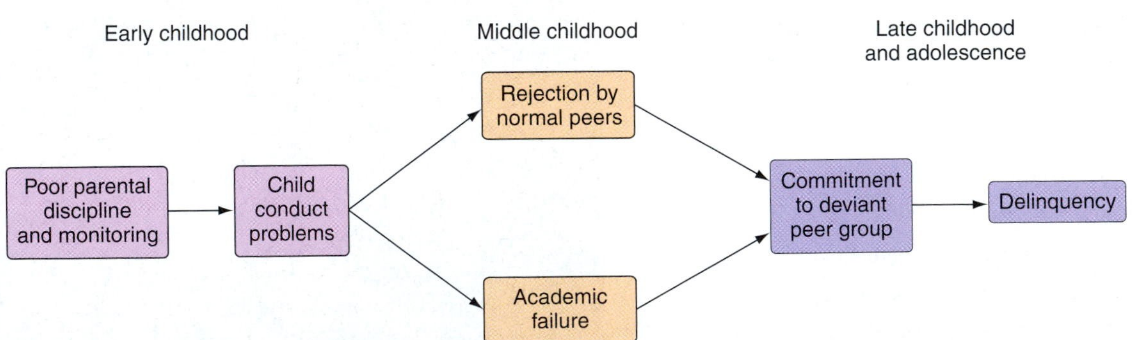

FIGURE 16.5 ***A Developmental Progression for Antisocial Behavior***

Gerald Patterson suggests that poor parental monitoring and discipline lead to child conduct problems, which in turn cause poor social and academic outcomes, leading to involvement with delinquent peers and subsequently juvenile delinquency.

From "A Developmental Perspective on Antisocial Behavior," by G. R. Patterson, B. D. DeBaryshe, & E. Ramsey, 1989, in *American Psychologist, 44,* 331. Used by permission.

Teenage Suicide

Another emotional concern in adolescence is the tragic loss of life due to suicide. In general, adolescent suicide rates in the United States are comparable to those in Australia, Belgium, and Great Britain (Orbach, 1997). Rates are lower in Canada, Italy, Norway, the Netherlands, New Zealand, and Ireland (Drummond, 1997). However, the rates are substantially higher in Austria, Denmark, Hungary, Japan, and Switzerland. In the United States, European Americans are more likely to commit suicide; African American and Latino adolescents have a slightly lower suicide rate. The rates of suicide among Latinos, however, are steadily increasing (Allen & Mitchell, 1998). The suicide rate for Native Americans is higher than for African Americans, Latinos, and European Americans (see Table 16.3). Native Americans have the highest rate of completed suicide, and suicide is the leading cause of death in this group (Centers for Disease Control, 1997; Rudd & Joiner, 1998).

No single fact about adolescents arouses more attention than the dramatic rise in the suicide rate of young people over the past 25 years. In the United States, the present adolescent suicide rate is about twice as high as 10 years ago and three times as high as 20 years ago, although the nation's overall suicide rate has not significantly varied in the past half century (D'Attilio, Campbell, Lubold, Jacobson, & Richard, 1992). The increase has been over 250 percent for young women (ages 15–24) and over 300 percent among young men (Wagner, Cole, & Schwartzman, 1995).

Young people in the 15- to 24-year-old age group now constitute one-fifth of the suicides in the United States each year—a number that reaches over 5000 a year at a near epidemic rate of 13 a day. Similarly, suicides in the 10–14 age group have increased 32 percent since 1968; it is now the third leading cause of death for this group, behind accidents and homicide. Completed suicide rates are higher for boys than girls, but three times as many girls attempt suicide (D'Attilio et al., 1992). Boys tend to use firearms and other very serious methods leading to completion. Poisoning via overdoses is used by adolescent female attempters—serious but generally not lethal.

Moreover, thoughts of committing suicide increase rapidly during adolescence—over 75 percent of adolescents have contemplated suicide at one point in their lives (Wong, 1999). The statistics on actual suicides may not be complete. There has always been a stigma attached to suicide. As a result, it may be concealed and not accurately reported. For example, in upper- and middle-class families, a death may be reported as an accident, when in fact a suicide has occurred. For this reason, suicide statistics may be higher than actually reported. Still, the reported figures provide compelling reasons for attempting to understand the nature of suicidal behavior in adolescents. It is important for parents, teachers, counselors, and all persons who have a great influence upon young people to understand this tragic waste of life.

TABLE 16.3

Suicide Rates of 15- to 19-Year-Olds by Ethnic Group

Rank	Ethnic Group	Suicides per 100,000
1	Native American males	36.4
2	European American males	19.3
3	Asian American males	12.0
4	African American males	11.5
5	Hispanic American males	10.9
6	Native American females	6.5
7	Asian American females	4.0
8	European American females	4.0
9	Hispanic females	3.2
10	African American females	1.9

From *Suicide in the United States: 1980–1992* (Violence Surveillance Summary Series No. 1), by S. P. Kachur, L. B. Potter, S. P. James, & K. E. Powell, 1995. Atlanta: National Center for Injury Prevention and Control. Used by permission.

APPLICATIONS:

Warning Signs of a Potentially Suicidal Teenager

When young people kill themselves one question always surfaces, Why? Suicide is as varied in its dynamics as are people, but research has identified some common reasons for suicide in young people. Those individuals who attempt suicide are significantly more likely than nonsuicidal youths to have experienced physical or sexual abuse by an adult caretaker, to have experienced sexual victimization, and to have a friend who has attempted suicide (Yoder, 1999). Further, the recency of onset and degree of stress may contribute to suicidal behavior (Huff, 1999). Findings also suggest that the accumulation of these risk factors greatly increases the chance that these youths will engage in suicidal behavior. Being aware of these factors and knowing the possible danger signals will help adults identify the teenager who needs help and allow the adolescent to get professional help before it is too late.

Depression

The most prevalent symptom of suicide is depression (Janos, Sandor, Emoke, Judit, & Katalin, 1999). Approximately 20 percent of adolescents experience intense depressive difficulties (Hauser & Bowlds, 1990), but it is probable that many of these adolescents were already having adjustment difficulties as children (Garber, Little, Hilsman, & Weaver, 1998). Not all suicidal adolescents, however, manifest depressive symptoms. Masked symptoms of depression may be the use of drugs and sexual promiscuity, as well as such problem behavior as acting out, stealing, and lying (Petersen, Sarigiani, & Kennedy, 1991). Minor depression can be expressed as a negative mood; major depression impairs the adolescent's functioning with associated complaints of worthlessness, suicidal wishes, and lethargy (Kovacs, 1990). Cognitive theorists have noted that whether depression is minor or major, a critical variable accounting for the relationship between depression and suicide is *hopelessness* (Flisher, 1999; Kerr, 1995; Klimes-Dougan, 1998).

One of the most prevalent symptoms of suicidal teens is a pervasive loss of interest or pleasure and persistent anxiety and dissatisfaction.

Threats of Suicide

Verbal statements, such as "I want to die. How does one go about donating organs to science?" should not be overlooked as empty threats (Flisher, 1999). They may be a danger signal. Many people mistakenly believe that individuals who talk about committing suicide do not go through with it. This does not appear to be true. Such behavioral clues as previous attempts to commit suicide should be considered serious; a history of suicidal thinking, gestures, or attempts represent high risk.

Situational Cues

Some presuicidal adolescents may seem calmer and happier than they have been in weeks (Collins & Angen, 1997). This temporary mood of exhilaration is what is known as the presuicidal mood. This could signal that the young person has come to terms with death and is ready to take his or her life. Another situational cue that needs immediate attention is the unexplained "setting one's affairs in order," in which the adolescent gives away prized possessions—like a stereo and CD collection. He or she may make out a will. These actions could indicate impending death (Oldenburg & Kerns, 1997). In addition, many adolescents are intoxicated before death; in some cases, this may indicate an attempt to disinhibit themselves in order to commit suicide.

When a parent, teacher, or concerned adult becomes aware of warning signals from an adolescent, the most critical preventive measure is to notify the appropriate mental health authorities so that the individual can receive counseling. Parents and teachers can also play a vital role by listening to the adolescent. Communication may play a larger role in preventing suicide among younger people than it does among older people. In adults, for example, suicidal behavior more frequently represents a wish to die, whereas in younger people the suicidal behavior tends to reflect a wish to bring about changes in how others treat them. The way in which one responds to the adolescent, then, is of extreme importance. Experts advise that it is best not to belittle their comments but to take them seriously. Statements such as "You're being silly"

"You're just kidding I know" "Everybody says that they want to die" need to be avoided (Angement & de Man, 1993). If adults act in a concerned manner and show that they really want to help, there is a much better chance that the adolescent will not commit suicide (Oldenburg & Kerns, 1997).

Concept Checks

1. Male juvenile delinquents are more apt to commit such offenses as ____________; female delinquents, however, are more likely to commit such offenses as ____________________.
2. ***True or False:*** Suicide rates for girls are at lower levels than boys; however, more girls attempt suicide.
3. Amilio experiences angry moods and is often violent; Ivan is shy and feels he has let his family down because he is not athletic; Marc who is generally happy has been depressed for days. Of these three teenagers, who is the most probable candidate for suicide?
   a. Amilio
   b. Ivan
   c. Marc

Moral Development

Before Beginning ...

After reading this section, you will be able to

- explain moral reasoning during adolescence.
- understand guilt and moral reasoning.
- discuss peer-approved and parent-approved values.
- understand the role of peers and adolescent conformity.

Moral Reasoning in Adolescence

The study of moral development is one of the oldest topics of interest to those curious about human nature. Moral development concerns rules and conventions centered around what people should do in their interactions with other people. The cognitive developmental model of Lawrence Kohlberg, revisited here in adolescence, is oriented toward the intellectual structures that the adolescent uses in determining behavior. Recall from Chapter 13 that Kohlberg's developmental sequence of moral reasoning consists of three levels, each comprising two stages. Level 1, preconventional morality, consists of stage 1 in which moral behavior is based on fear of punishment and stage 2 in which one's immediate self-interests dominate the child's moral behavior. In the preconventional, or moral realism, stages of moral reasoning, children in early and middle childhood see rules as absolutes emanating from such authorities as parents or teachers, and judgments of right and wrong are made according to concrete rules.

During adolescence, moral reasoning shifts to the moral relativism stage, in which absolutes and rules are questioned and the adolescent begins to see that moral standards are subjective and based on points of view that are subject to disagreement. In late adolescence, we see the emergence of reasoning that is based on such moral principles as equality, justice, or fairness—abstract concepts that transcend concrete situations (Bukatko & Daehler, 1995). Culture is also an important context for shaping adolescents' moral reasoning. (See Cultural Variations.)

Stages of Moral Reasoning in Adolescence

Lawrence Kohlberg (1976) described most adolescents as functioning at what he termed a "conventional level," in which individuals are able to understand and conform to social conventions, consider the motives of others, and engage in appropriate behavior to please significant others or to follow the rules of society. Kohlberg's level 2, conventional morality, comprises stages 3 and 4. Level 3, postconventional morality, comprises stages 5 and 6.

Stage 3: Good-Boy/Nice-Girl Adolescents' moral reasoning may be based on stage 3, *good-boy/nice-girl* morality, which focuses on mutual interpersonal expectations, relationships, and conformity. In responding to the Heinz dilemma (a man named Heinz considers whether or not to steal a drug that he cannot afford to buy to save the life of his wife), Amy, age 16, replies in this way:

> Well, I don't think he should steal the drug. I think there might be other ways besides stealing it, like if he could borrow the money or make a loan or something, but his wife should not die either.

Amy envisions the wife's continuing need for her husband and the husband's continuing concern for his wife and seeks to respond to the druggist's need in a way that would sustain rather than sever the connection. A stage 3 moralist lives up to what is expected by

Cultural Variations

Culture as a Context for Moral Development

Cultural expectations have a substantial effect on moral reasoning and moral behavior. In Japan, there is a strong connection between adolescents' aims and those of their parents. Relatedly, when discussing moral issues, Japanese youths quite often use expressions such as "ought to" or "should," reflecting a rule-oriented morality of fulfilling one's duties to parents (Mizuno, 1999). Japanese children often experience shame and guilt if they act in ways displeasing to parents.

All societies include morality as a form of internal control based on ideas of what is right or wrong, but this does not preclude differences in moral systems (Damon, 1999). Would you stop to help a stranded motorist? Would you return a wallet containing several hundred dollars? Would you not attend a party because your father did not want you to attend? It is highly probable that you would request more information about these situations so you could make some personal considerations about what you might do. However, Hindu Indian adolescents generally do not view moral matters as judgments of individual choice and discretion but, rather, as a moral obligation and would probably, without reservation, answer "yes" to these questions (Miller, 1997; Miller, Bersoff, & Harwood, 1990).

Moreover, if the situation is such that one person is dominant (such as a parent) and one person is subordinate (adolescent), as in the case of a father not wanting his child to attend a party, Hindu Indian adolescents generally believe that adults should have the decision-making power and adolescents should refrain from making independent decisions. In India, compared with the United States, there is greater concern with social roles and social positions. Thus, in non-life-threatening situations, U.S. adolescents tend to consider meeting the needs of others as a matter of personal decision making, whereas Indians tend to treat moral behavior as a matter of unquestionable duty.

Both Hindu Indian and U.S. adolescents, however, think that deceitful acts (a father breaking a promise to a child) and uncharitable acts (ignoring a beggar with a sick child) are wrong. They also share a repugnance toward theft, vandalism, and harming innocent victims, although there is some disagreement on what constitutes innocence (Shweder, Jensen, & Goldstein, 1995). Among these judgments is found a universal moral sense—based on common human aversions—reflecting core values of benevolence, fairness, and honesty.

Similarly, adolescents from myriad cultures show a deep moral concern for humanity. Peter Kahn Jr. (1997) explores the moral significance of protecting the environment, which is quite original, as most previous work on morality has focused on individuals' rights and justice. Kahn proposed various ecological problems to adolescents from Houston, Texas, and Manaus, Brazil, the largest Brazilian city within the vast Amazon rain forest. As an example, he asked them about throwing garbage into the river:

> It is not all right to throw garbage in the river because it causes pollution that is dangerous for us. Because we now have cholera, a very dangerous disease, and there are others attacking us like malaria. (Brazilian child)

> It's not right because we depend on rivers for fish or drinking water and if people drank from these polluted waters they could die because they get all that dirt and stuff inside their bodies. (Houston child)

I find these to be marvelous passages because not only do they emphasize the ecology's impact on humans, but they demonstrate that concerns for human welfare appear to be very much a part of the adolescent's moral reasoning in a wide variety of cultures, including India (Madden, 1992), Nigeria (Hollos, Leis, & Turiel, 1986), and Korea (Song, Smetana, & Kim, 1987). Kahn also found that African American adolescents who were living in an urban environment that limits their opportunities to observe natural ecological development also expressed a strong understanding of ecology and its importance to the welfare of mankind. Cross-cultural research makes us aware of both the distinctive strengths as well as collective representations of moral reasoning in various cultures. Both uniqueness and shared understandings go hand in hand in looking at, and understanding, culture.

significant others or what is generally expected of people in the role of daughter, brother, friend, and so on; "being good" is important and being good means having good motives and showing concern for others. Reasons for doing right center on the need to be a good person in one's own eyes and those of others, caring for others, belief in the Golden Rule, and a desire to maintain rules and authority that support stereotypical good behavior.

Stage 4: Law and Order Adolescents reasoning at stage 4, *law and order*, are concerned with order in society. They obey their conscience, which tells them that honor and duty come from keeping the rules of society. Civil and criminal law codes represent a more stable and comprehensive system of resolving moral dilemmas than attempting to solve such questions on the basis of social conventions or community popularity. What is right is fulfilling duties to which one has agreed; laws are to be upheld except in extreme cases in which they conflict with other fixed social duties; and right also means contributing to society, the group, or institution. A typical response at this level might be, "Heinz should not steal the drug because stealing is against the law."

Stage 5: Social Contract Level 3, postconventional morality, consists of stages 5 and 6. Stage 5, *social contract*, involves being aware that people hold a variety of values and opinions, and that most values and rules are relative to the group. Rules, however, should usually be upheld in the interest of impartiality and because they form the social contract. Some nonrelative values and rights such as life and liberty, however, must be upheld in any society and regardless of majority opinion. Reasons for doing right involve a sense of obligation to law because of the social contract to make and abide by laws for the welfare of all and for the protection of all people's rights. A stage 5 moralist might respond to the Heinz dilemma by saying, "You cannot completely blame Heinz for stealing; he probably was right to do so because of the extenuating circumstances."

Stage 6: Universal Ethical Principles Stage 6, *universal ethical principles,* is only achieved by a very few, such as Mother Teresa and Abraham Lincoln. These exceptional people follow self-chosen ethical principles; particular laws or social agreements that are valid because they rest on universal principles of justice; the equality of human rights; and respect for the dignity of human beings as individual persons. Reasons for doing right relate to the belief in the validity of universal moral principles and a sense of personal commitment to them. Someone reasoning at this stage might say, "Heinz is faced with the decision of whether to consider the other people who need the drug just as badly as his wife. Heinz ought to act according to his particular feelings toward his wife, but he needs to consider all the other lives that may be affected by his actions."

In Different Voices

Kohlberg's theory has not gone without strong criticism. The question of gender differences in moral reasoning, particularly related to stages 3 and 4, has attracted much debate. Carol Gilligan and her colleagues (Gilligan, 1992, 1998; Gilligan & Attanucci, 1998) have extensively studied adolescents' moral reasoning and found gender differences. In particular, they found that females are more likely to focus on issues related to caring and a connection between people, whereas males tend to resolve moral dilemmas by referring to principles of justice and fairness. Males, according to Gilligan, favor a justice perspective, in which the core notion is not to treat others unfairly, whereas females favor a care orientation, in which the focus is not to turn away from others. To Gilligan, neither way of reasoning is better than the other or sufficient by itself.

According to Kohlberg's theory, men tend to advocate equality, reciprocity, autonomy, and individuation, and thus, progress to stage 4 with its emphasis on the maintenance of social order; women stay at stage 3, a less sophisticated stage of moral reasoning. Gilligan argues that Kohlberg's model is insensitive to typically feminine concerns for welfare, caring, interpersonal obligations, and responsibility.

The empirical support for Gilligan's claims, however, has been mixed. Lawrence Walker (1997) finds that a nonsignificant pattern of sex differences in levels of moral reasoning exists. Moreover, girls and women can and do use fairness and justice reasoning when the problem calls for it. For example, Eva Skoe and her colleagues (Skoe, Hansen, Morch, Bakke, Hoffmann, Larsen, & Aasheim, 1999) found in a sample of Norwegian adolescents that both boys and girls resorted more to the care orientation than to justice when discussing relational real-life dilemmas, and both tended to use justice more than care when discussing nonrelational dilemmas.

Further, the differences between the moral reasoning of men and women are not absolute. For example, in one study of 80 subjects, 27 males and

Thought
CHALLENGE
If you were a college professor, how much of your work would be guided by stage 3, the ethics of caring, and how much by stage 4, the ethics of justice?

females in the sample chose both caring and justice responses to a moral dilemma. Walker has demonstrated that there is far more similarity between male and female moral orientations than differences. This evidence presents some serious problems for Gilligan's criticisms. Gilligan's ultimate contribution may lie in her broadening of assumptions about male's and female's moral reasoning and her redefining of the understanding that the really moral person must integrate the concept of abstract justice with the concern for particular others.

Moral Feelings: Guilt

Most adolescents experience some degree of guilt when they have lied, cheated, or stolen something. At an adaptive level, guilt promotes prosocial, and inhibits antisocial, behaviors. Guilt involves a sense of feeling responsible for your actions and an ability to sense that your actions have brought psychological or physical harm to another. It results from wrongdoing or from breaking a rule or violating our standards or beliefs. Guilt refers to our sense of wrongdoing, whether or not we are caught, and guilt feelings can be evoked by real or imagined wrongdoing.

The Development of Guilt

There are distinct stages in the development of guilt that are dependent on the individual's cognitive and social skills and experiences (Bybee, 1998; Bybee, Merisca, & Velasco, 1998). Perhaps the simplest case of feeling guilty occurs in younger children when they commit a *physically harmful act* such as hitting another child. Because the consequences are immediate and observable, this form is minimally demanding, cognitively speaking. In addition, an adult is usually around to point out the harmful effect of the child's act. Thus, the first rudimentary feelings of guilt occur when children believe that they have caused some kind of physical harm to another.

A second kind of guilt, *guilt over inaction*, becomes a possibility once children acquire the additional capacity to construct a mental representation of an event that might have occurred but did not. Guilt over not taking any action (omission) is more cognitively demanding. In such a situation, children must be able to imagine something that might have happened and to be aware of the consequences of not doing anything.

Martin Hoffman (1988) asked fifth and seventh graders to complete the following story:

> A child who is hurrying with a friend to an important sports event encounters a small child who seems lost. He suggests that they stop and help, but his friend talks him out of it. The next day he finds out that the small child, who had been left alone by an irresponsible baby-sitter, had run into the street and was badly injured after he was hit by a car.

The transgression in this story was one of omission: not stopping to help. The protagonist actually did nothing wrong, and there was no reason for him to anticipate the tragic consequences of his inaction. Despite these reasons for deserving little blame, most of the childrens' responses indicated that they would feel very guilty in similar situations. Hoffman's findings suggest that children from about age 11 typically respond with guilt feelings when they believe they have harmed others by neglecting to take action.

Even more demanding cognitively is guilt over contemplating a harmful act or *anticipatory guilt*. To experience anticipatory guilt, children must have the capacity to visualize not only an act that they have not performed, but may be contemplating, but also the other person's probable distress in response as well. Preadolescent children, starting at around age 12, may experience anticipatory guilt (Bybee, 1998).

For example, a young preadolescent may experience anticipatory guilt when she thinks about stealing the social studies notes from another student. She realizes that if she does, the other student will not do well on the exam.

Survivor guilt occurs when the individual has neither done nor contemplated doing anything wrong but feels somehow to blame for a bad event, even though the circumstances were beyond his or her control. The experience of guilt, even when no wrong has been done, is exemplified by an individual who wrestles with a sense of guilt over the problem of homelessness.

Is Guilt Good or Bad?

On the negative side, guilt feelings can be highly threatening to children's and adolescent's self-image. An overdeveloped sense of guilt or too low a threshold of guilt may lead to serious adjustment problems. Excessive guilt may cause fears and anxieties that can, in turn, bring on a galaxy of illnesses, ranging from chronic fatigue to drug abuse. In contrast, guilt may be a good thing in the sense that it makes us aware that we have done something wrong. In short, guilt is society's regulator. Guilt may also be responsible, in part, for keeping us true to the values we hold—despite temptation from peers.

Morality and Peers

What kinds of influences do peers have on an adolescent's behavior? Do they play an active role in shaping one's values? Values are normative ideas that guide behavior and provide external and internal moral standards that adolescents strive toward. Consider these dilemmas:

1. Your parents are not very fond of two of your friends who have bad haircuts, wear outlandish clothes, play loud music, and have pierced everything. They believe you should break off your friendship with them.
2. A friend at school who is bored with life suggests that both of you drop out and move to Peru.

The negative influence of the adolescent peer culture has received a great deal of attention from the popular press and research. The press consistently links association with bad peers and antisocial behavior. Research, however, presents a more complicated picture.

Lifestyle Versus Basic Family Values

Research findings indicate that peers are likely to be more influential than parents in value areas involving social activities and friendship choices, known as *lifestyle values*. These values relate to daily living and matters of taste, dress, speech, and social behavior. In responding to the first dilemma, you may have decided to keep your friends. In general, however, adolescents are in sync with their parents about *basic family values*. Adolescents have values similar to their parents in basic areas such as scholastic goals or future-oriented decisions and aspirations (Girdner, Eisenman, & Tracy, 1996). Adolescents continue to side with parents on issues that relate to the larger society and ethical questions. As such, you may have decided to stay in school and avoid the excursion to Peru. Still, answers to the questions raised in Table 16.4 may make it clear that parents and adolescents typically do hold different lifestyle views.

Positive Peer Influence

Data also support the view that peers can have a positive influence on an adolescent's behavior. They can encourage positive study habits and getting good grades, involvement in community service, or abstention from drinking (Newcomb & Keefe, 1997). Other researchers have found that peer influences during junior and senior high school seem to be generally positive, with encouragement to engage in prosocial behaviors exceeding that for misconduct or inappropriate activities (Grusec & Kuczynski, 1997). For example, succumbing to friends' encouragement to engage in potentially self-destructive behaviors, such as unprotected sexual activity or the use of illicit drugs, can be contrasted with athletic team members' pressure to maintain academic achievement sufficient to remain active in athletic activities or friends' insistence on the use of a designated driver when a peer has consumed alcoholic beverages. Underestimating the influence of friends would be as serious a mistake as overestimating it.

APPLICATIONS:

Morality and the Power of Parents

This is not to suggest that peers do not play an important role in modeling and encouraging antisocial and anti-authority behavior but simply that the

TABLE 16.4

Values

How closely do your ideas agree with your parents' about the following?

	Very Similar	Mostly Similar	Very Different
1. What you should do with your life	_____	_____	_____
2. How you should dress or what clothes you wear	_____	_____	_____
3. How you spend your money	_____	_____	_____
4. Whether it is okay to drink	_____	_____	_____
5. The value of education	_____	_____	_____
6. Racial issues	_____	_____	_____
7. Religion	_____	_____	_____
8. What you do in your leisure time	_____	_____	_____
9. The people you hang out with	_____	_____	_____
10. Completing college	_____	_____	_____

Typically, you will be "Very Similar" on basic values (items 1, 3, 6, 7, and 10) more often than on lifestyle choices (items 2, 4, 5, 8, and 9). This would generally be true for your younger adolescent counterparts as well.

negative influence is not as omnipresent and one-sided as many of us think (Urberg, 1999). Whether adolescents conform to negative peer pressure depends on the quality of their relationship to their parents, whether the adolescent or parents possess certain characteristics, and the adolescent's age and maturity.

AP/World Wide Photos

Although education and career goals may be in line with parental values, lifestyle values, such as hairstyle, are more peer-oriented.

Quality of the Parent–Child Relationship

The quality of the relationship between adolescents and their parents is a primary variable in determining the relative influence of parents and peers. When interaction is of high quality, and parents are perceived as competent, adolescents generally do not differ from parents on significant issues. As such, those who have a close relationship with their parents may choose peers with a similar rather than conflicting value system.

Characteristics of Adolescents and Parents

Autonomous adolescents who are not highly dependent on peers are the least likely to be influenced by peers. Adolescents who are highly peer-oriented are more likely to conform to peer pressure. Relatedly, the parents of nonconforming adolescents provide moderate to high levels of support and nurturance for their sons and daughters. They are firm but not oppressive in their level of control. Moreover, these parents tend to demonstrate democratic decision making. In contrast, highly conforming adolescents tend to come from homes that are either high on permissiveness or high on punitiveness. Adolescents in these family situations receive less support and less control from their parents and therefore may seek support and direction from peers.

Supervision problems have been implicated in the adolescent's associating with antisocial peers. For example, children whose parents do not know their whereabouts are more susceptible to negative peer pressure (Katz, 1997). Lax supervision, in combination with rejection by normal peers, is thought to put the child, especially boys, at risk for association with peers who have nonconventional, or deviant, orientations (Dishion, Patterson, Stoolmiller, & Skinner, 1991). In addition, lax supervision becomes a strong predictor of more serious forms of noncompliance, such as delinquency and drug use (Chamberlain & Patterson, 1995).

Age and Maturity

In studying developmental trends in peer conformity, peers appear to have their greatest influence in early to middle adolescence—especially with regard to antisocial behavior (Berndt, Hawkins, & Jiao, 1999). But, peer pressures have their strongest effects for those individuals with a propensity toward conformity with peers (Santor, Messervey, & Kusumakar, 2000). Adolescents, for example, who spend the most time with peers and prefer gangs are more likely to go along with the crowd in deviant acts than adolescents who do not spend as much time with peers and prefer to be with their best friends.

Such conflicts between adult and peer values, however, are not a general thrust throughout adolescence, or for all adolescents. Although the influence of peer groups and friendships increases across adolescence, parents retain primary influence over decision making regarding life values, goals, and future decisions (Newcomb & Keefe, 1997).

Concept Checks

1. "Heinz should steal the drug to save his wife; his wife's family will be grateful to him" is an example of reasoning at Kohlberg's stage of ________________.
2. An African American student at Stanford University wrestles with a keen sense of guilt about families struggling in the ghetto; this would be labeled ____________ guilt.
3. Vicki dresses in baggy jeans and loose-fitting sweatshirts and thinks her mother's way of dressing is boring and conventional. These differences reflect __________ values.
4. Whether adolescents conform to parental or to peer values is dependent on
   a. the quality of the parent–adolescent relationship.
   b. the age of the parents.
   c. the quality of the adolescent–peer relationship.

Family Influences During Adolescence

Before Beginning ...

After reading this section, you will be able to

- conceptualize emotionality in adolescence.
- examine emotional separateness issues.
- understand the importance of connectedness in the separation process.

Whereas most adolescents perceive this developmental period in generally positive ways (Montemayor, Adams, & Gullotta, 1990) and emotional problems do not seem to characterize the adolescent years for most teens (Wagner, 1997), most parents, however, perceive adolescence as a time of "storm and stress." Teenagers do experience a wider range of emotional states than during the preadolescent years—and so do their parents.

Emotionality

If emotionality is a distinguishing trait, then adolescents should report wider daily emotional variations than do children. Reed Larson's (Larson, 1997; Richards, Crowe, Larson, & Swarr, 1998) experiment with children, grades 5 through 9, carrying electronic pagers showed that they experienced more positive and negative emotional states than their younger counterparts. Not only do adolescents experience more frequent emotional highs and lows; parents do as well (Montemayor, Adams, & Gullotta, 1990). Some researchers have attributed parents' negative mood states to dissatisfaction reflecting midlife issues they may be experiencing (Wilson & Gottman, 1995). Whether these indexes of dissatisfaction reflect midlife issues of the parent, the stresses of parenting an adolescent, or a combination of the two is not known.

During this time, some parents become increasingly negative toward their adolescents; there is more criticism, whining, frustration, anger, and defensiveness on the part of both adolescents and their parents (Harter, 1990). Challenges and conflicts promote these negative emotions and actions.

Parents may also feel less satisfied with their parenting role as teenagers spend more time away from home and with their peers. Fathers have difficulty separating from their adolescents, mostly because they feel regret about the time they have not spent with them (Rutter, 1995). The separation may be more painful for mothers, however, who are generally more emotionally engaged with their children. Although parents continue to be a source of support for their adolescents, emotional issues between parents and adolescents do arise, which may center around adolescents' beliefs in their rights to have control over their lives—referred to as self-determination rights. Many adolescents believe that they should have an active part in many of the decisions regarding their own lives.

emotional autonomy Self-governance, autonomy from peers, and autonomy in relation to parents; it is the degree to which the adolescent has managed to cast off infantile ties to the family.

"Soon you will be entering a phase, son, in which you will no longer pay attention to anything I have to say. Please let me know when that changeover occurs."

Emotional Separateness from Parents

Adolescence has been characterized as a period of emotional separateness, or emotional autonomy. **Emotional autonomy** is defined as self-governance, as autonomy from peers, and as autonomy in relation to parents. It is the degree to which the adolescent has managed to cast off infantile ties to the family.

The development of emotional autonomy is related to the adolescent's developing a sense of individuation. Individuation implies that the growing person takes increasing responsibility for what he does and what he is rather than depositing this responsibility on the shoulders of his parents. The process of emotional autonomy or individuation does not begin in adolescence, but, rather from infancy on, individuals gradually and progressively sharpen their sense of self as autonomous and competent beings. Adolescents who have been successful in establishing a sense of individuation can accept responsibility for their choices and actions instead of relying on their parents to do it for them.

Emotional Connectedness to Peers and Parents

When comparing levels of intimacy between adolescents and their best friends, their mothers, and their fathers, one finds that intimacy between adolescents and their best friends increases. From age 12 on, adolescents describe their relationships with best friends as more intimate than with their mothers or fathers (Azmitia, Kamprath, & Linnet, 1998). But this difference between parent and peer intimacy is due to increases in intimacy with peers, not to decreases in intimacy with parents.

As with emotional autonomy, adolescents who perceive their parents as being warm and nurturant engage in significantly more self-disclosure about a variety of topics (Ruck, Abramovitch, & Keating, 1998). Adolescents from the most affectionate families disclose more not only to their parents but with their peers as well. Thus, emotional self-disclosure during adolescence appears to be influenced by the affective and communicative quality of the family context. Interestingly, adolescents from East Asian, Filipino, and Latin American backgrounds reported more cohesion and closeness with their parents and greater discussion with them when they were able to communicate with them in their native tongue. Adolescents who spoke in a second language (generally English) with their parents reported less cohesion and discussion with their parents.

Emotional self-disclosure among adolescents is lowest when families are perceived by adolescents as being closed to communication and emotionally detached and there is dissatisfaction with the affective quality of family relationships. Emotional connectedness with parents helps the adolescent with identity issues that arise during the adolescent years.

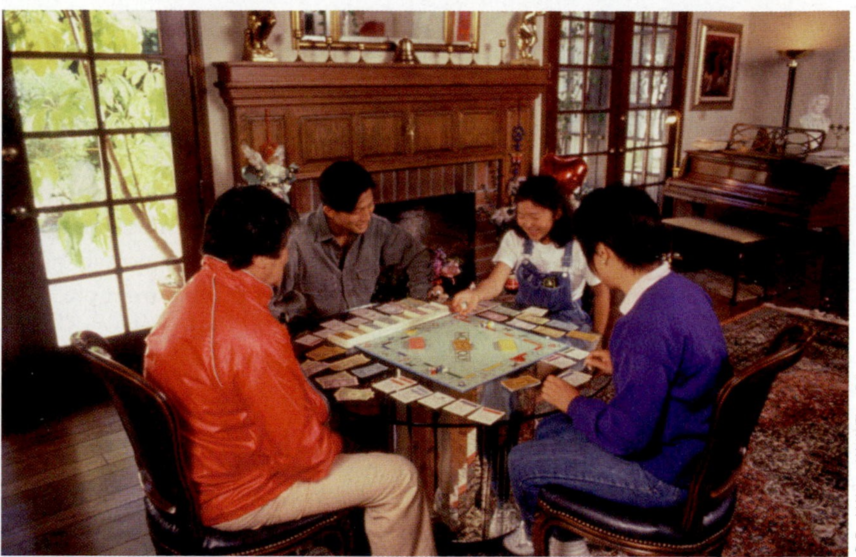

Intimacy with parents does not decrease during adolescence.

APPLICATIONS:

Fostering the Adolescent's Emancipation Proclamation

Morally, adolescence may appear to be a time of parental values clashing with the adolescent's values. What may be surprising, however, is that the two are not as contradictory as you might think. Emotionally, adolescents are in search of emotional separateness from their parents and seek to exert their independence as they attempt to establish a distinct sense of self. Many issues arising during adolescence center on independence and adolescents' desire to exercise their self-determination rights. The problem arises over what these self-determination rights are. For example, do you believe that an adolescent, age 16, should be granted the following rights or denied them?

- *Voting:* Jamie's parents are going out to vote in the presidential election. Jamie wants to go with them and vote also. She is told that only adults can vote. Should Jamie be able to vote if she wants to?
- *Keeping a diary:* Pat kept a diary and said that no one else could read it—not even her parents. Her parents, however, are quite concerned that Pat has a drug problem. Under these circumstances, should Pat's parents read her diary?
- *Choosing friends:* Fernando has fallen in with a group of adolescents, and his parents do not approve of the type of friends he is making. Should his parents intervene and tell him that he cannot see these friends anymore?
- *Access to school file:* Lee knows that he has a file in the school office, and he wants to know what it says about him. The teacher told Lee that he is not allowed to see his file. Should he be allowed to see his own file?

Is "it's my life and I can do want I want" the rallying cry of most adolescents? Do adults then need to be very strict and put up a kind of "tough love" facade? What is the best way for adults to foster the adolescent's emancipation proclamation?

The Process of Individuation

Adolescence is a time when individuals push for autonomy and gradually develop the wherewithal to take that control. The process of individuation from parents involves two phases: practicing and the rapprochement. In the *practicing phase,* adolescents revel in feelings of separateness and autonomy, defining themselves oppositionally to their parents and other authority figures. The practicing phase is characterized by an unambivalent assertion of will as adolescents define themselves. Power relations between adolescents and their parents are typically still asymmetrical, and parents may appropriately continue to make behavioral demands while allowing psychological freedom. During the practicing phase, immediately following puberty, both sons and daughters report less cohesion with parents—particularly mothers (Steinberg, 1993). But, in the second, *rapprochement phase,* adolescents attempt to reestablish bonds with their parents provided that their parents give them room to grow. An amicable relationship can be restored when parents provide recognition of their adolescent's autonomy (Baumrind, 1991). This is particularly true in the mother–daughter relationship.

Parenting Styles

The style of parenting is an important determinant influencing the extent to which adolescents are likely to have adjustment problems or to make a smooth and positive transition through adolescence. Obtaining adolescents' cooperation is more crucial than obtaining their obedience. Adolescents who feel comfortable with their relationship with their parents are more likely to reflect their parents' values, to disclose to them, and to cooperate with them (Darling & Steinberg, 1993). When adolescents cooperate with their parents, obedience becomes a nonissue.

Adolescents cope much better when they feel accepted by their parents, when they feel free to talk to parents about their problems, and they are able to negotiate changes in rules and roles with their parents. Authoritative adults use reasoning with adolescents, display flexibility and adaptability, use firm but fair control, and have a high degree of acceptance of the adolescent. These families are characterized by a high degree of democracy and a high degree of parental control. Research consistently shows that authoritative parents have adolescents who are more cooperative and experience fewer adjustment difficulties, and subsequently they have an easier time in performing their tasks (Maccoby, 1999).

Rebellion is most likely to occur when the authority structure is patriarchal and unequal, when discipline is excessive and inconsistent, and when demands are arbitrarily made and inflexible (Baumrind, 1991). Evidence seems clear that the best environment for adolescents involves limited control combined with encouragement to be an autonomous individual. A good environment also involves the ability to adjust to the adolescent's needs rather than to be rigid and inflexible.

Each stage of adolescence, however, requires a different mix of parental control and encouragement of emancipation. In early adolescence, coinciding with the middle school period, young people assume an exaggerated pseudoindependent stance, which adults should respond to by continuing to enforce age-appropriate limits. During middle adolescence, coinciding with the high school years, adolescents achieve cognitive and social gains that enable adults to increase both responsibilities and rights in the domains of money management and individual liberty. It is only in late adolescence, following graduation from high school, sometimes with an intervening moratorium in the form of college or apprenticeship, that a nearly symmetrical adult–adolescent relationship becomes a possibility. Continuing bonds between adolescent and parent, although now transformed, provide a crucial backdrop for growth through adolescence and into adulthood.

Adolescents who have achieved independence from parents experience satisfaction with whom they are and with the directions their lives are taking (Lamborn & Steinberg, 1993). Self-confidence is evidenced by a stability in their relationships and self-presentation to others. There are some young people, however, who have a fear of being on their own and of growing up. Adolescents who wish to remain children have excessive dependency needs, intense fear of their inability to assume responsibilities and demands of adulthood, intense fear of sexual impulses, low self-esteem, and poor peer relations; are academic underachievers; and feel that adults are unacceptable role models.

Separateness and Connectedness

Most theorists now believe that healthy individuation is fostered by close, not distant, family relationships. Emotional autonomy develops best under conditions that encourage both individuation and closeness. In this sense, individuation is not something that happens *from* parents but rather *with* them. Individuation involves adults' helping adolescents achieve independence and individuality while still helping them feel included and connected. The effective family system is one that avoids both enmeshment, in which individuality is discouraged in favor of exaggerated family harmony, and disengagement, in which family members are so separate that they have little effect on each other.

Connectedness between parents and adolescents also tends to enhance the life satisfaction and psychological well-being of adolescents. *Life satisfaction* refers to the adolescent's subjective perception of the quality of his or her life. *Psychological well-being* consists of multiple subdimensions such as self-esteem, locus of control, anxiety, loneliness, and sociability. Individuals who exhibit high self-esteem, an internal locus of control, low anxiety and loneliness, and high sociability are considered to have a strong psychological well-being.

A study on a sample of adolescents from Hong Kong, China, offers a unique look at the parent–adolescent relationship in a rapidly developing society. Adolescents who were oriented toward their peers and their parents were satisfied with school and their acceptance by others. However, those adolescents who were most oriented toward their parents were additionally satisfied with life and exhibited more positive states of psychological well-being (Man, 1991). In a sample of adolescents from Iran, those who perceived their relationship with their parents as "distant" were more likely to experience lower self-esteem and lower sociabilities than were adolescents who perceived the parent–adolescent relationship as being emotionally connected (Hojat, Borenstein, & Shapurian, 1990).

In addition, researchers found that Mexican American adolescents who described their relationships with their parents as being emotionally close were more likely to display more positive life satisfaction and tended to be less involved with drugs and drug-oriented peers (Coombs, Paulson, & Richardson, 1991). Similarly, in a sample of Native American Ojibway adolescents, a close relationship with their parents and tribal elders appeared to protect these youths from negative behaviors such as drug use and delinquent behaviors (Zitzow, 1990). The implications of these cross-cultural/ethnic studies are that, universally, an adolescent's individuation process is enhanced when he or she achieves a balance between *separation* from and *connectedness* with parents.

Concept Checks

1. Which statement best describes "emotionality" during adolescence?
   a. Adolescents typically experience a breach in relations with parents.
   b. Adolescents do not confide their emotional concerns to their parents.
   c. Adolescents experience wide mood swings, both positive and negative.
2. When adolescents revel in feelings of separateness and autonomy and define themselves oppositionally to their parents and other authority figures, they are in the ________________ of individuation.
3. ***True or False:*** Separation or independence is fostered when adolescents and parents maintain a sense of closeness.

Reviewing Key Points

Understanding Self and Others

- Adolescents tend to describe the self in terms of social and psychological constructs. This shift in ways of conceiving the self reflects greater cognitive abstractness as well as a search for a new understanding of the self. During adolescence, we observe a reorganization of the self. Studies seem to indicate that in early adolescence self-esteem becomes less stable and more negative, particularly for girls who mature earlier, begin dating, and start attending a new junior high school.
- Friends are defined as relationships in which parties care for one another, share their thoughts and feelings, and comfort one another. Adolescents are able to take a detached, third-person, view of the dyadic relationship.
- Adolescent's tasks involve achieving a stable sense of self-identity; achieving independence from parents; achieving a comfortable body image; developing a personal value system; developing cooperative relationships with peers; and gaining skills necessary for economic independence.
- Higher scores on masculinity for males and higher scores on androgyny for females (perhaps the masculine component of androgyny) have been positively correlated with heightened self-esteem in each gender.
- Androgynous youths become the most well-adjusted adults. The key factor that appears to promote androgynous behavior in girls is having a mother and a father who value and actively encourage their children's intellectual pursuits. The key factor in producing androgynous males is warm, nurturing parents and exposure to competent, achievement-oriented women.

Emotional Concerns in Adolescence

- Adolescent delinquency is a result of complex factors: Family factors, a sense of alienation, antisocial behavior, poor academic performance, rejection by the conventional peer group, and association with antisocial peers are salient factors that lead to committing delinquent acts.
- Why youths take their own lives has been related to a number of causes: relief from an intolerable situation or state of mind, an attempt to make others understand how desperate they feel, getting back at loved ones for the hurt they have caused, family disorganization, family disharmony, and academic failures.
- Warning signs of a potentially suicidal adolescent include clinical depression (characterized by a pervasive loss of interest or pleasure and persistent anxiety or dissatisfaction); threats of suicide; situational cues (family strife, setting one's affairs in order; giving away prized possessions); and feelings of hopelessness.

Moral Development

- During adolescence moral reasoning tends to be based on abstract guidelines that transcend concrete situations and can be applied across a variety of moral situations. The conventional level stresses conformity and loyalty to the family and the priority of interpersonal relationships (stage 3). It also stresses conformity and loyalty to the larger society, the fulfillment of duties, and unquestioning obedience to the law (stage 4). The postconventional level involves an emphasis on basic nonrelative values. These include liberty, the belief that laws are a service to society and subject to change (stage 5), the preeminence of self-chosen ethical principles, and the domination of conscience in making moral decisions (stage 6).

- Children first experience a rudimentary form of guilt in situations in which they have physically harmed another child. With further cognitive and social advancements, children and adolescents begin to feel guilt over inaction, because they are aware that they could have done something to prevent a bad situation but did not. Finally, adolescents begin to feel guilty over their harmful actions (or inactions) beyond their immediate situations.
- Adolescent values are surprisingly similar to parental values in terms of basic values (the value of education, for example). Adolescent values on lifestyle (dress, choice of friends), however, are more similar to their peers.
- When there is a conflict between adolescents' values and parental values, whether adolescents go against parental values depends on whether the adolescent or parents possess certain characteristics, the quality of the parent–adolescent relationship, and the adolescent's age.

Family Influences During Adolescence

- Adolescence has been characterized as a period of emotionality, in which emotional states are more extreme, more variable, and more intense than earlier or later periods.
- During adolescence emotional autonomy emerges as adolescents become emotionally independent from parents. Adolescents increasingly accept responsibility for their choices and actions rather than depositing this responsibility on their parents' shoulders.
- A key task during adolescence is to help teenagers achieve a sense of separateness by encouraging assertion and freedom to disagree, helping them assume responsibility for their own behavior, and allowing them to play an active role in decision making. At the same time, adults need to help adolescents feel connected to the family by being open and responsive to their views and ideas, offering guidance and support, and being warm and accepting.

Answers to Concept Checks

Understanding Self and Others

1. achievement/leadership; congeniality/sociability
2. defining friendship in more abstract, internal dispositional relationship; intimacy

3. c 4. c 5. c

Emotional Concerns in Adolescence

1. larceny-theft, robbery, forcible rape; running away or illicit sexual behavior

2. true 3. c

Moral Development

1. good-boy/nice-girl 2. anticipatory guilt
3. lifestyle 4. a

Family Influences During Adolescence

1. c 2. practicing phase 3. true

Key Terms

androgyny
clique
crowd
emotional autonomy
gender intensification hypothesis
identity achievers
identity crisis
identity diffusion
identity foreclosure
juvenile delinquent
moratorium

InfoTrac College Edition

For additional readings, explore InfoTrac College Edition, your online library. Go to **http://www.infotrac-college.com/wadsworth** and use the passcode that came on the card with your book. Try these search terms: cliques, friendship in adolescence, interpersonal relationships in adolescence, peer pressure and adolescence, moral development.

Child Development CD-ROM

Go to the Wadsworth Child Development CD-ROM for further study of the concepts in this chapter. The CD-ROM also includes quizzes and additional activities to expand your learning experience.

GLOSSARY

accommodation According to Piaget, the process of modifying a scheme or adding a new one.

acquired immunodeficiency syndrome (AIDS) The shutting down of the immune system; caused by human immunodeficiency virus (HIV).

active listening Involves paraphrasing the often unspoken emotions that may accompany the speaker's verbal message.

acute illnesses Illnesses having a sudden onset and a strong possibility of ending quickly.

adaptation The process of adjusting our schemes and experiences to each other to maintain a state of equilibrium.

adolescence Begins with the biological changes of puberty and ends with the assumption of adult work and family roles.

aftercare Follow-up intensive, partial-day programs, weekly meetings, or both.

agility The ability to change the direction of the body rapidly and accurately.

allele One of two or more alternative forms of a gene that exist at a specific gene location on a chromosome, giving rise to alternative hereditary characteristics.

amae Refers to one's inclination to depend on or accept another's nurturing and indulgence, including one's dependency; typically used to describe the mother–child relationship in Japan.

anabolic steroids Strength enhancers that come in many chemical structures; the prime one is testosterone. Although used to increase muscle mass, they carry potentially negative side effects such as liver infection and damage to the reproductive system.

anaclitic identification Little girls, fearing their mother's resentment and loss of love, resolve their anxiety by identifying with her.

androgyny Being able to behave in ways traditionally associated with both sexes as the situation warrants.

anemia A nutritional deficiency in which the body lacks sufficient hemoglobin, or red blood cells, to carry oxygen from lungs to all parts of the body.

animistic thinking According to Piaget, the tendency of young children to assume that nonliving objects like the sun or the wind have thoughts, motives, or feelings.

anorexia nervosa A condition in which girls starve themselves until they lose 15 to 25 percent of their body weight. Sufferers have an extreme fear of fatness and intake only 300 to 600 calories a day.

anxious-avoidant attachment relations The quality of insecure attachment that characterizes infants who are usually not distressed by parental separation and who avoid the parent when she returns.

anxious-resistant attachment relations An insecure infant–caregiver bond, characterized by strong separation protest and a tendency of the child to remain near but resist contact initiated by the caregiver, particularly after separation.

assimilation The process of taking in new information and fitting it into an already existing notion about objects and the world. In this sense, to assimilate is to use what we already know how to do to do something new.

associative play A form of play when children engage in true social participation; they interact by exchanging toys and commenting on each other's activities.

attachment A strong physical and emotional bond between the infant and the principal caregiver.

attachment Q-sort An alternative method of assessing attachment security that is based on observations of the child's attachment-related behaviors at home; it can be used with preschool children.

attention The amount and type of information to which one attends.

attention deficit hyperactivity disorder A learning disability characterized by impulsivity, lack of attention, and hyperactivity.

authoritarian parenting styles Parents exhibit high levels of demandingness and receive low levels of responsiveness.

authoritative parenting styles Parents exhibit a high level of demandingness and receive high level of responsiveness.

autism A condition in which children are unable to interact with others normally, their language development is retarded, and their behavior is often compulsive and ritualistic.

autosome Any chromosome that is not a sex chromosome.

axon The long extension from the cell body that transmits messages away from the cell body to other neurons across the synapse.

babbling By the fifth or sixth month, infants combine various sounds, including consonants and vowels.

balance The ability to maintain the equilibrium of one's body when it is placed in various positions; it is basic to all movement.

behavioral genetics Focuses on the nature and organization of genetic material and the way in which it controls the development of traits during the life of an individual.

behavior modification A technique, defined by B. F. Skinner, that would shape children's behavior by reinforcing desired actions and ignoring undesirable ones.

blastocyst The zygote three days after fertilization; the tiny mass of cells forms a hollow, fluid-filled sphere that looks like a miniature mulberry.

Broca's area Our verbal speech center; located in the fontal lobe of the brain.

bulimia nervosa An eating disorder in which the individual (usually female) alternates between dieting and binge eating followed by self-induced vomiting or purging.

canalized traits Traits that are fated or predetermined on a virtually fixed, developmental pathway.

case studies Research done on a sample of one: one person, one institution, one society, and so on.

center care Group care that takes place outside a home setting and offers care in a school-like setting.

cephalocaudal An organized pattern of physical growth, which literally means from "head to foot"; that is, the body develops from the head end downward.

cerebellum The part of the brain that allows growing coordination and advanced motor skills.

cerebrum and cerebral cortex Higher centers of the brain implicated in higher-order thinking, complex reasoning, and problem solving.

chromosome Threadlike structures in the body's cells made up of genes.

chronic illnesses Illnesses having a gradual onset and long duration.

classical conditioning Learning that involves the modification of a reflex; the conditioning stimulus, which is neutral at the start, eventually initiates the same behavioral response as the unconditioned stimulus (reflex reaction).

classification Organizing and ordering what is immediately present; a skill necessary to concrete operational thinking.

class inclusion The child's knowledge that a superordinate class (flowers) is always larger than any of its subordinate classes (tulips, daffodils).

cohort A generation of individuals used to make comparisons in cross-sectional research.

cohort effect Differences between cohorts that reflect unidentified cultural or historical factors.

colic An extremely fussy period of crying usually disappearing between 5 and 10 months.

collectivism A cultural philosophy that emphasizes the interconnectedness of persons; valuing the social and the group. Collective societies tend to emphasize obedience, reliability, and proper behavior in children.

combinatorial analysis Refers to being able to organize an array of all possible combinations inherent in a problem.

competency self-esteem Feelings of worthiness based on demonstrated competencies, behaviors, and skills.

computer-assisted instruction Learning in which students use the computer and instructional programs in fairly controlled conditions to master a typical school subject matter.

concrete operational thinker Between the ages of 7 and 11 children move into Piaget's third stage of cognitive development. These children are able to classify, reverse thought, understand class inclusion, go from centration to decentration, and develop the skill of conservation of thought.

confounding variables Factors that could confuse or confound the effects of the independent variable.

conservation The understanding that a quantity remains the same despite its appearance.

context This refers to the social relationships in which children are involved, the features of their particular society or culture, and the social institutions that affect the beliefs and behavior of parents and other caregivers.

control group In an experimental design, the group of subjects that does not receive the experimental treatment; they are used for comparison.

convergent thinking Produces one correct answer and is characteristic of the kind of thinking on IQ tests or standardized tests.

cooing Vocalizations infants make at 3 to 4 months, consisting of long, open vowel sounds.

cooperative play A more sophisticated type of play, in which children work toward a common goal with the same product.

coordination Skills that all require considerable amounts of visual input integrated with motor output.

corpus callosum The part of the brain responsible for cross talk between the two hemispheres.

correlational method A method that attempts to measure the relationship between two or more variables. The association does not imply a causal link between the variables.

co-sleeping When young children share the same bed with their parents.

conventional moral reasoning Consists of mutual social expectations and following rules to maintain law and order.

creativity The ability to think about something in unusual ways, generate many responses, and come up with unique solutions.

critical period Denotes a particular interval of time in which the development of attachment behaviors must take place; after this time, it is extremely difficult if not impossible for bonding to take place.

crossing over Creation of new genetic information in offspring through the exchanging of places by male and female chromosome strands during meiosis.

cross-sectional research design A study that compares groups of individuals of different ages on some particular behavior at one point in time.

cross-sequential research design A study that incorporates cross-sectional and longitudinal designs.

crowd A larger, more interpersonal, peer group consisting of 10 to 20 members who share common interests in social activities.

culture Reflects the values, ideals, and beliefs of a particular group of people that are passed on from one generation to the next.

daily hassles The irritating and frustrating demands that occur on a day-to-day basis.

decentration The ability to focus on several dimensions of a problem at once and relate them.

defensive identification According to Freud, little boys, out of fear of castration anxiety, repress a desire to possess their mother and identify with their father.

deferred imitation The imitation of actions that have occurred at an earlier time.

demandingness Refers to the extent to which parents expect and demand mature, responsible behavior from children.

dendrites Fine, wirelike extensions that receive messages from adjacent neurons and conduct them to the soma, or cell body.

deoxyribonucleic acid, or DNA DNA is a long threadlike molecule shaped like a double helix that runs along the length of each chromosome.

dependent variable The performance or behavior of the subjects in the experimental research design.

depressants Drugs that slow down the activity of the central nervous system; examples include alcohol, inhalants, tranquilizers, and sedatives. Also known as downers.

deprivation dwarfism A growth-related disorder that appears to be caused by environmental factors.

difficult temperament Temperament in which the child is irregular in its biological functions, is irritable, and often responds intensely and negatively to new situations or tries to withdraw from them.

diploid cell A cell containing two full sets of chromosomes.

discipline Comes from the word *disciple,* meaning "one who gives instruction." Discipline goes beyond the confines of short-term, immediate behavioral gains; it influences children's future behavior.

dishabituation The recovery of attention to a novel stimulus.

disorganized–disoriented attachment relations The quality of insecure attachment that characterizes infants who respond in a confused, contradictory fashion when reunited with their caregiver.

divergent thinking Produces many answers to the same question and is characteristic of creative thinking.

dizygotic twins Fraternal twins.

dominant Said of an allele that expresses its phenotype even in the presence of a recessive allele.

Down syndrome A genetic disorder that leads to mental retardation caused by an extra chromosome on the 21st pair.

drug Any substance, other than food, that by its chemical nature affects the structure or function of the living organism.

drug abuse Using a drug(s) to such an extent that everyday functioning is impaired.

dysfluency A disorder of communication in which sounds or whole words are repeated as the child speaks, interrupting the flow of his communication; stammering or stuttering.

easy temperament Temperament in which the child quickly establishes regular routines in infancy, is generally cheerful, and adapts to new experiences.

ecological approach Bronfenbrenner's model, which emphasizes five environmental subsystems that influence the child's development.

ego Freud's rational level of personality that slowly emerges and becomes noticeable after the child's first birthday. It is the executive branch of personality, mediating between the id and superego.

egocentric speech Piaget's term for self-talk in children; it plays no functional role in cognitive development and disappears at the end of the preoperational stage.

egocentrism The tendency of young children to view the world from their own perspective while failing to recognize that others may have different points of view.

embryonic period The third to eighth weeks of gestation; the growing organism is no longer a blastocyst but an embryo. The prominent task of this period is differentiation and development of organs.

emic When conducting research from an *emic* perspective, the objective is to describe behavior *within* a certain cultural setting.

emotional autonomy Self-governance, autonomy from peers, and autonomy in relation to parents; it is the degree to which the adolescent has managed to cast off infantile ties to the family.

equilibrium A Piagetian term that refers to the cognitive balance between assimilation and accommodation.

estrogen Female hormone responsible for sexual maturation during puberty.

ethnicity, or ethnic group Groups having a unique system of beliefs and practices that overlap but differ in some respects from that of other ethnic groups.

ethnocentrism The belief that one's culture is preferable or superior.

ethnolinguistics The study of the relationship between language and culture.

etic Refers to *outside* the cultural setting. Researchers interested in studying political leadership across several cultures might adopt an *etic* approach.

evolutionary psychology The study of evolution of behavior using the principles of natural selection. Certain behavioral traits and ways of thinking are selected by conferring a reproductive advantage upon them. Those traits, over time, come to prevail.

executive processing space Refers to the maximum number of schemes children can activate at any one time.

expansion Rephrasing a child's communications in correct grammatical form. Also describes young children's broadening sense of who they are as they enter middle childhood.

experimental group In experimental research design, the group of subjects who receives the experimental treatment.

experimental method A method in which one can manipulate the environment to provide a precise test of the hypothesis; the only experimental method that allows us to draw cause-and-effect relationships.

explicit rules Rules of grammar that are taught, such as identifying the eight parts of speech.

external locus of control When children believe that they do not exercise power over events and outcomes affecting their academic achievement.

false belief The ability to attribute to another individual a belief that differs both from reality and what is known to be true.

family day care An arrangement in which the child is cared for by a family child care provider in her home.

family systems model A theory that emphasizes that each member of the family influences other members and is influenced by them. It underscores the bidirectional and reciprocal nature of family relationships.

fetal alcohol syndrome (FAS) A condition in which a child suffers from growth deficiency, dysmorphogenic characteristics, and central nervous system manifestations; caused by alcohol consumption during pregnancy.

fetal period Lasts from the ninth week of gestation until delivery; a period marked by the continued elaboration and growth of the basic systems and ossification.

fine motor development Behavior that depends primarily on small muscles that control fingers and hands.

fixation According to Freud, leaving too much libido in one psychosexual stage results in stagnation, or fixation, within that stage.

food allergies Condition in which the body's immune system reacts to a food substance as if it were an attacking system.

formal operational thinking Thinking that is more hypothetical, future-oriented; adolescents can think abstractly.

fragile X syndrome A genetic disorder resulting from an abnormal chromosomal structure.

friendship Refers to the establishment of a particular dyadic relationship between two children characterized by strong mutual liking.

gamete A haploid reproductive cell—for example, a sperm or an egg cell—in sexually reproducing organisms.

gender consistency/constancy The realization that biological sex is invariant despite superficial changes in appearance.

gender identity Correct labeling of self and others as males and females.

gender intensification hypothesis Theory that during early adolescence individuals hold very rigid gender-role conceptions and behaviors.

gender schema A pattern of beliefs and stereotypes about gender that children use to organize information about gender-related characteristics, experiences, and expectations.

gender stability Understanding that a person's sex remains constant throughout life.

gene The basic physical and functional unit of heredity that is transmitted from one generation to the next.

generalizability Refers to the extent to which research findings may be applied to broader populations or settings.

generative fathering Refers to fathering that meets the needs of the next generation with fathers becoming sensitive, nurturing, and involved parents.

genetic screening The process of systematically scanning individual genotypes for possible defects or abnormalities.

genome All the genetic information encoded in a complete strand of DNA as it lies coiled inside a cell.

genotype An individual's genetic makeup underlying a specific trait or constellation of traits.

germinal period In the first two weeks of gestation, the process of cell division begins; implantation is the major developmental task of this period.

gestures Nonverbal means of conveying messages that are conventional in form and universally recognized.

gifted children Those who are generally in the top 3 to 5 percent of their class academically and have an IQ of 125 or above.

goodness-of-fit Development is likely to be optimized when parents' child-rearing practices are sensitively adapted to the child's temperamental characteristics.

gonadotrophic hormones In males, these hormones stimulate the testes and adrenal glands to manufacture the hormone testosterone, which brings about the manufacture of sperm. In females, these hormones stimulate the ovaries to manufacture the hormones estrogen and progesterone, which trigger numerous physical events, including the release of mature ova from the ovaries; this eventually allows for reproduction.

gonads Primary sex organs; the ovaries in females and the testes in males.

gonorrhea Sexually transmitted disease contracted through vaginal, anal, and oral intercourse; in women symptoms are burning when urinating, menstrual irregularities, pelvic pain, and yellow-green discharge from vagina; in men, it is a puslike discharge from the urethra or pain during urination. Oral antibiotics are used for treatment.

grammar of language The study of the three branches of language development: phonology, semantics, and syntactics.

gross motor development Behavior that involves the movement of the entire body or major parts of the body (large muscles controlling arms and legs, for example).

growth hormone (GH) A pituitary hormone that affects all body tissues, except the central nervous system and the genitals. Produced throughout life in varying amounts, it is directly related to gradual increases in body size and weight over the childhood years. During adolescence, the system is flooded with this hormone, causing an acceleration of growth known as the growth spurt.

growth spurt The rapid growth in height during adolescence, triggered by the so-called growth hormone.

habituation The gradual decrease of attention paid to a repeated stimulus.

hallucinogens Mind-distorting drugs that create altered perceptions; they include marijuana and lysergic acid diethylamide (LSD).

haploid cell A cell containing only one set, or half the usual diploid number, of chromosomes.

hemophilia An X-linked disorder that prevents blood from clotting.

heritability The relative contribution of genes to a given trait, which tells us what proportion of individual differences in a population can be ascribed to genes.

heterozygous An individual whose genotype is characterized by two different alleles of a gene.

holophrastic The notion that children's words sometimes serve as entire sentences.

homologous chromosomes Matched chromosomes that are virtually identical in shape, size, and function and that pair during meiotic cell division.

homozygous An individual whose genotype is characterized by identical alleles of a gene.

horizontal decalage Asynchronous development within a Piagetian stage; for example, gradual understanding of conservation beginning with number and later volume.

hormones Literally means "to set in motion." The sex hormones, testosterone in males, and estrogen in females, are responsible for sexual maturation.

human immunodeficiency virus (HIV) HIV infections weaken the body's ability to fight disease and lead to acquired immune deficiency syndrome (AIDS). Symptoms may include weight loss, lack of appetite, diarrhea, night sweats, fever, whitish coating of yeast on the tongue, and purplish growths on the skin.

Huntington's disease A dominant autosomal disorder that leads to death.

hyperactivity A constant high level of activity in situations where it is clearly inappropriate coupled with an inability to inhibit activity on demand.

hypertext/hypermedia Hypertext—which consists of written material—and hypermedia—a more general term for a mixture of sound, graphics, and text—describe nonlinear programs.

hypothesis A specific prediction of behavior based on scientific theory that can be tested.

hypothetico-deductive reasoning Involves identifying all the various alternative hypotheses by moving from the specific to the general, followed by deducing a conclusion.

id Freud's level of personality that contains all human motives and emotions such as love, aggression, fear, and so on. It is primitive and illogical and wants immediate gratification.

identity achievers An identity status that characterizes adolescents who questioned alternatives and made a decision; these adolescents experience an optimal sense of identity.

identity crisis A sense of confusion about who one is and what one wants out of life and the ensuing effort to "discover" or "find" one's self.

identity diffusion An identity status that indicates that these adolescents have made no commitment nor are they attempting to arrive at a commitment about their lives.

identity foreclosure An identity status characterizing adolescents who have not actively questioned alternatives but have made a commitment.

imaginary audience Hypersensitivity to social evaluation or perception that the self is like an actor on stage.

imitation According to social learning theory, children learn gender roles by observing and imitating others of the same sex.

implantation Takes place during the germinal period when the trophoblast burrows itself into the uterine wall to obtain nourishment.

implicit rules Language rules that are innately known.

independent variable In an experimental design, the variable that is manipulated and controlled by the experimenter. It is received by the experimental group.

indifferent parenting styles Parents are low on demandingness and low on responsiveness.

individualism A cultural philosophy that emphasizes independence, self-assertiveness, and competitiveness.

indulgent parenting styles Parents are minimally controlling but affectionate; low levels of demandingness and high levels of responsiveness.

infanticide During antiquity, the deliberate murdering of young children.

infertility When a couple is unable to conceive after one year of unprotected intercourse; also when a woman is unable to carry a pregnancy to term.

information-processing theory A branch of cognitive psychology that is interested in studying the nature of information that children pick up and the series of stages they pass through as they absorb and transform this information.

inner speech Self-guiding and self-directing speech; an important cognitive tool for intellectual growth according to Vygotsky's thinking.

inpatient treatment A structured, time-limited stay in a treatment center.

intelligence According to Piagetian theorists, organization and adaptation, or the ability to deal with the complexities of one's environment; according to information-processing theorists, the ability to solve problems and adapt effectively to the environment; according to psychometric theorists, information a child possesses at a given point in time.

intermodal perception Relating or coordinating two or more senses such as hearing and vision.

internal locus of control When children perceive a causal relationship between their personal actions in an academic setting and the resultant outcomes.

internal working model A mental model that infants build as a result of their experience with their caregivers that they use to guide their behavior in other relationships.

intracytoplasmic sperm injection Technique in which a sperm cell is injected into an egg; used for infertile couples.

in vitro fertilization Ova are removed from the woman when they are just about to rupture; they are then mixed with the sperm and if the eggs develop and begin to divide, they are placed inside the woman's uterus.

IQ Intelligence quotient measured by the ratio of children's chronological age and their mental age.

irreversibility An impediment to logical thinking that is the inability to reverse an operation cognitively.

juvenile delinquent Refers to a young person, under the age of 18, who has been apprehended and convicted for transgression of established laws.

Klinefelter's syndrome A chromosomal abnormality that usually results from the presence of two X chromosomes and one Y chromosome. Children with this syndrome are male but never produce sperm.

knowledge base What children know; their background of information.

kwashiorkor Malnutrition found in toddlers whose diet consists of carbohydrates and little or no protein.

Lamaze method A series of exercises designed to teach breathing techniques associated with different stages of labor to ease the pain of delivery.

language An ordered system of rules that people comprehend in speaking, listening, and writing.

language acquisition device (LAD) According to Chomsky, this refers to an innate capacity to acquire language. It is a universal linguistic structure found in the brain.

lateralization The process by which brain functions become specialized either in the left or the right hemisphere.

learned helplessness When children are exposed to repeated failure, they develop a feeling that they are unable to handle tasks presented to them and perceive themselves as unable to surmount failure.

learning disability Refers to a specific disorder in language, perception, behavior, reading, spelling, writing, or mathematical reasoning.

levels of aspiration Expectations and goals set by children in the academic setting.

libido The sexual energy that Freud believed children expended during each of their five psychosexual stages.

linguistics Begins when children utter their first words, followed by the two-word stage, and then simple sentences.

locus The term in genetics for the position of a specific gene on a chromosome.

logical knowledge The development of concepts such as relationships of objects through size, shape, and color; the development of numbers and quantity such as less, more, equal; and notions about space and time.

longitudinal studies Study done on a group of subjects over a period of time.

long-term-memory (LTM) According to information-processing theory, this is our permanent storehouse of information

marasmus A form of starvation found in children under 1 who are severely deprived of necessary proteins and calories.

masturbation Self-stimulation that produces erotic arousal.

meiosis A mode of cell division in which a diploid parent cell gives rise to haploid reproductive cells or gametes.

menarche A girl's first menstrual period.

mentally challenged children A label that describes a child's position in relation to other children on the basis of some standard of performance—usually an IQ test. The most common form of mental retardation is Down syndrome, in which the child's IQ is between 20 and 80.

meritocracy Plato's belief that regardless of the child's position in life or gender, each should be educated to the full extent of his or her abilities.

metacognition Monitoring and evaluating one's current memory capabilities.

metamemory Knowledge of memory skills or of when it is most appropriate to use these strategies.

mitosis A mode of cell division in which a single parent cell gives rise to two genetically identical daughter cells.

molecular genetics The study of the molecular basis of gene structure and function.

monozygotic twins Identical twins.

moral relativism Cognitively more mature stage of moral reasoning characterized by an understanding that morality depends on mutual respect rather than on unquestioned obedience to authority.

moratorium An identity status in which adolescents are in the process of selecting alternatives, actively seeking information, and looking to make a decision.

morphemes When phonemes are combined, they form meaningful structures known as words.

multivariate analysis Experimental designs that utilize information about the relationship among two or more variables.

mutation A heritable change in a DNA molecule.

myelination The process of covering the axon of the neuron with a protein covering called the myelin sheath. The slow buildup of fatty sheaths around axons in the brain, which enables neurons to conduct messages at faster rates and allows actions and thoughts to be automatic.

myopia Nearsightedness.

naturalistic observation A study in which the researcher observes subjects in their natural habitat.

nature Genetic and biological influences on children's development.

negative reinforcement Removing a condition previously in effect to increase the probability of a response.

neglect The failure of the caregiver to properly provide an atmosphere in which the child has responsible safeguards for physical health, safety, and general well-being.

neglected children Children who receive little attention from their peers but are not necessarily disliked by their peers.

neurons Brain cells.

nightmares Frightening dreams that usually occur toward the early morning hours.

night terrors Less common and more intense than nightmares and characterized by a sudden arousal from sleep; they are accompanied by physiological changes (rapid heart beat; crying). The child usually does not remember night terrors.

nocturnal enuresis Repeated bed-wetting during the night.

nonattachment The failure of the infant–caregiver bond to form.

nonshared family environment Experiences and the effect of experiences that are unique to each family member.

nonsocial activity The simplest form of play, which is reflected in *onlooker, unoccupied,* and *solitary* play.

nucleotide A chemical subunit composed of a sugar, phosphate, and base; it makes up the nucleic acids of DNA and RNA.

nurture Environmental influences on children's development.

obesity A child who weighs more than 20 percent of what is considered to be normal for his or her height and weight.

object permanence Over six substages in the first two years of life, children realize that objects continue to exist even though they are out of sight.

operant conditioning According to Skinner, a process of learning in which reinforced behaviors tend to be repeated and occur more frequently.

operations To Piaget, mental representations carried out through logical thinking.

opiates Drugs that have an analgesic effect and are used to relieve physical and mental pain; most are derived from the opium poppy (morphine, codeine, heroin).

organization The innate process of synthesizing or consolidating existing information.

overachievers Those whose academic performance (in English, science, mathematics, and social science) exceeds what would have been anticipated statistically on the basis of their IQs.

ovulation Producing and discharging ova.

parallel play Playing near other children with similar toys but not trying to interact with them.

parentese A simplistic way of speaking to young children, using shorter sentences, emphasis on certain words, and repetition.

peer acceptance Refers to a child's inclusion in the group.

perception The process by which children extract meaningful information from physical stimuli.

perceptual centration The tendency to attend to only one attribute of what one observes and to ignore others.

perceptual-motor movements A combination of what the child sees or perceives through her senses and the body movements that respond to those perceptions.

personal fable An overdifferentiation of self from others in which the adolescent fails to see similarities in the experiences of self and others, leaving him or her with an exaggerated feeling of personal uniqueness.

petting A variety of mutually sexually stimulating acts that do not involve intercourse.

phenotype The detectable characteristics associated with a particular genotype.

phenylketonuria (PKU) An autosomal recessive disorder that leads to an excess of phenylalanine. If untreated through proper diet, children will suffer from severe mental retardation.

pheromones Chemical signals given off by others of the same species that communicate various messages such as fear and identification.

phonemes The smallest units of sound in a spoken language.

phonology The study of the meaning of sounds that compose the English language.

physical abuse Characterized by overt physical violence to the child.

pica A pattern of eating nonfood (paper, paint, plaster); it is found in young children and individuals with profound or severe mental retardation.

placenta The membranous structure that supplies the fetus with nourishment before its birth and to which the fetus is attached by the umbilical cord.

polygenetic (polygenic) inheritance The joint operation of several genes in producing a particular phenotype.

popular children Often engage in prosocial behavior, are seldom aggressive, and are able to pick up on the emotions of others and how their behavior is affecting other children.

poorness-of-fit Development is not likely to be optimized when parents' child-rearing practices are not sensitively adapted to the child's temperamental characteristics.

positive reinforcement A consequent event that occurs after a desired behavior, increasing the probability the behavior will recur.

postpartum period Refers to the first several weeks after giving birth when the mother undergoes intensified positive and negative emotions.

power The ability to perform a maximum effort in as short a period as possible.

pragmatics Learning the purposes and ways in which words and sentences are used in conversation.

preconventional moral reasoning Involves avoiding punishment or gaining a fair exchange.

preimplantation genetic testing In this experimental procedure, ova and sperm from the parents are collected, fertilized, and grown in the laboratory. Then a number of developing preembryonic cells are subjected to DNA analysis. A healthy preembryo is selected and implanted into the mother, where it can complete its prenatal development.

prelinguistics Communication that precedes intelligible words; crying, cooing, and babbling.

premoral period The first of Piaget's three-stage moral development periods; during this time, children (up to age 4) have little conception of what a rule is and what purpose it serves.

preoperational stage Ages 2 to 7; thinking is perception bound—that is, children focus on what strikes them first perceptually and error accordingly.

pretend play Play in which children take on imaginary roles like, Mommy and baby. Also known as symbolic play.

private speech Vygotsky's term for children's self-talk; a precursor to inner speech.

prosocial behaviors Generous, helping, and caring behaviors that promote a society's values.

proximodistal Development proceeds from the middle of the organism out to the periphery; that is, growth proceeds from the midline of the body outward.

psychometric approach Concerned with quantifying individual differences in children's intelligence.

psychosexual stages Freud's notion of five stages in which sexual instincts are associated with different erogenous zones.

psychosocial stages Erikson's notion that during our life span, we pass through eight psychosocial stages, each representing a turning point with a potential for growth as well as vulnerability.

puberty Biological developments that transform individuals from a state of physical immaturity to one in which they are mature and capable of reproduction.

race Technically, a race is an interbreeding population whose members share a greater number of traits with one another than they do with people outside the group.

reaction range The degree to which variations in environments can affect the development of children within the boundaries of the genetic code.

recall A type of memory that involves remembering a stimulus that is not present.

recasting Rephrasing something the child said to reflect the complexity of speech.

receptive speech The meaning infants attach to what others say.

recessive Said of an allele that must be present in a homozygous pair to be phenotypically expressed.

recognition A type of memory that involves noticing whether a stimulus is identical or similar to one previously experienced.

reflexes Unlearned responses that involve a reaction of an organism to a specific, eliciting stimulus.

rehearsal A memory strategy that involves repeating the words or information to be remembered either aloud or mentally.

rejected-aggressive children Actively disliked by peers, they are argumentative, disruptive, inattentive, and unsociable. These children are most at-risk for pathological problems.

rejected children Actively disliked by their peers. Some rejected children are aggressive and some are nonaggressive.

representation The understanding that an object in a model stands for a corresponding object in a real-life setting.

resilient children Children able to bounce back from those unwanted curves life sometimes throws us; they are positive in mood and adaptive to change.

responsiveness Refers to the degree to which parents respond to children's needs in an accepting, supportive manner.

retrieval A class of strategies aimed at getting information out of long-term memory.

reversibility Consists of two types negation (or inversion)—if $5 + 2 = 7$, then $7 - 2 = 5$—and compensation (or reciprocity)—for any operation there exists another operation that compensates for the effects of the first.

Rh factor A protein that when present in the fetus's blood but not in the mother's causes the mother to build up antibodies. In any subsequent pregnancies, these antibodies can be passed on to the fetus, destroying its red blood cells and reducing oxygen supplies to vital organs and tissues.

ribonucleic acid (RNA) An RNA molecule that has been transcribed from a gene-bearing DNA molecule and will later be translated into a protein.

role-sharing families Families of teenage mothers where each member shares in the responsibilities of raising the infant.

scaffolding Temporary assistance provided by one person to a lesser-skilled person when learning a new task.

schemes Mental patterns or systems that describe the way people think about the world. A particular system, in Piaget's theory, that reflects what the child knows—his or her arsenal of knowledge.

secondary sex characteristics The anatomical and physiological signs that outwardly distinguish males from females. They make their appearance as the primary sexual organs are maturing.

secular trend A trend toward earlier maturation, in which children at all ages are growing larger than those from earlier generations.

secure base The use of the familiar caregiver as a base from which the infant confidently explores the environment and for emotional support.

securely attached attachment relations An infant–caregiver bond in which the child welcomes contact with a close companion and uses this person as a secure base from which to explore the environment.

self-concept The acquisition of categories that define the self; how children describe themselves.

self-conscious emotions Emotions such as embarrassment, empathy, pride, shame, and envy emerge when children become self-aware of a standard of behavior against which the self can evaluate its own action.

self-esteem How individuals evaluate their conceptions of self.

semantics A branch of linguistics that studies the meaning of words and sentences.

semen The sticky fluid that men ejaculate, containing sperm, which is capable of fertilizing eggs and making a woman pregnant.

sensorimotor period (from birth to age 2) Period during which children solve problems using senses and motor activities; they are action thinkers—meaning they think and do at the same time.

sensory register A part of the memory sequence that picks up sights and sounds and allows them to persist for a brief period of time after they have been removed.

separation anxiety The distress that infants show when their mother leaves the room.

set point The weight the child maintains when no effort is made to gain or lose weight.

sex chromosome See *gamete.*

sex-linked characteristics Those that depend on X and Y chromosomes.

sexual abuse The involvement of a developmentally immature child or adolescent and an adult in sexual activities that violate social mores.

sexually transmitted diseases Any disease that can be transmitted through sexual contact.

shared family environment Factors such as parental attitudes, education, socioeconomic factors, experiences, and the effects of those experiences that family members have in common.

short-term memory (STM) The temporary, active, conscious memory; our attention span or working memory.

shy children Nonassertive, they tend to be uncomfortable around strangers and prefer solitary activities.

sickle-cell disease An inherited disorder that affects predominantly African Americans; it is accompanied by severe anemia and markedly reduces life expectancy. A genetic disorder in which the blood cells become curved or sickle-shaped, causing clotting in joints or body organs.

simulations Models that combine content and problem-solving, immersing students in experiences that would be difficult to duplicate in real life.

slow-to-warm-up temperament Descriptive of babies who are low in activity level; their responses are typically mild; and they tend to withdraw from new situations.

social cognition When infants possess thoughts and feelings about their own and other people's motives and behaviors.

social competence Refers to a set of skills that collectively result in successful social functioning with peers.

socialization Refers to how parents rear their children and how children learn to become acceptable members of society.

social learning theory A theory by Bandura that emphasizes social variables as determinants of behavior and personality.

social referencing Relying on a trusted person's emotional reaction to decide how to respond in an ambiguous situation.

soma The cell body of the neuron.

speed The ability to cover a short distance in as brief a time as possible.

spermarche Around the age of 12 or 13, boys experience their first ejaculation of semen.

sprouting The extensiveness of dendrite branching in the neurons.

stimulants Drugs that stimulate activity, suppress the appetite, and ameliorate emotional depression: examples include caffeine, nicotine, Methedrine, and cocaine; also known as uppers.

stranger anxiety A wary or fretful reaction that infants often display when approached by an unfamiliar person.

Strange Situation test A series of eight separation and reunion episodes to which infants are exposed to determine the quality of their attachments.

stress A feeling of high emotional tension that children experience when they encounter an event or situation that they perceive as a threat to their well-being.

stressors Environmental forces or events that make children feel they lack adequate coping strategies.

sudden infant death syndrome (SIDS) The unexplainable death of an infant. It is the leading cause of infant mortality.

superego Freud's level of personality that represents ideals on morals and manners.

survey A research design that investigates many cases at once via questionnaires and/or interviews.

symbolic play Pretend play; substituting imaginary situations for real ones.

synapses Microscopic gaps that exist between neurons; where communication between neurons takes place.

synaptogenesis The formation of synapses or connectivity between neurons; implicated in behavior functions and higher-order mental functioning.

syntax A branch of linguistics that studies the way words come together to form sentences.

syphilis Sexually transmitted disease contracted through vaginal, anal, and oral intercourse and kissing; symptoms are sores and ulcers and, 3 to 6 weeks later, body rashes, fatigue, and sore throat. If untreated with antibiotics, death may result.

tabula rasa Locke argued that children's minds were like a "blank tablet" on which experience writes, creating their personalities.

Tay-Sachs disease (TSD) A fatal genetic disorder in children that causes the progressive destruction of the central nervous system.

telegraphic speech Early utterances by young children that leave out words not essential for communicating meaning.

temperament Stable individual differences in quality and intensity of emotional reaction.

teratogens External agents, such as viruses, drugs, chemicals, and radiation, that can impair prenatal development and lead to abnormalities, disabilities, or even death.

testosterone A hormone associated in boys with the development of secondary sex characteristics.

theory of mind Ideas about mental states like thoughts, beliefs, or dreams and the relations among those states.

theory of multiple intelligences Howard Gardner theory that dismisses the idea of general intelligence and proposes eight independent intelligences.

thyroid-stimulating hormone (TSH) A pituitary hormone that stimulates the thyroid gland to release its hormone thyroxine, which is necessary for normal brain development and body growth.

toddlers The term applied to infants from the period when they begin to walk until they achieve a stable pattern at about 24 months.

transductive reasoning Preoperational thinkers' tendency to reason from one particular instance to another.

Turner's syndrome A chromosomal abnormality that results from the presence of only one sex chromosome, an X. Children with this syndrome are female but sterile.

unconscious mind Freud defined it as a sort of mental receptacle for ideas too anxiety-producing for the conscious mind to acknowledge.

underachievers Individuals whose performance falls below expected IQ levels.

variance The percentage of individual differences on certain traits that can be accounted for or explained by another factor or factors is something behavioral geneticists try to explain.

vicarious reinforcement A central tenet of social learning theory that says learning will take place even when reinforcement is indirectly applied; children observe others being reinforced and then emulate that behavior with the anticipation that they, too, will receive reinforcement and praise.

visual cortex The part of the brain that controls vision, visual thoughts, and images.

Wernicke's area A language area located in the temporal lobe of the brain; it assists with understanding expressive speech.

word processing Using the computer as a sophisticated typewriter, adding the flexibility of revising and editing into the learning process.

zone of proximal development Vygotsky's phrase for range of various kinds of support and assistance provided by a more skilled adult or peer who helps children to carry out activities they currently are unable to complete but will later be able to accomplish independently.

REFERENCES

Aaronson, L. S., & Macnee, C. L. (1989). Tobacco, alcohol, and caffeine use during pregnancy. *JOGNN, 22,* 279–286.

Abel, E. L. (1998). *Fetal alcohol abuse syndrome.* New York: Plenum Press.

Aboud, F. E., & Mendelson, M. J. (1998). Determinants of friendship selection and quality: Developmental perspectives. In W. M. Bukowski & A. F. Newcomb (Eds.), *The company they keep: Friendship in childhood and adolescence* (pp. 87–112). New York: Cambridge University Press.

Ackerman, C. M. (1997). Identifying gifted adolescent's using personality characteristics: Dabrowski's overexcitabilities. *Roeper Review, 19,* 229–236.

Adams, G. R. (1991). Physical attractiveness and adolescent development. In R. Lerner, A. Petersen, & J. Brooks-Gunn (Eds.), *Encyclopedia of adolescence* (pp. 785–794). New York: Garland.

Adams, G. R., Ryan, J. H., Hoffman, J. J., Dobson, W. R., & Nielson, E. C. (1985). Ego-identity status, conformity behavior, and personality in late adolescence. *Journal of Personality and Social Psychology, 47,* 1091–1104.

Adams, M. J. (1990). *Learning to read: Thinking and learning about print.* Cambridge, MA: MIT Press.

Adler, S. A., Gerhardstein, P., & Rovee-Collier, C. (1998). Levels of processing effects in infant memory. *Child Development, 69,* 280–294.

Adolph, K. E., Vereijken, B., & Denny, M. A. (1998). Learning to crawl, *Child Development, 69,* 1299–1312.

Agnihotri, R. K., & Khanna, A. L. (1997). The social psychological perspective on second language learning: A critique. In R. Singh (Ed.), *Grammar, language, and society: Contemporary Indian contributions* (pp. 325–342). Thousands Oaks, CA: Sage.

Ahluwalia, J., Grummer-Strawn, L., & Scanlon, K. (1997). Exposure to environmental tobacco smoke and birth outcome: Increased effects on pregnant women aged 30 years or older. *American Journal of Epidemiology, 46,* 42–47.

Ahmed, A., & Ruffman, T. (2000). Why do infants make A not B errors in a search task, yet show memory for the location of hidden in a nonsearch task? In D. Muir & A. Slater (Eds.), *Infant development: The essential readings* (pp. 213–237). Malden, MA: Blackwell.

Ahnert, L., Meischner, T., & Schmidt, A. (2000). Maternal sensitivity and attachment in East German and Russian family networks. In P. Crittenden & A. H. Claussen (Eds.), *The organization of attachment relationships* (pp. 61–74). Cambridge, MA: Cambridge University Press.

Aiken, L. R. (2001). *Dying, death, and bereavement.* Mahwah, NJ: Erlbaum.

Ainsworth, M. (1967). *Infancy in Uganda.* Baltimore: Johns Hopkins.

Ainsworth, M. (1973). The development of infant–mother attachment. In B. M. Caldwell & H. N. Ricciuti (Eds.), *Review of child development research* (Vol. 3, pp. 1–94). Chicago: University of Chicago Press.

Ainsworth, M., Blehar, M., Waters, E., & Wall, S. (1978). *Patterns of attachment.* Hillsdale, NJ: Erlbaum.

Ajayi, J. F. A. (1993). On the politics of being mortal. *Transition, 59,* 32–44.

Akan, G. E., & Grilo, C. M. (1995). Sociocultural influences on eating attitudes and behaviors, body image, and psychological functioning: A comparison of African-American, Asian-American, and Caucasian college women. *International Journal of Eating Disorders, 18,* 181–187.

Alan Guttmacher Institute. (1994). *Facts in brief: Teenage reproductive health in the United States.* New York: Author.

Alexander, C. S., Allen, P., Crawford, M. A., & McCormick, L. K. (1999). Taking a first puff: Cigarette smoking experiences among ethnically diverse adolescents. *Ethnicity and Health, 4,* 245–257.

Allan, A. M., Weeber, E. J., Savage, D. D., & Caldwell, K. K. (1997). Effects of prenatal ethanol exposure on phospholipase C-betal and phospholipase A-sub-Z in hippocampus and medial frontal cortex of adult rate offspring. *Alcoholism: Clinical and Experimental Research, 21,* 1534–1541.

Allan, J. D. (1997). Explanatory models of overweight among African American, Euro-American, and Mexican American women. *Western Journal of Nursing Research, 20*(1), 45–66.

Allen, K. E., & Marotz, L. R. (1999). *Developmental profiles.* Albany, NY: Delmar Publishers.

Allen, L., & Mitchell, C. (1998). Racial and ethnic differences in patterns of problematic and adaptive development: An epidemiological review. In V. C. McLoyd & L. Steinberg (Eds.), *Studying minority adolescents: Conceptual, methodological, and theoretical issues* (pp. 9–54). Mahwah, NJ: Erlbaum.

Allen, R. (1992). Social factors associated with the amount of school week sleep lag for seniors in an early-starting suburban high school. *Sleep Research, 21,* 114.

Altschuler, J. L., & Ruble, D. N. (1989). Developmental changes in children's awareness of strategies for coping with uncontrollable stress. *Child Development, 60,* 1337–1349.

Amato, P. R. (1998). More than money? Men's contributions to their children's lives. In A. Booth & A. C. Crouter (Eds.), *Men in families: When do they get involved? What difference does it make?* (pp. 241–279). Mahwah, NJ: Erlbaum.

Amato, P. R. (2000). Diversity within single-parent families. In D. H. Demo & K. R. Allen (Eds.), *Handbook of family diversity* (pp. 149–172). New York: Oxford University Press.

Amato, P. R., & Booth, A. (1996). A prospective study of divorce and parent–child relationships. *Journal of Marriage and the Family, 58,* 356–365.

Amato, P. R., & Rezac, S. J. (1994). Contact with nonresidential parents, interparental conflict, and children's behavior. *Journal of Family Issues, 15,* 191–207.

American Academy of Pediatrics, Committee on Nutrition. (1999). Iron-fortified infant formulas. *Pediatrics, 94,* 114–115.

American Association of University Women (1992). *The AAUW report: How schools shortchange girls.* Washington, DC: Author.

American Association of University Women. (1999). *Gender gaps.* New York: Marlow & Co.

American Psychiatric Association (APA). (1994). *Diagnostic and Statistical manual of mental disorders* (4th ed.). Washington, DC: Author.

Amoateng, A. Y., & Heaton, T. B. (1989). The sociodemographic correlates of the timing of divorce in Ghana. *Journal of Comparative Family Studies, 20,* 79–96.

Anandalaksmy, S., & Bajaj, M. (1988). Childhood in the weaver's community in Varanasi: Socialization for adult roles. In D. Sinha (Ed.), *Socialization of the Indian child* (pp. 31–38). New Delhi: Concept Publishing.

Anastasi, A. (1958). Heredity, environment, and the question of "how?" *Psychological Review, 65,* 350–360.

Anastasi, A. (1989). *Psychological testing* (6th ed.). New York: Macmillan.

Anderson, E. R., & Greene, S. M. (1999). Children of stepparents and blended families. In W. K. Silverman & T. H. Ollendick (Eds.), *Developmental issues in the clinical treatment of children* (pp. 342–357). Boston: Allyn & Bacon.

Anderson, R. C., Wilson, P. T., & Fielding, L. G. (1988). Growth in reading and how children spend their free time. *Reading Research Quarterly, 23,* 285–303.

Andujo, E. (1988). Ethnic identity of transethnically adopted Hispanic adolescents. *Social Work, 33,* 531–535.

Angement, H., & de Man, A. (1993). *Child rearing, personality development, and deviant behavior*. New York: Thompson Educational Publishing, Co.

Anisfeld, E., Casper, V., Nozyce, M., & Cunningham, N. (1990). Does infant carrying promote attachment? An experimental study of the effects of increased physical contact on the development of attachment. *Child Development, 61*, 1617–1627.

Apgar, V. (1953). A proposal for a new method of evaluation of the newborn infant. *Current Research in Anesthesia and Analgesia, 32*, 260–267.

Arcia, E., & Johnson, A. (1998). When respect means to obey: Immigrant Mexican mothers' values for their children. *Journal of Child and Family Studies, 7*, 79–95.

Arendell, T. (1997). A social constructionist approach to parenting. In T. Arendell (Ed.), *Contemporary parenting: Challenges and issues* (pp. 1–44). Thousand Oaks, CA: Sage.

Aries, P. (1962). *Centuries of childhood*. New York: Knopf.

Armistead, L., Forehand, R., Steele, R., & Kotchick, B. (1998). Pediatric AIDS. In T. H. Ollendick & M. Hersen (Eds.), *Handbook of child psychopathology* (pp. 463–481). New York: Plenum.

Arnett, J. J. (1999). Adolescent storm and stress, reconsidered. *American Psychologist, 54*, 317–326.

Arthur, L. B. (1999). Dress and the social construction of gender in two sororities. *Clothing and Textiles Research Journal, 17*, 84–93.

Ary, D. V., Duncan, T. E., Duncan, S. C., & Hops, H. (1999). Adolescent problem behavior: The influence of peers and parents. *Behaviour Research and Therapy, 37*, 217–230.

Asamen, J. K., & Berry, G. L. (Eds.). (1998). *Research paradigms, television, and social behavior.* Thousand Oaks, CA: Sage.

Asendorpf, J. B. (1993). Beyond temperament. In K. H. Rubin & J. B. Asendorpf (Eds.), *Social withdrawal, inhibition, and shyness in childhood* (pp. 265–289). Hillsdale, NJ: Erlbaum.

Asendorpf, J. B. (1998). Personality effects on social relationships. *Journal of Personality and Social Psychology, 74*, 1531–1544.

Asher, S. R., & Coie, J. D. (Eds.). (1990). *Peer rejection in childhood*. New York: Cambridge University Press.

Asher, S. R., Parker, J. G., & Walker, D. L. (1998). Distinguishing friendship from acceptance: Implications for intervention and assessment. In W. H. Bukowski, A. F. Newcomb, & W. W. Hartup (Eds.), *The company they keep: Friendship in childhood and adolescence* (pp. 366–405). New York: Cambridge University Press.

Asher, S. R., & Rose, A. J. (1997). Promoting children's social–emotional adjustment with peers. In P. Salovey & D. J. Sluyter (Eds.), *Emotional development and emotional intelligence: Educational implications* (pp. 196–230). New York: Basic Books.

Ashland Daily Tidings (1993, November 18), p. 14.

Assaiante, C. (1998). Development of locomotor balance control in healthy children. *Neuroscience and Biobehavioral Reviews, 22*, 527–532.

Association of Black Social Workers and Allied Professions. (1993). *Black children in care: Evidence to the House of Commons Social Services Committee.* London: Author.

Astington, J. W. (1993). The child's discovery of the mind. Cambridge, MA: Harvard University Press.

Astington, J. W. (1998). Theory of mind, Humpty Dumpty, and the icebox. *Human Development, 41*, 30–39.

Astington, J. W., & Gopnik, A. (1988). Knowing you've changed your mind: Children's understanding of representational change. In J. W. Astington, P. L. Harris, & D. R. Olson (Eds.), *Developing theories of mind*. Cambridge, England: Cambridge University Press.

Astington, J. W., & Olson, D. R. (1995). The cognitive revolution in children's understanding of mind. *Human Development, 38*, 179–189.

Attili, G., Vermigli, P., & Schneider, B. H. (1997). Peer acceptance and friendship patterns among Italian schoolchildren within a cross-cultural perspective. *International Journal of Behavioral Development, 21*, 277–288.

Au, T. K. (1990). Children's use of information in word learning. *Journal of Child Language, 17*, 393–416.

Au, T. K., Dapretto, M., & Song, Y. K. (1994). Input vs. constraints: Early word acquisition in Korean and English. *Journal of Memory and Language, 33*, 567–582.

Austin, E. W., Roberts, D. F., & Nass, C. I. (1990). Influences of family communication on children's television-interpretation processes. *Communication Research, 17*, 545–564.

Averett, S. L., Gennetian, L. A., & Peters, H. E. (2000). Patterns and determinants of paternal child care during a child's first three years of life. *Marriage and Family Review, 29*, 115–136.

Aviezer, D., van IJzendoorn, M. H., Sagi, A., & Schuengel, C. (1994). "Children of the dream" revisited: 70 years of collective early child care in an Israeli Kibbutz. *Psychological Bulletin, 116*, 99–116.

Avis, J., & Harris, P. L. (1991). Belief-desire reasoning among Baka children: Evidence for a universal conception of mind. *Child Development, 62*, 460–467.

Azar, S. T. (1998). A cognitive behavioral approach to understanding and treating parents who physically abuse their children. In D. A. Wolfe & R. J. McMahon (Eds.), *Child abuse: New directions in prevention and treatment across the lifespan* (pp. 79–101). Thousand Oaks, CA: Sage.

Azar, S. T., & Bober, S. L. (1999). Children of abusive parents. In W. K. Silverman & T. H. Ollendick (Eds.), *Developmental issues of the clinical treatment of children* (pp. 371–389). Boston: Allyn & Bacon.

Azar, S. T., Breton, S. J., & Miller, L. R. (1998). Cognitive-behavioral group work and physical child abuse: Intervention and prevention. In K. C. Stoiber & T. R. Kratochwill (Eds.), *Handbook of group intervention for children and families* (pp. 376–400). Boston: Allyn & Bacon.

Azmitia, M., Kamprath, N. A., & Linnet, J. (1998). Intimacy and conflict: The dynamics of boys' and girls' friendships during middle childhood and early adolescence. In L. H. Meyer, H. S. Park, M. Grenot-Scheyer, I. S. Schwartz, & B. Harry (Eds.), *Making friends: The influence of culture and development* (pp. 171–187). Baltimore: Paul H. Brookes.

Azuma, H. (1994). Two modes of cognitive socialization in Japan and the United States. In. P. M. Greenfield & R. R. Cocking (Eds.), *Cross-cultural roots of minority child development* (pp. 275–284). Hillsdale, NJ: Erlbaum.

Azuma, H. (1998). Japanese collectivism and education. In S. G. Paris & H. M. Wellman (Eds.), *Global prospects for education: Development, culture, and schooling* (pp. 291–307). Washington, DC: American Psychological Association.

Azzarto, J. (1997). A young women's support group: Prevention of a different kind. *Health and Social Work, 22*, 299–305.

Bagwell, C. L., Newcomb, A. F., & Bukowski, W. M. (1998). Preadolescent friendship and peer rejection as predictors of adult adjustment. *Child Development, 69*, 140–153.

Baharudin, R., & Luster, T. (1998). Factors related to the quality of the home environment and children's achievement. *Journal of Family Issues, 19*, 375–403.

Bahrick, L. E. (1995). Intermodal origins of self-perception. In P. Rochat (Ed.), *The self in infancy: Theory and research* (pp. 349–373). Amsterdam: North Holland-Elsevier.

Bailey, C. E., & Piercy, F. P. (1997). Enhancing ethical decision making in sexuality and AIDS education. *Adolescence, 32*, 989–998.

Bailey, G. W. (1998). Current perspectives on substance abuse in youth. *Journal of the American Academy of Adolescent Psychiatry, 28*, 151–162.

Bailey, J. M., & Zucker, K. (1995). Childhood sex-typed behavior and sexual orientation: A conceptual analysis and quantitative review. *Developmental Psychology, 50*, 43–55.

Baillargeon, R. (1994). How do infants learn about the physical world? *Current Directions in Psychological Science, 3*, 133–140.

Baillargeon, R. (2000). How do infants learn about the physical world? In D. Muir & A. Slater (Eds.), *Infant development: The essential readings* (pp. 193–212). Malden, MA: Blackwell.

Balaban, M. T., Snidman, N., & Kagan, J. (1997). Attention, emotion, and reactivity in infancy and early childhood. In P. J. Lang & R. F. Simons (Eds.),

Attention and orienting: Sensory and motivational processes (pp. 369–391). Mahwah, NJ: Erlbaum.

Bandura, A. (1977). *Social learning theory.* Englewood Cliffs, NJ: Prentice-Hall.

Bandura, A. (1991). Social cognitive theory of moral thought and action. In W. M. Kurtines & J. W. Gewirtz (Eds.), *Handbook of moral behavior and development* (pp. 45–103). Hillsdale, NJ: Erlbaum.

Bandura, A. (1997). *Self-efficacy: The exercise of control.* New York: W. H. Freeman.

Bangert-Drowns, R. L. (1993). The word processor as an instructional tool. A meta-analysis of word-processing in writing instruction. *Review of Educational Psychology, 53,* 143–158.

Barker, G., & Loewenstein, I. (1997). Where the boys are: Attitudes related to masculinity, fatherhood, and violence toward women among low-income adolescent and young adult males in Rio de Janeiro, Brazil. *Youth and Society, 29,* 166–196.

Barker, S. E., & O'Neil, P. M. (1999). Anorexia and bulimia nervosa. In A. J. Goreczny & M. Hersen (Eds.), *Handbook of pediatric and adolescent health psychology* (pp. 71–86). Boston: Allyn & Bacon.

Barlow, D. H., & Durand, V. M. (1999). *Abnormal psychology: An integrative approach.* Brooks/Cole.

Barnat, S. B., Klein, P. J., & Meltzoff, A. N. (1996). Deferred imitation across changes in context and object: Memory and generalization in 14-month-old infants. *Infant Behavior and Development, 19,* 241–251.

Barnett, D., Manly, J. T., & Cicchetti, D. (1993). Continuing toward an operational definition of psychological maltreatment. *Development and Psychopathology, 3,* 19–30.

Barnett, W. S., & Boocock, S. S. (Eds.). (1998). *Early childcare and education for children in poverty: Promises, programs, and long-term results.* Albany, NY: State University of New York Press.

Bar-Or, O., Foreyt, J., Bouchard, C., Brownell, K. D., Dietz, W. H., Ravussin, E., Salbe, A. D., Schwenger, S., St.Jeor, S., & Torun, B. (1998). Physical activity, genetic, and nutritional considerations in childhood weight management. *Medicine and Science in Sports and Exercise, 30,* 2–10.

Barr, H. M., Streissguth, A., Darby, B., & Sampson, P. (1990). Prenatal exposure to alcohol, caffeine, tobacco, and aspirin: Effects on fine and gross motor performance in 4-year-old children. *Developmental Psychology, 26,* 339–348.

Barrett, K. C. (Ed.). (1997). *The communication of emotion: Current research from diverse perspectives.* San Francisco: Jossey-Bass.

Barrett, K. C., & Ferguson, T. (2001, April 19–22). *Personality patterns and violent tendencies in adolescence.* Paper presented at the biennial meeting of the Society for Research in Child Development, Minneapolis.

Barrett, K. C., & Nelson-Goens, G. C. (1997). Emotion communication and the development of the social emotions. In K. C. Barrett (Ed.), *The communication of emotion: Current research from diverse perspectives. New directions for child development* (No. 77, pp. 69–88). San Francisco: Jossey-Bass.

Barr-Zisowitz, C. (2000). "Sadness." Is there such a thing? In M. Lewis & J. M. Haviland- Jones (Eds.), *Handbook of emotions* (pp. 607–622). New York: Guilford Press.

Barth, J., & Parke, R. D. (1993). Parent–child relationship influences on children's transition to school. *Merrill-Palmer Quarterly, 39,* 173–195.

Barth, R. P. (1998). Abusive and neglecting parents and the care of their children. In M. A. Mason & A. Skolnick (Eds.), *All our families: New policies for a new century* (pp. 217–235). New York: Oxford University Press.

Barth, R. P. (2001). Policy implications of foster family characteristics. *Family Relations: Interdisciplinary Journal of Applied Family Studies, 50*(1), 16–19.

Barton, M. E., & Tomasello, M. (1991). Joint attention and conversation in mother-infant-sibling triads. *Child Development, 62,* 517–529.

Basow, S. A., & Rubin, L. R. (1999). Gender influences on adolescent development. In N. Johnson & M. C. Roberts (Eds.), *Beyond appearance: A new look at adolescent girls* (pp. 25–52). Washington, DC: American Psychological Association.

Bates, E. (1979). *The emergence of symbols.* New York: Academic Press.

Bates, E. (1995). *Modularity, domain specificity, and the development of language.* Cambridge, England: Cambridge University Press.

Bates, E., Bretherton, I., & Snyder, L. (1988). *From first words to grammar* (pp. 1–92). Cambridge, England: Cambridge University Press.

Bates, E., & Elman, J. (1996). Learning rediscovered. *Science, 274,* 1849–1850.

Bates, E., O'Connell, B., & Shore, C. (1987). Language and communication in infancy. In J. D. Osofsky (Ed.), *Handbook of infant development* (pp. 149–203). New York: Wiley.

Bates, E., Marchman, V., Thal, D., Fenson, L., Dale, P., Reznick, J., Reilly, J., & Hartung, J. (1994). Developmental and stylistic variation in the composition of early vocabulary. *Journal of Child Language, 21,* 85–123.

Batshaw, M. L. (1997). PKU and other inborn errors of metabolism. In M. L. Batshaw (Ed.), *Children with disabilities* (pp. 389–404). Baltimore: Paul H. Brookes.

Batshaw, M. L., & Conlon, C. J. (1997). Substance abuse: A preventable threat to development. In M. L. Batshaw (Ed.), *Children with disabilities* (pp. 143–162). Baltimore: Paul H. Brookes.

Batshaw, M. L., & Rose, N. C. (1997). Birth defects, prenatal diagnosis, and fetal therapy. In M. L. Batshaw (Ed.), *Children with disabilities* (pp. 35–52). Baltimore: Paul H. Brookes.

Baumeister, R. F. (2001, April 19–22). *Nature and structure of the self.* Paper presented at the biennial meeting of the Society for Research in Child Development, Minneapolis.

Baumrind, D. (1971). Current patterns of parental authority. *Developmental Psychology Monographs, 4*(1, Serial No. 2).

Baumrind, D. (1989). Rearing competent children. In W. Damon (Ed.), *Child development: Today and tomorrow* (pp. 349–375). San Francisco: Jossey-Bass.

Baumrind, D. (1991). Effective parenting during the early adolescent transition. In P. A. Cowan & E. M. Hetherington (Eds.), *Family transitions* (pp. 111–163). Hillsdale, NJ: Erlbaum.

Baumrind, D. (1993). The average expectable environment is not good enough. A response to Scarr. *Child Development, 54,* 1299–1317.

Baumrind, D. (1997). Necessary distinctions. *Psychological Inquiries, 8*(3), 176–182.

Baumwell, L., Tamis-LaMondaLeMonda, C. S., & Bornstein, M. H. (1997). Maternal verbal sensitivity and child language comprehension. *Infant Behavior and Development, 20,* 247–258.

Baydar, N., Brooks-Gunn, J., & Furstenberg, F. F. (1993). Early warning signs of functional illiteracy: Predictors in childhood and adolescence. *Child Development, 64,* 815–829.

Baydar, N., Brooks-Gunn, J., & Senior, A. M. (1995). How do living arrangements affect the development of black infants? *Family Relations: Interdisciplinary Journal of Applied Family Studies, 44,* 385–393.

Baydar, N., Greek, A., & Gritz, R. M. (1999). Young mothers' time spent at work and time spent caring for children. *Journal of Family and Economic Issues, 20,* 61–84.

Bayley, N. (1933). Mental growth during the first three years. *Genetic Psychology Monographs, 14,* 1–92.

Bayley, N. (1993). *Bayley scales of infant development.* (2nd ed.). San Antonio, TX: Psychological Foundation.

Beach, S. R. H. (1998). Attachment. In E. A. Blechman & K. D. Brownell (Eds.), *Behavioral medicine and women* (pp. 103–107). New York: Guilford Press.

Beale, E. W. (1998). Identification of culturally diverse children with Attention Deficit/Hyperactivity Disorder: A school-based survey. *Dissertation Abstracts International, 59,* Humanities and Social Sciences.

Bear, G. G. (1998). School discipline in the United States: Prevention, correction, and long-term social development. *Educational and Child Psychology, 15,* 15–39.

Beaty, L. A. (1999). Identity development of homosexual youth and parental and familial influences on the coming out process. *Adolescence, 34*(135), 597–601.

Beauvais, F., Chavez, E .L., Oetting, E. R., & Deffenbacher, J. L. (1996). Drug use, violence, and victimization among white American, Mexican American, and American Indian dropouts, students with academic problems, and students in good academic standing. *Journal of Counseling Psychology, 43,* 292–299.

Becker, G. (1997). *Helping the infertile family: Strengthening your relationship in the search for parenthood.* Berkeley, CA: University of California Press.

Bedi, A. (2000). *Path to the soul.* York Beach, ME: Samuel Weiser, Inc.

Beekman, D. (1977). *The mechanical baby.* Westport, CT: Lawrence Hills.

Behnke, M., Eyler, E., Conlon, M., Casanova, O., & Woods, N. (1997). How fetal cocaine exposure increases neonatal hospital costs. *Pediatrics, 99,* 204–208.

Behrens, K. (2001, April 19–22). *Representational models of parenting: The case of Japanese mothers.* Paper presented at the biennial meeting of the Society for Research in Child Development, Minneapolis.

Bell, C. C., & Jenkins, E. J. (1993). Community violence and children on Chicago's southside. In D. Reiss, J. E. Richters, M. Radke-Yarrow, & D. Scharff (Eds.), *Children and violence* (pp. 46–54). New York: Guilford Press.

Bell, M. A. (1998). Frontal lobe function during infancy: Implications for the development of cognition and attention. In J. E. Richards (Ed.), *Cognitive neuroscience of attention: A developmental perspective* (pp. 287–316). Mahwah, NJ: Erlbaum.

Bell, R. Q. (1979). Parent–child and reciprocal influences. *American Psychologist, 34,* 821–826.

Bellenir, K. (Ed.), (1996). *Genetic disorders sourcebook.* Detroit: Omnigraphics, Inc.

Belsky, J. (1996). Parent, infant, and social-contextual antecedents of father–son attachment security. *Developmental Psychology, 32,* 905–913.

Belsky, J. (1998). Paternal influence and children's well-being: Limits of, and new directions for, understanding. In A. Booth & A. C. Crouter (Eds.), *Men in families: When do they get involved? What difference does it make?* (pp. 279–294). Mahwah, NJ: Erlbaum.

Belsky, J., Campbell, S. B., Cohn, J. F., & Moore, G. (1996). Instability of infant–parent attachment security. *Developmental Psychology, 32,* 921–924.

Bem, S. L. (1981). Gender schema theory: A cognitive account of sex-typing. *Psychological Bulletin, 88,* 354–364.

Bem, S. L. (1993). *The lenses of gender: Transforming the debate on sexual inequality.* New Haven, CT: Yale University Press.

Bem, S. L. (1995). Dismantling gender polarization and compulsory heterosexuality: Should we turn the volume down or up? *Journal of Sex Research, 32*(4), 329–334.

Bem, S. L. (1998). *An unconventional family.* New Haven, CT: Yale University Press.

Benda, B. B., & Corwyn, R. F. (1998). Testing theoretical elements as predictors of sexual behavior by race among urban adolescents. *Social Work Research, 22*(2), 75–88.

Bender, D. L., Leone, B., Szumski, B., Wekesser, C., Biskup, M. D., & Cozic, C. P. (1992). *Youth violence.* San Diego: Greenhaven Press.

Bergen, D. (1998). Development of the sense of humor. In W. Ruch (Ed.), *The sense of humor: Explorations of a personality charactaeristics* (pp. 329–358). Berlin, Germany: Walter De Gruyter & Co.

Berggren, N. (1997). Rhetoric or reality? An economic analysis of the effects of religion in Sweden. *Journal of Socio-Economics, 26,* 571–596.

Berk, L. S., Tan, S. A., Fry, W. F., Napier, B. J., Lee, J. W., Hubbard, R. W., Lewis, J. W., & Eby, W. C. (1989). Neuroendocrine and stress hormone changes during mirthful laughter. *American Journal of the Medical Sciences, 298,* 390–396.

Berko, J. (1958). The child's learning of English morphology. *Word, 14,* 150–177.

Berko-Gleason, J. (1997). Language development: An overview and a preview. In J. Berko-Gleason (Ed.), *The development of language* (4th ed., pp. 1–39). Boston: Allyn & Bacon.

Bernbaum, J. C., & Batshaw, M. L. (1997). Born too soon, born too small. In M. L. Batshaw (Ed.), *Children with disabilities* (pp. 115–142). Baltimore: Paul H. Brookes.

Berndt, T. J. (1994). Intimacy and competition in friendships of adolescent boys and girls. In M. R. Stevenson (Ed.), *Gender roles through the life span: A multidisciplinary perspective.* Muncie, IN: Ball State University.

Berndt, T. J., Hawkins, J. A., & Jiao, Z. (1999). Influences of friends and friendships on adjustment to junior high school. *Merrill-Palmer Quarterly, 45,* 13–41.

Berndt, T. J., & Perry, T. B. (1990). Distinctive features and effects of early adolescent friendships. In R. Montemayor, G. Adams, & T. Gullotta (Eds.), *Advances in adolescent development: From childhood to adolescence: A transitional period?* (Vol. 2, pp. 269–287). Beverly Hills, CA: Sage.

Bernhardt, E. M. (1987). The choice of part-time work among Swedish one-child mothers. *Stockholm Research Reports in Demography, No. 41.* Stockholm: University of Stockholm.

Berry, G. L., & Asamen, J. K. (Eds.). (1993). *Children and television: Images in a changing cultural world.* Newbury Park, CA: Sage.

Berry, M., Dylla, D. J. C., Barth, R. P., & Needell, B. (1998). The role of open adoption in the adjustment of adopted children and their families. *Child and Youth Services Review, 20,* 151–171.

Bertenthal, B. I., Campos, J. J., & Barrett, K. C. (1984). Self-produced locomotions: An organizer of emotional, cognitive, and social development in infancy. In. R. Emde & R. Harmon (Eds.), *Continuities and discontinuities in development.* New York: Plenum.

Berzins, J., Welling, M., & Wetter, R. (1975). *The PRF Andro scale user's manual.* Unpublished manuscript. University of Kentucky.

Bettes, B. A., Dusenbury, L., Kerner, J., James-Ortiz, S., & Botvin, G. J. (1990). Ethnicity and psychosocial factors in alcohol and tobacco use in adolescence. *Child Development, 61,* 557–565.

Beverly, C. L. (1995). Providing a safe environment for children infected with the human immunodeficiency virus. *Topics in Early Childhood Special Education, 15,* 100–110.

Bidwell, C., Schneider, B., & Borman, K. (1998). Working: Perceptions and experiences of American teenagers. In K. Borman & B. Schneider (Eds.), *The adolescent years: Social influences and educational challenges* (pp. 142–159). Chicago: National Society for the Study of Education.

Bierman, K. L., Smoot, D. L., & Aumiller, K. (1993). Characteristics of aggressive-rejected, aggressive (nonrejected), and rejected (nonaggressive) boys. *Child Development, 64,* 139–151.

Bild, E. R., & Swain, M. (1989). Minority language students in a French immersion program: Their French proficiency. *Journal of Multilingual and Multicultural Development, 10,* 255–274.

Biller, H. B. (1993). *Fathers and families.* Westport, CT: Auburn House.

Binder, R. L. (1998). American Psychiatric Association resource document on controversies in child custody: Gay and lesbian parenting, transracial adoptions, joint versus sole custody, and custody gender issues. *Journal of the American Academy of Psychiatry and the Law, 26,* 267–276.

Binet, A., & Simon, T. (1905). *The intelligence of the feeble-minded.* (E. S. Kite, Trans.). Baltimore: Williams & Wilkins.

Binghma, C. R., Miller, B. C., & Adams, G. R. (1990). Correlates of age at first sexual intercourse in a national sample of women. *Journal of Adolescent Research, 5,* 18–33.

Binion, V. J. (1990). Psychological androgyny: A black female perspective. *Sex Roles, 22,* 487–507.

Birch, S. H., & Ladd, G. W. (1998). Children's interpersonal behaviors and the teacher–child relationship. *Developmental Psychology, 34,* 934–946.

Birch, S. H., & Ladd, G. W. (1997). The teacher–child relationship and children's early school adjustment. *Journal of School Psychology, 35,* 61–79.

Bird-David, N. (1999). Animism revisited: Personhood, environment, and relational epistemology, *Current Anthropology, 40,* S67–S91.

Birdsong, D. (1999). Age of learning and second language speech. In D. Birdsong (Ed.), *Second language acquisition and the Critical Theory Hypothesis. Second language acquisition research* (pp. 101–131). Mahwah, NJ: Erlbaum.

Bjoenberg, U. (1998). Well-being among Swedish employed mothers with preschool children. In K. Orth-Gomer & M. Chesney (Eds.), *Women, stress, and heart disease* (pp. 133–149). Mahwah, NJ: Erlbaum.

Bjorklund, D. F., & Brown, R. D. (1998). Physical play and cognitive development: Integrating activity, cognition, and education. *Child Development, 69*(3), 604–606.

Blackbill, W., & Fitzgerald, H. E. (1969). Development of the sensory analyzers during infancy. In L. P. Lipsitt & H. W. Reese (Eds.), *Advances in child development and behavior* (pp. 173–208). New York: Academic Press.

Blake, I. K. (1994). Language development and socialization in young African-American children. In P. M. Greenfield & R. R. Cocking (Eds.), *Cross-cultural roots of minority child development* (pp. 147–166). Hillsdale, NJ: Erlbaum.

Bloch, M. N., & Adler, S. M. (1998). African children's play and the emergence of the sexual division of labor. In J. L. Roopnarine, J. E. Johnson, & F. H. Hooper (Eds.), *Children's play in diverse cultures* (pp. 148–178). New York: State University of New York Press.

Block, J., & Robins, R. W. (1993). A longitudinal study of consistency and change in self-esteem from early adolescence to early adulthood. *Child Development, 64,* 90–93.

Bloom, L. (1993). *The transition from infancy to language.* New York: Cambridge University Press.

Bloom, L., Margulis, C., Tinker, & Fujita, N. (1996). Early conversations and word learning: Contributions from child and adult. *Child Development, 67,* 3154–3175.

Blum, N. J., & Mercugliano, M. (1997). Attention-hyperactivity disorder. In M. L. Batshaw (Ed.), *Children with disabilities* (pp. 449–470). Baltimore: Paul H. Brookes.

Blyth, D. A., Simmons, R. G., & Carlton-Ford, S. (1998). The adjustment of early adolescents to school transitions. In R. E. Muuss & H. D. Porton (Eds.), *Adolescence behavior and society* (pp. 178–188). New York: McGraw-Hill.

Blyth, D., & Traeger, C. (1991). The self-concept and self-esteem of early adolescents. In N. Lauter-Klatell (Ed.), *Readings in child development* (pp. 130–135). Mountain View, CA: Mayfield.

Bogenschneider, K., Wu, M., Raffaelli, M., & Tsay, J. (1998). Parent influences on adolescent peer orientation and substance use: The interface of parenting practices and values. *Child Development, 69,* 1672–1688.

Bolger, K. E., Patterson, C. J., & Kupersmidt, J. B. (1998). Peer relationships and self-esteem among children who have been maltreated. *Child Development, 69,* 1171–1197.

Bolig, E. E., Borkowski, J., & Brandenberger, J. (1999). Poverty and health across the life span. In T. L. Whitman, T. V. Merluzzi, & R. D. White (Eds.), *Life-span perspectives on health and illness* (pp. 67–87). Mahwah, NJ: Erlbaum.

Bond, N. W. (2000). Using computers to teach learning. In M. E. Ware & D. E. Johnson (Eds.), *Handbook of demonstrations and activities in the teaching of psychology: Physiological-comparative, perception, learning, cognitive, and developmental* (pp. 149–151). Mahwah, NJ: Erlbaum.

Bon De Matte, L. (1998). Anorexic syndrome in adolescence and anorexia. In P. Bria & A. Ciocca (Eds.), *Psychotherapeutic issues on eating disorders: Models, methods, and results* (pp. 41–48). Rome, Italy: Abramowicz.

Bonnafont, G. (1992, October). *Video games and the child.* Paper presented at a seminar on Myths and Realities of Play, London.

Booth, C. L. (2001, April 19–22). *Mother–infant "quality time." Comparison of infants at home versus full-time child care.* Paper presented at the biennial meeting of the Society for Research in Child Development, Minneapolis.

Bornstein, M. H. (1992). Perception across the life cycle. In M. H. Bornstein & M. E. Lamb (Eds.), *Developmental psychology: An advanced textbook* (pp. 155–209). Hillsdale, NJ: Erlbaum.

Bornstein, M. H. (1995). Information processing (habituation) in infancy and stability in cognitive development. *Human Development, 32,* 129–136.

Bornstein, M. H. (1996). Origins of communication in infancy. In B. M. Velichkovsky & D. M. Rumbaugh (Eds.), *Communicating meaning: The evolution and development of language* (pp. 139–172). Mahwah, NJ: Erlbaum.

Bornstein, M. H., Haynes, O. M., Azuma, H., Galperin, C., Maital, S., Ogino, M., Painter, K., Pascual, L., Pecheus, M. G., Rahn, C., Toda, S., Venuti, P., Vyt, A., & Wright, B. (1998). A cross-national study of self-evaluations and attributions in parenting: Argentina, Belgium, France, Israel, Italy, Japan, and the United States. *Developmental Psychology, 34,* 662–676.

Bornstein, M. H., Haynes, O. M., Pascual, L., Painter, K. M., & Galperin, C. (1999). Play in two societies: Pervasiveness of process, specificity of structure. *Child Development, 70,* 317–331.

Bornstein, M. H., Slater, A., Brown, E., Roberts, E., & Barrett, J. (1997). *Stability of mental development from infancy to later childhood: Three "waves" of research.* In G. Bremner, A. Slater, & G. Butterworth (Eds.), *Infant development: Recent advances* (pp. 191–215). East Sussex, UK: Psychology Press.

Borowsky, D., & Rovee-Collier, C. (1990). Contextual constraints on memory retrieval at six months. *Child Development, 61,* 1569–1583.

Borstelmann, L. J. (1983). Children before psychology: Ideas about children from antiquity to the late 1800s. In P. H. Mussen (Ed.), *Child psychology handbook.* New York: Wiley.

Bortolotti, S., D'Elia, P., & Whissell, C. (1993). When children talk about the causes of emotions, how well do adults and other children understand which emotion they are talking about? *Perceptual and Motor Skills, 77,* 67–78.

Bost, K. K., Vaugh, B. E., Washington, W. M., Cielinski, K. L., & Bradbard, M. R. (1998). Social competence, social support, and attachment: Demarcation of construct domains, measurement, and paths of influence for preschool children attending Head Start. *Child Development, 69,* 192–218.

Botstein, D. (1999). Of genes and genomes. In D. C. Grossman & H. Valtin (Eds.), *Great issues for medicine in the twenty-first century: Ethical and social issues arising out of advances in the biomedical sciences. Annals of the New York Academy of Sciences* (Vol. 882, pp. 32–41). New York: New York Academy of Sciences.

Bouchard, T. J. (1990). Sources of human psychological differences: The Minnesota study of twins reared apart. *Science, 250,* 223–228.

Bouchard, T. J. (1997). The genetics of personality. In K. Blum & E. P. Nobel (Eds.), *Handbook of psychiatric genetics* (pp. 273–296). Boca Raton, FL: Orc Press, Inc.

Bouchard, T. J., & Pedersen, N. (1999). Twins reared apart: Nature's double experiment. In M. C. LaBuda & E. L. Grigorenko (Eds.), *On the way to individuality: Current methodological issues in behavior genetics* (pp. 71–93). Commack, NY: Nova Science Publishers.

Bowey, J. A. (1994). Phonological sensitivity in novice readers and nonreaders. *Journal of Experimental Child Psychology, 58,* 134–159.

Bowlby, J. (1969). *Attachment and loss: Vol. 1. Attachment.* New York: Basic Books.

Bowlby, J. (1973). *Separation: Anxiety and anger.* London: Hogarth.

Bowlby, J. (1980). *Attachment.* New York: Basic Books.

Bowlby, J. (1981). *Attachments, separation, and loss.* New York: Basic Books.

Bowlby, J. (1989). *Secure attachment.* New York: Basic Books.

Boyd-Franklin, N. (1989). *Black families in therapy: A multisystems approach.* New York: Guilford.

Boyes, M. C., & Chandler, M. (1992). Cognitive development, epistemic doubts, and identity formation during adolescence. *Journal of Youth Adolescence, 21,* 277–304.

Boyle, F. M., Vance, J. C., Najman, J. M., & Thearle, M. J. (1996). The mental health impact of stillbirth, neonatal death, or SIDS: Prevalence and patterns of distress among mothers. *Social Science and Medicine, 43,* 1273–1282.

Bradley, C. R. (1998). Child rearing in African American families: A study of the disciplinary practices of African American parents. *Journal of Multicultural Counseling and Development, 26,* 273–281.

Bradley, R. H. (1995). Environment and parenting. In M. H. Bornstein (Ed.), *Handbook on parenting* (pp. 325–262). New York: Erlbaum.

Braet, C., Mervielde, I., & Vandereycken, W. (1997). Psychological aspects of childhood obesity: A controlled study in a clinical and nonclinical sample. *Journal of Pediatric Psychology, 22,* 59–71.

Brainerd, C. J., Stein, L. M., & Reyna, V. F. (1998). On the development of conscious and unconscious memory. *Developmental Psychology, 34,* 342–357.

Brannen, J. (1992). Money, marriage, and motherhood: Dual earner households after maternity leave. In S. Arber & N. Gilbert (Eds.), *Women and working lives* (pp. 54–70). London: Macmillan.

Brannon, L. (2001). Gender: *Psychological perspectives.* Boston: Allyn & Bacon.

Braude, J. (1957). *Encyclopedia of stories, quotations, and anecdotes.* Englewood Cliffs, NJ: Prentice Hall.

Braungart, J. M., Plomin, R., DeFries, J. C., & Fulker, D. W. (1992). Genetic influence tester-rater infant temperament as assessed by Bayley's Infant Behavior Record: Nonadoptive and adoptive siblings and twins. *Developmental Psychology, 28,* 40–47.

Bray, J. H. (1990, August). *The developing stepfamily II: Overview and previous findings.* Paper presented at the 98th Annual Convention of the American Psychological Association, Boston.

Bray, J. H., & Berger, S. H. (1993). Developmental issues in stepfamilies research project: Family relationships and parent–child interactions. *Journal of Family Psychology, 7,* 1–17.

Brazelton, T. B. (1984). *Neonatal behavioral assessment scale.* Philadelphia: Spastics International.

Brazelton, T. B. (1992). *Touchpoints: Your child's emotional and behavioral development.* Addison-Wesley, Reading, MA.

Brenner, V., & Fox, R. A. (1998). Parental discipline and behavior problems in young children. *Journal of Genetic Psychology, 159,* 251–256.

Brent, D., May, D. C., & Kundert, D. K. (1996). The incidence of delayed school entry: A twelve-year review. *Early Education and Development, 7,* 121–135.

Bretherton, J. (1996). Attachment theory and research in historical and personal context. *Contemporary Psychology, 41,* 236–237.

Brewster, K. L. (1994). Race differences in sexual activity among adolescent women: The role of neighborhood characteristics, *American Sociological Review, 59,* 408–424.

Brezina, T. (1998). Adolescent maltreatment and delinquency: The question of intervening processes. *Journal of Research in Crime and Delinquency, 35,* 71–99.

Brickle, G. (1997). Argumentativeness and the facets of the big five. *Psychological Reports, 81,* 1379–1385.

Brockington, I. (1996). *Motherhood and mental health.* Oxford, England: Oxford University Press.

Brodman, M., Thacker, J., & Kranz, R. (1998). *Straight talk about sexually transmitted diseases.* New York: Facts on File, Inc.

Brody, G. H., & Flor, D. L. (1998). Maternal resources, parenting practices, and child competence in rural, single-parent African American families. *Child Development, 69,* 803–816.

Brody, N. (1997). Malleability and change in intelligence. In H. Nyborg (Ed.), *The scientific study of human nature: Tribute to Hans J. Eysenck at eighty* (pp. 311–330). Oxford, England: Pergamon/Elsevier (UK).

Brody, S., & Axelrod, S. (1978). *Mothers, fathers, and children.* New York: International Universities Press.

Brodzinsky, D. M., Smith, D. W., & Brodzinsky, A. B. (1998). *Children's adjustment to adoption: Developmental and clinical issues.* Thousand Oaks, CA: Sage.

Brondolo, E., DiGiuseppe, R., & Tafrate, R. C. (1997). Exposure-based treatment for anger problems: Focus on the feeling. *Cognitive and Behavioral Practice, 4,* 75–98.

Bronfenbrenner, U. (1974). Is early intervention effective? *Columbia Teachers College Record, 76,* 279–303.

Bronfenbrenner, U. (1989). *The ecology of human development.* Cambridge, MA: Harvard University Press.

Bronfenbrenner, U. (1995). The bioecological model from a life course perspective: Reflections of a participant observer. In P. Moen, G. H. Elder, & K. Lüscher (Eds.), *Examining lives in context* (pp. 599–618). Washington, DC: American Psychological Association.

Bronstein, P. (1999). Differences in mothers' and fathers' behaviors toward children: A cross-cultural comparison. In L. A. Peplau & S. C. DeBro (Eds.), *Gender, culture, and ethnicity: Current research about women and men* (pp. 70–82). Mountain View, CA: Mayfield.

Brooks-Gunn, J. (1991). How stressful is the transition to adolescence for girls? In M. E. Colton & S. Gore (Eds.), *Adolescent stress: Causes and consequences* (pp. 131–149). New York: Aldine de Gruyter.

Brooks-Gunn, J., Britto, P. R., & Brady, C. (1999). Struggling to make ends meet: Poverty and child development. In M. E. Lamb (Ed.), *Parenting and child development in "nontraditional" families* (pp. 279–304). Mahwah, NJ: Erlbaum.

Brooks-Gunn, J., & Chase-Lansdale, P. L. (1995). Adolescent parenthood. In M. H. Bornstein (Ed.), *Handbook on parenting* (pp. 113–150). Hillsdale, NJ: Erlbaum.

Brooks-Gunn, J., & Duncan, G. J. (2001). The effects of poverty on children. In E. N. Junn & C. J. Boyatzis (Eds.), *Annual editions: Child growth and development* (pp. 186–200). Guilford, CT: Duskin/McGraw-Hill.

Brooks-Gunn, J., Duncan, G. J., Klebanov, P. K., & Sealand, N. (1993). Do neighborhoods influence child and adolescent development? *American Journal of Sociology, 99*(2), 353–395.

Brooks-Gunn, J., & Paikoff, R. L. (1992). Changes in self-feelings during the transition toward adolescence. In H. McGurk (Ed.), *Childhood social development: Contemporary issues* (pp. 63–97). Hillsdale, NJ: Erlbaum.

Brooks-Gunn, J., & Paikoff, R. L. (1997). Sexuality and developmental transitions during adolescence. In J. Schulenberg & J. L. Maggs, *Health risks and developmental transitions during adolescence* (pp. 190–219). New York: Cambridge University Press.

Broom, B. L. (1998). Parental differences and changes in marital quality, psychological well-being, and sensitivity with first-born children. *Journal of Family Nursing, 4,* 97–112.

Broschart, K. (1992). Women under glasnost: An analysis of "women's place" in contemporary Soviet society. In S. Arber & N. Gilbert (Eds.), *Women and working lives* (pp. 18–127). London: Macmillan.

Brown, I. C. (1963). *Understanding cultures.* Englewood Cliffs, NJ: Prentice-Hall.

Brown, L. M., & Gilligan, C. (1992). *Meeting at the crossroads: Women's psychology and girl's development.* Cambridge, MA: Cambridge University Press.

Brown, R. (1973). The development of language in children. In G. A. Miller (Ed.), *Communication, language, and meaning.* New York: Basic Books.

Brown, R. (1977). Introduction. In C. A. Snow & C. Ferguson (Eds.), *Talking to children.* New York: Cambridge University Press.

Brown, R. (1987). Roger Brown: An autobiography in the third person. In F. S. Kessel (Ed.), *The development of language and language researchers: Essays in honor of Roger Brown* (pp. 395–404). Hillsdale, NJ: Erlbaum. [6]

Brown, R. (1988). Roger Brown: An autobiography in the third person. In F. S. Kessel (Ed.), *The development of language and language researchers: Essays in honor of Roger Brown* (pp. 395–404). Hillsdale, NJ: Erlbaum.

Brown, R. (1996). The language of social relationship. In D. I. Slobin & J. Gerhardt (Eds.), *Social interaction, social context, and language: Essays in honor of Susan Ervin-Tripp* (pp. 39–52). Mahwah, NJ: Erlbaum.

Brown, R., & Bellugi, U. (1964). Three processes in the child's acquisition of syntax. *Harvard Educational Review, 34,* 133–151.

Brown, T. A. (1999). *Genomes.* New York: Wiley-Liss.

Brownell, K. D., & Fairburn, C. G. (Eds.). (1995). *Eating disorders and obesity: A comprehensive handbook.* New York: Guilford Press.

Bruer, J. T., Johnson, M. L., Kirlik A., North, D. C., Rissland, E. L., Bray, N. W., Reilly, K. D., Huffman, L. F., Grupe, L. A., Villan, M. F., Fletcher, K. L., Anumolu, V., Brewer, W. F., & Mishra, P. (1998). Cognitive science in the real world. In W. Bechtel & G. Graham (Eds.), *A companion to cognitive science* (pp. 681–749). Malden, MA: Blackwell.

Bryant, B. K. (1998). Children's scoping at school: The relevance of "failure" and cooperative learning for enduring peer and academic success. In L. H. Meyer, H. S. Park, M. Grenot-Scheyer, I. S. Schwartz, & B. Harry (Eds.), *Making friends: The influences of culture and development* (pp. 353–367). Baltimore: Paul H. Brookes.

Bryant, J. (Ed.). (1990). *Television and the American family.* Hillsdale, NJ: Erlbaum.

Bryant, P. E., MacLean, M., Bradley, L. L., & Crossland, J. (1990). Rhyme and alliteration, phoneme detection, and learning to read. *Developmental Psychology, 26,* 429–438.

Buchanan, C. M., Eccles, J. S., & Becker, J. B. (1992). Are adolescents the victims of raging hormones: Evidence for activational effects of hormones on moods and behavior at adolescence. *Psychological Bulletin, 111,* 62–107.

Bu-Haroon, A., Eapen, V., & Bener, A. (1999). The prevalence of hyperactivity symptoms in the United Arab Emirates. *Nordic Journal of Psychiatry, 53,* 439–442.

Bukatko, D., & Daehler, M. W. (1995). Child development: A thematic approach. Boston: Houghton Mifflin.

Bukowski, W., Newcomb, A. F., & Hartup, W. W. (Eds.). (1998). *The company they keep: Friendship in childhood and adolescence.* New York: Cambridge University Press.

Bull, N. L. (1992). Dietary habits, food consumption, and nutrient intake during adolescence. *Journal of Adolescent Health, 13*(6), 384–388.

Bullock, M. (1985). Animism in childhood thinking: A new look at an old question. *Developmental Psychology, 21,* 217–225.

Bullock, M., & Lutkenhaus, P. (1990). Who am I? Self-understanding in toddlers. *Merrill-Palmer Quarterly, 36,* 217–238.

Buntaine, R. L., & Costenbader, V. K. (1997). The effectiveness of a transitional prekindergarten program on later academic achievement. *Psychology in the Schools, 34,* 41–50.

Burciaga, J. A. (1985, November). A day to laugh at death. *San Jose Mercury News.*

Burhmester, D. (1998). Need fulfillment, interpersonal competence, and the developmental contexts of early adolescent friendship. In W. M. Bukowski, A. F. Newcomb, & W. W. Hartup (Eds.), *The company they keep: Friendship in childhood and adolescence* (pp. 158–185). New York: Cambridge University Press.

Buriel, R., Mercado, R., Rodriguez, J., & Chavez, D. V. (1991). Mexican American disciplinary practices and attitudes toward child maltreatment: A comparison of foreign- and native-born mothers. *Hispanic Journal of Behavioral Sciences, 13,* 78–94.

Burnham, D. K., & Harris, M. B. (1992). Effects of real gender and labeled gender on adults' perceptions of infants. *Journal of Genetic Psychology, 153,* 165–183.

Bush, D. M., & Simmons, R. G. (1987). Gender and coping with the entry into early adolescence. In R. C. Barnett, L. Biener, & G. K. Baruch (Eds.), *Gender and stress* (pp. 185–217). New York: Free Press.

Buss, A. H., & Plomin, R. (1984). Temperament: *Early developing personality traits.* Hillsdale, NJ: Erlbaum.

Buss, D. M. (1989). Sex differences in human mate preferences: Evolutionary hypotheses tested in 37 cultures. *Behavioral and Brain Sciences, 12,* 1–49.

Bussey, K., & Bandura, A. (1992). Self-regulatory mechanisms governing gender development. *Child Development, 63,* 1236–1250.

Butcher, J. E. (1989). Adolescent girls' sex role development: Relationship with sports participation, self-esteem, and age at menarche. *Sex Roles, 20,* 575–593.

Buzzelli, C. A. (1992). Popular and rejected children's social reasoning: Linking social status and social knowledge. *Journal of Genetic Psychology, 153,* 331–342.

Bybee, J. (Ed.). (1998). *Guilt and children.* San Diego: Academic Press.

Bybee, J., Merisca, R., & Velasco, R. (1998). The development of reactions of guilt-producing events. In J. Bybee (Ed.), *Guilt and children* (pp. 185–213). San Diego: Academic Press.

Byne, W. (1996). Biology and homosexuality: Implications of neuroendocrinological and neuroanatomical studies. In R. P. Cabaj & T. S. Stein (Eds.), *Textbook of homosexuality and mental health* (pp. 129–146). Washington, DC: American Psychiatric Press.

Caffero-Rouget, A., Long, R., & Van Santen, V. (1989). The impact of sexual abuse on victims' adjustment. *Annals of Sex Research, 2,* 29–47.

Cahill, L., & McGaugh, J. L. (1997). Commentary on the amygdala and individual differences in human fear conditions. *Neuroreport: An International Journal for the Rapid Communication of Research in Neuroscience, 8,* i.

Cain, K. M., & Dweck, C. S. (1995). The relation between motivational patterns and achievement cognitions through the elementary school years. *Merrill-Palmer Quarterly, 41,* 25–52.

Cairns, R. B. (1998). Multiple metaphors for a single idea. *Developmental Psychology, 27,* 23–26.

Cairns, R. B., & Hood, K. E. (1983). Continuity is social development. In P. Baltes & O. G. Brim (Eds.), *Life span development* (pp. 301–358). New York: Academic Press.

Cairns, R. B., Mahoney, J. L., Xie, H., & Cadwallader, T. W. (1999). Issues across development. In W. K. Silverman & T. H. Ollendick (Eds.), *Developmental issues of the clinical treatment of children* (pp. 108–124). Boston: Allyn & Bacon.

Caldera, Y. M., Huston, A. C., & O'Brien, M. (1989). Social interactions and play patterns of parents and toddlers with feminine, masculine, and neutral toys. *Child Development, 60,* 70–76.

Caldera, Y. M., & Sciaraffa, M. A. (1998). Parent–toddler play with feminine toys: Are all dolls the same? *Sex Roles, 39,* 657–668.

Calkins, S. D., & Fox, N. A. (1992). The relations among infant temperament, security of attachment, and behavioral inhibition at twenty-four months. *Child Development, 63,* 1456–1472.

Campbell, J. (1997). *NAEP 1996 Trends in Academic Progress.* Washington, DC: U.S. Department of Education, Office of Educational Research and Improvement, National Center for Education Statistics.

Campero, L., Garcia, C., Diaz, C., Ortiz, O., Reynoso, S., & Langer, A. (1998). "Alone, I wouldn't have known what to do": A qualitative study on social support during labor and delivery in Mexico. *Social Science and Medicine, 47,* 395–403.

Camras, L. A., Oster, H., Campos, J. J., Miyake, K., & Bradshaw, D. (1992). Japanese and American infants' responses to arm restraints. *Developmental Psychology, 28,* 578–583.

Camras, L. A., Oster, H., Joseph, J., Campos, R., Capose, T. U., Kazuo, M., Wang, L., & Meng, Z. (1997). Observer judgments of emotion in American, Japanese, and Chinese infants. In K. C. Barrett (Ed.), *The communication of emotion: Current research from diverse perspectives* (pp. 89–106). San Francisco: Jossey-Bass.

Capelli, C. A., Nakagawa, N., & Madden, C. M. (1990). How children understand sarcasm: The role of context and intonation. *Child Development, 61,* 1824–1841.

Cardon, L. R., Smith, S. D., Fulker, D. W., Kimberling, W. J., Pennington, B. F., & Defries, J. C. (1994). Quantitative trait locus for reading disability on chromosome 6. *Science, 266,* 276–279.

Carey, W. B., McCane-Sanford, T., & Davidson, E. C. (1991). Adolescent age and obstetric risk. *Seminars in Perinatology, 5,* 9–17.

Carlisle, J. F., Beeman, M., Davis, L. H., & Spharim, G. (1999). Relationship of meta-linguistic capabilities and reading achievement for children who are becoming bilingual. *Applied Psycholinguistics, 20,* 459–478.

Carlson, C., Uppal, S., & Prosser, E. C. (2000). Ethnic differences in processes contributing to self-esteem of early adolescent girls. *Journal of Early Adolescence, 20,* 44–67.

Carlson, E. A. (1998). A prospective longitudinal study of attachment disorganization/disorientation. *Child Development, 69,* 1107–1128.

Carlson, E. A., & Sroufe, L. A. (1995). Contribution of attachment theory to developmental psychopathology. In D. Cicchetti & D. J. Cohen (Eds.), *Developmental psychopathology,* (pp. 581–617). New York: Wiley.

Carnegie Task Force. (1994). *Starting points: Meeting the needs of our youngest children.* Carnegie Corporation of New York.

Carroll, J. L., & Shmidt, J. L., Jr. (1992). Correlation between humorous coping style and health. *Psychological Reports, 70,* 402.

Carroll, L. (1995). *Alice in wonderland.* New York: Grammercy. (Originally published in 1865)

Carskadon, M. A. (1990). Patterns of sleep and sleepiness in adolescents. *Pediatrician, 17,* 5–12.

Carskadon, M. A., & Mancuso, J. (1998). Sleep habits in high school adolescents: Boarding versus day students. *Sleep Research, 17,* 74.

Carson, D. K., & Bittner, M. T. (1994). Temperament and school-aged children's coping abilities and responses to stress. *Journal of Genetic Psychology, 155*(3), 289–302.

Carter, B. (1992). Stonewalling feminism. *Family Therapy Networker, 16,* 64–69.

Caruso, D. A. (1996). Maternal employment status, mother–infant interaction, and infant development in daycare and non-daycare groups. *Child and Youth Care Forum, 25,* 125–134.

Case, R. (1985). *Intellectual development: Birth to adulthood.* New York: Academic Press.

Case, R. (1996). Changing views of knowledge and their impact on educational research and practice. In D. R. Olson & N. Torrance (Eds.), *The handbook of education and human development* (pp. 75–99). Oxford, England: Blackwell Publishers.

Case, R. (1996, November 16–17). *Some thoughts about cognitive development.* Computers and Cognitive Development: Invitations Workshop. University of California, Berkeley.

Case, R. (1999). Conceptual development in the child and in the field: A personal view of the Piagetian legacy. In E. K. Scholnick & K. Nelson (Eds.), *Conceptual development: Piaget's legacy* (pp. 23–51). Mahwah, NJ: Erlbaum.

Casiglia, A. C., LoCoco, A., & Zappulla, C. (1998). Aspects of social reputation and peer relationships in Italian children: A cross-cultural perspective. *Developmental Psychology, 34,* 723–730.

Casper, V., Cuffaro, H. K., Schultz, S., & Silin, J. G. (1996). Toward a most thorough understanding of the world: Sexual orientation in early childhood education. *Harvard Educational Review, 66,* 271–293.

Catalyst. (1984). *Why I may or may not want to have children.* New York, 10803.

Cenoz, J., & Valencia, J. F. (1994). Ethnolinguistic vitality, social networks, and motivation in second language acquisition: Some data from the Basque country. *Language, Culture and Curriculum, 6,* 1–15.

Centerwall, B. S. (1995). Television and violent crime. In R. L. DelCampo & D. S. DelCampo (Eds.), *Taking sides: Clashing views on controversial issues in childhood and society* (pp. 180–187). Guilford, CT: Dushkin.

Centers for Disease Control. (1997, May 7). *AIDS weekly surveillance report.* Atlanta. Author.

Centers for Disease Control. (1997). Youth risk behavior surveillance—United States, 1995. *Morbidity and Mortality Report, 46,* 193–199.

Cesare, S. J. (1996). Subjective judgment and the selection interview: A methodological review. *Public Personnel Management, 25,* 291–306.

Chamberlain, P., & Patterson, G. R. (1995). Discipline and child compliance in parenting. In M. H. Bornstein (Ed.), *Handbook on parenting* (pp. 205–226). Hillsdale, NJ: Erlbaum.

Chambers, D. W. (1993). Stereotypic images of the scientist: The draw-a-scientist test. *Science Education, 67,* 255–265.

Chan, D., & Chan, L. K. (1999). Implicit theories of creativity: Teachers' perception of student characteristics in Hong Kong. *Creativity Research Journal, 12,* 185–195.

Chan, H., & Lee, R. P. L. (1995). Hong Kong families: At the crossroads of modernism and traditionalism. *Journal of Comparative Family Studies, 26*(1), 83–99.

Chan, J. (1996). Chinese intelligence. In M. H. Bond (Ed.), *The Handbook of Chinese Psychology* (pp. 93 –108). New York: Oxford University Press.

Chan, R.W., Raboy, B., & Patterson, C. J. (1998). Psychosocial adjustment among children conceived via donor insemination by lesbian and heterosexual mothers. *Child Development, 69,* 443–457.

Chandler, M., & LaLonde, C. (1996). Shifting to an interpretive theory of mind: 5- to 7-year-olds' changing conceptions of mental life. In A. J. Sameroff & M. M. Haith (Eds.), *The five to seven shift: The age of reason and responsibility* (pp. 141–160). Chicago: University of Chicago Press.

Chandra, A., & Stephen, E. (1998). Impaired fecundity in the United States: 1982–1995. *Family Planning Perspectives, 30,* 34–42.

Chang, H. C. (1997). Language and words: Communication in the *"Analects of Confucius." Journal of Language and Social Psychology, 16,* 107–131.

Chang, L. (2001, April 19–22). *Punitive parenting and child aggression in schools: Direct and mediating effects in relation to parents and child gender.* Paper presented at the biennial meeting for the Society for Research in Child Development, Minneapolis.

Chapman, S. (1997, July). Making "I do" stick. *The Oregonian,* 177, C8.

Charman, T., Swettenham, J., Baron-Cohen, S., Cox, A., Baird, G., & Drew, A. (1998). An experimental investigation of social-cognitive abilities of infants with autism: Clinical implications. *Infant Mental Health Journal, 19,* 260–275.

Charpentier, P. (1998). Eating disorders among adolescents: An overview. *Psychiatria Fennica, 29,* 65–77.

Chase-Lansdale, P. L., & Brooks-Gunn, J. (1994). Correlates of adolescent pregnancy. In C. B. Fisher & R. M. Lerner (Eds.), *Applied Developmental Psychology.* Cambridge, MA: McGraw-Hill.

Chase-Lansdale, P. L., & Brooks-Gunn, J. (Eds.). (1995). *Escape from poverty: What makes a difference for children?* New York: Cambridge University Press.

Chasnoff, I., Anson, A., Hatcher, R., Stenson, H., Iaukea, K., & Randolph, L. A. (1998). Prenatal exposure to cocaine and other drugs. Outcome at four to six years. In J. A. Harvey & B .E. Kosofsky (Eds.), *Cocaine: Effects on the developing brain. Annals of the New York Academy of Sciences* (pp. 314–328). New York: New York Academy of Sciences.

Chassin, L., Presson, C. C., Rose, J. S., & Sherman, S. J. (1998). Maternal socialization of adolescent smoking: Intergenerational transmission of smoking-related beliefs. *Psychology of Addictive Behaviors, 12,* 206–216.

Chavkin, W., & Breitbart, V. (1997). Substance abuse and maternity: The United States as a case study. *Addiction, 92,* 1201–1205.

Cheah, C., & Li, M. (2001, April 19–22). *Maternal socialization beliefs regarding preschoolers' social skills: A cross-cultural study of Euro-Americans and mainland Chinese mothers.* Paper presented at the biennial meeting of the Society for Research in Child Development, Minneapolis.

Chen, H., & Sanson, A. (1997). Children's social development as reported by parents: A cross culture comparative study in China and Australia. *Psychological Science China, 20*(6), 490–493, 513.

Chen, K., & Kandel, D. B. (1998). Predictors of cessation of marijuana use: An event history analysis. *Drug and Alcohol Dependence, 50,* 109–121.

Chen, S., & Miyake, K. (1986). Japanese studies of child development. In H. Stevenson, H. Azuma, & K. Hakuta (Eds.), *Child development and education in Japan* (pp. 112–124). New York: Freeman.

Chen, W. J. A., & West, J. R. (1999). Alcohol-induced brain damage during development: Potential risk factors. In J. H. Hannigan & L. P. Spear (Eds.), *Alcohol and alcoholism: Effects on brain development* (pp. 17–37). Mahwah, NJ: Erlbaum.

Chen, X., Hastings, P. D., Rubin, K. H., Chen, H., Cen, G., & Stewart, S. L. (1998). Child-rearing attitudes and behavioral inhibition in Chinese and Canadian toddlers: A cross-cultural study. *Developmental Psychology, 34,* 677–686.

Chen, X., & Rubin, K. H. (1993, July). *Family capital and psychological resources, parental behavior, and children's social competence.* Paper presented at the 12th biennial meetings of the International Society for the Study of Behavioral Development, Recife, Brazil.

Chen, X., Rubin, K. H., & Li, B. S. (1997). Maternal acceptance and social and school adjustment in Chinese children: A four-year longitudinal study. *Merrill-Palmer Quarterly, 43,* 663–681.

Chen, X., Rubin, K. H., Li, B. S., & Li, D. (1999). Adolescent outcomes of social functioning in Chinese children. *International Journal of Behavioral Development, 23,* 199–223.

Chen, X., Rubin, K. H., & Sun, Y. (1992). Social reputation and peer relationships in Chinese and Canadian children: A cross-cultural study. *Child Development, 63,* 1336–1343.

Cherlin, A. J., & Furstenberg, F. F. (1994). Stepfamilies in the United States: A reconsideration. In J. Blake & J. Hagen (Eds.), *Annual review of sociology* (pp. 359–381). Palo Alto, CA: Annual Reviews.

Cherny, S. S., Fulker, D. W., & Hewitt, J. K. (1997). Cognitive development from infancy to middle childhood. In R. J. Sternberg & E. L. Grigorenko (Eds.), *Intelligence, heredity, and environment.* Cambridge, MA: Cambridge University Press.

Chess, S. (1997). The temperament program. In J. K. Zeig (Ed.), *The evolution of psychotherapy: The third conference* (pp. 323–335). Philadelphia: Brunner/Mazel.

Chess, S., & Thomas, A. (1996). *Temperament: Theory and practice.* New York: Brunner/Mazel.

Cheung, C. K., & Liu, E. S. C. (1997). Parental distress and children's problems among single-parent families in China. *Journal of Genetic Psychology, 158,* 245–260.

Chi, M. (1997). Quantifying qualitative analyses of verbal data: A practical guide. *Journal of the Learning Sciences, 6,* 271–315.

Chi, M., deLeeuw, N., Chiu, M., & LaVancher, C. (1994). Eliciting self-explanations improves learning. *Cognitive Science, 18,* 439–477.

Chia, R. C., Allred, L. J., Grossnickle, W. F., & Lee, G. W. (1998). Effects of attractiveness and gender on the perception of achievement-related variables. *Journal of Social Psychology, 138,* 471–477.

Chisholm, J. S. (1983). *Navajo infancy.* New York: Aldine.

Chisholm, J. S. (1989). Biology, culture, and the development of temperament: A Navajo example. In J. K. Nugent, B. M. Lester, & T. B. Brazelton (Eds.), *The cultural context of infancy* (Vol. 1, pp. 341–364). Norwood, NJ: Ablex.

Chisholm, J. S. (1996). Learning "respect for everything": Navajo images. In C. P. Hwang, M. E. Lamb, & I. E. Sigel (Eds.), *Images of childhood* (pp. 167–184). Mahwah, NJ: Erlbaum.

Chodorow, N. J. (1989). *Feminism and psychoanalytical theory.* New Haven, CT: Yale University Press.

Chomitz, V. R., Cheung, L. W. Y., & Lieberman, E. (1995). The role of lifestyle in preventing low birth weight. In *The Future of Children* (pp. 121–138). Center for the Future of Children of the David and Lucile Packard Foundation.

Chomsky, N. (1968). *Language and mind.* New York: Harcourt Brace Jovanovich.

Chomsky, N. (1986). *Knowledge of language: Its nature, origin, and use.* New York: Praeger.

Christianson, R. E. (1990). The relationship between maternal smoking and the incidence of congenital anomalies. *American Journal of Epidemiology, 112,* 684–695.

Chuang, S. (2001, April 19–22). *Chinese mothers' beliefs about the personal domain for young children.* Paper presented at the biennial meeting of the Society for Research in Child Development, Minneapolis.

Chugani, H. T. (1996). Neuroimaging of developmental nonlinearity and development pathologies. In R. W. Thatcher & G. R. Lyon (Eds), *Developmental neuroimaging: Mapping the development of brain and behavior* (pp. 187–195). San Diego: Academic Press.

Chugani, H. T., & Phelps, M. E. (1986). Maturational changes in cerebral function in infants determined by positive emission tomography. *Science, 231,* 840–843. [5]

Chugani, H. T., & Phelps, M. E. (1996). Maturational changes in cerebral function in infants determined by positive emission tomography. *Science, 231,* 840–843. [9]

Chung, S. W., & Doh, H. S. (1997). Parental sociability, parenting behaviors, and shyness in children. *Korean Journal of Child Studies, 18,* 149–161.

Clark, A. G., & Harned, M. S. (2001, April 19–22). *Interpersonal strain and the development of weight concerns in adolescence. The mediating role on social functioning.* Paper presented at the biennial meeting of the Society for Research in Child Development, Minneapolis.

Clark, E. V. (Ed.). (1998). *The proceedings of the twenty-ninth annual child language research forum.* Stanford, CA: Center for the Study of Language and Information.

Clark, H. H. (2001, April 19–22). *Learning to use gestures in utterances.* Paper presented at the biennial meeting of the Society for Research in Child Development, Minneapolis.

Clark, M. L., & Ayers, M. (1991). Friendship similarity during early adolescence: Gender and racial patterns. *Journal of Psychology, 126,* 393–405.

Clarke, A. C. (2000). Of genes and stars. *CMAJ: Canadian Medical Association Journal, 163,* 381–383.

Clarke, A. S. (1997). The American Indian child: Victims of the culture of poverty or cultural discontinuity? In R. D. Taylor & M. C. Wang (Eds.), *Social and emotional adjustment and family relations in ethnic minority families* (pp. 63–82). Mahwah, NJ: Erlbaum.

Clarke-Stewart, K. A. (1992). Consequences of child care for children's development. In A. Booth (Ed.), *Child care in the 1990s: Trends and consequences* (pp. 63–82). Hillsdale, NJ: Erlbaum.

Clarke-Stewart, K. A., Gruber, C. P., & Fitzgerald, L. M. (1994). *Children at home and in day care.* Hillsdale, NJ: Erlbaum.

Clarke-Stewart, K. A., Vandell, D. L., McCartney, K., Owen, M. T., & Booth, C. (2000). Effects of parental separation and divorce on very young children. *Journal of Family Psychology, 14,* 304–326.

Clatts, M. C., Davis, W. R., Sotheran, J. L., & Atillasoy, A. (1998). Correlates and distribution of HIV risk behaviors among homeless youths in New York City: Implications for prevention and policy. *Child Welfare, 77,* 195–207.

Claussen, C. (1993). *Worlds of sense.* London: Routledge.

Clerkx, L. E., & van Ijzendoorn, M. H. (1992). Child care in a Dutch context: On the history, current status, and evaluation of nonmaternal child care in the Netherlands. In M. E. Lamb, K. J. Sternberg, C. Hwang, & A.G. Broberg (Eds.), *Child care in context* (pp. 55–80). Hillsdale, NJ: Erlbaum.

Clinchy, B., & Norem, J. K. (Eds.). (1998). *The gender and psychology reader.* New York: New York University Press.

Cochran, D. L. (1997). African American fathers: A decade review of the literature. *Families in Society, 78,* 340–350.

Cochran, S., Mays, V., & Leung, L. (1991). Sexual practices of heterosexual Asian American young adults: Implications for risk of HIV infection. *Archives of Sexual Behavior, 20,* 381–392.

Cogan, J. C., Bhalla, S. K., Sefa-Dedeh, A., & Rothblum, E. D. (1996). A comparison study of United States and African students' perceptions of obesity and thinness. *Journal of Cross-Cultural Psychology, 27,* 98–113.

Cohen, D. B. (1999). *Stranger in the nest: Do parents really shape their children's personality, intelligence, or character?* New York: Wiley.

Cohen, J. (1997). How many genes are there? *Science, 275,* 769.

Cohen, L. L., & Shotland, R. L. (1996). Timing of first sexual intercourse in relationship: Expectations, experiences, and perceptions of others. *Journal of Sex Research, 33*(4), 291–299.

Cohen, T. F. (1993). What do fathers provide? Reconsidering the economic and nurturant dimensions of men as parents. In J. C. Hood (Ed.), *Men, work, and family* (pp. 1–22). Newbury Park: Sage.

Cohn, J. F., & Tronick, E. Z. (1989). Specificity of infants' response to mothers' affective behavior. *Journal of the American Academy of Child and Adolescent Psychiatry, 28,* 550–559.

Coie, J. D. (1990). Toward a theory of peer rejection. In S. R. Asher & J. D. Coie (Eds.), *Peer rejection in childhood* (pp. 365–401). New York: Cambridge University Press.

Coie, J. D., & Dodge, K. A. (1988). Multiple sources of data on social behavior and social status in school: A cross-age comparison. *Child Development, 59,* 815–829.

Coie, J. D., Terry, R., Lenox, K., Lochman, J., & Hyman, C. (1998). Childhood peer rejections and aggression as predictors of stable patterns of adolescent disorder: Erratum. *Development and Psychopathology, 10,* 587–588.

Cole, D. A., Martin, J. M., Peeke, L. A., Seroczynski, S. D., & Fier, J. (1999). Children's over- and underestimation of academic competence: A longitudinal study of gender differences, depression, and anxiety. *Child Development, 70,* 459–473.

Cole, J. G. (1991). High-risk infants: Prenatal drug exposure (PDE), prematurity, and AIDS. In Lauter-Klatell (Ed.), *Readings in child development* (pp. 36–42). Mountain View, CA: Mayfield.

Cole, M. (1999). Culture in development. In M. H. Bornstein & M. E. Lamb (Eds.), *Developmental psychology: An advanced textbook* (pp. 73–124). Mahwah, NJ: Erlbaum.

Cole, M., & Cole, S. R. (1993). *The development of children.* New York: Scientific American Books.

Cole, P. M., & Tamang, B. L. (1998). Nepali children's ideas about emotional displays in hypothetical challenges. *Developmental Psychology, 34,* 640–646.

Coleman, E. (1997). Child physical and sexual abuse among chemically dependent individuals. *Journal of Chemical Dependency, 1,* 27–38.

Coles, R. (1970). *Erik H. Erikson: The growth of his work.* Boston: Little, Brown.

Coles, R. (1971). *Migrants, sharecroppers, and mountaineers* (pp. 435–436). Children of Crisis Series. Boston: Little, Brown.

Coley, R. L., & Chase-Lansdale, P. L. (1998). Adolescent pregnancy and parenthood: Recent evidence and future directions. *American Psychologist, 53,* 152–166.

Coley, R. L., & Chase-Lansdale, P. L. (1999). Stability and change in paternal involvement among urban African American fathers. *Journal of Family Psychology, 13,* 416–435.

Colin, A. (2000). Coping with attention-deficit/hyperactivity disorder. In D. N. Sattler, G. P. Kramer, V. Shabatay, & D. A. Bernstein (Eds.), *Child development in context* (pp. 56–62). Boston: Houghton Mifflin.

Colin, V. L. (1996). *Human attachment.* New York: McGraw-Hill.

Coll, C. G. (1990). Developmental outcome of minority infants: A process-oriented look into our beginnings. *Child Development, 61,* 270–289.

Coll, C. G., Lamberty, G., Jenkins, R., McAdoo, H. P., Crnic, K., Wasik, B. H., & Garcia, H. V. (1998). An integrative model for the study of developmental competencies in minority children. In M. E. Hertzig & E. A. Farber (Eds.), *Annual progress in child psychiatry and child development: 1997* (pp. 437–463). Philadelphia: Brunner/Mazel.

Colligan, J. (1983). Musical creativity and social rules in four cultures. *Creative Child and Adult Quarterly, 8,* 39–47.

Collins, J. W., Jr., & David, R. J. (1990). The differential effect of traditional risk factors on infant birthweight among blacks and whites in Chicago. *American Journal of Public Health, 80,* 679.

Collins, N. L., Dunkel-Schetter, C., Lobel, M., & Scrimshaw, S. C. M. (1993). Social support in pregnancy: Psychosocial correlates of birth outcomes and postpartum depression. *Journal of Personality and Social Psychology, 65,* 1243–1248.

Collins, S., & Angen, M. (1997). Adolescents voice their needs: Implications for health promotion and suicide prevention. *Canadian Journal of Counselling, 31*(1), 53–66.

Coltrane, S. (1995). *Family man.* New York: Oxford.

Coltrane, S. (1998). Gender, power, and emotional expression: Social and historical contexts for a process model of men in marriages and families. In A. Booth & A. C. Crouter (Eds.), *Men in families: When do they get involved? What difference does it make?* (pp. 193–212). Mahwah, NJ: Erlbaum.

Comas-Diaz, L., & Greene, B. (Eds.). (1994). *Women of color.* New York: Guilford.

Compas, B., Howell, D. C., Phares, V., Williams, R. A., & Ledoux, N. (1989). Parent and child stress and symptoms: An integrative analysis. *Developmental Psychology, 25,* 550–559.

Coney, N. S., & Mackey, W. C. (1998). Motivations toward fathering: Two minority profiles within the majority's context. *Journal of Men's Studies, 6,* 169–188.

Connell, J. P., Spencer, M. B., & Aber, J. L. (1996). Educational risk and resilience in African-American youth: Context, self, action, and outcomes in school. *Child Development, 65*(2), 493–506.

Cook, T. H., Nies, M. A., & Hepworth, J. T. (2000). Race differences in the relationships between dietary nutrients and overweight in women. *Health Care for Women International, 21,* 41–51.

Cooley, C. H. (1909). *Social organization.* New York: Schocken Books.

Coombs, R. H., Paulson, M. J., & Richardson, M. A. (1991). Peer vs. parental influence in substance use among Hispanic and Anglo children and adolescents. *Journal of Youth and Adolescence, 20,* 73–88.

Cooney, R. (2001, April 19–22). *Success in early elementary school: The role of parenting practices.* Paper presented at the biennial meeting of the Society for Research in Child Development, Minneapolis.

Cooper, C. R., & Cooper, R. G. (1992). Links between adolescent's relationships with their parents and peers: Models, evidence, and mechanisms. In R. D. Parke & G. W. Ladd (Eds.), *Family-peer relationships: Modes of linkage.* Hillsdale, NJ: Erlbaum.

Cooper, R. P., Abraham, J., Berman, S., & Staska, M. (1997). The development of infants' preference for motherese. *Infant Behavior and Development, 20,* 477–488.

Coopersmith, S. (1967). *Antecedents of self-esteem.* San Francisco: Freeman.

Cordell, A. S. (1999). Self-esteem in children. In C. J. Carlock (Ed.), *Enhancing self-esteem* (pp. 287–376). Philadelphia: Accelerated Development, Inc.

Cornbleth, C. (1998). An American curriculum? *Teachers College Record, 99,* 622–646.

Cornelius, M. D., Day, N. L., Richardson, G. A., & Taylor, P. M. (1999). Epidemiology of substance abuse during pregnancy. In P. J. Ott, R. E. Tarter, & R. T. Ammerman (Eds.), *Sourcebook on substance abuse: Etiology, epidemiology, assessment, and treatment* (pp. 1–13). Boston: Allyn & Bacon.

Cornwell, A. C. (1992). Sex differences in the maturation of sleep/wake patterns in high risk for SIDS infants. *Neuropediatrics, 23,* 8–14.

Corsaro, W. A. (1997). *The sociology of childhood.* Thousand Oaks, CA: Sage.

Corsaro, W. A., & Emiliani, F. (1992). Child care, early education, and children's peer culture in Italy. In M. E. Lamb, K. Sternberg, C. P. Hwang, & A. G. Broberg (Eds.), *Child care in context: Cross-cultural perspectives* (pp. 81–118). Hillsdale: NJ: Erlbaum.

Corsaro, W. A., & Rizzo, T. A. (1990). *Conflict talk.* Cambridge, England: Cambridge University Press.

Coverdale, J. H., & Gruenbaum, H. (1998). Sexuality and family planning. In K. T. Muesser & N. Tarrier (Eds.), *Handbook of social functioning in schizophrenia* (pp. 224–237). Boston: Allyn & Bacon.

Covington, M. V. (1985). The role of self-processes in applied social psychology. *Journal for the Theory of Social Behaviour, 15,* 355–392.

Cowan, C. P., & Cowan, P. A. (1992). *When partners become parents: The big life change for couples.* New York: Basic Books.

Cowan, C. P., Cowan, P. A., Heming, G., & Miller, N. (1991). Becoming a family: Marriage, parenting, and child development. In P. A. Cowan & M. Hetherington (Eds.), *Family transitions.* Hillsdale, NJ: Erlbaum.

Cowan, C. P., Cowan, P. A., Schulz, M., & Heming, G. (1994). Prebirth to preschool family factors predicting children's adaptation to kindergarten. In R. Parke & S. Kellam (Eds.), *Exploring family relationships with other social contexts: Advances in family research* (pp. 75–114). Hillsdale, NJ: Erlbaum.

Cowan, P. A. (1997). Beyond meta analysis: A plea for a family systems view of attachment. *Child Development, 68,* 601–603.

Cowan, P. A., & Cowan, C. P. (1988). Changes in marriage during the transition to parenthood: Must we blame the baby? In G. Y. Michaels & W. A. Goldberg (Eds.), *The transition to parenthood: Current theory and research.* Cambridge: Cambridge University Press.

Cowan, P. A, & Cowan, C. P. (1992). *When partners become parents.* New York: Basic Books.

Cowan, P. A., & Cowan, C. P. (1997). Working with couples during stressful transitions. In S. Dreman (Ed.), *The family on the threshold of the 21st century: Trends and implications* (pp. 17–47). Mahwah, NJ: Erlbaum.

Cowan, P. A., & Cowan, C. P. (1998a). Interventions to ease the transition to parenthood: Why they are needed and what they can do. *Journal of Applied Family and Child Studies, 44,* 412–423.

Cowan, P. A., & Cowan, C. P. (1998b). New families: Modern couples as new pioneers. In M. A. Mason, A. Skolnick, & S. D. Sugarman (Eds.), *All our families: New policies for a new century* (pp. 169–192). New York: Oxford University Press.

Cox, B. D., Ornstein, P. A., Naus, M. J., Maxfield, D., & Zimler, J. (1989). Children's concurrent use of rehearsal and organizational strategies. *Developmental Psychology, 25,* 619–627.

Cox, M. J., & Paley, B. (1997). Families as systems. *Annual Review of Psychology, 48,* 243–267.

Crain, L. S., & Bennett, B. (1996). Prenatal causes of atypical infant development. In M. J. Hanson (Ed.), *Atypical infant development* (pp. 529–545). Austin TX: Pro-Ed, Inc.

Crane, J. (1991). The epidemic theory of ghettos and neighborhood effects on dropping out and teenage childbearing. *American Journal of Sociology, 96*(5), 1226–1259.

Cratty, B. J. (1986). *Perceptual and motor development in infants and children.* Englewood Cliffs, NJ: Prentice Hall.

Creasey, G. L., Jarvis, P. A., & Berk, L. E. (1998). Play and social competence. In O. N. Saracho & B. Spodek (Eds.), *Multiple perspectives on play in early childhood education. SUNY series, Early childhood education: Inquiries and insights* (pp. 116–143). Albany, NY: State University of New York Press.

Crews, H. (2000). Fantasy and storytelling: Children at play. In D. N. Sattler, G. P. Kramer, V. Shabatay, & D. A. Bernstein (Eds.), *Child development in context* (pp. 43–47). Boston: Houghton Mifflin.

Crick, N. R., & Grotpeter, J. K. (1998). Children's treatment by peers: Victims of relational and overt aggression. In M. E. Hertzig & E. A. Farber (Eds.), *Annual progress in child psychiatry and child development* (pp. 79–92). Bristol, PA: Brunner/Mazel.

Crockenberg, S., & Forgays, D. K. (1996). The role of emotion in children's understanding and emotional reactions to marital conflict. *Merrill Palmer Quarterly, 42,* 22–47.

Crockenberg, S., Jackson, S., & Langrock, A. M. (1996). *Autonomy and goal attainment: Parenting, gender, and children's social competence.* San Francisco: Jossey-Bass.

Crocker, J., Luhtanen, R., Blaine, B., & Broadnax, S. (1994). Collective self-esteem and psychological well-being among White, Black, and Asian college students. *Personality and Social Psychology Bulletin,* 20, 503–513.

Crooks, R., & Baur, K. (1999). *Our sexuality.* Pacific Grove, CA: Brooks/Cole.

Cross, W. E. (1991). *Shades of black: Diversity in African-American identity.* Philadelphia: Temple University Press.

Crystal, D. S., Watanabe, H., Weinfurt, K., & Wu, C. (1998). Concepts of human differences: A comparison of American, Japanese, and Chinese children and adolescents. *Developmental Psychology, 34,* 714–722.

Csikszentmihalyi, M., Rathunde, K., & Whalen, S. (1993). *Talented teenagers: The roots of success and failure.* New York: Cambridge University Press.

Culp, R. E., Culp, A. M., Osofsky, J. D., & Osofsky, H. J. (1991). Adolescent and toddler mothers' interaction patterns with their six-month-old infants. *Journal of Adolescence, 14*(2), 195–200.

Cunningham, A. E., & Stanovich, K. E. (1998, Spring/Summer). What reading does for the mind. *American Educator,* 8–15.

Cunningham-Burley, S., & Boulton, M. (2000). The social context of the new genetics. In G. L. Albrecht & R. Fitzpatrick (Eds.), *The handbook of social studies in health and medicine* (pp. 173–187). London: Sage.

Curran, C. P. (1998). *Sexually transmitted diseases.* Springfield, NJ: Easlow Publishers, Inc.

Curtis, K., Savitz, D., & Arbuckle, T. (1997). Effects of cigarette smoking, caffeine consumption, and alcohol intake on fecundability. *American Journal of Epidemiology, 146,* 32–41.

Dai, D. Y., Moon, S. M., & Feldhusen, J. F. (1998). Achievement motivation and gifted students: A social cognitive perspective. *Educational Psychologist, 33,* 45–63.

Damon, W. (1998). The lifelong transformation of moral goals through social influence. In P. B. Baltes & W. M. Staudinger (Eds.), *Life-span perspectives on the social foundation of cognition* (pp. 198–220). New York: Cambridge University Press.

Damon, W. (1999, August). The moral development of children. *Scientific American,* 72–78.

Daniels, T. (2001, April 19–22). *Neighborhood violence and child outcomes in high-risk families: The role of child and family factors.* Paper presented at the biennial meeting of the Society for Research in Child Development, Minneapolis.

Darling, N., & Steinberg, L. (1993). Parenting style as context: An integrative model. *Psychological Bulletin, 113,* 487–496.

Darwin, C. (1965). *The expression of the emotions in man and animals.* London: Murray. (Original work published in 1872)

Darwin, C. (1998). *The expressions of the emotions in man and animals* (3rd ed.). (P. Ekman, Ed.). New York: Oxford University Press. (Original work published 1872)

Dasen, P. R. (1975). Concrete operational development in three cultures. *Journal of Cross-Cultural Psychology, 6,* 156–172.

Dasen, P. R. (1984). The cross-cultural study of intelligence: Piaget and the Baoule. *International Journal of Psychology, 19,* 407–434.

Dasgupta, S. D. (1998). Gender roles and cultural continuity in the Asian Indian immigrant community in the U.S. *Sex Roles, 38,* 953–974.

D'Attilio, J. P., Campbell, B. M., Lubold, P., Jacobson, T., & Richard, J. (1992). Social support and suicide potential: Preliminary findings for adolescent populations. *Psychological Reports, 70,* 76–78.

D'Augelli, A., & Hershberger, S. (1993). Lesbian, gay, and bisexual youth in community settings: Personal challenges and mental health problems. *American Journal of Community Psychology, 21,* 421–447.

Davis, D. (1998). Child development: A practitioner's guide. New York: Guilford Press.

Davis, J. O., Phelps, J. A., & Bracha, S. (1995). Prenatal development of monozygotic twins and concordance for schizophrenia. *Schizophrenia Bulletin, 21,* 357–366.

Davis, P. T., & Cummings, M. (1998). Exploring children's emotional security as a mediator of the link between marital relations and child adjustment. *Child Development, 69,* 124–139.

Day, R. D., Peterson, G. W., & McCracken, C. (1998). Predicting spanking of younger and older children by mothers and fathers. *Journal of Marriage and the Family, 60,* 79–94.

Deater-Deckard, K., & Dodge, K. A. (1997). Spare the rod, spoil the authors: Emerging themes on parenting and child development. *Psychological Inquire, 8,* 230–235.

Deater-Deckard, K., Dodge, K. A., & Bates, J. E. (1998). Multiple risk factors in the development of externalizing behavior problems: Group and individual differences. *Development and Psychopathology, 10,* 469–493.

Deater-Deckard, K., Dodge, K. A., Bates, J. E., & Pettit, G. S. (1996). Physical discipline among African American and European American mothers: Links to children's externalizing behaviors. *Developmental Psychology, 32,* 1065–1072.

DeBerry, K. M., Scarr, S., & Weinberg, R. (1996). Family racial socialization and ecological competence: Longitudinal assessments of African-American transracial adoptees. *Child Development, 67,* 2375–2399.

DeBoysson-Bardies, B. (1989). A cross-linguistic investigation of vowel formants in babbling. *Journal of Child Language, 16,* 1–17.

DeCasper, A. J., & Fifer, W. P. (1999). Of human bonding: Newborns prefer their mothers' voices. In A. Slater & D. Muir (Eds.), *Developmental psychology* (pp. 99–105). Oxford, England: Blackwell Publishers.

DeCasper, A. J., Lecanuet, J. P., Busnel, M. C., Granier-Deferre, C., & Naugeais, R. (1994). Fetal reactions to recurrent maternal speech. *Infant Behavior and Development, 17,* 159–164.

De Gaston, J. F., Weed, S., & Jensen, L. (1996). Understanding gender differences in adolescent sexuality. *Adolescence, 31*(121), 217–231.

Delaney, C. H. (1995). Rites of passage in adolescence. *Adolescence, 30,* 891–897.

DeLoach, J., & Brown, A. L. (1997). Looking for Big Bird: Studies in memory of young children. In M. Cole & Y. Engestroem (Eds.), *Mind, culture, and activity: Seminal papers from the Laboratory of Comparative Human Cognition* (pp. 79–89). New York: Cambridge University Press.

Delgado-Gaitan, C. (1994). Socializing young children in Mexican-American families: An intergenerational perspective. In P. M. Greenfield & R. R. Cocking (Eds.), *Cross-cultural roots of minority child development* (pp. 55–86). Hillsdale, NJ: Erlbaum.

De Mause, L. (1995). The evolution of childhood. In L. de Mause (Ed.), *The history of childhood* (pp. 1–74). Northvale, NJ: Jason Aronson Inc.

DeMarrais, K. B., Nelson, J. A., & Baker, J. H. (1994). Meaning in mud: Yup'ik Eskimo girls at play. In J. L. Roopnarine, J. E. Johnson, & F. H. Hooper (Eds.), *Children's play in diverse cultures* (pp. 179–209). New York: State University of New York Press.

Demorest, S. M., & Serlin, R. C. (1997). The integration of pitch and rhythm in musical judgment: Testing age-related trends in novice listeners. *Journal of Research in Music Education, 45,* 67–79.

Denham, S. A., & Couchoud, E. A. (1990). Young preschoolers' understanding of emotions. *Child Study Journal, 20,* 171–192.

Denmark, F. L. (1999). Enhancing the development of adolescent girls. In N. G. Johnson, M. C. Roberts, & J. Worell (Eds.), *Beyond appearance: A new look at adolescent girls* (pp. 377–404). Washington, DC: American Psychological Association.

Dennis, W. (1943). Animism and related tendencies in Hopi children. *Journal of Abnormal and Social Psychology, 38,* 21–36.

Dermer, A. (1998). Breastfeeding and women's health. *Journal of Women's Health, 7*(4), 427–433.

Desmond, R. J., Singer, J. L., & Singer, D. G. (1990). Family mediation: Parental communication patterns and the influences of television on children. In J. Bryant (Ed.), *Television and the American family* (pp. 293–309). Hillsdale, NJ: Erlbaum.

DeSpelder, L. A., & Strickland, A. L. (1999). *The last dance: Encountering death and dying.* Mountain View, CA: Mayfield.

Deutsch, F. M., Lozy, J. L., & Saxon, S. (1993). Taking credit: Couples' reports of contributions to child care. *Journal of Family Issues, 14,* 421–437.

DeVries, M. W. (1984). Temperament and infant mortality among the Masai of East Africa. *American Journal of Psychiatry, 141,* 1189–1194.

DeVries, M. W. (1997). Optimal foetal growth in the reduction of learning and behaviour disorder and the prevention of sudden infant death syndrome (SIDS) after the first month: Commentary. *International Journal of Psychophysiology, 27,* 123–124.

De Waal, F. B. M. (1999, December). The end of nature versus nurture. *Scientific American,* 94–99.

Dews, S., Winner, E., Kaplan, J., & Rosenblatt, E. (1996). Children's understanding of the meaning and functions of verbal irony. *Child Development, 67,* 3071–3085.

Diamond, M. (1995). Biological aspects of sexual orientation and identity. In L. Diamant & R. D. McAnulty (Eds.), *The psychology of sexual orientation, behavior, and identity.* Westport, CT: Greenwood Press.

Diamond, M. D., & Hopson, J. (1998). *Magic trees of the mind.* New York: Plume/Penguin.

DiBlasio, F. A., & Benda, B. B. (1992). Gender differences in theories of adolescent sexual activities. *Sex Roles, 27,* 221–239.

Dick-Read, G. (1959). *Childbirth without fear: The principles and practice of natural childbirth* (2nd ed.). New York: Harper & Row.

Diebel, P. (1990). Effects of cigarette smoking on maternal nutrition and the fetus. *Journal of Obstetrics Gynecology Neonatal Nursing, 9,* 333–336.

Dienhart, A., & Daly, K. (1997). Men and women co-creating father involvement in a nongenerative culture. In A. J. Hawkins & D. C. Dollahite (Eds.), *Generative fathering: Beyond deficit perspectives. Current issues in the family series* (Vol. 3, pp. 147–164). Thousand Oaks, CA: Sage.

DiGirolamo, A. M., Geis, H. K., & Walker, C. E. (1998). Developmental issues. In R. T. Ammerman & J. V. Campo (Eds.), *Handbook of pediatric psychology and psychiatry. Vol. 1: Psychological and psychiatric issues in the pediatric setting* (pp. 1–22). Boston: Allyn & Bacon.

Dilworth-Anderson, P., & Marshall, S. (1996). Social support in its cultural context. In G. R. Pierce & B. R. Sarason (Eds.), *Handbook of social support and the family* (pp. 67–79). New York: Plenum.

Dishion, T. J., Patterson, G. R., Stoolmiller, M., & Skinner, M. L. (1991). Family, school, and behavioral antecedents to early adolescent involvement with antisocial peers. *Developmental Psychology, 27,* 172–180.

Dittman, L. L. (2000). *Finding the best care for your infant or toddler.* [Brochure]. Washington, DC: National Association for the Education of Young Children (NAEYC).

Dixey, R. (1998). Healthy eating in schools: Overweight and "eating disorders": Are they connected? *Educational Review, 50,* 29–35.

Dodge, K. A., Coie, J. D., Pettit, G. S., & Price, J. M. (1990). Peer status and aggression in boys' groups: Developmental and contextual analyses. *Child Development, 61,* 1289–1309.

Dodge, K. A., & Schwartz, D. (1998). Social information processing mechanisms in aggressive behavior. In D. M. Stoff & J. Breiling (Eds.), *Handbook of antisocial behavior* (pp. 171–180). New York: Wiley.

Doh, H. S., & Falbo, T. (1999). Social competence, maternal attentiveness, and overprotectiveness: Only children in Korea. *International Journal of Behavioral Development, 23,* 149–162.

Dohn, H. (1992). "Drop-out" in the Danish high school (gymnasium): An investigation of psychological, sociological, and pedagogical factors. *International Review of Education, 37,* 415–428.

Dollahite, D. C., & Hawkins, A. J. (1998). A conceptual ethic of generative fathering. *Journal of Men's Studies, 7,* 109–132.

Dollahite, D. C., Hawkins, A. J., & Brotherson, S. E. (1997). Fatherwork: A conceptual ethic of fathering as generative work. In A. J. Hawkins & D. C. Dollahite (Eds.), *Generative fathering* (pp. 17–35). Thousand Oaks, CA: Sage.

Dolto, F. (1998). On feminine sexuality. *Journal of European Psychoanalysis, 6,* 123–141.

Donahue, M. L. (1997). Beliefs about listening in students with learning disabilities: "Is the speaker always right?" *Topics in Language Disorders, 17,* 41–61.

Donaldson, M. (1996). Humanly possible: Education and the scope of the mind. In D. R. Olson & N. Torrance (Eds.), *New models of learning, teaching, and schooling* (pp. 324–344). Oxford, England: Blackwell Publishers (UK).

Donegan-Johnson, A. (1992). *The value of responsibility.* Los Angeles: Value Tales.

Donnerstein, E., Slaby, R. G., & Eron, L. D. (1994). The mass media and youth aggression. In L. D. Eron, J .H. Gentry, & P. Schlegel (Eds.), *Reason to hope: A psychosocial perspective on violence and youth* (pp. 219–250). Washington, DC: American Psychological Association.

Dorney, J. (1995). Educating towards resistance: A task for women teaching girls. *Youth & Society, 27,* 55–72.

Dorr, A. (1993). Media literacy for modern America. In *Media competency as a challenge to school and education* (pp. 217–237). Gutersloh, Germany: Bertelsmann Foundation Publishers.

Dorr, A., & Rabin, B. E. (1995). Parents, children, and television. In M. H. Bornstein (Ed.), *Handbook on parenting* (pp. 323 –352). Hillsdale, NJ: Erlbaum.

Dosanjh, J. S., & Ghuman, A. S. (1996). The cultural context of child-rearing: A study of indigenous and British Punjabis. *Early Child Development and Care, 126,* 39–55.

Doswell, W. M., Millor, G. K., Thompson, H., & Braxter, B. (1998). Self-image and self-esteem in African-American preteen girls: Implications for mental health. *Issues in Mental Health Nursing, 19,* 71–94.

Douthitt, V. L. (1998). Exercise for adolescents. In E. A. Blechman & K. D. Brownell (Eds.), *Behavioral medicine and women* (pp. 274–279). New York: Guilford Press.

Dowling, J. E. (1998). *Creating mind.* New York: W. W. Norton.

Downey, G., Lebolt, A., Rincon, C., & Freitas, A. L. (1998). Rejection sensitivity and children's interpersonal difficulties. *Child Development, 69,* 1074–1091.

Drake, D. D. (1997). Medical trends and issues in learning disabilities. In D. D. Duane & C. K. Leong (Eds.), *Understanding learning disabilities: International and multidisciplinary views* (pp. 39–46). New York: Plenum Press.

Dreikurs, R., & Soltz, V. (1995). *Happy children: A challenge to parents.* New York: Duell, Soloan, & Pearce.

Dresser, N. (1996). *Multicultural manners.* New York: Wiley.

Drews, C., Yeargin-Allsopp, M., Decoufle, P., & Murphy, C. (1995). Variation in the influence of selected sociodemographic risk factors for mental retardation. *American Journal of Public Health, 85,* 329–334.

Drucker, R. R., Hammer, L. D., Agras, W. S., & Bryson, S. (1999). Can mothers influence the child's eating behavior? *Journal of Developmental and Behavioral Pediatrics, 20,* 88–92.

Drummond, W. J. (1997). Adolescents at risk: Causes of youth suicide in New Zealand. *Adolescence, 32,* 925–934.

Dryfoos, J. G. (1997). Adolescents at risk: Shaping programs to fit the need. *Journal of Negro Education, 65,* 5–18.

DuBois, D. L., & Hirsch, B. (1993). School/nonstop friendship patterns in early adolescence. *Journal of Early Adolescence, 13,* 102–122.

DuBois, D. L., Tevendale, H. D., Burk-Braxton, C., Swenson, L. P., & Hardesty, J. L. (2000). Self-system influences during early adolescence: Investigation of an integrative model. *Journal of Early Adolescence, 20,* 12–43.

Duindam, V. P. J., & Spruijt, A. P. (1998). Child care and fathers. *Kind en Adolescent, 19,* 78–92.

Dukes, R. L., & Martinez, R. (1994). The impact of gender on self-esteem among adolescents. *Adolescence, 29,* 105–115.

Dulmus, C. N., & Wodarski, J. S. (2000). Trauma-related symptomatology among children of parents victimized by urban community violence. *American Journal of Orthopsychiatry, 70*(2), 272–277.

Duncan, G. J., & Brooks-Gunn, J. (1997). *Consequences of growing up poor.* New York: Russell Sage Foundation.

Duncan, G. J., Yeung, W., Brooks-Gunn, J., & Smith, J. R. (1998). How much does childhood poverty affect the life chances of children? *American Sociological Review, 63,* 406–423.

Duncan, S. C., Duncan, T. E., & Hops, H. (1998). Progressions of alcohol, cigarette, and marijuana use in adolescence. *Journal of Behavioral Medicine, 21,* 375–388.

Dunn, J., Brown, J., & Beardsall, L. (1991). Family talk about feeling states and children's later understanding of others' emotions. *Developmental Psychology, 65,* 1385–1397.

Dunn, J., & Plomin, R. (1998). *Separate lives: Why are siblings so different?* New York: Basic Books.

Dunphy, D. C. (1963). The social structure of urban adolescent peer groups. *Sociometry, 26,* 36.

Du Pre, A. (1998). *Humor and the healing arts.* Mahwah, NJ: Erlbaum.

Duran-Aydintug, C. (1998). Emotional support during separation: Its sources and determinants. *Journal of Divorce and Remarriage, 29,* 121–141.

Durbin, D. L., Darling, N., Steinberg, L., & Brown, B. B. (1993). Parenting style and peer group membership among European-American adolescents. *Journal of Research on Adolescence, 3,* 87–100.

Durkin, D. (1990). *Children who read early.* New York: Teachers College Press.

Durrant, J. E., Broberg, A. G., & Rose-Krasnor, L. (1999). Predicting mother's use of physical punishment during mother–child conflicts in Sweden and Canada. In C. C. Piotrowski & P. D. Hastings (Eds.), *Conflict as a context for understanding maternal beliefs about child rearing and children's misbehavior* (pp. 25–41). San Francisco: Jossey-Bass.

Duyff, R. L., Giarratano, S. C., & Zuzich, M. F. (1995). *Nutrition, health, and safety for preschool children.* New York: McGraw-Hill.

Eastman, M. (1994). *Taming the dragon in your child.* New York: Wiley.

Eaves, L. J., Eysenck, H. J., & Martin, N. G. (1989). *Genes, culture, and personality.* New York: Academic Press.

Eccles, J. S., & Bryan, J. (1994). Adolescence: Critical crossroad in the path of gender-role development. In M. R. Stevenson (Ed.), *Gender roles through the life span: A multidisciplilnary perspective* (pp. 111–147). Muncie, IN: Ball State University.

Eccles, J. S., Midgley, C., Wigfield, A., Buchanan, C. M., Reuman, D., Flanagan, C., & MacIver, D. (1993). Development during adolescence: The impact of stage-environment fit in young adolescents' experiences in schools and in families. *American Psychologist, 48,* 90–101.

Eccles, J. S., Wigfield, A., Harold, R. D., & Blumenfeld, P. (1993). Age and gender differences in children's self- and task perceptions during elementary school. *Child Development, 64,* 830–847.

Eccles, J. S., Wigfield, A., & Schiefele, U. (1997). Motivation to succeed. In W. Damon & N. Eisenberg (Eds.), *Handbook of child psychology* (pp. 1017–1096). New York: Wiley.

Eckenrode, J., Laird, M., & Doris, J. (1993). School performance and disciplinary problems among abused and neglected children. *Developmental Psychology, 29,* 53–62.

Eckensberger, L. H., & Zimba, R. F. (1997). The development of moral judgment. In J. W. Berry, P. R. Dasen, & T. S. Saraswathi (Eds.), *Handbook of cross-cultural psychology* (pp. 299–338). Boston: Allyn & Bacon.

Eddy, J. M., Heyman, R. E., & Weiss, R. L. (1991). An empirical evaluation of the Dyadic Adjustment Scale: Exploring differences between marital "satisfaction" and "adjustment." *Behavioral Assessment, 13,* 199–220.

Eder, R. A. (1990). Uncovering young children's psychological selves: Individual and developmental differences. *Child Development, 61,* 849–863.

Eder, R. A., & Mangelsdorf, S. C. (1997). The emotional basis of early personality development: Implications for the emergent self-concept. In R. Hogan & J. A. Johnson (Eds.), *Handbook of personality psychology* (pp. 209–240). San Diego: Academic Press.

Edlund, B., Halvarsson, K., Gebre-Medhin M., & Sjoeden, P. O. (1999). Psychological correlates of dieting in Swedish adolescents: A cross-sectional study. *European Eating Disorders Review, 7,* 47–61.

Edlund, B., Halvarsson, K., & Sjoeden, P. O. (1996). Eating behaviors and attitudes in eating, dieting, and body image in 7-year-old Swedish girls. *European Eating Disorders Review, 4,* 40–53.

Edmondson, J. H., & White, J. (1998). A tutorial and counseling program: Helping students at risk of dropping out of school. *Professional School Counseling, 1,* 43–47.

Edmunds, H., & Hill, A. J. (1999). Dieting and the family context of eating in young adolescent children. *International Journal of Eating Disorders, 25,* 435–440.

Edwards, C. P. (1995). Parenting toddlers. In M. H. Bornstein (Ed.), *Handbook on parenting* (pp. 41–63). Hillsdale, NJ: Erlbaum.

Efran, J. S., & Greene, M. A. (2000). The limits of change: Heredity, temperament, and family influence. In W. C. Nichols & M. A. Pace-Nichols (Eds.), *Handbook of family dynamics and treatment* (pp. 41–64). New York: Wiley.

Egeland, B., Carlson, E., & Sroufe, L. A. (1993). Resilience as a process. *Development and Psychopathology, 5,* 517–528.

Egeland, B., & Erickson, M. F. (1993). Attachment theory and findings: Implications for prevention and intervention. In S. Kramer & H. Paren (Eds.), *Prevention in mental health: Now, tomorrow, ever?* (pp. 21–25). Northvale, NJ: Jason Aronson.

Eimas, P. D. (1999). Segmental and syllabic representations in the perception of speech by young infants. *Journal of the Acoustical Society of America, 105,* 1901–1911.

Eimas, P. D., Sigueland, E. R., Jusczyk, P., & Vigorito, J. (1971). Speech percepetion in infants. *Science, 71,* 303–306.

Eisenberg, N. (2000). Empathy and sympathy. In M. Lewis & J. M. Haviland-Jones (Eds.), *Handbook of emotions* (pp. 677–697). New York: Guilford.

Eisenberg, N., & Murphy, W. M. (1995). Parenting and children's moral development. In M. H. Bornstein (Ed.), *Handbook on parenting* (pp. 227–258). Hillsdale, NJ: Erlbaum.

Eisenberg, N., Shepard, S. A., Fabes, R. A., Murphy, B. C., & Guthrie, I. K. (1998). Shyness and children's emotionality, regulation, and coping: Contemporaneous, longitudinal, and across-context relations. *Child Development, 69,* 767–790.

Eisikovits, Z., Winstok, Z., & Enosh, G. (1998). Children's experience of interparental violence: A heuristic model. *Children and Youth Services Review, 20,* 547–568.

Ekman, P. (1973). Cross-cultural studies of facial expression. In P. Ekman (Ed.), *Darwin and facial expression: A century of research in review* (pp. 169–222). New York: Academic Press.

Ekman, P. (1998). Introduction. In C. Darwin (1872/1998). *The expression of the emotions in man and animals* (pp. xxi–xxxvi). New York: Oxford University Press.

Elkind, D. (1967). Egocentrism in adolescence. *Child Development, 38,* 1025–1034.

Elkind, D. (1978). Understanding the young adolescent. *Adolescence, 13,* 127–134.

Elkind, D. (1998). *All grown up and no place to go: Teenagers in crisis.* Reading, MA: Addison-Wesley.

Elkind, D. (1998). Egocentrism in adolescence. In R. E. Muuss & H. D. Porton (Eds.), *Adolescent behavior and society* (pp. 91–101). New York: McGraw-Hill.

Elkind, D., & Bowen, R. (1979). Imaginary audience behavior in children and adolescents. *Developmental Psychology, 15,* 38–44.

Ellickson, P., Bui, K., Bell, R., & McGuigan, K. A. (1998). Does early drug use increase the risk of dropping out of high school? *Journal of Drug Issues, 28,* 357–380.

Elliott, J. G. (1999). School refusal: Issues of conceptualisation, assessment, and treatment. *Journal of Child Psychology and Psychiatry and Allied Disciplines, 40,* 1001–1012.

Elliott, L., & Brantley, C. (1997). *Sex on campus.* New York: Random Books.

El-Sheikh, M., & Cummings, E. M. (1997). Marital conflict, emotional regulation, and the adjustment of children of alcoholics. In K. C. Barrett (Ed.), *The communication of emotions: Current research from diverse perspectives* (pp. 25–44). San Francisco: Jossey-Bass.

Elvin-Nowak, Y. (1999). The meaning of guilt: A phenomenological description of employed mothers' experiences of guilt. *Scandinavian Journal of Psychology, 40,* 73–83.

Engel, J. (1998). Japanese and American housewives' attitudes toward the employment of women. In E. Goldsmith (Ed.), *Work and family: Theory, research, and applications* (pp. 363–372). Corte Madera, CA: Select Press.

Ephron, N. (2000). Shaping up absurd. In D. N. Sattler, G. P. Kramer, V. Shabatay, & D. A. Bernstein (Eds.), *Child development in context* (pp. 76–80). Boston: Houghton Mifflin.

Epstein, L. H., Saelens, B. E., Myers, M. D., & Vito, D. (1997). Effects of decreasing sedentary behaviors on activity choice in obese children. *Health Psychology, 16,* 107–113.

Epstein, Y. M., & Rosenberg, H. S. (1997). He does, she doesn't: She does, he doesn't: Couple conflicts about infertility. In S. R. Leiblum (Ed.), *Infertility: Psychological issues and counseling strategies* (pp. 129–148). New York: Wiley.

Eriksen, K. (2001). Infertility and the search for family. *Family Journal Counseling and Therapy for Couples and Families, 9*(1), 55–61.

Erikson, E. (1950). *Childhood and society.* New York: Norton.

Erikson, E. (1959). Identity and the life cycle: Selected papers [Monograph 1]. *Psychological Issues, 1.*

Erikson, E. (1963). *Childhood and society* (2nd ed.). New York: Norton.

Erikson, E. (1968). *Identity: Youth in adolescence and crisis.* New York: W. W. Norton.

Eron, L. D. (1997). The development of antisocial behavior from a learning perspective. In D. M. Stoff & J. Breiling (Eds.), *Handbook of antisocial behavior* (pp. 140–147). New York: Wiley.

Erwin, E. J., & Kontos, S. (1998). Parents' and kindergarten teachers' beliefs about the effects of child care. *Early Education and Development, 9,* 141–146.

Estes, D. (1998). Young children's awareness of their mental ability: The case of mental rotation. *Child Development, 69,* 1345–1360.

Etaugh, C., & Folger, D. (1998). Perceptions of parents whose work and parenting behaviors deviate from role expectations. *Sex Roles, 39,* 215–223.

Etringer, B., Altmaier, E., & Bowers, W. (1998). An investigation into the cognitive functioning of bulimic women. *Journal of Counseling and Development, 68,* 216–219.

Eugster, A., & Vingerhoets, A. J. M. (1999). Psychological aspects of in vitro fertilization. *Social Science and Medicine, 48,* 575–589.

Evans, C. A., & Docking, J. (1996). Improving the quality of supportive measures for children with learning disabilities. *Early Child Development and Care, 121,* 107–118.

Evans, L. D. (2000). Functional school refusal subtypes: Anxiety, avoidance, and malingering. *Psychology in the Schools, 37,* 183–191.

Ewing, C. K., Loffredo, C. A., & Beaty, T. H. (1997). Paternal risk factors for isolated membranous ventricular septal defects. *American Journal of Medical Genetics, 71,* 42–46.

Eyre, S. L., & Millstein, S. G. (1999). What leads to sex? Adolescent preferred partners and reasons for sex. *Journal of Research on Adolescence, 9,* 277–307.

Eysenck, H. J. (1998). *A new look intelligence.* New Brunswick, NJ: Transaction Publishers.

Eysenck, H. J., & Eysenck, S. B. G. (1969). *Personality structure and measurement.* London: Routledge & Kegan Paul.

Fabes, R. A., & Eisenberg, N. (1992). Young children's coping with interpersonal anger. *Child Development, 63,* 116–128.

Fagan, J. (1997). Patterns of mother and father involvement in day care. *Child and Youth Care Forum, 26,* 113–126.

Fagan, J. F., III, & Haiken-Vasen, J. (1997). Selective attention to novelty as a measure of information processing across the lifespan. In J. A. Burack & J. T. Enns (Eds.), *Attention, development, and psychopathology* (pp. 55–73). New York: Guilford Press.

Fagen, D. B., Cowen, E. L., Wyman, P. A., & Work, W. C. (1996). Relationships between parent–child relational variables and child test variables in highly stressed urban families. *Child Study Journal, 26*(2), 87–108.

Fagot, B. I. (1998). Social problem solving: Effect of context and parent sex. *International Journal of Behavioral Development, 22,* 389–401.

Fagot, B. I., & Hagen, R. (1991). Observations of parents' reactions to sex-stereotyped behaviors: Age and sex effects. *Child Development, 62,* 617–628.

Fagot, B. I., & Leinbach, M. (1995). Gender knowledge in egalitarian and traditional families. *Sex Roles, 32*(7–8), 513–526.

Faison, S. (1997, August 17). One-child limitation eases in China. *The Oregonian,* A8.

Falbo, T., & Poston, D. L. (1993). The academic, personality, and physical outcomes of only children in China. *Child Development, 64,* 18–35.

Fantz, R. (1961). The origin of form perception. *Scientific American, 204,* 5, 66–72.

Fantz, R., Fagan, J. F., & Miranda, S. (1975). Early visual selectivity. In L. Cohen & P. Salapatek (Eds.), *Infant perception: From sensation to cognition. Vol. 1: Basic visual processes.* New York: Academic Press.

Farrar, M. J. (1990). Discourse and the acquisition of grammatical morphemes. *Journal of Child Language, 17,* 607–624.

Farrington, D. P. (1991). Childhood aggression and adult violence: Early precursors and later life outcomes. In D. J. Pepler & K. H. Rubin (Eds.), *The development and treatment of childhood aggression* (pp. 5–29). Hillsdale, NJ: Erlbaum.

Farruggia, S. P., Dmitrieva, J., & Tally, S. (2001, April 19–22). *Self-esteem in cross-cultural perspective: Measurement equivalence and relations to parental warmth and depression.* Paper presented at the biennial meeting of the Society for Research in Child Development, Minneapolis.

Fauber, R., Forehand, R., Thomas, A., & Wierson, M. (1990). A mediational model of the impact of marital conflict on adolescent adjustment in intact and divorced families: The role of disrupted parenting. *Child Development, 61,* 1112–1123.

Favaro, P. J. (1993). *The effects of video game play on mood, physiological arousal, and psycho-motor performance.* Unpublished doctoral dissertation. Hempstead, NY: Hofstra University.

Fehr, M. J. (1981). The communication of evaluation through the use of interpersonal gaze in same- and inter-racial dyads. *Dissertation Abstracts International, 41,* 4307.

Feldman, D. H., & Goldsmith, L. (1991). *Nature's gambit: Child prodigies and the development of human potential.* New York: Teachers College Press.

Feldman, D. H., & Piirto, J. (1995). Parenting talented children. In M. H. Bornstein (Ed.), *Handbook on parenting* (pp. 285–304). Hillsdale, NJ: Erlbaum.

Feldman, M. W., & Otto, S. P. (1997). Twin studies, heritability, and intelligence. *Science, 278,* 1383.

Feldman, S. S., Turner, R. A., & Araujo, K. (1999). Interpersonal context as an influence on sexual timetables of youths: Gender and ethnic effects. *Journal of Research on Adolescence, 9,* 25–52.

Fenton, S. (1999). *Ethnicity: Racism, class, and culture.* New York: Rowman & Littlfield.

Ferrari, A. M. (1999). Child rearing practices and definitions of maltreatment: How they vary according to cultural attitudes and values. *Dissertation Abstracts International,* Section B: The Sciences and Engineering.

Ferraro, G. (2001). *Cultural anthropology: An applied perspective.* Belmont, CA: Wadsworth.

Feuerstein, R., Rand, Y., & Rynders, J. (1998). *Don't accept me as I am: Helping "retarded" people to excel.* New York: Plenum.

Field, T. (1995). Psychologically depressed parents. In M. H. Bornstein (Ed.), *Handbook on parenting* (pp. 85–100). Hillsdale, NJ: Erlbaum.

Field, T. (1998). Maternal cocaine use and fetal development. In E. A. Blechman & K. D. Brownell (Eds.), *Behavioral medicine and women* (pp. 27–31). New York: Guilford Press.

Finch, M. D., Mortimer, J. T., & Rhy, S. (1997). Transition into part-time work: Health risks and opportunities. In J. Schulenberg & J. L. Maggs (Eds.), *Health risks and developmental transitions during adolescence* (pp. 321–344). New York: Cambridge University Press.

Fincham, F. D., & Linfield, K. (1997). A new look at marital quality: Can spouses be positive and negative about their marriage? *Journal of Family Psychology, 11,* 489–502.

Fine, D. S., & Grun, J. (1998). Anxiety disorders. In B. T. Walsh (Ed.), *Child psychopharmacology. Review of psychiatry series* (pp. 1115–1148). Washington, DC: American Psychiatric Press, Inc.

Fine, R. (1979). *A history of psychoanalysis.* New York: Columbia University Press.

Finn, J. D., & Rock, D. A. (1997). Academic success among students at risk for school failure. *Journal of Applied Psychology, 82*(2), 221–234.

Fischer, C. S., Hout, M., Jankowski, M. S., Lucas, S. R., Swidler, A., & Voss, K. (1996). *Inequality by design: Cracking the bell curve myth.* Princeton, NJ: Princeton University Press.

Fischer, K. W. (1980). A theory of cognitive development: The control and construction of hierarchies of skills. *Psychological Review, 87,* 477–525.

Fischer, K. W. (1994). Research: Brain spurts and Piagetian periods. *Educational Leadership, 41,* 70–78.

Fischer, K. W. (1997). Relations between brain and cognitive development. *Child Development, 68,* 623–632.

Fischer, K. W., & Farrar, M. J. (1988). Generalizations about generalization: How a theory of skill development explains both generality and specificity. In A. Demetriou (Ed.), *The neo-Piagetian theories of cognitive development: Toward an integration.* Amsterdam: Elsevier.

Fischer, K. W., & Rose, S. P. (1996). Dynamic growth cycles of brain and cognitive development. In R. W. Thatcher & G. R. Lyon (Eds.), *Developmental neuroimaging: Mapping the development of brain and behavior* (pp. 263–279). San Diego: Academic Press.

Fitzgibbon, M. L., Stolley, M. R., & Kirschenbaum, D. S. (1995). An obesity prevention pilot program for African-American mothers and daughters. *Journal of Nutritional Education, 27,* 93–99.

Flavell, J. H. (1996). Piaget's legacy. *Psychological Science, 7,* 200–202.

Flavell, J. H., Green, F. L., & Flavell, E. R. (1997). The development of children's knowledge about inner speech. *Child Development, 68,* 39–47.

Flavell, J. H., Green, F. L., & Flavell, E. R. (1998). The mind has a mind of its own: Developing knowledge about mental uncontrollability. *Cognitive Development, 13,* 127–138.

Flavell, J. H., Miller, P. H., & Miller, S. A. (1993). *Cognitive development.* Englewood Cliffs, NJ: Prentice-Hall.

Fletcher-Flinn, C. M., & Suddendorf, T. (1996). Do computers affect "The Mind"? *Journal of Educational Computing Research, 15,* 97–112.

Flisher, A. J. (1999). Mood disorder in suicidal children and adolescents: Recent developments. *Journal of Child Psychology and Psychiatry and Applied Disciplines, 40,* 315–324.

Floyd, F. J., Stein, T. S., Harter, K. S. M., Allison, A., & Nye, C. L. (1999). Gay, lesbian, and bisexual youths. Separation-individuation, parental attitudes, identity consolidation, and well-being. *Journal of Youth and Adolescence, 28*(6), 719–739.

Flynn, J. M., & Rabar, M. H. (1994). Prevalence of reading failure in boys compared to girls. *Psychology in the Schools, 31,* 66.

Flynn, J. R. (1998). Israeli military IQ tests: Gender differences small; IQ gains large. *Journal of Biosocial Science, 30,* 541–553.

Flynn, J. R. (1999). Searching for justice: The discovery of IQ gains over time. *American Psychologist, 54,* 5–20.

Flyr, M. L., & Wild, M. N. (2001, April 19–22). *Exposure to marital conflict in young adolescents: Self-reports and teacher and peer observations.* Paper presented at the biennial meeting of the Society for Research in Child Development, Minneapolis.

Foote, D. (1998, February 2). And baby makes one. *Newsweek, 68,* 70.

Fordham, S. (1993). "Those loud black girls": (Black) women, silence, and gender "passing" in the academy. *Anthropology and Education Quarterly, 24,* 3–32.

Fordham, S., & Ogbu, J. T. (1998). Black students' school success: Coping with the "burden of 'acting white.'" In R. E. Muuss & H. D. Porton (Eds.), *Adolescent behavior and society* (pp. 189–207). New York: McGraw-Hill.

Franco, F., & Butterworth, G. (1996). Pointing and social awareness: Declaring and requesting in the second year. *Journal of Child Language, 23,* 307–336.

Frankenburg, W. K. (1992). The Denver II: A major revision and restandardization of the Denver Developmental Screening Test. *Pediatrics, 89,* 91–97.

Frankenburg, W. K., & Dodds, J. B. (1967). The Denver Developmental Screening Test. *Journal of Pediatrics, 71,* 181–191.

Frazier, J. A., & Morrison, F. J. (1998). The influence of extended-year schooling on growth of achievement and perceived competence in early elementary school. *Child Development, 69,* 495–517.

Freedman, D. A. (1997). *On infancy and toddlerhood.* Madison, CT: International Universities Press, Inc.

Freedman, D. G. (1969). Ethnic differences in babies. *Human Nature, 2,* 36–43.

Freedman, D. G. (1979). *Human infancy: An evolutionary perspective.* Hillsdale, NJ: Erlbaum.

Freedman-Doan, C. R., Arbreton, A. J. A., Harold, R. D., & Eccles, J. S. (1993). Looking forward to adolescence: Mothers' and fathers' expectations for affective and behavioral change. *Journal of Early Adolescence, 13,* 472–502.

French, D. (1990). Heterogeneity of peer-rejected girls. *Child Development, 61,* 2028–2031.

Freud, A. (1974). *The writings of Anna Freud.* New York: International Universities Press.

Freud, S. (1916). *Jokes and their relation to the unconscious.* New York: Moffat Ward.

Freud, S. (1938). *An outline of psychoanalysis.* London: Hogarth.

Freud, S. (1957). Beyond the pleasure principle. In J. Strachey (Ed.), *The standard edition of the complete psychological works of Sigmund Freud* (Vol. 18). London: Hogarth. (Original work published in 1920)

Freud, S. (1960). *Jokes and their relation to the unconscious.* New York: W.W. Norton. (Originally published in 1905)

Freud, S. (1973). *An outline of psychoanalysis.* London: Hogarth. (Original work published in 1938)

Freud, S. (1974). *The ego and the id.* London: Hogarth. (Original work published in 1923)

Fricker, H. S., & Segal, S. (1988). Narcotic addiction, pregnancy, and the newborn. *American Journal of Diseases of Children, 132,* 360–366.

Fried, P. A. (1989). Postnatal consequences of maternal marijuana use in humans. In D. E. Hutchings (Ed.), *Prenatal abuse of licit and illicit drugs* (Vol. 562, pp. 123–132). New York: Annals of the New York Academy of Sciences.

Fried, P. A., & Watkinson, B. (1990). Thirty-six- and 48-month neurobehavioral follow-up of children prenatally exposed to marijuana, cigarettes, and alcohol. *Developmental and Behavioral Pediatrics, 11,* 49–58.

Fried, P. A., Watkinson, B., & Siegel, L. S. (1997). Reading and language in 9- to 12-year-olds prenatally exposed to cigarettes and marijuana. *Neurotoxicology and Teratology, 19,* 171–183.

Friedberg, R. D., & Taylor, L. A. (1997). Imaginary friends and amazing stories: Clinical implications of children's metaphorical communications. In L. VandeCreek & S. Knapp (Eds.), *Innovations in clinical practice: A source book* (pp. 97–109). Sarasota, FL: Professional Resource Press.

Friedler, G. (1996). Paternal exposures: Impact on reproductive and developmental outcome: An overview. *Pharmacology, Biochemistry, and Behavior, 55*, 691–700.

Friedman, L. (1998). Erik H. Erikson's critical themes and voices: The task of synthesis. In R. S. Wallerstein & L. Goldberger (Eds.), *Ideas and identities: The life work of Erik Erikson* (pp. 353–377). Madison, CT: International Universities Press.

Friedman, R. M., Sandler, J., Hernandez, M., & Wolfe, D. A. (1991). Child abuse. In E. J. Mash & L. G. Terdal (Eds.), *Behavioral assessment of childhood disorders.* New York: Guilford Press.

Friedrichsen, J. E. (1998). *Self-concept and self-esteem development in the context of adolescence and genders.* Dissertation Abstracts International. Vol. 58. Humanities and Social Sciences.

Fritschy, M. N., & Grzanna, R. (1992). Degeneration of rat locus coeruleus neurons is not accompanied by an irreversible loss of ascending projections. *Annals of the New York Academy of Sciences, 648*, 275–278.

Fromm, E. (1980). *Greatness and limitations of Freud's thought.* New York: New American Library.

Frone, M. R. (1999). Developmental consequences of youth employment. In J. Barling & E. K. Kelloway (Eds.), *Young workers: Varieties of experience* (pp. 89–128). Washington, DC: American Psychological Association.

Fuligni, A. J. (1998). Authority, autonomy, and parent–adolescent conflict and cohesion: A study of adolescents from Mexican, Chinese, Filipino, and European backgrounds. *Developmental Psychology, 34*, 782–792.

Fuligni, A. J., & Eccles, J. S. (1993). Perceived parent–child relationships and early adolescents' orientation toward peers. *Developmental Psychology, 29*, 622–632.

Fullilove, M., & Dieudonne, I. (1996). Substance abuse in pregnancy. *The Hatherleigh guide to treating substance abuse* (pp. 93–117). New York: Hatherleigh Press.

Fulroth, R. F., Phillips, B., & Durant, D. J. (1989). Perinatal outcome of infants exposed to cocaine and/or heroin in utero. *American Journal of Diseases in Children, 143*, 905–910.

Funk, J. B. (2001, April 19–22). *The effects of video games on youth.* Paper presented at the biennial meeting of the Society for Research in Child Development, Minneapolis.

Funk, J. B., & Buckman, D. D. (1996). Playing violent video and computer games and adolescent self-concept. *Journal of Communication, 46*, 19–32.

Funk, J. B., Flores, G., Buchman, D. D., & Germann, J. N. (1999). Rating electronic games: Violence is in the eye of the beholder. *Youth and Society, 30*, 283–312.

Furham, A., Fong, G., & Martin, N. (1999). Sex and cross-cultural differences in the estimated multifaceted intelligence quotient score for self, parents, and siblings. *Personality and Individual Differences, 26*, 1024–1034.

Furman, E. (1998). *Relationships in early childhood: Helping children grow.* Madison, CT: International Universities Press, Inc.

Furman, E. (1999). The role of the father in earliest childhood. In T. B. Cohen & E. M. Hossein (Eds.), *The vulnerable child* (pp. 269–279). Madison, CT: International Universities Press.

Furman, W. (1999). Friends and lovers: The role of peer relationships in adolescent romantic relationships. In W. A. Collins & B. Laursen (Eds.), *Relationships as developmental contexts. The Minnesota Symposia on Child Psychology* (pp. 133–154). Mahwah, NJ: Erlbaum.

Furr, L. A., & Seger, R. E. (1998). Psychosocial predictors of interest in prenatal genetic screening. *Psychological Reports, 82*, 235–244.

Furstenberg, F. F., Jr., (1991). As the pendulum swings: Teenage childbearing and social concern. *Family Relations, 40*(2), 127–138.

Furstenberg, F. F., Jr. (1998). Social capital and the role of fathers in the family. In A. Booth & A. C. Crouter (Eds.), *Men in families: When do they get involved? What difference does it make?* (pp. 296–301). Mahwah, NJ: Erlbaum.

Furstenberg, F. F., Jr., Hughes, M. E., & Brooks-Gunn, J. (1992). The next generation: Children of teenage mothers grow up. In M. K. Rosenheim & M. F. Testa (Eds.), *Early parenthood* (pp. 113–135). New Brunswick, NJ: Rutgers University Press.

Gabrenya, W. E., Jr., & Hwang, K. K. (1996). Chinese social interaction: Harmony and hierarchy on the good earth. In M. H. Bond (Ed.), *The handbook of Chinese psychology* (pp. 309–321). Hong Kong: Oxford University Press.

Gabriel, K., Hofmann, C., Glavas, M., & Weinberg, J. (1998). The hormonal effects of alcohol use on the mother and fetus. *Alcohol Health and Research World, 22*, 170–177.

Gaines, R., & Price-Williams, D. (1990). Dreams and imaginative processes in American and Balinese artists. *Psychiatric Journal of the University of Ottawa, 15*, 107–110.

Galambos, N. L., Almeida, D. M., & Petersen, A. C. (1990). Masculinity, femininity, and sex roles attitudes in early adolescence: Exploring gender intensification. *Child Development, 61*, 1905–1914.

Gallagher, S. A. (1997). Problem-based learning: Where did it come from, what does it do, and where is it going? *Journal for the Education of the Gifted, 20*, 332–362.

Gallahue, D. L. (1993). Motor development and movement skill acquisition in early childhood education. In B. Spodek (Ed.), *Handbook of research on education of young children* (pp. 24–41). New York: Maxwell Macmillan.

Gallahue, D. L., & Ozmun, J. C. (1998). *Understanding motor development: Infants, children, adolescents, and adults.* Boston: McGraw-Hill.

Galton, F. (1978). *Hereditary genius.* London: Julian Friedman. (Originally published in 1869)

Gan, L., & Chong, S. (1998). The rhythm of language: Fostering oral and listening skills in Singapore preschool children through an integrated music and language arts program. *Early Child Development and Care, 144*, 39–45.

Garbarino, J. (1993). Reinventing fatherhood. *Families in society: Journal of Contemporary Human Services, 74*, 51–55.

Garber, J., Little, S., Hilsman, R., & Weaver, K. R. (1998). Family predictors of suicidal symptoms in young adolescents. *Journal of Adolescence, 21*, 445–457.

Garcia, S. D., & Rivera, S. M. (1999). Perceptions of Hispanic and African-American couples at the friendship or engagement stage of a relationship. *Journal of Social and Personal Relationships, 16*, 65–86.

Garcia-Preto, N. (1996). Latino families: An overview. In M. McGoldrick & J. Giordan (Eds.), *Ethnicity and family therapy* (2nd ed., pp. 141–154). New York: Guilford Press.

Gardner, H. (1983). *Frames of mind: The theory of multiple intelligence.* New York: Basic Books.

Gardner, H. (1997). Six afterthoughts: Comments on "Varieties of intellectual talent." *Journal of Creative Behavior, 31*, 120–124.

Gardner, H. (1999). The vehicle and the vehicles of leadership. *American Behavioral Scientist, 42*, 1009–1023.

Gardner, H., Hatch, T., & Torff, B. (1997). A third perspective: The symbol systems approach. In R. J. Sternberg & E. L. Grigorenko (Eds.), *Intelligence, heredity, and environment* (pp. 243–268). New York: Cambridge University Press.

Garmezy, N., & Rutter, M. (1983). *Stress, coping, and development in children.* New York: McGraw-Hill.

Garrison, E. G., Roy, I. S., & Azar, V. (1999). Responding to the mental health needs of Latino children and families through school-based services. *Clinical Psychology Review, 19*, 199–219.

Gatmon, D. M. (1999). Cultural and parental role models for combining work and family roles in Sweden and the United States. *Dissertation Abstracts International, 59*(9), 5165B. (University Microfilms No. AAM99-07438)

Ge, X., Conger, R. D., & Elder, G. H., Jr. (1996). Coming of age too early: Pubertal influences on girls' vulnerability to psychological stress. *Child Development, 67*, 3386–3400.

Geddes, A. (1994). Socrates, Plato, and Therapeia. *Australian Journal of Psychotherapy, 13*, 41–52.

Gelman, R. (1998). Domain specificity in cognitive development: Universals and nonuniversals. In M. Sabourin & F. Craik (Eds.), *Advances in psychological science. Vol. 2: Biological and cognitive aspects* (pp. 557–579). Hove, England: Psychology Press/Erlbaum (UK).

Gelman, R., & Kit-Fong, T. (Eds.). (1996). *Perceptual and cognitive development.* San Diego: Academic Press.

Gendall, K. A., Sullivan, P. F., Joyce, P. R., Fear, J. L., & Bulik, C. M. (1997). Psychopathology and personality of young women who experience food cravings. *Addictive Behaviors, 22,* 545–555.

Gergen, K. J. (1996). Technology and the self: From the essential to the sublime. In D. Grodin & T. R. Lindlof (Eds.), *Constructing the self in a mediated world: Inquiries in social construction* (pp. 127–140). Thousand Oaks, CA: Sage.

Gerrard, L. E., Poteat, G. M., & Ironsmith, M. (1996). Promoting children's creativity: Effects of competition, self-esteem, and immunization. *Creativity Research Journal, 9*(4), 339–346.

Gesell, A. (1925). *The mental growth of the preschool child.* New York: Macmillan.

Gesell, A. (1972). *The embryology of behavior: The beginnings of the human mind.* Westport, CT: Greenwood.

Gesell, A., & Ames, L. B. (1940). The ontogenetic organization of prone behavior in human infancy. *Journal of Genetic Psychology, 56,* 247–263.

Getzels, J. S., & Jackson, P .W. (1962). *Creativity and intelligence.* New York: Wiley.

Gibbs, J. T., & Huang, L. N. (Eds.). (1998). *Beating the odds: Raising academically successful African American males.* New York: Oxford University Press.

Giguere, J., Fortin, C., & Sabourin, S. (1999). Determinants de satisfaction conjugale chez des personnes vivant une premiere ou une seconde union conjugale. *International Journal of psychology, 34,* 119–132.

Gilbert, N. (1997). *Combatting child abuse: International perspective and trends.* New York: Oxford University Press.

Gilbreath, B., & Cicchetti, D. (1990). *Psychopathology in maltreating mothers.* Unpublished manuscript.

Gill, N. E., Behnke, M., Conlon, M., NcNeely, J. B., & Anderson, G. C. (1988). Effect of non-nutritive sucking on behavioral sate in premature infants before feeding. *Nursing Research, 37,* 347–350.

Gilligan, C. (1992, May). *Joining the resistance: Girls' development in adolescence.* Paper presented at the Symposium on Development and Vulnerability in Close Relationships, Montreal.

Gilligan, C. (1993). Adolescent development reconsidered. In A. Garrod (Ed.), *Approaches to moral development: New research and emerging themes.* New York: Teachers College Press.

Gilligan, C. (1998). Exit-voice dilemmas in adolescent development. In R. E. Muuss & H. W. Porton (Eds.), *Adolescent behavior and society: A book of readings* (pp. 352–362). New York: McGraw-Hill.

Gilligan, C., & Attanucci, J. (1998). Two moral orientations. In R. E. Muuss & H. W. Porton (Eds.), *Adolescent behavior and society: A book of readings* (pp. 241–251). New York: McGraw-Hill.

Ginsberg, H. P., Choi, Y., Lopez, S., Netley, R., & Chao-Yuan, C. (1997). Happy birthday to you: Early mathematical thinking of Asian, South American, and U.S. children. In T. Nunes & P. Bryant (Eds.), *Learning and teaching mathematics: An international perspective* (pp. 163–207). Hove, England: Psychology Press/Erlbaum (UK).

Ginsburg, H., & Opper, S. (1988). *Piaget's theory of intellectual development* (3rd. ed.). Englewood Cliffs, NJ: Prentice-Hall.

Girdner, E. J., Eisenman, R., & Tracy, N. (1996). Contemporary lifestyles and values of students in Louisiana, USA, and North Cyprus: A cross-cultural study. *International Journal of Adolescence and Youth, 6*(3), 205–222.

Glazer, J. P., Goldfarb, J., & James, R. S. (1998). Infectious diseases. In R. T. Ammerman & J. V. Campo (Eds.), *Handbook of pediatric psychology and psychiatry* (pp. 347–368). Boston: Allyn & Bacon.

Glissov, P., Siann, G., & Durndell, A. (1994). Chips with everything: Personal attributes of heavy computer users. *Educational Studies, 20,* 367–377.

Glover, V. (1997). Maternal stress or anxiety in pregnancy and emotional development of the child. *British Journal of Psychiatry, 171,* 105–106.

Goddard, C., & Wierzbicka, A. (1997). Discourse and culture. In L. A. van Uijk (Ed.), *Discourse as social interaction: Discourse studies: A multidisciplinary introduction.* London: Sage.

Goicoehea-Balbona, A. (1998). Children with HIV/AIDS and their families: A successful social work intervention based on the culturally specific health care model. *Heath and Social Work, 23,* 61–69.

Golding, J., Rogers, I. S., & Emmett, P. M. (1997). Association between breast feeding, child development, and behaviour. *Early Human Development, 49,* 5175–5184.

Goldman, G., Pineault, R., Potvin, L., Blais, R., & Bilodeau, H. (1993). Factors influencing the practice of vaginal birth after cesarean section. *American Journal of Public Health, 83,* 1104–1108.

Goldsmith, H. H., & Campos, J. J. (1990). Fundamental issues in the study of early temperament: The Denver twin temperament study. In M. E. Lamb, A. L. Brown, & B. Rogoff (Eds.), *Advances in developmental psychology* (pp. 231–283). Hillsdale, NJ: Erlbaum.

Goldsmith, H. H., & Campos, J. J. (1990). The structure of temperamental fear and pleasure in infants: A psychometric perspective. *Child Development, 61,* 1944–1964.

Goldstein, J. (1998). *Why we watch: The attractions of violent entertainment.* New York: Oxford University Press.

Gonzalez-Mena, J. (1991, July/August). Do you have cultural tunnel vision? *Child Care Information Exchange,* 29–31.

Goodenow, C., & Grady, K. (1995). The relationship of school belonging and friends' values to academic motivation among urban adolescent students. *Journal of Experimental Education, 62,* 60–71.

Goodlin-Jones, B. L., Eiben, L. A., & Anders, T. F. (1997). Maternal well-being and sleep-wake behaviors in infants: An intervention using maternal odor. *Infant Mental Health Journal, 18,* 378–393.

Goodman, J. C., McDonough, L., & Brown, N. B. (1998). The role of semantic context and memory in the acquisition of novel nouns. *Child Development, 69,* 1330–1344.

Goodnow, J. J. (1995). Parents' knowledge and expectations. In M. H. Bornstein (Ed.), *Handbook on parenting* (pp. 305–332). Hillsdale, NJ: Erlbaum.

Goodnow, J. J. (1998). Contexts of achievement. In S. G. Paris & H. M. Wellman (Eds.), *Global prospects for education: Development, culture, and schooling* (pp. 105–127). Washington, DC: American Psychological Association.

Goodwin, T., & Tang, C. (1998). The transition to uncertainty?: The impacts of Hong Kong 1997 on personal relationships. *Personal Relationships, 5,* 183–190.

Gopaul-McNicol, S. A., & Thomas-Presswood, T. (1998). *Working with linguistically and culturally different children: Innovative clinical and educational approaches.* Boston: Allyn & Bacon.

Gopnik, A., & Wellman, H. M. (1994). The theory theory. In L. Hirschfeld & S. Gelman (Eds.), *Mapping the mind: Domain specificity in cognition and culture* (pp. 257–293). Cambridge: Cambridge University Press.

Gordon, T. (1970). *Parent effectiveness training: The tested new way to raise responsible children.* New York: David McKay.

Goreczny, A. J., & Hersen, M. (Eds.). (1999). *Handbook of pediatric and adolescent health psychology.* Boston: Allyn & Bacon.

Gottfried, A. E., Fleming, J. S., & Gottfried, A. W. (1998). Role of cognitive stimulating home environment in children's academic intrinsic motivation: A longitudinal study. *Child Development, 69,* 1148–1460.

Gottfried, A. E., Gottfried, A. W., & Bathurst, K. (1995). Maternal and dual-earner employment status and parenting. In M. H. Bornstein (Ed.), *Handbook on parenting* (pp. 139–160). Hillsdale, NJ: Erlbaum.

Gottlieb, G. (1991). Experiential canalization of behavioral development: Theory. *Developmental Psychology, 27,* 4–13.

Gottman, J. M. (1998). Toward a process model of men in marriages and families. In A. Booth & A. C. Crouter (Eds.), *Men in families: When do they get involved? When do they make a difference?* (pp. 149–192). Mahwah, NJ: Erlbaum.

Goubet, N., & Clifton, R. K. (1998). Object and event representation in 6½-month-old infants. *Developmental Psychology, 34,* 63–76.

Gough, B., & Reavey, P. (1997). Parental accounts regarding the physical punishment of children: Discourses of disempowerment. *Child Abuse and Neglect, 21,* 417–430.

Gould, E. (1999). Serotonin and hippocampal neurogenesis. *Neuropsychopharmacology, 21,* 46S–51S.

Gould, E., Reeves, A. J., Graziano, S. A., & Gross, C. G. (1999). Neurogenesis in the neocortex of adult primates. *Science, 286,* 548–551.

Graber, J. A., & Brooks-Gunn, J. (1996). Prevention of eating problems and disorders: Including parents. *Eating Disorders, 4,* 348–363.

Graber, J. A., & Brooks-Gunn, J. (1998). Puberty. In E. A. Blechman & K. D. Brownell (Eds.), *Behavioral medicine and women* (pp. 51–58). New York: Guilford Press.

Graham, J. A., & Cohen, R. (1997). Race and sex as factors in children's sociometric ratings and friendship choices. *Social Development, 6,* 355–372.

Graham, J. A., Cohen, R., Zbikowski, S. M., & Secrist, M. E. (1998). A longitudinal investigation of race and sex as factors in children's classroom friendship choices. *Child Study Journal, 28,* 245–266.

Graham, S. (1997). Using attribution theory to understand social and academic motivation in African American youth. *Educational Psychologist, 32,* 21–34.

Graham, S., Taylor, A. Z., & Hudley, C. (1998). Exploring achievement values among ethnic minority early adolescents. *Journal of Educational Psychology, 90,* 606–620.

Gray, W. Q., & Wandersman, L. P. (1990). The methodology of home-based intervention studies: Problems and promising strategies. *Child Development, 51,* 993–1009.

Greb, A. (1998). Multiculturalism and the practice of genetic counseling. In D. L. Baker & J. L. Schuette (Eds.), *A guide to genetic counseling* (pp. 171–198). New York: Wiley-Liss.

Gredler, G. R. (1997). Issues in early childhood screening and assessment. *Psychology in the Schools, 34,* 99–106.

Greenberg, D. R., & LaPorte, D. L. (1996). Racial differences in body type preferences of men for women. *International Journal of Eating Disorders, 19,* 275–278.

Greenberg, M., & Morris, N. (1974). Engrossment: The newborn's impact upon the father. *American Journal of Orthopsychiatry, 44,* 520–531.

Greene, B. (1994). Ethnic minority lesbians and gay men: Mental health and treatment issues. *Journal of Consulting and Clinical Psychology, 62,* 243–251.

Greenfield, P. M. (1994). Independence and interdependence as developmental scripts: Implications for theory, research, and practice. In P. M. Greenfield & R. R. Cocking (Eds.), *Cross-cultural roots of minority child development* (pp. 1–37). Hillsdale, NJ: Erlbaum.

Greenfield, P. M. (1998). The cultural evolution of IQ. In U. Neisser (Ed.), *The rising curve: Long-term gains in IQ and related measures* (pp. 81–123). Washington, DC: American Psychological Association.

Greenfield, P. M. (1998). Language, tools, and brain revisited. *Behavioral and Brain Sciences, 21,* 159–163.

Greenfield, P. M. (1999). Cultural change and human development. *New Directions of Child and Adolescent Development, 83,* 37–45.

Greenfield, P. M. (1999). Cultural change and human development. In E. Turiel (Ed.), *Development and cultural change: Reciprocal processes* (pp. 37–59). San Francisco: Jossey-Bass.

Greenfield, P. M., Brannon, C., & Lohr, D. (1994). Two-dimensional representation of movement through three-dimensional space: The role of video game expertise. *Journal of Applied Developmental Psychology, 15,* 87–104.

Greenfield, P. M., Camaioni, L., Ercolani, P., Weiss, L., Lauber, B. A., & Perucchini, P. (1994). Cognitive socialization by computer games in two cultures: Inductive discovery or mastery of an iconic code? *Journal of Applied Developmental Psychology, 15,* 59–86.

Greenfield, P. M., deWinstanley, P., Kilpatarick, H., & Kaye, D. (1994). Action video games and informal education: Effects on strategies for dividing visual attention. *Journal of Applied Developmental Psychology, 115,* 105–123.

Greenleaf, B. (1978). *Children through the ages: A history of childhood.* New York: Barnes and Noble Books.

Greenough, W. (2001, April 19–22). *Nature and nurture in the brain development process.* Paper presented at the biennial meeting of the Society for Research in Child Development, Minneapolis.

Greenspan, S. I. (1998). *The growth of the mind.* Reading, MA: Addison-Wesley.

Greenspan, S. I., Wieder, S., & Simons, R. (1998). *The child with special needs: Encouraging intellectual and emotional growth.* Reading, MA: Addison-Wesley.

Greenstein, T. M. (1993). Maternal employment and child behavioral outcomes. *Journal of Family Issues, 14,* 323–354.

Greenstein, T. M. (1995). Are the "most advantaged" children truly disadvantaged by early maternal employment? Effects on child cognitive outcomes. *Journal of Family Issues, 16,* 149–169.

Greil, A. L. (1997). Infertility and psychological distress: A critical review of the literature. *Social Science and Medicine, 45,* 1669–1704.

Griffiths, M. (1997). Immortal kombat: War toys and violent video games. In J. H. Goldstein (Ed.), *Why we watch: The attractions of violent entertainment* (pp. 53–68). New York: Oxford University Press.

Griffiths, P., Smith, C., & Harvie, A. (1997). Transitory hyperphenylalaninemia in children with continuously treated phenylketonuria. *American Journal on Mental Retardation, 102,* 27–36.

Griswold, R. L. (1997). Generative fathering: A historical perspective. In A. J. Hawkins & D. C. Dollahite (Eds.), *Generative fathering: Beyond deficit perspectives. Current issues in the family series* (Vol. 3, pp. 71–86). Thousand Oaks, CA: Sage.

Grolnick, W., & Slowiaczek, M. L. (1994). Parents' involvement in children's schooling: Multidimensional conceptualization and motivational model. *Child Development, 65,* 237–252.

Gross, C. G. (1998). *Brain, vision, memory: Tales in the history of neuroscience.* Cambridge, MA: MIT Press.

Grossman, F. K., Eichler, L. S., Winickoff, S. A., Anzalone, M. K., Gorseyeff, M., & Sargent, S. P. (1990). *Pregnancy, birth, and parenthood.* San Francisco: Jossey-Bass.

Grossmann, K., Fremmer-Bombik, E., & Rudolph, J. (1988). Maternal attachment representations as related to patterns of infant–mother attachment and maternal care during the first year. In R. A. Hinde & J. Stevenson-Hinde (Eds.), *Relationships within families: Mutual influences* (pp. 241–260). Oxford: Clarendon Press.

Grow, L. J., & Shapiro, D. (1974). *Black children–white parents.* New York: Child Welfare League of America.

Gruber, E., Anderson, M. M., Ponton, L., & DiClemente, R. (1995). Overweight and obesity in Native-American adolescents: Comparing nonreservation youths with African-American and Caucasian peers. *American Journal of Preventive Medicine, 11*(5), 306–310.

Gruber, E., DiClemente, R. J., & Anderson, M. M. (1996). Risk-taking behavior among Native American adolescents in Minnesota public schools: Comparisons with black and white adolescents. *Ethnicity and Health, 1,* 261–267.

Grunbaum, J. A., Base-Engquist, K., & Pandey, D. (1998). Association between violent behaviors and substance use among Mexican-American and non-Hispanic white high school students. *Journal of Adolescent Health, 23,* 153–159.

Grusec, J. E., & Kuczynski, L. (Eds.). (1997). *Parenting and children's internalization of values: A handbook of contemporary theory.* New York: Wiley.

Grych, J. H., & Fincham, F. D. (1993). Children's appraisals of marital conflict: Initial investigations of the cognitive-contextual framework. *Child Development, 64,* 215–230.

Grych, J. H., & Fincham, F. D. (1999). Children of single parents and divorce. In W. K. Silverman & T. H. Ollendick (Eds.), *Developmental issues of the clinical treatment of children* (pp. 321–344). Boston: Allyn & Bacon.

Gu, H., Cen, G., Li, D., Gao, X., Li, Z., & Chen, X. (1997). Two-year-old children's social behavior development and related family factors. *Psychological Science China, 20,* 519–524.

Guerra, N., & Jagers, R. (1998). The importance of culture in the assessment of children and youth. In V. C. McLoyd & L. Steinberg (Eds.), *Studying minority adolescents: Conceptual, methodological, and theoretical issues* (pp. 167–181). Mahwah, NJ: Erlbaum.

Guilford, J. P. (1967). *The structure of intellect.* New York: McGraw-Hill.

Gullone, E., & King, N. J. (1993). The fears of youth in the 1990s: Contemporary normative data. *Journal of Genetic Psychology, 154,* 137–153.

Guralnick, M. J., & Groom, J. M. (1990). The relationship between parent-rated behavior problems and peer relations in preschool children. *Early Education and Development, 1,* 266–278.

Gustafsson, S. S., & Stafford, F. P. (1998). Equity-efficiency trade-offs and government policy in the United States, the Netherlands, and Sweden. In W. S. Barnett & S. S. Boocock (Eds.), *Early care and education for children in poverty: Promises, programs, and long-term results* (pp. 211–244). Albany, New York: State University of New York Press.

Guthrie, S. (2000). On animism. *Current Anthropology, 41,* 106–107.

Gutierrez, J., & Sameroff, A. (1990). Determinants of complexity in Mexican-American and Anglo-American mothers' conceptions of child development. *Child Development, 61,* 384–394.

Haas, L. (1993). Nurturing fathers and working mothers: Changing gender roles in Sweden. In J. Hood (Ed.), *Men, work, and family* (pp. 238–261). Newbury Park, CA: Sage.

Hagerman, R. J., & Silverman, A. C. (Eds.). (1991). *Fragile X syndrome: Diagnosis, treatment, and research.* Baltimore: The Johns Hopkins University Press.

Haight, W. L., & Miller, P. J. (1993). *Pretending at home.* Albany: University of New York Press.

Haith, M. M., Wass, T. S., & Adler, S. A. (1997). Infant visual expectations: Advances and issues. *Monographs of the Society for Research in Child Development, 62,* 150–160.

Hakim-Larson, J., Voelker, S., Thomas, C., & Reinstein, L. (1997). Feeding and eating disorders. In C. A. Essau & F. Petermann (Eds.), *Developmental psychopathology: Epidemiology, diagnostics, and treatment* (pp. 351–410). Amsterdam, Netherlands: Harwood Academic Publishers.

Hala, S. (1991, April). *The role of personal involvement in facilitating false belief understanding.* Paper presented at the biennial meeting of the Society for Research in Child Development, Seattle, WA.

Hala, S., Chandler, M., & Fritz, A. (1991). Fledgling theories of mind: Deception as a marker of three-year-olds' understanding of false belief. *Child Development, 61,* 83–97.

Hales, R. E. (Ed.). (1996). *Synopsis of psychiatry.* Washington, DC: American Psychiatric Press.

Halfe, L. B. (1989). The circle: Death and dying from a native perspective. *Journal of Palliative Care, 5,* 437–441.

Hall, G. S. (1904). *Adolescence: Its psychology and its relations to physiology, anthropology, sex, crime, religion, and education.* New York: Appleton.

Hamburg, D. A., & Lunde, T. D. (1966). Sex hormones in the development of sex differences in human behavior. In E. E. Maccoby (Ed.), *The development of sex differences* (pp. 1–24). Palo Alto, CA: Stanford University Press.

Hamer, D., & Copeland P. (1998). *Living with our genes.* New York: Doubleday.

Hamilton, V. L., & Sanders, J. (1992). *Everyday justice.* New Haven, CT: Yale University Press.

Hamm, J. V. (1992, March). *Black–white and beyond: Cross-ethnic friendship patterns and dynamics of adolescents in multi-ethnic high schools.* Paper presented at the fourth biennial meeting of the Society for Research on Adolescence, Washington, DC.

Hamm, J. V. (1993, March). *The nature of African-American, Asian-American, and Hispanic-American adolescents' perceived crowd affiliations in multi-ethnic high schools.* Paper presented at the 60th biennial meetings of the Society for Research in Child Development, New Orleans.

Hamm, J. V. (1998). Negotiating the maze: Adolescents' cross-ethnic peer relations in ethnically diverse schools. In L. H. Meyer, H. S. Park, M. Grenot-Scheyer, I. S. Schwartz, & B. Harry (Eds.), *Making friends: The influences of culture and development* (pp. 243–262). Baltimore: Paul H. Brookes.

Hampson, J., & Nelson, K. (1993). The relation of maternal language to variation in rate and style of language acquisition. *Journal of Child Language, 20,* 313–342.

Hanley, W. B., Demshar, H., Preston, M. A., & Borczyk, A., et al. (1997). Newborn phenylketonuria (PKU) Guthrie (BIA) screening and early hospital discharge. *Early Human Development, 47,* 87–96.

Hanna, N. A. (1998). Predictors of friendship quality and peer group acceptance at summer camp. *Journal of Early Adolescence, 18,* 291–318.

Hannigan, J. H., Saunders, D. E., Treas, L. M., & Sperry, M. A. (1999). Modification of alcohol-related neurodevelopmental disorders: In vitro and in vivo studies of neuroplasticity. In J. H. Hannigan & L. P. Spear (Eds.), *Alcohol and alcoholism: Effects on brain development* (pp. 39–58). Mahwah, NJ: Erlbaum.

Hannon, P. R., Willis, S. K., Bishop-Townsend, V., Martinez, I. M., & Scrimshaw, S. C. (2000). African-American and Latino adolescent mothers' infant-feeding decisions and breastfeeding practices: A qualitative study. *Journal of Adolescent Health, 26,* 399–407.

Hansen, C., Sanders, S. L., Massaro, S., & Last, C. G. (1998). Predictors of severity of absenteeism in children with anxiety-based school refusal. *Journal of Clinical Child Psychology, 27,* 246–254.

Happe, F., & Frith, U. (1996). Theory of mind and social impairment in children with conduct disorder. *British Journal of Developmental Psychology, 14,* 385–398.

Hara, H., & Minagawa, M. (1996). From productive dependents to precious guests: Historical changes in Japanese children. In D. W. Shwalb & B. J. Shwalb (Eds.), *Japanese childrearing: Two generations of scholarship* (pp. 9–30). New York: Guilford Press.

Hardy, J. B. (1998). Teenage and adolescent pregnancy. In E. A. Blechman & K. D. Brownell (Eds.), *Behavioral medicine and women* (pp. 63–69). New York: Guilford Press.

Harkness, S., & Super, C. M. (1995). Culture and parenting. In M. H. Bornstein (Ed.), *Children and parenting* (Vol. 2). Hillsdale, NJ: Erlbaum.

Harlow, H. F., Harlow, M. K., & Suomi, S. J. (1971). From thought to therapy: Lessons from a primate laboratory. *American Scientist, 59,* 538–549.

Harman, M. J., & Johnson, J. A. (1995). Cross-cultural sex education. Aspects of age, source, and sex equity. *TCA Journal, 23,* 1–11.

Harold, G. T., Fincham, F. D., Osborne, L. N., & Conger, R. D. (1997). Mom and Dad are at it again: Adolescent perceptions of marital conflict and adolescent psychological distress. *Developmental Psychology, 33,* 333–350.

Harper, D. C. (1997). Children's attitudes toward physical disability in Nepal: A field study. *Journal of Cross Cultural Psychology, 26,* 710–729.

Harrell, J. S., Gansky, S. A., & Bradley, C. B. (1997). Leisure time activities of elementary school children. *Nursing Research, 46,* 246–253.

Harris, G. (1997). Development of taste perception and appetite regulation. In G. Bremner, A. Slater, & G. Butterworth (Eds.), *Infant development: Recent advances* (pp. 9–30). East Sussex, UK: Psychology Press.

Harris, P. L. (1995). Developmental constraints on emotion categories. In J. Russell, J. M. Fernandez Dols, A. S .R. Manstead, & J. Wellenkamp (Eds.), *Everyday conceptions about emotions* (pp. 353–372). Dordrecht, The Netherlands: Kluwer.

Hart, B., & Ridley, T. (1995). *Meaningful differences in the everyday experiences of young American children.* Baltimore: Paul H. Brookes.

Hart, D., Fegley, S., Chan, Y. H., Mulvey, D., & Fischer, L. (1993). Judgments about personal identity in childhood and adolescence. *Social Development, 2,* 66–81.

Harter, S. (1990). Causes, correlates, and the functional role of global self-worth: A life-span perspective. In J. Kolligian & R. Sternberg (Eds.), *Perceptions of competence and incompetence across the life-span* (pp. 67–948). New Haven: Yale University Press.

Harter, S. (1993). Causes and consequences of low self-esteem in children and adolescents. In R. F. Baumeister (Ed.), *Self-esteem: The puzzle of low self-regard.* New York: Plenum.

Harter, S. (1996). Developmental changes in self-understanding across the 5 to 7 shift. In A. J. Sameroff & M. M. Haith (Eds.), *The five to seven year shift: The age of reason and responsibility* (pp. 207–236). Chicago: Chicago University Press.

Harter, S. (1997). The personal self in social context: Barriers to authenticity. In R. D. Ashmore & L. J. Jussim (Eds.), *Self and identity: Fundamental issues. Rutgers series on self and social identity* (pp. 81–105). New York: Oxford University Press.

Harter, S. (1999). *The construction of the self: A developmental perspective.* New York: Guilford.

Harter, S., Stocker, C., & Robinson, N. (1996). The perceived directionality of the link between approval and self-worth: The liabilities of a looking glass self orientation among young adolescents. *Journal of Adolescence, 6,* 285–308.

Harter, S., Waters, P., & Whitesell, N. R. (1998). Relationship self-worth: Differences in perceived worth as a person across interpersonal contexts among adolescents. *Child Development, 69,* 756–766.

Harter, S., Waters, P., Whitesell, N. R., & Kastelic, D. (1998). Level of voice among female and male high school students: Relational context, support, and gender orientation. *Developmental Psychology,* 34, 892–901.

Hartley, P. (1998). Eating disorders and health education. *Psychology, Health, and Medicine, 3,* 133–140.

Hartup, W. W. (1998). The company they keep: Friendships and their developmental significance. In M. E. Hertaig & E. A. Farber (Eds.), *Annual progress in child psychiatry and child development* (pp. 63–77). Bristol, PA: BrunnerMazel.

Haselager, G. J. T., Hartup, W. W., van Lieshout, C. F. M., & Riksen-Walraven, J. M. A. (1998). Similarities between friends and nonfriends in middle childhood. *Child Development, 69,* 1198–1208.

Hatta, T., Kawakami, A., Goto, Y., Kadobayashi, S., & Iwamoto, T. (1999). Interpersonal constructs or pregnant women during the perinatal period: Their perceptions of medical staff. *Social Behavior and Personality, 27*(2), 165–176.

Hattie, J., & Marsh, H. W. (1996). Future directions in self-concept research. In B. Bracken (Ed.), *Handbook of self-concept.* New York: Wiley.

Hauser, S. T., & Bowlds, M. K. (1990). Stress, coping, and adaptation. In S. S. Feldman & G. L. Elliott (Eds.), *At the threshold: The developing adolescent* (pp. 388–413). Cambridge, MA: Harvard University Press.

Haussler, A. (1999). Parents' attitudes and experiences regarding treatment for children with autism: A cross-national study. *Dissertation Abstracts International, 59*(7), 3734B. (University Microfilms No. AAM98–40922)

Haveman, R., & Wolfe, B. (1994). *Succeeding generations: On the effect of investments of children.* New York: Russell Sage Foundation.

Haveman, R., & Wolfe, B. (1995). The determinants of children's attainments: A review of methods and findings. *Journal of Economic Literature, 3,* 1829–1878.

Havighurst, R. J., & Neugarten, B. L. (1955). *American Indian and white children: A sociological investigation.* Chicago: University Press.

Haviland, W. A. (1999). *Cultural anthropology.* New York: Harcourt Brace College Publishers.

Hawkins, A. J., & Dollahite, D. C. (1997). Beyond the role-inadequacy perspective of fathering. In A. J. Hawkins & D. C. Dollahite (Eds.), *Generative fathering: Beyond deficit perspectives* (pp. 3–16). Thousand Oaks, CA: Sage.

Hawkins, A. J., & Dollahite, D. C. (Eds.). (1997). *Generative fathering: Beyond deficit perspectives.* Thousand Oaks, CA: Sage.

Hayashi, H. (1991). Legal issues in Japan on wages of women workers. *International Review of Comparative Public Policy, 3,* 243–260.

Hayward, C., Killen, J. D., Wilson, D. M., & Hammer, L. D. (1997). Psychiatric risk associated with early puberty in adolescent girls. *Journal of the American Academy of Child and Adolescent Psychiatry, 36,* 255–262.

He, J., Zha, Z., & Xie, G. (1997). A research on creative thinking and tendency of creation in 10- and 12-year-old children. *Psychological Science China, 20,* 176–178.

Healy, J. M. (1998). *Failure to connect: How computers affect our children's mind—for better and worse.* New York: Simon & Schuster.

Hebert, T. P. (1998). Gifted black males in an urban high school: Factors that influence achievement and underachievement. *Journal for the Education of the Gifted, 21,* 385–414.

Hecht, D. B., Inderbitzen, H. M., & Bukowski, A. L. (1998). The relationship between peer status and depressive symptoms in children and adolescents. *Journal of Abnormal Child Psychology, 26,* 153–160.

Heckhausen, J., & Dweck, C. S. (Eds.). (1998). *Motivation and self-regulation across the life span.* New York: Cambridge University Press.

Hedgepeth, E., & Helmich, J. (1996). *Teaching about sexuality and HIV: Principles and methods for effective education.* New York: New York University Press.

Heffernan, K. (1998). Bulimia nervosa. In E. A. Blechman & K. D. Brownell (Eds.), *Behavioral medicine and women* (pp. 358–363). New York: Guilford Press.

Heide, K. M. (1999). *Young killers: The challenge of juvenile homicide.* Thousand Oaks, CA: Sage.

Henderson, A. S., Jorm, A. F., Christensen, H., Jacomb, P. A., & Korten, A. E. (1997). Aspirin, anti-inflammatory drugs, and risk of dementia. *International Journal of Geriatric Psychiatry, 12,* 926–930.

Henderson, N. D. (1982). Human behavior genetics. *Annual Review of Psychology, 33,* 403–440.

Hendrick, J. (1996). *The whole child.* Englewood Cliffs, NJ: Prentice-Hall.

Herbert, B. (1996, March 4). In trouble after school. *New York Times,* p. A15.

Herman, M. A., & McHale, S. M. (1993). Coping with parental negativity: Links with parental warmth and child adjustment. *Journal of Applied Developmental Psychology, 14,* 121–136.

Herman-Giddens, M., Slora, E., Wasserman, R., Bourdony, C., Bhapkar, M., Koch, G., & Hesemeier, C. (1997). Secondary sexual characteristics and menses in young girls seen in office practice: A study from the pediatric research office settings network. *Pediatrics, 99,* 505–512.

Hess, R. D., Kashiwagi, K., Azuma, H., Price, G., & Dickinson, W. P. (1980). Maternal expectations of mastery of developmental tasks in Japan and the United States. *International Journal of Psychology, 15,* 259–271.

Hess, U., & Kirouac G. (2000). Emotion expression in groups. In M. Lewis & J. M. Haviland-Jones (Eds.), *Handbook of emotions* (pp. 368–381). New York: Guilford.

Hetherington, E. M. (1993). An overview of the Virginia longitudinal study of divorce and remarriage: A focus on early adolescence. *Journal of Family Psychology, 7,* 39–56.

Hetherington, E. M., Bridges, M., & Isabella, G. M. (2000). What matters? What does not? In E. N. Junn & C. J. Boyatzis (Eds.), *Annual editions: Child growth and development* (pp. 131–148). Guilford, CT: Dushkin/McGraw-Hill.

Hetherington, E. M., & Clingempeel, W. G. (1992). Coping with marital transitions. *Monographs of the Society for Research in Child Development, 57* (Serial No. 227).

Hetherington, E. M., & Stanley-Hagan, M. M. (1995). Parenting in divorced and remarried families. In M. H. Bornstein (Ed.), Handbook on parenting (pp. 233–254). Hillsdale, NJ: Erlbaum.

Hewlett, B. S. (1991). *Intimate fathers.* Ann Arbor, MI: University of Michigan Press.

Hewlett, B. S. (2001). The cultural nexus of Aka father–infant bonding. In C. B. Brettell & C. F. Sargent (Eds.), *Gender in cross-cultural perspective* (pp. 45–56). Upper Saddle River, NJ: Prentice-Hall.

Heyman, G. D., & Dweck, C. S. (1998). Children's thinking about traits: Implications for judgments of the self and others. *Child Development, 64,* 391–403.

Hickman, S., & Morales, J. R. (2001, April 19–22). *Longitudinal findings on aggression: Parenting qualities and social adjustment.* Paper presented at the biennial meeting of the Society for Research in Child Development, Minneapolis.

Hill, A. J., & Franklin, J. A. (1998). Mothers, daughters, and dieting: Investigating the transmission of weight control. *British Journal of Clinical Psychology, 37*(1), 3–13.

Hill, H. M., & Madhere, S. (1995). *Exposure to community violence and African American children: A multidimensional model.* Unpublished manuscript. Washington, DC: Howard University.

Hinde, R. A. (1989). Temperament as an intervening variable. In G. A. Kohnstamm, J. E. Bates, & M. K. Rothbart (Eds.), *Temperament in childhood* (pp. 27–34). Chichester, England: Wiley.

Hinde, R. A., Tamplin, A., & Barret, J. (1993). Social isolation in 4-year-olds. *British Journal of Child Psychology, 11,* 211–236.

Hintzman, D. L., Caulton, D. A., & Levitin, D. J. (1998). Retrieval dynamics in recognition and list discrimination: Further evidence of separate processes of familiarity and recall. *Memory and Cognition, 26,* 449–462.

Hirayama, J. (1999). A study of "family care." *Japanese Journal of Family Psychology, 13,* 47–61.

Hirsch, J. (1997). The coming of genetics in the control of ingestion. *Appetite, 29,* 115–117.

Ho, D. Y. F. (1996). Filial piety and its psychological consequences. In M. H. Band (Ed.), *The handbook of Chinese psychology.* New York: Oxford University Press.

Ho, D.Y. F. (1998). Indigenous psychologies: Asian perspectives. *Journal of Cross Cultural Research, 29,* 88–103.

Hobson, R. P. (1988). Beyond cognition: A theory of autism. In G. Dawson (Ed.), *Autism: New perspectives on diagnosis, nature, and treatment.* New York: Guilford.

Hock, E., & Lutz, W. J. (1998). Psychological meaning of separation anxiety in mothers and fathers. *Journal of Family Psychology, 12,* 41–55.

Hoff-Ginsberg, E. (1990). Mother–child conversation in different social classes and communicative settings. *Child Development, 62,* 782–796.

Hoffman, L. B. (1999). Predictors of HIV/AIDS conceptualization in early adolescence. *Dissertation Abstracts International: The Sciences and Engineering.*

Hoffman, L. W. (2000). Maternal employment: Effects of social context. In R. D. Taylor & M. C. Wang (Eds.), *Resilience across contexts: Family, work, culture, and community* (pp. 147–176). Mahwah, NJ: Erlbaum.

Hoffman, M. L. (1988). Moral development. In M. H. Bornstein & M. E. Lamb (Eds.), *Developmental psychology: An advanced textbook* (pp. 497–548). Hillsdale, NJ: Erlbaum.

Hofstede, G. (1998). Comparative studies of sexual behavior: Sex as achievement or as relationship? In G. Hofstede (Ed.), *Masculinity and femininity: The taboo dimension of national cultures* (pp. 153–178). Thousand Oaks, CA: Sage.

Hofstede, G. (1998). The cultural construction of gender. In G. Hofstede (Ed.), *Masculinity and femininity: The taboo dimension of national cultures* (pp. 77–105). Thousand Oaks, CA: Sage.

Hogan, D. P., Hao, L. X., & Parish, W. L. (1990). Race, kin networks, and assistance to mother-headed families. *Social Forces, 68,* 797–812.

Hojat, M., Borenstein, B. D., & Shapurian, R. (1990). Perception of childhood dissatisfaction with parents and selected personality traits in adulthood. *Journal of General Psychology, 117,* 241–253.

Holahan, C., & Moos, R. (1987). "Personal and contextual determinants of coping strategies." *Journal of Personality and Social Psychology, 52,* 946–955.

Hollan, D. (1996). Cultural and experiential aspects of spirit beliefs among the Toraja. In J. Mageo & A. Howard (Eds.), *Spirits in culture, history, and mind* (pp. 213–236). New York: Routledge.

Holland, J. (1987). Current status of Holland's theory of careers: Another perspective. *Career Development Quarterly, 36,* 24–30.

Holland, V. (1998). Underachieving boys: Problems and solutions. *Support for Learning, 13,* 174–178.

Hollingsworth, L. D. (1998). Adoptee dissimilarity from the adoptive family: Clinical practice and research implications. *Child and Adolescent Social Work Journal, 15,* 303–319.

Hollos, M., Leis, P. E., & Turiel, E. (1986). Social reasoning in Ijo children and adolescents in Nigerian communities. *Journal of Cross Cultural Research, 17,* 352–374.

Holmbeck, G. N., Paikoff, R. L., & Brooks-Gunn, J. (1995). Parenting adolescents. In M. H. Bornstein (Ed.), *Handbook on parenting* (pp. 91–118). Hillsdale, NJ: Erlbaum.

Honer, W. G. (1999). Assessing the machinery of mind: Synapses in neuropsychiatric disorders. *Journal of Psychiatry and Neuroscience, 24,* 116–121.

Honig, A. (1991). Compliance, control, and discipline. In N. Lauter-Klatell (Ed.), *Readings in child development* (pp. 56–61). Mountain View, CA: Mayfield.

Honig, A., & Chung, M. (1989). Children-rearing practices of urban poor mothers of infants and three-year-olds in five cultures. *Early Child Development and Care, 50,* 75–97.

Hood, B. M., Murray, L., King, F., & Hooper, R. (1996). Habituation changes in early infancy: Longitudinal measures from birth to 6 months. *Journal of Reproductive and Infant Psychology, 14,* 177–185.

Hopkins, B., & Westra, T. (1989). Maternal expectations of their infants' development: Some cultural differences. *Developmental Medicine and Child Neurology, 31,* 384–390.

Hopkins, K. (1998). A descriptive study of African-American professionals' attitudes toward corporal punishment. *Dissertation Abstracts International, 58.* The Sciences and Engineering.

Hopp, J. W., & Herring, P. (1999). Promoting health among black American populations: An overview. In R. M. Huff & M. V. Kline (Eds.), *Promoting health in multicultural populations* (pp. 201–222). Thousand Oaks, CA: Sage.

Horn, J. L., & Trickett, P. K. (1999). Community violence and children's development: A review of the research. In P. K. Trickett & C. J. Schellenbach (Eds.), *Violence against children in the family and the community* (pp. 103–138). Washington, DC: American Psychological Association.

Horn, J. M., Loehlin, J. C., & Willerman, L. (1979). Intellectual resemblance among adoptive and biological relatives: The Texas Adoption Project. *Behavioral Genetics, 9,* 177–207.

Horowitz, T. R. (1992). Dropout-Mertonian or reproduction scheme? *Adolescence, 27,* 451–459.

Householder, J., Hatcher, R., Burns, W., & Chasnoff, I. (1992). Infants born to narcotic-addicted mothers. *Psychological Bulletin, 92,* 453–468.

Howes, C. (1998). The earliest friendships. In W. M. Bukowski, A. F. Newcomb, & W. W. Hartup (Eds.), *The company they keep: Friendship in childhood and adolescence* (pp. 66–86). New York: Cambridge University Press.

Howes, C., Hamilton, C. E., & Philipsen, L. C. (1998). Stability and continuity of child–caregiver and child–peer relationships. *Child Development, 69,* 418–426.

Hrabowski, F. A. III, Maton, K. I., & Greif, G. L. (1998). *Beating the odds: Raising academically successful African American males.* New York: Oxford University Press.

Hser, Y., Anglin, M. D., & Powers, K. (1993). A 24-year follow-up of California narcotics addicts. *Archives of General Psychiatry, 50,* 577–584.

Hudley, C., & Graham, S. (1995). School-based interventions for aggressive African-American boys. *Applied and Preventive Psychology, 4,* 185–195.

Hudson, J. A. (1990). The emergence of autobiographic memory in mother–child conversation. In R. Fivosh and J. A. Hudson (Eds.), *Knowledge and remembering in young children* (pp. 166–196). New York: Cambridge University Press.

Hudson, J. A., & Sheffield, E. G. (1998). Deja vu all over again: Effects of reenactment on toddlers' event memory. *Child Development, 69,* 51–67.

Huesmann, L. R. (1997). No simple relation. *Psychological Inquiry, 8,* 200–204.

Huff, C. O. (1999). Source, recency, and degree of stress in adolescence and suicide ideation. *Adolescence, 34,* 81–89.

Hughey, M. J., McElin, T., & Young, T. (1988). Maternal and fetal outcome of Lamaze-prepared patients. *Journal of Obstetrics and Gynecology, 5,* 643–647.

Hui, C. H. (1988). Measurement of individualism–collectivism. *Journal of Research in Personality, 22,* 17–36.

Huizinga, D., & Jakob-Chien, C. (1998). The contemporaneous co-occurrence of serious and violent juvenile offending and other problem behaviors. In R. Loeber & D. P. Farrington (Eds.), *Serious and violent juvenile offenders: Risk factors and successful interventions* (pp. 47–67). Thousand Oaks, CA: Sage.

Hull, J. D. (1993, August 2). A boy and his gun. *Time,* p. 22.

Huntsinger, C., Jose, P. E., Liaw, F. R., & Ching, W. D. (1997). Cultural differences in early mathematics learning: A comparison of Euro-American, Chinese-American, and Taiwan-Chinese families. *International Journal of Behavioral Development, 21,* 371–388.

Huon, G. F., Roncolato, W. G., Ritchie, J. E., & Braganza, C. (1997). Prevention of dieting-induced disorders: Findings and implications of a pilot study. *Eating Disorders: Journal of Treatment and Prevention, 5,* 280–293.

Hur, Y. M., & Bouchard, T. J. (1997). The genetic correlation between impulsivity and sensation seeking traits. *Behavior Genetics, 27,* 455–463.

Huston, A. C., Watkins, B. A., & Kunkel, D. (1989). Public policy and children's television. *American Psychologist, 44,* 424–433.

Huston, A. C., & Wright, J. C. (1996). Television and socialization of young children. In T. M. MacBeth (Ed.), *Tuning in to young viewers: Social science perspectives on television* (pp. 37–60). Thousand Oaks, CA: Sage.

Huston, A. C., Wright, J. C., Rice, M. L., Kerkman, D., & St. Peters, M. (1990). Development of television viewing patterns in early childhood: A longitudinal investigation. *Developmental Psychology, 26,* 409–420.

Hutchins, E. (1997). Drug use during pregnancy. *Journal of Drug Issues, 27,* 463–485.

Huttenlocher, J. (1998). Language input and language growth. *Preventive Medicine, 27,* 185–199.

Hwang, C. P. (1997). The changing role of Swedish fathers. In M. Lamb (Ed.), *The father's role: Cross-cultural perspectives* (pp. 115–138). Hillsdale, NJ: Erlbaum.

Hwang, C. P., Lamb, M. E., & Sigel, I. E. (Eds.). (1996). *Images of childhood.* Mahwah, NJ: Erlbaum.

Hyche, J., Bakeman, R., & Adamson, L. (1992). Understanding communicative cues of infants with Down syndrome: Effects of mothers' experience and infants' age. *Journal of Applied Developmental Psychology, 13,* 1–16.

Hyde, J. S., Essex, M. J., & Horton, F. (1993). Fathers and parental leave: Attitudes and experiences. *Journal of Family Issues, 14,* 616–638.

Ignico, A. A. (1991). Physical education for Head Start children: A field-based study. *Early Child Development and Care, 77,* 77–92.

Imbens-Bailey, A. L. (2000). Ancestral language acquisition: Implications for aspects of ethnic identity among Armenian American children and adolescents. *Journal of Language and Social Psychology, 15,* 422–443.

Inciardi, J. A., McBride, D. C., & Surratt, H. L. (1998). The heroin street addict: Profiling a national population. In J. A. Inciardi & L. D. Harrison (Eds.), *Heroin in the age of crack-cocaine. Drugs, health, and social policy series* (pp. 31–50). Thousand Oaks, CA: Sage.

Inciardi, J. A., Surratt, H. L., & Saum, C. A. (1997). *Cocaine-exposed infants: Social, legal, and public health issues.* Thousand Oaks, CA: Sage.

Ingoldsby, B. B. (1995). Marital structure. In B. B. Ingoldsby & S. Smith (Eds.), *Families in multicultural perspective* (pp. 117–138). New York: Guilford.

Ingoldsby, B. B., & Smith, S. (Eds.). (1995). *Families in multicultural perspective.* New York: Guilford Press.

Inhelder, B. B., & Piaget, J. (1958). *The growth of logical thinking from childbirth to adolescence.* New York: Basic Books.

International Association for the Evaluation of Educational Achievement. (1998). *Science achievement in seventeen countries: A preliminary report.* New York: Pergamon.

Intons-Peterson, M. J. (1988). *Gender concepts of Swedish and American youths.* Hillsdale, NJ: Erlbaum.

Isabella, R. A., & Belsky, J. (1991). Interactional synchrony and the origins of infant–mother attachment: A replication study. *Child Development, 62,* 373–384.

Ishii-Kuntz, M. (1995). Paternal involvement and perception toward fathers' role: A comparison between Japan and the United States. In W. Marsiglio (Ed.), *Fatherhood: Contemporary theory, research, and social policy* (pp. 102–118). Thousand Oaks, CA: Sage.

Izard, C. E. (1977). *Human emotions.* New York: Plenum Press.

Izard, C. E., & Ackerman, B. P. (1998). Emotions and self-concept across the life span. In K. W. Schaia & M. P. Lawton (Eds.), *Annual review of gerontology and geriatrics. Vol. 17: Focus on emotions and adult development* (pp. 1–28). New York: Springer.

Izard, C. E., & Ackerman, B. P. (2000). Motivation, organization, and regulatory functions of discrete emotions. In M. Lewis & J. M. Haviland-Jones (Eds.), *Handbook of emotions* (pp. 253–264). New York: Guilford Press.

Izard, C. E, Haynes, M., Chisholm, G., & Baak, K. (1991). Emotional determinants of infant–mother attachment. *Child Development, 62,* 906–917.

Izard, C. E., Libero, D. Z., Putman, P., & Haynes, O. M. (1993). Stability of emotion experience and their relations to traits of personality. *Journal of Personality and Social Psychology, 64,* 847–860.

Jaccard, J. (1995, October). *Adolescent contraceptive behavior: Conceptual and Applied Issues.* Paper presented at the Improving Contraceptive Use in the United States: Assessing Past Efforts and Setting New Directions, Conference, Bethesda, MD.

Jaccard, J., Dittus, P. J., & Gordon, V. V. (1998). Parent–adolescent congruency in reports of adolescent sexual behavior and in communications about sexual behavior. *Child Development, 69,* 247–261.

Jackendoff, R. (1994). *Patterns in the mind: Language and human nature.* New York: Harvester Wheatsheaf.

Jacklin, C. N. (1989). Female and male: Issues of gender. *American Psychologist, 44,* 127–133.

Jackson, D. W., & Tein, J. Y. (1998). Adolescents' conceptualization of adult roles: Relationships with age, gender, work goals, and maternal employment. *Sex Roles, 38,* 987–1008.

Jackson, R., Jr. (1998). The effects of cooperative learning on the development of cross-racial friendships. *Dissertation Abstracts International, 59*(4), 1068A. (University Microfilms No. AAM98–31801)

Jacobson, S. W., & Frye, K. F. (1991). Effect of maternal social support on attachment: Experimental evidence. *Child Development, 62,* 572–582.

Jacobvitz, D. B., Hazen, N. L., & Riggs, S. (1997, April). *Disorganized mental processes in mothers, frightening/frightened caregiving, and disoriented, disorganized behavior in infancy.* Paper presented at the biennial meeting of the Society for Research in Child Development, Washington, DC.

Jahoda, G. (1958). Child animism: I. A critical survey of cross-cultural research: II. A study in West Africa. *Journal of Social Psychology, 47,* 197–212, 213–222.

Jahoda, G. (1998). Cultural influences on development. In A. Campbell & S. Muncer (Eds.), *The social child* (pp. 85–110). Psychology Press.

Jahoda, G. (2000). Piaget and Levy-Bruhl. *History of psychology, 3,* 218–238.

James, W. (1890). *Principles of psychology* (Vol.1). New York: Henry Holt.

James, W. (1907). *Principles of psychology.* New York: Henry Holt. (Original work published in 1890)

James, W. (1950). *Principles of psychology.* New York: Dover. (Original work published in 1890)

Janos, C., Sandor, R., Emoke, S., Judit, M., & Katalin, S. (1999). Oengyilkossagi kiserlete elkoevetell fantazialo es nem-szuicid depresszios serduelok oesszehasonlit vizgalata. *Psychiatria Hungarica, 14,* 32–38.

Janowsky, J. S., & Carper, R. (1996). Is there a neural basis for cognitive transitions in school-age children? In A. J. Sameroff & M. M. Haith (Eds.), *The five to seven shift: The age of reason and responsibility* (pp. 33–62). Chicago: University of Chicago Press.

Jansen, B. R. J., & van der Maas, H. L. J. (1997). Statistical test of the rules assessment methodology by latent class analysis. *Developmental Review, 17,* 321–357.

Janssen, A. W. H., Janssen, J. M. A., & Gerris, J. R. M. (1992). Parents' and children's levels of moral reasoning: Antecedents and consequences of parental discipline strategies. In J. M. A. Janssen & J. R. M. Gerris (Eds.), *Child rearing: Influence on prosocial and moral development* (pp. 57–75). Amsterdam: Swets & Zeitlinger.

Janus, L., & Dowling, T. (1997). The enduring effects of the prenatal experience: Echoes from the womb. Northvale, NJ: Jason Aronson, Inc.

Jarrett, R. (1995). Growing up poor: The family experiences of socially mobile youth in low-income African American neighborhoods. *Journal of Adolescent Research, 10,* 111–135.

Jason, L. A., & Hanaway, L. K. (1997). *Remote control: A sensible approach to kids, TV, and the new electronic media.* Sarasota, FL: Professional Resource Press.

Jeammet, P., & Corcos, M. (1998). Psychodynamic comprehension of adolescent eating disorders: Consequences on therapeutic approach. In P. Bria & A. Ciocca (Eds.), *Psychotherapeutic issues on eating disorders: Models, methods, and results* (pp. 27–40). Rome, Italy: Abramowizc.

Jekielek, S. M. (1998). Parental conflict, marital disruption, and children's emotional well-being. *Social Forces, 76,* 905–936.

Jencks, C. (1972). *Inequality: A reassessment of the effect of family and schooling in America.* New York: Basic Books.

Jenkins, J. M., Oatley, K., & Stein, N. L. (Eds.). (1998). *Human emotions: A reader.* Malden, MA: Blackwell Publishers.

Jensen, A. A. (1998). Parenthood and childhood in the Scandinavian countries: Challenges of responsibility. *Childhood: A Global Journal of Child Research, 5,* 55–57.

Jensen, A. R. (1969). How much can we boost IQ and scholastic achievement? *Harvard Educational Review, 39,* 1–123.

Jensen, A. R. (1985). The nature of the black–white difference on various psychometric tests: Spearman's hypothesis. *Behavioral and Brain Sciences, 8,* 193–219.

Jessee, P. O., Nagy, M. C., Gresham, C. L., & Poteet-Johnson, D. (1996). Pediatric AIDS: Are physicians ready? *Children's Health Care, 25,* 175–189.

Jessor, R., Turbin, M. S., & Costa, F. M. (1998). Protective factors in adolescent health behavior. *Journal of Personality and Social Psychology, 75,* 788–800.

Ji, C. H. C. (1997). Collectivism in moral development. *Psychological Reports, 80,* 967–975.

Jiang, J., Xia, X., Hui, J., & Cheng, X. (1997). Comprehensive family based modification for obese children. *Chinese Mental Health Journal, 11,* 242–244.

Jiao, S., Ji, G., & Jing, Q. (1996). Cognitive development of Chinese urban only children and children with siblings. *Child Development, 67,* 387–395.

Joe, J. R. (1994). Revaluing Native-American concepts of development and education. In P. M. Greenfield & R. R. Cocking (Eds.), *Cross-cultural roots of minority child development* (pp. 107–115). Hillsdale, NJ: Erlbaum.

Joe, J. R., & Malach, R. S. (1992). Families with Native American roots. In E. W. Lynch & M. J. Hanson (Eds.), *Developing cross-cultural competence: A guide for working with young children and their families* (pp. 89–119). Baltimore: Paul H. Brookes.

John, O. P., Donahue, E. M., & Kentle, R. L. (1991). *The "Big Five" inventory—versions 4a and 54* (Tech. Report). Berkeley, CA: Institute of Personality Assessment and Research.

Johnson, C. A., & Johnson, D. L. (1998). Working with Native American families. In H. Lefley (Ed.), *Families coping with mental illness: The cultural context.* San Francisco: Jossey-Bass Inc.

Johnson, M. H., Dziurawiec, S., Ellis, H. D., & Morton, J. (1991). *Biology and cognitive development: The case of face recognition.* Oxford, England: Blackwell Publishers.

Johnson, R. (Ed.). (1995). African American voices: African American health educators speak out. New York: National League for Nursing.

Johnston, R. S., Anderson, M., & Holligan, C. (1996). Knowledge of the alphabet and explicit awareness of phonemes in prereaders: The nature of the relationship. *Reading and Writing: An Interdisciplinary Journal, 8,* 217–234.

Jones, A., & Selby, C. (1997). The use of computers for self-expression and communication. *Journal of Computing in Childhood Education, 8,* 199–214.

Jones, D. C., Lee, Y., & Vigfusdottir, T. R. (2001, April 19–22). *Peers, media, and body image during adolescence.* Paper presented at the biennial meeting of the Society for Research in Child Development, Minneapolis.

Jones, G. P., & Dembo, M. H. (1998). Age and sex role differences in intimate friendships during childhood and adolescence. *Merrill-Palmer Quarterly, 35,* 445–457.

Jordan, P. L. (1990). Laboring for relevance: Expectant and new fatherhood. *Nursing Research, 39,* 11–16.

Jordan, W. J., Lara, J., & McPartland, J. M. (1996). Exploring the causes of early dropout among race–ethnic and gender groups. *Youth and Society, 28,* 62–94.

Joseph, J. M. (1994). *The resilient child.* New York: Insight Books.

Joseph, R. M. (1998). Intention and knowledge in preschoolers' conception of pretend. *Child Development, 69,* 966–980.

Juarabe, T. C. (1996). The state of Hispanic health: Cardiovascular disease and health. In S. Torres (Ed.), *Hispanic voices* (pp. 93–113). New York: NLN Press.

Juel, C. (1998). Learning to read and write: A longitudinal study of fifty-four children from first to fourth grade. *Journal of Educational Psychology, 80,* 437–447.

Jusczyk, P. W., Kennedy, L. J., & Jusczyk, A. (1995). Young infants' retention of information about syllables. *Infant Behavior and Development, 18,* 24–41.

Kachur, S. P., Potter, L. B., James, S. P., & Powell, K. E. (1995). *Suicide in the United States: 1980–1992* (Violence surveillance summary series, No. 1). Atlanta: National Center for Injury Prevention and Control.

Kaemingk, K., & Paquette, A. (1999). Effects of prenatal alcohol exposure on neuropsychological functioning. *Developmental Neuropsychology, 15,* 111–140.

Kagan, J. (1996). Three pleasing ideas. *American Psychologist, 51,* 901–908.

Kagan, J. (1997). Biology and the child. In N. Eisenberg (Ed.), W. Damon (Series Ed.), *Handbook of child psychology. Vol. 3: Social, emotional, and personality development* (5th ed., pp. 177–235). New York: Wiley.

Kagan, J. (1997). Temperament contributors to the development of social behavior. In D. Magnusson (Ed.), The lifespan development of individuals: Behavioral, neurobiological, and psychosocial perspectives: A synthesis (pp. 376–393). New York: Cambridge University Press.

Kagan, J. (1999). Biological basis of childhood shyness. In A. Slater & D. Muir (Eds.), *The Blackwell reader in development psychology* (pp. 65–78). Malden, MA: Blackwell Publishers.

Kagan, J., Snidman, N., & Arcus, D. (1998). Childhood derivatives of high and low reactivity in infancy. *Child Development, 69,* 1483–1493.

Kagitcibasi, C. (1994). Human development and societal development. In A. M. Boovy, F. J. R. Vijver, & P. Boski (Eds.), *Journeys in cross-cultural psychology* (pp. 3–24). Lisse, Netherlands: Swets & Zeitlinger.

Kagitcibasi, C. (1996). *Family and human development across cultures.* Mahwah, NJ: Erlbaum.

Kahn, P. H., Jr. (1997). Bayous and jungle rivers: Cross-cultural perspectives on children's environmental moral reasoning. In H. D. Saltzstein (Ed.), *Culture as a context for moral development: New perspectives on the particular and the universal* (pp. 23–36). San Francisco: Jossey-Bass.

Kail, R. (1996). Nature and consequences of developmental change in speed of processing. *Swiss Journal of Psychology, 55,* 133–138.

Kakar, S. (1978). *The inner world: A psychoanalytic study of childhood and society in India.* Oxford, England: Oxford University Press.

Kallen, K. (1997). Maternal smoking during pregnancy and limb reduction malformations in Sweden. *American Journal of Public Health, 87,* 29–32.

Kam, W. K., & Lee, S. (1998). The variable manifestations and contextual meanings of anorexia nervosa: Two case illustrations from Hong Kong. *International Journal of Eating Disorders, 23,* 227–231.

Kamm, R. L. (1998). A developmental and psychoeducational approach to reducing conflict and abuse in little league and youth sports: The sport psychiatrist's role. *Child and Adolescent Psychiatric Clinics of North America, 7,* 891–918.

Kandel, D. B., & Andrews, K. (1987). Processes of adolescent socialization by parents and peers. *International Journal of the Addictions, 22,* 319–342.

Kandel, D. B., & Lesser, G. S. (1969). Parent–adolescent relationships and adolescent independence in the U.S. and Denmark. *Journal of Marriage and the Family, 69,* 348–358.

Kanner, L. (1943). Autistic disturbances of affective contact. *Nervous Child, 2,* 217–250.

Kanno, K. (1998). The stability of UG principles in second-language acquisition: Evidence from Japanese. *Linguistics, 36,* 1125–1146.

Kantrowitz, B., & Wingert, P. (1994). How kids learn. In E. N. Junn & C. J. Boyatzis (Eds.), *Annual editions: Child growth and development* (pp. 89–95). Guilford, CT: Dushkin.

Karasaw, M., Little, T. D., Miyashita, T., & Mashima, M. (1997). Japanese children's action-control beliefs about school performance. *International Journal of Behavioral Development, 20,* 405–423.

Karr, C., & Wesley, F. (1966). Comparison of German and U.S. childrearing practices. *Child Development, 37,* 715–723.

Katz, P. (1997). Adolescence, authority, and change. In L. T. Flaherty & H. A. Horowitz (Eds.), *Adolescent psychiatry. Vol. 21: Developmental and clinical studies. Annals of the American Society for Adolescent Psychiatry* (pp. 18–85). Hillsdale, NJ: Analytic Press.

Kavanaugh, R. D., & Engel, S. (1998). The development of pretense and narrative in early childhood education. In O. N. Saracho & B. Spodek (Eds.), *Multiple perspectives on play in early childhood education* (pp. 80–99). Albany, NY: University of New York Press.

Katzman, M. A., & Lee, S. (1998). Beyond body image: The integration of feminist and transcultural theories in the understanding of self-starvation. *International Journal of Eating Disorders, 22,* 385–394.

Kazui, M. (1997). The influence of cultural expectations on mother–child relationships in Japan. *Journal of Applied Developmental Psychology, 18,* 485–496.

Kearney, C. A., & Roblek, T. L. (1998). Parent training in the treatment of school refusal behavior. In J. M. Briesmeister & C. E. Schaefer (Eds.), *Handbook of parent training: Parents as co-therapists for children's behavior problems* (pp. 225–256). New York: Wiley.

Keating, D. P. (1990). Adolescent thinking. In S. S. Feldman & G. L. Elliott (Eds.), *At the threshold: The developing adolescent* (pp. 54–89). Cambridge, MA: Harvard University Press.

Keats, D. M. (1997). *Culture and the child: A guide for professionals in child care and development.* Chichester, England: Wiley (UK).

Kelley, M. L., Power, T. G., & Wimbush, D. D. (1992). Determinants of disciplining practices on low-income black mothers. *Child Development, 63,* 575–582.

Kelley, M. L., & Tseng, H. (1992). Cultural differences in child rearing: A comparison of immigrant Chinese and Caucasian American mothers. *Journal of Cross-Cultural Psychology, 23*(4), 444–455.

Kellman, P. H., & Arterberry, M E. (1998). *The cradle of knowledge: Development of perception in infancy.* Cambridge, MA: MIT Press.

Kellogg, R. (1967). *The psychology of children's art.* Del Mar, CA: CRM.

Kellogg, R., & O'Dell, S. (1969). *Analyzing children's art,* Palo Alto: CA: National Press Books.

Kelloway, E. K., & Harvey, S. (1999). Learning to work: The development of work beliefs. In J. Barling & E. K. Kelloway (Eds.), *Young workers: Varieties of experience* (pp. 37–58). Washington, DC: American Psychological Association.

Kemple, K. M., David, G. M., & Wang, Y. (1996). Preschoolers' creativity, shyness, and self-esteem. *Creativity Research Journal, 9*(4), 317–326.

Kenyon, P. M., & Barker, M. E. (1998). Attitudes towards meat-eating in vegetarian and non-vegetarian teenage girls in England. *Appetite, 30,* 185–198.

Keogh, B. K., Gallimore, R., & Weisner, T. (1997). A sociocultural perspective on learning and learning disabilities. *Learning Disabilities Research and Practice, 12,* 107–113.

Kephart, W., & Jedlicka, D. (1991). *The family, society, and the individual.* New York: HarperCollins.

Kernis, M. H. (1993). The roles of stability and level of self-esteem in psychological functioning. In R. F. Baumeister (Eds.), *Self-esteem: The puzzle of low self-regard* (pp. 167–180). New York: Plenum.

Kerr, J. (1995). A study on suicide. *Crisis, 16*(3), 132–134.

Kessler, C. J., & Graham, T. A. (2001, April 19–22). *School adjustment: Do parents matter?* Paper presented at the biennial meeting of the Society for Research in Child Development, Minneapolis.

Kessler, R. C., McGonagle, K. A., Zhao, S., Nelson, C. B., Hughes, M., Eshleman, S., Wittchen, H., & Kendler, K. A. (1994). Lifetime and 12-month prevalence of DSM-III-R psychiatric disorders in the United States. *Archives of General Psychiatry, 51,* 8–19.

Khanam, M., & Sen, A. K. (1998). The influence of creativity, sex, and type of school on creative self-perception. *Social Science International, 14,* 60–70.

Killen, J. D. (1998). Smoking prevention. In E. A. Blechman & K. D. Brownell (Eds.), *Behavioral medicine and women* (pp. 228–232). New York: Guilford Press.

Kim, U., & Choi, S. H. (1994). Individualism, collectivism, and child development. In P. M. Greenfield & R. R. Cocking (Eds.), *Cross-cultural roots of minority child development* (pp. 227–258). Hillsdale, NJ: Erlbaum.

Kim, W. J., Kim, L. I., & Rue, D. S. (1997). Korean American children. In G. Johnson-Powell & J. Yamamoto (Eds.), *Transcultural child development: Psychological assessment and treatment* (pp. 183–207). New York: Wiley.

Kimball, G. (1988). *50–50 parenting.* Lexington, MA: Lexington Books.

King, A. R. (1998). Family environment scale predictors of academic performance. *Psychological Reports, 83,* 1319–1327.

King, B. M. (1999). *Human sexuality today.* Upper Saddle River, NJ: Prentice-Hall.

King, N., Ollendick, T. H., Tonge, B. J., Heyne, D., Pritchard, M., Rollings, S., Young, D., & Myerson, N. (1998). School refusal: An overview. *Behaviour Change, 15,* 5–15.

Kirsh, S. J. (1998). Seeing the world through Mortal Kombat-colored glasses: Violent video games and the development of a short-term hostile attribution bias. *Childhood: A Global Journal of Child Research, 5,* 177–184.

Kisilevsky, B. S., Hains, S. M. J., Lee, K., Muir, D. W., Xu, F., & Fu, G. (1998). The still-face effect in Chinese and Canadian 3- to 6-month-old infants. *Developmental Psychology, 34,* 629–639.

Kitson, G. C., with Holmes, W. M. (1992). *Portrait of divorce: Adjustment to marital dissolution.* New York: Guilford.

Klaczynski, P. A., Fauth, J. M., & Swanger, A. (1998). Adolescent identity: Rational vs. experiential processing, formal operations, and critical thinking beliefs. *Journal of Youth and Adolescence, 27,* 185–207.

Klebanoff, M. A., & Berendes, H. W. (1988). Aspirin exposure during the first 20 weeks of gestation and IQ at four years of age. *Teratology, 37,* 249–255.

Klee, H. (Ed.). (1997). *Amphetamine misuse: International perspectives on current trends.* Amsterdam: Harwood.

Klimes-Dougan, B. (1998). Screening for suicidal ideation in children and adolescents: Methodological considerations. *Journal of adolescence, 21,* 435–444.

Klin, A., Volkmar, F. R., Sparrow, S. S., Cicchetti, D. V., et al. (1996). Validity and neuropsychological characterization of Asperger Syndrome: Convergence with Nonverbal Learning Disabilities syndrome. *Annual Progress in Child Psychiatry and Child Development,* 241–259.

Knight, G. P., Tein, J. Y., Shell, R., & Roosa, M. (1992). The cross-ethnic equivalence of parenting and family interaction measures among Hispanic and Anglo-American families. *Child Development, 63,* 1392–1403.

Kobayashi, Y. (1994). Conceptual acquisition and change through social interaction. *Human Development, 37,* 233–241.

Kochanska, G. (1993). Toward a synthesis of parental socialization and child temperament in early development of conscience. *Child Development, 64,* 325–347.

Kochanska, G., Coy, K. C., Tjebkes, T. L., & Husarek, S. J. (1998). Individual differences in emotionality in infancy. *Child Development, 64,* 375–390.

Kochanska, G., De Vet, K., Goldman, M., Murray, K., & Putman, S. P. (1994). Maternal reports of conscience development and temperament in young children. *Child Development, 65,* 852–868.

Kochanska, G., Murray, K. T., & Harlan, E. T. (2000). Effortful control in early childhood: Continuity and change, antecedents, and implications for social development. *Developmental Psychology, 36*(2), 220–232.

Kochanska, G., & Thompson, R. A. (1997). The emergence and development of conscience in toddlerhood and early childhood. In J. E. Grusec & L. Kuczynski (Eds.), *Parenting and children's internalization of values: A handbook of contemporary theory* (pp. 53–77). New York: Wiley.

Kohlberg, L. (1966). A cognitive-developmental analysis of children's sex-role concepts and attitudes. In E. E. Maccoby (Ed.), *The development of sex differences* (pp. 82–173). Palo Alto, CA: Stanford University Press.

Kohlberg, L. (1971). From is to ought: How to commit the naturalistic fallacy and get away with it in the study of moral development. In T. Mischel (Ed.), *Cognitive development and epistemology* (pp. 131–145). New York: Gordon and Breach.

Kohlberg, L. (1976). Moral stages and moralization: The cognitive-developmental approach. In T. Lickona (Ed.), *Moral development and behavior: Theory, research, and social issues* (pp. 31–53). New York: Holt, Rinehart, & Winston.

Kohlberg, L. (1978). *The meaning and measurement of moral development.* Invited address at the meetings of the American Psychological Association, Toronto.

Kohlberg, L. (1981). *The philosophy of moral development.* San Francisco: Harper & Row.

Kohlberg, L., Yaeger, J., & Hjertholm, E. (1999). Private speech: Four studies and a review of theories. In P. Llyod & C. Fernyhough (Eds.), *Lev Vygotsky: Critical assessments: Thought and language* (Vol. II, pp. 185–229). New York: Routledge.

Kolata, G. B. (1995, February 28). Man's word, woman's world? Brain studies point to differences. *New York Times.*

Kopp, C. B. (1989). Regulation of distress and negative motions: A developmental view. *Developmental Psychology, 25,* 343–354.

Korenman, S., Miller, J. E., & Sjaastad, J. E. (1995). Long-term poverty and child development in the United States: Results from the National Longitudinal Survey of Youth. *Children and Youth Services Review, 17,* 127–151.

Kovacs, M., (1990). Affective disorders in children and adolescents. *American Psychologist 44,* 209–215.

Kposowa, A. J. (1998). The impact of race on divorce in the United States. *Journal of Comparative Family Studies, 29,* 529–548.

Kramer, L., Locke, G., Ogunyemi, A., & Nelson, L. (1990). Neonatal cocaine-related seizures. *Journal of Child Neurology, 5,* 60–64.

Kraus, N., McGee, T. J., Carrell, T. D., Zecker, S. G., Nicol, T. G., & Koch, D. B. (1996). Auditory neurophysiologic responses and discrimination deficits in children with learning problems. *Science, 273,* 971–973.

Krispen, O., Sternberg, K. J., & Lamb, M. E. (1992). The dimensions of peer evaluations in Israel: A cross-cultural perspective. *International Journal of Behavioral Development, 15,* 299–314.

Kronk, C. M. (1994). Private speech in adolescents. *Adolescence, 29,* 781–804.

Kubey, R., & Csikszentmihalyi, M. (1990). *Television and the quality of life: How viewing shapes everyday experience.* Hillsdale, NJ: Erlbaum.

Kuhn, P. K. (1993). Developmental speech perception: Implications for models of language impairment. *Annals of New York Academy of Sciences, 682,* 248–263.

Kuhn, P. K. (1994). Learning and representation in speech and language. *Current opinions in Neurobiology, 4,* 812–822.

Kuhn, P. K., & Meltzoff, A. M. (1996). Infant vocalizations in response to speech: Vocal imitation and developmental change. *Journal of the Acoustical Society of America, 100,* 2425–2438.

Kuhn, P. K., Williams, K. A., & Lacerda, F. (1992). Linguistic experience alters phonetic perceptions in infants by 6 months of age. *Science, 255,* 606–608.

Kuiper, N. A., & Martin, R A. (1993). Human and self-concept. *International Journal of Humor Research, 6,* 251–270.

Kuo, Y. Y. (1996). Taoistic pschology and creativity. *Journal of Creative Behavior, 30,* 197–212.

Kupersmidt, J. B., & Coie, J. D. (1990). Preadolescent peer status, aggression, and school adjustment as predictors of externalizing problems in adolescence. *Child Development, 61,* 1350–1362.

Kwok, D. C., & Lytton, H. (1993, April). *Perceptions of mathematics ability and mathematic performance: Canadian and Hong Kong Chinese children.* Paper presented at biennial meeting of the Society for Research in Child Development, New Orleans.

Kyei, A. K., Acker, D. B., & MacBain, D. (1998). The effect of post detoxification drug-free residential living on birth outcome in the pregnant drug abuser. *Substance Abuse, 19,* 123–128.

Ladd, G. W., & Coleman, C. C. (1997). Children's classroom peer relationships and early school attitudes: Concurrent and longitudinal associations. *Early Education and Development, 8,* 51–66.

Ladd, G. W., & Kochenderfer, B. J. (1998). Linkages between friendship and adjustment during early school transition. In W. M. Bukowski, A. F. Newcomb, & W. W. Hartup (Eds.), *The company they keep: Friendship in childhood and adolescence. Cambridge studies in social and emotional development* (pp. 32–345). New York: Cambridge University Press.

Ladd, G. W., Kochenderfer, B. J., & Coleman, C. C. (1997). Classroom peer acceptance, friendship, and victimization: Distinct relational systems that contribute uniquely to children's adjustment? *Child Development, 68,* 1181–1197.

Ladd, G. W., & LeSieur, K. D. (1995). Parents and children's peer relationships. In M. H. Bornstein (Ed.), *Handbook on parenting* (pp. 377–410). Hillsdale, NJ: Erlbaum.

Ladd, G. W., Profilet, S. M., & Hart, C. H. (1992). Parents' management of children's peer relations: Facilitating and supervising children's activities in the peer culture. *Journal of Early Adolescence, 10,* 399–415.

Ladson-Billings, G. (1994). *The dreamkeepers: Successful teachers of African American children.* San Francisco: Jossey-Bass.

Lagattuta, K. H., Wellman, H. M., & Flavell, J. H. (1997). Preschoolers' understanding of the link between thinking and feeling: Cognitive cuing and emotional change. *Child Development, 68,* 1081–1104.

Lalonde, C., Chandler, M., Hallett, D., & Paul, D. (2001, April 19–22). *A longitudinal study of identity formation processes in Native American youth.* Paper presented at the biennial meeting of the Society for Research in Child Development, Minneapolis.

Lamb, M. E. (1997). The development of father–infant relationships. In M .E. Lamb (Ed.), *The role of the father in child development* (pp. 104–120). New York: Wiley.

Lamb, M. E. (1998). Fatherhood then and now. In A. Booth & A. C. Crouter (Eds.), *Men in families: When do they get involved? What difference does it make?* (pp. 47–52). Mahwah, NJ: Erlbaum.

Lamb, M. E. (1999). Nonparental child care. In M. E. Lamb (Ed.), *Parenting and child development in "nontraditional" families* (pp. 39–55). Mahwah, NJ: Erlbaum.

Lamb, M. E., Hwang, C. P., Ketterlinus, R. D., & Fracasso, M. P. (1999). Parent–child relationships: Development in the context of the family. In M. H. Bornstein & M. E. Lamb (Eds.), *Developmental psychology: An advanced textbook* (pp. 411–450). Mahwah, NJ: Erlbaum.

Lamb, M. E., & Oppenheim, D. (1989). Fatherhood and father–child relationships: Five years of research. In S. Cath, A. Gurwitt, & L. Gunsberg. (Eds.), *Fathers and their families* (pp. 11–26). Hillsdale, NJ: Analytic Press.

Lamb, M. E., & Sternberg, K. J. (1992). Sociocultural perspectives in nonparental childcare. In. M. E. Lamb, K. J. Sternberg, C. Hwang, & A. G. Broberg (Eds.), *Child care in context.* Hillsdale, NJ: Erlbaum.

Lamborn, S. D., & Steinberg, L. (1993). Emotional autonomy: Revisiting Ryan and Lynch. *Child Development, 64,* 483–499.

Lamson, S. R. (1995). Media violence has increased the murder rate. In C. Wekesser (Ed.), *Violence in the media* (pp. 25–27). San Diego: Greenhaven Press.

Landa, R., & Goldberg, M. (2001, April 19–22). *Language and executive functions in high-functioning autistic children.* Paper presented at the biennial meeting of the Society for Research in Child Development, Minneapolis.

Landau, S., & McAninch, C. (1993). Young children with attention deficits. *Young Children, 21,* 49–58.

Lang, P. J., Simons, R. F., & Balaban, M. T. (Eds.). (1997). *Attention and orienting: Sensory and motivational processes.* Mahwah, NJ: Erlbaum.

Lange, C. M. (1998). Characteristics of alternative schools and programs serving at-risk students. *High School Journal, 81,* 183–198.

Langer, W. L. (1973). Infanticide: A historical survey. *History of Childhood Quarterly, 1,* 353–367.

Langfield, P. A., & Pasley, K. (1997). Understanding stress associated with adolescent pregnancy and early childbearing. In S. A. Wolchik & I. N. Sandler (Eds.), *Handbook of children's coping: Linking theory and intervention* (pp. 245–274). New York: Plenum.

Langlois, J. H., Rutter, J. M., Roggman, L. A., & Vaugh, L. S. (1991). Facial diversity and infant preferences for attractive faces. *Developmental Psychology, 27,* 79–84.

Lanham, B. B., & Garrick, R. J. (1996). Adult to child in Japan: Interaction and relations. In D. W. Shwalb & B. J. Shwalb (Eds.), *Japanese childrearing: Two generations of scholarship* (pp. 97–124). New York: Guilford Press.

Lapsley, D. K., & Murphy, M. M. (1985). Another look at the theoretical assumptions of adolescent egocentrism. *Developmental Review, 5,* 201–217.

LaRossa, R., & Reitzes, D. C. (1996). Gendered perceptions of father involvement in early 20th century America. *Journal of Marriage and the Family, 57,* 223–229.

Larson, R. W. (1997). The emergence of solitude as a constructive domain of experience in early adolescence. *Child Development, 68,* 80–93.

Larson, R. W., Gillman, S. A., & Richards, M. H. (1997). Divergent experiences of family leisure: Fathers, mothers, and young adolescents. *Journal of Leisure Research, 29,* 78–97.

Larson, R. W., & Richards, M. H. (1994). *Divergent realities: The emotional lives of mothers, fathers, and adolescents.* New York: Basic Books.

Lask, B., & Bryant-Waugh, R. (1999). Review of anorexia and bulimia. *Journal of the American Academy of Child and Adolescent Psychiatry, 38,* 109.

Laursen, B., & Bukowski, W. M. (1997). A developmental guide to the organisation of close relationships. *International Journal of Behavioral development, 21,* 747–770.

Laursen, B., Coy, D. C., & Collins, W. A. (1998). Reconsidering changes in parent–child conflict across adolescence: A meta-analysis. *Child Development, 69,* 817–832.

Lavee, Y., Sharlin, S., & Katz, R. (1996). The effect of parenting stress on marital quality. *Journal of Family Issues, 17,* 114–135.

Lazarus, R. S. (1993). Coping theory and research: Past, present, and future. *Psychosomatic Medicine, 55,* 234–247.

Leadbeater, B. J. R., & Way, N. (1996). *Urban girls: Resisting stereotypes, creating identities.* New York: New York University Press.

Leap, W. (1989). *Written Ute English: Texture, construction, and point of view.* Proceedings of the Ninth Annual International Native American Language Issues (NALI) Institute. Billings, Montana, June 8–9.

Leary, M. R., & Downs, D. L. (1995). Interpersonal functions of the self-esteem motive: The self-esteem system as a sociometer. In M. H. Kernis (Ed.), *Efficacy, agency, and self-esteem* (Vol. 6, pp. 123–140). New York: Plenum.

Leboyer, F. (1975). *Birth without violence.* New York: Knopf.

Lebra, T. S. (1994). Mother and child in Japanese socialization: A Japan–U.S. comparison. In P. M. Greenfield & R. R. Cocking (Eds.), *Cross-cultural roots of minority child development* (pp. 259–274). Hillsdale, NJ: Erlbaum.

Le Couteur, A., Bailey, A., Goode, S., Robertson, S., Gottesman, I. I., Schmidt, D., & Rutter, M. (1993). *A broader phenotype of autism: The clinical spectrum in twins.* Unpublished manuscript.

LeDoux, J. E. (1994). Emotion, memory, and the brain. *Scientific American, 370,* 50–57.

LeDoux, J. E. (1996). *The emotional brain: The mysterious underpinnings of emotional life.* New York: Simon & Schuster.

Lee, B., & Goerge, R. M. (1999). Poverty, early childbearing, and child maltreatment: A multinomial analysis. *Children and Youth Services Review, 21,* 755–780.

Lee, C. (1997). Social context, depression, and the transition to motherhood. *British Journal of Health Psychology, 2,* 93–108.

Lee, E. (1996). Asian American families: An overview. In M. McGoldrick & J. Giordano (Eds.), *Ethnicity and family therapy* (2nd ed., pp. 227–248). New York: Guilford Press.

Lee, L. C. (1999). An overview. In L. C. Lee & N. W. S. Zane (Eds.), *The handbook of Asian psychology* (pp. 1–20). Thousand Oaks, CA: Sage.

Lee, L. C., & Zane, N. W. S. (1999). *Handbook of Asian American psychology.* Thousand Oaks, CA: Sage.

Lee, S. Y. (1998). Mathematics learning and teaching in the school context: Reflections from cross-cultural comparisons. In S. G. Paris & H. M. Wellman (Eds.), *Global prospects for education: Development, culture, and schooling* (pp. 45–77). Washington, DC: American Psychological Association.

LeFore, P. C., & Warren, J. R. (1997). A comparison of single sex and coeducational Catholic secondary schooling: Evidence from the National Educational Longitudinal Study. *American Educational Research Journal, 34,* 405–511.

Legerstee, M. (1997). Contingency effects of people and objects on subsequent cognitive functioning in three-month-old infants. *Social Development, 6,* 307–321.

Legerstee, M., Anderson, D., & Schaffer, A. (1998). Five- and eight-month-old infants recognize their faces and voices as familiar and social stimuli. *Child Development, 69,* 37–50.

Leiblum, S. R., & Greenfeld, D. A. (1997). The course of infertility: Immediate and long-term reactions. In S. R. Leiblum (Ed.), *Infertility: Psychological issues and counseling strategies* (pp. 83–102). New York: Wiley.

Lemerise, E. A, & Dodge, K. A. (2000). The development of anger and hostile interactions. In M. Lewis & J. M. Haviland-Jones (Eds.), *Handbook of emotions* (pp. 594–606). New York: Guilford Press.

Lempert, H. (1989). Animacy constraints on preschool children's acquisition of syntax. *Child Development, 60,* 237–245.

Lenarduzzi, G., & McLaughlin, R. F. (1996). Working on GPA, test accuracy, and attendance of high-school dropouts. *Psychological Reports, 78,* 42–52.

Lerman, R. I. (1993). A national profile of young unwed fathers. In R. I. Lerman & T. J. Ooms (Eds.), *Young unwed fathers* (pp. 27–51). Philadelphia: Temple University Press.

Lerner, J. V., & Galambos, N. L. (1991). *Employed mothers and their children.* New York: Garland.

Lerner, R. M., & Galambos, N. L. (1998). Adolescent development: Challenges and opportunities for research, programs, and policies. *Annual Review of Psychology, 49,* 413–446.

Leung, K., Lau, S., & Lam, W. L. (1998). Parenting styles and academic achievement: A cross-cultural study. *Merrill Palmer Quarterly, 44,* 157–172.

Levenkron, S. (1992). *Treating and overcoming anorexia nervosa.* New York: Scribner's Sons.

Levine, L. J., Stein, N. L., & Liwag, M. D. (1999). Remembering children's emotions: Sources of concordant and discordant accounts between parents and children. *Developmental Psychology, 35,* 790–801.

LeVine, R. A. (1984). Properties of culture: An ethnographic view. In R. A. Shweder & R. A. LeVine (Eds.), *Culture, theory: Essays on mind, self, and emotion* (pp. 67–87). Cambridge, England: Cambridge University Press.

LeVine, R. A., Dixon, S., LeVine, S., Richman, A., Leiderman, P. H., Keefer, C. H., & Brazelton, T. B. (1994). *Childcare and culture: Lessons from Africa.* Cambridge, UK: Cambridge University Press.

LeVine, S. (1979). *Mothers and wives.* Chicago: University of Chicago Press.

Levine, S. B. (1995). A variety of measures could combat media violence. In C. Wekesser (Ed.), *Violence in the media* (pp. 142–147). San Diego: Greenhaven Press.

Levy, R. I. (1984). Emotion, knowing, and culture. In R. Shweder & R. Levine (Eds.), *Culture theory: Mind, self, and emotion* (pp. 214–237). Cambridge, England: Cambridge University Press.

Lewis, C. C. (1995). *Educating hearts and minds.* New York: Cambridge University Press.

Lewis, M. (2000). The emergence of human emotions. In M. Lewis & J. M. Haviland-Jones (Eds.), *Handbook of emotions* (pp. 265–280). New York: Guilford Press.

Lewis, R. A., Piercy, F. P., Sprenkle, D. H., & Trepper, T. S. (1990). Family-based interventions for helping drug-abusing adolescents. *Journal of Adolescent Research, 5,* 82–95.

Li, C. Y., Copeland, E. P., & Martin, J. D. (1995). Peer relations of children in Taiwan with characateristics of attention deficit hyperactivity disorder. *School Psychology International, 16,* 379–388.

Li, L., & Moore, D. (1998). Acceptance of disability and its correlates. *Journal of Social Psychology, 138,* 13–25.

Lightfoot, C. (1997). *The culture of adolescent risk-taking.* New York: Guilford Press.

Lillard, A. S. (1998). Ethnopsychologies: Cultural variations in theories of mind. *Psychological Bulletin, 123,* 3–32.

Lillard, A. S., Zeljo, A., & Harlan, D. (1998). *Developing cultural schemas: Behavior explanation in Taipei, the rural U.S., and the urban U.S.* University of Virginia. Typescript paper.

Lin, S., & Lepper, M. R. (1987). Correlates of children's usage of video games and computers. *Journal of Applied Social Psychology, 17,* 72–93.

Lincoln, A., Courchesne, E., Allen, M., Hanson, E., & Ene, M. (1998). Neurobiology of Asperger syndrome: Seven case studies and quantitative magnetic resonance imaging findings. In E. Schopler & G. B. Mesibov (Eds.), *Asperger syndrome or high-functioning autism? Current issues in autism* (pp. 145–163). New York: Plenum.

Linn, S., Schoenbaum, S. C., Monson, R. R., Rosner, B., Stubblefield, P. G., & Ryan, K. J. (1992). No association between coffee consumption and adverse outcomes of pregnancy. *New England Journal of Medicine, 306,* 141–145.

Lipsitt, L. P. (1990). Learning and memory in infants. *Merrill-Palmer Quarterly, 36,* 53–66.

Llyod, P., & Fernyhough, C. (1999). *Lev Vygotsky: Critical assessments: The zone of proximal development.* New York: Routledge.

Lochman, J. E., & Dodge, K. E. (1998). Distorted perceptions in dyadic interactions of aggressive and nonaggressive boys: Effects of prior expectations, context, and boys' age. *Development and Psychopathology, 10,* 495–512.

Locke, J. (1964). *Some thoughts concerning education.* F. W. Garforth (Ed.), Woodbury, NY: Barron's Educational Series. (Original work published in 1693)

Lockwood, V. (2001). The impact of development on women: The interplay of material conditions and gender ideology. In C. B. Brettell & C. F. Sargent (Eds.), *Gender in cross-cultural perspective* (pp. 529–543). Upper Saddle River, NJ: Prentice-Hall.

LoConte, J. S., O'Leary. A., & Labouvie, E. (1997). Psychosocial correlates of HIV-related sexual behavior in an inner city STD clinic. *Psychology and Health, 12,* 589–601.

Locuy, M. I. (1999). Suggestions for working with fat children in the schools. *Professional School Counseling, 1,* 18–22.

Loeber, R., Farrington, D. P., Stouthamer-Loeber, M., & Van Kammen, W. B. (1998). *Antisocial behavior and mental health problems: Explanatory factors in childhood and adolescence.* Mahwah, NJ: Erlbaum.

Loehlin, J. C. (1992). *Genes and environment in personality development.* Newbury Park, CA: Sage.

Loehlin, J. C. (1997). Genes and environment. In D. Magnusson (Ed.), *The life-span development of individuals: Behavioral, neurobiological, and psychological perspectives: A synthesis* (pp. 38–51). New York: Cambridge University Press.

Loehlin, J. C., Willerman, L., & Horn, J. M. (1982). Personality resemblances between unwed mothers and their adopted-away offspring. *Journal of Personality and Social Psychology, 42,* 1089–1099.

Loehlin, J. C., Willerman, L., & Horn, J. M. (1997). Heredity, environment, and IQ in the Texas Adoption Project. In R. J. Sternberg & E. L. Grigorenko (Eds.), *Intelligence, heredity, and environment* (pp. 105–125). New York: Cambridge University Press.

Lohaus, A., Klein-Hessling, J., & Shebar, S. (1997). Stress management for elementary school children: A comparative evaluation of different approaches. *European Review of Applied Psychology, 47,* 157–162.

Loken, E. (2001, April 19–22). *Temperamental types: Converging evidence from diverse approaches.* Paper presented at the biennial meeting of the Society for Research in Child Development, Minneapolis.

Lonner, W. J., Dinnel, D. L., Forgays, D. K., & Hayes, S. A. (Eds.). (1999). *Merging past, present, and future in cross-cultural psychology.* Selected papers from the Fourteenth International Congress of the International Association for Cross-Cultural Psychology. Lisse, Netherlands: Swets and Zeitlinger.

Lorenz, K. Z. (1965). *Evolution and the modification of behavior.* Chicago: University of Chicago Press.

Lowe, G. S., & Krahn, H. (1999). Reconceptualizing youth unemployment. In J. Barling & E. K. Kelloway (Eds.), *Young workers: Varieties of experience* (pp. 201–234). Washington, DC: American Psychological Association.

Lowenthal, B. (1997). Pediatric HIV infection: Effects on development, learning, and interventions. *Early Child Development and Care, 136,* 17–26.

Lubart, T. I. (1999). Creativity across cultures. In R. J. Sternberg (Ed.), *Handbook of creativity* (pp. 339–350). New York: Cambridge University Press.

Lucente, R. L. (1996). Sexual identity: Conflict and confusion in a male adolescent. *Child and Adolescent Social Work Journal, 13*(2), 97–114.

Ludemann, P. M. (1991). Generalized discrimination of positive facial expressions by seven- and ten-month-old infants. *Child Development, 62,* 55–67.

Ludwig, J., Ladd, H., & Duncan, G. (2001, April 19–22). *The effects of urban poverty on educational outcomes.* Paper presented at the biennial meeting of the Society for Research in Child Development, Minneapolis.

Lundy, D. E., Tan, J., & Cunningham, M. R. (1998). Heterosexual romantic preferences: The importance of humor and physical attractiveness for different types of relationships. *Personal Relationships, 5,* 311–325.

Luthar, S. (1991). Vulnerability and resilience: A study of high-risk adolescents. *Child Development, 62*(3), 600–616.

Lutz, D., & Sternberg, R. J. (1999). Cognitive development. In M. H. Bornstein & M. E. Lamb (Eds.), *Developmental psychology: An advanced textbook* (pp. 275–312). Mahwah, NJ: Erlbaum.

Lynn, R. (1982). IQ in Japan and the United States shows a growing disparity. *Nature, 297,* 222–223.

Lynn, R. (1989). Positive correlation between height, head size, and IQ: A nutrition theory of the secular increases in intelligence. *British Journal of Educational Psychology, 59,* 372–377.

Lynn, R. (1997). Geographic variation in intelligence. In H. Nyborg (Ed.), *The scientific study of human nature: Tribute to Hans J. Eysenck at eighty* (pp. 259–281). Oxford, England: Pergamon/Elsevier Science (UK).

Lynn, R. (1998). Has the black–white intelligence difference in the United States been narrowing over time? *Personality and Individual Differences, 25,* 999–1002.

Lyon, T. D., & Flavell, J. H. (1993). Young children's understanding of forgetting over time. *Child Development, 64,* 789–800.

Lyons-Ruth, K., Connell, D. B., Grunebaum, H. V., & Botein, S. (1990). Infants at social risk: Maternal depression and family support services as mediators of infant development and security of attachment. *Child Development, 61,* 85–98.

Lyons-Ruth, K., Repacholi, B., McLeod, S., & Silva, E. (1991). Disorganized attachment behavior in infancy: Short-term stability, maternal and infant correlates, and risk-related subtypes. *Development and Psychopathology, 3,* 377–396.

Lyons-Ruth, K., Zeanah, C. H., & Benoit, D. (1996). Discord and risk for disorder during infancy and toddlerhood. In E. J. Mash & R. A. Barkley (Eds.), *Child psychopathology* (pp. 457–491). New York: Guilford Press.

Lytton, H., & Pyryt, M. (1998). Predictors of achievement in basic skills: A Canadian effective schools study. *Canadian Journal of Education, 23,* 281–301.

Lytton, H., & Romney, D. M. (1992). Parents' differential socialization of boys and girls: A meta-analysis. *Psychological Bulletin, 109,* 267–296.

Maccoby, E. E. (1998). *The two sexes: Growing up apart, coming together.* Cambridge, MA: Harvard University Press.

Maccoby, E. E. (1999). The uniqueness of the parent–child relationship. In W. A. Collins & B. Laursen (Eds.), *Relationships as developmental contexts. The Minnesota Symposia on Child Psychology* (pp. 157–176). Mahwah, NJ: Erlbaum.

Maccoby, E. E., & Martin, J. A. (1983). Socialization, personality, and social development. In. E. M. Hetherington (Ed.), *Handbook of child psychology* (Vol. IV, p. 39). New York: Wiley.

MacGregor, S. K. (1999). Hypermedia navigation profiles: Cognitive characteristics and information-processing strategies. *Journal of Educational Computing Research, 20,* 189–206.

MacPhee, D., Fritz, J. J., & Miller-Heyl, J. (2001, April 19–22). *Teen mothers' hopes and fears.* Paper presented at the biennial meeting of the Society for Research in Child Development, Minneapolis.

Macro. (1993). *Ailedecocuk egitimi arastirmasi* (Child training in the family). Istanbul.

Madden, T. (1992). *Cultural factors and assumptions in social reasoning in India.* Unpublished doctoral dissertation, University of California, Berkeley.

Madon, S., Jussim, L., Keiper, S., Eccles, J., Smith, A., & Palumbo, P. (1998). The accuracy and power of sex, social class, and ethnic stereotypes: A naturalistic study in person perception. *Personality and Social Psychology Bulletin, 24,* 1304–1318.

Mael, F. A., Morath, R. A., & McLellan, J. A. (1997). Dimensions of adolescent employment. *Career Development Quarterly, 45,* 351–368.

Magnus, K. B., Cowen, E. L., Wyman, P. A., Fagen, D. B., & Work, W. C. (1999). Parent–child relationship qualities and child adjustment in highly stressed urban black and white families. *Journal of Community Psychology, 27*(1), 55–71.

Magnus, M. H. (1991). Cardiovascular health among African-Americans: A review of the health status, risk reduction, and intervention strategies. *American Journal of Health Promotion, 5,* 282–290.

Maher, F. A., & Tetreault, M. K. T. (1994). *The feminist classroom.* New York: Basic Books.

Mahler, M. S. (1968). *On human symbiosis and the vicissitudes of individuation. Vol. 1: Infantile psychosis.* New York: International Universities Press.

Mahon, M. H., Goldberg, E., & Washington, S. K. (1999). Concept of death in a sample of Israeli kibbutz children. *Death Studies, 23,* 43–59.

Mahoney, J. L., & Cairns, R. B. (1997). Do extracurricular activities protect against early school dropout? *Developmental Psychology, 33*(2), 241–251.

Maier, S. E., Chen, W. J. A., Miller, J. A., & West, J. R. (1997). Fetal alcohol exposure and temporal vulnerability: Regional differences in alcohol-induced microencephaly as a function of timing of binge-like alcohol exposure during rat brain development. *Alcoholism: Clinical and Experimental Research, 21,* 1418–1420.

Main, M., & Hesse, E. (1990). Parents' unresolved traumatic experiences are related to infant disorganized attachment status: Is frightened and/or frightening parental behavior the linking mechanism? In M. T. Greenberg, D. Cicchetti, & E. M. Cummings (Eds.), *Attachment in the preschool years* (pp. 161–182). Chicago: University of Chicago Press.

Main, M., & Morgan, H. (1996). Disorganization and disorientation in infant strange situation behavior: Phenotypic resemblance to dissociative states. In L. K. Michelson & W. J. Ray (Eds.), *Handbook of dissociation: Theoretical, empirical, and clinical perspectives* (pp. 197–138). New York: Plenum.

Major, B., Spencer, S., Schmader, T., Wolfe, C., & Crocker, J. (1998). Coping with negative stereotypes about intellectual performance: The role of psychological disengagement. *Personality and Social Psychology Bulletin, 24,* 34–50.

Makarenko, N. V., Chaichenko, G. M., & Bogutskaya, T. A. (1999). Children's psychophysiological readiness for school education. *Human Physiology, 25,* 156–161.

Makin, J., Fried, P. A., & Watkinson, B. (1991). A comparison of active and passive smoking during pregnancy: Long-term effects. *Neurotoxicology and Teratology, 13*(1), 5–12.

Males, M. (1993). School-age pregnancy: Why hasn't prevention worked? *Journal of School Health, 63,* 429–432.

Malgady, R. G., & Costantino, G. (1999). Ethnicity and culture: Hispanic youth. In W. K. Silverman & T. H. Ollendick (Eds.), *Developmental issues of the clinical treatment of children* (pp. 231–246). Boston: Allyn & Bacon.

Malina, R. M., (1988). Racial/ethnic variation in the motor development and performance of American children. *Canadian Journal of Sport Sciences,* 136–143.

Malinowski, B. (1953). *Sex and repression in a savage society.* London: Routledge & Kegan Paul.

Mallard, A. R. (1998). Using problem-solving procedures in family management of stuttering. *Journal of Fluency Disorders, 23,* 127–135.

Man, P. (1991). The influence of peers and parents on youth life satisfaction in Hong Kong. *Social Indicators Research, 24,* 347–365.

Manber, R., Pardee, R. E., Bootzin, R. R., Kuo, T., Rider, A. M., Rider, S. P., & Bergstrom, L. (1995). Changing sleep patterns in adolescence. *Sleep Research, 24,* 106.

Mandinach, E. B., & Kline, H. F. (1996). Classroom dynamics: The impact of a technology-based curriculum innovation of teaching and learning. *Journal of Educational Computing Research, 14,* 83–102.

Mang, M. E. (1998). *The social origins of preschoolers private speech: Self regulation via internalized social discourse.* Dissertation Abstracts International; Humanities and Social Sciences.

Mangelsdorf, S., Gunnar, M., Kestenbaum, R., Lang, S., & Andreas, D. (1990). Infant proneness-to-distress temperament, maternal personality and mother–infant attachment: Associations and goodness-of-fit. *Child Development, 61,* 820–831.

Manzano, J., Righetti-Veltema, M., & Perreard, E. C. (1997). Post-partum depression syndrome: Results of research concerning early warning signs. *Psychiatrie de l'Enfant, 40,* 533–552.

Marchman, V. A. (1990). The acquisition of language in normally developing children. Some basic strategies and approaches. In I. P. Martins (Ed.), *Acquired aphasia in children: Acquisition and breakdown of language in the developing brain* (pp. 15–23). Drodrecht: Kluwer.

Marcia, J. E. (1988). *Identity diffusions differentiated.* Paper presented at the XXIV Meeting of the International Congress of Psychology, Sydney, Australia.

Margolin, G. (1999). Effects of domestic violence on children. In P. K. Trickett & C. J. Schellenbach (Eds.), *Violence against children in the family and the community* (pp. 58–102). Washington, DC: American Psychological Association.

Markus, H. R., & Kitayama, S. (1991). Culture and the self: Implications for cognition, emotion, and motivation. *Psychological Review, 98,* 224–253.

Marseille, E., Kahn, J. G., Mmiro, F., Guay, L., Musoke, P., Fowler, M. G., & Jackson, J. B. (1999). Cost effectiveness of single-dose nevirapine regimen for mothers and babies to decrease vertical HIV-1 transmission in sub-Saharan Africa. *Lancet, 354,* 803–309.

Marsh, H. W. (1989). Age and sex effects in multiple dimensions of self-concept: Preadolescence to early adulthood. *Journal of Educational Psychology, 81,* 417–430.

Marsh, H. W., Craven, R., & Debus, R. (1998). Structure, stability, and development of young children's self-concepts: A multicohort–multioccasion study. *Child Development, 69,* 1030–1053.

Marshall, H. H. (1994). The development of self-concept. In E. N. Junn & C. J. Boyatzis (Eds.), *Annual editions: Child growth and development* (pp. 115–120). Guilford, CT: Dushkin.

Marsiglio, W. (1993). Contemporary scholarship on fatherhood: Culture, identity, and conduct. *Journal of Family Issues, 14,* 484–509.

Martin, C. A. (1983). *Children's self-perceptions in relation to mothers' developmental beliefs and mothers' perceptions of the child.* Unpublished doctoral dissertation. University of Wisconsin, Madison.

Martin, C. A., & Johnson, J. E. (1992). Children's self-perceptions and mothers' beliefs about development and competence. In I. E. Sigel & A. V. McGillicuddy-Delisi (Eds.), *Parental belief systems: The psychological consequences for children* (pp. 95–113). Hillsdale, NJ: Erlbaum.

Martin, C. L., & Halverson, C. (1981). A schematic processing model of sex typing and stereotyping in young children. *Child Development, 52,* 1119–1134.

Martin, C. L., & Halverson, C. (1987). The roles of cognition in sex roles acquisition. In D. B. Carter (Ed.), *Current conceptions of sex roles and sex typing: Theory and research* (pp. 123–137). New York: Praeger.

Martin, C. L., Wood, C. H., & Little, J. K. (1990). The development of gender stereotype components. *Child Development, 61,* 891–1904.

Martin, J. C., Barr, H. M., Martin, D. C., & Streissguth, A. P. (1996). Neonatal neurobehavioral outcome following prenatal exposure to cocaine. *Neurotoxicology and Teratology, 18,* 617–625.

Martin, R. A. (1998). Approaches to the sense of humor: A historical view. In W. Ruch (Ed.), *The sense of humor: Explorations of a personality characteristic* (pp. 15–62). New York: Mouton de Gruyter.

Martini, M. (1994). Peer interactions in Polynesia: A view from the Marquesas. In J. L. Roopnarine, J. E. Johnson, & F. H. Hooper (Eds.), *Children's play in diverse cultures* (pp. 73–103). New York: State University of New York Press.

Marzolf, D. P., & DeLoache, J. (1997). Search tasks as measures of cognitive development. In N. Foreman & R. Gillet (Eds.), *A handbook of spatial research paradigms and methodologies. Vol. 1: Spatial cognition in adult and child* (pp. 131–152). Hove, England: Psychology Press/Erlbaum (UK).

Mash, E. J., & Barkley, R. A. (Eds.). (1998). *Treatment of childhood disorders.* New York: Guilford Press.

Mason, M. A., Skolnick, A., & Sugarman, S. D. (Eds.). (1998). *All our families: New policies for a new century.* New York: Oxford University Press.

Masten, A. S. (Ed.). (1999). *Cultural processes in child development. The Minnesota symposia on child psychology.* Mahwah, NJ: Erlbaum.

Masten, A. S., Hubbard, J. J., Gest, S. D., Tellegen, A., Garmezy, N., & Ramirez, M. (1999). Competence in the context of adversity: Pathways to resilience and maladaption from childhood to late adolescence. *Development and Psychopathology, 11,* 143–159.

Masur, E. F. (2000). Infants' verbal imitation and their language development: Controversies, techniques, and consequences. In L. Menn & N. Bernstein Ratner (Eds.), *Methods for studying language production* (pp. 27–44). Mahwah, NJ: Erlbaum.

Mattay, V. S., Berman, K. F., Ostrem, J. L., Esposito, G., Van-Horn, J. D., Bigelow, L. B., & Weinberger, D. R. (1996). Dextroamphetamine enhances "neural network-specific" physiological signals: A positron-emission tomography rCBF study. *Journal of Neuroscience, 16,* 4816–4822.

Mattson, S. N., Riley, E. P., Gramling, L., Delis, D. C., & Jones, K. L. (1998). Neuropsychological comparison of alcohol-exposed children with or without physical features of fetal alcohol syndrome. *Neuropsychology, 12,* 146–153.

Mauldon, J. (1998). Families started by teenagers. In M. A. Mason & A. Skolnick (Eds.), *All our families: New policies for a new century* (pp. 39–65). New York: Oxford University Press.

Mauthner, N. S. (1999). "Feeling low and feeling really bad about feeling low": Women's experiences of motherhood and postpartum depression. *Canadian Psychology, 40,* 143–161.

May, D. C., & Kundert, D. K. (1997). School readiness practices and children at-risk: Examining the issues. *Psychology in the Schools, 34,* 73–84.

May, D. C., Kundert, D. K., Nikoloff, O., Welch, E., Garrett, M., & Brent, D. (1994). School readiness: An obstacle to intervention and inclusion. *Journal of Early Intervention, 18,* 308–319.

Mayes, L. C. (1995). Substance abuse and parenting. In M. H. Bornstein (Ed.), *Handbook on parenting* (pp. 101–125). Hillsdale, NJ: Erlbaum.

Mayes, L. C. (1999). Reconsidering the concept of vulnerability in children using the model of prenatal cocaine exposure. In T. B. Cohen & M. H. Etezady (Eds.), *The vulnerable child* (pp. 35–54). Madison, CT: International Universities Press.

Mayes, L. C., Feldman, R., Granger, R. M., Haynes, O. M., Bornstein, M. H. & Schottenfeld, R. (1997). The effects of polydrug use with and without cocaine on mother–infant interaction at 3 and 6 months. *Infant Behavior and Development*, 20, 489–502.

Mayne, T. J., & Ambrose, T. E. (1999). Research review on anger in psychotherapy. *Journal of Clinical Psychology, 55,* 353–363.

Mayo, L. H., Florentine, M., & Buss, S. (1997). Age of second-language acquisition and perception of speech in noise. *Journal of Speech and Hearing Research, 40,* 686–693.

Mazzocco, M. M. M., Kates, W. R., Baumgardner, T. L., Freund, L. S., & Reiss, A. L. (1997). Autistic behaviors among girls with fragile X syndrome. *Journal of Autism and Developmental Disorders, 27,* 415–435.

McAdoo, H. P. (1997). *Black families.* Thousand Oaks, CA: Sage.

Mcbride, L. R. (1999). A comparison of postformal operations in diverse adult populations: Contrasting African-Americans and standard-average-European-Americans. *Dissertation Abstracts International, 59, The Sciences and Engineering.*

McCaul, M. E. (1998). Drug abuse. In E. A. Blechman & K. D. Brownell (Eds.), *Behavioral medicine and women* (pp. 414–419). New York: Guilford Press.

McCord, J. (1990). Problem behaviors. In S. S. Feldman & G. R. Elliott (Eds.), *At the threshold: The developing adolescent* (pp. 414–430). Cambridge, MA: Harvard University Press.

McCord, J. (1997). On discipline. *Psychological Inquiry, 8,* 215–217.

McCourt, F. (2000). *Angela's Ashes: Memoir of a childhood.* In D. N. Sattler, G. P. Kramer, V. Shabatay, & D. A. Bernstein (Eds.), *Child development in context* (pp. 48–52). Boston: Houghton Mifflin.

McCrae, R. R., & Costa, P. T. (1996). *Personality in adulthood.* New York: Guilford Press.

McCubbin, H. I., Thompson, E. A., & Thompson, A. I. (Eds.). (1998). *Resiliency in Native American and immigrant families.* Thousand Oaks, CA: Sage.

McDonald, D. L., & McKinney, J. P. (1994). Steady dating and self-esteem in high school students. *Journal of Adolescence, 17*(6), 557–564.

McDougall, P., & Hymel, S. (1998). Moving into middle school: Individual differences in the transition experience. *Canadian Journal of Behavioural Science, 30,* 108–120.

McEwen, A., Knipe, D., & Gallagher, T. (1997). The impact of single sex and coeducational schooling on participation and achievement in science: A 10-year perspective. *Research in Science and Technological Education, 15,* 223–233.

McGoldrick, M. & Giordan, J. (Eds.). (1996). *Ethnicity and family therapy* (2nd ed.). (pp 141–154). New York: Guilford Press.

McKay, S., & Yager Smith, S. (1993). What are they talking about? Is something wrong? Information sharing during the second stage of labor. *Birth, 20,* 142–147.

Mckenna, E. R. (1999). The relationship between parenting style, level of culture change, and depression in Chinese living in the United States. *Dissertation Abstracts International, 59*(7), 3703B. (University Microfilms No. AAM98–39241)

McKenna, J. J. (1996). Sudden infant death syndrome in cross-cultural perspective. Infant–parent cosleeping protective? *Annual Review of Anthropology, 25,* 201–216.

McKenry, P. C., & Price, S. J. (1995). Divorce: A comparative perspective. In B. B. Ingoldsby & S. Smith (Eds.), *Families in multicultural perspective* (pp. 187–212). New York: Guilford Press.

McKenzie, L., & Stephenson, P. A. (1993). Variation in cesarean section rates among hospitals in Washington state. *American Journal of Public Health, 83,* 1109–1112.

McLanahan, S., & Sandefur, G. (1994). *Growing up with a single parent: What hurts, what helps.* Cambridge, MA: Harvard University Press.

McLaughlin, S. C., & Saccuzzo, D. P. (1997). Ethnic and gender differences in locus of control in children referred for gifted programs: The effects of vulnerability factors. *Journal for the Education of the Gifted, 20,* 268–283.

McLoyd, V. C. (1999). Culture and development in our postcultural age. In A. S. Masten (Ed.), *Cultural processes in child development. The Minnesota Symposia on Child Psychology* (pp. 123–135). Mahwah, NJ: Erlbaum.

McNeal, C., & Amato, P. R. (1998). Parents' marital violence: Long-term consequences for children. *Journal of Family Issues, 19,* 123–139.

McNeil, D. (1970). *The acquisition of language.* New York: Harper & Row.

Mead, G. H. (1934). *Mind, self, and society.* Chicago: University of Chicago Press.

Mebert, C. J., & Leonard, C. J. (2001, April 19–22). *Why do adolescents have sex and why does it matter?* Paper presented at the biennial meeting of the Society for Research in Child Development, Minneapolis.

Medvescek, C. R. (1994). Toddler talk. In E. N. Junn & C. J. Boyatzis (Eds.), *Annual editions: Child growth and development* (pp. 43–45). Guilford, CT: Dushkin.

Meins, E. (1997). *Security of attachment and the social development of cognition.* Hove, England: Psychology Press/Erlbaum (UK).

Meisels, S. J. (1996). Performance in context: Assessing children's achievement at the outset of school. In A. J. Sameroff & M. M. Haith (Eds.), *The five-to-seven-year shift: The age of reason and responsibility* (pp. 407–431). Chicago: University of Chicago Press.

Meltzoff, A. N. (1988). Infant imitation and memory: Nine-month-old infants in immediate and deferred tests. *Child Development, 59,* 217–225.

Meltzoff, A. N. (1996). Understanding the intentions of others: Re-enactment of intended acts by 18-month-old children. *Annual Progress in Child Psychiatry and Child Development,* 67–98.

Meltzoff, A. N., & Moore, M. K. (1999). Imitation of facial and manual gestures by human neonates. In A. Slater & D. Muir (Eds.), *Developmental psychology* (pp. 143–150). Oxford, England: Blackwell Publishers.

Menchu, R. (2000). Birth ceremonies of the Quiche community. In D. N. Sattler, G. P. Kramer, V. Shabatay, & D. A. Bernstein (Eds.), *Child development in context* (pp. 11–15). Boston: Houghton Mifflin.

Mendel, G. (1866). Experiments with plant hybrids. *Proceedings of the Brunn Natural History Society.*

Menon, S. (2001). Male authority and female autonomy: A study of matrilineal Nayars of Kerala, South India. In C. B. Brettell & C. F. Sargent (Eds.), *Gender in cross-cultural perspective* (pp. 352–360). Upper Saddle River, NJ: Prentice-Hall.

Menon, U., & Shweder, R. A. (1994). Kali's tongue: Cultural psychology and the power of shame in Orissa, India. In S. Kitayama & H. Markus (Eds.), *Emotion and culture* (pp. 185–241). Washington, DC: American Psychological Association.

Mercer, J. (1998). *Infant development: A multidisciplinary introduction.* Pacific Grove, CA: Brooks/Cole.

Mesch, G. S., & Manor, O. (1998). Social ties, environmental perception, and local attachment. *Environment and Behavior, 30,* 501–519.

Mesquita, B., Frijda, N. H., & Scherer, K. R. (1997). Culture and emotion. In J. W. Berry (Ed.), *Handbook of cross-cultural psychology. Vol. 2: Basic processes and human development* (pp. 254–297). Boston: Allyn & Bacon.

Meyer, L. H., Park, H. S., Grenot-Scheyer, M., Schwartz, I. S., & Harry, B. (Eds.). (1998). *Making friends: The influences of culture and development.* Baltimore: Paul H. Brookes.

Meyer-Bahlburg, H., Ehrhardt, A., Rosen, L., Gruen, R., Veridiano, N., Vann, F., & Neuwalder, H. (1995). Prenatal estrogens and the development of homosexual orientation. *Developmental Psychology, 31,* 12–21.

Miettinen, R. (1999). Transcending traditional school learning: Teachers' work and networks of learning. In V. Engestroem & R. Miettinen (Eds.), *Perspectives on activity theory. Learning in doing: Social, cognitive, and computational perspectives* (pp. 325–344). New York: Cambridge University Press.

Milbrath, C., & Houston, T. (1998). *Patterns of artistic development in children: Comparative studies of talent.* San Francisco: University of California, Department of Psychiatry.

Miller, A. (1995). A developmental study of the cognitive basis of performance impairment after failure. *Journal of Personality and Social Psychology, 49,* 529–538.

Miller, B., & Sollie, D. (1990). Normal stresses during the transition to parenthood. *Family Relations, 29,* 459–465.

Miller, J. G. (1997). Agency and context in cultural psychology: Implications for moral theory. In H. D. Saltzstein (Ed.), *Culture as a context for moral development: New perspectives on the particular and the universal* (pp. 69–86). San Francisco: Jossey-Bass.

Miller, J. G., Bersoff, D., & Harwood, R. (1990). Perceptions of social responsibilities in India and the United States: Moral imperatives or personal decisions? *Journal of Personality and Social Psychology, 58,* 33–47.

Miller, J. L., & Levy, G. D. (1996). Gender role conflict, gender-typed characteristics, self-concepts, and sport socialization in female athletes and nonathletes. *Sex Roles, 35,* 111–122.

Miller, L. H., & Smith, A. D. (1987). *Vulnerability scale.* Brookline, MA: Biobehavioral Associates.

Miller, L. K., & Clausen, H. (1997). Pitch identification in children and adults: Naming and discrimination. *Psychology of Music, 25,* 4–17.

Mills, J. L. (1999). Cocaine, smoking, and spontaneous abortion. *New England Journal of Medicine, 340,* 380–381.

Millstein, S. G., & Halpern-Felsher, B. L. (1998). Adolescent sexuality. In E. A. Blechman & K. D. Brownell (Eds.), *Behavioral medicine and women* (pp. 59–64). New York: Guilford Press.

Millstein, S. G., & Igra, V. (1995). Theoretical models of adolescent risk-taking behavior. In J. L. Wallander & L. J. Siegel (Eds.), *Adolescent health problems: Behavioral perspectives* (pp. 52–71). New York: Guilford Press.

Miltner, W. H. R., Braun, C., Arnold, M., Witte, H., & Taub, E. (1999). Coherence of gamma-band EEG activity as a basis for associative learning. *Nature, 397,* 434–436.

Min, P. G. (1998). The Korean American family. In C. H. Mindel, R. W. Habenstein, & R. Wright (Eds.), *Ethnic families in America: Patterns and variations* (pp. 199–229). New York: Elsevier.

Minde, K. (1992). Aggression in preschoolers: Its relation to socialization. *Journal of the American Academy of Child and Adolescent Psychiatry, 31,* 853–862.

Miner, K. (1998). The etiology and epidemiology of HIV disease. In M. D. Knox & C. H. Sparks (Eds.), *HIV and community mental healthcare* (pp. 19–36). Baltimore: Johns Hopkins University Press.

Minturn, L., & Lambert, W. (1964). *Mothers of six cultures: Antecedents of child rearing.* New York: Wiley.

Mintz, S. (1998). From patriarchy to androgyny and other myths: Place men's family roles in historical perspective. In A. Booth & A. C. Crouter (Eds.), *Men in families: When do they get involved? What difference does it make?* (pp. 3–30). Mahwah, NJ: Erlbaum.

Minuchin, P. (1985). Families and individual development: Provocations from the field of family therapy. *Child Development, 56,* 289–302.

Minuchin, P. (1988). Relationships within the family: A systems perspective on development. In R. A. Hinde & J. Stevenson-Hinde (Eds.), *Relationships within families* (pp. 7–26). New York: Oxford University Press.

Mirochnick, M., Meyer, J., Cole, J. G., & Zuckerman, B. (1991). *Circulating catecholamine in cocaine-exposed neonates.* Boston: Boston City Hospital.

Mischel, W., & Ebbesen, E. B. (1970). Attention in delay of gratification. *Journal of Personality and Social Psychology, 34,* 942–950.

Mitchell, J. J. (1996). *Adolescent vulnerability: A sympathetic look at the frailties and limitations of youth.* Calgary, AB, Canada: Detselig Enterprises Ltd.

Mizuno, S. (1999). Psychosocial development and moral development: An exploratory comparison of adolescents in Japan and America. *Psychological Reports, 84,* 51–62.

Moen, P. (1989). *Working parents: Transformations in gender roles and public policies in Sweden.* Madison, WI: University of Wisconsin Press.

Mohanty, A. K., Panda, S., & Misra, B. (1999). Language socialization in a multilingual society. In T. S. Saraswathi (Ed.), *Culture, socialization, and human development: Theory, research, and applications in India* (pp. 125–144). Thousand Oaks, CA: Sage.

Mohanty, A. K., & Perregaux, C. (1997). Language acquisition and bilingualism. In J. W. Berry & P. R. Dasen (Eds.), *Handbook of cross-cultural psychology. Vol. 2: Basic processes and human development* (2nd ed., pp. 217–253). Needham Heights, MA: Allyn & Bacon.

Mohanty, A. K., & Perregaux, C. (2000). Language acquisition and bilingualism. In J. W. Berry, P. R. Dasen, & T. S. Saraswathi (Eds.), *Handbook of cross-cultural psychology* (pp. 217–254). Boston: Allyn & Bacon.

Molnar, B. (2001, April 19–22). *Child sexual abuse: Links to subsequent psychopathology.* Paper presented at the biennial meeting for the Society for Research in Child Development, Minneapolis.

Money, J., & Lehne, G. K. (1999). Gender identity disorders. In R. T. Ammerman & M. Hersen (Eds.), *Handbook of prescriptive treatments for children and adolescents* (pp. 214–228). Boston: Allyn & Bacon.

Monsour, M. (1997). Communication and cross-sex friendships across a life cycle: A review of the literature. In B. R. Burleson & A. Kunkel (Eds.), *Communication yearbook* (pp. 375–414). Thousand Oaks, CA: Sage.

Montague, A. (1963). *Race, science, and humanity.* Princeton, NJ: D. Van Nostrand.

Montemayor, R. (1998). Parents and adolescents in conflict. In R. E. Muuss & H. D. Porton (Eds.), *Adolescent behavior and society* (pp. 102–117). New York: McGraw-Hill.

Montemayor, R., Adams, G. R., & Gullotta, T. P. (1990). *From childhood to adolescence: A transitional period?* Newbury Park, CA: Sage.

Montessori, M. (1948). *To educate the human potential.* Thiruvanmiyur, Madras: Kalashetra Publications.

Moore, K. L. (1993). *Before we were born* (5th ed.). New York: W. B. Saunders.

Moore, K. L., & Persaud, T. V. M. (1998). *The developing human: Clinically oriented embryology.* Philadelphia: W. B. Saunders.

Moreau-Gruet, F., Ferron, C., Jeannin, A., & Dubois-Arber, F. (1996). Adolescent sexuality: The gender gap. *AIDS-Care, 8*(6), 641–653.

Morinaga, Y. (1995). Women's vocational behavior in Japan: A different perspective. *Japanese Psychological Review, 38,* 424–440.

Morley, L. (1992). Women's studies, difference, and internalised oppression. *Women's Studies International Forum, 15,* 517–525.

Morrison, D. M., McGee, R., & Stanton, W. R. (1992). Sleep problems in adolescence. *Journal of the American Academy of Child and Adolescent Psychiatry, 31,* 94–99.

Morrison, D. R., & Cherlin, A. J. (1995). The divorce process and young children's well-being: A prospective analysis. *Journal of Marriage and the Family, 57,* 800–812.

Morrison, F. J., Griffith, E. M., & Alberts, D. M. (1997). Nature–nurture in the classroom: Entrance age, school readiness, and learning in children. *Developmental Psychology, 33,* 254–262.

Morrongiello, B. A., & Dawber, T. (1998). Toddlers' and mothers' behaviors in an injury-risk situation: Implications for sex differences in childhood injuries. *Journal of Applied Developmental Psychology, 19,* 625–639.

Mortimer, J. T., & Johnson, M. K. (1998). Adolescent part-time work and educational achievement. In K. Borman & B. Schneider (Eds.), *The adolescent years: Social influences and educational challenges* (pp. 183–206). Chicago: The National Society for the Study of Education.

Mortimer, J. Y., Finch, M. D., Scongryeol, R., Shanahan, M. J., & Call, K. T. (1996). The effects of work intensity on adolescent mental health, achievement, and behavioral adjustment: New evidence from a prospective study. *Child Development, 67,* 1243–1261.

Mueller, C. M., & Dweck, C. S. (1998). Praise for intelligence can undermine children's motivation and performance. *Journal of Personality and Social Psychology, 75,* 33–52.

Mueller, R. A., Rothermel, R. D., Behen, M. E., Muzik, O., Mangner, T. J., & Chugani, H. T. (1997). Receptive and expressive language activations for sentences: A PET study. *Neuroreport: An International Journal for the Rapid Communication of Research in Neuroscience, 8,* 3767–3770.

Mueller, R. A., Rothermel, R. D., Behen, M. E., Muzik, O., Mangner, T. J., & Chugani, H. T. (1998). Developmental changes of cortical and cerebellar motor control: A clinical positron emission tomography study with children and adults. *Journal of Child Neurology, 13,* 550–556.

Mueller, W. H., Joos, S. K., Hanis, C. L., Zavaleta, A. N., Eichner, J., & Schull, W. J. (1994). The diabetes alert study: Growth, fatness and fat patterning, adolescence through adulthood in Mexican-Americans. *American Journal of Physical Anthropology, 64,* 389–399.

Mukhamedrakhimov, R. Z. (1996). Forms of interaction of mother and infant. *Journal of Russian and East European Psychology, 34,* 68–85.

Mukhopadhyay, P., & Dash, B. B. (1999). Cognitive style: Its relationship to intelligence and locus of control in children. *Social Science International, 15,* 81–85.

Muncer, S., & Campbell, A. (1999). Concluding remarks. In A. Campbell & S. Muncer (Eds.), *The social child* (pp. 393–403). Hove, England: Psychology Press/Erlbaum (UK).

Munroe, R. H., Munroe, R. L., & Shimmin, H. S. (1984). Children's work in four cultures: Determinants and consequences. *American Anthropologist, 86,* 369–379.

Muris, P., Merckelbach, H., van Brakel, A., Mayer, B., & van Dongen, L. (1998). The Screen for Child Anxiety Related Emotional Disorders (SCARED): Relationship with anxiety and depression in normal children. *Personality and Individual Differences, 24,* 451–458.

Murphy, D. A., Rotheram-Borus, M. J., & Reid, H. M. (1998). Adolescent gender differences in HIV-related sexual risk acts, social–cognitive factors, and behavioral skills. *Journal of Adolescence, 21,* 197–228.

Murray, M., Swan, A. V., Johnson, M. R. D., & Bewley, B. R. (1993). Some factors associated with increased risk of smoking by children. *Journal of Child Psychology and Psychiatry, 24,* 223–232.

Murray, J. P. (1997). Media violence and youth. In J. D. Osofsky (Ed.), *Children in a violent society* (pp. 72–96). New York: Guilford Press.

Murry-McBride, V. (1996). An ecological analysis of coital timing among middle-class African American adolescent females. *Journal of Adolescent Research, 11,* 261–279.

Muuss, R. E. (1998). Marcia's expansion of Erikson's theory of identity formation. In R. E. Muuss & H. W. Porton (Eds.), *Adolescent behavior and society: A book of readings* (pp. 260–270). New York: McGraw-Hill.

Muzi, M. J. (2000). *The experience of parenting.* New York: Prentice-Hall.

Mwageni, E. A., Ankomah, A., & Powell, R. A. (1998). Attitudes of men toward family planning in Mbeya region, Tanzania: A rural–urban comparison of qualitative data. *Journal of Biosocial Science,* 30, 381–392.

Mwamwenda, T. S. (1991). Sex differences in self-concept among African adolescents. *Perceptual and Motor Skills, 73,* 191–194.

Naeye, K. L. (1998). Fetal complications of maternal heroin addition: Abnormal growth, infections, and episodes of stress. *Journal of Pediatrics,* 83, 1055–1061.

Nahas, G. G., Sutin, K. M., Harvey, D., Agurell, S., Pace, N., & Cancro, R. (Eds.). (1999). *Marihuana and medicine.* Clifton, NJ: Humana Press.

Nakazima, S. (1992). A comparative study of the speech development of Japanese and American English in children. *Studies in Phonology, 2,* 27–39.

Namerow, P. B., Kaimuss, D., & Cushman, L. F. (1997). The consequences of placing versus parenting among young unmarried women. *Marriage and Family Review, 25,* 175–197.

Nason, R. B. (1991). Retaining children: Is it the right decision? *Childhood Education, 32,* 300–304.

National Association for Year-Round Education (NAYRE). (1996). *Twenty-third reference directory of year-round education programs for the 1996–97 school year.* San Diego: Author.

National Center for Health Statistics. (1993, September 9). *Advance report of final natality statistics,* Monthly Vital Statistics Report, Vol. 42, No. 3, Suppl. Hyattsville, MD: Public Health Service.

National Institute on Drug Abuse. (1997). *National household survey on drug abuse: Main findings.* Washington, DC: U.S. Government Printing Office.

Needham, A., Baillargeon, R., & Kaufman, L. (1997). Object segregation in infancy. *Advances in Infancy Research, 11,* 1–44.

Neisser, E., Boodoo, G., Bouchard, T. J., Jr., Boykin, A. W., Brody, N., Ceci, S. J., Halpern, D., Loehlin, J. C., Sternberg, R. J., & Urbina, S. (1998). Intelligence: Knowns and unknowns. In M. E. Hertzig & E. A. Farber (Eds.), *Annual progress in child psychiatry and child development* (pp. 95–133). Bristol, PA: Brunner/Mazel.

Neisser, U. (1995). Criteria for an ecological self. In P. Rochat (Ed.), *The self in infancy: Theory and research* (pp. 17–34). Amsterdam: North Holland-Elsevier.

Neisser, U. (1998). Introduction: Rising test scores and what they mean. In U. Neisser (Ed.), *The rising curve: Long-term gains in IQ and related measures* (pp. 3–22). Washington, DC: American Psychological Association.

Neisser, U., Boodoo, G., Bouchard, T. J., Boykin, A. W., Brody, N., Ceci, S. J., Halpern, D. F., Loehlin, J. C., Perloff, R., Sternberg, R. J., & Urbina, S. (1996). Intelligence: Knowns and unknowns. *American Psychologist, 51,* 77–101.

Nelson, C. A. (1996). *Language in cognitive development: Emergence of the mediated mind.* New York: Cambridge University Press.

Nelson, C. A. (1998). The nature of early memory. *Preventive Medicine: An International Devoted to Practice and Theory, 27,* 172–178.

Nelson, C. A., & Collins, P. E. (1991). Event-related potential and looking-time analysis of infants' responses to familiar and novel events: Implications for visual recognition memory. *Developmental Psychology, 27,* 50–58.

Nelson, K., Hampson, J., & Shaw, L. K. (1993). Nouns in early lexicons: Evidence, explanations, and implications. *Journal of Child Language, 20,* 61–84.

Nettles, S. M., & Pleck, J. H. (1993). *Risk, resilience, and development: The multiple ecologies of black adolescents* (Rep. No. 44). Baltimore: Johns Hopkins University, Center for Research on Effective Schooling for Disadvantaged Students.

Neumark-Sztainer, D., Story, M., & Faibisch, L. (1998). Perceived stigmatization among overweight African-American and Caucasian adolescent girls. *Journal of Adolescent Health, 23,* 264–270.

Newcomb, A. F., Bukowski, W. M., & Bagwell, C. L. (1999). Knowing the sounds: Friendship as a developmental context. In W. A. Collins & B. Laursen (Eds.), *Relationships as developmental contexts. The Minnesota Symposia on Child Psychology* (pp. 63–84). Mahwah, NJ: Erlbaum.

Newcomb, M. D., & Keefe, K. (1997). Social support, self-esteem, social conformity, and gregariousness: Developmental patterns across 12 years. In G. R. Pierce & B. Lakey (Eds.), *Sourcebook of social support and personality: The Plenum series in social/clinical psychology* (pp. 303–333). New York: Plenum.

Newcombe, N. S., & Huttenlocher, J. (2000). *Making space: the development of spatial representation and reasoning.* Cambridge, MA: MIT Press.

Newman, L. S. (1990). Intentional versus unintentional memory in children: Remembering versus playing. *Journal of Experimental Child Psychology, 50,* 243–258.

Newton, C. R. (1999). Counseling the infertile couple. In L. H. Burns & S. N. Covington (Eds.), *Infertile counseling: A comprehensive handbook for clinicians* (pp. 105–111). New York: Parthenon.

Newton, M. (1995). *Adolescence: Guiding youth through the perilous journey.* New York: W. W. Norton.

NICHD—Early Child Care Research Network. (1997). The effects of infant child care on infant–mother attachment security: Results of the NICHD study of early child care. *Child Development, 68,* 860–879.

Nicholas, L. M., Lancer, M. E., & Silva, S. G. (1997). Short stature, growth hormone deficiency, and social anxiety. *Psychosomatic Medicine, 59,* 372–375.

Nichols, R. C. (1979). Heredity and environment: Major findings from twin studies of ability, personality, and interests. *Homo, 29,* 158–173.

Nicklas, T. A., Webber, L. S., Jonson, C. S., Srinivasan, S. R., & Berenson, G. S. (1995). Foundations for health promotion with youth. A review of observations of the Bogalusa Heart Study. *Journal of Health Education, 26,* 518–526.

Nicoladis, E., & Secco, G. (2000). The role of a child's productive vocabulary in the language choice of a bilingual family. *First Language, 20,* 3–28.

Nicolaisen, I. (1997). Concepts and learning among the Punan Bah of Sarawak. In G. Jahoda & I. M. Lewis (Eds.), *Acquiring culture: Cross cultural studies in child development* (pp. 193–222). London: Croom Helm.

Ninio, A. (1979). The naive theory of the infant and other maternal attitudes in two subgroups in Israel. *Child Development, 50,* 976–980.

Nippold, M. A. (2000). Language development during the adolescent years: Aspects of pragmatics, syntax, and semantics. *Topics in Language Disorders, 20,* 15–28.

Nisbett, R. E. (1998). Race, genetics, and IQ. In C. Jencks & M. Phillips (Eds.), *The black–white test score gap* (pp. 86–102). Washington, DC: Brookings Institution.

Nolen-Hoeksem, S., & Larson, J. (1999). *Coping with loss.* Mahwah, NJ: Erlbaum.

Nolte, J. (1998). *The human brain.* St. Louis: Mosby.

Norman, J., & Harris, M. (1981). *The private life of the American teenager.* New York: Fawson-Wade.

Norwicki, S., & Strickland, B. R. (1973). A locus of control scale for children. *Journal of Consulting and Clinical Psychology, 40,* 148–154.

Oatley, K., & Jenkins, J. M. (1996). *Understanding emotions.* Oxford, England: Blackwell.

Ochs, E. (1988). *Culture and language development.* Cambridge, England: Cambridge University Press.

Ochs, E. (1990). Indexicality and socialization. In J. W. Stigler, R. A. Shweder, & G. Herdt (Eds.), *Cultural psychology,* Cambridge, UK: Cambridge University Press.

Ochse, R. (1998). Toward a prediction and stimulation of creativity. *South African Journal of Psychology, 19,* 113–121.

Ogbu, J. (1986). The consequences of the American caste system. In U. Neisser (Ed.), *The school achievement of minority children: New perspectives* (pp. 19–56). Hillsdale, NJ: Erlbaum.

Ogbu, J. (1988). Black education: A cultural–ecological perspective. In H. P. McAdoo (Ed.), *Black families* (pp. 169–186). Beverly Hills: Sage.

Ogbu, J. (1992). Understanding cultural diversity and learning. *Educational Researcher, 21,* 5–14.

Ogbu, J. (1997). Understanding the school performance of urban blacks: Some essential background knowledge. In H. J. Walberg & O. Reyes (Eds.), *Children and youth: Interdisciplinary perspectives. Issues in children's and families' lives* (pp. 190–222). Thousand Oaks, CA: Sage.

Ogbu, J. (1999). Cultural context of human development: A challenge to research. In M. E. Fitzgerald, B. M. Lister, & B. S. Zuckerman (Eds.), *Children of color: Research, health, and policy issues* (pp. 73–92). New York: Garland.

Ogbu, J. (2000). Personal communication.

Ogbu, J., & Simons, H. D. (1998). Voluntary and involuntary minorities: A cultural–ecological theory of school performance with some implications for education. *Anthropology and Education Quarterly, 29,* 155–188.

Ohman, A. (2000). Fear and anxiety: Evolutionary, cognitive, and clinical perspectives. In M. Lewis & J. M. Haviland-Jones (Eds.), *Handbook of emotions* (pp. 573–593). New York: Guilford Press.

Okamura, A., Heras, P., & Wong-Kerberg, L. (1995). Asian, Pacific Island, and Filipino Americans and sexual child abuse. In L. A. Fontes (Ed.), *Sexual abuse in nine North American cultures* (pp. 67–96). Thousand Oaks, CA: Sage.

Okonkwo, R. U. N. (1997). Moral development and culture in Kohlberg's theory: A Nigerian (Igbo) evidence. *IFE Psychological: An International Journal, 5,* 117–128.

Oldenburg, C. M., & Kerns, K. A. (1997). Associations between peer relationships and depressive symptoms: Testing moderator effects of gender and age. *Journal of Early Adolescence, 17,* 319–337.

Ollech, D., & McCarthy, J. (1997). Impediments to identity formation in female adolescents. *Psychoanalytic Psychology, 14*(1), 65–80.

Olson, H. C. (1998). Maternal alcohol use and fetal development. In E. A. Blechman & K. D. Brownell (Eds.), *Behavioral medicine and women* (pp. 31–38). New York: Guilford Press.

Olson, H. C., Sampson, P. S., Barr, H., Streissguth, A. P., & Bookstein, F. L. (1992). Prenatal exposure to alcohol and school problems in late childhood: A longitudinal prospective study. *Development and Psychopathology, 4,* 341–359.

Olver, R. R., Aries, E., & Batgos, J. (1990). Self-other differentiation and the mother- child relationship: The effects of sex and birth order. *Journal of Genetic Psychology,* 150, 311–321.

O'Malley, P. M., Johnston, L. D., & Bachman, J. G. (1999). Epidemiology of substance abuse in adolescence. In P. J. Ott, R. E. Tarter, & R. T. Ammerman (Eds.), *Sourcebook on substance abuse: Etiology, epidemiology, assessment, and treatment* (pp. 14–32). Boston: Allyn & Bacon.

Oppenheim, D. (1998). Perspectives on infant mental health from Israel: The case of change in collective sleeping in the kibbutz. *Infant Mental Health Journal, 19,* 76–86.

Orbach, T. (1997). Suicidal behavior in adolescents. *Giornale Italiano di Suicidologia, 7,* 87–98.

Orenstein, A., & Ullman, A. (1996). Characteristics of alcoholic families and adolescent substance use. *Journal of Alcohol and Drug Education, 42*(3), 86–101.

Orenstein, P. (1994). *School girls: Young women, self-esteem, and the confidence gap.* New York: Doubleday.

Orfield, G. (1997). Going to work: Weak preparation, little help. In K. R. Wong (Ed.), *Advances in educational policy. Vol. 3: The Indiana Youth Opportunity Study: A symposium* (pp. 3–31). Greenwich, CT: Jai Press.

Orlandi, M. A., & Dalton, L .T. (1998). Lifestyle interventions for the young. In S. A. Shumaker & E. B. Schron (Eds.), *The handbook of health behavior change* (pp. 335–356). New York: Springer.

Orme, J. G., & Buehler, C. (2001). Foster family characteristics and behavioral and emotional problems of foster children: A narrative review. *Family Relations: Interdisciplinary Journal of Applied Family Studies, 50*(1), 3–15.

Osborne, L. M., & Fincham, F. D. (1996). Marital conflict, parent–child relations, and child adjustment: Does gender matter? *Merrill Palmer Quarterly, 42,* 48–75.

Osherson, D. N., & Markman, E. M. (1975). Language and the ability to evaluate contradictions and tautologies, *Cognition, 2,* 213–226.

Osofsky, J. D. (1997). Children and youth violence: An overview of the issue. In J. D. Osofsky (Ed.), *Children in a violent society* (pp. 1–8). New York: Guilford Press.

Osofsky, J. D. (1998). "On the outside: Interventions with infants and families at risk." *Infant Mental Health Journal, 19,* 101–110.

Osone, A. (1997). The personality traits of adolescent girls and young women with eating disorders. *Seishin Igaku Clinical Psychiatry, 39,* 617–624.

Osterweil, Z., & Nagano, K. N. (1991). Maternal views on autonomy: Japan and Israel. *Psychological Reports, 67,* 1273–1274.

O'Sullivan, L. F., Jaramillo, B. M. S., Moreau, D., & Meyer-Bahlburg, H. F. L. (1999). Mother–daughter communication about sexuality in a clinical sample of Hispanic adolescent girls. *Hispanic Journal of Behavioral Sciences, 21,* 447–469.

Ott, P. J., Tarter, R. E., & Ammerman, R. T. (Eds.) (1999). *Sourcebook on substance abuse: Etiology, epidemiology, assessment, and treatment.* Boston, MA: Allyn & Bacon.

Overbay, J. D., & Purath, J. (1997). Self-concept and health status in elementary-school-aged children. *Issues in Comprehensive Pediatric Nursing, 20,* 89–101.

Overstreet, S., & Braun, S. (2000). Exposure to community violence and post-traumatic stress symptoms: Mediating factors. *American Journal of Orthopsychiatry, 70*(2), 263–271.

Owens, K. (1995). *Raising your child's inner self-esteem.* New York: Plenum.

Owens, K. (1996, August). Self-esteem: The secret to academic success. *Parent Guide,* 25–29.

Owens, K. (1997). Six myths about self-esteem. *Journal of Invitational Theory and Practice, 4,* 115–129.

Palkovitz, R. (1998). Reconstructing "involvement": Expanding conceptualizations of men's caring in contemporary families. In A. J. Hawkins & D. C. Dollahite (Eds.), *Generative fathering: Beyond deficit perspectives. Current issues in the family series.* (Vol. 3, pp. 200–216). Thousand Oaks, CA: Sage.

Palumbo, J. (1996). The diagnosis and treatment of children with non-verbal learning disabilities. *Child and Adolescent Social Work, 13*(4), 311–332.

Panter-Brick, C. (1998). *Biosocial perspectives on children.* New York: Cambridge University Press.

Papousek, M., Bornstein, M. H., Nuzzo, C., Papousek, H., & Symmes, D. (1990). Infant responses to protypical melodic contours in parental speech. *Infant Behavior and Development, 13,* 539–545.

Pardes, G. (1991). Childhood in China. In J. M. Hawes & N. R. Hiner (Eds.), *Childhood in historical and comparative perspectives* (pp. 75–94). New York: Greenwood.

Parish, S. (1991). The sacred mind: Newar cultural representations of mental life and the production of moral consciousness. *Ethos, 19,* 313–351.

Park, E. H. M., & Dimigen, G. (1997). A cross-cultural comparison of attributional style: Korean versus Scottish mothers. *Psychologia: An International Journal of Psychology in the Orient, 40*(3), 201–208.

Parke, R. D. (1995). Fathers and families. In M. H. Bornstein (Ed.), *Handbook on parenting* (pp. 27–63). Hillsdale, NJ: Erlbaum.

Parke, R. D. (1996). *Fatherhood.* Cambridge, MA: Harvard University Press.

Parke, R. D., MacDonald, K. B., Burks, V. M., Bhavnagri, N., Barth, J. M., & Beitel, A. (1989). Family and peer systems: In search of the linkages. In K. Kreppner & M. Lerner (Eds.), *Family systems of life-span development* (pp. 65–92). Hillsdale, NJ: Erlbaum.

Parke, R. D., O'Neil, R., Spitzer, S., Isley, S., Welsh, M., Wang, S., Lee, J., Strand, C., & Cupp, R. (1997). A longitudinal assessment of sociometric stability and the behavioral correlates of children's social acceptance. *Merrill Palmer Quarterly, 43,* 635–662.

Parker, J. G., & Asher, S. R. (1993). Friendship and friendship quality in middle childhood: Links with peer group acceptance and feelings of loneliness and social dissatisfaction. *Developmental Psychology, 29,* 611–621.

Parten, M. (1932). Social participation among preschool children. *Journal of Abnormal and Social Psychology, 27,* 243–269.

Pascual, L., Haynes, O. M., Galperin, C. Z., & Bornstein, M. H. (1995). Psychosocial determinants of whether and how much new mothers work: A study in the United States and Argentina. *Journal of Cross Cultural Psychology, 26,* 314–330.

Patenaude, R., & Baillargeon, J. (1996). Evaluation des fonctions executives a l'aide du chez des parkinsonians non dements. *Revue de Neuropsychologie, 6,* 443–469.

Pathak, Z., & Rajan, R. S. (1989). Shahbano. *Journal of Women in Culture and Society, 14,* 558–582.

Patterson, C. J., & Redding, R. E. (1996). Lesbian and gay families with children: Implications of social science research for policy. *Journal of Social Issues, 52,* 29–50.

Patterson, G. R. (1982). *Coercive family process.* Eugene, OR: Castilia Press.

Patterson, G. R., DeBaryshe, B. D., & Ramsey, F. (1989). A developmental perspective on antisocial behavior. *American Psychologist, 44,* 329–335.

Paul, M. (1997). Occupational reproductive hazards. *Lancet, 349,* 1385–1388.

Payne, V. G., & Rink, J .E. (1997). Physical education in the developmentally appropriate integrated curriculum. In C. H. Hart & D. C. Burts (Eds.), *Integrated curriculum and developmentally appropriate practice: Birth to age 8* (pp. 145–170). Albany, NY: State University of New York Press.

Pearson, J. L., Hunter, A. G., Ensminger, M. E., & Kellam S. G. (1990). Black grandmothers in multigenerational households: Diversity in family structure and parenting involvement in the Woodlawn community. *Child Development, 61,* 434–442.

Pedlow, R., Sanson, A. V., Prior, M., & Oberklaid, F. (1993). The stability of temperament from infancy to eight years. *Developmental Psychology, 29,* 998–1007.

Penfield, W., & Rasmussen, T. (1968). *The cerebral cortex of man: A clinical study of localization of function.* New York: Hafner.

Perani, D., Vallar, C., Paulesu, E., Alberoni, M., & Fazio, F. (1993). Left and right hemisphere contributions to recovery from neglect after right hemisphere damage. *Neuropsychologia, 31,* 115–125.

Perl, M. A., Mandic, M., Primorac, L., Klapec, T., & Perl, A. (1998). Adolescent acceptance of different foods by obesity status and by sex. *Physiology and Behavior, 65,* 241–245.

Perlmutter, M. (Ed.). (1980). *Children's memory: New directions in child development.* San Francisco: Jossey-Bass.

Pernice-Ducas, F., Harrison, A., & Martin, A. M. (2001, April 19–22). *Ethnic socialization and perceptions of family and social support among African American, Caucasian, and Latino adolescents.* Paper presented at the biennial meeting of the Society for Research in Child Development, Minneapolis.

Petersen, A. C. (1998). Adolescence. In E. A. Blechman & K. D. Brownell (Eds.), *Behavioral medicine and women* (pp. 45–50). New York: Guilford Press.

Petersen, A. C., Compas, B. E., Brooks-Gunn, J., Stemmler, M., Ey, S., & Grant, K. E. (1993). Depression in adolescence. *American Psychologist, 48,* 155–168.

Petersen, A. C., Sarigiani, P. A., & Kennedy, R. E. (1991). Adolescent depression: Why more girls? *Journal of Youth and Adolescence, 20,* 247–271.

Peterson, J. S., & Colangelo, N. (1996). Gifted achievers and underachievers: A comparison of patterns found in school files. *Journal of Counseling and Development, 74,* 399–407.

Pettit, G. S., Bates, J. E., & Dodge, K. A. (1997). Supportive parenting, ecological context, and children's adjustment: A seven-year longitudinal study. *Child Development, 68,* 908–923.

Pettit, G. S., Brown, E. G., Mize, J., & Lindsey, E. (1998). Mothers' and fathers' socializing behaviors in three contexts: Links with children's peer competence. *Merrill Palmer Quarterly, 44,* 173–193.

Phelan, P., Davidson, A. L., & Yu, H. C. (1996). *Adolescents' worlds.* New York: Teachers College Press.

Phillips, J. R. (1973). Syntax and vocabulary of mother's speech to young children: Age and sex comparisons. *Child Development, 44,* 182–185.

Phinney, J. S. (1998). Stages of ethnic identity development in minority group adolescents. In R. E. Muuss & H. W. Porton (Eds.), *Adolescent behavior and society: A book of readings* (pp. 271–280). New York: McGraw-Hill.

Phinney, J. S., & Rosenthal, D. A. (1992). Ethnic identity in adolescence: Process, context, and outcome. In G. R. Adams, T. P. Gullota, & R. Montemighter (Eds.), *Advances in adolescent development. Vol. 4: Adolescent identity formation* (pp. 145–172). Thousand Oaks, CA: Sage.

Piaget, J. (1929). *The child's conception of physical causality*. New York: Harcourt, Brace.

Piaget, J. (1950). *The origins of intelligence.* (M. Piercy & D. E. Berlyne, Trans.). New York: Harcourt, Brace & Co.

Piaget, J. (1952). Autobiography. In E. G. Boring (Ed.), *A history of psychology in autobiography* (Vol. 4). New York: Russell and Russell.

Piaget, J. (1952). *The origins of intelligence in children.* (M. Cook, Trans.). New York: International Universities Press. (Original work published 1936)

Piaget, J. (1955). *The language and thought of the child.* New York: Meridian Books.

Piaget, J. (1962). *Play, dreams, and imitation in childhood.* New York: W. W. Norton.

Piaget, J. (1965). *The moral judgment of the child.* (M. Gabain, Trans.). New York: Free Press.

Piaget, J. (1969). *The mechanisms of perception.* New York: Basic Books. (Original work published in 1932)

Piaget, J. (1970). *Science of education and psychology of the child.* New York: Orion Press.

Piaget, J. (1972). *Psychology and epistemology.* London: Penguin.

Piaget, J. (1973). *The child and reality.* New York: Viking Press.

Piaget, J. (1976). *The grasp of consciousness. Action and concept in the young child.* (Susan Wedgewood, Trans.). Cambridge, MA: Harvard University Press.

Piaget, J. (1976). *Judgment and reasoning in the child.* London: Routledge & Kegan Paul. (Originally published in 1928)

Piaget, J. (1995). *Sociological studies.* New York: Routledge. (Original work published in 1965)

Piaget, J., & Inhelder, B. (1958). *The growth of logical thinking.* New York: Basic Books.

Piaget, J., & Inhelder, B. (1969). *The child's conception of space* (F. J. Langdon & J. L. Lullnzer Trans.). New York: W. W. Norton.

Pianta, R. C. (1999). Early childhood. In W. K. Silverman & T. H. Ollendick (Eds.), *Developmental issues of the clinical treatment of children* (pp. 88–107). Boston: Allyn & Bacon.

Pianta, R. C., Nimetz, S. L., & Bennett, E. (1997). Mother–child relationships, teacher–child relationships, and school outcomes in preschool and kindergarten. *Early Childhood Research Quarterly, 12,* 263–280.

Picke, F. N. (1991). Chinese educational achievement and folk theories of success. *Anthropology and Educational Quarterly, 22,* 162–180.

Pierrehumbert, B., Ramstein, T., Karmaniola, A., & Halfon, O. (1996). Child care in the preschool years: Attachment, behaviour problems and cognitive development. *European Journal of Psychology of Education, 11,* 201–214.

Pilgrim, C. (1998). Close friend's drug use, authoritative parenting, and sensation-seeking effects on drug use among European-American and African-American adolescents. *Dissertation Abstracts International.* Sciences and Engineering.

Pilgrim, C., Luo, Q., Urberg, K. A., & Fang, X. (1999). Influence of peers, parents, and individual characteristics on adolescent drug use in two cultures. *Merrill-Palmer Quarterly, 45,* 85–107.

Pinker, S. (1995). *The language instinct.* New York: HarperPerennial.

Plato. (1952). "Cratylus" dialogues. In R. M. Hutchins (Ed.), *Great books of the Western world* (Vol. 7, pp. 85–114). Chicago: Encyclopedia Britannica. (Original work published in 350 B.C.)

Plomin, R. (1990). *Development, genetics, and psychology.* Pacific Grove, CA: Brooks/Cole.

Plomin, R. (1996). Beyond nature versus nurture. In L. L. Hall (Ed.), *Genetics and mental illness: Evolving issues for research and society* (pp. 29–50). New York: Plenum.

Plomin, R. (1997). Identifying genes for cognitive abilities and disabilities. In R. J. Sternberg & E. L. Grigorenko (Eds.), *Intelligence, heredity, and environment* (pp. 89–104). Cambridge, MA: Cambridge University Press.

Plomin, R. (1998). Using DNA in health psychology. *Health Psychology, 17,* 53–55.

Plomin, R., & Caspi, A. (1998). DNA and personality. *European Journal of Personality, 12,* 387–407.

Plomin, R., DeFries, J. C., McClearn, G. E., & Rutter, M. (1997). *Behavioral genetics.* New York: W. H. Freeman.

Plomin, R., & Petrill, S. (1997). Genetics and intelligence: What's new? *Intelligence, 24,* 63–77.

Plomin, R., & Rutter, M. (1998). Child development, molecular genetics, and what to do with genes once they are found. *Child Development, 69,* 1223–1242.

Polce-Lynch, M., Myers, B. J., Kilmartin, C. T., Forssman-Falck, R., & Kliewer, W. (1998). Gender and age patterns in emotional expression, body image, and self-esteem: A qualitative analysis. *Sex Roles, 38,* 1025–1048.

Pomerantz, E. M., & Ruble, D. N. (1997). Distinguishing multiple dimensions of conceptions of ability: Implications for self-evaluation. *Child Development, 68,* 1165–1180.

Pomerleau, A., Bolduc, D., Malcuit, G., & Cossette, L. (1990). Pink or blue: Environmental gender stereotypes in the first two years of life. *Sex Roles, 22,* 359–365.

Pomerleau, A., Malcuit, G., & Sabatier, C. (1991). Child-rearing practices and parental beliefs in three cultural groups of Montreal-Quebecois, Vietnamese, Haitian. In M. H. Bornstein (Ed.), *Cultural approaches to parenting* (pp. 45–68). Hillsdale, NJ: Erlbaum.

Pomeroy, J. C. (1998). Subtyping pervasive developmental disorder: Issues of validity and implications for child psychiatric diagnosis. In E. Schopler & G. B. Mesibov (Eds.), *Asperger syndrome or high-functioning autism? Current issues in autism* (pp. 29–60). New York: Plenum.

Popenoe, D. (1998, December). What is happening to the family in Sweden? *Social Change in Sweden, No. 366.* Stockholm: Swedish Information Service.

Potts, S., Farrell, M., & O'Toole, J. (1999). Treasure weekend: Supporting bereaved siblings. *Palliative Medicine, 13,* 51–56.

Powers, N. G. (1997). Cosleeping (bedsharing) among infants and toddlers. *Journal of Developmental and Behavioral Pediatrics, 18*(6), 411.

Powledge, T. M. (2000, September). Beyond the first draft. *Scientific American, 283,* 16–18.

Prior, M. (2001). Matrifocality, power, and gender relations in Jamaica. In C. B. Brettell & C. F. Sargent (Eds.), *Gender in cross-cultural perspective* (pp. 371–378). Upper Saddle River, NJ: Prentice-Hall.

Pruett, K. D. (1995). The paternal presence. In J. L. Shapiro, M. J. Diamond, & M. Greenberg (Eds.), *Becoming a father: Contemporary, social, developmental, and clinical perspectives* (pp. 36–42). New York: Springer.

Pryor, T., & Wiederman, M. W. (1998). Personality features and expressed concerns of adolescents with eating disorders. *Adolescence, 33,* 291–300.

Public Health Service. (1999). *Healthy people 2000: National health promotion and disease objectives.* U.S. Department of Health & Human Services.

Quiggle, N. L., Garber, J., Panak, W. F., & Dodge, K. A. (1992). Social information processing in aggressive and depressed children. *Child Development, 63,* 1305–1320.

Quirk, A., Rhodes, T., & Stimson, G. V. (1998). "Unsafe protected sex": Qualitative insights on measures of sexual risk. *AIDS Care, 10,* 105–114.

Raag, T., & Rackliff, C. L. (1998). Preschoolers' awareness of social expectations of gender: Relationships to toy choices. *Sex Roles, 38,* 685–700.

Rahdert, E. R., & Grabowski, J. (Eds.). (1988). *Adolescent drug abuse: Analysis of treatment research.* Washington, DC: U.S. Department of Health and Human Services, Public Health Service, Alcohol, Drug Abuse, and Mental Health Administration, National Institute on Drug Abuse.

Ramey, C. T., Breitmayer, V. J., Goldman, B. D., & Wakeley, A. (1996). Learning and cognition during infancy. In M. J. Hanson (Ed.), *Atypical infant development* (pp. 311–363). Austin, TX: Pro-Ed, Inc.

Ramey, C. T., & Ramey, S. L. (1998). Early intervention and early experience. *American Psychologist, 53,* 109–120.

Ramey, C. T., & Ramey, S. L. (1998). Prevention of intellectual disabilities: Early interventions to improve cognitive development. *Preventative Medicine: An International Devoted to Practice and Theory, 27,* 224–232.

Ransdell, L. B., & Wells, C. L. (1998). Physical activity in urban, white, African-American, and Mexican-American women. *Medicine and Science in Sports and Exercise, 30,* 1608–1615.

Ratner, C. (2000). A cultural–psychological analysis of emotions. *Culture and Psychology, 6,* 5–39.

Raty, H., & Snellman, L. (1997). Children's images of an intelligent person. *Journal of Social Behavior and Personality, 12,* 773–781.

Rauh, H., Ziegenhain, T., Mueller, B., & Wijnroks, L. (2000). Stability and change in infant–mother attachment in the second year of life: Relations to parenting quality and varying degrees of day-care experience. In P. Crittenden & A. H. Claussen (Eds.), *The organization of attachment relationships: Maturation, culture, and context* (pp. 251–276). New York: Cambridge University Press.

Read, D., Adams, G. R., & Dobson, W. R. (1985). Ego-identity status, personality, and social-influence style. *Journal of Personality and Social Psychology, 46,* 169–177.

Reardon, S. F., Brennan, R., & Buka, S. (2001, April 19–22). *Person or place? Explaining lower rates of cigarette use among minority youth.* Paper presented at the biennial meeting of the Society for Research in Child Development, Minneapolis.

Reddy, V., Hay, D., Murray, L., & Trevarthen, C. (1997). Communication in infancy: Mutual regulation of affect and attention. In G. Bremner, A. Slater, & G. Butterworth (Eds.), *Infant development: Recent advances* (pp. 247–271). East Sussex, UK: Psychology Press.

Red Horse, J. (1988). Cultural evolution of American Indian families. In C. Jacobs & D. C. Bowles (Eds.), *Ethnicity and race: Critical concepts in social work* (pp. 86–102). Silver Spring, MD: National Association of Social Workers.

Reeve, A. (1998). "Cerebral lateralization": Commentary. *Journal of Psychosomatic Research, 44,* 641–642.

Reeve, R. E., & Kauffman, J. M. (1988). Learning disabilities. In V. B. Van Hasselt, P. S. Strain, & M. Hersen (Eds.), *Handbook of developmental and physical disabilities* (pp. 316–335). Elmsford, NY: Pergamon Press.

Regan, P. C. (1996). Sexual outcasts: The perceived impact of body weight and gender on sexuality. *Journal of Applied Social Psychology, 26*(20), 1803–1815.

Reis, S. M., & Callahan, C. M. (1996). My boyfriend, my girlfriend, or me: The dilemma of talented teenage girls. *Journal of Secondary Gifted Education, 7,* 434–446.

Reis, S. M., & Gavin, M. K. (1998). *Why Jane doesn't think she can do math: How teachers encourage talented girls in mathematics.* Reston, VA: National Council of Teachers of Mathematics.

Reiss, D. (1995). Genetic influence on family systems: Implications for development. *Journal of Marriage and the Family, 57,* 543–560.

Reitzle, M., Vondracek, F. W., & Silbereisen, R. K. (1998). Timing of school-to-work transitions: A developmental-contextual perspective. *International Journal of Behavioral Development, 22,* 7–28.

Renk, K., Phares, V., & Epps, J. (1999). The relationship between parental anger and behavior problems in children and adolescents. *Journal of Family Psychology, 13,* 209–227.

Reynolds, A. J., & Temple, J. A. (1998). Extended early childhood intervention and school achievement: Age thirteen findings from the Chicago Longitudinal Study. *Child Development, 69,* 231–246.

Reznick, J. S. (1999). Can prenatal caffeine exposure affect behavioral inhibition? *Review of General Psychology, 3,* 118–132.

Rhodes, G., Sumich, A., & Byatt, G. (1999). Are average facial configurations attractive only because of their symmetry? *Psychological Science, 10,* 52–58.

Rice, F. P. (1999). *Intimate relationships, marriages, and families.* Mountain View, CA: Mayfield.

Rice, M. L., Huston, A. C., Truglio, R., & Wright, J. C. (1990). Words from *Sesame Street:* Learning vocabulary while viewing. *Developmental Psychology, 26,* 421–428.

Rich, A. (1976). *Of woman born.* New York: W. W. Norton.

Richards, H. (1997). The teaching of Afrocentric values by African American parents. *Western Journal of Black Studies, 21,* 42–50.

Richards, M. H., Crowe, P. A., Larson, R., & Swarr, A. (1998). Developmental patterns and gender differences in the experience of peer companionship during adolescence. *Child Development, 69,* 154–163.

Richards, M. H., & Larson, R. (1989). The life space and socialization of the self: Sex differences in the young adolescent. *Journal of Youth and Adolescence, 79,* 555–566.

Richardson, G. A., Conroy, M. L., & Day, N. L. (1996). Prenatal cocaine exposure: Effects on the development of school-age children. *Neurotoxicology and Teratology, 18,* 627–634.

Richardson, J. L. (1998). HIV infection. In E. A. Blechman & K. D. Brownell (Eds.), *Behavioral medicine and women* (pp. 659–664). New York: Guilford Press.

Richman, A. I., Miller, P. M., & LeVine, R. (1992). Cultural and educational variations in maternal responses. *Developmental Psychology, 28,* 614–621.

Richman, C. L., Bovelsky, S., Kroovand, N., Vacca, J., & West, T. (1997). Racism 102: The classroom. *Journal of Black Psychology, 23,* 378–387.

Richters, J. E., & Martinez, P. (1993). Violent communities, family choices, and children's chances: An algorithm for improving the odds. *Development and Psychopathology, 5,* 609–627.

Rickel, A. U., & Becker, E. (1997). *Keeping children from harm's way: How national policy affects psychological development.* Washington, DC: American Psychological Association.

Ritenbaugh, C., Shissiak, C., Teufel, N., & Leonard-Green, T. K. (1998). Eating and sexual disorders. In J. E. Mezzich & A. Kleinman (Eds.), *Cultural and psychiatric diagnosis: A DSM-IV perspective* (pp. 174–211). Washington, DC: American Psychiatric Press.

Roberts, K. (1997). Linguistic and nonlinguistic factors influencing infant categorization: Studies of the relationship between cognition and language. *Advances in Infant Research, 11,* 45–107.

Robertson, P. (1995). Home as a nest: Middle-class childhood in nineteenth-century Europe. In L. de Mause (Ed.), *The history of childhood* (pp. 407–432). Northvale, NJ: Jason Aronson.

Robinson, A., & Clinkenbeard, P. R. (1998). Giftedness: An exceptionality examined. *Annual Review of Psychology, 49,* 117–139.

Rochat, P., & Coubet, J. (1995). Development of sitting and reaching in 5- to 6-month-old infants. *Infant Behavior and Development, 18,* 53–68.

Rocheleau, B. (1996). Computer use by school-age children: Trends, patterns, and predictors. *Journal of Educational Computing Research, 12,* 1–17.

Rockett, H. R. H., Breitenbach, M., Frazier, A. L., Witschi, J., Wolf, A. M., Field, A. E., & Colditz, G. (1997). Validation of a youth/adolescent food frequency health questionnaire. *Preventative Medicine, 26,* 808–816.

Rodning, C., Beckwith, L., & Howard, J. (1991). Characteristics of attachment organization and play organization in prenatally drug-exposed toddlers. *Development and Psychopathology, 1,* 277–289.

Rodriguez, C., & Cordero-Gusman, H. (1992). Place race in context. *Ethnic and Racial Studies, 15,* 523–542.

Rodriguez, R. (2000). A bilingual childhood. In D. N. Sattler, G. P. Kramer, V. Shabatay, & D. A. Bernstein (Eds.), *Child development in context* (pp. 76–80). Boston: Houghton Mifflin.

Roebuck, T. M., Mattson, S. M., & Riley, E. P. (1999). Prenatal exposure to alcohol: Effects on brain structure and neuropsychological functioning. In J. H. Hannigan & L. P. Spear (Eds.), *Alcohol and alcoholism: Effects on brain and development* (pp. 1–16). Mahwah, NJ: Erlbaum.

Roebuck, T. M., Simmons, R. W., Mattson, S. M., & Riley, E. P. (1998). Prenatal exposure to alcohol affects the ability to maintain postural balance. *Alcoholism: Clinical and Experimental Research, 22,* 252–258.

Roenkae, A., & Pulkkinen, L. (1998). Work involvement and timing of motherhood in the accumulation of problems in social functioning in young women. *Journal of Research on Adolescence, 8,* 221–239.

Roeser, R. W., & Eccles, J. S. (1998). Adolescents' perceptions of middle school: Relation to longitudinal changes in academic and psychological adjustment. *Journal of Research on Adolescence, 8,* 123–158.

Roffman, R. A., & Barnhart, R. (1987). Assessing need for marijuana dependence treatment through an anonymous telephone interview. *International Journal of Addictions, 22,* 639–651.

Rogers, S. J., & White, L. K. (1998). Satisfaction with parenting: The role of marital happiness, family structure, and parents' gender. *Journal of Marriage and the Family, 60,* 293–308.

Rogoff, B. (1998). Cognition as a collaborative process. In D. Kuhn & R. S. Siegler (Eds.), *Handbook of child psychology: Vol. 2. Cognition, perception, and language* (pp. 523–574). New York: Wiley.

Rogoff, B., & Chavajay, P. (1995). What's become of the cultural basis of cognitive development? *American Psychologist, 50,* 859–877.

Rogoff, B., Mistry, J., Goncu, A., & Mosier, C. (1993). Adjustment of adult–child instruction according to child's age and task. *Monographs of the Society for Research in Child Development, 58* (8, Serial No. 179).

Rohner, R. P. (1986). *The warmth dimension: Foundations of parental acceptance–rejection theory.* Beverly Hills, CA: Sage.

Roopnarine, J. L., & Johnson, J. E. (1998). The need to look at play in diverse cultural settings. In J. L. Roopnarine, J. E. Johnson, & F. H. Hooper, (Eds.), *Children's play in diverse cultures* (pp. 1–9). Albany, NY: State University of New York Press.

Roopnarine, J. L., Lasker, J., Sacks, M., & Stores, M. (1998). The cultural context of play. In O. N. Saracho & B. Spodek (Eds.), *Multiple perspectives on play in early childhood education* (pp. 194–219). Albany, NY: State University of New Press.

Roopnarine, J. L., Lu, M. W., & Ahmeduzzaman, M. (1989). Parental reports of early patterns of caregiving, play, and discipline in India and Malaysia. *Early Child Development and Care, 50,* 109–120.

Roosa, M. W., Lein, J. Y., Reinholtz, C., & Angelini, P. J. (1997). The relationship of childhood sexual abuse to teenage pregnancy. *Journal of Marriage and Family, 59,* 119–130.

Root, M. P. P. (1990). Disordered eating in women of color. *Sex Roles, 22,* 525–536.

Rose, A. J. (1995). *The relationship between children's social goals, social strategies, and friendship adjustment.* Unpublished master's thesis, University of Illinois, Urbana-Champaign.

Rose, S. P., & Fischer, K. W. (1998). Models and rulers in dynamical development. *British Journal of Developmental Psychology, 16,* 123–131.

Rosenbaum, J. E., & Kariya, T. (1989). From high school to work: Market and institutional mechanisms in Japan. *American Journal of Sociology, 94,* 1334–1365.

Rosenblum, G. D., & Lewis, M. (1999). The relations among body image, physical attractiveness, and body mass in adolescence, *Child Development, 70,* 50–64.

Rosenblum O., Mazet, P., & Benony, H. (1997). Mother and infant affective involvement states and maternal depression. *Infant Mental Health Journal, 18,* 350–363.

Rosenheck, R., & Fontana, A. (1998). Warrior fathers and warrior sons: Intergenerational aspects of trauma. In Y. Danieli (Ed.), *International handbook of multigeneration legacies of trauma* (pp. 225–242). New York: Plenum Press.

Rosenthal, D. A., & Feldman, S. S. (1991). The influence of perceived family and personal factors on self-reported school performance of Chinese and Western high school students. *Journal of Research on Adolescence, 1,* 135–154.

Rosenthal, E. (1994). When a pregnant woman drinks. In E. N. Junn & C. J. Boyatzis (Eds.), *Annual editions: Child growth and development* (pp. 20–22). Guilford, CT: Dushkin.

Rosenthal, M. B., & Goldfard, J. (1997). Infertility and assisted reproductive technology: An update for mental health professions. *Harvard Review of Psychiatry, 5,* 169–172.

Rosenthal, M. B., & Kingsberg, S. A. (1999). The older infertile patient. In L. H. Burns & S. N. Covington (Eds.), *Infertility counseling: A comprehensive handbook for clinicians* (pp. 283–295). New York: Parthenon.

Rothbart, M. K. (1996). Incongruity, problem-solving, and laughter. In A. J. Chapman & H. C. Foot (Eds.), *Humor and laughter: Theory, research, and applications* (pp. 37–54). Brunswick, NJ: Transaction Publishers.

Rothbart, M. K., & Ahadi, S. A. (1994). Temperament and social behavior in childhood. *Merrill-Palmer Quarterly, 40,* 21–39.

Rothbart, M. K., & Bates, J. E. (1997). Temperament. In N. Eisenberg (Ed.), W. Damon (Series Ed.), *Handbook of child psychology: Vol. 3. Social, emotional, and personality development* (5th ed., pp. 105–176). New York: Wiley.

Rotheram-Borus, M. J., Dopkins, S., Sabate, S., & Lightfoot, M. (1996). Personal and ethnic identity, values, and self-esteem among black and Latino adolescent girls. In B. J. R. Leadbeater & N. Way (Eds.), *Urban girls: Resisting stereotypes, creating identities* (pp. 35–52). New York: New York University Press.

Rothi, L. J. G., & Heilman, K. M. (Eds). (1997). Apraxia: The neuropsychology of action. In *Brain damage, behaviour, and cognition* series (pp. 19–28). Hove, England: Psychology Press/Erlbaum (UK).

Rotter, J. (1966). Generalized expectancies for internal versus external locus of control of reinforcement. *Psychological Monographs: General and Applied, 80,* 1–28.

Roush, W. (1995). Arguing over why Johnny can't read. *Science, 267,* 196–198.

Rousseau, J. (1911). *Emile, or on education* (B. Foxley, Trans.). London: Dent. (Original work published in 1762)

Rovee-Collier, C. (1996). Measuring infant memory: A critical commentary. *Developmental Review, 16*(3), 301–310.

Rovee-Collier, C. (1996). Shifting the focus from what to why. *Infant Behavior and Development, 19,* 385–400.

Rovee-Collier, C. (2000). Shifting the focus from what to why. In D. Muir & A. Slater (Eds.), *Infant development: The essential readings* (pp. 5–34). Malden, MA: Blackwell Publishers.

Rovee-Collier, C., & Gerhardstein, P. (1997). The development of infant memory. In N. Cowan (Ed.), *The development of memory in childhood: Studies in developmental psychology* (pp. 5–39). Hove, England: Erlbaum (UK).

Rowe, D. C. (1997). A place at the policy table? Behavior genetics and estimates of family environmental effects on IQ. *Intelligence, 24,* 133–158.

Rowe, D. C. (1998). Genes, environment, and psychological development. In A. Campbell & S. Muncer (Eds.), *The social child* (pp. 51–83). Hove, England: Psychology Press/Erlbaum (UK).

Rowlinson, R. T., & Felner, R. D. (1998). Major life events, hassles, and adaptation in adolescence: Confounding in the conceptualization and measurement of life stress and adjustment revisited. *Journal of Personality and Social Psychology, 55,* 432–444.

Rubin, K. H., & Coplan, R. J. (1998). Social and nonsocial play in childhood: An individual differences perspective. In O. N. Saracho & B. Spodek (Eds.), *Multiple perspectives on play in early childhood education* (pp. 144–170). Albany, NY: State University of New York Press.

Rubin, K. H., Coplan, R. J., Nelson, L. J., Cheah, C. S. L., & Lagace-Seguin, D. G. (1999). Peer relationships in childhood. In M. H. Bornstein & M. E. Lamb (Eds.), *Developmental psychology: An advanced textbook* (pp. 451–502). Mahwah, NJ: Erlbaum.

Rubin, R. R., & Fisher, J. J. (1982). *Ages 3 and 4: Your preschooler.* New York: Macmillan.

Rubin, K. H., LeMare, L., & Lollis, S. (1990). Social withdrawal in childhood: Developmental pathways to peer rejection. In S. R. Asher & J. D. Coie (Eds.), *Peer rejection in childhood.* New York: Cambridge University Press.

Rubinstein, S., & Caballero, B. (2000). Is Miss America an undernourished role model? *Journal of the American Medical Association, 283,* 1569.

Ruble, D. M., Feldman, U. S., & Boggiano, A. K. (1976). Young children in achievement situations. *Developmental Psychology, 12,* 192–197.

Ruble, D. N., & Goodnow, J. J. (1998). Social development in childhood and adulthood. In D. T. Gilbert & S. T. Fiske (Eds.), *The handbook of social psychology* (4th ed., pp. 741–787). New York: McGraw-Hill.

Ruck, M. D., Abramovitch, R., & Keating, D. P. (1998). Children's and adolescents' understanding of rights: Balancing nurturance and self-determination. *Child Development, 69,* 404–417.

Rudd, M. D., & Joiner, T. E., Jr. (1998). An integrative conceptual framework for assessing and treating suicidal behavior in adolescents. *Journal of Adolescence, 21,* 489–498.

Ruff, H. A. (1998). Summary and commentary. Selective attention: Its measurement in a developmental framework. In J. E. Richards (Ed.), *Cognitive neuroscience of attention: A developmental perspective* (pp. 419–425). Mahwah, NJ: Erlbaum.

Runco, M. A. (1997). Is every child gifted? *Roeper Review, 19,* 220–224.

Rushton, J. P., Fulker, D. W., Neale, M. C., Nias, D. K. B., & Eysenck, H. J. (1986). Altruism and aggression: To what extent are individual differences inherited? *Journal of Personality and Social Psychology, 50,* 1192–1198.

Russell, A. T. (1995). Transracial adoptions should be forbidden. In D. Bender & B. Leone (Eds.), *Adoption: Opposing viewpoints* (pp.188–196). San Diego: Greenhaven Press.

Russell, G. (1999). Primary caregiving fathers. In M. E. Lamb (Ed.), *Parenting and child development in "nontraditional" families* (pp. 57–81). Mahwah, NJ: Erlbaum.

Russell, G., & Radojevic, M. (1992). The changing role of fathers? Current understandings and future directions for research and practice. *Infant Mental Health Journal, 13,* 296–311.

Russell, J. A. (1990). The preschooler's understanding of the causes and consequences of emotion. *Child Development, 61,* 1872–1881.

Russell, J. A. (1994). Is there universal recognition of emotion from facial expression? A review of cross-cultural studies. *Psychological Bulletin, 115,* 102–141.

Rutstein, R. M., Conlon, C. J., & Batshaw, M. L. (1997). HIV and AIDS: From mother to child. In M. L. Batshaw (Eds.), *Children with disabilities* (pp. 163–181). Baltimore: Paul H. Brookes.

Rutter, M. (1994). Psychiatric genetics: Research challenges and pathways forward. *American Journal of Medical Genetics (Neuropsychiatric Genetics), 54,* 185–198.

Rutter, M. (1995). Maternal deprivation. In M. H. Bornstein (Ed.), *Handbook of parenting. Vol. 4: Applied and practical parenting* (pp. 3–32). Mahwah, NJ: Erlbaum.

Rutter, M. (1996). Stress research: Accomplishments and tasks ahead. In R. J. Haggerty & L. R. Sherrod (Eds.), *Stress, risk, and resilience in children and adolescents: Processes, mechanisms, and interventions* (pp. 384–385). New York: Cambridge University Press.

Rycek, R. F., Stuhr, S. L., McDermott, J., Benker, J., & Schwartz, M. D. (1998). Adolescent egocentrism and cognitive functioning during late adolescence. *Adolescence, 33,* 745–749.

Rydell, A. M., Hagekull, B., & Bohlin, G. (1997). Measurement of two social competence aspects in middle childhood. *Developmental Psychology, 33,* 824–833.

Saarni, C. (1999). *The development of emotional competence.* New York: Guilford Press.

Sabbadini, L. L. (1995). *Matrimonie e convivenze nell' opione publica in Italia.* Rome: IRP, WP 02.

Sadker, M., & Sadker, D. F. (1994). *Failing at fairness: How our schools treat girls.* New York: Charles Scribner's Sons.

Sage, N. A., & Kindermann, T. A. (1999). Peer networks: Behavior contingencies and children's engagement. *Merrill Palmer Quarterly, 45,* 109–143.

Sagi, A., van IJzendoorn, M. H., Aviezer, O., Donnell, F., & Mayseless, O. (1994). Sleeping out of the home in a kibbutz communal arrangement: It makes a difference for infant–mother attachment. *Child Development, 65,* 992–1004.

Sagi, A., van IJzendoorn, M. H., Scharf, M., & Joels, T. (1997). Ecological constraints for intergenerational transmission of attachment. *International Journal of Behavioral Development, 20,* 287–299.

Sahibzada, N. R. (1992). The use of reward and punishment for fostering discipline among children of different cultures. *Journal of Behavioural Sciences, 3,* 45–58.

Saldinger, A., Cain, A., Kalter, N., & Lohnes, K. (1999). Anticipating parental death in families with young children. *American Journal of Orthopsychiatry, 89,* 35–48.

Salny, A. F. (1988). *The Mensa book of words, word games, puzzles, and oddities.* New York: HarperCollins.

Salomon, G. (1993). On the nature of pedagogic computer tools: The case of Writing Partner. In S. P. Lajoie & S. J. Derry (Eds.), *Computers as cognitive tools.* New York: Cambridge University Press.

Salzer, L. P. (1999). Adoption after infertility. In L. H. Burns & S. N. Covington (Eds.), *Infertility counseling: A comprehensive handbook for clinicians* (pp. 391–409). New York: Parthenon Publishing Group.

Salzinger, S., Feldman, R. S., Hammer, M., & Rosario, M. (1993). The effects of physical abuse on children's social relationships. *Child Development, 64,* 169–187.

Samango-Sprouse, C. (1999). Frontal lobe development in children. In B. L. Miller & J. L. Cummings (Eds.), *The human frontal lobes: Functions and disorders. The science and practice of neuropsychology series* (pp. 584–603). New York: Guilford Press.

Sampson, R. J., & Laub, J. H. (1998). Urban poverty and the family context of delinquency. In R. E. Muuss & H. D. Porton (Eds.), *Adolescent behavior and society* (pp. 118–135). New York: McGraw-Hill.

Samuel, V. J., Curtis, S., Thornell, A., George, P., Taylor, A., Brome, D. R., Biederman, J., & Faraone, S. V. (1997). The unexplored void of ADHD and African-American research: A review of the literature. *Journal of Attention Disorders, 1*(4), 197–207.

Samuels, C. A., Butterworth, G., Roberts, T., & Graupner, L. (1994). Babies prefer attractiveness to symmetry. *Perception, 23,* 823–831.

Sanchez-Ayendez, M. (1988). The Puerto Rican American family. In C. H. Mindel, R. W. Habenstein, & R. W. Wright, Jr. (Eds.), *Ethnic families in America: Patterns and variations* (pp. 173–195). New York: Elsevier.

Sandberg, S. (Ed.). (1996). Hyperactivity disorders of childhood. *Cambridge monographs on child and adolescent psychiatry, 2.* New York: Cambridge University Press.

Sanders, M. J., Kapphahn, C. J., & Steiner, H. (1998). Eating disorders. In R. T. Ammerman & J. V. Campo (Eds.), *Handbook of pediatric psychology and psychiatry* (pp. 287–312). Boston: Allyn & Bacon.

Sanderson, C. A., & Cantor, N. (1995). Social dating goals in late adolescence: Implications for safer sexual activity. *Journal of Personality and Social Psychology, 68*(6), 1121–1134.

Sanders-Thompson, V. L. (1999). Variables affecting racial-identity salience among African Americans. *Journal of Social Psychology, 139*(6), 748–761.

Sandqvist, K. (1997). Swedish family policy and attempts to change paternal roles. In C. Lewis & M. O'Brien (Eds.), *Reassessing fatherhood: New observations on fathers and the modern family* (pp. 144–160). London: Sage Publications.

Sands, R., Tricker, J., Sherman, C., & Armatas, C. (1997). Disorder eating patterns, body image, self-esteem, and physical activity in preadolescent school children. *International Journal of Eating Disorders, 21*(2), 159–166.

Sanson, A., Pedlow, R., Cann, W., & Prior, M. (1996). Shyness ratings: Stability and correlates in early childhood. *International Journal of Behavioral Development, 19,* 705–724.

Sanson, A., & Rothbart, M. K. (1995). Child temperament and parenting. In M. H. Bornstein (Ed.), *Handbook on parenting* (pp. 299–321). Hillsdale, NJ: Erlbaum.

Santor, D. A., Messervey, D., & Kusumakar, V. (2000). Measuring peer pressure, popularity, and conformity in adolescent boys and girls: Predicting school performance, sexual attitudes, and substance abuse. *Journal of Youth and Adolescence, 29*(2), 163–182.

Santos, R. A. (1997). Filipino American children. In G. Johnson-Powell & J. Yamamoto (Eds.), *Transcultural child development: Psychological assessment and treatment* (pp. 128–142). New York: Wiley.

Saracho, O. N., & Spodek, B. (Eds.). (1998). Multiple perspectives on play in early childhood education. Albany, NY: University of New York Press.

Saraswathi, T. S., & Pai, S. (1997). Socialization in the Indian context. In H. S. R. Kao & D. Durganand (Eds.), *Asian perspectives on psychology. Cross-cultural research and methodology series* (pp. 74–92). New Delhi, India: Sage.

Sastry, J., & Ross, C. E. (1998). Asian ethnicity and sense of personal control. *Social Psychology Quarterly, 6,* 101–120.

Saudino, K. J. (1997). Moving beyond the heritability question: New directions in behavioral genetic studies of personality. *Current Directions in Psychological Science, 6,* 86–90.

Saugstad, L. F. (1997). Optimal foetal growth in the reduction of learning and behaviour disorder and prevention of sudden infant death (SIDS) after the first month. *International Journal of Psychophysiology, 27,* 107–121.

Scarr, S. (1992). Developmental theories for the 1990s: Development and individual differences. *Child Development, 63,* 1–19.

Scarr, S. (1998). American child care today. *American Psychologist, 53,* 95–108.

Scarr, S. (1998). How do families affect intelligence? Social environmental and behavior genetic predictions. In J. J. McArdle & R. W. Woodcock (Eds.), *Human cognitive abilities in theory and practice* (pp. 113–136). Mahwah, NJ: Erlbaum.

Schaal, B. (1986). Presumed olfactory exchanges between mother and neonate in humans. In J. LeCamus & R. Campan (Eds.), *Ethologie et Psychologie de l'Enfant* (pp. 100–110). Toulouse: Prival.

Schaefer, R. T. (1988). *Racial and ethnic groups.* Glenview, IL: Scott, Foresman.

Schaffer, H. R. (1998). *Social development.* Malden, MA: Blackwell Publishers.

Schaffer, H. R., & Emerson, P. E. (1964). The development of social attachments in infancy. *Monographs of the Society for Research in Child Development, 29* (Serial No. 94).

Schmidt, L. A., Fox, N. A., Rubin, K. H., & Sternberg, E. M. (1997). Behavioral and neuroendocrine response in shy children. *Developmental Psychobiology, 30,* 127–140.

Schmidt, U. (1998). Eating disorders and obesity. In P. J. Graham (Ed.), *Cognitive-behaviour therapy for children and families* (pp. 262–281). New York: Cambridge University Press.

Schnitzer, P. G., Olshan, A. F., & Erickson, J. D. (1995). Paternal occupation and risk of birth defects in offspring. *Epidemiology, 6,* 577–583.

Schoelmerich, A., & van Aken, M. A. G. (1996). Attachment security and maternal concepts of ideal children in Northern and Southern Germany. *International Journal of Behavioral Development, 19,* 725–738.

Schoenhals, M., Tienda, M., & Schneider, B. (1998). The educational and personal consequences of adolescent employment. *Social Forces, 77,* 723–762.

Schopler, E., & Mesibov, G. B. (Eds.). (1998). *Asperger syndrome or high-functioning autism? Current issues in autism.* New York: Plenum.

Schreiber, G. B., Robins, M., Striegel-Moore, R. H., Obarzanek, E., Morrison, J. A., & Wright, D. J. (1996). Weight modification efforts reported by black and white preadolescent girls. *Pediatrics, 98,* 63–70.

Schuengel, C., van IJzendoorn, M. H., Bakermans-Kranenburg, M. J., & Blom, M. (1997, April). *Frightening, frightened, and dissociated behavior; unresolved loss; and infant disorganization.* Paper presented at the biennial meeting of the Society for Research in Child Development, Washington, DC.

Schuetze, P., & Zeskind, P. S. (1997). Relation between reported maternal caffeine consumption during pregnancy and neonatal state and heart rate. *Infant Behavior and Development, 20,* 559–562.

Scopesi, A., Zanobini, M., & Carossino, P. (1997). Childbirth in different cultures: psychophysical reactions of women delivering in U.S., German, French, and Italian hospitals. *Journal of Reproductive and Infant Psychology, 15,* 9–30.

Scott, B., & Melin, L. (1998). Psychometric properties and standardised data for questionnaires measuring negative affect, dispositional style, and daily hassles: A nationwide sample. *Scandinavian Journal of Psychology, 39,* 381–387.

Seachrist, L. (1994). Allergy gene nothing to sneeze at. *Science, 264,* 1533.

Segal, N. (1990). The importance of twin studies for individual differences in research. *Journal of Counseling and Development, 68,* 612–622.

Segal, N. (1997). Twin research perspective on human development. In N. L. Segal & G. E. Weisfeld (Eds.), *Uniting psychology and biology: Integrative perspectives on human development* (pp. 145–173). Washington, DC: American Psychological Association.

Segall, M. H., Dasen, P. R., Berry, J. W., Poortinga, Y. H. (1999). *Human behavior in global perspective: An introduction to cross-cultural psychology.* Needham Heights, MA: Allyn & Bacon.

Selman, R. (1980). *The growth of interpersonal understanding.* New York: Academic Press.

Selye, H. (1976). *The stress of life.* New York: McGraw-Hill. (Original work published in 1956)

Selye, H. (1980). The stress concept today. In I. Kutash (Ed.), *Handbook on stress and anxiety.* San Francisco: Jossey-Bass.

Senechal, M., LeFevre, J., Hudson, E., & Lawson, E. P. (1996). Knowledge of storybooks as a predictor of young children's vocabulary. *Journal of Educational Psychology, 88,* 520–536.

Serpell, R. (1989). Dimensions endogenes de l'intelligence chez les A-chews et autres peuples African. In J. Retschitzky, M. Bossel-Lagos, & P. Dasen (Eds.), *La recherche interculturelle.* Paris: L'Harmattan.

Serra, M., Jackson, A. E., van Geert, R. L. C., & Minderaa, R. B. (1998). Brief report: Interpretation of facial expressions, postures and gestures in children with a pervasive developmental disorder not otherwise specified. *Journal of Autism and Developmental Disorders, 28,* 257–263.

Sewell, G. (1999). Involuntary childlessness: Deciding to remain child-free. In L. H. Burns & S. N. Covington (Eds.), *Infertility counseling: A comprehensive handbook for clinicians* (pp. 411–422). New York: Parthenon.

Shaffer, D. R. (1999). *Developmental psychology: Childhood and adolescence* (4th ed.). Pacific Grove, CA: Brooks/Cole.

Shahinfar, A., Fox, N. A., & Leavitt, L. A. (2000). Preschool children's exposure to violence: Relation of behavior problems to parent and child reports. *American Journal of Orthopsychiatry, 70*(1), 115–125.

Shanahan, M. J., Elder, G. H., Jr., Burchinal, M., & Conger, R. D. (1996). Adolescents' earnings and relationships with parents. In J. T. Mortimer & M. D. Finch (Eds.), *Adolescents, work, and family: An intergenerational developmental analysis* (pp. 97–128). Thousand Oaks, CA: Sage.

Shapiro, J. L. (1995). When men are pregnant. In J. L. Shapiro, M. J. Diamond, & M. Greenberg (Eds.), *Becoming a father: Contemporary, social, developmental, and clinical perspectives* (pp. 118–134). New York: Springer.

Shapiro, S., Newcomb, M., & Loeb, T .B. (1997). Fear of fat, disregulated-restrained eating, and body-esteem: Prevalence and gender differences among eight- to ten-year-old children. *Journal of Clinical Child Psychology, 26,* 358–365.

Sharma, P. (1998). Attitudes of academic achievers. *Psycho Lingua, 25,* 103–110.

Shaw, D. S., Winslow, E. B., & Flanagan, C. (1999). A prospective study of the effects of marital status and family relations on young children's adjustment among African American and European Amerian families. *Child Development, 70,* 742–755.

Shaw, S. M., Kleiber, D. A., & Caldwell, L. L. (1995). Leisure and identity formation in male and female adolescents: A preliminary investigation. *Journal of Leisure Research, 27,* 245–263.

Shek, D. T. L. (1998). Life satisfaction of working women and "nonemployed" housewives in a Chinese context. *Psychological Reports, 83,* 702.

Shek, D. T. L. (2000). Differences between fathers and mothers in the treatment of, and relationship with, their teenage children: Perceptions of Chinese adolescents. *Adolescence, 35,* 135–146.

Shek, D. T. L., & Chan, L. K. (1999). Hong Kong Chinese parents' perceptions of the ideal child. *Journal of Psychology, 133,* 291–302.

Shepard, L. A. (1997). Children not ready to learn? The invalidity of school readiness testing. *Psychology in the Schools, 34,* 85–97.

Sher, K. J. (1987, December 2). *What we know and do not know about COAs: A research update.* Paper presented at the MacArthur Foundation Meeting on Children of Alcoholics. Princeton, NJ.

Sherrill, J. T., O'Leary, S. G., Albertson-Kelly, J. A., & Kendziora, K. T. (1996). When reprimand consistency may and may not matter. *Behavior Modification, 20,* 226–236.

Sheynkin, Y., & Schlegel, J. P. (1997). Sperm retrieval for assisted reproductive technologies. *Contemporary Ob/Gyn,* April, 15, 113–129.

Shifren, K., & Bauserman, R. L. (1996). The relationships between instrumental and expressive traits, health behaviors, and perceived physical health. *Sex Roles, 34,* 841–864.

Shimonaka, Y., Nakazato, K., Kawaai, C., & Sato, S. (1997). Androgyny and successful adaptation across the life span among Japanese adults. *Journal of Genetic Psychology, 158,* 389–400.

Shiono, P. (1995). Low birth weight. *The Future of Children, 5,* 231–237.

Shireman, J., & Johnson, P. (1986). A longitudinal study of black adoptions: Single parent, transracial, and traditional. *Social Work, 31,* 172–176.

Shisslak, C. M., Crago, M., McKnight, K. M., Estes, L. S., Gray, N., & Parnaby, O. G. (1998). Potential risk factors associated with eight control behaviors in elementary and middle school girls. *Journal of Psychosomatic Research, 44,* 301–313.

Shoda, Y., Mischel, W., & Peake, P. K. (1990). Predicting adolescent cognitive and self-regulatory competencies from preschool delay of gratification: Identifying diagnostic conditions. *Developmental Psychology, 26,* 978–986.

Shore, R. (1997). *Rethinking the brain.* New York: Families and Work Institute.

Shotton, G. (1998). A circles of friends approach with socially neglected children. *Educational Psychology in Practice, 14,* 22–25.

Shulman, S., Laursen, B., Kalman, Z., & Karpovsky, S. (1997). Adolescent intimacy revisited. *Journal of Youth and Adolescence, 26,* 597–617.

Shwalb, D. W., Kawai, H., Shoji, J., & Tsunetsugu, K. (1997). The middle-class father: A survey of parents of preschoolers. *Journal of Applied Developmental Psychology, 18,* 497–511.

Shwalb, D. W., & Shwalb, B. J. (Eds.). (1996). *Japanese childrearing: Two generations of scholarship.* New York: Guilford Press.

Shwe, H. I. (1999). Gricean pragmatics in preschoolers: Young children's understanding of sarcasm and irony. *Dissertation Abstracts Internations, 59,* Sciences and Engineering.

Shweder, R. A. (1999). Culture and development in our postcultural age. In A. S. Masten (Ed.), *Cultural processes in child development. The Minnesota Symposia on Child Psychology,* (Vol. 29, pp. 137–148). Mahwah, NJ: Erlbaum.

Shweder, R. A., Jensen, L. A., & Goldstein, W. M. (1995). Who sleeps by whom revisited: A method for extracting the moral goods implicit in practice. In J. J. Goodnow, P. J. Miller, & F. Kessel (Eds.), *Cultural practices as contexts for development. New directions for child development* (Vol. 67, pp. 21–39). San Francisco: Jossey-Bass.

Siano, B. (1994). Frankenstein must be destroyed: Chasing the monster of TV violence. *Humanist, 54,* 17–22.

Siegal, M. (1997). *Knowing children: Experiments in conversation and cognition.* Hove, England: Psychological Press/Erlbaum.

Siegel, B. (1996). *The world of the autistic child.* New York: Oxford University Press.

Siegel, M. (1997). *Knowing children: Experiments in conversation and cognition* (2nd ed.). Hove, England: Psychology Press/Erlbaum (UK).

Siegler, R. S. (1997). Beyond competence—toward development. *Cognitive Development, 12,* 323–332.

Siegler, R. S. (1997). Concepts and methods for studying cognitive development. In E. Amsel & K. A. Renninger (Eds.), *Change and development: Issues of theory, method, and application* (pp. 77–97). Mahwah, NJ: Erlbaum.

Siegler, R. S. (2001, April 19–22). *Relations between learning and development.* Paper presented at the biennial meeting of the Society for Research in Child Development, Minneapolis.

Siegler, R. S., & Chen, Z. (1998). Developmental differences in rule learning: A microgenetic analysis. *Cognitive Psychology, 36,* 273–310.

Siegmund, R., Tittel, M., Schiefenhoevel, W. (1994). Time patterns in parent–child interactions in a Trobriand village. *Biological Rhythm Research, 25,* 241–251.

Sigelman, C. K., Maddock, A., Epstein, J., & Carpenter, W. (1993). Age differences in understandings of disease causality: AIDS, colds, and cancer. *Child Development, 64,* 272–284.

Sigelman, C. K., & Shaffer, D. R. (1995). *Life-span human development* (2nd ed.). Pacific Grove, CA: Brooks/Cole.

Sigman, M., Cohen, S. E., & Beckwith, L. (1997). Why does infant attention predict adolescent intelligence? *Infant Behavior and Development, 20,* 133–140.

Sigman, M., Cohen, S. E., & Beckwith, L. (2000). Why does infant attention predict adolescent intelligence? In D. Muir & A. Slater (Eds.), *Infant development: The essential readings. Essential readings in development psychology* (pp. 239–253). Malden, MA: Blackwell.

Signorielli, N., & Lears, M. (1992). Television and children's conceptions of nutrition: Unhealthy messages. *Health Communication 1*(1), 245–257.

Signorielli, N., & Staples, J. (1997). Television and children's conceptions of nutrition. *Health Communication, 9,* 289–301.

Silverstein, L. B. (1991). Transforming the debate about child care and maternal employment. *American Psychologist, 46,* 1025–1032.

Silverstein, L. B. (1996). Fathering is a feminist issue. *Psychology of Women, 20,* 3–37.

Silverman, P. R. (2000). Children as part of the family drama: An integrated view of childhood bereavement. In R. Malkinson & S. S. Shimshon (Eds.), *Traumatic and nontraumatic loss and bereavement: Clinical theory and practice* (pp. 67–90). Madison, CT: International Universities Press.

Silverman, W. K., La Greca, A. M., & Wasserstein, S. (1995). What do children worry about? Worries and their relation to anxiety. *Child Development, 66,* 671–686.

Simion, F., & Butterworth, G. (Eds.). (1998). *The development of sensory, motor, and cognitive capacities in early infancy: From perception to cognition.* Hove, England: Psychology Press/Erlbaum.

Simon, R. J., & Alstein, H. (1977). *Transracial adoption.* New York: Wiley.

Simon, R. J., & Alstein, H. (1987). *Transracial adoptees and their families: A study of identity and commitment.* New York: Praeger.

Simon, R. J., Alstein, H., & Melli, M. S. (1995). Transracial adoptions should be encouraged. In D. Bender & B. Leone (Eds.), *Adoption: Opposing viewpoints* (pp. 197–204). San Diego: Greenhaven Press.

Simons, R. L., Whitbeck, L. B., Conger, R. D., & Chyi-In, W. (1991). Intergenerational transmission of harsh parenting. *Developmental Psychology, 27,* 159–171.

Singer, J. L., & Singer, D. G. (1998). *Barney & Friends* as entertainment and education: Evaluating the quality and effectiveness of a television series for preschool children. In J. K. Asamen & G. L. Berry (Eds.), *Research paradigms, television, and social behavior* (pp. 305–367). Thousand Oaks, CA: Sage.

Skevington, S., & Baker, D. (1989). *The social identity of women.* Beverly Hills, CA: Sage.

Skinner, B. F. (1948). *Walden two.* New York: Macmillan.

Skinner, B. F. (Ed.). (1972). *Cumulative record: A selection of papers* (3rd ed.). New York: Appleton.

Skinner, B. F. (1974). *About behaviorism.* New York: Knopf.

Skinner, B. F. (1981). Are theories of learning necessary? Psychological Review, 57, 193–216.

Skinner, E. A., Zimmer-Gembeck, M. J., & Connell, J. P. (1998). Individual differences and the development of perceived control. *Monographs of the Society for Research in Child Development, 63*(Serial No. 220).

Skodak, M., & Skeels, H. (1949). A final follow-up of one hundred adopted children. *Journal of Genetic Psychology, 73,* 85–125.

Skoe, E. E. A., Hansen, K. L., Morch, W. T., Bakke, I., Hoffmann, T., Larsen, B., & Aasheim, M. (1999). Care-based moral reasoning in Norwegian and Canadian early adolescents: A cross-national comparison. *Journal of Early Adolescence, 19,* 280–291.

Skorikov, V. B., & Vondracek, F. W. (1997). Longitudinal relationships between part-time work and career development in adolescents. *Career Development Quarterly, 45*(3), 221–235.

Slater, A., Brown, E., Mattock, A., & Bornstein, M. H. (1996). Continuity and change in habituation in the first 4 four months from birth. *Journal of Reproductive and Infant Psychology, 14,* 187–194.

Slater, A., Von der Schulenburg, C., Brown, E., Badenoch, M., Butterworth, G., Parsons, S., & Samuels, C. (1998). Newborn infants prefer attractive faces. *Infant Behavior and Development, 21,* 345–354.

Slaughter-Defoe, D. T., Nakagawa, K., Takanishi, R., & Johnson, D. J. (1990). Toward cultural/ecological perspectives on schooling and achievement in African- and Asian-American children. *Child Development, 61,* 363–383.

Slater, A. (1997). Visual perception and its organisation in early infancy. In G. Bremner, A. Slater, & G. Butterworth (Eds.), *Infant development: Recent advances* (pp. 31–54), East Sussex, UK: Psychology Press.

Slobin, D. I. (1971). *Psycholinguistics.* Glenview, IL: Scott, Foresman.

Slobin, D. I. (1985). Crosslinguistic evidence of the language-making capacity. In D. I. Slobin (Ed.), *The crosslinguistic study of language acquisition. Vol. 2: Theoretical issues* (pp. 1157–1256). Hillsdale, NJ: Erlbaum.

Slobin, D. I. (1988, April). *Confessions of a wayward Chomskyan. Papers and reports on child development* (Vol. 27, pp. 131–138). Proceedings of the Annual Language Research Forum: Papers and Reports on Child Development. Palo Alto, CA: Stanford University.

Slotboom, A. M., Havill, V. L., Pavlopoulous, V., & De Fruyt, F. (1998). Developmental changes in personality descriptions of children: A cross-national comparison of parental descriptions of children. In G. A. Kohnstramm & C. F. Halverson, Jr. (Eds.), *Parental descriptions of child personality: Developmental antecedents of the Big Five: The LEA series in personality and clinical psychology* (pp. 127–153). Mahwah, NJ: Erlbaum.

Smedley, B. (1999). Child protection: Facing up to fear. In P. Milner & B. Carolin (Eds.), *Time to listen to children: Personal and professional communication* (pp. 112–125). New York: Routledge.

Smetana, J. G. (1989). Adolescents' and parents' reasoning about actual family conflict. *Child Development, 60,* 1052–1067.

Smetana, J. G. (1996). Adolescent–parent conflict: Implications for adaptive and maladaptive development. In D. Cicchetti & S. L. Toth (Eds.), *Rochester Symposium on Developmental Psychopathology. Vol. 7: Adolescence opportunities and challenges.* Rochester, NY: University of Rochester Press.

Smilansky, S. (1968). *The effects of sociodramatic play on disadvantaged preschool children.* New York: Wiley.

Smith, J. R., Brooks-Gunn, J., & Klebanov, P. (1997). The consequences of living in poverty for young children's cognitive and verbal ability and early school achievement. In G. J. Duncan & J. Brooks-Gunn, (Eds.), *Consequences of growing up poor.* New York: Russell Sage Foundation.

Smith, L. (1983). A conceptual model of families incorporating and adolescent mother and child into the household. *Advances in Nursing Science, 6,* 45–60.

Smith, P. K., Cowie, H., & Blades, M. (1998). *Understanding children's development.* Oxford, England: Blackwell Publishers.

Smith, S. (1995). Family theory and multicultural family studies. In B. B. Ingoldsby & S. Smith (Eds.), *Families in multicultural perspective* (pp. 5–36). New York: Guilford Press.

Smith, S. (1995). Women and households in the Third World. In B. B. Ingoldsby & S. Smith (Eds.), *Families in multicultural perspective* (pp. 235–267). New York: Guilford Press.

Snarey, J. (1993). *How fathers care for the next generation.* Cambridge, MA: Harvard University Press.

Smolak, L., Levine, M. P., & Schermer, F. (1999). Parental input and weight concerns among elementary school children. *International Journal of Eating Disorders, 25,* 263–271.

Snow, M. E., Jacklin, C. N., & Maccoby, E. E. (1983). Sex of child differences in father–child interaction at one year of age. *Child Development, 54,* 227–232.

Socha, T. J., & Diggs, R. C. (Eds.). (1999). *Communication, race, and family: Exploring in black, white, and biracial families.* Mahwah, NJ: Erlbaum.

Sogolow, E. D., Kay, L. S., Doll, L. S., Neumann, M. S., Mezoff, J. S., Eke, A. N., Semann, S., & Anderson, J. R. (2000, October). *AIDS Education and Prevention, 12*(Suppl 15), 21–32.

Sokol, M. S., & Gray, N. S. (1998). Anorexia nervosa. In E. A. Blechman & K. D. Brownell (Eds.), *Behavioral medicine and women* (pp. 350–357). New York: Guilford Press.

Solis, C. R. P., & Fox, R. A. (1996). Parenting practices and expectations among Mexican mothers with young children. *Journal of Genetic Psychology, 157,* 465–576.

Song, M. J., Smetana, J. G., & Kim, S. J. (1987). Korean children's conceptions of moral and conventional transgressions. *Developmental Psychology, 23,* 577–582.

Sorce, J. F., Emde, R. N., Campos, J., & Klinnert, M. D. (2000). Maternal emotional signaling: Its effect on the visual cliff behavior of 1-year-olds. In D. Muir & A. Slater (Eds.), *Infant development: The essential readings. Essential readings in development psychology* (pp. 282–292). Malden, MA: Blackwell Publishers.

Southwest Educational Development Laboratory (SEDL). (1992). *Follow through: A bridge to the future.* Developed through SEDL Follow-through Project.

Spearman, C. (1927). *The abilities of man.* New York: Macmillan.

Spelke, E. S. (1991). Physical knowledge in infancy: Reflections on Piaget's theory. In S. Carey & R. Gelman (Eds.), *The epigenesis of mind: Essays on biology and cognition.* Hillsdale, NJ: Erlbaum.

Spelke, E. S., & Hermer, L. (1996). Early cognitive development: Objects and space. In R. Gelman, & T. Kit-Fong (Eds.), *Perceptual and cognitive development. Handbook of perception and cognition* (pp. 71–114). San Diego: Academic Press, Inc.

Spence, J. T. (1985). Achievement American style: The rewards and costs of individualism. *American Psychologist, 40,* 1285–1295.

Spence, S. H., & McCathie, H. (1993). The stability of fears in children: A two-year prospective study: A research note. *Journal of Child Psychology and Psychiatry, 34,* 579–585.

Spencer, M. B., Dupree, D. V., Swanson, D. P., & Cunningham, M. (1998). The influence of physical maturation and hassles on African American adolescents' learning behaviors. *Journal of Comparative Family Studies, 29,* 189–200.

Spencer, M. B., & Markstrom-Adams, C. (1990). Identity processes among racial and ethnic minority children in America. *Child Development, 61,* 290–300.

Spieker, S. J., Larson, N. C., Lewis, S. M., Keller, T. E., & Gilchrist, L. (1999). Developmental trajectories of disruptive behavior problems in preschool children of adolescent mothers. *Child Development, 70,* 443–458.

Spinello, T. M. (1998). Exploration of the relationships between female adolescent anorexics/bulimics and their mothers. *Dissertation Abstracts International, 59,* The Sciences and Engineering.

Spitz, R. A. (1945). Hospitalism: An inquiry into the genesis of psychiatric conditions in early childhood. *Psychoanalytic Study of the Child, 1,* 113–117.

Springer, S. P., & Deutsch, G. (1998). *Left brain, right brain: Perspectives from cognitive neuroscience* (5th ed.). New York: W. H. Freeman.

Sroufe, L. A. (1996). *Emotional development.* New York: Cambridge University Press.

Sroufe, L. A., Egeland, B., & Carlson, E. A. (1999). One social world: The integrated development of parent–child and peer relationships. In W. A. Collins & B. Laursen (Eds.), *Relationships as developmental contexts. The Minnesota Symposia on Child Psychology* (pp. 241–261). Mahwah, NJ: Erlbaum.

Sroufe, L. A., Carlson, E. A., Levy, A. K., & Egeland, B. (1999). Implications of attachment theory for developmental psychopathology. *Development and Psychopathology, 11,* 1–13.

Stake, J. E. (1997). Integrating expressiveness and instrumentality in real-life settings: A new perspective on the benefits of androgyny. *Sex Roles, 37,* 541–564.

Staso, W. H. (1995). *Brain under construction: Experiences that promote the intellectual capabilities of young toddlers.* Orcutt, CA: Great Beginnings Press.

Stattin, H., & Klackenberg-Larsson, I. (1991). The short- and long-term implications for parent–child relations of parents' prenatal preferences for their child's gender. *Developmental Psychology, 27,* 141–147.

Steele, C. M. (1997). A threat in the air: How stereotypes shape intellectual identity and performance. *American Psychologist, 52,* 613–629.

Steele, R. G., Forehand, R., Armistead, L., Morse, E., Simon, P., & Clark, L. (1999). Coping strategies and behavior problems of urban African-American children: Concurrent and longitudinal relationships. *American Journal of Orthopsychiatry, 69,* 182–193.

Steighner, J. (2001, April 19–22). *A longitudinal investigation of the relationship between academic achievement and extra-curriculum involvement.* Paper presented at the biennial meeting of the Society for Research in Child Development, Minneapolis.

Stein, M. T. (1996). Beyond infant colic. *Journal of Developmental and Behavioral Pediatrics, 17,* 38–47.

Stein, M. T. (1997). Cosleeping (bedsharing) among infants and toddlers. *Journal of Developmental and Behavioral Pediatrics, 18,* 408–409.

Steinberg, L. D. (1993). *Adolescence.* New York: Knopf.

Steinberg, L. D., Dornbusch, S. M., & Brown, B. B. (1998). Ethnic differences in adolescent achievement: An ecological perspective. In R. E. Muuss & H. D. Porton (Eds.), *Adolescent behavior and society* (pp. 208–231). New York: McGraw-Hill.

Steinberg, L. D., Greenberger, E., Garduque, L., Ruggiero, M., & Vaux, A. (1992). Effects of working on adolescent development. *Developmental Psychology, 18,* 385–395.

Stephens, D. P., & Willert, A. (2001, April 19–22). *Risk and protective factors associated with sexual risk taking of African American girls.* Paper presented at the biennial meeting of the Society for Research in Child Development, Minneapolis.

Stephenson, J. (1999). Perinatal HIV prevention. *JAMA, 282,* 625.

Stern, S. B. (1999). Anger management in parent–adolescent conflict. *American Journal of Family Therapy, 27,* 181–193.

Sternberg, R. J. (1997). Educating intelligence: Infusing the Triarchic theory into school instruction. In R. J. Sternberg & E. L. Grigorenko (Eds.), *Intelligence, heredity, and environment* (pp. 343–362). Cambridge, MA: Cambridge University Press.

Sternberg, R. J. (2000). *Handbook of intelligence.* New York: Cambridge University Press.

Sternberg, R. J., & Williams, W. M. (1995). Parenting toward cognitive competence. In M. H. Bornstein (Ed.), *Handbook on parenting* (pp. 259–275). Hillsdale, NJ: Erlbaum.

Sternberg, R. J., & Williams, W. M. (Eds.). (1998). *Intelligence, instruction, and assessment: Theory into practice.* Mahwah, NJ: Erlbaum.

Stevens, E. (1983). *Erik Erikson.* New York: St. Martin's Press.

Stevenson, D. L., Kochanek, J., & Schneider, B. (1998). Making the transition from high school: Recent trends and policies. In K. Borman & B. Schneider (Eds.), *The adolescent years: Social influences and educational challenges* (pp. 207–226). Chicago: National Society for the Study of Education.

Stevenson, H. W. (1998). Cultural interpretations of giftedness: The case of East Asia. In R. C. Friedman & K. B. Rogers (Eds.), *Talent in context: Historical and social perspectives on giftedness* (pp. 61–77). Washington, DC: American Psychological Association.

Stevenson, H. W., & Lee, S. (1990). Contexts of achievement. *Monographs of the Society for Research in Child Development, 55* (Serial No. 221).

Stevenson, H. W., & Lee, S. (1997). The academic achievement of Chinese students. In M. H. Bond (Ed.), *The handbook of Chinese psychology* (pp. 124–142). New York: Oxford University Press.

Stevenson, H. W., Chen, C., & Lee, S. Y. (1993). Mathematics achievement of Chinese, Japanese, and American children: Ten years later. *Science, 259,* 53–58.

Stevenson, W., Maton, K. J., & Teti, D. M. (1998). School importance and dropout among pregnant adolescents. *Journal of Adolescent Health, 22,* 376–382.

Steward, O., Bakker, C. E., Wilems, P. J., & Oostra, B. A. (1998). No evidence for disruption of normal patterns of mRNA localization in dendrites of dendritic transport of recently synthesized mRNA in FMR1 knockout mice, a model for human fragile X mental retardation syndrome. *Neuroreport: An International Journal for the Rapid Communication of Research in Neuroscience, 9,* 477–481.

Stewart, A. J., Copeland, A. P., Chester, N. L., Malley, J. E., & Barenbaum, N. B. (1997). *Separating together: How divorce transforms families.* New York: Guilford Press.

Stice, E., & Agras, W. S. (1998). Predicting onset and cessation bulimic behaviors during adolescence: A longitudinal grouping analysis. *Behavior Therapy, 29,* 257–276.

Stice, R., Agras, W. S., & Hammer, L. D. (1999). Risk factors for the emergence of childhood eating disturbances: A five-year prospective study. *International Journal of Eating Disorders, 25,* 375–387.

Stifter, C. A., & Braungart, J. (1992). Infant colic: A transient condition with no apparent effects. *Journal of Applied Developmental Psychology, 13,* 447–462.

Stifter, C. A., Coulehan, C. M., & Fish, M. (1993). Linking employment to attachment: The mediating effects of maternal separation anxiety and interactive behavior. *Child Development, 64,* 1451–1460.

Stigler, J. W., & Stevenson, H. W. (1999). How Asian teachers polish each lesson to perfection. *Child Growth and Development* (6th ed., pp. 66–77). Guilford, CT: Dushkin/McGraw-Hill.

Stipek, D. J., Recchia, S., & McClintic, S. (1992). Self-evaluations in young children. *Monographs of the Society for Research in Child Development, 57* (Serial No. 226).

Stoff, D. M., Breiling, J., & Maser, J. D. (Eds.). (1997). *Handbook of antisocial behavior.* New York: Wiley.

Stone, M. (2001, April 19–22). *How to succeed in high school by really trying: Does activity participation benefit students at all levels of social competence?* Paper presented at the biennial meeting of the Society for Research in Child Development, Minneapolis.

Story, M., French, S. A., Resnick, M. D., & Blum, R. W. (1995). Ethnic/racial and socioeconomic differences in dieting behaviors and body image perceptions in adolescence. *International Journal of Eating Disorders, 18*(2), 173–179.

Straus, M. A., & McCord, J. (1998). Do physically punished children become violent adults? In S. Nolen-Hoeksema (Ed.), *Clashing views on abnormal psychology: A taking sides custom reader* (pp. 130–155). Guilford, CT: Dushkin/McGraw-Hill.

Straus, M. A., & Stewart, J. H. (1999). Corporal punishment by American parents: National data on prevalence, chronicity, severity, and duration, in relation to child and family characteristics. *Clinical Child and Family Psychology, 2,* 55–70.

Straus, M. B. (1994). Suicidal adolescents. In M. B. Straus (Ed.), *Violence in the lives of adolescents* (pp. 31–53). New York: W. W. Norton.

Strauss, R. (2001, April 19–22). *Fathers' involvement in children's lives: Examining relationships with children's school success.* Paper presented at the biennial meeting of the Society for Research in Child Development, Minneapolis.

Streeter, L. A. (1976). Language perception of 2-month-old infants. *Nature, 259,* 39–41.

Streissguth, A., Sampson, P. D., & Barr, H. (1989). Neurobehavioral dose-response effects of prenatal alcohol exposure in humans from infancy to adulthood. In D. E. Hutchings (Ed.), *Prenatal abuse of licit and illicit drugs* (Vol. 562, pp. 145–158). New York: Annals of the New York Academy of Sciences.

Streissguth, A., Treder, R. P., Barr, H. M., Shepard, T. H., Bleyer, W. A., Sampson, P. D., & Martin, D. C. (1987). Aspirin and acetaminophen used by pregnant women and subsequent child IQ and attention decrements. *Teratology, 35,* 211–219.

Streitmatter, J. (1994). *Toward gender equity in the classroom.* New York: State University of New York Press.

Striegel-Moore, R. H., Schreiber, G. V., Pike, K. M., & Wilfley, D. E. (1995). Drive for thinness in black and white preadolescent girls. *International Journal of Eating Disorders, 18*(1), 59–69.

Strom, K., Oguinick, C. M., & Singer, M. I. (1995). What do teenagers want? What do teenagers need? *Child and Adolescent Social Work Journal, 12*(5), 345–359.

Stromshak, E .A., Bierman, K. L., Coie, J. D., & Dodge, K. A. (1998). The implications of different developmental patterns of disruptive behavior problems for school adjustment. *Development and Psychopathology, 10,* 451–467.

Strong, K. G., & Huon, G. F. (1998). An evaluation of a structural model for studies of the initiation of dieting among adolescent girls. *Journal of Psychosomatic Research,* 44, 315–326.

Stuart, M. (1999). Getting ready for reading: Early phoneme awareness and phonics teaching improves reading and spelling in inner-city second language learners. *British Journal of Educational Psychology, 69,* 587–605.

Stunkard, A. J., Sorensen, I.T.A., Hanis, C., Teasdale, T. W., Chakraborty, R., Schull, W. J., & Schulinger, F. (1986). An adoption study of human obesity. *New England Journal of Medicine,* 314, 193–198.

Subhi, T. (1997). Who is gifted? A computerized identification procedure. *High-Ability Studies, 8,* 189–211.

Subrahmanyam, K., & Greenfield, P. M. (1998). Computer games for girls: What makes them play? In J. Cassell & H. Jenkins (Eds.), *From Barbie to Mortal Kombat: Gender and computer games* (pp. 46–71). Cambridge, MA: MIT Press.

Sue, S., & Zane, N. (1987). The role of culture and cultural techniques in psychotherapy: A critique and reformulation. *American Psychologist, 42,* 37–45.

Sullivan, H. S. (1953). *The interpersonal theory of psychiatry.* New York: W. W. Norton.

Sullivan, P. F., Bulik, C. M., & Kendler, K. S. (1998). Genetic epidemiology of binging and vomiting. *British Journal of Psychiatry, 173,* 75–79.

Summers, P., Forehand, R., Armistead, L., & Tannenbaum, L. (1998). Parental divorce during early adolescence in Caucasian families: The role of family process variables in predicting the long-term consequences for early adult psychosocial adjustment. *Journal of Consulting and Clinical Psychology, 66,* 327–336.

Sun, S. L. (1995). *The development of social networks of Chinese children in Taiwan.* Poster presented in the biennial meeting of Society for Research in Child Development, Indianapolis.

Super, C. M., & Harkness, S. (1997). The cultural structuring of child development. In J. W. Berry, P. R. Dasen, & T. S. Saraswathi (Eds.), *Handbook of cross-cultural psychology* (pp. 1–40). Needham Heights, MA: Allyn & Bacon.

Super, C. M., & Harkness, S. (1999). The environment as culture in developmental research. In S. L. Freidman & T. D. Wachs (Eds.), *Measuring environment across the life span: Emerging methods and concepts* (pp. 279–323). Washington, DC: American Psychological Association.

Sutton, J. (1998). *Philosophy and memory traces: Descartes to connectionism.* New York: Cambridge University Press.

Suzuki, D., & Knudtson, P. (1989). *Genethics: The clash between the new genetics and human values.* Cambridge, MA: Cambridge University Press.

Suzuki, L. A., Hashimoto, Y., & Ishii, K. (1997). Measuring information behavior: A time budget survey in Japan. *Social Indicators Research, 42,* 151–169.

Suzuki, L. A., & Valencia, R. R. (1997). Race-ethnicity and measured intelligence: Educational implications. *American Psychologist, 52,* 1103–1114.

Svensson, A. K. (2000). Computers in school: Socially isolating or a tool to promote collaboration? *Journal of Educational Computing Research, 22*(4), 437–453.

Swaab, D. F., & Gofman, M. A. (1995). Sexual differentiation of the human hypothalamus in relation to gender and sexual orientation. *Trends in Neurosciences, 18,* 264–270.

Swanson, D. P., Spencer, M. B., & Petersen, A. (1998). Identity formation in adolescence. In. K. Borman & B. Schneider (Eds.), *The adolescent years: Social influences and educational challenges: Ninety-seventh yearbook of the National Society for the Study of Education. Part I.* (pp 18–41). Chicago: National Society for the Study of Education.

Szatmari, P. (1998). Differential diagnosis of Asperger disorder. In E. Schopler & G. B. Mesibov (Eds.), *Asperger syndrome or high-functioning autism?* Current issues in autism (pp. 61–76). New York: Plenum.

Takahashi, K. (1990). Are the key assumptions of the "Strange Situation" procedure universal? A view from Japanese research. *Human Development, 30,* 23–30.

Takeuchi, M. (1994). Children's play in Japan. In J. L. Roopnarine, J. E. Johnson, & F. H. Hooper (Eds.), *Children's play in diverse cultures* (pp. 51–72). Albany, NJ: State University of New York.

Tamis-LeMonda, C. S., Bornstein, M. H., Cyphers, L., Toda, S., & Ogino, M. (1992). Language and play at one year: A comparison of toddlers and mothers in the United States and Japan. *International Journal of Behavioral Development, 15,* 19–42.

Tanner, J. M. (1962). *Growth at adolescence* (2nd ed.). Oxford, England: Black Scientific Publications.

Tanner, J. M. (1978). *Education and physical growth.* London: Hoddler and Stoughton.

Tanner, J. M. (1990). *Fœtus into man.* Cambridge, MA: Harvard University Press.

Tanner, J. M. (1998). Sequence, tempo, and individual variation in growth and development of boys and girls aged twelve to sixteen. In R. Muuss & H. Porton (Eds.), *Adolescent behavior and society: A book of readings* (pp. 34–46). New York: McGraw-Hill.

Tao, S., Dong, Q., Lin, L., & Zeng, Q. (1997). A comparative study of maternal sensitivity and response to child's physical and mental needs. *Psychological Science China, 20,* 146–150.

Tardif, T., & Wellman, H. M. (2000). Acquisition of mental state language in Mandarin- and Cantonese-speaking children. *Developmental Psychology, 36,* 25–43.

Taylor, M. (1996). A theory of mind perspective on social cognitive development. In R. Gelman & T. Kit-Fong (Eds.), *Perceptual and cognitive development: Handbook of perception and cognition* (pp. 283–329). San Diego: Academic Press.

Taylor, R. L. (1997). Who's parenting? Trends and patterns. In T. Arendell (Ed.), *Contemporary parenting: Challenges and issues* (pp. 68–91). Thousand Oaks, CA: Sage.

Taylor, W. C., Beech, B. M., & Cummings, S. S. (1998). Increasing physical activity levels among youth: A public health challenge. In D. K. Wilson & J. R. Rodriguez, (Eds.), *Health-promoting and health-compromising behaviors among minority adolescents. Application and practice in health psychology* (pp. 107–128). Washington, DC: American Psychological Association.

Telama, R., Yang, X., Laakso, L., & Viikari, J. (1997). Physical activity in childhood and adolescence as predictor of physical activity in young adulthood. *American Journal of Preventative Medicine, 13,* 317–323.

Tellegen, A., Lykken, D. T., Bouchard, T. J., Wilcox, K., Segal, N. L., & Rich, S. (1988). Personality similarity in twins reared apart and together. *Journal of Social and Personality Psychology, 54,* 1031–1039.

Tencer, H. L. (2001, April 19–22). *Friendship behavior among harshly punished children.* Paper presented at the biennial meeting for the Society for Research in Child Development, Minneapolis.

Tesman, J., & Hills, A. (1994). Developmental effects of lead exposure in children. *Social Policy Report: Society for Research on Child Development, 8*(3).

Teti, D. M., & Teti, L. O. (1996). Infant–parent relationships. In N. Vanzetti & S. Duck (Eds.), *A lifetime of relationships* (pp. 77–104). Pacific Grove, CA: Brooks/Cole.

Thatcher, R. W. (1998). Normative EEG databases and EEG biofeedback. *Journal of Neurotherapy, 2,* 8–39.

Thelen, E. (1998). Berstein's legacy for motor development: How infants learn to reach. In M. L. Latash (Ed.), *Progress in motor control. Vol. 1: Bernstein's traditions in movement studies* (pp. 267–288). Champaign, IL: Human Kinetics.

Thienemann, M. (1998). Toilet training, enuresis, and encopresis. In H. Steiner (Ed.), *Treating preschool children* (pp. 83–112). San Francisco, CA: Jossey-Bass.

Thomas, A., & Chess, S. (1980). *The dynamics of psychological development.* New York: Brunner/Mazel.

Thomas, A., Chess, S., & Birch, H. (1968). *Temperament and behavior disorders in children.* New York: New York University Press.

Thompson, A. D. (1999). Perceived social support and adult attachment styles: Relationship with view of self, view of others, and helping tendencies. *Disseration Abstracts International, 60*(6), 3022B. (University Microfilms No. AAI99–33017)

Thompson, L. A., & Fagan, J. F. (1991). Longitudinal prediction of specific cognitive abilities from infant novelty preference. *Child Development, 62,* 530–538.

Thompson, R. A. (1999). The individual child: Temperament, emotion, self, and personality. In M. H. Bornstein & M. E. Lamb (Eds.), *Developmental psychology: An advanced textbook* (pp. 377–411). Mahwah, NJ: Erlbaum.

Thorn, A. S. C., & Gathercole, S. E. (1999). Language-specific knowledge and short-term memory performance in bilingual and non-bilingual children. *Quarterly Journal of Experimental Psychology, 52A,* 303–324.

Thornberry, T. P. (1998). Membership in youth gangs and involvement in serious and violent offending. In R. Loeber & D. P. Farrington (Eds.), *Serious and violent juvenile offenders: Risk factors and successful interventions* (pp. 147–166). Thousand Oaks, CA: Sage.

Thorne, B. (2001). Girls and boys together . . . But mostly apart: Gender arrangements in elementary schools. In R. Satow (Ed.), *Gender and social life* (pp. 153–166). Boston: Allyn & Bacon.

Thornton, M. C., Chatters, L. M., Taylor, R. J., & Allen, W. R. (1990). Sociodemographic and environmental correlates of racial socialization by black parents. *Child Development, 61,* 401–409.

Tincoff, R., & Jusczyk, P. W. (2000). Some beginnings of word comprehension in 6-month-olds. In D. Muir & A. Slater (Eds.), *Infant development: The essential readings. Essential readings in development psychology* (pp. 270–278). Malden, MA: Blackwell.

Tizard, B., & Rees, J. (1975). The effect of early institutional rearing on behaviour problems and affectional relationships of four-year-old children. *Journal of Child Psychology and Psychiatry and Allied Disciplines, 16,* 61–73.

Toda, S., Fogel, A., & Kawai, M. (1990). Maternal speech to three-month-old infants in the United States and Japan. *Journal of Child Language, 17,* 279–294.

Tomasello, M., & Merriman W. (Ed.). (1995). *Beyond names for things: Young children's acquisition of verbs* (pp. 377–404). Hillsdale, NJ: Erlbaum.

Tonkin, R. S. (1997). Evaluation of a summer camp for adolescents with eating disorders. *Journal of Adolescent Health, 20,* 412–413.

Torrance, E. P. (1962). Education and creativity. In C. W. Taylor (Ed.), *Creativity: Progress and potential.* New York: McGraw-Hill.

Towell, D. (1997). Promoting a better life for people with learning disabilities and their families: A practical agenda for the new government. *British Journal of Learning Disabilities, 25,* 90–94.

Townsend, B. L. (1998). Social friendships and networks among African American children and youth. In L. H. Meyer, H. S. Park, M. Grenot-Scheyer, I. S. Schwartz, & B. Harry, (Eds.), *Making friends: The influences of culture and development* (pp. 225–242). Baltimore: Paul H. Brookes.

Travis, J. (2000). Work reaches milestone. *Science News, 158,* 4–6.

Trehub, S. E., Schneider, B. A., Thorpe, L. A., & Judge, P. (1991). Observational measures of auditory sensitivity in early infancy. *Developmental Psychology, 27,* 40–49.

Tremble, B., Schneider, M., & Appathurai, C. (1989). Growing up gay or lesbian in multicultural context. *Journal of Homosexuality, 17,* 253–267.

Triandis, H. C. (1997). A cross-cultural perspective on social psychology. In C. McGarty & S. A. Haslam (Eds.), *The message of social psychology: Perspectives on mind in society* (pp. 342–351). Oxford, England: Blackwell Publishers.

Trickett, P. K., Aber, J. L., Carlson, V., & Cicchetti, D. (1991). Relationship of socioeconomic status to the etiology and developmental sequelae of physical child abuse. *Developmental Psychology, 27,* 148–158.

Troiden, R. R. (1989). The formation of homosexual identities. *Journal of Homosexuality, 17,* 43–73.

Tronick, E .A. (1989). Emotions and emotional communication in infants. *American Psychologist, 44,* 112–119.

Tronick, E. A., Morelli, G., & Ivey, P. (1992). The Efe forager infant and toddler's pattern of social relationships: Multiple and simultaneous. *Developmental Psychologist, 28,* 568–577.

Troseth, G. L., & DeLoache, J. S. (1998). The medium can obscure the message: Young children's understanding of video. *Child Development, 69,* 950–965.

Trudge, J., & Rogoff, B. (1999). Peer influences on cognitive development: Piagetian and Vygotskian perspectives. In P. Llyod & C. Fernyhough (Eds.), *Lev Vygotsky: Critical assessment: The zone of proximal development* (pp. 32–56). New York: Routledge.

Trull, T. J., & Geary, D. C. (1997). Comparison of the Big-Five factor across samples of Chinese and American adults. *Journal of Personality Assessment, 69,* 324–341.

Trusty, J., Watts, R. E., & Erdman, P. (1997). Predictors of parents' involvement in their teens' career development. *Journal of Career Development, 23*(3), 189–201.

Tucker, C. M. (1999). *African American children: A self-empowerment approach to modifying behavior problems and preventing academic failure.* Boston: Allyn & Bacon.

Tucker, C. M., Harris, V. R., Brady, B. A., & Herman, K. C. (1996). The association of selected parent behaviors with the academic achievement of African-American children and European American children. *Child Study Journal, 26*(4), 253–277.

Tucker, J. A. (1998). Preventing alcohol problems. In E. A. Blechman & K. D. Brownell (Eds.), *Behavioral medicine and women* (pp. 238–245). New York: Guilford Press.

Tuckman, B. W. (1999). The effects of exercise on children and adolescents. In A. J. Gorczny & M. Hersen (Eds.), *Handbook of pediatric and adolescent health psychology* (pp. 275–286). Boston: Allyn & Bacon.

Tudge, J. R. H., Hogan, D. M., Snezhkova, I. A., Kulakova, N. N., & Etz, K. E. (2000). Parents' child-rearing beliefs in the United States and Russia: The impact of culture and social class. *Infant and Child Development, 9,* 105–121.

Tuohy, G. (2000). Digital revolution. *Modern Physician, 4,* 56–58.

Turkheimer, E., & Waldron, M. (2000). Nonshared environment: A theoretical, methodological, and quantitative review. *Psychological Bulletin, 126,* 78–108.

Underwood, M. K. (1997). Peer social status and children's understanding of the expression and control of positive and negative emotions. *Merrill Palmer Quarterly, 43,* 610–634.

United Nations. (1991). *Women: Challenges to the year 2000.* New York: Author.

United Nations International Children's Emergency Fund. (1995). *The state of the world's children: 1995.* New York: Oxford University Press.

Urberg, K. A. (1999). Introduction to invitational issue: Some thoughts about studying the influences of peers on children and adolescents. *Merrill-Palmer Quarterly, 45,* 1–13.

Urberg, K. A., Degirmencioclu, S. M., & Pilgrim, C. (1997). Close friend and group influence on adolescent cigarette smoking, and alcohol use. *Developmental Psychology, 33,* 834–844.

U.S. Bureau of the Census. (1996). *Statistical abstract of the United States, 1996* (116th ed.). Washington, DC: Government Printing Office.

U.S. Bureau of the Census. (1997). *Current Population Reports,* (Series P, 20). No. 413, School enrollment—social and economic characteristics of students. Washington, DC: U.S. Government Printing Office.

U.S. Bureau of the Census. (1998). *Statistical abstract of the United States, 1998.* Washington, DC: U.S. Government Printing Office.

U.S. Bureau of the Census. (1999). Child support for custodial mothers and fathers. In *Current population reports* (Series P, 60–187). Washington, DC: U.S. Government Printing Office.

U.S. Department of Commerce. (1995). *Statistical abstract of the United States, 1994.* Washington, DC: U.S. Government Printing Office.

U.S. Department of Education. (1999). *America 2000: An education strategy.* Washington, DC: U.S. Government Printing Office.

Valente, E., & Dodge, K. A. (1997). Evaluations of preventative programs for children. In R. P. Wissberg & T. P. Gullotta (Eds.), *Healthy children 2010: Establishing preventive services. Issues in children's and families' lives.* Thousand Oaks, CA: Sage.

Valkenburg, P. M., & Janssen, S. C. (1999). What do children value in entertainment programs? A cross-cultural investigation. *Journal of Communication, 49,* 3–21.

Vallano, G., & Slomka, G. T. (1998). Attention-deficit hyperactivity disorder. In R. T. Ammerman & J. V. Campo (Eds.), *Handbook of Pediatric Psychology & Psychiatry* (pp. 227–247). Boston: Allyn & Bacon.

Vallerand, R. J., Fortier, M. S., & Guay, F. (1997). Self-determination and persistence in real-life setting: Toward a motivational model of high school dropout. *Journal of Personality and Social Psychology, 72*(5), 1161–1176.

Van Balen, F., Verdurmen, J., & Ketting, E. (1997). Choices and motivations for infertile couples. *Patient Education and Counseling, 31,* 19–27.

Van Dam, M., & van IJzendoorn, M. H. (1990). *Are infants of working mothers insecurely attached?* Leiden: Center for Child and Family Studies.

Vandenberg, B. (1998). Real and not real: A vital developmental dichotomy. In O. N. Saracho & B. Spodek (Eds.), *Multiple perspectives on play in early childhood education* (pp. 295–305). Albany, NY: University of New York Press.

Van Dongen-Melman, J.E.W.M., Koot, H. N., & Verhulst, F. C. (1993). Cross-cultural validation of Harter's self-perception profile for children in a Dutch sample. *Educational and Psychological Measurement, 53,* 739–753.

Van Evra, J. P. (1998). *Television and child development.* Mahwah, NJ: Erlbaum.

Van IJzendoorn, M. H., Juffer, F., & Duyvesteyn, M. G. C. (1995). Breaking the intergenerational cycle of insecure attachment: A review of the effects of attachment-based interventions on maternal sensitivity and infant security. *Journal of Child Psychology and Psychiatry, 36,* 225–248.

Van IJzendoorn, M. H., & Kroonenbert, P. M. (1988). Cross-cultural patterns of attachment: A meta-analysis of the strange situation. *Child Development, 59,* 147–156.

Van Lieshout, C. F. M., Cillessen, A. H. N., & Haselager, G. J. T. (1999). Interpersonal support and individual development. In W. A. Collins & B. Laursen (Eds.), *Relationships as developmental contexts. The Minnesota Symposia on Child Psychology* (pp. 37–60). Mahwah, NJ: Erlbaum.

Van Stegeren, A. H., Everaerd, W., Cahill, L., McGaugh, J. L., & Gooren, L. J. G. (1998). Memory for emotional events: Differential effects of centrally versus peripherally acting beta-blocking agents. *Psychopharmacology, 138,* 305–310.

Vartanian, L. R. (1997). Separation-individuation, social support, and adolescent egocentrism: An exploratory study. *Journal of Early Adolescence, 17,* 245–257.

Vartanian, L. R., & Powlishta, K. K. (1996). A longitudinal examination of the social–cognitive foundations of adolescent egocentrism. *Journal of Early Adolescence, 16,* 157–178.

Vasquez-Nuttal, E., Romero-Garcia, I., & De Leon, B. (1987). Sex roles and perceptions of femininity and masculinity of Hispanic women: A review of the literature. *Psychology of Women Quarterly, 11,* 409–425.

Veatch, T. C. (1998). A theory of humor. *Humor: International Journal of Humor Research, 11,* 161–215.

Vega, W. A. (1995). The study of Latino families. In R. E. Zambrana (Ed.), *Understanding Latino families* (p. 1017). Thousand Oaks, CA: Sage.

Vereijken, C.M.J.L., Riksen-Walraven, J. M., & Van Lieshout, C. F. M. (1997). Mother–infant relationships in Japan: Attachment, dependency, and amae. *Journal of Cross-Cultural Psychology, 28,* 442–462.

Vernon, P. A. (1997). Behavioral genetic and biological approaches to intelligence. In H. Nyborg (Ed.), *The scientific study of human nature: Tribute to Hans J. Eysenck at eighty* (pp. 240–258). Oxford, England UK: Pergamon/Elsevier Science.

Veroff, J., Douvan, E., & Kulka, R. A. (1981). *Mental health in America: Patterns of help-seeking from 1957–1976.* New York: Basic Books.

Veron-Guidry, S., Williamson, D. A., & Netemeyer, R. G. (1997). Structural modeling analysis of body dysphoria and eating disorder symptoms in preadolescent girls. *Eating Disorders Journal of Treatment and Prevention, 5*(1), 15–27.

Viemero, V., & Paajanen, S. (1990). The role of fantasies and dreams in the TV viewing-aggression relationship. *Aggressive Behavior, 18,* 109–116.

Vik, P., & Brown, S. A. (1998). Life events and substance abuse during adolescence. In T. W. Miller (Ed.), *Children of trauma: Stressful life events and their effects on children and adolescents. International Universities Press stress and health series. Monograph 8* (pp. 179–204). Madison, CT: International Universities Press.

Vikan, A., & Claussen, C. J. (1994). *Barns oppfatninger (Children's perception).* Oslo, Norway: Universitetsforlaget.

Vinden, P. G. (1996). Junin Quecha children's understanding of mind. *Child Development, 67,* 1707–1716.

Vinden, P. G. (1999). Children's understanding of mind and emotion: A multi-culture study. *Cognition and Emotion, 13,* 19–48.

Visscher, W. D., Bray, R. M., & Kroutil, L. A. (1999). Drug use and pregnancy. In R. M. Bray & M. E. Marsden (Eds.), *Drug use in metropolitan America* (pp. 235–265). Thousand Oaks, CA: Sage.

Vogel, E. F. (1996). Japan's old time new middle class. In D. W. Shwalb & B. J. Shwalb (Eds.), *Japanese childrearing: Two generations of scholarship* (pp. 201–207). New York: Guilford Press.

Vogel, S. H. (1996). Urban middle-class Japanese family life, 1958–1996: A personal and evolving perspective. In D. W. Shwalb & B. J. Shwalb (Eds.), *Japanese childrearing* (pp. 177–200). New York: Guilford Press.

Vogt, C. J. (1999). A model of risk factors involved in childhood and adolescent obesity. In A. J. Gorcezny & M. Hersen (Eds.), *Handbook of pediatric and adolescent health psychology* (pp. 221–234). Boston: Allyn & Bacon.

Von der Lippe, A. L. (1998). Are conflict and challenge sources of personality development? Ego development and family communication. In E. E. A. Skoe & A. L. von der Lippe (Eds.), *Personality development in adolescence: A cross national and life span perspective* (pp. 38–60). New York: Routledge.

Vygotsky, L. (1962). *Thought and language.* (E. Hanfmann & G. Vakar, Trans.). Cambridge, MA: MIT Press.

Vygotsky, L. (1978). *Mind in society: The development of higher psychological processes.* Cambridge, MA: Harvard University Press.

Vygotsky, L. (1994). Imagination and creativity of the adolescent. In R. van der Veer & J. Valsiner (Eds.), *The Vygotsky reader.* Cambridge, MA: Blackwell.

Wachs, T. (1992). *The nature of nurture.* Beverly Hills, CA: Sage.

Wachs, T., & King, B. (1995). Behavioral research in the brave new world of neuroscience and temperament: A guide to the biologically perplexed. In J. E. Bates & T. D. Wachs (Eds.), *Temperament: Individual differences at the interface of biology and behavior* (pp. 307–336). Washington, DC: American Psychological Association.

Wachtel, P. L. (1999). *Race in the mind of America: Breaking the vicious circle between blacks and whites.* New York: Routledge.

Waddington, C. H. (1968). *Principles of development and differentiation.* New York: Macmillan.

Wagner, B. M. (1997). Family risk factors for child and adolescent suicidal behavior. *Psychological Bulletin, 121*(2), 246–298.

Wagner, B. M., Cole, R. E., & Schwartzman, P. (1995). Psychosocial correlates of suicide attempts among junior and senior high school youth. *Suicide and Life Threatening Behavior, 25*(3), 358–372.

Wagner, R. F., & Wells, K. A. (1985). A refined neurobehavioral inventory of hemispheric preference. *Journal of Clinical Psychology, 41,* 672–673.

Wagner, R. K., & Torgesen, J. K. (1997). The nature of phonological processing and its causal role in the acquisition of reading skills. *Psychological Bulletin, 101,* 192–212.

Wakschlag, L. S., Lahey, B. B., Loeber, R., Green, S. M., Gordon, R. A., & Leventhal, B. L. (1997). Maternal smoking during pregnancy and the risk of conduct disorder in boys. *Archives of General Psychiatry, 54,* 670–676.

Walco, G. A. (1997). Growing pains. *Journal of Developmental and Behavioral Pediatrics, 18,* 107–109.

Walden, T. A., & Field, T. M. (1990). Preschool children's social competence and production and discrimination of affective expressions. *British Journal of Developmental Psychology, 8,* 65–76.

Walker, L. J. (1997). Is morality gendered in early parent–child relationships? *Merrill-Palmer Quarterly, 43,* 148–159.

Walker, L. J., & Taylor, J. H. (1991). Family interactions and the development of moral reasoning. *Child Development, 62,* 264–283.

Walker, S. Y. (1991). *The survival guide for parents of gifted children.* Minneapolis: Free Spirit Publishing.

Walkins, R. V., & Bunce, B. H. (1996). National literacy: Theory and practice for preschool intervention programs. *Topics in Early Childhood Special Education, 16,* 191–212.

Wallace, B. A., Serafica, F. C., & Osipow, S. H. (1994). Adolescent career development: Relationships to self-concept and identity status. *Journal of Research Adolescence, 4,* 127–149.

Wallerstein, J. S. (1998). Children of divorce: A society in search of policy. In M. A. Mason, A. Skolnick, & S. D. Sugarman (Eds.), *All our families: New policies for a century* (pp. 66–94). New York: Oxford University Press.

Wallerstein, J. S., & Corbin, S. B. (1999). The child and the vicissitudes of divorce. In R. M. Galatzer-Levy & L. Kraus (Eds.), *The scientific basis of child custody decisions* (pp. 73–95). New York: Wiley.

Wallis, C. (1994, July 18). Life in overdrive. *Time.*

Wang, P. P., & Baron, M. A. (1997). Language: A code for communicating. In M. L. Batshaw (Ed.), *Children with disabilities* (pp. 275–292). Baltimore: Paul H. Brookes.

Wang, V., & Marsh, F. H. (1992). Ethical principles and cultural integrity in health care delivery: Asian ethnocultural perspectives. *Journal of Genetic Counseling, 1,* 81–92.

Ward, L. M., & Greenfield, P. M. (1998). Designing experiments on television and social behavior: developmental perspectives. In J. K. Asamen & G. L. Berry (Eds.), *Research paradigms, televisions, and social behavior* (pp. 67–108). Thousand Oaks, CA: Sage.

Ward, S., Levinson, D., & Wackman, D. (1992). Children's attention to television commercials. In E. Rubinstein, G. Comstock, & J. Murray (Eds.), *Television and social behavior. 4. Television in day-to-day life: Patterns of use.* Washington, DC: U.S. Government Printing Office.

Warren, A. R., & Tate, C. S. (1992). Egocentrism in children's telephone conversations. In R. M. Diaz & L. E. Berk (Eds.), *Private speech: From social interaction to self-regulation* (pp. 245–264). Hillsdale, NJ: Erlbaum.

Wartner, U. G., Grossman, K., Fremmer-Bombik, E., & Suess, G. (1994). Attachment patterns at age six in south Germany: Predictability from infancy and implications for preschool behavior. *Child Development, 65,* 1014–1027.

Washington, A. C. (1992). A cultural and historical perspective on pregnancy-related activity among U.S. teenagers. *Journal of Black Psychology, 9,* 1–28.

Wasik, B. H., Ramey, C. T., Bryant, D. M., & Sparling, J. J. (1990). A longitudinal study of two early intervention strategies: Project CARE. *Child Development, 61,* 1682–1696.

Waters, E., & Deane, K. E. (1985). Defining and assessing individual differences in attachment relationships: Q-methodology and the organization of behavior in infancy and early childhood. In I. Bretherton & E. Waters (Eds.), Growing points in attachment theory and research (pp. 39–40). *Monographs of the Society for Research in Child Development, 50* (1–2, Serial No. 209).

Waterson, E. J., & Murray-Lyon, I. M. (1990). Preventing alcohol related birth damage: A review. *Social Science Medicine, 30,* 349–364.

Watkins, D., & Akande, A. (1992). The internal structure of the self-description questionnaire: A Nigerian investigation. *British Journal of Educational Psychology, 62,* 120–125.

Watkins, D., & Dahlin, B. (1997). Assessing study approaches in Sweden. *Psychological Reports, 81,* 131–136.

Watson, J. B. (1914). *Behavior: An introduction to comparative psychology.* New York: Holt.

Watson, J. B. (1928). *Psychological care of infant and child.* New York: W. W. Norton.

Watson, J. B, & Crick, F. H. (1953). Molecular structure of nucleic acids: A structure for deoxyribonucleic acid. *Nature, 171,* 737–738.

Waxman, S. R., & Kosowski, T. D. (1990). Nouns mark category relations: Toddlers and preschoolers' word-learning biases. *Child Development, 61,* 1461–1473.

Way, N. (2001, April 19–22). *Friendship patterns among Asian American, African American, and Latino adolescents.* Paper presented at the biennial meeting of the Society for Research in Child Development, Minneapolis.

Webster-Stratton, C. (1992). *The incredible years.* Toronto: Umbrella Press.

Wehrfritz, G. (1996). Joining the party. *Newsweek.* April 1, 46, 48.

Weinberg, K. (1989). *The relation between facial expressions of emotion and behavior in 6-month-old infants.* Unpublished master's thesis. Amherst, MA: University of Massachusetts.

Weinfield, N. S., Ogawa, J. R., & Sroufe, L. A. (1997). Early attachment as a pathway to adolescent peer competence. *Journal of Research on Adolescence, 7,* 241–265.

Weinraub, M., & Gringlas, M. B. (1995). Single parenthood. In M. H. Bornstein (Ed.), *Handbook on parenting* (pp. 65–88). Hillsdale, NJ: Erlbaum.

Weis, L., & Fine, M. (1993). *Beyond silenced voices.* Albany, NJ: State University of New York Press.

Weisfeld, G. (1997). Puberty rites as clues to the nature of human adolescence. *Cross-Cultural Research the Journal of Comparative Social Science, 31,* 27–54.

Weisz, V., & Tomkins, A. J. (1996). The right to a family environment for children with disabilities. *American Psychologist,* 1239–1245.

Welles, N. B. (1997). The meaning of postponed motherhood for women in the United States and Sweden: Aspects of feminism and radical timing strategies. *Health Care for Women International, 18,* 279–299.

Wellman, H. W. (1990). *The child's theory of mind.* Cambridge, MA: MIT Press.

Wellman, H. W. (1993). Early understanding of mind: The normal case. In S. Baron-Cohen, H. Tager-Flusberg, & D. Cohen (Eds.), *Understanding other minds* (pp. 10–39). New York: Oxford University Press.

Wellman, H. W. (1998). Culture, variation, and levels of analysis in folk psychologies: comment on Lillard. *Psychological Bulletin, 123,* 33–36.

Wellman, H. W., & Banerjee, M. (1991). Mind and emotion: Children's understanding of the emotional consequences of beliefs and desires. *British Journal of Developmental Psychology, 9,* 191–214.

Wellman, H. W., & Gelman, S. A. (1992). Cognitive development: Foundational theories of core domains. *Annual Review of Psychology, 43,* 337–375.

Werker, J. F., Lloyd, V. L., Pegg, J. E., & Polka, L. (1996). Putting the baby in the bootstraps: Toward a more complete understanding of the role of input in infant speech processing. In J. L. Morgan & K. Demuth (Eds.), *Signal to syntax: Bootstrapping from speech to grammar in early acquisition* (pp. 427–447). Mahwah, NJ: Erlbaum.

Werner, E. E. (1995). Resilience in development. *Current Directions in Psychological Science,* 81–85.

Wessels, H., Lamb, M. E., Hwang, C. P., & Broberg, A. G. (1997). Personality development between 1 and 8 years of age in Swedish children with varying child care experiences. *International Journal of Behavioral Development, 21,* 771–794.

West, P., & Michell, L. (1999). Smoking and peer influence. In A. J. Goreczny & M. Hersen, (Eds.), *Handbook of pediatric and adolescent health psychology* (pp. 179–202). Boston: Allyn & Bacon.

Weymann, A. (1999). From education to employment: Occupations and careers in the social transformation of East Germany. In W. R. Heinz (Ed.), *From education to work: Cross-national perspectives* (pp. 87–108). New York: Cambridge University Press.

Whaley, L. F., & Wong, D. L. (1991). *Nursing care of infants and children.* St. Louis: Mosby.

Wheaton, B. (1999). The nature of stressors. In A. V. Horwitz & L. T. Scheid (Eds.), *A handbook for the study of mental health: Social contexts, theories, and systems* (pp. 176–197). New York: Cambridge University Press.

Whitaker, R. C., Wright, J. A., Pepe, M. S., Seidel, K. D., & Dietz, W. H. (1997). Predicting obesity in young adulthood from childhood and parental obesity. *New England Journal of Medicine, 337,* 869–873.

White, M. J., & Kaufman, G. (1997). Language usage, social capital, and school completion among immigrants and native-born ethnic groups. *Social Science Quarterly, 78,* 385–398.

White, S. A., Duda, J. L., & Keller, M. R. (1998). The relationship between goal orientation and perceived purposes of sport among young sport participants. *Journal of Sport Behavior, 21,* 474–483.

Whitehurst, G. J., Arnold, D. H., Epstein, J. N., Angell, A. L., Smith, M., & Fischel, J. E. (1994). A picture book reading intervention in daycare and home for children from low-income families. *Developmental Psychology, 30,* 679–689.

Whitehurst, G. J., & Lonigan, C. J. (1998). Child development and emergent literacy. *Child Development, 69*, 848–872.

Whiting, J., & Whiting, B. (1975). *Children of six cultures.* Cambridge, MA: Harvard University Press.

Whitman, T. L., White, R. D., O'Mara, K. M., & Goeke-Morey, M. C. (1999). Environmental aspects of infant health and illness. In T. L. Whitman & T. V. Merluzzi (Eds.), *Life-span perspectives on health and illness* (pp. 105–124). Mahwah, NJ: Erlbaum.

Widener, A. J. (1998). Beyond Ritalin: The importance of therapeutic work with parents and children diagnosed ADD/ADHD. *Journal of Child Psychotherapy, 24*, 267–281.

Wiegman, O., & van Schie, E. G. M. (1998). Video game playing and its relations with aggressive and prosocial behaviour. *British Journal of Social Psychology, 37*, 367–378.

Wiener, L. S., & Taylor-Brown, S. (1998). Services for children and families. In D. M. Aronstein, & B. J. Thompson (Eds.), *HIV and social work: A practitioner's guide.* New York: Harrington Park Press.

Wigfield, A., Eccles, J., Mac Iver, D., Reuman, D., & Midgley, C. (1991). Transitions during early adolescence: Changes in children's domain-specific self-perceptions and general self-esteem across the transition to junior high school. *Developmental Psychology, 27*, 552–565.

Wilcox, A., Weinberg, C., & Baird, D. (1995). Timing of sexual intercourse in relation to ovulation. Effects on the probability of conception, survival of the pregnancy, and sex of the baby. *New England Journal of Medicine, 333*, 1517–1521.

Wilcox, M. (1993). Partner-based prelinguistic intervention: A preliminary report. *Office of Special Education and Rehabilitative Services: News in Print, 5*, 4–9.

Wiley, A. R., Rose, A. J., Burger, L. K., & Miller, P. J. (1998). Constructing autonomous selves through narrative practices: A comparative study of working-class and middle-class families. *Child Development, 69*, 833–847.

Wilgosh, L., Meyer, M., & Mueller, H. H. (1995). Longitudinal study of effects on academic achievement for early and late age of school entry. *Canadian Journal of School Psychology, 11*, 43–51.

Wille, D. E. (1998). Longitudinal analysis of mothers' and fathers' responses on the maternal separation anxiety scale. *Merrill-Palmer Quarterly, 44*(2), 216–233.

Williams, D. R. (1992). Black–white differences in blood pressure: The role of social factors. *Ethnicity and Disease, 2*, 125–141.

Williams, J. E., & Best, D. L. (1994). Cross-cultural views of men and women. In W. J. Lonner & R. S. Malpass (Eds.), *Psychology and Culture.* Needham, MA: Allyn & Bacon.

Williams, J. W., & Stith, M. (1980). *Middle childhood: Behavior and development.* New York: Macmillan.

Williams, W. (1998). Are we raising smarter kids today? School- and home-related influences on IQ. In U. Neisser (Ed.), *The rising curve: Long-term gains in IQ and related measures* (pp. 125–154). Washington, DC: American Psychological Association.

Willinger, M., Hoffman, H. J., & Hartford, R. B. (1994). Infant sleep position and risk for sudden infant death syndrome: Report of meeting held January 13 and 14, 1994, National Institutes of Health, Bethesda, MD. *Pediatrics, 93*, 814–819.

Wilson, B. J., & Gottman, J. M. (1995). Marital interaction and parenting. In M. H. Bornstein (Ed.), *Handbook on parenting* (pp. 33–56). Hillsdale, NJ: Erlbaum.

Wilson, G. S. (1989). Clinical studies of infants exposed prenatally to heroine. In D. E. Hutchings (Ed.), *Prenatal abuse of licit and illicit drugs* (Vol. 562, pp. 183–194). New York: Annals of the New York Academy of Sciences.

Wilson, R. S. (1983). The Louisville twin study: Developmental synchronies in behavior. *Child Development, 54*, 298–316.

Wilson, R. S., & Matheny, A. P. (1986). Behavior-genetics research in infant temperament: The Louisville twin study. In R. Plomin & J. Dunn (Eds.), *The study of temperament: Changes, continuities, and challenges.* Hillsdale, NJ: Erlbaum.

Wing, L. (1990). Diagnosis of autism. In C. Gillberg (Ed.), *Autism: Diagnosis and treatment.* New York: Plenum Press.

Winner, E., Kaplan, J., & Rosenblatt, E. (1989, April). *Discrimination and interpretation of metaphor and irony: Evidence for a dissociation.* Paper presented at the meeting of the Society for Research in Child Development, Kansas City, MO.

Winner, H., & Sullivan, K. (1993, March). *Young 3-year-olds' understanding of false belief when observing or participating in deception.* Poster session presented at the biennial meeting of the Society for Research in Child Development, New Orleans, LA.

Winsler, A., Diaz, R. M., Espinosa, L., & Rodriguez, J. L. (1999). When learning a second language does not mean losing the first: Bilingual language development in low-income, Spanish-speaking children attending bilingual preschool. *Child Development, 70*, 349–362.

Winters, K. C., Latimer, W. L., & Stinchfield, R. D. (1999). Adolescent treatment. In P. J. Ott, R. E. Tarter, & R. T. Ammerman (Eds.), *Sourcebook on substance abuse: Etiology, epidemiology, assessment, and treatment* (pp. 350–361). Boston: Allyn & Bacon.

Wisnicwski, L., & Marcus, M. C. (1999). Childhood obesity. In V. B. Van Masselt & M. Hersen (Eds.), *Handbook of psychological treatment protocols for children and adolescents* (pp. 179–201). Mahwah, NJ: Erlbaum.

Witkowski, T. (1997). Performance level in situations of helplessness threat and group affiliation: Egotistic mechanisms in helplessness deficits. *Journal of Social Psychology, 137*, 229–234.

Witt, S. D. (1997). Parental influence on children's socialization to gender roles. *Adolescence, 32*, 253–259.

Wo, J., Shen, J., & Lin, C. (1997). Sources of age differences at stages of information processing. *Psychological Science, 20*, 13–118.

Wolf, A. M., Gortmaker, S. L., Cheung, L., & Gray, H. M. (1993). Activity, inactivity, and obesity: Racial, ethnic, and age differences among schoolgirls. *American Journal of Public Health, 83*, 1625–1627.

Wolf, A. W., Lozoff, B., Latz, S., & Paludetto, R. (1996). Parental theories in the management of sleep routines in Japan, Italy, and the United States. In S. Harkness & C. M. Super (Eds.), *Parents' cultural belief systems* (pp. 364–385). New York: Guilford.

Wolfe, D. A., Wekerle, C., Reitzel-Jaffe, D., & Lefebvre, L. (1998). Factors associated with abusive relationships among maltreated and nonmaltreated youth. *Developmental Psychopathology, 10*, 61–85.

Wolfe, P., & Brandt, R. (1998, November). What do we know from brain research? *Educational Leadership*, 8–13.

Wolfson, A. R. (1996). Sleeping patterns of children and adolescents: Developmental trends, disruptions, and adaptations. *Child and Adolescent Psychiatric Clinics of North America, 5*, 549–568.

Wolfson, A. R., & Carskadon, M. A. (1998). Sleep schedules and daytime functioning in adolescents. *Child Development, 69*, 875–887.

Wong, E. K. N. (1999). An examination of multiple variables of teenage suicide in a general adolescent population. *Dissertation Abstracts International, 59*, The Sciences and Engineering.

Wood, D., Flower, P., & Black, D. (1998). Should parents take charge of their child's eating disorder? Some preliminary findings and suggestions for future research. *International Journal of Psychiatry in Clinical Practice, 2*, 295–301.

Woods, B. T., & Rosenstein, L. D. (1998). Brain and behavioral development. In E. A. Blechman & K. D. Brownell (Eds)., *Behavioral medicine and women* (pp. 20–26). New York: Guilford Press.

Woods, N. S., Eyler, F. S., Behnke, M., & Conlon, M. (1993). Cocaine use during pregnancy: Maternal depressive symptoms and infant neurobehavior over the first month. *Infant Behavior and Development, 16*, 83–98.

Woolfson, R. (1972). Language, thought, and culture. In V. P. Clark, P. A. Escholz, & A. F. Rosa (Eds.), *Language* (p. 4). New York: St. Martin's Press.

Worden, J. W., Davies, B., & McCown, D. (1999). Comparing parent loss with sibling loss. *Death Studies, 23*, 1–15.

Work, W. C., Parker, G. R., & Cowen, E. L. (1990). The impact of life stressors on childhood adjustment: Multiple perspectives. *Journal of Community Psychology, 18,* 73–78.

World Health Organization. (1995). *World health statistics annual.* 1994. Author.

Worley, L. P. (1995). Working adolescents: Implications for counselors. *School Counselor, 42*(3), 218–223.

Wren, D. J. (1999). School culture: Exploring the hidden curriculum. *Adolescence, 34,* 593–596.

Wright, J. C., St. Peters, M., & Huston, A. C. (1990). Family television use and its relation to children's cognitive skills and social behavior. In J. Bryant (Ed.), *Television and the American family* (pp. 227–251). Hillsdale, NJ: Erlbaum.

Wright, W. (1999). *Born that way: Genes-behavior-personality.* New York: Knopf.

Wu, D. Y. H. (1992). Early childhood education in China. In S. Feeney (Ed.), *Early childhood education in Asia and the Pacific: A source book* (pp. 1–26). New York: Garland.

Wu, D. Y. H. (1996). Chinese childhood socialization. In M. H. Bond (Ed.), *The handbook of Chinese psychology* (pp. 143–154). Hong Kong: Oxford University Press.

Wulff, M. B., & Steitz, J. A. (1997). Curricular track, career choice, and androgyny among adolescent females. *Adolescence, 32,* 43–49.

Wyly, M. V. (1997). *Infant assessment.* Boulder, CO: Westview Press.

Xiao, H. (1999). Independence and obedience: An analysis of child socialization values in the United States and China. *Journal of Comparative Family Studies, 30,* 641–657.

Yamamoto, N., & Wallhagen, M. L. (1997). The continuation of family caregiving in Japan. *Journal of Health and Social Behavior, 38,* 164–176.

Yarnold, B. M. (1998). Peers and the body cult. *Psychological Reports, 82,* 19–24.

Yi, S. H., & Lee, S. E. (1997). Video game experience and children's abilities of self-control and visual information processing. *Korean Journal of Child Studies, 18,* 105–120.

Yi Qing, L. (1999). Personal communication.

Yoder, K. A. (1999). Comparing suicide attempters, suicide ideators, and nonsuicidal homeless and runaway adolescents. *Suicide and Life Threatening Behavior, 29,* 25–36.

Young, E. R., & Fouts, J. T. (1993). Field dependence/independence and the identification of gifted students. *Journal for the Education of the Gifted, 16,* 229–310.

Young, S., Young, B., & Ford, D. (1997). Parents with a learning disability: Research issues and informed practice. *Disability and Society, 12*(1), 57–68.

Youngblade, L. M., & Dunn, J. (1995). Individual differences in young children's pretend play with mother and sibling: Links to relationships and understanding of other people's feelings and beliefs. *Child Development, 66,* 1472–1492.

Youngblade, L. M., Thurling, S., Tapia, T., Ruiz, A., & Reed, S. (2001, April 19–22). *Attachment security, peer group acceptance, friendship quality, and conceptions of friendship: Direct and mediated connections.* Paper presented at the biennial meeting of the Society for Research in Child Development, Minneapolis.

Yu, G. (1987). *The urban family in flux. New trends in Chinese marriage and the family.* Beijing: Women of China.

Yuen-Tsang, A. W. K. (1999). Chinese communal support networks. *International Social Work, 42,* 359–372.

Zahn-Waxler, C., Friedman, R. J., Cole, P. M., & Mizuta, I. (1996). Japanese and United States preschool children's responses to conflict and distress. *Child Development, 67,* 2462–2477.

Zahn-Waxler, C., & McBride, A. (1998). Current perspectives on social and emotional development. In J. G. Adair & D. Belanger (Eds.), *Advances in psychological science* (pp. 513–546). Hove, England: Psychology Press/Erlbaum (UK).

Zakriski, A., Jacobs, M., & Coie, J. (1997). Coping with childhood peer rejection. In S. A. Wolchik & I. M. Sandler (Eds.), *Handbook of children's coping: Linking theory and intervention. Issues in clinical child psychology* (pp. 423–451). New York: Plenum.

Zaslow, M. J. (1989). Sex differences in children's response to parental divorce. Vol. 2: Samples, variables, ages, and sources. *American Journal of Orthopsychiatry, 59,* 118–140.

Zeidenstein, S., & Moore, K. (Eds.). (1996). Learning about sexuality: A practical beginning. New York: Population Council.

Zeig, J. K. (Ed.). (1997). *The evolution of psychotherapy: The third conference.* Philadelphia: Brunner/Mazel.

Zelazo, N. A., Zelazo, P. R., Cohen, K. M., & Zelazo, P. D. (1993). Specificity of practice effects on elementary neuromotor patterns. *Developmental Psychology, 29,* 686–691.

Zeman, J., Penza, S., Shipman, K., & Young, G. (1997). Preschoolers as functionalists: The impact of social context on emotion regulation. *Child Study Journal, 27,* 41–67. In C. H. Mindel, R. W. Habenstein, & R. Wright (Eds.), *Ethnic families in America: Patterns and variations* (pp. 173–193). New York: Elsevier.

Zhang, K., & Liao, F. (1998). La garde des jeunes enfants dans la Republique Populaire de China, *Enfance, 2,* 17–23.

Ziegler, E. (1998). School should begin at age 3 years for American children. *Journal of Developmental and Behavioral Pediatrics, 19,* 38–40.

Zigler, E. F., & Finn-Stevenson, M. (1999). Applied developmental psychology. In M. H. Bornstein & M. E. Lamb (Eds.), *Developmental psychology: An advanced textbook* (pp. 555–598). Mahwah, NJ: Erlbaum.

Zigler, E. F., & Styfco, S. J. (1998). Applying the findings of developmental psychology to improve early childhood intervention. In S. G. Paris & H. M. Wellman (Eds.), *Global prospects for education: Development, culture, and schooling* (pp. 345–365). Washington, DC: American Psychological Association.

Zitzow, D. (1990). Ojibway adolescent time spent with parents/elders as related to delinquency and court adjudication experiences. *American Indian and Alaska Native Mental Health Research, 4,* 53–63.

Ziv, M., & Frye, D. (2001, April 19–22). *Intention and outcome in children's theory of mind: Their application to deception.* Paper presented at the biennial meeting of the Society for Research in Child Development, Minneapolis.

Ziv, S. (1984). *Personality and sense of humor.* New York: Springer.

Zuckerman, M. (1994). *Behavioral expressions and biosocial bases of sensation seeking.* New York: Cambridge University Press.

Zuger, R. (1989). Homosexuality in families of boys with early effeminate behavior: An epidemiological study. *Archives of Sexual Behavior, 18,* 155–165.

PHOTO CREDITS

CHAPTER ONE

2: Courtesy of John U. Ogbu; **4:** Courtesy of Karen Owens; **7:** © Superstock; **8:** © Lawrence Migdale; **11:** AP/Wide World Photos; **14:** American Museum, Bath, Avon, UK/Bridgeman Art Library; **20:** Courtesy of Professor Benjamin Harris; **26:** © Laura Dwight; **30:** © Sean Spragne/Stock, Boston; **34:** © Mary Kate Denny/Photo Edit; **37:** © Dwayne Newton/Photo Edit

CHAPTER TWO

48: © Laura Dwight/Photo Edit; **51:** © Danny Lehman/CORBIS; **55:** © Jennie Woodcock-Reflections PhotoLibrary/CORBIS; **55:** © Michael S. Yamashita/CORBIS; **58:** © Elizabeth Crews; **64:** © Rhoda Sidney/Stock, Boston; **66:** © Superstock; **68:** © Will Hart/Photo Edit; **71:** © Taeke Henstra/Petit Format/Photo Researchers, Inc.; **72:** © Bill Bachman/The Image Works; **73:** © Robin L. Sachs/Photo Edit; **76:** © James Schaffer/Photo Edit

CHAPTER THREE

80: Courtesy of Robert Plomin; **82:** © Raoul Minsart/CORBIS; **88:** © Science Photo Library/Photo Researchers; **89:** © Laura Dwight; **91:** © Meckes/Ottawa/Photo Researchers, Inc.; **95:** STONE © MacNeal Hospital; **98:** © Ann Clark; **98:** © Ann Clark; **103:** © Bob Daemmrich/The Image Works; **107:** © Tony Freemann/Photo Edit

CHAPTER FOUR

114: STONE/Richard Shock; **122:** © David Young-Wolfe/Photo Edit; **127:** STONE/Christopher Amesen; **132:** © David Young-Wolfe/Photo Edit; **133:** © George Steinmetz; **137:** © Francis Leroy/Photo Researchers, Inc.; **139:** STONE/Yorgos Nikas; **141:** © Science Pictures Limited/CORBIS; **144:** © Lennart Nilsson/Albert Bonniers Forlag AB, A Child is Born; **145:** © Lawrence Migdale/Photo Researchers, Inc.

CHAPTER FIVE

154: Courtesy of Michael E. Lamb; **156:** © Elizabeth Crews; **162:** © Bronwyn Kidd/PhotoDisc, Inc.; **164:** © Nancy Sheehan/Photo Edit; **173:** © Iven DeVore/AnthroPhoto File; **175:** © Sotographs/Liaison Agency; **176:** © Elizabeth Crews; **179:** © Anna Lundgren/Superstock; **179:** © Enrico Ferorelli; **183:** © Bill Horsman/Stock, Boston; **186:** © Nubar Alexanian/Stock, Boston; **191:** © Myrleen Ferguson/Photo Edit

CHAPTER SIX

194: © www.comstock.com; **199:** © Laura Dwight; **203:** © Laura Dwight; **206:** © Rutgers University/Dr. Carolyn Royee-Collier, Department of Psychology, Busch campus; **207:** © Myrleen Ferguson Cate/Photo Edit; **215:** © Laura Dwight; **219:** © Alan Farnsworth/The Image Works; **221:** © Myrleen Ferguson/Photo Edit; **222:** © I. DeVore/AnthroPhoto File; **223:** © Owen Franken/CORBIS

CHAPTER SEVEN

226: STONE/Dale Durfee; **230:** © Jeff Greenberg/Photo Edit; **235:** © David R. Austen/Stock, Boston; **236:** © Mary Kate Denny/Photo Edit; **237:** Courtesy of Karen Owens; **242:** © Myrleen Ferguson Cate/Photo Edit; **245:** © Laura Dwight; **246:** © Michael Newman/Photo Edit; **249:** © Spencer Grant/Photo Edit; **260:** © Dorothy Littell Greco/Stock, Boston

CHAPTER EIGHT

264: Courtesy of K. Alison Clarke Stewart; **266:** © Paul Conklin/Photo Edit; **269:** © Merrritt Vincent/Photo Edit; **270:** © Elizabeth Crews; **277:** © Felicia Martinez/Photo Edit; **277:** © Robert Ginn/Photo Edit; **281:** © John Dewaele/Stock, Boston; **282:** © Laura Dwight; **283:** © Margaret Ross/Stock, Boston; **289:** © Myrleen Cate/Photo Edit; **291:** © J. Berndt/Stock, Boston; **294:** © Elizabeth Crews

CHAPTER NINE

298: © Elizabeth Crews; **307:** © Farrell Greehan/CORBIS; **307:** Archives of the History of American Psychology, University of Akron, Akron, Ohio; **308:** © Steven Rubin/The Image Works; **311:** © Lawrence Migdale/Stock, Boston; **320:** © Elizabeth Crews; **329:** © Laura Dwight; **332:** © Robert Rathe/Stock, Boston; **334:** © Elizabeth Crews; **335:** © Mary Kate Denny/Photo Edit

CHAPTER TEN

338: © CORBIS; **342:** © Clave Bryant/Photo Edit; **343:** © Joe Carini/Bear Productions/Pacific Stock; **346:** © Elizabeth Crews; **349:** © Elizabeth Crews; **351:** © Lawrence Migdale/Stock, Boston; **353:** © Tony Freeman/Photo Edit; **354:** © David Young-Wolff/Photo Edit; **360:** © Myrleen Cate/Photo Edit; **363:** © Elizabeth Crews; **371:** © Robert Eckert/Stock, Boston

CHAPTER ELEVEN

376: Courtesy of James Garbarino; **378:** © David Young-Wolff/Photo Edit; **381:** © Richard Hutchings/Photo Edit; **383:** © Phyllis Picardi/Stock, Boston; **389:** © Bob Daemmrich/Stock, Boston; **391:** © David Young-Wolff/Photo Edit; **392:** © Karen Su/Stock, Boston; **393:** © CORBIS; **394:** © Charles Gupton/Stock, Boston

CHAPTER TWELVE

412: © Myrleen Cate/Photo Edit; **418:** © Charles Gupton/Stock, Boston; **423:** © David Young-Wolff/Photo Edit; **426:** © Elena Rooraid/Photo Edit; **427:** © Monika Graff/The Image Works;

431: © Jonathan Nourak/Photo Edit; **434:** © Charles Gupton/Stock, Boston; **439:** © Michael Newman/Photo Edit; **443:** © Spencer Grant/Photo Edit; **447:** © Myrleen Ferguson/Photo Edit

CHAPTER THIRTEEN

454: © Richard Hutchings/Photo Edit; **458:** © Myrleen Cate/Photo Edit; **460:** © Mary Kate Denny/Photo Edit; **462:** © Will Hart/Photo Edit; **463:** © Bob Daemmrich/Stock, Boston; **465:** © Richard Hutchings/Photo Edit; **470:** © Spencer Grant/Photo Edit; **471:** © Bill Aron/Photo Edit; **478:** © Myrleen Ferguson/Photo Edit

CHAPTER FOURTEEN

488: Courtesy of Jeanne Brooks-Gunn; **490:** © Will Hart/Photo Edit; **495:** © Jeff Greenberg/Photo Edit; **499:** © Mary Kate Denny/Photo Edit; **505:** Courtesy of Karen Owens; **509:** © David Young-Wolff/Photo Edit; **512:** © Jeffry W. Myers/Stock, Boston; **514:** © Tom Pettyman/Photo Edit; **520:** © Michael Newman/Photo Edit; **521:** © Tony Freeman/Photo Edit

CHAPTER FIFTEEN

530: © Peter Cade/The Image Bank; **535:** © David Young-Wolff/Photo Edit; **539:** © Michael Newman/Photo Edit; **541:** © Jose Galvez/Photo Edit; **546:** © Spencer Grant/Photo Edit; **548:** © Bob Daemmrich/Stock, Boston; **550:** © Robert Brenner/Photo Edit; **551:** © David Young-Wolff/Photo Edit; **557:** © Michael Newman/Photo Edit; **562:** © Michael Newman/Photo Edit

CHAPTER SIXTEEN

568: © G & M David de Lossy/The Image Bank/Gettyone; **576:** © Deborah Davis/Photo Edit; **581:** © Alan Oddie/Photo Edit; **582:** © Dwayne Newton/Photo Edit; **585:** © Myrleen Cate/Photo Edit; **586:** © Spencer Grant/Photo Edit; **587:** © Shelley Gazin/CORBIS; **590:** © Jeff Greenberg/Photo Edit; **594:** © Mary Kate Denny/Photo Edit; **596:** AP/Wide World Photos; **599:** © David Young-Wolff/Photo Edit

NAME INDEX

Aaronson, L. S., 132
Aasheim, M., 593
Abel, E. L., 133
Aber, J. L., 372, 547, 548
Aboud, F. E., 504
Abraham, J., 221
Abramovitch, R., 598
Acker, D. B., 137
Ackerman, B. P., 360, 571
Ackerman, C. M., 443, 444
Adams, G. R., 504, 508, 570, 579, 597
Adams, M. J., 332
Adamson, L., 442
Adler, S. A., 166, 206
Adler, S. M., 392
Adolph, K. E., 169
Agnihotri, R. K., 321
Agras, W. S., 399, 401, 500
Agurell, S., 136
Ahadi, S. A., 253
Ahluwalia, J., 132
Ahmed, A., 201
Ahmeduzzaman, M., 393
Ahnert, L., 237
Aiken, L. R., 396
Ainsworth, M., 228–229, 230, 232, 234, 235, 236
Ajayi, J. F. A., 397
Akan, G. E., 572
Akande, A., 573
Alberoni, M., 385
Alberts, D. M., 328
Albertson-Kelly, J. A., 369
Alexander, C. S., 523
Allan, A. M., 134
Allan, J. D., 400, 401
Allen, B. P., 12–13
Allen, K. E., 274, 275, 276, 287
Allen, L., 560, 589
Allen, M., 247
Allen, P., 523
Allen, R., 496
Allen, W. R., 68, 72
Allison, A., 511
Allred, L. J., 504
Almeida, D. M., 582
Alstein, H., 70, 71
Altmaier, E., 501
Altschuler, J. L., 408
Amato, P. R., 260, 481, 482, 484
Ambrose, T. E., 363
Ames, L. B., 172
Ammerman, R. T., 134
Amoateng, A. Y., 482
Anandalaksmy, S., 54
Anastasi, A., 97, 107
Anders, T. F., 184
Anderson, D., 176
Anderson, E. R., 485
Anderson, G. C., 189
Anderson, J. R., 128
Anderson, M., 332
Anderson, M. M., 399, 509
Andreas, D., 208
Andrews, K., 527
Andujo, E., 70
Angelini, P. J., 514
Angell, A. L., 331
Angement, H., 591
Angen, M., 590
Anglin, M. D., 522
Anisfeld, E., 241
Ankomah, A., 126
Anson, A., 135
Anumolu, V., 161
Anzalone, M. K., 121
Apgar, V., 149
Appathurai, C., 510
Araujo, K., 506, 507
Arbreton, A. J. A., 496
Arbuckle, T., 123
Arcia, E., 32
Arcus, D., 463
Arendell, T., 485
Aries, E., 571, 572
Aries, P., 7
Armatas, C., 399
Armistead, L., 68, 129, 481
Arnett, J. J., 508
Arnold, D. H., 331
Arnold, M., 387
Arterberry, M. E., 178
Arthur, L. B., 574
Ary, D. V., 508
Asamen, J. K., 332
Asendorpf, J. B., 463, 469
Asher, S. R., 458, 460, 464, 465, 468, 469, 574, 575
Assaiante, C., 276
Astington, J. W., 313, 314, 315
Atillasoy, A., 128
Attanucci, J., 593
Attili, G., 464
Au, T. K., 219, 318
Aumiller, K., 465
Austin, E. W., 470
Averett, S. L., 255
Aviezer, D., 245
Aviezer, O., 239
Avis, J., 314
Axelrod, S., 236
Ayers, M., 574
Azar, S. T., 372, 373, 374
Azar, V., 439
Azmitia, M., 460, 461, 576, 598
Azuma, H., 54, 58, 59, 222, 316, 326, 365, 434
Azzarto, J., 516

Baak, K., 237
Bachman, J. G., 498, 524
Badenoch, M., 504
Bagwell, C. L., 467, 576
Baharudin, R., 439
Bahrick, L. E., 176
Bailey, A., 248
Bailey, C. E., 513
Bailey, G. W., 525
Bailey, J. M., 511
Baillargeon, J., 202
Baillargeon, R., 200, 201, 202
Baird, D., 138
Baird, G., 248
Bajaj, M., 54
Bakeman, R., 442
Baker, D., 461
Baker, J. H., 340
Bakermans-Kranenburg, M. J., 233
Bakke, I., 593
Bakker, C. E., 90
Balaban, M. T., 211, 463
Bandura, A., 21, 46, 349, 351, 354, 458, 570
Banerjee, M., 315
Bangert-Drowns, R. L., 428
Barenbaum, N. B., 480
Barker, G., 582, 586
Barker, M. E., 498
Barker, S. E., 500, 503
Barkley, R. A., 503
Barlow, D. H., 379
Barnat, S. B., 207
Barnett, D., 372
Barnett, W. S., 66
Barnhart, R., 522
Baron, M. A., 212
Baron-Cohen, S., 248
Bar-Or, O., 400, 401
Barr, H., 133, 134
Barr, H. M., 131, 135
Barret, J., 469
Barrett, J., 206, 211
Barrett, K. C., 35–36, 360, 361, 588
Barr-Zisowitz, C., 359
Barth, J., 334
Barth, J. M., 334
Barth, R. P., 71, 371, 373
Barton, M. E., 222
Base-Engquist, K., 519
Basow, S. A., 582
Bates, E., 182, 216, 220, 223, 449
Bates, J. E., 246, 369, 469, 471
Batgos, J., 571, 572
Bathurst, K., 221, 255, 256
Batshaw, M. L., 91, 92, 132, 133, 135, 151
Baumeister, R. F., 458
Baumgardner, T. L., 90
Baumrind, D., 101, 102, 367, 368, 369, 573, 599, 600
Baumwell, L., 223
Baur, A., 204
Baur, K., 507, 510
Bauserman, R. L., 584
Baydar, N., 257, 329, 514
Bayley, N., 168, 209
Beach, S. R. H., 236
Bear, G. G., 43
Beardsall, L., 316
Beaty, L. A., 511
Beaty, T. H., 137
Beauvais, F., 560
Becker, E., 210
Becker, G., 123
Becker, J. B., 496
Beckwith, L., 211, 223, 234
Bedi, A., 420
Beech, B. M., 394
Beekman, D., 7
Beeman, M., 321
Behen, M. E., 162, 383, 384
Behnke, M., 135, 189

Behrens, K., 59
Beitel, A., 334
Bell, C. C., 518
Bell, M. A., 268
Bell, R., 561
Bell, R. Q., 27
Bellenir, K., 90
Belsky, J., 229, 233, 236, 255
Bem, S. L., 358, 583, 584, 585, 586
Benda, B. B., 506, 508
Bender, D. L., 519
Bener, A., 447
Benker, J., 550
Bennett, B., 131
Bennett, E., 335
Benoit, D., 241
Benony, H., 234
Berendes, H. W., 131
Berenson, G. S., 401
Bergen, D., 450
Berger, S. H., 480
Berggren, N., 65
Bergstrom, L., 496
Berk, L. E., 343
Berk, L. S., 451
Berko, J., 318
Berko-Gleason, J., 318
Berman, K. F., 447
Berman, S., 221
Bernbaum, J. C., 151
Berndt, T. J., 504, 527, 576, 597
Bernhardt, E. M., 65
Berry, G. L., 332
Berry, J. W., 24, 344, 416, 465, 582
Berry, M., 71
Bersoff, D., 592
Bertenthal, B. I., 35–36
Berzins, J., 584
Best, D. L., 582, 583
Bettes, B. A., 524
Beverly, C. L., 128
Bewley, B. R., 523
Bhalla, S. K., 399, 502
Bhapkar, M., 495
Bhavnagri, N., 334
Bidwell, C., 558
Biederman, J., 447
Bierman, K. L., 465, 469
Bigelow, L. B., 447
Bild, E. R., 321
Biller, H. B., 260
Bilodeau, H., 148
Binder, R. L., 70
Binet, A., 109
Binghma, C. R., 508
Binion, V. J., 571
Birch, H., 251
Birch, S. H., 333, 334, 335
Bird-David, N., 303
Birdsong, D., 320
Bishop-Townsend, V., 187
Biskup, M. D., 519
Bittner, M. T., 409
Bjoenberg, U., 65
Bjorklund, D. F., 341
Black, D., 503
Blackbill, W., 182
Blades, M., 536
Blaine, B., 571
Blais, R., 148
Blake, I. K., 316
Blehar, M., 232
Bleyer, W. A., 131
Bloch, M. N., 392
Block, J., 572
Blom, M., 233
Bloom, L., 219
Blum, N. J., 448
Blum, R. W., 399
Blumenfeld, P., 571
Blyth, D. A., 557, 572
Bober, S. L., 372, 374
Bodley, J., 57
Bogenschneider, K., 527
Bogutskaya, T. A., 328
Bohlin, G., 66
Bolduc, D., 356
Bolger, K. E., 373
Bolig, E. E., 285
Bond, N. W., 428
Bon De Matte, L., 500
Bonnafont, G., 426, 428
Boocock, S. S., 66
Boodoo, G., 107, 541
Bookstein, F. L., 133
Booth, A., 484
Booth, C., 482
Booth, C. L., 256
Bootzin, R. R., 496
Borczyk, A., 91
Borenstein, B. D., 601
Borkowski, J., 285
Borman, K., 558
Bornstein, M. H., 134, 177, 181, 184, 206, 211, 221, 223, 254, 342, 344, 365
Borowsky, D., 206
Borstelmann, L. J., 7
Bortolotti, S., 360
Bost, K. K., 347
Botein, S., 241
Botstein, D., 92
Botvin, G. J., 525
Bouchard, C., 400, 401
Bouchard, T. J., 97, 101, 103, 106, 107, 541
Bouchard, T. J., Jr., 107
Boulton, M., 100
Bourdony, C., 495
Bovelsky, S., 437
Bowen, R., 550
Bowers, W., 501
Bowey, J. A., 332
Bowlby, J., 228–229, 233, 235, 236, 361, 398
Bowlds, M. K., 590
Boyd-Franklin, N., 69, 128
Boyes, M. C., 579
Boykin, A. W., 107, 541
Boyle, F. M., 185
Bracha, S., 92
Bradbard, M. R., 347
Bradley, C. B., 425
Bradley, C. R., 370
Bradley, L. L., 332
Bradley, R. H., 110
Bradshaw, D., 359
Brady, B. A., 561
Brady, C., 284
Braet, C., 402
Braganza, C., 400
Brainerd, C. J., 313
Brandenberger, J., 285
Brandt, R., 210
Brannen, J., 254
Brannon, C., 428
Brannon, L., 587
Brantley, C., 507
Braude, J., 551
Braun, C., 387
Braun, S., 518
Braungart, J. M., 182, 251
Braxter, B., 572
Bray, J. H., 480, 483
Bray, N. W., 161
Bray, R. M., 135
Brazelton, T. B., 135, 171, 172, 177, 181, 184
Breiling, J., 466
Breitbart, V., 134
Breitenbach, M., 499
Breitmayer, V. J., 165, 208
Brennan, R., 524
Brenner, V., 370
Brent, D., 328
Bretherton, I., 182
Bretherton, J., 257
Breton, S. J., 373
Brewer, W. F., 161
Brewster, K. L., 506
Brezina, T., 587
Brickle, G., 554
Bridges, M., 480, 483, 485
Britto, P. R., 284
Broadnax, S., 571
Broberg, A. G., 22, 325
Brockington, I., 273
Brodman, M., 511
Brody, G. H., 68, 72
Brody, N., 107, 211, 541
Brody, S., 236
Brodzinsky, A. B., 70
Brodzinsky, D. M., 70
Brome, D. R., 447
Brondolo, E., 363
Bronfenbrenner, U., 28–29, 46, 212
Bronstein, P., 60, 77
Brooks-Gunn, J., 284, 285, 329, 403, 488–489, 497, 508, 510, 513, 514, 516, 517, 552, 553, 570
Broom, B. L., 121
Broschart, K., 254
Brotherson, S. E., 60, 257
Brown, A. L., 313
Brown, B. B., 536, 556, 558
Brown, C., 165
Brown, E., 206, 211, 504
Brown, E. G., 237
Brown, I. C., 50
Brown, J., 316
Brown, L. M., 572
Brown, N. B., 317
Brown, R., 317, 318
Brown, R. D., 341
Brown, S. A., 522
Brown, T. A., 100
Brownell, K. D., 400, 401, 501
Bruer, J. T., 161
Bryan, J., 430
Bryant, B. K., 422, 424
Bryant, D. M., 212
Bryant, J., 333
Bryant, P. E., 332
Bryant-Waugh, R., 400
Bryson, S., 401
Buchanan, C. M., 496, 571
Buchman, D. D., 426
Buckman, D. D., 466
Buehler, C., 373
Bu-Haroon, A., 447
Buhrmester, D., 573, 575
Bui, K., 561
Buka, S., 524
Bukatko, D., 591
Bukowski, A. L., 468
Bukowski, W. M., 461, 467, 554, 576
Bulik, C. M., 502
Bull, N. L., 401
Bullock, M., 304, 347
Bunce, B. H., 210
Buntaine, R. L., 328
Burchinal, M., 558
Buriel, R., 22
Burk-Braxton, C., 573
Burks, V. M., 334
Burnham, D. K., 354
Burns, W., 134
Bush, D. M., 431
Busnel, M. C., 177
Buss, A. H., 250
Buss, D. M., 504
Buss, S., 320

Bussey, K., 354
Butcher, J. E., 586
Butterworth, G., 176, 177, 242, 504
Buzzelli, C. A., 478
Byatt, G., 176
Bybee, J., 290, 594
Byne, W., 511

Caballero, B., 501
Cadwallader, T. W., 466
Caffero-Rouget, A., 373
Cahill, L., 163
Cain, A., 398
Cain, K. M., 422
Cairns, R. B., 27, 42, 466, 562
Caldera, Y. M., 356
Caldwell, K. K., 134
Caldwell, L. L., 586
Calkins, S. D., 236
Call, K. T., 559
Callahan, C. M., 430
Calvin, J., 7
Camaioni, L., 428
Campbell, A., 415
Campbell, B. M., 589
Campbell, J., 430
Campbell, S. B., 236
Campero, L., 146
Campos, J. J., 35–36, 103, 179, 250, 251, 359, 360
Campos, R., 360
Camras, L. A., 359
Cancro, R., 136
Cann, W., 462
Cantor, N., 504
Capelli, C. A., 449
Capose, T. U., 360
Cardon, L. R., 445
Carey, W. B., 515
Carlisle, J. F., 321
Carlson, C., 573
Carlson, E., 285
Carlson, E. A., 42, 235, 344
Carlson, V., 372
Carlton-Ford, S., 557
Carossino, P., 146
Carpenter, W., 512
Carper, R., 419
Carrell, T. D., 445
Carroll, J. L., 451
Carroll, L., 578
Carskadon, M. A., 496
Carson, D. K., 409
Carter, B., 121
Caruso, D. A., 256
Casanova, O., 135
Case, R., 166, 305
Casiglia, A. C., 464
Casper, V., 241, 292
Caspi, A., 101
Caulton, D. A., 311
Ceci, S. J., 107, 541
Cen, G., 61, 464
Cenoz, J., 321
Centerwall, B. S., 466
Cesare, S. J., 504
Chaichenko, G. M., 328
Chakraborty, R., 274
Chamberlain, P., 597
Chambers, D. W., 437
Chan, D., 420
Chan, H., 62
Chan, J., 434
Chan, L. K., 62, 420
Chan, R. W., 485
Chan, Y. H., 457
Chandler, M., 76, 314, 315, 579
Chandra, A., 123
Chang, H. C., 6
Chang. L., 370
Chao-Yuan, C. K., 432, 433, 435
Chapman, S., 120
Charman, T., 248
Charpentier, P., 502
Chase-Lansdale, P. L., 257, 285, 508, 513, 515, 517
Chasnoff, I., 134, 135
Chassin, L., 523
Chatters, L. M., 68, 72
Chavajay, P., 109, 415
Chavez, D. V., 22
Chavez, E. L., 560
Chavkin, W., 134
Cheah, C., 73
Cheah, C. S. L., 464, 465, 468
Chen, C., 434, 435
Chen, H., 359, 464
Chen, K., 522
Chen, S., 359
Chen, W. J. A., 133
Chen, X., 61, 63, 461, 462, 464, 466
Chen, Z., 537
Cheng, X., 402
Cherlin, A. J., 480, 482
Cherny, S. S., 106, 107
Chess, S., 251, 252
Chester, N. L., 480
Cheung, C. K., 54, 61
Cheung, L. W. Y., 150
Chi, M., 307, 539
Chia, R. C., 504
Ching, W. D., 102
Chisholm, G., 237
Chisholm, J. S., 74, 75, 131
Chiu, M., 307
Chodorow, N. J., 17
Choi, S. H., 59, 61
Choi, Y., 432, 433, 435
Chomitz, V. R., 150
Chomsky, N., 215–216
Chong, S., 321
Christensen, H., 131
Christianson, R. E., 132
Chuang, S., 62
Chugani, H. T., 162, 163, 269, 320, 383, 384, 387
Chung, M., 366
Chung, S. W., 463
Chyi-In, W., 372
Cicchetti, D., 372, 373
Cicchetti, D. V., 447
Cielinski, K. L., 347
Cillessen, A. H. N., 575
Clark, A. G., 502
Clark, E. V., 317
Clark, H. H., 218
Clark, L., 68
Clark, M. L., 574
Clarke, A. C., 100
Clarke, A. S., 76
Clarke-Stewart, K. A., 255, 264–265, 324, 325, 482
Clatts, M. C., 128
Clausen, H., 386
Claussen, C., 178
Claussen, C. J., 583
Clerkx, L. E., 256
Clifton, R. K., 201
Clinchy, B., 581
Clingempeel, W. G., 483
Clinkenbeard, P. R., 444
Cochran, D. L., 72
Cochran, S., 507
Cogan, J. C., 399, 502
Cohen, B. M., 124
Cohen, D. B., 101, 105, 106
Cohen, J., 100
Cohen, K. M., 172
Cohen, L. L., 509
Cohen, R., 459
Cohen, S. E., 211, 223
Cohen, T. F., 482, 484
Cohn, J. F., 236, 244
Coie, J. D., 465, 468, 469, 470
Colangelo, N., 548
Colditz, G., 499
Cole, D. A., 540
Cole, J. G., 129, 135
Cole, M., 60, 109, 147, 210, 221
Cole, P. M., 58, 359, 362
Cole, R. E., 589
Cole, S. R., 210
Coleman, C. C., 333, 334, 335
Coleman, E., 372
Coles, R., 18, 284
Coley, R. L., 257, 515
Colin, A., 446
Colin, V. L., 231, 236
Coll, C. G., 53, 439
Colligan, J., 420
Collins, J. W., Jr., 150
Collins, P. E., 206
Collins, S., 590
Collins, W. A., 552
Coltrane, S., 258, 357
Compas, B., 407
Compas, B. E., 570
Coney, N. S., 117
Conger, R. D., 372, 481, 497, 558
Conlon, C. J., 132, 135
Conlon, M., 135, 189
Connell, D. B., 241
Connell, J. P., 423, 547, 548
Conroy, M. L., 135
Cook, T. H., 401
Cooley, C. H., 349
Coombs, R. H., 601
Cooney, R., 331
Cooper, C. R., 527
Cooper, R. G., 527
Cooper, R. P., 221
Coopersmith, S., 349
Copeland, A. P., 480
Copeland, E. P., 447
Copeland, P., 249, 251
Coplan, R. J., 464, 465, 468
Corbin, S. B., 481
Corcos, M., 500
Cordell, A. S., 348
Cordero-Gusman, H., 51
Cornbleth, C., 556
Cornelius, M. D., 134
Cornwell, A. C., 185
Corsaro, W. A., 325, 365, 464
Corwyn, R. F., 506
Cossette, L., 356
Costa, F. M., 498
Costa, P. T., 103
Costantino, G., 77
Costenbader, V. K., 328
Coubet, J., 170
Couchoud, E. A., 360
Coulehan, C. M., 256
Courchesne, E., 247
Coverdale, J. H., 511
Covington, M. V., 424
Cowan, C. P., 116, 120, 121, 122, 123, 334, 480, 481
Cowan, P. A., 116, 120, 121, 122, 123, 237, 334, 480, 481
Cowen, E. L., 406, 407, 408
Cowie, H., 536
Cox, A., 248
Cox, B. D., 419
Coy, D. C., 552
Coy, K. C., 244
Cozic, C. P., 519
Crago, M., 400
Crain, L. S., 131
Crane, J., 513
Cratty, B. J., 389

Craven, R., 347
Crawford, M. A., 523
Creasey, G. L., 343
Crews, H., 341
Crnic, K., 439
Crockenberg, S., 366, 481
Crocker, J., 439, 571
Crooks, R., 507, 510
Cross, W. E., 431
Crossland, J., 332
Crowe, P. A., 597
Crystal, D. S., 58, 59, 73
Csikszentmihalyi, M., 42, 333, 562
Cuffaro, H. K., 292
Culp, A. M., 514
Culp, R. E., 514
Cummings, E. M., 362
Cummings, M., 481
Cummings, S. S., 394
Cunningham, A. E., 329, 331
Cunningham, M., 406
Cunningham, M. R., 504
Cunningham, N., 241
Cunningham-Burley, S., 100
Cupp, R., 468
Curran, C. P., 512
Curtis, K., 123
Curtis, S., 447
Cushman, L. F., 516
Cyphers, L., 342

Daehler, M. W., 591
Dahlin, B., 295
Dai, D. Y., 443
Dale, P., 223
Dalton, L. T., 512
Daly, K., 257
Damon, W., 570, 592
Daniels, T., 518
Dapretto, M., 219
Darby, B., 134
Darling, N., 536, 600
Darwin, C., 41, 358, 451
Dasen, P. R., 23–24, 344, 416, 465, 582
Dasgupta, S. D., 457
Dash, B. B., 423
D'Atillio, J. P., 589
D'Augelli, A., 510
David, G. M., 348
David, R. J., 150
Davidson, A. L., 576
Davidson, E. C., 515
Davies, B., 398
Davis, D., 168
Davis, J. O., 92
Davis, L. H., 321
Davis, M. H., 479
Davis, P. T., 481
Davis, W. R., 128
Dawber, T., 282
Day, N. L., 134, 135
Day, R. D., 370
Deane, K. E., 232
Deater-Deckard, K., 369, 469
DeBaryshe, B. D., 471, 588
DeBerry, K. M., 71
DeBoysson-Bardies, B., 217
Debus, R., 347
DeCasper, A. J., 177
Decoufle, P., 442
Deffenbacher, J. L., 560
DeFries, J. C., 92, 106, 107, 251
Defries, J. C., 445
De Fruyt, F., 101
De Gaston, J. F., 510
Degirmencioclu, S. M., 527
Delaney, C. H., 580, 581
deLeeuw, N., 307
De Leon, B., 571
Delgado-Gaitan, C., 53–54, 77
D'Elia, P., 360
Delis, D. C., 134
DeLoach, J., 313
DeLoache, J., 312
DeLoache, J. S., 332
de Man, A., 591
DeMarrais, K. B., 340
De Mause, L., 7, 9
Dembo, M. H., 576
Demorest, S. M., 386
Demshar, H., 91
Denham, S. A., 360
Denmark, F. L., 572
Dennis, W., 304
Denny, M. A., 169
Dermer, A., 187
Desmond, R. J., 333
DeSpelder, L. A., 399
Deutsch, F. M., 121
Deutsch, G., 270
De Vet, K., 251
DeVries, M. W., 186, 252
De Waal, F. B. M., 41
deWinstanley, P., 428
Dews, S., 449
Diamond, M., 511
Diamond, M. D., 140, 161, 163, 165, 268, 276, 532
Diaz, C., 146
Diaz, R. M., 320
DiBlasio, F. A., 508
Dickinson, W. P., 327
Dick-Read, G., 145
DiClemente, R. J., 399, 509
Diebel, P., 132
Dienhart, A., 257
Dietz, W. H., 400, 401, 402, 426
Dieudonne, I., 132, 133, 134
Diggs, R. C., 564
DiGirolamo, A. M., 167, 272, 380, 382
DiGiuseppe, R., 363
Dilworth-Anderson, P., 8
Dinnel, D. L., 54
Dishion, T. J., 597
Dittman, L. L., 326
Dittus, P. J., 517
Dixey, R., 400
Dixon, S., 171, 172, 177
Dmitrieva, J., 571
Dobson, W. R., 579
Docking, J., 448
Dodds, J. B., 279
Dodge, K. A., 362, 369, 465, 467, 468, 469–470, 471
Dodge, K. E., 465
Doh, H. S., 64, 463
Dohn, H., 561
Doll, L. S., 128
Dollahite, D. C., 60, 257, 260, 515
Dolto, F., 505
Donahue, E. M., 101
Donahue, J. O. P., 105
Donahue, M. L., 448
Donaldson, M., 304
Donegan-Johnson, A., 409
Dong, Q., 63
Donnell, F., 239
Donnerstein, E., 466
Dopkins, S., 572
Doris, J., 374
Dornbusch, S. M., 556, 558
Dorney, J., 572
Dorr, A., 332, 333
Dosanjh, J. S., 126
Doswell, W. M., 572
Douthitt, V. L., 523
Douvan, E., 33
Dowling, J. E., 269, 270
Dowling, T., 131
Downey, G., 470
Downs, D. L., 572
Drake, D. D., 444
Dreikurs, R., 368
Dresser, N., 220
Drew, A., 248
Drews, C., 442
Drucker, R. R., 401
Drummond, W. J., 589
Dryfoos, J. G., 508
DuBois, D. L., 460, 573
Dubois-Arber, F., 509
Duda, J. L., 391
Duindam, V. P. J., 325
Dukes, R. L., 572
Dulmus, C. N., 518
Duncan, G. J., 284, 285, 510
Duncan, S. C., 508, 527
Duncan, T. E., 508, 527
Dunn, J., 105, 106, 316
Dunphy, D. C., 575
Du Pre, A., 451
Dupree, D. V., 406
Duran-Aydintug, C., 485
Durand, V. M., 379
Durant, D. J., 135
Durbin, D. L., 536
Durkin, D., 331
Durndell, A., 428
Durrant, J. E., 22
Dusenbury, L., 524
Duyff, R. L., 286, 288
Duyvesteyn, M. G. C., 241
Dweck, C. S., 421, 422, 425
Dylla, D. J. C., 71
Dziurawiec, S., 175

Eapen, V., 447
Eaves, L. J., 101
Ebbesen, E. B., 363
Eby, W. C., 451
Eccles, J., 572
Eccles, J. S., 422, 423, 430, 496, 527, 571, 572
Eckenrode, J., 374
Eckensberger, L. H., 473, 476
Eddy, J. M., 481
Eder, R. A., 346, 457
Edlund, B., 399, 400
Edmondson, J. H., 560
Edmunds, H., 400
Edwards, C. P., 319
Efran, J. S., 100
Egeland, B., 236, 285, 344
Ehrhardt, A., 511
Eiben, L. A., 184
Eichler, L. S., 121
Eichner, J., 401
Eimas, P. D., 213, 214
Einstein, A., 443
Eisenberg, N., 362, 468, 469, 477, 478
Eisenman, R., 595
Eisikovits, Z., 520
Eke, A. N., 128
Ekman, P., 358, 359, 360
Elder, G. H., Jr., 497, 558
Elkind, D., 10–11, 508, 549, 550, 552
Ellickson, P., 561
Elliott, J. G., 330
Elliott, L., 507
Ellis, H. D., 175
Elman, J., 449
El-Sheikh, M., 362
Elvin-Nowak, Y., 256
Emde, R. N., 179
Emiliani, F., 325
Emmett, P. M., 189
Emoke, S., 590
Ene, M., 247
Engel, J., 58
Engel, S., 341

Enosh, G., 520
Ensminger, M. E., 72
Ephron, N., 498
Epps, J., 363
Epstein, J., 512
Epstein, J. N., 331
Epstein, L. H., 401, 403
Epstein, Y. M., 124
Ercolani, P., 428
Erdman, P., 561
Erickson, J. D., 137
Erickson, M. F., 236
Eriksen, K., 123, 124
Erikson, E., 15–18, 25, 46, 157, 268, 550, 557, 577, 578, 580
Eron, L. D., 466, 519
Erwin, E. J., 324
Eshleman, S., 240
Espinosa, L., 320
Esposito, G., 447
Essex, M. J., 259
Estes, D., 313
Estes, L. S., 400
Etaugh, C., 256
Etringer, B., 500
Etz, K. E., 254
Eugster, A., 124
Evans, C. A., 448
Evans, J. R., 185
Evans, L. D., 330
Everaerd, W., 163
Ewing, C. K., 137
Ey, S., 570
Eyler, E., 135
Eyler, F. S., 135
Eyre, S. L., 506
Eysenck, H. J., 101, 103, 108, 110
Eysenck, S. B. G., 108

Fabes, R. A., 362, 468, 469
Fagan, J. F., 176, 211
Fagan, J. F., III, 176
Fagen, D. B., 408
Fagot, B. I., 354, 431
Faibisch, L., 402
Fairburn, C. G., 501
Faison, S., 126
Falbo, T., 64
Fang, X., 527
Fantz, R., 175, 176
Faraone, S. V., 447
Farrar, M. J., 301, 319
Farrell, M., 398
Farrington, D. P., 465, 588
Farruggia, S. P., 571
Fauber, R., 481
Fauth, J. M., 536
Fazio, F., 385
Fear, J. L., 502
Fegley, S., 457
Fehr, M. J., 563
Feldhusen, J. F., 443
Feldman, D. H., 443, 444
Feldman, M. W., 107
Feldman, R., 134
Feldman, S. S., 432, 506, 507
Felner, R. D., 406
Fenson, L., 223
Fenton, S., 52
Ferguson, T., 588
Fernyhough, C., 309
Ferrari, A. M., 372
Ferraro, G., 52
Ferron, C., 509
Feuerstein, R., 102
Field, A. E., 499
Field, T., 135, 208
Field, T. M., 246, 360
Fier, J., 540
Fifer, W. P., 177
Finch, M. D., 558, 559
Fincham, F. D., 481, 482, 484
Fine, D. S., 245
Fine, M., 431
Fine, R., 14
Finn, J. D., 561
Finn-Stevenson, M., 254, 284, 481
Fischel, J. E., 331
Fischer, C. S., 108
Fischer, K. W., 163–164, 269, 301, 305, 384
Fischer, L., 457
Fish, M., 256
Fisher, J. J., 217
Fitzgerald, H. E., 182
Fitzgerald, L. M., 324, 325
Fitzgibbon, M. L., 402
Flanagan, C., 481, 571
Flavell, E. R., 304, 311, 312
Flavell, J. H., 202, 303, 311, 312, 313, 419
Fleming, J. S., 425
Fletcher, K. L., 161
Fletcher-Flinn, C. M., 426
Flisher, A. J., 590
Flor, D. L., 68, 72
Florentine, M., 320
Flores, G., 426
Flower, P., 503
Floyd, F. J., 511
Flynn, J. M., 444
Flynn, J. R., 432, 436
Flyr, M. L., 481
Fogel, A., 221
Folger, D., 256
Fong, G., 541
Fontana, A., 137
Foote, D., 125
Ford, D., 447
Fordham, S., 547, 560, 561, 579
Forehand, R., 68, 129, 481
Foreyt, J., 400, 401
Forgays, D. K., 54, 481
Forssman-Falck, R., 585, 586
Fortier, M. S., 561
Fortin, C., 123
Fouts, J. T., 443
Fowler, M. G., 129
Fox, N. A., 236, 463, 518
Fox, R. A., 32, 370
Fracasso, M. P., 480
Franco, F., 242
Frankenburg, W. K., 279, 280
Franklin, J. A., 400
Frazier, A. L., 499
Frazier, J. A., 434
Freedman, D. A., 238
Freedman, D. G., 75
Freedman-Doan, C. R., 496
Freitas, A. L., 470
Fremmer-Bombik, E., 238
French, D., 465
French, S. A., 399
Freud, A., 14, 350
Freud, S., 13–17, 25, 42, 46, 228, 236, 350, 351, 451
Freund, L. S., 90
Fricker, H. S., 134
Fried, P. A., 132, 135
Friedberg, R. D., 346
Friedler, G., 136
Friedman, L., 18
Friedman, R. J., 58, 362
Friedman, R. M., 371
Friedrichsen, J. E., 571
Frijda, N. H., 359, 360
Frith, U., 316
Fritschy, M. N., 385
Fritz, A., 314
Fritz, J. J., 514
Fromm, E., 26
Frone, M. R., 558
Fry, W. F., 451
Frye, D., 315
Frye, K. F., 241
Fu, G., 176
Fujita, N., 219
Fuligni, A. J., 527, 553
Fulker, D. W., 103, 106, 107, 251, 445
Fullilove, M., 132, 133, 134
Fulroth, R. F., 135
Funk, J. B., 393, 426, 466
Furham, A., 541
Furman, E., 60, 335
Furman, W., 576
Furr, L. A., 94
Furstenberg, F. F., Jr., 257, 329, 480, 514

Gabrenya, W. E., Jr., 6
Gabriel, K., 134
Gaines, R., 420
Galambos, N. L., 256, 513, 582
Gallagher, T., 543
Gallagher,S. A., 536
Gallahue, D. L., 274, 277, 278, 281
Gallimore, R., 447
Galperin, C., 344, 365
Galperin, C. Z., 254
Galton, F., 96, 414, 442
Gan, L., 321
Gansky, S. A., 425
Gao, X., 61
Garbarino, J., 143, 259, 260, 376–377
Garber, J., 465, 490
Garcia, C., 146
Garcia, H. V., 439
Garcia, S. D., 460
Garcia-Preto, N., 77
Gardner, H., 109, 385–387, 410
Garduque, L., 559
Garmezy, N., 404, 409
Garrett, M., 328
Garrick, R. J., 60
Garrison, E. G., 439
Gathercole, S. E., 321
Gatmon, D. M., 256, 259
Gavin, M. K., 430
Ge, X., 497
Geary, D. C., 101
Gebre-Medhin, M., 399
Geddes, A., 6
Geis, H. K., 167, 272, 380, 382
Gelman, R., 304, 310, 318, 417
Gelman, S. A., 312
Gendall, K. A., 502
Gennetian, L. A., 255
George, P., 447
Gerardi, J., 390
Gergen, K. J., 347
Gerhardstein, P., 206
Germann, J. N., 426
Gerrard, L. E., 421
Gerris, J. R. M., 477
Gesell, A., 172, 209, 328
Gest, S. D., 409
Getzels, J. S., 420
Ghuman, A. S., 126
Giarrantano, S. C., 286, 288
Gibbs, J. T., 438
Giguere, J., 123
Gilbert, N., 372
Gilbreath, B., 373
Gill, N. E., 189
Gilligan, C., 476, 572, 585, 593, 594
Gillman, S. A., 393
Ginsberg, H. P., 432, 433, 435
Ginsburg, H., 303
Giordano, J., 579
Girdner, E. J., 595
Glavas, M., 134

Glazer, J. P., 129
Glissov, P., 428
Glover, V., 131
Goddard, C., 359
Goeke-Morey, M. C., 188
Goerge, R. M., 372
Gofman, M. A., 511
Goicoehea-Balbona, A., 129
Goldberg, E., 398
Goldberg, M., 247
Goldfarb, J., 124, 129
Golding, J., 189
Goldman, B. D., 165, 208
Goldman, G., 148
Goldman, M., 251
Goldsmith, H. H., 103, 250, 251
Goldsmith, L., 444
Goldstein, J., 425
Goldstein, W. M., 184, 592
Goncu, A., 308
Gonzalez-Mena, J., 183
Goode, S., 248
Goodenow, C., 437
Goodlin-Jones, B. L., 184
Goodman, J. C., 317
Goodnow, J. J., 54, 243, 364, 365, 457
Goodwin, T., 62
Gooren, L. J. G., 163
Gopaul-McNicol, S. A., 321
Gopnik, A., 313, 422
Gordon, R. A., 132
Gordon, T., 564
Gordon, V. V., 517
Goreczny, A. J., 500, 502
Gorseyeff, M., 121
Goto, Y., 146
Gottesman, I. I., 248
Gottfried, A. E., 221, 255, 256, 425
Gottfried, A. W., 221, 255, 256, 425
Gottlieb, G., 97
Gottman, J. M., 358, 598
Goubet, J., 170
Goubet, N., 201
Gough, B., 370
Gould, E., 160
Graber, J. A., 403, 495
Grabowski, J., 525
Grady, K., 437
Graham, J. A., 459
Graham, S., 437, 438, 470
Graham, T. A., 326
Gramling, L., 134
Granger, R. M., 134
Granier-Deferre, C., 177
Grant, K. E., 570
Graupner, L., 176
Gray, N., 400
Gray, N. S., 500, 501
Gray, W. Q., 212
Graziano, S. A., 160
Greb, A., 94
Gredler, G. R., 328, 329
Greek, A., 257
Green, F. L., 303, 311, 312
Green, S. M., 132
Greenberg, D. R., 501
Greenberger, E., 559
Greene, B., 510, 511
Greene, M. A., 100
Greene, S. M., 485
Greenfeld, D. A., 124
Greenfield, P. M., 55, 68, 138, 393, 394, 426, 428, 432
Greenleaf, B., 9
Greenough, W., 162
Greenspan, S. I., 110, 163, 166, 248, 249, 446
Greenstein, T. M., 255, 256
Greif, G. L., 69, 439
Greil, A. L., 123
Grenot-Scheyer, M., 459, 574
Gresham, C. L., 129
Griffith, E. M., 328
Griffiths, M., 426
Griffiths, P., 91
Grilo, C. M., 572
Gringlas, M. B., 485
Griswold, R. L., 257
Gritz, R. M., 257
Grolnick, W., 547
Groom, J. M., 468
Gross, C. G., 160
Grossman, F. K., 121
Grossman, K., 238
Grossmann, K., 238
Grossnickle, W. F., 504
Grow, L. J., 70
Gruber, C. P., 324, 325
Gruber, E., 399, 509
Gruen, R., 511
Gruenbaum, H., 511
Grummer-Strawn, L., 132
Grun, J., 245
Grunbaum, J. A., 519
Grunebaum, H. V., 241
Grupe, L. A., 161
Grusec, J. E., 595
Grych, J. H., 481, 482, 484
Grzanna, R., 385
Gu, H., 61
Guay, F., 561
Guay, L., 129
Guerra, N., 68
Guilford, J. P., 419
Gullone, E., 361
Gullotta, T. P., 570, 597
Gunnar, M., 208
Guralnick, M. J., 468
Gustafsson, S. S., 66
Guthrie, I. K., 468, 469
Guthrie, S., 303
Gutierrez, J., 77

Haas, L., 65
Hagekull, B., 66
Hagen, R., 354
Hagerman, R. J., 248
Haight, W. L., 341
Haiken-Vasen, J., 176
Hains, S. M. J., 176
Haith, M. M., 166
Hala, S., 314, 315
Hales, R. E., 446, 448
Halfe, L. B., 397
Halfon, O., 325
Hall, G. S., 543
Hallett, D., 76
Halpern, D., 107, 541
Halpern-Felsher, B. L., 507
Halvarsson, K., 399, 400
Halverson, C., 352
Halverson, H. M., 171
Hambleton, C., 259
Hamburg, D. A., 353
Hamer, D., 249, 251
Hamilton, C. E., 236, 346
Hamilton, V. L., 315
Hamm, J. V., 574
Hammer, L. D., 399, 401, 497
Hampson, J., 219
Hanaway, L. K., 333, 426
Hanis, C., 274
Hanis, C. L., 401
Hanley, W. B., 91
Hanna, N. A., 504
Hannon, P. R., 187
Hansen, C., 330
Hansen, K. L., 593
Hanson, E., 247
Hao, L. X., 507
Happe, F., 316
Hara, H., 58, 59
Hardesty, J. L., 573
Hardy, J. B., 513
Harkness, S., 53, 109, 184, 244
Harlan, D., 316
Harlan, E. T., 362
Harlow, H. F., 228
Harlow, M. K., 228
Harman, M. J., 517
Harned, M. S., 502
Harold, G. T., 481
Harold, R. D., 496, 571
Harper, D. C., 401
Harrell, J. S., 425
Harris, G., 178
Harris, M., 525
Harris, M. B., 354
Harris, P. L., 314, 315
Harris, V. R., 561
Harrison, A., 77
Harry, B., 459, 574
Hart, B., 162–163
Hart, C. H., 257
Hart, D., 457
Harter, K. S. M., 511
Harter, S., 347, 456, 457, 458, 570, 571, 572, 573, 598
Hartford, R. B., 186
Hartley, P., 400
Hartung, J., 223
Hartup, W. W., 345, 459, 461, 469, 554
Harvey, D., 136
Harvey, S., 558
Harvie, A., 91
Harwood, R., 592
Haselager, G. J. T., 459, 576
Hashimoto, Y., 425
Hastings, P. D., 464
Hatch, T., 387
Hatcher, R., 134, 135
Hatta, T., 146
Hattie, J., 571
Hauser, S. T., 590
Haussler, A., 248
Haveman, R., 284, 285
Havighurst, R. J., 473
Haviland, W. A., 212, 220
Havill, V. L., 101
Hawkins, A. J., 60, 257, 260, 515
Hawkins, J. A., 527, 597
Hay, D., 221, 242, 246
Hayashi, H., 58
Hayes, S. A., 54
Haynes, M., 237
Haynes, O. M., 134, 254, 344, 365
Hayward, C., 497
Hazen, N. L., 233
He, J., 420
Healey, J. M., 220
Healy, J. M., 165, 166, 428
Heaton, T. B., 482
Hebert, T. P., 547
Hecht, D. B., 468
Heckhausen, J., 422
Hedgepeth, E., 293
Heffernan, K., 500
Heide, K. M., 519, 520
Heilman, K. M., 270
Helmich, J., 293
Heming, G., 122, 123, 334, 480, 481
Henderson, A. S., 131
Henderson, N. D., 103
Hendrick, J., 275, 281
Hepworth, J. T., 401
Heras, P., 371
Herbert, B., 466
Herman, K. C., 561
Herman, M. A., 563
Herman-Giddens, M., 495

Hermer, L., 200
Hernandez, M., 371
Herring, P., 400
Hersen, M., 500, 502
Hershberger, S., 510
Hesemeier, C., 495
Hess, R. D., 326, 327
Hess, U., 360
Hesse, E., 234
Hetherington, E. M., 480, 481, 483, 484, 485
Hewitt, J. K., 106, 107
Hewlett, B. S., 18, 258
Heyman, G. D., 421, 422, 425
Heyman, R. E., 481
Heyne, D., 330
Hickman, S., 465
Higgins, A. M., 445
Hill, A. J., 400
Hill, H. M., 518
Hills, A., 282
Hilsman, R., 590
Hinde, R. A., 253, 469
Hintzman, D. L., 311
Hirayama, J., 58
Hirsch, B., 460
Hirsch, J., 191
Hjertholm, E., 307
Ho, D. Y. F., 61, 63, 359
Hock, E., 242, 257
Hoff-Ginsberg, E., 220
Hoffman, H. J., 186
Hoffman, J. J., 579
Hoffman, L. B., 512
Hoffman, L. W., 254, 256
Hoffman, M. L., 594
Hoffmann, T., 593
Hofmann, C., 134
Hofstede, G., 355, 506
Hogan, D. M., 254
Hogan, D. P., 507
Hojat, M., 601
Holahan, C., 526
Hollan, D., 359
Holland, J., 557
Holland, V., 548
Holligan, C., 332
Hollingsworth, L. D., 70
Hollos, M., 592
Holmbeck, G. N., 553
Holmes, W. M., 480
Honer, W. G., 161
Honig, A., 354, 366
Hood, B. M., 206
Hood, K. E., 42
Hooper, R., 206
Hopkins, B., 172
Hopkins, K., 369
Hopp, J. W., 400
Hops, H., 508, 527
Hopson, J., 140, 161, 163, 165, 268, 276, 532
Horn, J. L., 518
Horn, J. M., 101, 107
Horowitz, T. R., 561
Horton, F., 259
Householder, J., 134
Houston, T., 443
Hout, M., 108
Howard, J., 234
Howell, D. C., 407
Howes, C., 236, 346
Hrabowski, F. A., III, 69, 439
Hser, Y., 522
Huang, L. N., 438
Hubbard, J. J., 409
Hubbard, R. W., 451
Hudley, C., 437, 438, 470
Hudson, E., 329
Hudson, J. A., 310, 312
Huesmann, L. R., 369
Huff, C. O., 589
Huffman, L. F., 161
Hughes, M., 240
Hughes, M. E., 514
Hughey, M. J., 146
Hui, C. H., 56
Hui, J., 402
Huizinga, D., 520
Hull, J. D., 520
Hunter, A. G., 72
Huntsinger, C., 39, 102
Huon, G. F., 400, 498
Hur, Y. M., 103
Husarek, S. J., 244
Huston, A. C., 222, 332, 333, 356, 470
Hutchins, E., 131
Huttenlocher, J., 162, 304, 383
Hwang, C. P., 7, 75, 258, 325, 480
Hwang, K. K., 6
Hyche, J., 442
Hyde, J. S., 259
Hyman, C., 465
Hymel, S., 572

Iaukea, K., 135
Ignico, A. A., 281
Igra, V., 508
Imbens-Bailey, A. L., 320
Inciardi, J. A., 135, 521
Inderbitzen, H. M., 468
Ingoldsby, B. B., 52, 65, 120, 130
Inhelder, B., 302, 415, 508, 534
Insabella, G. M., 480, 485
Intons-Peterson, M. J., 583
Ironsmith, M., 421
Isabella, R. A., 233, 483
Ishii, K., 425
Ishii-Kuntz, M., 258
Isley, S., 468
Ivey, P., 56–57
Iwamoto, T., 146
Izard, C. E., 237, 359, 360, 571

Jaccard, J., 517
Jackendoff, R., 221
Jacklin, C. N., 354, 355
Jackson, A. E., 246
Jackson, D. W., 585
Jackson, J. B., 129
Jackson, P. W., 420
Jackson, R., Jr., 574
Jackson, S., 366
Jacobs, M., 468, 470
Jacobson, S. W., 241
Jacobson, T., 589
Jacobvitz, D. B., 233
Jacomb, P. A., 131
Jagers, R., 68
Jahoda, G., 23, 304
Jakob-Chien, C., 520
James, R. S., 129
James, S. P., 589
James, W., 96, 155, 158, 349
James-Ortiz, S., 525
Jankowski, M. S., 108
Janos, C., 590
Janowsky, J. S., 419
Jansen, B. R. J., 419
Janssen, A. W. H., 477
Janssen, J. M. A., 477
Janssen, S. C., 333
Janus, L., 131
Jaramillo, B. M. S., 563, 564
Jarrett, R., 482
Jarvis, P. A., 343
Jason, L. A., 333, 426
Jeammet, P., 500
Jeannin, A., 509
Jedlicka, D., 77
Jekielek, S. M., 481
Jenkins, E. J., 518
Jenkins, J. M., 242, 360
Jenkins, R., 439
Jensen, A. A., 65
Jensen, A. R., 108
Jensen, L., 510
Jensen, L. A., 184, 592
Jessee, P. O., 129
Jessor, R., 498
Ji, C. H. C., 475
Ji, G., 64
Jiang, J., 402
Jiao, S., 64
Jiao, Z., 527, 597
Jing, Q., 64
Joe, J. R., 74, 75
Joels, T., 239
John, O. P., 101
Johnson, A., 32
Johnson, D. J., 73
Johnson, J. A., 517
Johnson, J. E., 197, 392
Johnson, M. H., 175
Johnson, M. L., 161
Johnson, M. R. D., 523
Johnson, M.K., 558, 559
Johnson, P., 71
Johnson, R., 396
Johnston, L. D., 498, 524
Johnston, R. S., 332
Joiner, T. E., Jr., 589
Jones, A., 426
Jones, D. C., 502
Jones, G. P., 576
Jones, K. L., 134
Jonson, C. S., 401
Joos, S. K., 401
Jordan, P. L., 257
Jordan, W. J., 560
Jorm, A. F., 131
Jose, P. E., 102
Joseph, J., 360
Joseph, J. M., 409
Joseph, R. M., 313
Joyce, P. R., 502
Juarabe,T. C., 401
Judge, P., 177
Judit, M., 590
Juel, C., 329
Juffer, F., 241
Jusczyk, A., 177
Jusczyk, P., 177, 213
Jusczyk, P. W., 218

Kachur, S. P., 589
Kadobayashi, S., 146
Kaemingk, K., 133
Kagan, J., 42, 253, 300, 463, 469
Kagitcibasi, C., 53
Kahn, J. G., 129
Kahn, P. H., Jr., 592
Kail, R., 538
Kaimuss, D., 516
Kakar, S., 53
Kallen, K., 132
Kalman, Z., 554
Kalter, N., 398, 399
Kam, W. K., 499
Kamm, R. L., 391
Kamprath, N. A., 460, 461, 576, 598
Kandel, D. B., 522, 527, 554
Kanner, L., 246
Kanno, K., 321
Kantrowitz, B., 334
Kaplan, J., 449
Kapphahn, C. J., 498
Karasaw, M., 423
Kariya, T., 556
Karmaniola, A., 325
Karpovsky, S., 554
Karr, C., 555

Kashiwagi, K., 326, 327
Kastelic, D., 572
Katalin, S., 590
Kates, W. R., 90
Katz, P., 597
Katz, R., 121
Katzman, M. A., 500
Kauffman, J. M., 445
Kaufman, G., 560
Kaufman, L., 200
Kavanaugh, R. D., 341
Kawaai, C., 584
Kawai, H., 58
Kawai, M., 221
Kawakami, A., 146
Kay, L. S., 128
Kaye, D., 428
Kazui, M., 59
Kazuo, M., 360
Kearney, C. A., 330
Keating, D. P., 538, 539, 598
Keats, D. M., 322
Keefe, K., 595, 597
Keefer, C. H., 171, 172, 177
Kellam, S. G., 72
Keller, M. R., 391
Kelley, M. L., 69, 72, 73
Kellman, P. H., 178
Kellogg, R., 278, 279
Kelloway, E. K., 558
Kemple, K. M., 348
Kendler, K. A., 240
Kendler, K. S., 502
Kendziora, K. T., 369
Kennedy, L. J., 177
Kennedy, R. E., 590
Kentle, R. L., 101, 105
Kenyon, P. M., 498
Keogh, B. K., 447
Kephart, W., 77
Kerkman, D., 332
Kerner, J., 524
Kernis, M. H., 572
Kerns, K. A., 590, 591
Kerr, J., 590
Kessler, C. J., 326
Kessler, R. C., 240
Kestenbaum, R., 208
Ketterlinus, R. D., 480
Ketting, E., 124
Khanam, M., 420
Khanna, A. L., 321
Killen, J. D., 497, 523
Kilmartin, C. T., 585, 586
Kilpatrick, H., 428
Kim, L. I., 126
Kim, S. J., 592
Kim, U., 59, 61
Kim, W. J., 126
Kimball, G., 261
Kimberling, W. J., 445
Kindermann, T. A., 547
King, A. R., 548
King, B., 252
King, B. M., 137, 138
King, F., 206
King, N., 330
King, N. J., 361
Kingsberg, S. A., 124
Kirlik, A., 161
Kirouac, G., 360
Kirschenbaum, D. S., 402
Kirsh, S. J., 426
Kisilevsky, B. S., 176
Kitayama, S., 571
Kit-Fong, T., 417
Kitson, G. C., 480
Klackenberg-Larsson, I., 354
Klaczynski, P. A., 536
Klapec, T., 401
Klebanoff, M. A., 131
Klebanov, P., 284
Klebanov, P. K., 510
Klee, H., 521
Kleiber, D. A., 586
Klein, P. J., 207
Klein-Hessling, J., 408
Kliewer, W., 585, 586
Klimes-Dougan, B., 590
Klin, A., 447
Kline, H. F., 427
Klinnert, M. D., 179
Knight, G. P., 77
Knipe, D., 543
Knudtson, P., 92
Kobayashi, Y., 308
Koch, D. B., 445
Koch, G., 495
Kochanek, J., 556
Kochanska, G., 244, 251, 362, 474
Kochenderfer, B. J., 333, 334, 335, 345, 469
Kohlberg, L., 307, 352, 474–477, 486, 591, 593
Kolata, G. B., 401
Kontos, S., 324
Koot, H. N., 573
Kopp, C. B., 360
Korenman, S., 284
Korten, A. E., 131
Kosowski, T. D., 219
Kotchick, B., 129
Kovacs, M., 590
Kposowa, A. J., 480
Krahn, H., 558
Kramer, L., 135
Kranz, R., 511
Kraus, N., 445
Krispen, O., 464
Kronk, C. M., 306
Kroonenbert, P. M., 233
Kroovand, N., 437
Kroutil, L. A., 135
Kubey, R., 333
Kuczynski, L., 595
Kuhl, P. K., 163
Kuhn, P. K., 214, 217
Kuiper, N. A., 451
Kulakova, N. N., 254
Kulka, R. A., 33
Kundert, D. K., 328
Kuo, T., 496
Kuo, Y. Y., 420
Kupersmidt, J. B., 373, 468
Kusumakar, V., 597
Kwok, D. C., 432
Kyei, A. K., 137

Laakso, L., 394
Labouvie, E., 512
Lacerda, F., 163
Ladd, G. W., 257, 333, 334, 335, 345, 461, 469
Ladd, H., 284
Ladson-Billings, G., 440
Lagace-Seguin, D. G., 464, 465, 468
Lagattuta, K. H., 313
La Greca, A. M., 405
Lahey, B. B., 132
Laird, M., 374
LaLonde, C., 76, 315
Lam, W. L., 548
Lamb, M. E., 7, 42, 60, 75, 120, 123, 154–155, 237, 240, 256, 259, 260, 325, 354, 464, 480
Lambert, W., 22
Lamberty, G., 439
Lamborn, S. D., 600
Lamson, S. R., 467
Lancer, M. E., 493
Landa, R., 247
Landau, S., 446
Lang, P. J., 211
Lang, S., 208
Lange, C. M., 557
Langer, A., 146
Langer, W. L., 7
Langfield, P. A., 506, 517
Langlois, J. H., 176
Langrock, A. M., 366
Lanham, B. B., 60
LaPorte, D. L., 501
Lara, J., 560
LaRossa, R., 257
Larsen, B., 593
Larson, J., 398
Larson, R. W., 34–35, 393, 574, 582, 597
Lasin, G., 96
Lask, B., 400
Lasker, J., 390, 393
Last, C. G., 330
Latimer, W. L., 25
Latz, S., 183
Lau, S., 548
Laub, J. H., 552
Lauber, B. A., 428
Laursen, B., 552, 554
LaVancher, C., 307
Lavee, Y., 121
Lawson, E. P., 329
Lazarus, R. S., 403, 407
Leadbeater, B. J. R., 506
Leap, W., 214
Lears, M., 401, 403
Leary, M. R., 572
Leavitt, L. A., 518
Lebolt, A., 470
Leboyer, F., 148
Lebra, T. S., 58, 59
Lecanuet, J. P., 177
Le Couteur, A., 248
LeDoux, J. E., 163
Ledoux, N., 407
Lee, B., 372
Lee, C., 151
Lee, E., 73
Lee, G. W., 504
Lee, J. W., 451, 468
Lee, K., 176
Lee, L. C., 62, 64, 381, 382, 392
Lee, R. P. L., 62
Lee, S., 430, 432, 433, 434, 435, 499, 500
Lee, S. E., 425
Lee, S. Y., 435
Lee, Y., 502
Lefebvre, L., 372
LeFevre, J., 329
LeFore, P. C., 540, 543
Legerstee, M., 176
Lehne, G. K., 510
Leiblum, S. R., 124, 138
Leiderman, P. H., 171, 172, 177
Lein, J. Y., 514
Leinbach, M., 431
Leis, P. E., 592
LeMare, L., 462, 468
Lemerise, E. A., 362
Lempert, H., 318
Lenarduzzi, G., 559
Lenox, K., 465
Leonard, C. J., 510
Leonard-Green, T. K., 502
Leone, B., 519
Lepper, M. R., 426
Lerman, R. I., 515
Lerner, J. V., 256
Lerner, R. M., 513
LeSieur, K. D., 461
Lesser, G. S., 554
Leung, K., 548
Leung, L., 507

Levenkron, S., 500
Leventhal, B. L., 132
Levine, L. J., 361
Levine, M. P., 400
Le Vine, R., 222, 315
Le Vine, R. A., 171, 172, 177
Le Vine, S., 171, 172, 177, 315
Levine, S. B., 467
Levinson, D., 401
Levitin, D. J., 311
Levy, A. K., 344
Levy, G. D., 586
Levy, R. I., 359
Lewis, C. C., 315
Lewis, J. W., 451
Lewis, M., 360, 501
Lewis, R. A., 525
Li, B. S., 63, 462, 464
Li, C. Y., 447
Li, D., 464
Li, M., 73
Li, Z., 61
Liao, F., 65
Liaw, F. R., 102
Lieberman, E., 150
Lightfoot, C., 508, 509
Lightfoot, M., 572
Lillard, A. S., 315, 316
Lin, C., 538
Lin, L., 63
Lin, S., 426
Lincoln, A., 247
Lindsey, E., 237
Linfield, K., 481
Linn, S., 131
Linnet, J., 460, 461, 576, 598
Lipsitt, L. P., 185
Little, J. K., 353
Little, S., 590
Little, T. D., 423
Liu, E. S. C., 54, 61
Liu, Y. Q., 61, 63
Liwag, M. D., 361
Lloyd, V. L., 221
Llyod, P., 309
Lochman, J., 465
Lochman, J. E., 465
Locke, G., 135
Locke, J., 8, 41, 46
Lockwood, V., 17
LoCoco, A., 464
LoConte, J. S., 512
Locuy, M. I., 402
Loeb, T. B., 400
Loeber, R., 132, 588
Loehlin, J. C., 101, 106, 107, 108, 541
Loewenstein, I., 582, 586
Loffredo, C. A., 137
Loftus, E., 205
Lohaus, A., 408
Lohnes, K., 398, 399
Lohr, D., 428
Loken, E., 251
Lollis, S., 462, 468
Long, R., 373
Lonigan, C. J., 331
Lonner, W. J., 54
Lopez, S., 432, 433, 435
Lorenz, K. Z., 231
Lowe, G. S., 558
Lowenthal, B., 128
Lozoff, B., 183
Lozy, J. L., 121
Lu, M. W., 393
Lubart, T. I., 420
Lubold, P., 589
Lucas, S. R., 108
Lucente, R. L., 578
Ludemann, P. M., 244
Ludwig, J., 284
Luhtanen, R., 571
Lunde, T. D., 353
Lundy, D. E., 504
Luo, Q., 527
Luster, T., 439
Luthar, S., 409
Lutkenhaus, P., 304, 347
Lutz, D., 201
Lutz, W. J., 242, 257
Lykken, D. T., 101
Lynn, R., 432
Lyon, T. D., 312
Lyons-Ruth, K., 234, 241
Lytton, H., 354, 432, 436

MacBain, D., 137
Maccoby, E. E., 355, 367, 600
MacDonald, K. B., 334
MacGregor, S. K., 428
Mac Iver, D., 571, 572
Mackey, W. C., 117
MacLean, M., 332
Macnee, C. L., 132
MacPhee, D., 514
Madden, C. M., 449
Madden, T., 592
Maddock, A., 512
Madhere, S., 518
Mael, F. A., 559
Magnus, K. B., 408
Magnus, M. H., 401
Maher, F. A., 431
Mahler, M. S., 243
Mahon, M. H., 398
Mahoney, J. L., 466, 562
Maier, S. E., 133
Main, M., 234
Maital, S., 365
Major, B., 439
Makarenko, N. V., 328
Makin, J., 132
Malach, R. S., 74
Malcuit, G., 327, 356
Males, M., 515
Malgady, R. G., 77
Malina, R. M., 171
Malinowski, B., 16–17
Mallard, A. R., 319
Malley, J. E., 480
Man, P., 600
Manber, R., 496
Mancuso, J., 496
Mandic, M., 401
Mandinach, E. B., 427
Mang, M. E., 307
Mangelsdorf, S. C., 208, 457
Mangner, T. J., 162, 383, 384
Manly, J. T., 372
Manor, O., 238
Manzano, J., 151
Marchman, V., 223
Marchman, V. A., 220
Marcia, J. E., 577, 578, 579
Marcus, M. C., 401
Margolin, G., 518
Margulis, C., 219
Markman, E. M., 533
Markstrom-Adams, C., 579
Markus, H. R., 571
Marotz, L. R., 274, 275, 276, 287
Marseille, E., 129
Marsh, F. H., 94
Marsh, H. W., 347, 571
Marshall, H. H., 348
Marshall, S., 8
Marsiglio, W., 258
Martin, A. M., 77
Martin, C. A., 197
Martin, C. L., 352, 353
Martin, D. C., 131, 135
Martin, J. A., 367
Martin, J. C., 135
Martin, J. D., 447
Martin, J. M., 540
Martin, N., 541
Martin, N. G., 101
Martin, R. A., 451
Martinez, I. M., 187
Martinez, P., 518
Martinez, R., 572
Martini, M., 342
Marzolf, D. P., 312
Maser, J. D., 466
Mash, E. J., 503
Mashima, M., 423
Mason, M. A., 480
Massaro, S., 330
Masten, A. S., 68, 409
Matheny, A. P., 103
Maton, K. I., 69, 439
Maton, K. J., 560
Mattay, V. S., 447
Mattock, A., 206
Mattson, S. M., 133, 134
Mattson, S. N., 134
Mauldon, J., 513, 515
Mauthner, N. S., 151
Maxfield, D., 419
May, D. C., 328
Mayer, B., 245
Mayes, L. C., 134, 135
Mayne, T. J., 363
Mayo, L. H., 320
Mays, V., 507
Mayseless, O, 239
Mazet, P., 234
Mazzocco, M. M. M., 90
McAdoo, H. P., 69, 439
McAninch, C., 446
McBride, D. C., 521
Mcbride, L. R., 536
McCane-Sanford, T., 515
McCarthy, J., 571, 572
McCartney, K., 482
McCathie, H., 361
McCaul, M. E., 524
McClearn, G. E., 92, 106, 107
McClintic, S., 422
McCord, J., 365, 370, 525
McCormick, L. K., 523
McCourt, F., 285
McCown, D., 398
McCracken, C., 370
McCrae, R. R., 103
McCubbin, H. I., 76
McDermott, J., 550
McDonald, D. L., 505
McDonough, L., 317
McDougall, P., 572
McElin, T., 146
McEwen, A., 543
McGaugh, J. L., 163
McGee, R., 496
McGee, T. J., 445
McGoldrick, M., 579
McGonagle, K. A., 240
McGuigan, K. A., 561
McHale, S. M., 563
McKay, S., 146
Mckenna, E. R., 235
McKenna, J. J., 186
McKenry, P. C., 480
McKenzie, L., 148
McKinney, J. P., 505
McKnight, K. M., 400
McLanahan, S., 511
McLaughlin, R. F., 559
McLaughlin, S. C., 423
McLellan, J. A., 559
McLeod, S., 234
McLoyd, V. C., 67
McNeal, C., 481
McNeely, J. B., 189

McPartland, J. M., 560
Mead, G. H., 349
Mead, M., 27
Mebert, C. J., 510
Medvescek, C. R., 317
Meins, E., 236
Meischner, T., 237
Meisels, S. J., 328
Melin, L., 406
Melli, M. S., 70
Meltzoff, A. M., 217
Meltzoff, A. N., 206, 207
Menchu, R., 144, 149, 171
Mendel, G., 85, 96
Mendelson, M. J., 504
Meng, Z., 360
Menon, S., 18
Menon, U., 359
Mercado, R., 22
Mercer, J., 188
Merckelbach, H., 245
Mercugliano, M., 448
Merisca, R., 594
Merriman, W., 221
Mervielde, I., 402
Mesch, G. S., 238
Mesibov, G. B., 248, 249
Mesquita, B., 359, 360
Messervey, D., 597
Meyer, J., 135
Meyer, L. H., 459, 574
Meyer, M., 328
Meyer-Bahlburg, H., 511
Meyer-Bahlburg, H. F. L., 563, 564
Mezoff, J. S., 128
Michell, L., 523
Midgley, C., 571, 572
Miettinen, R., 294
Milbrath, C., 443
Miller, A., 422
Miller, B., 121
Miller, B. C., 508
Miller, J. A., 133
Miller, J. E., 284
Miller, J. G., 592
Miller, J. L., 586
Miller, L. H., 404
Miller, L. K., 386
Miller, L. R., 373
Miller, N., 122, 123
Miller, P. H., 419
Miller, P. J., 341
Miller, P. M., 222
Miller, S. A., 419
Miller-Heyl, J., 514
Millor, G. K., 572
Mills, J. L., 132
Millstein, S. G., 506, 507, 508
Miltner, W. H. R., 387
Min, P. G., 480
Minagawa, M., 58, 59
Minde, K., 466
Minderaa, R. B., 246
Miner, K., 512
Minturn, L., 22
Mintz, S., 259
Minuchin, P., 27–28
Miranda, S., 176
Mirochnick, M., 135
Mischel, W., 363, 364
Mishra, P., 161
Misra, B., 220
Mistry, J., 308
Mitchell, C., 560, 589
Miyake, K., 359
Miyashita, T., 423
Mize, J., 237
Mizuno, S., 592
Mizuta, I., 58, 362
Mmiro, F., 129
Moen, P., 65
Mohanty, A. K., 218, 220
Molnar, B., 373
Money, J., 510
Monson, R. R., 131
Monsour, M., 345
Montague, A., 52
Montemayor, R., 551, 554, 570, 597
Montessori, M., 321
Moon, S. M., 443
Moore, G., 236
Moore, K., 126
Moore, K. L., 128
Moore, M. K., 206, 207
Moos, R., 526
Morales, J. R., 465
Morath, R. A., 559
Morch, W. T., 593
Moreau, D., 563, 564
Moreau-Gruet, F., 509
Morelli, G., 56–57
Morgan, H., 234
Morinaga, Y., 59
Morley, L., 461
Morrison, D. M., 496
Morrison, D. R., 482
Morrison, F. J., 328, 434
Morrison, J. A., 502
Morrongiello, B. A., 282
Morse, E., 68
Mortimer, J. T., 558
Mortimer, J. Y., 559
Morton, J., 175
Mosier, C., 308
Mueller, B., 232
Mueller, C. M., 422
Mueller, H. H., 328
Mueller, R. A., 162, 383, 384
Mueller, W. H., 401
Muir, D. W., 176
Mukhamedrakhimov, R. Z., 231
Mukhopadhyay, P., 422
Mulvey, D., 457
Muncer, S., 415
Munroe, R. H., 477
Munroe, R. L., 477
Muris, P., 245
Murphy, B. C., 468, 469
Murphy, C., 442
Murphy, D. A., 512
Murphy, W. M., 477
Murray, J. P., 466
Murray, K., 251
Murray, K. T., 362
Murray, L., 206, 221, 242, 246
Murray, M., 523
Murry-McBride, V., 506
Musoke, P., 129
Muuss, R. E., 502, 552, 578
Muzi, M. J., 52, 59, 72, 77
Muzik, O., 162, 383, 384
Mwageni, E. A., 126
Mwamwemba, T. S., 572
Myers, B. J., 585, 586
Myers, M. D., 401, 403
Myerson, N., 330

Naeye, K. L., 133
Nagano, K. N., 21
Nagy, M. C., 129
Nahas, G. G., 136
Najman, J. M., 185
Nakagawa, K., 73
Nakagawa, N., 449
Nakazato, K., 584
Nakazima, S., 217
Namerow, P. B., 516
Napier, B. J., 451
Nason, R. B., 329
Nass, C. I., 470
Naugeais, R., 177
Naus, M. J., 419
Neale, M. C., 103
Needell, B., 71
Needham, A., 200
Neisser, U., 107, 176, 432, 541
Nelson, C. A., 162, 206, 218
Nelson, C. B., 240
Nelson, J. A., 340
Nelson, K., 219
Nelson, L., 135
Nelson, L. J., 464, 465, 468
Nelson-Goens, G. C., 361
Netemeyer, R. G., 399
Netley, R., 432, 433, 435
Nettles, S. M., 285
Neugarten, B. L., 473
Neumann, M. S., 128
Neumark-Sztainer, D., 402
Neuwalder, H., 510
Newcomb, A. F., 461, 467, 554, 576
Newcomb, M., 400
Newcomb, M. D., 595, 597
Newcombe, N. S., 304
Newman, L. S., 307
Newton, C. R., 124
Newton, M., 524
Nias, D. K. B., 103
Nicholas, L. M., 493
Nichols, R. C., 422
Nicklas, T. A., 401
Nicol, T. G., 445
Nicoladis, E., 320
Nielson, E. C., 579
Nies, M. A., 401
Nikoloff, O., 328
Nimetz, S. L., 335
Ninio, A., 327
Nippold, M. A., 563
Nisbett, R. E., 108
Nolen-Hoeksem, S., 398
Nolte, J., 268
Norem, J. K., 581
Norman, J., 525
North, D. C., 161
Norwicki, S., 423
Nozyce, M., 241
Nuzzo, C., 221
Nye, C. L., 511

Oatley, K., 242, 360
Obarzanek, E., 502
Oberklaid, F., 237
O'Brien, M., 356
Ochs, E., 223, 315
Ochse, R., 420
O'Connell, B., 220
O'Dell, S., 279
Oetting, E. R., 560
Ogawa, J. R., 236
Ogbu, J. T., 2–3, 52, 53, 68, 69, 70, 74, 435, 436, 437, 438, 440, 547, 560, 561, 579
Ogino, M., 342, 365
Oguinick, C. M., 517
Ogunyemi, A., 135
Ohman, A., 361
Okamura, A., 371
Okonkwo, R. U. N., 476
Oldenburg, C. M., 590, 591
O'Leary, A., 512
O'Leary, S. G., 369
Ollech, D., 571, 572
Ollendick, T. H., 330
Olshan, A. F., 137
Olson, D. R., 313, 315
Olson, H. C., 133
Olver, R. R., 571, 572
O'Malley, P. M., 498, 524
O'Mara, K. M., 188
O'Neil, P. M., 500, 503
O'Neil, R., 468

Oostra, B. A., 90
Oppenheim, D., 238, 239, 256
Opper, S., 303
Orbach, T., 589
Orenstein, A., 522
Orenstein, P., 429, 431
Orfield, G., 556
Orlandi, M. A., 512
Orme, J. G., 373
Ornstein, P. A., 419
Ortiz, O., 146
Osborne, L. M., 482
Osborne, L. N., 481
Osherson, D. N., 533
Osipow, S. H., 579
Osofsky, H. J., 514
Osofsky, J. D., 466, 514, 516
Osone, A., 499
Oster, H., 359, 360
Osterweil, Z., 21
Ostrem, J. L., 447
O'Sullivan, L. F., 563, 564
O'Toole, J., 398
Ott, P. J., 134
Otto, S. P., 107
Overbay, J. D., 394
Overstreet, S., 518
Owen, M. T., 482
Owens, K., 348, 349, 572
Ozmun, J. D., 274, 277, 278, 281

Paajanen, S., 466
Pace, N., 136
Pai, S., 53
Paikoff, R. L., 516, 552, 553
Painter, K., 344, 360
Palkovitz, R., 258
Paludetto, R., 183
Palumbo, J., 448
Panak, W. F., 465
Panda, S., 220
Pandey, D., 519
Panter-Brick, C., 41
Papousek, H., 221
Papousek, M., 221
Paquette, A., 133
Pardee, R. E., 496
Parish, S., 359
Parish, W. L., 507
Park, H. S., 459, 574
Parke, R. D., 237, 240, 259, 260, 334, 468
Parker, G. R., 406, 407
Parker, J. G., 458, 460, 465, 469, 574, 575
Parnaby, O. G., 400
Parsons, S., 504
Parten, M., 341
Pascual, L., 254, 344, 365
Pasley, K., 506, 517
Patenaude, R., 202
Pathak, Z., 482
Patterson, C. J., 373, 485
Patterson, G. R., 471, 588, 597
Paul, D., 76
Paul, M., 137
Paulesu, E., 385
Paulson, M. J., 601
Pavlopoulous, V., 101
Pavlov, I., 19
Payne, V. G., 274, 394
Peake, P. K., 364
Pearson, J. L., 72
Pecheus, M. G., 365
Pedersen, N., 97, 107
Pedlow, R., 237, 462
Peeke, L. A., 540
Pegg, J. E., 221
Pennington, B. F., 445
Penza, S., 362
Pepe, M. S., 402
Perani, D., 385
Perl, A., 401
Perl, M. A., 401
Perlmutter, M., 311, 312
Perloff, R., 107, 541
Pernice-Ducas, F., 77
Perreard, E. C., 151
Perregaux, C., 218
Perry, T. B., 504
Persaud, T. V. M., 128
Perucchini, P., 428
Peters, H. E., 255
Petersen, A. C., 493, 570, 580, 582, 590
Peterson, G. W., 370
Peterson, J. S., 548
Petrill, S., 108
Pettit, G. S., 237, 369, 465, 471
Phares, V., 363, 407
Phelan, P., 576
Phelps, J. A., 92
Phelps, M. E., 162, 320
Philipsen, L. C., 236, 346
Phillips, B., 135
Phillips, J. R., 220
Phinney, J. S., 579
Piaget, J., 22–23, 25–26, 33, 46, 195–204, 300–307, 309–310, 313, 343, 352, 414–416, 472–474, 477, 508, 534
Pianta, R. C., 335, 344
Picasso, P., 414, 443
Picke, F. N., 432
Piercy, F. P., 513, 525
Pierrehumbert, B., 325
Piirto, J., 443, 444
Pike, K. M., 399
Pilgrim, C., 527
Pineault, R., 148
Pinker, S., 220
Plato, 6, 41–42, 583
Pleck, J. H., 285
Plomin, R., 80–81, 90, 91, 92, 94, 101, 103, 105, 106, 107, 108, 111, 249, 250, 251, 272, 353
Polce-Lynch, M., 585, 586
Polka, L., 221
Pomerantz, E. M., 348
Pomerleau, A., 327, 356
Pomeroy, J. C., 247
Ponton, L., 399
Poortinga, Y. H., 24, 344, 416, 465, 582
Popenoe, D., 65
Porton, H. W., 502, 552
Poston, D. L., 64
Poteat, G. M., 421
Poteet-Johnson, D., 129
Potkay, C. R., 12–13
Potter, L. B., 589
Potts, S., 398
Potvin, L., 148
Powell, K. E., 589
Powell, R. A., 126
Power, T. G., 69, 72
Powers, K., 522
Powers, N. G., 186
Powledge, T. M., 100
Powlishta, K. K., 550
Presson, C. C., 523
Preston, M. A., 91
Price, G., 326, 327
Price, J. M., 465
Price, S. J., 480
Price-Williams, D., 420
Primorac, L., 401
Prior, M., 17, 237, 462
Pritchard, M., 330
Profilet, S. M., 257
Prosser, E. C., 573
Pruett, K. D., 143
Pryor, T., 501
Pulkkinen, L., 121
Purath, J., 394
Putman, S. P., 251
Pyryt, M., 436

Quiggle, N. L., 465
Quirk, A., 512

Raag, T., 354
Rabar, M. H., 444
Rabin, B. E., 332
Raboy, B., 485
Rackliff, C. L., 354
Radojevic, M., 259
Raffaelli, M., 527
Rahdert, E. R., 525
Rahn, C., 365
Rajan, R. S., 482
Ramey, C. T., 165, 208, 210, 212, 384
Ramey, S. L., 165, 210, 384
Ramirez, M., 409
Ramsey, E., 588
Ramsey, F., 471
Ramstein, T., 325
Rand, Y., 102
Randolph, L. A., 135
Ransdell, L. B., 394
Rathunde, K., 562
Ratner, C., 30
Raty, H., 437
Rauh, H., 232
Ravussin, E., 400, 401
Rayner, R., 20
Read, D., 579
Reardon, S. F., 524
Reavey, P., 370
Recchia, S., 422
Reddy, V., 221, 242, 246
Red Horse, J., 74
Reed, S., 236
Rees, J., 235
Reeve, A., 270
Reeve, R. E., 445
Reeves, A. J., 160
Regan, P. C., 504
Reid, H. M., 512
Reilly, J., 223
Reilly, K. D., 161
Reinholtz, C., 514
Reis, S. M., 430
Reiss, A. L., 90
Reiss, D., 106
Reitzel-Jaffe, D., 372
Reitzes, D. C., 257
Reitzle, M., 556
Renk, K., 363
Repacholi, B., 234
Resnick, M. D., 399
Reuman, D., 571, 572
Reyna, V. F., 313
Reynolds, A. J., 210
Reynoso, S., 146
Rezac, S. J., 482
Reznick, J., 223
Reznick, J. S., 131
Rhodes, G., 176
Rhodes, T., 512
Rhy, S., 558
Rice, F. P., 123
Rice, M. L., 222, 332, 333
Rich, S., 101
Richard, J., 589
Richards, H., 68, 71
Richards, M. H., 34, 393, 574, 582, 597
Richardson, G. A., 134, 135
Richardson, J. L., 512
Richardson, M. A., 601
Richman, A., 171, 172, 177
Richman, A. I., 222

Richman, C. L., 437
Richters, J. E., 518
Rickel, A. U., 210
Rider, A. M., 496
Rider, S. P., 496
Ridley, T., 162–163
Riggs, S., 233
Righetti–Veltema, M., 151
Riksen-Walraven, J. M. A., 238, 459
Riley, E. P., 133, 134
Rincon, C., 470
Rink, J. E., 274, 394
Rissland, E. L., 161
Ritchie, J. E., 400
Ritenbaugh, C., 502
Rivera, S. M., 460
Rizzo, T. A., 464
Roberts, D. F., 470
Roberts, E., 206, 211
Roberts, K., 217
Roberts, T., 176
Robertson, P., 9
Robertson, S., 248
Robins, M., 502
Robins, R. W., 572
Robinson, A., 444
Robinson, N., 570, 573
Roblek, T. L., 330
Rochat, P., 170
Rocheleau, B., 428
Rock, D. A., 561
Rockett, H. R. H., 499
Rodning, C., 234
Rodriguez, C., 51
Rodriguez, J., 22
Rodriguez, J. L., 320
Rodriguez, R., 320
Roebuck, T. M., 133, 134
Roenkae, A., 121
Roeser, R. W., 572
Roffman, R. A., 522
Rogers, I. S., 189
Rogers, S. J., 131
Roggman, L. A., 176
Rogoff, B., 109, 308, 415, 418
Rohner, R. P., 57
Rollings, S., 330
Romero-Garcia, I., 571
Romney, D. M., 354
Roncolato, W. G., 400
Roopnarine, J. L., 390, 392, 393
Roosa, M., 77
Roosa, M. W., 514
Root, M. P. P., 573
Rose, A. J., 464, 468
Rose, J. S., 523
Rose, N. C., 92
Rose, S. P., 269, 301, 305
Rose-Krasnor, L., 22
Rosen, L., 511
Rosenbaum, J. E., 234, 556
Rosenberg, H. S., 124
Rosenblatt, E., 449
Rosenblum, G. D., 501
Rosenblum, O., 234
Rosenheck, R., 137
Rosenstein, L. D., 269
Rosenthal, D. A., 432, 579
Rosenthal, E., 133
Rosenthal, M. B., 124
Rosner, B., 131
Ross, C. E., 54
Rothbart, M. K., 246, 253, 451
Rothblum, E. D., 399, 502
Rotheram-Borus, M. J., 512, 572
Rothermel, R. D., 162, 383, 384
Rothi, L. J. G., 270
Rotter, J., 424
Roush, W., 444
Rousseau, J., 8, 46
Rousseau, R., 508
Rovee-Collier, C., 165, 187, 206
Rowe, D. C., 101
Rowlinson, R. T., 406
Roy, I. S., 439
Rubin, K. H., 61, 63, 462, 463, 464, 465, 466, 468
Rubin, L. R., 582
Rubin, R. R., 217
Rubinstein, S., 501
Ruble, D. N., 348, 364, 365, 408, 457
Ruck, M. D., 598
Rudd, M. D., 589
Rudolph, J., 238
Rue, D. S., 126
Ruff, H. A., 417
Ruffman, T., 201
Ruggiero, M., 559
Ruiz, A., 236
Runco, M. A., 442
Rushton, J. P., 103
Russell, A. T., 70
Russell, G., 259, 354
Russell, J. A., 359, 361
Rutter, J. M., 176
Rutter, M., 92, 106, 107, 235, 248, 404, 407, 598
Ryan, J. H., 579
Ryan, K. J., 131
Rycek, R. F., 550
Rydell, A. M., 66
Rynders, J., 102

Saarni, C., 363
Sabate, S., 572
Sabatier, C., 327
Sabbadini, L. L., 482
Sabourin, S., 123
Saccuzzo, D. P., 423
Sacks, M., 390, 393
Sadker, D. F., 429, 540, 543
Sadker, M., 429, 540, 543
Saelens, B. E., 401, 403
Sage, N. A., 547
Sagi, A., 239, 245
Sahibzada, N. R., 369
Salbe, A. D., 400, 401
Saldinger, A., 398
Salgado, C., 286
Salny, A. F., 545
Salomon, G., 428
Salzer, L. P., 125
Samango-Sprouse, C., 385, 419
Sameroff, A., 77
Sampson, P., 134
Sampson, P. D., 131
Sampson, P. S., 133, 134
Sampson, R. J., 552
Samuel, V. J., 447
Samuels, C., 504
Samuels, C. A., 176
Sanchez-Ayendez, M., 77, 480
Sandberg, S., 447
Sandefur, G., 511
Sanders, J., 315
Sanders, M. J., 498
Sanders, S. L., 330
Sanderson, C. A., 504
Sanders-Thompson, V. L., 573
Sandler, J., 371
Sandor, R., 590
Sandqvist, K., 65
Sands, R., 399
Sanson, A., 359, 462
Sanson, A. V., 237
Santor, D. A., 597
Santos, R. A., 126
Saracho, O. N., 344
Saraswathi, T. S., 53
Sargent, S. P., 121
Sarigiani, P. A., 590
Sastry, J., 54
Sato, S., 584
Saudino, K. J., 106
Saugstad, L. F., 186
Saum, C. A., 135
Savage, D. D., 134
Savitz, D., 123
Saxon, S., 121
Scanlon, K., 132
Scarr, S., 71, 101, 102, 240, 254, 256
Schaal, B., 178
Schaefer, R. T., 51
Schaffer, A., 176
Schaffer, H. R., 408, 459
Scharf, M., 239
Scherer, K. R., 359, 360
Schermer, F., 400
Schiefele, U., 422, 423
Schiefenhoevel, W., 126
Schlegel, J. P., 123
Schmader, T., 439
Schmidt, A., 237
Schmidt, D., 248
Schmidt, L. A., 463
Schmidt, U., 403
Schneider, B., 556, 558, 559
Schneider, B. A., 177
Schneider, B. H., 464
Schneider, M., 510
Schnitzer, P. G., 137
Schoelmerich, A., 238
Schoenbaum, S. C., 131
Schoenhals, M., 559
Schopler, E., 248, 249
Schottenfeld, R., 134
Schreiber, G. B., 502
Schreiber, G. V., 399
Schuengel, C., 233, 239, 245
Schuetze, P., 130, 131
Schulinger, F., 274
Schull, W. J., 274, 401
Schultz, S., 292
Schulz, M., 334, 480, 481
Schwartz, D., 467
Schwartz, I. S., 459, 574
Schwartz, M. D., 550
Schwartzman, P., 589
Schwenger, S., 400, 401
Sciaraffa, M. A., 356
Scongryeol, R., 559
Scopesi, A., 146
Scott, B., 406
Scrimshaw, S. C. M., 187
Seachrist, L., 187
Sealand, N., 510
Secco, G., 320
Secrist, M. E., 459
Sefa-Dedeh, A., 399, 502
Segal, M. H., 24, 344, 416, 465, 582
Segal, N., 103
Segal, N. L., 101
Segal, S., 134
Seger, R. E., 94
Seidel, K. D., 402
Selby, C., 426
Selman, R., 345, 461, 573, 575
Selye, H., 405, 407, 408
Semann, S., 128
Sen, A. K., 420
Senechal, M., 329
Senior, A. M., 514
Serafica, F. C., 579
Serlin, R. C., 386
Seroczynski, S. D., 540
Serpell, R., 222
Serra, M., 246
Sewell, G., 117, 124
Shaffer, D. R., 151, 478, 577, 583, 585

Shahinfar, A., 518
Shanahan, M. J., 558, 559
Shapiro, D., 70
Shapiro, J. L., 143
Shapiro, S., 400
Shapurian, R., 601
Sharlin, S., 121
Shaw, D. S., 481
Shaw, L. K., 219
Shaw, S. M., 586
Shebar, S., 408
Sheffield, E. G., 312
Shek, D. T. L., 62, 256, 563, 564
Shell, R., 77
Shen, J., 538
Shepard, L. A., 328, 329
Shepard, S. A., 468, 469
Shepard, T. H., 131
Sherman, C., 399
Sherman, S. J., 523
Sherrill, J. T., 369
Sheynkin, Y., 123
Shifren, K., 584
Shimmin, H. S., 477
Shimonaka, Y., 584
Shiono, P., 284
Shipman, K., 362
Shireman, J., 71
Shissiak, C., 502
Shisslak, C. M., 400
Shmidt, J. L., Jr., 451
Shoda, Y., 364
Shoji, J., 58
Shore, C., 220
Shore, R., 141
Shotland, R. L., 509
Shotton, G., 469
Shulman, S., 554
Shwalb, B. J., 58
Shwalb, D. W., 58
Shwe, H. I., 449
Shweder, R. A., 184, 359, 432, 592
Siann, G., 428
Siano, B., 467
Siegal, M., 311
Siegel, B., 247, 248
Siegel, L. S., 135
Siegler, R. S., 416, 537
Siegmund, R., 126
Sigel, I. E., 7, 75
Sigelman, C. K., 512, 577, 583, 585
Sigman, M., 211, 223
Signorielli, N., 288, 401, 403
Sigueland, E. R., 213
Silbereisen, R. K., 556
Silin, J. G., 292
Silva, E., 234
Silva, S. G., 493
Silverman, A. C., 248
Silverman, P. R., 396
Silverman, W. K., 405
Silverstein, L. B., 258, 259
Simion, F., 177
Simmons, R. G., 431, 557
Simmons, R. W., 133, 134
Simon, P., 68
Simon, R. J., 70, 71
Simon, T., 109
Simons, H. D., 435, 436, 440
Simons, R., 166, 446
Simons, R. F., 211
Simons, R. L., 372
Singer, D. G., 333
Singer, J. L., 333
Singer, M. I., 517
Sjaastad, J. E., 284
Sjoeden, P. O., 399, 400
Skeels, H., 107
Skevington, S., 461
Skinner, B. F., 20–21, 24, 25, 46, 83, 214
Skinner, E. A., 423
Skinner, M. L., 597
Skodak, M., 107
Skoe, E. E. A., 593
Skolnick, A., 480
Skorikov, V. B., 558
Slaby, R. G., 466
Slater, A., 175, 206, 211, 504
Slaughter-Defoe, D. T., 73
Slife, B., 15
Slobin, D. I., 216
Slomka, G. T., 447
Slora, E., 495
Slotboom, A. M., 101
Slowiaczek, M. L., 547
Smedley, B., 361, 362
Smetana, J. G., 555, 592
Smilansky, S., 343
Smith, A. D., 404
Smith, C., 91
Smith, D. W., 70
Smith, J. R., 284
Smith, L., 516
Smith, M., 331
Smith, P. K., 536
Smith, S., 52, 54, 65, 120, 147
Smith, S. D., 445
Smolak, L., 400
Smoot, D. L., 465
Snellman, L., 437
Snezhkova, I. A., 254
Snidman, N., 463
Snow, C. W., 219
Snow, M. E., 355
Snyder, L., 182
Socha, T. J., 564
Socrates, 41, 551
Sogolow, E. D., 128
Sokol, M. S., 500, 501
Solis, C. R. P., 32
Sollie, D., 121
Soltz, V., 368
Song, M. J., 592
Song, Y. K., 219
Sorce, J. F., 179
Sorensen, I.T.A., 274
Sotheran, J. L., 128
Sparling, J. J., 212
Sparrow, S. S., 447
Spearman, C., 109
Spelke, E. S., 180, 200
Spence, J. T., 55
Spence, S. H., 361
Spencer, M. B., 406, 547, 548, 579, 580
Spencer, S., 439
Spharim, G., 321
Spinello, T. M., 400
Spitz, R. A., 235
Spitzer, S., 468
Spodek, B., 344
Sprenkle, D. H., 525
Springer, S. P., 270
Spruijt, A. P., 325
Srinivasan, S. R., 401
Sroufe, L. A., 42, 236, 285, 344
St. Peters, M., 332, 470
Stafford, F. P., 66
Stake, J. E., 584
Stanley-Hagan, M. M., 481, 483
Stanovich, K. E., 329, 331
Stanton, W. R., 496
Staples, J., 288
Staska, M., 221
Staso, W. H., 166
Stattin, H., 354
Steele, C. M., 429, 437, 438, 441
Steele, R., 129
Steele, R. G., 68
Steighner, J., 560
Stein, L. M., 313
Stein, M. T., 182, 183
Stein, N. L., 360, 361
Stein, T. S., 511
Steinberg, L., 536, 600
Steinberg, L. D., 556, 558, 559, 599
Steiner, H., 498
Steitz, J. A., 586
Stemmler, M., 570
Stenson, H., 135
Stephen, E., 123
Stephens, D. P., 506
Stephenson, J., 129
Stephenson, P. A., 148
Stern, S. B., 554
Sternberg, E. M., 463
Sternberg, K. J., 42, 464
Sternberg, R. J., 106, 107, 108, 109, 201, 276, 443, 541
Stevens, E., 18
Stevenson, D. L., 556
Stevenson, H. W., 32, 53, 61, 108, 422, 430, 431, 432, 433, 434, 435, 436
Stevenson, W., 560
Steward, O., 90
Stewart, A. J., 480
Stewart, J. H., 370
Stewart, S. L., 464
Stice, E., 500
Stice, R., 399
Stifter, C. A., 182, 256
Stigler, J. W., 435, 436
Stimson, G. V., 512
Stinchfield, R. D., 525
Stipek, D. J., 422
St. Jeor, S., 400, 401
Stocker, C., 570, 573
Stoff, D. M., 466
Stolley, M. R., 402
Stone, M., 562
Stoolmiller, M., 597
Stores, M., 390, 393
Story, M., 399, 402
Stouthamer-Loeber, M., 588
Strand, C., 468
Straus, M. A., 370
Strauss, R., 260
Streeter, L. A., 214
Streissguth, A., 131
Streissguth, A. P., 133, 134, 135
Streitmatter, J., 543
Strickland, A. L., 399
Strickland, B. R., 423
Striegel-Moore, R. H., 399, 502
Strom, K., 517
Stromshak, E. A., 465, 469
Strong, K. G., 498
Stuart, M., 321
Stubblefield, P. G., 131
Stuhr, S. L., 550
Stunkard, A. J., 274
Styfco, S. F., 210
Subhi, T., 443
Subrahmanyam, K., 426
Suddendorf, T., 426
Sue, S., 94
Suess, G., 238
Sugarman, S. D., 480
Sullivan, H. S., 242
Sullivan, K., 315
Sullivan, P. F., 502
Sumich, A., 176
Summers, P., 481
Sun, S. L., 467
Sun, Y., 61, 462, 464
Suomi, S. J., 228
Super, C. M., 53, 109, 184, 244
Surratt, H. L., 135, 521
Sutin, K. M., 136
Suzuki, D., 92

Suzuki, L. A., 425, 436
Svensson, A. K., 324, 428
Swaab, D. F., 511
Swain, M., 321
Swan, A. V., 523
Swanger, A., 536
Swanson, D. P., 406, 580
Swarr, A., 597
Swenson, L. P., 573
Swettenham, J., 248
Swidler, A., 108
Symmes, D., 221
Szatmari, P., 247
Szumski, B., 519

Tafrate, R. C., 363
Takahashi, K., 239
Takanishi, R., 73
Takeuchi, M., 393, 394
Tally, S., 571
Tamang, B. L., 359
Tamis-LeMonda, C. S., 223, 342
Tamplin, A., 469
Tan, J., 504
Tan, S. A., 451
Tang, C., 62
Tannenbaum, L., 481
Tanner, J. M., 167, 168, 272, 274, 381, 493–494, 496, 497
Tao, S., 63
Tapia, T., 236
Tardif, T., 314
Tarter, R. E., 134
Tate, C. S., 302
Taub, E., 387
Taylor, A., 447
Taylor, A. Z., 437, 438
Taylor, J. H., 476
Taylor, L. A., 346
Taylor, M., 313
Taylor, P. M., 134
Taylor, R. J., 68, 72
Taylor, R. L., 483
Taylor, W. C., 394
Taylor-Brown, S., 129
Teasdale, T. W., 274
Tein, J. Y., 77, 585
Telama, R., 394
Tellegen, A., 101, 409
Temple, J. A., 210
Tencer, H. L., 370
Terry, R., 465
Tesman, J., 282
Teti, D. M., 251, 560
Teti, L. O., 251
Tetreault, M. K. T., 431
Teufel, N., 502
Tevendale, H. D., 573
Thacker, J., 511
Thal, D., 223
Thatcher, R. W., 384
Thearle, M. J., 185
Thelen, E., 172
Thienemann, M., 173
Thomas, A., 251, 252, 481
Thomas-Presswood, T., 321
Thompson, A. D., 457, 573
Thompson, A. I., 76
Thompson, E. A., 76
Thompson, H., 572
Thompson, L. A., 211
Thompson, R. A., 245, 250, 474
Thorn, A. S. C., 321
Thornberry, T. P., 520
Thorne, B., 429
Thornell, A., 447
Thornton, M. C., 68, 72
Thorpe, L. A., 177
Thurling, S., 236
Tienda, M., 559
Tincoff, R., 218
Tinker, 219
Tittel, M., 126
Tizard, B., 235
Tjebkes, T. L., 244
Toda, S., 221, 342, 365
Tomasello, M., 221, 222
Tomkins, A. J., 448
Tonge, B. J., 330
Tonkin, R. S., 402
Torff, B., 387
Torgesen, J. K., 332
Torrance, E. P., 420
Torun, B., 400, 401
Towell, D., 446
Townsend, B. L., 459
Tracy, N., 595
Traeger, C., 572
Travis, J., 100
Treder, R. P., 131
Trehub, S. E., 177
Tremble, B., 510
Trepper, T. S., 525
Trevarthen, C., 221, 242, 246
Triandis, H. C., 85
Tricker, J., 399
Trickett, P. K., 372, 518
Troiden, R. R., 510
Tronick, E. A., 56–57, 244
Tronick, E. Z., 244
Troseth, G. L., 332
Trudge, J., 418
Truglio, R., 222, 333
Trull, T. J., 101
Trusty, J., 561
Tsay, J., 527
Tseng, H., 73
Tsunetsugu, K., 58
Tucker, C. M., 69, 561
Tucker, J. A., 522
Tuckman, B. W., 393
Tudge, J. R. H., 254
Tuohy, G., 100
Turbin, M. S., 498
Turiel, E., 592
Turkheimer, E., 105
Turner, R. A., 506, 507

Ullman, A., 522
Underwood, M. K., 470
Uppal, S., 573
Urberg, K. A., 527, 596
Urbina, S., 107, 541

Vacca, J., 437
Valencia, J. F., 321
Valencia, R. R., 436
Valente, E., 469
Valkenburg, P. M., 332
Vallano, G., 447
Vallar, C., 385
Vallerand, R. J., 561
van Aken, M. A. G., 238
Van Balen, F., 124
van Brakel, A., 245
Vance, J. C., 185
Van Dam, M., 256
Vandell, D. L., 482
Vandenberg, B., 341
Vandereycken, W., 402
van der Maas, H. L. J., 419
van Dongen, L., 245
Van Dongen-Melman, J. E. W. M., 573
Van Evra, J. P., 333, 467
van Geert, R. L. C., 246
Van-Horn, J. D., 447
van IJzendoorn, M. H., 233, 239, 241, 245, 256
Van Kammen, W. B., 588
Van Lieshout, C. F. M., 238, 459, 575
Vann, F., 510
Van Santen, V., 373
van Schie, E. G. M., 425
Van Stegeren, A. H., 163
Vartanian, L. R., 550
Vasquez-Nuttal, E., 571
Vaugh, B. E., 347
Vaugh, L. S., 176
Vaux, A., 559
Veatch, T. C., 451
Vega, W. A., 573
Velasco, R., 594
Venuti, P., 365
Verdurmen, J., 124
Vereijken, B., 169
Vereijken, C. M. J. L., 238
Verhulst, F. C., 573
Veridiano, N., 510
Vermigli, P., 464
Vernon, P. A., 108
Veroff, J., 33
Veron-Guidry, S., 399
Viemero, V., 466
Vigfusdottir, T. R., 502
Vigorito, J., 213
Viikari, J., 394
Vik, P., 522
Vikan, A., 583
Villan, M. F., 161
Vinden, P. G., 314, 315
Vingerhoets, A. J. M., 124
Visscher, W. D., 135
Vito, D., 401, 403
Vogel, S. H., 22, 59, 73
Vogt, C. J., 400, 401
Volkmar, F. R., 447
Von der Lippe, A. L., 552
Von der Schulenburg, C., 504
Vondracek, F. W., 556, 558
Voss, K., 108
Vygotsky, L., 30–32, 46, 109, 202, 306–310, 321, 336, 508
Vyt, A., 365

Wachs, T., 164, 251, 252
Wachtel, P. L., 437
Wackman, D., 401
Waddington, C. H., 97
Wagner, B. M., 589, 597
Wagner, R. F., 271
Wagner, R. K., 332
Wakeley, A., 165, 208
Wakschlag, L. S., 132
Walco, G. A., 381, 382
Walden, T. A., 246, 360
Waldron, M., 105
Walker, C. E., 167, 272, 380, 382
Walker, D. L., 460, 465, 574
Walker, L. J., 476, 593, 594
Walker, S. Y., 443, 444
Walkins, R. V., 210
Wall, S., 232
Wallace, B. A., 579
Wallerstein, J. S., 481, 482, 484
Wallhagen, M. L., 238
Wallis, C., 447
Wandersman, L. P., 212
Wang, L., 360
Wang, P. P., 212
Wang, S., 468
Wang, V., 94
Wang, Y., 348
Ward, L. M., 394
Ward, S., 401
Warren, A. R., 302
Warren, J. R., 540, 543
Wartner, U. G., 238
Washington, A. C., 516
Washington, S. K., 398
Washington, W. M., 347
Wasik, B. H., 212, 439
Wass, T. S., 166

Wasserman, R., 495
Wasserstein, S., 405
Watanabe, H., 59, 73
Waters, E., 232
Waters, P., 456, 458, 570, 572
Watkins, D., 295, 573
Watkinson, B., 132, 135
Watson, J. B., 19–20, 26, 46
Watts, R. E., 561
Waxman, S. R., 219
Way, N., 506, 574
Weaver, K. R., 590
Webber, L. S., 401
Webster-Stratton, C., 208
Weeber, E. J., 134
Weed, S., 510
Wehrfritz, G., 505
Weinberg, C., 138
Weinberg, J., 134
Weinberg, K., 245
Weinberg, R., 71
Weinberger, D. R., 447
Weinfield, N. S., 236
Weinfurt, K., 59, 73
Weinraub, M., 485
Weis, L., 431
Weisfeld, G., 580
Weisner, T., 447
Weiss, L., 428
Weiss, R. L., 481
Weisz, V., 448
Wekerle, C., 372
Wekesser, C., 519
Welch, E., 328
Welles, N. B., 131
Welling, M., 584
Wellman, H. M., 313, 314, 422
Wellman, H. W., 218, 312, 313, 315
Wells, C. L., 394
Wells, K. A., 271
Welsh, M., 468
Werker, J. F., 221
Werner, E. E., 409
Wesley, F., 555
Wessels, H., 325
West, J. R., 133
West, P., 523
West, T., 437
Westra, T., 172
Wetter, R., 584
Weymann, A., 556
Whalen, S., 562
Whaley, L. F., 287
Wheaton, B., 403
Whissell, C., 360
Whitaker, R. C., 402
Whitbeck, L. B., 372
White, J., 560
White, L., K., 131
White, M. J., 560
White, R. D., 188
White, S. A., 391
Whitehurst, G. J., 331
Whitesell, N. R., 456, 458, 570, 572
Whiting, B., 477
Whiting, J., 477
Whitman, T. L., 188
Widener, A. J., 447
Wieder, S., 166, 248, 249, 446
Wiederman, M. W., 501
Wiegman, O., 425
Wiener, L. S., 129
Wierson, M., 481
Wierzbicka, A., 359
Wigfield, A., 422, 423, 571, 572
Wijnroks, L., 232
Wilcox, A., 138
Wilcox, K., 101
Wilcox, M., 222
Wild, M. N., 481
Wilems, P. J., 90
Wilfley, D. E., 399
Wilgosh, L., 328
Wille, D. E., 245
Willerman, L., 101, 107
Willert, A., 506
Williams, D. R., 401
Williams, J. E., 582, 583
Williams, K. A., 163
Williams, R. A., 407
Williams, W., 432
Williams, W. M., 276, 443, 541
Williamson, D. A., 399
Willinger, M., 186
Willis, S. K., 187
Wilson, B. J., 598
Wilson, D. M., 497
Wilson, G. S., 134
Wilson, R. S., 103, 107, 111–112
Wimbush, D. D., 69, 72
Wing, L., 247
Wingert, P., 334
Winickoff, S. A., 121
Winner, E., 449
Winner, H., 315
Winsler, A., 320
Winslow, E. B., 481
Winstok, Z., 520
Winters, K. C., 525
Wisnicwski, L., 401
Witkowski, T., 423
Witschi, J., 499
Witt, S. D., 586
Wittchen, H., 240
Witte, H., 387
Wo, J., 538
Wodarski, J. S., 518
Wolf, A. M., 499
Wolf, A. W., 183
Wolfe, B., 284, 285
Wolfe, C., 439
Wolfe, D. A., 371, 372
Wolfe, P., 210
Wolfson, A. R., 184, 496
Wong, D. L., 287
Wong, E. K. N., 589
Wong-Kerberg, L., 371
Wood, C. H., 353
Wood, D., 503
Woods, B. T., 269
Woods, N., 135
Woods, N. S., 135
Woolfson, R., 213
Worden, J. W., 398
Work, W. C., 406, 407, 408
Worley, L. P., 559
Wren, D. J., 430
Wright, B., 365
Wright, D. J., 502
Wright, J. A., 402
Wright, J. C., 222, 332, 333, 470
Wright, W., 106
Wu, C., 59, 73
Wu, D. Y. H., 65
Wu, M., 527
Wulff, M. B., 586
Wyman, P. A., 408

Xia, X., 402
Xiao, H., 63
Xie, G., 420
Xie, H., 466
Xu, F., 176

Yaeger, J., 307
Yager Smith, S., 146
Yamamoto, N., 238
Yang, K., 62
Yang, X., 394
Yarnold, B. M., 498
Yeargin-Allsopp, M., 442
Yeung, W., 284, 285
Yi, S. H., 425
Yi Qing, L., 325
Yoder, K. A., 589
Young, B., 447
Young, D., 330
Young, E. R., 443
Young, G., 362
Young, S., 447
Young, T., 146
Youngblade, L. M., 236, 316
Yu, G., 62
Yu, H. C., 576
Yuen-Tsang, A. W. K., 256

Zahn-Waxler, C., 58, 362
Zakriski, A., 468, 470
Zane, N., 94
Zane, N. W. S., 392
Zanobini, M., 146
Zappulla, C., 464
Zaslow, M. J., 483
Zavaleta, A. N., 401
Zbikowski, S. M., 459
Zeanah, C. H., 241
Zecker, S. G., 445
Zeidenstein, S., 126
Zelazo, N. A., 172
Zelazo, P. D., 172
Zelazo, P. R., 172
Zeljo, A., 316
Zell, Jennifer, 125
Zeman, J., 362
Zeng, Q., 63
Zeskind, P. S., 130, 131
Zha, Z., 420
Zhang, K., 64
Zhao, S., 240
Ziegenhain, T., 232
Ziegler, E., 328, 329
Zigler, E. F., 210, 254, 284, 481
Zimba, R. F., 473, 476
Zimler, J., 419
Zimmer-Gembeck, M. J., 423
Zitzow, D., 601
Ziv, M., 315
Ziv, S., 421
Zucker, K., 511
Zuckerman, B., 135
Zuckerman, M., 509
Zuger, R., 511
Zuzich, M. F., 286, 288

SUBJECT INDEX

Abecedarian Project, 210
abortion, 126, 516
accommodation, 23, 198
achievement tests, 540–542, 566
acquired immunodeficiency syndrome (AIDS), 127–129, 512–514
active listening, 565
activity levels, 103
acute illnesses, 395–396
adaptation, 198, 252, 409
adaptation executors, 41
adipose tissue, 191
adolescence. *See also* puberty
  adult responses to, 564–566
  argumentativeness, 551–555
  body image, 498
  cognitive development, 536–539, 566
  dating, 505
  definition, 492–493
  divorce of parents, 481
  drug abuse, 521–527
  early maturation effects, 497
  education, 555–562
  employment, 558–559
  friendships, 573–576
  gender roles, 582–587
  guilt feelings, 594–595
  idealism, 550–551
  independence, 493, 599–601
  juvenile delinquency, 587–588
  language development, 562–563
  moral development, 591–597
  nutrition, 498–499
  parent relationships, 493, 496, 551–555, 595–601
  perceptions, 44
  planning for the future, 535
  pregnancy, 131, 150, 295, 506, 513–517, 528
  privacy, 493
  self understanding, 570–573, 577–582
  sexuality, 503–517
  sexually transmitted diseases, 511–514
  sleep deprivation, 496
  suicide, 498, 589–591
  violence and, 518–521
adoption, 70–71, 516
adoption studies, 98–99, 101, 107
adrenaline, 361
affection, need for, 189
AFP (alpha-fetoprotein) test, 95–96
African Americans
  accommodation without assimilation, 440
  body-build proportions, 274
  child care, 255
  child-rearing practices, 69–72, 78
  co-sleeping of infants, 183
  drug abuse, 524, 527
  education, 431, 435–439, 560
  emotion talk in, 316
  ethnic identity, 68
  families, 67, 69, 480
  friendships, 460, 574
  identity issues, 579
  IQ tests, 107–108
  low birth weight, 150
  minority status difficulties, 68–69
  moral development, 592
  motor skill development, 171
  puberty, 495
  punishment, 370
  self-esteem, 571–572
  sexuality, 506
  sexually transmitted diseases, 128, 512
  sickle-cell anemia, 91–92, 396
  stress, 405
  television viewing, 394, 401
  transethnic adoption of, 70–71
  unemployment, 560
  violence, 518–519
  weight issues, 400–401, 501
African children
  attachment in, 235
  body image, 399, 502
  breast feeding, 188
  childbirth rate, 120
  cognitive development, 23–24, 313–315
  infant emotions, 244
  intelligence, 109
  language development, 213, 214, 222
  nutrition and development, 498–499
  play, 344, 392
  praise by parents, 53
  rites of passage, 580
  sickle-cell anemia, 91–92, 396
  socialization, 32
  temperament, 252
  understanding of death, 397
afterbirth, 149
aftercare, 525
Agent Orange, 137
aggression
  anabolic steroids, 498
  child factors, 465
  cultural variations, 464
  father–child relationship, 465
  hostile attributions, 469–470
  media violence and, 426, 466–467, 470–471, 520
  parent responses, 466–467
  peer factors, 466–467
  physical punishment and, 369, 471
  rejected-aggressive children, 465–471
  underachievers, 546
agility, 389–390
AIDS, 127–129, 512–514
Aka pygmy children, 18
Albert, conditioning experiment on, 19–20
Alcoholics Anonymous (AA), 525
alcohol use
  driving and, 522
  effects, 521–522
  infertility and, 123
  multiculturalism, 521
  Plato on, 508
  during pregnancy, 133–134, 136
  statistics, 522–523
  treatment, 525
alleles, 85
alpha-fetoprotein test (AFP), 95–96
altruism, 103–104
amae, 59
American College Test (ACT), 540, 542
amniocentesis, 95
amphetamines, 136
anabolic steroids, 498
anaclitic identification, 350
anal stage, 15, 16
anandamide, 522
androgens, 353
androgyny, 583–587
anemia, 130, 149, 287
anemia, sickle-cell, 91–92, 112, 396
anger, 362–364. *See also* aggression; violence
animistic thinking, 302–304
anorexia nervosa, 379, 399, 499–503
antibiotics, 136
antigens/antibodies, 187
anxiety. *See also* stress
  castration, 350
  in infants, 245

post-traumatic stress disorder, 518
school phobia, 330–331
anxious-avoidance attachment relations, 232–233, 344
anxious-resistant attachment relations, 232–234
Apgar Scale, 149
aphasia, 444
Argentinian children, 365
argumentativeness, 551–555
arhythmicity, 252
artificial fertilization, 124–125
Asian Americans
achievement in school, 39, 102, 431–432
composition of, 72
families, 72–73, 480
friendships, 460
genetic screening, 94
Asian children. *See* Chinese children; Japanese children; Thai children
Asperger's disorder, 247
aspirin, 131, 136
assertiveness, aggression and, 465
assimilation, 23, 198
associative play, 341
athletic games. *See* sports
attachment
assessment, 230–232
child care and, 255–256
classifications, 232–235, 261
critical period, 229, 231
cultural variations, 233, 238–239
examples of, 227–228
factors affecting, 256–257
fostering strong relations, 240–241
insecure, 232–235, 236, 344
nonattachment, 235
preschool friendships and, 344
progression of, 228–229
Q-sort, 232
separation anxiety, 229, 245, 257, 330–331
significance of, 235–236
social and cognitive skills, 236
Strange Situation test, 230–232, 261
attachment Q-sort, 232
attention, 416–418
attention deficit hyperactivity disorder (ADHD), 446–448
attractiveness
eating disorders and, 399, 499
employment advantages, 504
as ideal, 503–504
infant preferences for, 175–177
Australian Aborigines, 149
authoritative/authoritarian parents, 367–368, 370, 548, 554–555, 573, 601
autism, 246–249, 262
automobile accidents, 282, 396, 522
autosomes, 88, 91–92
axons, 159–160, 385
babbling, 217–218
Babinski reflex, 169
baby talk, 220–221
balance, 277, 388–389
balance beam problem, 537
Balinese children, 420
ball skills, 277–278
Bandura, Albert, 21, 26, 351–352
Baoule children, 23–24
barbiturates, 136
baths, for newborns, 148
Baumrind, Diana, 367–368
Bayley Scales of Infant Development (BSID), 171, 209, 211
beauty, as ideal, 503–504
bed-wetting, 289–290
behaviorism
culture and, 21–22
discipline, 369
language development, 214–215, 225
Skinner on, 20–21, 24–26, 214–215
Watson on, 19–20, 26, 46
weakness of theory, 26
behavior modification, 21, 447
benzene, 136
benzodiazepines, 136
bilingualism, 320–321
biological theory, gender roles in, 353
birth. *See* childbirth
birth defects
from AIDS and measles, 127–129
cocaine, 135
fetal alcohol syndrome, 133–134
genetic disorders, 89–91
Rh factor, 129–130
birthing centers, 146–147
blacks. *See* African Americans
blastocysts, 139
blended families, 482–485, 487
blood
cardiovascular system, 272
childbirth, 149
hemophilia, 88, 93
Rh factor, 129–130
sickle-cell anemia, 91–92, 396
body image
"beauty is good" hypothesis, 504
in early childhood, 174–175, 347
eating disorders and, 399, 501
ideal physiques, 399, 498, 528
names for body parts, 290–291
physical attractiveness, 503–504
respect for bodies, 291
self-worth and, 573
boys. *See also* gender differences
androgynous, 586–587
early maturation effects, 497
gender role lessons, 354–357
growth rates, 274, 381, 493–494
ideal physique, 498
motor development, 388–389
puberty, 494–495
self-esteem, 571–573
brain development
in adolescence, 532–536
Broca's/Wernicke's areas, 216, 269, 384
in early childhood, 268–270, 272
emotions and, 163
environmental input, 162–163
fostering growth, 164–165
growth spurts, 163–164, 384–385
hemispheric activity, 270–271, 384
homosexuality and, 511
in infants, 158–161, 192
language and, 216, 220
memory, 161, 205, 310–313, 419, 538–539, 566
in middle childhood, 383–387, 410, 419
musical abilities, 386–387
plasticity, 163, 384
prenatal, 141, 150–151
pruning process, 161–163, 383–384
repair of damage, 384–385
structure, 161
Braxton Hicks contractions, 148
Brazelton Neonatal Assessment Scale (NBAS), 135, 149–150
breast feeding, 187–189
British children, 254, 394
Broca's area, 216, 269, 384
bulimia nervosa, 399, 499–503
burns, 282

caffeine, 130–131, 136, 523
Cameroon, 5–6
canalized traits, 97
cardiovascular endurance, 394
cardiovascular system, 272, 394
caregivers. *See also* parents
attachment and, 236, 255
cultural variations, 238–239
insensitive, 241
perception of role, 53–54
case studies, features of, 33, 38
castration anxiety, 350
catching skills, 278
catecholamines, 451
Caucasian children. *See* European American children
cell division, 86–87
cell migration, 141
center care, 322–324. *See also* day care
center stage syndrome, 550
central nervous system, 134, 158–162, 268–269, 272
centration, 301, 304, 415–416
cephalocaudal, 168
cerebellum, 268
cerebral cortex, 161, 164, 268, 383, 387
cerebrum, 164

cesarean section, 148
child abuse, 371–374
childbirth. *See also* newborns
afterbirth, 149
birthing center choice, 146–147
father present at, 237–240
postpartum period, 151, 153
premature, 150–151, 153
relaxed, painless, 145–146, 152–153
stages of, 147–149
child care. *See* day care
child development. *See* cognitive development; developmental theories; physical development
Child Development Issues
adaptability of the human brain, 384–385
adolescent risk-taking, 508–509
are girls getting shortchanged in school?, 542–543
breast or bottle?, 189
critical period for attachment, 231
do smart infants become smart children?, 211
expectant fathers, 143
extending the school year, 434
fathers—the forgotten parent?, 143
how adaptable is the human brain?, 384–385
media violence and aggression, 466–467
mixed-ethnic adoption, 70–71
poverty and development outcomes, 284–285
rites of passage and identity status, 580–581
school phobia, 330–331
socialization of gender roles, 355
childhood, historical attitudes toward, 6–10
childhood disintegrative disorder, 247
chimney sweeps, 9
Chinese American children. *See also* Asian Americans
body-build proportions, 274
child-rearing practices, 73, 78–79
drug use, 527
infants' interaction with faces, 176
mathematics skills, 39
parent–adolescent conflict, 553
Chinese children
academic achievement, 433–434
attachment, 256
change toward individualism, 61–62
creativity, 420
day care, 325
emotions, 359
4-2-1 syndrome, 64–65
one-child policy, 50, 63–64, 78
parent relationships, 54, 600
sex preferences for firstborn children, 126–127
sexual behavior, 505
social skills, 462, 464
teachers, 435
weakening of the family, 62–63
chlamydia, 513
chorionic villus sampling, 95
chromosomes. *See also* genetics
autosomes, 88, 91–92
DNA replication, 87–88
Down syndrome, 442
gene-linkage studies, 99
overview, 84, 112
preimplantation genetic testing, 137
sex, 88–90, 93
chronic illnesses, 396
chronosystem, 29
circular reactions, 199–200
circumcision, 178
classical conditioning, 19–20
classification skills, 415
class inclusion, 416
climbing skills, 278
cliques, 574
cocaine, 135, 136, 523
coffee drinking, 130–131
cognitive development. *See also* intelligence
active manipulation, 204
in adolescence, 492, 532–548
attachment and, 236
attention, 416–418
centration, 301, 304, 415–416
classification, 415
class inclusion, 416
combinatorial analysis, 534
conservation, 416–417
definition, 45
developmental quotient, 209
in early childhood, 299–337
equilibrium, 196–198
habituation, 205–206, 211
hypothetico-deductive reasoning, 534–535
imaginary audience, 549–550
imitation, 206–207, 224, 246
importance of play, 203–204
in infancy, 195–225
intrinsic motivation, 202
knowledge base, 539
logical knowledge, 203–204, 301–303
memory, 161, 205, 310–313, 419, 538–539, 566
metacognition, 538, 566
in middle childhood, 413–453
object permanence, 200–202
organization and adaptation, 198
overstimulation, 207–208
personal fables, 549–550
Piaget's stages, 199–200, 224, 300–305, 414–417
postformal thinking, 536
poverty and, 284
problem-finding thinkers, 536
propositional thinking, 533
psychometric assessment, 208–212, 224
relativistic thinking, 533
reversibility, 301, 415
sarcasm, 449–450
schemes, 23, 198, 305
self-awareness, 243, 570–573
Siegler's model, 537–538
social cognition, 461
theory of mind in young children, 313–316
transformations, understanding of, 301, 305
video games and, 426
cognitive-developmental theory, 22–26, 352
cohabitation, in Sweden, 65
cohort effect, 38–39
colds, 283, 395
colic, 182
collectivism, 54–56, 58, 78, 508
Colorado Adoption Study, 107
color blindness, 89, 93
colors, seen by infants, 177
colostrum, 144
combinatorial analysis, 534
communication. *See also* language
I messages, 565
with infants, 222–223
listening, 565
patterns, 563–564
prelinguistic, 216–218
put-down messages, 564–565
solution-type messages, 564
suicide prevention and, 590
competency self-esteem, 349
competition, 391
computer-assisted instruction (CAI), 427
computers, 165–166, 425, 427–429
conception, 138–140, 152. *See also* fertilization
concrete operational thinkers, 414–416, 533
conditioning, classical, 19–20
condoms, 513
confounding variables, 36
Confucius, 6, 46
connectivity, of neurons, 162, 192
conscience, 14
conservation, 416–417
consistency, 369–370, 570
contexts, 28, 31, 109
contextual models. *See also* developmental theories
Bell, 27
Bronfenbrenner, 28–29, 46
Minuchin, 27–28
Vygotsky, 30–32, 46
continuity *vs.* discontinuity, 41–42
contraception, 63–64, 517
contractions, 148
control groups, 35
conventional moral reasoning, 474–475
convergent thinking, 419
cooing, 217
cooperative play, 341

coordination, 383, 388–389
corporal punishment, 7–8. *See also* punishment
corpus callosum, 270
correlational method, 37, 38
cortisol, 451, 463
co-sleeping, 183–184, 186
crack cocaine, 523
cradleboards, 74–75
creativity, 419–421, 444
crib death (SIDS), 132, 135, 184–186, 193
critical periods, in attachment, 229, 231
crossed eyes, 382
crossing over, of chromosomes, 87
cross-sectional studies, 38, 40
cross-sequential studies, 39
crowds, 574
crying, 181–182, 192, 243
cultural diversity. *See* multiculturalism
Cultural Variations. *See also* multiculturalism
  assessing intelligence, 109
  attachment relations, 238–239
  child care, 325
  communicating with infants, 222–223
  cultural meanings of social behavior, 464
  culture and moral development, 592
  do parents matter?, 102
  fathers around the world, 60
  games and sports, 392–393
  meanings of social behavior, 464
  in motor development, 172–173
  occupational training, 556
  play, 342–343
  sex education, 294–295
  sex preferences for firstborn children, 126–127
  sexuality, 506
  teachers, 436–437
  Vygotsky on the importance of cultural contexts, 32
culture. *See also* multiculturalism
  behaviorism and, 21–22
  competency and, 52–54
  definition, 3, 30, 49
  emotions and, 21, 358–360
  importance in child development, 18, 30, 202
  Piaget on, 23–24
  Vygotsky on, 30–32
Cylert, 447

Danish children, 554–555
dating, 505
day care
  advantages and disadvantages, 324
  center care, 322–323
  effects on attachment, 255–256
  family, 255, 322
  public benefits for, 66–67, 324
  quality criteria, 324–326
deafness, 180–181, 221–222
death
  causes of, 397
  cultural views on, 396–397
  of infants, 185
  reactions to grief, 398–399
  stages of grief, 398
  from teenage pregnancy, 514–515
  understanding by children, 398, 410
decentration, 301, 304, 415–416
defensive identification, 350
deferred imitation, 207, 303
degree of fit, 251–252
delayed gratification, 363–364
delivery stage, 148, 150
demandingness, 102, 367
dendrites, 158–160, 162, 385
Denver II Developmental Screening Test (DDST), 279–280, 296
dependent variables, 35–36
depressants, 521–522
depression
  from child abuse, 373
  eating disorders, 400
  genetic factors, 92
  of mothers, 240
  postpartum, 151
  suicide and, 590
deprivation dwarfism, 273
depth perception, 178–179
desensitization, 330–331, 467
determinism, 42, 84
developmental issues
  attachment, 235–236
  continuity *vs.* discontinuity, 41–42
  effects of poverty, 284–285
  importance of early experiences, 42–43
  improving children's lives, 43–44
  nature *vs.* nurture, 40–41
developmental quotient (DQ), 209
developmental theories. *See also* contextual models
  ancient Chinese, 115–116
  assessment of, 24–26
  Bandura, 21, 26, 351–352
  behaviorism, 18–22
  Erikson, 15–18, 24–26, 46, 157
  Freud, 13–17, 25, 26, 46, 228, 350–351
  information-processing, 204–208, 224, 310–313, 352–353, 416–419, 536–539
  Kohlberg, 352, 474–478, 486, 591–594
  multiple intelligences, 385–387, 410
  Navajo, 75
  Piaget, 22–26, 199–200, 224, 300–305, 414–417, 472–474
  psychometric assessment, 208–212, 224
  Skinner, 20–21, 24–26, 214–215
  Vygotsky, 30–32, 46, 109, 202, 306–310, 336
  Watson, 19–20, 26, 46
development domains, 45–46
Dexedrine, 447
el Dia de los Muertos, 397
dialogic reading, 331
diaschisis, 385
diet. *See* nutrition
difficult temperaments, 251
dioxins, 137
diploid cells, 87
directed groping, 200
disabilities, learning, 444–445
discipline. *See also* punishment
  in blended families, 483–485
  consistency in, 369–370
  cultural variations, 59–61, 73
  definition, 365
  parenting styles and, 366–368
  punishment *vs.*, 370
  questionnaire on, 366
  reinforcement, 369
dishabituation, 205–206, 211
disorganized-disoriented attachment relations, 234–235
distractibility, 252
divergent thinking, 419
diversity, cultural. *See* multiculturalism
divorce, 65, 480–482, 487
dizygotic twins, 98–99
DNA (deoxyribonucleic acid), 84, 86–87, 100, 112. *See also* genetics
DNA testing, 137
Doll Preference Test, 71
domestic violence, 518
dominant genes, 85–86
Down syndrome, 89–90, 102, 131, 442
drawing ability, 274–275, 278–279
dreams, 289
dropping out of school, 559–562
drownings, 282–283, 396
drug abuse. *See also* alcohol use
  amphetamines, 136
  anabolic steroids, 498
  cocaine, 135
  definition, 521
  heroin, 134
  infertility and, 123
  marijuana, 135–136
  progression, 524
  rates, 523–524
  reasons, 524–525
  risk factors, 468
  selling drugs, 524
  treatment, 525
  types of drugs, 521–523
drugs, definition, 521
Dutch children, 256, 325
dyscalculia, 444
dysfluency, 319
dysgraphia, 444
dyslexia, 444, 448

early childhood
  attention, 417–418
  body image, 174–175
  brain development, 268–270, 272
  divorce during, 480–481
  emotional understanding, 360–362
  expansion in, 340–341
  gender roles, 349–358
  height and weight, 271–272
  humor, 451
  intervention programs, 211–212
  kindergarten, 326, 328–329, 334–336
  language development, 269, 306–310, 317–321, 336
  memory, 310–313
  motor development, 276–281
  nutrition, 284–288
  perceptual skills, 44, 275–276, 345, 418
  preoperational stage, 300–305
  safety concerns, 282–283, 326
  self-concept, 347–349
  sex education, 291–295
  sleeping patterns, 288–289
  theory of mind in, 313–316
early failure syndrome, 329
easy temperament, 251
eating disorders
  anorexia nervosa, 379, 399, 499–500
  bulimia nervosa, 399, 499–501
  causes, 501–502
  early dieting, 400
  ideal body and, 399, 499
  low self-esteem and depression, 400
  parents and, 400
  treatment, 502–503
  warning signs, 499
ecological approach, 28–29
economic factors, 482, 484, 506, 558. *See also* poverty
education
  academic failure, 423–424, 559–560
  academic success, 334, 421–425, 440, 559
  academic tracking, 433–434
  attention deficit hyperactivity disorder, 446–448
  computers in, 165–166, 427–428
  day cares, 322–323
  effects of employment on, 559
  extracurricular activities, 561–562
  family factors, 102, 212, 241
  friendships and, 334
  gender differences, 430–432, 540–543
  gender preferences, 429–431
  gifted children, 423, 442–444, 452
  for girls, 8–9, 429–431
  high school curriculum, 555–556
  for insensitive caregivers, 241
  kindergarten, 326, 328–329, 334–336
  learning disabilities, 444–445, 452
  length of school year, 434
  mentally challenged children, 441–442, 452
  multicultural, 439–441
  Navajo, 75–76
  occupational training, 556–557
  overachievers, 541–542
  poverty and school achievement, 284–285
  praise for ability *vs.* effort, 422
  preschools, 61, 64–65, 321, 323, 334, 357
  readiness, 326–329
  role models, 440
  scaffolding, 308
  school phobia, 330–331
  single-sex, 543
  social adjustment at school, 333–334
  teachers, 335, 435–437
  television and video games, 333, 426
  underachievers, 543–548
  zone of proximal development, 30, 307–309
Efe children, 56–57
egg donation, 124
eggs, 87
ego, Freudian definition, 14
egocentric speech, 306
egocentrism, 301, 304, 508, 549
Electra complex, 350
embryonic period, 139–141, 152
emic perspective, 55, 57
emotional abuse, 371–372
emotions
  anger, 362–364
  autism, 246–249, 262
  autonomy, 21, 598, 600
  belief-dependent, 315
  brain development, 163
  classification, 358–359
  culture and, 21, 358–360
  early childhood, 360–362
  emergence in infants, 244–245, 262
  emotionality, 597–598
  endocrine system and, 131
  expectant fathers, 143
  facial expressions, 359–360
  fears, 330–331, 361–362
  gender roles, 358
  imitation of, in infants, 246
  parental relationship, 597–599
  of parents, 240
  poverty and, 285
  self-control, 363
  social referencing, 245–246
  stability in, 103, 105
  support for teenage mothers, 516–517
  temperament and, 249–254
empathy, 478–479
employment
  of adolescents, 558–559, 567
  attractiveness and, 504
  occupational training, 556–557
  unemployment, 559–560
endocrine system, 131
endorphins, 451
English as a second language, 321
equilibrium, 196–198
erogenous zones, 14
Eskimo children, 340–341
estrogen, 494
ethics. *See* moral development
ethics, of Human Genome Project, 100
ethnic groups. *See also* minority groups; multiculturalism
  ADHD and, 447
  child abuse, 372
  definition, 52
  drug abuse, 527
  ethnic identity, 68, 71
  growth rates, 381
  identity differences, 579
  IQ and, 107–108
  obesity in, 400–401
  puberty, 495
  risk-taking behavior, 508–509
  self-esteem, 571
  suicide, 589
  violence and, 519
ethnicity, definition, 52
ethnocentrism, 50, 57
ethnolinguistics, 212–213
ethnosensitivity, 76
etic perspective, 56–57
European-American children
  body image, 501
  divorce of parents, 480–481
  drug abuse, 524
  friendships, 437, 460, 462, 574
  identity issues, 579
  language, 53
  parent–adolescent conflicts, 552–553
  proportion of, 52
  puberty, 495
  school success, 39, 560
  self-esteem, 571–572
  sexuality, 506
  smoking, 523–524
  stress, 405
  teenage pregnancy, 513
  use of term, 52
evolutionary psychology, 41
executive processing space, 305
exosystems, 28–29
expansions, 319
experienced canalization theory, 97
experimental groups, 35
experimental method, 35–36, 38
explicit rules, 213
explosions, 396
external locus of control, 423–424
extracurricular activities, 561–562
extroversion, 101–103, 105
eye-hand coordination, 383, 388

facial expressions, 359–360
FAE (fetal alcohol effects), 133
false beliefs, 313–315
families
aggressive children and, 465
blended, 482–485, 487
changes with children, 120–121
Chinese, 62–63
day care by, 255, 322
divorce, 480–482
dropping out of school and, 561
drug abuse and, 525, 527
dual-wage, 256–260
eating disorders and, 502–503
ethnic minority, 68–69
gifted children, 443–444
intelligence of children and, 110
juvenile delinquency and, 588
Latino, 76–77
leave policies, 259
in middle childhood 480–485, 465, 487
moral behavior and, 476–477
sexual abuse, 371
single-parent, 481, 482, 484–485, 487
stress and, 406, 408
teenage parents, 516–517
violence in, 518
family care, 255, 322. *See also* day care
family systems model, 27–28
FAS (fetal alcohol syndrome), 133–134
fathers. *See also* parents
African American, 69, 72
aggressive children and, 465
attachment to, 229, 231, 237–241, 262
during childbirth process, 146
in child development, 27
Chinese, 63
conflicts with adolescents, 553
cultural variations, 60
in dual-wage families, 256–260
expectant, 142–143, 152
gender roles and, 354–355
generative fathering, 258–260, 262
Japanese, 58–59
Mexican American, 77
on-the-job training, 240
reasons to become, 116–120, 152
self-esteem of, 121
Swedish, 65
teenage, 515
fats, dietary, 286
fatty acids, 186
fears
early childhood, 361–362
of punishment, 370
school phobia, 330–331
shyness, 463, 468–469
femininity, 583–587
fertility drugs, 138–139
fertilization, 88, 124–125, 138–140
fetal alcohol effects (FAE), 133
fetal alcohol syndrome (FAS), 133–134
fetal period, 139, 141–142
field experiments, 36
50-50 parenting, 260–261
Filipino-American children, 553
finances, personal, 558
fine motor development, 278–279
First Person
being physically fit, 390
best disciplinarian ever, 369
breaking away from poverty, 286
child care in Sweden, 324
Chris, a stay-at-home dad, 259
cliques and friendships, 574
everyday learning, 204
geniuses of tomorrow, 165
identical twins, 99
in vitro fertilization, 125
learning disabled children, 445
longitudinal research, 39
making money the wrong way, 524
mother and daughter communication, 565
single parenting after divorce, 485
a visit to Peking University, 63
working with learning disabled children, 445
fixation, 14
flexibility, of caregivers, 253
flexibility, physical, 395
flu, 395
fontanelles, 150
food. *See* nutrition
food allergies, 287
foot withdrawal reflex, 169
formal operational thinking, 532–536
foster care, for abused children, 373
4-2-1 syndrome, 64–65
fragile X syndrome, 90, 162
French children, 325, 394
Freud, Sigmund
attachment, 228
child development advice, 16
gender-role development, 350–351
humor, 451
legacy of, 13–14
psychosexual stages, 14–15, 25–26, 46
universality of ideas, 16
women, 17
friendships. *See also* social skills
adolescence, 573–576
benefits, 458–459
children's understandings of, 345–346
cliques and crowds, 574
cross-sex and cross-ethnic, 459–460
defining, 458–459
descriptions of, 460
developmental stages, 461
imaginary friends, 346–347
intimacy, 575–576
lack of, 459
making and keeping, 460–461
neglected children, 462–463, 468–469, 486
peer acceptance, 346–347, 458, 486
preschool, 344–347
rejected children, 462, 464–466, 468
school success and, 334
triads, 460–461

GABA system, 522
games. *See* sports
gametes, 87, 112
gay adolescents, 15, 510–511
gender consistency/constancy, 352
gender differences
achievement tests, 540–542
aggression, 466–467, 519
blended families, 483
cultural prescriptions for, 43
early maturation effects, 497
in education, 429–431, 542–543
effects of divorce, 481–482
employment status, 254–255
friendships, 460–461, 576
gender role process, 354–356
growth rates, 272, 274, 296, 381–383, 493
masturbation, 507
moral reasoning, 593
motor development, 277, 388–389
self-esteem, 571–573
sexual attitudes, 509–510
in socialization of infants, 242–243
stress, 405
television preferences, 333
temperament, 251
weight and attractiveness, 504
gender identity, 351–352, 510. *See also* gender roles
gender intensification hypothesis, 582
gender roles
androgyny, 583–587
development theories, 350–353
engendering process, 353–356
examples of, 349–350
gender equality, 356–358
gender intensification, 582
homosexuality and, 511
prenatal hormones and, 353
questionnaire on, 584
rewards for, 354–355
rewriting, 583–587
stereotypes, 352–355, 582–583
through education process, 429–431
toys, 356
gender schema, 352–353
gender stability, 352
gene-linkage analysis, 99

generalizability, 28
generative fathering, 258–260, 262
genes, 85–86
genetic disorders
  color blindness, 89, 93
  diagnosis of, 93–96
  Down syndrome, 89–90, 102, 131, 442
  fragile X syndrome, 90, 162
  hemophilia, 88, 93, 125
  Huntington's disease, 92, 99, 112
  Klinefelter's syndrome, 93, 112
  phenylketonuria, 90–91, 97
  preimplantation genetic testing, 137
  sickle-cell anemia, 91–92, 112, 396
  Tay-Sachs disease, 92, 94, 112
  Turner's syndrome, 93, 112
genetics
  age influences, 108, 111
  canalized traits, 97
  determination of sex, 88
  directness and indirectness, 97
  DNA replication, 86–88
  dominant and recessive traits, 85
  effects on rearing environment, 11
  intelligence, 106–108
  molecular, 99–100
  nature *vs.* nurture, 40–41, 96–97
  obesity and, 401
  overview, 84–86
  personality, 100–106
  schizophrenia and, 80–81
  twin and adoption studies, 98–99
  X-linked inheritance, 88–89
genetic screening, 93–94, 100, 137
genomes, 100
genotypes, 86
German children, 238–239, 554–556
German measles, 129
germinal period, 139
gestation period, 139–142, 167
gestures, 218
g factor, 109
Ghanaian children, 399. *See also* African children
gifted children, 423, 442–444, 452
girls. *See also* gender differences
  androgynous, 585–586
  early maturation effects, 497
  education differences, 542–543
  friendships, 460–461
  gender role lessons, 354–357
  growth rates, 274, 381–382, 493–494
  historical views on education of, 8–9
  ideal physique, 498
  motor development, 388–389
  parenting types and, 102
  puberty, 494–495
  self-esteem, 571–573
glial cells, 161
gonadotrophic hormones, 494
gonads, 494
gonorrhea, 511, 513
goodness-of-fit, 251, 253
grammar, of language, 213–214
grasping skills, 170–171
The Grasp of Consciousness (Piaget), 203
grief, 398–399
gross motor development, 276–278, 296
growth. *See* physical development
growth hormone (GH), 273, 296, 493
growth spurts, 493–494
Guatemalan children, 109, 144
guilt, 594–595

habituation, 205–206, 211
hallucinogens, 522
handedness, 270, 387
hand-eye coordination, 383, 388
hand grasp reflex, 169
haploid cells, 87
head control, in infants, 168
Head Start, 210, 281
health care, 283–284
hearing
  deafness, 180–181, 319
  in early childhood, 272
  by infants, 177, 180–181, 192, 272
  in middle childhood, 382
heart diseases, 382, 394
heart rates, 131, 394
height, 271–272, 380–382
Heinz dilemma, 474, 591–593
hemophilia, 88, 93, 125
hepatitus B virus, 513
heredity. *See* genetics
heritability, 97
heroin, 134, 136
herpes, 513
heterozygous individuals, 85–86
hex-A, 92
high blood pressure, 131
Hindu children
  caregiver roles, 53–54
  divorce of parents, 482
  emotions, 359
  formal education of girls, 54
  moral development, 592
  punishment of, 22
  sex preferences for firstborn children, 126
Hispanic American children
  academic achievement, 435–439, 560
  AIDS, 128
  birth weight, 150
  child care, 53–54, 255
  child-rearing practices, 77, 79
  composition of, 76–77
  co-sleeping, 183
  families, 67, 77, 480
  friendships, 460, 574
  identity issues, 579
  obesity, 400
  parent–adolescent relationships, 553, 601
  punishment, 22
  self-esteem, 571–572
  sexuality, 506
  stress, 405
  television viewing, 394
  violence and, 519
historical attitudes toward children, 6–10, 46
HIV infection, 127–129, 512–514
holophrastic speech, 219
homologous chromosomes, 84
homosexuality, 15, 510–511
homozygous individuals, 85–86
Hopi language, 304
horizontal decalage, 416, 538
horizontality tests, 23–24
hormones
  definition, 494
  emotions and, 131, 361
  estrogen, 494
  gender roles and, 353
  gonadotrophic, 494
  growth, 273, 296
  homosexuality and prenatal, 510–511
  humor and, 451
  testosterone, 494
HPV (human papillomavirus), 513
Human Genome Project, 100
human immunodeficiency virus (HIV), 127–129, 512–514
humanistic views of children, 8–9
human papillomavirus (HPV), 513
humor, 450–451
Huntington's disease, 92, 99, 112
hyperactivity, 446–448
hypersomnolence, 135
hypertext/hypermedia, 427–428
hypothesis, 32, 35
hypothetico-deductive reasoning, 534–535

id, 14
idealism, 550–551, 566
idealization, 493
identity
  crises, 577
  ethnic, 68, 579
  gender, 351–352, 510
  individuation, 599–600
  multicultural differences, 579
  parental relationships and, 578–579
  promoting sense of, 579–582
  rites of passage and, 580–581
  statuses, 577–579
identity achievers, 578–579
identity diffusion, 578–579
identity foreclosure, 577–579
identity moratorium, 578–579
ideographic development, 46

illnesses
acute/chronic, 395–396
immune system, 187
infectious diseases, 283, 296, 395–396
in middle childhood, 407, 410
post-traumatic stress disorder, 518
sexually transmitted diseases, 511–514
stress and, 407
imaginary audience, 549–550
imagination, 269, 316, 343–344, 346–347
imitation, 21, 224, 246, 303, 351
immune system, 187, 272, 407, 451
immunizations, 187, 188, 283–284
implantation, 139–140
implicit rules, 213
imprinting, 231. *See also* attachment
incest, 371–373
independent variables, 35–36
Indian children. *See* Hindu children; Native American children
indifferent parents, 368
individualism
in China, 61–62, 64–65
collectivism *vs.*, 54–56
definition, 78
risk-taking behavior, 508
individuation, 599–600
Indonesian children, 321
indulgent parents, 368
Industrial Revolution, childhood during, 9–10
infanticide, in ancient times, 7, 9
infants. *See also* newborns; toddlers
attachment, 227–241
autistic, 246–249
behavioral states, 181–186
brain development stages, 163–164, 192
co-sleeping, 183–184, 186
crying, 181–182, 192, 243
day care, 323
death, 7, 132, 135, 184–186, 193
developmental milestones, 159, 209
divorce and, 480
emotional development, 244–245
facial preferences, 175–177
gestation period stages, 139–142, 167
growth patterns, 167–168
habituation and memory, 205–206, 211
hearing, 177, 180–181, 192, 272
imitation, 206–207, 224, 246
immunizations, 187–188
increasing intelligence, 165–166
intervention programs, 210–212
language development, 212–225
laughter, 450–451
learning to walk, 169–170, 172
motor development, 168–173, 192
nutrition, 187–191, 193
overstimulation, 207–208
overweight, 190–191
perception, 44, 177, 178–179
preference for attractive faces, 504
reaching, grasping, and manipulative skills, 170–171
self-awareness, 155, 158, 243–244
self-comforting behaviors, 184
sense of trust, 155, 158, 244, 398
senses, 178
sleep, 168, 181–186, 192–193
social referencing, 245–246
tactile stimulation, 178
of teenage parents, 515–516
temperament, 249–254
visual development, 174–177
infectious diseases. *See also* illnesses
course of, 283, 296
immunizations, 283–284
in middle childhood, 395–396
infertility, 122–124, 136–137, 152
information-processing theory
adolescence, 536–539
early childhood, 310–313
gender roles, 352–353
infancy, 204–208, 224
middle childhood, 416–419
injuries, 282–283, 396
inner speech, 306–307, 309
inpatient treatment, 525
Institutes for the Achievement of Human Potential, 165
intelligence. *See also* cognitive development
achievement tests, 540–542
adopted children, 107
assessment of, 109, 540–541
convergent *vs.* divergent thinking, 419–421
cultural variations, 109
definitions, 106, 196, 204
ethnicity and, 107–108
family factors, 212
gender differences, 541
gifted children, 423, 442–444, 452
incremental view, 421–422
infant and toddler education, 165–166
intervention programs, 210–212
IQ tests, 106–109, 131, 210, 541
logical knowledge, 203–204
optimal environments for, 109–111
overachievers, 541–542
questionnaire, 544–545
stereotypes, 437
theory of multiple intelligences, 385–387, 410
twins, 106–107
underachievers, 543–548
intelligence tests
Bayley Scales of Infant Development, 171, 209, 211
developmental quotient, 209
gifted children, 442–443
infants *vs.* preschoolers, 211
IQ, 106–109, 131, 210, 541
intermodal perception, 179–180
internal locus of control, 421–424
internal working model, 236
Internet, 428
intervention programs
child abuse, 374
infants and toddlers, 210–212
prior to kindergarten, 335
interviews, as research tools, 33, 38
intimacy, 575–576
intracytoplasmic sperm injection (ICSI), 125
Inuit children, 23–24
in vitro fertilization, 124–125
IQ (intelligence quotient), 106–109, 131, 141, 210, 432
irreversibility, 301
Islamic children, 505
Israeli children, 21, 213, 238–239, 464
Italian children, 325, 365, 464, 482

Jamaican children, 172
Japanese children
academic achievement, 57–59, 432–435
attachment relations, 238–239
childbirth, 146
child-rearing goals, 59–61, 78
collectivism, 58
creativity, 420
day care, 325
emotions, 21, 359–360, 362
growth rates compared to Japanese American children, 381
hearing, in infants, 177
lack of punishment of, 22
language development, 214, 222–223
moral development, 592
occupational training, 556
parents of, 28, 59–61, 258, 435
play, 342, 393
scaffolding, 308
school readiness, 326
self-effacement, 571
teachers, 435
television, 393–394
theory of mind in, 315–316
Jewish children, 92
jobs. *See* employment
jumping, 277–278, 388–389
juvenile delinquency, 587–588

Kenyan children, 53, 172, 177, 214, 222
kindergarten, 326, 328–329, 334–336
Klinefelter's syndrome, 93, 112
knowledge base, 539
Korean children, 394
!Kung women, 147, 222
kwashiorkor, 190

labor, child, 9–10
labor, childbirth, 147–148

Lamaze method, 145–146
Lamb, Michael E., 154–155
language. *See also* communication
  in adolescence, 562–566
  autistic children, 247, 249, 262
  behavioral theory, 214–215
  bilingualism, 320–321
  brain development, 162–163, 177, 306, 384
  of caregivers, 220–223
  cultural setting, 212–213
  definition, 213
  delayed development, 219–220
  in early childhood, 269, 303, 306–310, 317–321, 336
  egocentric, private, and inner speech, 306–307, 309
  encouragement of, 221–224
  expansions and recastings, 319
  holophrastic speech, 219
  inadequacy of television, 221–222, 333
  in infancy, 216–220, 317–319
  in middle childhood, 449–452
  nativistic theory, 215–216, 225
  natural selection and, 41
  nonverbal, 218, 563
  phonemes, 213–214, 320–321
  receptive, 218
  as rule-governed system, 213–214, 318
  sarcasm, 449–450
  sexism in, 222–223
  sleep talking, 289
  social interactionist theory, 216, 225, 306–310
  speech and hearing problems, 319
  telegraphic speech, 317
language acquisition device (LAD), 215–216
latency stage, 15–17
lateralization, 270, 387
Latin American children. *See also* Mexican children
  games, 393
  motor skills, 171
  newborn welcoming, 149
  sex preferences, 126
Latino children. *See* Hispanic American children
laughter, 450–451
lead poisoning, 282
learned helplessness, 423
learning. *See* cognitive development; intelligence
learning, beliefs about, 197
learning disabilities, 444–445, 452
learning-experience model, 172
left and right concepts, 275–276, 387
lesbian adolescents, 15, 510–511
levels of aspiration, 423
libido, 14
linguistics, 212–213, 216
listening, 565
lithium, 136
Locke, John, 8, 41
locus, 86
logical knowledge, 203–204, 533
longitudinal studies, 38–40
long-term memory (LTM), 205, 310–312
Louisville twin study, 107
low birth weight babies, 150–151
LSD (lysergic acid diethylamide), 522
lungs, in premature infants, 150
lysergic acid diethylamide (LSD), 522

macrosystems, 28–29
Malaysian children, 392
malnutrition, 190
marasmus, 190
marijuana, 135–136, 522–523
marriage
  changes with children, 120–121
  divorce, 65, 480–482, 487
  remarriage, 482–485, 487
marshmallow challenge, 363–364
masculinity, 583–587
masturbation, 290, 507
mathematics education, 430–432, 536, 542
matrifocal societies, 17
matrilineal descent, 17, 74, 126
maturation, definition, 279
mean length utterance (MLU), 318
measles, during pregnancy, 129
Medicaid, 284
meiosis, 86–87
memory
  brain development, 161
  early childhood, 310–313
  infants, 205–206, 211
  knowledge base, 539
  long-term/short-term, 205, 310–312
  metacognition, 538, 566
  metamemory, 312–313
  middle childhood, 419
men. *See also* fathers; gender differences
  decision to have children, 116–120
  infertility in, 123
  reproductive system, 138
menarche, 494–495
menstruation, onset of, 494–495, 580
mental age (MA), 106
mental retardation
  education, 441–442, 452
  genetic disorders, 89–91, 93, 102, 112, 131, 442
  prenatal effects, 134
meritocracy, 6, 43
mesosystems, 28–29
metacognition, 538, 566
metamemory, 312–313
methadone, 134, 136
Mexican American children. *See* Hispanic American children
Mexican children, 32, 146, 171, 187, 393, 397
microsystems, 28–29
middle childhood
  attention, 416–418
  brain development, 383–387
  classification skills, 415
  concrete operational thinkers, 414–416, 533
  creativity, 419–421
  decentration, 415–416
  divorce, 481–482, 487
  education, 429–431
  friendships, 458–461
  growth spurts, 384–385
  guilt, 594
  height and weight, 380–382
  humor, 450–451
  illnesses, 395–396
  information-processing skills, 416–419
  language development, 449–451, 452
  memory, 419
  moral development, 472–478
  motor skills, 387–390, 410
  perceptions, 44
  play, 390–391
  popularity, 461–462
  reversibility, 415
  self-concept, 456–458
  skeletal and muscular growth, 382
  stress, 403–409
  television, 392–394
midwives, 146
minority groups. *See also* ethnic groups
  academic achievement, 436–441
  AIDS, 128
  composition of, 52
  ethnic identity, 68, 579
  homosexuals, 510
  negative stereotyping, 437–439
  voluntary *vs.* involuntary, 435–436
  vulnerability of families, 68–69
mitosis, 86–87
mixed-ethnic adoptions, 68, 70–71
molecular genetics, 99–100
money management, 558
monkeys, brain development in, 160
monozygotic twins, 98
Montessori schools, 323
moral development
  cultural and gender contexts, 475–476, 592
  empathy, 478–479
  family factors, 476–477
  gender differences, 593–594
  guilt, 594–595
  Kohlberg's theory, 352, 474–478, 486, 591–594
  parents and, 595–597
  peer factors, 477–478, 595
  Piaget's theory, 472–474, 486
morality, definition of, 472
moral realism, 472, 477

moral relativism, 472–473, 477, 591
moratorium identity status, 578
Moro reflex, 168, 169
morphemes, 214
morphine, 136
mothers. *See also* parents
abuse by, 372
attachment to, 229, 234–237, 240–241, 255, 262
Chinese American, 73
communication with daughters, 553, 564, 565
cultural diversity in responses of, 32, 53
differences from father in child interactions, 257–258
eating disorders and, 400
Japanese, 57–61
Mexican American, 77
outside employment of, 58, 65–66, 254–261, 262
pregnancy trimesters, 142–144
reasons to become, 116–120, 152
sensitivity, 236–237, 253, 255, 554
single, 254, 484–485
surrogate, 125
teenage, 514–515
motivation
to become parents, 116–120, 152
individual-oriented, 62
Piaget on, 202
for school success, 547–548, 561
motor skill development
agility, 389–390
assessment, 279–280
balance, 277, 388–389
complex, 281
coordination, 388–389
enhancing, 279, 281
ethnic groups, 171–173
fine motor, 278–279
gross motor, 276–278, 296
heredity and, 387
importance of, 390
in middle childhood, 387–390, 410
need for variety, 281
perceptual-motor movements, 275–276
power, 390
speed, 389
twin studies, 172
multiculturalism. *See also* ethnic groups
achievement in school, 308–309, 431–432, 437–439
animistic thinking, 304
attachment relations, 233, 238–239, 256
childbirth, 146, 149
child-rearing goals, 53–54, 57–61
collectivism *vs.* individualism, 54–56, 58
communication patterns, 563–564
conflicts with parents, 552–553
creativity, 420
cross-cultural research, 55–57
cultural sensitivity, 439
day care, 255, 325
decision to have children, 120
drug use, 521, 527
eating disorders, 399
effect of language on brain development, 163
emotions, 358–360, 362
families, 67–68
fathers, 257–258
formal operational thinking, 536
friendships, 460, 461–462
gender roles, 582–583
goals of, 50–51
intelligence tests, 107–109
language development, 212–213, 220–221
moral development, 475–476, 592
motor skill development, 171–173
Navajo education, 75–76
negative stereotyping, 437–439
occupational training, 556
outside employment of mothers, 254–255
parenting styles, 554–555
personality traits, 101
play, 340–343
risk-taking behaviors, 508–509
rites of passage, 580–581
self-esteem, 573
sex education, 293–295
sex preferences for firstborn children, 126–127
socialization differences, 52–54, 59
stress, 405
television viewing, 394
temperaments, 252
theories of mind in children, 315
transracial adoptions, 68, 70–71
video games, 425
within-group variations, 51–52
multivariate analysis, 36–37
Mundugumor children, 126
musical abilities, 386–387
mutations, 88
myelination, 161, 186, 268
myopia, 382

Native American children
animistic thinking, 304
creativity, 420
education, 30, 75–76, 560
extended families, 68, 73–74, 79
games, 392
inherent worth of, 8
language development, 214
moral reasoning, 473
parental relationships, 601
risk-taking behavior, 509
suicide, 589
understanding of death, 397
natural childbirth, 145. *See also* childbirth
naturalistic observation, 34–35, 38
natural selection, 41
nature *vs.* nurture, 40–41, 96–97, 107–108
Navajo nation, 8, 74–76. *See also* Native American children
neglect, 371–372
neglected children, 462–463, 468–469, 486
Nepalese children, 401
nervous system, 134, 158–162, 272, 384
neurons, 158–162, 268–269, 384
nevirapine, 129
newborns. *See also* infants
appearance, 150
birth defects, 89–91, 127–130, 133–135
Leboyer practices, 148
neonatal assessment techniques, 149–150
premature, 150–151, 153
nicotine, 132–133
nightmares, 289
night terrors, 289
nocturnal enuresis, 289–290
nonattachment, 235
nonshared family environment, 105, 111
nonsocial activity, 341
nonverbal behaviors, 563
nonviolence, 476
noradrenaline, 361
normative development, 46
Norwegian children, 393, 593
nucleotides, 84. *See also* genetics
nurture *vs.* nature, 40–41
nutrition. *See also* eating disorders
adolescents, 498–499
deficiencies, 287
early childhood, 284–288, 296
emotional eating, 401, 403
food allergies, 287
infants, 187–191, 193
intelligence and, 110
need for variety, 287–288
overnutrition, 190–191
during pregnancy, 130–132, 186
SIDS and, 186
smoking and, 132
snacks, 288, 499
television and, 288, 401, 403
undernutrition, 190
vegetarian diets, 498

OAE test, 180
obesity
causes, 401, 403, 410
definition, 400
in ethnic groups, 400–401
exercise programs, 402–403
family factors, 402
in infants, 190–191, 193
school prevention programs, 403
object permanence, 200–202

observer bias, 35
occupational training, 556–557
Oedipal complex, 350
operant conditioning, 20
operations, definition, 301
opiates, 522–523
oral stage, 14–15
organization, in intelligence, 198
orienting responses, 205
ossification, 140
outpatient treatment, 525
ovarian follicles, 138
overachievers, 541–542
overpopulation, 63–64
overprotectiveness, 469
overstimulation, 207–208
overweight children. *See* obesity; weight
ovulation, 138–139

parallel play, 341
parentese, 220–221
parents. *See also* fathers; mothers
  abusing, 372
  academic expectations, 434–435
  adaptability, 240
  aggressive children, 466–467
  authoritative/authoritarian, 367–368, 370, 548, 554–555, 573, 601
  of autistic children, 248
  child-centered *vs.* self-centered, 240
  childrens' intelligence and, 110–111
  conflicts with, 551–555, 566
  decision to become, 116–121, 152
  demandingness and responsiveness, 102, 367
  democratic, 477
  division of labor, 121, 123, 257, 260–261
  divorce, 480–482
  dropouts and, 561
  drug abuse and, 525–527
  eating disorders and, 400
  education of, 43–44
  gender role process, 354–357, 430
  identity statuses of adolescents, 578–579
  language development role, 220–224
  moral behavior in children, 476–477, 595–597
  on-the-job training, 240
  overprotective, 469
  paid/unpaid leave for, 66–67
  perception of role, 53–54
  physical contact with infants, 241
  positive transitions to, 122–123
  praise of children, 53, 422
  relational styles, 207–208
  relationship between, 121, 291–292
  relationship to adolescents, 493, 496, 595–597, 600–601
  relationship with own parents, 121
  relative importance of, 101–102
  self-esteem of, 121
  self-esteem of children and, 348–349
  sensitivity of, 236–237, 240–241, 253, 255, 554
  sexual behavior of adolescents and, 508
  stepparents, 482–485
  teenage, 514–517
  of teenage mothers, 516
  temperament of children, 252–254
  of underachievers, 546–548
  verbal responsiveness of, 32, 53
  video games and, 426
peer acceptance. *See also* social skills
  characteristics of popular children, 461–462
  cliques and crowds, 574
  conflicts, 554
  definition, 458
  drug abuse, 525–527
  imaginary audiences, 549–550
  juvenile delinquency, 588
  morality and, 477–478, 595
  parental supervision, 596–597
  risk-taking behavior, 509
pendulum problem, 534–535
penis envy, 350
perception. *See also* sensory perception, in infants
  of body, 274–275
  of colors, 177
  definition, 418
  depth, 178–179
  intermodal, 179–180
  in middle childhood, 382–383, 418
  perceptual centration, 301, 304, 415
  perceptual-motor movements, 275–276
  by rejected-aggressive children, 465, 469–470
  at stages of childhood, 44–45
  of stress, 403
  Turner's syndrome and, 93
  video games and, 426
perceptual centration, 301, 304, 415–416
perceptual-motor movements, 275–276
perfect pitch, 387
personal fables, 549–550
personality. *See also* temperaments
  Big Five traits, 101–105
  Chinese children, 61–62
  Erikson on, 15–18, 25, 46
  genetic factors in, 92, 101–102
  questionnaire on, 12–13, 104–105
  vocational choice and, 557
perspective taking, stages of, 345
petting, 505
phallic stage, 15–16
phenotypes, 86
phenylalanine, 91
phenylketonuria (PKU), 90–91, 97
pheromones, 178
phonemes, 213–214, 320–321, 332
phonology, 213
physical abuse, 371–372
physical contact, with infants, 241
physical development. *See also* brain development; motor skill development
  cardiovascular endurance, 394
  definition, 45
  early childhood, 270–273
  environmental factors, 273
  genetic factors, 273
  growth spurts, 272, 384–385, 493–494
  height and weight, 271–272, 380–382, 494
  infants, 167–174, 192
  middle childhood, 380–387
  nutrition and, 498–499
  physical fitness, 392–395
  poverty and, 284
  prenatal, 139–144
  proportions, 272, 274, 381, 383
  sensory systems, 174–181, 382, 386–387
  sexual maturity, 494–497
Piaget, Jean
  active manipulation, 204
  assimilation and accommodation, 23, 198
  child's theory of mind, 313
  compared to Vygotsky, 309
  concrete operational thinkers, 414–416, 533
  criticisms of theory of, 200–202, 305
  evaluation of theory of, 303–304
  formal operational thinking, 532–536
  fostering cognitive competence, 203–204
  interview technique of, 33
  mechanisms of thought, 196–198
  moral development, 472–474, 486
  object permanence, 200–202
  observations by infants, 195–196
  organization and adaptation, 198
  preoperational thinking, 300–305
  schemes, 23, 198, 305
  sensorimotor thinking, 199–200, 224
  stages of cognitive development, 22–23, 25–26, 46
  three mountains problem, 302, 304
pica, 287, 296
PKU (phenylketonuria), 90–91, 97
placenta, 127, 141, 149
Plato, 6–7, 41–43, 508
play
  afterschool free time, 392–394
  cognitive levels, 343–344
  cultural variations, 342–343, 392–393
  games and sports, 390–393
  importance of, 203–204, 334, 340–341
  pretend, 316, 343–344
  symbolic, 303, 307
  types of, 341–343
pointing gestures, 218
poisoning, 396
polar bodies, 137
Polish children, 359

polygenetic inheritance, 85
Polynesian children, 342–343
poorness-of-fit, 251
popularity. *See* peer acceptance
popular/unpopular children, 461–463, 468
positive reinforcement, 20–21
postconventional moral reasoning, 474–475
postformal thinking, 536
postpartum period, 151, 153
post-traumatic stress disorder, 518
posture, in infants, 168–169
poverty. *See also* economic factors
  breaking away from, 286
  child abuse, 372
  development outcomes, 284–285
  effects of divorce, 482, 484
  ethnic minorities, 68
  obesity, 401
  sexual activity, 506
  stress, 408
  violence, 519
  working adolescents, 558
power, 390
pragmatics, 563
praise of children, 53, 422, 429
preconventional moral reasoning, 474–475
pregnancy. *See also* prenatal period
  abortion, 126, 516
  age and emotions, 131
  alcohol use during, 133–134
  caffeine during, 130–131
  development of primary organs, 128
  diagnostic tests, 94–96
  drug use, 131, 134–136
  effect of androgens on gender roles, 353
  embryonic period, 139–141, 152
  environmental hazards, 127–137, 152
  fetal period, 141–142
  first trimester, 142–143
  germinal period, 139
  motivation for, 513
  nutrition during, 130–132, 186, 191
  postpartum period, 151, 153
  Rh factor, 129–130
  second trimester, 143–144
  sex preferences for firstborn children, 126–127
  smoking during, 132–133
  teenage, 131, 150, 295, 506, 513–517, 528
  third trimester, 144
preimplantation genetic testing, 137
Preliminary Scholastic Assessment Test (PSAT), 540
prelinguistics, 216
premature infants, 150–151, 153
premoral period, 473–474
prenatal period. *See also* pregnancy
  AIDS and measles during, 127–129
  genetic screening, 94
  perceptions, 44
  physical growth patterns, 167
preoperational stage, 300–305
preschoolers. *See* early childhood
preschools
  bilingual, 321
  Chinese, 64–65
  education at, 323
  gender roles and, 357
  Japanese, 61
  social readiness for school, 334
prescription drugs. *See also* drug abuse
  against HIV in unborn children, 129
  during pregnancy, 131, 136
  Rh factor during pregnancy, 130
  use of genome catalog in, 100
pretend play, 316, 343–344
pretense, 314
preterm delivery, 150–151, 153
privacy, need for, 493
private speech, 306–307, 309
problem-finding thinkers, 536
prosocial behaviors, 477
protein intake requirements, 130
proximodistal, 168
psychoanalytical theories, 13–15, 26, 46, 350–351
psychometric approach, 208–212, 224
psychosocial stages, 15–18, 25, 46
puberty. *See also* adolescence
  age of, 381
  definition, 492
  effects of early maturation, 497
  growth spurt, 493–494
  rites of passage, 580–581
  secular trend, 495–496
  sexual maturity, 494–496
Puerto Rican children, 252, 480
punishment. *See also* discipline
  aggression and, 369, 471
  behaviorism and, 21–22
  child abuse, 371–374
  cultural variability, 22, 370
  discipline *vs.*, 370
  in history, 265
  negativism and, 370
  physical, 370–371
  stages of perspective taking and, 345
  whipping, 7–8
Punnett squares, 86
Puritan children, 7–8

quasi-experimental designs, 36
questionnaires, as research tools, 33–34. *See also* Self-Insights

race, 51, 52
reaction range, 97
reading
  developing an early love for, 329
  gender roles in books, 358
  knowledge of letters, 332
  reading readiness, 10, 329, 337
  shared, 331
  writing and, 331–332
recall, 311–312
recastings, 319
receptive speech, 218
recessive genes, 85–86
reciprocating influences, 27
recognition, 311–312
Recommended Dietary Allowances (RDAs), 285. *See also* nutrition
referential communication, 218–219
reflexive actions, 168–169, 199–200
rehearsal, 311–312
reinforcement. *See also* behaviorism
  Bandura on, 21
  gender roles, 351
  as guidance strategy, 369
  Skinner on, 20–21
  vicarious, 21, 351
rejected-aggressive children
  help for, 469–471
  media violence, 466–467, 470–471
  parental responses, 466
  peer interactions, 465–467, 469–470
  relationships with fathers, 465
  stability of peer status, 468
  undercontrol in, 465
rejected children, 462, 464–466, 468
relativistic thinking, 533
REM sleep, 183
representation, 303
representational mapping, 269
research designs, 38–39, 46–47
research strategies
  case studies, 33, 38
  combinatorial analysis, 534
  correlational method, 37–38
  cross-cultural, 55–57
  experimental method, 35–36, 38
  field experiments, 36
  gene-linkage analysis, 99
  hypotheses, 32, 35
  molecular genetics, 99–100
  multivariate analysis, 36–37
  naturalistic observation, 34–35, 38
  quasi-experimental designs, 36
  shared and nonshared family environment, 105
  surveys, 33–34, 38
  twin and adoption studies, 98–99, 106–107
resilient children, 408–409
responsiveness, 102, 367
retrieval, 311–312
Rett's disorder, 247
reversibility, 301, 415
rewards, 20–21
rheumatic fever, 382
Rh factor, 129–130

Rhogam, 130
rhythmicity, 252
risk-taking behaviors, 508
Ritalin, 447
rites of passage, 580–581
RNA (ribonucleic acid), 86
role models, 440
role-sharing families, 516
rolling, in infants, 168
rooting reflex, 169
Rough Rock Navajo School, 75–76
rubella, 129
running, 276–278, 388–389
Russian children, 254–255

safety concerns, early childhood, 282–283, 326
salt, 286
Samoan children, 420
sarcasm, 449–450
scaffolding, 308
schemes, 23, 198, 200, 305, 352
schizophrenia, 13, 80–81, 92
Scholastic Assessment Test (SAT), 540, 542
science education, 430–431, 536, 542
seat belts, 282
secondary sex characteristics, 494
secular trends, 495–496
secure base, 232
securely attached attachment relations, 232
sedatives, 136
self-awareness, 243–244, 314
self-concept
  adolescence, 570–571
  consistency of, 458, 570
  early childhood, 347–348
  middle childhood, 456–458, 486
self-conscious emotions, 360
self-control, 363
self-efficacy, 155, 158, 240, 243
self-esteem
  academic failure, 424
  adolescence, 571–573
  competency, 349
  developmental changes in, 347
  early childhood, 348–349
  early maturation and, 497
  eating disorders, 400
  gender differences, 571–572
  identity status and, 577–578
  middle childhood, 457–458
  transracial adoptions, 70–71
Self-Insights
  analyzing your own temperament, 250
  assessing parenting styles, 366
  Big Five inventory, 104–105
  child development expectations, 327
  collectivism-individualism scale, 56
  coping with stress, 526
  how androgynous are you?, 584
  how empathic are you?, 479
  how smart are you?, 544–545
  internal locus of control, 424
  learning about learning, 197
  personal theory on personality, 12–13
  reasons for and against having children, 118–119
  recognizing infants' competencies, 159
  sexuality comfort inventory, 292–293
  stress test, 404–405
semantics, 214
semen, 495
sensitivity of caregivers, 236–237, 240, 253, 255
sensorimotor thinking, 199–200, 224
sensory perception, in infants
  depth perception, 178–179
  hearing, 177, 180–181, 192
  intermodal, 179–180
  novel stimuli, 155
  olfactory system, 178
  tactile stimulation, 178
  taste, 178
  visual system, 174–177, 382
sensory registers, 205
separation anxiety, 229, 245, 257, 330–331. *See also* attachment
set point, 401
sex, determination of, 88, 125, 126
sex chromosomes, 88–90, 93
sex education
  cultural variations, 294–295, 506
  by parents, 291–292, 564
  for preschoolers, 291
  teenage pregnancy and, 506, 517
sexism, 222–223, 429–431, 476
sex-linked characteristics, 88–90, 93
sex preferences, 126–127
sex roles. *See* gender roles
sexual abuse, 371–373
sexual activity
  age of, 506
  decision-making, 507–508
  homosexuality, 15, 510–511
  masturbation, 290, 507
  multiculturalism, 506
  risk-taking, 507–508
  sexual attitudes, 509–510
  sexually transmitted diseases and, 511–514
  teenage pregnancy and, 513
sexual awakenings, 505–507
sexual identity, 510
sexual instincts, Freud on, 14–15
sexuality
  in early childhood, 290–295
  multiculturalism, 506
  names for body parts, 290–291
  physical attractiveness, 503–504
  questionnaire, 292–293
  respect for bodies, 291
sexually transmitted diseases (STDs), 511–514
sexual maturity, 494–496
sexual orientation, 15, 510–511
shared family environment, 105, 111
short-term memory (STM), 205, 310
shyness, 462–464, 468–469
sickle-cell anemia, 91–92, 112, 396
Sioux children, 18
sitting, in infants, 168
skipping, 277
sleeping
  active and passive, 183
  apnea, 184–186
  bed-wetting and, 289–290
  co-sleeping, 183–184, 186
  deprivation during adolescence, 496
  dreams, 289
  early childhood, 288–289
  infants, 181–186, 192–193
  position of infants, 168, 186
  staying dry at night, 173
  talking during, 289
slow-to-warm-up temperament, 251
smell, by infants, 178
smiling, infants and, 175, 244–245
smoking, 123, 132–133, 136, 523
social cognition, 242. *See also* socialization
social competence, 461–462
social interactionist theory, 216, 225, 306–310
socialization
  attachment and, 236
  child abuse and, 373–374
  cultural differences, 52–54, 365
  friendships, 334
  gender roles, 242–243, 353–356
  how infants learn, 242
  prosocial behaviors, 477
  at school, 333–334
  social expectancies, 243–244
  social referencing, 245–246
  stages of self-awareness, 243, 262
  symbolic play, 303, 307
  teacher relationships, 335
social learning theory, 21, 26, 351–352
social referencing, 245–246
social skills. *See also* friendships; peer acceptance
  computers and, 428
  cultural variations, 464
  help with, 468–471
  importance of, 468–469
  juvenile delinquency and, 588
  neglected children, 462–463, 468–469, 486
  popularity, 461–462, 468
  prosocial behavior, 477
  rejected children, 462, 464–466, 468
  shyness, 462–464, 468–469
  social self-concept, 457
  stability of status, 468
  video games and, 426
socioemotional development, 45

soma, 158–159
somatic cells, 86
spatial abilities, video games and, 426
speech, learning, 41
speed, 389
sperm, 87, 125, 136–137, 138
spermarche, 495
sports
  cultural variations, 392–393
  dropping out of school and, 561–562
  heart muscle growth rates and, 382
  in middle childhood, 390–391
  rewriting gender roles, 586
sprouting, 162, 384–385
stammering, 319
startle reflex, 168
statistics
  alcohol use, 522, 523
  on children, 43–44
  combinatorial analysis, 534
  correlational method, 37, 38
  television viewing, 332, 393–394
  variance, 105–106
  violence, 466–467
stepping reflex, 168–169, 172
stereotyping
  gender roles, 352–355, 582–583
  negative, 437–439
  sexual, 506
  social, 504
stimulants, 523
stranger anxiety, 229, 245
Strange Situation test, 230–232, 261
Stravinsky, Igor, 443
stress
  common childhood stressors, 405–407
  daily hassles, 406–407
  definition, 403
  employment and, 558–559
  family and, 408
  illnesses, 407, 451
  management, 407–409, 526
  middle childhood, 403–409, 411
  peer relationships, 468–469
  during pregnancy, 131
  questionnaire, 404
  shyness and, 463
  varying responses to events, 403–405
stressors, 403, 405–407
stretching, 395
stuttering, 319
substance abuse. *See* drug abuse
sucking reflex, 169
sudden infant death syndrome (SIDS), 132, 135, 184–186, 193
suffocation, 283
sugar, 286, 288
suicide, 498, 589–591
superego, 14
superovulation, 139
surfactin, 150
surrogate mothers, 125
surveys, strategy of, 33–34, 38
survivor guilt, 595
Swedish children
  child care, 324–325
  eating disorders, 399
  games, 393
  sex education, 293–295
  social welfare policies, 28, 66–67, 78, 259
  with unmarried parents, 65
  working mothers, 65–66, 256
swimming instruction, 283
Swiss children, 325
symbolic play, 303, 307
synapses, 160–161, 269
synaptogenesis, 162
syntax, 214–215
syphilis, 511, 513
systematic observation, 35

tabula rasa, 8
tactile stimulation, in infants, 178
Tahitian children, 359
taste, in infants, 178
Tay-Sachs disease, 92, 94, 112
teachers, 335, 435–437
technology
  computers, 165–166, 425, 427–429
  educational technology software, 427–428
  video games, 425–426
teenagers. *See* adolescence
telegraphic speech, 317
television
  advantages and disadvantages, 333
  established viewing patterns, 332–333
  lack of language development from, 221–222
  in middle childhood, 393
  obesity and, 401, 403
  preference for unhealthy foods and, 288
  statistics on viewing, 332, 393–394
  violence and, 466–467, 520
temperaments. *See also* personality
  degree of fit, 251–252, 253
  differences in, 249–251
  difficult, 252–253
  dimensions of, 251–252, 262
  questionnaire on, 250
  recognizing and accepting, 252–254
teratogens, 127, 136–137
testes-determining factor, 88
testosterone, 494
test-tube babies, 124
tetrahydrocannabinol (THC), 522
Texas Adoption Study, 101, 107
Thai children, 394
thalidomide, 136
theory of mind, in children, 313–316
therapy
  for drug abuse, 525
  for eating disorders, 502–503
thinking skills. *See* cognitive development
three mountains problem, 302, 304
throwing, 278
thyroid-stimulating hormone (TSH), 273
thyroxin, 273
tobacco, 123, 132–133, 136, 523
toddlers
  day care, 323
  definition, 169
  education of, 165–166
  intervention programs, 210–212
  learning to walk, 169–170, 172
  nutrition, 188–190
  toilet training, 16, 171–174
toilet training, 16, 171–174. *See also* bed-wetting
toys, 341–342, 356. *See also* play
tranquilizers, 136
transductive reasoning, 303–304
transracial adoptions, 68, 70–71
Trisomy 21, 89
Trobriand Islanders, 16–17, 505–507
trust
  in infants, 155, 158, 244, 398
  in multicultural education, 440
Turkish children, 53
Turner's syndrome, 93, 112
12-step programs, 525
twins, conception of, 138–139
twin studies
  first person account, 99
  intelligence, 106–107
  motor skill development, 172
  overview, 98–99
  personality, 101, 103–104
  schizophrenia, 80–81

Ugandan children, 120, 222. *See also* African children
ultrasound tests, 94–95
unconscious mind, 14
underachievers, 543–548
United States
  access to health care, 283–284
  adolescent employment, 558
  childcare benefits in, 28
  colonial attitudes toward children, 7–8, 46
  cultural beliefs in, 67–68, 78
  outside employment of mothers, 254
  praise of children, 53
  role of fathers, 258
  role of mothers, 54
  teenage pregnancies, 575
  verbal responsiveness of parents, 32
Ute language, 214

vaccinations, 187, 188, 283–284
variance, 105–106
vegetarian diets, 498
verbal abilities, IQ and, 107
vicarious reinforcement, 21, 351
video games, 425–426, 466–467

violence. *See also* aggression
  causes, 520
  community, 518
  domestic, 518
  gangs, 520
  homicide rate, 519
  in the media, 466–467, 470–471, 520
  as social toxicity, 376–377
  solutions, 520–521
  statistics on, 466–467
  in video games, 425–426
vision
  in early childhood, 269, 272, 275
  in infants, 174–176, 272
  in middle childhood, 382, 385
visual cortex, 269
vitamins, 136

Wagner Preference Inventory, 271
Walden Two (Skinner), 21
walking, 169–170, 172, 277–278
walking reflex, 169, 172
water breaking, 148
weight
  attractiveness and, 504
  in early childhood, 271–272
  in middle childhood, 380–382
  obesity, 190–191, 193, 400–403, 410
  set point, 401
  smoking and, 523
Wernicke's area, 216, 269
white children. *See* European American children
withdrawn underachievers, 546
within-group variations, 51–52, 107–108
women. *See also* gender differences; mothers
  advice to good wives, 228
  decision to have children, 116–120
  infertility in, 123–124
  in matrifocal societies, 17
  Navajo, 74
  reproductive system, 138
word processing, 427–428
working. *See* employment
writing, 331–332

X chromosomes, 88–90, 93
X-linked inheritance, 88–90, 125
XXY males, 93, 112

Y chromosomes, 88–90, 93
Yoruba children, 188. *See also* African children

zidovudine, 129
Zinacanteco Indians, 30
zone of proximal development, 30, 307–309

TO THE OWNER OF THIS BOOK:

I hope that you have found *Child and Adolescent Development: An Integrated Approach* useful. So that this book can be improved in a future edition, would you take the time to complete this sheet and return it? Thank you.

School and address: ____

____

Department: ____

Instructor's name: ____

1. What I like most about this book is: ____

____

____

2. What I like least about this book is: ____

____

____

3. My general reaction to this book is: ____

____

____

4. The name of the course in which I used this book is: ______________________________

____

5. Were all of the chapters of the book assigned for you to read? ______________________

   If not, which ones weren't? ____

6. In the space below, or on a separate sheet of paper, please write specific suggestions for improving this book and anything else you'd care to share about your experience in using this book.

____

____

____

____

____

____

OPTIONAL:

Your name: ________________________________ Date: ____________________

May we quote you, either in promotion for *Child and Adolescent Development: An Integrated Approach*, or in future publishing ventures?

Yes: __________ No: __________

Sincerely yours,

Karen Owens

FOLD HERE

NO POSTAGE NECESSARY IF MAILED IN THE UNITED STATES

BUSINESS REPLY MAIL

FIRST CLASS PERMIT NO. 34 BELMONT, CA

POSTAGE WILL BE PAID BY ADDRESSEE

ATTN: *Edith Beard Brady, Psychology*

WADSWORTH/THOMSON LEARNING
10 DAVIS DRIVE
BELMONT, CA 94002-9801

FOLD HERE